MERGENT'S DIVIDEND ACHIEVERS

W9-BEE-388

2002 Edition

Published by:

MERGENT

MERGENT'S DIVIDEND ACHIEVERS

Mergent, Inc.

CHIEF EXECUTIVE OFFICER: Bruce E. Rogoff

CHIEF OPERATING OFFICER: Bimal Gandhi

CHIEF FINANCIAL OFFICER: Laizer Kornwasser

CHIEF INFORMATION OFFICER: Timothy E. Roche

SENIOR VICE PRESIDENT-SALES: John W. Condon

ASSOCIATE PUBLISHER: Thomas Wecera

Staff for *MERGENT'S DIVIDEND ACHIEVERS*

ASST. VICE PRES. AND EDITOR: Suzanne Wittebort

EDITORS: Brad A. Armbruster, Stacy M. Cleeland

ASSOCIATE EDITORS: Reggie D. Cain, Kevin D. Heckert

SENIOR BUSINESS ANALYSTS: Christalyn Y. Daniel, Richard K. Dee, Jr., Melissa A. Francis, Andrew J. Kalinski

BUSINESS ANALYSTS: Troy Gaunt, Anthony E. Harp, Ava J. Oszlanyi, Talvi S. Young

TABLE OF CONTENTS

Page

SPECIAL FEATURES

COMPANY REPORTS   Arranged Alphabetically

INTRODUCTION

Defying miserable market conditions, **Mergent's Dividend Achiever** companies once again delivered the goods in 2001. While the S&P 500 earned a negative total return of -11.89% for the year, the average Dividend Achiever total return was a robust 10.6%. All told, 80 Dividend Achievers returned 20.0% or more in 2001, and well over three-quarters of them beat the S&P. This happy result built on 2000's impressive average return of 19.7%, against a similarly bleak S&P 500 performance of -9.10%.

Mergent has been highlighting companies with outstanding dividend records since 1979. For this edition, Mergent has identified and profiled 282 companies that have increased their regular cash dividends for at least ten consecutive calendar years through 2001.

Why are these companies so attractive now? Investors, unsettled by turbulent markets and disturbing world events, may be turning to Dividend Achievers in a trend that could be called comfort investing. Like comfort food, comfort investments favor the traditional and familiar and are particularly appealing in tough times. Companies that may be categorized as comfort investments supply homey, uncomplicated products and anxiety-relieving services.

But truly comforting investments are nourishing as well, turning in consistent operating and investment results through difficult times. Most of the 2002 Dividend Achievers decisively delivered the operating results to support their dividend payouts. In 2001, a year of recession and national trauma, more than 95% of the Dividend Achievers posted profits, while more than 85% recorded payout ratios of less than 100%, meaning they paid dividends with profits to spare. Long records of dividend increases are generally possible only if earnings increase as well, suggesting capable management. Furthermore, as longtime dividend payers, these companies have earmarked in advance a portion of those profits to send back to investors.

Companies that are definitely *not* comfort investments include the highest of high-tech, Internet and other life-on-the-edge ventures. If a company's business description requires interpretation from your technology department (or the nearest teenager), it's not a comfort investment. If a company has never made a profit, it's not a comfort investment. If a company has "one-time" charges every quarter, it's not a comfort investment. If a company trumpets its pro forma results and buries its actual losses pages later in its reports, it's not a comfort investment. Few if any companies with these traits will be found in this book.

After getting unkindly cut on the cutting edge of technology investments, many investors are forsaking the world of dizzying possibilities for treasures closer to home. And that's precisely where many Dividend Achievers can be found. Picture this scenario (with Dividend Achievers in boldface): you spend a Saturday shopping at **Wal-Mart, Home Depot, Lowe's, Pier 1** and **Target**. You stop by **McDonald's** for lunch, and fill up your gas tank at the **Exxon Mobil** station. Later in the day, you drop by your local **Walgreen's** to pick up some **Wrigley's** gum and your prescriptions, manufactured by **Merck, Lilly** and **Pfizer**. Once home, you raid your **General Electric** refrigerator for a **Coke** or **Pepsi**, or perhaps a Budweiser from **Anheuser-Busch**. Then you kick back in your **La-Z-Boy** to watch the local news on a television station owned by **Belo Corp.** or **Jefferson-Pilot**.

After a hearty dinner of Ball Park franks from **Sara Lee**, garnished with **Heinz** ketchup, you treat yourself to a **Hershey** bar, or maybe a **Tootsie Roll**. At bedtime, you brush your teeth with **Procter & Gamble's** Crest toothpaste and blow your nose with a Kleenex from **Kimberly-Clark**. Once in bed, you sleep soundly, secure in the knowledge your money is safe in one of more than 50 Dividend Achiever banks, and you and your possessions are insured by one of nearly 30 Dividend Achiever insurance companies.

The point is that many Dividend Achievers are tightly woven into everyday American life. Add their familiar brand names to their strong operating results and concern for shareholders shown in their dividend policies, and it's no wonder their attractions are particularly potent in uncertain times - the ultimate comfort investments, the financial equivalent of a big old bowl of macaroni and cheese.

Once again, **Paychex, Inc.** takes the top spot in the ranking of average annual compound dividend growth rates for 1991 through 2001. With a ten-year average annual compound growth rate of 46.77%, the Rochester, New York provider of payroll and benefit services has led the pack for four years straight. The tops in total return for 2001 is **Raven Industries, Inc.**, which returned a whopping 112.9%. The Sioux Falls, South Dakota company, which manufactures products ranging from global positioning systems for farmers to hot-air balloons, is benefiting from a series of strategic acquisitions and divestitures. Also topping 100% with 109.0% in total return is **Lowe's Companies, Inc.**, the Wilkesboro, North Carolina owner of the fast-growing home supplies chain with 744 stores in 42 states.

The distinction of the most consecutive years of dividend increases was retained by **Aon Corp.**, which increased its dividend for the 50th consecutive year in April 2001. This astonishing corporate achievement could not have been sustained over such a long period of time without sound management and highly effective and dedicated employees. Tragically, on September 11, 2001 Aon lost 175 employees of its retail insurance brokerage in the World Trade Center attacks. Another Dividend Achiever, **Marsh & McLennan Companies, Inc.**, lost 295 employees in the terrorist strikes. Other Dividend Achievers also lost employees on that terrible day. We salute their achievements and mourn their loss.

Will the Dividend Achievers continue to perform well in 2002? It's anyone's guess, but for the 12 months ending March 30, 2002, more than 80% of the Dividend Achievers' stocks had outperformed the NYSE on price alone. Looks like for now macaroni and cheese is still the blue-plate special.

Suzanne Wittebort
Asst. Vice President & Editor
Mergent's Dividend Achievers
Charlotte, NC
April, 2002

Ranking the 2002 Dividend Achievers

Companies are listed by the ten-year average annual compound growth rate of their dividends. Also shown are total numbers of consecutive years of dividend growth.

Rank	Company	10-Year Growth Rate %	No. of Yrs.	Rank	Company	10-Year Growth Rate %	No. of Yrs.
1.	[2] Paychex, Inc. (NS)	46.77	13	49.	F.N.B. Corp. (NS)	16.034	17
2.	First Federal Capital Corp (NS)	40.30	10	50.	[1] Leggett & Platt, Inc. (NY)	16.032	32
3.	Community First Bankshares (NS)	32.75	10	51.	[1] General Dynamics Corp. (NY)	15.97	10
4.	[1] Citigroup Inc. (NY)	31.95	15	52.	[1] Brady Corp. (NY)	15.92	17
5.	[1] Home Depot, Inc. (The) (NY)	30.13	14	53.	[1] Automatic Data Processing (NY)	15.91	26
6.	[2] SEI Investments Co. (NS)	26.86	10	54.	[1] AFLAC Inc. (NY)	15.90	19
7.	[1] Schwab (Charles) Corp. (NY)	26.48	12	55.	[1] Gillette Co. (The) (NY)	15.79	24
8.	[1] Pier 1 Imports, Inc. (NY)	26.05	10	56.	[1] BB&T Corp. (NY)	15.60	30
9.	[1] Dollar General Corporation (NY)	25.58	11	57.	[1] Wells Fargo & Co. (NY)	15.58	14
10.	First Indiana Corp. (NS)	23.97	10	58.	[1] State Street Corp. (NY)	15.48	21
11.	[1] Washington Mutual Inc. (NY)	23.69	12	59.	[1] Transatlantic Holdings, Inc. (NY)	15.39	11
12.	[2] Applebee's International, Inc. (NS)	23.49	10	60.	[1] Golden West Financial Corp. (NY)	15.17	18
13.	[1] Raymond James Finl. Inc. (NY)	23.18	15	61.	[1] Illinois Tool Works, Inc. (NY)	15.15	39
14.	[1] Sysco Corp. (NY)	23.11	25	62.	[1] Morgan (J.P.) Chase & Co. (NY)	14.93	10
15.	[1] Medtronic, Inc. (NY)	22.69	24	63.	United Mobile Homes, Inc. (AM)	14.91	11
16.	[2] T. Rowe Price Group, Inc. (NS)	22.32	15	64.	[1] Pfizer Inc. (NY)	14.87	34
17.	[1] Charter One Financial, Inc. (NY)	21.83	13	65.	Cousins Properties Inc. (NY)	14.69	10
18.	CVB Financial Corp. (AM)	21.78	11	66.	Corus Bankshares, Inc. (NS)	14.68	15
19.	[1] M & T Bank Corp. (NY)	21.73	21	67.	[1] Schering-Plough Corp. (NY)	14.60	16
20.	[1] Eaton Vance Corp. (NY)	21.42	20	68.	[1] Baldor Electric Co. (NY)	14.55	18
21.	[2] Cintas Corp. (NS)	21.38	19	69.	[2] McGrath Rentcorp (NS)	14.51	11
22.	[1] Wal-Mart Stores, Inc. (NY)	20.85	20	70.	[1] Kaydon Corp. (NY)	14.40	14
23.	[2] Virco Manufacturing Corp. (AM)	20.76	19	71.	[1] ConAgra Foods, Inc. (NY)	14.26	24
24.	Irwin Financial Corp. (NY)	20.58	12	72.	[1] General Electric Co. (NY)	14.18	26
25.	[1] Synovus Financial Corp. (NY)	20.39	25	73.	[1] Legg Mason, Inc. (NY)	14.09	18
26.	[1] Tootsie Roll Industries, Inc. (NY)	19.90	38	74.	[1] Old Republic International (NY)	13.82	20
27.	[2] Jack Henry & Associates, Inc. (NS)	19.62	11	75.	[1] Johnson & Johnson (NY)	13.78	39
28.	Pacific Capital Bancorp (NS)	18.85	32	76.	[1] Valspar Corp. (NY)	13.67	23
29.	Hudson United Bancorp (NY)	18.66	11	77.	[1] Philip Morris Cos., Inc. (NY)	13.62	36
30.	State Auto Financial Corp. (NS)	18.27	10	78.	1st Source Corp. (NS)	13.58	14
31.	WestAmerica Bancorporation (NS)	18.25	12	79.	National Penn Bancshares (NS)	13.57	23
32.	National Commerce Finl. Corp.	18.22	27	80.	[1] Merck & Co., Inc. (NY)	13.53	18
33.	Mercury General Corp. (NY)	18.15	15	81.	[1] Unitrin, Inc. (NY)	13.52	11
34.	[2] Fifth Third Bancorp (NS)	17.91	29	82.	[2] Associated Banc-Corp. (NS)	13.50	28
35.	[1] Nucor Corp. (NY)	17.87	29	83.	[2] Compass Bancshares Inc. (NS)	13.44	20
36.	[2] Trustco Bank (NS)	17.81	25	84.	[2] SouthTrust Corp. (NS)	13.15	31
37.	S & T Bancorp, Inc. (NS)	17.79	12	85.	[1] Abbott Laboratories (NY)	13.07	29
38.	[1] Merrill Lynch & Co. (NY)	17.74	10	86.	[1] Pitney Bowes, Inc. (NY)	13.06	18
39.	[2] Cohu Inc. (NS)	17.46	14	87.	[1] SunTrust Banks, Inc. (NY)	13.03	16
40.	[1] Archer Daniels Midland Co. (NY)	17.20	27	88.	[1] Franklin Resources, Inc. (NY)	12.99	12
41.	[1] Superior Industries Int'l, Inc. (NY)	17.05	16	89.	[1] Teleflex Inc. (NY)	12.97	24
42.	[1] Freddie Mac (NY)	16.98	11	90.	[2] Lancaster Colony Corp. (NS)	12.90	32
43.	Commerce Bancorp, Inc. (NY)	16.94	10	91.	[1] Myers Industries Inc. (NY)	12.76	25
44.	Park National Corp. (AM)	16.59	14	92.	[1] Jefferson-Pilot Corp. (NY)	12.71	34
45.	[1] Fannie Mae (NY)	16.53	16	93.	[1] Family Dollar Stores, Inc. (NY)	12.60	25
46.	[1] MBNA Corp. (NY)	16.047	10	94.	[1] Avery Dennison Corp. (NY)	12.46	26
47.	[2] Northern Trust Corp. (NS)	16.045	16	95.	[2] Trustmark Corp. (NS)	12.37	28
48.	[1] Fidelity National Financial (NY)	16.04	14	96.	[1] Gallagher (Arthur J.) & Co. (NY)	12.36	17

Rank	Company	10-Year Growth Rate %	No. of Yrs.
97.	[1] American International Grp. (NY)	12.30	16
98.	Chemical Financial Corp. (NS)	12.18	26
99.	[1] Pall Corp. (NY)	11.95	21
100.	[1] Bank of America Corp. (NY)	11.91	24
101.	[2] Cincinnati Financial Corp. (NS)	11.87	41
102.	First Commonwealth Finl. (NY)	11.81	14
103.	[2] Raven Industries, Inc. (NS)	11.76	14
104.	[1] Federal Signal Corp. (NY)	11.65	14
105.	[1] Alberto-Culver Co. (NY)	11.61	17
	[1] Coca-Cola Co. (The) (NY)	11.61	39
	[2] Sigma-Aldrich Corp. (NS)	11.61	20
108.	[1] USA Education, Inc. (NY)	11.551	21
109.	[1] MBIA Inc. (NY)	11.549	14
110.	[1] AmSouth Bancorporation (NY)	11.44	31
111.	[1] Procter & Gamble Co. (NY)	11.31	48
112.	[1] Hillenbrand Industries, Inc. (NY)	11.22	31
113.	[2] Mercantile Bankshares Corp. (NS)	11.15	25
114.	[2] Huntington Bancshares, Inc. (NS)	11.09	35
115.	[1] Comerica, Inc. (NY)	11.07	18
	[1] McCormick & Co., Inc. (NY)	11.07	15
117.	Community Bank System, Inc. (NY)	11.01	10
118.	[1] Albertson's, Inc. (NY)	10.90	30
119.	BancorpSouth, Inc. (NY)	10.84	15
	[2] Nordson Corp. (NS)	10.84	21
121.	[1] ABM Industries Inc. (NY)	10.82	37
122.	First Financial Bancorp (NS)	10.79	18
123.	[1] Interpublic Group of Cos. (NY)	10.77	20
124.	[1] Sherwin-Williams Co. (NY)	10.69	22
125.	Wausau-Mosinee Paper Corp. (NY)	10.61	17
126.	[1] Wrigley (Wm.) Jr. Co. (NY)	10.48	21
127.	[2] Modine Manufacturing Co. (NS)	10.454	14
128.	[2] Commerce Bancshares, Inc. (NS)	10.448	33
129.	[1] Protective Life Corp. (NY)	10.37	12
130.	[1] HON Industries Inc. (NY)	10.31	13
131.	[2] Donegal Group Inc. (NS)	10.30	12
132.	[1] Colgate-Palmolive Co. (NY)	10.22	39
133.	[1] Marshall & Ilsley Corp. (NY)	10.19	28
134.	[2] Alfa Corp. (NS)	10.14	16
135.	[1] Becton, Dickinson & Co. (NY)	10.11	29
136.	[1] Valley National Bancorp	10.05	10
137.	[1] Anheuser-Busch Cos., Inc. (NY)	10.042	27
138.	[1] Carlisle Companies Inc. (NY)	10.040	25
139.	[1] PepsiCo, Inc. (NY)	9.99	30
140.	[1] First Virginia Banks Inc. (NY)	9.97	24
141.	[2] Regions Financial Corp. (NS)	9.90	30
142.	[1] KeyCorp (NY)	9.88	22
143.	[1] Harleysville Group, Inc. (NS)	9.85	15
144.	[1] Dover Corp. (NY)	9.76	46
145.	Citizens Banking Corp. (NS)	9.70	18
146.	[1] McDonald's Corp. (NY)	9.52	25
147.	[1] Hershey Foods Corp. (NY)	9.50	27
148.	[1] Sara Lee Corp. (NY)	9.46	25
149.	[1] Hormel Foods Corp. (NY)	9.45	34
150.	Fulton Financial Corp. (NS)	9.42	28
151.	[1] Beckman Coulter, Inc. (NY)	9.28	10
152.	[1] Banta Corp. (NY)	9.19	23
153.	[1] Crawford & Co. (NY)	9.15	21
154.	[1] Heinz (H.J.) Co. (NY)	9.14	38
155.	[1] Bemis Co., Inc. (NY)	9.06	18
156.	[1] Walgreen Co. (NY)	9.049	26
157.	[1] Wilmington Trust Corp. (NY)	9.046	20
158.	[1] Marsh & McLennan Cos. Inc. (NY)	9.04	40
159.	[2] FirstMerit Corp. (NS)	8.77	19
160.	[1] Belo Corp. (NY)	8.72	14
161.	[1] Emerson Electric Co. (NY)	8.68	45
162.	[1] Pentair, Inc. (NY)	8.60	25
163.	[1] Grainger (W.W.) Inc. (NY)	8.58	30
164.	[1] Worthington Industries, Inc. (NY)	8.53	19
165.	[2] United Bankshares, Inc. (NS)	8.46	20
166.	[1] Lilly (Eli) & Co. (NY)	8.40	34
167.	[2] Weyco Group, Inc. (NS)	8.33	21
168.	[1] Lowe's Cos., Inc. (NY)	8.309	24
169.	[1] Household International Inc. (NY)	8.307	49
170.	Community Trust Bancorp (NS)	8.30	13
171.	[1] Bandag, Inc. (NY)	8.29	25
172.	[1] Clorox Co. (NY)	8.18	25
173.	[1] American Water Works Co. (NY)	8.13	26
174.	[1] Avon Products, Inc. (NY)	8.06	11
175.	RLI Corp. (NY)	7.97	25
176.	Stepan Co. (NY)	7.92	35
177.	[1] Cedar Fair, L.P. (NY)	7.83	14
178.	[2] Midland Co. (NS)	7.70	15
179.	[2] Fuller (H.B.) Co. (NS)	7.63	34
180.	[1] Air Products & Chemicals (NY)	7.60	19
181.	[1] GATX Corp. (NY)	7.53	16
182.	[2] Susquehanna Bancshares, Inc. (NS)	7.52	31
183.	WesBanco, Inc. (NS)	7.46	16
184.	National Security Group, Inc. (NS)	7.35	11
185.	[1] Diebold, Inc. (NY)	7.31	48
186.	[1] Sonoco Products Co. (NY)	7.22	18
187.	[1] Johnson Controls, Inc. (NY)	7.18	26
	[1] NiSource, Inc. (NY)	7.18	13
	[2] North Pittsburgh Systems, Inc. (NS)	7.18	39
190.	[1] Old National Bancorp (NY)	7.06	18
191.	[1] PPG Industries, Inc. (NY)	6.93	30
192.	[1] Hubbell, Inc. (NY)	6.84	41
193.	[1] Rohm & Haas Co. (NY)	6.83	24
194.	Health Care Prop. Investors (NY)	6.72	16
195.	[1] Aon Corp. (NY)	6.69	50
196.	[1] La-Z-Boy Inc. (NY)	6.60	20
197.	[1] ALLTEL Corp. (NY)	6.55	41
198.	[1] Donnelley (R.R.) & Sons Co. (NY)	6.52	32
199.	[1] Kellogg Co. (NY)	6.511	45
200.	Hilb, Rogal & Hamilton Co. (NY)	6.507	15
201.	[1] Chubb Corp. (NY)	6.49	37
202.	[1] RPM, Inc. (NY)	6.32	28
203.	[1] Masco Corp. (NY)	6.30	43
204.	[2] Mine Safety Appliances Co. (AM)	6.29	31

Rank	Company	10-Year Growth Rate %	No. of Yrs.	Rank	Company	10-Year Growth Rate %	No. of Yrs.
	[1] Pacific Century Financial (NY)	6.29	24	244.	[1] Stanley Works (NY)	4.42	34
	[2] United Fire & Casualty Co. (NS)	6.29	16	245.	[1] Minnesota Mining & Mfg. Co. (NY)	4.40	43
207.	[1] Bristol-Myers Squibb Co. (NY)	6.25	29	246.	[1] Kimberly-Clark Corp. (NY)	4.35	27
	[1] Target Corp. (NY)	6.25	30	247.	Semco Energy Inc. (NY)	4.23	23
209.	Bard (C.R.) Inc. (NY)	6.21	30	248.	[1] NACCO Industries, Inc. (NY)	4.22	18
210.	[1] VF Corp. (NY)	6.19	29	249.	[1] Vectren Corporation (NY)	4.01	26
211.	[1] PNC Financial Services Grp. (NY)	6.12	10	250.	[2] Wesco Financial Corp. (AM)	3.89	30
212.	[2] Telephone & Data Systems (AM)	6.05	27	251.	Florida Public Utilities Co. (AM)	3.86	33
213.	[1] Lincoln National Corp. (NY)	6.02	18	252.	[1] SBC Communications Inc. (NY)	3.79	17
214.	[1] Lee Enterprises, Inc. (NY)	5.99	41	253.	Atmos Energy Corp. (NY)	3.74	14
215.	[1] McGraw-Hill Cos., Inc. (NY)	5.95	28	254.	Gorman-Rupp Co. (AM)	3.71	29
216.	EnergySouth, Inc. (NS)	5.94	24	255.	[1] Gannett Co., Inc. (NY)	3.68	30
217.	[1] Genuine Parts Corp. (NY)	5.91	45	256.	Black Hills Corp. (NY)	3.65	21
218.	[1] Brown-Forman Corp. (NY)	5.86	17	257.	[1] Energen Corp. (NY)	3.59	19
219.	[2] Energy West Inc. (NS)	5.78	15	258.	MDU Resources Group Inc. (NY)	3.42	11
220.	[1] May Department Stores Co. (NY)	5.77	26	259.	[1] Questar Corp. (NY)	3.39	22
221.	[1] DQE, Inc. (NY)	5.76	12	260.	[1] Progress Energy, Inc. (NY)	3.38	13
222.	[1] Piedmont Natural Gas Co. (NY)	5.74	22	261.	[1] National Fuel Gas Co. (NY)	3.18	30
223.	[1] St. Paul Cos., Inc. (NY)	5.70	15	262.	[1] Exxon Mobil Corp. (NY)	3.00	19
224.	Frisch's Restaurants, Inc. (AM)	5.69	18	263.	SJW Corp. (AM)	2.96	35
225.	United Dominion Rlty. Trust (NY)	5.60	16	264.	Tennant Co. (NY)	2.92	29
226.	[1] Weis Markets, Inc. (NY)	5.37	27	265.	Health Care REIT, Inc. (NY)	2.83	12
227.	[1] Universal Corp. (NY)	5.35	31	266.	[1] CLECO Corp. (NY)	2.82	20
228.	Washington R.E.I.T. (NY)	5.233	40	267.	[2] Middlesex Water Co. (NS)	2.80	29
229.	[2] American National Insurance (NS)	5.229	28	268.	[1] UGI Corp. (NY)	2.67	14
230.	Haverty Furniture Cos., Inc. (NY)	5.17	31	269.	[2] Otter Tail Power Co. (NS)	2.66	26
231.	Weingarten Realty Investors (NY)	5.11	13	270.	Clarcor Inc. (NY)	2.56	21
232.	[1] ChevronTexaco Corp. (NY)	5.01	14	271.	Federal Realty Invest. Trust (NY)	2.41	34
233.	[1] TECO Energy Inc. (NY)	4.92	42	272.	[1] XCEL Energy, Inc. (NY)	2.39	26
234.	[1] Progressive Corp. (NY)	4.91	32	273.	[1] California Water Service Co. (NY)	2.17	34
235.	[1] SUPERVALU Inc. (NY)	4.87	29	274.	[1] WPS Resources Corp. (NY)	2.16	43
236.	[1] ServiceMaster Co. (NY)	4.81	31	275.	Universal Health Rlty. Inc. Tr. (NY)	1.99	14
237.	Quaker Chemical Corp. (NY)	4.660	30	276.	[1] WGL Holdings, Inc. (NY)	1.87	25
238.	[1] Northwestern Corp. (NY)	4.658	18	277.	[1] Peoples Energy Corp. (NY)	1.76	18
239.	Philadelphia Suburban Corp. (NY)	4.657	10	278.	Commercial Net Lease Realty (NY)	1.74	12
240.	[2] Bowl America Inc. (AM)	4.63	29	279.	[1] Consolidated Edison, Inc. (NY)	1.69	27
241.	[1] CenturyTel, Inc. (NY)	4.62	28	280.	American States Water Co. (NY)	1.68	48
242.	[1] NICOR Inc. (NY)	4.61	14	281.	[2] Madison Gas & Electric Co. (NS)	1.32	26
243.	[1] Briggs & Stratton Corp. (NY)	4.48	10	282.	[2] Connecticut Water Service (NS)	1.24	26

[1] Appears in Mergent's Handbook of Common Stocks [2] Appears in Mergent's Handbook of Nasdaq Stocks
(NY) New York Stock Exchange (NS) Nasdaq Stock Market (AM) American Stock Exchange

Longest Records of Dividend Achievement

These Dividend Achievers boast the longest records of consecutive annual dividend increases.

Rank	Company	No. of Yrs.
1.	Aon Corp.	50
2.	Household International Inc.	49
3.	American States Water Co.	48
	Diebold, Inc.	48
	Procter & Gamble Co.	48
6.	Dover Corp.	46
7.	Emerson Electric Co.	45
	Genuine Parts Corp.	45
	Kellogg Co.	45
10.	Masco Corp.	43
	Minnesota Mining & Mfg. Co.	43
	WPS Resources Corp.	43
13.	TECO Energy Inc.	42
14.	ALLTEL Corp.	41
	Cincinnati Financial Corp.	41
	Hubbell, Inc.	41
	Lee Enterprises, Inc.	41
18.	Marsh & McLennan Cos. Inc.	40
	Washington R.E.I.T.	40
20.	Coca-Cola Co. (The)	39
	Colgate-Palmolive Co.	39
	Illinois Tool Works, Inc.	39
	Johnson & Johnson	39
	North Pittsburgh Systems, Inc.	39
25.	Heinz (H.J.) Co.	38
	Tootsie Roll Industries, Inc.	38
27.	ABM Industries Inc.	37
	Chubb Corp.	37
29.	Philip Morris Cos., Inc	36
30.	Huntington Bancshares, Inc.	35
	SJW Corp.	35
	Stepan Co.	35
33.	California Water Service Co.	34
	Federal Realty Invest. Trust	34

Rank	Company	No. of Yrs.
	Fuller (H.B.) Co.	34
	Hormel Foods Corp.	34
	Jefferson-Pilot Corp.	34
	Lilly (Eli) & Co.	34
	Pfizer Inc.	34
	Stanley Works	34
41.	Commerce Bancshares, Inc	33
	Florida Public Utilities Co.	33
43.	Donnelley (R.R.) & Sons Co.	32
	Lancaster Colony Corp.	32
	Leggett & Platt, Inc.	32
	Pacific Capital Bancorp	32
	Progressive Corp.	32
48.	AmSouth Bancorporation	31
	Haverty Furniture Cos., Inc.	31
	Hillenbrand Industries, Inc.	31
	Mine Safety Appliances Co.	31
	ServiceMaster Co.	31
	SouthTrust Corp.	31
	Susquehanna Bancshares, Inc.	31
	Universal Corp.	31
56.	Albertson's, Inc.	30
	Bard (C.R.) Inc.	30
	BB&T Corp.	30
	Gannett Co., Inc.	30
	Grainger (W.W.) Inc.	30
	National Fuel Gas Co.	30
	PepsiCo, Inc.	30
	PPG Industries, Inc.	30
	Quaker Chemical Corp.	30
	Regions Financial Corp.	30
	Target Corp.	30
	Wesco Financial Corp.	30

INTERPUBLIC GROUP OF COMPANIES, INC.

YIELD 1.1%
P/E RATIO ...

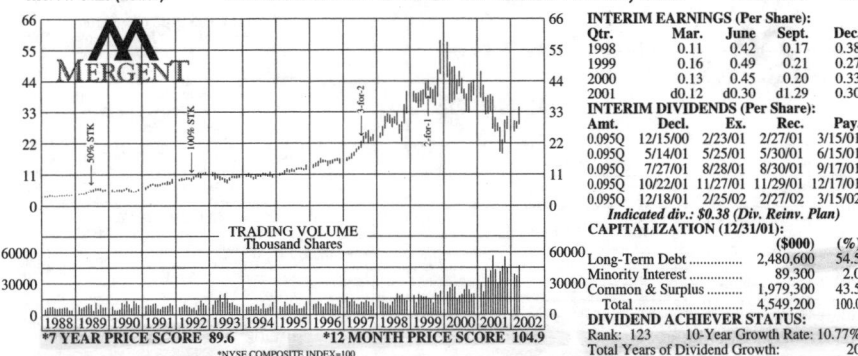

*7 YEAR PRICE SCORE 89.6   *12 MONTH PRICE SCORE 104.9
*NYSE COMPOSITE INDEX=100

INTERIM EARNINGS (Per Share):

Qtr.	Mar.	June	Sept.	Dec.
1998	0.11	0.42	0.17	0.38
1999	0.16	0.49	0.21	0.27
2000	0.13	0.45	0.20	0.33
2001	d0.12	d0.30	d1.29	0.30

INTERIM DIVIDENDS (Per Share):

Amt.	Decl.	Ex.	Rec.	Pay.
0.095Q	12/15/00	2/23/01	2/27/01	3/15/01
0.095Q	5/14/01	5/25/01	5/30/01	6/15/01
0.095Q	7/27/01	8/28/01	8/30/01	9/17/01
0.095Q	10/22/01	11/27/01	11/29/01	12/17/01
0.095Q	12/18/01	2/25/02	2/27/02	3/15/02

Indicated div.: $0.38 (Div. Reinv. Plan)

CAPITALIZATION (12/31/01):

	($000)	(%)
Long-Term Debt	2,480,600	54.5
Minority Interest	89,300	2.0
Common & Surplus	1,979,300	43.5
Total	4,549,200	100.0

DIVIDEND ACHIEVER STATUS:
Rank: 123   10-Year Growth Rate: 10.77%
Total Years of Dividend Growth: 20

RECENT DEVELOPMENTS: For the year ended 12/31/01, IPG incurred a net loss of $505.3 million versus net income of $420.3 million in the prior year. Earnings for 2001 and 2000 included costs of $303.1 million and $44.7 million related to asset impairments, and pre-tax restructuring costs of $645.6 million and $133.0 million, respectively. Total revenue decreased 6.3% to $6.73 billion. Comparisons were made with restated prior-year figures.

PROSPECTS: IPG has taken steps to improve its operating performance and to lower costs. The restructuring plan undertaken in the second half of 2001 has begun to yield cost savings, which are expected to exceed $250.0 million on an annualized basis. As of 12/31/01, IPG had reduced its staff by 7,900, or 12.7%, versus 2001. Going forward, IPG expects double-digit earnings per share growth in 2002, excluding nonrecurring items.

BUSINESS

INTERPUBLIC GROUP OF COMPANIES, INC. is a large organization of advertising agencies and marketing services companies. Its four global operating groups are McCann-Erickson WorldGroup, The Partnership, FCB Group and Advanced Marketing Services. Major global brands include Draft Worldwide, Deutsch, Foote, Cone & Belding Worldwide, Golin/Harris International, Initiative Media, Lowe & Partners Worldwide, McCann-Erickson, Octagon, Universal McCann, and Weber Shandwick. IPG also offers advertising agency services through association arrangements with local agencies in various parts of the world. Other activities conducted by the Company within the area of marketing communications include public relations, graphic design and market research. On 6/22/01, the Company acquired True North Communications, Inc.

ANNUAL FINANCIAL DATA

	12/31/01	12/31/00	12/31/99	12/31/98	12/31/97	12/31/96	12/31/95
Earnings Per Share	⑤ d1.37	③④ 1.15	③ 1.11	1.11	0.95	② 0.85	① 0.55
Cash Flow Per Share	d0.15	2.11	1.86	1.74	1.43	1.28	0.94
Tang. Book Val. Per Share	...	...	...	...	0.32	0.50	0.47
Dividends Per Share	0.38	0.37	0.33	0.29	0.25	0.22	0.20
Dividend Payout %	...	32.2	29.7	26.2	26.5	26.0	36.5

INCOME STATEMENT (IN MILLIONS):

Total Revenues	6,726.8	5,625.8	4,561.5	3,968.7	3,125.8	2,537.5	2,179.7
Costs & Expenses	6,483.7	4,653.6	3,694.1	3,168.0	2,504.3	2,036.2	1,796.4
Depreciation & Amort.	451.2	299.5	215.9	179.1	130.8	103.4	91.2
Operating Income	d208.1	672.7	651.5	621.6	490.7	397.9	292.2
Net Interest Inc./(Exp.)	d121.6	d109.1	d66.4	d58.7	d49.4	d40.8	d38.0
Income Before Income Taxes	d524.3	657.9	585.1	562.9	441.3	357.1	254.2
Income Taxes	cr43.9	273.0	236.3	232.0	184.9	150.0	122.7
Equity Earnings/Minority Int.	d24.9	d26.2	d26.8	d21.0	d17.2	d1.9	d1.6
Net Income	⑤ d505.3	③④ 358.7	③ 321.9	309.9	239.1	② 205.2	① 129.8
Cash Flow	d54.1	658.2	537.9	489.0	370.0	308.6	221.0
Average Shs. Outstg. (000)	369,000	312,653	289,548	281,050	259,088	240,879	234,540

BALANCE SHEET (IN MILLIONS):

Cash & Cash Equivalents	935.2	748.1	1,018.2	840.5	745.9	503.9	457.4
Total Current Assets	6,467.2	6,026.1	5,767.8	4,776.9	4,025.7	3,353.5	2,974.4
Net Property	850.3	660.4	534.3	439.6	348.8	307.0	279.3
Total Assets	11,514.7	10,238.2	8,727.3	6,942.8	5,702.5	4,765.1	4,259.8
Total Current Liabilities	6,433.9	6,106.1	5,636.9	4,658.4	3,751.6	3,199.0	2,826.7
Long-Term Obligations	2,480.6	1,505.1	867.3	506.6	452.7	347.0	283.5
Net Stockholders' Equity	1,979.3	2,046.4	1,628.1	1,265.1	1,107.2	872.0	749.7
Net Working Capital	33.3	d80.0	130.9	118.6	274.0	154.4	147.7
Year-end Shs. Outstg. (000)	378,500	314,672	287,658	279,070	261,638	243,396	238,884

STATISTICAL RECORD:

Operating Profit Margin %	...	12.0	14.3	15.7	15.7	15.7	13.4
Net Profit Margin %	...	6.4	7.1	7.8	7.7	8.1	6.0
Return on Equity %	...	17.5	19.8	24.5	21.6	23.5	17.3
Return on Assets %	...	3.5	3.7	4.5	4.2	4.3	3.0
Debt/Total Assets %	21.5	14.7	9.9	7.3	7.9	7.3	6.7
Price Range	47.44-18.25	57.69-32.69	58.38-34.41	40.31-22.56	26.50-15.67	16.75-13.21	14.46-10.58
P/E Ratio	...	50.2-28.4	52.6-31.0	36.5-20.4	27.9-16.5	19.6-15.5	26.1-19.1
Average Yield %	1.2	0.8	0.7	0.9	1.2	1.5	1.6

Statistics are as originally reported. Adj. for stk splits: 2-for-1, 7/99; 3-for-2, 7/97. ① Incl. aft.-tax chg. $38.2 mill. for write-down of assets. ② Incl. $8.1 mill. gain fr. sale of a portion of IPG's int. in CKS Group, Inc. ③ Incl. pre-tax restruct. & other merger-rel. chrgs. of $645.6 mill., 2001; $116.1 mill., 2000; $84.2 mill., 1999. ④ Incl. pre-tax non-recurr. costs of $44.7 mill. ⑤ Incl. restr. chrgs. of $645.6 mill. & non-recurr. costs of $303.1 mill.

QUARTERLY DATA

(12/31/2001)($000)	REV	INC
1st Quarter	1,658,200	(28,800)
2nd Quarter	1,743,400	(110,200)
3rd Quarter	1,605,700	(477,500)
4th Quarter	1,719,500	111,200

OFFICERS:
J. J. Dooner Jr., Chmn, Pres., C.E.O.
S. F. Orr, Exec. V.P., C.F.O.

INVESTOR CONTACT: Susan V. Watson, Sr. V.P.-Inv. Rel., (212) 399-8000

PRINCIPAL OFFICE: 1271 Avenue of the Americas, New York, NY 10020

TELEPHONE NUMBER: (212) 399-8000
FAX: (212) 399-8130
WEB: www.interpublic.com

NO. OF EMPLOYEES: 54,100 (approx.)

SHAREHOLDERS: 17,872

ANNUAL MEETING: In May

INCORPORATED: DE, Sept., 1930

INSTITUTIONAL HOLDINGS:
No. of Institutions: 463
Shares Held: 307,852,426
% Held: 81.5

INDUSTRY: Advertising agencies (SIC: 7311)

TRANSFER AGENT(S): EquiServe, Jersey City, NJ

IRWIN FINANCIAL CORP.

	YIELD	1.4%
	P/E RATIO	9.4

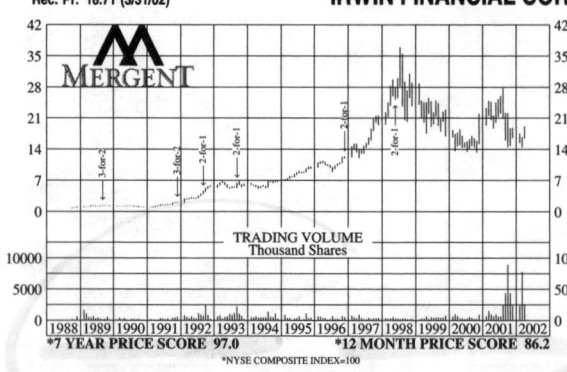

*7 YEAR PRICE SCORE 97.0 *NYSE COMPOSITE INDEX=100 ***12 MONTH PRICE SCORE 86.2**

INTERIM EARNINGS (Per Share):

Qtr.	Mar.	June	Sept.	Dec.
1998	0.31	0.32	0.46	0.29
1999	0.41	0.35	0.40	0.36
2000	0.40	0.41	0.43	0.46
2001	0.40	0.56	0.50	0.53

INTERIM DIVIDENDS (Per Share):

Amt.	Decl.	Ex.	Rec.	Pay.
0.065Q	4/26/01	6/06/01	6/08/01	6/22/01
0.065Q	8/30/01	9/05/01	9/07/01	9/21/01
0.065Q	10/19/01	12/05/01	12/07/01	12/21/01
0.068Q	2/27/02	3/06/02	3/08/02	3/22/02

Indicated div.: $0.27 (Div. Reinv. Plan)

CAPITALIZATION (12/31/01):

	($000)	(%)
Total Deposits	2,309,018	83.6
Long-Term Debt	29,654	1.1
Redeemable Pfd. Stock	190,948	6.9
Preferred Stock	1,386	0.1
Common & Surplus	230,937	8.4
Total	2,761,943	100.0

DIVIDEND ACHIEVER STATUS:
Rank: 24   10-Year Growth Rate: 20.58%
Total Years of Dividend Growth: 12

RECENT DEVELOPMENTS: For the year ended 12/31/01, income was $45.3 million, before an accounting change gain of $175,000, versus net income of $35.7 million the previous year. Net interest income rose 61.7% to $147.1 million. Provision for loan and lease losses climbed to $17.5 million from $5.4 million in 2000, reflecting general economic conditions, portfolio growth and increased charge-offs. Total other income grew 28.2% to $271.4 million. Total other expense rose 37.6% to $327.4 million.

PROSPECTS: Changes in IFC's securitization practices are expected to significantly affect the financial results of the Company's home equity line of business in 2002. However, after the initial transition period IFC expects to be in a position to resume profitable growth in this line of business. Accordingly, IFC expects consolidated net income to decline in 2002 and to increase significantly in 2003. IFC estimates that consolidated net income will be about $36.0 million in 2002 and about $54.0 million in 2003.

BUSINESS

IRWIN FINANCIAL CORP. is a diversified financial services company with $3.44 billion in assets at 12/31/01. IFC primarily focuses on the extension of credit to consumers and small businesses as well as providing the ongoing servicing of those customer accounts. The Company currently operates five major lines of business through its direct and indirect subsidiaries. IFC's major lines of business are: commercial banking, mortgage banking, home equity lending, equipment leasing and venture capital. Direct and indirect major subsidiaries include Irwin Union Bank and Trust, a commercial bank, which together with Irwin Union Bank, F.S.B., a federal savings bank, conducts the Company's commercial banking activities; Irwin Mortgage Corporation, a mortgage banking company; Irwin Home Equity Corporation, a consumer home equity lending company; Irwin Capital Holdings Corporation, an equipment leasing subsidiary; and Irwin Ventures LLC, a venture capital company.

ANNUAL FINANCIAL DATA

	12/31/01	12/31/00	12/31/99	12/31/98	12/31/97	12/31/96	12/31/95
Earnings Per Share	[2] 1.99	1.67	1.51	[1] 1.38	1.08	0.97	0.88
Tang. Book Val. Per Share	10.84	8.97	7.55	6.70	5.82	2.26	2.24
Dividends Per Share	0.26	0.24	0.20	0.16	0.14	0.12	0.11
Dividend Payout %	13.1	14.4	13.2	11.6	13.0	12.4	12.6
INCOME STATEMENT (IN MILLIONS)							
Total Interest Income	268.2	184.5	126.6	122.4	99.4	89.4	64.2
Total Interest Expense	121.1	93.5	54.8	59.2	44.6	41.6	28.6
Net Interest Income	147.1	91.0	71.8	63.2	54.9	47.8	35.6
Provision for Loan Losses	17.5	5.4	4.4	6.0	6.2	4.5	3.1
Non-Interest Income	271.4	211.7	204.1	243.7	174.6	153.6	115.8
Non-Interest Expense	327.4	238.0	214.1	245.4	176.5	159.7	115.9
Income Before Taxes	73.6	59.3	57.3	55.5	46.7	37.3	32.4
Equity Earnings/Minority Int.	0.4	...	...	...	...	...	...
Net Income	[2] 45.3	35.7	37.9	[1] 35.1	28.9	22.4	20.1
Average Shs. Outstg. (000)	24,173	21,593	21,886	22,139	22,722	23,219	22,973
BALANCE SHEET (IN MILLIONS)							
Cash & Cash Equivalents	158.3	83.5	47.2	68.9	56.5	71.4	49.3
Total Loans & Leases	2,195.5	1,266.4	733.9	558.2	626.3	540.1	423.5
Allowance for Credit Losses	80.0	44.6	9.0	11.1	24.0	17.6	15.6
Net Loans & Leases	2,115.5	1,221.8	724.9	547.1	602.3	522.5	407.9
Total Assets	3,439.8	2,422.4	1,680.8	1,946.2	1,496.8	1,303.9	1,038.3
Total Deposits	2,309.0	1,443.3	870.3	1,009.2	719.6	640.2	564.0
Long-Term Obligations	29.7	29.6	29.8	2.8	7.1	17.6	21.6
Total Liabilities	3,207.5	2,232.5	1,473.5	1,752.5	1,320.9	1,185.0	939.1
Net Stockholders' Equity	232.3	189.9	159.3	145.2	128.0	118.9	99.2
Year-end Shs. Outstg. (000)	21,305	21,026	21,105	21,673	22,001	22,738	22,660
STATISTICAL RECORD:							
Return on Equity %	19.5	18.8	23.8	24.2	22.6	18.9	20.2
Return on Assets %	1.3	1.5	2.3	1.8	1.9	1.7	1.9
Equity/Assets %	6.8	7.8	9.5	7.5	8.6	9.1	9.6
Non-Int. Exp./Tot. Inc. %	78.2	78.6	77.6	80.0	76.9	79.3	76.5
Price Range	27.70-14.49	22.00-13.25	28.88-16.88	37.00-19.50	21.56-12.00	12.38-8.94	10.13-6.88
P/E Ratio	13.9-7.3	13.2-7.9	19.1-11.2	26.8-14.1	20.1-11.2	12.8-9.3	11.6-7.9
Average Yield %	1.2	1.4	0.9	0.6	0.8	1.1	1.3

Statistics are as originally reported. Adj. for stk. splits: 2-for-1, 5/98 & 12/96. [1] Incl. gain from sale of leasing assets of $5.2 mill. [2] Bef. acctg. chge. gain of $175,000.

OFFICERS:	TELEPHONE NUMBER: (812) 376-1909	INSTITUTIONAL HOLDINGS:
W. I. Miller, Chmn.	FAX: (812) 376-1709	No. of Institutions: 79
J. A. Nash, Pres.	WEB: www.irwinfinancial.com	Shares Held: 8,307,640
G. F. Ehlinger, Sr. V.P., C.F.O.	NO. OF EMPLOYEES: 2,941 (avg.)	% Held: 39.0
INVESTOR CONTACT: Suzie Singer, Corp. Comm., (812) 376-1917	SHAREHOLDERS: 1,805 (approx.)	INDUSTRY: State commercial banks (SIC: 6022)
PRINCIPAL OFFICE: 500 Washington Street, Columbus, IN 47201	ANNUAL MEETING: In Apr. INCORPORATED: IN, May, 1972	TRANSFER AGENT(S): National City Bank, Cleveland, OH

JACK HENRY & ASSOCIATES, INC.

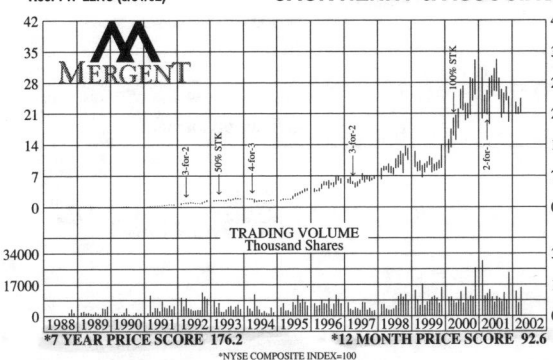

TRADING VOLUME
Thousand Shares

*7 YEAR PRICE SCORE 176.2   *12 MONTH PRICE SCORE 92.6
*NYSE COMPOSITE INDEX=100

INTERIM EARNINGS (Per Share):

Qtr.	Sept.	Dec.	Mar.	June
1997-98	0.06	0.07	0.07	0.10
1998-99	0.11	0.09	0.10	0.10
1999-00	0.11	0.10	0.12	0.13
2000-01	0.14	0.14	0.17	0.17
2001-02	0.16	0.14	...	...

INTERIM DIVIDENDS (Per Share):

Amt.	Decl.	Ex.	Rec.	Pay.
2-for-1	1/29/01	3/05/01	2/15/01	3/02/01
0.03Q	4/27/01	5/01/01	5/03/01	5/18/01
0.03Q	8/28/01	9/04/01	9/06/01	9/20/01
0.03Q	10/31/01	11/16/01	11/20/01	12/04/01
0.035Q	1/28/02	2/11/02	2/13/02	2/28/02

Indicated div.: $0.14 (Div. Reinv. Plan)

CAPITALIZATION (6/30/01):

	($000)	(%)
Long-Term Debt	228	0.1
Deferred Income Tax	7,857	2.5
Common & Surplus	302,504	97.4
Total	310,589	100.0

DIVIDEND ACHIEVER STATUS:
Rank: 27   10-Year Growth Rate: 19.62%
Total Years of Dividend Growth: 11

RECENT DEVELOPMENTS: For the quarter ended 12/31/01, net income climbed 1.2% to $13.0 million versus $12.9 million in the corresponding prior-year quarter. Total revenues rose 13.4% to $91.5 million from $80.7 million a year earlier. Support and services revenues jumped 29.8% to $41.9 million from $32.3 million in 2000. Software licensing and installation revenues declined 6.8% to $22.9 million from $24.5 million, while hardware sales increased 11.9% to $26.8 million from $23.9 million in the 2000 quarter. Gross profit increased 12.2% to $39.0 million, or 42.6% of total revenues, from $34.8 million, or 43.1% of total revenues, in the previous year. Operating income was unchanged at $19.8 million versus 2000. Backlog increased 19.2% to $132.1 million versus $110.8 million in the second quarter of 2000. Separately, on 1/3/02, JKHY completed the acquisition of Transcend Systems Group, Inc.

BUSINESS

JACK HENRY & ASSOCIATES, INC. is a provider of integrated computer systems that perform data processing for banks and credit unions. The Company's developed proprietary applications software for IBM AS/400 computers is offered under two systems: CIF 20/20™ typically for banks with less than $400.0 million in assets, and the Silverlake System®, for banks with assets up to $10.00 billion. JKHY has developed several banking applications software systems that it markets, along with computer hardware, to financial institutions in the United States and overseas. As of 1/16/02, JKHY had more than 2,800 banks and credit unions as customers. JKHY also performs data conversion, software installation and software customization for the implementation of its systems, and provides continuing customer maintenance/support services. Additionally, JKHY processes ATM and debit card transactions through its subsidiary, CommLink Corp., and provides Internet banking applications for financial institutions.

ANNUAL FINANCIAL DATA

	6/30/01	6/30/00	6/30/99	6/30/98	6/30/97	6/30/96	6/30/95
Earnings Per Share	0.61	Ⓘ 0.41	Ⓘ 0.39	Ⓘ 0.28	Ⓘ 0.21	Ⓘ 0.16	0.11
Cash Flow Per Share	0.85	0.58	0.48	0.35	0.26	0.21	0.14
Tang. Book Val. Per Share	2.20	0.48	1.07	0.73	0.49	0.27	0.14
Dividends Per Share	0.12	0.10	0.08	0.07	0.055	0.047	0.04
Dividend Payout %	19.7	24.7	20.8	23.0	26.2	29.4	34.8

INCOME STATEMENT (IN THOUSANDS):

Total Revenues	345,468	225,300	184,497	113,423	82,600	67,558	46,124
Costs & Expenses	237,840	158,817	127,233	74,542	54,288	44,790	32,244
Depreciation & Amort.	21,888	15,473	7,858	5,105	4,071	3,562	2,077
Operating Income	85,740	51,010	49,406	33,776	24,241	19,206	11,803
Net Interest Inc./(Exp.)	466	d1,047	1,571	1,221	660	541	746
Income Before Income Taxes	86,923	51,765	51,347	35,364	25,087	19,873	12,642
Income Taxes	31,292	17,415	18,821	13,127	9,332	7,605	4,664
Net Income	55,631	Ⓘ 34,350	Ⓘ 32,526	Ⓘ 22,237	Ⓘ 15,755	Ⓘ 12,268	7,978
Cash Flow	77,519	49,823	40,384	27,342	19,826	15,830	10,055
Average Shs. Outstg.	91,344	85,278	84,448	79,044	76,288	74,904	72,294

BALANCE SHEET (IN THOUSANDS):

Cash & Cash Equivalents	19,574	6,132	9,887	26,523	13,867	8,080	8,073
Total Current Assets	172,050	104,000	79,842	69,138	42,729	28,146	27,474
Net Property	138,439	93,285	65,595	26,855	21,869	13,612	10,302
Total Assets	433,121	321,082	174,721	115,286	82,069	60,401	58,721
Total Current Liabilities	107,018	151,140	57,666	39,260	27,239	21,251	28,140
Long-Term Obligations	228	320	...	...	...	...	...
Net Stockholders' Equity	302,504	154,545	114,469	73,500	52,782	37,418	29,484
Net Working Capital	65,032	d47,140	22,176	29,878	15,490	6,895	d666
Year-end Shs. Outstg.	88,847	82,716	80,400	75,740	74,068	71,208	70,392

STATISTICAL RECORD:

Operating Profit Margin %	24.8	22.6	26.8	29.8	29.3	28.4	25.6
Net Profit Margin %	16.1	15.2	17.6	19.6	19.1	18.2	17.3
Return on Equity %	18.4	22.2	28.4	30.3	29.8	32.8	27.1
Return on Assets %	12.8	10.7	18.6	19.3	19.2	20.3	13.6
Debt/Total Assets %	0.1	0.1	...	...	...	...	...
Price Range	33.24-18.56	33.13-12.06	14.13-6.61	13.75-6.19	7.56-4.38	6.96-3.40	4.25-1.46
P/E Ratio	54.5-30.4	81.8-29.8	36.7-16.9	48.7-21.9	36.5-21.1	42.7-20.8	38.6-13.2
Average Yield %	0.5	0.4	0.8	0.7	0.9	0.9	1.3

Statistics are as originally reported. Adj. for stk. splits: 2-for-1, 3/2/01; 100% div., 3/2/00; 3-for-2, 3/13/97. Ⓘ Bef. disc. oper. loss 6/30/00: $332,000; 6/30/99: $758,000; 6/30/98: $668,000; 6/30/97: $450,000; 6/30/96: $2.6 mill.

OFFICERS:
M. E. Henry, Chmn., C.E.O.
T. W. Thompson, Pres., C.O.O.
K. D. Williams, C.F.O., Treas.

INVESTOR CONTACT: K. D. Williams, C.F.O., Treas., (417) 235-6652

PRINCIPAL OFFICE: 663 Highway 60, P.O. Box 807, Monett, MO 65708

TELEPHONE NUMBER: (417) 235-6652
FAX: (417) 235-4281
WEB: www.jackhenry.com

NO. OF EMPLOYEES: 1,910

SHAREHOLDERS: 25,283

ANNUAL MEETING: In Oct.

INCORPORATED: MO, Aug., 1977; reincorp., DE, Nov., 1985

INSTITUTIONAL HOLDINGS:
No. of Institutions: 178
Shares Held: 49,384,778
% Held: 55.3

INDUSTRY: Computer integrated systems design (SIC: 7373)

TRANSFER AGENT(S): UMB Bank, N.A. Kansas City, MO

JEFFERSON-PILOT CORP. ✓

	YIELD	2.4%
	P/E RATIO	15.0

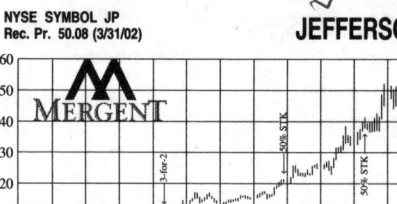
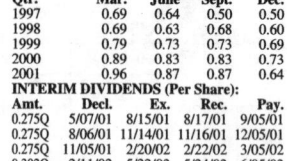

INTERIM EARNINGS (Per Share):

Qtr.	Mar.	June	Sept.	Dec.
1997	0.69	0.64	0.50	0.50
1998	0.69	0.63	0.68	0.60
1999	0.79	0.73	0.73	0.69
2000	0.89	0.83	0.83	0.73
2001	0.96	0.87	0.87	0.64

INTERIM DIVIDENDS (Per Share):

Amt.	Decl.	Ex.	Rec.	Pay.
0.275Q	5/07/01	8/15/01	8/17/01	9/05/01
0.275Q	8/06/01	11/14/01	11/16/01	12/05/01
0.275Q	11/05/01	2/20/02	2/22/02	3/05/02
0.302Q	2/11/02	5/22/02	5/24/02	6/05/02

Indicated div.: $1.21 (Div. Reinv. Plan)

CAPITALIZATION (12/31/01):

	($000)	(%)
Long-Term Debt	150,000	3.9
Deferred Income Tax	291,000	7.6
Common & Surplus	3,391,000	88.5
Total	3,832,000	100.0

DIVIDEND ACHIEVER STATUS:

Rank: 92   10-Year Growth Rate: 12.71%
Total Years of Dividend Growth: 34

TRADING VOLUME
Thousand Shares

*7 YEAR PRICE SCORE 111.1   *12 MONTH PRICE SCORE 109.2
*NYSE COMPOSITE INDEX=100

RECENT DEVELOPMENTS: For the year ended 12/31/01, net income rose slightly to $537.4 million, before an accounting gain of $1.0 million, from $536.6 million in the previous year. Total revenue grew 2.8% to $3.33 billion versus $3.24 billion in 2000. Revenue for 2001 and 2000 included realized investment gains of $65.5 million and $102.1 million, respectively. Premiums and other considerations revenue improved 7.1% to $770.0 million, while net investment income increased 6.4% to $1.54 billion.

PROSPECTS: Earnings are being negatively affected by lower profitability at JP's broker-dealer due to a relatively poor environment for investment product sales, modest and expected investment-spread compression in fixed annuities and reduced surrender-charge income. However, this decline is being partially offset by strong fixed annuity sales. Looking ahead, JP will continue to focus on its Premier Partnering strategy, which builds life insurance sales via new products and increased field sales support.

BUSINESS

JEFFERSON-PILOT CORP. is a holding company that conducts insurance, investment, broadcasting and other business through its subsidiaries. Jefferson-Pilot Life Insurance Company offers both group and individual life insurance, health insurance, annuity and pension products. Other subsidiaries provide fire and casualty insurance, title insurance and mutual fund sales and management services. Jefferson-Pilot Communications Company provides information and entertainment services through three network television and 17 radio stations, and produces and syndicates sports programming. On 12/30/99, JP acquired The Guarantee Life Companies Inc. Contributions to revenues in 2001 were as follows: premiums & other, 42.7%; net investment income, 46.1%; realized investment gains, 2.0%; communications sales, 5.9%; and broker-dealer concessions and other, 3.3%.

ANNUAL FINANCIAL DATA

	12/31/01	12/31/00	12/31/99	12/31/98	12/31/97	12/31/96	12/31/95
Earnings Per Share	③ 3.34	3.29	2.95	2.61	2.31	1.82	① 1.58
Tang. Book Val. Per Share	20.53	18.38	15.80	17.77	15.73	13.89	13.02
Dividends Per Share	1.07	0.96	0.86	0.77	0.69	0.62	0.55
Dividend Payout %	32.1	29.2	29.1	29.4	30.0	34.2	35.1
INCOME STATEMENT (IN MILLIONS):							
Total Premium Income	1,424.0	1,365.0	903.0	1,049.0	1,135.0	994.0	810.0
Net Investment Income	1,533.0	1,430.0	1,272.0	1,202.0	1,103.0	893.0	540.8
Other Income	373.0	443.0	386.0	359.0	340.0	238.0	218.6
Total Revenues	3,330.0	3,238.0	2,561.0	2,610.0	2,578.0	2,125.0	1,569.4
Policyholder Benefits	1,796.0	1,660.0	1,208.0	1,307.0	1,399.0	1,211.0	842.3
Income Before Income Taxes	800.0	814.0	751.0	670.0	591.0	443.0	380.8
Income Taxes	263.0	277.0	256.0	226.0	195.0	149.0	125.4
Net Income	② 537.0	537.0	495.0	446.0	396.0	294.0	① 255.3
Average Shs. Outstg. (000)	153,411	155,922	159,348	160,578	160,189	159,917	161,312
BALANCE SHEET (IN MILLIONS):							
Cash & Cash Equivalents	139.0	26.0	62.0	21.0	9.0	105.0	122.5
Premiums Due	1,433.0	1,450.0	1,576.0	1,342.0	1,526.0	1,260.0	1,583.7
Invst. Assets: Fixed-term	17,467.0	16,108.0	15,182.0	14,503.0	13,945.0	10,550.0	9,985.6
Invst. Assets: Equities	511.0	551.0	737.0	949.0	893.0	929.0	862.8
Invst. Assets: Loans	4,005.0	3,694.0	3,449.0	3,408.0	3,138.0	2,535.0	2,201.4
Invst. Assets: Total	22,135.0	20,499.0	19,536.0	18,978.0	18,094.0	14,143.0	13,168.1
Total Assets	28,996.0	27,321.0	26,446.0	24,338.0	23,131.0	17,562.0	16,478.0
Long-Term Obligations	150.0	139.0	290.0	327.0	331.0	148.0	137.1
Net Stockholders' Equity	3,391.0	3,159.0	2,753.0	3,052.0	2,732.0	2,297.0	2,156.1
Year-end Shs. Outstg. (000)	150,007	154,306	155,016	158,844	159,417	159,179	160,229
STATISTICAL RECORD:							
Return on Revenues %	16.1	16.6	19.3	17.0	15.4	13.8	16.3
Return on Equity %	15.8	17.0	18.0	14.5	14.5	12.8	11.8
Return on Assets %	1.9	2.0	1.9	1.8	1.7	1.7	1.5
Price Range	49.67-38.00	50.59-33.25	53.09-40.79	52.25-32.45	38.56-22.89	26.50-20.06	21.45-14.96
P/E Ratio	14.9-11.4	15.4-10.1	18.0-13.8	20.0-12.4	16.7-9.9	14.6-11.0	13.6-9.5
Average Yield %	2.4	2.3	1.8	1.8	2.3	2.7	3.0

Statistics are as originally reported. Adj. for stk. splits: 3-for-2, 4/01; 4/98; 12/95 ① Bef. disc. oper gain $18.5 mill. ② Bef. acctg. gain $1.0 mill.

JOHNSON & JOHNSON

YIELD	1.1%
P/E RATIO	34.9

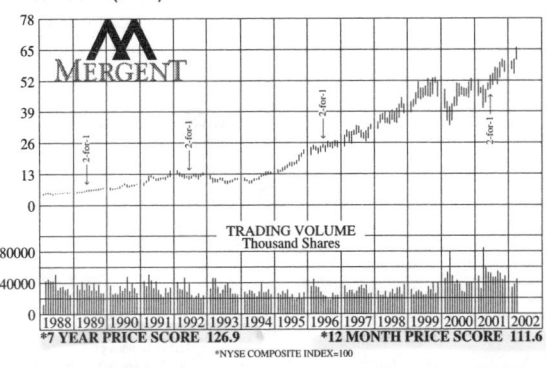

INTERIM EARNINGS (Per Share):

Qtr.	Mar.	June	Sept.	Dec.
1997	0.34	0.34	0.32	0.24
1998	0.37	0.37	0.35	0.25
1999	0.41	0.42	0.40	0.27
2000	0.47	0.47	0.45	0.32
2001	0.53	0.48	0.49	0.36

INTERIM DIVIDENDS (Per Share):

Amt.	Decl.	Ex.	Rec.	Pay.
0.36Q	4/26/01	5/18/01	5/22/01	6/12/01
2-for-1	4/26/01	6/13/01	5/22/01	6/12/01
0.18Q	7/16/01	8/17/01	8/21/01	9/11/01
0.18Q	10/18/01	11/16/01	11/20/01	12/11/01
0.18Q	1/02/02	2/14/02	2/19/02	3/12/02

Indicated div.: $0.72 (Div. Reinv. Plan)

CAPITALIZATION (12/30/01):

	($000)	(%)
Long-Term Debt	2,217,000	8.2
Deferred Income Tax	493,000	1.8
Common & Surplus	24,233,000	89.9
Total	26,943,000	100.0

DIVIDEND ACHIEVER STATUS:

Rank: 75   10-Year Growth Rate: 13.78%
Total Years of Dividend Growth: 39

*7 YEAR PRICE SCORE 126.9   *12 MONTH PRICE SCORE 111.6

*NYSE COMPOSITE INDEX=100

RECENT DEVELOPMENTS: For the year ended 12/31/01, net earnings improved 14.4% to $5.67 billion versus $4.95 billion in 2000. Results for 2001 and 2000 included pre-tax in-process research and development charges of $105.0 million and $66.0 million, respectively. Sales increased 10.6% to $33.00 billion. Pharmaceutical segment sales advanced 17.3% to $14.85 billion. Comparisons were made with restated prior-year figures.

PROSPECTS: On 3/22/02, the Company announced that it signed a definitive agreement to acquire all of the assets of Tibotec-Virco NV, a privately-held biopharmaceutical company for about $320.0 million in cash and debt. Meanwhile, the Company should continue to benefit from strong results in its Pharmaceutical and Medical Device and Diagnostics businesses.

BUSINESS

JOHNSON & JOHNSON is engaged in the manufacture and sale of a broad range of products in the health care field. The pharmaceutical segment, 45.0% of 2001 sales, consists of prescription drugs in the antifungal, anti-infective, cardiovascular, dermatology, gastrointestinal, hematology, immunology, neurology, oncology, pain management, psychotropic and women's health fields. Major pharmaceutical products include NIZORAL, SPORANOX, TERAZOL, DAKTARIN, FLOXIN, LEVAQUIN, RETAVASE, REOPRO, RETIN-A MICRO, ACIPHEX, IMODIUM, MOTILIUM®, REMICADE, PROCRIT, ORTHOCLONE OKT-3, REMINYL, TOPAMAX, STUGERON, DOXIL®, ERGAMISOL, LEUSTATIN, DURAGESIC, ULTRAM, RISPERDAL, HALDOL, ORTHO-NOVUM and TRICILEST. The consumer segment, 21.1% of 2001 sales, consists of personal care and hygienic products. Major consumer brands include BAND-AID, BENECOL, CAREFREE, CLEAN & CLEAR, IMODIUM A-D, LACTAID, MONISTAT, MOTRIN IB, MYLANTA, NEUTROGENA, STAYFREE and TYLENOL. The Medical Devices and Diagnostics segment, 33.9% of 2001 sales, includes a broad range of products used by or under the direction of health care professionals. JNJ acquired ALZA Corp. on 6/22/01.

ANNUAL FINANCIAL DATA

	12/30/01	12/31/00	1/2/00	1/3/99	12/28/97	12/29/96	12/31/95
Earnings Per Share	④ 1.84	③ 1.70	② 1.47	① 1.12	1.21	1.09	0.93
Cash Flow Per Share	2.35	2.23	1.98	1.57	1.60	1.68	1.26
Tang. Book Val. Per Share	4.97	4.15	3.11	2.37	3.38	2.90	2.36
Dividends Per Share	0.70	0.62	0.55	0.48	0.42	0.37	0.32
Dividend Payout %	38.0	36.5	37.1	43.5	35.3	33.9	34.4

INCOME STATEMENT (IN MILLIONS):

Total Revenues	33,004.0	29,464.0	27,717.0	23,493.0	22,629.0	21,620.0	18,842.0
Costs & Expenses	23,514.0	21,114.0	20,101.0	17,979.0	16,940.0	16,308.0	14,474.0
Depreciation & Amort.	1,605.0	1,515.0	1,444.0	1,246.0	1,067.0	1,009.0	857.0
Operating Income	8,236.0	6,835.0	6,172.0	4,268.0	4,622.0	4,303.0	3,511.0
Net Interest Inc./(Exp.)	d153.0	d146.0	d197.0	152.0	83.0	14.0	d28.0
Income Before Income Taxes	7,898.0	6,622.0	5,753.0	4,269.0	4,576.0	4,033.0	3,317.0
Income Taxes	2,230.0	1,822.0	1,586.0	1,210.0	1,273.0	569.0	914.0
Net Income	④ 5,668.0	③ 4,800.0	② 4,167.0	① 3,059.0	3,303.0	3,464.0	2,403.0
Cash Flow	7,273.0	6,315.0	5,611.0	4,305.0	4,370.0	4,473.0	3,260.0
Average Shs. Outstg. (000)	3,099,300	2,834,800	2,836,400	2,743,200	2,739,800	2,666,000	2,584,000

BALANCE SHEET (IN MILLIONS):

Cash & Cash Equivalents	7,972.0	5,744.0	3,879.0	2,578.0	2,899.0	2,136.0	1,364.0
Total Current Assets	18,473.0	15,450.0	13,200.0	11,132.0	10,563.0	9,370.0	7,938.0
Net Property	7,719.0	6,971.0	6,719.0	6,240.0	5,810.0	5,651.0	5,196.0
Total Assets	38,488.0	31,321.0	29,163.0	26,211.0	21,453.0	20,010.0	17,873.0
Total Current Liabilities	8,044.0	7,140.0	7,454.0	8,162.0	5,283.0	5,184.0	4,388.0
Long-Term Obligations	2,217.0	2,037.0	2,450.0	1,269.0	1,126.0	1,410.0	2,107.0
Net Stockholders' Equity	24,233.0	18,808.0	16,213.0	13,590.0	12,359.0	10,836.0	9,045.0
Net Working Capital	10,429.0	8,310.0	5,746.0	2,970.0	5,280.0	4,186.0	3,550.0
Year-end Shs. Outstg. (000)	3,047,215	2,781,874	2,779,366	2,688,000	2,690,000	2,664,000	2,588,000

STATISTICAL RECORD:

Operating Profit Margin %	25.0	23.2	22.3	18.2	20.4	19.9	18.6
Net Profit Margin %	17.2	16.3	15.0	13.0	14.6	16.0	12.8
Return on Equity %	23.4	25.5	25.7	22.5	26.7	32.0	26.6
Return on Assets %	14.7	15.3	14.3	11.7	15.4	17.3	13.4
Debt/Total Assets %	5.8	6.5	8.4	4.8	5.2	7.0	11.8
Price Range	60.97-40.25	52.97-33.06	53.44-38.50	44.88-31.69	33.66-24.31	27.00-20.78	23.09-13.41
P/E Ratio	33.1-21.9	31.2-19.4	36.3-26.2	40.2-28.4	27.9-20.2	24.9-19.2	24.8-14.4
Average Yield %	1.4	1.4	1.2	1.3	1.5	1.5	1.8

Statistics are as originally reported. Adjusted for 2-for-1 stock split, 6/96 & 6/01. ① Incl. a pre-tax in-process R&D chrg. of $164.0 mill. & a pre-tax restruct. chrg. of $613.0 mill. ② Incl. nonrecurr. after-tax chrg. of $42.0 mill. ③ Incl. pre-tax chrg. of $54.0 mill. for in-proc. res. & devel. ④ Incl. pre-tax chrg. of $105.0 mill. for in-proc. res. & devel.

OFFICERS:
R. S. Larsen, Chmn., C.E.O.
R. N. Wilson, Sr. Vice-Chmn.
W. C. Weldon, Vice-Chmn.
J. T. Lenehan, Vice-Chmn.

INVESTOR CONTACT: Helen E. Short, Vice President, (800) 950-5089

PRINCIPAL OFFICE: One Johnson & Johnson Plaza, New Brunswick, NJ 08933

TELEPHONE NUMBER: (732) 524-0400
FAX: (732) 214-0332
WEB: www.jnj.com

NO. OF EMPLOYEES: 101,800 (approx.)

SHAREHOLDERS: 164,158

ANNUAL MEETING: In Apr.

INCORPORATED: NJ, Nov., 1887

INSTITUTIONAL HOLDINGS:
No. of Institutions: 1,322
Shares Held: 1,890,150,149
% Held: 62.0

INDUSTRY: Pharmaceutical preparations
(SIC: 2834)

TRANSFER AGENT(S): First Chicago Trust Company, c/o EquiServe, Jersey City, NJ

JOHNSON CONTROLS, INC.

YIELD 1.5%
P/E RATIO 16.7

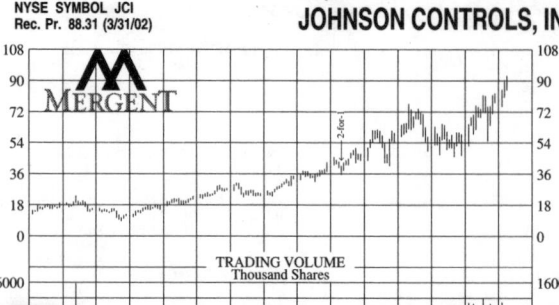

INTERIM EARNINGS (Per Share):

Qtr.	Dec.	Mar.	June	Sept.
1997-98	0.70	0.56	0.90	1.47
1998-99	0.86	1.05	1.19	1.38
1999-00	1.06	0.95	1.45	1.63
2000-01	1.10	0.89	1.45	1.67
2001-02	1.27	...	...	...

INTERIM DIVIDENDS (Per Share):

Amt.	Decl.	Ex.	Rec.	Pay.
0.31Q	1/24/01	3/07/01	3/09/01	3/30/01
0.31Q	5/17/01	6/13/01	6/15/01	6/29/01
0.31Q	7/25/01	9/17/01	9/14/01	9/28/01
0.33Q	11/14/01	12/12/01	12/14/01	1/02/02
0.33Q	1/23/02	3/06/02	3/08/02	3/29/02

Indicated div.: $1.32 (Div. Reinv. Plan)

CAPITALIZATION (9/30/01):

	($000)	(%)
Long-Term Debt	1,394,800	30.4
Minority Interest	207,300	4.5
Preferred Stock	123,200	2.7
Common & Surplus	2,862,200	62.4
Total	4,587,500	100.0

DIVIDEND ACHIEVER STATUS:

Rank: 187   10-Year Growth Rate: 7.18%
Total Years of Dividend Growth: 26

TRADING VOLUME
Thousand Shares

*7 YEAR PRICE SCORE 124.3   *12 MONTH PRICE SCORE 118.4
*NYSE COMPOSITE INDEX=100

RECENT DEVELOPMENTS: For the quarter ended 12/31/01, net income rose 17.0% to $119.9 million compared with $102.5 million in the same period of 2000. Net sales were $4.82 billion, up 8.2% from $4.45 billion in the prior-year period. Sales in the Automotive Systems Group grew 7.9% to $3.66 billion from $3.39 billion, while sales in the Controls Group rose 8.9% to $1.16 billion from $1.07 billion a year earlier.

PROSPECTS: On 1/24/02, the Company announced plans to acquire the remaining 45.0% interest that it does not already own in Yokogawa Johnson Controls Corporation, a building controls business in Japan. Yokogawa, which is expected to become a fully-owned subsidiary of the Company, plans to sell all of its shares to JCI. The transaction is expected to be slightly accretive to the Company's earnings in 2002.

BUSINESS

JOHNSON CONTROLS, INC. operates in two business segments. The Automotive segment is engaged in the design and manufacture of complete seat systems, seating components and interior trim systems for North American and European manufacturers of cars, vans and light trucks. The Controls segment is a worldwide supplier of control systems, services and products providing energy management, temperature and ventilation control, security and fire safety for non-residential buildings. Revenues (and operating income) for fiscal 2001 were derived: Automotive Systems Group, 73.9% (75.0%); and Controls Group, 26.1% (25.0%). On 7/1/98, JCI acquired Becker Group, Inc., a supplier of automotive interior systems, which include door systems and instrument panels.

ANNUAL FINANCIAL DATA

	9/30/01	9/30/00	9/30/99	9/30/98	9/30/97	9/30/96	9/30/95
Earnings Per Share	5.11	5.09	④4.48	③3.63	②2.48	①2.55	2.27
Cash Flow Per Share	10.60	10.06	9.25	7.78	6.67	6.49	5.76
Tang. Book Val. Per Share	3.41	3.65	0.45	...	...	9.70	8.04
Dividends Per Share	1.24	1.12	1.00	0.92	0.86	0.82	0.78
Dividend Payout %	24.3	22.0	22.3	25.3	34.7	32.2	34.4
INCOME STATEMENT (IN MILLIONS):							
Total Revenues	18,427.2	17,154.6	16,139.4	12,586.8	11,145.4	9,210.0	8,330.3
Costs & Expenses	16,950.2	15,727.8	14,838.9	11,538.6	10,263.4	8,401.4	7,593.0
Depreciation & Amort.	515.9	461.8	445.6	384.2	354.9	329.7	288.5
Operating Income	961.1	965.0	854.9	664.0	527.1	478.9	448.8
Net Interest Inc./(Exp.)	d110.0	d111.5	d136.0	d118.7	d112.8	d65.5	d4.8
Income Before Income Taxes	835.3	855.7	769.9	616.8	425.6	421.5	387.9
Income Taxes	335.5	338.9	311.7	256.0	180.9	171.8	162.9
Equity Earnings/Minority Int.	d53.3	d44.4	d38.6	d23.1	d24.1	d27.0	d29.2
Net Income	478.3	472.4	④419.6	③337.7	②220.6	①222.7	195.8
Cash Flow	985.4	924.4	852.2	712.4	565.9	542.9	474.9
Average Shs. Outstg. (000)	93,000	91,900	92,100	91,600	84,800	83,600	82,400
BALANCE SHEET (IN MILLIONS):							
Cash & Cash Equivalents	374.6	275.6	276.2	134.0	111.8	165.2	103.8
Total Current Assets	4,544.0	4,277.2	3,848.5	3,404.2	2,529.3	2,849.1	2,063.9
Net Property	2,379.8	2,305.0	1,996.0	1,882.9	1,533.0	1,320.2	1,518.8
Total Assets	9,911.5	9,428.0	8,614.2	7,942.1	6,048.6	4,991.2	4,320.9
Total Current Liabilities	4,579.7	4,510.0	4,266.6	4,288.4	2,972.7	2,182.6	1,909.5
Long-Term Obligations	1,394.8	1,315.3	1,283.3	997.5	706.4	752.2	630.0
Net Stockholders' Equity	2,985.4	2,576.1	2,270.0	1,941.4	1,687.9	1,507.8	1,340.2
Net Working Capital	d35.7	d232.8	d418.1	d884.2	d443.4	666.5	154.4
Year-end Shs. Outstg. (000)	87,499	85,989	85,395	84,700	84,100	83,000	82,200
STATISTICAL RECORD:							
Operating Profit Margin %	5.2	5.6	5.3	5.3	4.7	5.2	5.4
Net Profit Margin %	2.6	2.8	2.6	2.7	2.0	2.4	2.4
Return on Equity %	16.0	18.3	18.5	17.4	13.1	14.8	14.6
Return on Assets %	4.8	5.0	4.9	4.3	3.6	4.5	4.5
Debt/Total Assets %	14.1	14.0	14.9	12.6	11.7	15.1	14.6
Price Range	82.70-51.94	65.13-45.81	76.69-49.00	61.88-40.50	51.00-35.38	42.69-31.25	34.88-22.88
P/E Ratio	16.2-10.2	12.8-9.0	17.1-10.9	17.0-11.2	20.6-14.3	16.7-12.3	15.4-10.1
Average Yield %	1.8	2.0	1.6	1.8	2.0	2.2	2.7

Statistics are as originally reported. Adj. for 100% stk. div., 3/97. ① Bef. $12.0 mill. chg. fr. disc. ops. ② Bef. $67.9 mill. disc. ops. ③ Incl. $35.0 mill. after-tax gain fr. sale of bus. ④ Incl. $32.5 mill. net one-time gain on sale of bus.

OFFICERS:
J. H. Keyes, Chmn., C.E.O.
J. M. Barth, Pres., C.O.O.
S. A. Roell, Sr. V.P., C.F.O.

INVESTOR CONTACT: Arlene Gumm, Investor Relations, (414) 228-1200

PRINCIPAL OFFICE: 5757 North Green Bay Avenue, Milwaukee, WI 53201

TELEPHONE NUMBER: (414) 524-1200
FAX: (414) 524-2070
WEB: www.johnsoncontrols.com
NO. OF EMPLOYEES: 112,000 (approx.)
SHAREHOLDERS: 59,311 (record)
ANNUAL MEETING: In Jan.
INCORPORATED: WI, July, 1900

INSTITUTIONAL HOLDINGS:
No. of Institutions: 374
Shares Held: 57,424,023
% Held: 65.5

INDUSTRY: Public building & related furniture (SIC: 2531)

TRANSFER AGENT(S): Firstar Trust Company, Milwaukee, WI

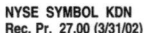

NYSE SYMBOL KDN
Rec. Pr. 27.00 (3/31/02)

KAYDON CORPORATION

YIELD 1.8%
P/E RATIO ...

TRADING VOLUME
Thousand Shares

*7 YEAR PRICE SCORE 80.2 ***12 MONTH PRICE SCORE 111.1**
*NYSE COMPOSITE INDEX=100

INTERIM EARNINGS (Per Share):

Qtr.	Mar.	June	Sept.	Dec.
1998	0.55	0.57	0.54	0.51
1999	0.50	0.50	0.41	0.44
2000	0.44	0.19	0.24	0.45
2001	0.35	0.22	d0.81	0.12

INTERIM DIVIDENDS (Per Share):

Amt.	Decl.	Ex.	Rec.	Pay.
0.12Q	2/15/01	3/08/01	3/12/01	4/02/01
0.12Q	5/03/01	6/07/01	6/11/01	7/02/01
0.12Q	8/20/01	9/06/01	9/10/01	10/01/01
0.12Q	11/15/01	12/06/01	12/10/01	1/02/02
0.12Q	2/19/02	3/07/02	3/11/02	4/01/02

Indicated div.: $0.48

CAPITALIZATION (12/31/01):

	($000)	(%)
Long-Term Debt	112,194	27.0
Common & Surplus	303,804	73.0
Total	415,998	100.0

DIVIDEND ACHIEVER STATUS:
Rank: 70   10-Year Growth Rate: 14.40%
Total Years of Dividend Growth: 14

RECENT DEVELOPMENTS: For the year ended 12/31/01, income fell 29.2% to $28.5 million, before a loss of $32.5 million from discontinued operations, versus income of $40.2 million, a net gain of $892,000 from discontinued operations, in 2000. Results for 2001 included a special charge of $38.1 million and a net gain of $200,000. Results for 2000 included unusual litigation-related charges of $21.7 million. Net sales increased 2.5% to $285.6 million from $278.8 million a year earlier.

PROSPECTS: Effective 12/31/01, the Company sold the assets of the Fluid Power Products Group for approximately $16.0 million in cash to a private ownership group. Looking ahead, the Company expects to continue to experience weakness in the semiconductor manufacturing equipment, construction equipment, and other heavy industrial equipment markets for the next five to six months. In an effort to improve results, the Company will continue to focus on improving operating performance.

BUSINESS

KAYDON CORPORATION designs, manufactures and sells custom-engineered products for a broad and diverse customer base primarily in the domestic industrial, aerospace, medical, and electronic equipment markets. The Company's principal products include antifriction bearings, bearing systems and components, filters and filter housings, specialty retraining rings, specialty balls, custom rings, shaft seals, metal castings and various types of slip-rings. These products are used by customers in a wide variety of medical, instrumentation, material handling, machine tool positioning, aerospace, defense, construction and other industrial applications. On 12/31/01, the Company sold the assets of its Fluid Power Products Group.

ANNUAL FINANCIAL DATA

	12/31/01	12/31/00	12/31/99	12/31/98	12/31/97	12/31/96	12/31/95
Earnings Per Share	② 0.95	① 1.30	1.85	2.17	1.86	1.53	1.14
Cash Flow Per Share	1.46	1.88	2.34	2.59	2.24	1.88	1.47
Tang. Book Val. Per Share	5.98	7.22	7.78	7.68	6.57	5.42	3.91
Dividends Per Share	0.48	0.44	0.40	0.36	0.28	0.24	0.22
Dividend Payout %	50.5	33.8	21.6	16.6	15.1	15.7	19.3
INCOME STATEMENT (IN THOUSANDS):							
Total Revenues	285,603	339,246	325,696	376,172	329,036	290,670	229,924
Costs & Expenses	224,676	264,833	220,894	251,748	220,599	199,967	159,462
Depreciation & Amort.	15,430	17,367	15,634	14,044	12,756	11,749	11,176
Operating Income	45,497	57,046	89,168	110,380	95,681	78,954	59,286
Net Interest Inc./(Exp.)	d292	5,072	4,877	4,434	3,780	2,662	2,505
Income Before Income Taxes	45,205	62,118	94,045	114,814	99,461	81,616	61,791
Income Taxes	16,725	22,771	35,266	43,630	37,795	31,095	23,588
Net Income	② 28,480	① 39,347	58,779	71,184	61,666	50,521	38,203
Cash Flow	43,910	56,714	74,413	85,228	74,422	62,270	49,379
Average Shs. Outstg.	29,982	30,166	31,775	32,871	33,163	33,098	33,482
BALANCE SHEET (IN THOUSANDS):							
Cash & Cash Equivalents	152,570	114,965	89,749	96,802	96,802	83,267	47,159
Total Current Assets	261,774	241,185	211,553	229,800	214,778	186,056	135,454
Net Property	84,273	105,304	98,844	99,259	85,510	76,176	72,345
Total Assets	497,798	475,552	406,749	413,808	383,985	331,538	267,675
Total Current Liabilities	31,645	59,999	54,183	71,200	71,015	66,824	44,047
Long-Term Obligations	112,194	47,518	...	...	...	4,000	18,059
Net Stockholders' Equity	303,804	322,435	316,950	311,656	283,596	232,056	187,905
Net Working Capital	230,129	181,186	157,370	158,600	143,763	119,232	91,407
Year-end Shs. Outstg.	30,428	30,355	31,097	32,150	32,992	32,934	35,266
STATISTICAL RECORD:							
Operating Profit Margin %	15.9	16.8	27.4	29.3	29.1	27.2	25.8
Net Profit Margin %	10.0	11.6	18.0	18.9	18.7	17.4	16.6
Return on Equity %	9.4	12.2	18.5	22.8	21.7	21.8	20.3
Return on Assets %	5.7	8.3	14.5	17.2	16.1	15.2	14.3
Debt/Total Assets %	22.5	10.0	...	...	...	1.2	3.0
Price Range	28.25-17.80	29.31-19.94	41.06-23.00	45.94-22.81	34.94-20.88	24.75-14.44	15.81-11.38
P/E Ratio	29.7-18.7	22.5-15.3	22.2-12.4	21.2-10.5	18.8-11.2	16.2-9.5	13.9-10.0
Average Yield %	2.1	1.8	1.2	1.0	1.2	1.2	1.6

Statistics are as originally reported. Adj. for stk. split: 2-for-1, 10/97. ① Incl. nonrecurr. pre-tax chrg. of $21.7 mill. for special litigation-related charges. ② Bef. loss of $32.5 mill. from disc. opers.; incl. net special charge of $37.9 mill.

OFFICERS:
B. P. Campbell, Chmn., Pres., C.E.O., C.F.O.
J. F. Brocci, V.P., Admin., Sec.

INVESTOR CONTACT: Brian P. Campbell (734) 747-7025 ext. 129

PRINCIPAL OFFICE: 315 East Eisenhower Parkway, Suite 300, Ann Arbor, MI 48108

TELEPHONE NUMBER: (734) 747-7025
FAX: (734) 747-6565
WEB: www.kaydon.com

NO. OF EMPLOYEES: 1,850 (avg.)

SHAREHOLDERS: 1,151 (record)

ANNUAL MEETING: In May

INCORPORATED: DE, Oct., 1983

INSTITUTIONAL HOLDINGS:
No. of Institutions: 119
Shares Held: 22,472,805
% Held: 73.9

INDUSTRY: Ball and roller bearings (SIC: 3562)

TRANSFER AGENT(S): Continental Stock Transfer and Trust Company, New York, NY

KELLOGG COMPANY

YIELD 3.0%
P/E RATIO 28.2

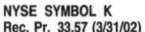

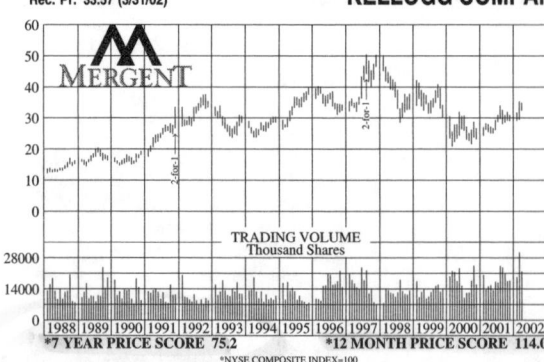

INTERIM EARNINGS (Per Share):

Qtr.	Mar.	June	Sept.	Dec.
1997	0.39	0.40	0.50	0.08
1998	0.42	0.35	0.35	0.11
1999	0.29	0.38	d0.08	0.25
2000	0.40	0.37	0.45	0.23
2001	0.23	0.28	0.37	0.31

INTERIM DIVIDENDS (Per Share):

Amt.	Decl.	Ex.	Rec.	Pay.
0.253Q	4/27/01	5/29/01	5/31/01	6/15/01
0.253Q	7/27/01	8/29/01	8/31/01	9/14/01
0.253Q	10/26/01	11/28/01	11/30/01	12/14/01
0.253Q	2/22/02	2/28/02	3/04/02	3/15/02

Indicated div.: $1.01 (Div. Reinv. Plan)

CAPITALIZATION (12/31/01):

	($000)	(%)
Long-Term Debt	5,619,000	86.6
Common & Surplus	871,500	13.4
Total	6,490,500	100.0

TRADING VOLUME
Thousand Shares

DIVIDEND ACHIEVER STATUS:
Rank: 199   10-Year Growth Rate: 6.51%
Total Years of Dividend Growth: 45

*7 YEAR PRICE SCORE 75.2   ***12 MONTH PRICE SCORE 114.0**
*NYSE COMPOSITE INDEX=100

RECENT DEVELOPMENTS: For the year ended 12/31/01, earnings totaled $482.0 million, before a $7.4 million extraordinary loss and a $1.0 million accounting change charge, versus net earnings of $587.7 million in 2000. Results included net pre-tax restructuring charges of $33.3 million and $86.5 million in 2001 and 2000, respectively. Net sales jumped 27.3% to $8.85 billion from $6.95 billion a year earlier, reflecting the 3/26/01 acquisition of Keebler.

PROSPECTS: The integration of Keebler Foods Company is progressing smoothly and on schedule, while synergistic cost savings are being realized faster than originally anticipated. The Company is targeting full-year 2002 earnings per share of $1.73 per share. Over the long term, the Company anticipates low single-digit revenue growth, mid single-digit operating profit growth and high single-digit earnings per share growth.

BUSINESS

KELLOGG COMPANY is a producer of ready-to-eat cereal products and convenience foods such as cookies, crackers, toaster pastries, cereal bars, frozen waffles, meat alternatives, pie crusts, and ice cream cones. Brand names include KELLOGG'S, KEEBLER, POP-TARTS, EGGO, CHEEZ-IT, NUTRI-GRAIN, RICE KRISPIES, MORNINGSTAR FARMS, MURRAY, AUSTIN, FAMOUS AMOS, CARR'S, READY CRUST, PLANTATION, and KASHI. Products are manufactured in 19 countries and distributed in 160 countries in Asia, Australia, Europe, Africa and Latin America. Contributions to sales (and operating profit) in 2001 were: United States, 69.2% (64.5%); Europe, 15.4% (16.8%); Latin America, 7.4% (11.7%); and Other, 8.0% (7.0%). On 3/26/01, K acquired Keebler Foods Co. for $4.56 billion.

ANNUAL FINANCIAL DATA

	12/31/01	12/31/00	12/31/99	12/31/98	12/31/97	12/31/96	12/31/95
Earnings Per Share	④ 1.18	② 1.45	② 0.83	② 1.23	②③ 1.36	① 1.25	① 1.12
Cash Flow Per Share	2.26	2.17	1.54	1.91	2.06	1.84	1.71
Tang. Book Val. Per Share	2.14	2.21	2.01	2.20	2.43	3.06	3.67
Dividends Per Share	1.01	0.99	0.96	0.92	0.87	0.81	0.75
Dividend Payout %	85.6	68.3	115.6	74.8	64.0	64.8	67.0
INCOME STATEMENT (IN MILLIONS):							
Total Revenues	8,853.3	6,954.7	6,984.2	6,762.1	6,830.1	6,676.6	7,003.7
Costs & Expenses	7,246.8	5,674.3	5,867.4	5,588.9	5,533.7	5,466.2	5,907.4
Depreciation & Amort.	438.6	290.6	288.0	278.1	287.3	251.5	258.8
Operating Income	1,167.9	989.8	828.8	895.1	1,009.1	958.9	837.5
Net Interest Inc./(Exp.)	d351.5	d137.5	d118.8	d119.5	d108.3	d65.6	d62.6
Income Before Income Taxes	804.1	867.7	536.7	782.5	904.5	859.9	796.0
Income Taxes	322.1	280.0	198.4	279.9	340.5	328.9	305.7
Net Income	④ 482.0	② 587.7	② 338.3	② 502.6	②③ 564.0	① 531.0	① 490.3
Cash Flow	920.6	878.3	626.3	780.7	851.3	782.5	749.1
Average Shs. Outstg. (000)	407,200	405,600	405,700	408,600	414,100	424,900	438,300
BALANCE SHEET (IN MILLIONS):							
Cash & Cash Equivalents	231.8	204.4	150.6	136.4	173.2	243.8	221.9
Total Current Assets	1,902.0	1,606.8	1,569.2	1,496.5	1,467.7	1,528.6	1,428.8
Net Property	2,952.8	2,526.9	2,640.9	2,888.8	2,773.3	2,932.9	2,784.8
Total Assets	10,368.6	4,896.3	4,808.7	5,051.5	4,877.6	5,050.0	4,414.6
Total Current Liabilities	2,207.6	2,492.6	1,587.8	1,718.5	1,657.3	2,199.0	1,265.4
Long-Term Obligations	5,619.0	709.2	1,612.8	1,614.5	1,415.4	726.7	717.8
Net Stockholders' Equity	871.5	897.5	813.2	889.8	997.5	1,282.4	1,590.9
Net Working Capital	d305.6	d885.8	d18.6	d222.0	d189.6	d670.4	163.4
Year-end Shs. Outstg. (000)	406,611	405,639	405,500	405,000	410,800	419,296	433,410
STATISTICAL RECORD:							
Operating Profit Margin %	13.2	14.2	11.9	13.2	14.8	14.4	12.0
Net Profit Margin %	5.4	8.5	4.8	7.4	8.3	8.0	7.0
Return on Equity %	55.3	65.5	41.6	56.5	56.5	41.4	30.8
Return on Assets %	4.6	12.0	7.0	9.9	11.6	10.5	11.1
Debt/Total Assets %	54.2	14.5	33.5	32.0	29.0	14.4	16.3
Price Range	34.00-24.25	32.00-20.75	42.25-30.00	50.19-28.50	50.50-32.00	40.31-31.00	39.75-26.25
P/E Ratio	28.8-20.5	22.1-14.3	50.9-36.1	40.8-23.2	37.1-23.5	32.2-24.8	35.5-23.4
Average Yield %	3.5	3.8	2.7	2.3	2.1	2.3	2.3

Statistics are as originally reported. Adj. for 2-for-1 stk. split, 8/97. ① Incl. discont. opers. loss $120.1 mil, 1996; & loss $271.3 mil, 1995. ② Incl. $64.2 mil ($0.16/sh) after-tax restr. chg., 2000; $244.6 mil pre-tax non-recur. chg. & $168.5 mil pre-tax disposition-related chgs., 1999; $46.3 mil ($0.12/sh) after-tax, 1998; $140.5 mil ($0.34/sh) chgs., 1997. ③ Bef. $18.0 mil ($0.04/sh) chg. for acctg. change. ④ Bef. $7.4 mil extraord. chg., $1.0 mil chg. for acctg. change & incl. $33.3 mil restr. chg.

OFFICERS:
C. M. Gutierrez, Chmn., Pres., C.E.O.
J. A. Bryant, Sr. V.P., C.F.O.
J. L. Kelly, Exec. V.P., Sec., Gen. Couns.

INVESTOR CONTACT: John P. Renwick, (616) 961-6365

PRINCIPAL OFFICE: One Kellogg Square, Battle Creek, MI 49016-3599

TELEPHONE NUMBER: (616) 961-2000
FAX: (616) 961-2871
WEB: www.kelloggs.com
NO. OF EMPLOYEES: 26,424 (approx.)
SHAREHOLDERS: 46,126 (record)
ANNUAL MEETING: In Apr.
INCORPORATED: DE, Dec., 1922

INSTITUTIONAL HOLDINGS:
No. of Institutions: 354
Shares Held: 334,706,052
% Held: 82.3

INDUSTRY: Cereal breakfast foods (SIC: 2043)

TRANSFER AGENT(S): Wells Fargo Shareowner Services, South St. Paul, MN

KEYCORP

YIELD 4.5%
P/E RATIO 74.0

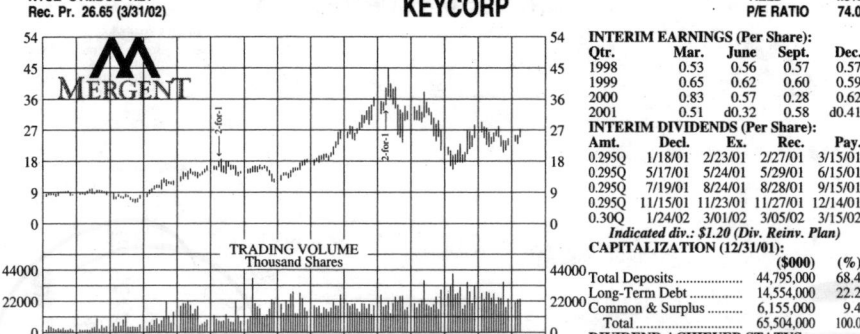

INTERIM EARNINGS (Per Share):

Qtr.	Mar.	June	Sept.	Dec.
1998	0.53	0.56	0.57	0.57
1999	0.65	0.62	0.60	0.59
2000	0.83	0.57	0.28	0.62
2001	0.51	d0.32	0.58	d0.41

INTERIM DIVIDENDS (Per Share):

Amt.	Decl.	Ex.	Rec.	Pay.
0.295Q	1/18/01	2/23/01	2/27/01	3/15/01
0.295Q	5/17/01	5/24/01	5/29/01	6/15/01
0.295Q	7/19/01	8/24/01	8/28/01	9/15/01
0.295Q	11/15/01	11/23/01	11/27/01	12/14/01
0.30Q	1/24/02	3/01/02	3/05/02	3/15/02

Indicated div.: $1.20 (Div. Reinv. Plan)

CAPITALIZATION (12/31/01):

	($000)	(%)
Total Deposits	44,795,000	68.4
Long-Term Debt	14,554,000	22.2
Common & Surplus	6,155,000	9.4
Total	65,504,000	100.0

DIVIDEND ACHIEVER STATUS:
Rank: 142 10-Year Growth Rate: 9.88%
Total Years of Dividend Growth: 22

TRADING VOLUME Thousand Shares

7 YEAR PRICE SCORE 83.5   *12 MONTH PRICE SCORE 104.6*
NYSE COMPOSITE INDEX=100

RECENT DEVELOPMENTS: For the year ended 12/31/01, income was $157.0 million, before an accounting change charge of $25.0 million, versus net income of $1.00 billion in 2000. Results for 2001 and 2000 included restructuring gains of $4.0 million and charges of $102.0 million, respectively. Net interest income grew 3.5% to $2.83 billion, while provision for loan losses advanced to $1.35 billion. Total non-interest income fell 21.4% to $1.73 billion, while total non-interest expense rose slightly to $2.94 billion.

PROSPECTS: The Company continues to implement a series of initiatives, including exiting the automobile leasing business, de-emphasizing indirect prime automobile lending and discontinuing certain non-relationship, profit-only commercial lending. Moreover, KEY will focus on strengthening its loan loss reserve and balance sheet. Separately, the Company's business-to-business e-marketplace, KeyProcure, added five more suppliers.

BUSINESS

KEYCORP (formerly Society Corporation) is a multi-line financial services company, with assets of $80.94 billion as of 12/31/01. The Company provides investment management, retail and commercial banking, consumer finance, and investment banking products and services to individuals and companies throughout the U.S. and, for certain businesses, internationally, through its three lines of business: Key Consumer Banking, Key Corporate Finance and Key Capital Partners. The Company operates throughout the U.S. with a network of approximately 2,333 ATMs, a Web site named Key.com, and telephone banking centers. In October 1998, the Company acquired McDonald & Company Investments, Inc. On 1/31/00, the Company sold its credit card business.

ANNUAL FINANCIAL DATA

	12/31/01	12/31/00	12/31/99	12/31/98	12/31/97	12/31/96	12/31/95
Earnings Per Share	⑤ 0.37	④ 2.30	③ 2.45	② 2.23	② 2.07	① 1.69	1.65
Tang. Book Val. Per Share	11.85	12.42	11.14	10.30	9.14	7.97	8.77
Dividends Per Share	1.18	1.12	1.04	0.94	0.84	0.76	0.72
Dividend Payout %	318.9	48.7	42.4	42.2	40.6	45.1	43.6

INCOME STATEMENT (IN MILLIONS):

Total Interest Income	5,627.0	6,277.0	5,695.0	5,525.0	5,262.0	4,951.0	5,121.0
Total Interest Expense	2,802.0	3,547.0	2,908.0	2,841.0	2,468.0	2,234.0	2,484.3
Net Interest Income	2,825.0	2,730.0	2,787.0	2,684.0	2,794.0	2,717.0	2,636.7
Provision for Loan Losses	1,350.0	490.0	348.0	297.0	320.0	197.0	100.5
Non-Interest Income	1,725.0	2,194.0	2,294.0	1,575.0	1,306.0	1,087.0	933.0
Non-Interest Expense	2,941.0	2,917.0	3,049.0	2,483.0	2,435.0	2,464.0	2,311.6
Income Before Taxes	259.0	1,517.0	1,684.0	1,479.0	1,345.0	1,143.0	1,157.7
Net Income	⑤ 157.0	④ 1,002.0	③ 1,107.0	② 996.0	② 919.0	① 783.0	789.2
Average Shs. Outstg. (000)	429,573	435,573	452,363	447,437	444,544	459,810	469,574

BALANCE SHEET (IN MILLIONS):

Cash & Due from Banks	2,891.0	3,189.0	2,816.0	3,296.0	3,651.0	3,444.0	3,443.8
Securities Avail. for Sale	7,244.0	9,213.0	8,525.0	7,252.0	9,636.0	8,424.0	8,742.3
Total Loans & Leases	63,309.0	66,905.0	64,222.0	62,012.0	53,380.0	49,235.0	47,691.7
Allowance for Credit Losses	1,677.0	1,001.0	930.0	900.0	900.0	870.0	876.0
Net Loans & Leases	61,632.0	65,904.0	63,292.0	61,112.0	52,480.0	48,365.0	46,815.7
Total Assets	80,938.0	87,270.0	83,395.0	80,020.0	73,699.0	67,621.0	66,339.1
Total Deposits	44,795.0	48,649.0	43,233.0	42,583.0	45,073.0	45,317.0	47,281.9
Long-Term Obligations	14,554.0	14,161.0	15,881.0	12,967.0	7,446.0	4,213.0	4,003.6
Total Liabilities	74,783.0	80,647.0	77,006.0	73,853.0	68,518.0	62,740.0	61,186.5
Net Stockholders' Equity	6,155.0	6,623.0	6,389.0	6,167.0	5,181.0	4,881.0	5,152.5
Year-end Shs. Outstg. (000)	425,005	423,254	443,427	452,452	438,064	491,888	447,406

STATISTICAL RECORD:

Return on Equity %	2.6	15.1	17.3	16.2	17.7	16.0	15.3
Return on Assets %	0.2	1.1	1.3	1.2	1.2	1.2	1.2
Equity/Assets %	7.6	7.6	7.7	7.7	7.0	7.2	7.8
Non-Int. Exp./Tot. Inc. %	64.6	59.2	60.0	58.3	59.4	64.8	64.8
Price Range	29.25-20.49	28.50-15.56	38.13-21.00	44.88-23.38	36.59-23.94	27.13-16.69	18.63-12.38
P/E Ratio	79.1-55.4	12.4-6.8	15.6-8.6	20.1-10.5	17.7-11.6	16.1-9.9	11.3-7.5
Average Yield %	4.7	5.1	3.5	2.8	2.8	3.5	4.6

Statistics are as originally reported. Adj. for 2-for-1 splits 3/98. ① Incl. pre-tax SAIF chg. & restr. chgs. totaling $17.0 mill. ② Incl. pre-tax gain fr. sale of branch: $148.0 mill., 1999; $89.0 mill., 1998; $151.0 mill., 1997. ③ Incl. various pre-tax net gains of $448.0 mill. & restr. chgs. of $98.0 mill. ④ Incl. pre-tax gains from divest. of $332.0 mill. & pre-tax restr. chgs. of $102.0 mill. ⑤ Bef. acctg. chrg. of $25.0 mill.; incl. pre-tax restr. gains of $4.0 mill.

OFFICERS:
H. L. Meyer III, Chmn., Pres, C.E.O.
K. B. Somers, Sr. Exec. V.P., C.F.O.

INVESTOR CONTACT: Bernon L. Patterson, Investor Relations, (216) 689-4520

PRINCIPAL OFFICE: 127 Public Square, Cleveland, OH 44114-1306

TELEPHONE NUMBER: (216) 689-6300
FAX: (216) 689-3595
WEB: www.key.com

NO. OF EMPLOYEES: 21,230

SHAREHOLDERS: 45,340

ANNUAL MEETING: In May

INCORPORATED: OH, Dec., 1958

INSTITUTIONAL HOLDINGS:
No. of Institutions: 394
Shares Held: 238,477,476
% Held: 56.1

INDUSTRY: National commercial banks
(SIC: 6021)

TRANSFER AGENT(S): Computershare Investor Services, Chicago, IL

KIMBERLY-CLARK CORPORATION

YIELD	1.9%
P/E RATIO	21.1

INTERIM EARNINGS (Per Share):

Qtr.	Mar.	June	Sept.	Dec.
1998	0.53	0.54	0.62	0.44
1999	0.75	0.73	0.89	0.77
2000	0.86	0.79	0.81	0.85
2001	0.81	0.78	0.79	0.68

INTERIM DIVIDENDS (Per Share):

Amt.	Decl.	Ex.	Rec.	Pay.
0.28Q	2/22/01	3/07/01	3/09/01	4/03/01
0.28Q	4/26/01	6/06/01	6/08/01	7/03/01
0.28Q	8/01/01	9/05/01	9/07/01	10/02/01
0.28Q	11/13/01	12/05/01	12/07/01	1/03/02
0.30Q	2/19/02	3/06/02	3/08/02	4/02/02

Indicated div.: $1.20 (Div. Reinv. Plan)

CAPITALIZATION (12/31/01):

	($000)	(%)
Long-Term Debt	2,424,000	25.8
Deferred Income Tax	1,004,600	10.7
Minority Interest	309,400	3.3
Common & Surplus	5,646,900	60.2
Total	9,384,900	100.0

TRADING VOLUME
Thousand Shares

1988 1989 1990 1991 1992 1993 1994 1995 1996 1997 1998 1999 2000 2001 2002

*7 YEAR PRICE SCORE 101.3   ***12 MONTH PRICE SCORE 105.6**
*NYSE COMPOSITE INDEX=100

DIVIDEND ACHIEVER STATUS:
Rank: 246   10-Year Growth Rate: 4.35%
Total Years of Dividend Growth: 27

RECENT DEVELOPMENTS: For the year ended 12/31/01, net income declined 10.6% to $1.61 billion compared with $1.80 billion in 2000. Earnings for 2001 and 2000 included non-recurring items that resulted in a net charge of $179.7 million and a net gain of $1.1 million, respectively. Net sales improved 3.9% to $14.52 billion from $13.98 billion a year earlier. Gross profit slipped to $1.47 billion from $1.48 billion the prior year.

PROSPECTS: KMB expects results to be enhanced by a comprehensive marketing program designed to bolster volume growth for its consumer products. KMB expects the rollout of new and improved products to drive future growth. Results in KMB's personal care business continue to be adversely affected by weakness in Argentina and Brazil. Meanwhile, KMB's consumer tissues business is posting solid results despite competitive market conditions.

BUSINESS

KIMBERLY-CLARK CORPORATION is a global manufacturer of consumer products. The Company's global brands include HUGGIES, PULL-UPS, LITTLE SWIMMERS, GOODNITES, KOTEX, LIGHTDAYS, DEPEND, POISE, KLEENEX, SCOTT, COTTONELLE, VIVA, ANDREX, SCOTTEX, PAGE, KIMBERLY-CLARK, KIMWIPES, WYPALL, SURPASS, SAFESKIN, TECNOL and BALLARD. Kimberly-Clark also is a major producer of premium business, correspondence and technical papers. The Company has manufacturing operations in 42 countries and sells its products in more than 150 countries. Net sales (and operating profit) for 2001 were derived from the following: personal care, 38.7% (41.6%); consumer tissue, 36.7% (34.5%); and business-to-business, 24.6% (23.9%).

ANNUAL FINANCIAL DATA

	12/31/01	12/31/00	12/31/99	12/31/98	12/31/97	12/31/96 ☑	12/31/95
Earnings Per Share	☑ 3.02	3.31	☑ 3.09	☑ 2.13	☑ 1.58	☑ 2.49	☑ 0.06
Cash Flow Per Share	4.41	4.55	4.25	3.11	2.49	3.48	1.10
Tang. Book Val. Per Share	7.10	7.04	7.12	6.13	6.36	7.96	6.11
Dividends Per Share	1.11	1.07	1.03	0.99	0.95	0.92	0.90
Dividend Payout %	36.8	32.3	33.3	46.5	60.1	36.7	N.M.
INCOME STATEMENT (IN MILLIONS):							
Total Revenues	14,524.4	13,982.0	13,006.8	12,297.8	12,546.6	13,149.1	13,373.0
Costs & Expenses	11,446.6	10,674.8	9,943.4	10,079.2	10,735.7	10,534.4	12,578.3
Depreciation & Amort.	739.6	673.4	628.0	542.5	507.7	561.0	581.7
Operating Income	2,338.2	2,633.8	2,435.4	1,676.1	1,303.2	2,053.7	213.0
Net Interest Inc./(Exp.)	d173.8	d197.8	d183.7	d174.4	d133.4	d158.6	d212.2
Income Before Income Taxes	2,164.4	2,436.0	2,251.7	1,626.1	1,187.5	2,002.3	104.4
Income Taxes	645.7	758.5	730.2	561.9	433.1	700.8	153.5
Equity Earnings/Minority Int.	91.2	123.1	146.6	112.8	129.6	102.3	82.3
Net Income	☑ 1,609.9	1,800.6	☑ 1,668.1	☑ 1,177.0	☑ 884.0	☑ 1,403.8	☑ 33.2
Cash Flow	2,349.5	2,474.0	2,296.1	1,719.5	1,391.7	1,964.8	614.6
Average Shs. Outstg. (000)	533,200	543,800	540,100	553,100	559,300	564,000	559,000
BALANCE SHEET (IN MILLIONS):							
Cash & Cash Equivalents	405.2	206.5	322.8	144.0	90.8	83.2	221.6
Total Current Assets	3,922.2	3,789.9	3,561.8	3,366.9	3,489.0	3,539.2	3,813.8
Net Property	7,326.5	6,918.5	6,222.0	5,845.0	5,600.6	6,813.3	6,053.3
Total Assets	15,007.6	14,479.8	12,815.5	11,510.3	11,266.0	11,845.7	11,439.2
Total Current Liabilities	4,168.3	4,573.9	3,845.8	3,790.7	3,698.3	3,686.9	3,869.6
Long-Term Obligations	2,424.0	2,000.6	1,926.6	2,068.2	1,803.9	1,738.6	1,984.7
Net Stockholders' Equity	5,646.9	5,767.3	5,093.1	3,887.2	4,133.3	4,483.1	3,650.4
Net Working Capital	d246.1	d784.0	d284.0	d423.8	d209.3	d147.7	d55.8
Year-end Shs. Outstg. (000)	521,000	533,400	540,600	538,300	556,300	563,400	597,000
STATISTICAL RECORD:							
Operating Profit Margin %	16.1	18.8	18.7	13.6	10.4	15.6	1.6
Net Profit Margin %	11.1	12.9	12.8	9.6	7.0	10.7	0.2
Return on Equity %	28.5	31.2	32.8	30.3	21.4	31.3	0.9
Return on Assets %	10.7	12.4	13.0	10.2	7.8	11.9	0.3
Debt/Total Assets %	16.2	13.8	15.0	18.0	16.0	14.7	17.3
Price Range	72.19-52.06	73.25-42.00	69.56-44.81	59.44-35.88	56.88-43.25	49.81-34.31	41.50-23.63
P/E Ratio	23.9-17.2	22.1-12.7	22.5-14.5	27.9-16.8	36.0-27.4	20.0-13.8	690.5-393.1
Average Yield %	1.8	1.9	1.8	2.1	1.9	2.2	2.7

Statistics are as originally reported. Adj. for stk. split: 2-for-1, 4/97. ① Incl. gain $72.6 mill., 1996. ② Refl. acq. of Scott Paper Co. on 12/15/95. ③ Incl. $1.44 bill. chrg. for merger & incl. $40.0 mill. gain. ④ Bef. extraord. cr. $17.5 mill. & incl. restruct. chrg. $481.1 mill. ⑤ Bef. acctg. chrg. of $11.2 mill. ⑥ Incl. restruct. cr. $27.0 mill. ⑦ Incl. net chrg. of $179.7 mill.

OFFICERS:
W. R. Sanders, Chmn., C.E.O.
T. J. Falk, Pres., C.O.O.
J. W. Donehower, Sr. V.P., C.F.O.

INVESTOR CONTACT: Michael D. Masseth, V.P.-Investor Relations, (800) 639-1352

PRINCIPAL OFFICE: P.O. Box 619100, Dallas, TX 75261-9100

TELEPHONE NUMBER: (972) 281-1200
FAX: (972) 281-1435
WEB: www.kimberly-clark.com
NO. OF EMPLOYEES: 66,300 (avg.)
SHAREHOLDERS: 48,090
ANNUAL MEETING: In Apr.
INCORPORATED: DE, June, 1928

INSTITUTIONAL HOLDINGS:
No. of Institutions: 772
Shares Held: 384,054,925
% Held: 72.1

INDUSTRY: Paper mills (SIC: 2621)

TRANSFER AGENT(S): Bank Boston NA, Boston, MA

LANCASTER COLONY CORPORATION

YIELD	1.9%
P/E RATIO	17.8

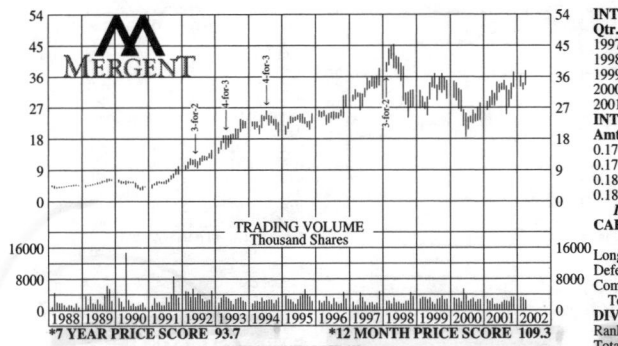

*7 YEAR PRICE SCORE 93.7   *12 MONTH PRICE SCORE 109.3
*NYSE COMPOSITE INDEX=100

INTERIM EARNINGS (Per Share):

Qtr.	Sept.	Dec.	Mar.	June
1997-98	0.48	0.67	0.52	0.55
1998-99	0.48	0.67	0.53	0.61
1999-00	0.56	0.83	0.51	0.61
2000-01	0.57	0.78	0.52	0.54
2001-02	0.55	0.47	...	...

INTERIM DIVIDENDS (Per Share):

Amt.	Decl.	Ex.	Rec.	Pay.
0.17Q	5/23/01	6/07/01	6/11/01	6/29/01
0.17Q	8/29/01	9/06/01	9/10/01	9/28/01
0.18Q	11/19/01	12/06/01	12/10/01	12/31/01
0.18Q	2/27/02	3/06/02	3/08/02	3/29/02

Indicated div.: $0.72 (Div. Reinv. Plan)

CAPITALIZATION (6/30/01):

	($000)	(%)
Long-Term Debt	1,095	0.2
Deferred Income Tax	11,301	2.4
Common & Surplus	459,901	97.4
Total	472,297	100.0

DIVIDEND ACHIEVER STATUS:
Rank: 90   10-Year Growth Rate: 12.90%
Total Years of Dividend Growth: 32

RECENT DEVELOPMENTS: For the three months ended 12/31/01, net income fell 41.6% to $17.4 million compared with $29.9 million in the corresponding prior-year quarter. Net sales totaled $311.9 million versus $311.1 million a year earlier. Specialty foods net sales advanced 11.3% to $149.7 million from $134.5 million the year before, reflecting increased demand for the Company's frozen bread and foodservice products. Glassware and candles net sales slid 12.1% to $103.9 million from $118.2 million in 2000. Automotive net sales slipped to $58.2 million from $58.4 million a year earlier. Gross profit declined 8.9% to $70.4 million, or 22.6% of net sales, from $77.2 million, or 24.8% of net sales, in the previous year. Operating income dropped 42.7% to $28.0 million from $48.9 million the prior year, primarily due to pricing pressures, lower production, and reduced inventory levels in the glassware and candles segment. In addition, results were hampered by a labor strike at a glassware production facility, which was settled in January 2002.

BUSINESS

LANCASTER COLONY CORPORATION operates in three business segments: Specialty Foods, Glassware and Candles, and Automotive. The Specialty Foods segment manufactures and sells salad dressings and sauces, frozen unbaked pies, frozen breads, refrigerated chip and produce dips, dairy snacks and desserts, premium dry egg noodles, frozen noodles, pastas and specialty items, croutons, and caviar. The Glassware and Candles segment produces a broad range of machine-pressed and machine-blown consumer glassware, technical glass products, and candles and other home fragrances of all sizes, forms and fragrance. The Automotive segment manufactures and sells rubber, vinyl and carpeted car mats, pickup truck bed mats, running boards, bed liners, tool boxes, and other accessories. The Specialty Foods, Glassware and Candles, and Automotive business segments accounted for 47.5%, 30.7%, and 21.8%, respectively, of consolidated net sales for the fiscal year ended 6/30/01.

ANNUAL FINANCIAL DATA

	6/30/01	6/30/00	6/30/99	6/30/98	6/30/97	6/30/96	6/30/95
Earnings Per Share	① 2.40	2.51	2.28	2.22	2.01	1.71	1.57
Cash Flow Per Share	3.34	3.38	3.13	2.97	2.62	2.25	2.07
Tang. Book Val. Per Share	10.38	10.03	9.35	8.74	8.00	6.83	5.89
Dividends Per Share	0.69	0.65	0.61	0.57	0.51	0.46	0.41
Dividend Payout %	28.7	25.9	26.8	25.7	25.2	26.9	26.0
INCOME STATEMENT (IN MILLIONS):							
Total Revenues	1,098.5	1,104.3	1,045.7	1,008.8	922.8	855.9	795.1
Costs & Expenses	915.3	908.0	854.4	820.3	751.5	705.8	655.9
Depreciation & Amort.	35.5	34.3	35.6	32.6	27.0	24.4	22.7
Operating Income	147.7	161.9	155.7	155.9	144.4	125.7	116.5
Net Interest Inc./(Exp.)	d1.2	d1.6	d2.7	d2.6	d2.6	d2.9	d2.7
Income Before Income Taxes	145.9	160.2	153.5	154.4	142.5	123.2	114.8
Income Taxes	55.6	60.9	58.3	59.2	53.8	47.1	44.3
Net Income	① 90.2	99.3	95.1	96.1	88.7	76.1	70.5
Cash Flow	125.8	133.6	130.7	128.7	115.7	100.5	93.2
Average Shs. Outstg. (000)	37,636	39,554	41,799	43,364	44,108	44,624	45,057
BALANCE SHEET (IN MILLIONS):							
Cash & Cash Equivalents	4.9	2.7	18.9	23.2	32.1	4.7	8.2
Total Current Assets	317.6	315.9	328.4	311.5	308.8	273.3	249.8
Net Property	173.2	172.4	175.6	170.8	151.3	139.1	113.2
Total Assets	571.9	531.8	550.0	529.4	484.4	435.4	379.9
Total Current Liabilities	92.3	96.5	116.2	76.5	73.7	69.4	60.5
Long-Term Obligations	1.1	3.0	3.6	29.1	30.7	31.2	31.8
Net Stockholders' Equity	459.9	415.5	414.9	410.6	368.0	323.6	277.1
Net Working Capital	225.3	219.4	212.2	235.0	235.1	204.0	189.3
Year-end Shs. Outstg. (000)	37,253	37,962	40,548	42,753	43,526	44,345	44,744
STATISTICAL RECORD:							
Operating Profit Margin %	13.4	14.7	14.9	15.5	15.6	14.7	14.7
Net Profit Margin %	8.2	9.0	9.1	9.5	9.6	8.9	8.9
Return on Equity %	19.6	23.9	22.9	23.4	24.1	23.5	25.4
Return on Assets %	15.8	18.7	17.3	18.2	18.3	17.5	18.6
Debt/Total Assets %	0.2	0.6	0.6	5.5	6.3	7.2	8.4
Price Range	37.36-24.96	34.75-18.50	37.00-24.69	45.38-24.06	38.50-26.17	30.67-22.00	25.33-19.17
P/E Ratio	15.6-10.4	13.8-7.4	16.2-10.8	20.4-10.8	19.1-13.0	18.0-12.9	16.2-12.2
Average Yield %	2.2	2.4	2.0	1.6	1.6	1.7	1.8

Statistics are as originally reported. Adj. for stk. splits: 3-for-2, 1/27/98. ① Excl. accounting change chrg. $998,000.

OFFICERS: J. B. Gerlach, Jr., Chmn., Pres., C.E.O. J. L. Boylan, V.P., C.F.O., Treas., Asst. Sec. **INVESTOR CONTACT:** Investor Relations, (614) 224-7141 **PRINCIPAL OFFICE:** 37 West Broad Street, Columbus, OH 43215	**TELEPHONE NUMBER:** (614) 224-7141 **FAX:** (614) 469-8219 **WEB:** www.lancastercolony.com **NO. OF EMPLOYEES:** 6,000 (approx.) **SHAREHOLDERS:** 9,000 (approx.) **ANNUAL MEETING:** In Nov. **INCORPORATED:** DE, 1961; reincorp., OH, Jan., 1992	**INSTITUTIONAL HOLDINGS:** No. of Institutions: 157 Shares Held: 17,112,527 % Held: 46.5 **INDUSTRY:** Frozen specialties, nec (SIC: 2038) **TRANSFER AGENT(S):** American Stock Transfer and Trust Company, Brooklyn, NY

TRADING VOLUME
Thousand Shares

LA-Z-BOY INCORPORATED

YIELD 1.3%
P/E RATIO 35.6

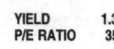

INTERIM EARNINGS (Per Share):

Qtr.	July	Oct.	Jan.	Apr.
1997-98	0.03	0.31	0.21	0.37
1998-99	0.13	0.35	0.33	0.43
1999-00	0.25	0.44	0.41	0.49
2000-01	0.21	0.48	0.27	0.17
2001-02	0.05	0.20	0.35	...

INTERIM DIVIDENDS (Per Share):

Amt.	Decl.	Ex.	Rec.	Pay.
0.09Q	2/12/01	2/21/01	2/23/01	3/09/01
0.09Q	5/11/01	5/23/01	5/25/01	6/08/01
0.09Q	7/30/01	8/22/01	8/24/01	9/10/01
0.09Q	11/14/01	11/21/01	11/26/01	12/10/01
0.09Q	2/12/02	2/22/02	2/26/02	3/11/02

Indicated div.: $0.36 (Div. Reinv. Plan)

CAPITALIZATION (4/28/01):

	($000)	(%)
Long-Term Debt	196,923	20.9
Capital Lease Obligations..	2,496	0.3
Deferred Income Tax	45,709	4.9
Common & Surplus	695,146	73.9
Total	940,274	100.0

DIVIDEND ACHIEVER STATUS:
Rank: 196 10-Year Growth Rate: 6.60%
Total Years of Dividend Growth: 20

TRADING VOLUME
Thousand Shares

*7 YEAR PRICE SCORE 115.1   *12 MONTH PRICE SCORE 130.7
*NYSE COMPOSITE INDEX=100

RECENT DEVELOPMENTS: For the quarter ended 1/26/02, net income increased 34.4% to $21.7 million compared with $16.1 million in the corresponding 2001 period. Results for 2001 included a loss on divestiture of $11.7 million. Sales declined 1.3% to $545.0 million from $552.0 million a year earlier. Upholstery segment sales increased 6.7% to $397.4 million. Casegoods segment sales decreased 18.0% to $147.9 million.

PROSPECTS: The Company expects results to improve in 2002 as the economy begins to stabilize. LZB expects low interest rates and other more localized economic forces to strengthen housing turnover and home remodeling, which are both strong drivers of retail furniture demand. The Company expects to report diluted net income per share for the fiscal year ending 4/27/02 between $1.20 to $1.06.

BUSINESS

LA-Z-BOY INCORPORATED (formerly La-Z-Boy Chair Company) is one of the largest furniture manufacturers in the U.S. LZB is comprised of two business groups: upholstery and casegoods. The upholstery segment includes recliners, sofas, occasional chairs, reclining sofas and office and health care seating. The casegoods segment includes dining room tables and chairs, bed frames and bed boards, dressers, coffee tables and end tables manufactured using hardwood or hardwood veneer, as well as hospitality and assisted-living furniture. Brand names include LA-Z-BOY, ENGLAND, SAM MOORE, BAUHAUS, CENTURION, PENN-SYLVANIA HOUSE, CLAYTON MARCUS, KINCAID, HAMMARY, ALEXVALE, AMERICAN DREW, HICKORY MARK, LA-Z-BOY CONTRACT FURNITURE, and LEA. As of 2/13/02, the Company operated 295 La-Z-Boy Furniture Galleries® and 324 in-store galleries.

ANNUAL FINANCIAL DATA

	4/28/01	4/29/00	4/24/99	4/25/98	4/26/97	4/27/96	4/29/95
Earnings Per Share	①1.13	1.60	1.24	0.93	0.83	0.71	0.67
Cash Flow Per Share	1.88	2.15	1.66	1.32	1.21	1.07	0.95
Tang. Book Val. Per Share	7.40	6.70	7.03	6.33	5.97	5.49	5.06
Dividends Per Share	0.34	0.32	0.30	0.28	0.25	0.24	0.23
Dividend Payout %	30.1	20.0	24.2	30.1	30.4	33.9	33.8
INCOME STATEMENT (IN MILLIONS):							
Total Revenues	2,256.2	1,717.4	1,287.6	1,108.0	1,005.8	947.3	850.3
Costs & Expenses	2,089.7	1,542.8	1,158.7	1,009.8	911.5	859.6	772.6
Depreciation & Amort.	45.7	30.3	22.1	21.0	20.4	20.1	15.2
Operating Income	120.8	144.3	106.8	77.2	73.9	67.5	62.5
Net Interest Inc./(Exp.)	d16.2	d7.7	d2.3	d2.1	d2.6	d3.3	d1.7
Income Before Income Taxes	112.0	140.3	107.2	79.3	73.8	66.2	62.0
Income Taxes	43.7	52.7	41.1	29.4	28.5	26.9	25.7
Net Income	①68.3	87.6	66.1	49.9	45.3	39.3	36.3
Cash Flow	114.0	118.0	88.2	70.9	65.7	59.4	51.5
Average Shs. Outstg. (000)	60,692	54,860	53,148	53,821	54,324	55,494	54,132
BALANCE SHEET (IN MILLIONS):							
Cash & Cash Equivalents	23.6	14.4	33.6	28.7	25.4	27.1	27.0
Total Current Assets	708.8	692.4	425.6	383.0	342.8	337.1	325.4
Net Property	230.3	227.9	126.0	121.8	114.7	116.2	117.2
Total Assets	1,222.5	1,218.3	629.8	580.4	528.4	517.5	503.8
Total Current Liabilities	249.9	237.0	132.4	108.3	97.7	96.5	88.1
Long-Term Obligations	199.4	236.1	62.7	67.3	54.7	61.3	76.4
Net Stockholders' Equity	695.1	663.1	414.9	388.2	359.3	343.4	323.6
Net Working Capital	458.9	455.4	293.2	274.7	245.1	240.6	237.3
Year-end Shs. Outstg. (000)	60,501	61,328	52,340	53,551	53,724	55,155	55,686
STATISTICAL RECORD:							
Operating Profit Margin %	5.4	8.4	8.3	7.0	7.4	7.1	7.4
Net Profit Margin %	3.0	5.1	5.1	4.5	4.5	4.1	4.3
Return on Equity %	9.8	13.2	15.9	12.9	12.6	11.4	11.2
Return on Assets %	5.6	7.2	10.5	8.6	8.6	7.6	7.2
Debt/Total Assets %	16.3	19.4	10.0	11.6	10.3	11.8	15.2
Price Range	17.81-13.00	24.56-15.38	22.63-14.08	14.96-9.88	11.33-8.96	11.17-8.54	13.33-8.42
P/E Ratio	15.8-11.5	15.4-9.6	18.2-11.4	16.1-10.6	13.6-10.8	15.8-12.1	19.9-12.6
Average Yield %	2.2	1.6	1.6	2.3	2.5	2.4	2.1

Statistics are as originally reported. Adj. for stk split: 200%, 9/98. ① Incl. restruct. chrg. of $11.2 mill.

OFFICERS:
P. H. Norton, Chmn.
G. L. Kiser, Pres., C.E.O., C.O.O.
D. M. Risley, Sr. V.P., C.F.O.

INVESTOR CONTACT: Gene M. Hardy, Sec. & Treas., (734) 241-4414

PRINCIPAL OFFICE: 1284 North Telegraph Road, Monroe, MI 48162

TELEPHONE NUMBER: (734) 241-4414
FAX: (734) 241-4422
WEB: www.la-z-boy.com
NO. OF EMPLOYEES: 19,700 (approx.)
SHAREHOLDERS: 23,600
ANNUAL MEETING: In July
INCORPORATED: MI, May, 1941

INSTITUTIONAL HOLDINGS:
No. of Institutions: 122
Shares Held: 34,417,043
% Held: 56.5

INDUSTRY: Wood household furniture (SIC 2511)

TRANSFER AGENT(S): American Stock Transfer & Trust Company, New York, NY

LEE ENTERPRISES, INC.

YIELD 1.8%
P/E RATIO 28.6

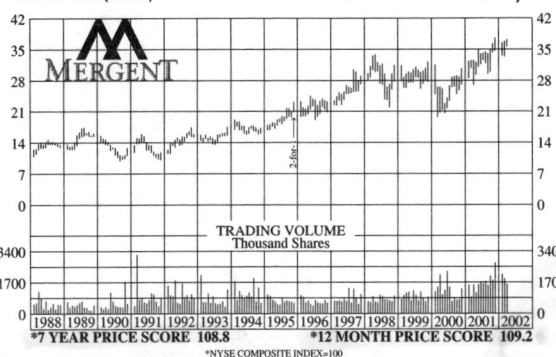

INTERIM EARNINGS (Per Share):				
Qtr.	Dec.	Mar.	June	Sept.
1998-99	0.44	0.27	0.43	0.38
1999-00	0.68	0.27	0.36	0.36
2000-01	0.48	0.30	0.36	0.22
2001-02	0.41	...	...	...

INTERIM DIVIDENDS (Per Share):				
Amt.	Decl.	Ex.	Rec.	Pay.
0.17Q	5/17/01	5/30/01	6/01/01	7/02/01
0.17Q	8/23/01	8/29/01	8/31/01	9/28/01
0.17Q	11/15/01	11/29/01	12/03/01	1/02/02
0.17Q	1/23/02	2/27/02	3/01/02	4/01/02
Indicated div.: $0.68 (Div. Reinv. Plan)				

CAPITALIZATION (9/30/01):		
	($000)	(%)
Long-Term Debt	161,800	18.8
Deferred Income Tax	18,336	2.1
Common & Surplus	681,944	79.1
Total	862,080	100.0

TRADING VOLUME
Thousand Shares

*7 YEAR PRICE SCORE 108.8   *12 MONTH PRICE SCORE 109.2
*NYSE COMPOSITE INDEX=100

DIVIDEND ACHIEVER STATUS:
Rank: 214   10-Year Growth Rate: 5.99%
Total Years of Dividend Growth: 41

RECENT DEVELOPMENTS: For the quarter ended 12/31/01, net income dropped 93.4% to $18.0 million versus income from continuing operations of $21.0 million in 2000. Results for 2001 and 2000 included amortization of intangibles of $1.9 million and $3.9 million, respectively. Results for 2000 also excluded a gain of $250.9 million from discontinued operations. Total operating revenue was $111.6 million, down 6.0% from $118.7 million the year before.

PROSPECTS: On 4/1/02, the Company completed the acquisition of 16 daily newspapers from Howard Publications, including one that is jointly owned. In addition, the Company gained a half interest in another daily newspaper through its affiliate in Madison, WI. The acquisitions increased the Company's daily circulation to more than 1.1 million dailies in 45 newspapers in 18 states. The transactions are expected to be accretive to earnings in the first full fiscal year, beginning on 10/1/02.

BUSINESS

LEE ENTERPRISES, INC. owns 23 daily newspapers and more than 100 other weekly, classified, shopper and specialty publications, along with associated Internet services, primarily from the Midwest to the Pacific Northwest. Jointly with The Capital Times Co., LEE also owns five daily newspapers and more than a dozen other publications operated by Madison Newspapers Inc. in Wisconsin. In fiscal 2001, revenues were as follows: advertising, 65.5%; circulation, 19.6%; and other, 14.9%.

ANNUAL FINANCIAL DATA

	9/30/01	9/30/00	9/30/99	9/30/98	9/30/97	9/30/96	9/30/95
Earnings Per Share	④1.35	③1.58	1.52	1.37	②1.33	①1.33	1.24
Cash Flow Per Share	2.08	2.51	2.40	2.19	1.95	1.79	1.80
Tang. Book Val. Per Share	8.42	1.43	...	...	...	1.68	...
Dividends Per Share	0.68	0.64	0.60	0.56	0.52	0.48	0.44
Dividend Payout %	50.4	40.5	39.5	40.9	39.1	42.9	35.5
INCOME STATEMENT (IN THOUSANDS):							
Total Revenues	441,153	431,513	536,333	517,293	446,686	427,369	443,188
Costs & Expenses	322,979	287,783	379,845	366,870	312,954	300,469	313,782
Depreciation & Amort.	32,158	41,263	39,748	37,576	29,581	32,159	25,974
Operating Income	86,016	102,467	116,740	112,847	104,151	94,741	103,432
Net Interest Inc./(Exp.)	16,585	d9,384	d10,043	d2,715	d2,929	d7,039	d8,198
Income Before Income Taxes	92,434	110,215	106,535	100,132	101,222	87,702	95,234
Income Taxes	32,977	40,340	38,562	37,899	38,477	34,032	36,775
Net Income	④59,457	③69,875	67,973	62,233	②62,745	①53,670	58,459
Cash Flow	91,615	111,138	107,721	99,809	92,326	85,829	84,433
Average Shs. Outstg.	44,089	44,360	44,861	45,557	47,312	47,991	46,962
BALANCE SHEET (IN THOUSANDS):							
Cash & Cash Equivalents	483,390	29,427	10,536	16,941	14,163	19,267	10,883
Total Current Assets	537,677	251,566	102,543	99,591	93,967	146,708	104,509
Net Property	119,061	127,356	139,203	128,372	120,026	104,705	108,196
Total Assets	1,000,397	746,233	679,513	660,585	650,963	527,416	559,849
Total Current Liabilities	125,139	117,627	79,448	98,061	248,908	97,777	116,527
Long-Term Obligations	161,800	173,400	187,005	186,028	26,114	52,290	75,511
Net Stockholders' Equity	681,944	395,167	354,329	319,759	319,390	324,954	311,042
Net Working Capital	412,538	133,939	23,095	1,530	d154,941	48,931	d12,018
Year-end Shs. Outstg.	44,038	43,810	44,259	44,350	45,508	47,022	47,366
STATISTICAL RECORD:							
Operating Profit Margin %	19.5	23.7	21.8	21.8	23.3	22.2	23.3
Net Profit Margin %	13.5	16.2	12.7	12.0	14.0	12.6	13.2
Return on Equity %	8.7	17.7	19.2	19.5	19.6	16.5	18.8
Return on Assets %	5.9	9.4	10.0	9.4	9.6	10.2	10.4
Debt/Total Assets %	16.2	23.2	27.5	28.2	4.0	9.9	13.5
Price Range	37.60-26.94	31.56-19.69	32.25-26.13	33.88-21.81	30.50-22.25	24.50-19.00	23.13-16.75
P/E Ratio	27.8-20.0	20.0-12.5	21.2-17.2	24.7-15.9	22.9-16.7	21.9-17.0	18.6-13.5
Average Yield %	2.1	2.5	2.1	2.0	2.0	2.2	2.2

Statistics are as originally reported. Adj. for 2-for-1 stock split, 12/95. ① Excl. $7.7 mill. ($0.16/sh) income fr. disc. ops. ② Excl. $1.0 mill. ($0.02/sh) income fr. disc. ops. ③ Excl. $13.8 mill. net income fr. disc. ops., 2000; $250.9 mill., 2001. ④ Incl. $15.8 mill. amort. of intang. and excl. $254.8 mill. gain fr. disc. ops.

OFFICERS:
M. E. Junck, Chmn., Pres., C.E.O.
C. G. Schmidt, V.P., C.F.O., Treas.
C. Wahlig, V.P., C.A.O.

INVESTOR CONTACT: D. Hayes, (563) 383-2163

PRINCIPAL OFFICE: 400 Putnam Building, 215 N. Main Street, Davenport, IA 52801

TELEPHONE NUMBER: (563) 383-2100
FAX: (563) 326-2972
WEB: www.lee.net
NO. OF EMPLOYEES: 3,600 full-time (approx.); 1,300 part-time (approx.)
SHAREHOLDERS: 2,954 (common); 1,954 (class B common)
ANNUAL MEETING: In Jan.
INCORPORATED: DE, Sept., 1950

INSTITUTIONAL HOLDINGS:
No. of Institutions: 146
Shares Held: 25,829,302
% Held: 58.5

INDUSTRY: Newspapers (SIC: 2711)

TRANSFER AGENT(S): EquiServe First Chicago Trust Division, Jersey City, NJ

LEGG MASON, INC.

YIELD 0.8%
P/E RATIO 25.0

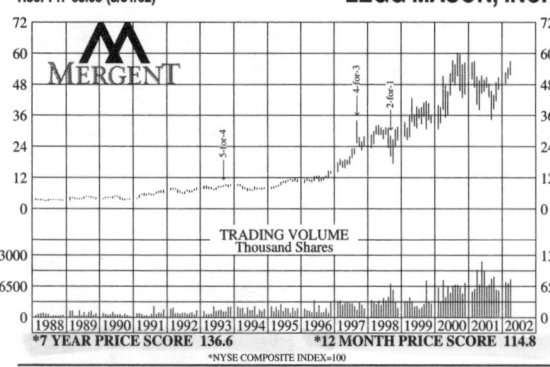

TRADING VOLUME
Thousand Shares

*7 YEAR PRICE SCORE 136.6   *12 MONTH PRICE SCORE 114.8
*NYSE COMPOSITE INDEX=100

INTERIM EARNINGS (Per Share):

Qtr.	June	Sept.	Dec.	Mar.
1997-98	0.31	0.36	0.39	0.40
1998-99	0.42	0.37	0.39	0.43
1999-00	0.54	0.47	0.55	0.78
2000-01	0.60	0.55	0.61	0.55
2001-02	0.52	0.45	0.60	...

INTERIM DIVIDENDS (Per Share):

Amt.	Decl.	Ex.	Rec.	Pay.
0.09Q	1/23/01	3/06/01	3/08/01	4/09/01
0.09Q	4/24/01	6/08/01	6/12/01	7/09/01
0.10Q	7/24/01	10/02/01	10/04/01	10/22/01
0.10Q	10/23/01	12/10/01	12/12/01	1/07/02
0.10Q	1/22/02	3/05/02	3/07/02	4/08/02

Indicated div.: $0.40

CAPITALIZATION (3/31/01):

	($000)	(%)
Long-Term Debt	218,970	19.1
Common & Surplus	927,720	80.9
Total	1,146,690	100.0

DIVIDEND ACHIEVER STATUS:
Rank: 73   10-Year Growth Rate: 14.09%
Total Years of Dividend Growth: 18

RECENT DEVELOPMENTS: For the quarter ended 12/31/01, net income decreased to $41.1 million from $41.3 million in the corresponding period of the previous year. Net revenues grew 7.4% to $374.8 million from $349.1 million in the prior year. Investment advisory and related fees increased 25.6% to $208.0 million, while principal transactions revenues improved 26.0% to $37.9 million. Interest revenues fell 54.3% to $33.5 million.

PROSPECTS: The Company continues to report record revenues from its asset management activities primarily as a result of the acquisitions of Private Capital Management and Royce & Associates, as well as the strong investment performance and client cash flows at Western Asset Management. Assets under management continue to grow primarily due to the positive investment performance at all of LM's domestic equity managers.

BUSINESS

LEGG MASON, INC. provides securities brokerage, investment advisory, corporate and public finance, and mortgage banking services to individuals, institutions, corporations and municipalities. As of 3/31/01, the Company serves brokerage clients through 146 offices. As investment advisors, the Company manages approximately $170.10 billion in assets as of 12/31/01. LM's mortgage-banking subsidiaries have direct and master servicing responsibility for commercial mortgages. For the fiscal year ended 3/31/01, revenues were derived as follows: investment advisory and related fees, 42.6%; commissions, 23.3%; principal transactions, 8.1%; investment banking, 4.3%; interest, 18.4%; and other, 3.3%. On 5/26/00, the Company acquired Perigee, Inc.

ANNUAL FINANCIAL DATA

	3/31/01	3/31/00	3/31/99	3/31/98	3/31/97	3/31/96	3/31/95
Earnings Per Share	2.30	2.33	1.55	1.32	1.17	0.93	⑴ 0.49
Cash Flow Per Share	2.84	2.83	1.92	1.69	1.53	1.28	0.80
Tang. Book Val. Per Share	12.38	10.60	8.83	7.97	7.33	5.64	4.71
Dividends Per Share	0.33	0.28	0.23	0.20	0.18	0.17	0.15
Dividend Payout %	14.3	11.8	14.8	15.3	15.7	18.1	31.6

INCOME STATEMENT (IN MILLIONS):

Total Revenues	1,536.3	1,370.8	1,046.0	889.1	639.7	516.0	371.6
Costs & Expenses	1,105.8	991.7	682.2	594.4	425.1	354.9	267.3
Depreciation & Amort.	36.5	29.3	21.6	22.0	17.2	14.2	10.5
Operating Income	393.9	349.7	342.2	272.7	197.3	146.9	93.8
Net Interest Inc./(Exp.)	d175.4	d134.3	d94.9	d73.7	d43.4	d26.2	d17.1
Income Before Income Taxes	265.8	239.1	148.8	128.4	95.2	63.9	27.7
Income Taxes	109.6	96.6	59.4	52.3	38.6	26.0	11.4
Net Income	156.2	142.5	89.3	76.1	56.6	37.9	⑴ 16.3
Cash Flow	192.7	171.8	110.9	98.1	73.8	52.1	26.7
Average Shs. Outstg. (000)	67,916	60,787	57,657	58,006	48,157	40,728	33,411

BALANCE SHEET (IN MILLIONS):

Cash & Cash Equivalents	2,627.5	2,058.1	1,740.6	1,334.3	793.1	450.1	173.9
Total Current Assets	4,087.8	3,813.4	2,805.9	2,129.2	1,399.4	932.7	532.7
Net Property	71.6	60.5	55.8	52.0	35.8	33.3	25.9
Total Assets	4,687.6	4,785.1	3,473.7	2,832.3	1,879.0	1,314.5	816.7
Total Current Liabilities	3,397.4	3,532.6	2,718.4	2,147.2	1,303.4	798.0	451.3
Long-Term Obligations	219.0	339.0	99.7	99.6	99.6	167.5	102.5
Net Stockholders' Equity	927.7	751.9	554.2	500.1	418.6	298.9	226.5
Net Working Capital	690.0	280.8	87.5	d18.1	96.0	134.7	81.4
Year-end Shs. Outstg. (000)	62,850	58,599	56,376	55,050	48,723	41,021	32,667

STATISTICAL RECORD:

Operating Profit Margin %	25.6	25.5	32.7	30.7	30.8	28.5	25.2
Net Profit Margin %	10.2	10.4	8.5	8.6	8.8	7.3	4.4
Return on Equity %	16.8	19.0	16.1	15.2	13.5	12.7	7.2
Return on Assets %	3.3	3.0	2.6	2.7	3.0	2.9	2.0
Debt/Total Assets %	4.7	7.1	2.9	3.5	5.3	12.7	12.5
Price Range	60.25-30.69	42.88-26.44	32.28-17.31	33.97-14.16	14.77-9.94	11.77-7.69	9.47-6.80
P/E Ratio	26.2-13.3	18.4-11.3	20.8-11.2	25.8-10.8	12.6-8.5	12.7-8.3	19.4-14.0
Average Yield %	0.7	0.8	0.9	0.8	1.5	1.7	1.9

Statistics are as originally reported. Adj. for 2-for-1 split, 9/98; 4-for-3 split, 9/97. ⑴ Incl. $2.0 mill. ($0.06 sh.) pre-tax chg. for litigation.

OFFICERS:
R. A. Mason, Chmn., Pres., C.E.O.
C. J. Daley Jr., Sr. V.P., C.F.O.
R. F. Price, Sr. V.P., Sec., Gen. Couns.

INVESTOR CONTACT: F. Barry Bilson, Investor Relations, (410) 539-0000

PRINCIPAL OFFICE: 100 Light Street, Baltimore, MD 21202

TELEPHONE NUMBER: (410) 539-0000
FAX: (410) 539-8010
WEB: www.leggmason.com

NO. OF EMPLOYEES: 5,380 (approx.)

SHAREHOLDERS: 2,331

ANNUAL MEETING: In July

INCORPORATED: MD, 1981

INSTITUTIONAL HOLDINGS:
No. of Institutions: 207
Shares Held: 43,777,484
% Held: 68.1

INDUSTRY: Security brokers and dealers (SIC: 6211)

TRANSFER AGENT(S): First Union National Bank, Charlotte, NC

LEGGETT & PLATT, INCORPORATED

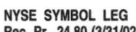

YIELD 1.9%
P/E RATIO 26.4

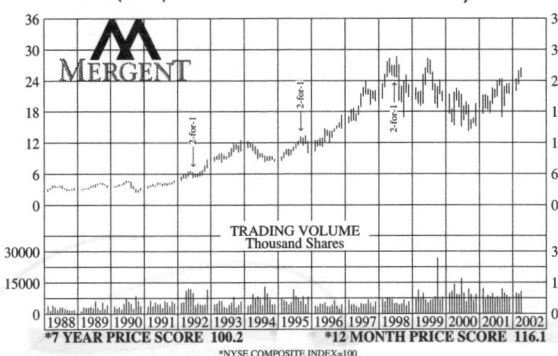

TRADING VOLUME
Thousand Shares

*7 YEAR PRICE SCORE 100.2   *12 MONTH PRICE SCORE 116.1
*NYSE COMPOSITE INDEX=100

INTERIM EARNINGS (Per Share):

Qtr.	Mar.	June	Sept.	Dec.
1998	0.29	0.32	0.32	0.31
1999	0.33	0.36	0.39	0.37
2000	0.37	0.38	0.34	0.23
2001	0.23	0.25	0.28	0.18

INTERIM DIVIDENDS (Per Share):

Amt.	Decl.	Ex.	Rec.	Pay.
0.12Q	2/14/01	2/28/01	3/02/01	3/15/01
0.12Q	5/09/01	5/23/01	5/25/01	6/15/01
0.12Q	8/08/01	8/22/01	8/24/01	9/14/01
0.12Q	11/14/01	12/12/01	12/14/01	1/15/02
0.12Q	2/13/02	3/13/02	3/15/02	4/15/02

Indicated div.: $0.48

CAPITALIZATION (12/31/01):

	($000)	(%)
Long-Term Debt	977,600	33.6
Deferred Income Tax	64,700	2.2
Common & Surplus	1,866,600	64.2
Total	2,908,900	100.0

DIVIDEND ACHIEVER STATUS:
Rank: 50   10-Year Growth Rate: 16.03%
Total Years of Dividend Growth: 32

RECENT DEVELOPMENTS: For the year ended 12/31/01, net income dropped 29.0% to $187.6 million from $264.1 million in 2000. Results for 2001 and 2000 included costs related to restructuring and plant closures of approximately $18.0 million and $9.0 million, respectively. Net sales declined 3.8% to $4.11 billion from $4.28 billion a year earlier due to continued weak market demand. Gross profit as a percentage of net sales was 24.1% versus 25.4% in 2000.

PROSPECTS: Looking ahead, LEG should continue to be affected by decreased market demand and its adverse effect on sales at least until the economy recovers. Consequently, the Company expects about a $0.20 per share improvement in earnings for 2002, provided full-year same-store location sales are flat. However, if same-store location sales grow 5.0% in 2002, LEG expects an additional increase in earnings of approximately $0.20 per share.

BUSINESS

LEGGETT & PLATT INCORPO-RATED is a diversified manufacturer that conceives, designs and produces a broad variety of engineered components and products for customers worldwide. The Company serves a wide array of manufacturers and retailers. Main operations include metal stamping, forming, casting, manufacturing, coating, welding, wire drawing, and assembly. Leggett & Platt is a major independent manufacturer of the following: a) components for residential furniture and bedding; b) retail store fixtures and point-of-purchase displays; c) components for office furniture; d) non-automotive aluminum die casting; e) drawn steel wire; f) automotive seat support and lumbar systems; and g) bedding industry machinery for wire forming, sewing and quilting. Primary raw materials include steel and aluminum, followed by smaller amounts of chemicals, wood, and plastics. LEG's international division is involved primarily in the sale of machinery and equipment designed to manufacture LEG's MiraCoil innersprings. As of 1/30/02, LEG was composed of 29 business units and more than 300 facilities located in 16 countries.

ANNUAL FINANCIAL DATA

	12/31/01	12/31/00	12/31/99	12/31/98	12/31/97	12/31/96	12/31/95
Earnings Per Share	③ 0.94	② 1.32	1.45	1.24	1.08	① 0.84	0.80
Cash Flow Per Share	1.92	2.18	2.19	1.87	1.62	1.34	1.19
Tang. Book Val. Per Share	4.81	4.58	4.50	4.59	3.88	3.37	3.45
Dividends Per Share	0.47	0.40	0.35	0.30	0.26	0.22	0.18
Dividend Payout %	50.0	30.3	24.1	24.6	24.1	26.3	22.6
INCOME STATEMENT (IN MILLIONS):							
Total Revenues	4,113.8	4,276.3	3,779.0	3,370.4	2,909.2	2,466.2	2,059.3
Costs & Expenses	3,555.4	3,616.4	3,129.4	2,815.6	2,441.9	2,070.4	1,756.0
Depreciation & Amort.	196.6	173.3	149.3	127.9	105.6	92.2	67.1
Operating Income	361.8	486.6	500.3	426.9	361.7	303.6	236.2
Net Interest Inc./(Exp.)	d53.9	d62.2	d39.9	d33.5	d31.8	d30.0	d11.5
Income Before Income Taxes	297.3	418.6	462.6	395.6	333.3	249.7	220.7
Income Taxes	109.7	154.5	172.1	147.6	125.0	96.7	85.8
Net Income	③ 187.6	② 264.1	290.5	248.0	208.3	① 153.0	134.9
Cash Flow	384.2	437.4	439.8	375.9	313.9	245.2	202.0
Average Shs. Outstg. (000)	200,435	200,388	200,938	200,670	193,190	183,600	170,000
BALANCE SHEET (IN MILLIONS):							
Cash & Cash Equivalents	187.2	37.3	20.6	83.5	7.7	3.7	6.7
Total Current Assets	1,421.9	1,405.3	1,256.2	1,137.1	944.6	763.3	571.9
Net Property	961.9	1,018.4	915.0	820.4	693.2	582.9	451.8
Total Assets	3,412.9	3,373.2	2,977.5	2,535.3	2,106.3	1,712.9	1,218.3
Total Current Liabilities	457.0	476.6	431.5	401.4	372.5	292.8	226.8
Long-Term Obligations	977.6	988.4	787.4	574.1	466.2	388.5	191.9
Net Stockholders' Equity	1,866.6	1,793.8	1,646.2	1,436.8	1,174.0	941.1	734.1
Net Working Capital	964.9	928.7	824.7	735.7	572.1	470.5	345.1
Year-end Shs. Outstg. (000)	196,298	196,097	196,880	197,684	192,754	184,216	167,520
STATISTICAL RECORD:							
Operating Profit Margin %	8.8	11.4	13.2	12.7	12.4	12.3	11.5
Net Profit Margin %	4.6	6.2	7.7	7.4	7.2	6.2	6.6
Return on Equity %	10.1	14.7	17.6	17.3	17.7	16.3	18.4
Return on Assets %	5.5	7.8	9.8	9.8	9.9	8.9	11.1
Debt/Total Assets %	28.6	29.3	26.4	22.6	22.1	22.7	15.8
Price Range	24.45-16.85	22.56-14.19	28.31-18.63	28.75-16.88	23.88-15.75	17.38-10.31	13.44-8.50
P/E Ratio	26.0-17.9	17.1-10.7	19.5-12.8	23.2-13.6	22.1-14.6	20.8-12.3	16.9-10.7
Average Yield %	2.3	2.2	1.5	1.3	1.3	1.3	1.6

Statistics are as originally reported. Adj. for stk. split: 2-for-1, 9/95 and 6/98. ① Bef. extraord. chrg. $12.5 mill. ② Incl. pre-tax chrg. of $6.2 mill. for plant closures. ③ Incl. nonrecurr. chrg. of $18.0 mill.

OFFICERS:
F. E. Wright, Chmn. & C.E.O.
D. S. Haffner, Pres. & C.O.O.
K. G. Glassman, Exec. V.P.

INVESTOR CONTACT: Investor Relations, (417) 358-8131

PRINCIPAL OFFICE: No. 1 Leggett Road, Carthage, MO 64836

TELEPHONE NUMBER: (417) 358-8131
FAX: (417) 359-5114
WEB: www.leggett.com

NO. OF EMPLOYEES: 31,000 (approx.)

SHAREHOLDERS: 16,356

ANNUAL MEETING: In May

INCORPORATED: MO, 1901

INSTITUTIONAL HOLDINGS:
No. of Institutions: 252
Shares Held: 117,924,325
% Held: 60.0

INDUSTRY: Diversified Manufacturing

TRANSFER AGENT(S): UMB Bank, n.a., Kansas City, MO

LILLY (ELI) & COMPANY

YIELD	1.6%
P/E RATIO	29.5

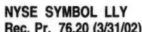

INTERIM EARNINGS (Per Share):

Qtr.	Mar.	June	Sept.	Dec.
1997	0.40	d1.57	0.41	0.40
1998	0.48	0.44	0.46	0.51
1999	0.40	0.52	0.67	0.73
2000	0.77	0.61	0.71	0.70
2001	0.74	0.76	0.54	0.54

INTERIM DIVIDENDS (Per Share):

Amt.	Decl.	Ex.	Rec.	Pay.
0.28Q	4/16/01	5/11/01	5/15/01	6/11/01
0.28Q	6/25/01	8/13/01	8/15/01	9/10/01
0.28Q	10/15/01	11/13/01	11/15/01	12/10/01
0.31Q	12/17/01	2/13/02	2/15/02	3/08/02
0.31Q	4/15/02	5/13/02	5/15/02	6/10/02

Indicated div.: $1.24 (Div. Reinv. Plan)

CAPITALIZATION (12/31/01):

	($000)	(%)
Long-Term Debt	3,132,100	30.6
Common & Surplus	7,104,000	69.4
Total	10,236,100	100.0

DIVIDEND ACHIEVER STATUS:
Rank: 166   10-Year Growth Rate: 8.40%
Total Years of Dividend Growth: 34

TRADING VOLUME
Thousand Shares

*7 YEAR PRICE SCORE 112.7   *12 MONTH PRICE SCORE 98.2
*NYSE COMPOSITE INDEX=100

RECENT DEVELOPMENTS: For the year ended 12/31/01, income was $2.81 billion, before an extraordinary charge of $29.4 million, compared with net income of $3.06 billion in the previous year. Results for 2001 included an acquired in-process technology charge of $190.5 million and asset impairment and other site charges of $121.4 million. Net sales grew 6.3% to $11.54 billion due to higher sales of ZYPREXA®, GEMZAR®, HUMALOG®, ACTOS® and EVISTA®.

PROSPECTS: LLY anticipates earnings per share for 2002 in the range of $2.70 to $2.80, excluding any unusal items. LLY expects to post sales growth in the low to mid-single digits in 2002. Several key products are expected to contribute to this growth, including ZYPREXA®, GEMZAR®, EVISTA® and XIGRIS®. Growth in all these products is anticipated to more than offset the decline in PROZAC® sales and anti-infectives. LLY has plans to launch a number of new products, including FORTEO® and CIALIS®.

BUSINESS

LILLY (ELI) & COMPANY. discovers, develops, manufactures and markets pharmaceuticals and animal health products. Neuroscience products (46.2% of 2001 sales) include PROZAC®, ZYPREXA®, DARVON®, PERMAX® and SARAFEM™. Endocrine products (26.9%) include HUMULIN®, HUMALOG®, ILETIN®, ACTOS®, EVISTA® and HUMATROPE®. Anti-infective products (6.5%) include CECLOR®, KEFLEX®, KEFTAB®, LORABID®, DYNABAC®, NEBCIN®, TAZIDIME®, KEFUROX®, KEFZOL® and VANCOCIN®. Oncology products (6.4%) include GEMZAR®, ONCOVIN®, VELBAN® and ELDISINE®. Animal Health products (5.9%) include TYLAN®, RUMENSIN®, COBAN®, MONTEBAN®, MAXIBAN®, APRALAN®, MICOTIL®, PULMOTIL®, SURMAX® and PAYLEAN®. Cardiovascular products (5.1%) include REOPRO®, DOBUTREX®, XIGRIS™, CYNT™ and AXID®. Other pharmaceutical products, (3.0%).

ANNUAL FINANCIAL DATA

	12/31/01	12/31/00	12/31/99	12/31/98	12/31/97	12/31/96	12/31/95
Earnings Per Share	⑥2.58	⑤2.79	④2.30	③1.87	②d0.35	1.39	①1.15
Cash Flow Per Share	2.99	3.18	2.70	2.31	0.11	1.89	1.63
Tang. Book Val. Per Share	6.32	5.37	4.49	2.86	2.79	1.87	1.21
Dividends Per Share	1.12	1.04	0.92	0.80	0.74	0.69	0.66
Dividend Payout %	43.4	37.3	40.0	42.8	...	49.3	57.0
INCOME STATEMENT (IN MILLIONS):							
Total Revenues	11,542.5	10,862.2	10,002.9	9,236.8	8,517.6	7,346.6	6,763.8
Costs & Expenses	7,548.3	6,866.7	6,199.5	6,049.4	5,549.5	4,756.3	4,228.3
Depreciation & Amort.	454.9	435.8	439.7	490.4	509.8	543.5	553.7
Operating Income	3,539.3	3,559.7	3,363.7	2,697.0	2,458.3	2,046.8	1,981.8
Net Interest Inc./(Exp.)	d146.5	d182.3	d183.8	d181.3	d234.1	d288.8	d286.3
Income Before Income Taxes	3,552.1	3,858.7	3,245.4	2,665.0	5,396.2	2,031.3	1,765.6
Income Taxes	742.7	800.9	698.7	568.7	895.3	507.8	459.0
Net Income	⑥2,809.4	⑤3,057.8	④2,546.7	③2,096.3	②d385.1	1,523.5	①1,306.6
Cash Flow	3,264.3	3,493.6	2,986.4	2,586.7	124.7	2,067.0	1,860.3
Average Shs. Outstg. (000)	1,090,793	1,097,725	1,106,055	1,121,486	1,101,099	1,093,654	1,138,052
BALANCE SHEET (IN MILLIONS):							
Cash & Cash Equivalents	3,731.0	4,618.2	3,836.0	1,597.1	2,024.6	955.1	1,084.1
Total Current Assets	6,938.9	7,943.0	7,055.5	5,406.8	5,320.7	3,891.4	4,138.6
Net Property	4,532.4	4,176.6	3,981.5	4,096.3	4,101.7	4,307.0	4,239.3
Total Assets	16,434.1	14,690.8	12,825.2	12,595.5	12,577.4	14,307.2	14,412.5
Total Current Liabilities	5,203.0	4,960.7	3,935.4	4,607.2	4,191.6	4,222.2	4,967.0
Long-Term Obligations	3,132.1	2,633.7	2,811.9	2,185.5	2,326.1	2,516.5	2,592.9
Net Stockholders' Equity	7,104.0	6,046.9	5,013.0	4,429.6	4,645.6	6,100.1	5,432.6
Net Working Capital	1,735.9	2,982.3	3,120.1	799.6	1,129.1	d330.9	d828.4
Year-end Shs. Outstg. (000)	1,123,349	1,125,560	1,090,238	1,019,090	1,110,522	1,105,646	1,101,506
STATISTICAL RECORD:							
Operating Profit Margin %	30.7	32.8	33.6	29.2	28.9	27.9	29.3
Net Profit Margin %	24.3	28.2	25.5	22.7	...	20.7	19.3
Return on Equity %	39.5	50.6	50.8	47.3	...	25.0	24.1
Return on Assets %	17.1	20.8	19.9	16.6	...	10.6	9.1
Debt/Total Assets %	19.1	17.9	21.9	17.4	18.5	17.6	18.0
Price Range	95.00-70.01	109.00-54.00	97.75-60.56	91.31-57.69	70.31-35.56	40.19-24.69	28.50-15.63
P/E Ratio	36.8-27.1	39.1-19.4	42.5-26.3	48.8-30.8	...	28.9-17.8	24.8-13.6
Average Yield %	1.4	1.3	1.2	1.4	...	1.4	3.0

Statistics are as originally reported. Adj. for 2-for-1 stock split, 10/97 & 12/95. ① Bef. inc. fr. dis. ops. of $984.3 mill. ② Incl. net gain of $631.8 mill. & non-cash chg. of $2.40 bill. ③ Excl. net gain of $1.6 mill. fr. disc. opers.; incl. a pre-tax chg. of $127.5 mill. ④ Incl. net gain of $30.4 mill.; excl. a net gain of $174.3 mill. fr. disc. opers. ⑤ Incl. net one-time gain of $214.4 mill. ⑥ Bef extraord. chrg. of $29.4 mill., incl. net chrgs. of $311.9 mill.

OFFICERS:
S. Taurel, Chmn., Pres., C.E.O.
C. E. Golden, Exec. V.P., C.F.O.
R. O. Kendall, Sr. V.P., Gen. Couns.

INVESTOR CONTACT: R. B. Graper, Dir. Inv. Rel., (317) 276-2506

PRINCIPAL OFFICE: Lilly Corporate Center, Indianapolis, IN 46285

TELEPHONE NUMBER: (317) 276-2000
FAX: (317) 276-6331
WEB: www.lilly.com
NO. OF EMPLOYEES: 41,100 (approx.)
SHAREHOLDERS: 57,700
ANNUAL MEETING: In Apr.
INCORPORATED: IN, Jan., 1901; reincorp., IN, Jan., 1936

INSTITUTIONAL HOLDINGS:
No. of Institutions: 846
Shares Held: 726,384,600
% Held: 64.6

INDUSTRY: Pharmaceutical preparations (SIC: 2834)

TRANSFER AGENT(S): Wells Fargo Shareowner Services, South St. Paul, MN

LINCOLN NATIONAL CORPORATION

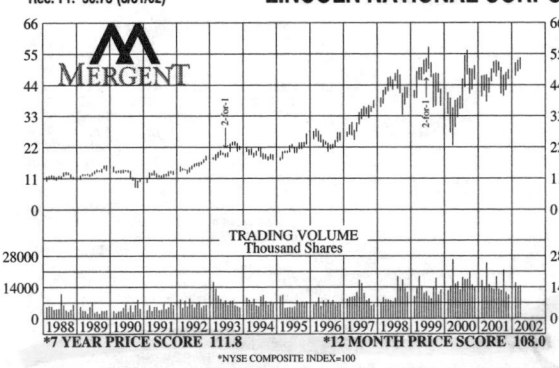

INTERIM EARNINGS (Per Share):

Qtr.	Mar.	June	Sept.	Dec.
1998	0.60	0.73	0.56	0.62
1999	0.71	0.73	0.66	0.18
2000	0.87	0.84	0.71	0.76
2001	0.85	0.74	0.61	0.88

INTERIM DIVIDENDS (Per Share):

Amt.	Decl.	Ex.	Rec.	Pay.
0.305Q	3/08/01	4/06/01	4/10/01	5/01/01
0.305Q	5/10/01	7/06/01	7/10/01	8/01/01
0.305Q	8/09/01	10/05/01	10/10/01	11/01/01
0.32Q	11/09/01	1/08/02	1/10/02	2/01/02
0.32Q	3/14/02	4/08/02	4/10/02	5/01/02

Indicated div.: $1.28 (Div. Reinv. Plan)

CAPITALIZATION (12/31/01):

	($000)	(%)
Long-Term Debt	861,754	13.1
Redeemable Pfd. Stock	474,656	7.2
Preferred Stock	762	0.0
Common & Surplus	5,262,722	79.7
Total	6,599,894	100.0

TRADING VOLUME Thousand Shares

*7 YEAR PRICE SCORE 111.8 *12 MONTH PRICE SCORE 108.0

*NYSE COMPOSITE INDEX=100

DIVIDEND ACHIEVER STATUS:
Rank: 213   10-Year Growth Rate: 6.02%
Total Years of Dividend Growth: 18

RECENT DEVELOPMENTS: For the year ended 12/31/01, income was $605.8 million, before an accounting charge of $15.6 million, versus net income of $621.4 million in the previous year. Results for 2001 included a gain on the sale of subsidiaries of $12.8 million. Total revenue declined 6.9% to $6.38 billion from $6.85 billion in the prior year. Net investment income decreased 2.5% to $2.68 billion. Insurance premiums declined 6.0% to $1.70 billion and insurance fees fell 7.1% to $1.54 billion.

PROSPECTS: The Company's near-term outlook appears to be positive. Results in the life insurance segment are being driven by solid business growth and reduced expenses. Total individual life insurance in-force increased 9.0% over the prior year reaching $234.40 billion at 12/31/01. Meanwhile, although earnings have declined in its annuities segment, LNC is beginning to benefit from increasing deposits, and in the fourth quarter, achieved substantial positive net cash flows.

BUSINESS

LINCOLN NATIONAL CORPORATION, a multi-line holding company, is one of the nation's largest diversified financial services companies. Through its subsidiaries, the Company provides annuities, life insurance, 401(k) plans, mutual funds, managed accounts, institutional investment management and financial planning and advisory services. In 1994, the Company sold its employee life health benefit operations. In 1997, the Company sold its property-casualty operations. In January 1998, the Company acquired the individual life insurance and annuities business of CIGNA Corporation for $1.40 billion. On 12/7/01, the Company sold Lincoln Re for $2.00 billion.

ANNUAL FINANCIAL DATA

	12/31/01	12/31/00	12/31/99	12/31/98	12/31/97	12/31/96	12/31/95
Earnings Per Share	③ 3.05	① 3.19	① 2.30	2.51	② 0.11	2.46	① 2.32
Tang. Book Val. Per Share	14.11	11.06	5.59	10.16	19.38	15.97	16.20
Dividends Per Share	1.22	1.16	1.10	1.04	0.98	0.92	0.86
Dividend Payout %	40.0	36.4	47.8	41.4	932.4	37.5	37.1
INCOME STATEMENT (IN MILLIONS):							
Total Premium Income	1,704.0	1,813.1	1,881.5	1,620.6	1,328.7	3,182.0	3,253.8
Other Income	4,676.6	5,038.4	4,922.2	4,466.4	3,569.7	3,539.3	3,379.4
Total Revenues	6,380.6	6,851.5	6,803.7	6,087.1	4,898.5	6,721.3	6,633.3
Policyholder Benefits	3,409.7	3,557.2	3,805.0	3,328.9	3,191.7	3,921.3	4,113.1
Income Before Income Taxes	764.1	836.3	570.0	697.4	34.9	712.3	626.6
Income Taxes	158.4	214.9	109.6	187.6	12.7	179.2	144.4
Equity Earnings/Minority Int.	...	...	...	...	d19.6	...	...
Net Income	③ 605.8	① 621.4	① 460.4	509.8	② 22.2	513.6	① 482.2
Average Shs. Outstg. (000)	193,303	194,921	200,418	203,262	207,992	209,122	208,232
BALANCE SHEET (IN MILLIONS):							
Cash & Cash Equivalents	3,095.5	1,927.4	1,895.9	2,433.4	3,794.7	1,231.7	1,572.9
Premiums Due	6,445.6	4,252.0	4,559.0	3,577.4	2,548.3	3,915.9	3,033.2
Invst. Assets: Fixed-term	28,345.7	27,449.8	27,688.6	30,232.9	24,066.4	27,906.4	25,834.5
Invst. Assets: Equities	470.5	549.7	604.0	542.8	660.4	992.7	1,164.8
Invst. Assets: Loans	6,475.2	6,623.9	6,627.8	6,233.1	4,051.3	4,031.1	3,789.4
Invst. Assets: Total	36,121.2	35,375.0	35,604.2	37,948.3	29,839.8	34,066.2	31,942.0
Total Assets	98,001.3	99,844.1	103,095.7	93,836.3	77,174.7	71,713.4	63,257.7
Long-Term Obligations	861.8	712.2	712.0	712.2	511.0	626.3	659.3
Net Stockholders' Equity	5,263.5	4,954.1	4,263.9	5,387.9	4,982.9	4,470.0	4,378.1
Year-end Shs. Outstg. (000)	186,944	190,748	195,495	202,112	201,718	207,318	208,370
STATISTICAL RECORD:							
Return on Revenues %	9.4	9.1	6.8	8.4	0.5	7.6	7.3
Return on Equity %	11.4	12.5	10.8	9.5	0.4	11.5	11.0
Return on Assets %	0.6	0.6	0.4	0.5	...	0.7	0.8
Price Range	52.75-38.00	56.38-22.63	57.50-36.00	49.44-33.50	38.56-24.50	28.50-20.38	26.88-17.31
P/E Ratio	17.3-12.5	17.7-7.1	25.0-15.7	19.7-13.3	366.9-233.1	11.6-8.3	11.6-7.5
Average Yield %	2.7	2.9	2.4	2.5	3.1	3.8	3.9

Statistics are as originally reported. Adj. for stk. split: 2-for-1, 6/99. ① Incl. non-recur. chrg. $80.2 mill., 12/00; $18.9 mill., 12/99; credit $54.2 mill., 12/95. ② Bef. disc. oper. gain $911.8 mill. ③ Bef. acctg. change chrg. $15.6 mill. & incl. gain of $12.8 mill. fr. sale of subsids.

OFFICERS:
J. A. Boscia, Chmn., Pres., C.E.O.
R. C. Vaughan, Exec. V.P., C.F.O.
D. L. Schoff, Sr. V.P., Gen. Couns.

INVESTOR CONTACT: Investor Relations, (215) 448-1422

PRINCIPAL OFFICE: 1500 Market Street, Suite 3900, Philadelphia, PA 19102-2112

TELEPHONE NUMBER: (215) 448-1400
WEB: www.lfg.com

NO. OF EMPLOYEES: 6,780 (avg.)

SHAREHOLDERS: 10,609 (record)

ANNUAL MEETING: In May

INCORPORATED: IN, Jan., 1968

INSTITUTIONAL HOLDINGS:
No. of Institutions: 399
Shares Held: 130,500,604
% Held: 69.6

INDUSTRY: Life insurance (SIC: 6311)

TRANSFER AGENT(S): First Chicago Trust Company of New York, Jersey City, NJ

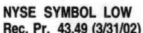

NYSE SYMBOL LOW
Rec. Pr. 43.49 (3/31/02)

LOWE'S COMPANIES, INC.

YIELD 0.2%
P/E RATIO 33.2

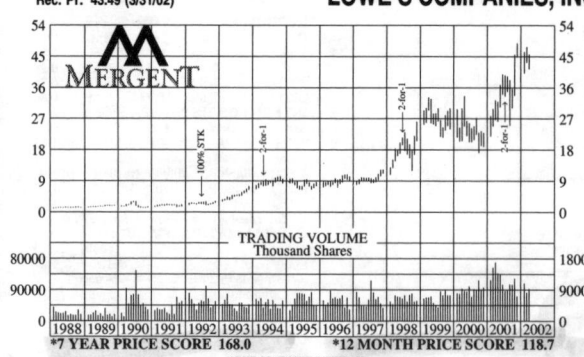

TRADING VOLUME
Thousand Shares

| 1988 | 1989 | 1990 | 1991 | 1992 | 1993 | 1994 | 1995 | 1996 | 1997 | 1998 | 1999 | 2000 | 2001 | 2002 |

*7 YEAR PRICE SCORE 168.0   ***12 MONTH PRICE SCORE 118.7**
*NYSE COMPOSITE INDEX=100

INTERIM EARNINGS (Per Share):

Qtr.	Apr.	July	Oct.	Jan.
1998-99	0.14	0.24	0.17	0.15
1999-00	0.17	0.30	0.22	0.20
2000-01	0.25	0.37	0.27	0.19
2001-02	0.29	0.42	0.32	0.28

INTERIM DIVIDENDS (Per Share):

Amt.	Decl.	Ex.	Rec.	Pay.
2-for-1	5/25/01	7/02/01	6/08/01	6/29/01
0.02Q	5/25/01	7/18/01	7/20/01	8/03/01
0.02Q	9/25/01	10/17/01	10/19/01	11/02/01
0.02Q	1/03/02	1/16/02	1/18/02	2/01/02
0.02Q	4/09/02	4/17/02	4/19/02	5/03/02

Indicated div.: $0.08 (Div. Reinv. Plan)

CAPITALIZATION (2/1/02):

	($000)	(%)
Long-Term Debt	3,734,011	34.9
Deferred Income Tax	304,697	2.8
Common & Surplus	6,674,442	62.3
Total	10,713,150	100.0

DIVIDEND ACHIEVER STATUS:
Rank: 168   10-Year Growth Rate: 8.31%
Total Years of Dividend Growth: 24

RECENT DEVELOPMENTS: For the 52 weeks ended 2/1/02, net earnings jumped 26.3% to $1.02 billion from $809.9 million in the corresponding 53-week period the year before. Net sales climbed 17.8% to $22.11 billion from $18.78 billion the previous year. Comparable-store sales rose 2.4% year-over-year. Gross margin was $6.37 billion, or 28.8% of net sales, versus $5.29 billion, or 28.2% of net sales, a year earlier. Earnings before taxes advanced 26.8% to $1.62 billion from $1.28 billion in the prior year.

PROSPECTS: Going forward, sales and earnings growth should be fueled by strengthening economic conditions and LOW's aggressive store expansion program. During fiscal 2001, the Company opened 115 new stores, including fourteen store relocations. Seven stores were closed during the year. LOW plans to open 123 stores in fiscal 2002, which would boost total square-footage by about 18.0%. The Company is projecting full fiscal 2002 sales growth of between 18.0% and 19.0% and earnings of $1.55 to $1.58 per share.

BUSINESS

LOWE'S COMPANIES, INC. is a specialty retailer that combines the merchandise, sales and service of a home improvement center, a building materials supplier and a consumer-durables retailer to serve the do-it-yourself home improvement and construction markets. As of 2/1/02, LOW operated 744 retail stores in 42 states with approximately 80.7 million square feet of selling space. Each store is stocked with more than 40,000 separate items, while the Company's special order program features more than 400,000 additional items. On 4/2/99, the Company acquired Eagle Hardware & Garden, Inc.

ANNUAL FINANCIAL DATA

	p2/1/02	2/2/01	1/28/00	1/29/99	1/30/98	1/31/97	1/31/96
Earnings Per Share	1.30	1.06	⬚ 0.88	0.68	0.52	0.44	0.35
Cash Flow Per Share	1.96	1.59	1.32	1.07	0.86	0.73	0.59
Tang. Book Val. Per Share	...	7.17	6.14	4.45	3.71	3.20	2.57
Dividends Per Share	0.08	0.07	0.06	0.058	0.055	0.05	0.047
Dividend Payout %	6.2	6.6	6.8	8.5	10.6	11.4	13.4
INCOME STATEMENT (IN MILLIONS):							
Total Revenues	22,111.1	18,778.6	15,905.6	12,244.9	10,136.9	8,600.2	7,075.4
Costs & Expenses	...	16,966.8	14,419.8	11,139.5	9,271.7	7,897.8	6,531.7
Depreciation & Amort.	534.1	409.5	337.8	272.2	241.1	199.8	153.6
Operating Income	...	1,402.3	1,148.0	833.2	624.1	502.7	390.1
Net Interest Inc./(Exp.)	d173.5	d120.8	d84.9	d74.7	d65.6	d49.1	d38.0
Income Before Income Taxes	1,624.3	1,281.4	1,063.1	758.4	558.5	453.6	352.1
Income Taxes	601.0	471.6	390.3	276.0	201.1	161.5	126.1
Net Income	1,023.3	809.9	⬚ 672.8	482.4	357.5	292.2	226.0
Cash Flow	1,557.4	1,219.4	1,010.6	754.6	598.6	491.9	379.6
Average Shs. Outstg. (000)	794,597	768,950	767,708	707,590	697,518	670,712	641,812
BALANCE SHEET (IN MILLIONS):							
Cash & Cash Equivalents	853.2	468.5	568.8	243.1	211.3	70.5	171.3
Total Current Assets	4,920.4	4,175.0	3,709.5	2,585.7	2,109.6	1,851.5	1,603.7
Net Property	8,653.4	7,035.0	5,177.2	3,636.9	3,005.2	2,494.4	1,858.3
Total Assets	13,736.2	11,375.8	9,012.3	6,344.7	5,219.3	4,435.0	3,556.4
Total Current Liabilities	3,016.8	2,928.6	2,386.0	1,765.3	1,449.3	1,348.5	949.9
Long-Term Obligations	3,734.0	2,697.7	1,726.6	1,283.1	1,045.6	767.3	866.2
Net Stockholders' Equity	6,674.4	5,494.9	4,695.5	3,136.0	2,600.6	2,217.5	1,656.7
Net Working Capital	1,903.6	1,246.4	1,323.6	820.3	660.3	502.9	653.8
Year-end Shs. Outstg. (000)	775,714	766,484	764,718	705,286	701,264	693,616	643,672
STATISTICAL RECORD:							
Operating Profit Margin %	...	7.5	7.2	6.8	6.2	5.8	5.5
Net Profit Margin %	4.6	4.3	4.2	3.9	3.5	3.4	3.2
Return on Equity %	15.3	14.7	14.3	15.4	13.7	13.2	13.6
Return on Assets %	7.4	7.1	7.5	7.6	6.8	6.6	6.4
Debt/Total Assets %	27.2	23.7	19.2	20.2	20.0	17.3	24.4
Price Range	48.88-21.88	33.63-17.13	33.22-21.50	26.09-10.80	12.28-7.91	10.88-7.16	9.72-6.50
P/E Ratio	37.6-16.8	31.9-16.2	38.0-24.6	38.4-15.9	23.8-15.3	25.0-16.4	27.6-18.5
Average Yield %	0.2	0.3	0.2	0.3	0.5	0.6	0.6

Statistics are as originally reported. Adj. for 2-for-1 stk. split, 6/01 & 6/98. ⬚ Incl. $24.4 mil pre-tax, non-recur. chg.

OFFICERS:
R. L. Tillman, Chmn., Pres., C.E.O.
R. A. Niblock, Exec. V.P., C.F.O.
S. A. Hellrung, Sr. V.P., Sec., Gen. Couns.
INVESTOR CONTACT: Marshall Croom, (336) 658-4022
PRINCIPAL OFFICE: 1605 Curtis Bridge Road, Wilkesboro, NC 28697

TELEPHONE NUMBER: (336) 658-4000
FAX: (336) 658-4766
WEB: www.lowes.com
NO. OF EMPLOYEES: 100,000 (approx.)
SHAREHOLDERS: 16,885
ANNUAL MEETING: In May
INCORPORATED: NC, Aug., 1952

INSTITUTIONAL HOLDINGS:
No. of Institutions: 639
Shares Held: 606,008,833
% Held: 78.1
INDUSTRY: Lumber and other building materials (SIC: 5211)
TRANSFER AGENT(S): EquiServe Trust Company, N.A., Boston, MA

M&T BANK CORPORATION

YIELD	1.2%
P/E RATIO	18.4

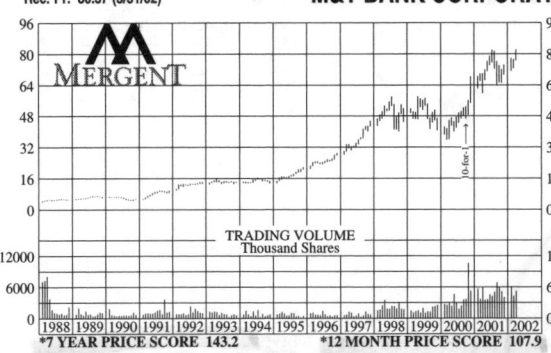

MERGENT

TRADING VOLUME
Thousand Shares

7 YEAR PRICE SCORE 143.2   *12 MONTH PRICE SCORE 107.9*
NYSE COMPOSITE INDEX=100

INTERIM EARNINGS (Per Share):

Qtr.	Mar.	June	Sept.	Dec.
1998	0.70	0.53	0.68	0.71
1999	0.83	0.80	0.83	0.82
2000	0.86	0.97	0.94	0.76
2001	1.14	0.94	1.24	1.05

INTERIM DIVIDENDS (Per Share):

Amt.	Decl.	Ex.	Rec.	Pay.
0.25Q	4/18/01	5/30/01	6/01/01	6/29/01
0.25Q	7/17/01	8/30/01	9/04/01	9/28/01
0.25Q	10/17/01	11/29/01	12/03/01	12/31/01
0.25Q	2/20/02	2/26/02	2/28/02	3/29/02

Indicated div.: $1.00 (Div. Reinv. Plan)

CAPITALIZATION (12/31/01):

	($000)	(%)
Total Deposits	21,580,400	77.1
Long-Term Debt	3,461,769	12.4
Common & Surplus	2,939,451	10.5
Total	27,981,620	100.0

DIVIDEND ACHIEVER STATUS:
Rank: 19   10-Year Growth Rate: 21.73%
Total Years of Dividend Growth: 21

RECENT DEVELOPMENTS: For the year ended 12/31/01, net income rose 32.1% to $378.1 million from $286.2 million the year before. Earnings for 2001 and 2000 included after-tax merger-related expenses of $4.8 million and $16.4 million, respectively. Net interest income grew 35.6% to $1.16 billion from $854.2 million a year earlier. Provision for credit losses surged to $103.5 million from $38.0 million a year earlier, reflecting the downturn in the economy. Total other income grew 47.0% to $477.4 million, while total other expense increased 36.6% to $948.3 million.

PROSPECTS: In 2002, diluted earnings per share are expected to be approximately $4.89. Separately, the Company and Benefit Resource, Inc. announced eTRAC, a stored value card program that enables individuals to purchase transit passes and fares with pre-tax dollars through employer-sponsored, Qualified Transportation Expense Programs. Employers offering this plan to their employees may save $90 per employee per year in payroll taxes. eTRAC will be initially launched in New York, Chicago, Boston, Philadelphia and Washington D.C.

BUSINESS

M&T BANK CORPORATION, with assets of $31.45 billion as of 12/31/01, is a bank holding company with two wholly-owned bank subsidiaries, Manufacturers and Traders Trust Company and M&T Bank, National Association. The banks collectively offer commercial banking, trust and investment services to their customers. The Company's five reportable segments are Commercial Banking, Commercial Real Estate, Discretionary Portfolio, Residential Mortgage Banking and Retail Banking. On 2/10/01, the Company acquired Premier National Bancorp, Inc.

ANNUAL FINANCIAL DATA

	12/31/01	12/31/00	12/31/99	12/31/98	12/31/97	12/31/96	12/31/95
Earnings Per Share	⑪ 3.82	⑪ 3.44	⑪ 3.28	⑪ 2.62	2.53	2.13	1.88
Tang. Book Val. Per Share	17.84	16.10	14.88	13.72	15.59	13.55	12.53
Dividends Per Share	1.00	0.63	0.45	0.38	0.32	0.28	0.25
Dividend Payout %	26.2	18.2	13.7	14.5	12.7	13.1	13.3
INCOME STATEMENT (IN MILLIONS)							
Total Interest Income	2,101.9	1,772.8	1,478.6	1,351.8	1,065.0	997.4	928.2
Total Interest Expense	943.6	918.6	719.2	687.5	508.1	466.4	441.7
Net Interest Income	1,158.3	854.2	759.4	664.3	556.9	531.0	486.4
Provision for Loan Losses	103.5	38.0	44.5	43.2	46.0	43.3	40.4
Non-Interest Income	477.4	324.7	282.4	270.6	193.1	170.2	149.5
Non-Interest Expense	948.3	694.5	579.0	566.1	421.8	409.0	374.4
Income Before Taxes	583.9	446.4	418.3	325.6	282.2	249.0	221.2
Net Income	⑪ 378.1	⑪ 286.2	⑪ 265.6	⑪ 208.0	176.2	151.1	131.0
Average Shs. Outstg. (000)	99,024	83,171	80,900	79,500	69,770	70,480	67,810
BALANCE SHEET (IN MILLIONS)							
Cash & Due from Banks	965.7	750.3	592.8	493.8	333.8	324.7	363.1
Securities Avail. for Sale	2,702.1	3,071.7	2,321.9	2,756.9	1,640.6	1,434.0	1,541.6
Total Loans & Leases	25,395.5	22,970.3	17,572.9	16,005.7	11,765.5	11,120.2	9,873.7
Allowance for Credit Losses	632.7	602.2	482.3	520.5	543.6	668.6	580.2
Net Loans & Leases	24,762.8	22,368.1	17,090.6	15,485.2	11,221.9	10,451.7	9,293.5
Total Assets	31,450.2	28,949.5	22,409.1	20,583.9	14,002.9	12,943.9	11,955.9
Total Deposits	21,580.4	20,232.7	15,373.6	14,737.2	11,163.2	10,514.5	9,469.6
Long-Term Obligations	3,461.8	3,414.5	1,775.1	1,567.5	427.8	178.0	192.8
Total Liabilities	28,510.7	26,249.0	20,612.1	18,981.5	12,972.7	12,038.3	11,109.6
Net Stockholders' Equity	2,939.5	2,700.5	1,797.0	1,602.4	1,030.3	905.7	846.3
Year-end Shs. Outstg. (000)	93,684	93,244	77,238	76,980	66,100	66,860	64,330
STATISTICAL RECORD:							
Return on Equity %	12.9	10.6	14.8	13.0	17.1	16.7	15.5
Return on Assets %	1.2	1.0	1.2	1.0	1.3	1.2	1.1
Equity/Assets %	9.3	9.3	8.0	7.8	7.4	7.0	7.1
Non-Int. Exp./Tot. Inc. %	58.0	58.9	55.6	60.6	56.2	58.3	58.9
Price Range	82.11-59.80	68.42-35.70	58.25-40.60	58.20-40.00	45.50-28.10	28.96-20.90	21.80-13.60
P/E Ratio	21.5-15.7	19.9-10.4	17.7-12.4	22.2-15.3	18.0-11.1	13.6-9.8	11.6-7.2
Average Yield %	1.4	1.2	0.9	0.8	0.9	1.1	1.4

Statistics are as originally reported. Adj. for 10-for-1 stk. split, 10/5/00. ⑪ Incl. after-tax nonrecurr. merger & acq. chrgs.: $4.8 mill., 2001; $16.4 mill., 2000; $3.0 mill., 12/31/99; $14.0 mill., 12/31/98.

OFFICERS:
R. G. Wilmers, Chmn., Pres., C.E.O.
M. P. Pinto, Exec. V.P., C.F.O.
A. C. Kugler, Exec. V.P., Treas.

INVESTOR CONTACT: Shareholder Relations/Corp. Fin. Dept., (716) 842-5445

PRINCIPAL OFFICE: One M&T Plaza, 5th Floor, Buffalo, NY 14203

TELEPHONE NUMBER: (716) 842-5445
FAX: (716) 842-5177
WEB: www.mandtbank.com
NO. OF EMPLOYEES: 8,139 full-time; 1,152 part-time
SHAREHOLDERS: 12,565
ANNUAL MEETING: In Apr.
INCORPORATED: NY, Nov., 1969

INSTITUTIONAL HOLDINGS:
No. of Institutions: 243
Shares Held: 52,129,733
% Held: 56.1

INDUSTRY: State commercial banks (SIC: 6022)

TRANSFER AGENT(S): BankBoston, N.A. c/o EquiServe, Boston, MA

MADISON GAS & ELECTRIC COMPANY

YIELD 4.7%
P/E RATIO 17.4

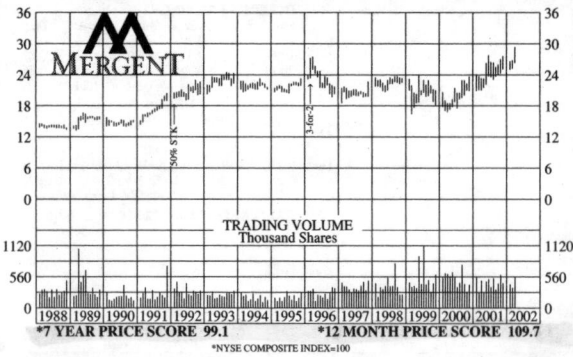

TRADING VOLUME
Thousand Shares

| 1988 | 1989 | 1990 | 1991 | 1992 | 1993 | 1994 | 1995 | 1996 | 1997 | 1998 | 1999 | 2000 | 2001 | 2002 |

*7 YEAR PRICE SCORE 99.1   ***12 MONTH PRICE SCORE 109.7**

*NYSE COMPOSITE INDEX=100

INTERIM EARNINGS (Per Share):

Qtr.	Mar.	June	Sept.	Dec.
1996	0.46	0.19	0.34	d0.59
1997	0.50	0.16	0.35	0.39
1998	0.53	0.15	0.36	0.34
1999	0.56	0.15	0.38	0.39
2000	0.62	0.15	0.51	0.39
2001	0.58	0.32	0.36	0.37

INTERIM DIVIDENDS (Per Share):

Amt.	Decl.	Ex.	Rec.	Pay.
0.331Q	5/22/01	5/30/01	6/01/01	6/15/01
0.333Q	8/17/01	8/29/01	9/01/01	9/15/01
0.333Q	11/16/01	11/28/01	12/01/01	12/15/01
0.333Q	2/22/02	2/27/02	3/01/02	3/15/02

Indicated div.: $1.33 (Div. Reinv. Plan)

CAPITALIZATION (12/31/01):

	($000)	(%)
Long-Term Debt	157,600	36.6
Deferred Income Tax	56,198	13.1
Common & Surplus	216,292	50.3
Total	430,090	100.0

DIVIDEND ACHIEVER STATUS:

Rank: 281   10-Year Growth Rate: 1.32%
Total Years of Dividend Growth: 26

RECENT DEVELOPMENTS: For the twelve months ended 12/31/01, income was unchanged at $27.4 million, before an after-tax accounting charge of $117,000, compared with net income in 2000. Total operating revenues climbed 3.0% to $333.7 million from $324.1 million a year earlier. Electric revenue was unchanged at $203.2 million versus the prior year. Gas revenues rose 7.9% to $130.5 million due to increased gas commodity costs and a rise in gas rates.

However, gas deliveries were down in 2001 due to unseasonably mild weather conditions in November and December. Electric operating expenses grew 8.8% due to a rise in fuel costs, increased transmission wheeling costs paid to American Transmission Company and higher distribution expense. Operating income decreased 13.5% to $34.7 million compared with $40.1 million in the previous year.

BUSINESS

MADISON GAS & ELECTRIC COMPANY is a public utility that generates, transmits and distributes electricity to 127,000 customers in Dane County, Wisconsin (250 sq. miles) as of 2/7/02. MDSN also purchases, transports and distributes natural gas to 120,000 customers in seven Wisconsin counties: Columbia, Crawford, Dane, Iowa, Juneau, Monroe and Vernon (1,325 sq. miles). Of the total number of electric customers, approximately 110,000 are residential and 17,000 are commercial and industrial.

ANNUAL FINANCIAL DATA

	12/31/01	12/31/00	12/31/99	12/31/98	12/31/97	12/31/96	12/31/95
Earnings Per Share	☐1.63	1.67	1.48	1.38	1.40	0.40	1.49
Cash Flow Per Share	3.79	3.90	3.78	3.54	3.21	2.07	3.15
Tang. Book Val. Per Share	12.67	12.05	11.49	11.34	11.25	11.14	12.01
Dividends Per Share	1.33	1.32	1.31	1.30	1.29	1.27	1.26
Dividend Payout %	81.5	78.9	88.4	94.1	91.9	318.2	84.6
INCOME STATEMENT (IN THOUSANDS):							
Total Revenues	333,711	324,108	274,034	249,752	264,648	253,291	248,590
Costs & Expenses	248,302	228,927	191,127	170,014	191,842	182,545	176,074
Depreciation & Amort.	36,459	36,548	37,053	34,759	29,081	26,816	26,787
Maintenance Exp.	14,279	18,532	13,304	15,167	12,735	12,414	11,858
Operating Income	34,671	40,101	32,550	29,812	30,990	31,516	33,871
Net Interest Inc./(Exp.)	d13,572	d14,129	d12,039	d10,855	d10,724	d10,891	d11,507
Net Income	☐27,362	27,355	23,746	22,230	22,523	6,427	23,970
Cash Flow	63,821	63,903	60,799	56,989	51,604	33,243	50,693
Average Shs. Outstg.	16,819	16,382	16,084	16,080	16,080	16,080	16,080
BALANCE SHEET (IN THOUSANDS):							
Gross Property	741,909	952,035	879,253	814,286	770,695	739,514	715,487
Accumulated Depreciation	340,660	510,381	484,428	446,984	407,602	374,315	348,254
Net Property	401,249	441,654	394,825	367,302	363,093	365,199	367,233
Total Assets	541,451	571,604	495,510	466,265	471,790	484,169	493,876
Long-Term Obligations	157,600	183,437	148,599	159,761	129,923	128,886	129,048
Net Stockholders' Equity	216,292	200,312	185,686	182,275	180,923	179,089	193,137
Year-end Shs. Outstg.	17,072	16,619	16,161	16,080	16,080	16,080	16,080
STATISTICAL RECORD:							
Operating Profit Margin %	10.4	12.4	11.9	11.9	11.7	12.4	13.6
Net Profit Margin %	8.2	8.4	8.7	8.9	8.5	2.5	9.6
Net Inc./Net Property %	6.8	6.2	6.0	6.1	6.2	1.8	6.5
Net Inc./Tot. Capital %	6.4	6.4	6.3	5.8	6.3	1.8	6.4
Return on Equity %	12.7	13.7	12.8	12.2	12.4	3.6	12.4
Accum. Depr./Gross Prop. %	45.9	53.6	55.1	54.9	52.9	50.6	48.7
Price Range	27.80-20.88	23.69-16.75	23.88-16.38	23.75-20.63	22.75-18.50	27.50-19.63	23.33-20.33
P/E Ratio	17.1-12.8	14.2-10.0	16.1-11.1	17.2-14.9	16.2-13.2	68.7-49.1	15.7-13.6
Average Yield %	5.5	6.5	6.5	5.9	6.2	5.4	5.8

Statistics are as originally reported. Adj. for stk. split: 3-for-2, 2/20/96. ☐ Bef. acctg. change chrg. of $117,000.

OFFICERS:
G. J. Wolter, Chmn., Pres., C.E.O.
D. C. Mebane, Vice-Chmn.
T. A. Hanson, V.P., C.F.O.

INVESTOR CONTACT: Shareholder Services, (800) 356-6423

PRINCIPAL OFFICE: 133 South Blair St., P.O. Box 1231, Madison, WI 53701

TELEPHONE NUMBER: (608) 252-7000
FAX: (608) 252-7098
WEB: www.mge.com

NO. OF EMPLOYEES: 676

SHAREHOLDERS: 18,000 (approx.)

ANNUAL MEETING: In Mar.

INCORPORATED: WI, Apr., 1896

INSTITUTIONAL HOLDINGS:
No. of Institutions: 69
Shares Held: 3,678,791
% Held: 21.5

INDUSTRY: Electric and other services combined (SIC: 4931)

TRANSFER AGENT(S): Continental Stock Transfer & Trust Company, New York, NY

MARSH & McLENNAN COMPANIES, INC.

YIELD 1.9%
P/E RATIO 33.4

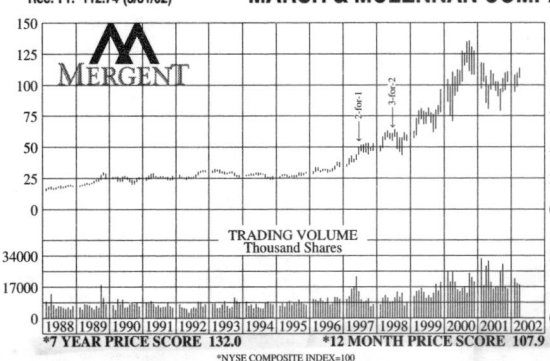

TRADING VOLUME
Thousand Shares

*7 YEAR PRICE SCORE 132.0   *12 MONTH PRICE SCORE 107.9
*NYSE COMPOSITE INDEX=100

INTERIM EARNINGS (Per Share):

Qtr.	Mar.	June	Sept.	Dec.
1997	0.75	0.58	0.55	d0.19
1998	0.87	0.72	0.69	0.70
1999	1.03	0.63	0.81	0.16
2000	1.19	0.96	0.97	0.98
2001	1.27	1.02	0.58	0.51

INTERIM DIVIDENDS (Per Share):

Amt.	Decl.	Ex.	Rec.	Pay.
0.53Q	5/17/01	7/05/01	7/09/01	8/15/01
0.53Q	9/20/01	10/11/01	10/15/01	11/15/01
0.53Q	11/15/01	1/03/02	1/07/02	2/15/02
0.53Q	3/21/02	4/05/02	4/09/02	5/15/02

Indicated div.: $2.12 (Div. Reinv. Plan)

CAPITALIZATION (12/31/01):

	($000)	(%)
Long-Term Debt	2,334,000	31.1
Common & Surplus	5,173,000	68.9
Total	7,507,000	100.0

DIVIDEND ACHIEVER STATUS:
Rank: 158   10-Year Growth Rate: 9.04%
Total Years of Dividend Growth: 40

RECENT DEVELOPMENTS: For the year ended 12/31/01, net income declined 17.5% to $974.0 million from $1.18 billion in the prior year. Results for 2001 included a net non-recurring charges of $396.0 million related to a change in value of investments and the events of 9/11/01, while results for 2000 included a net non-recurring gain of $2.0 million. Total revenue decreased 2.1% to $9.94 billion from $10.16 billion in 2000. Revenue from risk and insurance services grew 7.7% to $5.15 billion, while consulting revenue rose 1.2% to $2.16 billion.

PROSPECTS: Looking ahead, future prospects are mixed. Earnings continue to be hampered by a slumping stock market. In the fourth quarter of 2001, Putnam's average assets under management were $304.00 billion, down from $381.00 billion in the year-earlier period. However, many of the Company's consulting practices are benefiting from positive market conditions as premiums continued to rise and capacity, particularly for large risks, are becoming more scarce.

BUSINESS

MARSH & McLENNAN COMPANIES, INC. is engaged in the worldwide business of providing retail and wholesale insurance services, principally as a broker or consultant for insurers, insurance underwriters and other brokers. MMC subsidiaries include Marsh Inc., a risk and insurance services firm; Putnam Investments, one of the largest investment management companies in the U.S.; and Mercer Consulting Group, a major global provider of consulting services. Other subsidiaries render advisory services in the area of employee benefits and compensation consulting, management consulting, economic consulting and environmental consulting. Contributions to revenues by type of service in 2001 were as follows: insurance services, 51.8%; consulting, 21.7%; and investment management, 26.5%.

ANNUAL FINANCIAL DATA

	12/31/01	12/31/00	12/31/99	12/31/98	12/31/97	12/31/96	12/31/95
Earnings Per Share	[1] 3.39	4.10	[2] 2.62	2.98	[1] 1.59	2.11	1.84
Tang. Book Val. Per Share	...	...	...	...	3.07	6.19	4.29
Dividends Per Share	2.06	1.90	1.70	1.47	1.27	1.10	0.99
Dividend Payout %	60.8	46.3	64.9	49.2	79.5	52.1	53.8
INCOME STATEMENT (IN MILLIONS):							
Total Revenues	9,943.0	10,157.0	9,157.0	7,190.0	6,008.6	4,149.0	3,770.3
Income Before Income Taxes	1,590.0	1,955.0	1,247.0	1,305.0	662.4	668.0	649.8
Income Taxes	599.0	753.0	521.0	509.0	263.0	208.7	246.9
Equity Earnings/Minority Int.	d17.0	d21.0	...	...	...	...	...
Net Income	[2] 974.0	1,181.0	[2] 726.0	796.0	[1] 399.4	459.3	402.9
Average Shs. Outstg. (000)	286,000	284,000	272,000	264,000	250,800	217,200	218,700
BALANCE SHEET (IN MILLIONS):							
Cash & Cash Equivalents	537.0	240.0	428.0	610.0	424.3	299.6	328.1
Premiums Due	2,692.0	2,812.0	2,323.0	1,909.0	1,498.2	1,085.8	1,132.5
Invst. Assets: Total	826.0	976.0	687.0	828.0	720.2	573.3	411.8
Total Assets	13,293.0	13,769.0	13,021.0	11,871.0	7,914.2	4,545.2	4,329.5
Long-Term Obligations	2,334.0	2,347.0	2,357.0	1,590.0	1,239.8	458.2	410.6
Net Stockholders' Equity	5,173.0	5,228.0	4,170.0	3,659.0	3,198.8	1,888.6	1,665.5
Year-end Shs. Outstg. (000)	274,327	276,026	267,026	257,000	254,925	216,957	218,322
STATISTICAL RECORD:							
Return on Revenues %	9.8	11.6	7.9	11.1	6.6	11.1	10.7
Return on Equity %	18.8	22.6	17.4	21.8	12.5	24.3	24.2
Return on Assets %	7.3	8.6	5.6	6.7	5.0	10.1	9.3
Price Range	118.06-79.00	135.69-70.50	96.75-57.13	64.31-43.38	53.33-34.21	38.29-28.08	30.04-25.38
P/E Ratio	34.8-23.3	33.1-17.2	36.9-21.8	21.6-14.6	33.5-21.5	18.1-13.3	16.3-13.8
Average Yield %	2.1	1.8	2.2	2.7	2.9	3.3	3.6

Statistics are as originally reported. Adj. for stk. splits: 3-for-2, 6/98; 2-for-1, 6/97 [1] Incl. non-recurr. chrg. 2001, $396.0 mill.; 1997, $296.8 mill. [2] Incl. special chrg. $337.0 mill.

OFFICERS:
J. W. Greenberg, Chmn., Pres., C.E.O.
M. Cabiallavetta, Vice-Chmn.
C. A. Davis, Vice-Chmn.
S. S. Wijnberg, Sr. V.P., C.F.O.

PRINCIPAL OFFICE: 1166 Avenue of the Americas, New York, NY 10036-2774

TELEPHONE NUMBER: (212) 345-5000
FAX: (212) 345-4809
WEB: www.mmc.com
NO. OF EMPLOYEES: 57,800 (approx.)
SHAREHOLDERS: 10,927
ANNUAL MEETING: In May
INCORPORATED: DE, March, 1969

INSTITUTIONAL HOLDINGS:
No. of Institutions: 636
Shares Held: 188,220,744
% Held: 68.5
INDUSTRY: Insurance agents, brokers, & service (SIC: 6411)
TRANSFER AGENT(S): The Bank of New York, New York, NY

NYSE SYMBOL MI
Rec. Pr. 62.24 (3/31/02)

MARSHALL & ILSLEY CORPORATION

YIELD 1.9%
P/E RATIO 20.2

TRADING VOLUME
Thousand Shares

*7 YEAR PRICE SCORE 106.5   ***12 MONTH PRICE SCORE 108.5**
*NYSE COMPOSITE INDEX=100

INTERIM EARNINGS (Per Share):

Qtr.	Mar.	June	Sept.	Dec.
1998	0.66	0.54	0.70	0.72
1999	0.75	0.77	0.81	0.81
2000	0.81	0.83	0.47	0.78
2001	0.80	0.55	0.75	0.98

INTERIM DIVIDENDS (Per Share):

Amt.	Decl.	Ex.	Rec.	Pay.
0.265Q	2/22/01	3/02/01	3/06/01	3/14/01
0.29Q	4/24/01	5/29/01	5/31/01	6/14/01
0.29Q	8/15/01	8/29/01	8/31/01	9/17/01
0.29Q	10/18/01	11/28/01	11/30/01	12/14/01
0.29Q	2/21/02	2/26/02	2/28/02	3/14/02

Indicated div.: $1.16 (Div. Reinv. Plan)

CAPITALIZATION (12/31/01):

	($000)	(%)
Total Deposits	16,493,047	80.3
Long-Term Debt	1,560,177	7.6
Preferred Stock	336	0.0
Common & Surplus	2,492,632	12.1
Total	20,546,192	100.0

DIVIDEND ACHIEVER STATUS:
Rank: 133   10-Year Growth Rate: 10.19%
Total Years of Dividend Growth: 28

RECENT DEVELOPMENTS: For the year ended 12/31/01, income, before accounting changes, increased 6.5% to $337.9 million from $317.4 million in the previous year. Earnings for 2001 and 2000 included after-tax non-recurring net charges related to various items of $68.1 million and $46.5 million, respectively. Net interest rose 25.2% to $842.8 million from $673.0 million the year before. Provision for credit losses soared 78.3% to $54.1 million from $30.4 million in 2000.

PROSPECTS: On 3/1/02, the Company completed the acquisitions of Richfield State Agency, Inc., a bank holding company in Richfield, MN and Century Bancshares, Inc., a financial holding company in Eden Prairie, MN. The transactions are expected to enhance MI's existing offices in downtown Minneapolis and Edina, MN. In addition, the acquisitions are expected to be accretive to earnings in 2002.

BUSINESS

MARSHALL & ILSLEY CORPO-RATION, a multi-bank holding company with assets of $27.25 billion as of 12/31/01, is headquartered in Milwaukee, Wisconsin. The Company's principal subsidiary is Metavante Corporation (formerly MI's M&I Data Services Division), a provider of integrated financial transaction processing, outsourcing services, software, and consulting services. The Company has 215 banking offices in Wisconsin, and 25 locations throughout Arizona and offices in Minneapolis, Minnesota; Las Vegas, Nevada; and Naples, Florida. The Company also provides trust and investment management, equipment leasing, data processing, mortgage banking, financial planning, investments, and insurance services from offices throughout the U.S. and on the Internet.

ANNUAL FINANCIAL DATA

	12/31/01	12/31/00	12/31/99	12/31/98	12/31/97	12/31/96	12/31/95
Earnings Per Share	①② 3.09	①② 2.91	3.14	② 2.61	2.42	2.07	1.96
Tang. Book Val. Per Share	18.32	18.44	16.54	17.98	18.90	14.23	13.44
Dividends Per Share	1.14	1.03	0.94	0.86	0.79	0.72	0.65
Dividend Payout %	36.7	35.6	29.9	32.9	32.4	34.8	32.9
INCOME STATEMENT (IN MILLIONS):							
Total Interest Income	1,709.1	1,748.0	1,496.6	1,434.0	1,143.7	971.4	924.7
Total Interest Expense	866.3	1,075.0	791.3	758.0	579.6	465.7	433.2
Net Interest Income	842.8	673.0	705.3	676.1	564.0	505.7	491.5
Provision for Loan Losses	54.1	30.4	25.4	27.1	17.3	15.2	16.2
Non-Interest Income	1,002.8	928.4	845.8	1,424.2	598.9	503.3	424.2
Non-Interest Expense	1,290.4	1,100.7	997.7	944.9	775.4	680.7	599.6
Income Before Taxes	501.0	470.4	527.9	465.3	370.3	313.1	299.9
Net Income	①② 337.9	①② 317.4	354.5	② 964.3	245.1	203.4	193.3
Average Shs. Outstg. (000)	109,132	108,883	113,005	115,240	101,510	98,482	98,757
BALANCE SHEET (IN MILLIONS):							
Cash & Due from Banks	617.2	760.1	705.3	760.4	800.1	780.6	745.9
Securities Avail. for Sale	4,216.8	4,801.2	4,477.0	4,247.2	4,182.2	3,213.9	2,677.8
Total Loans & Leases	19,295.4	17,587.1	16,335.1	13,996.2	12,542.3	9,301.9	8,868.9
Allowance for Credit Losses	268.2	235.1	225.9	226.1	202.8	155.9	161.4
Net Loans & Leases	19,027.2	17,352.0	16,109.2	13,770.1	12,339.5	9,146.0	8,707.5
Total Assets	27,253.7	26,077.7	24,369.7	21,566.3	19,477.5	14,763.3	13,343.1
Total Deposits	16,493.0	19,248.6	16,435.2	15,919.9	14,356.0	10,952.4	10,280.8
Long-Term Obligations	1,560.2	921.3	665.0	794.5	791.2	336.1	422.6
Total Liabilities	24,760.8	23,835.6	22,252.8	19,322.5	17,557.4	13,502.1	12,085.5
Net Stockholders' Equity	2,493.0	2,242.2	2,116.9	2,243.8	1,920.1	1,261.2	1,257.6
Year-end Shs. Outstg. (000)	103,949	102,847	105,816	106,103	101,537	88,584	93,526
STATISTICAL RECORD:							
Return on Equity %	13.6	14.2	16.7	43.0	12.8	16.1	15.4
Return on Assets %	1.2	1.2	1.5	4.5	1.3	1.4	1.4
Equity/Assets %	9.1	8.6	8.7	10.4	9.9	8.5	9.4
Non-Int. Exp./Tot. Inc. %	69.9	68.7	64.3	45.0	66.7	67.5	65.5
Price Range	64.24-47.07	62.25-38.25	72.75-54.38	62.25-39.38	60.50-32.38	35.63-24.38	26.50-18.00
P/E Ratio	20.8-15.2	21.4-13.1	23.2-17.3	23.8-15.1	25.0-13.4	17.2-11.8	13.5-9.2
Average Yield %	2.0	2.1	1.5	1.7	1.7	2.4	2.9

Statistics are as originally reported. ① Bef. acctg. change chrg., $436,000, 2001; $2.3 mill., 2000. ② Incl. non-recur. net chrgs. of $68.1 mill., 2001; $16.7 mill., 2000; $23.4 mill., 1998.

OFFICERS:
J. B. Wigdale, Chmn.
D. J. Kuester, Pres., C.E.O.
M. F. Furlong, Exec. V.P., C.F.O., Sec.

INVESTOR CONTACT: M.A. Hatfield, Secretary, (414) 765-7801

PRINCIPAL OFFICE: 770 North Water Street, Milwaukee, WI 53202

TELEPHONE NUMBER: (414) 765 7801
FAX: (414) 765 8026
WEB: www.micorp.com

NO. OF EMPLOYEES: 11,657 (approx.)

SHAREHOLDERS: 19,311 (approx.)

ANNUAL MEETING: In Apr.

INCORPORATED: WI, Feb., 1959

INSTITUTIONAL HOLDINGS:
No. of Institutions: 238
Shares Held: 36,180,647
% Held: 34.8

INDUSTRY: National commercial banks (SIC: 6021)

TRANSFER AGENT(S): BankBoston, N.A., Boston, MA

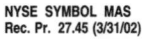

MASCO CORPORATION

	YIELD	2.0%
	P/E RATIO	65.4

INTERIM EARNINGS (Per Share):

Qtr.	Mar.	June	Sept.	Dec.
1998	0.33	0.34	0.37	0.36
1999	0.36	0.41	0.15	0.40
2000	0.39	0.41	0.41	0.10
2001	0.25	0.30	d0.39	0.26

INTERIM DIVIDENDS (Per Share):

Amt.	Decl.	Ex.	Rec.	Pay.
0.13Q	3/16/01	4/04/01	4/06/01	5/08/01
0.13Q	6/29/01	7/11/01	7/13/01	8/13/01
0.135Q	11/02/01	11/07/01	11/09/01	11/19/01
0.135Q	12/05/01	1/09/02	1/11/02	2/11/02
0.135Q	3/15/02	4/03/02	4/05/02	5/07/02

Indicated div.: $0.54 (Div. Reinv. Plan)

CAPITALIZATION (12/31/01):

	($000)	(%)
Long-Term Debt	3,627,630	46.8
Preferred Stock	20	0.0
Common & Surplus	4,119,810	53.2
Total	7,747,460	100.0

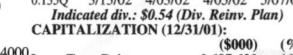

DIVIDEND ACHIEVER STATUS:
Rank: 203   10-Year Growth Rate: 6.30%
Total Years of Dividend Growth: 43

*7 YEAR PRICE SCORE 94.8   *12 MONTH PRICE SCORE 115.9
*NYSE COMPOSITE INDEX=100

TRADING VOLUME Thousand Shares

RECENT DEVELOPMENTS: For the year ended 12/31/01, net income declined 66.4% to $198.5 million from $591.7 million in 2000. Results for 2001 included a $530.0 pre-tax, non-cash charge related to the write-down of certain long-term investments. Net sales increased 15.4% to $8.36 billion from $7.24 billion in 2000. Gross profit as a percentage of net sales was 30.5% in 2001 versus 32.3% in 2000.

PROSPECTS: Going forward, the Company may continue to benefit from an improvement in sales and incoming orders. The Company noted that the first quarter is seasonally one of its lowest quarters. As a result, the Company expects earnings per common share in the last three quarters of 2002 will average higher than first quarter results, thereby improving earnings for the full-year 2002.

BUSINESS

MASCO CORPORATION manufactures faucets, cabinets, architectural coatings, locks and other consumer brand-name home improvement and building products. MAS' principal product and service categories are kitchen and bathroom cabinets, faucets, other kitchen and bath products, architectural coatings, builders' hardware products and other specialty products and services. Brand-names include MERILLAT, KRAFTMAID, and QUALITY CABINETS kitchen and bathroom cabinets; DELTA and PEERLESS faucets; WEISER and BALDWIN locks; and BEHR architectural coatings. Sales in 2001 were derived as follows: cabinets and related products, 30.9%; plumbing products, 21.0%; installation and other services, 20.2%; decorative architectural products, 18.1%; and other specialty products, 9.8%.

ANNUAL FINANCIAL DATA

	12/31/01	12/31/00	12/31/99	12/31/98	12/31/97	12/31/96	12/31/95
Earnings Per Share	⑤ 0.42	④ 1.31	③ 1.28	1.39	1.15	0.92	① 0.63
Cash Flow Per Share	0.99	1.84	1.68	1.78	1.48	1.23	0.91
Tang. Book Val. Per Share	1.30	2.78	3.14	4.99	4.53	4.30	4.09
Dividends Per Share	0.53	0.49	0.45	0.43	0.41	0.39	0.36
Dividend Payout %	125.0	37.4	35.2	30.9	35.2	41.8	58.4
INCOME STATEMENT (IN MILLIONS):							
Total Revenues	8,358.0	7,243.0	6,307.0	4,345.0	3,760.0	3,237.0	2,927.0
Costs & Expenses	7,048.7	6,038.0	5,213.8	3,528.2	3,056.9	2,656.8	2,434.6
Depreciation & Amort.	269.5	238.3	181.8	136.3	116.1	99.7	90.1
Operating Income	1,039.8	966.7	911.4	680.5	587.1	480.5	402.3
Net Interest Inc./(Exp.)	d239.3	d191.4	d120.4	d85.3	d79.8	d74.7	d73.8
Income Before Income Taxes	300.7	893.4	904.1	755.0	630.9	502.7	351.8
Income Taxes	102.2	301.7	334.5	279.0	248.5	207.5	151.7
Equity Earnings/Minority Int.	6.2	19.5	23.9	29.2	24.1	20.1	26.2
Net Income	⑤ 198.5	④ 591.7	③ 569.6	476.0	382.4	295.2	① 200.1
Cash Flow	468.0	830.0	751.4	612.3	498.5	394.9	290.1
Average Shs. Outstg. (000)	474,900	451,800	446,200	343,700	337,600	321,200	319,200
BALANCE SHEET (IN MILLIONS):							
Cash & Cash Equivalents	312.0	169.4	230.8	541.7	441.3	473.7	60.5
Total Current Assets	2,626.9	2,308.2	2,109.8	1,862.6	1,626.7	1,429.8	964.5
Net Property	2,016.7	1,906.8	1,624.4	1,164.3	1,037.3	940.6	856.7
Total Assets	9,183.1	7,744.0	6,634.9	5,167.4	4,333.8	3,701.7	3,778.6
Total Current Liabilities	1,236.6	1,078.1	846.4	846.6	620.0	518.4	445.9
Long-Term Obligations	3,627.6	3,018.2	2,431.3	1,391.4	1,321.5	1,236.3	1,577.1
Net Stockholders' Equity	4,119.8	3,426.1	3,136.5	2,728.6	2,229.0	1,839.8	1,655.4
Net Working Capital	1,390.4	1,230.1	1,263.3	1,016.0	1,006.7	911.3	518.6
Year-end Shs. Outstg. (000)	459,050	444,750	443,510	339,330	331,140	321,740	320,760
STATISTICAL RECORD:							
Operating Profit Margin %	12.4	13.3	14.5	15.7	15.6	14.8	13.7
Net Profit Margin %	2.4	8.2	9.0	11.0	10.2	9.1	6.8
Return on Equity %	4.8	17.3	18.2	17.4	17.2	16.0	12.1
Return on Assets %	2.2	7.6	8.6	9.2	8.8	8.0	5.3
Debt/Total Assets %	39.5	39.0	36.6	26.9	30.5	33.4	41.7
Price Range	26.94-17.76	27.00-14.50	33.69-22.50	33.00-20.75	26.91-16.88	18.44-13.25	15.75-11.25
P/E Ratio	64.1-42.3	20.6-11.1	26.3-17.6	23.7-14.9	23.4-14.7	20.0-14.4	25.2-18.0
Average Yield %	2.3	2.4	1.6	1.6	1.9	2.4	2.7

Statistics are as originally reported. Adj. for stk. split: 2-for-1, 7/98. ① Incl. non-recurr. chrg. $47.9 mill.; bef. discont. oper. loss $641.7 mill. ② Reflects the sale of the Masco Home Furnishings Group businesses. ③ Incl. aftertax non-recurr. chrg. of approx. $126.0 mill. ④ Incl. pre-tax chrg. of $55.0 mill. for the write-down of assets and $90.0 mill. for the planned dispos. of assets. ⑤ Incl. a pretax, noncash write-down charge of $530.0 mill.

OFFICERS:
R. A. Manoogian, Chmn., C.E.O.
R. F. Kennedy, Pres., C.O.O.
T. Wadhams, V.P., C.F.O.
R. B. Rosowski, V.P., Treas.

INVESTOR CONTACT: Investor Relations, (313) 274-7400

PRINCIPAL OFFICE: 21001 Van Born Road, Taylor, MI 48180

TELEPHONE NUMBER: (313) 274-7400
FAX: (313) 792-6135
WEB: www.masco.com

NO. OF EMPLOYEES: 55,400 (approx.)

SHAREHOLDERS: 6,000 (approx.)

ANNUAL MEETING: In May

INCORPORATED: MI, Dec., 1929; reincorp., DE, 1968

INSTITUTIONAL HOLDINGS:
No. of Institutions: 373
Shares Held: 361,329,621
% Held: 78.7

INDUSTRY: Plumbing fixture fittings and trim (SIC: 3432)

TRANSFER AGENT(S): Bank of New York, New York, NY

MAY DEPARTMENT STORES COMPANY (THE)

YIELD 2.7%
P/E RATIO 15.7

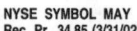
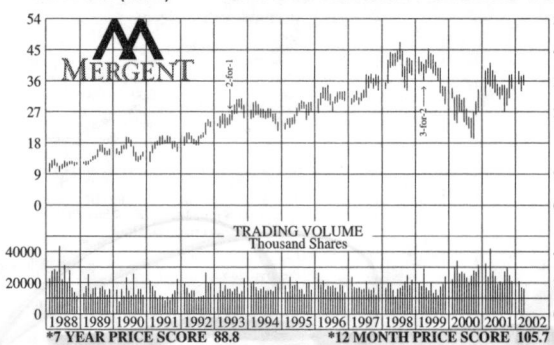

TRADING VOLUME
Thousand Shares

*7 YEAR PRICE SCORE 88.8   *12 MONTH PRICE SCORE 105.7
*NYSE COMPOSITE INDEX=100

INTERIM EARNINGS (Per Share):

Qtr.	Apr.	July	Oct.	Jan.
1998-99	0.29	0.35	0.35	1.31
1999-00	0.34	0.43	0.38	1.45
2000-01	0.35	0.41	0.27	1.59
2001-02	0.34	0.35	0.17	1.36

INTERIM DIVIDENDS (Per Share):

Amt.	Decl.	Ex.	Rec.	Pay.
0.235Q	8/17/01	8/29/01	9/01/01	9/15/01
0.235Q	11/09/01	11/28/01	12/01/01	12/15/01
0.237Q	2/14/02	2/27/02	3/01/02	3/15/02
0.237Q	3/15/02	5/29/02	6/01/02	6/15/02

Indicated div.: $0.95 (Div. Reinv. Plan)

CAPITALIZATION (2/2/02):

	($000)	(%)
Long-Term Debt	4,403,000	49.3
Deferred Income Tax	696,000	7.8
Common & Surplus	3,841,000	43.0
Total	8,940,000	100.0

DIVIDEND ACHIEVER STATUS:

Rank: 220   10-Year Growth Rate: 5.77%
Total Years of Dividend Growth: 26

RECENT DEVELOPMENTS: For the 52 weeks ended 2/2/02, earnings totaled $706.0 million, before a $3.0 million extraordinary charge, compared with net income of $858.0 million in the corresponding 53-week period the year before. Revenues slipped 2.3% to $14.18 billion from $14.51 billion a year earlier. Comparable-store sales declined 4.6% year over year. Earnings before income taxes fell 18.4% to $1.14 billion from $1.40 billion the previous year.

PROSPECTS: The Company is expanding its bridal and formal-wear operations through acquisitions. On 2/1/02, MAY announced that it had acquired Priscilla of Boston, a retailer of upscale bridal gowns with ten locations in major metropolitan markets. On 12/19/01, the Company acquired After Hours Formalwear, Inc., a major tuxedo retailer in the U.S. After Hours, with annual sales of more than $110.0 million, operates about 240 stores in 19 states.

BUSINESS

THE MAY DEPARTMENT STORES COMPANY operated 439 department stores in 44 states, the District of Columbia and Puerto Rico as of 2/2/02 under the following names: Lord & Taylor, Hecht's, Strawbridge's, Foley's, Robinsons-May, Filene's, Kaufmann's, Famous-Barr, L.S. Ayers, The Jones Store and Meier & Frank. In addition, MAY operated 150 David's Bridal stores, 240 After Hours stores and ten Priscilla of Boston stores. Thalhimers was acquired for $317.0 million in 1990, and was consolidated with the Hecht's division in January 1992. On 5/4/96, the Company completed its spin-off of Payless ShoeSource, Inc. On 8/11/00, MAY acquired David's Bridal, Inc.

QUARTERLY DATA

(2/2/2002)($000)	REV	INC
1st Quarter................	3,153,000	109,000
2nd Quarter...............	3,173,000	111,000
3rd Quarter................	3,202,000	55,000
4th Quarter................	4,647,000	431,000

ANNUAL FINANCIAL DATA

	2/2/02	2/3/01	1/29/00	1/30/99	1/31/98	2/1/97 ☑3	☑2/3/96
Earnings Per Share	☑1 2.22	2.62	2.60	2.30	☑1 2.07	☑1 1.96	☑2 1.82
Cash Flow Per Share	3.98	4.18	3.93	3.51	3.19	3.01	2.75
Tang. Book Val. Per Share	7.76	8.53	9.51	8.67	8.82	8.09	10.48
Dividends Per Share	0.94	0.93	0.89	0.85	0.80	0.77	0.74
Dividend Payout %	42.3	35.5	34.2	36.8	38.6	39.3	40.8
INCOME STATEMENT (IN MILLIONS):							
Total Revenues	14,175.0	14,511.0	13,866.0	13,413.0	12,685.0	12,000.0	10,952.0
Costs & Expenses	12,123.0	12,253.0	11,587.0	11,301.0	10,695.0	10,118.0	9,209.0
Depreciation & Amort.	559.0	511.0	469.0	439.0	412.0	373.0	333.0
Operating Income	1,493.0	1,747.0	1,810.0	1,673.0	1,578.0	1,509.0	1,410.0
Net Interest Inc./(Exp.)	d349.0	d345.0	d287.0	d278.0	d299.0	d277.0	d250.0
Income Before Income Taxes	1,144.0	1,402.0	1,523.0	1,395.0	1,279.0	1,232.0	1,160.0
Income Taxes	438.0	544.0	596.0	546.0	500.0	483.0	460.0
Net Income	☑1 706.0	858.0	927.0	849.0	☑1 779.0	☑1 749.0	☑2 700.0
Cash Flow	1,246.0	1,351.0	1,377.0	1,270.0	1,173.0	1,104.0	1,014.0
Average Shs. Outstg. (000)	317,600	327,700	355,600	367,400	373,600	373,050	375,000
BALANCE SHEET (IN MILLIONS):							
Cash & Cash Equivalents	52.0	156.0	41.0	112.0	199.0	102.0	159.0
Total Current Assets	4,925.0	5,270.0	5,115.0	4,987.0	4,878.0	5,035.0	5,097.0
Net Property	5,264.0	4,899.0	4,769.0	4,513.0	4,224.0	4,159.0	3,744.0
Total Assets	11,920.0	11,574.0	10,935.0	10,533.0	9,930.0	10,059.0	10,122.0
Total Current Liabilities	2,538.0	2,214.0	2,415.0	2,059.0	1,866.0	1,923.0	1,602.0
Long-Term Obligations	4,403.0	4,534.0	3,560.0	3,825.0	3,512.0	3,849.0	3,333.0
Net Stockholders' Equity	3,841.0	3,855.0	4,077.0	3,836.0	3,809.0	3,650.0	4,585.0
Net Working Capital	2,387.0	3,056.0	2,700.0	2,928.0	3,012.0	3,112.0	3,495.0
Year-end Shs. Outstg. (000)	287,200	298,200	325,500	334,700	346,500	355,350	373,500
STATISTICAL RECORD:							
Operating Profit Margin %	10.5	12.0	13.1	12.5	12.4	12.6	12.9
Net Profit Margin %	5.0	5.9	6.7	6.3	6.1	6.2	6.4
Return on Equity %	18.4	22.3	22.7	22.1	20.5	20.5	15.3
Return on Assets %	5.9	7.4	8.5	8.1	7.8	7.4	6.9
Debt/Total Assets %	36.9	39.2	32.6	36.3	35.4	38.3	32.9
Price Range	41.25-27.00	33.94-19.19	45.38-29.19	47.25-33.17	38.09-29.08	34.84-26.67	30.25-21.92
P/E Ratio	18.6-12.2	13.0-7.3	17.5-11.2	20.5-14.4	18.4-14.0	17.8-13.6	16.6-12.0
Average Yield %	2.8	3.5	2.4	2.1	2.4	2.5	2.8

Statistics are as originally reported. Adj. for 3-for-2 stk. split, 3/99. ☑1 Bef. $3 mil ($0.01/sh) extraord. loss, 2002; $4 mil extraord. loss, 1997; & bef. $5 mil extraord. loss & cr$11 mil from discont. opers., 1996. ☑2 Bef. discont. opers. cr$55 mil; bef. $3 mil extraord. loss; & incl. $44 mil non-recur. chg. ☑3 Excl. results of spun-off PayLess ShoeSource, Inc.

OFFICERS:

E. S. Kahn, Chmn., C.E.O.
J. L. Dunham, Pres.
T. D. Fingleton, Exec. V.P., C.F.O.

INVESTOR CONTACT: Sharon L. Bateman, Investor Relations, (314) 342-6494

PRINCIPAL OFFICE: 611 Olive Street, St. Louis, MO 63101-1799

TELEPHONE NUMBER: (314) 342-6300
FAX: (314) 342-6497
WEB: www.maycompany.com
NO. OF EMPLOYEES: 60,000 full-time (approx.); 67,000 part-time (approx.)
SHAREHOLDERS: 41,000 (approx.)
ANNUAL MEETING: In May
INCORPORATED: NY, June, 1910; reincorp., DE, May, 1996

INSTITUTIONAL HOLDINGS:
No. of Institutions: 431
Shares Held: 220,225,776
% Held: 76.9

INDUSTRY: Department stores (SIC: 5311)

TRANSFER AGENT(S): The Bank of New York, New York, NY

MBIA INC.

YIELD 1.2%
P/E RATIO 14.0

7 YEAR PRICE SCORE 117.9   **12 MONTH PRICE SCORE 108.6**
NYSE COMPOSITE INDEX=100

TRADING VOLUME
Thousand Shares

INTERIM EARNINGS (Per Share):

Qtr.	Mar.	June	Sept.	Dec.
1997	0.69	0.68	0.72	0.72
1998	0.67	0.78	0.72	0.69
1999	0.06	0.37	0.85	0.85
2000	0.89	0.87	0.88	0.92
2001	0.87	0.96	1.03	1.05

INTERIM DIVIDENDS (Per Share):

Amt.	Decl.	Ex.	Rec.	Pay.
0.15Q	6/18/01	6/21/01	6/25/01	7/16/01
0.15Q	9/14/01	9/20/01	9/24/01	10/15/01
0.15Q	12/06/01	12/17/01	12/19/01	1/15/02
0.17Q	3/15/02	3/22/02	3/26/02	4/15/02

Indicated div.: $0.68

CAPITALIZATION (12/31/01):

	($000)	(%)
Long-Term Debt	805,062	13.7
Deferred Income Tax	272,665	4.7
Common & Surplus	4,782,638	81.6
Total	5,860,365	100.0

DIVIDEND ACHIEVER STATUS:
Rank: 109   10-Year Growth Rate: 11.55%
Total Years of Dividend Growth: 14

RECENT DEVELOPMENTS: For the year ended 12/31/01, income was $583.2 million, before an accounting change charge of $13.1 million, versus net income of $528.6 million in 2000. Results for 2001 and 2000 included net realized gains of $8.9 million and $32.9 million, respectively. Results for 2001 also included a loss on the change in fair value of derivative instruments of $3.9 million. Total revenues grew 10.2% to $1.13 billion. Total insurance revenues grew 12.4% to $975.9 million, while investment revenues rose 5.9% to $125.9 million.

PROSPECTS: Earnings continue to be fueled by strong growth in the Company's structured finance and international sectors. In the global finance business, more than a third of the global public finance adjusted direct premiums are now coming from the Company's international operations compared with 10.0% in 2000. Going forward, earnings should be positively affected by the Company's continued focus on credit quality, price, expense control, and capital management.

BUSINESS

MBIA INC. is the holding company of MBIA Insurance Corporation, a major company in the municipal bond and structured finance insurance business. MBIA's principal business is to guarantee timely payment of principal and interest for new municipal bond issues, asset-backed securities, bonds traded in the secondary market and those held in unit investment trusts and mutual funds. In addition, it provides equity and fixed-income investment services for the public and private sectors. MBIA serves state and local governments and other agencies, issuers of asset-backed securities, financial advisors, investment banking firms, bond traders, sponsors of unit investment trusts and mutual funds and the investing public. MBI's operations take place in North America, Europe, Asia and Australia. MBI acquired CapMAC Holdings, Inc. on 2/17/98 and 1838 Investment Advisors on 7/31/98.

ANNUAL FINANCIAL DATA

	12/31/01	12/31/00	12/31/99	12/31/98	12/31/97	12/31/96	12/31/95
Earnings Per Share	① 3.82	3.55	③ 2.13	② 2.88	2.81	2.48	2.14
Tang. Book Val. Per Share	31.56	27.86	22.79	24.59	21.82	18.28	16.88
Dividends Per Share	0.59	0.55	0.53	0.52	0.51	0.47	0.42
Dividend Payout %	15.4	15.4	25.1	18.2	18.1	19.0	19.8
INCOME STATEMENT (IN MILLIONS):							
Total Premium Income	523.9	446.4	442.8	424.6	297.4	251.7	215.1
Net Investment Income	412.8	394.0	359.5	331.8	281.5	247.6	219.9
Other Income	199.2	184.2	162.2	164.7	75.1	46.3	27.3
Total Revenues	1,135.8	1,024.6	964.4	921.0	654.0	545.5	462.2
Income Before Income Taxes	791.0	714.9	387.9	565.0	479.6	408.1	345.0
Income Taxes	207.8	186.2	67.4	132.3	105.4	86.0	345.0
Net Income	① 583.2	528.6	③ 320.5	② 432.7	374.2	322.2	271.4
Average Shs. Outstg. (000)	149,283	148,669	150,604	150,245	133,121	130,044	126,720
BALANCE SHEET (IN MILLIONS):							
Cash & Cash Equivalents	7,210.2	5,901.4	5,264.3	4,217.2	4,099.4	3,722.8	2,978.0
Premiums Due	700.0	487.8	459.0	402.2	266.3	217.8	207.0
Invst. Assets: Fixed-term	7,421.0	6,740.1	5,784.0	5,884.1	4,867.3	4,149.7	3,652.6
Invst. Assets: Total	14,516.2	12,547.6	10,954.8	10,080.5	8,943.4	7,865.2	6,607.3
Total Assets	16,199.7	13,894.3	12,263.9	11,796.6	9,810.8	8,562.0	7,267.5
Long-Term Obligations	805.1	795.1	689.2	689.0	473.9	374.0	373.9
Net Stockholders' Equity	4,782.6	4,223.4	3,513.1	3,792.3	3,048.3	2,479.7	2,234.3
Year-end Shs. Outstg. (000)	148,434	147,846	149,328	149,322	134,192	129,882	126,012
STATISTICAL RECORD:							
Return on Revenues %	51.3	51.6	33.2	47.0	57.2	59.1	58.7
Return on Equity %	12.2	12.5	9.1	11.4	12.3	13.0	12.1
Return on Assets %	3.6	3.8	2.6	3.7	3.8	3.8	3.7
Price Range	57.49-36.00	50.79-24.21	47.92-30.08	53.96-30.71	44.84-30.29	34.88-23.33	25.83-18.46
P/E Ratio	15.0-9.4	14.3-6.8	22.5-14.1	18.7-10.7	15.9-10.8	14.1-9.4	12.1-8.6
Average Yield %	1.3	1.5	1.4	1.2	1.4	1.6	1.9

Statistics are as originally reported. Adj. for stk. splits: 3-for-2, 4/01; 2-for-1, 10/97 ① Bef. acctg. chrg. $13.1 mill. ② Incl. non-recurr. chrg. of $36.1 mill. ③ Incl. non-recurr. chrg. of $105.0 mill.

OFFICERS:
J. W. Brown Jr., Chmn., C.E.O.
G. C. Dunton, Pres., C.O.O.
N. G. Budnick, C.F.O., Treas.

INVESTOR CONTACT: Judith C. Radasch, Dir. Inv. Rel., (914) 765-3014

PRINCIPAL OFFICE: 113 King Street, Armonk, NY 10504

TELEPHONE NUMBER: (914) 273-4545
FAX: (914) 765-3163
WEB: www.mbia.com

NO. OF EMPLOYEES: 601

SHAREHOLDERS: 851

ANNUAL MEETING: In May

INCORPORATED: CT, Nov., 1986

INSTITUTIONAL HOLDINGS:
No. of Institutions: 413
Shares Held: 131,273,312
% Held: 88.5

INDUSTRY: Surety insurance (SIC: 6351)

TRANSFER AGENT(S): Mellon Investor Services, Ridgefield Park, NJ

MBNA CORPORATION

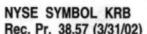

		YIELD	1.0%
		P/E RATIO	20.1

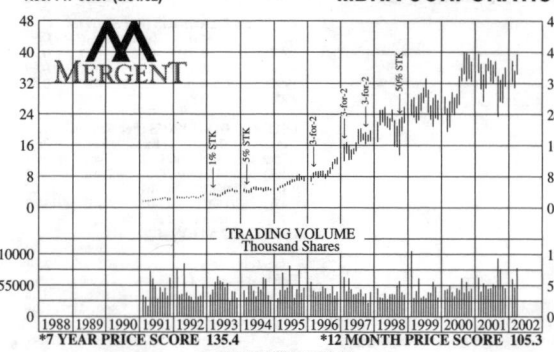

INTERIM EARNINGS (Per Share):

Qtr.	Mar.	June	Sept.	Dec.
1998	0.18	0.21	0.27	0.30
1999	0.22	0.27	0.34	0.38
2000	0.28	0.34	0.43	0.48
2001	0.35	0.43	0.54	0.60

INTERIM DIVIDENDS (Per Share):

Amt.	Decl.	Ex.	Rec.	Pay.
0.09Q	4/11/01	6/13/01	6/15/01	7/01/01
0.09Q	7/12/01	9/17/01	9/15/01	10/01/01
0.09Q	10/11/01	12/12/01	12/14/01	1/01/02
0.10Q	1/10/02	3/13/02	3/15/02	4/01/02
0.10Q	4/11/02	6/12/02	6/14/02	7/01/02
Indicated div.: $0.40				

CAPITALIZATION (12/31/01):

	($000)	(%)
Total Deposits	27,094,745	64.9
Long-Term Debt	6,867,033	16.4
Preferred Stock	86	0.0
Common & Surplus	7,798,632	18.7
Total	41,760,496	100.0

TRADING VOLUME Thousand Shares

*7 YEAR PRICE SCORE 135.4   *12 MONTH PRICE SCORE 105.3

*NYSE COMPOSITE INDEX=100

DIVIDEND ACHIEVER STATUS:
Rank: 46   10-Year Growth Rate: 16.05%
Total Years of Dividend Growth: 10

RECENT DEVELOPMENTS: For the year ended 12/31/01, net income advanced 29.1% to $1.69 billion compared with $1.31 billion in 2000. Net interest income increased 18.0% to $1.39 billion. Provision for possible credit losses more than doubled to $1.14 billion from $547.3 million. Non-interest income improved 35.1% to $6.94 billion, while non-interest expense rose 22.7% to $4.47 billion. Comparisons were made with restated prior-year figures.

PROSPECTS: As of 12/31/01, total managed loans increased 17.4% to $90.90 billion from $77.44 billion in the prior year. In addition, during 2001, KRB added 11.2 million new customers and 9.5 million new accounts. Moreover, KRB expects to continue to benefit from its on-line service, MBNA.com, which currently serves more than 5.6 million customers. During the fourth quarter, KRB added 600,000 new customers via the Internet.

BUSINESS

MBNA CORPORATION is a registered bank holding company, with assets of $45.45 billion as of 12/31/01. The Corporation is the parent company of MBNA America Bank, N.A. and has two wholly-owned foreign bank subsidiaries, MBNA International Bank Limited, located in the United Kingdom, and MBNA Canada Bank. The Corporation is an independent credit card lender and an issuer of affinity credit cards, marketed primarily to members of associations and customers of financial institutions. In addition to its credit card lending, the Corporation also makes other consumer loans and offers insurance and deposit products.

ANNUAL FINANCIAL DATA

	12/31/01	12/31/00	12/31/99	12/31/98	12/31/97	12/31/96	12/31/95
Earnings Per Share	1.92	1.53	1.21	0.97	0.77	① 0.59	② 0.46
Tang. Book Val. Per Share	6.12	4.55	5.24	3.18	2.62	2.27	1.68
Dividends Per Share	0.35	0.31	0.27	0.23	0.21	0.18	0.16
Dividend Payout %	18.2	20.3	22.3	24.1	27.0	31.1	35.1
INCOME STATEMENT (IN MILLIONS):							
Total Interest Income	3,205.1	2,775.7	2,262.3	1,966.2	1,711.0	1,383.3	1,140.8
Total Interest Expense	1,814.1	1,691.7	1,328.5	1,223.8	1,018.6	742.8	596.6
Net Interest Income	1,391.0	1,084.0	933.8	742.3	692.4	640.5	544.2
Provision for Loan Losses	1,140.6	409.0	408.9	310.0	260.0	178.2	138.2
Non-Interest Income	6,939.6	5,093.2	4,207.8	3,229.0	2,812.9	1,895.9	1,424.6
Non-Interest Expense	4,474.8	3,647.7	3,077.2	2,407.2	2,223.1	1,626.9	1,246.1
Income Before Taxes	2,715.2	2,120.4	1,655.0	1,254.1	1,022.1	785.6	584.6
Net Income	1,694.3	1,312.5	1,024.4	776.3	622.5	① 474.5	② 353.1
Average Shs. Outstg. (000)	876,153	846,531	837,038	789,421	789,801	778,473	770,465
BALANCE SHEET (IN MILLIONS):							
Cash & Due from Banks	962.1	971.5	488.4	382.9	263.1	225.1	291.9
Total Loans & Leases	14,703.6	11,682.9	7,971.1	11,776.1	8,261.9	7,659.1	4,967.5
Allowance for Credit Losses	833.4	386.6	356.0	216.9	162.5	118.4	104.9
Net Loans & Leases	13,870.2	11,296.3	7,615.1	11,559.2	8,099.4	7,540.7	4,862.6
Total Assets	45,447.9	38,673.9	30,859.1	25,806.3	21,305.5	17,035.3	13,228.7
Total Deposits	27,094.7	24,343.6	18,714.8	15,407.0	12,913.2	10,151.7	8,608.9
Long-Term Obligations	6,867.0	5,735.6	5,708.9	5,939.0	5,478.9	3,950.4	2,657.6
Total Liabilities	37,649.2	32,050.8	26,659.7	23,415.2	19,335.5	15,331.0	11,963.8
Net Stockholders' Equity	7,798.7	6,627.3	4,199.4	2,391.0	1,970.1	1,704.3	1,265.1
Year-end Shs. Outstg. (000)	851,804	851,804	801,781	751,796	751,782	751,781	751,781
STATISTICAL RECORD:							
Return on Equity %	21.7	19.8	24.4	32.5	31.6	27.8	27.9
Return on Assets %	3.7	3.4	3.3	3.0	2.9	2.8	2.7
Equity/Assets %	17.2	17.1	13.6	9.3	9.2	10.0	9.6
Non-Int. Exp./Tot. Inc. %	53.7	59.1	59.9	60.6	63.4	64.1	62.9
Price Range	39.56-23.43	40.13-19.50	33.25-20.81	25.88-13.50	20.39-11.95	12.96-6.72	8.62-4.42
P/E Ratio	20.6-12.2	26.2-12.7	27.5-17.2	26.7-13.9	26.6-15.6	21.9-11.4	18.9-9.7
Average Yield %	1.1	1.0	1.0	1.2	1.3	1.9	2.5

Statistics are as originally reported. Adj. for 3-for-2 splits: 10/98, 10/97, 2/97 & 2/96. ① Incl. pre-tax exp. fr. termination of mktg. agreement: $54.3 mill. ② Incl. pre-tax gain on invest. securities sold: $39,000.

OFFICERS:
A. Lerner, Chmn., C.E.O.
C. M. Cawley, Pres.
M. S. Kaufman, Sr. Exec. V.P., C.F.O., Treas.

INVESTOR CONTACT: Brian D. Dalphon, Director, Investor Relations, (800) 362-6255

PRINCIPAL OFFICE: 1100 North King Street, Wilmington, DE 19884-0141

TELEPHONE NUMBER: (302) 456-8588
FAX: (302) 456-8541
WEB: www.mbna.com

NO. OF EMPLOYEES: 28,000 (approx.)

SHAREHOLDERS: 2,723

ANNUAL MEETING: In May

INCORPORATED: MD, Dec., 1990

INSTITUTIONAL HOLDINGS:
No. of Institutions: 592
Shares Held: 629,122,333
% Held: 73.9

INDUSTRY: National commercial banks (SIC: 6021)

TRANSFER AGENT(S): National City Bank, Cleveland, OH

MCCORMICK & COMPANY, INC.

YIELD	1.6%
P/E RATIO	23.2

TRADING VOLUME
Thousand Shares

*7 YEAR PRICE SCORE 123.3   *12 MONTH PRICE SCORE 113.6
*NYSE COMPOSITE INDEX=100

INTERIM EARNINGS (Per Share):

Qtr.	Feb.	May	Aug.	Nov.
1998-99	0.13	0.04	0.18	0.38
1999-00	0.18	0.18	0.23	0.42
2000-01	0.19	0.19	0.25	0.42
2001-02	0.24	…	…	…

INTERIM DIVIDENDS (Per Share):

Amt.	Decl.	Ex.	Rec.	Pay.
0.20Q	6/19/01	6/27/01	6/29/01	7/12/01
0.20Q	9/18/01	9/26/01	9/28/01	10/11/01
0.21Q	11/20/01	12/27/01	12/31/01	1/22/02
2-for-1	2/19/02	4/09/02	3/25/02	4/08/02
0.105Q	3/06/02	3/21/02	3/25/02	4/12/02

Indicated div.: $0.42 (Div. Reinv. Plan)

CAPITALIZATION (11/30/01):

	($000)	(%)
Long-Term Debt	454,100	48.2
Deferred Income Tax	25,800	2.7
Common & Surplus	463,100	49.1
Total	943,000	100.0

DIVIDEND ACHIEVER STATUS:
Rank: 115   10-Year Growth Rate: 11.07%
Total Years of Dividend Growth: 15

RECENT DEVELOPMENTS: For the quarter ended 2/28/02, net income was $33.8 million, up 27.3% versus $26.6 million a year earlier. Results for the recent period included one-time pre-tax special charges of $367,000. Net sales rose 3.9% to $518.9 million from $499.4 million the year before. Gross profit was $185.3 million, or 35.7% of net sales, versus $169.6 million, or 34.0% of net sales, the prior year. Operating income grew 15.9% to $52.1 million.

PROSPECTS: Sales growth is being fueled by strong demand for the Company's products by warehouse clubs and its restaurant customers, along with robust sales of snack seasonings. Meanwhile, earnings are being positively affected by favorable raw material costs and MKC's efforts to improve efficiencies. In 2002, the Company is targeting sales growth in the range of 4.0% to 6.0% and earnings per share growth of between 9.0% and 11.0%.

BUSINESS

MCCORMICK & COMPANY, INC. is a diversified specialty food company primarily engaged in the manufacture of spices, seasonings, flavors and other specialty food products. The Company operates in three business segments: consumer, industrial, and packaging. The consumer segment sells spices, herbs, extracts, proprietary seasoning blends, sauces and marinades to the consumer food market under a variety of brands, including the MCCORMICK brand, the CLUB HOUSE brand in Canada, and the SCHWARTZ brand in the U.K. The industrial segment sells spices, herbs, extracts, proprietary seasonings, condiments, coatings and compound flavors to food processors, restaurant chains, distributors, warehouse clubs and institutional operations. The packaging segment sells plastic packaging products to the food, personal care and other industries, primarily in the U.S.

ANNUAL FINANCIAL DATA

	11/30/01	11/30/00	11/30/99	11/30/98	11/30/97	11/30/96	11/30/95
Earnings Per Share	① 1.05	① 0.99	① 0.72	① 0.71	② 0.65	③ 0.27	① 0.54
Cash Flow Per Share	1.57	1.43	1.12	1.07	0.97	0.67	0.99
Tang. Book Val. Per Share	…	…	1.70	1.57	1.59	1.82	2.08
Dividends Per Share	0.40	0.38	0.34	0.32	0.30	0.28	0.26
Dividend Payout %	38.3	38.4	47.5	45.4	46.5	103.7	48.6
INCOME STATEMENT (IN MILLIONS):							
Total Revenues	2,372.3	2,123.5	2,006.9	1,881.1	1,801.0	1,732.5	1,858.7
Costs & Expenses	2,058.7	1,837.2	1,772.6	1,643.5	1,580.8	1,575.4	1,590.0
Depreciation & Amort.	73.0	61.3	57.4	54.8	49.3	63.8	63.7
Operating Income	240.6	225.0	176.9	182.8	170.8	93.3	205.0
Net Interest Inc./(Exp.)	d52.9	d39.7	d32.4	d36.9	d36.3	d33.8	d55.3
Income Before Income Taxes	190.4	186.0	150.0	152.5	142.3	61.7	149.2
Income Taxes	62.9	66.6	60.1	54.9	52.7	23.9	53.7
Equity Earnings/Minority Int.	19.1	18.1	13.4	6.2	7.8	5.9	2.1
Net Income	① 146.6	① 137.5	① 103.3	① 103.8	② 97.4	③ 43.5	① 97.5
Cash Flow	219.6	198.8	160.7	158.6	146.8	107.3	161.2
Average Shs. Outstg. (000)	140,200	139,200	144,000	147,600	151,316	161,282	162,362
BALANCE SHEET (IN MILLIONS):							
Cash & Cash Equivalents	31.3	23.9	12.0	17.7	13.5	22.4	12.5
Total Current Assets	635.8	620.0	490.6	503.8	506.5	534.4	670.7
Net Property	424.5	373.0	363.3	377.0	380.0	400.4	524.8
Total Assets	1,772.0	1,659.9	1,188.8	1,259.1	1,256.2	1,326.6	1,614.3
Total Current Liabilities	713.7	1,027.2	470.6	518.0	498.2	499.3	646.9
Long-Term Obligations	454.1	160.2	241.4	250.4	276.5	291.2	349.1
Net Stockholders' Equity	463.1	359.3	382.4	388.1	393.1	450.0	519.3
Net Working Capital	d77.9	d407.2	20.0	d14.2	8.3	35.1	23.9
Year-end Shs. Outstg. (000)	138,400	136,600	140,800	145,000	148,048	156,410	162,436
STATISTICAL RECORD:							
Operating Profit Margin %	10.1	10.6	8.8	9.7	9.5	5.4	11.0
Net Profit Margin %	6.2	6.5	5.1	5.5	5.4	2.5	5.2
Return on Equity %	31.7	38.3	27.0	26.7	24.8	9.7	18.8
Return on Assets %	8.3	8.3	8.7	8.2	7.8	3.3	6.0
Debt/Total Assets %	25.6	9.7	20.3	19.9	22.0	22.0	21.6
Price Range	23.27-17.08	18.88-11.88	17.31-13.31	18.22-13.53	14.19-11.31	12.69-9.44	13.31-9.06
P/E Ratio	22.3-16.3	19.1-12.0	24.2-18.6	25.8-19.2	22.0-17.5	47.0-34.9	24.9-16.9
Average Yield %	2.0	2.5	2.2	2.0	2.4	2.5	2.3

Statistics are as originally reported. Adj. for 2-for-1 stk. split, 4/02. ① Incl. $10.8 mill. pre-tax chrg., 2001; $1.1 mil pre-tax chrg., 2000; $18.4 mill. after-tax chrg., 1999; $2.3 mill. pre-tax chrg., 1998; $3.9 mill. pre-tax credit, 1995. ② Bef. $1.0 mill. disc. oper. gain & incl. $3.2 mill. pre-tax credit. ③ Bef. $7.8 mill. extraord. chrg., $6.2 mill. disc. oper. gain & incl. $58.1 mill. pre-tax chrg.

OFFICERS:
R. J. Lawless, Chmn., Pres., C.E.O.
F. A. Contino, Exec. V.P., C.F.O.
C. J. Kurtzman, V.P., Treas.

INVESTOR CONTACT: Chris Kurtzman, V.P., Treas., (410) 771-7244

PRINCIPAL OFFICE: 18 Loveton Circle, P.O Box 6000, Sparks, MD 21152

TELEPHONE NUMBER: (410) 771-7301
FAX: (410) 771-7462
WEB: www.mccormick.com
NO. OF EMPLOYEES: 8,493 (approx.)
SHAREHOLDERS: 2,000 (approx. common); 10,000 (approx. non-voting common)
ANNUAL MEETING: In Mar.
INCORPORATED: MD, Nov., 1915

INSTITUTIONAL HOLDINGS:
No. of Institutions: 247
Shares Held: 88,369,984 (Adj.)
% Held: 63.7

INDUSTRY: Food preparations, nec (SIC: 2099)

TRANSFER AGENT(S): Wells Fargo Shareowner Services, South St. Paul, MN

MCDONALD'S CORPORATION

YIELD 0.8%
P/E RATIO 22.0

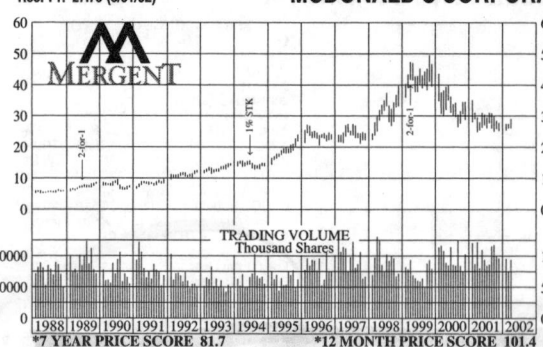

7 YEAR PRICE SCORE 81.7   **12 MONTH PRICE SCORE 101.4**
*NYSE COMPOSITE INDEX=100

INTERIM EARNINGS (Per Share):

Qtr.	Mar.	June	Sept.	Dec.
1998	0.26	0.25	0.35	0.25
1999	0.29	0.37	0.39	0.35
2000	0.33	0.39	0.41	0.34
2001	0.29	0.34	0.42	0.21

INTERIM DIVIDENDS (Per Share):

Amt.	Decl.	Ex.	Rec.	Pay.
0.215A	9/12/00	11/13/00	11/15/00	12/01/00
0.225A	10/29/01	11/13/01	11/15/01	12/03/01

Indicated div.: $0.23 (Div. Reinv. Plan)

CAPITALIZATION (12/31/01):

	($mill.)	(%)
Long-Term Debt	8,555.5	44.7
Deferred Income Tax	1,112.2	5.8
Common & Surplus	9,488.4	49.5
Total	19,156.1	100.0

DIVIDEND ACHIEVER STATUS:
Rank: 146   10-Year Growth Rate: 9.52%
Total Years of Dividend Growth: 25

RECENT DEVELOPMENTS: For the year ended 12/31/01, net income declined 17.2% to $1.64 billion versus $1.98 billion in 2000. Results for 2001 included net after-tax charges totaling $142.5 million. Systemwide sales increased 1.1% to $40.63 billion from $40.18 billion in 2000. Total revenues advanced 4.4% to $14.87 billion from $14.24 billion a year earlier. Company operated restaurant revenue rose 5.5% to $11.04 billion, while revenue from franchised and affiliated restaurants grew 1.4% to $3.83 billion.

PROSPECTS: In 2002, MCD plans to add approximately 1,300 to 1,400 restaurant units and 100 to 150 Partner Brand restaurants. MCD expects earnings per share in the range of $1.47 to $1.54 for 2002. Ongoing restaurant initiatives in the U.S. include streamlining operations by reducing the number of divisions and regions. These and other initiatives should result in annual savings of about $100.0 million beginning in 2002. Also, MCD plans to dispose of its Aroma Cafe business during the first half of 2002.

BUSINESS

MCDONALD'S CORPORATION develops, licenses, leases and services a worldwide system of restaurants. Units serve a mostly uniform menu of moderately priced food consisting of hamburgers, cheeseburgers, chicken sandwiches, french fries, salads, milk shakes, desserts and beverages. As of 12/31/01, there were 17,321 units operated by franchisees, 8,452 units operated by the Company, and 4,320 units operated by affiliates. In addition to its McDonald's units, MCD also operated 197 Donatos Pizzas, 177 Chipotle Mexican Grills, 44 Aroma Cafes and 657 Boston Markets. In addition, MCD has a minority interest in Pret A Manger in the U.K. Systemwide sales in 2001 were derived from: franchised restaurants, 61.1%; Company-owned units' sales, 27.2%; and affiliated restaurants, 11.7%. On 5/26/00, MCD acquired approximately 750 Boston Market restaurants from Boston Chicken, Inc.

ANNUAL FINANCIAL DATA

	12/31/01	12/31/00	12/31/99	12/31/98	12/31/97	12/31/96	12/31/95
Earnings Per Share	② 1.25	1.46	① 1.39	① 1.10	1.15	1.11	0.99
Cash Flow Per Share	2.08	2.20	2.07	1.73	1.73	1.66	1.52
Tang. Book Val. Per Share	6.30	5.95	6.20	6.26	4.83	5.48	4.98
Dividends Per Share	0.23	0.21	0.20	0.18	0.16	0.15	0.13
Dividend Payout %	18.0	14.7	14.0	16.0	14.1	13.2	13.3
INCOME STATEMENT (IN MILLIONS):							
Total Revenues	14,870.0	14,243.0	13,259.3	12,421.4	11,408.8	10,686.5	9,794.5
Costs & Expenses	10,829.3	10,099.0	9,107.5	8,678.6	7,920.2	7,356.8	6,589.9
Depreciation & Amort.	1,086.3	1,010.7	956.3	881.1	793.8	742.9	709.0
Operating Income	2,697.0	3,329.7	3,319.6	2,761.9	2,808.3	2,632.6	2,601.3
Net Interest Inc./(Exp.)	d452.4	d429.9	d396.3	d413.8	d364.4	d342.5	d340.2
Income Before Income Taxes	2,329.7	2,882.3	2,884.1	2,307.4	2,407.3	2,174.2	2,072.6
Income Taxes	693.1	905.0	936.2	757.3	764.8	678.4	741.8
Equity Earnings/Minority Int.	...	...	...	...	...	76.8	96.5
Net Income	② 1,636.6	1,977.3	① 1,947.9	① 1,550.1	1,642.5	1,572.6	1,427.3
Cash Flow	2,722.9	2,988.0	2,904.2	2,431.2	2,411.0	2,287.9	2,095.8
Average Shs. Outstg. (000)	1,309,300	1,356,500	1,404,200	1,405,700	1,410,200	1,396,400	1,403,000
BALANCE SHEET (IN MILLIONS):							
Cash & Cash Equivalents	418.1	421.7	419.5	299.2	341.4	329.9	334.8
Total Current Assets	1,819.1	1,662.4	1,572.3	1,309.4	1,142.3	1,102.5	955.8
Net Property	17,289.5	17,047.6	16,324.5	16,041.6	14,961.4	14,352.1	12,811.3
Total Assets	22,534.5	21,683.5	20,983.2	19,784.4	18,241.5	17,386.0	15,414.6
Total Current Liabilities	2,248.3	2,360.9	3,274.3	2,497.1	2,984.5	2,135.3	1,794.9
Long-Term Obligations	8,555.5	7,843.9	5,632.4	6,188.6	4,834.1	4,830.1	4,257.8
Net Stockholders' Equity	9,488.4	9,204.4	9,639.1	9,464.7	8,851.6	8,718.2	7,861.3
Net Working Capital	d429.0	d698.5	d1,702.0	d1,187.7	d1,842.2	d1,032.8	d839.1
Year-end Shs. Outstg. (000)	1,280,700	1,304,900	1,350,800	1,356,200	1,660,600	1,389,200	1,399,400
STATISTICAL RECORD:							
Operating Profit Margin %	18.1	23.4	25.0	22.2	24.6	24.6	26.6
Net Profit Margin %	11.0	13.9	14.7	12.5	14.4	14.7	14.6
Return on Equity %	17.2	21.5	20.2	16.4	18.6	18.0	18.2
Return on Assets %	7.3	9.1	9.3	7.8	9.0	9.0	9.3
Debt/Total Assets %	38.0	36.2	26.8	31.3	26.5	27.8	27.6
Price Range	35.06-24.75	43.63-26.38	49.56-35.94	39.75-22.31	27.44-21.06	27.13-20.50	24.00-14.31
P/E Ratio	28.0-19.8	29.9-18.1	35.7-25.9	36.1-20.3	24.0-18.4	24.5-18.6	24.4-14.5
Average Yield %	0.8	0.6	0.5	0.6	0.7	0.6	0.7

Statistics are as originally reported. Adj. for stk. splits: 2-for-1, 3/99. ① Incl. non-recurr. chrg. of $18.9 mill., 1999; $321.6 mill., 1998. ② Incl. an after-tax gain on McDonalds's Japan initial public offering of $137.1 million and after-tax non-recurring chrgs. totaling $279.6 mill.

OFFICERS:
F. L. Turner, Sr. Chmn.
J. M. Greenberg, Chmn., C.E.O.
M. A. Paul, Exec. V.P., C.F.O.

INVESTOR CONTACT: Investor Relations Service Center, (630) 623-7428

PRINCIPAL OFFICE: McDonald's Plaza, Oak Brook, IL 60523

TELEPHONE NUMBER: (630) 623-3000
FAX: (630) 623-5027
WEB: www.mcdonalds.com

NO. OF EMPLOYEES: 395,000 (approx.)

SHAREHOLDERS: 1,027,000 (approx.)

ANNUAL MEETING: In May

INCORPORATED: DE, March, 1965

INSTITUTIONAL HOLDINGS:
No. of Institutions: 787
Shares Held: 810,651,753
% Held: 63.3

INDUSTRY: Eating places (SIC: 5812)

TRANSFER AGENT(S): EquiServe, First Chicago Trust Division, Jersey City, NJ

MCGRATH RENT CORP.

YIELD 2.1%
P/E RATIO 14.2

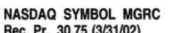

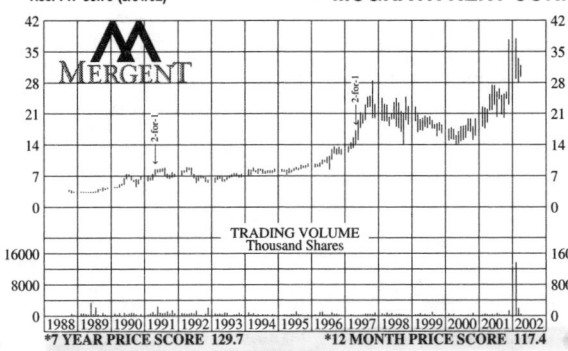

INTERIM EARNINGS (Per Share):

Qtr.	Mar.	June	Sept.	Dec.
1998	0.33	0.42	0.50	0.41
1999	0.38	0.43	0.51	0.47
2000	0.45	0.52	0.73	0.50
2001	0.54	0.62	0.58	0.42

INTERIM DIVIDENDS (Per Share):

Amt.	Decl.	Ex.	Rec.	Pay.
0.16Q	7/03/01	7/11/01	7/13/01	7/31/01
0.16Q	10/03/01	10/11/01	10/15/01	10/31/01
0.16Q	1/03/02	1/11/02	1/15/02	1/31/02
0.16Q	4/05/02	4/11/02	4/15/02	4/30/02

Indicated div.: $0.64

CAPITALIZATION (12/31/01):

	($000)	(%)
Long-Term Debt	104,140	34.1
Deferred Income Tax	66,985	21.9
Minority Interest	2,946	1.0
Common & Surplus	131,595	43.1
Total	305,666	100.0

DIVIDEND ACHIEVER STATUS:
Rank: 69   10-Year Growth Rate: 14.51%
Total Years of Dividend Growth: 11

TRADING VOLUME
Thousand Shares

*7 YEAR PRICE SCORE 129.7   *12 MONTH PRICE SCORE 117.4
*NYSE COMPOSITE INDEX=100

RECENT DEVELOPMENTS: For the year ended 12/31/01, net income declined 2.1% to $26.7 million compared with $27.2 million in 2000. Total revenues slipped 2.9% to $159.4 million from $164.2 million a year earlier. Revenues from rental operations improved 5.7% to $18.5 million, while sales dropped 22.5% to $39.5 million. Revenues from other operations were $1.3 million versus $1.0 million the year before. Gross profit rose 0.7% to $77.0 million

from $76.5 million, while gross profit as a percentage of total revenues grew to 48.3% from 46.6% in the prior year. Income from operations decreased 7.9% to $52.0 million compared with $56.5 million in the previous year. Separately, on 12/20/01, the Company entered into a definitive agreement to be acquired by a subsidiary of Tyco International Ltd. in a transaction valued at about $482.0 million. The sale is subject to shareholder and regulatory approvals.

BUSINESS

MCGRATH RENT CORP. rents and sells modular offices designed to fill customers' temporary and permanent space needs under the trade name "Mobile Modular Management Corp." The Company also rents electronic test and measurement instruments. MGRC's rental and sales operations are conducted from branch offices in San Lorenzo and Corona, California and Houston, Texas. Electronic test and measurement instrument rental and sales operations are conducted from the San Lorenzo facility as well as from a facility in Richardson, Texas. On 10/30/00, the Company changed the name of its McGrath-RenTelco division to RenTelco.

ANNUAL FINANCIAL DATA

	12/31/01	12/31/00	12/31/99	12/31/98	12/31/97	12/31/96	12/31/95
Earnings Per Share	2.14	2.19	[1] 1.78	1.67	1.58	1.02	0.86
Cash Flow Per Share	4.51	4.26	3.39	2.98	2.62	1.88	1.63
Tang. Book Val. Per Share	10.67	8.99	7.60	7.54	6.79	5.99	5.53
Dividends Per Share	0.62	0.54	0.46	0.38	0.31	0.27	0.23
Dividend Payout %	29.0	24.7	25.8	22.8	19.6	26.6	27.5
INCOME STATEMENT (IN THOUSANDS):							
Total Revenues	159,394	164,158	129,962	135,428	134,976	89,005	71,273
Costs & Expenses	77,717	81,926	62,924	69,398	73,755	47,561	32,994
Depreciation & Amort.	29,632	25,716	21,474	18,794	15,771	13,285	12,442
Operating Income	52,045	56,516	45,564	47,236	45,450	28,159	25,837
Net Interest Inc./(Exp.)	d7,078	d8,840	d6,606	d6,326	d4,070	d2,887	d2,831
Income Before Income Taxes	44,967	47,676	38,958	40,910	41,379	25,272	23,006
Income Taxes	17,807	19,762	14,874	16,010	16,323	9,750	9,163
Equity Earnings/Minority Int.	d482	d670	d251	d1,005	d1,011	. . .	. . .
Net Income	26,678	27,244	[1] 23,833	23,895	24,045	15,522	13,843
Cash Flow	56,310	52,960	45,307	42,689	39,816	28,807	26,285
Average Shs. Outstg.	12,495	12,428	13,383	14,349	15,181	15,306	16,168
BALANCE SHEET (IN THOUSANDS):							
Cash & Cash Equivalents	4	643	490	857	538	686	221
Total Current Assets	36,900	46,330	25,585	22,668	22,332	20,606	13,422
Net Property	307,304	299,938	268,149	250,441	223,503	177,032	159,810
Total Assets	354,884	357,246	297,722	278,676	252,392	200,035	175,149
Total Current Liabilities	30,745	37,012	24,811	22,964	27,047	15,281	11,701
Long-Term Obligations	104,140	126,876	110,300	97,000	82,000	53,850	37,080
Net Stockholders' Equity	131,595	108,958	95,403	105,394	98,646	88,808	85,893
Net Working Capital	6,155	9,318	774	d296	d4,715	5,326	1,721
Year-end Shs. Outstg.	12,335	12,125	12,546	13,970	14,522	14,820	15,540
STATISTICAL RECORD:							
Operating Profit Margin %	32.7	34.4	35.1	34.9	33.7	31.6	36.3
Net Profit Margin %	16.7	16.6	18.3	17.6	17.8	17.4	19.4
Return on Equity %	20.3	25.0	25.0	22.7	24.4	17.5	16.1
Return on Assets %	7.5	7.6	8.0	8.6	9.5	7.8	7.9
Debt/Total Assets %	29.3	35.5	37.0	34.8	32.5	26.9	21.2
Price Range	37.69-17.63	19.88-14.00	22.50-15.88	24.75-13.88	28.50-12.25	13.63-8.38	9.75-7.25
P/E Ratio	17.6-8.2	9.1-6.4	12.6-8.9	14.8-8.3	18.0-7.8	13.4-8.3	11.4-8.5
Average Yield %	2.2	3.2	2.4	2.0	1.5	2.5	2.8

Statistics are as originally reported. Adj. for stk. splits: 2-for-1, 4/25/97. [1] Bef. acctg. chrg. of $1.4 mill.

OFFICERS:
R. P. McGrath, Chmn., C.E.O.
D. C. Kakures, Pres., C.O.O.
T. J. Sauer, V.P., C.F.O.

INVESTOR CONTACT: Tom Sauer, C.F.O.,
(925) 606-9200

PRINCIPAL OFFICE: 5700 Las Positas Road,
Livermore, CA 94550

TELEPHONE NUMBER: (925) 606-9200
WEB: www.mgrc.com

NO. OF EMPLOYEES: 418 (avg.)

SHAREHOLDERS: 95 (approx.)

ANNUAL MEETING: In May

INCORPORATED: CA, Mar., 1979

INSTITUTIONAL HOLDINGS:
No. of Institutions: 55
Shares Held: 5,853,945
% Held: 47.0

INDUSTRY: Equipment rental & leasing, nec
(SIC: 7359)

TRANSFER AGENT(S): U.S. Stock Transfer,
Glendale, CA

MCGRAW-HILL COMPANIES, INC. (THE)

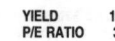

	YIELD	1.5%
	P/E RATIO	35.5

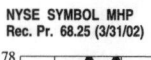

INTERIM EARNINGS (Per Share):

Qtr.	Mar.	June	Sept.	Dec.
1998	0.10	0.39	0.86	0.38
1999	0.12	0.45	0.96	0.61
2000	0.29	0.55	1.11	0.50
2001	0.10	0.61	1.22	d0.01

INTERIM DIVIDENDS (Per Share):

Amt.	Decl.	Ex.	Rec.	Pay.
0.245Q	1/31/01	2/22/01	2/26/01	3/12/01
0.245Q	4/25/01	5/24/01	5/29/01	6/12/01
0.245Q	7/25/01	8/24/01	8/28/01	9/12/01
0.245Q	10/31/01	11/26/01	11/28/01	12/12/01
0.255Q	1/30/02	2/22/02	2/26/02	3/12/02

Indicated div.: $1.02 (Div. Reinv. Plan)

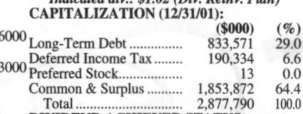

TRADING VOLUME
Thousand Shares

CAPITALIZATION (12/31/01):

	($000)	(%)
Long-Term Debt	833,571	29.0
Deferred Income Tax	190,334	6.6
Preferred Stock	13	0.0
Common & Surplus	1,853,872	64.4
Total	2,877,790	100.0

*7 YEAR PRICE SCORE 127.4   ***12 MONTH PRICE SCORE 109.0**
*NYSE COMPOSITE INDEX=100

DIVIDEND ACHIEVER STATUS:
Rank: 215   10-Year Growth Rate: 5.95%
Total Years of Dividend Growth: 28

RECENT DEVELOPMENTS: For the year ended 12/31/01, MHP reported net income of $377.0 million versus income of $471.9 million, before an after-tax accounting charge of $68.1 million, in 2000. Earnings for 2001 included a net pre-tax loss of $166.1 million related to various one-time items. Earnings for 2000 included a pre-tax gain of $16.6 million on the disposition of Tower Group International. Operating revenue rose 8.5% to $4.65 billion.

PROSPECTS: In 2002, MHP expects to report double-digit earnings growth. Separately, on 1/17/02, MHP's Construction Information Group (CIG) acquired several former Construction-zone.com key business assets. CIG will integrate the construction-zone.com content, applications and services into its construction.com Building Product Center, which will establish an Internet construction product database and search engine.

BUSINESS

THE MCGRAW-HILL COMPANIES, INC., a multimedia publishing and information services company, serves worldwide markets in education, finance and business information. As of 12/31/01, the Company had 335 offices worldwide. The Company provides information in print through books, newsletters, and magazines, including Business Week; on-line over electronic networks; over the air by television, satellite and FM sideband; and on software, videotape, facsimile and compact disks. Among the Company's business units are Standard & Poor's Financial Information Services and Standard & Poor's Ratings Services divisions.

ANNUAL FINANCIAL DATA

	12/31/01	12/31/00	12/31/99	12/31/98	12/31/97	12/31/96	12/31/95
Earnings Per Share	⑥ 1.92	⑤ 2.41	④ 2.14	③ 1.71	② 1.46	① 2.48	1.14
Cash Flow Per Share	4.07	4.25	3.70	3.22	2.93	3.67	2.30
Tang. Book Val. Per Share	0.18	0.33	2.24	1.48	0.64	0.28	0.38
Dividends Per Share	0.98	0.94	0.86	0.78	0.72	0.66	0.60
Dividend Payout %	51.0	39.0	40.2	45.8	49.5	26.6	52.6
INCOME STATEMENT (IN MILLIONS):							
Total Revenues	4,645.5	4,281.0	3,992.0	3,729.1	3,534.1	3,074.7	2,935.3
Costs & Expenses	3,554.8	3,098.5	2,943.7	2,821.5	2,716.8	1,973.7	2,258.8
Depreciation & Amort.	420.6	362.3	308.3	299.2	293.5	238.6	231.4
Operating Income	670.1	820.2	740.0	608.4	523.8	862.5	445.0
Net Interest Inc./(Exp.)	d55.1	d52.8	d42.0	d48.0	d52.5	d47.7	d58.8
Income Before Income Taxes	615.1	767.3	698.0	560.4	471.3	814.8	386.3
Income Taxes	238.0	295.4	272.2	218.6	180.6	319.1	159.1
Net Income	⑥ 377.0	⑤ 471.9	④ 425.8	③ 341.9	② 290.7	① 495.7	227.2
Cash Flow	797.6	834.2	734.1	641.1	584.2	734.3	458.6
Average Shs. Outstg. (000)	195,873	196,072	198,557	199,104	199,504	199,994	199,504
BALANCE SHEET (IN MILLIONS):							
Cash & Cash Equivalents	53.5	3.2	6.5	10.5	4.8	3.4	10.3
Total Current Assets	1,812.9	1,801.7	1,553.7	1,428.8	1,464.4	1,349.6	1,239.8
Net Property	454.9	431.9	430.4	364.0	273.6	311.5	336.1
Total Assets	5,161.2	4,931.4	4,088.8	3,788.1	3,724.5	3,642.2	3,104.4
Total Current Liabilities	1,876.4	1,780.8	1,525.5	1,291.5	1,206.2	1,218.7	1,046.5
Long-Term Obligations	833.6	817.5	354.8	452.1	607.0	556.9	557.4
Net Stockholders' Equity	1,853.9	1,761.0	1,691.5	1,551.8	1,434.7	1,361.1	1,035.1
Net Working Capital	d63.4	20.9	28.3	137.3	258.2	130.9	193.3
Year-end Shs. Outstg. (000)	193,218	194,285	195,709	197,111	198,204	199,062	200,286
STATISTICAL RECORD:							
Operating Profit Margin %	14.4	19.2	18.5	16.3	14.8	28.1	15.2
Net Profit Margin %	8.1	11.0	10.7	9.2	8.2	16.1	7.7
Return on Equity %	20.3	26.8	25.2	22.0	20.3	36.4	21.9
Return on Assets %	7.3	9.6	10.4	9.0	7.8	13.6	7.3
Debt/Total Assets %	16.2	16.6	8.7	11.9	16.3	15.3	18.0
Price Range	70.87-48.70	67.69-41.88	63.13-47.13	51.66-34.25	37.38-22.44	24.63-18.63	21.91-15.91
P/E Ratio	36.9-25.4	28.1-17.4	29.5-22.0	30.2-20.0	25.7-15.4	9.9-7.5	19.2-14.0
Average Yield %	1.6	1.7	1.6	1.8	2.4	3.1	3.2

Statistics are as originally reported. Adj. for 2-for-1 splits 3/99 & 4/96. ① Incl. $260.5 mill. net gain fr. the exch. of its legal publish. unit for Times Mirror Higher Education Group. ② Incl. nonrecurr. gain of $40.1 mill. ③ Bef. extraord. chrg. of $8.7 mill. ④ Incl. after-tax gain of $24.2 mill. fr. sale of Co.'s Petrochemical publications. ⑤ Bef. acctg. chrg. of $68.1 mill.; incl. a gain of $10.2 mill. fr. sale of Tower Group Int'l. ⑥ Incl. a prov. of $159.0 mill. for restruct. & asset write-down & a pre-tax net chrg. of $7.1 mill. rel. to various one-time items.

OFFICERS:
H. McGraw III, Chmn., Pres., C.E.O.
R. J. Bahash, Exec. V.P., C.F.O.

INVESTOR CONTACT: Steven H. Weiss, V.P.-Corp. Comm., (212) 512-2247

PRINCIPAL OFFICE: 1221 Avenue Of The Americas, New York, NY 10020

TELEPHONE NUMBER: (212) 512-2000
FAX: (212) 512-2305
WEB: www.mcgraw-hill.com
NO. OF EMPLOYEES: 17,135
SHAREHOLDERS: 5,122 (approx.)
ANNUAL MEETING: In April
INCORPORATED: NY, Dec., 1925

INSTITUTIONAL HOLDINGS:
No. of Institutions: 455
Shares Held: 137,871,379
% Held: 71.2

INDUSTRY: Book publishing (SIC: 2731)

TRANSFER AGENT(S): Mellon Investor Services, New York, NY

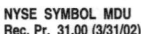

MDU RESOURCES GROUP, INC.

YIELD 3.0%
P/E RATIO 13.6

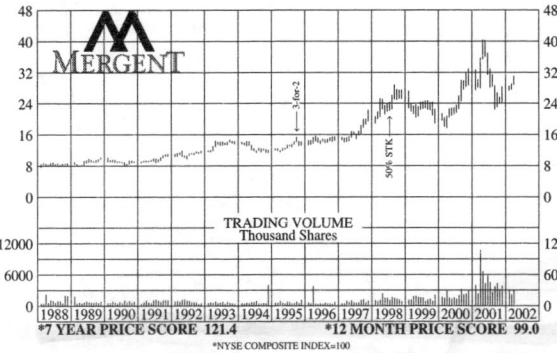

TRADING VOLUME
Thousand Shares

*7 YEAR PRICE SCORE 121.4   *12 MONTH PRICE SCORE 99.0
*NYSE COMPOSITE INDEX=100

INTERIM EARNINGS (Per Share):

Qtr.	Mar.	June	Sept.	Dec.
1998	0.39	d0.12	0.42	d0.01
1999	0.23	0.33	0.52	0.44
2000	0.23	0.35	0.63	0.56
2001	0.49	0.63	0.74	0.42

INTERIM DIVIDENDS (Per Share):

Amt.	Decl.	Ex.	Rec.	Pay.
0.22Q	5/17/01	6/12/01	6/14/01	7/01/01
0.23Q	8/16/01	9/11/01	9/13/01	10/01/01
0.23Q	11/15/01	12/11/01	12/13/01	1/01/02
0.23Q	2/14/02	3/12/02	3/14/02	4/01/02

Indicated div.: $0.92 (Div. Reinv. Plan)

CAPITALIZATION (12/31/01):

	($000)	(%)
Long-term Debt...............	783,709	34.8
Deferred Income Tax	342,412	15.2
Redeemable Pfd. Stock	1,300	0.1
Preferred Stock................	15,000	0.6
Common & Surplus	1,109,771	49.3
Total	2,252,192	100.0

DIVIDEND ACHIEVER STATUS:
Rank: 258   10-Year Growth Rate: 3.42%
Total Years of Dividend Growth: 11

RECENT DEVELOPMENTS: For the year ended 12/31/01, net income advanced 40.4% to $155.8 million versus $111.0 million in 2000. Total revenues increased 18.7% to $2.22 billion. On a segment basis, electric revenue rose 4.5% to $168.8 million, while natural gas distribution revenue grew 9.6% to $255.4 million. Utility services revenue soared 115.3% to $364.7 million, and construction materials and mining revenue jumped 29.8% to $801.9 million. Pipeline and energy services revenues fell 17.3% to $479.1 million.

PROSPECTS: On 2/5/02, MDU's Centennial Power, Inc. subsidiary announced its purchase of Rocky Mountain Power, Inc., a Montana energy development company. The deal enables Centennial to construct a 113-megawatt, coal-fired electric generation facility near Hardin, Montana. The plant will provide electricity to Montana Power Company under a long-term power purchase agreement. On 3/13/02, MDU's Knife River Corporation subsidiary acquired Thorson, Inc. a asphalt and aggregate company in Minnesota.

BUSINESS

MDU RESOURCES GROUP, INC. is a diversified natural resource company. The Company, through its public utility division, Montana-Dakota Utilities Co., generates, transmits and distributes electricity, distributes natural gas and provides related value-added products and services in North Dakota, Montana, South Dakota and Wyoming. Great Plains Natural Gas Co., another public utility division of the company, distributes natural gas in southeastern North Dakota and western Minnesota. Also the Company, through its wholly-owned subsidiary, Centennial Energy Holdings, Inc., owns WBI Holdings, Inc., a provider of pipeline and energy services and a natural gas and oil producer; Knife River Corporation, a producer of construction materials; Utility Services, Inc., a utility infrastructure company; and Centennial Holdings Capital Corp.

REVENUES

(12/31/2001)	($000)	(%)
Electric	168,837	7.6
Natural Gas..................	255,389	11.5
Utility Service	364,746	16.5
Pipeline & Energy	479,108	21.6
Oil & Natural Gas Production	148,653	6.7
Construction Material & Mining................	801,833	36.1
Total	2,218,616	100.0

ANNUAL FINANCIAL DATA

	12/31/01	12/31/00	12/31/99	12/31/98	12/31/97	12/31/96	12/31/95
Earnings Per Share	2.29	1.80	1.52	0.66	1.24	1.05	0.95
Cash Flow Per Share	4.35	3.60	3.01	2.19	2.75	2.51	2.24
Tang. Book Val. Per Share	16.12	13.55	11.74	10.39	8.84	8.21	7.90
Dividends Per Share	0.89	0.85	0.81	0.78	0.75	0.73	0.71
Dividend Payout %	38.9	47.2	53.3	117.4	60.2	69.7	75.0
INCOME STATEMENT (IN MILLIONS):							
Total Revenues	2,223.6	1,873.7	1,279.8	896.6	607.7	514.7	464.2
Costs & Expenses	1,810.4	1,545.8	1,038.2	747.9	430.3	340.5	318.8
Depreciation & Amort.	139.9	110.9	81.8	77.8	65.8	62.7	54.8
Operating Income	273.3	217.0	159.8	70.9	111.6	111.5	90.6
Net Interest Inc./(Exp.)	d45.9	d48.0	d36.0	d30.3	d30.2	d28.8	d24.7
Income Taxes	98.3	69.7	49.3	17.5	30.7	16.1	23.1
Net Income	155.8	111.0	84.1	34.1	54.6	45.5	41.6
Cash Flow	295.0	221.2	165.1	111.1	119.6	107.3	95.7
Average Shs. Outstg. (000)	67,869	61,390	54,870	50,837	43,478	42,716	42,716
BALANCE SHEET (IN MILLIONS):							
Gross Property	2,756.7	2,496.1	2,042.3	1,810.8	1,510.3	1,370.3	1,287.2
Accumulated Depreciation	947.4	895.1	794.1	726.1	670.8	617.7	570.9
Net Property	1,809.3	1,601.0	1,248.2	1,084.7	839.5	752.6	716.3
Total Assets	2,623.1	2,313.0	1,766.3	1,452.8	1,113.9	1,089.2	1,056.5
Long-Term Obligations	783.7	728.2	563.5	413.3	298.6	280.7	237.4
Net Stockholders' Equity	1,124.8	896.0	684.4	565.7	401.2	365.6	352.2
Year-end Shs. Outstg. (000)	69,777	65,028	57,038	53,033	43,715	42,716	42,716
STATISTICAL RECORD:							
Operating Profit Margin %	12.3	11.6	12.5	7.9	18.4	21.7	19.5
Net Profit Margin %	7.0	5.9	6.6	3.8	9.0	8.8	9.0
Net Inc./Net Property %	8.6	6.9	6.7	3.1	6.5	6.0	5.8
Net Inc./Tot. Capital %	6.9	5.8	5.7	3.0	6.7	5.9	5.9
Return on Equity %	13.9	12.4	12.3	6.0	13.6	12.4	11.8
Accum. Depr./Gross Prop. %	34.4	35.9	38.9	40.1	44.4	45.1	44.3
Price Range	40.37-22.38	33.00-17.63	27.19-18.81	28.88-18.83	22.33-14.00	15.67-13.25	15.39-11.45
P/E Ratio	17.6-9.8	18.3-9.8	17.9-12.4	43.7-28.5	18.0-11.3	15.0-12.7	16.1-12.0
Average Yield %	2.8	3.4	3.5	3.2	4.1	5.0	5.3

Statistics are as originally reported. Adj. for 3-for-2 stk. split, 7/13/98.

OFFICERS:
M. A. White, Chmn., Pres., C.E.O.
W. L. Robinson, Exec. V.P., C.F.O., Treas.

INVESTOR CONTACT: Nicole Kivisto, Investor Relations, (701) 222-7937

PRINCIPAL OFFICE: Schuchart Building, 918 East Divide Avenue, P.O. Box 5650, Bismarck, ND 58506-5650

TELEPHONE NUMBER: (701) 222-7900
FAX: (701) 222-7607
WEB: www.mdu.com
NO. OF EMPLOYEES: 6,568
SHAREHOLDERS: 14,000 (approx.)
ANNUAL MEETING: In April
INCORPORATED: DE, March, 1924

INSTITUTIONAL HOLDINGS:
No. of Institutions: 178
Shares Held: 21,771,143
% Held: 31.2

INDUSTRY: Gas and other services combined (SIC: 4932)

TRANSFER AGENT(S): Wells Fargo Shareowner Services, South St. Paul, MN

MEDTRONIC, INC.

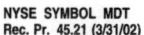
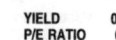

	YIELD	0.5%
	P/E RATIO	66.5

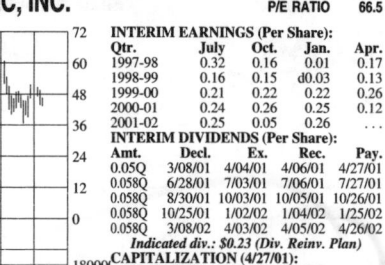

INTERIM EARNINGS (Per Share):

Qtr.	July	Oct.	Jan.	Apr.
1997-98	0.32	0.16	0.01	0.17
1998-99	0.16	0.15	d0.03	0.13
1999-00	0.21	0.22	0.22	0.26
2000-01	0.24	0.26	0.25	0.12
2001-02	0.25	0.05	0.26	...

INTERIM DIVIDENDS (Per Share):

Amt.	Decl.	Ex.	Rec.	Pay.
0.05Q	3/08/01	4/04/01	4/06/01	4/27/01
0.058Q	6/28/01	7/03/01	7/06/01	7/27/01
0.058Q	8/30/01	10/03/01	10/05/01	10/26/01
0.058Q	10/25/01	1/02/02	1/04/02	1/25/02
0.058Q	3/08/02	4/03/02	4/05/02	4/26/02

Indicated div.: $0.23 (Div. Reinv. Plan)

CAPITALIZATION (4/27/01):

	($000)	(%)
Long-Term Debt	13,300	0.2
Common & Surplus	5,509,500	99.8
Total	5,522,800	100.0

DIVIDEND ACHIEVER STATUS:
Rank: 15   10-Year Growth Rate: 22.69%
Total Years of Dividend Growth: 24

TRADING VOLUME
Thousand Shares

*7 YEAR PRICE SCORE 125.2   *12 MONTH PRICE SCORE 104.7
*NYSE COMPOSITE INDEX=100

RECENT DEVELOPMENTS: For the third quarter ended 1/25/02, net earnings rose 4.0% to $314.9 million compared with $302.8 million in the corresponding period of the prior year. Results for 2001 included after-tax non-recurring charges of $49.1 million, while results for 2000 included after-tax non-recurring charges of $11.1 million. Net sales increased 17.0% to $1.59 billion from $1.36 billion the year before.

PROSPECTS: MDT is benefiting from broad-based growth, particularly the cardiac rhythm management segment, which reported an increase in revenues due to strong demand for MDT's tachyarrhythmia and heart failure product lines. Separately, on 1/3/02, MDT announced that it has acquired Paceart from GE Medical Systems Information Technologies. Paceart is a computerized pacemaker follow-up system. Terms of the transaction were not disclosed.

BUSINESS

MEDTRONIC, INC. is a medical technology company specializing in implantable and interventional therapies. Primary products include those for bradycardia pacing, tachyarrhythmia management, atrial fibrillation management, heart failure management, coronary and peripheral vascular disease, heart valve replacement, extracorporeal cardiac support, minimally invasive cardiac surgery, malignant and non-malignant pain, movement disorders, neurosurgery, neurodegenerative disorders and ear, nose and throat (ENT) surgery. As of 2/12/02, MDT operated business in more than 120 countries and reports on four primary product line platforms: Cardiac Rhythm Management; Cardiac Surgery; Vascular, Neurological and Diabetes; and Spinal and ENT.

ANNUAL FINANCIAL DATA

	4/27/01	4/30/00	4/30/99	4/30/98	4/30/97	4/30/96	4/30/95
Earnings Per Share	[1] 0.85	[3] 0.90	[2] 0.40	[1] 0.48	0.56	0.47	0.32
Cash Flow Per Share	1.10	1.10	0.57	0.63	0.68	0.59	0.43
Tang. Book Val. Per Share	3.53	2.61	1.99	1.68	1.34	1.41	1.05
Dividends Per Share	0.18	0.14	0.12	0.10	0.08	0.06	0.05
Dividend Payout %	21.2	16.1	30.4	21.3	14.4	12.4	14.7

INCOME STATEMENT (IN MILLIONS):

	4/27/01	4/30/00	4/30/99	4/30/98	4/30/97	4/30/96	4/30/95
Total Revenues	5,551.8	5,014.6	4,134.1	2,604.8	2,438.2	2,169.1	1,742.4
Costs & Expenses	3,714.9	3,157.7	3,121.2	1,744.0	1,536.9	1,410.2	1,199.6
Depreciation & Amort.	297.3	243.3	213.1	137.6	116.9	111.8	106.5
Operating Income	1,539.6	1,613.6	799.8	723.2	784.5	647.2	436.3
Net Interest Inc./(Exp.)	74.2	15.4	22.2	14.8	24.7	21.2	5.8
Income Before Income Taxes	1,549.4	1,629.0	822.0	702.0	809.1	668.4	442.1
Income Taxes	503.4	530.5	353.6	244.6	279.2	230.6	148.1
Net Income	[1] 1,046.0	[3] 1,098.5	[2] 468.4	[1] 457.4	530.0	437.8	294.0
Cash Flow	1,343.3	1,341.8	681.5	594.9	646.9	549.6	400.5
Average Shs. Outstg. (000)	1,226,000	1,220,800	1,185,800	951,168	954,772	932,628	921,920

BALANCE SHEET (IN MILLIONS):

	4/27/01	4/30/00	4/30/99	4/30/98	4/30/97	4/30/96	4/30/95
Cash & Cash Equivalents	1,231.7	558.1	375.9	425.9	250.6	460.8	323.6
Total Current Assets	3,756.8	3,013.4	2,395.2	1,551.6	1,237.9	1,343.2	1,103.9
Net Property	1,176.5	946.5	748.8	508.8	487.2	415.3	331.1
Total Assets	7,038.9	5,669.4	4,870.3	2,774.7	2,409.2	2,503.3	1,946.7
Total Current Liabilities	1,359.3	991.5	990.3	572.0	518.7	525.0	456.1
Long-Term Obligations	13.3	14.1	17.6	16.2	14.0	15.3	14.2
Net Stockholders' Equity	5,509.5	4,491.5	3,654.6	2,044.2	1,746.2	1,789.3	1,335.0
Net Working Capital	2,397.5	2,021.9	1,404.9	979.6	719.2	818.2	647.8
Year-end Shs. Outstg. (000)	1,209,515	1,197,698	1,170,452	938,090	935,256	937,272	924,072

STATISTICAL RECORD:

	4/27/01	4/30/00	4/30/99	4/30/98	4/30/97	4/30/96	4/30/95
Operating Profit Margin %	27.7	32.2	19.3	27.8	32.2	29.8	25.0
Net Profit Margin %	18.8	21.9	11.3	17.6	21.7	20.2	16.9
Return on Equity %	19.0	24.5	12.8	22.4	30.4	24.5	22.0
Return on Assets %	14.9	19.4	9.6	16.5	22.0	17.5	15.1
Debt/Total Assets %	0.2	0.2	0.4	0.6	0.6	0.6	0.7
Price Range	62.00-32.75	44.63-29.94	38.38-22.72	26.38-14.41	17.47-11.13	15.00-6.55	6.98-4.32
P/E Ratio	72.9-38.5	49.6-33.3	97.1-57.5	54.9-30.0	31.5-20.0	31.9-13.9	21.9-13.5
Average Yield %	0.4	0.4	0.4	0.5	0.6	0.6	0.8

Statistics are as originally reported. Adj. for 2-for-1 stk split, 9/99, 9/97 & 9/95. [1] Incl. a pre-tax chrg. of $169.3 mill., 1998; $338.8 mill., 2001. [2] Incl. a pre-tax nonrecur. chg. of $371.3 mill. & a pre-tax chg. of $150.9 mill. for pchsd. in-process R&D. [3] Incl. a pre-tax nonrecur. chrg. of $14.7 mill. for the Xomed acquis.

OFFICERS:
W. W. George, Chmn.
G. D. Nelson M.D., Vice-Chmn.
A. D. Collins Jr., Pres., C.E.O.

INVESTOR CONTACT: Rachel Scherer,
Investor Relations, (763) 505-2694

PRINCIPAL OFFICE: 710 Medtronic
Parkway, Minneapolis, MN 55432

TELEPHONE NUMBER: (763) 514-4000
FAX: (763) 514-4879
WEB: www.medtronic.com

NO. OF EMPLOYEES: 23,290 full-time; 2,760
part-time

SHAREHOLDERS: 45,500 (approx.)

ANNUAL MEETING: In Aug.

INCORPORATED: MN, 1957

INSTITUTIONAL HOLDINGS:
No. of Institutions: 901
Shares Held: 801,317,290
% Held: 66.0

INDUSTRY: Electromedical equipment (SIC:
3845)

TRANSFER AGENT(S): Wells Fargo Bank
Shareowner Services, South St. Paul, MN

MERCANTILE BANKSHARES CORPORATION

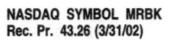

	YIELD	2.6%
	P/E RATIO	17.0

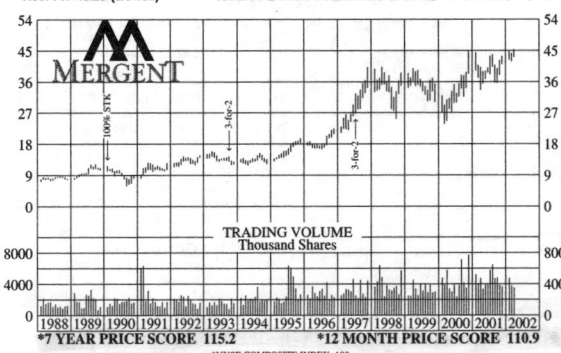

7 YEAR PRICE SCORE 115.2 **12 MONTH PRICE SCORE 110.9**
*NYSE COMPOSITE INDEX=100

TRADING VOLUME
Thousand Shares

INTERIM EARNINGS (Per Share):

Qtr.	Mar.	June	Sept.	Dec.
1997	0.45	0.46	0.48	0.45
1998	0.49	0.50	0.52	0.53
1999	0.53	0.55	0.59	0.59
2000	0.60	0.62	0.64	0.64
2001	0.65	0.62	0.65	0.63

INTERIM DIVIDENDS (Per Share):

Amt.	Decl.	Ex.	Rec.	Pay.
0.26Q	3/13/01	3/21/01	3/23/01	3/30/01
0.28Q	6/12/01	6/20/01	6/22/01	6/29/01
0.28Q	9/11/01	9/19/01	9/21/01	9/28/01
0.28Q	12/11/01	12/20/01	12/24/01	12/31/01
0.28Q	3/12/02	3/20/02	3/22/02	3/29/02

Indicated div.: $1.12 (Div. Reinv. Plan)

CAPITALIZATION (12/31/01):

	($000)	(%)
Total Deposits	7,447,372	83.2
Long-Term Debt	269,437	3.0
Common & Surplus	1,230,206	13.7
Total	8,947,015	100.0

DIVIDEND ACHIEVER STATUS:

Rank: 113	10-Year Growth Rate: 11.15%

Total Years of Dividend Growth: 25

RECENT DEVELOPMENTS: For the year ended 12/31/01, net income climbed 3.5% to $181.3 million compared with $175.2 million the year before. Results for 2001 and 2000 included amortization of goodwill of $9.1 million and $5.2 million, respectively. Net interest income increased 2.2% to $418.2 million from $409.4 million in the prior year due to average loan growth. Provision for loan losses dropped 22.0% to $13.4 million. Total interest income improved to $649.8 million from $646.5 million a year earlier. Interest and fees on loans totaled $543.0 million, down from $547.9 million the year before. Total interest and dividends on investment securities increased 4.0% to $100.5 million. Other interest income advanced to $6.2 million from $1.9 million in 2000. Total non-interest income rose 15.9% to $145.5 million, while total non-interest expenses grew 8.4% to $264.0 million. For the quarter ended 12/31/01, net income slipped 3.3% to $44.2 million and net interest income fell 2.4% to $104.8 million.

BUSINESS

MERCANTILE BANKSHARES CORPORATION is a bank holding company that owns substantially all of the outstanding shares of capital stock of twenty-one banks as of 12/31/01. The affiliated banks are engaged in general commercial and retail banking business, including acceptance of demand, savings and time deposits and the making of various types of loans. Mercantile-Safe Deposit and Trust Company offers a full range of personal trust services, investment management services and, for corporate and institutional customers, investment advisory, financial and pension and profit sharing services, including Mercantile Capital Advisors, Inc. The Company also owns all of the outstanding shares of Mercantile Mortgage Corporation, a mortgage banking company, MBC Agency, Inc., an insurance agency, Hopkins Plaza Agency, Inc., an agent in the sale of fixed rate annuities, Hopkins Plaza Securities, Inc., a broker-dealer, MBC Leasing, Inc., a leasing company, and MBC Realty, LLC, which owns and operates various properties used by Mercantile Safe Deposit and Trust Company.

ANNUAL FINANCIAL DATA

	12/31/01	12/31/00	12/31/99	12/31/98	12/31/97	12/31/96	12/31/95
Earnings Per Share	2.55	2.51	2.25	2.04	1.84	1.64	1.46
Tang. Book Val. Per Share	16.03	15.03	13.51	13.36	12.50	11.35	10.55
Dividends Per Share	1.10	1.02	0.94	0.86	0.77	0.65	0.57
Dividend Payout %	43.1	40.6	41.8	42.2	42.0	39.8	39.3
INCOME STATEMENT (IN MILLIONS)							
Total Interest Income	649.8	646.5	559.2	555.4	534.0	498.1	467.3
Total Interest Expense	231.5	237.1	190.1	202.0	197.9	187.6	180.5
Net Interest Income	418.2	409.4	369.1	353.4	336.0	310.6	286.8
Provision for Loan Losses	13.4	17.2	12.1	11.5	13.7	14.7	8.0
Non-Interest Income	145.5	125.5	122.0	108.7	98.7	89.4	80.9
Non-Interest Expense	264.0	243.5	230.4	219.0	213.4	198.4	193.7
Income Before Taxes	286.3	274.2	248.6	231.6	207.6	186.9	166.0
Net Income	181.3	175.2	157.7	147.1	132.0	117.4	104.4
Average Shs. Outstg. (000)	71,199	69,719	70,020	72,237	71,904	71,477	71,652
BALANCE SHEET (IN MILLIONS)							
Cash & Due from Banks	290.2	244.9	219.4	255.0	337.2	257.3	247.3
Securities Avail. for Sale	2,288.7	1,676.6	1,743.9	1,880.5	1,607.3	1,596.7	1,551.7
Total Loans & Leases	6,906.2	6,693.3	5,718.9	5,220.9	4,978.5	4,582.7	4,301.3
Allowance for Credit Losses	141.5	138.6	118.0	112.4	106.1	97.7	91.4
Net Loans & Leases	6,764.8	6,554.7	5,600.9	5,108.5	4,872.4	4,485.0	4,209.9
Total Assets	9,928.8	8,938.0	7,895.0	7,609.6	7,170.7	6,642.7	6,349.1
Total Deposits	7,447.4	6,796.5	5,925.1	5,958.3	5,693.9	5,339.7	5,169.4
Long-Term Obligations	269.4	92.5	82.7	40.9	50.0	49.4	25.6
Total Liabilities	8,698.6	7,764.7	6,921.0	6,610.2	6,235.7	5,806.6	5,555.3
Net Stockholders' Equity	1,230.2	1,173.3	974.0	999.4	935.0	836.0	793.8
Year-end Shs. Outstg. (000)	69,776	71,099	68,646	71,027	71,874	71,153	72,408
STATISTICAL RECORD:							
Return on Equity %	14.7	14.9	16.2	14.7	14.1	14.0	13.2
Return on Assets %	1.8	2.0	2.0	1.9	1.8	1.8	1.6
Equity/Assets %	12.4	13.1	12.3	13.1	13.0	12.6	12.5
Non-Int. Exp./Tot. Inc. %	46.8	45.5	46.9	47.4	49.1	49.6	52.7
Price Range	44.50-33.63	45.13-23.75	39.94-30.00	40.25-25.25	40.25-21.17	22.50-16.50	19.67-13.00
P/E Ratio	17.5-13.2	18.0-9.5	17.7-13.3	19.7-12.4	21.9-11.5	13.7-10.1	13.5-8.9
Average Yield %	2.8	3.0	2.7	2.6	2.5	3.4	3.5

Statistics are as originally reported. Adj. for 3-for-2 stock split, 7/97.

OFFICERS:
H. F. Baldwin, Chmn.
E. J. Kelly III, Pres., C.E.O.
T. L. Troupe, C.F.O., Treas.

INVESTOR CONTACT: Investor Relations, (410) 347-8039

PRINCIPAL OFFICE: Two Hopkins Plaza, P.O. Box 1477, Baltimore, MD 21203

TELEPHONE NUMBER: (410) 237-5900
FAX: (410) 347-8493
WEB: www.mrbk.com

NO. OF EMPLOYEES: 2,949 (approx.)

SHAREHOLDERS: 8,740

ANNUAL MEETING: In Apr.

INCORPORATED: MD, May, 1969

INSTITUTIONAL HOLDINGS:
No. of Institutions: 200
Shares Held: 29,019,380
% Held: 41.6

INDUSTRY: State commercial banks (SIC: 6022)

TRANSFER AGENT(S): The Bank of New York, New York, NY

MERCK & CO., INC.

YIELD 2.4%
P/E RATIO 18.3

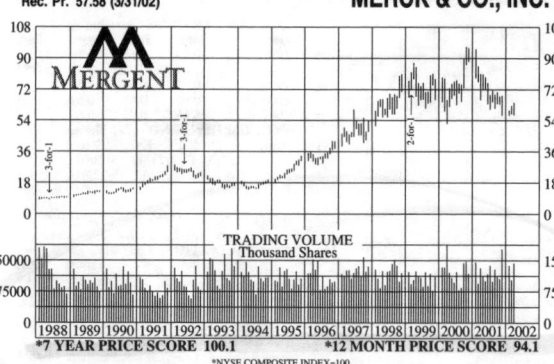

TRADING VOLUME
Thousand Shares

*7 YEAR PRICE SCORE 100.1   *12 MONTH PRICE SCORE 94.1

*NYSE COMPOSITE INDEX=100

INTERIM EARNINGS (Per Share):

Qtr.	Mar.	June	Sept.	Dec.
1997	0.42	0.48	0.50	0.51
1998	0.48	0.54	0.56	0.58
1999	0.54	0.61	0.64	0.66
2000	0.63	0.73	0.78	0.75
2001	0.71	0.78	0.84	0.81

INTERIM DIVIDENDS (Per Share):

Amt.	Decl.	Ex.	Rec.	Pay.
0.34Q	2/27/01	3/07/01	3/09/01	4/02/01
0.34Q	5/22/01	5/31/01	6/04/01	7/02/01
0.35Q	7/24/01	8/30/01	9/04/01	10/01/01
0.35Q	11/27/01	12/05/01	12/07/01	1/02/02
0.35Q	2/26/02	3/06/02	3/08/02	4/01/02

Indicated div.: $1.40 (Div. Reinv. Plan)

CAPITALIZATION (12/31/01):

	($000)	(%)
Long-Term Debt	4,798,600	18.7
Minority Interest	4,837,500	18.8
Common & Surplus	16,050,100	62.5
Total	25,686,200	100.0

DIVIDEND ACHIEVER STATUS:
Rank: 80   10-Year Growth Rate: 13.53%
Total Years of Dividend Growth: 18

RECENT DEVELOPMENTS: For the year ended 12/31/01, net income advanced 6.7% to $7.28 billion compared with $6.82 billion in 2000. Sales increased 18.2% to $47.72 billion from $40.36 billion in the prior year. Sales growth was attributed to a 26.0% improvement in key growth products, ZOCOR, VIOXX, COZAAR, HYZAAR, FOSAMAX, and SINGULAIR. Expenses for materials and production rose 29.1% to $29.0 million from $22.4 million a year earlier.

PROSPECTS: In the near term, top-line growth is expected to continue, while bottom-line results should remain at the same level as 2001 due to the patent expiration of Prilosec. Separately, on 1/29/02, the Company announced plans to establish its subsidiary, Merck-Medco, as a separate, publicly-traded company. Also, the Company expects to file or launch 11 new medicines and vaccines between 2002 and 2006.

BUSINESS

MERCK & CO., INC. is a research pharmaceutical company that discovers, develops, manufactures and markets human and animal health products, directly and through its joint ventures, and provides pharmaceutical benefit services through Merck-Medco Managed Care LLC. The Merck Pharmaceuticals segment (44.7% of 2001 sales) consists of therapeutic and preventive agents, generally sold by prescription, for the treatment of human disorders. Human health products include ZOCOR, a cholesterol-lowering medicine, FOSAMAX, a treatment for osteoporosis, VIOXX, a prescription arthritis medicine, SINGULAIR, for the treatment of chronic asthma, and COZAAR and HYZAAR for the treatment of high blood pressure. The Merck-Medco segment (55.3% of 2001 sales) primarily includes sales of non-Merck products and Merck-Medco pharmaceutical benefit services for more than 65.0 million customers.

ANNUAL FINANCIAL DATA

	12/31/01	12/31/00	12/31/99	12/31/98	12/31/97	12/31/96	12/31/95
Earnings Per Share	3.14	2.90	④ 2.45	③ 2.15	② 1.87	1.60	① 1.35
Cash Flow Per Share	3.77	3.44	2.93	2.57	2.21	2.00	1.74
Tang. Book Val. Per Share	3.77	3.23	2.43	1.91	2.44	2.17	2.00
Dividends Per Share	1.37	1.21	1.10	0.94	0.84	0.71	0.62
Dividend Payout %	43.6	41.7	44.9	44.0	45.2	44.4	45.9
INCOME STATEMENT (IN MILLIONS):							
Total Revenues	47,715.7	40,363.2	32,714.0	26,898.2	23,636.9	19,828.7	16,681.1
Costs & Expenses	36,193.5	29,677.7	23,708.7	20,282.3	16,936.1	13,916.9	11,593.3
Depreciation & Amort.	1,463.8	1,277.3	1,144.8	1,015.1	837.1	730.9	667.2
Operating Income	10,058.4	9,408.2	7,860.5	5,600.8	5,863.7	5,180.9	4,420.6
Income Before Income Taxes	9,716.7	9,059.2	7,857.5	7,248.8	5,734.4	5,180.9	5,103.5
Income Taxes	3,120.8	3,002.4	2,729.0	2,884.9	1,848.2	1,659.5	1,462.0
Equity Earnings/Minority Int.	685.9	764.9	762.0	884.3	727.9	600.7	...
Net Income	7,281.8	6,821.7	④ 5,890.5	③ 5,248.2	② 4,614.1	4,122.1	① 3,641.5
Cash Flow	8,745.6	8,099.0	7,035.3	6,263.3	5,451.2	4,853.0	4,308.7
Average Shs. Outstg. (000)	2,322,300	2,353,200	2,404,600	2,441,100	2,469,400	2,427,200	2,472,200
BALANCE SHEET (IN MILLIONS):							
Cash & Cash Equivalents	3,286.6	4,254.6	3,202.4	3,355.7	2,309.3	2,181.6	3,349.8
Total Current Assets	12,961.6	13,353.4	11,259.2	10,228.5	8,213.0	7,726.6	8,617.5
Net Property	13,103.4	11,482.1	9,676.7	7,843.8	6,609.4	5,926.7	5,269.1
Total Assets	44,006.7	39,910.4	35,634.9	31,853.4	25,735.9	24,293.1	23,831.8
Total Current Liabilities	11,544.2	9,709.6	8,758.8	6,068.8	5,568.6	4,829.2	5,689.5
Long-Term Obligations	4,798.6	3,600.7	3,143.9	3,220.8	1,346.5	1,155.9	1,372.8
Net Stockholders' Equity	16,050.1	14,832.4	13,241.6	12,801.8	12,594.6	11,970.5	11,735.7
Net Working Capital	1,417.4	3,643.8	2,500.4	4,159.7	2,644.4	2,897.4	2,928.0
Year-end Shs. Outstg. (000)	2,272,729	2,307,599	2,329,078	2,360,453	2,387,296	2,413,204	2,457,698
STATISTICAL RECORD:							
Operating Profit Margin %	21.1	23.3	24.0	20.8	24.8	26.1	26.5
Net Profit Margin %	15.3	16.9	18.0	19.5	19.5	20.8	21.8
Return on Equity %	45.4	46.0	44.5	41.0	36.6	34.4	31.0
Return on Assets %	16.5	17.1	16.5	16.5	17.9	17.0	15.3
Debt/Total Assets %	10.9	9.0	8.8	10.1	5.2	4.8	5.8
Price Range	95.25-56.80	96.69-52.00	87.38-60.94	80.88-50.69	60.31-39.00	42.13-28.25	33.63-18.19
P/E Ratio	30.3-18.1	33.3-17.9	35.7-24.9	37.6-23.6	32.3-20.9	26.3-17.7	24.9-13.5
Average Yield %	1.8	1.6	1.5	1.4	1.7	2.0	2.4

Statistics are as originally reported. Adj. for 2-for-1 stock split, 2/99 ① Incl. a net pre-tax gain of $169.4 mill. ② Inc. a nonrecurr. pre-tax gain of $213.0 mill. & non-recurr. pre-tax chgs. totaling $207.0 mill. ③ Incl. a pre-tax gain of $2.15 bill. from the sale of businesses, and a pre-tax charge of $1.04 bill. for acquired research and development. ④ Incl. a pre-tax chg. of $51.1 mill. for acquired research.

OFFICERS:
R. V. Gilmartin, Chmn., Pres., C.E.O.
J. C. Lewent, Exec. V.P., C.F.O.
C. A. Colbert, V.P., Sec., Asst. Gen. Couns.

INVESTOR CONTACT: Investor Relations, (908) 423-5881

PRINCIPAL OFFICE: One Merck Drive, Whitehouse Station, NJ 08889-0100

TELEPHONE NUMBER: (908) 423-1000
FAX: (908) 735-1500
WEB: www.merck.com

NO. OF EMPLOYEES: 78,100 (avg.)

SHAREHOLDERS: 256,200

ANNUAL MEETING: In Apr.

INCORPORATED: NJ, June, 1927

INSTITUTIONAL HOLDINGS:
No. of Institutions: 1,272
Shares Held: 1,258,167,320
% Held: 55.4

INDUSTRY: Pharmaceutical preparations (SIC: 2834)

TRANSFER AGENT(S): Wells Fargo Shareowner Services, South St. Paul, MN

MERCURY GENERAL CORPORATION

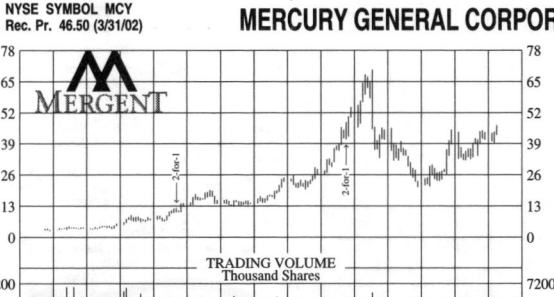

YIELD 2.6%
P/E RATIO 24.0

TRADING VOLUME
Thousand Shares

| | 1988|1989|1990|1991|1992|1993|1994|1995|1996|1997|1998|1999|2000|2001|2002 |
7 YEAR PRICE SCORE 100.4   *12 MONTH PRICE SCORE 113.1*
NYSE COMPOSITE INDEX=100

INTERIM EARNINGS (Per Share):

Qtr.	Mar.	June	Sept.	Dec.
1998	0.93	0.90	0.75	0.63
1999	0.73	0.60	0.51	0.60
2000	0.55	0.48	0.51	0.48
2001	0.45	0.49	0.59	0.41

INTERIM DIVIDENDS (Per Share):

Amt.	Decl.	Ex.	Rec.	Pay.
0.265Q	4/27/01	6/13/01	6/15/01	6/28/01
0.265Q	7/27/01	9/17/01	9/14/01	9/27/01
0.265Q	10/29/01	12/12/01	12/14/01	12/27/01
0.30Q	1/25/02	3/13/02	3/15/02	3/28/02

Indicated div.: $1.20 (Div. Reinv. Plan)

CAPITALIZATION (12/31/01):

	($000)	(%)
Long-Term Debt	129,513	10.8
Common & Surplus	1,069,711	89.2
Total	1,199,224	100.0

DIVIDEND ACHIEVER STATUS:
Rank: 33   10-Year Growth Rate: 18.15%
Total Years of Dividend Growth: 15

RECENT DEVELOPMENTS: For the year ended 12/31/01, net income declined 3.7% to $105.3 million versus $109.4 million in 2000. Total revenues rose 10.3% to $1.51 billion from $1.37 billion a year earlier. Earned premiums climbed 10.5% to $1.38 billion, while net investment income increased 7.6% to $114.5 million. Other revenues fell 15.0% to $5.4 million. Revenues included net realized investment gains of $6.5 million and $3.9 million in 2001 and 2000, respectively. The loss ratio grew to 73.2% from 72.2% in 2000.

PROSPECTS: In California, MCY received approval for rate increases on its non-good driver private passenger automobile premiums. The Company also recently received a 4.1% rate increase for private passenger automobile insurance in Mercury Insurance Company, which represents about 55.0% of MCY's premiums written, and a 6.9% combined rate increase for Mercury Casualty Company and California Automobile Insurance Company, which represents 24.0% of MCY's premiums written. MCY plans to make additional filings for rate increases.

BUSINESS

MERCURY GENERAL CORPORATION, through its subsidiaries, engages primarily in writing all risk classifications of automobile insurance in a number of states, principally in California. The Company offers automobile policyholders the following types of coverage: bodily injury liability, underinsured and uninsured motorist, personal injury protection, property damage liability, comprehensive, collision and other hazards specified in the policy. The Company sells its policies through independent agents in California, Florida, Georgia, Illinois, New York, Oklahoma, Texas and Virginia. In addition, MCY writes other lines of insurance in various states, including mechanical breakdown and homeowners insurance.

REVENUES

(12/31/2001)	($000)	(%)
Earned Premiums	1,380,561	91.6
Net Investment Income	114,511	7.6
Net Real Investment Gains	6,512	0.4
Other Revenues	5,396	0.4
Total	1,506,980	100.0

ANNUAL FINANCIAL DATA

	12/31/01	12/31/00	12/31/99	12/31/98	12/31/97	12/31/96	12/31/95
Earnings Per Share	1.94	2.02	2.44	3.21	2.82	1.93	1.66
Tang. Book Val. Per Share	19.71	19.06	16.71	16.78	14.51	11.66	10.30
Dividends Per Share	1.06	0.96	0.84	0.70	0.58	0.48	0.40
Dividend Payout %	54.6	47.5	34.4	21.8	20.6	24.9	24.2
INCOME STATEMENT (IN MILLIONS):							
Total Premium Income	1,380.6	1,249.3	1,188.3	1,121.6	1,031.3	754.7	616.3
Net Investment Income	114.5	106.5	99.4	96.2	86.8	70.2	63.0
Other Income	11.9	10.3	d7.0	4.4	9.9	0.1	4.4
Total Revenues	1,507.0	1,366.0	1,280.7	1,222.1	1,127.9	825.0	683.7
Income Before Income Taxes	124.8	128.6	168.5	235.3	209.8	136.6	114.3
Income Taxes	19.5	19.2	34.8	57.8	53.5	30.8	24.0
Net Income	105.3	109.4	133.7	177.5	156.3	105.8	90.3
Average Shs. Outstg. (000)	54,382	54,258	54,815	55,354	55,383	54,794	54,624
BALANCE SHEET (IN MILLIONS):							
Cash & Cash Equivalents	75.8	38.9	51.6	47.9	62.8	69.7	31.4
Premiums Due	191.6	173.7	178.6	152.5	144.3	125.8	76.7
Invst. Assets: Fixed-term	1,586.4	1,509.5	1,322.1	1,324.9	1,215.0	954.1	779.8
Invst. Assets: Equities	277.8	252.5	209.8	219.7	173.5	148.1	114.9
Invst. Assets: Total	1,936.2	1,795.0	1,575.5	1,590.6	1,448.2	1,168.3	923.2
Total Assets	2,316.5	2,142.3	1,906.4	1,877.0	1,725.5	1,419.9	1,081.7
Long-Term Obligations	129.5	107.9	92.0	78.0	75.0	75.0	25.0
Net Stockholders' Equity	1,069.7	1,032.9	909.6	917.4	799.6	641.2	565.2
Year-end Shs. Outstg. (000)	54,277	54,193	54,425	54,684	55,125	55,014	54,886
STATISTICAL RECORD:							
Return on Revenues %	7.0	8.0	10.4	14.5	13.9	12.8	13.2
Return on Equity %	9.8	10.6	14.7	19.4	19.5	16.5	16.0
Return on Assets %	4.5	5.1	7.0	9.5	9.1	7.4	8.3
Price Range	44.50-32.00	44.88-21.06	45.50-20.94	70.00-33.00	54.44-26.13	29.13-19.88	24.88-14.13
P/E Ratio	22.9-16.5	22.2-10.4	18.6-8.6	21.8-10.3	19.3-9.3	15.1-10.3	15.0-8.5
Average Yield %	2.8	2.9	2.5	1.4	1.4	2.0	2.1

Statistics are as originally reported. Adj. for 2-for-1 stk. split, 10/97.

OFFICERS:
G. Joseph, Chmn., C.E.O.
G. Tirador, Pres., C.O.O.
T. R. Stalick, V.P., C.F.O.
INVESTOR CONTACT: Investor Relations, (323) 857-4973
PRINCIPAL OFFICE: 4484 Wilshire Boulevard, Los Angeles, CA 90010

TELEPHONE NUMBER: (323) 937-1060
FAX: (323) 857-7116
WEB: www.mercuryinsurance.com
NO. OF EMPLOYEES: 2,800 (approx.)
SHAREHOLDERS: 241 (approx.); 7,700 (approx. beneficial)
ANNUAL MEETING: In May
INCORPORATED: CA, 1961

INSTITUTIONAL HOLDINGS:
No. of Institutions: 131
Shares Held: 19,619,497
% Held: 36.2
INDUSTRY: Fire, marine, and casualty insurance (SIC: 6331)
TRANSFER AGENT(S): The Bank of New York, New York, NY

MERRILL LYNCH & CO., INC.

YIELD 1.2%
P/E RATIO 135.1

7 YEAR PRICE SCORE 124.6   **12 MONTH PRICE SCORE 95.4**
*NYSE COMPOSITE INDEX=100

INTERIM EARNINGS (Per Share):

Qtr.	Mar.	June	Sept.	Dec.
1998	0.65	0.67	d0.25	0.43
1999	0.72	0.79	0.67	0.90
2000	1.19	1.01	0.94	0.93
2001	0.92	0.56	0.44	d1.51

INTERIM DIVIDENDS (Per Share):

Amt.	Decl.	Ex.	Rec.	Pay.
0.16Q	1/22/01	1/31/01	2/02/01	2/28/01
0.16Q	4/27/01	5/09/01	5/11/01	5/30/01
0.16Q	7/23/01	8/01/01	8/03/01	8/22/01
0.16Q	10/22/01	10/31/01	11/02/01	11/21/01
0.16Q	1/29/02	2/06/02	2/08/02	2/28/02

Indicated div.: $0.64 (Div. Reinv. Plan)

CAPITALIZATION (12/28/01):

	($000)	(%)
Long-Term Debt	76,572,000	79.3
Preferred Stock	425,000	0.4
Common & Surplus	19,583,000	20.3
Total	96,580,000	100.0

DIVIDEND ACHIEVER STATUS:
Rank: 38   10-Year Growth Rate: 17.74%
Total Years of Dividend Growth: 10

RECENT DEVELOPMENTS: For the year ended 12/28/01, net income decreased 84.9% to $573.0 million from $3.78 billion in the prior year. Earnings for 2001 included after-tax restructuring and other charges of $1.73 billion and after-tax expenses of $83.0 million related to the events of 9/11/01. Total net revenues declined 18.3% to $21.88 billion from $26.77 billion the year before. Interest and dividend revenues slid 4.7% to $20.18 billion from $21.18 billion a year earlier.

PROSPECTS: On 1/9/02, MER announced a restructuring plan aimed at improving profitability and growth, with expected annualized expense savings of about $1.40 billion. The plan includes, among other things, workforce reductions of about 9,000 through a combination of divestitures, voluntary separation and managed reductions, and real estate initiatives, including the consolidation of private client offices in the U.S., Europe, Asia and Australia.

BUSINESS

MERRILL LYNCH & CO. INC. provides investment, financing, insurance and related services. Merrill Lynch, Pierce, Fenner & Smith, Inc. (MLPF&S), its largest subsidiary, is one of the largest securities firms in the world. MLPF&S is a broker and a dealer in various financial instruments, and an investment banker. MER is also engaged in asset management, investment counseling, and is a dealer in U.S. government and federal agency obligations. As of 12/28/01, client assets totaled $1.46 trillion, including $529.00 billion under management.

ANNUAL FINANCIAL DATA

	12/28/01	12/29/00	12/31/99	12/25/98	12/26/97	12/27/96	12/29/95
Earnings Per Share	② 0.57	4.11	3.09	① 1.50	2.42	2.05	1.36
Cash Flow Per Share	2.93	5.83	4.70	2.50	2.99	2.58	1.83
Tang. Book Val. Per Share	18.39	16.67	10.09	6.09	3.65	9.47	7.87
Dividends Per Share	0.64	0.60	0.53	0.46	0.38	0.29	0.25
Dividend Payout %	112.3	14.7	17.0	30.7	15.5	14.1	18.6
INCOME STATEMENT (IN MILLIONS):							
Total Revenues	38,757.0	44,872.0	34,879.0	35,853.0	31,731.0	25,011.0	21,513.0
Costs & Expenses	35,161.0	37,582.0	29,450.0	32,946.0	28,235.0	22,034.0	19,335.0
Depreciation & Amort.	2,219.0	1,573.0	1,351.0	811.0	446.0	411.0	367.0
Operating Income	1,377.0	5,717.0	4,078.0	2,096.0	3,050.0	2,566.0	1,811.0
Income Before Income Taxes	1,182.0	5,522.0	3,883.0	1,972.0	3,003.0	2,566.0	1,811.0
Income Taxes	609.0	1,738.0	1,265.0	713.0	1,097.0	947.0	697.0
Net Income	② 573.0	3,784.0	2,618.0	① 1,259.0	1,906.0	1,619.0	1,114.0
Cash Flow	2,754.0	5,318.0	3,931.0	2,031.0	2,313.0	1,983.0	1,433.0
Average Shs. Outstg. (000)	938,555	911,416	836,262	812,600	773,498	767,344	783,988
BALANCE SHEET (IN MILLIONS):							
Cash & Cash Equivalents	93,357.0	78,548.0	26,852.0	23,725.0	20,725.0	11,183.0	10,868.0
Total Current Assets	369,056.0	361,556.0	289,777.0	266,992.0	272,874.0	199,595.0	164,664.0
Net Property	2,873.0	3,444.0	3,117.0	2,761.0	2,074.0	1,670.0	1,605.0
Total Assets	419,419.0	407,200.0	328,071.0	299,804.0	292,819.0	213,016.0	176,857.0
Total Current Liabilities	316,407.0	312,051.0	254,950.0	225,163.0	236,057.0	174,685.0	147,934.0
Long-Term Obligations	76,572.0	70,223.0	53,465.0	57,563.0	43,090.0	26,102.0	17,340.0
Net Stockholders' Equity	20,008.0	18,304.0	12,802.0	10,132.0	8,329.0	6,892.0	6,141.0
Net Working Capital	52,649.0	49,505.0	34,785.0	41,829.0	36,817.0	24,910.0	16,730.0
Year-end Shs. Outstg. (000)	843,474	807,955	735,531	712,568	670,164	662,500	701,604
STATISTICAL RECORD:							
Operating Profit Margin %	3.6	12.7	11.7	5.8	9.6	10.3	8.4
Net Profit Margin %	1.5	8.4	7.5	3.5	6.0	6.5	5.2
Return on Equity %	2.9	20.7	20.4	12.4	22.9	23.5	18.1
Return on Assets %	0.1	0.9	0.8	0.4	0.7	0.8	0.6
Debt/Total Assets %	18.3	17.2	16.3	19.2	14.7	12.3	9.8
Price Range	80.00-33.50	74.63-36.31	51.25-31.00	54.56-17.88	39.09-19.63	21.28-12.34	16.19-8.66
P/E Ratio	140.3-58.8	18.2-8.8	16.6-10.0	36.4-11.9	16.2-8.1	10.4-6.0	11.9-6.4
Average Yield %	1.1	1.1	1.3	1.3	1.3	1.7	2.0

Statistics are as originally reported. Adj. for 2-for-1 stk. split, 8/00 & 5/97. ① Incl. after-tax provision of $430.0 million for costs related to staff reductions. ② Incl. after-tax restruct. & oth. chrgs. of $1.73 bill. & after-tax exps. of $83.0 mill. rel. to 9/11/01 events.

OFFICERS:
D. H. Komansky, Chmn., C.E.O.
S. L. Hammerman, Vice-Chmn., Gen. Coun.
E. S. O'Neal, Pres., C.O.O.
T. H. Patrick, Exec. V.P., , C.F.O.

INVESTOR CONTACT: Martin Wise, Investor Relations, (212) 449-7119

PRINCIPAL OFFICE: 4 World Financial Center, New York, NY 10080

TELEPHONE NUMBER: (212) 449-1000
FAX: (212) 449-7461
WEB: www.ml.com

NO. OF EMPLOYEES: 57,400 (approx.)

SHAREHOLDERS: 13,955 (approx.)

ANNUAL MEETING: In April

INCORPORATED: DE, May, 1973

INSTITUTIONAL HOLDINGS:
No. of Institutions: 694
Shares Held: 541,044,614
% Held: 63.4

INDUSTRY: Security brokers and dealers (SIC: 6211)

TRANSFER AGENT(S): Mellon Investor Services, LLC, New York, NY

NASDAQ SYMBOL MSEX
Rec. Pr. 23.28 (3/31/02)

MIDDLESEX WATER COMPANY

YIELD 3.6%
P/E RATIO 26.5

*7 YEAR PRICE SCORE 114.3 *12 MONTH PRICE SCORE 75.4
*NYSE COMPOSITE INDEX=100

TRADING VOLUME
Thousand Shares

INTERIM EARNINGS (Per Share):

Qtr.	Mar.	June	Sept.	Dec.
1998	0.19	0.23	0.34	0.19
1999	0.19	0.33	0.36	0.13
2000	0.11	0.17	0.19	0.19
2001	0.11	0.24	0.30	0.23

INTERIM DIVIDENDS (Per Share):

Amt.	Decl.	Ex.	Rec.	Pay.
0.31Q	4/26/01	5/11/01	5/15/01	6/01/01
0.31Q	7/26/01	8/13/01	8/15/01	8/31/01
0.315Q	10/25/01	11/13/01	11/15/01	11/30/01
3-for-2	12/14/01	1/03/02	12/14/01	1/02/02
0.21Q	1/28/02	2/13/02	2/15/02	3/01/02

Indicated div.: $0.84 (Div. Reinv. Plan)

CAPITALIZATION (12/31/01):

	($000)	(%)
Long-Term Debt	88,140	49.7
Deferred Income Tax	12,716	7.2
Preferred Stock	4,063	2.3
Common & Surplus	72,290	40.8
Total	177,210	100.0

DIVIDEND ACHIEVER STATUS:
Rank: 267   10-Year Growth Rate: 2.80%
Total Years of Dividend Growth: 29

RECENT DEVELOPMENTS: For the year ended 12/31/01, net income increased 31.1% to $7.0 million compared with $5.3 million in 2000. Operating revenues advanced 9.5% to $59.6 million from $54.5 million a year earlier. The improvement in revenues was primarily attributed to higher consumption in the Company's New Jersey service areas, increased consumption and customer growth in Delaware, and benefits from rate increases, primarily in New Jersey.

Operating income rose 15.6% to $11.5 million versus $9.9 million in 2000. Looking ahead, the Company's revenues are expected to continue to grow in 2002. The full impact of the Middlesex and Pinelands rate increases approved in 2001 and the phased-in rate relief in Delaware should provide additional revenues. Anticipated customer growth in Delaware should also enhance operating results.

BUSINESS

MIDDLESEX WATER COMPANY operates water utility systems in central and southern New Jersey and in Delaware as well as a wastewater utility in southern Delaware. The Company's New Jersey subsidiaries are Bayview Water Company, Pinelands Water Company, Pinelands Wastewater Company, Middlesex Water Company, and Utility Service Affiliates, Inc. The Company's Delaware subsidiary is Tidewater Utilities, Inc. The Middlesex System treats, stores and distributes water for residential, commercial, industrial and fire prevention purposes, and produced approximately 75.0% of the Company's total revenue in 2001. Water services are furnished to approximately 57,000 retail customers, and under special contract, to a total population of approximately 267,000. Bayview Water Company provides water services to about 300 retail customers in Cumberland County, New Jersey. Pinelands Water Company and Pinelands Wastewater Company service approximately 2,300 retail customers and, under contract, one municipal wastewater system in Burlington County, New Jersey. Tidewater Utilities, Inc. provides water services to nearly 17,000 retail customers in Kent, Sussex and New Castle counties in Delaware. Utility Service Affiliates, Inc. provides contract operations and maintenance services for non-affiliated water and wastewater systems.

ANNUAL FINANCIAL DATA

	12/31/01	12/31/00	12/31/99	12/31/98	12/31/97	12/31/96	12/31/95
Earnings Per Share	0.88	0.67	1.01	0.94	0.89	0.80	0.91
Cash Flow Per Share	1.53	1.28	1.54	1.46	1.34	1.28	1.38
Tang. Book Val. Per Share	9.48	9.33	9.40	9.08	8.00	7.80	7.68
Dividends Per Share	0.83	0.82	0.79	0.77	0.75	0.74	0.72
Dividend Payout %	94.3	121.3	78.3	81.6	84.5	92.1	79.7
INCOME STATEMENT (IN THOUSANDS):							
Total Revenues	59,638	54,477	53,497	43,058	40,294	38,025	37,847
Costs & Expenses	40,123	37,038	35,910	28,397	26,614	25,263	24,323
Depreciation & Amort.	5,304	4,945	4,303	3,797	3,145	3,011	2,926
Maintenance Exp.	2,719	2,555	2,619	1,715	1,741	1,528	1,686
Operating Income	11,493	9,938	10,665	9,149	8,793	8,222	8,912
Net Interest Inc./(Exp.)	d5,042	d4,997	d4,695	d4,424	d3,337	d3,280	d3,115
Net Income	6,953	5,305	7,881	6,521	5,861	5,167	5,704
Cash Flow	12,002	9,995	11,883	9,999	8,780	8,020	8,471
Average Shs. Outstg.	7,856	7,791	7,722	6,870	6,574	6,254	6,118
BALANCE SHEET (IN THOUSANDS):							
Gross Property	239,734	227,135	214,896	191,484	165,323	149,707	144,335
Accumulated Depreciation	43,671	38,857	35,175	32,368	30,252	28,463	26,402
Net Property	199,060	191,196	181,809	162,827	137,109	123,019	119,668
Total Assets	236,374	219,400	215,036	203,501	159,761	148,660	144,822
Long-Term Obligations	88,140	82,109	82,330	78,032	52,918	52,961	52,960
Net Stockholders' Equity	76,353	74,698	74,552	71,725	56,221	51,882	50,310
Year-end Shs. Outstg.	7,626	7,573	7,501	7,346	6,404	6,307	6,205
STATISTICAL RECORD:							
Operating Profit Margin %	19.3	18.2	19.9	21.2	21.8	21.6	23.5
Net Profit Margin %	11.7	9.7	14.7	15.1	14.5	13.6	15.1
Net Inc./Net Property %	3.5	2.8	4.3	4.0	4.3	4.2	4.8
Net Inc./Tot. Capital %	3.9	3.1	4.7	4.0	4.8	4.4	5.0
Return on Equity %	9.1	7.1	10.6	9.1	10.4	10.0	11.3
Accum. Depr./Gross Prop. %	18.2	17.1	16.4	16.9	18.3	19.0	18.3
Price Range	37.45-29.38	33.94-25.00	39.50-21.00	25.75-19.25	22.25-16.38	19.25-15.50	18.75-15.25
P/E Ratio	42.6-33.4	50.4-37.1	39.0-20.7	27.4-20.5	25.1-18.5	24.1-19.4	20.7-16.8
Average Yield %	2.5	2.8	2.6	3.4	3.9	4.2	4.3

Statistics are as originally reported. Adj. for 3-for-2 stk. split, 1/2/02.

OFFICERS:
J. R. Tompkins, Chmn., C.E.O.
D. Sullivan, Pres., C.O.O.
A. B. O'Connor, V.P., Contr.

INVESTOR CONTACT: Marion F. Reynolds, V.P., Sec. & Treas., (732) 634-1500

PRINCIPAL OFFICE: 1500 Ronson Road, Iselin, NJ 08830-3020

TELEPHONE NUMBER: (732) 634-1500
FAX: (732) 750-5981
WEB: www.middlesexwater.com

NO. OF EMPLOYEES: 139

SHAREHOLDERS: 2,051 (common); 23 (preferred)

ANNUAL MEETING: In May
INCORPORATED: NJ, 1897

INSTITUTIONAL HOLDINGS:
No. of Institutions: 39
Shares Held: 921,970
% Held: 12.1

INDUSTRY: Water supply (SIC: 4941)

TRANSFER AGENT(S): Registrar and Transfer Company, Cranford, NJ

MIDLAND COMPANY (THE)

YIELD 0.8%
P/E RATIO 14.1

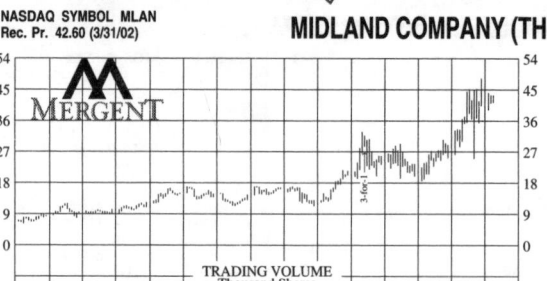

7 YEAR PRICE SCORE 145.5   **12 MONTH PRICE SCORE 110.1**
NYSE COMPOSITE INDEX=100

INTERIM EARNINGS (Per Share):

Qtr.	Mar.	June	Sept.	Dec.
1997	0.46	0.55	0.66	0.96
1998	0.64	0.39	0.77	1.06
1999	0.83	0.55	0.77	1.15
2000	0.97	0.78	0.83	1.20
2001	1.07	0.68	0.20	1.08

INTERIM DIVIDENDS (Per Share):

Amt.	Decl.	Ex.	Rec.	Pay.
0.08Q	1/25/01	3/08/01	3/12/01	4/16/01
0.08Q	4/26/01	6/20/01	6/22/01	7/06/01
0.08Q	7/26/01	9/19/01	9/21/01	10/04/01
0.08Q	10/25/01	12/19/01	12/21/01	1/03/02
0.087Q	1/31/02	3/08/02	3/12/02	4/04/02

Indicated div.: $0.35 (Div. Reinv. Plan)

CAPITALIZATION (12/31/01):

	($000)	(%)
Long-Term Debt	48,619	13.1
Deferred Income Tax	31,803	8.5
Common & Surplus	291,876	78.4
Total	372,298	100.0

DIVIDEND ACHIEVER STATUS:
Rank: 178   10-Year Growth Rate: 7.70%
Total Years of Dividend Growth: 15

RECENT DEVELOPMENTS: For the year ended 12/31/01, net income dropped 23.2% to $27.2 million from $35.5 million in the previous year. Results were adversely affected by higher-than-normal fire losses and ongoing challenges in the manufactured housing industry. Total revenues increased 9.8% to $586.5 million from $534.4 million a year earlier. Revenues for 2001 and 2000 included net realized investment gains of $2.0 million and $4.6 million, respectively. Insurance premiums earned rose 11.4% to $508.2 million versus $456.1 million in 2000. Net investment income improved 9.8% to $33.8 million. Other insurance income fell 18.3% to $7.2 million, while transportation revenues increased 5.2% to $34.8 million. Total costs and expenses climbed 13.7% to $549.8 million compared with $483.8 million the year before. Going forward, MLAN expects 2002 revenues to be only slightly ahead of 2001 as property and casualty premium and investment income are expected to grow in the low single-digits.

BUSINESS

THE MIDLAND COMPANY is a provider of specialty insurance products and services through two wholly-owned subsidiaries, American Modern Insurance Group and M/G Transport Group. American Modern specializes in writing physical damage insurance and related coverages on manufactured housing and has expanded to other areas of insurance, including homeowners, lower valued homes, dwelling fire, mortgage fire, collateral protection, watercraft, specialty automobile, motorcycle, snowmobile, recreational vehicle, long-haul truck, commercial and excess and surplus lines. The Company's other subsidiary, M/G Transport, charters barges and brokers freight for the movement of commodities on the inland waterways.

ANNUAL FINANCIAL DATA

	12/31/01	12/31/00	12/31/99	12/31/98	12/31/97	12/31/96	12/31/95
Earnings Per Share	3.03	3.78	3.30	2.86	① 2.63	0.12	1.04
Tang. Book Val. Per Share	33.06	31.46	27.11	26.61	21.11	17.50	17.28
Dividends Per Share	0.32	0.29	0.27	0.25	0.23	0.21	0.20
Dividend Payout %	10.4	7.7	8.0	8.6	8.8	182.2	19.6
INCOME STATEMENT (IN THOUSANDS):							
Total Premium Income	508,233	456,120	400,991	375,478	311,159	303,175	282,104
Other Income	78,310	78,302	68,135	66,884	64,271	67,317	68,856
Total Revenues	586,543	534,422	469,126	442,362	375,430	370,492	350,960
Income Before Income Taxes	36,704	50,669	43,713	37,527	34,703	d769	12,516
Income Taxes	9,482	15,206	12,534	10,595	10,336	cr1,837	2,964
Net Income	27,222	35,463	31,179	26,932	① 24,367	1,068	9,552
Average Shs. Outstg.	8,995	9,379	9,463	9,412	9,291	9,099	9,216
BALANCE SHEET (IN THOUSANDS):							
Cash & Cash Equivalents	715,295	701,048	620,957	593,857	504,106	404,079	373,439
Premiums Due	88,108	70,396	60,426	d753	58,739	57,949	93,315
Invst. Assets: Total	704,009	692,657	610,859	590,170	498,829	400,462	367,054
Total Assets	1,053,942	993,850	888,057	837,220	760,463	659,539	604,703
Long-Term Obligations	48,619	40,025	44,288	54,563	62,518	62,470	62,470
Net Stockholders' Equity	291,876	283,177	258,002	248,832	197,026	159,688	156,595
Year-end Shs. Outstg.	8,830	9,000	9,516	9,352	9,333	9,126	9,060
STATISTICAL RECORD:							
Return on Revenues %	4.6	6.6	6.6	6.1	6.5	0.3	2.7
Return on Equity %	9.3	12.5	12.1	10.8	12.4	0.7	6.1
Return on Assets %	2.6	3.6	3.5	3.2	3.2	0.2	1.6
Price Range	48.27-25.00	30.50-18.50	29.31-19.25	32.83-19.17	21.71-12.33	16.92-11.25	17.00-14.33
P/E Ratio	15.9-8.3	8.1-4.9	8.9-5.8	11.5-6.7	8.3-4.7	144.5-96.1	16.4-13.8
Average Yield %	0.9	1.2	1.1	0.9	1.4	1.5	1.3

Statistics are as originally reported. Adj. for 3-for-1 stk. split, 5/98. ① Bef. loss from disc. ops. of $6.8 mill.

OFFICERS:
J. P. Hayden III, Chmn., C.O.O.
J. W. Hayden, Pres., C.E.O.
J. I. Von Lehman, Exec. V.P., C.F.O., Sec.

INVESTOR CONTACT: James Von Lehman, Exec. V.P., C.F.O., (513) 943-7100

PRINCIPAL OFFICE: 7000 Midland Blvd., Amelia, OH 45102-2607

TELEPHONE NUMBER: (513) 943-7100
FAX: (513) 943-7111
WEB: www.midlandcompany.com

NO. OF EMPLOYEES: 1,032 (avg.)

SHAREHOLDERS: 2,100 (approx.)

ANNUAL MEETING: In April

INCORPORATED: OH, 1938

INSTITUTIONAL HOLDINGS:
No. of Institutions: 55
Shares Held: 1,867,105
% Held: 21.3

INDUSTRY: Insurance carriers, nec (SIC: 6399)

TRANSFER AGENT(S): Fifth Third Bank, Cincinnati, OH

ASE SYMBOL MSA
Rec. Pr. 37.55 (3/31/02)

MINE SAFETY APPLIANCES COMPANY

YIELD 1.5%
P/E RATIO 14.4

7 YEAR PRICE SCORE 136.8   **12 MONTH PRICE SCORE 108.6**
*NYSE COMPOSITE INDEX=100

INTERIM EARNINGS (Per Share):

Qtr.	Mar.	June	Sept.	Dec.
1998	0.41	0.36	0.23	0.37
1999	0.20	0.05	0.33	0.67
2000	0.58	0.22	0.33	0.76
2001	0.66	0.58	0.64	0.73

INTERIM DIVIDENDS (Per Share):

Amt.	Decl.	Ex.	Rec.	Pay.
0.14Q	5/03/01	5/10/01	5/14/01	6/08/01
0.14Q	8/14/01	8/22/01	8/24/01	9/10/01
0.14Q	11/02/01	11/20/01	11/23/01	12/10/01
0.14Q	1/16/02	2/20/02	2/22/02	3/10/02

Indicated div.: $0.56 (Div. Reinv. Plan)

CAPITALIZATION (12/31/01):

	($000)	(%)
Long-Term Debt	67,381	17.9
Deferred Income Tax	56,053	14.9
Preferred Stock.................	3,569	0.9
Common & Surplus	249,935	66.3
Total	376,938	100.0

DIVIDEND ACHIEVER STATUS:
Rank: 204   10-Year Growth Rate: 6.29%
Total Years of Dividend Growth: 31

RECENT DEVELOPMENTS: For the year ended 12/31/01, net income climbed 36.1% to $31.6 million from $23.2 million in the previous year. Results were enhanced by a strong performance in North America, particularly the Company's focus on new and improved products in the fire service segment, MSA's largest segment, and ongoing projects to streamline operations, especially in Europe. Earnings for 2001 and 2000 included facilities consolidation and restructuring charges of $2.3 million and $2.4 million, respec-

tively. Net sales grew 8.5% to $542.9 million from $500.4 million in the prior year. Other income rose 13.9% to $2.8 million. Costs of products sold as a percentage of sales declined to 60.0% versus 62.6% a year earlier. On 12/26/01, MSA agreed to acquire CGF Gallet of France, a major European manufacturer of protective helmets for the fire service, police and military. The transaction is expected to be completed in the first half of 2002.

BUSINESS

MINE SAFETY APPLIANCES COMPANY's primary business is the manufacture and sale of products designed to guard the safety and health of workers throughout the world. Principal products include respiratory protective equipment that is air-purifying, air-supplied and self-contained in design. MSA also produces instruments that monitor and analyze workplace environments and control industrial processes. Personal protective products include head, eye and face, body and hearing protectors. For the mining industry, MSA provides mine lighting, rockdusting equipment, fire-fighting foam and foam application equipment. MSA health-related products include emergency care items, hospital filters and instruments and heart pacemaker power cells. MSA also manufactures specialized high-efficiency space filters with applications ranging from safeguarding clean rooms to the protection of sophisticated electronic equipment. Many of these products have wide application for workers in industries that include manufacturing, public utilities, chemicals, petroleum, construction, transportation, municipal fire departments, the military and hazardous materials clean-up.

ANNUAL FINANCIAL DATA

	12/31/01	12/31/00	12/31/99	12/31/98	12/31/97	12/31/96	12/31/95
Earnings Per Share	① 2.61	① 1.88	② 1.25	① 1.37	① 1.60	① 1.58	① 1.11
Cash Flow Per Share	4.81	3.87	3.07	3.05	3.18	3.12	2.28
Tang. Book Val. Per Share	17.87	18.85	18.55	18.21	17.79	17.20	16.08
Dividends Per Share	0.54	0.47	0.45	0.44	0.41	0.37	0.35
Dividend Payout %	20.7	25.2	36.3	32.4	25.8	23.2	31.9
INCOME STATEMENT (IN THOUSANDS):							
Total Revenues	545,666	502,833	498,051	497,207	499,409	506,855	491,859
Costs & Expenses	459,051	440,168	447,662	443,028	438,833	445,485	435,762
Depreciation & Amort.	26,471	24,557	23,625	22,398	21,516	22,373	20,002
Operating Income	60,144	38,108	26,764	31,781	39,060	38,997	36,095
Net Interest Inc./(Exp.)	d6,061	d4,502	d4,273	d3,258	d2,781	d1,595	d1,730
Income Before Income Taxes	52,886	34,050	23,185	28,208	36,239	36,667	33,132
Income Taxes	21,255	10,811	6,859	9,933	14,385	13,606	14,220
Net Income	① 31,631	① 23,239	① ② 16,326	① 18,275	① 21,854	① 23,061	① 18,912
Cash Flow	58,054	47,747	39,901	40,624	43,333	45,370	38,861
Average Shs. Outstg.	12,079	12,356	13,005	13,341	13,647	14,556	17,043
BALANCE SHEET (IN THOUSANDS):							
Cash & Cash Equivalents	26,992	26,541	17,108	24,020	19,921	25,096	31,950
Total Current Assets	217,686	201,153	203,090	229,209	219,613	228,407	228,625
Net Property	152,968	159,586	163,509	164,561	155,184	147,058	151,106
Total Assets	520,698	489,683	451,741	456,716	406,404	407,682	406,600
Total Current Liabilities	82,500	86,978	80,005	110,006	103,240	91,814	71,984
Long-Term Obligations	67,381	71,806	36,550	11,919	12,270	13,278	14,746
Net Stockholders' Equity	253,504	226,465	242,457	242,846	241,449	241,432	253,540
Net Working Capital	135,186	114,175	123,085	119,203	116,373	136,593	156,641
Year-end Shs. Outstg.	12,101	11,828	12,875	13,137	13,368	13,833	15,549
STATISTICAL RECORD:							
Operating Profit Margin %	11.0	7.6	5.4	6.4	7.8	7.7	7.3
Net Profit Margin %	5.8	4.6	3.3	3.7	4.4	4.5	3.8
Return on Equity %	12.5	10.3	6.7	7.5	9.1	9.6	7.5
Return on Assets %	6.1	4.7	3.6	4.0	5.4	5.7	4.7
Debt/Total Assets %	12.9	14.7	8.1	2.6	3.0	3.3	3.6
Price Range	51.90-22.00	26.50-18.63	27.00-16.83	29.00-19.08	24.58-17.83	18.50-13.67	18.33-13.67
P/E Ratio	19.9-8.4	14.1-9.9	21.6-13.5	21.2-14.0	15.4-11.1	11.7-8.6	16.6-12.3
Average Yield %	1.5	2.1	2.1	1.8	1.9	2.3	2.2

Statistics are as originally reported. Adj. for stk. split: 3-for-1, 5/24/00. ① Incl. restr. chrgs.: $2.3 mill., 12/31/01; $2.4 mill., 12/31/00; $4.0 mill., 12/31/99; $1.0 mill., 12/31/98; $2.2 mill., 12/31/97; $5.3 mill., 12/31/96; $730,000, 12/31/95. ② Bef. acctg. chrg. of $1.2 mill.

OFFICERS:
J. T. Ryan, III, Chmn., C.E.O.
T. B. Hotopp, Pres.
D. L. Zeitler, V.P., Treas.

INVESTOR CONTACT: Investor Relations, (412) 967-3000

PRINCIPAL OFFICE: 121 Gamma Drive, RIDC Industrial Park, O'Hara Township, Pittsburgh, PA 15238

TELEPHONE NUMBER: (412) 967-3000
FAX: (412) 967-3451
WEB: www.msanet.com
NO. OF EMPLOYEES: 4,100 (approx.)
SHAREHOLDERS: 1,000 (approx.)
ANNUAL MEETING: In May
INCORPORATED: PA, Jan., 1917

INSTITUTIONAL HOLDINGS:
No. of Institutions: 50
Shares Held: 4,040,474
% Held: 33.5

INDUSTRY: Men's and boys' work clothing (SIC: 2326)

TRANSFER AGENT(S): Wells Fargo Shareowner Services, South St.Paul, MN

NYSE SYMBOL MMM
Rec. Pr. 115.01 (3/31/02)

MINNESOTA MINING & MANUFACTURING COMPANY

YIELD 2.2%
P/E RATIO 32.1

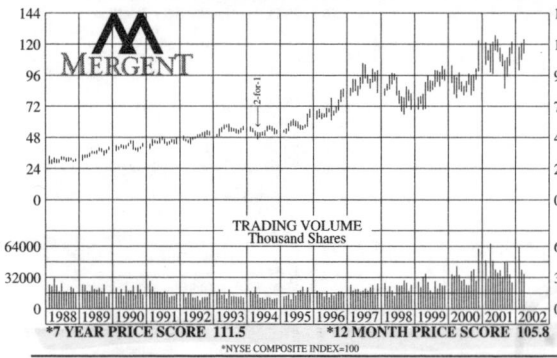

TRADING VOLUME
Thousand Shares

*7 YEAR PRICE SCORE 111.5   *12 MONTH PRICE SCORE 105.8
*NYSE COMPOSITE INDEX=100

INTERIM EARNINGS (Per Share):

Qtr.	Mar.	June	Sept.	Dec.
1998	0.98	0.94	0.44	0.61
1999	0.95	1.17	1.13	1.10
2000	1.21	1.18	1.25	1.00
2001	1.13	0.50	0.99	0.96

INTERIM DIVIDENDS (Per Share):

Amt.	Decl.	Ex.	Rec.	Pay.
0.60Q	2/12/01	2/21/01	2/23/01	3/12/01
0.60Q	5/08/01	5/16/01	5/18/01	6/12/01
0.60Q	8/13/01	8/22/01	8/24/01	9/12/01
0.60Q	11/12/01	11/20/01	11/23/01	12/12/01
0.62Q	2/11/02	2/20/02	2/22/02	3/12/02

Indicated div.: $2.48 (Div. Reinv. Plan)

CAPITALIZATION (12/31/01):

	($000)	(%)
Long-Term Debt	1,520,000	20.0
Common & Surplus	6,086,000	80.0
Total	7,606,000	100.0

DIVIDEND ACHIEVER STATUS:
Rank: 245   10-Year Growth Rate: 4.40%
Total Years of Dividend Growth: 43

RECENT DEVELOPMENTS: For the year ended 12/31/01, the Company reported net income of $1.43 billion versus income of $1.86 billion, before an accounting change charge of $75.0 million, the year before. Results for 2001 and 2000 included non-recurring net charges of $504.0 million and $23.0 million, respectively, related to various items. Net sales decreased 3.9% to $16.08 billion from $16.72 billion in the prior year.

PROSPECTS: The Company expects earnings per share, excluding non-recurring items, to range between $4.60 and $5.05 for the full-year 2002. Meanwhile, the Company expects to benefit from its strategic and selective restructuring program. On 2/7/02, MMM announced that it will phase out most of its production operations on St. Paul's East Side over the next twelve months, eliminating about 500 out of 1,500 employees.

BUSINESS

MINNESOTA MINING & MANU-FACTURING COMPANY, also known as 3M, is a worldwide producer of a diverse variety of industrial and consumer products. 3M operates in six business sectors: Transportation, Graphics and Safety (22% of 2001 sales) provides reflective sheeting, high-performance graphics, respirators, automotive components, and optical films; Health Care (21%) provides skin health products, medical/surgical supplies and devices, infection control, cardiovascular systems, health care information systems, pharmaceuticals, and dental products; Industrial (20% of sales) provides telecommunications products, industrial tapes, and industrial abrasives; Consumer and Office (17%) provides consumer and office products; Electro and Communications (14%) provides electronic and electrical products; and Specialty Material (6%) provides specialty materials, including protective material for furniture and fabrics, firefighting agents and engineering fluids.

ANNUAL FINANCIAL DATA

	12/31/01	12/31/00	12/31/99	12/31/98	12/31/97	12/31/96	12/31/95
Earnings Per Share	⑥ 3.58	⑤ 4.64	④ 4.34	③ 2.97	② 5.06	3.63	① 3.11
Cash Flow Per Share	6.30	7.21	6.55	5.10	7.14	5.74	5.15
Tang. Book Val. Per Share	15.55	16.49	15.77	14.80	14.63	15.07	16.43
Dividends Per Share	2.40	2.32	2.24	2.20	2.12	1.92	1.88
Dividend Payout %	67.0	50.0	51.6	74.1	41.9	52.9	60.4

INCOME STATEMENT (IN MILLIONS):

	12/31/01	12/31/00	12/31/99	12/31/98	12/31/97	12/31/96	12/31/95
Total Revenues	16,079.0	16,724.0	15,659.0	15,021.0	15,070.0	14,236.0	13,460.0
Costs & Expenses	12,717.0	12,641.0	11,803.0	12,116.0	11,525.0	10,862.0	10,380.0
Depreciation & Amort.	1,089.0	1,025.0	900.0	866.0	870.0	883.0	859.0
Operating Income	2,273.0	3,058.0	2,956.0	2,039.0	2,675.0	2,491.0	2,221.0
Net Interest Inc./(Exp.)	d87.0	d111.0	d109.0	d139.0	d94.0	d79.0	d102.0
Income Before Income Taxes	2,186.0	2,974.0	2,880.0	1,952.0	3,440.0	2,479.0	2,168.0
Income Taxes	702.0	1,025.0	1,032.0	685.0	1,241.0	886.0	785.0
Equity Earnings/Minority Int.	d54.0	d92.0	d85.0	d54.0	d78.0	d77.0	d77.0
Net Income	⑥ 1,430.0	1,857.0	④ 1,763.0	③ 1,213.0	② 2,121.0	1,516.0	① 1,306.0
Cash Flow	2,519.0	2,882.0	2,663.0	2,079.0	2,991.0	2,399.0	2,165.0
Average Shs. Outstg. (000)	399,900	399,900	406,500	408,000	419,000	418,000	420,000

BALANCE SHEET (IN MILLIONS):

	12/31/01	12/31/00	12/31/99	12/31/98	12/31/97	12/31/96	12/31/95
Cash & Cash Equivalents	616.0	302.0	441.0	448.0	477.0	744.0	772.0
Total Current Assets	6,296.0	6,379.0	6,066.0	6,318.0	6,168.0	6,486.0	6,395.0
Net Property	5,615.0	5,823.0	5,656.0	5,566.0	5,034.0	4,844.0	4,638.0
Total Assets	14,606.0	14,522.0	13,896.0	14,153.0	13,238.0	13,364.0	14,183.0
Total Current Liabilities	4,509.0	4,754.0	3,819.0	4,386.0	3,983.0	3,606.0	6,096.0
Long-Term Obligations	1,520.0	971.0	1,480.0	1,614.0	1,015.0	851.0	1,203.0
Net Stockholders' Equity	6,086.0	6,531.0	6,289.0	5,936.0	5,926.0	6,284.0	6,884.0
Net Working Capital	1,787.0	1,625.0	2,247.0	1,932.0	2,185.0	2,880.0	299.0
Year-end Shs. Outstg. (000)	391,304	396,085	398,700	401,000	405,000	417,000	419,000

STATISTICAL RECORD:

	12/31/01	12/31/00	12/31/99	12/31/98	12/31/97	12/31/96	12/31/95
Operating Profit Margin %	14.1	18.3	18.9	13.6	17.8	17.5	16.5
Net Profit Margin %	8.9	11.1	11.3	8.1	14.1	10.6	9.7
Return on Equity %	23.5	28.4	28.0	20.4	35.8	24.1	19.0
Return on Assets %	9.8	12.8	12.7	8.6	16.0	11.3	9.2
Debt/Total Assets %	10.4	6.7	10.7	11.4	7.7	6.4	8.5
Price Range	127.00-85.86	122.94-78.19	103.38-69.31	97.88-65.63	105.50-80.00	85.88-61.25	69.88-50.75
P/E Ratio	35.5-24.0	26.5-16.9	23.8-16.0	33.0-22.1	20.8-15.8	23.7-16.9	22.5-16.3
Average Yield %	2.3	2.4	2.6	2.7	2.3	2.6	3.1

Statistics are as originally reported. ① Bef. disc. ops. loss $330.0 mill. ② Incl. $803.0 mill. gain. ③ Bef. extraord. chrg. $38.0 mill.; incl. pre-tax restruct. chrg. of $493.0 mill. & a gain on divest. of $10.0 mill. ④ Incl. pre-tax chrg. of $73.0 mill. rel. to litig., a gain on divest. $147.0 mill., & a $26.0 mill. gain. ⑤ Incl. a net after-tax chrg. of $15.0 mill. & excl. an acctg. chrg. $75.0 mill. ⑥ Incl. nonrecurr. net chrgs. of $504.0 mill.

OFFICERS:
W. J. McNerney Jr., Chmn., C.E.O.
P. D. Campbell, Sr. V.P., C.F.O.

INVESTOR CONTACT: Matt Ginter, Director, Investor Relations, (651) 733-8206

PRINCIPAL OFFICE: 3M Center, St. Paul, MN 55144

TELEPHONE NUMBER: (651) 733-1110
FAX: (651) 733-9973
WEB: www.3m.com
NO. OF EMPLOYEES: 71,669 (avg.)
SHAREHOLDERS: 127,196 (record)
ANNUAL MEETING: In May
INCORPORATED: MN, July, 1902; reincorp., DE, June, 1929

INSTITUTIONAL HOLDINGS:
No. of Institutions: 869
Shares Held: 272,867,079
% Held: 69.9

INDUSTRY: Adhesives and sealants (SIC: 2891)

TRANSFER AGENT(S): Wells Fargo Shareowner Services, St. Paul, MN

MODINE MANUFACTURING COMPANY

YIELD 1.9%
P/E RATIO 38.6

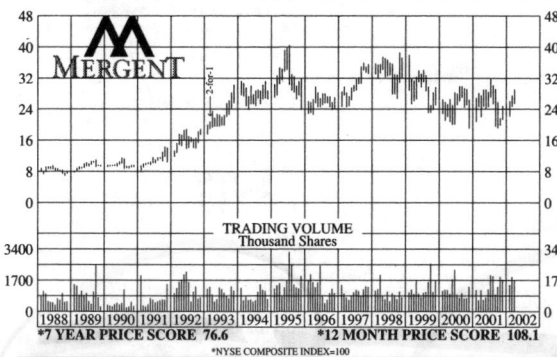

TRADING VOLUME
Thousand Shares

*7 YEAR PRICE SCORE 76.6 ***12 MONTH PRICE SCORE 108.1**
*NYSE COMPOSITE INDEX=100

INTERIM EARNINGS (Per Share):

Qtr.	June	Sept.	Dec.	Mar.
1998-99	0.67	0.63	0.58	0.58
1999-00	0.65	0.51	0.55	0.49
2000-01	0.61	0.65	0.20	0.15
2001-02	0.31	0.20	0.04	...

INTERIM DIVIDENDS (Per Share):

Amt.	Decl.	Ex.	Rec.	Pay.
0.25Q	1/17/01	2/22/01	2/26/01	3/08/01
0.25Q	5/16/01	5/24/01	5/29/01	6/07/01
0.25Q	7/18/01	8/22/01	8/24/01	9/06/01
0.25Q	10/17/01	11/20/01	11/23/01	12/06/01
0.125Q	1/16/02	2/20/02	2/22/02	3/07/02

Indicated div.: $0.50 (Div. Reinv. Plan)

CAPITALIZATION (3/31/01):

	($000)	(%)
Long-Term Debt	134,359	20.1
Deferred Income Tax	31,796	4.8
Common & Surplus	501,853	75.1
Total	668,008	100.0

DIVIDEND ACHIEVER STATUS:
Rank: 127   10-Year Growth Rate: 10.45%
Total Years of Dividend Growth: 15

RECENT DEVELOPMENTS: For the quarter ended 12/26/01, net earnings dropped 82.3% to $1.3 million versus $7.1 million in the equivalent 2000 quarter. Results for 2001 included an $8.5 million restructuring charge and other closure-related costs of $3.8 million associated with the Company's previously announced plans to reduce manufacturing capacity. Net sales improved 1.9% to $270.4 million from $265.4 million a year earlier. Gross profit decreased 4.8% to $66.8 million, or 24.7% of net sales, from $70.2 million, or 26.4% of net sales, in the previous year. Income from operations fell 66.6% to $4.5 million from $13.4 million the year before. Comparisons were made with restated results for the prior year. On 12/6/01, MODI announced that it was awarded a contract to provide engine cooling modules to BMW for future vehicle programs. The deal is expected to result in $135.0 million in annual revenue. Separately, on 2/19/02, MODI announced it was selected by DaimlerChrysler to supply the radiatior module for the 2002 Dodge Ram.

BUSINESS

MODINE MANUFACTURING COMPANY is engaged in heat-transfer technology serving vehicular, industrial, and building HVAC (heating, ventilating, air conditioning) markets. The Company develops, manufactures, and markets heat exchangers for use in various OEM (original equipment manufacturer) applications and for sale to the automotive aftermarket as replacement parts and to a wide array of building markets. MODI's products are used in light, medium and heavy-duty vehicles, HVAC equipment, industrial equipment, refrigeration systems, fuel cells and electronics. On 1/16/00, the Company announced the formation of an Engine Products Group for North America. The new business group focuses on the design and development of components, systems, and services in support of engine manufacturers' needs.

ANNUAL FINANCIAL DATA

	3/31/01	3/31/00	3/31/99	3/31/98	3/31/97	3/31/96	3/31/95
Earnings Per Share	① 1.62	2.20	2.46	2.39	2.10	2.02	2.24
Cash Flow Per Share	3.31	3.85	3.94	3.77	3.46	3.32	3.37
Tang. Book Val. Per Share	14.88	14.01	12.63	12.24	10.82	9.37	9.23
Dividends Per Share	0.98	0.90	0.82	0.74	0.66	0.58	0.51
Dividend Payout %	60.5	40.9	33.3	31.0	31.4	28.7	22.5
INCOME STATEMENT (IN MILLIONS):							
Total Revenues	1,065.4	1,139.3	1,111.4	1,040.4	999.0	990.5	913.0
Costs & Expenses	953.7	991.4	954.0	881.2	856.7	856.6	766.5
Depreciation & Amort.	49.9	48.8	44.2	41.8	41.5	39.6	34.5
Operating Income	61.7	99.0	113.3	117.5	100.9	94.3	112.1
Net Interest Inc./(Exp.)	d8.0	d8.5	d5.7	d4.0	d5.0	d6.8	d6.4
Income Before Income Taxes	78.3	95.3	118.1	116.0	97.8	99.1	108.8
Income Taxes	30.7	29.9	44.1	43.5	34.0	37.8	40.4
Net Income	① 47.6	65.4	73.9	72.5	63.8	61.4	68.4
Cash Flow	97.6	114.2	118.1	114.2	105.3	101.0	102.9
Average Shs. Outstg. (000)	29,444	29,703	30,015	30,289	30,420	30,416	30,534
BALANCE SHEET (IN MILLIONS):							
Cash & Cash Equivalents	20.4	31.1	49.2	36.4	34.8	18.0	32.7
Total Current Assets	387.5	429.6	453.1	393.2	366.1	351.3	340.4
Net Property	353.4	338.0	303.8	248.3	210.1	201.3	170.9
Total Assets	900.1	931.1	915.7	759.0	695.0	671.8	590.2
Total Current Liabilities	193.2	175.5	256.6	192.7	170.0	181.0	169.6
Long-Term Obligations	134.4	211.1	143.8	89.6	85.2	87.8	62.2
Net Stockholders' Equity	501.9	480.2	453.2	422.5	385.7	349.4	308.3
Net Working Capital	194.3	254.1	196.5	200.5	196.1	170.3	170.7
Year-end Shs. Outstg. (000)	29,530	29,261	29,525	29,664	29,833	29,759	29,700
STATISTICAL RECORD:							
Operating Profit Margin %	5.8	8.7	10.2	11.3	10.1	9.5	12.3
Net Profit Margin %	4.5	5.7	6.7	7.0	6.4	6.2	7.5
Return on Equity %	9.5	13.6	16.3	17.2	16.5	17.6	22.2
Return on Assets %	5.3	7.0	8.1	9.5	9.2	9.1	11.6
Debt/Total Assets %	14.9	22.7	15.7	11.8	12.3	13.1	10.5
Price Range	29.94-19.00	38.00-23.00	38.63-26.63	36.00-24.50	29.75-22.50	40.50-23.75	31.25-23.75
P/E Ratio	18.5-11.7	17.3-10.5	15.7-10.8	15.1-10.3	14.2-10.7	20.0-11.8	14.0-10.6
Average Yield %	4.0	3.0	2.5	2.4	2.5	1.8	1.8

Statistics are as originally reported. ① Incl. gain from patent settlement of $17.0 mill.

OFFICERS:
D. R. Johnson, Pres., C.E.O.
E. T. Thomas, Sr. V.P., C.F.O.
D. R. Zakos, V.P., Sec., Gen. Couns.
INVESTOR CONTACT: Mick Lucareli, (262) 636-8446
PRINCIPAL OFFICE: 1500 DeKoven Avenue, Racine, WI 53403-2552

TELEPHONE NUMBER: (262) 636-1200
FAX: (262) 636-1424
WEB: www.modine.com
NO. OF EMPLOYEES: 7,900 (approx.)
SHAREHOLDERS: 5,600 (approx.); 15,000 (approx. beneficial)
ANNUAL MEETING: In July
INCORPORATED: WI, June, 1916

INSTITUTIONAL HOLDINGS:
No. of Institutions: 96
Shares Held: 16,251,584
% Held: 48.7
INDUSTRY: Motor vehicle parts and accessories (SIC: 3714)
TRANSFER AGENT(S): Wells Fargo Shareowner Services, South St. Paul, MN

MORGAN (J.P.) CHASE & COMPANY

YIELD 3.8%
P/E RATIO 44.6

*7 YEAR PRICE SCORE 88.5   *12 MONTH PRICE SCORE 82.1

*NYSE COMPOSITE INDEX=100

INTERIM EARNINGS (Per Share):

Qtr.	Mar.	June	Sept.	Dec.
1998	0.53	0.80	0.63	0.87
1999	0.88	1.07	0.91	1.32
2000	1.06	0.85	0.66	0.34
2001	0.58	0.18	0.22	d0.18

INTERIM DIVIDENDS (Per Share):

Amt.	Decl.	Ex.	Rec.	Pay.
0.34Q	6/19/01	7/03/01	7/06/01	7/31/01
0.34Q	9/17/01	10/03/01	10/05/01	10/31/01
0.34Q	12/18/01	1/02/02	1/04/02	1/31/02
0.34Q	3/19/02	4/03/02	4/05/02	4/30/02

Indicated div.: $1.36 (Div. Reinv. Plan)

CAPITALIZATION (12/31/01):

	($000)	(%)
Total Deposits	293,650,000	77.5
Long-Term Debt	43,622,000	11.5
Redeemable Pfd. Stock	550,000	0.1
Preferred Stock	1,009,000	0.3
Common & Surplus	40,090,000	10.6
Total	378,921,000	100.0

DIVIDEND ACHIEVER STATUS:

Rank: 62   10-Year Growth Rate: 14.93%
Total Years of Dividend Growth: 10

RECENT DEVELOPMENTS: For the year ended 12/31/01, income fell 70.0% to $1.72 billion, before an accounting charge of $25.0 million, from $5.73 billion in the prior year. Earnings for 2001 and 2000 included restructuring and merger expenses of $2.52 billion and $1.43 billion, respectively. Net interest income rose 13.6% to $10.80 billion. Total non-interest revenue declined 22.1% to $18.25 billion from $23.42 billion the year before.

PROSPECTS: On 1/14/02, the Company announced that it has completed the acquisition of Systems & Service Technologies, Inc., which provides a complete line of asset services that include active and back-up servicing for various lending institutions, finance companies and banks. Separately, the Company continues to build its loan loss reserves in response to deteriorating market conditions.

BUSINESS

J.P. MORGAN CHASE & COMPANY (formerly Chase Manhattan Corporation) is a global financial services firm with assets of $693.58 billion as of 12/31/01. On 3/31/96, Chase Manhattan Corp. was acquired by Chemical Banking Corp., which then changed its name to Chase Manhattan Corp. JPM was formed on 12/31/00 as a result of the acquisition of J.P. Morgan & Co. Inc. by Chase Manhattan Corp., which then adopted its present name. JPM conducts financial services businesses through various bank and non-bank subsidiaries. JPM serves 32.0 million customers throughout the U.S., and has offices in more than 50 countries. On 12/10/99, JPM acquired Hambrecht & Quist Group, Inc.

ANNUAL FINANCIAL DATA

	12/31/01	12/31/00	12/31/99	12/31/98	12/31/97	12/31/96	12/31/95
Earnings Per Share	①③ 0.80	② 2.86	④ 4.18	④ 2.83	② 2.68	③ 1.67	⑤ 2.26
Tang. Book Val. Per Share	12.54	12.96	18.29	17.93	15.84	14.19	14.16
Dividends Per Share	1.34	1.23	1.06	0.93	0.81	0.73	0.63
Dividend Payout %	167.5	43.1	25.4	32.8	30.1	43.4	27.8
INCOME STATEMENT (IN MILLIONS):							
Total Interest Income	32,181.0	36,643.0	20,237.0	22,289.0	21,756.0	19,909.0	11,118.0
Total Interest Expense	21,379.0	27,131.0	11,493.0	13,723.0	13,598.0	11,569.0	6,429.0
Net Interest Income	10,802.0	9,512.0	8,744.0	8,566.0	8,158.0	8,340.0	4,689.0
Provision for Loan Losses	3,185.0	1,377.0	1,621.0	1,554.0	804.0	897.0	478.0
Non-Interest Income	18,248.0	23,422.0	13,473.0	10,301.0	8,625.0	7,512.0	3,766.0
Non-Interest Expense	23,299.0	22,824.0	12,221.0	11,383.0	10,069.0	11,144.0	5,001.0
Income Before Taxes	2,566.0	8,733.0	8,375.0	5,930.0	5,910.0	3,811.0	2,976.0
Net Income	⑥⑨ 1,719.0	⑤ 5,727.0	⑤ 5,446.0	④ 3,782.0	③ 3,708.0	② 2,461.0	②⑧ 1,816.0
Average Shs. Outstg. (000)	1,972,400	1,969,000	1,285,500	1,303,950	1,317,600	1,339,200	759,000
BALANCE SHEET (IN MILLIONS):							
Cash & Due from Banks	22,600.0	23,972.0	16,229.0	17,068.0	15,704.0	14,605.0	9,077.0
Securities Avail. for Sale	285,269.0	320,099.0	123,894.0	120,495.0	122,148.0	104,647.0	66,177.0
Total Loans & Leases	217,444.0	216,050.0	176,159.0	172,754.0	170,066.0	156,465.0	82,628.0
Allowance for Credit Losses	4,524.0	3,665.0	3,457.0	3,552.0	5,236.0	4,922.0	2,864.0
Net Loans & Leases	212,920.0	212,385.0	172,702.0	169,202.0	164,830.0	151,543.0	79,764.0
Total Assets	693,575.0	715,348.0	406,105.0	365,875.0	365,521.0	336,099.0	182,926.0
Total Deposits	293,650.0	279,365.0	241,745.0	212,437.0	193,688.0	180,921.0	98,417.0
Long-Term Obligations	43,622.0	47,238.0	20,140.0	18,375.0	15,127.0	13,314.0	7,329.0
Total Liabilities	652,476.0	673,010.0	382,488.0	342,037.0	343,779.0	315,105.0	171,014.0
Net Stockholders' Equity	41,099.0	42,338.0	23,617.0	23,838.0	21,742.0	20,994.0	11,912.0
Year-end Shs. Outstg. (000)	1,973,400	1,928,490	1,240,757	1,271,850	1,262,892	1,292,433	753,000
STATISTICAL RECORD:							
Return on Equity %	4.2	13.5	23.1	15.9	17.1	11.7	15.2
Return on Assets %	0.2	0.8	1.3	1.0	1.0	0.7	1.0
Equity/Assets %	5.9	5.9	5.8	6.5	5.9	6.2	6.5
Non-Int. Exp./Tot. Inc. %	80.2	69.3	55.0	60.3	60.0	70.3	59.1
Price Range	57.33-29.04	67.17-32.38	60.75-43.88	51.71-23.71	42.19-28.21	31.96-17.38	21.58-11.92
P/E Ratio	71.7-36.3	23.5-11.3	14.5-10.5	18.3-8.4	15.8-10.5	19.1-10.4	9.6-5.3
Average Yield %	3.1	2.5	2.0	2.5	2.3	2.9	3.7

Statistics are as originally reported. Adj. for 3-for-2 split, 6/00; 2-for-1 split, 6/98. ① Incl. restruct. chrg.: $2.52 bill., 2001; $1.43 bill., 2000; $48.0 mill., 1999; $192.0 mill., 1997; $1.81 bill., 1996. ② Bef. acctg. chrg. $25.0 mill., 2001; $11.0 mill., 1995. ③ Incl. $76.0 mill. gain. ④ Incl. net chrg. of $740.0 mill. related to various items. ⑤ Results are for Chase Manhattan Corp. for 1999 & earlier. ⑥ Reflects merger with J.P. Morgan & Co.

OFFICERS:
W. B. Harrison Jr., Chmn., C.E.O.
D. Dublon, C.F.O.

INVESTOR CONTACT: John Borden, Investor Relations, (212) 270-7318

PRINCIPAL OFFICE: 270 Park Avenue, New York, NY 10017

TELEPHONE NUMBER: (212) 270-6000
FAX: (212) 682-3761
WEB: www.chase.com

NO. OF EMPLOYEES: 95,812 (avg.)

SHAREHOLDERS: 135,359

ANNUAL MEETING: In May

INCORPORATED: DE, 1968

INSTITUTIONAL HOLDINGS:
No. of Institutions: 1,058
Shares Held: 1,255,355,614
% Held: 63.5

INDUSTRY: National commercial banks
(SIC: 6021)

TRANSFER AGENT(S): Mellon Investor Services, Ridgefield Park, NJ

MYERS INDUSTRIES, INC.

YIELD 1.7%
P/E RATIO 21.0

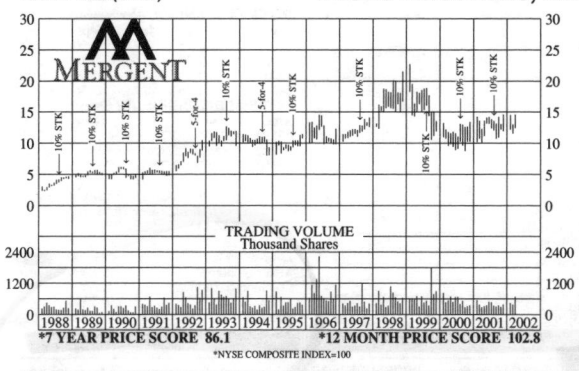

TRADING VOLUME
Thousand Shares

*7 YEAR PRICE SCORE 86.1 *12 MONTH PRICE SCORE 102.8
*NYSE COMPOSITE INDEX=100

INTERIM EARNINGS (Per Share):

Qtr.	Mar.	June	Sept.	Dec.
1997	0.20	0.21	0.15	0.34
1998	0.29	0.32	0.21	0.37
1999	0.34	0.37	0.16	0.41
2000	0.35	0.34	0.14	0.19
2001	0.37	0.15	0.07	0.10

INTERIM DIVIDENDS (Per Share):

Amt.	Decl.	Ex.	Rec.	Pay.
0.06Q	4/26/01	6/13/01	6/15/01	7/02/01
10% STK	6/21/01	8/08/01	8/10/01	8/31/01
0.06Q	6/21/01	9/05/01	9/07/01	10/01/01
0.06Q	9/25/01	12/05/01	12/07/01	1/02/02
0.06Q	2/19/02	3/06/02	3/08/02	4/01/02

Indicated div.: $0.24 (Div. Reinv. Plan)

CAPITALIZATION (12/31/01):

	($000)	(%)
Long-Term Debt	247,145	51.8
Deferred Income Tax	12,596	2.6
Common & Surplus	217,526	45.6
Total	477,267	100.0

DIVIDEND ACHIEVER STATUS:
Rank: 91   10-Year Growth Rate: 12.76%
Total Years of Dividend Growth: 25

RECENT DEVELOPMENTS: For the year ended 12/31/01, net income plummeted 36.7% to $15.2 million compared with $24.0 million in 2000. Earnings were negatively affected by lower demand, mainly from MYE's industrial markets. Results for 2000 included an after-tax restructuring charge of $1.9 million for closing the Company's Dayton, Ohio manufacturing facility. Net sales declined 6.9% to $608.0 million from $652.7 million a year earlier. Gross profit slid 5.8% to $204.9 million.

PROSPECTS: In an effort to remain profitable, the Company has moderated capital spending and reduced inventory and receivables. In addition, the Company lowered its employment levels by 7.0% to just over 4,100 by the end of 2001. At the end of 2001, the Company's total debt was $264.9 million, down 11.8% from $300.2 million at the end of 2000. Looking ahead, MYE may continue to be adversely affected by reduced demand in nearly all of its end markets, particularly its industrial markets.

BUSINESS

MYERS INDUSTRIES, INC. is comprised of two segments: the manufacturing business and the distribution business. The manufacturing business designs, manufactures and markets plastic and rubber products for the industrial, agricultural, automotive, commercial and consumer markets. As of 12/31/01, the Company operated 25 manufacturing facilities in Europe and North America and marketed reusable plastics under the brand names NESTIER, AKROBINS and BUCK-HORN. MYE also manufactures and sells molded rubber products and other materials used primarily in the tire and tire repair industries and for various other uses. As of 12/31/01, the distribution business, primarily conducted by the Myers Tire Supply division through 43 U.S. and five international branches, was engaged in the distribution of equipment, tools and supplies used for tire servicing and automotive underbody repair.

ANNUAL FINANCIAL DATA

	12/31/01	12/31/00	12/31/99	12/31/98	12/31/97	12/31/96	12/31/95
Earnings Per Share	0.64	①1.01	1.28	1.18	0.91	0.85	0.65
Cash Flow Per Share	2.48	2.80	2.82	1.90	1.45	1.30	1.07
Tang. Book Val. Per Share	1.12	0.70	0.34	6.68	6.32	5.89	5.06
Dividends Per Share	0.22	0.20	0.18	0.16	0.14	0.12	0.10
Dividend Payout %	34.9	20.1	14.4	13.4	15.4	13.7	15.7

INCOME STATEMENT (IN THOUSANDS):

	12/31/01	12/31/00	12/31/99	12/31/98	12/31/97	12/31/96	12/31/95
Total Revenues	607,950	652,660	580,761	392,020	339,626	320,944	300,699
Costs & Expenses	518,106	546,563	473,711	325,129	288,098	273,733	262,408
Depreciation & Amort.	43,905	42,828	37,542	17,518	13,214	11,311	10,450
Operating Income	45,939	63,270	69,507	49,373	38,313	35,901	27,840
Net Interest Inc./(Exp.)	d18,699	d22,360	d15,206	d888	d248	d285	d784
Income Before Income Taxes	27,240	40,910	54,301	48,485	38,066	35,615	27,056
Income Taxes	12,049	16,909	23,125	19,806	15,727	14,612	11,087
Net Income	15,191	①24,001	31,176	28,679	22,339	21,003	15,969
Cash Flow	59,096	66,828	68,719	46,197	35,553	32,314	26,419
Average Shs. Outstg.	23,802	23,863	24,402	24,364	24,585	24,782	24,701

BALANCE SHEET (IN THOUSANDS):

	12/31/01	12/31/00	12/31/99	12/31/98	12/31/97	12/31/96	12/31/95
Cash & Cash Equivalents	7,075	2,178	1,094	34,832	6,298	5,600	3,388
Total Current Assets	196,619	219,307	206,991	153,650	107,427	106,310	101,087
Net Property	190,736	204,198	189,446	109,443	90,551	80,660	69,430
Total Assets	582,166	624,797	600,410	306,708	224,078	207,122	193,604
Total Current Liabilities	104,899	115,583	102,244	51,234	39,644	36,853	32,372
Long-Term Obligations	247,145	284,273	280,104	48,832	4,261	4,569	13,335
Net Stockholders' Equity	217,526	213,903	207,747	202,689	176,677	162,445	145,184
Net Working Capital	91,719	103,724	104,747	102,417	67,783	69,457	68,715
Year-end Shs. Outstg.	23,848	23,749	24,185	24,408	24,329	24,677	24,752

STATISTICAL RECORD:

	12/31/01	12/31/00	12/31/99	12/31/98	12/31/97	12/31/96	12/31/95
Operating Profit Margin %	7.6	9.7	12.0	12.6	11.3	11.2	9.3
Net Profit Margin %	2.5	3.7	5.4	7.3	6.6	6.5	5.3
Return on Equity %	7.0	11.2	15.0	14.1	12.6	12.9	11.0
Return on Assets %	2.6	3.8	5.2	9.4	10.0	10.1	8.2
Debt/Total Assets %	42.5	45.5	46.7	15.9	1.9	2.2	6.9
Price Range	14.58-10.01	13.41-8.75	22.73-10.54	21.55-12.30	14.09-10.25	14.51-9.82	11.44-8.15
P/E Ratio	22.8-15.6	13.3-8.7	17.7-8.2	18.3-10.4	15.5-11.3	17.1-11.6	17.6-12.6
Average Yield %	1.8	1.8	1.1	0.9	1.2	1.0	1.0

Statistics are as originally reported. Adj. for stk. splits: 10% div., 8/01, 8/00, 8/99 & 8/97.
① Incl. an after-tax restructuring chrg. of $1.9 mill.

OFFICERS:
S. E. Myers, Pres., C.E.O.
G. J. Stodnick, V.P., C.F.O.
M. I. Wiskind, Sr. V.P., Sec.
INVESTOR CONTACT: Max R. Barton, II, (330) 761-6106
PRINCIPAL OFFICE: 1293 South Main Street, Akron, OH 44301

TELEPHONE NUMBER: (330) 253-5592
FAX: (330) 761-6156
WEB: www.myersind.com
NO. OF EMPLOYEES: 4,114
SHAREHOLDERS: 2,200 (approx.)
ANNUAL MEETING: In Apr.
INCORPORATED: OH, Jan., 1955

INSTITUTIONAL HOLDINGS:
No. of Institutions: 82
Shares Held: 11,183,009
% Held: 46.9
INDUSTRY: Plastics products, nec (SIC: 3089)
TRANSFER AGENT(S): First Chicago Trust Company of New York, New York, NY

NYSE SYMBOL NC
Rec. Pr. 66.29 (3/31/02)

NACCO INDUSTRIES, INC.

YIELD 1.4%
P/E RATIO ...

TRADING VOLUME
Thousand Shares

*7 YEAR PRICE SCORE 78.5   *12 MONTH PRICE SCORE 96.0
*NYSE COMPOSITE INDEX=100

INTERIM EARNINGS (Per Share):

Qtr.	Mar.	June	Sept.	Dec.
1998	2.95	3.21	2.50	3.87
1999	1.59	2.00	0.86	2.22
2000	1.13	1.67	1.09	0.75
2001	1.76	0.74	d3.36	d3.38

INTERIM DIVIDENDS (Per Share):

Amt.	Decl.	Ex.	Rec.	Pay.
0.225Q	2/14/01	2/27/01	3/01/01	3/15/01
0.235Q	5/09/01	5/30/01	6/01/01	6/15/01
0.235Q	8/08/01	8/29/01	8/31/01	9/14/01
0.235Q	11/14/01	11/28/01	11/30/01	12/14/01
0.235Q	2/13/02	2/27/02	3/01/02	3/15/02

Indicated div.: $0.94

CAPITALIZATION (12/31/01):

	($000)	(%)
Long-Term Debt	519,400	49.4
Minority Interest	3,400	0.3
Common & Surplus	529,300	50.3
Total	1,052,100	100.0

DIVIDEND ACHIEVER STATUS:
Rank: 248   10-Year Growth Rate: 4.22%
Total Years of Dividend Growth: 18

RECENT DEVELOPMENTS: For the year ended 12/31/01, the Company incurred a loss of $34.7 million, before an accounting change charge of $1.3 million, compared with income of $37.8 million, before an extraordinary gain of $29.9 million, in the previous year. Results for 2001 included net charges totaling $23.9 million. Total revenues decreased 8.1% to $2.64 billion from $2.87 billion a year earlier.

PROSPECTS: NMHG Wholesale expects a $13.5 million after-tax benefit in 2002 due to restructuring and downsizing actions taken in 2001. Moreover, the Company expects new accounting rules eliminating goodwill amortization should result in an after-tax gain for NC about $15.8 million in 2002. Separately, North American coal anticipates record lignite coal deliveries in 2002.

BUSINESS

NACCO INDUSTRIES, INC., with assets of $2.16 billion as of 12/31/01, is a holding company with three operating subsidiaries: NACCO Materials Handling Group (NMHG), the Housewares Group, comprised of Hamilton Beach/Proctor-Silex, Inc. (HB/PS) and the Kitchen Collection, Inc., and The North American Coal Corp. NMHG (63.4% of 2001 sales) designs and manufactures forklift trucks, marketed under the HYSTER and YALE brand names. HB/PS (24.0%) is a manufacturer of small electric appliances, and the Kitchen Collection, Inc. is a national specialty retailer of kitchenware and electric appliances. North American Coal (12.6%) mines and markets lignite coal, primarily as fuel for power generation by electric utilities.

ANNUAL FINANCIAL DATA

	12/31/01	12/31/00	12/31/99	12/31/98	12/31/97	12/31/96	12/31/95
Earnings Per Share	⑧⑥ d4.24	①④ 4.63	③ 6.66	② 12.53	② 7.55	5.67	① 7.31
Cash Flow Per Share	10.12	17.62	19.41	23.43	18.37	15.22	16.13
Tang. Book Val. Per Share	12.37	20.01	11.51	9.52	...	...	...
Dividends Per Share	0.93	0.89	0.85	0.81	0.77	0.74	0.71
Dividend Payout %	...	19.2	12.8	6.5	10.2	13.1	9.7
INCOME STATEMENT (IN MILLIONS):							
Total Revenues	2,637.9	2,871.3	2,602.8	2,536.2	2,246.9	2,273.2	2,204.5
Costs & Expenses	2,514.6	2,647.3	2,367.5	2,249.1	2,026.3	2,056.7	1,974.2
Depreciation & Amort.	117.6	106.1	104.0	89.0	88.6	85.3	79.3
Operating Income	5.7	117.9	131.3	198.1	132.0	131.2	151.1
Net Interest Inc./(Exp.)	d56.9	d47.1	d43.3	d34.6	d36.6	d45.9	d50.0
Income Before Income Taxes	d45.4	60.0	86.6	166.0	89.1	86.3	103.5
Income Taxes	cr9.9	22.3	31.7	60.7	26.4	34.3	34.7
Equity Earnings/Minority Int.	0.8	0.1	d0.6	d3.0	d0.9	d1.4	d3.3
Net Income	⑧⑥ d34.7	①④ 37.8	③ 54.3	② 102.3	② 61.8	50.6	① 65.5
Cash Flow	82.9	143.9	158.3	191.3	150.4	135.9	144.8
Average Shs. Outstg. (000)	8,190	8,167	8,154	8,166	8,189	8,931	8,975
BALANCE SHEET (IN MILLIONS):							
Cash & Cash Equivalents	71.9	33.7	36.2	34.7	24.1	47.8	30.9
Total Current Assets	770.0	815.7	772.2	703.2	599.6	591.8	722.0
Net Property	732.0	710.7	625.4	593.4	541.7	550.3	534.4
Total Assets	2,161.9	2,193.9	2,013.0	1,898.3	1,729.1	1,708.1	1,833.8
Total Current Liabilities	874.3	650.2	583.1	548.6	506.5	416.0	523.7
Long-Term Obligations	519.4	732.7	615.5	569.6	558.2	674.8	666.7
Net Stockholders' Equity	529.3	606.4	562.2	518.3	425.1	379.3	370.1
Net Working Capital	d104.3	165.5	189.1	154.6	93.1	175.8	198.3
Year-end Shs. Outstg. (000)	8,196	8,171	9,804	8,120	8,154	8,186	8,952
STATISTICAL RECORD:							
Operating Profit Margin %	0.2	4.1	5.0	7.8	5.9	5.8	6.9
Net Profit Margin %	...	1.3	2.1	4.0	2.8	2.2	3.0
Return on Equity %	...	6.2	9.7	19.7	14.5	13.3	17.7
Return on Assets %	...	1.7	2.7	5.4	3.6	3.0	3.6
Debt/Total Assets %	24.0	29.6	30.6	30.0	32.3	39.5	36.4
Price Range	82.80-42.50	55.75-33.56	97.00-44.50	177.00-76.25	127.00-44.38	64.00-43.13	64.00-46.88
P/E Ratio	...	12.0-7.2	14.6-6.7	14.1-6.1	16.8-5.9	11.3-7.6	8.8-6.4
Average Yield %	1.5	2.0	1.2	0.6	0.9	1.4	1.3

Statistics are as originally reported. ① Bef. extra. gain $29.9 mill., 2000; $28.9 mill., 1995. ② Incl. restruct. chrgs. $21.5 mill., 2001; $1.6 mill., 1998; $8.0 mill., 1997. ③ Bef. acctg. chrg. $1.2 mill. & incl. non-recurr. chrg. of $1.9 mill. ④ Incl. an after-tax restruct. chrg. of $8.3 mill. & an after-tax write-off of assets of $1.5 mill. ⑤ Incl. loss on sale of dealers of $10.4 mill. & ins. recovery of $8.0 mill.; bef. acctg. chrg. of $1.3 mill.

OFFICERS:
A. M. Rankin Jr., Chmn., Pres., C.E.O.
J. C. Butler Jr., V.P., Treas.
C. A. Bittenbender, V.P., Gen. Couns., Sec.
INVESTOR CONTACT: Ira Gamm, Manager of Investor Relations, (440) 449-9676
PRINCIPAL OFFICE: 5875 Landerbrook Drive, Mayfield Heights, OH 44124-4017

TELEPHONE NUMBER: (440) 449-9600
FAX: (440) 449-9607
WEB: www.nacco.com
NO. OF EMPLOYEES: 13,300 (approx.)
SHAREHOLDERS: 500 (class A com,); 400 (class B com.)
ANNUAL MEETING: In May
INCORPORATED: DE, 1986

INSTITUTIONAL HOLDINGS:
No. of Institutions: 69
Shares Held: 3,626,005
% Held: 44.2
INDUSTRY: Industrial trucks and tractors (SIC: 3537)
TRANSFER AGENT(S): National City Bank, Cleveland, OH

NATIONAL COMMERCE FINANCIAL CORPORATION

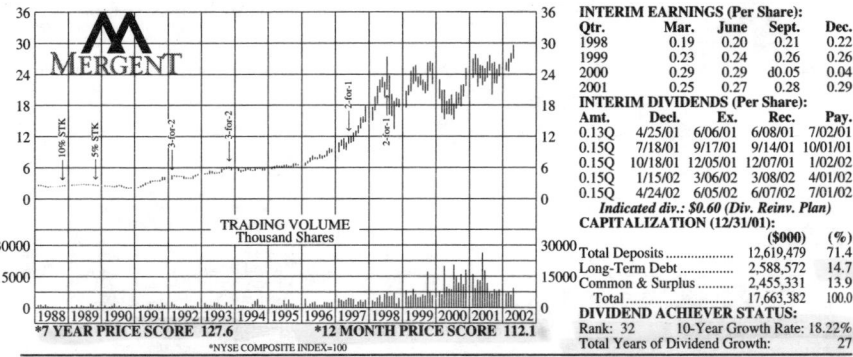

TRADING VOLUME
Thousand Shares

| | 1988 | 1989 | 1990 | 1991 | 1992 | 1993 | 1994 | 1995 | 1996 | 1997 | 1998 | 1999 | 2000 | 2001 | 2002 |

*7 YEAR PRICE SCORE 127.6   *12 MONTH PRICE SCORE 112.1
*NYSE COMPOSITE INDEX=100

INTERIM EARNINGS (Per Share):

Qtr.	Mar.	June	Sept.	Dec.
1998	0.19	0.20	0.21	0.22
1999	0.23	0.24	0.26	0.26
2000	0.29	0.29	d0.05	0.04
2001	0.25	0.27	0.28	0.29

INTERIM DIVIDENDS (Per Share):

Amt.	Decl.	Ex.	Rec.	Pay.
0.13Q	4/25/01	6/06/01	6/08/01	7/02/01
0.15Q	7/18/01	9/17/01	9/14/01	10/01/01
0.15Q	10/18/01	12/05/01	12/07/01	1/02/02
0.15Q	1/15/02	3/06/02	3/08/02	4/01/02
0.15Q	4/24/02	6/05/02	6/07/02	7/01/02

Indicated div.: $0.60 (Div. Reinv. Plan)

CAPITALIZATION (12/31/01):

	($000)	(%)
Total Deposits	12,619,479	71.4
Long-Term Debt	2,588,572	14.7
Common & Surplus	2,455,331	13.9
Total	17,663,382	100.0

DIVIDEND ACHIEVER STATUS:

Rank: 32	10-Year Growth Rate: 18.22%
Total Years of Dividend Growth:	27

RECENT DEVELOPMENTS: For the year ended 12/31/01, net income advanced to $225.3 million versus $45.3 million in 2000. Results for 2001 and 2000 included pre-tax acquisition charges of $11.4 million and $70.7 million, respectively. Net interest income soared 54.7% to $651.1 million. Provision for loan losses rose 77.4% to $29.2 million. Non-interest income soared 71.5% to $324.9 million, while non-operating expense increased 14.4% to $588.1 million. Comparisons were made with restated prior-year figures.

PROSPECTS: In February 2002, the Company's subsidiary National Bank of Commerce acquired 37 former Wachovia and First Union branches from Wachovia Bank, N.A. and First Union National Bank, including acquired loans of about $452.0 million and deposits of approximately $1.4 billion. On 4/28/02, NCF opened its first branch location in the Atlanta metro area. On 4/30/02, the Company announced it has purchased a free-standing branch building that will become its headquarters in metropolitan Atlanta.

BUSINESS

NATIONAL COMMERCE FINANCIAL CORPORATION is a bank holding company with assets of $19.27 billion as of 12/31/01. The Company's banking subsidiaries, National Bank of Commerce (NBC) and NBC Bank, Federal Savings Bank (FSB), provide commercial and retail banking, savings and trust services through 234 Central Carolina Bank offices located in North Carolina and South Carolina and 147 National Bank of Commerce offices located in Tennessee, Mississippi, Arkansas, Georgia, Virginia and West Virginia. NBC Bank operates two offices in DeSoto County, Mississippi. The Company also provides trust services through a subsidiary in Florida. NCF also owns 49.0% of First Market Bank, FSB. In addition to its banking subsidiaries, the Company operates several other non-banking financial businesses. In July 2000, the company acquired CCB Financial Corporation. In 2001 NCF acquired SouthBanc Shares, Inc. and First Vantage-Tennessee.

ANNUAL FINANCIAL DATA

	12/31/01	①12/31/00	12/31/99	12/31/98	12/31/97	12/31/96	12/31/95
Earnings Per Share	③1.09	②0.57	0.99	0.83	0.69	0.58	0.49
Tang. Book Val. Per Share	6.13	6.23	5.15	4.03	3.60	3.21	2.99
Dividends Per Share	0.54	0.45	0.36	0.29	0.22	0.19	0.17
Dividend Payout %	49.5	78.1	36.4	34.9	31.9	33.0	35.0
INCOME STATEMENT (IN MILLIONS):							
Total Interest Income	1,222.9	1,250.5	468.0	383.6	337.0	286.6	246.5
Total Interest Expense	571.8	664.7	231.5	191.0	174.2	151.1	126.4
Net Interest Income	651.1	585.7	236.5	192.6	162.8	135.5	120.0
Provision for Loan Losses	29.2	20.9	15.2	9.6	17.0	14.1	9.8
Non-Interest Income	324.9	247.5	92.5	84.9	82.4	70.9	53.9
Non-Interest Expense	588.1	627.9	155.3	140.3	123.5	105.2	91.8
Income Before Taxes	358.7	184.5	158.6	127.6	104.8	87.1	72.3
Net Income	③225.3	②117.5	107.2	85.1	69.8	57.5	48.0
Average Shs. Outstg. (000)	207,484	207,496	108,823	102,884	101,368	100,196	100,996
BALANCE SHEET (IN MILLIONS):							
Cash & Due from Banks	561.4	446.7	179.1	224.9	206.2	164.9	144.2
Securities Avail. for Sale	197.2	74.4	30.3	62.7	98.3	31.8	20.2
Total Loans & Leases	11,991.7	11,050.2	3,988.6	3,200.1	2,611.2	2,348.0	1,933.0
Allowance for Credit Losses	173.4	160.5	62.4	51.5	45.5	35.5	30.8
Net Loans & Leases	11,818.4	10,889.6	3,926.2	3,148.6	2,565.7	2,312.5	1,902.2
Total Assets	19,273.7	16,553.5	6,806.2	5,811.1	4,692.0	4,200.4	3,695.0
Total Deposits	12,619.5	11,982.3	4,495.9	3,947.3	3,251.2	2,976.4	2,574.8
Long-Term Obligations	2,588.6	1,696.5	720.7	738.0	546.1	552.2	379.2
Total Liabilities	16,818.4	15,225.0	6,198.9	5,352.6	4,290.0	3,887.1	3,398.4
Net Stockholders' Equity	2,455.3	1,278.6	557.4	408.5	352.1	313.3	296.7
Year-end Shs. Outstg. (000)	205,059	205,246	108,223	101,443	97,704	97,540	99,340
STATISTICAL RECORD:							
Return on Equity %	9.2	9.2	19.2	20.8	19.8	18.4	16.5
Return on Assets %	1.2	0.7	1.6	1.5	1.5	1.4	1.3
Equity/Assets %	12.7	7.7	8.2	7.0	7.5	7.5	8.0
Non-Int. Exp./Tot. Inc. %	60.3	75.4	47.2	50.6	50.3	51.0	52.8
Price Range	27.88-20.00	25.19-15.19	26.50-17.50	27.38-13.38	17.88-8.94	9.75-6.38	6.81-5.69
P/E Ratio	25.6-18.3	44.2-26.6	26.8-17.7	33.0-16.1	25.9-13.0	17.0-11.1	14.0-11.7
Average Yield %	2.3	2.2	1.6	1.4	1.6	2.4	2.7

Statistics are as originally reported. Adj. for stock splits: 2-for-1, 7/98, 5/97; 3-for-2, 10/93 ① Reflects the 7/00 acquisition of CCB Financial Corp. ② Incl. pre-tax acquisition chrg. of $122.9 mill. ③ Incl. pre-tax acquisition chrg. of $11.4 mill.

OFFICERS:	TELEPHONE NUMBER: (901) 523-3434	INSTITUTIONAL HOLDINGS:
T. M. Garrott, Chmn.	FAX: (901) 523-3310	No. of Institutions: 221
E. C. Roessler, Pres., C.E.O.	WEB: www.ncbccorp.com	Shares Held: 81,866,577
S. M. Fox, C.F.O.		% Held: 39.8
	NO. OF EMPLOYEES: 5,463	
INVESTOR CONTACT: Timothy K. Schools, Sr. V.P., (901) 523-3087	SHAREHOLDERS: 17,800	INDUSTRY: National commercial banks (SIC: 6021)
	ANNUAL MEETING: In April	
PRINCIPAL OFFICE: One Commerce Square, Memphis, TN 38150	INCORPORATED: TN, Feb., 1966	TRANSFER AGENT(S): Bank of New York, New York, NY

NATIONAL FUEL GAS COMPANY

YIELD 4.1%
P/E RATIO 43.5

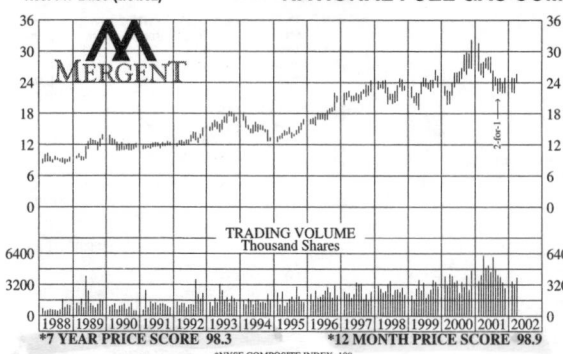

7 YEAR PRICE SCORE 98.3   *NYSE COMPOSITE INDEX=100*   **12 MONTH PRICE SCORE 98.9**

INTERIM EARNINGS (Per Share):

Qtr.	Dec.	Mar.	June	Sept.
1997-98	0.48	d0.28	0.25	d0.02
1998-99	0.49	0.79	0.15	0.06
1999-00	0.57	0.91	0.12	0.03
2000-01	0.66	0.94	0.45	d1.24
2001-02	0.41	...	...	...

INTERIM DIVIDENDS (Per Share):

Amt.	Decl.	Ex.	Rec.	Pay.
2-for-1	6/14/01	9/10/01	8/24/01	9/07/01
0.253Q	9/13/01	9/26/01	9/28/01	10/15/01
0.253Q	12/13/01	12/27/01	12/31/01	1/15/02
0.253Q	3/14/02	3/26/02	3/29/02	4/15/02

Indicated div.: $1.01 (Div. Reinv. Plan)

CAPITALIZATION (9/30/01):

	($000)	(%)
Long-Term Debt	1,046,694	43.4
Deferred Income Tax	340,559	14.1
Minority Interest	22,324	0.9
Common & Surplus	1,002,655	41.6
Total	2,412,232	100.0

DIVIDEND ACHIEVER STATUS:

Rank: 261   10-Year Growth Rate: 3.18%
Total Years of Dividend Growth: 30

RECENT DEVELOPMENTS: For the quarter ended 12/31/01, net income slid 37.3% to $33.2 million versus $53.0 million a year earlier. Operating revenues fell 28.3% to $394.1 million. The lower results were mainly due to a drop in commodity prices at NFG's Exploration and Production segment. During the quarter, NFG's weighted average price, after hedging, for natural gas fell 17.1% to $3.10 per thousand cubic feet, while the weighted average price for crude oil declined 26.1% to $17.01 per barrel.

PROSPECTS: Due to ongoing weakness in crude oil and natural gas prices, NFG has reduced its drilling budget and delayed production in its Canadian operations. As a result of the Company's lowered production expectations, NFG has revised its full-year fiscal 2002 earnings estimates from $1.70 to $1.80 per diluted share to $1.50 to $1.60 per diluted share. Meanwhile, NFG's long-term outlook remains solid, reflecting the Company's diverse business operations and growth opportunities.

BUSINESS

NATIONAL FUEL GAS COMPANY is a diversified energy company consisting of six business segments. The Utility segment operations (58.0% of 2001 revenues) are carried out by National Fuel Gas Distribution Corporation, which sells natural gas or provides natural gas transportation services to about 732,000 customers, as of 9/30/01, through a local distribution system located in western New York and northwestern Pennsylvania. The Pipeline and Storage segment operations (3.9%) are carried out by National Fuel Gas Supply Corporation and Seneca Independence Pipeline Corp. The Exploration and Production segment operations (19.0%) are carried out by Seneca Resources Corporation. The International segment operations (4.7%) are carried by Horizon Energy Development. The Energy Marketing segment operations (12.4%) are carried by National Fuel Resources, Inc. The Timber segment operations (2.0%) are carried out by Highland Forest Resources, Inc. and by a division of Seneca known as its Northeast Division.

ANNUAL FINANCIAL DATA

	9/30/01	9/30/00	9/30/99	9/30/98	9/30/97	9/30/96	9/30/95
Earnings Per Share	☐ 0.82	1.61	1.48	0.42	1.51	1.39	1.02
Cash Flow Per Share	2.99	3.40	3.13	1.95	2.97	2.70	1.97
Tang. Book Val. Per Share	12.63	12.55	12.09	11.38	12.02	11.31	10.69
Dividends Per Share	0.98	0.94	0.92	0.89	0.85	0.82	0.80
Dividend Payout %	120.1	58.9	62.0	210.7	56.8	59.3	78.8
INCOME STATEMENT (IN MILLIONS):							
Total Revenues	2,100.4	1,425.3	1,263.3	1,248.0	1,265.8	1,208.0	975.5
Costs & Expenses	1,746.1	1,041.4	917.7	1,019.4	960.1	925.9	753.6
Depreciation & Amort.	174.9	142.2	129.7	118.9	111.7	98.2	71.8
Maintenance Exp.	20.6	23.5	23.9	25.8	25.7	26.4	25.7
Operating Income	158.7	218.3	192.0	83.9	168.3	157.4	124.4
Net Interest Inc./(Exp.)	d107.1	d100.1	d87.7	d85.3	d56.8	d56.6	d53.9
Equity Earnings/Minority Int.	d1.3	d1.4	d1.6	d2.2	...	...	...
Net Income	☐ 65.5	127.2	115.0	32.3	114.7	104.7	75.9
Cash Flow	240.4	269.4	244.7	151.2	226.3	202.9	147.7
Average Shs. Outstg. (000)	80,361	79,166	78,084	77,406	76,168	75,226	74,794
BALANCE SHEET (IN MILLIONS):							
Gross Property	4,273.7	3,829.6	3,383.5	3,186.9	2,668.5	2,471.1	2,322.3
Accumulated Depreciation	1,493.0	1,146.2	1,029.6	938.7	849.1	761.5	673.2
Net Property	2,780.7	2,683.4	2,353.9	2,248.1	1,819.4	1,709.6	1,649.2
Total Assets	3,445.6	3,236.9	2,842.6	2,684.5	2,267.3	2,149.8	2,038.3
Long-Term Obligations	1,046.7	953.6	822.7	692.7	581.6	574.0	474.0
Net Stockholders' Equity	1,002.7	987.4	939.3	875.6	917.9	856.0	800.6
Year-end Shs. Outstg. (000)	79,406	78,660	77,674	76,938	76,332	75,704	74,868
STATISTICAL RECORD:							
Operating Profit Margin %	7.6	15.3	15.2	6.7	13.3	13.0	12.8
Net Profit Margin %	3.1	8.9	9.1	2.6	9.1	8.7	7.8
Net Inc./Net Property %	2.4	4.7	4.9	1.4	6.3	6.1	4.6
Net Inc./Tot. Capital %	2.7	5.6	5.6	1.7	6.4	6.1	4.9
Return on Equity %	6.5	12.9	12.2	3.7	12.5	12.2	9.5
Accum. Depr./Gross Prop. %	34.9	29.9	30.4	29.5	31.8	30.8	29.0
Price Range	31.59-21.95	32.25-19.69	26.47-18.75	24.81-19.81	24.44-19.69	22.06-15.69	16.94-12.50
P/E Ratio	38.5-26.8	20.1-12.3	17.9-12.7	59.1-47.2	16.2-13.1	15.9-11.3	16.7-12.3
Average Yield %	3.7	3.6	4.0	4.0	3.9	4.4	5.4

Statistics are as originally reported. Adj. for 2-for-1 stk. split, 9/01 ☐ Incl. after-tax impairment chrg. of $104.0 mill.

OFFICERS:
P. C. Ackerman, Chmn., Pres., C.E.O.
W. E. DeForest, Sr. V.P.
J. P. Pawlowski, Treas.

INVESTOR CONTACT: Margaret M. Suto, Director, Investor Relations, (716) 857-6987

PRINCIPAL OFFICE: 10 Lafayette Square, Buffalo, NY 14203

TELEPHONE NUMBER: (716) 857-7000
WEB: www.nationalfuelgas.com

NO. OF EMPLOYEES: 3,235

SHAREHOLDERS: 20,345

ANNUAL MEETING: In Feb.

INCORPORATED: NJ, Dec., 1902

INSTITUTIONAL HOLDINGS:
No. of Institutions: 181
Shares Held: 35,551,000
% Held: 44.6

INDUSTRY: Natural gas distribution (SIC: 4924)

TRANSFER AGENT(S): Mellon Investor Services, South Hackensack, NJ

NATIONAL PENN BANCSHARES, INC.

YIELD 3.6%
P/E RATIO 15.2

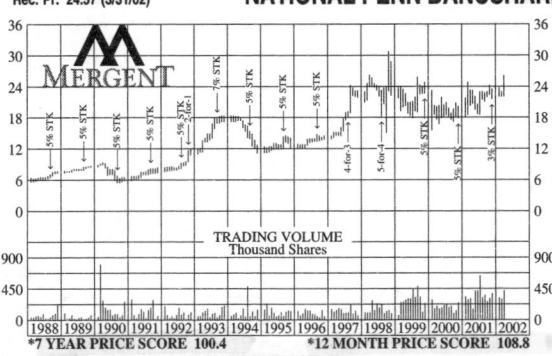

*7 YEAR PRICE SCORE 100.4   *12 MONTH PRICE SCORE 108.8
*NYSE COMPOSITE INDEX=100

TRADING VOLUME
Thousand Shares

INTERIM EARNINGS (Per Share):

Qtr.	Mar.	June	Sept.	Dec.
1998	0.35	0.34	0.32	0.33
1999	0.40	0.37	0.33	0.30
2000	0.41	0.39	0.37	0.35
2001	0.37	0.40	0.42	0.43

INTERIM DIVIDENDS (Per Share):

Amt.	Decl.	Ex.	Rec.	Pay.
0.21Q	6/27/01	7/27/01	7/31/01	8/17/01
0.22Q	9/26/01	10/29/01	10/31/01	11/17/01
3% STK	10/24/01	12/07/01	12/11/01	12/27/01
0.22Q	12/19/01	1/29/02	1/31/02	2/17/02
0.22Q	3/28/02	4/26/02	4/30/02	5/17/02

Indicated div.: $0.88 (Div. Reinv. Plan)

CAPITALIZATION (12/31/01):

	($000)	(%)
Total Deposits	2,076,795	86.1
Long-Term Debt	139,974	5.8
Common & Surplus	195,682	8.1
Total	2,412,451	100.0

DIVIDEND ACHIEVER STATUS:
Rank: 79   10-Year Growth Rate: 13.57%
Total Years of Dividend Growth: 23

RECENT DEVELOPMENTS: For the year ended 12/31/01, net income increased 17.8% to $32.7 million compared with $27.8 million in the prior year. Net interest income advanced 8.5% to $96.0 million from $88.4 million in the previous year. Total interest income slipped 2.0% to $188.5 million from $192.4 million the year before. Total interest expense decreased 11.0% to $92.5 million from $104.0 million a year earlier. Provision for loan and lease losses climbed 22.9% to $9.0 million from $7.3 million in 2000. Total noninterest income rose 24.7% to $34.5 million from $27.7 million the prior year. Total noninterest expense was $80.7 million, up 7.2% versus $75.3 million the previous year. Comparisons were made with restated prior-year financials reflecting the 1/3/01 acquisition of Community Independent Bank, Inc., which was accounted for as a pooling of interests.

BUSINESS

NATIONAL PENN BANCSHARES, INC. is a bank holding company with assets of $2.73 billion as of 12/31/01. The Company, primarily through its subsidiaries National Penn Bank and Panasia Bank, N.A., has been serving residents and businesses of southeastern Pennsylvania since 1874 and northern New Jersey since July 2000. The banks, which have in excess of 60 branch locations, are locally managed community banks providing commercial banking products, primarily loans and deposits. Trust services are provided through Investors Trust Company; brokerage services are provided through Penn Securities, Inc.; insurance services are provided through Penn Securities, Inc. and Link Financial Services, Inc.; and mortgage banking activities are provided through Penn 1st Financial Services, Inc. In addition, the Company has various wholly-owned, direct or indirect, nonbank subsidiaries engaged in activities related to the business of banking.

ANNUAL FINANCIAL DATA

	12/31/01	12/31/00	12/31/99	12/31/98	12/31/97	12/31/96	12/31/95
Earnings Per Share	1.62	1.52	1.40	1.34	1.21	1.12	1.03
Tang. Book Val. Per Share	9.82	9.22	8.08	8.72	8.17	7.59	7.08
Dividends Per Share	0.83	0.75	0.70	0.64	0.55	0.46	0.42
Dividend Payout %	50.9	49.4	49.8	47.6	45.6	41.3	40.6
INCOME STATEMENT (IN MILLIONS)							
Total Interest Income	188.5	184.7	164.3	131.9	119.0	106.6	99.0
Total Interest Expense	92.5	99.7	82.8	67.0	54.6	46.0	43.8
Net Interest Income	96.0	85.0	81.5	64.9	64.4	60.5	55.2
Provision for Loan Losses	9.0	5.6	6.0	5.1	4.6	3.9	3.2
Non-Interest Income	34.5	27.0	23.2	16.7	11.7	8.7	7.3
Non-Interest Expense	80.7	70.8	65.7	51.3	46.1	41.3	37.5
Income Before Taxes	40.8	35.7	33.2	25.5	25.8	24.5	22.1
Net Income	32.7	29.2	27.4	20.5	18.6	16.9	15.4
Average Shs. Outstg. (000)	20,223	19,351	19,548	15,325	15,476	15,092	14,960
BALANCE SHEET (IN MILLIONS)							
Cash & Due from Banks	101.8	80.9	63.0	46.6	40.0	40.2	39.2
Securities Avail. for Sale	658.6	593.3	516.0	443.3	321.8	236.8	240.9
Total Loans & Leases	1,856.4	1,720.3	1,570.5	1,248.0	1,122.8	1,051.1	939.1
Allowance for Credit Losses	42.2	37.1	34.1	27.3	25.1	22.7	20.4
Net Loans & Leases	1,814.2	1,683.2	1,536.4	1,220.7	1,097.7	1,028.3	918.7
Total Assets	2,727.5	2,512.5	2,242.4	1,811.6	1,534.4	1,358.0	1,251.4
Total Deposits	2,076.8	1,814.3	1,593.3	1,208.1	1,115.6	980.8	914.9
Long-Term Obligations	140.0	146.4	223.1	248.5	155.5	76.1	71.6
Total Liabilities	2,531.8	2,335.1	2,094.7	1,681.1	1,411.2	1,243.3	1,144.8
Net Stockholders' Equity	195.7	177.4	147.7	130.5	123.2	114.7	106.6
Year-end Shs. Outstg. (000)	19,927	19,251	18,269	14,953	15,085	15,109	15,053
STATISTICAL RECORD:							
Return on Equity %	16.7	16.5	18.6	15.7	15.1	14.8	14.4
Return on Assets %	1.2	1.2	1.2	1.1	1.2	1.2	1.2
Equity/Assets %	7.2	7.1	6.6	7.2	8.0	8.4	8.5
Non-Int. Exp./Tot. Inc. %	36.2	33.4	35.0	34.5	35.2	35.8	35.3
Price Range	24.88-17.96	23.29-15.49	25.87-17.83	30.82-14.97	24.31-13.81	14.80-11.95	14.60-11.15
P/E Ratio	15.4-11.1	15.4-10.2	18.5-12.8	23.0-11.2	20.2-11.4	13.2-10.6	14.2-10.8
Average Yield %	3.9	3.9	3.2	2.8	2.9	3.5	3.2

Statistics are as originally reported. Adj. for stk. splits: 3% div., 12/01; 5% div., 12/00; 5% div., 12/99; 5-for-4, 7/98; 4-for-3, 7/97; 5% div., 10/96; 5% div., 10/95.

OFFICERS:
W. R. Weidner, Chmn., Pres., C.E.O.
G. E. Moyer, Exec. V.P.
G. L. Rhoads, C.F.O., Treas.

INVESTOR CONTACT: Sandra L. Spayd, Sec., (610) 369-6291

PRINCIPAL OFFICE: Philadelphia & Reading Avenues, Boyertown, PA 19512

TELEPHONE NUMBER: (610) 369-6128
FAX: (610) 369-6349
WEB: www.natpennbank.com

NO. OF EMPLOYEES: 783 full-time; 80 part-time

SHAREHOLDERS: 3,338

ANNUAL MEETING: In Apr.

INCORPORATED: PA, Jan., 1982

INSTITUTIONAL HOLDINGS:
No. of Institutions: 47
Shares Held: 2,884,719
% Held: 14.4

INDUSTRY: National commercial banks
(SIC: 6021)

TRANSFER AGENT(S): Mellon Investor Services, L.L.C., Ridgefield Park, NJ

NATIONAL SECURITY GROUP, INC. (THE)

YIELD 5.7%
P/E RATIO 8.3

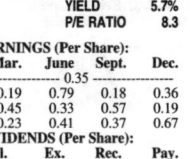

INTERIM EARNINGS (Per Share):

Qtr.	Mar.	June	Sept.	Dec.
1998	------------ 0.35 ------------			
1999	0.19	0.79	0.18	0.36
2000	0.45	0.33	0.57	0.19
2001	0.23	0.41	0.37	0.67

INTERIM DIVIDENDS (Per Share):

Amt.	Decl.	Ex.	Rec.	Pay.
0.22Q	4/19/01	5/03/01	5/07/01	5/31/01
20% STK	4/19/01	5/03/01	5/07/01	5/31/01
0.19Q	7/21/01	8/02/01	8/06/01	8/31/01
0.20Q	10/18/01	11/01/01	11/05/01	11/30/01
0.20Q	1/19/02	1/31/02	2/04/02	2/28/02

Indicated div.: $0.80

CAPITALIZATION (12/31/01):

	($000)	(%)
Long-Term Debt	2,108	4.2
Deferred Income Tax	3,083	6.2
Common & Surplus	44,884	89.6
Total	50,075	100.0

DIVIDEND ACHIEVER STATUS:
Rank: 184   10-Year Growth Rate: 7.35%
Total Years of Dividend Growth: 11

TRADING VOLUME
Thousand Shares

1988 1989 1990 1991 1992 1993 1994 1995 1996 1997 1998 1999 2000 2001 2002

*7 YEAR PRICE SCORE 94.0   *12 MONTH PRICE SCORE 113.8
*NYSE COMPOSITE INDEX=100

RECENT DEVELOPMENTS: For the twelve months ended 12/30/01, net income increased 9.4% to $4.1 million compared with $3.8 million in the equivalent prior-year period. Total revenues climbed 10.5% to $32.8 million from $29.7 million the year before. Net premiums earned rose 10.6% to $25.4 million. Property and casualty insurance premiums grew 10.2% to $20.2 million from $18.3 million a year earlier, while life and accident and health insurance premiums were up 12.3% to $5.2 million from $4.6 million in 2000. Net investment income totaled $4.5 million compared with $4.4 million in the prior year. Realized investment gains slipped 4.8% to $1.6 million from $1.7 million the year before. Other income more than doubled to $1.3 million from $597,000 a year earlier. The combined ratio of the Company's property and casualty operations decreased to 90.4% versus 96.4%, while its underwriting expense ratio increased to 36.1% from 34.8% in 2000.

BUSINESS

THE NATIONAL SECURITY GROUP, INC. is an insurance holding company that, through its subsidiaries, writes primarily dwelling fire and windstorm, homeowners, and personal non-standard automobile lines of insurance. The Company's property and casualty subsidiaries also write commercial lines of insurance for small businesses. The Company, through its life insurance subsidiary, offers a basic line of life, and health and accident insurance products. Property-casualty insurance is the most significant segment, accounting for 79.6%, as of 12/31/01, of total premium revenues. The Company's property and casualty insurance business is conducted through National Security Fire & Casualty Company, a wholly-owned subsidiary of the Company, and Omega One Insurance Company, a wholly-owned subsidiary of National Security Fire & Casualty Company.

REVENUES

(12/31/2001)	($000)	(%)
Net Premiums Earned..................	25,357	77.3
Net Investment Income..................	4,506	13.8
Net Realized Invest Gains.....................	1,640	5.0
Other Income............	1,280	3.9
Total	32,783	100.0

ANNUAL FINANCIAL DATA

	12/31/01	12/31/00	12/31/99	12/31/98	12/31/97	12/31/96	12/31/95
Earnings Per Share	1.67	1.53	1.53	0.35	1.07	0.48	0.08
Tang. Book Val. Per Share	18.20	17.75	16.98	17.05	16.70	14.55	14.26
Dividends Per Share	0.76	0.71	0.68	0.64	0.58	0.54	0.51
Dividend Payout %	45.3	46.2	44.3	183.3	54.7	112.1	676.9
INCOME STATEMENT (IN THOUSANDS):							
Total Premium Income	25,357	22,921	25,936	28,451	31,156	26,654	24,372
Net Investment Income	4,506	4,434	4,354	4,351	4,204	3,935	4,311
Other Income	2,920	2,320	2,336	4,502	3,415	2,421	2,155
Total Revenues	32,783	29,675	32,626	37,304	38,775	33,010	30,838
Policyholder Benefits	13,516	14,125	17,275	22,880	22,995	19,677	17,721
Income Before Income Taxes	5,470	4,844	4,516	1,106	3,360	1,621	276
Income Taxes	1,392	1,068	760	176	362	265	62
Equity Earnings/Minority Int.	52	...	...	...	...	...	...
Net Income	4,130	3,776	3,756	930	2,998	1,356	214
Average Shs. Outstg.	2,467	2,467	2,467	2,675	2,780	2,808	2,790
BALANCE SHEET (IN THOUSANDS):							
Cash & Cash Equivalents	61,039	54,277	53,124	55,308	56,707	37,438	30,268
Premiums Due	3,824	3,677	4,687	7,223	8,889	12,746	12,721
Invst. Assets: Fixed-term	23,135	28,875	30,911	30,807	29,995	35,413	38,427
Invst. Assets: Loans	1,001	808	781	780	968	1,027	1,111
Invst. Assets: Total	85,196	84,575	84,990	87,741	88,951	75,390	71,485
Total Assets	99,484	97,563	98,105	103,973	106,958	98,219	97,266
Long-Term Obligations	2,108	2,401	2,672	3,004	...	...	...
Net Stockholders' Equity	44,884	43,780	41,888	41,968	46,352	40,519	39,774
Year-end Shs. Outstg.	2,467	2,467	2,467	2,461	2,776	2,784	2,790
STATISTICAL RECORD:							
Return on Revenues %	12.6	12.7	11.5	2.5	7.7	4.1	0.7
Return on Equity %	9.2	8.6	9.0	2.2	6.5	3.3	0.5
Return on Assets %	4.2	3.9	3.8	0.9	2.8	1.4	0.2
Price Range	15.62-10.89	16.04-9.17	12.50-7.71	17.92-8.75	20.00-10.62	11.87-9.69	15.00-10.21
P/E Ratio	9.4-6.5	10.5-6.0	8.2-5.1	51.2-25.0	18.7-10.0	24.6-20.1	199.7-135.9
Average Yield %	5.7	5.6	6.7	4.8	3.8	5.0	4.0

Statistics are as originally reported. Adj. for stk. splits: 20% div., 5/01.

OFFICERS:
W. Baird, Chmn.
W. L. Brunson, Jr., Pres., C.E.O.
M. L. Murdock, C.O.O.

INVESTOR CONTACT: M. L. Murdock, C.O.O., (334) 897-2273

PRINCIPAL OFFICE: 661 East Davis Street, Elba, AL 36323

TELEPHONE NUMBER: (334) 897-2273
FAX: (334) 897-5694
WEB: www.nationalsecuritygroup.com

NO. OF EMPLOYEES: 150

SHAREHOLDERS: 1,100 (approx.)

ANNUAL MEETING: In Apr.

INCORPORATED: DE, Mar., 1990

INSTITUTIONAL HOLDINGS:
No. of Institutions: 4
Shares Held: 75,828
% Held: 3.1

INDUSTRY: Life insurance (SIC: 6311)

TRANSFER AGENT(S): The National Security Group, Inc., Elba, AL

NICOR INC.

	YIELD	4.0%
	P/E RATIO	14.3

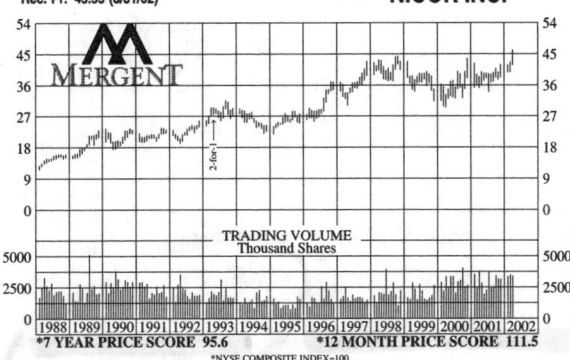

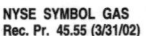

TRADING VOLUME
Thousand Shares

*7 YEAR PRICE SCORE 95.6   ***12 MONTH PRICE SCORE 111.5**
*NYSE COMPOSITE INDEX=100

INTERIM EARNINGS (Per Share):

Qtr.	Mar.	June	Sept.	Dec.
1997	0.82	0.58	0.40	0.81
1998	0.75	0.59	0.43	0.65
1999	0.82	0.56	0.42	0.83
2000	0.83	0.66	d1.37	0.87
2001	0.85	0.59	0.73	1.01

INTERIM DIVIDENDS (Per Share):

Amt.	Decl.	Ex.	Rec.	Pay.
0.44Q	3/15/01	3/28/01	3/30/01	5/01/01
0.44Q	4/19/01	6/27/01	6/29/01	8/01/01
0.44Q	7/19/01	9/26/01	9/28/01	11/01/01
0.44Q	11/15/01	12/27/01	12/31/01	2/01/02
0.46Q	3/21/02	3/26/02	3/28/02	5/01/02

Indicated div.: $1.84 (Div. Reinv. Plan)

CAPITALIZATION (12/31/01):

	($000)	(%)
Long-Term Debt	446,400	28.3
Deferred Income Tax	395,100	25.1
Redeemable Pfd. Stock	6,100	0.4
Common & Surplus	727,600	46.2
Total	1,575,200	100.0

DIVIDEND ACHIEVER STATUS:
Rank: 242   10-Year Growth Rate: 4.61%
Total Years of Dividend Growth: 14

RECENT DEVELOPMENTS: For the year ended 12/31/01, net income more than tripled to $143.7 million versus $46.7 million in 2000. The growth in earnings was primarily due to lower interest expenses. Operating revenues advanced 10.7% to $2.54 billion from $2.30 billion in the prior year. The cost of gas jumped 17.4% to $1.65 billion from $1.40 billion a year earlier. Operating income more than doubled to $243.5 million from $94.1 million in 2000.

PROSPECTS: GAS expects accelerated growth in its energy-related ventures. Meanwhile, the gas distribution and shipping segment results are expected to remain relatively unchanged in 2002 due to the negative effect of significantly lower 2001 pension plan returns, higher health care costs and continuing weak economic conditions. Moreover, GAS expects earnings per share to range from $3.10 and $3.25 in 2002, assuming normal weather.

BUSINESS

NICOR INC. is engaged in the purchase, storage, distribution, transportation, sale, and gathering of natural gas. The Company's natural gas unit, Northern Illinois Gas, is one of the nation's largest distributors of natural gas. As of 12/31/01, Northern Illinois served more than 2.0 million customers in the northern third of Illinois, excluding the city of Chicago. NICOR also owns Tropical Shipping Co., one of the largest containerized cargo carriers in the Carribean. Tropical Shipping's fleet consists of 11 owned vessels and six chartered vessels. In addition, the Company owns several unregulated energy-related ventures, including a 50.0% interest in Nicor Energy, a retail energy marketer. In 2001, operating revenues were derived: 84.6% gas distribution, 9.2% shipping and 9.2% other energy ventures.

ANNUAL FINANCIAL DATA

	12/31/01	12/31/00	12/31/99	12/31/98	12/31/97	12/31/96	12/31/95
Earnings Per Share	3.17	③ 1.00	② 2.62	2.42	2.61	① 2.42	1.96
Cash Flow Per Share	6.46	4.12	5.58	5.25	5.29	4.92	4.17
Tang. Book Val. Per Share	16.39	15.56	16.80	15.97	15.43	14.74	13.67
Dividends Per Share	1.74	1.64	1.54	1.46	1.37	1.31	1.27
Dividend Payout %	54.7	163.5	58.8	60.3	52.5	54.1	65.0
INCOME STATEMENT (IN MILLIONS):							
Total Revenues	2,544.1	2,298.1	1,615.2	1,465.1	1,992.6	1,850.7	1,480.1
Costs & Expenses	2,151.8	2,059.7	1,262.9	1,120.0	1,631.6	1,492.3	1,178.5
Depreciation & Amort.	148.8	144.3	140.3	136.5	131.2	125.3	111.8
Operating Income	243.5	94.1	212.0	208.6	229.8	233.1	189.8
Net Interest Inc./(Exp.)	d44.9	d48.6	d45.1	d46.6	d46.2	d46.2	d38.7
Income Taxes	73.4	14.4	65.7	61.1	69.0	67.7	54.4
Net Income	143.7	③ 46.7	② 124.4	116.4	127.9	① 121.2	99.8
Cash Flow	292.2	190.7	264.4	252.6	258.7	246.1	211.2
Average Shs. Outstg. (000)	45,200	46,300	47,400	48,100	48,900	50,000	50,700
BALANCE SHEET (IN MILLIONS):							
Gross Property	3,733.0	3,576.6	3,483.1	3,379.8	3,267.7	3,192.7	3,110.4
Accumulated Depreciation	1,964.4	1,847.0	1,747.9	1,648.0	1,531.9	1,420.8	1,331.1
Net Property	1,768.6	1,729.6	1,735.2	1,731.8	1,735.8	1,771.9	1,779.3
Total Assets	2,574.8	2,885.4	2,451.8	2,364.6	2,394.6	2,438.6	2,259.1
Long-Term Obligations	446.4	347.1	436.1	557.3	550.2	518.0	468.7
Net Stockholders' Equity	727.6	707.8	787.7	759.0	744.1	729.7	687.7
Year-end Shs. Outstg. (000)	44,398	45,491	46,890	47,514	48,217	49,492	50,302
STATISTICAL RECORD:							
Operating Profit Margin %	9.6	4.1	13.1	14.2	11.5	12.6	12.8
Net Profit Margin %	5.6	2.0	7.7	7.9	6.4	6.5	6.7
Net Inc./Net Property %	8.1	2.7	7.2	6.7	7.4	6.8	5.6
Net Inc./Tot. Capital %	9.1	3.3	7.9	7.1	8.0	7.8	6.8
Return on Equity %	19.7	6.6	15.8	15.3	17.2	16.6	14.5
Accum. Depr./Gross Prop. %	52.6	51.6	50.2	48.8	46.9	44.5	42.8
Price Range	42.38-34.00	43.88-29.38	42.94-31.19	44.44-37.13	42.94-30.00	37.13-25.38	28.50-21.75
P/E Ratio	13.4-10.7	43.9-29.4	16.4-11.9	18.4-15.3	16.5-11.5	15.3-10.5	14.5-11.1
Average Yield %	4.5	4.5	4.2	3.6	3.8	4.2	5.1

Statistics are as originally reported. ① Bef. inc. fr. dis. ops. of $150.0 mill. ② Incl. a pre-tax gain of $3.8 million on the sale of the Company's interest in QuickTrade. ③ Excls. one-time after-tax chrg. of $89.7 mill.

OFFICERS:
T. L. Fisher, Chmn., Pres., C.E.O.
G. M. Behrens, V.P., Treas.
R. M. Strobel, Exec. V.P., Gen. Couns., Sec.

INVESTOR CONTACT: Mark Knox, Investor Relations, (630) 305-9500 ext.2529

PRINCIPAL OFFICE: 1844 Ferry Road, Naperville, IL 60563-9600

TELEPHONE NUMBER: (630) 305-9500
FAX: (630) 983-9328
WEB: www.nicorinc.com

NO. OF EMPLOYEES: 3,400 (approx.)

SHAREHOLDERS: 27,500 (approx.)

ANNUAL MEETING: In Mar.

INCORPORATED: IL, 1976

INSTITUTIONAL HOLDINGS:
No. of Institutions: 233
Shares Held: 22,283,675
% Held: 50.3

INDUSTRY: Natural gas distribution (SIC: 4924)

TRANSFER AGENT(S): Computershare Investor Services, Chicago, IL

NISOURCE, INC.

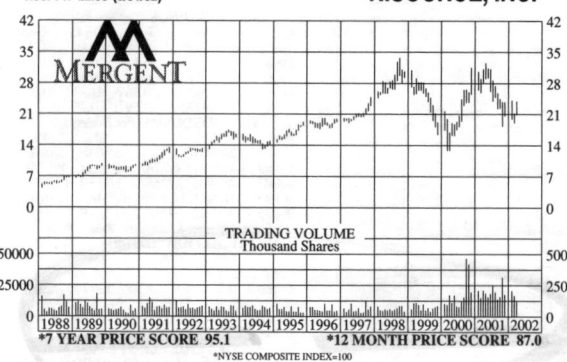

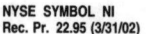

INTEREST EARNINGS (Per Share):

Qtr.	Mar.	June	Sept.	Dec.
1997	0.59	0.22	0.29	0.22
1998	0.48	0.24	0.35	0.51
1999	0.62	0.18	0.22	0.25
2000	0.62	0.18	0.42	Nil
2001	0.88	d0.03	d0.10	0.31

INTERIM DIVIDENDS (Per Share):

Amt.	Decl.	Ex.	Rec.	Pay.
0.29Q	5/22/01	7/27/01	7/31/01	8/20/01
0.29Q	8/28/01	10/29/01	10/31/01	11/20/01
0.29Q	1/03/02	1/29/02	1/31/02	2/20/02
0.29Q	3/27/02	4/26/02	4/30/02	5/20/02

Indicated div.: $1.16 (Div. Reinv. Plan)

CAPITALIZATION (12/31/01):

	($000)	(%)
Long-Term Debt	5,780,800	32.8
Deferred Income Tax	1,726,300	9.8
Redeemable Pfd. Stock	350,000	2.0
Preferred Stock	83,600	0.5
Common & Surplus	9,683,800	54.9
Total	17,624,500	100.0

DIVIDEND ACHIEVER STATUS:
Rank: 187   10-Year Growth Rate: 7.18%
Total Years of Dividend Growth: 13

TRADING VOLUME
Thousand Shares

1988 1989 1990 1991 1992 1993 1994 1995 1996 1997 1998 1999 2000 2001 2002
7 YEAR PRICE SCORE 95.1   **12 MONTH PRICE SCORE 87.0**
NYSE COMPOSITE INDEX=100

RECENT DEVELOPMENTS: For the year ended 12/31/01, income was $212.1 million, before an accounting change credit of $4.0 million, versus income from continuing operations of $141.1 million in 2000. Results included losses on impairment of $9.2 million in 2001 and $65.8 million in 2000. Earnings growth was due to increases in all revenue segments. Gross revenues advanced 56.8% to $9.46 billion from $6.03 billion in 2000.

PROSPECTS: NI and Acumentrics signed a stock purchase and a distribution and product purchase agreement. Under the stock purchase agreement, NI's subsidiary, NiSource Energy Technologies Inc., acquired about a 3.0% interest in Acumentrics. Under the distribution and product purchase agreement, NI agreed to purchase and distribute $10.0 million of Acumentrics' proprietary tubular solid-oxide fuel cell products.

BUSINESS

NISOURCE, INC. (formerly NIPSCO Industries, Inc.) is an energy-based holding company that provides electricity, natural gas, electricity and other products and services to 3.7 million customers from the Gulf Coast through the Midwest to New England as of 1/30/02. The Company's principal subsidiaries include Columbia Energy Resources, Inc., a natural gas distribution, transmission, storage and exploration and production holding company; Northern Indiana Public Service Company, a gas and electric company providing service to customers in northern Indiana; and Bay State Gas Company, a natural gas distribution company serving customers in New England. NI provides non-regulated energy marketing and services through its wholly-owned subsidiary, EnergyUSA, Inc. and develops power projects through its subsidiary, Primary Energy, Inc. In February 1999, NI acquired Bay State Gas Company. In November 2000, NI acquired Columbia Energy Group for approximately $6.00 billion.

ANNUAL FINANCIAL DATA

	12/31/01	12/31/00	12/31/99	12/31/98	12/31/97	12/31/96	12/31/95
Earnings Per Share	② 1.01	① 1.08	1.27	1.59	1.53	1.44	1.36
Cash Flow Per Share	4.21	3.84	4.05	3.71	3.56	3.20	2.95
Tang. Book Val. Per Share	28.93	46.25	29.68	34.41	28.92	29.01	28.86
Dividends Per Share	1.16	1.08	1.02	0.96	0.90	0.84	0.78
Dividend Payout %	114.8	100.0	80.3	60.4	58.8	58.3	57.3

INCOME STATEMENT (IN MILLIONS):

Total Revenues	9,458.7	6,030.7	3,144.6	2,932.8	2,586.5	1,821.6	1,722.3
Costs & Expenses	7,778.1	5,088.7	2,371.6	2,254.8	1,926.2	1,209.3	1,127.8
Depreciation & Amort.	671.7	374.2	311.4	256.5	249.8	215.0	201.1
Operating Income	1,008.9	567.8	461.5	421.5	410.6	397.3	393.4
Net Interest Inc./(Exp.)	d597.7	d304.5	d166.6	d128.8	d120.6	d106.5	d96.2
Income Before Income Taxes	395.3	277.2	286.2	294.7	295.9	287.7	283.9
Income Taxes	183.2	130.1	90.4	100.9	105.0	111.0	108.4
Net Income	② 212.1	① 147.1	195.8	193.9	190.8	176.7	175.5
Cash Flow	883.8	521.3	507.2	450.4	440.7	391.6	373.5
Average Shs. Outstg. (000)	209,800	135,811	125,339	121,335	123,849	122,382	126,562

BALANCE SHEET (IN MILLIONS):

Cash & Cash Equivalents	127.9	193.0	43.5	60.8	30.8	26.3	28.5
Total Current Assets	2,566.7	4,917.6	771.6	606.9	630.7	511.1	316.6
Net Property	9,554.7	9,546.7	13,471.5	10,378.9	10,168.2	9,083.1	8,936.2
Total Assets	17,374.1	19,696.8	6,835.2	4,986.5	4,937.0	4,274.3	3,999.5
Total Current Liabilities	4,728.6	6,893.4	1,473.7	886.1	750.3	1,022.2	669.2
Long-Term Obligations	5,780.8	5,802.7	1,975.2	1,668.0	1,667.9	1,127.1	1,175.7
Net Stockholders' Equity	9,767.4	13,194.4	3,898.9	4,195.0	4,427.6	3,551.6	3,681.5
Net Working Capital	d2,161.9	d1,975.8	d702.1	d279.2	d119.6	d511.1	d352.6
Year-end Shs. Outstg. (000)	205,553	205,553	124,139	117,531	147,784	119,612	124,760

STATISTICAL RECORD:

Operating Profit Margin %	10.7	9.4	14.7	14.4	15.9	21.8	22.8
Net Profit Margin %	2.2	2.4	6.2	6.6	7.4	9.7	10.2
Return on Equity %	2.2	1.1	5.0	4.6	4.3	5.0	4.8
Return on Assets %	1.2	0.7	2.9	3.9	3.9	4.1	4.4
Debt/Total Assets %	33.3	29.5	28.9	33.5	33.8	26.4	29.4
Price Range	32.55-18.25	31.50-12.75	30.94-16.38	33.75-24.66	24.94-19.00	20.13-17.63	19.25-14.63
P/E Ratio	32.2-18.1	29.2-11.8	24.4-12.9	21.2-15.5	16.3-12.4	14.0-12.2	14.2-10.8
Average Yield %	4.6	4.9	4.3	3.3	4.1	4.4	4.6

Statistics are as originally reported. Adj. for stk. split 2-for-1: 2/98. Results for 2000 and subsequent years reflect the acq. of Columbia Energy Group on 11/1/00. ① Excl. inc. from disc. oper. of $9.8 mill., but incl. loss on asset impair. of $65.8 mill. ② Bef. acctg. chng. cr. of $4.0 mill. & excl. gain of $100,000 from disc. ops., but incl. loss on impair. of $9.2

OFFICERS:
G. L. Neale, Chmn., Pres., C.E.O.
S. P. Adik, Vice-Chmn.
D. M. McFarland, V.P., Treas.

INVESTOR CONTACT: Investor Relations, (219) 647-5990

PRINCIPAL OFFICE: 801 East 86th Avenue, Merrillville, IN 46410

TELEPHONE NUMBER: (219) 647-5990
FAX: (219) 647-6085
WEB: www.nisource.com
NO. OF EMPLOYEES: 12,501
SHAREHOLDERS: 49,389
ANNUAL MEETING: In May
INCORPORATED: IN, Sept., 1987; reincorp., DE, Nov., 2000

INSTITUTIONAL HOLDINGS:
No. of Institutions: 302
Shares Held: 141,608,629
% Held: 68.2

INDUSTRY: Electric and other services combined (SIC: 4931)

TRANSFER AGENT(S): Computershare Investor Service, Chicago, IL

NORDSON CORPORATION

YIELD 1.9%
P/E RATIO 44.3

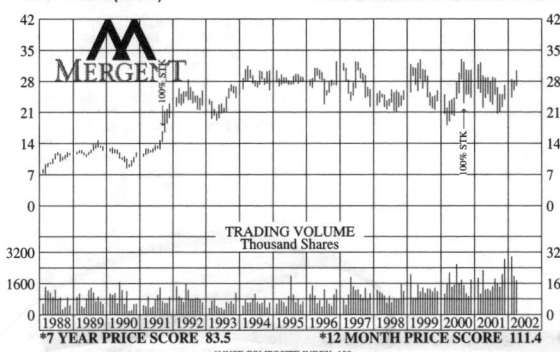

INTERIM EARNINGS (Per Share):

Qtr.	Jan.	Apr.	July	Oct.
1998	0.15	0.02	0.42	0.05
1999	0.21	0.39	0.40	0.43
2000	0.15	0.40	0.46	0.67
2001	0.23	0.27	0.17	0.07
2002	0.17	...	...	...

INTERIM DIVIDENDS (Per Share):

Amt.	Decl.	Ex.	Rec.	Pay.
0.14Q	1/31/01	2/21/01	2/23/01	3/13/01
0.14Q	5/24/01	6/04/01	6/06/01	6/19/01
0.14Q	8/01/01	8/29/01	8/31/01	9/18/01
0.14Q	11/07/01	12/12/01	12/14/01	1/03/02
0.14Q	1/30/02	2/20/02	2/22/02	3/12/02

Indicated div.: $0.56 (Div. Reinv. Plan)

CAPITALIZATION (10/28/01):

	($000)	(%)
Long-Term Debt	188,078	41.3
Capital Lease Obligations..	3,695	0.8
Common & Surplus	263,726	57.9
Total	455,499	100.0

DIVIDEND ACHIEVER STATUS:
Rank: 119   10-Year Growth Rate: 10.84%
Total Years of Dividend Growth: 21

TRADING VOLUME
Thousand Shares

*7 YEAR PRICE SCORE 83.5   *12 MONTH PRICE SCORE 111.4
*NYSE COMPOSITE INDEX=100

RECENT DEVELOPMENTS: For the first quarter ended 1/27/02, net income decreased 24.4% to $5.7 million compared with $7.5 million in the corresponding period of the previous year. Results for 2000 included goodwill amortization of $3.9 million and severance and restructuring costs of $126,000. Net sales decreased 17.3% to $145.0 million, primarily due to lower sales volume with unfavorable currency translations. Net sales for the adhesive dispensing and nonwoven fiber systems segment declined 7.4% to $90.8 million, while net sales for the coating and finishing systems segment fell 6.9% to $26.8 million. Net sales for the advanced technology systems segment dropped 43.6% to $27.4 million. On a geographic basis, North America sales declined 15.1% to $71.9 million, while sales in Europe fell 2.8% to $46.0 million. Sales in Japan decreased 37.0% to $12.5 million, while Pacific South sales slid 37.9% to $14.5 million.

BUSINESS

NORDSON CORPORATION designs, manufactures and markets systems that apply adhesives, sealants and coatings to a broad range of consumer and industrial products during manufacturing operations. The Company's value-added product line includes customized electronic controls for the precise application and curing of materials to meet customers' productivity, quality and environmental targets. NDSN's production operations include machining and assembly. The Company finishes specially designed parts and assembles components into finished equipment. Many components are made in standard modules that can be used in more than one product or in combination with other components for a variety of models. NDSN products are used around the world in the appliance, automotive, bookbinding, construction, container, converting, electronics, food and beverage, furniture, metal finishing, nonwovens, packaging and other diverse industries. NDSN has principal manufacturing facilities in Ohio, Georgia, Alabama, California, Connecticut, New Jersey, Florida, Germany, The Netherlands, and the United Kingdom.

ANNUAL FINANCIAL DATA

	10/28/01	10/29/00	10/31/99	11/1/98	11/2/97	11/3/96	10/29/95
Earnings Per Share	☐0.74	☐1.67	☐1.42	☐0.63	1.45	1.49	1.42
Cash Flow Per Share	2.01	2.59	2.32	1.38	2.18	2.14	1.97
Tang. Book Val. Per Share	...	4.73	2.45	3.90	4.76	5.10	5.54
Dividends Per Share	0.56	0.52	0.48	0.44	0.40	0.36	0.32
Dividend Payout %	75.7	31.1	33.8	70.4	27.7	24.2	22.5
INCOME STATEMENT (IN THOUSANDS):							
Total Revenues	731,416	740,568	700,465	660,900	636,710	609,444	581,444
Costs & Expenses	630,024	618,791	594,180	590,826	537,344	501,661	476,886
Depreciation & Amort.	41,855	30,325	29,300	25,003	25,307	23,522	20,614
Operating Income	59,537	91,452	76,985	45,071	74,059	84,261	83,944
Net Interest Inc./(Exp.)	d29,489	d11,665	d10,244	d9,647	d7,763	d5,955	d4,553
Income Before Income Taxes	37,716	83,408	71,438	38,927	71,745	81,061	80,642
Income Taxes	13,106	28,776	23,932	18,102	21,778	27,990	27,966
Net Income	☐24,610	☐54,632	☐47,506	☐20,825	49,967	53,071	52,676
Cash Flow	66,465	84,957	76,806	45,828	75,274	76,593	73,290
Average Shs. Outstg.	33,050	32,767	33,048	33,322	34,552	35,792	37,154
BALANCE SHEET (IN THOUSANDS):							
Cash & Cash Equivalents	7,943	815	16,060	6,850	1,717	9,531	1,584
Total Current Assets	362,177	369,238	341,316	328,476	318,815	317,702	285,941
Net Property	133,332	126,910	128,639	101,183	101,667	107,018	99,499
Total Assets	862,453	610,040	591,790	538,944	502,996	510,493	434,710
Total Current Liabilities	355,653	253,008	251,940	207,082	179,663	207,216	155,379
Long-Term Obligations	191,773	60,800	65,975	70,444	66,502	20,562	17,134
Net Stockholders' Equity	263,726	247,223	221,398	214,775	220,545	245,297	231,330
Net Working Capital	6,524	116,230	89,376	121,394	139,152	110,486	130,562
Year-end Shs. Outstg.	33,137	32,449	49,012	33,480	33,678	35,268	36,012
STATISTICAL RECORD:							
Operating Profit Margin %	8.1	12.3	11.0	6.8	11.6	13.8	14.4
Net Profit Margin %	3.4	7.4	6.8	3.2	7.8	8.7	9.1
Return on Equity %	9.3	22.1	21.5	9.7	22.7	21.6	22.8
Return on Assets %	2.9	9.0	8.0	3.9	9.9	10.4	12.1
Debt/Total Assets %	22.2	10.0	11.1	13.1	13.2	4.0	3.9
Price Range	32.25-20.67	32.99-18.06	32.97-21.50	26.19-21.13	32.50-22.19	32.50-22.75	30.50-26.88
P/E Ratio	43.6-27.9	19.8-10.8	23.2-15.1	41.9-33.8	22.5-15.4	21.9-15.3	21.5-18.9
Average Yield %	2.1	2.0	1.8	1.9	1.5	1.3	1.1

Statistics are as originally reported. Adj. for stk. split: 100% div., 9/12/00. ☐Incl. severance & restruct. costs of $13.3 mill., 10/01; $9.0 mill., 10/00; $3.0 mill., 10/99; $26.0 mill., 11/98.

OFFICERS:
W. P. Madar, Chmn.
E. P. Campbell, Pres., C.E.O.
R. L. Cushing, Treas.

INVESTOR CONTACT: Barbara T. Price, Mgr., Shldr. Svcs., (440) 414-5344

PRINCIPAL OFFICE: 28601 Clemens Road, Westlake, OH 44145-4551

TELEPHONE NUMBER: (440) 892-1580
FAX: (440) 892-9507
WEB: www.nordson.com
NO. OF EMPLOYEES: 3,902 (avg.)
SHAREHOLDERS: 2,511 (approx.)
ANNUAL MEETING: In March
INCORPORATED: OH, 1954

INSTITUTIONAL HOLDINGS:
No. of Institutions: 103
Shares Held: 11,937,260
% Held: 35.9

INDUSTRY: Adhesives and sealants (SIC: 2891)

TRANSFER AGENT(S): National City Bank, Cleveland, OH

NORTH PITTSBURGH SYSTEMS, INC.

YIELD 4.9%
P/E RATIO 20.0

TRADING VOLUME
Thousand Shares

| 1988 | 1989 | 1990 | 1991 | 1992 | 1993 | 1994 | 1995 | 1996 | 1997 | 1998 | 1999 | 2000 | 2001 | 2002 |

*7 YEAR PRICE SCORE N/A   *12 MONTH PRICE SCORE 108.3
*NYSE COMPOSITE INDEX=100

INTERIM EARNINGS (Per Share):

Qtr.	Mar.	June	Sept.	Dec.
1997	0.21	0.25	0.23	0.79
1998	0.28	0.27	0.21	0.21
1999	0.23	0.18	0.22	0.22
2000	0.16	0.22	0.08	0.07
2001	0.10	0.17	0.22	0.21

INTERIM DIVIDENDS (Per Share):

Amt.	Decl.	Ex.	Rec.	Pay.
0.17Q	3/21/01	3/29/01	4/02/01	4/16/01
0.17Q	5/18/01	6/28/01	7/02/01	7/16/01
0.17Q	9/05/01	9/27/01	10/01/01	10/15/01
0.17Q	12/06/01	12/28/01	1/02/02	1/15/02
0.17Q	3/18/02	3/27/02	4/01/02	4/15/02

Indicated div.: $0.68

CAPITALIZATION (12/31/01):

	($000)	(%)
Long-Term Debt	47,202	33.8
Capital Lease Obligations..	7,607	5.4
Deferred Income Tax	10,483	7.5
Common & Surplus	74,342	53.2
Total	139,634	100.0

DIVIDEND ACHIEVER STATUS:

Rank: 187   10-Year Growth Rate: 7.18%
Total Years of Dividend Growth: 39

RECENT DEVELOPMENTS: For the year ended 12/31/01, net income increased 31.3% to $10.4 million compared with $7.9 million a year earlier. Operating revenues advanced 11.0% to $86.4 million from $77.9 million the previous year. The Company attributed the improved results to continued growth in Incumbent Local Exchange (ILEC) services, an effective cost control program implemented and executed by the ILEC in 2001, continued penetration of broadband services, and the termination of costs related to the Nauticom Sports Network, which was shutdown in the fourth quarter of 2000. For the fourth quarter ended 12/31/01, the Company reported earnings per share of $0.21 versus earnings per share of $0.07 the year before. Revenues rose 13.4% to $22.1 million compared with $19.5 million in the corresponding year-earlier period.

BUSINESS

NORTH PITTSBURGH SYSTEMS, INC. is a holding company. Its subsidiaries include North Pittsburgh Telephone Company, Penn Telecom and Pinnatech Inc. North Pittsburgh Telephone Company is a telephone public utility. Penn Telecom, Inc.'s principal business activities consist of the sale, rental and servicing of telecommunications equipment to end users, the resale of bulk billed message toll services and high capacity intercity facilities. Penn Telecom is also certified as a Competitive Access Provider and a Competitive Local Exchange Carrier. Pinnatech, Inc., formed in 1995, provides Internet-related services including dial-up access, Web design and Web hosting.

REVENUES

(12/31/2001)	($000)	(%)
Local Network	20,142	23.3
Long Distance & Access	54,452	63.0
Dir. Adv., Billing & Other	2,324	2.7
Telecommunications Equipment	2,458	2.8
Other Operating Revenues	7,068	8.2
Total	86,444	100.0

ANNUAL FINANCIAL DATA

	12/31/01	12/31/00	12/31/99	12/31/98	12/31/97	12/31/96	12/31/95
Earnings Per Share	0.69	0.53	0.85	0.97	[1] 1.48	0.78	0.71
Cash Flow Per Share	1.84	1.64	1.75	1.76	2.18	1.41	1.26
Tang. Book Val. Per Share	4.95	4.94	5.16	4.93	4.57	3.68	3.43
Dividends Per Share	0.68	0.66	0.63	[2] 0.64	0.55	0.51	0.47
Dividend Payout %	98.5	124.5	74.1	66.0	37.2	65.4	66.2
INCOME STATEMENT (IN THOUSANDS):							
Total Revenues	86,444	79,021	70,888	66,788	66,207	59,933	52,757
Costs & Expenses	49,088	49,451	37,722	32,513	33,511	31,072	25,554
Depreciation & Amort.	17,311	16,725	13,622	11,864	10,579	9,407	8,194
Operating Income	20,045	12,845	19,544	22,411	22,117	19,454	19,009
Net Interest Inc./(Exp.)	d2,615	d1,773	d1,287	d576	d1,102	d444	d530
Income Taxes	7,474	6,008	8,833	9,264	14,186	7,909	7,054
Net Income	10,362	7,889	12,685	14,518	[1] 22,185	11,730	10,687
Cash Flow	27,673	24,614	26,307	26,382	32,764	21,137	18,881
Average Shs. Outstg.	15,005	15,005	15,005	15,005	15,019	15,040	15,040
BALANCE SHEET (IN THOUSANDS):							
Gross Property	200,958	203,254	174,437	155,184	140,500	125,927	111,291
Accumulated Depreciation	99,660	99,176	86,688	78,854	69,303	60,333	52,675
Net Property	101,298	104,078	87,749	76,330	71,197	65,594	58,616
Total Assets	168,963	160,954	147,792	135,315	127,833	99,523	96,156
Long-Term Obligations	54,809	52,514	38,940	32,196	27,037	21,311	21,694
Net Stockholders' Equity	74,342	74,194	77,247	73,806	68,560	55,306	51,527
Year-end Shs. Outstg.	15,005	15,005	14,970	14,970	15,005	15,040	15,040
STATISTICAL RECORD:							
Operating Profit Margin %	23.2	16.3	27.6	33.6	33.4	32.5	36.0
Net Profit Margin %	12.0	10.0	17.9	21.7	33.5	19.6	20.3
Net Inc./Net Property %	10.2	7.6	14.5	19.0	31.2	17.9	18.2
Net Inc./Tot. Capital %	7.4	5.8	10.1	12.7	21.7	14.2	13.5
Return on Equity %	13.9	10.6	16.4	19.7	32.4	21.2	20.7
Accum. Depr./Gross Prop. %	49.6	48.8	49.7	50.8	49.3	47.9	47.3
Price Range	18.97-9.63	15.06-10.56	19.25-12.06	18.75-11.00	25.00-14.38	60.00-23.00	33.50-20.50
P/E Ratio	27.5-13.9	28.4-19.9	22.6-14.2	19.3-11.3	16.9-9.7	76.9-29.5	47.2-28.9
Average Yield %	4.8	5.2	4.0	4.3	2.8	1.2	1.7

Statistics are as originally reported. Adj. for stk. split: 2-for-1, 5/96 [1] Incl. net gain of $14.5 mill. on the sale of investment. [2] Incl. spec. div. of $0.05 per share.

OFFICERS:
C. E. Thomas Jr., Chmn.
H. R. Brown, Pres.
A. P. Kimble, V.P., Treas.

INVESTOR CONTACT: Investor Relation, (724) 443-9600

PRINCIPAL OFFICE: 4008 Gibsonia Road, Gibsonia, PA 15044-9311

TELEPHONE NUMBER: (724) 443-9600
FAX: (724) 443-9431
WEB: www.northpittsburgh.com
NO. OF EMPLOYEES: 402
SHAREHOLDERS: 2,660 (approx.)
ANNUAL MEETING: In May
INCORPORATED: PA, May, 1985

INSTITUTIONAL HOLDINGS:
No. of Institutions: 39
Shares Held: 2,019,577
% Held: 13.5

INDUSTRY: Telephone communications, exc. radio (SIC: 4813)

TRANSFER AGENT(S): Wells Fargo Shareowner Services, South St. Paul, MN

NORTHERN TRUST CORPORATION

YIELD 1.1%
P/E RATIO 28.4

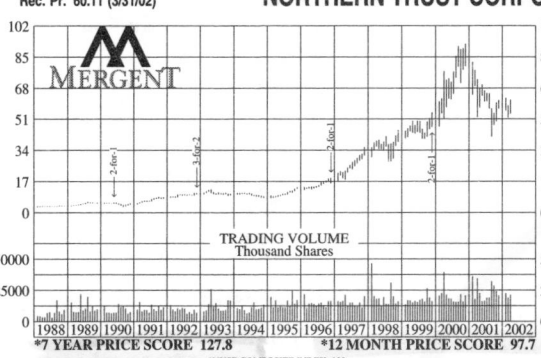

*7 YEAR PRICE SCORE 127.8   *12 MONTH PRICE SCORE 97.7

*NYSE COMPOSITE INDEX=100

TRADING VOLUME
Thousand Shares

INTERIM EARNINGS (Per Share):

Qtr.	Mar.	June	Sept.	Dec.
1997	0.31	0.33	0.35	0.35
1998	0.37	0.38	0.39	0.40
1999	0.41	0.43	0.45	0.46
2000	0.49	0.53	0.53	0.54
2001	0.55	0.57	0.55	0.45

INTERIM DIVIDENDS (Per Share):

Amt.	Decl.	Ex.	Rec.	Pay.
0.155Q	2/20/01	3/07/01	3/09/01	4/02/01
0.155Q	5/22/01	6/06/01	6/08/01	7/02/01
0.155Q	7/17/01	9/06/01	9/10/01	10/01/01
0.17Q	11/20/01	12/06/01	12/10/01	1/02/02
0.17Q	2/19/02	3/06/02	3/08/02	4/01/02

Indicated div.: $0.68 (Div. Reinv. Plan)

CAPITALIZATION (12/31/01):

	($000)	(%)
Total Deposits	25,019,300	85.5
Long-Term Debt	1,484,500	5.1
Preferred Stock	120,000	0.4
Common & Surplus	2,653,500	9.1
Total	29,277,300	100.0

DIVIDEND ACHIEVER STATUS:

Rank: 47   10-Year Growth Rate: 16.05%
Total Years of Dividend Growth: 16

RECENT DEVELOPMENTS: For the year ended 12/31/01, net income increased to $487.5 million compared with $485.1 million in the prior year. Net interest income advanced 4.2% to $595.3 million from $568.6 million the year before. Total non-interest income improved 2.8% to $1.58 billion from $1.54 billion in the previous year. Total non-interest expense grew 1.9% to $1.38 billion from $1.35 billion a year earlier. Provision for credit losses was $66.5 million compared with $24.0 million the year before. The Company increased its provision for credit losses due to its exposure to Enron Corporation, which filed for bankruptcy on 12/2/01, and other risks resulting from the economic recession. Total deposits amounted to $25.02 billion versus $22.83 billion in 2000. Total loans and leases were $17.98 billion compared with $18.14 billion the year before.

BUSINESS

NORTHERN TRUST CORPORA-TION is a Chicago-based multibank holding company. The Company's principal subsidiary is The Northern Trust Company, an Illinois banking corporation. NTRS also owns national bank subsidiaries in Arizona, California, Colorado, Florida and Texas; a federal savings bank with subsidiaries in Michigan, Missouri, Nevada, Ohio, Washington and Wisconsin; a trust company in New York; and various other nonbank subsidiaries, including an investment management company owned through NTRS, a securities brokerage firm, an international investment consulting firm and a retirement services company. With total assets of $39.66 billion as of 12/31/01, NTRS offers financial services including fiduciary, banking, investment and financial consulting services for individuals as well as credit operating, trust and investment management services for corporations, institutions and organizations. The Company is a provider of personal fiduciary, master trust/custody and global custody, and treasury management services. NTRS and its subsidiaries also provide corporate banking, automated clearing house and leasing services.

ANNUAL FINANCIAL DATA

	12/31/01	12/31/00	12/31/99	12/31/98	12/31/97	12/31/96	12/31/95
Earnings Per Share	2.11	2.08	1.74	1.52	1.33	1.11	0.94
Tang. Book Val. Per Share	11.97	10.54	9.25	8.18	7.27	6.40	5.76
Dividends Per Share	0.62	0.54	0.48	0.42	0.36	0.31	0.26
Dividend Payout %	29.4	26.0	27.6	27.6	27.1	28.1	27.7

INCOME STATEMENT (IN MILLIONS):

Total Interest Income	1,681.5	2,011.1	1,568.6	1,503.1	1,332.8	1,151.5	1,104.0
Total Interest Expense	1,086.2	1,442.5	1,049.8	1,025.9	894.6	763.2	746.4
Net Interest Income	595.3	568.6	518.8	477.2	438.2	388.3	357.6
Provision for Loan Losses	66.5	24.0	12.5	9.0	9.0	12.0	6.0
Non-Interest Income	1,580.0	1,537.0	1,235.2	1,071.6	934.5	777.9	678.1
Non-Interest Expense	1,376.9	1,351.5	1,125.0	997.1	891.8	766.8	709.2
Income Before Taxes	731.9	730.1	616.5	542.7	471.9	387.4	320.5
Net Income	487.5	485.1	405.0	353.9	309.4	258.8	220.0
Average Shs. Outstg. (000)	228,971	230,613	229,874	229,734	229,322	229,296	225,352

BALANCE SHEET (IN MILLIONS):

Cash & Due from Banks	2,592.3	2,287.8	1,977.9	2,366.0	1,738.9	1,292.5	1,308.9
Securities Avail. for Sale	5,667.5	6,491.2	5,491.0	5,384.3	3,741.8	4,316.5	5,225.2
Total Loans & Leases	17,979.9	18,144.6	15,374.5	13,646.9	12,588.2	10,937.4	9,906.0
Allowance for Credit Losses	161.6	162.9	150.9	146.8	147.6	148.3	147.1
Net Loans & Leases	17,818.3	17,981.7	15,223.6	13,500.1	12,440.6	10,789.1	9,758.9
Total Assets	39,664.5	36,022.3	28,708.2	27,870.0	25,315.4	21,608.3	19,933.5
Total Deposits	25,019.3	22,827.9	21,371.0	18,202.7	16,360.0	13,796.2	12,488.2
Long-Term Obligations	1,484.5	1,405.7	1,426.9	1,425.6	1,491.9	732.8	351.6
Total Liabilities	36,891.0	33,560.1	26,533.5	25,929.7	23,576.4	20,064.2	18,480.9
Net Stockholders' Equity	2,773.5	2,462.2	2,174.7	1,940.3	1,739.0	1,544.1	1,452.6
Year-end Shs. Outstg. (000)	221,647	222,232	222,162	222,430	222,734	222,496	222,656

STATISTICAL RECORD:

Return on Equity %	17.6	19.7	18.6	18.2	17.8	16.8	15.1
Return on Assets %	1.2	1.3	1.4	1.3	1.2	1.2	1.1
Equity/Assets %	7.0	6.8	7.6	7.0	6.9	7.1	7.3
Non-Int. Exp./Tot. Inc. %	63.3	64.2	64.1	64.4	64.5	64.8	68.5
Price Range	82.25-41.40	92.13-46.75	54.63-40.16	44.94-27.88	35.75-17.00	18.88-12.31	14.00-7.94
P/E Ratio	39.0-19.6	44.3-22.5	31.4-23.1	29.6-18.3	26.9-12.8	17.1-11.1	14.9-8.5
Average Yield %	1.0	0.8	1.0	1.2	1.4	2.0	2.4

Statistics are as originally reported. Adj. for stk. splits: 2-for-1, 12/9/96; 2-for-1, 12/11/99

OFFICERS:
W. A. Osborn, Chmn., C.E.O.
P. R. Pero, Vice-Chmn., C.F.O.
B. G. Hastings, Pres., C.O.O.
D. L. Eddy, Sr. V.P., Treas.
INVESTOR CONTACT: Laurie K. McMahon, (312) 444-7811
PRINCIPAL OFFICE: 50 South La Salle Street, Chicago, IL 60675

TELEPHONE NUMBER: (312) 630-6000
FAX: (312) 444-7843
WEB: www.northerntrust.com
NO. OF EMPLOYEES: 9,453
SHAREHOLDERS: 3,194
ANNUAL MEETING: In Apr.
INCORPORATED: DE, Aug., 1971

INSTITUTIONAL HOLDINGS:
No. of Institutions: 422
Shares Held: 143,865,742
% Held: 64.9

INDUSTRY: State commercial banks (SIC: 6022)

TRANSFER AGENT(S): Wells Fargo Shareowner Services, South St. Paul, MN

NORTHWESTERN CORPORATION

YIELD 5.8%
P/E RATIO 14.1

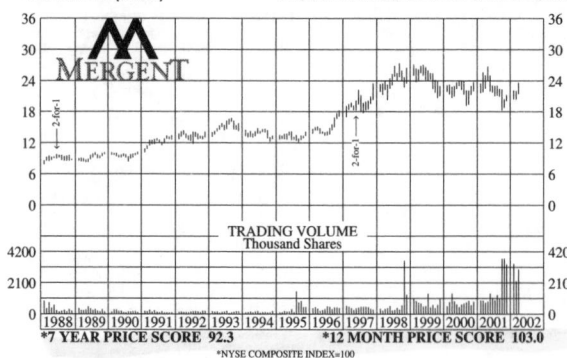

TRADING VOLUME
Thousand Shares

| 1988 | 1989 | 1990 | 1991 | 1992 | 1993 | 1994 | 1995 | 1996 | 1997 | 1998 | 1999 | 2000 | 2001 | 2002 |

*7 YEAR PRICE SCORE 92.3 *12 MONTH PRICE SCORE 103.0
*NYSE COMPOSITE INDEX=100

INTERIM EARNINGS (Per Share):

Qtr.	Mar.	June	Sept.	Dec.
1997	0.55	0.14	0.17	0.45
1998	0.58	0.15	0.20	0.48
1999	0.56	0.22	0.31	0.53
2000	0.62	0.26	0.35	0.60
2001	0.70	0.38	0.36	0.12

INTERIM DIVIDENDS (Per Share):

Amt.	Decl.	Ex.	Rec.	Pay.
0.297Q	2/07/01	2/13/01	2/15/01	3/01/01
0.297Q	5/03/01	5/11/01	5/15/01	6/01/01
0.297Q	8/02/01	8/13/01	8/15/01	9/01/01
0.318Q	11/07/01	11/13/01	11/15/01	12/01/01
0.318Q	2/06/02	2/13/02	2/15/02	3/01/02

Indicated div.: $1.27 (Div. Reinv. Plan)

CAPITALIZATION (12/31/01):

	($000)	(%)
Long-Term Debt	835,873	67.5
Deferred Income Tax	5,934	0.5
Common & Surplus	396,416	32.0
Total	1,238,223	100.0

DIVIDEND ACHIEVER STATUS:
Rank: 238   10-Year Growth Rate: 4.66%
Total Years of Dividend Growth: 18

RECENT DEVELOPMENTS: For the year ended 12/31/01, net income was $44.5 million versus income of $50.6 million, before an accounting change charge of $1.0 million, in 2000. Results for 2001 included a $24.9 million restructuring charge. Operating revenues dropped 40.6% to $4.24 billion from $7.13 billion in the prior year, due to the sale and exit of certain natural gas crude oil businesses of CornerStone Propane along with lower commodity prices.

PROSPECTS: NOR completed the acquisition of The Montana Power Company on 2/15/02, and subsequently renamed it Northwestern Energy on 3/12/02. The transaction was valued at about $1.09 billion, including $602.0 million in cash and the assumption of about $488.0 million in debt. NOR's mission is to grow NorthWestern Energy as a full-service energy provider. The acquisition should increase NOR's annual regulated revenues by more than $600.0 million.

BUSINESS

NORTHWESTERN CORPORATION (formerly Northwestern Public Service Company) provides integrated energy, communications, air conditioning, heating, ventilation, plumbing and related services and solutions to residential and business customers throughout North America. NOR distributes electricity in South Dakota and natural gas in South Dakota and Nebraska through its energy division, NorthWestern Energy, and electricity and natural gas in Montana through its wholly-owned subsidiary, NorthWestern Energy, L.L.C. NOR's partner entities include Expanets, Inc., a provider of integrated communication and data services to small and medium-sized businesses; Blue Dot Services, Inc., a provider of air conditioning, heating, plumbing and related services; and CornerStone Propane Partner L.P., a publicly-held retail propane and wholesale energy-related commodities distributor. On 4/1/00, NOR purchased Lucent Technologies' Growing and Emerging Markets business. On 3/12/02, NOR acquired The Montana Power Company and renamed it NorthWestern Energy.

ANNUAL FINANCIAL DATA

	12/31/01	12/31/00	12/31/99	12/31/98	12/31/97	12/31/96	12/31/95
Earnings Per Share	③ 1.53	② 1.87	1.62	1.44	1.31	① 1.28	1.11
Cash Flow Per Share	6.68	6.52	4.60	3.70	3.06	2.37	2.01
Tang. Book Val. Per Share	...	...	...	...	...	...	5.81
Dividends Per Share	1.21	1.13	1.05	0.98	0.93	0.89	0.86
Dividend Payout %	79.1	60.4	64.8	68.4	71.2	69.5	77.2

INCOME STATEMENT (IN MILLIONS):

Total Revenues	4,237.8	7,132.1	3,004.3	1,187.2	918.1	344.0	205.0
Costs & Expenses	4,196.0	6,982.5	2,856.5	1,070.6	827.8	274.2	146.2
Depreciation & Amort.	125.8	108.3	68.3	42.6	31.2	19.4	14.6
Maintenance Exp.	...	...	...	...	...	...	6.0
Operating Income	d84.0	41.3	79.6	73.9	59.0	50.4	38.1
Net Interest Inc./(Exp.)	d90.4	d77.2	d53.2	d35.7	d31.5	d18.7	d11.7
Income Taxes	cr47.4	cr4.1	14.5	13.2	11.1	15.4	10.1
Equity Earnings/Minority Int.	163.5	73.4	22.9	d0.8	d1.7	...	...
Net Income	③ 44.5	② 50.6	44.7	30.4	26.3	① 26.1	19.3
Cash Flow	163.3	152.1	106.2	69.7	54.6	42.3	32.6
Average Shs. Outstg. (000)	24,455	23,338	23,094	18,816	17,843	17,840	16,261

BALANCE SHEET (IN MILLIONS):

Gross Property	1,168.9	980.1	918.1	825.9	720.9	682.0	487.4
Accumulated Depreciation	350.5	284.1	236.4	196.6	175.3	162.9	150.5
Net Property	818.4	696.0	681.7	629.3	545.6	519.1	336.9
Total Assets	2,617.4	2,898.1	1,956.8	1,736.2	1,106.1	1,113.7	558.7
Long-Term Obligations	835.9	1,083.6	783.1	588.9	425.3	424.4	212.8
Net Stockholders' Equity	396.4	319.2	300.2	282.1	166.6	163.8	152.7
Year-end Shs. Outstg. (000)	27,241	23,411	23,109	23,017	17,843	17,840	17,840

STATISTICAL RECORD:

Operating Profit Margin %	...	0.6	2.6	6.2	6.4	14.7	18.6
Net Profit Margin %	1.1	0.7	1.5	2.6	2.9	7.6	9.4
Net Inc./Net Property %	5.4	7.3	6.6	4.8	4.8	5.0	5.7
Net Inc./Tot. Capital %	3.6	3.5	3.9	3.2	2.8	4.0	4.7
Return on Equity %	11.2	15.9	14.9	10.8	15.8	15.9	12.6
Accum. Depr./Gross Prop. %	30.0	29.0	25.8	23.8	24.3	23.9	30.9
Price Range	26.75-18.25	23.94-19.13	27.13-20.63	27.38-20.25	23.50-16.94	18.25-13.38	14.19-12.13
P/E Ratio	17.5-11.9	12.8-10.2	16.7-12.7	19.0-14.1	17.9-12.9	14.3-10.4	12.8-10.9
Average Yield %	5.4	5.2	4.4	4.1	4.6	5.6	6.5

Statistics are as originally reported. Adj. for 2-for-1 stock split, 5/97. ① Incl. a non-recurr., one-time gain of $0.09 a share. ② Excl. acctg. chrg. of $1.0 mill. ($0.04/sh.) ③ Inc. restr. chrg. of $24.9 mill.

OFFICERS:
M. D. Lewis, Chmn., C.E.O.
R. R. Hylland, Pres., C.O.O.
K. D. Orme, V.P., C.F.O.

INVESTOR CONTACT: Elizabeth A. Evans, Investor Relations, (605) 978-2929

PRINCIPAL OFFICE: 125 S. Dakota Ave., Suite 1100, Sioux Falls, SD 57104

TELEPHONE NUMBER: (605) 978-2908
FAX: (605) 353-7631
WEB: www.northwestern.com

NO. OF EMPLOYEES: 10,251 (avg.)

SHAREHOLDERS: 10,322

ANNUAL MEETING: In May

INCORPORATED: DE, Nov., 1923

INSTITUTIONAL HOLDINGS:
No. of Institutions: 120
Shares Held: 9,442,963
% Held: 34.5

INDUSTRY: Electric and other services combined (SIC: 4931)

REGISTRAR(S): Wells Fargo Shareowner Services, South St. Paul, MN

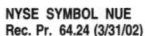

NUCOR CORPORATION

YIELD 1.2%
P/E RATIO 44.3

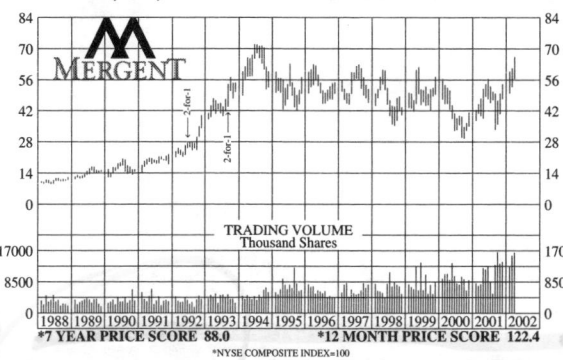

TRADING VOLUME
Thousand Shares

*7 YEAR PRICE SCORE 88.0   *12 MONTH PRICE SCORE 122.4
*NYSE COMPOSITE INDEX=100

INTERIM EARNINGS (Per Share):

Qtr.	Mar.	June	Sept.	Dec.
1997	0.74	0.83	0.91	0.87
1998	0.74	0.82	0.74	0.70
1999	0.32	0.58	0.78	1.12
2000	0.94	0.98	0.85	1.03
2001	0.42	0.43	0.26	0.34

INTERIM DIVIDENDS (Per Share):

Amt.	Decl.	Ex.	Rec.	Pay.
0.17Q	3/08/01	3/28/01	3/30/01	5/11/01
0.17Q	6/05/01	6/27/01	6/29/01	8/10/01
0.17Q	9/05/01	9/26/01	9/28/01	11/09/01
0.17Q	12/04/01	12/26/01	12/28/01	2/08/02
0.19Q	3/07/02	3/26/02	3/29/02	5/10/02

Indicated div.: $0.76 (Div. Reinv. Plan)

CAPITALIZATION (12/31/01):

	($000)	(%)
Long-Term Debt	460,450	15.6
Minority Interest	283,887	9.6
Common & Surplus	2,201,460	74.7
Total	2,945,797	100.0

DIVIDEND ACHIEVER STATUS:

Rank: 35   10-Year Growth Rate: 17.87%
Total Years of Dividend Growth: 29

RECENT DEVELOPMENTS: For the year ended 12/31/01, net income declined 63.7% to $113.0 million compared with $310.9 million a year earlier, reflecting pressure from steel imports on domestic steel prices. Earnings included charges for pre-operating and start-up costs of new facilities of $97.8 million and $50.0 million, in 2001 and 2000, respectively. Net sales decreased 9.7% to $4.14 billion from $4.59 billion a year earlier primarily due to a 16.0% decrease in composite sales price per ton.

PROSPECTS: On 2/14/02, NUE announced that it has offered to purchase substantially all of the assets of Birmingham Steel Corporation for $500.0 million in cash. Separately, the Company plans to spend over $200.0 million on capital projects over the next three years. With this new equipment, NUE's employees will be able to accelerate on-going programs to reduce operational costs, increase production yields and improve overall product quality.

BUSINESS

NUCOR CORPORATION manufactures steel products at operating facilities in 10 states. The Company's manufactured products include carbon and alloy steel, for use in bars, beams, sheet and plate; steel joists and joist girders; steel deck; cold finished steel; steel fasteners; metal building systems; and light gauge steel framing. The primary raw material is ferrous scrap, which is acquired from numerous sources throughout the U.S. Hot-rolled steel, cold-rolled steel, cold-finished steel, steel fasteners and steel-grinding balls are manufactured in standard sizes and inventories are maintained. Steel joists, joist girders and steel deck are sold to general contractors and fabricators throughout the U.S.

ANNUAL FINANCIAL DATA

	12/31/01	12/31/00	12/31/99	12/31/98	12/31/97	12/31/96	12/31/95
Earnings Per Share	ⓘ 1.45	3.80	2.80	3.00	3.34	2.83	3.14
Cash Flow Per Share	5.17	6.97	5.74	5.88	5.84	4.91	5.13
Tang. Book Val. Per Share	28.33	27.47	25.93	23.73	21.32	18.33	15.78
Dividends Per Share	0.66	0.58	0.51	0.46	0.38	0.31	0.26
Dividend Payout %	45.5	15.3	18.2	15.3	11.4	11.0	8.1
INCOME STATEMENT (IN MILLIONS):							
Total Revenues	4,139.2	4,586.1	4,009.3	4,151.2	4,184.5	3,647.0	3,462.0
Costs & Expenses	3,669.8	3,849.3	3,378.6	3,486.6	3,505.6	3,077.3	2,857.0
Depreciation & Amort.	289.1	259.4	256.6	253.1	218.8	182.2	173.9
Operating Income	180.4	477.5	374.1	411.5	460.1	387.5	431.2
Net Interest Inc./(Exp.)	d6.5	0.8	5.1	3.8	...	0.3	1.1
Income Before Income Taxes	173.9	478.3	379.2	415.3	460.2	387.8	432.3
Income Taxes	60.9	167.4	134.6	151.6	165.7	139.6	157.8
Net Income	ⓘ 113.0	310.9	244.6	263.7	294.5	248.2	274.5
Cash Flow	402.0	570.3	501.2	516.8	513.2	430.4	448.4
Average Shs. Outstg. (000)	77,783	81,777	87,287	87,878	87,922	87,686	87,430
BALANCE SHEET (IN MILLIONS):							
Cash & Cash Equivalents	462.3	490.6	572.2	308.7	283.4	104.4	201.8
Total Current Assets	1,373.7	1,381.4	1,538.5	1,129.5	1,125.5	828.4	830.7
Net Property	2,365.7	2,340.3	2,191.3	2,097.1	1,858.9	1,791.2	1,465.4
Total Assets	3,759.3	3,721.8	3,729.8	3,226.5	2,984.4	2,619.5	2,296.1
Total Current Liabilities	484.2	558.1	531.0	486.9	524.5	465.7	447.1
Long-Term Obligations	460.5	460.5	390.5	215.5	168.0	152.6	106.9
Net Stockholders' Equity	2,201.5	2,131.0	2,262.2	2,072.6	1,876.4	1,609.3	1,382.1
Net Working Capital	889.5	823.4	1,007.5	642.6	601.1	362.7	383.6
Year-end Shs. Outstg. (000)	77,708	77,583	87,247	87,353	87,997	87,796	87,599
STATISTICAL RECORD:							
Operating Profit Margin %	4.4	10.4	9.3	9.9	11.0	10.6	12.5
Net Profit Margin %	2.7	6.8	6.1	6.4	7.0	6.8	7.9
Return on Equity %	5.1	14.6	10.8	12.7	15.7	15.4	19.9
Return on Assets %	3.0	8.4	6.6	8.2	9.9	9.5	12.0
Debt/Total Assets %	12.2	12.4	10.5	6.7	5.6	5.8	4.7
Price Range	56.50-33.45	56.44-29.50	61.81-41.63	60.63-35.25	62.94-44.75	63.00-45.13	63.25-42.00
P/E Ratio	39.0-23.1	14.9-7.8	22.1-14.9	20.2-11.7	18.8-13.4	22.3-15.9	20.1-13.4
Average Yield %	1.5	1.3	1.0	1.0	0.7	0.6	0.5

Statistics are as originally reported. ⓘ Incl. chrg. of $97.8 mill. for pre-operating and start-up costs of new facilities.

OFFICERS:
P. C. Browning, Chmn.
D. R. DiMicco, Vice-Chmn., Pres., C.E.O.
T. S. Lisenby, Exec. V.P., C.F.O., Treas.

INVESTOR CONTACT: Terry S. Lisenby, Exec. V.P., (704) 366-7000

PRINCIPAL OFFICE: 2100 Rexford Road, Charlotte, NC 28211

TELEPHONE NUMBER: (704) 366-7000
FAX: (704) 362-4208
WEB: www.nucor.com
NO. OF EMPLOYEES: 8,400
SHAREHOLDERS: 47,000
ANNUAL MEETING: In May
INCORPORATED: MI, Jan., 1940; reincorp., DE, Mar., 1958

INSTITUTIONAL HOLDINGS:
No. of Institutions: 286
Shares Held: 55,537,442
% Held: 71.4

INDUSTRY: Blast furnaces and steel mills (SIC: 3312)

TRANSFER AGENT(S): American Stock Transfer & Trust Company, New York, NY

OLD NATIONAL BANCORP

YIELD 2.8%
P/E RATIO 16.4

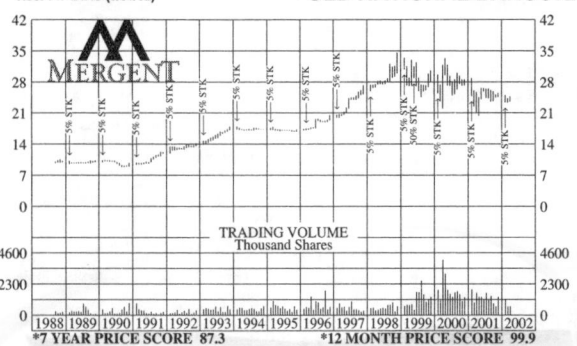

INTERIM EARNINGS (Per Share):

Qtr.	Mar.	June	Sept.	Dec.
1998	0.32	0.33	0.37	0.35
1999	0.36	0.39	0.39	0.37
2000	0.14	0.38	0.21	0.25
2001	0.35	0.31	0.43	0.40

INTERIM DIVIDENDS (Per Share):

Amt.	Decl.	Ex.	Rec.	Pay.
0.17Q	4/26/01	5/30/01	6/01/01	6/15/01
0.17Q	7/26/01	8/30/01	9/04/01	9/18/01
0.17Q	10/25/01	11/29/01	12/03/01	12/17/01
5% STK	12/06/01	1/02/02	1/04/02	1/25/02
0.17Q	1/24/02	2/27/02	3/01/02	3/15/02

Indicated div.: $0.68 (Div. Reinv. Plan)

CAPITALIZATION (12/31/01):

	($000)	(%)
Total Deposits	6,616,440	80.1
Long-Term Debt	1,000,046	12.1
Common & Surplus	639,235	7.7
Total	8,255,721	100.0

DIVIDEND ACHIEVER STATUS:
Rank: 190   10-Year Growth Rate: 7.06%
Total Years of Dividend Growth: 18

*7 YEAR PRICE SCORE 87.3   ***12 MONTH PRICE SCORE 99.9**
*NYSE COMPOSITE INDEX=100

RECENT DEVELOPMENTS: For the year ended 12/31/01, net income advanced 50.8% to $93.0 million versus $61.7 million in the prior year. Results for 2001 and 2000 included after-tax restructuring charges of $5.9 million and $25.7 million, respectively. Net interest income increased 7.9% to $291.3 million from $269.9 million the year before due to lower interest rates and ONB's balance sheet restructuring. Provision for loan losses increased 10.4% to $28.7 million. Total noninterest income climbed 11.1% to $113.0 million.

PROSPECTS: Results are being positively affected by increased deposit-related service charge revenues, stemming from growth in ONB's core deposit base, and strong mortgage banking revenues. Meanwhile, the Company is continuing to seek acquisition opportunities in its insurance brokerage business. Separately, ONB reached agreements to sell six branch offices in Indiana and Illinois and two branch offices in Kentucky. The transactions are expected to close mid-year 2002.

BUSINESS

OLD NATIONAL BANCORP is a financial holding company headquartered in Evansville, Indiana with banking activity in Indiana, Illinois, Kentucky, Tennessee, and Ohio. As of 12/31/01, the Company had total assets of $9.08 billion and over 140 community banking locations serving customers in both urban and rural markets. The Company's banking centers provide a wide range of financial services, such as commercial, real estate, and consumer loans; lease financing; checking, savings, time deposits and other depository accounts; letters of credit; cash management services; credit life, accident and health insurance; safe deposit facilities; investments and brokerage products; debit cards and other electronically accessed banking services; and Internet banking. The Company's non-bank affiliates provide additional financial or support services incidental to its operations, including issuance and reinsurance of credit life, accident, health, life, property, and casualty insurance; investment services; fiduciary and trust services; and property ownership.

ANNUAL FINANCIAL DATA

	12/31/01	12/31/00	12/31/99	12/31/98	12/31/97	12/31/96	12/31/95
Earnings Per Share	①1.49	①0.98	1.52	1.39	1.16	1.15	1.00
Tang. Book Val. Per Share	10.45	9.89	9.45	9.93	10.01	8.94	8.53
Dividends Per Share	0.65	0.62	0.57	0.50	0.48	0.46	0.44
Dividend Payout %	43.5	62.9	37.8	36.4	41.3	39.8	43.7
INCOME STATEMENT (IN MILLIONS):							
Total Interest Income	629.7	638.3	488.9	437.9	429.4	394.4	355.3
Total Interest Expense	338.4	368.4	250.5	223.1	210.2	190.6	174.1
Net Interest Income	291.3	269.9	238.4	214.8	219.2	203.8	181.2
Provision for Loan Losses	28.7	29.8	11.5	11.4	27.0	11.0	6.7
Non-Interest Income	113.0	101.7	67.5	54.6	47.1	44.8	39.2
Non-Interest Expense	254.8	265.5	185.6	158.1	154.4	152.3	142.8
Income Before Taxes	120.8	76.2	108.8	99.9	85.0	85.3	70.9
Net Income	①93.0	①61.7	82.7	71.7	60.7	60.2	51.7
Average Shs. Outstg. (000)	62,229	63,210	54,987	52,461	53,405	52,484	54,184
BALANCE SHEET (IN MILLIONS):							
Cash & Due from Banks	224.7	202.6	169.2	150.9	147.3	180.4	175.1
Securities Avail. for Sale	2,320.1	1,825.1	1,678.7	1,596.9	1,567.0	1,514.6	1,390.2
Total Loans & Leases	6,132.9	6,350.8	4,841.3	4,162.2	3,730.2	3,523.3	3,037.7
Allowance for Credit Losses	74.2	76.3	60.4	49.4	46.2	44.1	39.8
Net Loans & Leases	6,058.6	6,274.5	4,780.9	4,112.8	3,684.0	3,479.2	2,997.9
Total Assets	9,080.5	8,767.7	6,982.9	6,166.0	5,688.2	5,366.6	4,822.6
Total Deposits	6,616.4	6,583.9	5,071.3	4,443.5	4,298.7	4,268.0	3,973.7
Long-Term Obligations	1,000.0	863.2	663.0	629.9	388.8	74.6	81.5
Total Liabilities	8,441.2	8,141.4	6,490.2	5,671.4	5,211.0	4,908.1	4,394.6
Net Stockholders' Equity	639.2	626.3	492.7	494.6	477.2	458.5	428.1
Year-end Shs. Outstg. (000)	61,174	63,327	52,136	49,811	47,677	51,264	50,162
STATISTICAL RECORD:							
Return on Equity %	14.6	9.9	16.8	14.5	12.7	13.1	12.1
Return on Assets %	1.0	0.7	1.2	1.2	1.1	1.1	1.1
Equity/Assets %	7.0	7.1	7.1	8.0	8.4	8.5	8.9
Non-Int. Exp./Tot. Inc. %	63.0	71.5	60.7	58.7	58.0	61.3	64.8
Price Range	28.88-20.36	33.33-21.97	33.41-24.60	34.63-25.92	27.29-19.88	20.50-17.04	17.85-16.79
P/E Ratio	19.4-13.7	34.0-22.4	22.1-16.2	24.9-18.7	23.5-17.1	17.8-14.8	17.9-16.8
Average Yield %	2.6	2.2	2.0	1.7	2.0	2.4	2.5

Statistics are as originally reported. Adj. for stk. splits: 5% div., 1/02; 5% div., 1/01; 5% div., 1/00; 50% div., 5/24/99; 5% div., 1/29/98; 5% div., 1/97; 5% div., 2/96. ① Incl. after-tax merger and restruct. costs of $5.9 mill., 2001; $25.7 mill., 2000.

OFFICERS:
J. A. Risinger, Chmn., Pres., C.E.O.
J. S. Poelker, Exec. V.P., C.F.O.

INVESTOR CONTACT: Lynell J. Walton,
Asst. V.P., (812) 464-1366

PRINCIPAL OFFICE: 420 Main Street,
Evansville, IN 47708

TELEPHONE NUMBER: (812) 464-1434
FAX: (812) 464-1567
WEB: www.oldnational.com

NO. OF EMPLOYEES: 2,741

SHAREHOLDERS: 24,838

ANNUAL MEETING: In Apr.

INCORPORATED: IN, June, 1982

INSTITUTIONAL HOLDINGS:
No. of Institutions: 74
Shares Held: 9,199,013
% Held: 15.0

INDUSTRY: National commercial banks
(SIC: 6021)

TRANSFER AGENT(S): Old National
Bancorp, Evansville, IN

OLD REPUBLIC INTERNATIONAL CORPORATION

YIELD 2.0%
P/E RATIO 11.1

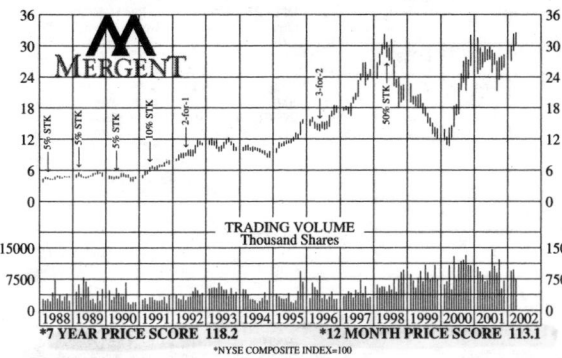

INTERIM EARNINGS (Per Share):

Qtr.	Mar.	June	Sept.	Dec.
1998	0.58	0.57	0.54	0.64
1999	0.55	0.48	0.31	0.39
2000	0.46	0.58	0.67	0.77
2001	0.70	0.76	0.69	0.74

INTERIM DIVIDENDS (Per Share):

Amt.	Decl.	Ex.	Rec.	Pay.
0.15Q	3/22/01	6/01/01	6/05/01	6/15/01
0.15Q	8/16/01	9/05/01	9/07/01	9/17/01
0.15Q	12/06/01	12/05/01	12/07/01	12/17/01
0.15Q	2/22/02	3/01/02	3/05/02	3/15/02
0.16Q	3/21/02	6/05/02	6/07/02	6/17/02

Indicated div.: $0.64 (Div. Reinv. Plan)

CAPITALIZATION (12/31/01):

	($000)	(%)
Long-Term Debt	159,000	4.8
Deferred Income Tax	376,500	11.3
Preferred Stock	300	0.0
Common & Surplus	2,783,600	83.9
Total	3,319,400	100.0

DIVIDEND ACHIEVER STATUS:

Rank: 74   10-Year Growth Rate: 13.82%
Total Years of Dividend Growth: 20

*7 YEAR PRICE SCORE 118.2   ***12 MONTH PRICE SCORE 113.1**

*NYSE COMPOSITE INDEX=100

RECENT DEVELOPMENTS: For the year ended 12/31/01, net income grew 16.6% to $346.9 million versus $297.6 million in the previous year. Total revenues grew 14.6% to $2.37 billion from $2.07 billion in the previous year. Revenues for 2001 included net realized investment gains of $29.7 million and $33.6 million, respectively. Net premiums earned grew 16.9% to $2.03 billion from $1.74 billion in 2000.

PROSPECTS: Earnings continue to benefit from positive trends in the General Insurance segment, which experienced further improvements in underwriting margins. Lower combined underwriting ratios and greater operating revenue growth also enhanced earnings of the Company's Mortgage Guaranty group. Meanwhile, accelerated growth in premiums and fees continues to drive the Company's Title segment.

BUSINESS

OLD REPUBLIC INTERNATIONAL CORPORATION is a multiple line insurance holding company with assets of approximately $7.92 billion and total capitalization of $3.32 billion as of 12/31/01. The Company's subsidiaries market, underwrite, and manage a wide range of specialty and general insurance programs in the property & liability, title, mortgage guaranty insurance and life & disability businesses. The Company primarily serves the insurance and related needs of major financial services and industrial corporations, with an emphasis on energy services, construction and forest products, transportation and housing industries. In 2001, revenues were derived as follows: general insurance, 51.0%; title insurance, 27.7%; mortgage guaranty, 18.6%; life and health insurance, 2.5% and other, 0.2%.

ANNUAL FINANCIAL DATA

	12/31/01	12/31/00	12/31/99	12/31/98	12/31/97	12/31/96	12/31/95
Earnings Per Share	2.88	2.47	1.75	2.33	2.10	① 1.64	1.61
Tang. Book Val. Per Share	22.78	20.08	19.65	17.27	15.59	14.57	13.58
Dividends Per Share	0.59	0.55	0.49	0.39	0.33	0.28	0.23
Dividend Payout %	20.5	22.3	28.0	16.6	15.9	16.9	14.1
INCOME STATEMENT (IN MILLIONS):							
Total Premium Income	1,786.8	1,550.3	1,567.2	1,568.1	1,464.6	1,360.4	1,251.7
Net Investment Income	274.7	273.9	263.2	273.1	270.8	260.5	251.9
Other Income	311.7	246.1	271.5	330.3	227.2	182.7	192.1
Total Revenues	2,373.2	2,070.3	2,101.9	2,171.5	1,962.6	1,803.6	1,695.7
Income Before Income Taxes	503.8	426.4	317.0	466.7	426.7	342.4	316.0
Income Taxes	159.6	131.0	92.9	145.7	129.1	108.5	103.5
Equity Earnings/Minority Int.	2.7	2.2	2.7	2.7	0.6	0.9	0.2
Net Income	346.9	297.5	226.8	323.8	297.6	① 234.6	212.7
Average Shs. Outstg. (000)	120,328	120,197	129,787	139,150	141,768	140,438	128,867
BALANCE SHEET (IN MILLIONS):							
Cash & Cash Equivalents	336.5	411.0	294.0	400.5	354.9	301.0	332.1
Premiums Due	1,835.3	1,660.4	1,626.3	1,572.2	1,634.3	1,677.9	1,714.4
Invst. Assets: Fixed-term	4,722.0	4,310.2	4,261.1	4,286.7	4,259.6	4,007.1	3,860.1
Invst. Assets: Equities	391.6	295.5	160.1	164.8	117.1	116.1	126.1
Invst. Assets: Total	5,472.9	5,038.9	4,739.4	4,854.2	4,720.1	4,414.0	4,325.8
Total Assets	7,919.8	7,280.9	6,937.7	7,018.9	6,922.8	6,655.6	6,592.8
Long-Term Obligations	159.0	238.0	208.3	145.1	142.9	154.0	320.5
Net Stockholders' Equity	2,783.9	2,439.3	3,078.7	2,305.4	2,153.0	1,901.1	1,667.8
Year-end Shs. Outstg. (000)	122,169	121,445	156,679	133,403	138,070	130,408	118,716
STATISTICAL RECORD:							
Return on Revenues %	14.6	14.4	10.8	14.9	15.2	13.0	12.5
Return on Equity %	12.5	12.2	7.4	14.0	13.8	12.3	12.8
Return on Assets %	4.4	4.1	3.3	4.6	4.3	3.5	3.2
Price Range	31.56-21.20	32.06-10.63	22.75-12.06	32.25-17.94	26.79-16.42	18.50-13.50	15.78-9.33
P/E Ratio	11.0-7.4	13.0-4.3	13.0-6.9	13.8-7.7	12.8-7.8	11.3-8.2	9.8-5.8
Average Yield %	2.2	2.6	2.8	1.5	1.5	1.7	1.8

Statistics are as originally reported. Adj. for stk. splits: 50% div., 5/98; 3-for-2, 5/96. ① Bef. extraord. chrg. $4.4 mill.

OFFICERS:
A. C. Zucaro, Chmn., Pres., C.E.O.
J. S. Adams, Sr. V.P., C.F.O.
S. LeRoy III, Sr. V.P., Gen. Couns., Sec.

INVESTOR CONTACT: A. C. Zucaro, Chmn., Pres., C.E.O., (312) 346-8100

PRINCIPAL OFFICE: 307 North Michigan Ave., Chicago, IL 60601

TELEPHONE NUMBER: (312) 346-8100
FAX: (312) 726-0309
WEB: www.oldrepublic.com

NO. OF EMPLOYEES: 6,135 (approx.)

SHAREHOLDERS: 3,120 (record)

ANNUAL MEETING: In May

INCORPORATED: DE, 1969

NASDAQ SYMBOL OTTR
Rec. Pr. 30.88 (3/31/02)

OTTER TAIL CORPORATION

YIELD 3.4%
P/E RATIO 18.7

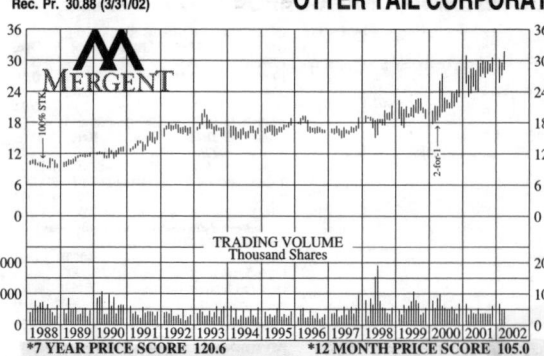

TRADING VOLUME
Thousand Shares

*7 YEAR PRICE SCORE 120.6   *12 MONTH PRICE SCORE 105.0
*NYSE COMPOSITE INDEX=100

INTERIM EARNINGS (Per Share):

Qtr.	Mar.	June	Sept.	Dec.
1997	0.43	0.21	0.31	0.34
1998	0.06	0.32	0.40	0.44
1999	0.37	0.28	0.41	0.75
2000	0.42	0.36	0.42	0.40
2001	0.45	0.34	0.43	0.43

INTERIM DIVIDENDS (Per Share):

Amt.	Decl.	Ex.	Rec.	Pay.
0.26Q	4/09/01	5/11/01	5/15/01	6/09/01
0.26Q	7/31/01	8/13/01	8/15/01	9/10/01
0.26Q	10/22/01	11/13/01	11/15/01	12/10/01
0.265Q	2/04/02	2/13/02	2/15/02	3/09/02
0.265Q	4/08/02	5/13/02	5/15/02	6/10/02

Indicated div.: $1.05 (Div. Reinv. Plan)

CAPITALIZATION (12/31/01):

	($000)	(%)
Long-Term Debt	227,360	37.4
Deferred Income Tax	85,591	14.1
Preferred Stock	15,500	2.6
Common & Surplus	279,308	46.0
Total	607,759	100.0

DIVIDEND ACHIEVER STATUS:
Rank: 269   10-Year Growth Rate: 2.66%
Total Years of Dividend Growth: 26

RECENT DEVELOPMENTS: For the year ended 12/31/01, net income climbed 6.2% to $43.6 million versus $41.0 million in 2000. Total operating revenues advanced 11.4% to $654.1 million from $586.9 million the year before. Total operating income grew 4.4% to $77.5 million compared with $74.2 million a year earlier. Strong operating results in the electric and manufacturing segments more than offset poor market conditions in the plastics division. Results for 2000 were restated to reflect the acquisitions of T.O. Plastics, Inc. on 2/28/01 and St. George Steel Fabrication, Inc. on 9/28/01. Looking ahead, the Company expects diluted earnings per share for 2002 to be in the range of $1.77 to $1.83. Also, the Company expects to complete additional acquisitions in 2002.

BUSINESS

OTTER TAIL CORPORATION (formerly Otter Tail Power Company) is an operating electric utility engaged in the production, transmission and distribution and sale of electric energy in western Minnesota, eastern North Dakota and northeastern South Dakota. In 2001, retail electric revenues from Minnesota were 50.9%; 41.2% from North Dakota; and 7.9% from South Dakota. Varistar Corporation, OTTR's diversification and growth business unit, operates manufacturing, plastics, health services, construction, transportation, telecommunications and entertainment businesses, with customers across the United States and Canada. Revenues for 2001 were derived: electric, 47.0%; plastics, 10.0%; manufacturing, 19.0%; health services, 12.0%; and other businesses, 12.0%.

ANNUAL FINANCIAL DATA

	12/31/01	12/31/00	12/31/99	12/31/98	12/31/97	12/31/96	12/31/95
Earnings Per Share	1.68	1.60	② 1.79	① 1.21	1.29	1.24	1.19
Cash Flow Per Share	3.37	3.20	3.25	2.68	2.98	2.79	2.47
Tang. Book Val. Per Share	9.31	9.06	9.32	8.58	8.07	7.64	7.39
Dividends Per Share	1.04	1.02	0.99	0.96	0.93	0.90	0.88
Dividend Payout %	61.9	63.7	55.3	79.7	72.1	72.9	73.9
INCOME STATEMENT (IN THOUSANDS):							
Total Revenues	654,132	559,445	464,577	431,078	394,279	361,739	326,329
Costs & Expenses	534,548	448,706	362,415	338,883	295,944	268,725	239,429
Depreciation & Amort.	42,100	38,249	34,796	34,965	39,302	34,788	28,602
Operating Income	77,484	72,490	67,366	57,230	59,033	58,226	58,298
Net Interest Inc./(Exp.)	d15,991	d16,583	d14,771	d15,566	d18,519	d16,601	d15,075
Income Taxes	20,083	17,515	23,915	15,140	14,308	14,040	16,159
Net Income	43,603	40,224	② 44,977	① 30,701	32,346	29,955	28,945
Cash Flow	83,710	76,595	77,545	63,308	69,290	62,385	55,189
Average Shs. Outstg.	24,832	23,928	23,831	23,596	23,278	22,364	22,360
BALANCE SHEET (IN THOUSANDS):							
Cash & Cash Equivalents	11,378	1,259	24,762	3,919	5,301	1,229	1,867
Gross Property	984,840	926,117	889,574	870,476	860,413	847,510	785,856
Accumulated Depreciation	441,863	410,188	386,618	370,290	350,647	327,672	308,174
Net Property	542,977	515,929	502,956	500,186	509,766	519,838	477,682
Total Assets	782,541	722,115	680,788	655,612	655,441	662,287	609,196
Long-Term Obligations	227,360	191,493	176,437	181,046	189,973	160,492	168,261
Net Stockholders' Equity	294,808	292,879	279,193	245,907	230,987	214,057	205,073
Year-end Shs. Outstg.	24,653	23,853	23,850	23,760	23,462	22,430	22,360
STATISTICAL RECORD:							
Operating Profit Margin %	11.8	13.0	14.5	13.3	15.0	16.1	17.9
Net Profit Margin %	6.7	7.2	9.7	7.1	8.2	8.3	8.9
Net Inc./Net Property %	8.0	7.8	8.9	6.1	6.3	5.8	6.1
Net Inc./Tot. Capital %	7.2	7.1	8.3	5.7	6.0	6.1	5.9
Return on Equity %	14.8	13.7	16.1	12.5	14.0	14.0	14.1
Accum. Depr./Gross Prop. %	44.9	44.3	43.5	42.5	40.8	38.7	39.2
Price Range	31.00-23.00	29.00-17.75	22.78-17.00	21.38-15.06	19.00-15.00	19.31-15.88	18.88-15.38
P/E Ratio	18.5-13.7	18.1-11.1	12.7-9.5	17.7-12.5	14.7-11.6	15.6-12.9	15.9-12.9
Average Yield %	3.9	4.4	5.0	5.3	5.5	5.1	5.1

Statistics are as originally reported. Adj. for stk. split: 2-for-1, 3/15/00. ① Incl. special chg. $9.5 mill. & bef. acctg. change credit $3.8 mill. ② Incl. net gain $8.1 mill.

OFFICERS:
J. C. MacFarlane, Chmn.
J. D. Erickson, Pres., C.E.O.
K. G. Moug, C.F.O., Treas.

INVESTOR CONTACT: Shareholder Services, (800) 664-1259

PRINCIPAL OFFICE: 215 S. Cascade St., P.O. Box 496, Fergus Falls, MN 56538-0496

TELEPHONE NUMBER: (218) 739-8200
FAX: (218) 739-8218
WEB: www.ottertail.com

NO. OF EMPLOYEES: 2,626

SHAREHOLDERS: 14,358

ANNUAL MEETING: In Apr.

INCORPORATED: MN, July, 1907

INSTITUTIONAL HOLDINGS:
No. of Institutions: 68
Shares Held: 5,063,318
% Held: 20.5

INDUSTRY: Electric services (SIC: 4911)

TRANSFER AGENT(S): Otter Tail Corp., Fergus Falls, MN

PACIFIC CAPITAL BANCORP

YIELD 2.9%
P/E RATIO 14.7

INTERIM EARNINGS (Per Share):

Qtr.	Mar.	June	Sept.	Dec.
1998	0.52	0.40	0.34	0.06
1999	0.59	0.37	0.40	0.43
2000	0.77	0.45	0.25	0.46
2001	0.86	0.43	0.42	0.39

INTERIM DIVIDENDS (Per Share):

Amt.	Decl.	Ex.	Rec.	Pay.
0.22Q	4/02/01	4/20/01	4/24/01	5/15/01
0.22Q	7/02/01	7/20/01	7/24/01	8/14/01
0.22Q	10/02/01	10/19/01	10/23/01	11/13/01
0.22Q	1/02/02	1/17/02	1/22/02	2/12/02
0.22Q	4/01/02	4/19/02	4/23/02	5/14/02

Indicated div.: $0.88

CAPITALIZATION (12/31/01):

	($000)	(%)
Total Deposits	3,365,575	86.7
Long-Term Debt	188,331	4.9
Common & Surplus	325,876	8.4
Total	3,879,782	100.0

DIVIDEND ACHIEVER STATUS:
Rank: 28   10-Year Growth Rate: 18.85%
Total Years of Dividend Growth: 32

TRADING VOLUME
Thousand Shares

7 YEAR PRICE SCORE N/A   **12 MONTH PRICE SCORE 106.6**
NYSE COMPOSITE INDEX=100

RECENT DEVELOPMENTS: For the year ended 12/31/01, net income increased 9.0% to $56.1 million compared with $51.5 million in 2000. Earnings for 2001 benefited from strong loan demand, especially from strong loan originations in the consumer, commercial and residential real estate segments of the portfolio. Net interest income grew 8.0% to $193.9 million from $179.4 million the year before. Provision for credit losses increased 84.7% to $26.7 million from $14.4 million a year earlier. Total interest income was $291.1 million versus $290.0 million in 2000. Total other income jumped 30.6% to $65.7 million from $50.3 million a year earlier. Total other operating expenses rose 8.5% to $143.2 million from $132.0 million in 2000. Looking ahead, SABB expects diluted earnings per share for fiscal 2002 to be in the range of $2.30 to $2.36. SABB's provision for credit losses in 2002 is expected to range from $33.0 million to $36.0 million, with a greater portion taken in the first half of the year.

BUSINESS

PACIFIC CAPITAL BANCORP (formerly Santa Barbara Bancorp) is a bank holding company. In 1998, Santa Barbara Bancorp merged with Pacific Capital Bancorp. Santa Barbara Bancorp was the surviving company, but took the name of Pacific Capital Bancorp. SABB's three banking subsidiaries are: Santa Barbara Bank and Trust (SBB&T), First National Bank of Central California (FNB) and Los Robles Bank (LRB). As of 12/31/01, SBB&T had grown to 29 banking offices with loan, trust and escrow offices. FNB has 12 banking offices in Monterey, Santa Cruz, Santa Clara and San Benito counties. LRB has three offices. During the fourth quarter of 2001, the Company applied for and received approval for a single national banking charter. The Company anticipates that SBB&T and FNB will be merged into this single charger at the end of the first quarter of 2002.

ANNUAL FINANCIAL DATA

	12/31/01	12/31/00	12/31/99	12/31/98	12/31/97	12/31/96	12/31/95
Earnings Per Share	2.11	1.93	1.79	1.21	1.29	1.03	0.68
Tang. Book Val. Per Share	12.43	11.19	9.55	8.84	7.75	7.09	6.58
Dividends Per Share	0.88	0.80	0.72	0.61	0.46	0.33	0.27
Dividend Payout %	41.7	41.4	40.2	50.4	35.7	32.0	39.2
INCOME STATEMENT (IN MILLIONS):							
Total Interest Income	291.1	290.9	211.6	193.5	114.9	89.6	82.2
Total Interest Expense	97.2	110.5	6.6	3.3	43.2	35.0	33.6
Net Interest Income	193.9	180.4	205.1	190.2	71.7	54.5	48.6
Provision for Loan Losses	26.7	14.4	6.4	9.1	7.0	4.3	9.9
Non-Interest Income	65.7	49.4	41.6	36.0	25.1	18.9	17.7
Non-Interest Expense	143.2	132.0	110.4	103.7	60.1	46.6	42.0
Income Before Taxes	89.8	83.4	129.9	113.3	29.8	22.6	14.4
Net Income	56.1	51.5	105.6	94.3	20.1	15.7	10.4
Average Shs. Outstg. (000)	26,639	26,609	24,790	24,447	15,584	15,270	15,354
BALANCE SHEET (IN MILLIONS):							
Cash & Due from Banks	136.5	176.3	121.5	114.2	67.8	51.2	74.7
Securities Avail. for Sale	72.0	139.3	153.3	194.8	222.4	276.4	0.5
Total Loans & Leases	2,799.1	2,517.1	1,981.9	1,582.8	881.5	684.2	558.8
Allowance for Credit Losses	48.9	35.1	28.7	29.3	21.1	16.6	12.3
Net Loans & Leases	2,750.2	2,482.0	1,953.2	1,553.5	860.4	667.6	546.5
Total Assets	3,960.9	3,677.6	2,879.3	2,649.4	1,592.4	1,301.3	1,212.4
Total Deposits	3,365.6	3,102.8	2,440.2	2,329.7	1,404.2	1,113.1	1,054.0
Long-Term Obligations	188.3	129.7	98.8	45.0	39.0	39.0	1.2
Total Liabilities	3,635.1	3,381.4	2,644.7	2,435.4	1,474.2	1,193.7	1,111.4
Net Stockholders' Equity	325.9	296.3	234.6	214.0	118.2	107.6	101.0
Year-end Shs. Outstg. (000)	26,207	26,481	24,554	24,209	15,242	15,176	15,358
STATISTICAL RECORD:							
Return on Equity %	17.2	17.4	45.0	44.1	17.0	14.6	10.3
Return on Assets %	1.4	1.4	3.7	3.6	1.3	1.2	0.9
Equity/Assets %	8.2	8.1	8.1	8.1	7.4	8.3	8.3
Non-Int. Exp./Tot. Inc. %	55.1	57.4	44.7	45.9	62.0	63.4	63.8
Price Range	30.62-24.09	30.75-21.38	38.00-20.13	34.38-22.00	24.50-13.75	14.38-9.88	11.17-9.08
P/E Ratio	14.5-11.4	15.9-11.1	21.2-11.2	28.4-18.2	19.0-10.7	14.0-9.6	16.4-13.4
Average Yield %	3.2	3.1	2.5	2.2	2.4	2.7	2.6

Statistics are as originally reported. Adj. for stk. split: 2-for-1, 4/98; 3-for-2, 2/96

OFFICERS:
D. W. Spainhour, Chmn.
C. C. Larson, Vice-Chmn.
D. V. Horton, Vice-Chmn.
W. S. Thomas Jr., Pres., C.E.O.

INVESTOR CONTACT: Debbie Lewis, V.P.,
(805) 884-6680

PRINCIPAL OFFICE: 200 E. Carrillo Street,
Suite 300, Santa Barbara, CA 93101

TELEPHONE NUMBER: (805) 564-6300
FAX: (805) 564-6293
WEB: www.pcbancorp.com

NO. OF EMPLOYEES: 1,200 (approx.)

SHAREHOLDERS: 10,000 (approx.)

ANNUAL MEETING: In Apr.

INCORPORATED: CA, July, 1982

INSTITUTIONAL HOLDINGS:
No. of Institutions: 70
Shares Held: 5,568,054
% Held: 21.2

INDUSTRY: State commercial banks (SIC: 6022)

TRANSFER AGENT(S): Mellon Investor Services, South Hackensack, NJ

NYSE SYMBOL BOH
Rec. Pr. 26.06 (3/31/02)

PACIFIC CENTURY FINANCIAL (BANK OF HAWAII CORP.)

YIELD 2.8%
P/E RATIO 18.0

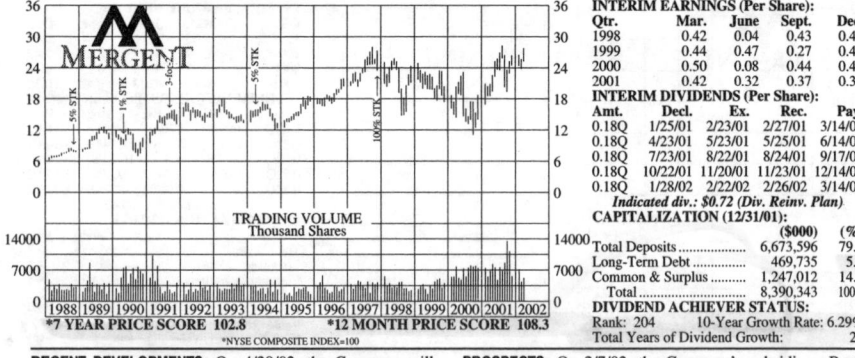

TRADING VOLUME Thousand Shares

*7 YEAR PRICE SCORE 102.8   *12 MONTH PRICE SCORE 108.3
*NYSE COMPOSITE INDEX=100

INTERIM EARNINGS (Per Share):

Qtr.	Mar.	June	Sept.	Dec.
1998	0.42	0.04	0.43	0.43
1999	0.44	0.47	0.27	0.47
2000	0.50	0.08	0.44	0.41
2001	0.42	0.32	0.37	0.34

INTERIM DIVIDENDS (Per Share):

Amt.	Decl.	Ex.	Rec.	Pay.
0.18Q	1/25/01	2/23/01	2/27/01	3/14/01
0.18Q	4/23/01	5/23/01	5/25/01	6/14/01
0.18Q	7/23/01	8/22/01	8/24/01	9/17/01
0.18Q	10/22/01	11/20/01	11/23/01	12/14/01
0.18Q	1/28/02	2/22/02	2/26/02	3/14/02

Indicated div.: $0.72 (Div. Reinv. Plan)

CAPITALIZATION (12/31/01):

	($000)	(%)
Total Deposits	6,673,596	79.5
Long-Term Debt	469,735	5.6
Common & Surplus	1,247,012	14.9
Total	8,390,343	100.0

DIVIDEND ACHIEVER STATUS:
Rank: 204   10-Year Growth Rate: 6.29%
Total Years of Dividend Growth: 24

RECENT DEVELOPMENTS: On 4/29/02, the Company will change its name to Bank of Hawaii Corporation. For the year ended 12/31/01, net income rose 3.6% to $117.8 million from $113.7 million in 2000. Earnings for 2001 included a pre-tax net gain of $173.4 million on the sale of banking operations and venture investments loss and pre-tax restructuring costs of $104.8 million. Earnings for 2000 included a nonrecurring pre-tax gain of $11.9 million. Net interest income fell 13.5% to $459.7 million.

PROSPECTS: On 2/7/02, the Company's subsidiary, Bank of Hawaii, announced its intention to divest its operations, consisting of four branches, in the Republic of the Marshall Islands and the Federated States of Micronedi by 6/30/02. In December 2001, Bank of Hawaii completed the sales of its Fiji operation as well as its operations in Papua New Guinea and Vanuatu to Australia-based ANZ for approximately $50.0 million.

BUSINESS

PACIFIC CENTURY FINANCIAL CORPORATION (new name as of 4/29/02: BANK OF HAWAII CORPORATION), with assets of $10.63 billion as of 12/31/01, is a bank holding company that was initially organized as Hawaii Bancorporation, Inc. In 1979, it changed its name to Bancorp Hawaii, Inc., and in 1997 to Pacific Century Financial Corp. BOH provides a broad range of products and services to businesses, consumers and governments in Hawaii, the West Pacific, and American Samoa. In a strategic shift in 2001, BOH sold its credit card portfolio to American Express Centurion Bank and its investment in the Bank of Queensland Ltd. in Australia, and closed branches in Hong Kong, Tokyo, Taipei, Seoul, Singapore, California and Arizona. BOH's principal subsidiary is the Bank of Hawaii.

ANNUAL FINANCIAL DATA

	12/31/01	12/31/00	12/31/99	12/31/98	12/31/97	12/31/96	12/31/95
Earnings Per Share	③ 1.46	② 1.42	① 1.64	① 1.32	1.72	1.63	1.45
Tang. Book Val. Per Share	16.16	13.93	12.57	12.07	11.47	12.13	11.69
Dividends Per Share	0.72	0.71	0.68	0.66	0.63	0.58	0.54
Dividend Payout %	49.3	50.0	41.5	49.8	36.3	35.6	37.4
INCOME STATEMENT (IN MILLIONS):							
Total Interest Income	828.3	1,057.5	1,026.5	1,099.8	1,062.6	982.1	896.7
Total Interest Expense	368.6	501.3	451.8	523.2	526.3	499.8	468.2
Net Interest Income	459.7	556.2	574.7	576.6	536.3	482.3	428.5
Provision for Loan Losses	74.3	142.9	60.9	84.0	30.3	22.2	17.0
Non-Interest Income	279.2	263.4	265.6	211.8	187.8	164.5	146.4
Non-Interest Expense	584.3	496.4	553.2	540.3	474.3	419.8	363.0
Income Before Taxes	240.0	180.0	225.7	163.6	218.0	203.3	193.8
Net Income	③ 117.8	② 113.7	① 133.0	① 107.0	139.5	133.1	121.8
Average Shs. Outstg. (000)	80,578	79,813	80,045	81,142	80,946	81,596	84,054
BALANCE SHEET (IN MILLIONS):							
Cash & Due from Banks	406.0	524.0	639.9	564.2	795.3	581.2	469.0
Securities Avail. for Sale	2,001.4	2,507.1	2,542.2	3,018.4	2,651.3	2,306.6	2,194.0
Total Loans & Leases	5,652.5	9,668.3	9,717.6	9,854.0	9,498.4	8,699.3	8,152.4
Allowance for Credit Losses	159.0	500.2	436.7	437.2	384.1	351.4	299.4
Net Loans & Leases	5,493.5	9,168.1	9,280.8	9,416.8	9,114.3	8,347.9	7,853.0
Total Assets	10,171.1	14,013.8	14,440.3	15,016.6	14,995.5	14,009.2	13,206.8
Total Deposits	6,673.6	9,080.6	9,394.2	9,576.3	9,621.3	8,684.1	7,576.8
Long-Term Obligations	469.7	997.2	727.7	585.6	705.8	932.1	1,063.4
Total Liabilities	9,380.8	12,712.5	13,228.0	13,831.0	13,878.3	12,943.0	12,152.3
Net Stockholders' Equity	1,247.0	1,301.4	1,212.3	1,185.6	1,117.2	1,066.1	1,054.4
Year-end Shs. Outstg. (000)	73,218	79,612	80,036	80,326	79,685	79,918	82,682
STATISTICAL RECORD:							
Return on Equity %	9.4	8.7	11.0	9.0	12.5	12.5	11.6
Return on Assets %	1.2	0.8	0.9	0.7	0.9	1.0	0.9
Equity/Assets %	12.3	9.3	8.4	7.9	7.5	7.6	8.0
Non-Int. Exp./Tot. Inc. %	82.8	60.4	67.0	68.9	65.8	65.0	63.4
Price Range	28.30-16.06	23.19-11.06	24.94-17.38	25.88-14.75	28.06-20.31	22.00-16.56	18.56-12.44
P/E Ratio	19.4-11.0	16.3-7.8	15.2-10.6	19.6-11.2	16.3-11.8	13.5-10.2	12.8-8.6
Average Yield %	4.5	4.1	3.2	3.2	2.6	3.0	3.5

Statistics are as originally reported. Adj. for stk. split: 100% div., 12/97. ① Incl. a restructuring charge of $22.5 mill., 1999; $19.4 mill., 1998. ② Incl. a pre-tax gain of $11.9 mill. on the settlement of pension obligations. ③ Incl. a pre-tax gain of $173.4 mill. on the sale of banking ops. & venture invest. loss & pre-tax restruct. & oth. rel. costs of $104.8 mill.

OFFICERS:
M. E. O'Neill, Chmn., C.E.O.
A. R. Landon, Vice-Chmn., C.F.O.
A. T. Kuioka, Vice-Chmn.

INVESTOR CONTACT: Cindy Wyrick, Investor Relations, (808) 537-8430

PRINCIPAL OFFICE: 130 Merchant Street, Honolulu, HI 96813

TELEPHONE NUMBER: (808) 537-8430
FAX: (808) 521-7602
WEB: www.boh.com
NO. OF EMPLOYEES: 3,175 (avg.)
SHAREHOLDERS: 10,918
ANNUAL MEETING: In Apr.
INCORPORATED: HI, Aug., 1971; reincorp., DE, Apr., 1998

INSTITUTIONAL HOLDINGS:
No. of Institutions: 175
Shares Held: 50,296,524
% Held: 68.6

INDUSTRY: State commercial banks (SIC: 6022)

TRANSFER AGENT(S): Continental Stock Transfer & Trust Company, New York, NY

PALL CORPORATION

YIELD 3.3%
P/E RATIO 25.0

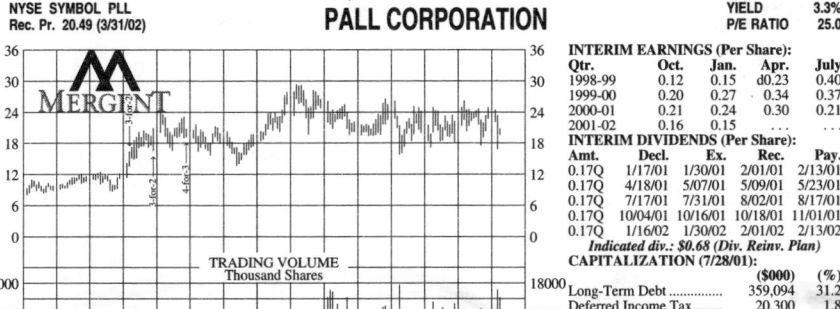

INTERIM EARNINGS (Per Share):

Qtr.	Oct.	Jan.	Apr.	July
1998-99	0.12	0.15	d0.23	0.40
1999-00	0.20	0.27	0.34	0.37
2000-01	0.21	0.24	0.30	0.21
2001-02	0.16	0.15	...	...

INTERIM DIVIDENDS (Per Share):

Amt.	Decl.	Ex.	Rec.	Pay.
0.17Q	1/17/01	1/30/01	2/01/01	2/13/01
0.17Q	4/18/01	5/07/01	5/09/01	5/23/01
0.17Q	7/17/01	7/31/01	8/02/01	8/17/01
0.17Q	10/04/01	10/16/01	10/18/01	11/01/01
0.17Q	1/16/02	1/30/02	2/01/02	2/13/02

Indicated div.: $0.68 (Div. Reinv. Plan)

CAPITALIZATION (7/28/01):

	($000)	(%)
Long-Term Debt	359,094	31.2
Deferred Income Tax	20,300	1.8
Common & Surplus	770,042	67.0
Total	1,149,436	100.0

DIVIDEND ACHIEVER STATUS:

Rank: 99   10-Year Growth Rate: 11.95%
Total Years of Dividend Growth: 21

TRADING VOLUME
Thousand Shares

| 1988 | 1989 | 1990 | 1991 | 1992 | 1993 | 1994 | 1995 | 1996 | 1997 | 1998 | 1999 | 2000 | 2001 | 2002 |

*7 YEAR PRICE SCORE 84.7   ***12 MONTH PRICE SCORE 93.6**
*NYSE COMPOSITE INDEX=100

RECENT DEVELOPMENTS: For the quarter ended 1/26/02, net income declined 38.4% to $18.4 million compared with the corresponding 2001 period. The decline in earnings reflected poor market conditions in the Company's Industrial segment. Net sales decreased 6.3% to $285.4 million. Total Life Sciences sales were $141.1 million compared with $140.7 million in 2000. Total Industrial sales declined 12.0% to $144.4 million.

PROSPECTS: The Company expects operating performance to remain modest until the microelectronics market and semiconductor manufacturers recover, which is expected to take place by early summer 2002. Meanwhile, the Company's Life Sciences Group should continue to perform well in the near-term, bolstered by a variety of actions taken to improve profitability.

BUSINESS

PALL CORPORATION is a supplier of fine filters mainly made by the Company using its proprietary filter media, and other fluid clarification and separations equipment for the removal of solid, liquid and gaseous contaminants from a wide variety of liquids and gases. The Company provides products for use in high-growth applications such as genomics, proteomics and biotechnology; in transfusion medicine; semiconductor; water; aerospace and a host of other industries. PLL is comprised of two operating segments: Life Sciences and Industrial. The Life Sciences segment is comprised of three sub-segments: Biosciences, BioPharmaceuticals and Medical. The Industrial sub-segments are Aerospace, Microelectronics and General Industrial.

ANNUAL FINANCIAL DATA

	7/28/01	7/29/00	7/31/99	8/1/98	8/2/97	8/3/96	7/29/95
Earnings Per Share	⑤ 0.95	1.18	② 0.41	④ 0.75	③ 0.53	1.21	① 1.04
Cash Flow Per Share	1.53	1.75	1.01	1.33	1.03	1.67	1.43
Tang. Book Val. Per Share	6.29	6.18	5.88	6.18	6.48	6.37	5.70
Dividends Per Share	0.68	0.66	0.64	0.62	0.56	0.49	0.42
Dividend Payout %	71.6	55.9	156.1	82.7	105.6	40.5	40.4

INCOME STATEMENT (IN MILLIONS):

Total Revenues	1,235.4	1,224.1	1,147.1	1,087.3	1,062.0	967.4	829.3
Costs & Expenses	997.0	949.7	1,000.4	871.4	910.2	706.0	606.1
Depreciation & Amort.	71.5	72.0	74.8	73.1	62.8	53.1	46.1
Operating Income	167.0	202.5	71.9	142.9	89.0	208.3	177.2
Net Interest Inc./(Exp.)	d16.6	d14.1	d13.0	d7.9	d2.8	d10.4	d9.5
Income Before Income Taxes	150.3	188.4	58.9	135.0	86.1	197.9	167.7
Income Taxes	32.3	41.8	7.4	41.4	18.8	59.4	48.5
Net Income	⑤ 118.0	146.6	② 51.5	④ 93.6	③ 67.3	138.5	① 119.2
Cash Flow	189.5	218.6	126.3	166.7	130.1	191.6	165.3
Average Shs. Outstg. (000)	123,735	124,709	124,800	125,681	126,319	114,839	115,184

BALANCE SHEET (IN MILLIONS):

Cash & Cash Equivalents	201.5	141.7	137.2	28.9	55.5	106.0	110.8
Total Current Assets	779.0	753.2	744.2	602.5	606.6	581.2	524.8
Net Property	503.0	503.8	507.0	520.6	504.0	463.9	427.9
Total Assets	1,548.5	1,507.3	1,488.3	1,346.9	1,265.6	1,185.0	1,074.9
Total Current Liabilities	313.8	437.7	558.3	394.1	301.0	303.2	287.7
Long-Term Obligations	359.1	223.9	116.8	111.5	62.1	46.7	68.8
Net Stockholders' Equity	770.0	761.3	730.7	765.6	824.8	732.3	651.8
Net Working Capital	465.1	315.5	185.9	208.4	305.6	251.0	237.0
Year-end Shs. Outstg. (000)	122,383	123,118	124,210	123,919	127,362	114,976	114,431

STATISTICAL RECORD:

Operating Profit Margin %	13.5	16.5	6.3	13.1	8.4	21.5	21.4
Net Profit Margin %	9.6	12.0	4.5	8.6	6.3	14.3	14.4
Return on Equity %	15.3	19.3	7.0	12.2	8.2	18.9	18.3
Return on Assets %	7.6	9.7	3.5	7.0	5.3	11.7	11.1
Debt/Total Assets %	23.2	14.9	7.8	8.3	4.9	3.9	6.4
Price Range	26.25-17.50	25.00-17.13	26.19-15.75	26.63-19.38	26.13-19.50	29.38-19.63	27.88-18.38
P/E Ratio	27.6-18.4	21.2-14.5	63.9-38.4	35.5-25.8	49.3-36.8	24.3-16.2	26.8-17.7
Average Yield %	3.1	3.1	3.1	2.7	2.5	2.0	1.8

Statistics are as originally reported. ① Bef. acctg. change chrg. $780,000. ② Incl. restruct. chrg. $89.4 mill., 1999; $9.9 mill., 2000. ③ Incl. merger (Gelman Sciences) restruct. chrgs. & other one-time chrgs. of $95.9 mill. ④ Incl. non-recurr. income of $5.0 mill. from litigation settlement & a chrg. of $27.0 mill. acq. related Rochem chrg. ⑤ Incl. restruct. & other chrgs. of $17.2 mill.

OFFICERS:
E. Krasnoff, Chmn., C.E.O.
J. Hayward-Surry, Pres.
J. Adamovich, Jr., V.P., C.F.O., Treas.

INVESTOR CONTACT: Diane Foster, Investor Relations, (516) 484-3600 ext. 6109

PRINCIPAL OFFICE: 2200 Northern Boulevard, East Hills, NY 11548

TELEPHONE NUMBER: (516) 484-5400
FAX: (516) 484-3649
WEB: www.pall.com

NO. OF EMPLOYEES: 9,400 (approx.)

SHAREHOLDERS: 5,600 (approx.)

ANNUAL MEETING: In Nov.

INCORPORATED: NY, July, 1946

INSTITUTIONAL HOLDINGS:
No. of Institutions: 290
Shares Held: 92,784,598
% Held: 75.8

INDUSTRY: General industrial machinery, nec (SIC: 3569)

TRANSFER AGENT(S): EquiServe, L.P. Providence, Rhode Island

PARK NATIONAL CORPORATION

INTERIM EARNINGS (Per Share):

Qtr.	Mar.	June	Sept.	Dec.
1997	1.02	1.01	1.10	0.93
1998	1.12	1.17	1.15	0.99
1999	1.24	1.29	1.27	1.06
2000	1.27	1.33	1.30	1.20
2001	1.34	1.45	1.45	1.34

INTERIM DIVIDENDS (Per Share):

Amt.	Decl.	Ex.	Rec.	Pay.
0.71Q	4/16/01	5/23/01	5/25/01	6/08/01
0.71Q	7/16/01	8/22/01	8/24/01	9/10/01
0.76Q	11/19/01	12/19/01	12/21/01	1/02/02
0.76Q	1/22/02	2/20/02	2/22/02	3/08/02

Indicated div.: $3.04 (Div. Reinv. Plan)

CAPITALIZATION (12/31/01):

	($000)	(%)
Total Deposits	3,314,203	79.4
Long-Term Debt	392,540	9.4
Common & Surplus	468,346	11.2
Total	4,175,089	100.0

DIVIDEND ACHIEVER STATUS:
Rank: 44   10-Year Growth Rate: 16.59%
Total Years of Dividend Growth: 14

TRADING VOLUME
Thousand Shares

*7 YEAR PRICE SCORE 103.0   *12 MONTH PRICE SCORE 107.8
*NYSE COMPOSITE INDEX=100

RECENT DEVELOPMENTS: For the year ended 12/31/01, net income increased 14.3% to $78.4 million compared with $68.5 million in the corresponding year-earlier period. Total interest income slipped to $320.3 million from $323.1 million the previous year; however, total interest expense declined 10.5% to $127.4 million, which resulted in a 6.7% rise in net interest income to $192.9 million. Provision for loan losses declined 11.7% to $13.1 million versus $14.8 million a year earlier. Total other income climbed 20.8% to $45.2 million, reflecting increased service charges on deposit accounts due to both fee increases and increases in the number of transaction accounts and higher income from fiduciary activities. PRK also benefited from increased fees from check card and ATM services. PRK reported a gain of $140,000 on the sale of securities in 2001 versus a loss of $889,000 in 2000. Results for 2000 have been restated to include the financial results of Security Banc Corporation and its subsidiaries, which were acquired effective 3/23/01 in a pooling-of-interests transaction.

BUSINESS

PARK NATIONAL CORPORATION is a bank holding company with $4.57 billion in total assets at 12/31/01. Through its subsidiaries, the Company is engaged in the commercial banking and trust business, generally in small to medium population Ohio communities. The Company's subsidiaries provide the following principle services: the acceptance of deposits for demand, savings and time accounts; commercial, industrial, consumer and real estate lending, including installment loans, credit cards, home equity lines of credit and commercial and auto leasing; trust services; cash management; safe deposit operations; electronic funds transfers; and a variety of additional banking-related services. As of 12/31/01, the Company had 107 financial services offices and a network of 109 automatic teller machines operating in 26 Ohio counties. On 3/23/01, the Company acquired Security Banc Corporation.

ANNUAL FINANCIAL DATA

	12/31/01	12/31/00	12/31/99	12/31/98	12/31/97	12/31/96	12/31/95
Earnings Per Share	5.58	5.10	4.67	4.22	3.81	3.43	2.94
Tang. Book Val. Per Share	33.60	29.66	24.60	23.50	22.52	19.89	18.21
Dividends Per Share	2.84	2.60	2.29	1.83	1.52	1.33	1.14
Dividend Payout %	50.9	51.0	48.9	43.3	40.0	38.9	38.8
INCOME STATEMENT (IN MILLIONS)							
Total Interest Income	320.3	249.3	191.9	185.9	180.5	122.3	113.2
Total Interest Expense	127.4	110.4	76.1	78.3	77.0	49.3	46.8
Net Interest Income	192.9	138.9	115.9	107.7	103.5	73.0	66.4
Provision for Loan Losses	13.1	8.7	7.0	6.8	7.0	4.5	4.7
Non-Interest Income	45.2	29.7	23.1	24.0	20.5	13.1	12.9
Non-Interest Expense	114.2	82.9	67.5	64.3	62.4	43.2	41.6
Income Before Taxes	110.9	76.9	64.4	60.5	54.6	38.3	33.0
Net Income	78.4	55.4	45.7	41.6	37.7	25.7	22.1
Average Shs. Outstg. (000)	14,051	10,877	9,811	9,856	9,908	7,494	7,524
BALANCE SHEET (IN MILLIONS):							
Cash & Due from Banks	169.1	109.9	104.2	100.3	93.6	61.5	92.8
Total Loans & Leases	2,806.3	2,293.0	1,850.7	1,654.0	1,603.6	1,123.6	1,036.3
Allowance for Credit Losses	70.5	63.7	58.0	50.5	47.3	38.8	36.6
Net Loans & Leases	2,735.8	2,229.3	1,792.7	1,603.5	1,556.3	1,084.8	999.7
Total Assets	4,569.5	3,211.1	2,634.3	2,460.8	2,288.4	1,614.8	1,476.2
Total Deposits	3,314.2	2,415.6	2,015.1	1,939.8	1,855.0	1,336.6	1,206.5
Long-Term Obligations	392.5	181.6	0.1	8.4	30.9	. . .	. . .
Total Liabilities	4,101.2	2,891.3	2,394.8	2,225.1	2,066.3	1,465.8	1,339.8
Net Stockholders' Equity	468.3	319.8	239.6	235.7	222.1	149.0	136.4
Year-end Shs. Outstg. (000)	13,941	10,779	9,740	10,031	9,862	7,490	7,492
STATISTICAL RECORD:							
Return on Equity %	16.7	17.3	19.1	17.6	17.0	17.2	16.2
Return on Assets %	1.7	1.7	1.7	1.7	1.6	1.6	1.5
Equity/Assets %	10.2	10.0	9.1	9.6	9.7	9.2	9.2
Non-Int. Exp./Tot. Inc. %	47.9	49.2	48.6	48.9	50.3	50.2	52.5
Price Range	102.50-74.50	106.00-77.50	116.00-86.67	102.62-80.95	93.87-48.69	50.60-44.17	51.91-40.36
P/E Ratio	18.4-13.4	20.8-15.2	24.8-18.6	24.3-19.2	24.6-12.8	14.8-12.9	17.6-13.7
Average Yield %	3.2	2.8	2.3	2.0	2.1	2.8	2.5

Statistics are as originally reported. Adj. for 5% stk. div. 12/99.

OFFICERS:
W. T. McConnell, Chmn.
H. O. Egger, Vice Chmn.
C. D. DeLawder, Pres., C.E.O.
INVESTOR CONTACT: David C. Bowers, Secretary, (740) 349-3708
PRINCIPAL OFFICE: 50 North Third Street, P.O. Box 3500, Newark, OH 43058-3500

TELEPHONE NUMBER: (740) 349-8451
FAX: (740) 349-3765
WEB: www.parknationalcorp.com
NO. OF EMPLOYEES: 1,551
SHAREHOLDERS: 5,092
ANNUAL MEETING: In Apr.
INCORPORATED: DE, July, 1986; reincorp., OH, 1992

INSTITUTIONAL HOLDINGS:
No. of Institutions: 58
Shares Held: 3,243,880
% Held: 23.3
INDUSTRY: National commercial banks (SIC: 6021)
TRANSFER AGENT(S): First-Knox National Bank, Mount Vernon, OH

PAYCHEX, INC.

YIELD 1.1%
P/E RATIO 54.4

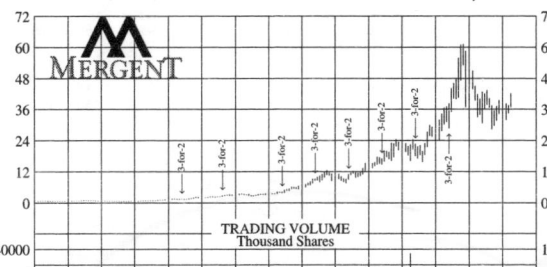

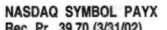

TRADING VOLUME
Thousand Shares

| | 1988 | 1989 | 1990 | 1991 | 1992 | 1993 | 1994 | 1995 | 1996 | 1997 | 1998 | 1999 | 2000 | 2001 | 2002 |

*7 YEAR PRICE SCORE 144.9   ***12 MONTH PRICE SCORE 106.4**
*NYSE COMPOSITE INDEX=100

INTERIM EARNINGS (Per Share):

Qtr.	Aug.	Nov.	Feb.	May
1997-98	0.06	0.07	0.07	0.07
1998-99	0.09	0.09	0.10	0.10
1999-00	0.11	0.12	0.13	0.14
2000-01	0.16	0.16	0.18	0.18
2001-02	0.19	0.18	0.18	...

INTERIM DIVIDENDS (Per Share):

Amt.	Decl.	Ex.	Rec.	Pay.
0.09Q	4/12/01	4/27/01	5/01/01	5/15/01
0.09Q	7/12/01	7/30/01	8/01/01	8/15/01
0.11Q	10/11/01	10/30/01	11/01/01	11/15/01
0.11Q	1/11/02	1/30/02	2/01/02	2/15/02
0.11Q	4/11/02	4/29/02	5/01/02	5/15/02

Indicated div.: $0.44 (Div. Reinv. Plan)

CAPITALIZATION (5/31/01):

	($000)	(%)
Common & Surplus	757,842	100.0
Total	757,842	100.0

DIVIDEND ACHIEVER STATUS:

Rank: 1   10-Year Growth Rate: 46.77%
Total Years of Dividend Growth: 13

RECENT DEVELOPMENTS: For the third quarter ended 2/28/02, net income inched up to $67.0 million compared with $66.4 million in the equivalent period of the previous year. Earnings were negatively affected by volatile interest rates and a lower number of checks per client, as existing clients reduce their work forces. Total revenues increased 5.9% to $242.8 million from $229.3 million in the prior-year quarter. Payroll service revenues advanced 10.1% to $195.8 million from $177.8 million, while human resource

and benefits revenue jumped 26.3% to $32.2 million from $25.5 million the year before. Interest on funds held for clients dropped 42.3% to $14.8 million from $25.9 million in the year-earlier period. Operating income increased slightly to $87.2 million from $86.9 million in 2000. Net investment income climbed 16.5% to $8.4 million from $7.2 million in the previous year. Looking ahead, the Company anticipates total revenue growth in the range of 9.0% to 10.0% for the full-year 2002.

BUSINESS

PAYCHEX, INC. is a national provider of payroll, human resource and benefits services for small-to-medium-sized businesses, those fewer than 200 employees. The Company is based in Rochester, New York and has more than 100 locations around the country, serving hundreds of thousands of clients nationwide. In 2001, the Company generated more than $870.0 million in service revenues. Services available to clients include 401(k) record keeping, workers' compensation administration, larger company payroll processing, and human resource outsourcing, called Paychex Administrative Services.

ANNUAL FINANCIAL DATA

	5/31/01	5/31/00	5/31/99	5/31/98	5/31/97	5/31/96	5/31/95
Earnings Per Share	0.68	0.51	0.37	0.28	0.21	0.15	0.12
Cash Flow Per Share	0.78	0.60	0.46	0.35	0.27	0.19	0.15
Tang. Book Val. Per Share	2.00	1.50	1.17	0.90	0.69	0.55	0.41
Dividends Per Share	0.27	0.18	0.12	0.08	0.05	0.04	0.02
Dividend Payout %	39.7	35.3	32.2	29.0	25.8	23.4	20.6
INCOME STATEMENT (IN MILLIONS):							
Total Revenues	869.9	728.1	597.3	493.7	734.7	325.3	267.2
Costs & Expenses	494.0	432.7	376.8	331.7	616.6	243.8	205.1
Depreciation & Amort.	39.1	36.5	32.9	27.3	21.4	13.9	11.0
Operating Income	336.7	258.9	187.6	134.7	96.6	67.5	51.0
Net Interest Inc./(Exp.)	27.3	16.5	12.6	9.5	7.0	5.2	3.4
Income Before Income Taxes	364.0	275.4	200.1	144.2	103.7	72.7	54.4
Income Taxes	109.1	85.4	61.0	42.0	28.5	20.4	15.3
Net Income	254.9	190.0	139.1	102.2	75.2	52.3	39.0
Cash Flow	294.0	226.5	172.0	129.5	96.6	66.3	50.1
Average Shs. Outstg. (000)	377,510	375,081	373,182	370,829	364,503	346,032	341,157
BALANCE SHEET (IN MILLIONS):							
Cash & Cash Equivalents	2,655.0	2,236.5	1,704.8	1,405.0	1,079.6	117.2	83.7
Total Current Assets	2,791.3	2,362.6	1,793.1	1,478.8	1,140.7	165.3	124.2
Net Property	96.1	75.4	65.9	64.7	54.2	50.0	43.7
Total Assets	2,907.2	2,455.6	1,873.1	1,549.8	1,201.3	220.2	168.4
Total Current Liabilities	2,143.8	1,886.9	1,432.3	1,215.7	946.0	28.1	26.7
Long-Term Obligations	...	...	...	...	...	...	0.5
Net Stockholders' Equity	757.8	563.4	435.8	329.6	251.5	190.8	139.9
Net Working Capital	647.4	475.6	360.8	263.1	194.6	137.2	97.6
Year-end Shs. Outstg. (000)	373,647	371,769	369,489	367,173	366,252	347,784	341,962
STATISTICAL RECORD:							
Operating Profit Margin %	38.7	35.6	31.4	27.3	13.2	20.8	19.1
Net Profit Margin %	29.3	26.1	23.3	20.7	10.2	16.1	14.6
Return on Equity %	33.6	33.7	31.9	31.0	29.9	27.4	27.9
Return on Assets %	8.8	7.7	7.4	6.6	6.3	23.8	23.2
Debt/Total Assets %	...	...	...	...	...	...	0.3
Price Range	61.25-24.17	29.92-15.71	24.47-13.37	15.33-7.56	12.57-6.03	6.57-3.39	3.58-2.50
P/E Ratio	90.1-35.5	58.7-30.8	65.6-35.8	55.5-27.4	60.7-29.1	43.2-22.3	31.1-21.7
Average Yield %	0.6	0.8	0.6	0.7	0.6	0.7	0.8

Statistics are as originally reported. Adj. for stk. splits: 3-for-2, 5/15/00; 5/21/99; 5/22/98; 5/29/97; 5/23/96; 5/25/95.

OFFICERS:
B. T. Golisano, Chmn., Pres., C.E.O.
J. M. Morphy, V.P., C.F.O., Sec.

INVESTOR CONTACT: Jan Shuler, Investor Relations, (585) 383-3406

PRINCIPAL OFFICE: 911 Panorama Trail South, Rochester, NY 14625-0397

TELEPHONE NUMBER: (585) 385-6666
FAX: (585) 383-3428
WEB: www.paychex.com

NO. OF EMPLOYEES: 7,000 full-time (approx.); 300 part-time (approx.)

SHAREHOLDERS: 13,894

ANNUAL MEETING: In Oct.

INCORPORATED: DE, June, 1979

INSTITUTIONAL HOLDINGS:
No. of Institutions: 423
Shares Held: 212,940,903
% Held: 56.8

INDUSTRY: Accounting, auditing, & bookkeeping (SIC: 8721)

TRANSFER AGENT(S): American Stock Transfer & Trust Co., New York, NY

PENTAIR, INC.

YIELD 1.6%
P/E RATIO 38.4

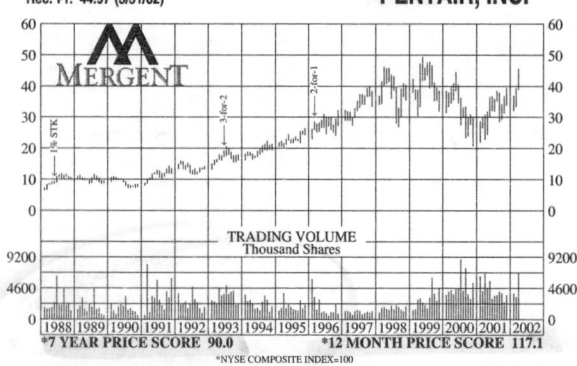

TRADING VOLUME
Thousand Shares

*7 YEAR PRICE SCORE 90.0   *12 MONTH PRICE SCORE 117.1
*NYSE COMPOSITE INDEX=100

INTERIM EARNINGS (Per Share):

Qtr.	Mar.	June	Sept.	Dec.
1997	0.48	0.50	0.54	0.68
1998	0.54	0.56	0.64	0.76
1999	0.05	0.66	0.69	0.90
2000	0.69	0.79	0.58	d0.38
2001	0.42	0.58	0.50	d0.33

INTERIM DIVIDENDS (Per Share):

Amt.	Decl.	Ex.	Rec.	Pay.
0.17Q	4/12/01	4/25/01	4/27/01	5/11/01
0.18Q	7/12/01	7/25/01	7/27/01	8/10/01
0.18Q	10/11/01	10/24/01	10/26/01	11/09/01
0.18Q	1/10/02	1/23/02	1/25/02	2/08/02
0.18Q	4/11/02	4/24/02	4/26/02	5/10/02

Indicated div.: $0.72 (Div. Reinv. Plan)

CAPITALIZATION (12/31/01):

	($000)	(%)
Long-Term Debt	714,977	40.5
Deferred Income Tax	34,128	1.9
Common & Surplus	1,015,002	57.5
Total	1,764,107	100.0

DIVIDEND ACHIEVER STATUS:
Rank: 162   10-Year Growth Rate: 8.60%
Total Years of Dividend Growth: 25

RECENT DEVELOPMENTS: For the twelve months ended 12/31/01, income from continuing operations was $57.5 million compared with income from continuing operations of $81.9 million in the corresponding year-earlier period. Results for 2001 and 2000 included pre-tax restructuring charges of $40.1 million and $24.8 million, respectively. Net sales declined 4.8% to $2.62 billion from $2.75 billion the previous year.

PROSPECTS: Results going forward should benefit from recent restructuring initiatives taken at the Company's Enclosures segment, which include plans to reduce manufacturing capacity by 20.0% and cut headcount by 25.0%. PNR expects that the Enclosures restructuring will be completed in the first half of 2002, and will result in an estimated $15.0 million in cost savings during 2002, and $21.0 million of saving annually thereafter.

BUSINESS

PENTAIR, INC. is a diversified manufacturer operating in three segments on a global basis. The Tools segment (39.7% of 2001 sales), manufactures and markets tool products, including woodworking machinery, portable power tools, compressors, generators, and pressure washers. The Water segment (33.9%), manufactures and markets water and wastewater pumps, control valves, pumps and pumping stations for thick fluid transfer applications, storage tanks, filtration systems, and pool and spa accessories. The Enclosures segment (26.4%), designs, manufactures, and markets customized and standard metal and composite enclosures. Products include metallic and composite enclosures, cabinets, cases, subracks, thermal management backplanes and power supplies.

ANNUAL FINANCIAL DATA

	12/31/01	12/31/00	12/31/99	12/31/98	12/31/97	12/31/96	12/31/95
Earnings Per Share	④1.17	③1.68	2.33	2.46	①2.11	①1.83	②1.48
Cash Flow Per Share	3.28	3.72	4.33	3.96	3.59	3.40	2.79
Tang. Book Val. Per Share	...	...	...	4.71	3.71	5.39	4.18
Dividends Per Share	0.70	0.66	0.64	0.60	0.54	0.50	0.40
Dividend Payout %	59.8	39.3	27.5	24.4	25.6	27.3	27.0

INCOME STATEMENT (IN MILLIONS):

Total Revenues	2,615.9	2,748.0	2,367.8	1,937.6	1,839.1	1,567.1	1,402.9
Costs & Expenses	2,353.8	2,447.0	2,064.8	1,676.0	1,601.4	1,364.6	1,237.7
Depreciation & Amort.	104.3	99.0	88.6	68.4	67.8	59.5	48.9
Operating Income	157.8	202.0	214.3	193.2	169.8	142.9	116.2
Net Interest Inc./(Exp.)	d61.5	d74.9	d47.8	d22.2	d21.7	d18.3	d14.6
Income Before Income Taxes	93.3	127.1	166.5	170.9	158.4	124.6	101.7
Income Taxes	35.8	45.3	63.2	64.1	66.8	50.1	41.2
Net Income	④57.5	③81.9	103.3	106.8	①91.6	①74.5	②60.5
Cash Flow	161.9	180.9	192.0	171.0	154.6	129.1	104.2
Average Shs. Outstg. (000)	49,297	48,645	44,287	43,149	43,067	37,949	37,300

BALANCE SHEET (IN MILLIONS):

Cash & Cash Equivalents	39.8	34.9	66.2	32.0	34.3	23.0	36.6
Total Current Assets	835.6	1,091.8	1,150.5	748.6	705.4	614.3	647.2
Net Property	329.5	353.0	403.8	308.3	293.6	298.8	266.7
Total Assets	2,372.2	2,644.0	2,803.0	1,554.7	1,472.9	1,289.0	1,252.5
Total Current Liabilities	428.4	648.8	760.9	394.8	392.2	301.6	396.8
Long-Term Obligations	715.0	781.8	857.3	288.0	294.5	279.9	219.9
Net Stockholders' Equity	1,015.0	1,010.6	993.2	709.4	630.6	563.9	502.9
Net Working Capital	407.2	443.0	389.5	353.8	313.2	312.6	250.4
Year-end Shs. Outstg. (000)	49,111	48,712	48,317	38,504	38,185	37,717	37,035

STATISTICAL RECORD:

Operating Profit Margin %	6.0	7.4	9.1	10.0	9.2	9.1	8.3
Net Profit Margin %	2.2	3.0	4.4	5.5	5.0	4.8	4.3
Return on Equity %	5.7	8.1	10.4	15.1	14.5	13.2	12.0
Return on Assets %	2.4	3.1	3.7	6.9	6.2	5.8	4.8
Debt/Total Assets %	30.1	29.6	30.6	18.5	20.0	21.7	17.6
Price Range	39.60-21.88	44.63-20.63	49.44-29.88	46.25-26.75	39.88-27.25	32.25-22.88	26.50-19.88
P/E Ratio	33.8-18.7	26.6-12.3	21.2-12.8	18.8-10.9	18.9-12.9	17.6-12.5	17.9-13.4
Average Yield %	2.3	2.0	1.6	1.6	1.6	1.8	1.7

Statistics are as originally reported. Adj. for 2-for-1 stk. split, 2/96. ① Incl. non-recurr. credit 12/31/97: $10.3 mill.; credit 12/31/96: $12.1 mill. ② Bef. disc. oper. gain $4.7 mill. ③ Incl. restruct. chrg. of $24.8 mill.; bef. loss fr. disc. ops. of $24.8 mill. ($0.51/sh.) & acctg. change chrg. of $1.2 mill. ($0.02/sh.) ④ Incl. restruct. chrg. of $40.1 mill.; bef. loss on sale of disc. ops. of $24.6 mill. ($0.50/sh.)

OFFICERS:
R. J. Hogan, Chmn., Pres., C.E.O.
D. D. Harrison, Exec. V.P., C.F.O.
L. L. Ainsworth, Sr. V.P., Gen. Couns., Sec.

INVESTOR CONTACT: Mark Cain, Investor Relations, (651) 639-5278

PRINCIPAL OFFICE: 1500 Country Road B2 West, Suite 400, St., MN 55113

TELEPHONE NUMBER: (651) 636-7920
FAX: (651) 639-5203
WEB: www.pentair.com

NO. OF EMPLOYEES: 11,700 (approx.)

SHAREHOLDERS: 4,229

ANNUAL MEETING: In May

INCORPORATED: MN, Aug., 1966

INSTITUTIONAL HOLDINGS:
No. of Institutions: 170
Shares Held: 33,037,689
% Held: 67.3

INDUSTRY: Woodworking machinery (SIC: 3553)

TRANSFER AGENT(S): Wells Fargo Shareowner Services, South St. Paul, MN

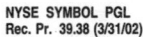

PEOPLES ENERGY CORPORATION

YIELD 5.3%
P/E RATIO 15.2

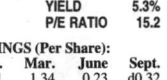

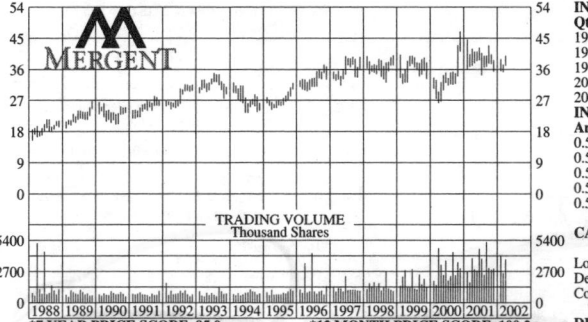

54 · 45 · 36 · 27 · 18 · 9 · 0

TRADING VOLUME
Thousand Shares

5400 · 2700 · 0

1988 1989 1990 1991 1992 1993 1994 1995 1996 1997 1998 1999 2000 2001 2002

*7 YEAR PRICE SCORE 95.0   *12 MONTH PRICE SCORE 100.2

*NYSE COMPOSITE INDEX=100

INTERIM EARNINGS (Per Share):

Qtr.	Dec.	Mar.	June	Sept.
1997-98	1.01	1.34	0.23	d0.32
1998-99	0.66	1.86	0.20	d0.11
1999-00	0.83	1.62	0.31	d0.32
2000-01	1.03	1.77	0.33	d0.38
2001-02	0.87	...	...	...

INTERIM DIVIDENDS (Per Share):

Amt.	Decl.	Ex.	Rec.	Pay.
0.51Q	2/07/01	3/20/01	3/22/01	4/13/01
0.51Q	5/30/01	6/20/01	6/22/01	7/13/01
0.51Q	8/01/01	9/19/01	9/21/01	10/15/01
0.51Q	12/05/01	12/19/01	12/21/01	1/15/02
0.52Q	2/06/02	3/20/02	3/22/02	4/15/02

Indicated div.: $2.08 (Div. Reinv. Plan)

CAPITALIZATION (9/30/01):

	($000)	(%)
Long-Term Debt	644,308	36.1
Deferred Income Tax	335,510	18.8
Common & Surplus	805,517	45.1
Total	1,785,335	100.0

DIVIDEND ACHIEVER STATUS:

Rank: 277   10-Year Growth Rate: 1.76%
Total Years of Dividend Growth: 18

RECENT DEVELOPMENTS: For the quarter ended 12/31/01, PGL reported net income of $31.0 million versus income of $35.2 million, before an accounting change charge of $34,000, in the equivalent period of 2000. Results for the 2001 period included a non-recurring charge of $1.2 million. Earnings were negatively affected by warmer weather, lower oil and natural gas commodity prices and the Enron bankruptcy. Operating revenues dropped 47.3% to $377.5 million from $717.0 million in 2000.

PROSPECTS: On 1/17/02, the Company and Dominion announced an alliance to market retail gas and electricity to the nearly 3.0 million residential consumers in Chicago and northern Illinois. Meanwhile, PGL expects earnings to be in the range of $2.75 to $2.90 per share for fiscal 2002. In the near-term, PGL should benefit from lowered utility operating costs by making profitable investments in its power generation and oil and gas segments.

BUSINESS

PEOPLES ENERGY CORPORA-TION is a diversified energy company comprised of five primary business segment: gas distribution, power generation, midstream services, oil and gas production, and retail energy services. These utilities distribute natural and synthetic gas to approximately 1.0 million customers in Chicago and northeastern Illinois. Other operations are conducted through PGL's subsidiaries engaged in non-regulated diversified energy operations. These subsidiaries consists of: Peoples District Energy Corp., a provider of district energy services; Peoples Energy Services, a provider of nonregulated retail energy sales; Peoples Energy Resources, a provider of gas-fired electric generation; Peoples NGV, a fueling station for natural gas fueled vehicles; and Peoples Energy Production Company, which acquires investments in oil and gas production properties.

ANNUAL FINANCIAL DATA

	9/30/01	9/30/00	9/30/99	9/30/98	9/30/97	9/30/96	9/30/95
Earnings Per Share	① 2.74	2.44	2.61	2.25	2.81	2.96	1.78
Cash Flow Per Share	5.42	5.29	4.96	4.44	4.93	4.98	3.68
Tang. Book Val. Per Share	22.66	21.86	21.66	20.94	20.43	19.48	18.38
Dividends Per Share	2.03	1.99	1.95	1.91	1.87	1.83	1.80
Dividend Payout %	74.1	81.6	74.7	84.9	66.5	61.8	101.1
INCOME STATEMENT (IN MILLIONS):							
Total Revenues	2,270.2	1,417.5	1,194.4	1,138.1	1,274.4	1,198.7	1,033.4
Costs & Expenses	2,013.2	1,157.4	954.8	858.4	964.5	893.4	788.0
Depreciation & Amort.	95.0	100.9	83.5	77.2	74.1	70.6	66.4
Maintenance Exp.	...	...	...	44.0	47.6	45.6	41.7
Operating Income	162.0	159.2	156.0	113.8	133.5	132.4	108.6
Net Interest Inc./(Exp.)	d72.1	d52.9	d39.5	d35.5	d33.1	d37.5	d43.8
Income Taxes	51.4	43.3	52.6	45.1	56.4	62.5	32.6
Net Income	① 97.1	86.4	92.6	79.4	98.4	103.4	62.2
Cash Flow	192.1	187.4	176.2	156.6	172.5	174.1	128.6
Average Shs. Outstg. (000)	35,439	35,413	35,490	35,276	35,000	34,942	34,901
BALANCE SHEET (IN MILLIONS):							
Gross Property	2,703.6	2,517.1	2,330.9	2,210.0	2,117.5	2,046.2	2,088.3
Accumulated Depreciation	949.7	871.8	811.1	763.3	715.3	665.1	715.2
Net Property	1,753.9	1,645.3	1,519.8	1,446.7	1,402.2	1,381.1	1,373.1
Total Assets	2,994.1	2,501.9	2,100.2	1,904.5	1,820.8	1,783.8	1,822.5
Long-Term Obligations	644.3	419.7	521.7	516.6	527.1	527.1	621.9
Net Stockholders' Equity	805.5	777.1	768.7	741.4	716.5	681.2	641.7
Year-end Shs. Outstg. (000)	35,544	35,544	35,489	35,402	35,070	34,960	34,913
STATISTICAL RECORD:							
Operating Profit Margin %	7.1	11.2	13.1	10.0	10.5	11.0	10.5
Net Profit Margin %	4.3	6.1	7.8	7.0	7.7	8.6	6.0
Net Inc./Net Property %	5.5	5.3	6.1	5.5	7.0	7.5	4.5
Net Inc./Tot. Capital %	5.4	5.6	5.9	5.2	6.6	7.2	4.2
Return on Equity %	12.0	11.1	12.1	10.7	13.7	15.2	9.7
Accum. Depr./Gross Prop. %	35.1	34.6	34.8	34.5	33.8	32.5	34.2
Price Range	44.63-34.35	46.94-26.19	40.25-31.75	40.13-32.13	39.88-31.25	37.38-29.63	32.00-24.25
P/E Ratio	16.3-12.5	19.2-10.7	15.4-12.2	17.8-14.3	14.2-11.1	12.6-10.0	18.0-13.6
Average Yield %	5.1	5.4	5.4	5.3	5.3	5.5	6.4

Statistics are as originally reported. ① Incls. special charges of $14.7 mill.

OFFICERS:
R. E. Terry, Chmn., C.E.O.
T. M. Patrick, Pres., C.O.O.
T. A. Nardi, C.F.O.

INVESTOR CONTACT: Mary Ann Wall, Mgr., Inv. Rel., (312) 240-7534

PRINCIPAL OFFICE: 130 East Randolph Drive, 24th Floor, Chicago, IL 60601-6207

TELEPHONE NUMBER: (312) 240-4000
FAX: (312) 240-4220
WEB: www.pecorp.com

NO. OF EMPLOYEES: 2,624

SHAREHOLDERS: 22,342

ANNUAL MEETING: In Feb.

INCORPORATED: IL, 1967

INSTITUTIONAL HOLDINGS:
No. of Institutions: 201
Shares Held: 17,377,574
% Held: 49.0

INDUSTRY: Natural gas distribution (SIC: 4924)

TRANSFER AGENT(S): Computershare Investor Services, Chicago, IL

NYSE SYMBOL PEP
Rec. Pr. 51.50 (3/31/02)

PEPSICO INC.

YIELD	1.1%
P/E RATIO	34.6

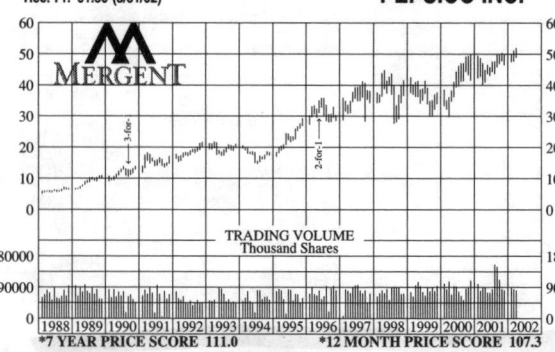

TRADING VOLUME
Thousand Shares

*7 YEAR PRICE SCORE 111.0   *12 MONTH PRICE SCORE 107.3
*NYSE COMPOSITE INDEX=100

INTERIM EARNINGS (Per Share):

Qtr.	Mar.	June	Sept.	Dec.
1998	0.24	0.33	0.50	0.24
1999	0.22	0.49	0.32	0.33
2000	0.29	0.38	0.40	0.41
2001	0.34	0.44	0.34	0.37

INTERIM DIVIDENDS (Per Share):

Amt.	Decl.	Ex.	Rec.	Pay.
0.145Q	5/02/01	6/06/01	6/08/01	6/29/01
0.145Q	7/26/01	9/05/01	9/07/01	9/28/01
0.145Q	11/16/01	12/05/01	12/07/01	1/02/02
0.145Q	2/01/02	3/06/02	3/08/02	3/29/02

Indicated div.: $0.58 (Div. Reinv. Plan)

CAPITALIZATION (12/29/01):

	($000)	(%)
Long-Term Debt	2,651,000	20.7
Deferred Income Tax	1,496,000	11.7
Common & Surplus	8,648,000	67.6
Total	12,795,000	100.0

DIVIDEND ACHIEVER STATUS:
Rank: 139   10-Year Growth Rate: 9.99%
Total Years of Dividend Growth: 30

RECENT DEVELOPMENTS: For the 52 weeks ended 12/29/01, net income was $2.66 billion versus $2.54 billion in the year-earlier period, which included 53 weeks. Results for 2001 and 2000 included after-tax other asset impairment and restructuring charges of $19.0 million and $111.0 million, respectively. Results for 2001 also included after-tax merger-related charges of $322.0 million. Net sales rose 5.7% to $26.94 billion from $25.48 billion the year before. Comparisons were made with restated 2000 results.

PROSPECTS: PEP's integration of The Quaker Oats Company is proceeding as planned, with realized synergies expected at the high end of the previously announced range of $140.0 million to $175.0 million. Meanwhile, new product introductions will be key to top-line growth in 2002. Roll-outs for 2002 include new salty snack platforms such as Munchies Snack Mix, Go Snacks and Ruffles 3D's, as well as Diet Code Red, and Mountain Dew's new energy drink, called AMP.

BUSINESS

PEPSICO INC. operates on a world-wide basis within the soft drinks, juice and snack-foods businesses. The Pepsi-Cola segment, which accounted for 23.9% of sales in 2001, manufactures concentrates, and markets PEPSI, PEPSI-COLA, DIET PEPSI, PEPSI ONE, MOUNTAIN DEW, MUG, FRUITWORKS, SIERRA MIST, AQUAFINA, MIRINDA, SLICE and allied brands worldwide, and 7-UP internationally. The Tropicana segment, 14.9%, manufactures and sells its products under trade-marks such as TROPICANA PURE PRE MIUM, and TROPICANA SEASONS BEST. The Frito-Lay segment, 53.8%, manufactures, markets, sells and distributes a varied line of salty and sweet snack foods. Trademarks include LAY'S, DORITOS, CHEETOS, ROLD GOLD and WOW! Quaker Foods, 7.4%, manufactures, markets and sells products that include ready-to-eat and hot cereals. On 8/2/01, PEP completed its acquisition of The Quaker Oats Company. As of 12/31/01, PEP maintained economic ownership of about 42.0% in The Pepsi Bottling Group.

ANNUAL FINANCIAL DATA

	12/29/01	12/30/00	12/25/99	12/26/98	12/27/97	12/28/96	12/30/95
Earnings Per Share	⑥1.47	1.48	④1.37	③1.31	①0.95	②0.72	①1.00
Cash Flow Per Share	2.07	2.13	2.06	2.12	1.65	1.79	2.08
Tang. Book Val. Per Share	2.17	1.91	1.47	...	0.72	...	...
Dividends Per Share	0.57	0.55	0.53	0.51	0.48	0.43	0.38
Dividend Payout %	38.8	37.2	38.7	38.9	50.5	59.7	38.0

INCOME STATEMENT (IN MILLIONS):

Total Revenues	26,935.0	20,438.0	20,367.0	22,348.0	20,917.0	31,645.0	30,421.0
Costs & Expenses	21,832.0	16,253.0	16,517.0	18,530.0	17,149.0	27,380.0	25,694.0
Depreciation & Amort.	1,082.0	960.0	1,032.0	1,234.0	1,106.0	1,719.0	1,740.0
Operating Income	4,021.0	3,225.0	2,818.0	2,584.0	2,662.0	2,546.0	2,987.0
Net Interest Inc./(Exp.)	d152.0	d145.0	d245.0	d321.0	d353.0	d499.0	d555.0
Income Before Income Taxes	4,029.0	3,210.0	3,656.0	2,263.0	2,309.0	2,047.0	2,432.0
Income Taxes	1,367.0	1,027.0	1,606.0	270.0	818.0	898.0	826.0
Net Income	⑥2,662.0	2,183.0	④2,050.0	③1,993.0	①1,491.0	②1,149.0	①1,606.0
Cash Flow	3,740.0	3,143.0	3,082.0	3,227.0	2,597.0	2,868.0	3,346.0
Average Shs. Outstg. (000)	1,807,000	1,475,000	1,496,000	1,519,000	1,570,000	1,606,000	1,608,000

BALANCE SHEET (IN MILLIONS):

Cash & Cash Equivalents	1,649.0	1,330.0	1,056.0	394.0	2,883.0	786.0	1,498.0
Total Current Assets	5,853.0	4,604.0	4,173.0	4,362.0	6,251.0	5,139.0	5,546.0
Net Property	6,876.0	5,438.0	5,266.0	7,318.0	6,261.0	10,191.0	9,870.0
Total Assets	21,695.0	18,339.0	17,551.0	22,660.0	20,101.0	24,512.0	25,432.0
Total Current Liabilities	4,998.0	3,935.0	3,788.0	7,914.0	4,257.0	5,139.0	5,230.0
Long-Term Obligations	2,651.0	2,346.0	2,812.0	4,028.0	4,946.0	8,439.0	8,509.0
Net Stockholders' Equity	8,648.0	7,249.0	6,881.0	6,401.0	6,936.0	6,623.0	7,313.0
Net Working Capital	855.0	669.0	385.0	d3,552.0	1,994.0	...	316.0
Year-end Shs. Outstg. (000)	1,756,000	1,446,000	1,455,000	1,471,000	1,502,000	1,545,000	1,576,000

STATISTICAL RECORD:

Operating Profit Margin %	14.9	15.8	13.8	11.6	12.7	8.0	9.8
Net Profit Margin %	9.9	10.7	10.1	8.9	7.1	3.6	5.3
Return on Equity %	30.8	30.1	29.8	31.1	21.5	17.3	22.0
Return on Assets %	12.3	11.9	11.7	8.8	7.4	4.7	6.3
Debt/Total Assets %	12.2	12.8	16.0	17.8	24.6	34.4	33.5
Price Range	50.46-40.25	49.94-29.69	42.56-30.13	44.81-27.56	41.31-28.25	35.88-27.25	29.38-16.94
P/E Ratio	34.3-27.4	33.7-20.1	31.1-22.0	34.2-21.0	43.5-29.7	49.8-37.8	29.4-16.9
Average Yield %	1.3	1.4	1.5	1.4	1.4	1.4	1.6

Statistics are as originally reported. Adj. for 2-for-1 stk. split, 5/96. ① Incl. non-recur. chrgs. of $290.0 mill.; bef. disc. oper. gain of $651.0 mill. ② Incl. non-recur. chrgs. 1/31/96, $716.0 mill.; chrg. 12/31/95, $520.0 mill. ③ Incl. non-recur. chrg. of $288.0 mill. ④ Incl. non-recur. chrg. of $65.0 mill. ⑤ Incl. aft.-tax merger-rel. chrgs. of $322.0 mill. and asset impairmnt. & restruct. chrgs. of $19.0 mill. ⑥ Refl. 10/6/97 spin-off of TRICON Global Restaurants.

OFFICERS:
S. S. Reinemund, Chmn., C.E.O.
R. S. Morrison, Vice-Chmn.
I. K. Nooyi, Pres., C.F.O.

INVESTOR CONTACT: Susan V. Watson, V.P., Inv. Rel., (914) 253-3035

PRINCIPAL OFFICE: 700 Anderson Hill Road, Purchase, NY 10577-1444

TELEPHONE NUMBER: (914) 253-2000
FAX: (914) 253-2070
WEB: www.pepsico.com
NO. OF EMPLOYEES: 143,000 (approx.)
SHAREHOLDERS: 227,000 (approx.)
ANNUAL MEETING: In May
INCORPORATED: DE, Sept., 1919; reincorp., NC, Dec., 1986

INSTITUTIONAL HOLDINGS:
No. of Institutions: 1,076
Shares Held: 1,145,439,909
% Held: 65.5

INDUSTRY: Bottled and canned soft drinks (SIC: 2086)

TRANSFER AGENT(S): The Bank of New York, Newark, NJ

PFIZER INC.

YIELD 1.3%
P/E RATIO 32.6

INTERIM EARNINGS (Per Share):

Qtr.	Mar.	June	Sept.	Dec.
1997	0.16	0.12	0.15	0.14
1998	0.18	0.16	0.13	0.08
1999	0.16	0.19	0.18	0.25
2000	0.31	0.18	0.21	0.23
2001	0.30	0.29	0.33	0.30

INTERIM DIVIDENDS (Per Share):

Amt.	Decl.	Ex.	Rec.	Pay.
0.11Q	12/18/00	2/14/01	2/16/01	3/08/01
0.11Q	4/26/01	5/16/01	5/18/01	6/07/01
0.11Q	6/28/01	8/15/01	8/17/01	9/06/01
0.11Q	10/25/01	11/14/01	11/16/01	12/06/01
0.13Q	12/18/01	2/13/02	2/15/02	3/07/02

Indicated div.: $0.52 (Div. Reinv. Plan)

CAPITALIZATION (12/31/01):

	($000)	(%)
Long-Term Debt	2,609,000	12.2
Deferred Income Tax	452,000	2.1
Common & Surplus	18,293,000	85.7
Total	21,354,000	100.0

DIVIDEND ACHIEVER STATUS:
Rank: 64   10-Year Growth Rate: 14.87%
Total Years of Dividend Growth: 34

7 YEAR PRICE SCORE 122.7   **12 MONTH PRICE SCORE 101.0**
NYSE COMPOSITE INDEX=100

RECENT DEVELOPMENTS: For the year ended 12/31/01, income from continuing operations more than doubled to $7.75 billion from $3.72 billion in the previous year. Results for 2001 and 2000 excluded income of $36.0 million and $8.0 million, respectively, from discontinued operations. The 2001 and 2000 results included pre-tax merger-related charges of $839.0 million and $3.26 billion, respectively. Revenues climbed 9.9% to $32.26 billion.

PROSPECTS: In 2002, PFE anticipates double-digit revenue growth at current foreign exchange rates, continuing strong investments in product support and research and development, and margin improvements. PFE plans to invest $5.30 billion in research and development in 2002, and expects diluted earnings per share in the range of $1.56 to $1.60, excluding special items and merger-related costs.

BUSINESS

PFIZER INC. is a global pharmaceutical company that develops, manufactures and markets innovative medicines for humans and animals. The products include NORVASC, a once-a-day calcium channel blocker for treatment of angina and hypertension, ZYRTEC, an anti-allergy medicine, VIAGRA, an oral medication for the treatment of erectile dysfunction, ZOLOFT, a selective serotonin re-uptake inhibitor for the treatment of depression, ZITHROMAX, an oral or injectable antibiotic, DIFLUCAN, used to treat various fungal infections, as well as non-prescription self-medications. The animal health segment includes anti-parasitic, anti-infective and anti-inflammatory medicines, and vaccines. Revenues for 2001 were derived 83.5% from the pharmaceutical segment and 16.5% from the consumer product segment. PFE acquired Warner-Lambert Co. on 6/19/00.

ANNUAL FINANCIAL DATA

	12/31/01	12/31/00	12/31/99	12/31/98	12/31/97	12/31/96	12/31/95
Earnings Per Share	④ 1.22	④ 0.59	③ 0.82	② 0.49	0.57	0.50	① 0.41
Cash Flow Per Share	1.39	0.74	0.96	0.62	0.69	0.61	0.51
Tang. Book Val. Per Share	2.64	2.26	2.11	2.06	1.71	1.43	1.12
Dividends Per Share	0.44	0.36	0.31	0.25	0.23	0.20	0.17
Dividend Payout %	36.1	61.0	37.4	51.7	40.0	40.2	42.1

INCOME STATEMENT (IN MILLIONS):

Total Revenues	32,259.0	29,574.0	16,204.0	13,544.0	12,504.0	11,306.0	10,021.4
Costs & Expenses	20,862.0	22,825.0	11,214.0	10,461.0	8,914.0	8,072.0	7,348.2
Depreciation & Amort.	1,068.0	968.0	542.0	489.0	502.0	430.0	374.0
Operating Income	10,329.0	5,781.0	4,448.0	2,594.0	3,088.0	2,804.0	2,299.2
Income Before Income Taxes	10,329.0	5,781.0	4,448.0	2,594.0	3,088.0	2,804.0	2,299.2
Income Taxes	2,561.0	2,049.0	1,244.0	642.0	865.0	869.0	738.0
Equity Earnings/Minority Int.	d16.0	d14.0	d5.0	d2.0	d10.0	d6.0	d7.0
Net Income	④ 7,752.0	④ 3,718.0	③ 3,199.0	② 1,950.0	2,213.0	1,929.0	① 1,554.2
Cash Flow	8,820.0	4,686.0	3,741.0	2,439.0	2,715.0	2,359.0	1,928.2
Average Shs. Outstg. (000)	6,361,000	6,368,000	3,884,000	3,945,000	3,909,000	3,864,000	3,777,000

BALANCE SHEET (IN MILLIONS):

Cash & Cash Equivalents	8,615.0	6,863.0	4,442.0	3,929.0	1,589.0	1,637.0	1,512.0
Total Current Assets	18,450.0	17,187.0	11,191.0	9,931.0	6,820.0	6,468.0	6,152.4
Net Property	10,415.0	9,425.0	5,343.0	4,415.0	4,137.0	3,850.0	3,472.6
Total Assets	39,153.0	33,510.0	20,574.0	18,302.0	15,336.0	14,667.0	12,729.3
Total Current Liabilities	13,640.0	11,981.0	9,185.0	7,192.0	5,305.0	5,640.0	5,187.2
Long-Term Obligations	2,609.0	1,123.0	525.0	527.0	729.0	687.0	833.0
Net Stockholders' Equity	18,293.0	16,076.0	8,887.0	8,810.0	7,933.0	6,954.0	5,506.6
Net Working Capital	4,810.0	5,206.0	2,006.0	2,739.0	1,515.0	828.0	965.2
Year-end Shs. Outstg. (000)	6,277,000	6,314,000	3,847,000	3,883,000	3,882,000	3,870,000	3,823,602

STATISTICAL RECORD:

Operating Profit Margin %	32.0	19.5	27.5	19.2	24.7	24.8	22.9
Net Profit Margin %	24.0	12.6	19.7	14.4	17.7	17.1	15.5
Return on Equity %	42.4	23.1	36.0	22.1	27.9	27.7	28.2
Return on Assets %	19.8	11.1	15.5	10.7	14.4	13.2	12.2
Debt/Total Assets %	6.7	3.4	2.6	2.9	4.8	4.7	6.5
Price Range	46.75-34.00	49.25-30.00	50.04-31.54	42.98-23.69	26.66-13.44	15.21-10.04	11.14-6.21
P/E Ratio	38.3-27.9	83.5-50.8	61.0-38.5	87.7-48.3	47.0-23.7	30.5-20.2	27.0-15.1
Average Yield %	1.1	0.9	0.8	0.8	1.1	1.6	2.0

Statistics are as originally reported. Adj. for stock splits: 200% div., 6/30/99; 2-for-1, 9/97, 6/95. ① Excl. gain of $18.8 mill. for dis. ops. ② Incl. unus. & nonrecurr. pre-tax chgs. total. $1.06 bill.; excl. a $1.40 bill. gain from disc. opers. ③ Incl. a one-time after-tax chrg. of $1.37 bill. for TROVAN inv. ④ Bef. inc. from disc. opers. of $36.0 mill., 2001; $8.0 mill., 2000 & incl. merger-rel. costs of $839.0 mill., 2001; $3.26 bill., 2000.

OFFICERS:
H. A. McKinnell, Chmn., C.E.O.
J. F. Niblack, Vice-Chmn.
D. Shedlarz, Exec. V.P., C.F.O.

INVESTOR CONTACT: Investor Relations, (212) 573-2323

PRINCIPAL OFFICE: 235 East 42nd Street, New York, NY 10017-5755

TELEPHONE NUMBER: (212) 573-2323
FAX: (212) 573-2641
WEB: www.pfizer.com

NO. OF EMPLOYEES: 90,000 (approx.)

SHAREHOLDERS: 202,365

ANNUAL MEETING: In Apr.

INCORPORATED: DE, 1942

INSTITUTIONAL HOLDINGS:
No. of Institutions: 1,316
Shares Held: 95,769,279
% Held: 60.3

INDUSTRY: Pharmaceutical preparations (SIC: 2834)

TRANSFER AGENT(S): First Chicago Trust Company of New York, Jersey City, NJ

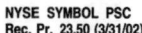
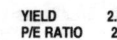

NYSE SYMBOL PSC
Rec. Pr. 23.50 (3/31/02)

PHILADELPHIA SUBURBAN CORPORATION

YIELD 2.3%
P/E RATIO 27.0

TRADING VOLUME
Thousand Shares

*7 YEAR PRICE SCORE 140.2   *12 MONTH PRICE SCORE 112.8
*NYSE COMPOSITE INDEX=100

INTERIM EARNINGS (Per Share):

Qtr.	Mar.	June	Sept.	Dec.
1998	0.13	0.17	0.21	0.15
1999	0.06	0.19	0.22	0.09
2000	0.16	0.21	0.25	0.18
2001	0.19	0.22	0.28	0.18

INTERIM DIVIDENDS (Per Share):

Amt.	Decl.	Ex.	Rec.	Pay.
0.155Q	5/01/01	5/11/01	5/15/01	6/01/01
0.155Q	8/07/01	8/15/01	8/17/01	9/01/01
0.166Q	8/07/01	11/14/01	11/16/01	12/01/01
25% STK	8/07/01	12/03/01	11/16/01	11/30/01
0.133Q	2/05/02	2/08/02	2/12/02	3/01/02

Indicated div.: $0.53 (Div. Reinv. Plan)

CAPITALIZATION (12/31/01):

	($000)	(%)
Long-Term Debt	516,520	52.2
Preferred Stock	1,116	0.1
Common & Surplus	471,930	47.7
Total	989,566	100.0

DIVIDEND ACHIEVER STATUS:
Rank: 239   10-Year Growth Rate: 4.66%
Total Years of Dividend Growth: 10

RECENT DEVELOPMENTS: For the year ended 12/31/01, net income increased 13.7% to $60.1 million compared with $52.9 million in 2000. Results for 2001 and 2000 included gains of $3.4 million and $5.1 million, respectively, on the sale of other assets. Results for 2000 included recovery of restructuring costs of $1.1 million and a recovery of merger transaction costs of $2.9 million. Operating revenues advanced 12.1% to $307.3 million.

PROSPECTS: On 3/13/02, PSC announced that its Consumers Pennsylvania Water Company and Suburban Wastewater Company subsidiaries have purchased the water and wastewater system assets of the White Haven Municipal Authority. White Haven collectively serves nearly 3,000 residents in Luzerne and Carbon counties of Pennsylvania. The transaction is valued at $2.7 million plus the assumption of White Haven's existing, low-interest loans.

BUSINESS

PHILADELPHIA SUBURBAN CORPORATION is a holding company for regulated utilities providing water or wastewater services to approximately 2 million people in Pennsylvania, Illinois, Ohio, New Jersey, Maine, and North Carolina as of 2/15/02. PSC's two primary subsidiaries are Pennsylvania Suburban Water Company, a regulated public utility that provides water or wastewater services to about 1.3 million residents in the suburban areas north and west of the City of Philadelphia and in ten other counties in Pennsylvania, and Consumers Water Company, a holding company for several regulated public utility companies that provide water or wastewater service to about 700,000 residents in various communities in four states. In addition, PSC provides water and wastewater service to approximately 35,000 people through operating and maintenance contracts with municipal authorities and other parties close to its operating companies' service territories. Some of PSC's subsidiaries provide wastewater collection, treatment and disposal services, primarily residential, to approximately 40,000 people in Pennsylvania, Illinois, New Jersey and North Carolina.

ANNUAL FINANCIAL DATA

	12/31/01	12/31/00	12/31/99	12/31/98	12/31/97	12/31/96	12/31/95
Earnings Per Share	② 0.87	③ 0.81	①⑤ 0.56	0.66	0.56	④ 0.67	④ 0.64
Cash Flow Per Share	1.46	1.33	1.06	1.03	0.92	1.11	1.05
Tang. Book Val. Per Share	6.90	6.38	5.69	5.34	4.46	5.98	5.49
Dividends Per Share	0.50	0.47	0.45	0.43	0.40	0.38	0.36
Dividend Payout %	58.0	58.1	79.6	64.6	70.8	57.0	57.0
INCOME STATEMENT (IN MILLIONS):							
Total Revenues	307.3	275.5	257.3	151.0	136.2	122.5	117.0
Costs & Expenses	132.8	123.1	124.4	68.2	64.8	59.9	59.4
Depreciation & Amort.	40.2	34.1	31.9	16.1	14.6	13.3	11.6
Operating Income	134.3	118.3	101.0	66.7	56.8	49.3	46.1
Net Interest Inc./(Exp.)	d39.9	d40.4	d33.7	d19.0	d17.9	d15.3	d14.9
Income Taxes	39.0	34.1	26.5	19.6	15.9	14.0	12.9
Net Income	② 60.1	③ 52.9	①⑤ 36.4	28.8	23.2	④ 19.8	④ 18.0
Cash Flow	100.2	86.9	68.2	44.7	37.6	33.1	29.6
Average Shs. Outstg. (000)	68,755	65,414	64,539	43,556	41,052	29,770	28,163
BALANCE SHEET (IN MILLIONS):							
Gross Property	1,677.1	1,536.2	1,393.0	745.5	656.0	612.8	529.4
Accumulated Depreciation	308.9	284.7	257.7	135.7	121.5	109.9	92.5
Net Property	1,368.1	1,251.4	1,135.4	609.8	534.5	502.9	436.9
Total Assets	1,560.3	1,414.0	1,280.8	701.5	618.5	582.9	518.1
Long-Term Obligations	516.5	468.8	413.8	261.8	232.5	217.5	175.4
Net Stockholders' Equity	473.0	429.5	366.3	234.8	194.7	180.0	157.0
Year-end Shs. Outstg. (000)	68,386	67,095	64,082	43,323	42,970	29,588	28,569
STATISTICAL RECORD:							
Operating Profit Margin %	43.7	42.9	39.3	44.2	41.7	40.2	39.4
Net Profit Margin %	19.6	19.2	14.1	19.1	17.0	16.1	15.4
Net Inc./Net Property %	4.4	4.2	3.2	4.7	4.3	3.9	4.1
Net Inc./Tot. Capital %	6.1	5.0	4.0	4.9	4.5	4.1	4.4
Return on Equity %	12.7	12.3	9.9	12.3	11.9	11.0	11.5
Accum. Depr./Gross Prop. %	18.4	18.5	18.5	18.2	18.5	17.9	17.5
Price Range	24.64-15.65	19.95-10.56	19.04-12.64	19.24-12.08	13.77-7.32	9.54-6.56	6.88-5.56
P/E Ratio	28.3-18.0	24.7-13.1	33.8-22.4	29.2-18.3	24.5-13.0	14.3-9.9	10.8-8.7
Average Yield %	2.5	3.1	2.8	2.7	3.8	4.7	5.9

Statistics are as originally reported. Adj. for stk. splits: 25% div., 11/01 & 12/00; 4-for-3, 1/98; 3-for-2, 7/96. ① Incl. restruct. recov. costs of $3.8 mill. ② Incl. gain on the sale of other assets of $3.4 mill. ③ Incl. restruct. recovery gain of $1.1 mill., merg. transac. costs of $2.9 mill., other asset sale gain of $5.1 mill. ④ Incl. reversal of reserve for discont. oper. of $965,000, 1996; $370,000, 1995. ⑤ Incl. merg. transac. costs of $6.3 mill.

OFFICERS:
N. DeBenedictis, Chmn., Pres.
D. P. Smeltzer, Sr V.P., C.F.O.
R. H. Stahl, Exec. V.P., Gen. Couns.

INVESTOR CONTACT: Keya W. Epps, Investor Relations, (610) 645-1084

PRINCIPAL OFFICE: 762 W. Lancaster Avenue, Bryn Mawr, PA 19010-3489

TELEPHONE NUMBER: (610) 525-1400
FAX: (610) 645-1061
WEB: www.suburbanwater.com

NO. OF EMPLOYEES: 951

SHAREHOLDERS: 21,056 (approx.)

ANNUAL MEETING: In May

INCORPORATED: PA, May, 1969

INSTITUTIONAL HOLDINGS:
No. of Institutions: 143
Shares Held: 13,804,159
% Held: 20.2

INDUSTRY: Water supply (SIC: 4941)

TRANSFER AGENT(S): EquiServe, L.P., Canton, MA

PHILIP MORRIS COMPANIES, INC.

YIELD 4.4%
P/E RATIO 13.6

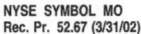

TRADING VOLUME	Thousand Shares

7 YEAR PRICE SCORE 111.4   **12 MONTH PRICE SCORE 111.1**
*NYSE COMPOSITE INDEX=100

INTERIM EARNINGS (Per Share):

Qtr.	Mar.	June	Sept.	Dec.
1998	0.57	0.74	0.81	0.11
1999	0.73	0.84	0.84	0.79
2000	0.87	0.95	1.03	0.90
2001	0.80	1.03	1.06	0.99

INTERIM DIVIDENDS (Per Share):

Amt.	Decl.	Ex.	Rec.	Pay.
0.53Q	5/30/01	6/13/01	6/15/01	7/10/01
0.58Q	8/29/01	9/17/01	9/17/01	10/10/01
0.58Q	12/12/01	12/20/01	12/24/01	1/10/02
0.58Q	2/27/02	3/13/02	3/15/02	4/10/02

Indicated div.: $2.32 (Div. Reinv. Plan)

CAPITALIZATION (12/31/01):

	($000)	(%)
Long-Term Debt	18,651,000	35.3
Deferred Income Tax	10,484,000	19.9
Minority Interest	4,013,000	7.6
Common & Surplus	19,620,000	37.2
Total	52,768,000	100.0

DIVIDEND ACHIEVER STATUS:

Rank: 77   10-Year Growth Rate: 13.62%
Total Years of Dividend Growth: 36

RECENT DEVELOPMENTS: For the year ended 12/31/01, earnings were $8.57 billion, before an accounting change charge of $6.0 million, versus net earnings of $8.51 billion a year earlier. Earnings for 2001 included non-recurring pre-tax charges of $101.0 million, while earnings for 2000 included non-recurring pre-tax gains of $239.0 million. Operating revenues rose 11.9% to $89.92 billion from $80.36 billion the previous year. Results for 2001 included the operating results of Nabisco Holdings Corp.

PROSPECTS: MO, in a bid to share in the growing flavored-alcohol malt beverage category, has entered into partnerships with Skyy Spirits LLC and Allied Domecq PLC to launch ready-to-drink malt beverages. The partnership with Skyy will introduce Skyy Blue, an alternative malt beverage with a citrus flavor. The partnership with Allied Domecq will introduce alternative malt beverages based on Allied Domecq's Stolichnaya™ vodka and Sauza™ tequila brands.

BUSINESS

PHILIP MORRIS COMPANIES, INC. is one of the world's largest consumer products companies. Tobacco is manufactured and sold through Philip Morris U.S.A., (27.6% of 2001 operating revenues and 30.1% of operating income) and Philip Morris International Inc. (29.6%, 30.9%). Retail packaged foods are processed and marketed through Kraft Foods North America (27.9%, 27.4%) in the U.S. and Canada and Kraft Foods International (9.7%, 7.1%) in Europe and the Asia/Pacific region. Miller Brewing Co. (4.7%, 2.8%) products include MILLER LITE, MILLER GENUINE DRAFT, MILLER HIGH LIFE, ICEHOUSE and FOSTER'S Lager beers. Philip Morris Capital Corporation (0.5%, 1.7%) engages in financing and investment activities. On 12/11/00, MO acquired Nabisco Holding Corp. for total consideration of $18.90 billion. As of 1/30/02, MO owned 83.9% of the outstanding common shares of Kraft Foods Inc. following Kraft Foods Inc.'s 6/13/01 initial public offering for a portion of its stock.

ANNUAL FINANCIAL DATA

	12/31/01	12/31/00	12/31/99	12/31/98	12/31/97	12/31/96	12/31/95
Earnings Per Share	⑤ 3.88	④ 3.75	③ 3.19	① 2.20	① 2.58	2.56	② 2.17
Cash Flow Per Share	4.93	4.50	3.90	2.89	3.25	3.25	2.83
Dividends Per Share	2.17	1.97	1.80	1.64	1.60	1.40	1.16
Dividend Payout %	55.9	52.5	56.4	74.5	62.0	54.7	53.5

INCOME STATEMENT (IN MILLIONS):

Total Revenues	89,924.0	80,356.0	78,596.0	74,391.0	72,055.0	69,204.0	66,071.0
Costs & Expenses	71,885.0	63,960.0	63,404.0	62,724.0	58,763.0	55,744.0	53,874.0
Depreciation & Amort.	2,337.0	1,717.0	1,702.0	1,690.0	1,629.0	1,691.0	1,671.0
Operating Income	15,702.0	14,679.0	13,490.0	9,977.0	11,663.0	11,769.0	10,526.0
Net Interest Inc./(Exp.)	d1,418.0	d719.0	d795.0	d890.0	d1,052.0	d1,086.0	d1,179.0
Income Before Income Taxes	14,284.0	13,960.0	12,695.0	9,087.0	10,611.0	10,683.0	9,347.0
Income Taxes	5,407.0	5,450.0	5,020.0	3,715.0	4,301.0	4,380.0	3,869.0
Equity Earnings/Minority Int.	d311.0	...	...	...	...	...	...
Net Income	⑤ 8,566.0	④ 8,510.0	③ 7,675.0	① 5,372.0	① 6,310.0	6,303.0	② 5,478.0
Cash Flow	10,903.0	10,227.0	9,377.0	7,062.0	7,939.0	7,994.0	7,149.0
Average Shs. Outstg. (000)	2,210,000	2,272,000	2,403,000	2,446,000	2,442,000	2,463,327	2,524,674

BALANCE SHEET (IN MILLIONS):

Cash & Cash Equivalents	453.0	937.0	5,100.0	4,081.0	2,282.0	240.0	1,138.0
Total Current Assets	17,275.0	17,238.0	20,895.0	20,230.0	17,440.0	15,190.0	14,879.0
Net Property	15,137.0	15,303.0	12,271.0	12,335.0	11,621.0	11,751.0	11,116.0
Total Assets	84,968.0	79,067.0	61,381.0	59,920.0	55,947.0	54,871.0	53,811.0
Total Current Liabilities	20,653.0	26,976.0	18,017.0	16,379.0	15,071.0	15,040.0	14,944.0
Long-Term Obligations	18,651.0	19,154.0	12,226.0	12,615.0	12,430.0	12,961.0	13,107.0
Net Stockholders' Equity	19,620.0	15,005.0	15,305.0	16,197.0	14,920.0	14,218.0	13,985.0
Net Working Capital	d3,378.0	d9,738.0	2,878.0	3,851.0	2,369.0	150.0	d65.0
Year-end Shs. Outstg. (000)	2,152,503	2,208,896	2,338,520	2,430,535	2,425,487	2,431,347	2,493,510

STATISTICAL RECORD:

Operating Profit Margin %	17.5	18.3	17.2	13.4	16.2	17.0	15.9
Net Profit Margin %	9.5	10.6	9.8	7.2	8.8	9.1	8.3
Return on Equity %	43.7	56.7	50.1	33.2	42.3	44.3	39.2
Return on Assets %	10.1	10.8	12.5	9.0	11.3	11.5	10.2
Debt/Total Assets %	22.0	24.2	19.9	21.1	22.2	23.6	24.4
Price Range	53.88-38.75	45.94-18.69	55.56-21.25	59.50-34.75	48.13-36.00	39.67-28.54	31.46-18.58
P/E Ratio	13.9-10.0	12.2-5.0	17.4-6.7	27.0-15.8	18.7-14.0	15.5-11.1	14.5-8.6
Average Yield %	4.7	6.1	4.7	3.5	3.8	4.1	4.6

Statistics are as originally reported. Adj. for 3-for-1 stk. split, 4/97. ① Incl. pre-tax non-recurr. chrg. 12/31/01, $3.38 bill.; 12/31/97, $1.46 bill. ② Bef. acctg. chge. chrg. of $28.0 mill. ③ Incl. non-recurr. chrgs. of $476.0 mill. ④ Incl. pre-tax gain of $139.0 mill. on sale of confect. business & $100.0 mill. gain on sale of beer rights. ⑤ Incl. pre-tax non-recurr. chrg. of $19.0 mill. & loss of $82.0 mill. rel. to fact. sale and integr. costs; bef. acctg. chge. chrg. of $6.0 mill.

OFFICERS:
G. C. Bible, Chmn.
W. H. Webb, Vice-Chmn., C.O.O.
L. C. Camilleri, Pres., C.E.O.

INVESTOR CONTACT: Nicholas M. Rolli, Inv. Rel., (917) 663-3460

PRINCIPAL OFFICE: 120 Park Avenue, New York, NY 10017

TELEPHONE NUMBER: (917) 663-5000
FAX: (917) 878-2167
WEB: www.philipmorris.com

NO. OF EMPLOYEES: 175,000 (approx.)

SHAREHOLDERS: 131,700 (approx.)

ANNUAL MEETING: In Apr.

INCORPORATED: VA, Mar., 1985

INSTITUTIONAL HOLDINGS:
No. of Institutions: 881
Shares Held: 1,432,936,771
% Held: 66.7

INDUSTRY: Cigarettes (SIC: 2111)

TRANSFER AGENT(S): First Chicago Trust Company, Jersey City, NJ

PIEDMONT NATURAL GAS COMPANY, INC.

YIELD 4.5%
P/E RATIO 20.6

7 YEAR PRICE SCORE 100.5   **12 MONTH PRICE SCORE 102.7**
*NYSE COMPOSITE INDEX=100

INTERIM EARNINGS (Per Share):

Qtr.	Jan.	Apr.	July	Oct.
1997-98	1.36	1.17	d0.20	d0.35
1998-99	1.32	1.12	0.26	d0.28
1999-00	1.40	1.18	d0.32	d0.23
2000-01	1.56	1.23	d0.52	d0.24
2001-02	1.26	...	...	...

INTERIM DIVIDENDS (Per Share):

Amt.	Decl.	Ex.	Rec.	Pay.
0.385Q	2/23/01	3/20/01	3/22/01	4/12/01
0.385Q	6/01/01	6/20/01	6/22/01	7/13/01
0.385Q	8/24/01	9/20/01	9/24/01	10/15/01
0.385Q	12/07/01	12/20/01	12/24/01	1/15/02
0.40Q	2/22/02	3/21/02	3/25/02	4/15/02

Indicated div.: $1.60 (Div. Reinv. Plan)

CAPITALIZATION (10/31/01):

	($000)	(%)
Long-Term Debt	509,000	42.0
Deferred Income Tax	143,211	11.8
Common & Surplus	560,379	46.2
Total	1,212,590	100.0

DIVIDEND ACHIEVER STATUS:
Rank: 222   10-Year Growth Rate: 5.74%
Total Years of Dividend Growth: 22

RECENT DEVELOPMENTS: For the quarter ended 1/31/02, net income declined 18.2% to $41.2 million compared with $50.3 million in the equivalent quarter of 2000. Operating revenues dropped 38.2% to $288.8 million from $467.6 million in the year-earlier quarter. The decrease in revenues and earnings was primarily due to unseasonably warm weather. Margin (revenues less the cost of gas) slipped 4.2% to $123.2 million from $128.6 million in 2000.

PROSPECTS: Going forward, the Company's results may continue to be negatively affected by a combination of unseasonable temperatures, weak economic conditions and lower consumer demand. As a result, the Company has lowered its earnings guidance for the fiscal year to between $1.90 and $2.00 per share. The Company's previous earnings guidance was between $2.10 to $2.20 per share for the fiscal year.

BUSINESS

PIEDMONT NATURAL GAS COMPANY, INC. is engaged in the transportation, distribution and sale of natural gas to over 710,000 residential, commercial and industrial customers in North Carolina, South Carolina and Tennessee. Non-utility subsidiaries and divisions are involved in the exploration, development, marketing and transportation of natural gas, oil, and propane. PNY's utility operations are subject to regulation by the North Carolina Utilities Commission, the Tennessee Public Service Commission and the Public Service Commission of South Carolina. PNY also owns Tennessee Natural Resources, Inc., and its subsidiaries.

ANNUAL FINANCIAL DATA

	10/31/01	10/31/00	10/31/99	10/31/98	10/31/97	10/31/96	10/31/95
Earnings Per Share	2.02	2.01	1.86	1.96	①1.81	1.67	1.45
Cash Flow Per Share	3.66	3.65	3.40	3.46	3.26	3.04	2.73
Tang. Book Val. Per Share	17.26	16.52	15.71	14.91	13.90	13.07	12.31
Dividends Per Share	1.52	1.44	1.36	1.28	1.21	1.15	1.08
Dividend Payout %	75.2	71.6	73.1	65.3	66.6	68.6	74.8
INCOME STATEMENT (IN MILLIONS)							
Total Revenues	1,107.9	830.4	686.5	765.3	775.5	685.1	505.2
Costs & Expenses	941.8	671.5	531.3	613.3	631.9	554.5	387.8
Depreciation & Amort.	53.1	52.1	47.9	46.1	43.4	40.1	35.7
Maintenance Exp.	19.1	17.1	15.6	14.7	16.2	15.8	16.4
Operating Income	94.0	89.7	91.7	91.2	84.0	74.6	65.3
Net Interest Inc./(Exp.)	d39.4	d40.3	d32.4	d33.2	d34.0	d31.1	d29.5
Income Taxes	7.3	...	...	...	...	...	...
Net Income	65.5	64.0	58.2	60.3	①54.1	48.6	40.3
Cash Flow	118.6	116.1	106.1	106.4	97.5	88.7	76.0
Average Shs. Outstg. (000)	32,420	31,779	31,242	30,717	29,883	29,161	27,890
BALANCE SHEET (IN MILLIONS)							
Gross Property	1,626.2	1,534.0	1,441.3	1,345.9	1,256.8	1,168.4	1,074.7
Accumulated Depreciation	511.5	463.0	420.1	381.6	342.4	306.4	273.4
Net Property	1,115.9	1,072.0	1,047.0	990.6	941.7	889.1	827.6
Total Assets	1,393.7	1,445.0	1,288.7	1,162.8	1,098.2	1,064.9	964.9
Long-Term Obligations	509.0	451.0	423.0	371.0	381.0	391.0	361.0
Net Stockholders' Equity	560.4	527.4	491.7	458.3	419.8	386.1	355.0
Year-end Shs. Outstg. (000)	32,463	31,914	31,295	30,738	30,193	29,549	28,835
STATISTICAL RECORD:							
Operating Profit Margin %	8.5	10.8	13.4	11.9	10.8	10.9	12.9
Net Profit Margin %	5.9	7.7	8.5	7.9	7.0	7.1	8.0
Net Inc./Net Property %	5.9	6.0	5.6	6.1	5.7	5.5	4.9
Net Inc./Tot. Capital %	5.4	5.7	5.6	6.4	6.0	5.6	5.0
Return on Equity %	11.7	12.1	11.8	13.2	12.9	12.6	11.4
Accum. Depr./Gross Prop. %	31.5	30.2	29.1	28.4	27.2	26.2	25.4
Price Range	38.00-29.19	39.44-23.69	36.63-28.63	36.13-27.88	36.44-22.00	25.75-20.50	24.88-18.25
P/E Ratio	18.8-14.4	19.6-11.8	19.7-15.4	18.4-14.2	20.1-12.2	15.4-12.3	17.2-12.6
Average Yield %	4.5	4.6	4.2	4.0	4.1	5.0	5.0

Statistics are as originally reported. ① Incl. pre-tax restruct. chg. of $1.8 mill.

OFFICERS:
J. H. Maxheim, Chmn.
W. F. Schiefer, C.E.O.
T. E. Skains, Pres., C.O.O.
T. C. Coble, V.P., Treas., Asst. Sec.

INVESTOR CONTACT: Stephen D. Connor, Investor Relations, (704) 364-3483 ext.6205

PRINCIPAL OFFICE: 1915 Rexford Road, Charlotte, NC 28211

TELEPHONE NUMBER: (704) 364-3120
FAX: (704) 365-8515
WEB: www.piedmontng.com

NO. OF EMPLOYEES: 1,657 (avg.)

SHAREHOLDERS: 16,620

ANNUAL MEETING: In Feb.

INCORPORATED: NY, May, 1950; reincorp., NC, Mar., 1994

INSTITUTIONAL HOLDINGS:
No. of Institutions: 140
Shares Held: 9,254,381
% Held: 28.3

INDUSTRY: Natural gas distribution (SIC: 4924)

TRANSFER AGENT(S): Wachovia Bank of North Carolina, NA, Boston, MA

PIER 1 IMPORTS, INC.

YIELD 1.0%
P/E RATIO 19.8

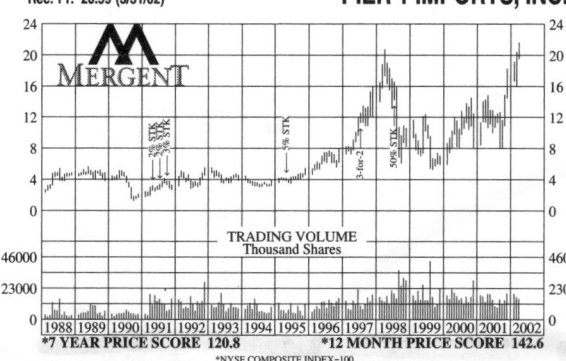

INTERIM EARNINGS (Per Share):

Qtr.	May	Aug.	Nov.	Feb.
1997-98	0.13	0.21	0.16	0.24
1998-99	0.15	0.17	0.19	0.27
1999-00	0.13	0.12	0.16	0.34
2000-01	0.17	0.18	0.24	0.38
2001-02	0.13	0.14	0.26	0.51

INTERIM DIVIDENDS (Per Share):

Amt.	Decl.	Ex.	Rec.	Pay.
0.04Q	6/28/01	7/30/01	8/01/01	8/15/01
0.04Q	9/27/01	10/30/01	11/01/01	11/15/01
0.04Q	12/06/01	2/04/02	2/06/02	2/20/02
0.05Q	4/05/02	5/06/02	5/08/02	5/22/02

Indicated div.: $0.20 (Div. Reinv. Plan)

CAPITALIZATION (3/3/01):

	($000)	(%)
Long-Term Debt	25,000	4.5
Common & Surplus	531,879	95.5
Total	556,879	100.0

TRADING VOLUME
Thousand Shares

46000

23000

0

1988 | 1989 | 1990 | 1991 | 1992 | 1993 | 1994 | 1995 | 1996 | 1997 | 1998 | 1999 | 2000 | 2001 | 2002

*7 YEAR PRICE SCORE 120.8   ***12 MONTH PRICE SCORE 142.6**
*NYSE COMPOSITE INDEX=100

DIVIDEND ACHIEVER STATUS:
Rank: 8   10-Year Growth Rate: 26.05%
Total Years of Dividend Growth: 10

RECENT DEVELOPMENTS: For the twelve months ended 3/2/02, net income climbed 5.9% to $100.2 million from $94.7 million in the corresponding period a year earlier. Net sales totaled $1.55 billion, up 9.7% versus $1.41 billion the previous year. Comparable-store sales increased 4.5% year over year. Cost of sales, including buying and store occupancy, rose 10.0% to $898.8 million from $817.0 million the year before. Operating income grew 4.8% to $158.8 million from $151.5 million in the prior year.

PROSPECTS: The Company's aggressive marketing efforts and new merchandise selections are helping boost customer traffic and average transaction values. Earnings are being positively affected by increased sales of regular-priced merchandise and PIR's cost-control initiatives. On 1/7/02, the Company signed an agreement to purchase a site for its new corporate headquarters that will better accommodate PIR's future growth. The Company anticipates relocating to the new facility in 2004.

BUSINESS

PIER 1 IMPORTS, INC. is a retailer of decorative home furnishings, furniture, dining and kitchen goods, bath and bedding accessories and other specialty items for the home imported from over 50 countries. As of 12/1/01, PIR operated 966 stores in 48 states, Canada, Puerto Rico, Mexico and Japan under the names "Pier 1 Imports" and "Cargo." In addition, PIR operates retail stores in the United Kingdom under the name "The Pier." In 1993, PIR sold its 49.5% ownership interest in Sunbelt Nursery Group to General Host Corporation. In 1997, PIR acquired a national bank and its assets in Omaha, Nebraska, which operates under the name of Pier 1 National Bank and holds the credit card accounts for the Company's proprietary credit card.

ANNUAL FINANCIAL DATA

	p3/2/02	3/3/01	2/26/00	2/27/99	2/28/98	3/1/97	3/2/96
Earnings Per Share	1.04	0.97	0.75	0.77	☐1 0.72	☐3 0.49	☐2 0.11
Cash Flow Per Share	1.49	1.41	1.11	1.02	0.90	0.69	0.30
Tang. Book Val. Per Share	6.27	5.53	4.70	4.14	3.86	3.19	2.56
Dividends Per Share	0.16	0.14	0.12	0.11	0.08	0.07	0.05
Dividend Payout %	15.4	14.4	16.0	14.3	11.4	14.5	47.4
INCOME STATEMENT (IN MILLIONS):							
Total Revenues	1,548.6	1,411.5	1,231.1	1,138.6	1,075.4	947.1	810.7
Costs & Expenses	1,346.9	1,216.8	1,067.9	972.8	929.7	837.1	720.8
Depreciation & Amort.	42.8	43.2	40.0	31.1	23.9	19.8	17.2
Operating Income	158.8	151.5	123.2	134.7	121.7	90.2	72.7
Net Interest Inc./(Exp.)	d2.3	d3.1	d6.9	d7.9	d8.7	d9.9	d13.8
Income Before Income Taxes	159.0	150.2	118.6	129.6	124.0	80.3	28.4
Income Taxes	58.8	55.6	43.9	49.3	46.0	32.1	18.4
Net Income	100.2	94.7	74.7	80.4	☐1 78.0	☐3 48.2	☐2 10.0
Cash Flow	143.0	137.8	114.7	111.5	102.0	68.0	27.3
Average Shs. Outstg. (000)	96,185	97,952	103,297	108,864	112,880	98,285	89,501
BALANCE SHEET (IN MILLIONS):							
Cash & Cash Equivalents	235.6	46.8	50.4	41.9	80.7	32.3	13.5
Total Current Assets	605.2	477.1	415.3	381.9	402.4	285.5	347.5
Net Property	210.0	211.8	213.0	226.3	216.3	216.8	144.6
Total Assets	862.7	735.7	670.7	654.0	653.4	570.3	531.1
Total Current Liabilities	208.4	144.1	176.0	128.9	121.6	110.4	100.7
Long-Term Obligations	25.4	25.0	25.0	96.0	114.9	111.3	180.1
Net Stockholders' Equity	585.7	531.9	440.7	403.9	392.7	323.0	227.9
Net Working Capital	396.8	333.0	239.3	252.1	280.8	175.1	246.8
Year-end Shs. Outstg. (000)	93,417	96,160	93,830	97,672	101,855	101,223	89,042
STATISTICAL RECORD:							
Operating Profit Margin %	10.3	10.7	10.0	11.8	11.3	9.5	9.0
Net Profit Margin %	6.5	6.7	6.1	7.1	7.3	5.1	1.2
Return on Equity %	17.1	17.8	17.0	19.9	19.9	14.9	4.4
Return on Assets %	11.6	12.9	11.1	12.3	11.9	8.5	1.9
Debt/Total Assets %	2.9	3.4	3.7	14.7	17.6	19.5	33.9
Price Range	18.30-7.97	14.50-5.88	12.38-5.25	20.75-6.06	15.96-7.22	7.95-4.61	5.50-3.45
P/E Ratio	17.6-7.7	14.9-6.1	16.5-7.0	26.9-7.9	22.2-10.0	16.2-9.4	49.5-31.0
Average Yield %	1.2	1.4	1.4	0.8	0.7	1.1	1.2

Statistics are as originally reported. Adj. for 3-for-2 stk. split, 7/98 & 7/97. ☐1 Incl. $9.1 mil ($0.08/sh) gain. ☐2 Incl. $9.6 mil non-recur. chg. ☐3 Bef. $4.1 mil extraord. chg.

OFFICERS:
M. J. Girouard, Chmn., C.E.O.
C. H. Turner, Sr. V.P., C.F.O., Treas.
R. Lawrence, Sr. V.P., Sec.

INVESTOR CONTACT: Cary Turner, Investor Relations, (817) 252-8400

PRINCIPAL OFFICE: 301 Commerce Street, Suite 600, Fort Worth, TX 76102

TELEPHONE NUMBER: (817) 252-8000
FAX: (817) 334-0191
WEB: www.pier1.com
NO. OF EMPLOYEES: 6,500 full-time (approx.); 8,100 part-time (approx.).
SHAREHOLDERS: 35,000 (approx.)
ANNUAL MEETING: In June
INCORPORATED: GA, May, 1978; reincorp., DE, Apr., 1979

INSTITUTIONAL HOLDINGS:
No. of Institutions: 208
Shares Held: 78,769,020
% Held: 84.3

INDUSTRY: Furniture stores (SIC: 5712)

TRANSFER AGENT(S): Mellon Investor Services, Ridgefield Park, NJ

PITNEY BOWES INC.

YIELD 2.8%
P/E RATIO 20.6

INTERIM EARNINGS (Per Share):

Qtr.	Mar.	June	Sept.	Dec.
1998	0.46	0.51	0.50	0.59
1999	0.52	0.58	0.69	0.66
2000	0.57	0.64	0.63	0.55
2001	0.42	0.76	0.49	0.41

INTERIM DIVIDENDS (Per Share):

Amt.	Decl.	Ex.	Rec.	Pay.
0.29Q	7/09/01	8/22/01	8/24/01	9/12/01
0.29Q	11/12/01	12/06/01	12/10/01	12/17/01
0.295Q	1/29/02	2/20/02	2/22/02	3/12/02
0.295Q	4/08/02	5/22/02	5/24/02	6/12/02

Indicated div.: $1.18 (Div. Reinv. Plan)

CAPITALIZATION (12/31/01):

	($000)	(%)
Long-Term Debt	2,419,150	52.8
Deferred Income Tax	1,273,593	27.8
Preferred Stock	1,627	0.0
Common & Surplus	889,728	19.4
Total	4,584,098	100.0

TRADING VOLUME
Thousand Shares

*7 YEAR PRICE SCORE 87.2   *12 MONTH PRICE SCORE 106.3
*NYSE COMPOSITE INDEX=100

DIVIDEND ACHIEVER STATUS:
Rank: 86   10-Year Growth Rate: 13.06%
Total Years of Dividend Growth: 18

RECENT DEVELOPMENTS: For the year ended 12/31/01, income from continuing operations was $514.3 million versus income from continuing operations of $563.1 million the prior year. Results for 2001 included a pre-tax restructuring charge of $116.1 million, a $268.3 million pre-tax charge related to new mailing technology and a $338.1 million pre-tax gain from litigation settlement. Results for 2000 included a pre-tax restructuring charge of $18.7 million. Total revenue rose 6.2% to $4.12 billion.

PROSPECTS: On 12/3/01, the Company announced that it has completed a tax-free spin-off of its office systems operations to PBI shareholders as an independent, publicly-traded company under the name Imagistics International Inc. (NYSE symbol: IGI). PBI shareholders of record on 11/19/01 received 0.08 shares of IGI stock for each PBI share owned. Meanwhile, the Company is targeting revenue growth of 7.0% to 9.0% and earnings of $2.37 to $2.40 per share in 2002.

BUSINESS

PITNEY BOWES INC. and its subsidiaries operate within three industry segments: Global Mailing, Enterprise Solutions, and Capital Services. Global Mailing, 69.0% of 2001 revenue (85.1% of operating profit), includes the sale, rental, and financing of mail finishing, mail creation and shipping equipment, related supplies and services, postal payment services, and software. Enterprise Solutions, 26.3% (7.7%), includes facilities management, through Pitney Bowes Management Services, Inc., and sales, service and financing of high-speed, software-enabled production mail systems, sorting equipment, incoming mail systems, electronic statement, billing and payment services, and mailing software. Capital Services, 4.7% (7.2%), includes large-ticket financing programs for a broad range of products.

ANNUAL FINANCIAL DATA

	12/31/01	12/31/00	12/31/99	12/31/98	12/31/97	12/31/96	12/31/95
Earnings Per Share	⑤ 2.08	④ 2.18	③ 2.42	① 2.03	1.80	③ 1.56	② 1.34
Cash Flow Per Share	3.36	3.42	3.94	3.32	2.82	2.51	2.25
Tang. Book Val. Per Share	1.05	4.34	5.28	5.26	5.96	6.86	6.20
Dividends Per Share	1.16	1.14	1.02	0.90	0.80	0.69	0.60
Dividend Payout %	55.8	52.3	42.1	44.3	44.4	44.2	44.8

INCOME STATEMENT (IN MILLIONS):

Total Revenues	4,122.5	3,880.9	4,432.6	4,220.5	4,100.5	3,858.6	3,554.8
Costs & Expenses	3,192.6	2,564.5	2,906.2	2,845.8	2,796.5	2,698.8	2,445.5
Depreciation & Amort.	317.4	321.2	412.1	361.3	300.1	278.2	271.6
Operating Income	612.5	995.2	1,114.3	1,013.4	1,003.8	881.6	837.6
Net Interest Inc./(Exp.)	d184.2	d192.4	d179.3	d149.2	d200.7	d197.2	d218.6
Income Before Income Taxes	766.4	802.8	984.6	864.2	803.1	684.4	618.9
Income Taxes	252.1	239.7	325.4	296.2	277.1	215.0	211.2
Net Income	⑤ 514.3	④ 563.1	③ 659.2	① 567.9	526.0	③ 469.4	② 407.7
Cash Flow	831.8	884.1	1,071.1	929.1	825.9	747.4	679.1
Average Shs. Outstg. (000)	247,616	258,602	272,006	279,657	292,517	298,234	302,280

BALANCE SHEET (IN MILLIONS):

Cash & Cash Equivalents	233.4	213.5	256.7	129.0	138.8	136.8	88.6
Total Current Assets	2,556.6	2,626.7	3,342.6	2,509.0	2,463.5	2,222.1	2,101.1
Net Property	1,008.3	1,114.5	1,306.1	1,287.8	1,289.7	1,307.2	1,276.2
Total Assets	8,008.5	7,591.3	7,912.7	7,350.9	7,593.4	7,955.7	7,644.6
Total Current Liabilities	3,083.0	2,881.6	2,872.8	2,721.8	3,373.2	3,305.3	3,501.6
Long-Term Obligations	2,419.2	1,881.9	1,997.9	1,712.9	1,068.4	1,300.4	1,048.5
Net Stockholders' Equity	891.4	1,285.0	1,625.6	1,648.0	1,872.6	2,239.0	2,071.1
Net Working Capital	d526.4	d254.9	469.8	d212.8	d909.7	d1,083.2	d1,400.5
Year-end Shs. Outstg. (000)	242,028	248,800	264,695	270,378	279,674	295,960	299,892

STATISTICAL RECORD:

Operating Profit Margin %	14.9	25.6	25.1	24.0	24.5	22.8	23.6
Net Profit Margin %	12.5	14.5	14.9	13.5	12.8	12.2	11.5
Return on Equity %	57.7	43.8	40.5	34.5	28.1	21.0	19.7
Return on Assets %	6.4	7.4	8.3	7.7	6.9	5.9	5.3
Debt/Total Assets %	30.2	24.8	25.2	23.3	14.1	16.3	13.7
Price Range	44.70-32.00	54.13-24.00	73.31-40.88	66.38-42.22	45.75-26.81	30.69-20.94	24.13-15.00
P/E Ratio	21.5-15.4	24.8-11.0	30.3-16.9	32.7-20.8	25.4-14.9	19.7-13.4	18.0-11.2
Average Yield %	3.0	2.9	1.8	1.7	2.2	2.7	3.1

Statistics are as originally reported. Adj. for 2-for-1 stk. split, 1/98. ① Bef. discont. opers. chg. $22.9 mil, 1999; $8.5 mil, 1998. ② Bef. discont. opers. cr$175.4 mil & incl. $155 mil nonrecur. gain. ③ Incl. $30 mil restr. chg. ④ Bef. $64.1 mil ($0.25/sh) discont. oper. gain & $4.7 mil ($0.02/sh) acctg. chg. ⑤ Bef. $26.0 mil ($0.10/sh) discont. oper. chg. & incl. $268.3 mil chg for new mailing technology, $116.1 mil restr. chg. and $338.1 mil gain fr. a lawsuit settlement.

OFFICERS:
M. J. Critelli, Chmn., C.E.O.
M. C. Breslawsky, Pres., C.O.O.
B. P. Nolop, Exec V.P, C.F.O.
INVESTOR CONTACT: Charles F. McBride, Exec. Dir., Invest. Rel., (203) 351-6349
PRINCIPAL OFFICE: One Elmcroft Road, Stamford, CT 06926-0700

TELEPHONE NUMBER: (203) 356-5000
FAX: (203) 351-7336
WEB: www.pitneybowes.com
NO. OF EMPLOYEES: 32,724 (avg.)
SHAREHOLDERS: 27,849
ANNUAL MEETING: In May
INCORPORATED: DE, Apr., 1920

INSTITUTIONAL HOLDINGS:
No. of Institutions: 469
Shares Held: 188,289,682
% Held: 77.8
INDUSTRY: Office machines, nec (SIC: 3579)
TRANSFER AGENT(S): EquiServe, Jersey City, NJ

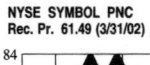

NYSE SYMBOL PNC
Rec. Pr. 61.49 (3/31/02)

PNC FINANCIAL SERVICES GROUP, INC.

YIELD 3.1%
P/E RATIO 34.9

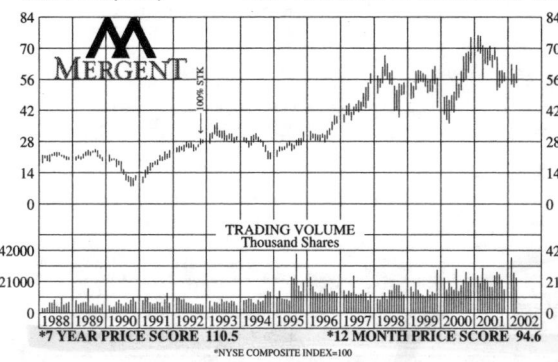

TRADING VOLUME
Thousand Shares

| 1988 | 1989 | 1990 | 1991 | 1992 | 1993 | 1994 | 1995 | 1996 | 1997 | 1998 | 1999 | 2000 | 2001 | 2002 |

*7 YEAR PRICE SCORE 110.5 ***12 MONTH PRICE SCORE 94.6**
*NYSE COMPOSITE INDEX=100

INTERIM EARNINGS (Per Share):

Qtr.	Mar.	June	Sept.	Dec.
1998	0.87	0.90	0.91	0.92
1999	1.05	1.03	1.06	1.01
2000	1.03	1.06	1.01	1.06
2001	0.89	1.00	1.02	d1.15

INTERIM DIVIDENDS (Per Share):

Amt.	Decl.	Ex.	Rec.	Pay.
0.48Q	4/05/01	4/10/01	4/13/01	4/24/01
0.48Q	7/05/01	7/11/01	7/13/01	7/24/01
0.48Q	10/03/01	10/10/01	10/12/01	10/24/01
0.48Q	1/03/02	1/09/02	1/11/02	1/24/02
0.48Q	4/02/02	4/10/02	4/12/02	4/24/02

Indicated div.: $1.92 (Div. Reinv. Plan)

CAPITALIZATION (12/31/01):

	($000)	(%)
Total Deposits	47,304,000	73.8
Long-Term Debt	10,969,000	17.1
Preferred Stock	1,000	0.0
Common & Surplus	5,822,000	9.1
Total	64,096,000	100.0

DIVIDEND ACHIEVER STATUS:
Rank: 211   10-Year Growth Rate: 6.12%
Total Years of Dividend Growth: 10

RECENT DEVELOPMENTS: For the year ended 12/31/01, PNC reported income from continuing operations of $377.0 million, before an accounting charge of $5.0 million, versus income from continuing operations of $1.21 billion in the prior year. Results for 2001 and 2000 excluded income of $5.0 million and $65.0 million, respectively, from discontinued operations. Results for 2001 included an after-tax repositioning cost of $615.0 million. Net interest income increased 3.8% to $2.27 billion.

PROSPECTS: In 2002, PNC expects diluted earnings per share of about $4.60, despite a difficult operating environment. Separately, PNC is repositioning its institutional lending businesses as a corporate services franchise and has elected to exit approximately $3.10 billion of loans and about $8.20 billion in exposure. As a result, PNC expects its non-credit revenue as a percentage of total revenue to exceed 60.0% of this business.

BUSINESS

PNC FINANCIAL SERVICES GROUP, INC. (formerly PNC Bank Corporation) is one of the largest diversified financial services companies in the nation with $69.57 billion in total assets as of 12/31/01. PNC operates seven major businesses engaged in regional banking, wholesale banking and asset management activities: PNC Bank-Regional Banking; PNC Bank-Corporate Banking; PNC Secured Finance; PNC Mortgage; PNC Advisors; BlackRock; and PFPC. The Company provides products and services nationally and in PNC's primary geographic markets in Pennsylvania, New Jersey, Delaware, Ohio and Kentucky. On 12/31/95, PNC acquired Midlantic Corp. On 12/1/98, PNC acquired Hilliard-Lyons, Inc. As of 12/31/01, assets under management totaled $284.00 billion.

ANNUAL FINANCIAL DATA

	12/31/01	12/31/00	12/31/99	12/31/98	12/31/97	12/31/96	12/31/95
Earnings Per Share	⑤ 1.26	④ 4.09	③ 4.15	3.60	3.28	② 2.90	① 1.19
Tang. Book Val. Per Share	12.19	14.42	6.20	11.49	12.47	18.09	17.06
Dividends Per Share	1.92	1.83	1.68	1.58	1.50	1.42	1.40
Dividend Payout %	52.4	44.7	40.5	43.9	45.7	49.0	117.6
INCOME STATEMENT (IN MILLIONS):							
Total Interest Income	4,137.0	4,732.0	4,921.0	5,313.0	5,051.0	4,938.0	5,149.4
Total Interest Expense	1,875.0	2,568.0	2,488.0	2,740.0	2,556.0	2,494.0	3,007.6
Net Interest Income	2,262.0	2,164.0	2,433.0	2,573.0	2,495.0	2,444.0	2,141.9
Provision for Loan Losses	903.0	136.0	163.0	225.0	70.0	...	6.0
Non-Interest Income	2,543.0	2,891.0	2,745.0	2,302.0	1,775.0	1,395.0	960.4
Non-Interest Expense	3,338.0	3,071.0	3,124.0	2,940.0	2,582.0	2,312.0	2,469.3
Income Before Taxes	564.0	1,848.0	1,891.0	1,710.0	1,618.0	1,527.0	627.0
Net Income	⑤ 377.0	④ 1,214.0	③ 1,264.0	1,115.0	1,052.0	② 992.0	① 408.1
Average Shs. Outstg. (000)	290,000	292,800	300,000	305,100	316,200	340,246	339,134
BALANCE SHEET (IN MILLIONS):							
Cash & Due from Banks	4,327.0	3,662.0	3,097.0	2,534.0	4,303.0	4,016.0	3,679.0
Securities Avail. for Sale	15,243.0	7,053.0	8,759.0	8,088.0	10,048.0	12,691.0	17,450.0
Total Loans & Leases	39,138.0	51,000.0	50,770.0	58,204.0	54,657.0	52,183.0	49,056.0
Allowance for Credit Losses	1,794.0	1,674.0	1,398.0	1,307.0	1,384.0	1,551.0	1,662.0
Net Loans & Leases	37,344.0	49,326.0	49,372.0	56,897.0	53,273.0	50,632.0	47,394.0
Total Assets	69,568.0	69,844.0	75,413.0	77,207.0	75,120.0	73,260.0	73,404.0
Total Deposits	47,304.0	47,664.0	46,668.0	47,496.0	47,649.0	45,676.0	46,899.0
Long-Term Obligations	10,969.0	9,666.0	16,944.0	18,887.0	15,276.0	15,186.0	11,642.0
Total Liabilities	62,727.0	62,340.0	68,619.0	70,316.0	69,086.0	67,041.0	67,636.0
Net Stockholders' Equity	5,823.0	6,656.0	5,946.0	6,043.0	5,384.0	5,869.0	5,768.0
Year-end Shs. Outstg. (000)	283,000	290,000	293,000	303,700	300,430	324,118	338,048
STATISTICAL RECORD:							
Return on Equity %	6.5	18.2	21.3	18.5	19.5	16.9	7.1
Return on Assets %	0.5	1.7	1.7	1.4	1.4	1.4	0.6
Equity/Assets %	8.4	9.5	7.9	7.8	7.2	8.0	7.9
Non-Int. Exp./Tot. Inc. %	68.8	60.8	60.3	60.3	60.5	60.2	79.6
Price Range	75.81-51.14	75.00-36.00	62.00-43.00	66.75-38.75	58.75-36.50	39.75-27.50	32.38-21.13
P/E Ratio	60.2-40.6	18.3-8.8	14.9-10.4	18.5-10.8	17.9-11.1	13.7-9.5	27.2-17.8
Average Yield %	3.0	3.3	3.2	3.0	3.1	4.2	5.2

Statistics are as originally reported. ① Incl. after-tax merger-rel. & restr. chgs. totaling $380.2 mill. ② Incl. pre-tax SAIF chg. of $35.1 mill. ③ Incl. various nonrecurr. after-tax net gains of $280.0 mill. ④ Excl. a gain fr. disc. ops. of $5.0 mill., 2001; $65.0 mill., 2000. ⑤ Bef. acct. change chrg. of $5.0 mill. & incl. an aft-tax strategic reposition. cost of $615.0 mill.

OFFICERS:
J. E. Rohr, Chmn., Pres., C.E.O.
W. E. Gregg Jr., Vice-Chmn.
R. L. Haunschild, C.F.O.

INVESTOR CONTACT: William H. Callihan, VP, Investor Relations, (412) 762-8257

PRINCIPAL OFFICE: One PNC Plaza, 249 Fifth Avenue, Pittsburgh, PA 15265

TELEPHONE NUMBER: (412) 762-1553
FAX: (412) 762-5798
WEB: www.pnc.com

NO. OF EMPLOYEES: 24,500 (avg.)

SHAREHOLDERS: 54,385

ANNUAL MEETING: In April

INCORPORATED: PA, Jan., 1983

PPG INDUSTRIES, INC.

YIELD 3.1%
P/E RATIO 24.0

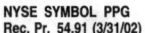

TRADING VOLUME
Thousand Shares

| 1988 | 1989 | 1990 | 1991 | 1992 | 1993 | 1994 | 1995 | 1996 | 1997 | 1998 | 1999 | 2000 | 2001 | 2002 |

7 YEAR PRICE SCORE 83.0   **12 MONTH PRICE SCORE 103.8**
*NYSE COMPOSITE INDEX=100

INTERIM EARNINGS (Per Share):

Qtr.	Mar.	June	Sept.	Dec.
1998	1.08	1.11	1.39	0.91
1999	0.70	1.05	0.56	0.92
2000	0.79	1.17	0.86	0.75
2001	0.33	0.92	0.55	0.49

INTERIM DIVIDENDS (Per Share):

Amt.	Decl.	Ex.	Rec.	Pay.
0.42Q	4/19/01	5/08/01	5/10/01	6/12/01
0.42Q	7/19/01	8/08/01	8/10/01	9/12/01
0.42Q	10/19/01	11/07/01	11/12/01	12/12/01
0.42Q	1/17/02	2/14/02	2/19/02	3/12/02

Indicated div.: $1.68 (Div. Reinv. Plan)

CAPITALIZATION (12/31/01):

	($000)	(%)
Long-Term Debt	1,699,000	31.9
Deferred Income Tax	552,000	10.4
Common & Surplus	3,080,000	57.8
Total	5,331,000	100.0

DIVIDEND ACHIEVER STATUS:

Rank: 191   10-Year Growth Rate: 6.93%
Total Years of Dividend Growth: 30

RECENT DEVELOPMENTS: For the year ended 12/31/01, net income fell 37.6% to $387.0 million compared with $620.0 million in 2000. Results for 2001 and 2000 included charges of $103.0 million and $5.0 million, respectively, for business realignments. Net sales were $8.17 billion, down 5.3% from $8.63 billion in the prior year. Results were hampered by volume declines and restructuring costs.

PROSPECTS: In an effort to continue to improve business processes, the Company announced additional restructuring and workforce reductions to take place beginning in the first quarter of 2002. These actions will result in pre-tax charges of between $60.0 million and $90.0 million, and will include workforce reductions and the closing of facilities or portions of facilities no longer needed.

BUSINESS

PPG INDUSTRIES, INC. is a supplier of products for manufacturing, construction, automotive, chemical processing and numerous other world industries. The diversified global manufacturer makes protective and decorative coatings, flat glass, fabricated glass products, continuous-strand fiberglass, and industrial and specialty chemicals. As of 12/31/01, PPG operates 70 major manufacturing facilities in countries including Canada, China, England, France, Germany, Ireland, Italy, Mexico, the Netherlands, Portugal, Spain, Taiwan, and the U.S. In 2001, revenues (and operating income) were derived: coatings, 54.0% (58.9%); glass, 27.4% (30.3%); and chemicals, 18.6% (10.8%).

ANNUAL FINANCIAL DATA

	12/31/01	12/31/00	12/31/99	12/31/98	12/31/97	12/31/96	12/31/95
Earnings Per Share	[7] 2.29	[5] 3.57	[4] 3.23	[3] 4.48	[2] 3.94	3.96	[1] 3.80
Cash Flow Per Share	4.96	6.19	5.62	6.63	5.99	5.89	5.54
Tang. Book Val. Per Share	9.12	8.61	8.30	13.17	21.29	13.55	13.21
Dividends Per Share	1.68	1.60	1.52	1.42	1.33	1.26	1.18
Dividend Payout %	73.4	44.8	47.1	31.7	33.8	31.8	31.1
INCOME STATEMENT (IN MILLIONS):							
Total Revenues	8,169.0	[8] 8,629.0	7,757.0	7,510.0	7,379.0	7,218.1	7,057.7
Costs & Expenses	6,726.0	6,907.0	6,418.0	5,851.0	5,690.0	5,561.3	5,405.5
Depreciation & Amort.	447.0	447.0	419.0	383.0	373.0	362.6	351.6
Operating Income	996.0	1,275.0	1,158.0	1,276.0	1,316.0	1,294.2	1,300.6
Net Interest Inc./(Exp.)	d241.0	d250.0	d182.0	d137.0	d105.0	d85.0	d74.0
Income Before Income Taxes	666.0	1,017.0	973.0	1,294.0	1,175.0	1,239.6	1,262.3
Income Taxes	247.0	369.0	377.0	466.0	435.0	471.0	479.7
Equity Earnings/Minority Int.	d32.0	d28.0	d28.0	d27.0	d26.0	d5.1	16.0
Net Income	[7] 387.0	[5] 620.0	[4] 568.0	[3] 801.0	[2] 714.0	744.0	[1] 767.6
Cash Flow	834.0	1,067.0	987.0	1,184.0	1,087.0	1,106.6	1,119.2
Average Int. Outstg. (000)	168,300	172,300	175,500	178,700	181,500	187,800	202,000
BALANCE SHEET (IN MILLIONS):							
Cash & Cash Equivalents	108.0	111.0	158.0	128.0	129.0	69.6	105.6
Total Current Assets	2,703.0	3,093.0	3,062.0	2,660.0	2,584.0	2,296.4	2,275.5
Net Property	2,752.0	2,941.0	2,933.0	2,905.0	2,855.0	2,913.5	2,834.8
Total Assets	8,330.0	9,125.0	8,914.0	7,387.0	6,868.0	6,441.4	6,194.3
Total Current Liabilities	1,955.0	2,543.0	2,384.0	1,912.0	1,662.0	1,768.9	1,629.4
Long-Term Obligations	1,699.0	1,810.0	1,836.0	1,081.0	1,257.0	833.9	735.5
Net Stockholders' Equity	3,080.0	3,097.0	3,106.0	2,880.0	2,509.0	2,482.6	2,569.2
Net Working Capital	748.0	550.0	678.0	748.0	922.0	527.5	646.1
Year-end Shs. Outstg. (000)	168,713	168,222	173,988	175,000	117,826	183,215	194,450
STATISTICAL RECORD:							
Operating Profit Margin %	12.2	14.8	14.9	17.0	17.8	17.9	18.4
Net Profit Margin %	4.7	7.2	7.3	10.7	9.7	10.3	10.9
Return on Equity %	12.6	20.0	18.3	27.8	28.5	30.0	29.9
Return on Assets %	4.6	6.8	6.4	10.8	10.4	11.6	12.4
Debt/Total Assets %	20.4	19.8	20.6	14.6	18.3	12.9	11.9
Price Range	59.75-38.99	65.06-36.00	70.75-47.94	76.63-49.13	67.50-48.63	62.25-42.88	47.88-34.88
P/E Ratio	26.1-17.0	18.2-10.1	21.9-14.8	17.1-11.0	17.1-12.3	15.7-10.8	12.6-9.2
Average Yield %	3.4	3.2	2.6	2.3	2.3	2.4	2.9

Statistics are as originally reported. [1] Incl $24.2 mil a-tax nonrecur. gain. [2] Incl $102 mil nonrecur. p-tx chg & $59 mil p-tx gain dvst chem busn. [3] Incl. $85.0 mill. p-tax gain fr. sale of bus. & $27.0 mill. p-tax restr. chg. and oth. chgs. [4] Incl. $110.0 mill. in p-tax chgs. [5] Incl. $5.0 mill. one-time chg. fr. bus. divestiture & realignments. [6] Incl. outgoing freight costs. [7] Incl. $103.0 mill. bus. alignments.

OFFICERS:
R. W. LeBoeuf, Chmn., C.E.O.
W. H. Hernandez, Sr. V.P., C.F.O.
J. C. Diggs, Sr. V.P., Gen. Couns.

INVESTOR CONTACT: Jeff Worden, Director of Investor Relations, (412) 434-3046

PRINCIPAL OFFICE: One PPG Place, Pittsburgh, PA 15272

TELEPHONE NUMBER: (412) 434-3131
FAX: (412) 434-2571
WEB: www.ppg.com

NO. OF EMPLOYEES: 34,900 (avg.)

SHAREHOLDERS: 29,005

ANNUAL MEETING: In Apr.

INCORPORATED: PA, Nov., 1883; reincorp., PA, Nov., 1920

INSTITUTIONAL HOLDINGS:
No. of Institutions: 419
Shares Held: 87,190,761
% Held: 51.7

INDUSTRY: Paints and allied products (SIC: 2851)

TRANSFER AGENT(S): Mellon Investor Services LLC, Ridgefield Park, NJ

PROCTER & GAMBLE COMPANY (THE)

YIELD 1.7%
P/E RATIO 42.5

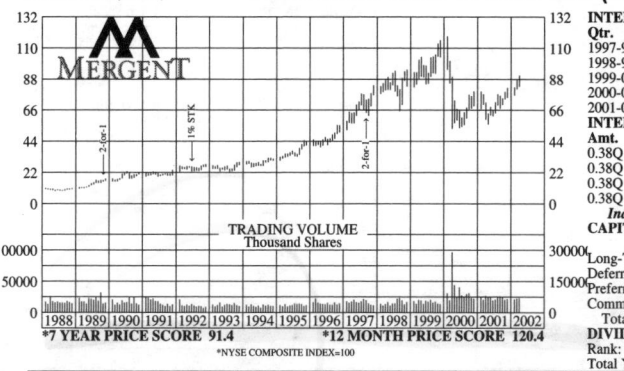

*7 YEAR PRICE SCORE 91.4 *12 MONTH PRICE SCORE 120.4
*NYSE COMPOSITE INDEX=100

TRADING VOLUME Thousand Shares

INTERIM EARNINGS (Per Share):

Qtr.	Sept.	Dec.	Mar.	June
1997-98	0.79	0.71	0.65	0.47
1998-99	0.80	0.78	0.72	0.29
1999-00	0.80	0.78	0.52	0.55
2000-01	0.82	0.84	0.63	d0.23
2001-02	0.79	0.93	...	...

INTERIM DIVIDENDS (Per Share):

Amt.	Decl.	Ex.	Rec.	Pay.
0.38Q	7/10/01	7/18/01	7/20/01	8/15/01
0.38Q	10/09/01	10/17/01	10/19/01	11/15/01
0.38Q	1/08/02	1/16/02	1/18/02	2/15/02
0.38Q	12/30/01	4/17/02	4/19/02	5/15/02

Indicated div.: $1.52 (Div. Reinv. Plan)

CAPITALIZATION (6/30/01):

	($000)	(%)
Long-Term Debt	9,792,000	43.1
Deferred Income Tax	894,000	3.9
Preferred Stock	1,701,000	7.5
Common & Surplus	10,309,000	45.4
Total	22,696,000	100.0

DIVIDEND ACHIEVER STATUS:
Rank: 111   10-Year Growth Rate: 11.31%
Total Years of Dividend Growth: 48

RECENT DEVELOPMENTS: For the three months ended 12/31/01, net income grew 8.8% to $1.30 billion from $1.19 billion in the equivalent prior-year period. Results included after-tax restructuring charges of $146.0 million and $120.0 million for 2001 and 2000, respectively. Net sales rose 2.2% to $10.40 billion from $10.18 billion in the previous year. In the fabric and homecare segment, net sales rose 1.0% to $2.97 billion. Operating income was $1.86 billion, up 8.9% from $1.71 billion the year before.

PROSPECTS: Earnings are benefiting from stronger sales in nearly all of PG's businesses, the exception being the baby, feminine and family care segment and the food and beverage segment. Unit volume in the health care segment is being fueled by the Clairol acquisition. Going forward, the proposed divestitures of the Jif peanut butter and Crisco cooking oils businesses coupled with new product introductions in the health care segment and the Clairol acquisition should drive earnings growth in 2002.

BUSINESS

THE PROCTER & GAMBLE COMPANY manufactures and markets more than 250 brands of consumer products including laundry, cleaning and personal-care products, pharmaceuticals, foods and beverages, and business and industrial products.

Leading brands are: DOWNY and TIDE cleansing compounds, BOUNTY paper towels, CREST toothpastes, ALWAYS sanitary napkins, HEAD AND SHOULDERS and PANTENE PRO-V shampoos. Other products include VICK'S cough and cold remedies, CHARMIN toilet tissue, PAMPERS diapers, OIL OF OLAY skin products, FOLGER'S coffee, PRINGLES potato chips, ACTONEL, a post-menopausal drug, and IAMS pet food. PG has operations in over 80 countries and markets to consumers in more than 140 countries. On 9/1/99, PG acquired The Iams Company, a global pet nutrition company. On 11/15/01, PG acquired the Clairol hair care business for $4.95 billion.

ANNUAL FINANCIAL DATA

	6/30/01	6/30/00	6/30/99	6/30/98	6/30/97	6/30/96	6/30/95
Earnings Per Share	☐ 2.07	☐ 2.47	☐ 2.59	2.56	2.43	2.15	1.86
Cash Flow Per Share	3.69	4.02	4.09	3.67	3.60	3.21	2.84
Tang. Book Val. Per Share	1.55	1.35	2.62	2.55	4.59	4.05	2.99
Dividends Per Share	1.46	1.34	1.21	1.07	0.95	0.85	0.75
Dividend Payout %	70.5	54.2	46.7	42.0	39.3	39.6	40.4

INCOME STATEMENT (IN MILLIONS):

	6/30/01	6/30/00	6/30/99	6/30/98	6/30/97	6/30/96	6/30/95
Total Revenues	39,244.0	39,951.0	38,125.0	37,154.0	35,764.0	35,284.0	33,434.0
Costs & Expenses	32,237.0	31,806.0	29,724.0	29,501.0	28,789.0	29,111.0	28,002.0
Depreciation & Amort.	2,271.0	2,191.0	2,148.0	1,598.0	1,487.0	1,358.0	1,253.0
Operating Income	4,736.0	5,954.0	6,253.0	6,055.0	5,488.0	4,815.0	4,179.0
Net Interest Inc./(Exp.)	d794.0	d722.0	d650.0	d548.0	d457.0	d484.0	d488.0
Income Before Income Taxes	4,616.0	5,536.0	5,838.0	5,708.0	5,249.0	4,669.0	4,000.0
Income Taxes	1,694.0	1,994.0	2,075.0	1,928.0	1,834.0	1,623.0	1,355.0
Net Income	☐ 2,922.0	☐ 3,542.0	☐ 3,763.0	3,780.0	3,415.0	3,046.0	2,645.0
Cash Flow	5,072.0	5,618.0	5,802.0	5,274.0	4,798.0	4,301.0	3,796.0
Average Shs. Outstg. (000)	1,405,600	1,427,200	1,446,800	1,465,500	1,360,000	1,372,000	1,372,000

BALANCE SHEET (IN MILLIONS):

	6/30/01	6/30/00	6/30/99	6/30/98	6/30/97	6/30/96	6/30/95
Cash & Cash Equivalents	2,518.0	1,600.0	2,800.0	2,406.0	3,110.0	2,520.0	2,178.0
Total Current Assets	10,889.0	10,069.0	11,358.0	10,577.0	10,786.0	10,807.0	10,842.0
Net Property	13,095.0	13,692.0	12,626.0	12,180.0	11,376.0	11,118.0	11,026.0
Total Assets	34,387.0	34,194.0	32,113.0	30,966.0	27,544.0	27,730.0	28,125.0
Total Current Liabilities	9,846.0	10,065.0	10,761.0	9,250.0	7,798.0	7,825.0	8,648.0
Long-Term Obligations	9,792.0	8,916.0	6,231.0	5,765.0	4,143.0	4,670.0	5,161.0
Net Stockholders' Equity	12,010.0	12,287.0	12,058.0	12,236.0	12,046.0	11,722.0	10,589.0
Net Working Capital	1,043.0	4.0	597.0	1,327.0	2,988.0	2,982.0	2,194.0
Year-end Shs. Outstg. (000)	1,295,700	1,305,900	1,319,800	1,337,400	1,360,000	1,372,000	1,374,000

STATISTICAL RECORD:

	6/30/01	6/30/00	6/30/99	6/30/98	6/30/97	6/30/96	6/30/95
Operating Profit Margin %	12.1	14.9	16.4	16.3	15.3	13.6	12.5
Net Profit Margin %	7.4	8.9	9.9	10.2	9.5	8.6	7.9
Return on Equity %	24.3	28.8	31.2	30.9	28.3	26.0	25.0
Return on Assets %	8.5	10.4	11.7	12.2	12.4	11.0	9.4
Debt/Total Assets %	28.5	26.1	19.4	18.6	15.0	16.8	18.4
Price Range	81.72-55.96	118.38-52.75	115.63-82.00	94.81-65.13	83.44-51.81	55.50-39.69	44.75-30.31
P/E Ratio	39.5-27.0	47.9-21.4	44.6-31.7	37.0-25.4	34.3-21.3	25.9-18.5	24.1-16.3
Average Yield %	2.1	1.6	1.2	1.3	1.4	1.8	2.0

Statistics are as originally reported. Adj. for stk. split: 2-for-1, 9/97 ☐ Incl. after-tax chrg. for organization 2005, $1.48 billion, 6/01; $688.0 mill., 6/00; $385.0 million, 6/99

OFFICERS:
J. E. Pepper, Chmn.
A. G. Lafley, Pres., C.E.O.
C. C. Daley Jr., C.F.O.

INVESTOR CONTACT: Inv. Rel., (513) 983-1100

PRINCIPAL OFFICE: One Procter & Gamble Plaza, Cincinnati, OH 45202

TELEPHONE NUMBER: (513) 983-1100
FAX: (513) 983-2062
WEB: www.pg.com

NO. OF EMPLOYEES: 106,000 (approx.)

SHAREHOLDERS: 1,090,000

ANNUAL MEETING: In Oct.

INCORPORATED: OH, May, 1905

INSTITUTIONAL HOLDINGS:
No. of Institutions: 1,065
Shares Held: 662,325,887
% Held: 51.1

INDUSTRY: Soap and other detergents (SIC: 2841)

TRANSFER AGENT(S): The Procter and Gamble Company, Cincinnati, OH

PROGRESS ENERGY, INC.

YIELD 4.4%
P/E RATIO 18.7

INTERIM EARNINGS (Per Share):

Qtr.	Mar.	June	Sept.	Dec.
1998	0.60	0.45	1.28	0.42
1999	0.63	0.43	0.97	0.51
2000	0.56	0.70	1.93	d0.07
2001	0.77	0.56	1.77	d0.42

INTERIM DIVIDENDS (Per Share):

Amt.	Decl.	Ex.	Rec.	Pay.
0.53Q	3/21/01	4/06/01	4/10/01	5/01/01
0.53Q	5/09/01	7/06/01	7/10/01	8/01/01
0.53Q	9/11/01	10/05/01	10/10/01	11/01/01
0.545Q	12/12/01	1/08/02	1/10/02	2/01/02
0.545Q	3/20/02	4/08/02	4/10/02	5/01/02

Indicated div.: $2.18 (Div. Reinv. Plan)

CAPITALIZATION (12/31/01):

	($000)	(%)
Long-Term Debt	9,483,745	55.7
Deferred Income Tax	1,434,506	8.4
Preferred Stock	92,831	0.5
Common & Surplus	6,003,533	35.3
Total	17,014,615	100.0

DIVIDEND ACHIEVER STATUS:
Rank: 260   10-Year Growth Rate: 3.38%
Total Years of Dividend Growth: 13

RECENT DEVELOPMENTS: For the year ended 12/31/01, net income increased 13.2% to $541.6 million versus $478.4 million in 2000. Earnings for 2001 included impairment charges of $164.2 million, while results for 2000 included a gain of $200.0 million from the sale of assets. Total revenues more than doubled to $8.46 billion from $4.10 billion a year earlier. Electric revenues soared 84.7% to $6.56 billion, while revenues from diversified businesses rocketed to $1.58 billion from $229.1 million the year before.

PROSPECTS: On 3/28/02, the Company's subsidiary, Florida Power, began construction of a new natural gas-fired combined-cycle power plant as the second phase of the planned growth of the Hines Energy Complex in Polk County, Florida. The new phase will add 395 megawatts of generating capacity by November 2003. Separately, PGN expects earnings to range from $3.90 to $4.10 per share in 2002, including about $0.45 per share due to the elimination of goodwill amortization in 2002.

BUSINESS

PROGRESS ENERGY, INC. (formerly CP&L Energy, Inc.) is a full-service utility holding company with more than 20,000 megawatts of generating capacity. PGN regulated subsidiaries include two major electric utility companies, Carolina Power & Light and Florida Power Corporation (FPC), as well as North Carolina Natural Gas Corporation. PGN's non-regulated businesses include Progress Telecommunications Corporation, Progress Rail Services Corporation and Progress Ventures, Inc. Progress Ventures manages fuel extraction, manufacturing and delivery; merchant generation; and energy marketing and trading. At 12/31/01, the Company served approximately 2.9 million electric and gas customers in portions of Florida, North Carolina and South Carolina. On 11/30/00, the Company acquired FPC for approximately $5.40 billion.

ANNUAL FINANCIAL DATA

	12/31/01	12/31/00	12/31/99	12/31/98	12/31/97	12/31/96	12/31/95
Earnings Per Share	③ 2.64	② 3.03	① 2.55	2.75	2.66	2.66	2.48
Cash Flow Per Share	8.46	8.36	10.44	10.74	10.32	9.35	9.16
Tang. Book Val. Per Share	10.58	8.60	...	19.49	18.63	17.77	16.93
Dividends Per Share	2.12	2.06	2.00	1.94	1.88	1.82	1.76
Dividend Payout %	80.3	68.0	78.4	70.5	70.7	68.4	71.0

INCOME STATEMENT (IN MILLIONS):

Total Revenues	8,461.5	4,118.9	3,357.6	3,130.0	3,024.1	2,995.7	3,006.6
Costs & Expenses	6,028.5	2,564.4	1,928.9	1,654.2	1,663.2	1,765.4	1,767.8
Depreciation & Amort.	1,189.2	835.0	588.1	578.3	565.2	446.5	446.7
Operating Income	1,243.8	719.6	840.5	897.5	795.6	783.9	792.1
Net Interest Inc./(Exp.)	d662.6	d235.3	d169.1	d164.7	d139.6	d167.5	d181.0
Income Taxes	cr151.6	202.8	258.4	257.5	253.0	269.8	259.2
Net Income	③ 541.6	② 478.4	① 382.3	399.2	388.3	391.3	372.6
Cash Flow	1,730.8	1,313.3	967.4	974.6	947.5	828.2	809.7
Average Shs. Outstg. (000)	204,683	157,169	148,344	143,941	143,645	143,621	146,232

BALANCE SHEET (IN MILLIONS):

Gross Property	21,011.3	19,786.9	11,740.2	10,796.2	10,474.6	10,196.5	9,821.6
Accumulated Depreciation	10,096.4	9,350.2	4,975.4	4,496.6	4,181.4	3,796.6	3,493.2
Net Property	10,914.9	10,436.7	6,764.8	6,299.5	6,293.2	6,399.9	6,328.5
Total Assets	20,739.8	20,091.0	9,494.0	8,347.4	8,220.4	8,369.2	8,227.1
Long-Term Obligations	9,483.7	5,890.1	3,028.6	2,614.4	2,415.7	2,525.6	2,610.3
Net Stockholders' Equity	6,096.4	5,517.0	3,472.0	3,008.7	2,878.2	2,834.3	2,718.5
Year-end Shs. Outstg. (000)	218,725	206,089	159,600	151,338	151,340	151,416	152,103

STATISTICAL RECORD:

Operating Profit Margin %	14.7	17.5	25.0	28.7	26.3	26.2	26.3
Net Profit Margin %	6.4	11.6	11.4	12.8	12.8	13.1	12.4
Net Inc./Net Property %	5.0	4.6	5.7	6.3	6.2	6.1	5.9
Net Inc./Tot. Capital %	3.2	3.6	8.1	5.5	5.5	5.4	5.3
Return on Equity %	8.9	8.7	9.1	13.3	13.5	13.8	13.7
Accum. Depr./Gross Prop. %	48.1	47.3	42.4	41.7	39.9	37.2	35.6
Price Range	49.25-38.78	49.38-28.25	47.88-29.25	49.63-39.19	42.69-32.75	38.75-33.75	34.63-26.13
P/E Ratio	18.7-14.7	16.3-9.3	18.8-11.5	18.0-14.2	16.0-12.3	14.6-12.7	14.0-10.5
Average Yield %	4.8	4.7	5.3	5.2	4.4	5.0	5.0

Statistics are as originally reported. ① Incl. one-time chrg. of $29.0 mill. ($0.14/sh.) related to storm damage. ② Incl. after-tax nonrecurr. chrg. of $118.3 mill. & an after-tax gain of $121.1 mill. fr. sale of an investment. ③ Incl. non-recurr. impairment chrg. of $164.2 mill.

OFFICERS:
W. Cavanaugh III, Chmn., Pres., C.E.O.
P. M. Scott III, Exec. V.P., C.F.O.

INVESTOR CONTACT: Robert F. Drennan Jr., Mgr., Inv. Rel., (919) 546-7474

PRINCIPAL OFFICE: 410 South Wilmington Street, Raleigh, NC 27601-1748

TELEPHONE NUMBER: (919) 546-6111
FAX: (919) 546-7678
WEB: www.progress-energy.com

NO. OF EMPLOYEES: 16,200

SHAREHOLDERS: 218,727,139

ANNUAL MEETING: In May

INCORPORATED: NC, April, 1926

INSTITUTIONAL HOLDINGS:
No. of Institutions: 370
Shares Held: 112,153,264
% Held: 51.3

INDUSTRY: Electric services (SIC: 4911)

TRANSFER AGENT(S): EquiServe Trust Company, Providence, RI

PROGRESSIVE CORPORATION (THE)

YIELD 0.2%
P/E RATIO 30.2

7 YEAR PRICE SCORE 126.0   **12 MONTH PRICE SCORE 116.0**
*NYSE COMPOSITE INDEX=100

INTERIM EARNINGS (Per Share):

Qtr.	Mar.	June	Sept.	Dec.
1997	0.34	0.45	0.51	0.46
1998	0.53	0.54	0.60	0.35
1999	0.47	0.50	0.33	0.02
2000	d0.21	d0.06	0.27	0.21
2001	0.39	0.46	0.43	0.56

INTERIM DIVIDENDS (Per Share):

Amt.	Decl.	Ex.	Rec.	Pay.
0.07Q	8/27/01	9/17/01	9/14/01	9/30/01
0.07Q	10/19/01	12/12/01	12/14/01	12/31/01
0.07Q	2/08/02	3/06/02	3/08/02	3/31/02
200% STK	3/19/02	4/23/02	4/01/02	4/22/02

Indicated div.: $0.093 (Adj.)

CAPITALIZATION (12/31/01):

	($000)	(%)
Long-Term Debt	1,095,700	25.2
Common & Surplus	3,250,700	74.8
Total	4,346,400	100.0

DIVIDEND ACHIEVER STATUS:

Rank: 234   10-Year Growth Rate: 4.91%
Total Years of Dividend Growth: 32

RECENT DEVELOPMENTS: For the year ended 12/31/01, net income rocketed to $411.4 million from $46.1 million in the previous year. Earnings benefited from higher premium rates coupled with a significant improvement in underwriting performance. Results for 2000 included a non-recurring charge of $4.2 million. Total revenues grew 10.6% to $7.49 billion from $6.77 billion in the prior year. Revenues included a net realized investment loss of $111.9 million in 2001 and a net realized investment gain of $16.9 million in 2000.

PROSPECTS: The Company continues to benefit from a significant reduction in total expense ratios and growth rates related to the Company's shift to six-month policies. Net premiums written for the fourth quarter of 2001 increased 16.0% to $1.90 billion, while the Company's combined expense ratio dropped 7.9 percentage points to 94.4%. Meanwhile, the Company recently announced that it has become the first auto insurance company approved by the Texas Department of Insurance to offer loan/lease payoff coverage to policyholders in the state.

BUSINESS

THE PROGRESSIVE CORPORATION is an insurance holding company that has 76 subsidiaries and 2 mutual insurance company affiliates. PGR, through its subsidiaries and affiliates, provides personal automobile insurance and other specialty property-casualty insurance and related services throughout the United States. The Company's personal lines segment writes insurance for private passenger automobiles and recreation vehicles. The Company's property-casualty insurance products protect its customers against collision and physical damage to their motor vehicles and liability to others for personal injury or property damage arising out of the use of those vehicles. The Company's other lines of business include the commercial vehicle business unit, United Financial Casualty Company, Professional Liability Group and Motor Carrier business unit.

ANNUAL FINANCIAL DATA

	12/31/01	12/31/00	12/31/99	12/31/98	12/31/97	12/31/96	12/31/95
Earnings Per Share	1.83	① 0.21	1.32	2.04	1.77	1.38	1.09
Tang. Book Val. Per Share	13.32	11.61	10.99	10.38	8.65	6.88	5.60
Dividends Per Share	0.093	0.090	0.087	0.083	0.080	0.077	0.073
Dividend Payout %	5.1	43.5	6.6	4.1	4.5	5.6	6.7
INCOME STATEMENT (IN MILLIONS):							
Total Premium Income	7,161.8	6,348.4	5,683.6	4,948.0	4,189.5	3,199.3	2,727.2
Other Income	326.4	422.6	440.6	344.4	418.7	279.1	284.7
Total Revenues	7,488.2	6,771.0	6,124.2	5,292.4	4,608.2	3,478.4	3,011.9
Policyholder Benefits	5,264.1	5,279.4	4,256.4	3,376.3	2,967.5	2,236.1	1,943.8
Income Before Income Taxes	587.6	31.8	412.2	661.1	578.5	441.7	345.9
Income Taxes	176.2	cr14.3	117.0	204.4	178.5	128.0	95.4
Net Income	411.4	① 46.1	295.2	456.7	400.0	313.7	250.5
Average Shs. Outstg. (000)	225,300	222,900	223,800	224,100	225,900	222,600	222,600
BALANCE SHEET (IN MILLIONS):							
Cash & Cash Equivalents	238.6	195.7	243.2	460.5	432.7	175.1	319.0
Premiums Due	1,698.6	1,804.7	2,015.5	1,737.2	1,478.3	1,130.8	988.0
Invst. Assets: Fixed-term	5,949.0	4,784.1	4,532.7	4,219.0	3,891.4	3,409.2	2,772.9
Invst. Assets: Equities	1,336.0	1,198.7	1,243.6	636.9	620.8	540.1	310.0
Invst. Assets: Total	8,226.3	6,983.3	6,427.7	5,674.3	5,270.4	4,450.6	3,768.0
Total Assets	11,122.4	10,051.6	9,704.7	8,463.1	7,559.6	6,183.9	5,352.5
Long-Term Obligations	1,095.7	748.8	1,048.6	776.6	775.9	775.7	675.9
Net Stockholders' Equity	3,250.7	2,869.8	2,752.8	2,557.1	2,135.9	1,676.9	1,475.8
Year-end Shs. Outstg. (000)	220,200	220,500	219,300	217,500	216,900	214,500	216,300
STATISTICAL RECORD:							
Return on Revenues %	5.5	0.7	4.8	8.6	8.7	9.0	8.3
Return on Equity %	12.7	1.6	10.7	17.9	18.7	18.7	17.0
Return on Assets %	3.7	0.5	3.0	5.4	5.3	5.1	4.7
Price Range	50.60-27.38	37.00-15.00	58.08-22.83	57.33-31.33	39.75-20.50	24.08-13.46	16.50-11.58
P/E Ratio	27.7-15.0	179.0-72.6	44.0-17.3	28.2-15.4	22.5-11.6	17.5-9.8	15.2-10.7
Average Yield %	0.2	0.3	0.2	0.2	0.3	0.4	0.5

Statistics are as originally reported. Adj. for stk. split: 200% div., 4/02 ① Incl. non-recurr. chrg. $4.2 mill.

OFFICERS:
P. B. Lewis, Chmn.
G. M. Renwick, Pres., C.E.O.
W. T. Forrester, C.F.O., Treas.
INVESTOR CONTACT: Investor Relations, (440) 446-2851
PRINCIPAL OFFICE: 6300 Wilson Mills Road, Mayfield Village, OH 44143

TELEPHONE NUMBER: (440) 461-5000
FAX: (440) 446-7168
WEB: www.progressive.com
NO. OF EMPLOYEES: 20,442
SHAREHOLDERS: 3,586
ANNUAL MEETING: In April
INCORPORATED: OH, Feb., 1965

INSTITUTIONAL HOLDINGS:
No. of Institutions: 295
Shares Held: 150,714,003 (Adj.)
% Held: 68.3
INDUSTRY: Fire, marine, and casualty insurance (SIC: 6331)
TRANSFER AGENT(S): National City Bank, Cleveland, OH

PROTECTIVE LIFE CORPORATION

YIELD	1.8%
P/E RATIO	15.3

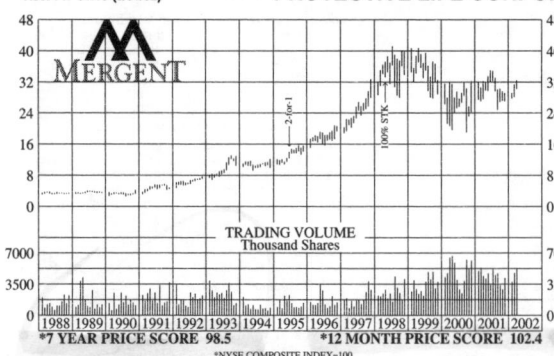

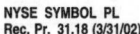
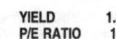

INTERIM EARNINGS (Per Share):

Qtr.	Mar.	June	Sept.	Dec.
1997	0.40	0.44	0.48	0.47
1998	0.47	0.52	0.52	0.53
1999	0.56	0.54	0.57	0.62
2000	0.65	0.59	0.52	0.56
2001	0.67	0.38	0.61	0.38

INTERIM DIVIDENDS (Per Share):

Amt.	Decl.	Ex.	Rec.	Pay.
0.14Q	5/07/01	5/16/01	5/18/01	6/01/01
0.14Q	8/06/01	8/15/01	8/17/01	8/31/01
0.14Q	11/05/01	11/14/01	11/16/01	11/30/01
0.14Q	2/04/02	2/13/02	2/15/02	3/01/02

Indicated div.: $0.56 (Div. Reinv. Plan)

CAPITALIZATION (12/31/01):

	($000)	(%)
Long-Term Debt	376,211	19.8
Deferred Income Tax	127,230	6.7
Common & Surplus	1,400,144	73.6
Total	1,903,585	100.0

DIVIDEND ACHIEVER STATUS:
Rank: 129   10-Year Growth Rate: 10.37%
Total Years of Dividend Growth: 12

TRADING VOLUME
Thousand Shares

*7 YEAR PRICE SCORE 98.5   *12 MONTH PRICE SCORE 102.4

*NYSE COMPOSITE INDEX=100

RECENT DEVELOPMENTS: For the year ended 12/31/01, PL reported income of $141.1 million, before an accounting change charge of $7.6 million and a loss from discontinuing operations of $30.5 million, versus net income of $153.5 million in the prior year. Results for 2001 included realized investment losses of $20.2 million. Net premiums earned grew 26.3% to $618.7 million from $489.8 million a year earlier. Net investment income rose 21.1% to $884.0 million versus $730.1 million the year before.

PROSPECTS: On 12/31/01, PL completed the sale of substantially all of its Dental Benefits Division to Fortis, Inc., and discontinued other remaining Dental Division related operations, primarily other health insurance lines. Meanwhile, PL plans to sharpen its focus on its core product lines and improve the quality and efficiency of its operations. Looking ahead, the Company expects its growth rate in 2002 to slow as PL refocuses and organizes its operations and deploys the proceeds from the Dental sale.

BUSINESS

PROTECTIVE LIFE CORPORATION is a holding company that provides financial services through the production, distribution and administration of insurance and investment products. The Company operates several divisions whose strategic focuses can be grouped into three segments: life insurance, specialty insurance products and retirement savings and investment products. The life insurance segment (68.3% of 2001 pre-tax operating income) includes the individual life, West Coast and acquisitions divisions. The specialty insurance products segment (14.7%) includes the financial institutions divisions, which markets credit life and disability insurance products. The retirement savings and the investment products segment (17.0%) includes the Stable Value products division, which markets guaranteed investment contracts, and investment products division, which sells variable annuities.

ANNUAL FINANCIAL DATA

	12/31/01	12/31/00	12/31/99	12/31/98	12/31/97	12/31/96	12/31/95
Earnings Per Share	② 2.01	2.32	① 2.32	2.04	1.78	1.47	1.34
Tang. Book Val. Per Share	19.72	·13.38	10.03	11.51	12.30	9.99	9.15
Dividends Per Share	0.55	0.51	0.47	0.43	0.39	0.35	0.31
Dividend Payout %	27.4	22.0	20.3	21.1	21.9	23.8	23.1
INCOME STATEMENT (IN MILLIONS):							
Total Premium Income	618.7	833.7	761.3	662.8	522.3	494.2	432.6
Net Investment Income	884.0	737.3	676.4	636.4	591.4	517.5	475.9
Other Income	111.5	163.0	96.2	67.2	33.6	26.4	13.4
Total Revenues	1,614.2	1,734.0	1,533.9	1,366.4	1,147.3	1,038.0	921.9
Income Before Income Taxes	209.6	253.8	255.8	220.7	179.4	139.7	121.0
Income Taxes	68.5	90.9	92.1	77.8	61.0	47.5	41.2
Equity Earnings/Minority Int.	...	d9.5	d10.6	d12.1	d6.4	d3.2	d3.2
Net Income	② 141.1	153.5	① 153.1	130.8	112.0	89.0	76.7
Average Shs. Outstg. (000)	69,950	66,281	66,161	64,088	62,850	61,608	57,320
BALANCE SHEET (IN MILLIONS):							
Cash & Cash Equivalents	363.7	244.7	165.3	225.7	123.6	235.3	65.0
Premiums Due	2,239.2	1,185.4	940.3	797.2	639.4	380.0	309.7
Invst. Assets: Fixed-term	9,838.1	7,415.8	6,311.8	6,437.8	6,374.3	4,686.1	3,892.0
Invst. Assets: Equities	76.8	58.7	36.4	12.3	15.0	35.3	38.7
Invst. Assets: Total	13,317.7	10,241.4	8,722.0	8,606.6	8,049.4	6,552.2	6,025.1
Total Assets	19,718.8	15,145.6	12,994.2	11,989.5	10,511.6	8,263.2	7,231.3
Long-Term Obligations	376.2	306.1	181.0	152.3	120.0	168.2	115.5
Net Stockholders' Equity	1,400.1	1,114.1	865.2	944.2	758.2	615.3	526.6
Year-end Shs. Outstg. (000)	68,555	64,558	64,502	64,435	61,642	61,608	57,550
STATISTICAL RECORD:							
Return on Revenues %	8.7	8.9	10.0	9.6	9.8	8.6	8.3
Return on Equity %	10.1	13.8	17.7	13.9	14.8	14.5	14.6
Return on Assets %	0.7	1.0	1.2	1.1	1.1	1.1	1.1
Price Range	35.00-24.80	32.25-19.00	40.75-27.81	41.25-28.00	32.75-18.81	20.81-15.06	15.69-10.69
P/E Ratio	17.4-12.3	13.9-8.2	17.6-12.0	20.2-13.7	18.4-10.6	14.2-10.2	11.7-8.0
Average Yield %	1.8	2.0	1.4	1.2	1.5	2.0	2.4

Statistics are as originally reported. Adj. for 100% stk. split, 4/98, 2-for-1, 6/95. ① Bef. extraord. loss of $1.8 mill. ② Bef. acctg. change chrg. $7.6 mill. & loss fr. disc. opers. of $30.5 mill.

OFFICERS:
D. Nabers Jr., Chmn.
J. D. Johns, Pres., C.E.O.
A. Ritchie, C.F.O.

INVESTOR CONTACT: John D. Johns, Pres., C.E.O., (205) 868-4400

PRINCIPAL OFFICE: 2801 Highway 280 South, Birmingham, AL 35223

TELEPHONE NUMBER: (205) 879-9230
FAX: (205) 868-3541
WEB: www.protective.com

NO. OF EMPLOYEES: 2,524 (approx.)

SHAREHOLDERS: 2,300 (approx.)

ANNUAL MEETING: In May

INCORPORATED: DE, Feb., 1981

INSTITUTIONAL HOLDINGS:
No. of Institutions: 217
Shares Held: 49,250,886
% Held: 71.7

INDUSTRY: Life insurance (SIC: 6311)

TRANSFER AGENT(S): Bank of New York, New York, NY

QUAKER CHEMICAL CORPORATION

YIELD 3.6%
P/E RATIO 27.5

7 YEAR PRICE SCORE 104.0   *12 MONTH PRICE SCORE 115.2*
NYSE COMPOSITE INDEX=100

INTERIM EARNINGS (Per Share):

Qtr.	Mar.	June	Sept.	Dec.
1998	0.33	0.39	0.40	0.08
1999	0.34	0.42	0.48	0.51
2000	0.49	0.53	0.53	0.39
2001	0.45	0.52	0.12	d0.17

INTERIM DIVIDENDS (Per Share):

Amt.	Decl.	Ex.	Rec.	Pay.
0.205Q	3/21/01	4/11/01	4/16/01	4/30/01
0.205Q	5/09/01	7/13/01	7/17/01	7/31/01
0.205Q	9/12/01	10/15/01	10/17/01	10/31/01
0.205Q	11/14/01	1/15/02	1/17/02	1/31/02
0.21Q	3/13/02	4/12/02	4/16/02	4/30/02

Indicated div.: $0.84 (Div. Reinv. Plan)

CAPITALIZATION (12/31/01):

	($000)	(%)
Long-Term Debt	19,380	19.1
Deferred Income Tax	1,233	1.2
Common & Surplus	80,899	79.7
Total	101,512	100.0

DIVIDEND ACHIEVER STATUS:
Rank: 237   10-Year Growth Rate: 4.66%
Total Years of Dividend Growth: 30

RECENT DEVELOPMENTS: For the year ended 12/31/01, net income fell 55.3% to $7.7 million compared with $17.2 million in 2000. Results for 2001 and 2000 included environmental charges of $500,000 and $1.5 million, respectively. Also, results for 2001 included a restructuring charge of $5.9 million, while results for 2000 included a net gain of $1.5 million from the exit of businesses. Net sales were $251.1 million, down 6.2% from $267.6 million a year earlier.

PROSPECTS: On 3/1/02, the Company completed the acquisition of United Lubricants Corporation, a North American manufacturer and distributor of specialty lubricant products and chemical management services, primarily for the steel industry. The transaction should strengthen the Company's position in the steel industry and is expected to be accretive to earnings in 2002. Terms of the transaction were not disclosed.

BUSINESS

QUAKER CHEMICAL CORPORATION develops, produces, and markets a broad range of formulated chemical specialty products for various heavy industrial and manufacturing applications and, in addition, offers and markets chemical management services. The Company's principal product lines include rolling lubricants, corrosion preventives, hydraulic fluids, machining and grinding compounds, forming compounds, chemical milling maskants, metal finishing compounds, technology for the removal of hydrogen sulfides, construction products and programs to provide chemical management services.

ANNUAL FINANCIAL DATA

	12/31/01	12/31/00	12/31/99	12/31/98	12/31/97	12/31/96	12/31/95
Earnings Per Share	⑤ 0.84	④ 1.93	③ 1.74	③ 1.20	② 1.45	① d0.88	0.76
Cash Flow Per Share	1.54	2.70	2.52	2.00	2.28	0.13	1.77
Tang. Book Val. Per Share	7.06	7.63	7.30	7.01	7.01	6.00	8.52
Dividends Per Share	0.82	0.79	0.77	0.73	0.70	0.69	0.68
Dividend Payout %	97.6	40.9	44.0	60.8	48.6	...	89.5
INCOME STATEMENT (IN THOUSANDS):							
Total Revenues	251,074	267,570	258,461	257,100	241,534	240,251	229,128
Costs & Expenses	230,503	235,610	224,224	232,719	213,122	235,574	206,958
Depreciation & Amort.	6,380	6,812	6,956	7,111	7,264	8,708	8,647
Operating Income	14,191	25,148	27,281	17,270	21,148	d4,031	13,523
Net Interest Inc./(Exp.)	d850	d1,096	d1,992	d1,589	d1,218	d1,474	d1,426
Income Before Income Taxes	14,430	26,486	27,151	16,797	19,735	d3,997	12,097
Income Taxes	4,473	8,211	10,860	6,719	7,893	664	4,887
Equity Earnings/Minority Int.	d2,292	d1,112	d640	572	769	d3,136	d522
Net Income	⑤ 7,665	④ 17,163	③ 15,651	③ 10,650	② 12,611	① d7,599	6,688
Cash Flow	14,045	23,975	22,607	17,761	19,875	1,109	15,335
Average Shs. Outstg.	9,114	8,896	8,975	8,860	8,707	8,635	8,664
BALANCE SHEET (IN THOUSANDS):							
Cash & Cash Equivalents	20,549	16,552	8,677	10,213	18,416	8,525	7,230
Total Current Assets	92,087	103,181	96,241	96,068	98,126	86,552	86,718
Net Property	38,244	42,459	44,752	49,622	40,654	43,560	56,309
Total Assets	170,387	188,161	182,213	189,903	170,640	165,608	185,408
Total Current Liabilities	44,663	50,200	44,657	50,432	47,759	64,034	60,868
Long-Term Obligations	19,380	22,295	25,122	25,344	25,203	5,182	9,300
Net Stockholders' Equity	80,899	84,907	81,199	83,735	75,642	74,254	93,992
Net Working Capital	47,424	52,981	51,584	45,636	50,367	22,518	25,850
Year-end Shs. Outstg.	9,137	8,851	8,934	8,894	8,720	9,664	8,803
STATISTICAL RECORD:							
Operating Profit Margin %	5.7	9.4	10.6	6.7	8.8	...	5.9
Net Profit Margin %	3.1	6.4	6.1	4.1	5.2	...	2.9
Return on Equity %	9.5	20.2	19.3	12.7	16.7	...	7.1
Return on Assets %	4.5	9.1	8.6	5.6	7.4	...	3.6
Debt/Total Assets %	11.4	11.8	13.8	13.3	14.8	3.1	5.0
Price Range	22.30-16.12	19.25-13.38	18.38-13.50	21.00-13.00	19.81-15.00	17.25-11.75	19.00-11.00
P/E Ratio	26.5-19.2	10.0-6.9	10.6-7.8	17.5-10.8	13.7-10.3	...	25.0-14.5
Average Yield %	4.3	4.8	4.8	4.3	4.1	4.7	4.5

Statistics are as originally reported. ① Incl. $16.9 mill. aft-tax spl. chg. ② Incl. $1.7 mill. aft-tax gain fr. sale of European bus. & $1.3 mill. aft-tax chg. for litigation. ③ Incl. $5.3 mill. aft-tax chgs. for reposit. and integration, 1998; $314,000, 1999. ④ Incl. $27,000 non-recur. gain. ⑤ Incl. $5.9 mill. restr. chg. & environmental chg. of $500,000.

OFFICERS:
R. J. Naples, Chmn., C.E.O.
J. W. Bauer, Pres., C.O.O.
M. F. Barry, V.P., C.F.O., Treas.
INVESTOR CONTACT: Irene M. Kisleiko, Shareholder Relations, (610) 832-4119
PRINCIPAL OFFICE: Elm and Lee Streets, Conshohocken, PA 19428-0809

TELEPHONE NUMBER: (610) 832-4000
FAX: (610) 832-8682
WEB: www.quakerchem.com
NO. OF EMPLOYEES: 955
SHAREHOLDERS: 810
ANNUAL MEETING: In May
INCORPORATED: PA, 1930

INSTITUTIONAL HOLDINGS:
No. of Institutions: 60
Shares Held: 4,355,569
% Held: 47.7
INDUSTRY: Lubricating oils and greases (SIC: 2992)
TRANSFER AGENT(S): American Stock Transfer & Trust Company, New York, NY

QUESTAR CORPORATION

YIELD 2.8%
P/E RATIO 13.3

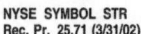
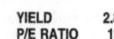
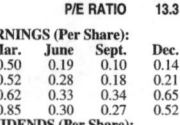
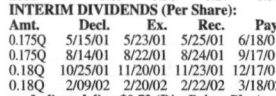

INTERIM EARNINGS (Per Share):

Qtr.	Mar.	June	Sept.	Dec.
1998	0.50	0.19	0.10	0.14
1999	0.52	0.28	0.18	0.21
2000	0.62	0.33	0.34	0.65
2001	0.85	0.30	0.27	0.52

INTERIM DIVIDENDS (Per Share):

Amt.	Decl.	Ex.	Rec.	Pay.
0.175Q	5/15/01	5/23/01	5/25/01	6/18/01
0.175Q	8/14/01	8/22/01	8/24/01	9/17/01
0.18Q	10/25/01	11/20/01	11/23/01	12/17/01
0.18Q	2/09/02	2/20/02	2/22/02	3/18/02

Indicated div.: $0.72 (Div. Reinv. Plan)

CAPITALIZATION (12/31/01):

	($000)	(%)
Long-Term Debt	997,423	41.2
Deferred Income Tax	324,309	13.4
Minority Interest	19,805	0.8
Common & Surplus	1,080,781	44.6
Total	2,422,318	100.0

DIVIDEND ACHIEVER STATUS:
Rank: 259   10-Year Growth Rate: 3.39%
Total Years of Dividend Growth: 22

TRADING VOLUME
Thousand Shares

*7 YEAR PRICE SCORE 108.2   *12 MONTH PRICE SCORE 96.1
*NYSE COMPOSITE INDEX=100

RECENT DEVELOPMENTS: For the twelve months ended 12/31/01, net income was $158.2 million compared with $149.5 million a year earlier. Results for 2001 and 2000 included an after-tax loss of $905,000 and an after-tax gain of $16.3 million, respectively, from securities transactions. Results also included an after-tax gain of $13.5 million and an after-tax loss of $700,000 for 2001 and 2000, respectively, from the sale of nonstrategic properties. Revenues rose 13.7% to $1.44 billion.

PROSPECTS: On 4/4/02, STR provided full-year 2002 earnings estimates of between $1.85 and $2.05 per share, based on the current forward price curves for gas and oil. The effect of possible future declines in natural gas and oil prices should be mitigated due to STR's hedging program, which extends through 2002. STR has also hedged about 47.0% of total gas production for 2003 at an average price of $3.39 per thousand cubic feet and about 52.0% of 2003 oil production at an average price of $21.80 per barrel.

BUSINESS

QUESTAR CORPORATION is a diversified energy services holding company with two divisions. Market Resources engages in energy development and production; gas gathering and processing; and wholesale gas and hydrocarbon liquids marketing, risk management, and storage. Regulated Services, through two subsidiaries, conducts interstate gas transmission and storage activities and retail gas distribution services. The Company is also involved in providing integrated information and communication services.

QUARTERLY DATA

(12/31/2001)($000)	Rev(%)	Inc(%)
First Quarter	562,638	110,386
Second Quarter	285,138	49,049
Third Quarter	225,142	47,045
Fourth Quarter	366,432	67,627

ANNUAL FINANCIAL DATA

	12/31/01	12/31/00	12/31/99	12/31/98	12/31/97	12/31/96	12/31/95
Earnings Per Share	④1.94	③1.94	①1.20	②0.93	1.26	1.20	1.03
Cash Flow Per Share	3.88	3.76	2.95	2.48	2.82	2.55	2.28
Tang. Book Val. Per Share	12.14	12.01	11.37	10.62	10.30	9.41	8.76
Dividends Per Share	0.70	0.69	0.67	0.65	0.62	0.59	0.58
Dividend Payout %	36.3	35.3	55.8	70.2	49.2	49.8	56.6
INCOME STATEMENT (IN MILLIONS):							
Total Revenues	1,439.4	1,266.2	924.2	906.3	933.3	818.0	649.3
Costs & Expenses	1,006.2	858.6	599.6	644.8	634.6	536.4	406.2
Depreciation & Amort.	159.0	147.6	144.7	128.7	128.5	110.0	101.1
Operating Income	274.1	259.9	179.9	132.8	170.2	171.6	142.0
Net Interest Inc./(Exp.)	d64.8	d63.5	d53.9	d48.0	d43.8	d41.1	d42.8
Income Taxes	88.3	85.4	47.8	29.0	45.6	45.4	32.7
Net Income	④158.2	③156.7	①98.8	②76.9	104.8	98.1	83.8
Cash Flow	317.2	304.4	243.5	205.6	233.1	207.8	184.4
Average Shs. Outstg. (000)	81,658	80,915	82,676	82,817	82,668	81,656	81,104
BALANCE SHEET (IN MILLIONS):							
Gross Property	4,089.4	3,544.3	3,258.8	3,104.5	2,741.9	2,575.4	2,330.9
Accumulated Depreciation	1,524.3	1,590.3	1,471.9	1,356.9	1,210.7	1,097.6	1,020.8
Net Property	2,565.1	1,954.0	1,786.9	1,747.6	1,531.2	1,477.3	1,310.1
Total Assets	3,235.7	2,539.0	2,238.0	2,161.3	1,945.0	1,816.2	1,584.6
Long-Term Obligations	997.4	714.5	735.0	615.8	542.0	555.5	421.7
Net Stockholders' Equity	1,080.8	991.1	925.8	878.0	845.8	772.1	712.7
Year-end Shs. Outstg. (000)	81,523	80,818	81,419	82,632	82,142	82,050	81,396
STATISTICAL RECORD:							
Operating Profit Margin %	19.0	20.5	19.5	14.7	18.2	21.0	21.9
Net Profit Margin %	11.0	12.4	10.7	8.5	11.2	12.0	12.9
Net Inc./Net Property %	6.2	8.0	5.5	4.4	6.8	6.6	6.4
Net Inc./Tot. Capital %	6.5	8.0	5.3	4.5	6.5	6.4	6.3
Return on Equity %	14.6	15.8	10.7	8.8	12.4	12.7	11.8
Accum. Depr./Gross Prop. %	37.3	44.9	45.2	43.7	44.2	42.6	43.8
Price Range	33.75-18.58	31.88-13.56	19.94-14.75	22.38-15.81	22.31-17.13	20.69-15.44	16.88-13.06
P/E Ratio	17.4-9.6	16.4-7.0	16.6-12.3	24.1-17.0	17.7-13.6	17.3-12.9	16.5-12.7
Average Yield %	2.7	3.0	3.9	3.4	3.1	3.3	3.9

Statistics are as originally reported. Adj. for 2-for-1 stk. split, 6/98. ① Incl. write-down of invst. in partnerships of $49.7 mill. ② Incl. $34.0 mill. write-down of oil & gas prop. ③ Incl. after-tax gain of $16.3 mill. ($0.20/sh.) on sale of securities. ④ Incl. after-tax loss of $905,000 on sale of securities & after-tax gain of $13.5 mill. on sales of nonstrategic properties.

OFFICERS:
R. D. Cash, Chmn.
K. O. Rattie, Pres., C.E.O., C.O.O.
C. C. Holbrook, Sr. V.P., Gen Coun., Corp. Sec.

INVESTOR CONTACT: Stephen E. Parks, V.P., C.F.O., Treas. (801) 324-5497

PRINCIPAL OFFICE: 180 East 100 South Street, Salt Lake City, UT 84145-0433

TELEPHONE NUMBER: (801) 324-5000
FAX: (801) 324-5483
WEB: www.questar.com

NO. OF EMPLOYEES: 2,221 (avg.)

SHAREHOLDERS: 11,299 (record)

ANNUAL MEETING: In May

INCORPORATED: UT, Oct., 1984

INSTITUTIONAL HOLDINGS:
No. of Institutions: 223
Shares Held: 52,478,177
% Held: 64.4

INDUSTRY: Gas transmission and distribution (SIC: 4923)

TRANSFER AGENT(S): Questar Corp., Salt Lake City, UT

RAVEN INDUSTRIES, INC.

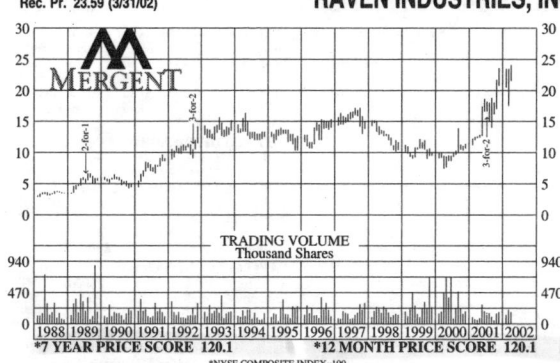

TRADING VOLUME
Thousand Shares

*7 YEAR PRICE SCORE 120.1   *12 MONTH PRICE SCORE 120.1
*NYSE COMPOSITE INDEX=100

INTERIM EARNINGS (Per Share):

Qtr.	Apr.	July	Oct.	Jan.
1998-99	0.14	0.21	0.29	0.23
1999-00	0.21	0.27	0.35	0.21
2000-01	0.29	0.23	0.33	0.39
2001-02	0.47	0.43	0.53	0.44

INTERIM DIVIDENDS (Per Share):

Amt.	Decl.	Ex.	Rec.	Pay.
3-for-2	5/23/01	7/16/01	6/25/01	7/13/01
0.13Q	5/23/01	6/21/01	6/25/01	7/13/01
0.13Q	8/23/01	9/21/01	9/25/01	10/15/01
0.13Q	11/19/01	12/20/01	12/24/01	1/15/02
0.14Q	3/18/02	3/26/02	3/28/02	4/15/02

Indicated div.: $0.56 (Div. Reinv. Plan)

CAPITALIZATION (1/31/01):

	($000)	(%)
Long-Term Debt	2,013	4.0
Common & Surplus	47,989	96.0
Total	50,002	100.0

DIVIDEND ACHIEVER STATUS:
Rank: 103   10-Year Growth Rate: 11.76%
Total Years of Dividend Growth: 14

RECENT DEVELOPMENTS: For the year ended 1/31/02, net income advanced 38.0% to $8.8 million compared with $6.4 million in 2001. Results for 2001 and 2000 included gains of $367,000 and $3.5 million, respectively, on the sale of businesses and assets. Net sales declined 10.8% to $118.5 million from $132.9 million a year earlier, reflecting the sale of the Plastic Tank division, which contributed $3.5 million in revenues in 2001, versus $16.2 million in 2000. Aerostar sales fell 33.7% to $16.3 million. Engineered Films net sales rose 0.7% to $40.3 million, while

Electronic Systems net sales increased 0.8% to $32.3 million. Flow Controls net sales advanced 38.3% to $23.2 million. Operating income increased 22.6% to $13.2 million versus $10.7 million in 2001. During the year, RAVN exited the storage tank business, closed a metal fabrication plant in Alabama and down-sized its Aerostar outerwear business. In the fourth quarter, the Company acquired Starlink, Inc., a developer of global positioning system devices, and Systems Integrators, Inc., an electronics manufacturing company.

BUSINESS

RAVEN INDUSTRIES, INC. is a manufacturing company that operates through four core divisions. The Engineered Films division (34.0% of sales for fiscal 2001) produces rugged reinforced plastic sheeting for manufactured housing and recreational vehicles, temporary grain covers for agriculture, temporary building construction enclosures, and pond lining and containment for oil exploration. This segment also manufactures high-altitude research balloons for NASA and universities. The Electronics Systems unit (27.2%) provides electronic manufacturing services primarily for industrial original equipment manufacturers in North America and companies that contract their small-volume, high-mix production. The Flow Controls division (19.6%) develops global positioning systems-based control systems, computerized control hardware and software for precision farming, and systems for the precision application of insecticides, fertilizer and road de-icers. Aerostar International Inc. (13.7%) produces custom-shaped advertising inflatables, hot-air sport balloons, and specialized sewing applications. As of 1/31/02, RAVN's Beta Raven Industrial Controls Division was being held for sale.

ANNUAL FINANCIAL DATA

	1/31/02	1/31/01	1/31/00	1/31/99	1/31/98	1/31/97	1/31/96
Earnings Per Share	⑪ 1.86	⑪ 1.24	1.03	0.87	1.10	1.07	0.87
Cash Flow Per Share	2.53	1.95	1.78	1.59	1.80	1.72	1.46
Tang. Book Val. Per Share	11.30	10.13	7.74	8.85	8.51	7.57	6.70
Dividends Per Share	0.50	0.46	0.43	0.41	0.36	0.33	0.29
Dividend Payout %	26.9	37.1	41.9	46.9	32.7	30.4	33.5

INCOME STATEMENT (IN THOUSANDS):

Total Revenues	118,515	132,858	147,906	152,798	149,619	139,441	120,444
Costs & Expenses	102,195	118,443	132,445	137,992	133,920	122,904	106,641
Depreciation & Amort.	3,145	3,667	4,884	5,133	5,137	4,566	4,242
Operating Income	13,175	10,748	10,577	9,673	10,562	11,971	9,561
Net Interest Inc./(Exp.)	d129	d258	d418	d474	d323	d310	d375
Income Before Income Taxes	13,565	10,924	10,503	9,649	12,540	11,915	9,566
Income Taxes	4,718	4,513	3,741	3,467	4,478	4,227	3,369
Net Income	⑪ 8,847	⑪ 6,411	6,762	6,182	8,062	7,688	6,197
Cash Flow	11,992	10,078	11,646	11,315	13,199	12,254	10,439
Average Shs. Outstg.	4,746	5,169	6,558	7,136	7,337	7,133	7,173

BALANCE SHEET (IN THOUSANDS):

Cash & Cash Equivalents	7,478	10,673	5,707	5,335	2,850	3,439	3,804
Total Current Assets	45,308	52,236	55,371	60,861	57,831	56,696	45,695
Net Property	14,059	11,647	15,068	19,563	19,817	18,142	18,069
Total Assets	67,836	65,656	74,047	83,674	82,590	80,662	67,553
Total Current Liabilities	13,810	13,935	14,702	16,792	19,375	20,016	14,771
Long-Term Obligations	280	2,013	3,024	4,572	1,128	3,181	2,816
Net Stockholders' Equity	52,032	47,989	54,519	62,293	61,563	56,729	49,151
Net Working Capital	31,498	38,301	40,669	44,069	38,456	36,680	30,924
Year-end Shs. Outstg.	4,606	4,739	7,041	7,041	7,236	7,254	7,074

STATISTICAL RECORD:

Operating Profit Margin %	11.1	8.1	7.2	6.3	7.1	8.6	7.9
Net Profit Margin %	7.5	4.8	4.6	4.0	5.4	5.5	5.1
Return on Equity %	17.0	13.4	12.4	9.9	13.1	13.6	12.6
Return on Assets %	13.0	9.8	9.1	7.4	9.8	9.5	9.2
Debt/Total Assets %	0.4	3.1	4.1	5.5	1.4	3.9	4.2
Price Range	24.10-11.17	13.91-7.42	12.17-9.00	15.17-10.17	17.17-13.00	15.33-10.67	14.00-10.33
P/E Ratio	12.96-6.00	11.2-6.00	11.8-8.7	17.5-11.7	15.6-11.8	14.3-9.9	16.2-11.9
Average Yield %	2.8	4.3	4.1	3.2	2.4	2.5	2.4

Statistics are as originally reported. Adj. for stk. split: 3-for-2, 7/01. ⑪ Incl. gain on sale of assets of $367,000, 1/01; $3.5 mill., 1/00.

OFFICERS:
C. J. Hoigaard, Chmn.
R. M. Moquist, Pres., C.E.O.
T. Iacarella, V.P., C.F.O.
INVESTOR CONTACT: Thomas Iacarella, V.P., C.F.O., (605) 336-2750
PRINCIPAL OFFICE: 205 East 6th Street, P.O. Box 5107, Sioux Falls, SD 57117-5107

TELEPHONE NUMBER: (605) 336-2750
FAX: (605) 335-0268
WEB: www.ravenind.com
NO. OF EMPLOYEES: 838 (avg.)
SHAREHOLDERS: 2,387
ANNUAL MEETING: In May
INCORPORATED: SD, Feb., 1956

INSTITUTIONAL HOLDINGS:
No. of Institutions: 25
Shares Held: 1,601,196
% Held: 34.5
INDUSTRY: Printed circuit boards (SIC: 3672)
TRANSFER AGENT(S): Wells Fargo Shareowner Services, South St. Paul, MN

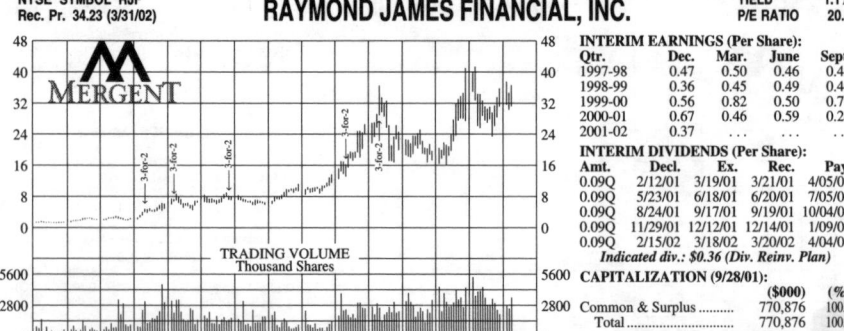

NYSE SYMBOL RJF
Rec. Pr. 34.23 (3/31/02)

RAYMOND JAMES FINANCIAL, INC.

YIELD 1.1%
P/E RATIO 20.4

INTERIM EARNINGS (Per Share):

Qtr.	Dec.	Mar.	June	Sept.
1997-98	0.47	0.50	0.46	0.45
1998-99	0.36	0.45	0.49	0.46
1999-00	0.56	0.82	0.50	0.79
2000-01	0.67	0.46	0.59	0.26
2001-02	0.37	...	...	...

INTERIM DIVIDENDS (Per Share):

Amt.	Decl.	Ex.	Rec.	Pay.
0.09Q	2/12/01	3/19/01	3/21/01	4/05/01
0.09Q	5/23/01	6/18/01	6/20/01	7/05/01
0.09Q	8/24/01	9/17/01	9/19/01	10/04/01
0.09Q	11/29/01	12/12/01	12/14/01	1/09/02
0.09Q	2/15/02	3/18/02	3/20/02	4/04/02

Indicated div.: $0.36 (Div. Reinv. Plan)

CAPITALIZATION (9/28/01):

	($000)	(%)
Common & Surplus	770,876	100.0
Total	770,876	100.0

DIVIDEND ACHIEVER STATUS:
Rank: 13   10-Year Growth Rate: 23.18%
Total Years of Dividend Growth: 15

TRADING VOLUME
Thousand Shares

*7 YEAR PRICE SCORE 127.6   *12 MONTH PRICE SCORE 109.6
*NYSE COMPOSITE INDEX=100

RECENT DEVELOPMENTS: For the quarter ended 12/28/01, net income decreased 43.8% to $18.1 million from $32.2 million in the corresponding period of the year before. Total revenues decreased 13.5% to $364.1 billion from $421.0 million a year earlier. Securities commissions and fees revenue declined 2.7% to $238.6 million versus $245.2 million in the previous year. Interest revenue fell 55.7% to $45.4 million from $102.5 million in the prior year.

PROSPECTS: The Company continues to be negatively affected by the sluggish economy and retail investors' caution. Moreover, net interest earnings continue to decline, reflecting lower interest rates. However, the Company expects to slowly resume growth as the market recovers, primarily due to the performance of its asset managers and its expense control efforts.

BUSINESS

RAYMOND JAMES FINANCIAL, INC., with assets totaling $6.61 billion as of 12/28/01, is a holding company primarily engaged in investment and financial planning, including securities brokerage, investment banking and asset management; banking and cash management; trust services; and life insurance. RJF's two broker/dealer subsidiaries, Raymond James & Associates and Raymond James Financial Services, serve more than 1.0 million accounts. RJF's asset management subsidiaries manage over $16.00 billion in financial assets for individuals, pension plans and municipalities. RJF operates from nearly 2,100 locations in the U.S., Canada and abroad. On 12/29/00, RJF acquired Vancouver-based brokerage Raymond James Ltd., formerly Goepel McDermid.

ANNUAL FINANCIAL DATA

	9/28/01	9/29/00	9/24/99	9/25/98	9/26/97	9/27/96	9/29/95
Earnings Per Share	1.98	③ 2.67	1.76	② 1.86	① 2.04	1.40	0.99
Cash Flow Per Share	2.62	3.18	2.17	2.18	2.32	1.63	1.20
Tang. Book Val. Per Share	14.71	13.35	11.08	10.56	8.87	6.67	5.74
Dividends Per Share	0.36	0.30	0.28	0.24	0.21	0.17	0.16
Dividend Payout %	18.2	11.2	15.9	12.9	10.2	12.1	16.1
INCOME STATEMENT (IN MILLIONS):							
Total Revenues	1,657.8	1,698.6	1,232.2	1,082.9	927.6	721.8	554.1
Costs & Expenses	1,469.1	1,470.1	1,074.6	916.4	753.8	601.9	469.9
Depreciation & Amort.	31.3	23.9	20.1	16.3	13.3	11.3	9.7
Operating Income	157.5	204.7	137.5	150.2	160.5	108.5	74.5
Income Before Income Taxes	157.5	204.7	137.5	150.2	160.5	108.5	74.5
Income Taxes	61.1	79.5	52.4	57.5	61.6	42.5	28.3
Net Income	96.4	③ 125.2	85.1	② 92.7	① 98.9	66.0	46.1
Cash Flow	127.7	149.0	105.1	109.0	112.2	77.3	55.8
Average Shs. Outstg. (000)	48,799	46,867	48,449	49,951	48,387	47,306	46,586
BALANCE SHEET (IN MILLIONS):							
Cash & Cash Equivalents	2,204.1	1,119.5	1,353.8	1,243.5	888.8	735.3	454.4
Total Current Assets	5,477.0	5,596.5	4,259.8	3,223.7	2,769.2	2,152.1	1,739.2
Net Property	104.7	91.1	91.3	81.4	51.7	39.6	40.9
Total Assets	6,372.1	6,308.8	5,030.7	3,852.7	3,278.6	2,566.4	2,012.7
Total Current Liabilities	5,601.2	5,658.3	4,472.2	3,298.1	2,841.2	2,214.9	1,733.4
Long-Term Obligations	...	...	...	44.8	14.2	24.9	13.1
Net Stockholders' Equity	770.9	650.5	558.5	509.9	423.3	326.6	266.2
Net Working Capital	d124.1	d61.8	d212.4	d74.4	d72.0	d62.7	5.8
Year-end Shs. Outstg. (000)	47,995	46,287	47,242	48,268	47,696	48,998	46,382
STATISTICAL RECORD:							
Operating Profit Margin %	9.5	12.0	11.2	13.9	17.3	15.0	13.4
Net Profit Margin %	5.8	7.4	6.9	8.6	10.7	9.1	8.3
Return on Equity %	12.5	19.2	15.2	18.2	23.4	20.2	17.3
Return on Assets %	1.5	2.0	1.7	2.4	3.0	2.6	2.3
Debt/Total Assets %	...	...	...	1.2	0.4	1.0	0.7
Price Range	41.35-23.36	41.00-16.00	25.19-16.69	36.50-16.75	26.50-12.45	13.67-8.45	11.22-6.11
P/E Ratio	20.9-11.8	15.4-6.0	14.3-9.5	19.6-9.0	13.0-6.1	9.8-6.1	11.3-6.2
Average Yield %	1.1	1.1	1.3	0.9	1.1	1.5	1.8

Statistics are as originally reported. Adj for 3-for-2 stock split, 4/98 & 4/97. ① Incl. $30.6 mill. gain fr. the sale of Liberty Investment Management, Inc. & a $2.5 mill. gin fr. the sale of the Company's former headquarters building. ② Incl. $1.7 mill. gain related to the sale of the real estate portfolio and property management subsidiaries & $2.4 mill. gain from the sale of the Company's specialist operations on the Chicago Exchange. ③ Incl. a pre-tax credit related to changes in litigation reserves of $16.0 mill., 9/01; d$20.0 mill., 9/00.

OFFICERS:
T. A. James, Chmn., C.E.O.
F. S. Godbold, Vice-Chmn.
C. Helck, Pres., C.O.O.
J. P. Julien, Sr. V.P., Fin., C.F.O.

INVESTOR CONTACT: Lawrence Silver, V.P., (727) 573-3800

PRINCIPAL OFFICE: 880 Carillon Parkway, St. Petersburg, FL 33716

TELEPHONE NUMBER: (727) 573-3800
FAX: (727) 573-8365
WEB: www.raymondjames.com

NO. OF EMPLOYEES: 5,811

SHAREHOLDERS: 12,000 (approx.)

ANNUAL MEETING: In Feb.

INCORPORATED: FL, 1974

INSTITUTIONAL HOLDINGS:
No. of Institutions: 172
Shares Held: 27,154,422
% Held: 55.9

INDUSTRY: Security brokers and dealers (SIC: 6211)

TRANSFER AGENT(S): Mellon Investor Services, Ridgefield Park, NJ

NASDAQ SYMBOL RGBK
Rec. Pr. 34.35 (3/31/02)

REGIONS FINANCIAL CORPORATION

YIELD 3.4%
P/E RATIO 15.3

INTERIM EARNINGS (Per Share):

Qtr.	Mar.	June	Sept.	Dec.
1997	0.52	0.54	0.56	0.57
1998	0.56	0.59	0.23	0.57
1999	0.61	0.63	0.59	0.59
2000	0.66	0.57	0.58	0.58
2001	0.57	0.49	0.59	0.60

INTERIM DIVIDENDS (Per Share):

Amt.	Decl.	Ex.	Rec.	Pay.
0.28Q	1/18/01	3/14/01	3/16/01	4/02/01
0.28Q	5/16/01	6/13/01	6/15/01	7/02/01
0.28Q	7/19/01	9/12/01	9/14/01	10/01/01
0.28Q	10/18/01	12/12/01	12/14/01	1/02/02
0.29Q	1/17/02	3/13/02	3/15/02	4/01/02

Indicated div.: $1.16 (Div. Reinv. Plan)

CAPITALIZATION (12/31/01):

	($000)	(%)
Total Deposits	31,548,323	78.2
Long-Term Debt	4,747,674	11.8
Common & Surplus	4,035,765	10.0
Total	40,331,762	100.0

DIVIDEND ACHIEVER STATUS:
Rank: 141   10-Year Growth Rate: 9.90%
Total Years of Dividend Growth: 30

TRADING VOLUME
Thousand Shares

*7 YEAR PRICE SCORE 89.6   *12 MONTH PRICE SCORE 109.3
*NYSE COMPOSITE INDEX=100

RECENT DEVELOPMENTS: RGBK plans to list its common stock on the New York Stock Exchange under the ticker symbol "RF", effective 5/3/02. For the year ended 12/31/01, net income decreased 3.5% to $508.9 million versus $527.5 million a year earlier. Net interest income climbed 2.6% to $1.43 billion. Provision for loan losses was $165.4 million, up 30.1% $127.1 million the year before. Total non-interest income jumped 63.3% to $981.9 million. Total non-interest expense increased 35.9% to $1.52 billion. Total deposits slipped 1.5% to $31.55 billion, while loans, net of unearned income, declined 1.6% to $30.89 billion. Separately, on 4/2/02, RGBK acquired Brookhollow Bancshares, Inc. in a cash transaction valued at $26.6 million.

BUSINESS

REGIONS FINANCIAL CORPORA-TION (formerly First Alabama Banc-shares, Inc.) is a bank holding company with assets of $45.38 billion as of 12/31/01. Serving customers throughout the South, the Company provides traditional commercial and retail banking services and other financial services in the fields of investment banking, asset management, trust, mutual funds, securities brokerage, insurance, leasing and mortgage banking. Its banking affiliate, Regions Bank, offers banking services from 677 full-service banking offices in Alabama, Arkansas, Florida, Georgia, Louisiana, North Carolina, South Carolina, Tennessee and Texas. The Company also provides investment and brokerage services from 142 offices of Morgan Keegan & Company, Inc., which was acquired in March 2001. Morgan Keegan is one of the South's largest investment firms. On 4/2/02, RGBK acquired Brookhollow Bancshares, Inc.

ANNUAL FINANCIAL DATA

	12/31/01	12/31/00	12/31/99	12/31/98	12/31/97	12/31/96	12/31/95
Earnings Per Share	2.24	2.38	2.35	1.88	2.15	1.85	1.88
Tang. Book Val. Per Share	17.54	15.73	13.89	13.61	13.99	12.76	12.37
Dividends Per Share	1.11	1.06	0.98	0.89	0.78	0.69	0.65
Dividend Payout %	49.6	44.5	41.7	47.3	36.0	37.3	34.4
INCOME STATEMENT (IN MILLIONS):							
Total Interest Income	3,055.6	3,234.2	2,854.7	2,597.8	1,653.1	1,386.1	1,017.3
Total Interest Expense	1,630.1	1,845.4	1,428.8	1,273.0	824.2	685.7	520.0
Net Interest Income	1,425.5	1,388.8	1,425.9	1,324.8	828.9	700.5	497.3
Provision for Loan Losses	165.4	127.1	113.7	60.5	41.8	29.0	20.7
Non-Interest Income	981.9	601.2	537.1	474.7	258.6	220.7	159.8
Non-Interest Expense	1,524.0	1,121.2	1,064.3	1,103.7	600.3	553.8	378.0
Income Before Taxes	718.0	741.7	785.0	635.3	445.3	338.4	258.5
Net Income	508.9	527.5	525.4	421.7	299.7	229.7	172.8
Average Shs. Outstg. (000)	227,063	221,989	223,967	223,781	139,421	124,272	92,194
BALANCE SHEET (IN MILLIONS):							
Cash & Due from Banks	1,239.6	1,210.9	1,393.4	1,619.0	726.1	774.8	484.1
Securities Avail. for Sale	8,555.0	5,468.4	6,873.3	4,893.4	1,576.6	1,797.5	1,609.3
Total Loans & Leases	31,137.0	31,472.7	28,221.2	24,430.1	16,427.6	13,335.5	9,564.4
Allowance for Credit Losses	670.8	472.7	414.9	379.9	227.0	199.8	148.3
Net Loans & Leases	30,466.2	31,000.0	27,806.3	24,050.2	16,200.6	13,135.6	9,416.1
Total Assets	45,382.7	43,688.3	42,714.4	36,831.9	23,034.2	18,930.2	13,708.6
Total Deposits	31,548.3	32,022.5	29,989.1	28,350.1	17,750.9	15,048.3	10,896.1
Long-Term Obligations	4,747.7	4,478.0	1,750.9	571.0	400.2	447.3	552.6
Total Liabilities	41,346.9	40,230.3	39,649.3	33,831.5	21,121.4	17,331.4	12,583.4
Net Stockholders' Equity	4,035.8	3,457.9	3,065.1	3,000.4	1,912.9	1,598.7	1,125.1
Year-end Shs. Outstg. (000)	230,081	219,769	220,636	220,454	136,696	125,310	90,920
STATISTICAL RECORD:							
Return on Equity %	12.6	15.3	17.1	14.1	15.7	14.4	15.4
Return on Assets %	1.1	1.2	1.2	1.1	1.3	1.2	1.3
Equity/Assets %	8.9	7.9	7.2	8.1	8.3	8.4	8.2
Non-Int. Exp./Tot. Inc. %	63.3	56.3	54.2	61.3	55.2	60.1	57.5
Price Range	32.99-25.73	28.00-18.31	41.63-23.19	45.63-28.88	45.00-25.69	27.00-20.25	22.50-15.50
P/E Ratio	14.7-11.5	11.8-7.7	17.7-9.9	24.3-15.4	20.9-11.9	14.6-10.9	12.0-8.3
Average Yield %	3.8	4.6	3.0	2.4	2.2	2.9	3.4

Statistics are as originally reported. Adj. for stk. splits: 2-for-1, 6/13/97.

OFFICERS:
C. E. Jones Jr., Chmn., Pres., C.E.O.
R. D. Horsley, Vice-Chmn., C.F.O.

INVESTOR CONTACT: Ronald C. Jackson, Sr. V.P. & Dir. of Inv. Rel., (205) 326-7374

PRINCIPAL OFFICE: 417 North 20th Street, Birmingham, AL 35203

TELEPHONE NUMBER: (205) 944-1300
FAX: (205) 326-7459
WEB: www.regionsbank.com

NO. OF EMPLOYEES: 15,921

SHAREHOLDERS: 54,512

ANNUAL MEETING: In May

INCORPORATED: DE, June, 1970

INSTITUTIONAL HOLDINGS:
No. of Institutions: 253
Shares Held: 61,357,606
% Held: 26.7

INDUSTRY: National commercial banks (SIC: 6021)

TRANSFER AGENT(S): First Chicago Trust Company of New York, Jersey City, NJ

RLI CORP.

YIELD 1.2%
P/E RATIO 17.1

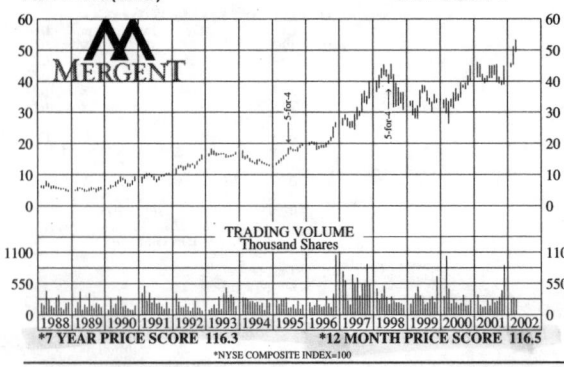

INTERIM EARNINGS (Per Share):

Qtr.	Mar.	June	Sept.	Dec.
1997	0.59	0.72	0.67	0.68
1998	0.52	0.57	0.42	0.62
1999	0.63	0.88	0.84	0.74
2000	0.66	0.70	0.74	0.78
2001	0.71	0.74	0.79	0.78

INTERIM DIVIDENDS (Per Share):

Amt.	Decl.	Ex.	Rec.	Pay.
0.15Q	3/05/01	3/28/01	3/30/01	4/13/01
0.16Q	5/03/01	6/27/01	6/29/01	7/13/01
0.16Q	9/05/01	9/26/01	9/28/01	10/15/01
0.16Q	12/14/01	12/27/01	12/31/01	1/15/02
0.16Q	3/08/02	3/26/02	3/29/02	4/15/02

Indicated div.: $0.64 (Div. Reinv. Plan)

CAPITALIZATION (12/31/01):

	($000)	(%)
Deferred Income Tax	43,151	11.4
Common & Surplus	335,432	88.6
Total	378,583	100.0

DIVIDEND ACHIEVER STATUS:
Rank: 175   10-Year Growth Rate: 7.97%
Total Years of Dividend Growth: 25

TRADING VOLUME
Thousand Shares

*7 YEAR PRICE SCORE 116.3   *12 MONTH PRICE SCORE 116.5
*NYSE COMPOSITE INDEX=100

RECENT DEVELOPMENTS: For the year ended 12/31/01, income was $30.2 million, before an accounting credit of $800,000, compared with net income of $28.7 million in the prior year. Total revenues advanced 17.4% to $309.4 million from $263.5 million in the previous year. Net premiums earned increased 17.9% to $273.0 million, net investment income climbed 10.8% to $32.2 million. Net realized investment gains jumped 46.4% to $4.2 million.

PROSPECTS: Going forward, the Company's property segment should continue to respond well to focused underwriting controls. In addition, RLI's surety postings, although still positive, are being hampered by higher-than-expected loss experience in the contract bond sector, which was affected by the economic slowdown of the last few quarters. Meanwhile, RLI believes that rising reinsurance costs will be offset by improving premiums.

BUSINESS

RLI CORP. is a holding company composed primarily of four main insurance companies. RLI Insurance Company, the principal subsidiary, writes multiple lines of insurance on an admitted basis in all 50 states, the District of Columbia and Puerto Rico. Mt. Hawley Insurance Company, a subsidiary of RLI Insurance Company, writes surplus lines of insurance in all 50 states, the District of Columbia, Puerto Rico, the Virgin Islands and Guam. Underwriters Indemnity Company, a subsidiary of RLI Insurance Company, has authority to write multiple lines of insurance on an admitted basis in 33 states and the District of Columbia and surplus lines of insurance in Ohio. Planet Indemnity Company (PIC), a subsidiary of Mt. Hawley, has authority to write multiple lines of insurance on an admitted basis in 40 states and the District of Columbia. PIC also has authority to write surplus lines of insurance in an additional three states. Other companies in the RLI Insurance Group include: Replacement Lens Inc., RLI Insurance Agency, Ltd., RLI Insurance Ltd., Underwriters Indemnity General Agency, Inc., and Safe Fleet Insurance Services, Inc.

ANNUAL FINANCIAL DATA

	12/31/01	12/31/00	12/31/99	12/31/98	12/31/97	12/31/96	12/31/95
Earnings Per Share	②3.02	2.89	3.08	2.65	①3.33	①2.60	0.81
Tang. Book Val. Per Share	30.73	29.98	26.23	28.25	30.87	20.46	16.16
Dividends Per Share	0.62	0.58	0.54	0.50	0.46	0.43	0.40
Dividend Payout %	20.5	20.1	17.5	18.9	13.9	16.6	49.5
INCOME STATEMENT (IN THOUSANDS):							
Total Premium Income	273,008	231,603	195,274	142,324	141,884	130,656	133,468
Net Investment Income	32,178	29,046	26,015	23,937	24,558	23,681	22,029
Other Income	4,168	2,847	4,467	1,853	2,982	1,018	35,052
Total Revenues	309,354	263,496	225,756	168,114	169,424	155,354	190,549
Policyholder Benefits	155,876	124,586	96,457	64,728	61,251	68,261	85,890
Income Before Income Taxes	38,173	35,314	41,422	36,384	40,571	35,009	8,268
Income Taxes	10,771	9,600	11,584	9,482	11,351	9,544	319
Equity Earnings/Minority Int.	2,845	2,979	1,613	1,337	951	231	...
Net Income	②30,247	28,693	31,451	28,239	①30,171	①25,696	7,950
Average Shs. Outstg.	10,002	9,945	10,222	10,638	9,371	9,871	9,812
BALANCE SHEET (IN THOUSANDS):							
Cash & Cash Equivalents	53,648	48,095	64,092	51,917	18,697	40,824	25,072
Premiums Due	449,049	398,994	361,795	274,708	242,106	255,889	286,594
Invst. Assets: Fixed-term	462,273	401,822	342,513	328,856	333,700	308,187	296,772
Invst. Assets: Equities	277,621	306,194	284,639	296,521	251,460	188,935	153,958
Invst. Assets: Total	814,435	774,159	706,314	690,751	617,422	546,917	474,590
Total Assets	1,390,970	1,281,323	1,170,363	1,012,685	911,741	845,474	814,647
Long-Term Obligations	...	...	...	...	...	46,000	46,000
Net Stockholders' Equity	335,432	326,654	293,069	293,959	266,552	200,039	158,608
Year-end Shs. Outstg.	9,913	9,804	9,873	10,406	8,634	9,777	9,814
STATISTICAL RECORD:							
Return on Revenues %	9.8	10.9	13.9	16.8	17.8	16.5	4.2
Return on Equity %	9.0	8.8	10.7	9.6	11.3	12.8	5.0
Return on Assets %	2.2	2.2	2.7	2.8	3.3	3.0	1.0
Price Range	46.15-38.75	45.06-26.25	38.81-27.88	45.63-30.69	40.20-24.40	26.80-17.90	20.00-13.04
P/E Ratio	15.3-12.8	15.6-9.1	12.6-9.0	17.2-11.6	12.1-7.3	10.3-6.9	24.7-16.1
Average Yield %	1.5	1.6	1.6	1.3	1.4	1.9	2.4

Statistics are as originally reported. Adjusted for 5-for-4 stock split 6/95. ① Incl. net realized gains of $0.21 per share, 1997; $0.07 per share, 1996. ② Bef. acctg. credit of $800,000

OFFICERS:
G. D. Stephens, Chmn.
J. E. Michael, Pres., C.E.O.
J. E. Dondanville, V.P., C.F.O.
M. A. Price, Treas.

INVESTOR CONTACT: Mike Price, Treas., (309) 693-5880

PRINCIPAL OFFICE: 9025 North Lindbergh Drive, Peoria, IL 61615

TELEPHONE NUMBER: (309) 692-1000
FAX: (309) 692-1068
WEB: www.rlicorp.com

NO. OF EMPLOYEES: 488 full-time; 67 part-time

SHAREHOLDERS: 4,168

ANNUAL MEETING: In May

INCORPORATED: DE, May, 1984; reincorp., IL, May, 1993

INSTITUTIONAL HOLDINGS:
No. of Institutions: 94
Shares Held: 5,251,211
% Held: 53.5

INDUSTRY: Fire, marine, and casualty insurance (SIC: 6331)

TRANSFER AGENT(S): Wells Fargo Shareowner Services, South St. Paul, MN

ROHM & HAAS COMPANY

YIELD 1.9%
P/E RATIO ...

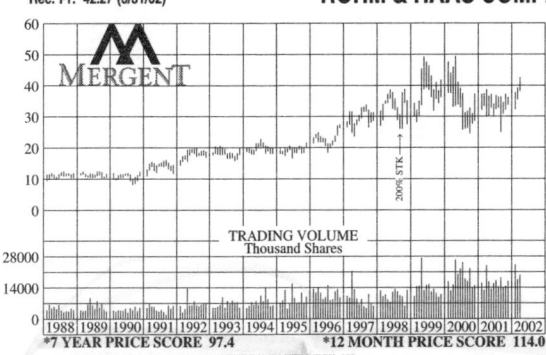

7 YEAR PRICE SCORE 97.4 **12 MONTH PRICE SCORE 114.0**
*NYSE COMPOSITE INDEX=100

INTERIM EARNINGS (Per Share):

Qtr.	Mar.	June	Sept.	Dec.
1999	0.64	d0.06	0.26	0.41
2000	0.56	0.35	0.38	0.32
2001	0.29	d0.94	0.24	0.17

INTERIM DIVIDENDS (Per Share):

Amt.	Decl.	Ex.	Rec.	Pay.
0.20Q	7/23/01	8/01/01	8/03/01	9/01/01
0.20Q	10/18/01	11/07/01	11/09/01	12/01/01
0.20Q	2/05/02	2/13/02	2/15/02	3/01/02

Indicated div.: $0.80 (Div. Reinv. Plan)

CAPITALIZATION (12/31/01):

	($000)	(%)
Long-Term Debt	2,720,000	34.7
Deferred Income Tax	1,278,000	16.3
Minority Interest	18,000	0.2
Common & Surplus	3,815,000	48.7
Total	7,831,000	100.0

DIVIDEND ACHIEVER STATUS:
Rank: 193   10-Year Growth Rate: 6.83%
Total Years of Dividend Growth: 24

RECENT DEVELOPMENTS: For the year ended 12/31/01, loss from continuing operations was $70.0 million versus income of $296.0 million in 2000. Results for 2001 and 2000 included non-recurring charges of $320.0 million and $26.0 million, and excluded income from discontinued operations of $468.0 million and $58.0 million, respectively. Net sales declined 10.8% to $5.67 billion.

PROSPECTS: ROH is beginning to see signs of stability in its end-use markets. As a result, the Company expects to see market demand beyond seasonal factors in the first half of 2002. Meanwhile, ROH remains on track to achieve savings of $200.0 million by October 2002. However, ROH will continue to spend money in the first half to dismantle closed plants and to move manufacturing capacity to more efficiently serve its customer base.

BUSINESS

ROHM & HAAS COMPANY is a multinational producer of specialty polymers and biologically active compounds. Products range from basic petrochemicals such as propylene, acetone and styrene to differentiated specialty products. ROH has developed acrylic plastics, a field that it pioneered with its development of plexiglas (used in outdoor signs, industrial lighting, skylights, and boat windshields). Other products include polymers, resins and monomers geared toward a wide variety of industrial applications. ROH also manufactures industrial chemicals. Contributions to sales in 2001 were as follows: performance polymers, 55.9%; chemical specialties, 14.2%; electronic materials, 16.7%; and salt, 13.2%. In January 1999, ROH acquired LeaRonal, an electronic materials firm.

ANNUAL FINANCIAL DATA

	12/31/01	12/31/00	12/31/99	12/31/98	12/31/97	12/31/96	12/31/95
Earnings Per Share	⑥d0.31	⑤1.61	④1.27	③2.52	2.13	①1.82	②1.41
Cash Flow Per Share	2.18	4.39	3.19	4.02	3.55	3.15	2.60
Tang. Book Val. Per Share	...	...	...	9.66	9.15	8.44	8.16
Dividends Per Share	0.80	0.78	0.74	0.69	0.63	0.57	0.52
Dividend Payout %	...	48.4	58.3	27.5	29.7	31.6	37.0
INCOME STATEMENT (IN MILLIONS):							
Total Revenues	5,666.0	6,879.0	5,339.0	3,720.0	3,999.0	3,982.0	3,884.0
Costs & Expenses	5,013.0	5,510.0	4,260.0	2,822.0	3,103.0	3,153.0	3,129.0
Depreciation & Amort.	562.0	613.0	451.0	276.0	279.0	262.0	242.0
Operating Income	91.0	756.0	628.0	622.0	617.0	567.0	513.0
Net Interest Inc./(Exp.)	d182.0	d241.0	d159.0	d34.0	d39.0	d32.0	d32.0
Income Before Income Taxes	d76.0	581.0	464.0	700.0	611.0	530.0	441.0
Income Taxes	6.0	227.0	215.0	247.0	201.0	167.0	149.0
Equity Earnings/Minority Int.	18.0	19.0	7.0	2.0	11.0	d17.0	d3.0
Net Income	⑥d70.0	⑤354.0	④249.0	③453.0	410.0	①363.0	②292.0
Cash Flow	480.0	967.0	698.0	723.0	682.0	618.0	527.0
Average Shs. Outstg. (000)	220,200	220,500	218,981	179,700	192,300	196,200	202,500
BALANCE SHEET (IN MILLIONS):							
Cash & Cash Equivalents	92.0	92.0	57.0	16.0	40.0	11.0	43.0
Total Current Assets	2,421.0	2,781.0	2,497.0	1,287.0	1,397.0	1,456.0	1,421.0
Net Property	2,916.0	3,339.0	3,496.0	1,908.0	2,008.0	2,066.0	2,048.0
Total Assets	10,350.0	11,267.0	11,256.0	3,648.0	3,900.0	3,933.0	3,916.0
Total Current Liabilities	1,624.0	2,194.0	2,510.0	875.0	850.0	886.0	828.0
Long-Term Obligations	2,720.0	3,225.0	3,122.0	409.0	509.0	562.0	606.0
Net Stockholders' Equity	3,815.0	3,653.0	3,475.0	1,561.0	1,797.0	1,728.0	1,781.0
Net Working Capital	797.0	587.0	d13.0	412.0	547.0	570.0	593.0
Year-end Shs. Outstg. (000)	220,427	219,937	218,981	154,000	182,700	189,300	201,900
STATISTICAL RECORD:							
Operating Profit Margin %	1.6	11.0	11.8	16.7	15.4	14.2	13.2
Net Profit Margin %	...	5.1	4.7	12.2	10.3	9.1	7.5
Return on Equity %	...	9.7	7.2	29.0	22.8	21.0	16.4
Return on Assets %	...	3.1	2.2	12.4	10.5	9.2	7.5
Debt/Total Assets %	26.3	28.6	27.7	11.2	13.1	14.3	15.5
Price Range	38.70-24.90	49.44-24.38	49.25-28.13	38.88-26.00	33.75-23.54	27.50-18.29	21.63-16.50
P/E Ratio	...	30.7-15.1	38.8-22.1	15.4-10.3	15.8-11.1	15.1-10.1	15.4-11.7
Average Yield %	2.5	2.1	1.9	2.2	2.2	2.5	2.7

Statistics are as originally reported. Adj. for 3-for-1 split, 9/98. ① Incl. $6.0 mill. non-recur. chgs. ② Incl. $17.0 mill. chg. ③ Excl. $13.0 mill. extraord. loss. ④ Incl. $105.0 mill. R&D chg., $22.0 mill. loss fr. disp. of jt. vent. & $36.0 mill. restr. chg. ⑤ Incl. $13.0 mill. R&D chg. & $13.0 mill. restr. chg. ⑥ Incl. $320.0 mill. restr. & excl. $468.0 mill. fr. disc. ops., $1.0 mill. extraord. loss & $2.0 mill. acctg. chg.

OFFICERS:
R. L. Gupta, Chmn., C.E.O.
J. M. Fitzpatrick, Pres., C.O.O.

INVESTOR CONTACT: Laura L. Hadden, Mgr. Bus. & Fin., (215) 592-3052

PRINCIPAL OFFICE: 100 Independence Mall West, Philadelphia, PA 19106

TELEPHONE NUMBER: (215) 592-3000
FAX: (215) 592-3377
WEB: www.rohmhaas.com

NO. OF EMPLOYEES: 18,210 (avg.)

SHAREHOLDERS: 9,234

ANNUAL MEETING: In May

INCORPORATED: DE, Apr., 1917

INSTITUTIONAL HOLDINGS:
No. of Institutions: 304
Shares Held: 169,174,375
% Held: 76.7

INDUSTRY: Plastics materials and resins (SIC: 2821)

TRANSFER AGENT(S): EquiServe, LP, Boston, MA

RPM, INC.

YIELD 3.2%
P/E RATIO 17.9

7 YEAR PRICE SCORE 78.8 *NYSE COMPOSITE INDEX=100 **12 MONTH PRICE SCORE 135.9**

INTERIM EARNINGS (Per Share):

Qtr.	Aug.	Nov.	Feb.	May
1997-98	0.29	0.22	0.06	0.33
1998-99	0.29	0.20	0.06	0.32
1999-00	0.07	0.19	0.04	0.09
2000-01	0.28	0.17	d0.07	0.24
2002-02	0.36	0.24	0.03	...

INTERIM DIVIDENDS (Per Share):

Amt.	Decl.	Ex.	Rec.	Pay.
0.125Q	4/02/01	4/10/01	4/13/01	4/30/01
0.125Q	7/02/01	7/11/01	7/13/01	7/31/01
0.125Q	10/12/01	10/18/01	10/22/01	10/31/01
0.125Q	1/04/02	1/10/02	1/14/02	1/31/02
0.125Q	4/01/02	4/10/02	4/12/02	4/30/02

Indicated div.: $0.50 (Div. Reinv. Plan)

CAPITALIZATION (5/31/01):

	($000)	(%)
Long-Term Debt	955,399	57.9
Deferred Income Tax	54,134	3.3
Common & Surplus	639,710	38.8
Total	1,649,243	100.0

DIVIDEND ACHIEVER STATUS:
Rank: 202   10-Year Growth Rate: 6.32%
Total Years of Dividend Growth: 28

RECENT DEVELOPMENTS: For the quarter ended 2/28/02, net income was $3.3 million versus a net loss of $7.0 million in the equivalent 2000 quarter. Results for 2002 included a non-cash charge of about $0.01 per diluted share relating to the devaluation of the Argentinean peso. Net sales were $407.5 million, up 0.5% from $405.4 million a year earlier. Gross profit as a percentage of net sales was 43.8% versus 42.2% in 2001. Selling, general and administrative expenses rose 0.6% to $166.0 million.

PROSPECTS: The Company plans to further reduce debt levels. During the past 12 months, the Company reduced debt levels with total debt payments approaching nearly $60.0 million. In addition, $55.0 million in senior unsecured notes were issued during RPM's fiscal second quarter, with the proceeds being used to reduce existing bank debt. Separately, earnings for RPM's current fiscal year are expected to be $0.93 per share.

BUSINESS

RPM, INC. is a manufacturer of protective coatings, with manufacturing facilities in the United States, Argentina, Belgium, Brazil, Canada, China, Colombia, Germany, Italy, Malaysia, Mexico, New Zealand, the Netherlands, Poland, South Africa, the United Arab Emirates and the United Kingdom. RPM participates in two broad market categories worldwide: industrial and consumer. As of 5/31/01, approximately 55.0% of RPM's sales were derived from the industrial market sectors, with the remainder in consumer products. RPM's industrial division consists of the StonCor Group, Tremco Group and RPM II Group product lines. The major product line groupings comprising RPM's consumer division include the Rust-Oleum Group, Zinsser Group, Wood Finishes Group, DAP/Bondex Group and Testor Hobby and Leisure Group. On 8/31/99, RPM acquired DAP Products Inc. and DAP Canada Corp.

ANNUAL FINANCIAL DATA

	5/31/01	5/31/00	5/31/99	5/31/98	5/31/97	5/31/96	5/31/95
Earnings Per Share	① 0.62	① 0.38	0.86	0.84	0.80	0.72	0.86
Cash Flow Per Share	1.41	1.12	1.41	1.30	1.32	1.17	1.37
Tang. Book Val. Per Share	...	...	0.77	...	...	0.18	0.71
Dividends Per Share	0.49	0.47	0.45	0.42	0.39	0.36	0.34
Dividend Payout %	79.4	125.0	52.7	50.5	49.0	50.7	39.6
INCOME STATEMENT (IN MILLIONS):							
Total Revenues	2,007.8	1,954.1	1,712.2	1,615.3	1,350.5	1,136.4	1,017.0
Costs & Expenses	1,759.6	1,699.5	1,457.6	1,372.0	1,131.1	948.1	849.7
Depreciation & Amort.	81.5	79.2	62.1	57.0	51.1	42.6	36.9
Operating Income	166.7	175.5	192.4	186.3	168.3	145.7	130.3
Net Interest Inc./(Exp.)	d65.2	d51.8	d32.8	d36.7	d32.6	d25.8	d23.4
Income Before Income Taxes	101.5	71.8	159.6	149.6	135.7	119.9	106.9
Income Taxes	38.5	30.8	65.1	61.7	57.4	51.0	45.8
Net Income	① 63.0	① 41.0	94.5	87.8	78.3	68.9	61.1
Cash Flow	144.5	120.1	156.7	144.8	129.5	111.5	98.0
Average Shs. Outstg. (000)	102,212	107,384	111,376	111,663	97,894	95,685	71,554
BALANCE SHEET (IN MILLIONS):							
Cash & Cash Equivalents	23.9	31.3	19.7	40.8	37.4	34.3	28.0
Total Current Assets	819.4	785.1	705.4	672.5	720.3	465.1	421.3
Net Property	362.0	366.2	339.7	305.9	270.3	224.7	204.0
Total Assets	2,078.5	2,099.2	1,737.2	1,683.3	1,633.2	1,155.1	959.1
Total Current Liabilities	375.8	376.2	302.5	285.8	241.8	189.4	151.1
Long-Term Obligations	955.4	959.3	582.1	715.7	784.4	447.7	406.4
Net Stockholders' Equity	639.7	645.7	742.9	567.1	493.3	445.8	347.6
Net Working Capital	443.7	408.9	402.9	386.7	478.5	275.7	270.2
Year-end Shs. Outstg. (000)	102,211	103,134	109,443	100,254	98,029	96,811	71,196
STATISTICAL RECORD:							
Operating Profit Margin %	8.3	9.0	11.2	11.5	12.5	12.8	12.8
Net Profit Margin %	3.1	2.1	5.5	5.4	5.8	6.1	6.0
Return on Equity %	9.8	6.3	12.7	15.5	15.9	15.5	17.6
Return on Assets %	3.0	2.0	5.4	5.2	4.8	6.0	6.4
Debt/Total Assets %	46.0	45.7	33.5	42.5	48.0	38.8	42.4
Price Range	11.31-7.75	16.50-9.94	18.00-12.75	16.80-12.50	14.90-11.50	13.80-11.36	12.56-10.40
P/E Ratio	18.2-12.5	43.4-26.1	20.9-14.8	20.0-14.9	18.6-14.4	19.2-15.8	14.7-12.1
Average Yield %	5.2	3.6	2.9	2.9	3.0	2.9	3.0

Statistics are as originally reported. Adj. for stk. splits: 5-for-4, 12/8/97; 25% div.; 12/8/95. ① Incl. restruct. chrg. of $52.0 mill., 5/01; $45.0 mill., 5/00.

OFFICERS:
T. C. Sullivan, Chmn., C.E.O.
J. A. Karman, Vice-Chmn.
F. C. Sullivan, Pres., C.O.O.
INVESTOR CONTACT: Investor Relations, (330) 273-5090
PRINCIPAL OFFICE: P.O. Box 777, 2628 Pearl Road, Medina, OH 44258

TELEPHONE NUMBER: (330) 273-5090
FAX: (330) 225-8743
WEB: www.rpminc.com
NO. OF EMPLOYEES: 7,928 (avg.)
SHAREHOLDERS: 42,036 (approx.)
ANNUAL MEETING: In Oct.
INCORPORATED: OH, May, 1947

INSTITUTIONAL HOLDINGS:
No. of Institutions: 223
Shares Held: 54,252,009
% Held: 53.0
INDUSTRY: Paints and allied products (SIC: 2851)
TRANSFER AGENT(S): Computershare Investor Services, Chicago, IL

S&T BANCORP, INC.

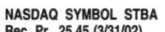
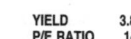

	YIELD	3.8%
	P/E RATIO	14.0

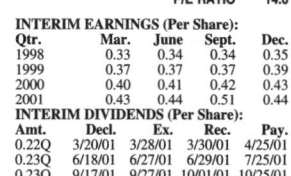

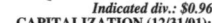

TRADING VOLUME
Thousand Shares

*7 YEAR PRICE SCORE 100.7 ***12 MONTH PRICE SCORE 107.9**
*NYSE COMPOSITE INDEX=100

INTERIM EARNINGS (Per Share):

Qtr.	Mar.	June	Sept.	Dec.
1998	0.33	0.34	0.34	0.35
1999	0.37	0.37	0.37	0.39
2000	0.40	0.41	0.42	0.43
2001	0.43	0.44	0.51	0.44

INTERIM DIVIDENDS (Per Share):

Amt.	Decl.	Ex.	Rec.	Pay.
0.22Q	3/20/01	3/28/01	3/30/01	4/25/01
0.23Q	6/18/01	6/27/01	6/29/01	7/25/01
0.23Q	9/17/01	9/27/01	10/01/01	10/25/01
0.24Q	12/17/01	12/27/01	12/31/01	1/25/02
0.24Q	3/18/02	3/27/02	4/01/02	4/25/02

Indicated div.: $0.96

CAPITALIZATION (12/31/01):

	($000)	(%)
Total Deposits	1,611,317	74.7
Long-Term Debt	251,226	11.7
Common & Surplus	293,327	13.6
Total	2,155,870	100.0

DIVIDEND ACHIEVER STATUS:

Rank: 37	10-Year Growth Rate: 17.79%
Total Years of Dividend Growth:	12

RECENT DEVELOPMENTS: For the year ended 12/31/01, income amounted to $49.2 million, before an extraordinary charge of $1.9 million, compared with net income of $45.0 million in the previous year. Net interest income was $90.0 million in both 2001 and 2000. STBA's provision for loan losses rose 25.0% to $5.0 million. Non-interest income jumped 40.9% to $31.2 million, while non-interest expenses climbed 2.9% to $47.0 million. Looking ahead,

STBA expects earnings in the range of $1.83 to $1.87 per share in 2002. On 3/20/02, the Company announced an agreement to acquire Peoples Financial Corp., Inc. the holding company for PFC Bank. Under the agreement, STBA will pay $52.50 in cash for each share of Peoples for an aggregate transaction value of $87.4 million. Peoples operates seven banking offices in the Pennsylvania counties of Armstrong, Butler, Clarion and Indiana.

BUSINESS

S&T BANCORP, INC. is a bank holding company with assets of $2.36 billion as of 12/31/01. The Company has two wholly-owned subsidiaries, S&T Bank and S&T Investment Company, Inc. S&T Bank offers a variety of services including time and demand deposit accounts, secured and unsecured commercial and consumer loans, letters of credit, discount brokerage services, personal finance planning and credit card services. S&T Investment Company, Inc. is an investment holding company, which manages investments previously owned by the bank. The Company operates through a branch network of 40 offices in 7 counties of Pennsylvania. Commonwealth Trust Credit Life Insurance Company is a joint venture that reinsures credit life, accident and health insurance policies sold by S&T Bank.

QUARTERLY DATA

(12/31/2001)($000)	REV	INC
1st Quarter	49,201	11,650
2nd Quarter	48,286	11,922
3rd Quarter	46,510	13,745
4th Quarter	44,245	11,868

ANNUAL FINANCIAL DATA

	12/31/01	12/31/00	12/31/99	12/31/98	12/31/97	12/31/96	12/31/95
Earnings Per Share	⅟1.82	1.66	1.51	1.35	1.17	1.05	0.91
Tang. Book Val. Per Share	11.01	10.28	8.88	9.38	9.20	7.96	7.42
Dividends Per Share	0.90	0.82	0.74	0.63	0.53	0.45	0.35
Dividend Payout %	49.4	49.4	49.0	46.7	45.3	42.9	38.5
INCOME STATEMENT (IN MILLIONS):							
Total Interest Income	166.7	176.2	156.7	151.4	141.1	111.4	107.0
Total Interest Expense	76.7	86.1	69.9	69.2	62.3	51.5	50.0
Net Interest Income	90.0	90.0	86.8	82.3	78.8	59.9	57.0
Provision for Loan Losses	5.0	4.0	4.0	10.6	5.0	4.3	3.8
Non-Interest Income	31.2	22.2	20.1	24.4	16.4	11.2	8.3
Non-Interest Expense	47.0	45.7	43.5	42.0	43.2	35.5	33.5
Income Before Taxes	69.2	62.5	59.4	54.2	47.1	31.3	28.0
Net Income	⅟49.2	45.0	41.4	38.0	33.4	23.2	20.5
Average Shs. Outstg. (000)	27,051	27,074	27,367	28,055	28,618	22,146	22,486
BALANCE SHEET (IN MILLIONS):							
Cash & Due from Banks	52.8	43.7	38.7	48.7	36.0	33.3	39.9
Securities Avail. for Sale	578.5	567.4	558.0	565.1	521.3	353.8	315.3
Total Loans & Leases	1,642.8	1,605.0	1,496.3	1,365.9	1,273.8	1,046.1	976.8
Allowance for Credit Losses	26.9	27.4	27.1	26.7	20.4	17.0	15.9
Net Loans & Leases	1,615.8	1,577.6	1,469.1	1,339.2	1,253.3	1,029.1	960.9
Total Assets	2,357.9	2,310.3	2,194.1	2,069.6	1,920.3	1,495.9	1,400.7
Total Deposits	1,611.3	1,525.3	1,435.1	1,380.1	1,284.7	1,032.3	979.6
Long-Term Obligations	251.2	378.0	364.1	240.1	144.2	136.6	96.6
Total Liabilities	2,064.5	2,033.2	1,954.4	1,810.0	1,660.2	1,319.7	1,233.8
Net Stockholders' Equity	293.3	277.1	239.7	259.6	260.1	176.3	166.9
Year-end Shs. Outstg. (000)	26,646	26,947	26,999	27,676	28,282	22,150	22,486
STATISTICAL RECORD:							
Return on Equity %	16.8	16.2	17.3	14.6	12.8	13.2	12.3
Return on Assets %	2.1	1.9	1.9	1.8	1.7	1.6	1.5
Equity/Assets %	12.4	12.0	10.9	12.5	13.5	11.8	11.9
Non-Int. Exp./Tot. Inc. %	38.7	40.7	40.7	39.4	45.3	50.0	51.3
Price Range	27.00-19.69	23.50-16.56	29.00-19.00	29.50-20.88	22.25-14.75	15.88-14.00	15.25-9.75
P/E Ratio	14.8-10.8	14.2-10.0	19.2-12.6	21.9-15.5	19.0-12.6	15.1-13.3	16.8-10.7
Average Yield %	3.9	4.1	3.1	2.5	2.9	3.0	2.8

Statistics are as originally reported. Adj. for 100% stk. split, 11/98. ⅟ Excl. extraord. chrg. of $1.9 mill.

OFFICERS:
R. D. Duggan, Chmn.
J. C. Miller, Pres., C.E.O.
R. E. Rout, Exec. V.P., C.F.O., Sec.

INVESTOR CONTACT: Sandy Ingmire, Shareholder Services, (724) 465-1466

PRINCIPAL OFFICE: 43 South Ninth Street, Indiana, PA 15701-3921

TELEPHONE NUMBER: (724) 465-1466
FAX: (724) 465-1488
WEB: www.stbank.com

NO. OF EMPLOYEES: 688

SHAREHOLDERS: 3,185 (record)

ANNUAL MEETING: In April

INCORPORATED: PA, March, 1983

INSTITUTIONAL HOLDINGS:
No. of Institutions: 54
Shares Held: 4,956,846
% Held: 18.5

INDUSTRY: State commercial banks (SIC: 6022)

TRANSFER AGENT(S): American Stock Transfer & Trust Company, New York, NY

SARA LEE CORPORATION

YIELD 2.9%
P/E RATIO 10.5

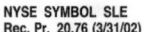

TRADING VOLUME
Thousand Shares

*7 YEAR PRICE SCORE 86.0   *12 MONTH PRICE SCORE 102.6
*NYSE COMPOSITE INDEX=100

INTERIM EARNINGS (Per Share):

Qtr.	Sept.	Dec.	Mar.	June
1998-99	0.35	0.34	0.26	0.31
1999-00	0.28	0.42	0.29	0.35
2000-01	0.27	0.17	0.28	1.19
2001-02	0.30	0.20	...	...

INTERIM DIVIDENDS (Per Share):

Amt.	Decl.	Ex.	Rec.	Pay.
0.145Q	4/26/01	5/30/01	6/01/01	7/02/01
0.145Q	6/28/01	8/29/01	9/03/01	10/01/01
0.15Q	10/25/01	11/29/01	12/03/01	1/02/02
0.15Q	1/31/02	2/27/02	3/01/02	4/01/02

Indicated div.: $0.60 (Div. Reinv. Plan)

CAPITALIZATION (6/30/01):

	($000)	(%)
Long-Term Debt	2,640,000	56.8
Deferred Income Tax	244,000	5.3
Minority Interest	625,000	13.5
Redeemable Pfd. Stock	238,000	5.1
Common & Surplus	899,000	19.3
Total	4,646,000	100.0

DIVIDEND ACHIEVER STATUS:
Rank: 148   10-Year Growth Rate: 9.46%
Total Years of Dividend Growth: 25

RECENT DEVELOPMENTS: For the quarter ended 12/29/01, net income was $160.0 million versus income from continuing operations of $151.0 million the year before. Results included pre-tax charges of $188.0 million and $320.0 million in 2001 and 2000, respectively, primarily related to business dispositions. Results for 2000 also included a $105.0 million pre-tax gain from the initial public offering of Coach, Inc. Net sales climbed 4.9% to $4.99 billion.

PROSPECTS: The Company is continuing to focus on streamlining its operations through the divestiture of non-core businesses and the closure or sale of certain high-cost manufacturing and distribution facilities. In addition, the Company is increasing its media advertising and promotional spending to help support new product launches, as well as boosting its investment in organizational and technology improvements.

BUSINESS

SARA LEE CORPORATION is a global manufacturer and marketer of brand-name foods and consumer products. Intimates & Underwear (43.6% of fiscal 2001 sales) is comprised of SLE's intimates, knit products, legwear and accessories businesses. Well-known brands include BALI, HANES HER WAY, and PLAYTEX. Sara Lee Foods (28.5%) is comprised of the packaged meats segment, which includes such brands as HILLSHIRE FARM, JIMMY DEAN, BALL PARK, and BRYAN, and the bakery segment. Beverage (16.2%) includes such brands as HILLS BROS., CHOCK FULL O'NUTS, DOUWE EGBERTS, MARCILLA and PICKWICK. Household Products (11.7%) is comprised of shoe care, body care, insecticides, air fresheners, and SLE's direct sales operations. On 12/4/00, SLE sold PYA/Monarch, its U.S. foodservice distributor. On 8/7/01, SLE acquired The Earthgrains Company.

ANNUAL FINANCIAL DATA

	6/30/01	7/1/00	7/3/99	6/27/98	6/27/97	6/29/96	7/1/95
Earnings Per Share	④ 1.87	③ 1.27	① 1.26	② d0.57	1.02	0.92	0.81
Cash Flow Per Share	2.58	1.92	1.83	0.09	1.71	1.57	1.44
Tang. Book Val. Per Share	...	...	...	...	0.35	0.46	0.02
Dividends Per Share	0.58	0.54	0.50	0.46	0.42	0.38	0.34
Dividend Payout %	31.0	42.5	39.7	...	41.4	41.5	42.0
INCOME STATEMENT (IN MILLIONS):							
Total Revenues	17,747.0	17,511.0	20,012.0	20,011.0	19,734.0	18,624.0	17,719.0
Costs & Expenses	15,556.0	15,166.0	17,708.0	17,620.0	17,411.0	16,439.0	15,709.0
Depreciation & Amort.	599.0	602.0	553.0	618.0	680.0	634.0	606.0
Operating Income	1,592.0	1,743.0	1,751.0	1,773.0	1,643.0	1,551.0	1,404.0
Net Interest Inc./(Exp.)	d180.0	d176.0	d141.0	d176.0	d159.0	d173.0	d185.0
Income Before Income Taxes	1,851.0	1,567.0	1,671.0	d443.0	1,484.0	1,378.0	1,219.0
Income Taxes	248.0	409.0	480.0	80.0	475.0	462.0	415.0
Net Income	④ 1,603.0	③ 1,158.0	① 1,191.0	② d523.0	1,009.0	916.0	804.0
Cash Flow	2,202.0	1,748.0	1,732.0	81.0	1,663.0	1,523.0	1,382.0
Average Shs. Outstg. (000)	854,000	912,000	944,000	939,000	970,000	970,000	960,000
BALANCE SHEET (IN MILLIONS):							
Cash & Cash Equivalents	548.0	314.0	279.0	273.0	272.0	243.0	202.0
Total Current Assets	5,083.0	5,974.0	4,987.0	5,220.0	5,391.0	5,081.0	4,928.0
Net Property	2,146.0	2,319.0	2,169.0	2,090.0	3,079.0	3,007.0	2,964.0
Total Assets	10,167.0	11,611.0	10,521.0	10,989.0	12,953.0	12,602.0	12,431.0
Total Current Liabilities	4,958.0	6,759.0	5,953.0	5,733.0	5,016.0	4,642.0	4,844.0
Long-Term Obligations	2,640.0	2,248.0	1,892.0	2,270.0	1,933.0	1,842.0	1,817.0
Net Stockholders' Equity	1,122.0	1,234.0	1,266.0	1,816.0	4,280.0	4,320.0	3,939.0
Net Working Capital	125.0	d785.0	d966.0	d513.0	375.0	439.0	84.0
Year-end Shs. Outstg. (000)	781,964	846,332	883,783	921,328	960,554	970,110	961,312
STATISTICAL RECORD:							
Operating Profit Margin %	9.0	10.0	8.7	8.9	8.3	8.3	7.9
Net Profit Margin %	9.0	6.6	6.0	...	5.1	4.9	4.5
Return on Equity %	142.9	93.8	94.1	...	23.6	21.2	20.4
Return on Assets %	15.8	10.0	11.3	...	7.8	7.3	6.5
Debt/Total Assets %	26.0	19.4	18.0	20.7	14.9	14.6	14.6
Price Range	24.75-18.26	25.31-13.38	28.75-21.06	31.81-22.16	28.91-18.25	20.25-14.94	16.88-12.13
P/E Ratio	13.2-9.8	19.9-10.5	22.8-16.7	...	28.5-18.0	22.1-16.3	20.8-15.0
Average Yield %	2.7	2.8	2.0	1.7	1.8	2.2	2.3

Statistics are as originally reported. Adj. for 2-for-1 stk. split, 12/98. ① Incl. $50 mil. ($0.05/sh) net chg. from product recall & incl. $97 mil ($0.10/sh) net gain on sale of intl. tobacco opers. ② Incl. $1.60 bil. ($1.72/sh) after-tax restr. chg. ③ Bef. $64.0 mil. ($0.07/sh) income fr. disc. oper. ④ Bef. $663 mil. ($0.78/sh) gain fr. disc. opers., incl. $967 mil. pre-tax gain fr. disposal of Coach business, and $554 mil. of other one-time pre-tax chgs.

OFFICERS:	**TELEPHONE NO.:** (312) 726-2600	**INSTITUTIONAL HOLDINGS:**
C. S. McMillan, Chmn., Pres., C.E.O.	**FAX:** (312) 558-4913	No. of Institutions: 583
L. M. DeKool, Exec. V.P., C.F.O.	**WEB:** www.saralee.com	Shares Held: 458,859,010
R. A. Palmore, Sr. V.P., Sec., Gen. Couns.		% Held: 58.4
	NO. OF EMPLOYEES: 141,500 (approx.)	
INVESTOR CONTACT: Janet Bergman, Sr.		**INDUSTRY:** Sausages and other prepared
V.P., Corp. Rel. (312) 558-8651	**SHAREHOLDERS:** 78,000 (approx.)	meats (SIC: 2013)
	ANNUAL MEETING: In Oct.	
PRINCIPAL OFFICE: Three First National	**INCORPORATED:** MD, Sept., 1941	**TRANSFER AGENT(S):** Sara Lee Corp.,
Plaza, Suite 4600, Chicago, IL 60602-4260		Chicago, IL

SBC COMMUNICATIONS INC.

YIELD 2.9%
P/E RATIO 17.6

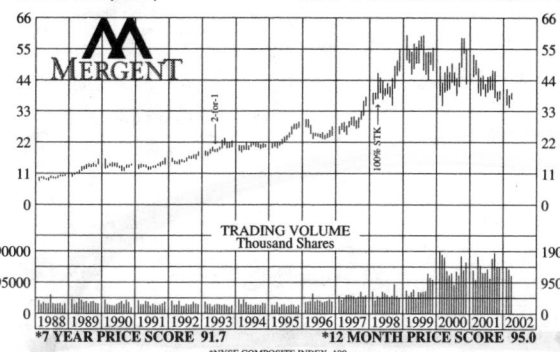

TRADING VOLUME
Thousand Shares

1988|1989|1990|1991|1992|1993|1994|1995|1996|1997|1998|1999|2000|2001|2002

*7 YEAR PRICE SCORE 91.7   ***12 MONTH PRICE SCORE 95.0**
*NYSE COMPOSITE INDEX=100

INTERIM EARNINGS (Per Share):

Qtr.	Mar.	June	Sept.	Dec.
1998	0.49	0.52	0.65	2.05
1999	0.56	0.59	0.64	0.50
2000	0.53	0.54	0.88	0.38
2001	0.54	0.61	0.61	0.37

INTERIM DIVIDENDS (Per Share):

Amt.	Decl.	Ex.	Rec.	Pay.
0.256Q	6/29/01	7/06/01	7/10/01	8/01/01
0.256Q	9/28/01	10/05/01	10/10/01	11/01/01
0.256Q	12/14/01	1/08/02	1/10/02	2/01/02
0.27Q	3/22/02	4/08/02	4/10/02	5/01/02

Indicated div.: $1.08 (Div. Reinv. Plan)

CAPITALIZATION (12/31/01):

	($000)	(%)
Long-Term Debt	17,133,000	29.4
Deferred Income Tax	8,578,000	14.7
Common & Surplus	32,491,000	55.8
Total	58,202,000	100.0

DIVIDEND ACHIEVER STATUS:

Rank: 252   10-Year Growth Rate: 3.79%
Total Years of Dividend Growth: 17

RECENT DEVELOPMENTS: For the year ended 12/31/01, income was $7.26 billion, before an extraordinary loss of $18.0 million, versus net income of $7.97 billion a year earlier. Results for 2001 and 2000 included a net non-recurring charge of $1.14 billion and a net non-recurring gain of $685.0 million, respectively. Operating revenues fell 10.6% to $45.91 billion, reflecting the sale of assets during 2001, including SBC's security-monitoring business, and the April 2000 formation of Cingular Wireless.

PROSPECTS: SBC's results continue to be pressured by the weak economy, regulatory uncertainty and competition in local phone markets. Looking ahead, SBC intends to focus on strengthening its core data, long-distance and wireless businesses. Expectations for 2002 include double-digit data revenue growth, long-distance approval in California and Cingular's service launch in New York City. SBC is targeting 5.0% to 7.0% full-year growth in earnings per share, before one-time items and the effect of accounting changes.

BUSINESS

SBC COMMUNICATIONS INC. (formerly Southwestern Bell) is one of seven regional holding companies divested by AT&T in 1984. SBC offers a variety of products and services under the SBC Ameritech, SBC Nevada Bell, SBC Pacific Bell, SBC SNET, and SBC Southwestern Bell brands, including local and long-distance voice, Internet services, telecommunications equipment, messaging, paging, directory advertising and publishing. As of 1/24/02, SBC had nearly 60.0 million network access lines in service and maintained a 60.0% equity interest in Cingular Wireless, which was formed in April 2000 and serves more than 21.0 million wireless customers. Internationally, SBC has telecommunications investments in 25 countries. On 4/1/97, SBC acquired Pacific Telesis Group. On 10/26/98, SBC acquired Southern New England Telecommunications Corporation. On 10/8/99, SBC acquired Ameritech Corp.

ANNUAL FINANCIAL DATA

	12/31/01	12/31/00	12/31/99	12/31/98	[1] 12/31/97	12/31/96	12/31/95
Earnings Per Share	[7] 2.14	[6] 2.32	[5] 1.90	[4] 2.05	[2][3] 0.80	1.73	1.55
Cash Flow Per Share	4.80	5.14	4.35	4.62	3.42	3.55	3.30
Tang. Book Val. Per Share	8.62	7.38	5.87	4.95	3.61	3.62	2.94
Dividends Per Share	1.02	1.00	0.96	0.93	0.89	0.85	0.82
Dividend Payout %	47.8	42.8	50.8	45.1	110.8	49.2	52.7
INCOME STATEMENT (IN MILLIONS)							
Total Revenues	45,908.0	51,476.0	49,489.0	28,777.0	24,856.0	13,898.0	12,670.0
Costs & Expenses	25,987.0	31,056.0	29,423.0	16,786.0	16,845.0	8,134.0	7,505.0
Depreciation & Amort.	9,033.0	9,677.0	8,468.0	5,105.0	4,841.0	2,208.0	2,128.0
Operating Income	10,888.0	10,743.0	11,598.0	6,886.0	3,170.0	3,556.0	3,037.0
Net Interest Inc./(Exp.)	d917.0	d1,313.0	d1,430.0	d993.0	d947.0	d472.0	d515.0
Income Before Income Taxes	11,357.0	12,888.0	10,853.0	6,374.0	2,337.0	3,267.0	2,792.0
Income Taxes	4,097.0	4,921.0	4,280.0	2,306.0	863.0	1,166.0	903.0
Net Income	[7] 7,260.0	[6] 7,967.0	[5] 6,573.0	[4] 6,068.0	[2][3] 1,474.0	2,101.0	1,889.0
Cash Flow	16,293.0	17,644.0	15,041.0	9,173.0	6,315.0	4,309.0	4,017.0
Average Shs. Outstg. (000)	3,396,000	3,433,000	3,458,000	1,984,000	1,844,000	1,214,000	1,218,000
BALANCE SHEET (IN MILLIONS)							
Cash & Cash Equivalents	703.0	643.0	495.0	460.0	398.0	242.0	490.0
Total Current Assets	12,580.0	23,216.0	11,930.0	7,538.0	7,062.0	3,912.0	3,679.0
Net Property	49,827.0	47,195.0	46,571.0	29,920.0	27,339.0	14,007.0	12,988.0
Total Assets	96,322.0	98,651.0	83,215.0	45,066.0	42,132.0	23,449.0	22,002.0
Total Current Liabilities	23,948.0	30,357.0	19,313.0	9,989.0	10,252.0	5,820.0	5,056.0
Long-Term Obligations	17,133.0	15,492.0	17,475.0	11,612.0	12,019.0	5,505.0	5,672.0
Net Stockholders' Equity	32,491.0	30,463.0	26,726.0	12,780.0	9,892.0	6,835.0	6,256.0
Net Working Capital	d11,368.0	d7,141.0	d7,383.0	d2,451.0	d3,190.0	d1,908.0	d1,377.0
Year-end Shs. Outstg. (000)	3,354,216	3,386,709	3,395,272	1,959,000	1,837,000	1,200,000	1,218,000
STATISTICAL RECORD:							
Operating Profit Margin %	23.7	20.9	23.4	23.9	12.8	25.6	24.0
Net Profit Margin %	15.8	15.5	13.3	14.1	5.9	15.1	14.9
Return on Equity %	22.3	26.2	24.6	31.8	14.9	30.7	30.2
Return on Assets %	7.5	8.1	7.9	9.0	3.5	9.0	8.6
Debt/Total Assets %	17.8	15.7	21.0	25.8	28.5	23.5	25.8
Price Range	53.06-36.50	59.00-34.81	59.94-44.06	54.88-35.00	38.06-24.63	30.13-23.00	29.25-19.81
P/E Ratio	24.8-17.1	25.1-14.8	31.5-23.2	26.8-17.1	47.6-30.8	17.4-13.3	18.9-12.8
Average Yield %	2.3	2.1	1.9	2.1	2.8	3.2	3.3

Statistics are as originally reported. Adj. for 100% stk. div., 3/98. [1] Incl. ops. of Pacific Telesis Group. [2] Incl. non-recurr. chrgs. $1.89 bill. [3] Bef. extraord. chrg. of $2.82 bill. [4] Bef. extraord. loss of $60.0 mill.; bef. acctg. chg. cr. of $15.0 mill. [5] Bef. extraord. gain of $1.38 bill. & acctg. chg. cr. of $207.0 mill.; incl. non-recurr. chrgs. of $866.0 mill. [6] Incl. non-recurr. chrg. of $659.0 mill. [7] Bef. extraord. chrg. of $18.0 mill.; incl. non-recurr. chrg. of $1.14 bill.

OFFICERS:
E. E. Whitacre, Jr., Chmn., C.E.O.
W. M. Daley, Pres.
R. Stephenson, Sr. Exec. V.P., C.F.O.

INVESTOR CONTACT: Larry L. Solomon, Investor Relations, (210) 351-3990

PRINCIPAL OFFICE: 175 E. Houston, P.O. Box 2933, San Antonio, TX 78205-2933

TELEPHONE NUMBER: (210) 821-4105
FAX: (210) 351-3553
WEB: www.sbc.com
NO. OF EMPLOYEES: 192,550 (approx.)
SHAREHOLDERS: 11,086,775
ANNUAL MEETING: In Apr.
INCORPORATED: DE, Oct., 1983

INSTITUTIONAL HOLDINGS:
No. of Institutions: 1,083
Shares Held: 1,545,588,569
% Held: 46.1

INDUSTRY: Telephone communications, exc. radio (SIC: 4813)

TRANSFER AGENT(S): EquiServe Trust Company, N.A., Jersey City, NJ

SCHERING-PLOUGH CORPORATION

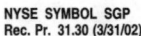

	YIELD	2.0%
	P/E RATIO	23.7

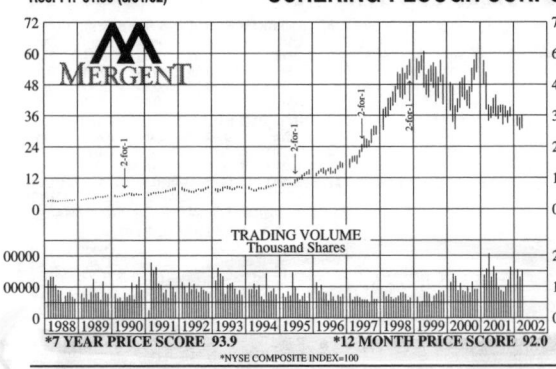

TRADING VOLUME
Thousand Shares

*7 YEAR PRICE SCORE 93.9   *12 MONTH PRICE SCORE 92.0
*NYSE COMPOSITE INDEX=100

INTERIM EARNINGS (Per Share):

Qtr.	Mar.	June	Sept.	Dec.
1997	0.26	0.26	0.24	0.24
1998	0.31	0.31	0.29	0.28
1999	0.36	0.37	0.35	0.34
2000	0.42	0.43	0.40	0.39
2001	0.38	0.43	0.41	0.10

INTERIM DIVIDENDS (Per Share):

Amt.	Decl.	Ex.	Rec.	Pay.
0.14Q	1/23/01	1/31/01	2/02/01	2/27/01
0.16Q	4/24/01	5/02/01	5/04/01	5/29/01
0.16Q	6/26/01	8/01/01	8/03/01	8/28/01
0.16Q	10/23/01	10/31/01	11/02/01	11/27/01
0.16Q	1/22/02	1/30/02	2/01/02	2/26/02

Indicated div.: $0.64 (Div. Reinv. Plan)

CAPITALIZATION (12/31/01):

	($000)	(%)
Deferred Income Tax	302,000	4.1
Common & Surplus	7,125,000	95.9
Total	7,427,000	100.0

DIVIDEND ACHIEVER STATUS:
Rank: 67   10-Year Growth Rate: 14.60%
Total Years of Dividend Growth: 16

RECENT DEVELOPMENTS: For the year ended 12/31/01, net income declined 19.8% to $1.94 billion compared with $2.42 billion in the previous year. Results for 2001 included a $500.0 million provision for a consent decree payment. Net sales decreased slightly to $9.80 billion from $9.82 billion in the prior year. Worldwide pharmaceutical sales grew to $8.37 billion from $8.35 billion in 2000.

PROSPECTS: Looking ahead, the Company's 2002 earnings remain subject to a number of factors, including the success of the U.S. launch of CLARINEX® tablets, a new nonsedating antihistamine, and potential trade inventory reductions of CLARITIN® nonsedating antihistamine, and the potential effect on product shipments as SGP continues to implement enhancements to manufacturing operations.

BUSINESS

SCHERING-PLOUGH CORPORA-TION is a is a global company primarily engaged in the discovery, development, manufacturing and marketing of pharmaceutical and consumer products. Pharmaceutical products include prescription drugs, over-the-counter medicines, vision-care products and animal health products promoted to the medical and allied professions. Prescription products include: CLARITIN, CLARITIN-D, NASONEX, PROVENTIL, VANCENASE and VANCERIL. The healthcare product segment consists of over-the-counter foot care products, including DR. SHOLLS, and sun care products, including COPPERTONE and BAIN DE SOLEIL. Healthcare products are sold primarily in the United States. In 2001, contributions to sales were pharmaceutical products, 85.4%; and healthcare products, 14.6%.

ANNUAL FINANCIAL DATA

	12/31/01	12/31/00	12/31/99	12/31/98	12/31/97	12/31/96	12/31/95
Earnings Per Share	[2] 1.32	1.64	1.42	1.18	0.97	0.83	[1] 0.71
Cash Flow Per Share	1.54	1.84	1.60	1.34	1.11	0.94	0.82
Tang. Book Val. Per Share	4.41	3.75	3.11	2.33	1.60	1.41	1.11
Dividends Per Share	0.62	0.55	0.48	0.42	0.37	0.32	0.28
Dividend Payout %	47.0	33.2	34.2	36.0	37.9	38.8	39.4
INCOME STATEMENT (IN MILLIONS):							
Total Revenues	9,802.0	9,815.0	9,176.0	8,077.0	6,778.0	5,656.0	5,104.0
Costs & Expenses	6,959.0	6,328.0	6,117.0	5,513.0	4,665.0	3,836.8	3,495.0
Depreciation & Amort.	320.0	299.0	264.0	238.0	200.0	173.2	157.0
Operating Income	2,523.0	3,188.0	2,795.0	2,326.0	1,913.0	1,646.0	1,452.0
Income Before Income Taxes	2,523.0	3,188.0	2,795.0	2,326.0	1,913.0	1,606.0	1,395.0
Income Taxes	580.0	765.0	685.0	570.0	469.0	393.0	342.0
Net Income	[2] 1,943.0	2,423.0	2,110.0	1,756.0	1,444.0	1,213.0	[1] 1,053.0
Cash Flow	2,263.0	2,722.0	2,374.0	1,994.0	1,644.0	1,386.2	1,210.0
Average Shs. Outstg. (000)	1,470,000	1,476,000	1,486,000	1,488,000	1,480,000	1,470,800	1,478,800
BALANCE SHEET (IN MILLIONS):							
Cash & Cash Equivalents	2,716.0	2,397.0	1,876.0	1,259.0	714.0	535.1	321.4
Total Current Assets	6,519.0	5,720.0	4,909.0	3,958.0	2,920.0	2,364.6	1,956.3
Net Property	3,814.0	3,362.0	2,939.0	2,675.0	2,526.0	2,246.3	2,098.9
Total Assets	12,174.0	10,805.0	9,375.0	7,840.0	6,507.0	6,253.2	5,505.9
Total Current Liabilities	3,917.0	3,645.0	3,209.0	3,032.0	2,891.0	3,454.2	3,203.4
Long-Term Obligations	...	...	...	...	46.0	46.4	87.1
Net Stockholders' Equity	7,125.0	6,119.0	5,165.0	4,002.0	2,821.0	2,059.9	1,622.9
Net Working Capital	2,602.0	2,075.0	1,700.0	926.0	29.0	d1,089.6	d1,247.1
Year-end Shs. Outstg. (000)	1,465,000	1,463,000	1,472,000	1,472,000	1,466,000	1,461,468	1,456,800
STATISTICAL RECORD:							
Operating Profit Margin %	25.7	32.5	30.5	28.8	28.2	29.1	28.4
Net Profit Margin %	19.8	24.7	23.0	21.7	21.3	21.4	20.6
Return on Equity %	27.3	39.6	40.9	43.9	51.2	58.9	64.9
Return on Assets %	16.0	22.4	22.5	22.4	22.2	19.4	19.1
Debt/Total Assets %	...	...	...	...	0.7	0.7	1.6
Price Range	57.25-32.35	60.00-30.50	60.81-40.25	57.75-30.34	32.00-15.88	18.28-12.63	15.19-8.88
P/E Ratio	43.4-24.5	36.6-18.6	42.8-28.3	48.9-25.7	33.0-16.4	22.2-15.3	21.3-12.4
Average Yield %	1.4	1.2	1.0	1.0	1.5	2.1	2.3

Statistics are as originally reported. Adjusted for 2-for-1 stock split, 12/98, 8/97 & 6/95. [1] Bef. dis. opers. loss of $166.4 mill. [2] Incl. $500.0 mill. provision for a consent decree payment.

OFFICERS:
R. J. Kogan, Chmn., Pres., C.E.O.
J. L. Wyszomierski, Exec. V.P., C.F.O.
E. K. Moore, V.P., Treas.
J. J. LaRosa, Staff V.P., Sec., Assoc. Gen. Couns.

INVESTOR CONTACT: Geraldine U. Foster, Sr. V.P., Inv. Rel., (908) 298-4000

PRINCIPAL OFFICE: 2000 Galloping Hill Road, Kenilworth, NJ 07033

TELEPHONE NUMBER: (908) 298-4000
FAX: (908) 298-7082
WEB: www.schering-plough.com

NO. OF EMPLOYEES: 29,800 (approx.)

SHAREHOLDERS: 47,900 (approx.)

ANNUAL MEETING: In Apr.

INCORPORATED: NJ, July, 1970

INSTITUTIONAL HOLDINGS:
No. of Institutions: 965
Shares Held: 984,047,620
% Held: 67.2

INDUSTRY: Pharmaceutical preparations (SIC: 2834)

TRANSFER AGENT(S): The Bank of New York, New York, NY

NYSE SYMBOL SCH
Rec. Pr. 13.09 (3/31/02)

SCHWAB (CHARLES) CORPORATION

YIELD 0.3%
P/E RATIO 218.2

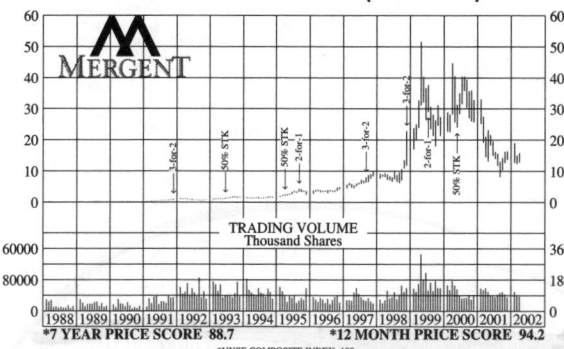

TRADING VOLUME Thousand Shares

| 1988 | 1989 | 1990 | 1991 | 1992 | 1993 | 1994 | 1995 | 1996 | 1997 | 1998 | 1999 | 2000 | 2001 | 2002 |

*7 YEAR PRICE SCORE 88.7   *12 MONTH PRICE SCORE 94.2
*NYSE COMPOSITE INDEX=100

INTERIM EARNINGS (Per Share):

Qtr.	Mar.	June	Sept.	Dec.
1998	0.06	0.07	0.12	0.09
1999	0.11	0.12	0.10	0.13
2000	0.33	0.09	0.10	0.10
2001	0.07	d0.01	0.01	d0.01

INTERIM DIVIDENDS (Per Share):

Amt.	Decl.	Ex.	Rec.	Pay.
0.011Q	1/25/01	2/07/01	2/09/01	2/23/01
0.011Q	4/26/01	5/07/01	5/09/01	5/23/01
0.011Q	7/18/01	8/07/01	8/09/01	8/23/01
0.011Q	10/25/01	11/07/01	11/09/01	11/23/01
0.011Q	1/23/02	2/06/02	2/08/02	2/22/02

Indicated div.: $0.04 (Div. Reinv. Plan)

CAPITALIZATION (12/31/01):

	($000)	(%)
Long-Term Debt	730,000	14.9
Common & Surplus	4,163,000	85.1
Total	4,893,000	100.0

DIVIDEND ACHIEVER STATUS:
Rank: 7   10-Year Growth Rate: 26.48%
Total Years of Dividend Growth: 12

RECENT DEVELOPMENTS: For the year ended 12/31/01, income was $78.0 million, before a $121.0 million extraordinary gain, versus net income of $718.0 million the year before. Results for 2001 included restructuring and other charges of $419.0 million. Results for 2000 included a $69.0 million merger-related charge. Total revenues slid 24.8% to $4.35 billion from $5.79 billion in 2000. Asset management and administration fees rose 5.8% to $1.68 billion from $4.158 billion the prior year.

PROSPECTS: On 2/13/02, SCH announced an agreement to sell its wholly-owned subsidiary, Charles Schwab Canada, Co., to the Scotiabank Group. Financial terms of the transaction were not disclosed. Separately, on 1/15/02, SCH announced a new Corporate Services division, which was created to deliver services, including retirement plans, equity compensation plans and specialized brokerage services, to corporations and their employees. This market is estimated at nearly $3.50 trillion in assets.

BUSINESS

THE CHARLES SCHWAB CORPORATION and its subsidiaries provide brokerage and related investment services to 7.8 million active investor accounts, with $846.00 billion in client assets as of 12/31/01. The Company's principal subsidiary, Charles Schwab & Co. Inc., is a securities broker-dealer and is the United States' largest on-line brokerage firm. Mayer & Schweitzer, Inc., a market-maker in Nasdaq securities, provides trade-execution services to institutional clients and broker-dealers. As of 12/31/01, SCH operated 429 domestic branch offices, 5 regional client telephone service centers and automated telephonic and on-line channels, in 48 states, Puerto Rico, and the U.S. Virgin Islands. SCH also has offices in Brazil, Canada, the Cayman Islands, Hong Kong, and the U.K. On 5/31/00, SCH acquired U.S. Trust Corporation.

REVENUES

(12/31/2001)	($000)	(%)
Asset management & administrative	1,675,000	38.5
Commissions	1,355,000	31.1
Interest revenue	929,000	21.3
Principal transactions	255,000	5.9
Other	139,000	3.2
Total	4,353,000	100.0

ANNUAL FINANCIAL DATA

	12/31/01	12/31/00	12/31/99	12/31/98	12/31/97	12/31/96	12/31/95
Earnings Per Share	③ 0.06	② 0.51	0.47	0.28	① 0.22	0.19	0.14
Cash Flow Per Share	0.34	0.73	0.59	0.39	0.32	0.28	0.20
Tang. Book Val. Per Share	2.58	2.69	1.81	1.15	0.90	0.66	0.47
Dividends Per Share	0.044	0.041	0.037	0.035	0.031	0.027	0.021
Dividend Payout %	73.2	8.0	8.0	12.7	14.1	13.8	14.4
INCOME STATEMENT (IN MILLIONS):							
Total Revenues	4,353.0	5,787.7	3,944.8	2,736.2	2,298.1	1,850.9	1,419.9
Costs & Expenses	3,814.0	4,245.3	2,816.9	2,021.2	1,726.8	1,358.5	1,074.0
Depreciation & Amort.	404.0	310.9	156.7	138.5	124.7	98.3	68.8
Operating Income	135.0	1,231.5	971.2	576.5	447.2	394.1	277.1
Income Before Income Taxes	135.0	1,231.5	971.2	576.5	447.2	394.1	277.1
Income Taxes	57.0	513.3	382.4	228.1	177.0	160.3	104.5
Net Income	③ 78.0	② 718.1	588.9	348.5	① 270.3	233.8	172.6
Cash Flow	482.0	1,029.0	745.6	486.9	395.0	332.1	241.4
Average Shs. Outstg. (000)	1,399,000	1,403,763	1,264,635	1,234,515	1,226,589	1,169,591	1,204,713
BALANCE SHEET (IN MILLIONS):							
Cash & Cash Equivalents	22,148.0	14,300.6	10,544.7	11,398.9	7,571.5	7,869.3	5,855.9
Total Current Assets	36,260.0	34,128.4	28,087.5	21,379.3	15,590.1	13,113.0	9,944.1
Net Property	1,058.0	1,132.6	597.8	396.2	342.3	315.4	243.5
Total Assets	40,464.0	38,154.0	29,299.1	22,264.4	16,481.7	13,778.8	10,552.0
Total Current Liabilities	35,571.0	33,154.0	26,570.1	20,484.8	14,975.5	12,640.4	9,673.0
Long-Term Obligations	730.0	770.2	455.0	351.0	361.0	283.8	246.1
Net Stockholders' Equity	4,163.0	4,229.7	2,273.9	1,428.6	1,145.1	854.6	632.9
Net Working Capital	689.0	974.3	1,517.4	894.6	614.5	472.6	271.2
Year-end Shs. Outstg. (000)	1,368,563	1,385,625	1,233,374	1,205,649	1,204,599	1,181,709	1,174,716
STATISTICAL RECORD:							
Operating Profit Margin %	3.1	21.3	24.6	21.1	19.5	21.3	19.5
Net Profit Margin %	1.8	12.4	14.9	12.7	11.8	12.6	12.2
Return on Equity %	1.9	17.0	25.9	24.4	23.6	27.4	27.3
Return on Assets %	0.2	1.9	2.0	1.6	1.6	1.7	1.6
Debt/Total Assets %	1.8	2.0	1.6	1.6	2.2	2.1	2.3
Price Range	33.00-8.13	44.75-22.46	51.67-16.96	22.83-6.17	9.83-4.50	4.87-2.67	4.30-1.64
P/E Ratio	549.1-135.3	87.7-44.0	110.6-36.3	80.7-21.8	44.7-20.4	25.2-13.8	29.8-11.4
Average Yield %	0.2	0.1	0.1	0.2	0.4	0.7	0.7

Statistics are as originally reported. Total revenues include interest income, net of interest expense; adj. for 3-for-2 split: 5/00, 12/98 & 9/97; 2-for-1 split, 7/99. ① Incl. $23.6 mill. chg. for litigation settlement. ② Incl. an after-tax chrg. of $22.0 mill. for merger retention programs, after-tax merger-rel. costs of $63.0 mill. & an after-tax chrg. of $46.0 mill. for amort. of goodwill & other intangibles assoc. with acquisions. ③ Bef. $121.0 mill. ($0.08/sh) extraord. gain & incl. $419.0 mill. restr. and other chgs.

OFFICERS:
C. R. Schwab, Chmn., Co-C.E.O.
D. S. Pottruck, Pres., Co-C.E.O.
S. L. Scheid, Exec. V.P., C.F.O.

INVESTOR CONTACT: Richard Fowler, Investor Relations, (415) 636-9869

PRINCIPAL OFFICE: 120 Kearny Street, San Francisco, CA 94108

TELEPHONE NUMBER: (415) 627-7000
FAX: (415) 627-8894
WEB: www.schwab.com

NO. OF EMPLOYEES: 19,600

SHAREHOLDERS: 12,918 (record)

ANNUAL MEETING: In May

INCORPORATED: DE, Nov., 1986

INSTITUTIONAL HOLDINGS:
No. of Institutions: 492
Shares Held: 685,365,132
% Held: 50.0

INDUSTRY: Security brokers and dealers (SIC: 6211)

TRANSFER AGENT(S): Wells Fargo Shareowner Services, St. Paul, MN

SEI INVESTMENTS COMPANY

	YIELD	0.2%
	P/E RATIO	39.3

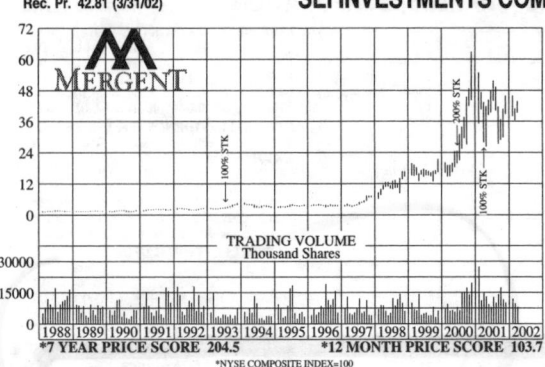

*7 YEAR PRICE SCORE 204.5   *12 MONTH PRICE SCORE 103.7
*NYSE COMPOSITE INDEX=100

INTERIM EARNINGS (Per Share):

Qtr.	Mar.	June	Sept.	Dec.
1996	0.05	0.04	0.05	0.06
1997	0.04	0.05	0.06	0.09
1998	0.07	0.08	0.10	0.13
1999	0.13	0.14	0.16	0.17
2000	0.18	0.20	0.24	0.25
2001	0.25	0.27	0.28	0.29

INTERIM DIVIDENDS (Per Share):

Amt.	Decl.	Ex.	Rec.	Pay.
0.08S	5/11/00	6/01/00	6/05/00	6/19/00
0.08S	12/14/00	1/04/01	1/08/01	1/25/01
100% STK	12/14/00	3/01/01	2/19/01	2/28/01
0.05S	5/29/01	6/08/01	6/12/01	6/26/01
0.05S	12/13/01	1/02/02	1/04/02	1/22/02

Indicated div.: $0.10

CAPITALIZATION (12/31/01):

	($000)	(%)
Long-Term Debt	43,055	13.6
Deferred Income Tax	2,925	0.9
Common & Surplus	270,593	85.5
Total	316,573	100.0

DIVIDEND ACHIEVER STATUS:
Rank: 6   10-Year Growth Rate: 26.86%
Total Years of Dividend Growth: 10

RECENT DEVELOPMENTS: For the year ended 12/31/01, net income increased 26.3% to $124.9 million compared with $99.0 million in the prior year. Total revenues grew 9.9% to $658.0 million from $598.8 million in the previous year. Private banking and trust revenue rose 6.4% to $360.1 million from $338.4 million the year before. Investment advisors revenue climbed 15.7% to $155.0 million from $134.0 million a year earlier. Enterprises revenue advanced 17.2% to $64.5 million from $55.0 million in the prior year. Money managers revenue rose 13.1% to $36.6 million from $32.3 million a year ago. Revenues from investments in new businesses grew 7.2% to $41.9 million from $39.0 million in the previous year. For the quarter ended 12/31/01, net income advanced 16.1% to $33.2 million from $28.6 million in the corresponding prior-year period. Revenues increased 4.3% to $164.8 million.

BUSINESS

SEI INVESTMENTS COMPANY is a provider of asset management and investment technology services with operations in five business segments. The Private Banking & Trust segment (54.7% of 2001 revenues, 69.8% of operating profits) provides investment processing services, fund processing services, and investment management programs to banks and private trust companies. The Investment Advisors segment (23.5%, 29.5%) provides investment management programs and investment processing services to investors through a network of financial intermediaries. The Enterprises segment (9.8%, 9.7%) provides retirement and treasury business services for corporations, unions, foundations and endowments, and other institutional investors. The Money Managers segment (5.6%, 2.4%) provides business services to U.S. investment managers, mutual fund companies and alternative investment managers worldwide. Investments in New Businesses (6.4%, -11.4%) include SEIC's global businesses, as well as initiatives in new U.S. markets. As of 1/31/02, SEIC operated 25 offices in 11 countries.

ANNUAL FINANCIAL DATA

	12/31/01	12/31/00	12/31/99	12/31/98	12/31/97	12/31/96	12/31/95
Earnings Per Share	1.09	0.87	0.59	0.38	0.23	① 0.20	① 0.18
Cash Flow Per Share	1.26	1.02	0.73	0.51	0.35	0.29	0.28
Tang. Book Val. Per Share	2.38	1.70	0.60	0.40	0.26	0.37	0.47
Dividends Per Share	0.09	0.07	0.06	0.05	0.043	0.037	0.03
Dividend Payout %	8.3	8.4	10.2	13.3	18.7	18.5	16.5
INCOME STATEMENT (IN THOUSANDS):							
Total Revenues	658,013	598,806	456,192	366,119	292,749	247,817	225,964
Costs & Expenses	455,177	433,542	337,905	282,546	233,169	201,691	179,647
Depreciation & Amort.	19,650	17,305	15,793	15,688	14,068	10,039	11,574
Operating Income	183,186	147,959	102,494	67,885	45,512	36,087	34,743
Net Interest Inc./(Exp.)	4,796	4,126	d90	d1,017	d1,505	760	764
Income Before Income Taxes	198,324	159,618	109,169	69,883	44,007	37,944	35,507
Income Taxes	73,380	60,655	42,030	26,904	17,163	14,798	14,381
Equity Earnings/Minority Int.	10,342	7,533	6,765	3,015	...	...	...
Net Income	124,944	98,963	67,139	42,979	26,844	① 23,146	① 21,126
Cash Flow	144,594	116,268	82,932	58,667	40,912	33,185	32,700
Average Shs. Outstg.	114,810	113,820	113,826	114,756	115,416	116,088	116,670
BALANCE SHEET (IN THOUSANDS):							
Cash & Cash Equivalents	173,685	159,576	73,206	52,980	16,891	13,167	10,256
Total Current Assets	266,142	249,031	146,992	113,509	83,995	64,956	54,075
Net Property	95,804	75,111	65,640	62,761	52,123	48,620	24,299
Total Assets	460,916	375,582	253,779	208,772	168,884	141,041	101,347
Total Current Liabilities	144,343	146,453	138,918	110,794	81,676	79,957	44,886
Long-Term Obligations	43,055	27,000	29,000	31,000	33,000	...	...
Net Stockholders' Equity	270,593	197,421	79,002	59,685	46,410	56,108	56,002
Net Working Capital	121,799	102,578	8,074	2,715	2,319	d15,001	9,189
Year-end Shs. Outstg.	109,180	108,560	106,152	107,166	106,602	110,988	110,550
STATISTICAL RECORD:							
Operating Profit Margin %	27.8	24.7	22.5	18.5	15.5	14.6	15.4
Net Profit Margin %	19.0	16.5	14.7	11.7	9.2	9.3	9.3
Return on Equity %	46.2	50.1	85.0	72.0	57.8	41.3	37.7
Return on Assets %	27.1	26.3	26.5	20.6	15.9	16.4	20.8
Debt/Total Assets %	9.3	7.2	11.4	14.8	19.5	...	...
Price Range	54.91-26.25	62.84-14.79	21.50-12.89	16.75-6.17	7.42-3.12	4.27-2.96	4.08-2.79
P/E Ratio	50.4-24.1	72.2-17.0	36.4-21.9	44.7-16.4	31.8-13.4	21.3-14.8	22.4-15.3
Average Yield %	0.2	0.2	0.4	0.4	0.8	1.0	0.9

Statistics are as originally reported. Adj. for stk. split: 2-for-1, 2/28/01; 3-for1, 6/19/00.
① Bef. disc. oper. loss $16.3 mill. ($0.84/sh.), 1996; $1.9 mill. ($0.10/sh.), 1995.

OFFICERS:	TELEPHONE NUMBER: (610) 676-1000	INSTITUTIONAL HOLDINGS:
A. P. West, Jr., Chmn., C.E.O.	FAX: (610) 676-1105	No. of Institutions: 224
T. B. Cipperman, Sr. V.P., Gen. Couns.	WEB: www.seic.com	Shares Held: 52,038,248
	NO. OF EMPLOYEES: 1,800 full-time	% Held: 48.2
INVESTOR CONTACT: Investor Relations,	(approx.); 90 part-time (approx.)	
(610) 676-1000	SHAREHOLDERS: 700 (approx.)	INDUSTRY: Security brokers and dealers
		(SIC: 6211)
PRINCIPAL OFFICE: 1 Freedom Valley	ANNUAL MEETING: In May	
Drive, Oaks, PA 19456-1100	INCORPORATED: PA, 1968	TRANSFER AGENT(S): American Stock
		Transfer & Trust Co., New York, NY

SEMCO ENERGY, INC.

YIELD 8.8%
P/E RATIO ...

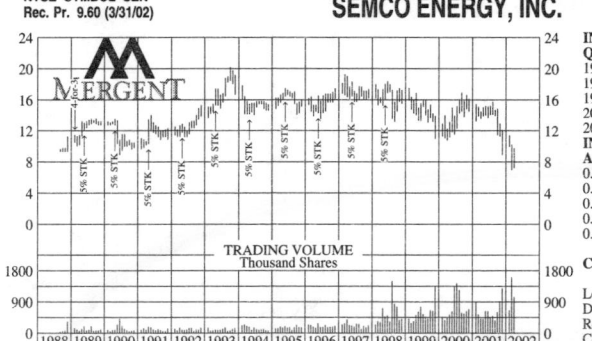

TRADING VOLUME
Thousand Shares

*7 YEAR PRICE SCORE 71.6   *12 MONTH PRICE SCORE 70.0
*NYSE COMPOSITE INDEX=100

INTERIM EARNINGS (Per Share):

Qtr.	Mar.	June	Sept.	Dec.
1997	0.70	0.01	d0.23	0.61
1998	0.59	d0.18	d0.18	0.37
1999	0.60	0.01	d0.12	0.52
2000	0.67	d0.17	d0.26	0.65
2001	0.52	d0.19	d0.36	0.01

INTERIM DIVIDENDS (Per Share):

Amt.	Decl.	Ex.	Rec.	Pay.
0.21Q	12/14/00	2/01/01	2/05/01	2/15/01
0.21Q	4/17/01	5/02/01	5/04/01	5/15/01
0.21Q	6/14/01	7/30/01	8/01/01	8/15/01
0.21Q	10/18/01	10/30/01	11/01/01	11/15/01
0.21Q	12/13/01	1/30/02	2/01/02	2/15/02

Indicated div.: $0.84 (Div. Reinv. Plan)

CAPITALIZATION (12/31/01):

	($000)	(%)
Long-Term Debt	338,966	54.2
Deferred Income Tax	33,149	5.3
Redeemable Pfd. Stock	139,394	22.3
Common & Surplus	113,810	18.2
Total	625,319	100.0

DIVIDEND ACHIEVER STATUS:
Rank: 247   10-Year Growth Rate: 4.23%
Total Years of Dividend Growth: 23

RECENT DEVELOPMENTS: For the year ended 12/31/01, SEN reported a loss from continuing operations of $239,000 versus income of continuing operations of $16.6 million in 2000. Results for 2001 excluded a loss of $6.1 million, while 2000 results excluded a gain of $95,000. The 2001 results also included restructuring and impairment charges of $6.1 million. Operating revenues rose 8.7% to $445.8 million from $410.3 million in 2000.

PROSPECTS: In 2001, the Company redirected its business strategy and, as a result, incurred restructuring and other charges that negatively affected earnings for the year. However, the redirection of the Company's business strategy is expected to increase future profitability. Looking ahead, SEN expects earnings per share for 2002 to be in the range of $0.82 and $0.90, including the effect of warmer-than-normal weather in January 2002.

BUSINESS

SEMCO ENERGY, INC. (formerly Southeastern Michigan Gas Company) operates four business segments: gas distribution, construction services, information technology services, and propane, pipelines and storage. The Company's gas distribution business segment distributes and transports natural gas to approximately 267,000 customers within the state of Michigan and approximately 108,000 customers in the state of Alaska. The construction services segment is comprised of six companies and operates in Florida, Georgia, Illinois, Iowa, Kansas, Michigan and Texas. Its primary service is the installation of underground natural gas mains and service lines. The information technology services business segment provides information technology infrastructure outsourcing services, and other information technology services with a focus on mid-range computers. The propane, pipelines and storage segment supplies propane to retail customers in Michigan's upper peninsula and northeast Wisconsin and operates natural gas transmission, gathering and storage facilities in Michigan.

ANNUAL FINANCIAL DATA

	12/31/01	12/31/00	12/31/99	12/31/98	12/31/97	12/31/96	12/31/95
Earnings Per Share	⑤ d0.01	0.90	1.00	①②0.63	1.09	③ d0.93	0.83
Cash Flow Per Share	2.00	3.07	2.13	1.52	2.06	0.98	2.49
Tang. Book Val. Per Share	...	...	...	7.61	6.82	6.33	8.00
Dividends Per Share	0.84	0.83	④0.86	0.78	0.75	0.71	0.67
Dividend Payout %	...	92.8	86.5	123.9	69.3	...	81.4
INCOME STATEMENT (IN THOUSANDS):							
Total Revenues	445,823	422,593	384,763	637,485	775,932	547,630	335,538
Costs & Expenses	364,473	323,863	322,867	597,941	733,902	505,847	290,552
Depreciation & Amort.	36,959	33,472	20,006	15,349	12,863	11,317	12,035
Maintenance Exp.	...	...	...	...	...	...	4,337
Operating Income	44,391	65,258	41,890	24,195	29,167	30,466	28,614
Net Interest Inc./(Exp.)	d31,784	d34,913	d20,575	d14,811	d13,059	...	...
Income Taxes	6,578	11,606	7,012	6,320	8,469	6,371	6,188
Net Income	⑤ d239	21,697	17,659	①⑤8,755	15,425	③2,088	22,069
Cash Flow	36,266	55,169	37,665	24,104	28,288	13,405	34,087
Average Shs. Outstg.	18,106	17,999	17,697	15,906	13,703	13,668	13,697
BALANCE SHEET (IN THOUSANDS):							
Gross Property	707,981	664,795	603,939	408,370	360,022	342,778	314,602
Accumulated Depreciation	183,436	154,769	129,593	118,132	102,790	96,391	87,308
Net Property	524,545	510,026	474,346	290,238	275,462	255,972	240,177
Total Assets	863,548	851,223	815,183	489,662	505,487	478,238	378,523
Long-Term Obligations	338,966	307,930	170,000	170,000	163,548	106,468	105,858
Net Stockholders' Equity	113,810	135,472	142,340	135,483	97,771	89,813	112,783
Year-end Shs. Outstg.	18,240	18,056	17,909	17,382	13,864	13,671	13,703
STATISTICAL RECORD:							
Operating Profit Margin %	10.0	15.4	10.9	3.8	3.8	5.6	8.5
Net Profit Margin %	1.9	5.1	4.6	1.4	2.0	0.4	6.6
Net Inc./Net Property %	1.6	4.3	3.7	3.0	5.6	0.8	9.2
Net Inc./Tot. Capital %	1.3	3.5	5.2	2.7	5.6	1.0	9.3
Return on Equity %	7.3	16.0	12.4	6.5	15.8	2.3	19.6
Accum. Depr./Gross Prop. %	25.9	23.3	21.5	28.9	28.6	28.1	27.8
Price Range	15.75-8.88	16.94-10.75	17.50-10.94	18.38-13.13	19.27-15.71	17.46-13.49	17.49-14.04
P/E Ratio	...	18.8-11.9	17.5-10.9	29.2-20.8	17.7-14.5	...	21.1-16.9
Average Yield %	6.8	6.0	6.1	5.0	4.3	4.6	4.3

Statistics are as originally reported. Adj. for stk. splits: 5% div., 5/15/99; 5% div., 5/15/97; 5% div., 5/96; 5% div., 5/95. ① Bef. extraord. chrg. 12/31/98: $499,000; 12/31/94: $1.3 mill. ($0.10/sh.) ② Bef. acctg. change credit $1.8 mill. ③ Incl. non-recurr. chrg. $21.0 mill. ④ Incl. spec. div. of $0.05 per share. ⑤ Excl. a loss of $6.1 mill. & incl. restruct. & impair. chrgs. of $6.1 mill.

OFFICERS:
M. Jackson, Chmn., Pres., C.E.O.
J. E. Schneider, Sr. V.P., C.F.O., Treas.

INVESTOR CONTACT: Investor Relations,
(810) 987-2200

PRINCIPAL OFFICE: 28470 13 Mile Road, Suite 300, Farmington Hills, MI 48334

TELEPHONE NUMBER: (810) 987-2200
FAX: (810) 987-4570
WEB: www.semcoenergy.com

NO. OF EMPLOYEES: 2,154 (approx.)

SHAREHOLDERS: 9,321

ANNUAL MEETING: In Apr.

INCORPORATED: MI, Nov., 1977

INSTITUTIONAL HOLDINGS:
No. of Institutions: 48
Shares Held: 2,797,981
% Held: 15.2

INDUSTRY: Natural gas distribution (SIC: 4924)

TRANSFER AGENT(S): Wells Fargo Shareowner Services, South St. Paul, MN

SERVICEMASTER COMPANY (THE)

YIELD 2.9%
P/E RATIO ...

INTERIM EARNINGS (Per Share):

Qtr.	Mar.	June	Sept.	Dec.
1998	0.10	0.19	0.19	0.16
1999	0.12	0.06	0.21	0.17
2000	0.13	0.22	0.16	0.11
2001	0.08	0.17	0.12	d0.86

INTERIM DIVIDENDS (Per Share):

Amt.	Decl.	Ex.	Rec.	Pay.
0.10Q	3/16/01	4/10/01	4/13/01	4/30/01
0.10Q	4/27/01	7/11/01	7/13/01	7/31/01
0.10Q	10/05/01	10/10/01	10/12/01	10/31/01
0.10Q	12/17/01	1/09/02	1/11/02	1/31/02
0.10Q	2/01/02	4/10/02	4/12/02	4/30/02

Indicated div.: $0.40 (Div. Reinv. Plan)

CAPITALIZATION (12/31/01):

	($000)	(%)
Long-Term Debt	1,105,518	42.7
Deferred Income Tax	263,000	10.2
Common & Surplus	1,220,961	47.2
Total	2,589,479	100.0

DIVIDEND ACHIEVER STATUS:
Rank: 236   10-Year Growth Rate: 4.81%
Total Years of Dividend Growth: 31

TRADING VOLUME
Thousand Shares

*7 YEAR PRICE SCORE 77.5   ***12 MONTH PRICE SCORE 117.3**
*NYSE COMPOSITE INDEX=100

RECENT DEVELOPMENTS: For the year ended 12/31/01, SVM reported a loss from continuing operations of $171.8 million compared with income from continuing operations of $136.8 million in 2000. Results for 2001 included impairment and other charges of $396.7 million. Revenues increased 3.3% to $3.60 billion from $3.49 billion a year earlier. Cost of services rendered and products sold amounted to $2.55 billion, or 70.7% of revenues, versus 2.49 billion, or 71.4% of revenues, the year before.

PROSPECTS: The Company expects earnings for 2002 to be in the range of $0.60 to $0.63 per share. This outlook anticipates costs of $20.0 million to implement Six Sigma and customer and employee satisfaction initiatives. In addition, SVM will make investments to improve sales and customer retention, and to rollout the recently announced pilot marketing program with Home Depot. Separately, the Company anticipates using excess cash to continue to reduce debt levels in 2002.

BUSINESS

THE SERVICEMASTER COMPANY (formerly ServiceMaster Limited Partnership) provides outsourcing services to more than 12.0 million residential and commercial customers worldwide. The core services of SVM include lawn care and landscape maintenance, termite and pest control, plumbing, heating and air conditioning maintenance and repair, cleaning, furniture repair and home warranty. These services are provided through a network of over 4,300 Company-owned and franchised service centers and business units, operating under brands including Terminix, TruGreen ChemLawn, TruGreen LandCare, American Residential Services, Rescue Rooter, American Mechanical Services, ServiceMaster Clean, American Home Shield, AmeriSpec, Merry Maids, Furniture Medic, and ServiceMaster Home Service Center. On 12/26/97, SVM converted from a publicly-traded partnership to a taxable corporation. On 11/30/01, SVM sold its management services business to ARAMARK Corp. for about $800.0 million.

ANNUAL FINANCIAL DATA

	12/31/01	12/31/00	12/31/99	12/31/98	12/31/97	12/31/96	12/31/95
Earnings Per Share	③ d0.54	① 0.61	② 0.55	0.64	0.55	0.76	0.64
Cash Flow Per Share	d0.14	1.12	0.99	1.42	1.19	0.99	0.88
Dividends Per Share	0.40	0.38	0.36	0.33	0.31	0.29	0.28
Dividend Payout %	74.1	62.3	65.4	51.6	56.4	38.2	43.8
INCOME STATEMENT (IN MILLIONS):							
Total Revenues	3,601.4	5,970.6	5,703.5	4,724.1	3,961.5	3,458.3	3,202.5
Costs & Expenses	3,561.9	5,396.0	5,181.9	4,223.1	3,524.5	3,084.1	2,884.6
Depreciation & Amort.	126.9	157.7	138.4	104.6	93.1	79.0	66.0
Operating Income	d87.4	416.9	383.2	396.4	343.9	295.2	251.9
Net Interest Inc./(Exp.)	d125.1	d136.8	d109.0	d92.9	d76.4	d38.3	d35.9
Income Bef. Income Taxes	d201.4	318.3	296.2	318.8	274.3	252.4	177.6
Income Taxes	cr29.6	133.3	122.6	128.8	10.2	7.3	5.6
Net Income	③ d171.8	① 185.0	② 173.6	190.0	329.1	245.1	172.0
Cash Flow	d44.8	342.7	312.0	294.6	422.3	324.1	238.0
Average Shs. Outstg. (000)	311,408	305,518	314,406	298,887	299,640	326,403	270,275
BALANCE SHEET (IN MILLIONS):							
Cash & Cash Equivalents	483.1	100.9	114.2	120.4	124.1	114.4	49.4
Total Current Assets	1,150.7	984.8	959.2	670.2	594.1	499.3	393.2
Net Property	189.0	306.0	318.1	212.2	158.3	146.4	145.9
Total Assets	3,674.7	3,967.7	3,870.2	2,914.9	2,475.2	1,846.8	1,649.9
Total Current Liabilities	814.4	833.4	845.8	753.7	558.2	425.6	372.9
Long-Term Obligations	1,105.5	1,756.8	1,697.6	1,076.2	1,247.8	482.3	411.9
Net Stockholders' Equity	1,221.0	1,161.6	1,205.7	956.5	524.4	796.8	746.7
Net Working Capital	336.3	151.3	113.4	d83.5	35.9	73.8	20.3
Year-end Shs. Outstg. (000)	300,531	298,474	307,530	298,030	279,944	331,196	275,144
STATISTICAL RECORD:							
Operating Profit Margin %	...	7.0	6.7	8.4	8.7	8.5	7.9
Net Profit Margin %	...	3.1	3.0	4.0	8.3	7.1	5.4
Return on Equity %	...	15.9	14.4	19.9	62.8	30.8	23.0
Return on Assets %	...	4.7	4.5	6.5	13.3	13.3	10.4
Debt/Total Assets %	30.1	44.3	43.9	36.9	50.4	26.1	25.0
Price Range	14.20-9.84	14.94-8.25	22.00-10.13	25.50-16.00	19.67-10.95	11.83-8.63	9.00-6.37
P/E Ratio	...	24.5-13.5	40.0-18.4	39.8-25.0	35.9-20.0	15.7-11.4	14.0-9.9
Average Yield %	3.3	3.3	2.2	1.6	2.0	2.9	3.6

Statistics are as originally reported. On 12/26/97, SVM converted from a publicly traded partnership to a taxable corporation. Prior to that date, net income was not subject to federal and state taxes. Adj. for stk. splits: 3-for-2, 8/98, 6/97, 6/96. ① Bef. acctg. change chrg. $11.2 mill., 2000. ② Incl. non-recurr. chrg. $85.5 mill., 1999. ③ Bef. income from disc. oper. of $330.2 mill. and extraord. chrg. of $3.4 mill.; incl. impair and oth. chrg. of $396.7 mill.

OFFICERS:
J. P. Ward, Chmn., Pres., C.E.O.
S. C. Preston, Exec. V.P., C.F.O.
J. L. Kaput, Sr. V.P., Gen.Couns.

INVESTOR CONTACT: Bruce J. Byots, V.P., Investor Relations, (630) 271-2906

PRINCIPAL OFFICE: One Servicemaster Way, Downers Grove, IL 60515-1700

TELEPHONE NUMBER: (630) 271-1300
FAX: (630) 271-2710
WEB: www. servicemaster.com

NO. OF EMPLOYEES: 37,000 (approx.)

SHAREHOLDERS: 50,000 (approx. record)

ANNUAL MEETING: In April

INCORPORATED: DE, Oct., 1986

INSTITUTIONAL HOLDINGS:
No. of Institutions: 235
Shares Held: 139,419,336
% Held: 46.4

INDUSTRY: Management services (SIC: 8741)

TRANSFER AGENT(S): Computershare Investor Services, Chicago, IL

SHERWIN-WILLIAMS COMPANY

YIELD 2.1%
P/E RATIO 17.0

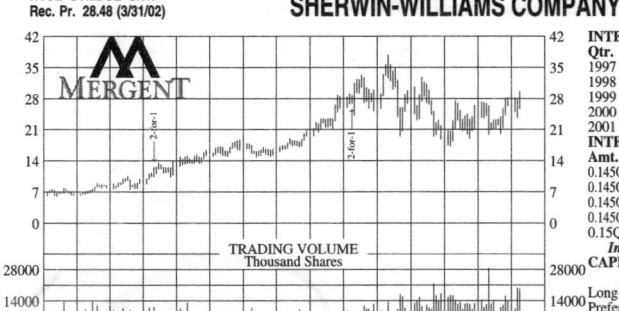

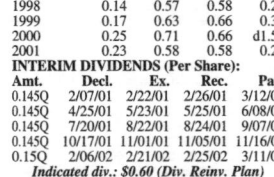

TRADING VOLUME
Thousand Shares

*7 YEAR PRICE SCORE 83.9   *12 MONTH PRICE SCORE 113.6

*NYSE COMPOSITE INDEX=100

INTERIM EARNINGS (Per Share):

Qtr.	Mar.	June	Sept.	Dec.
1997	0.13	0.54	0.57	0.26
1998	0.14	0.57	0.58	0.28
1999	0.17	0.63	0.66	0.34
2000	0.25	0.71	0.66	d1.55
2001	0.23	0.58	0.58	0.29

INTERIM DIVIDENDS (Per Share):

Amt.	Decl.	Ex.	Rec.	Pay.
0.145Q	2/07/01	2/22/01	2/26/01	3/12/01
0.145Q	4/25/01	5/23/01	5/25/01	6/08/01
0.145Q	7/20/01	8/22/01	8/24/01	9/07/01
0.145Q	10/17/01	11/01/01	11/05/01	11/16/01
0.15Q	2/06/02	2/21/02	2/25/02	3/11/02

Indicated div.: $0.60 (Div. Reinv. Plan)

CAPITALIZATION (12/31/01):

	($000)	(%)
Long-Term Debt ☐	503,517	25.3
Preferred Stock	168,305	8.5
Common & Surplus	1,319,459	66.3
Total	1,991,281	100.0

DIVIDEND ACHIEVER STATUS:
Rank: 124   10-Year Growth Rate: 10.69%
Total Years of Dividend Growth: 22

RECENT DEVELOPMENTS: For the year ended 12/31/01, net income amounted to $263.2 million versus $16.0 million in 2000. Results for 2000 included a charge for the impairment of long-lived assets of $352.0 million. Net sales decreased 2.8% to $5.07 billion. The decline in results was attributed to lower sales and production volume and, in the first half of 2001, high raw material costs. Gross profit as a percentage of net sales was 43.8% versus 44.3% in 2000.

PROSPECTS: SHW expects results for 2002 to continue to be challenged by difficult economic conditions. Meanwhile, SHW will be making investments in its Paint Stores division to enhance its operations and introduce an expanded color program starting in the first quarter of 2002. Separately, 2002 sales are expected to be flat to slightly higher year over year, while earnings are expected to be in the range of $1.88 to $2.03 per share.

BUSINESS

SHERWIN-WILLIAMS COMPANY is engaged in the manufacture, distribution and sale of coatings and related products. SHW has a network of 115 company-owned facilities, supported by an additional 2,300 SHW outlets throughout North America. The Paint Stores' division (63.4% of 2001 net sales) sells products through company-operated specialty paint stores in the U.S., Canada, the Virgin Islands and Puerto Rico. The Consumer segment (21.9%) manufactures and distributes architectural paints, stains, varnishes, wood finishing products, paint applicators, corrosion inhibitors, and paint-related products in the U.S. and Canada. The Automotive Finishes segment (9.2%) manufactures and distributes motor vehicle finish products throughout North and South America and the Caribbean Islands. The International Coatings segment (5.5%) manufactures and distributes architectural paints, stains, varnishes, and paint-related products worldwide. The Company's brands include SHERWIN WILLIAMS®, DUTCH BOY®, and KRYLON®.

ANNUAL FINANCIAL DATA

	12/31/01	12/31/00	12/31/99	12/31/98	12/31/97	12/31/96	12/31/95
Earnings Per Share	1.68	☐ 0.10	1.80	1.57	1.50	1.34	1.18
Cash Flow Per Share	2.62	1.08	2.72	2.42	2.30	1.92	1.62
Tang. Book Val. Per Share	2.59	3.18	2.32	1.76	0.70	3.65	5.85
Dividends Per Share	0.58	0.54	0.48	0.45	0.40	0.35	0.32
Dividend Payout %	34.5	539.5	26.7	28.7	26.8	26.1	27.1
INCOME STATEMENT (IN MILLIONS):							
Total Revenues	5,066.0	5,211.6	5,003.8	4,934.4	4,881.1	4,132.9	3,273.8
Costs & Expenses	4,428.1	4,836.4	4,273.0	4,254.9	4,218.7	3,610.6	2,874.6
Depreciation & Amort.	148.1	160.0	155.7	147.9	139.2	103.6	77.9
Operating Income	489.8	215.2	575.1	531.6	523.2	418.6	321.3
Net Interest Inc./(Exp.)	d54.6	d62.0	d61.2	d72.0	d80.8	d24.5	d2.5
Income Before Income Taxes	424.4	143.4	490.1	440.1	427.3	371.1	318.5
Income Taxes	161.3	127.4	186.3	167.2	166.7	146.2	117.8
Net Income	263.2	☐ 16.0	303.9	272.9	260.6	224.9	200.7
Cash Flow	411.3	176.1	459.6	420.8	399.9	328.5	278.6
Average Shs. Outstg. (000)	156,894	162,695	169,026	173,536	174,032	171,117	171,487
BALANCE SHEET (IN MILLIONS):							
Cash & Cash Equivalents	118.8	2.9	18.6	19.1	3.5	1.9	269.5
Total Current Assets	1,506.9	1,551.5	1,597.4	1,547.3	1,532.3	1,416.2	1,238.9
Net Property	672.7	722.4	711.7	718.9	692.3	549.4	456.4
Total Assets	3,627.9	3,750.7	4,052.1	4,065.5	4,035.8	2,994.6	2,141.1
Total Current Liabilities	1,141.4	1,115.2	1,189.9	1,110.0	1,115.7	1,051.0	618.9
Long-Term Obligations	503.5	623.6	624.4	730.3	843.9	142.7	24.0
Net Stockholders' Equity	1,487.8	1,471.9	1,698.5	1,715.9	1,592.2	1,401.2	1,212.1
Net Working Capital	365.6	436.3	407.5	435.3	416.6	365.2	620.0
Year-end Shs. Outstg. (000)	153,978	159,558	165,664	171,033	172,907	171,831	170,910
STATISTICAL RECORD:							
Operating Profit Margin %	9.7	4.1	11.5	10.8	10.7	10.1	9.8
Net Profit Margin %	5.2	0.3	6.1	5.5	5.3	5.4	6.1
Return on Equity %	17.7	1.1	17.9	15.9	16.4	16.1	16.6
Return on Assets %	7.3	0.4	7.5	6.7	6.5	7.5	9.4
Debt/Total Assets %	13.9	16.6	15.4	18.0	20.9	4.8	1.1
Price Range	28.23-19.73	27.63-17.13	32.88-18.75	37.88-19.44	33.38-24.13	28.88-19.50	20.75-16.00
P/E Ratio	16.8-11.7	276.0-171.1	18.3-10.4	24.1-12.4	22.2-16.1	21.5-14.6	17.6-13.6
Average Yield %	2.4	2.4	1.9	1.6	1.4	1.4	1.7

Statistics are as originally reported. Adj. for stk. splits: 2-for-1, 3/97. ☐ Incl. debentures conv. into common. ☐ Incl. impairment of long-lived assets chrg. of $352.0 mill.

OFFICERS:
C. M. Connor, Chmn., C.E.O.
J. M. Scaminace, Pres., C.O.O.
S. P. Hennessy, Sr. V.P., C.F.O.

INVESTOR CONTACT: Conway G. Ivy, Investor Relations, (216) 566-2000

PRINCIPAL OFFICE: 101 Prospect Avenue N.W., Cleveland, OH 44115-1075

TELEPHONE NUMBER: (216) 566-2000
FAX: (216) 566-3310
WEB: www.sherwin.com

NO. OF EMPLOYEES: 25,789 (avg.)

SHAREHOLDERS: 10,229

ANNUAL MEETING: In Apr.

INCORPORATED: OH, July, 1884

INSTITUTIONAL HOLDINGS:
No. of Institutions: 313
Shares Held: 105,035,432
% Held: 68.8

INDUSTRY: Paints and allied products (SIC: 2851)

TRANSFER AGENT(S): The Bank of New York, New York, NY

SIGMA-ALDRICH CORPORATION

YIELD 0.7%
P/E RATIO 25.1

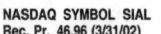

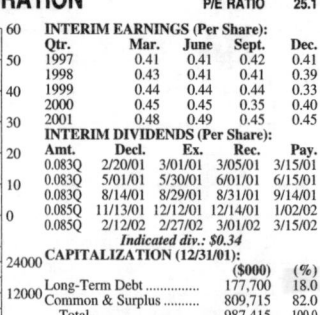

INTERIM EARNINGS (Per Share):

Qtr.	Mar.	June	Sept.	Dec.
1997	0.41	0.41	0.42	0.41
1998	0.43	0.41	0.41	0.39
1999	0.44	0.44	0.44	0.33
2000	0.45	0.45	0.35	0.40
2001	0.48	0.49	0.45	0.45

INTERIM DIVIDENDS (Per Share):

Amt.	Decl.	Ex.	Rec.	Pay.
0.083Q	2/20/01	3/01/01	3/05/01	3/15/01
0.083Q	5/01/01	5/30/01	6/01/01	6/15/01
0.083Q	8/14/01	8/29/01	8/31/01	9/14/01
0.085Q	11/13/01	12/12/01	12/14/01	1/02/02
0.085Q	2/12/02	2/27/02	3/01/02	3/15/02

Indicated div.: $0.34

CAPITALIZATION (12/31/01):

	($000)	(%)
Long-Term Debt	177,700	18.0
Common & Surplus	809,715	82.0
Total	987,415	100.0

DIVIDEND ACHIEVER STATUS:
Rank: 105   10-Year Growth Rate: 11.61%
Total Years of Dividend Growth: 20

TRADING VOLUME
Thousand Shares

1988 1989 1990 1991 1992 1993 1994 1995 1996 1997 1998 1999 2000 2001 2002

*7 YEAR PRICE SCORE 115.5   ***12 MONTH PRICE SCORE 104.5**
*NYSE COMPOSITE INDEX=100

RECENT DEVELOPMENTS: For the twelve months ended 12/31/01, net income climbed 1.2% to $140.7 million compared with income from continuing operations of $139.1 million in 2000. Results for 2001 and 2000 included purchased in-process research and development charges of $1.2 million and $6.7 million, respectively. Results for 2000 excluded income of $181.1 million from discontinued operations. Net sales climbed 7.6% to $1.18 billion from $1.10 billion in the previous year. The Company's operations benefited from higher sales, partially offset by the negative effect of a strong U.S. dollar and continued earnings hindrances from recent Diagnostics' acquisitions. Gross profit grew 6.5% to $566.4 million from $531.9 million, but slipped as a percentage of sales to 48.0% from 48.5%, the year before.

BUSINESS

SIGMA-ALDRICH CORPORATION develops, manufactures and distributes a broad range of biochemicals, organic chemicals, chromatography products and diagnostic reagents. The Company is organized into four business units: Scientific Research, Biotechnology, Diagnostics, and Fine Chemicals. Scientific Research and Biotechnology products are used by scientists in academia and industry performing research. The Company's Diagnostic products are used to help diagnose and treat diseases. Fine Chemical products are used primarily by pharmaceutical companies to produce medicines. On 5/1/00, the Company sold its B-Line Systems business to Cooper Industries, Inc. for $425.0 million.

ANNUAL FINANCIAL DATA

	12/31/01	12/31/00	12/31/99	12/31/98	12/31/97	12/31/96	12/31/95
Earnings Per Share	④ 1.87	③ 1.66	①② 1.47	1.64	1.62	1.48	1.32
Cash Flow Per Share	2.82	2.47	2.13	2.25	2.08	1.93	1.73
Tang. Book Val. Per Share	9.34	9.72	11.89	10.96	9.73	9.41	8.27
Dividends Per Share	0.33	0.31	0.29	0.28	0.25	0.22	0.18
Dividend Payout %	17.6	18.7	19.7	17.1	15.4	14.9	13.6
INCOME STATEMENT (IN MILLIONS):							
Total Revenues	1,179.4	1,096.3	1,037.9	1,194.3	1,127.1	1,034.6	959.8
Costs & Expenses	889.9	819.2	767.3	889.9	826.3	759.7	714.8
Depreciation & Amort.	71.4	67.6	66.9	61.8	48.1	45.2	40.9
Operating Income	218.2	209.5	203.7	242.6	252.8	229.7	204.2
Net Interest Inc./(Exp.)	d16.5	d6.6	...	...	...	...	...
Income Before Income Taxes	201.6	202.9	203.7	242.6	252.8	229.7	204.2
Income Taxes	60.9	63.9	55.1	76.2	86.7	81.8	72.5
Net Income	④ 140.7	③ 139.1	①② 148.6	166.3	166.1	147.9	131.7
Cash Flow	212.1	206.6	215.5	228.2	214.1	193.1	172.6
Average Shs. Outstg. (000)	75,175	83,585	100,984	101,188	102,804	99,930	99,714
BALANCE SHEET (IN MILLIONS):							
Cash & Cash Equivalents	37.6	31.1	43.8	24.3	46.2	103.7	84.0
Total Current Assets	727.3	713.6	774.6	772.7	706.7	666.6	610.0
Net Property	542.1	493.0	481.7	518.7	438.9	379.1	327.9
Total Assets	1,439.8	1,347.7	1,432.0	1,432.8	1,243.8	1,100.0	985.2
Total Current Liabilities	397.6	335.3	105.6	142.4	119.5	110.3	108.0
Long-Term Obligations	177.7	100.8	0.2	0.4	0.6	3.8	13.8
Net Stockholders' Equity	809.7	859.3	1,259.4	1,216.4	1,060.3	942.3	824.7
Net Working Capital	329.7	378.3	669.0	630.3	587.2	556.3	502.0
Year-end Shs. Outstg. (000)	73,014	76,216	98,292	100,623	100,377	100,100	99,754
STATISTICAL RECORD:							
Operating Profit Margin %	18.5	19.1	19.6	20.3	22.4	22.2	21.3
Net Profit Margin %	11.9	12.7	14.3	13.9	14.7	14.3	13.7
Return on Equity %	17.4	16.2	11.8	13.7	15.7	15.7	16.0
Return on Assets %	9.8	10.3	10.4	11.6	13.4	13.4	13.4
Debt/Total Assets %	12.3	7.5	...	...	...	0.3	1.4
Price Range	51.49-36.25	40.88-20.19	35.25-24.50	42.75-25.75	39.63-26.88	32.06-23.75	25.88-16.25
P/E Ratio	27.5-19.4	24.6-12.2	24.0-16.7	26.1-15.7	24.5-16.6	21.7-16.0	19.6-12.3
Average Yield %	0.8	1.0	1.0	0.8	0.8	0.8	0.9

Statistics are as originally reported. Adj. for stk. splits: 2-for-1, 1/2/97. ① Bef. disc. oper. gain $23.7 mill. ② Incl. non-recurr. net gain $2.6 mill. ③ Incl. in-process res. & dev. chrg. $6.7 mill. ④ Incl. $1.2 mill. purch. in-process R&D chg.

OFFICERS:
D. R. Harvey, Chmn., Pres., C.E.O.
M. Hogan, C.F.O., C.A.O., Sec.
L. Blazevich, V.P., C.I.O.

INVESTOR CONTACT: Investor Relations, (314) 771-5765

PRINCIPAL OFFICE: 3050 Spruce Street, St. Louis, MO 63103

TELEPHONE NUMBER: (314) 771-5765
FAX: (314) 286-7874
WEB: www.sigma-aldrich.com

NO. OF EMPLOYEES: 6,467 (avg.)

SHAREHOLDERS: 1,214 (record)

ANNUAL MEETING: In May

INCORPORATED: DE, July, 1975

INSTITUTIONAL HOLDINGS:
No. of Institutions: 288
Shares Held: 48,446,844
% Held: 66.0

INDUSTRY: Chemicals & allied products, nec (SIC: 5169)

TRANSFER AGENT(S): Computershare Investor Services, Chicago, IL

SJW CORP.

YIELD 3.4%
P/E RATIO 17.7

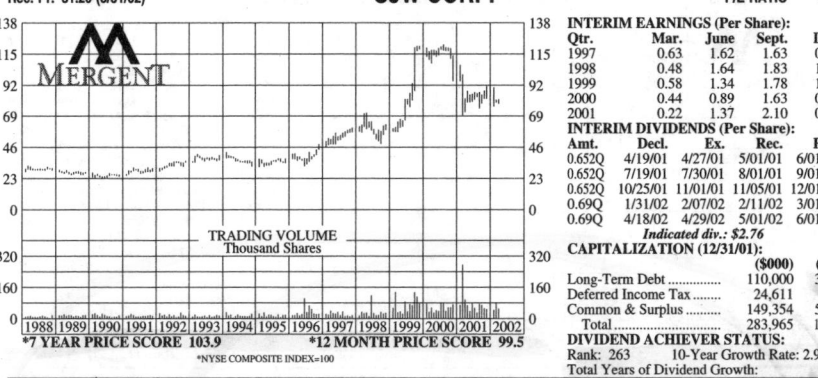

7 YEAR PRICE SCORE 103.9 **12 MONTH PRICE SCORE 99.5**
*NYSE COMPOSITE INDEX=100

INTERIM EARNINGS (Per Share):

Qtr.	Mar.	June	Sept.	Dec.
1997	0.63	1.62	1.63	0.92
1998	0.48	1.64	1.83	1.10
1999	0.58	1.34	1.78	1.52
2000	0.44	0.89	1.63	0.54
2001	0.22	1.37	2.10	0.91

INTERIM DIVIDENDS (Per Share):

Amt.	Decl.	Ex.	Rec.	Pay.
0.652Q	4/19/01	4/27/01	5/01/01	6/01/01
0.652Q	7/19/01	7/30/01	8/01/01	9/01/01
0.652Q	10/25/01	11/01/01	11/05/01	12/01/01
0.69Q	1/31/02	2/07/02	2/11/02	3/01/02
0.69Q	4/18/02	4/29/02	5/01/02	6/01/02

Indicated div.: $2.76

CAPITALIZATION (12/31/01):

	($000)	(%)
Long-Term Debt	110,000	38.7
Deferred Income Tax	24,611	8.7
Common & Surplus	149,354	52.6
Total	283,965	100.0

DIVIDEND ACHIEVER STATUS:
Rank: 263   10-Year Growth Rate: 2.96%
Total Years of Dividend Growth: 35

RECENT DEVELOPMENTS: For the year ended 12/31/01, net income increased 31.4% to $14.0 million compared with $10.7 million in 2000. Results for 2000 included merger-related costs of $1.6 million. Results for 2000 also included a non-recurring regulatory adjustment authorized by the California Public Utilities Commission of $541,000. Operating revenues advanced 10.5% to $136.1 million from $123.2 million a year earlier. The improvement in operat-ing revenues was primarily attributed to rate increases resulting from San Jose Water Company's general rate case application in April 2001 and an offset rate increase for production costs adjustments authorized in July 2001. In addition, operating revenues benefited from slightly higher overall water consumption. Operating income rose 21.6% to $19.8 million versus $16.3 million the year before.

BUSINESS

SJW CORP. is a holding company with two wholly-owned subsidiaries, San Jose Water Company and SJW Land Company. San Jose Water Company is a public utility in the business of providing water service to a population of approximately 988,000 in an area comprising about 138 square miles in the metropolitan San Jose area. SJW Land Company owns and operates a 900-space surface parking facility located adjacent to the San Jose Compaq Center, commercial properties and several undeveloped real estate parcels in San Jose, and a 70.0% limited partnership interest in 444 West Santa Clara Street, L.P. Crystal Choice Water Service LLC, a 75.0%-owned limited liability subsidiary formed in January 2001, engages in the sale and rental of water conditioning equipment. In addition, SJW owns 1,099,952 shares of California Water Service Group (formerly California Water Service Company), acquired through the liquidation of Western Precision, Inc., formerly a wholly-owned subsidiary of the Company.

QUARTERLY DATA

(12/31/2001)	REV	INC
1st Quarter	24,245	678
2nd Quarter	36,364	4,170
3rd Quarter	44,182	6,395
4th Quarter	31,292	2,774

ANNUAL FINANCIAL DATA

	12/31/01	12/31/00	12/31/99	12/31/98	12/31/97	12/31/96	12/31/95
Earnings Per Share	4.60	② 3.50	①② 5.20	① 5.05	① 4.80	① 5.75	3.55
Cash Flow Per Share	8.95	7.39	8.55	8.08	7.59	8.44	5.89
Tang. Book Val. Per Share	47.27	45.57	45.35	43.29	40.21	35.87	31.47
Dividends Per Share	2.57	2.46	2.40	2.34	2.28	2.22	2.16
Dividend Payout %	55.9	70.3	46.2	46.3	47.5	38.6	60.8
INCOME STATEMENT (IN THOUSANDS):							
Total Revenues	136,083	123,157	117,001	106,010	110,084	102,593	97,385
Costs & Expenses	88,535	79,095	71,515	60,975	64,726	60,399	60,335
Depreciation & Amort.	13,240	11,847	10,235	9,594	8,847	8,671	7,626
Maintenance Exp.	7,090	6,881	6,638	6,909	7,087	6,851	6,342
Operating Income	19,827	17,925	19,739	18,847	19,314	17,606	15,314
Net Interest Inc./(Exp.)	d6,737	d6,434	d6,552	d5,629	d5,695	d5,892	d4,888
Income Taxes	7,391	7,409	8,874	9,685	10,110	9,066	7,768
Net Income	14,017	② 10,665	①② 15,884	① 16,018	① 15,216	① 18,560	11,535
Cash Flow	34,648	29,921	34,993	35,297	34,113	36,297	26,529
Average Shs. Outstg.	3,045	3,045	3,055	3,170	3,170	3,227	3,251
BALANCE SHEET (IN THOUSANDS):							
Gross Property	507,227	462,892	432,262	403,227	371,200	342,368	324,098
Accumulated Depreciation	149,721	139,396	129,828	122,809	114,851	107,584	100,000
Net Property	367,815	333,475	312,567	291,778	263,663	242,071	230,722
Total Assets	431,017	391,930	372,427	359,380	323,223	296,536	280,497
Long-Term Obligations	110,000	90,000	90,000	90,000	75,000	75,000	76,500
Net Stockholders' Equity	149,354	144,325	143,894	143,149	133,553	120,028	108,854
Year-end Shs. Outstg.	3,045	3,045	3,045	3,168	3,170	3,170	3,251
STATISTICAL RECORD:							
Operating Profit Margin %	14.6	14.6	16.9	17.8	17.5	17.2	15.7
Net Profit Margin %	10.3	8.7	13.6	15.1	13.8	18.1	11.8
Net Inc./Net Property %	3.8	3.2	5.1	5.5	5.8	7.7	5.0
Net Inc./Tot. Capital %	4.9	4.2	6.1	6.2	6.6	8.8	5.8
Return on Equity %	14.3	12.5	17.2	18.0	19.0	23.0	17.7
Accum. Depr./Gross Prop. %	29.5	30.1	30.0	30.5	30.9	31.4	30.9
Price Range	107.00-69.50	122.00-95.00	121.00-57.25	71.50-48.50	60.50-46.00	48.25-32.00	37.88-31.25
P/E Ratio	23.3-15.1	34.9-27.1	23.3-11.0	14.2-9.6	12.6-9.6	8.4-5.6	10.7-8.8
Average Yield %	2.9	2.3	2.7	3.9	4.3	5.5	6.2

Statistics are as originally reported. ① Incl. non-recurr. gain $3.1 mill., 12/98; $9.4 mill., 12/97; $5.3 mill., 12/96; ② Incl. merger costs, 2000, $1.6 mill.; 1999, $1.6 mill.

OFFICERS:
J. W. Weinhardt, Chmn.
W. R. Roth, Pres., C.E.O.
A. Yip, C.F.O., Treas.

INVESTOR CONTACT: Angela Yip, (408) 279-7960

PRINCIPAL OFFICE: 374 West Santa Clara Street, San Jose, CA 95196

TELEPHONE NUMBER: (408) 279-7800
FAX: (408) 279-7934
WEB: www.sjwater.com

NO. OF EMPLOYEES: 289 (avg.)

SHAREHOLDERS: 793

ANNUAL MEETING: In Apr.

INCORPORATED: CA, Feb., 1985

INSTITUTIONAL HOLDINGS:
No. of Institutions: 40
Shares Held: 568,795
% Held: 18.7

INDUSTRY: Water supply (SIC: 4941)

TRANSFER AGENT(S): Boston EquiServe, Boston, MA

SONOCO PRODUCTS COMPANY

YIELD 2.8%
P/E RATIO 29.8

TRADING VOLUME
Thousand Shares

| 1988 | 1989 | 1990 | 1991 | 1992 | 1993 | 1994 | 1995 | 1996 | 1997 | 1998 | 1999 | 2000 | 2001 | 2002 |

*7 YEAR PRICE SCORE 85.5   *12 MONTH PRICE SCORE 111.4
*NYSE COMPOSITE INDEX=100

INTERIM EARNINGS (Per Share):

Qtr.	Mar.	June	Sept.	Dec.
1996	0.41	0.45	0.38	0.40
1997	0.39	0.43	0.39	d1.20
1998	0.48	0.70	0.39	0.31
1999	0.43	0.46	0.44	0.50
2000	0.45	0.47	0.39	0.37
2001	0.05	0.18	0.45	0.28

INTERIM DIVIDENDS (Per Share):

Amt.	Decl.	Ex.	Rec.	Pay.
0.20Q	4/18/01	5/16/01	5/18/01	6/08/01
0.20Q	7/18/01	8/15/01	8/17/01	9/10/01
0.20Q	10/17/01	11/14/01	11/16/01	12/10/01
0.20Q	2/06/02	2/20/02	2/22/02	3/08/02

Indicated div.: $0.80 (Div. Reinv. Plan)

CAPITALIZATION (12/31/01):

	($000)	(%)
Long-Term Debt	885,961	52.4
Common & Surplus	804,122	47.6
Total	1,690,083	100.0

DIVIDEND ACHIEVER STATUS:
Rank: 186   10-Year Growth Rate: 7.22%
Total Years of Dividend Growth: 18

RECENT DEVELOPMENTS: For the year ended 12/31/01, net income declined 44.9% to $91.6 million versus $166.3 million in 2000. Results for 2001 and 2000 included total pretax one-time charges of $53.3 million and $5.5 million, respectively. Sales decreased 3.9% to $2.61 billion from $2.71 billion. Interest expense declined 12.4% to $52.2 million, while interest income was flat at $3.8 million.

PROSPECTS: SON's seven acquisitions during 2001 have been accretive to earnings in the first year and are expected to add approximately $250.0 million in annual sales. The acquisitions should meet SON's cost of capital within the next five years. Over the next five years, SON anticipates generating approximately $800.0 million to $900.0 million of free cash flow.

BUSINESS

SONOCO PRODUCTS COMPANY is a multinational manufacturer of industrial and consumer packaging products. SON is also vertically integrated into paperboard production and recovered-paper collection. The paperboard utilized in SON's packaging products is produced substantially from recovered paper. As of 1/30/02, SON operated approximately 300 facilities in 33 countries serving customers in some 85 nations. The industrial packaging segment (50.3% of 2001 sales) includes engineered carriers (paper and plastic tubes and cores, paper manufacturing and recovered paper operations) and protective packaging (designed interior packaging and protective reels). The consumer packaging segment (49.7%) includes composite cans, flexible packaging (printing flexibles and high density bag and film products) and packaging services and specialty products (e-marketplace/supply chain management, graphics management, folding cartons, and paper glass covers and coasters).

ANNUAL FINANCIAL DATA

	12/31/01	12/31/00	12/31/99	12/31/98	12/31/97	12/31/96	12/31/95
Earnings Per Share	③ 0.96	③ 1.66	1.83	② 1.84	① Nil	1.64	1.56
Cash Flow Per Share	2.61	3.17	3.25	3.24	1.43	3.08	2.82
Tang. Book Val. Per Share	4.64	5.94	6.37	6.40	6.69	3.49	3.34
Dividends Per Share	0.80	0.79	0.75	0.70	0.64	0.59	0.53
Dividend Payout %	83.3	47.6	41.0	38.2	...	35.8	33.9
INCOME STATEMENT (IN MILLIONS):							
Total Revenues	2,606.3	2,711.5	2,546.7	2,557.9	2,847.8	2,788.1	2,706.2
Costs & Expenses	2,223.5	2,234.3	2,064.2	2,023.8	2,578.4	2,315.8	2,270.4
Depreciation & Amort.	158.6	150.8	145.8	145.7	153.5	142.9	125.8
Operating Income	224.2	326.4	336.7	388.5	115.9	329.4	309.9
Net Interest Inc./(Exp.)	d48.4	d55.8	d47.2	d48.9	d52.2	d49.3	d39.1
Income Before Income Taxes	175.8	270.6	289.6	339.6	63.7	280.1	270.8
Income Taxes	83.0	112.0	108.6	154.0	60.1	107.4	106.6
Equity Earnings/Minority Int.	d1.2	7.7	6.8	6.4	d1.0	d1.8	0.4
Net Income	③ 91.6	③ 166.3	187.8	② 192.0	① 2.6	170.9	164.5
Cash Flow	250.2	317.1	333.7	337.7	153.1	306.6	282.6
Average Shs. Outstg. (000)	95,807	99,900	102,780	104,275	107,350	99,564	100,253
BALANCE SHEET (IN MILLIONS):							
Cash & Cash Equivalents	36.1	35.2	36.5	57.2	53.6	71.3	61.6
Total Current Assets	665.2	695.8	723.1	661.4	873.0	737.6	661.8
Net Property	1,008.9	973.5	1,032.5	1,013.8	939.5	995.4	865.6
Total Assets	2,352.2	2,212.6	2,297.0	2,083.0	2,176.9	2,387.5	2,115.4
Total Current Liabilities	460.3	437.1	416.6	436.1	434.1	475.1	432.5
Long-Term Obligations	886.0	812.1	819.5	686.8	696.7	791.0	591.9
Net Stockholders' Equity	804.1	801.5	901.2	821.6	848.8	920.6	918.7
Net Working Capital	204.9	258.7	306.4	225.3	438.9	262.5	229.3
Year-end Shs. Outstg. (000)	95,713	95,006	101,448	101,683	105,417	98,850	100,229
STATISTICAL RECORD:							
Operating Profit Margin %	8.6	12.0	13.2	15.2	4.1	11.8	11.5
Net Profit Margin %	3.5	6.1	7.4	7.5	0.1	6.1	6.1
Return on Equity %	11.4	20.7	20.8	23.4	0.3	18.6	17.9
Return on Assets %	3.9	7.5	8.2	9.2	0.1	7.2	7.8
Debt/Total Assets %	37.7	36.7	35.7	33.0	32.0	33.1	28.0
Price Range	26.88-19.20	23.50-16.56	30.50-20.69	40.00-22.13	32.27-22.61	28.07-22.61	26.14-17.37
P/E Ratio	28.0-20.0	14.2-10.0	16.7-11.3	21.7-12.0	N.M.	17.1-13.8	16.7-11.1
Average Yield %	3.5	3.9	2.9	2.3	2.3	2.3	2.4

Statistics are as originally reported. Adj. for stk. splits: 5% div., 6/95; 10%, 6/98. ① Incl. non-recurr. after-tax chrg. $174.5 mill. for asset write-down. ② Bef. exraord. loss of $11.8 mill. and net gain on sale of divested assets of $85.4 mill. ③ Incl. nonrecurr. chrg. of $53.3 mill., 2001; $5.5 mill., 2000.

OFFICERS:
C. W. Coker, Chmn.
H. E. DeLoach, Jr., Pres., C.E.O.
C. J. Hupfer, V.P., C.F.O., Treas., Corp. Sec.

INVESTOR CONTACT: Allan V. Cecil, V.P. Investor Relations & Corp. Affairs, (843) 383-7524

PRINCIPAL OFFICE: North Second Street, Post Office Box 160, Hartsville, SC 29550

TELEPHONE NUMBER: (843) 383-7000
FAX: (843) 383-7008
WEB: www.sonoco.com

NO. OF EMPLOYEES: 17,900 (approx.)

SHAREHOLDERS: 43,000 (approx.)

ANNUAL MEETING: In Apr.

INCORPORATED: SC, May, 1899

INSTITUTIONAL HOLDINGS:
No. of Institutions: 202
Shares Held: 47,087,796
% Held: 49.2

INDUSTRY: Paperboard mills (SIC: 2631)

TRANSFER AGENT(S): EquiServe, Boston, MA

SOUTHTRUST CORPORATION

YIELD	2.6%
P/E RATIO	16.4

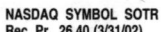

TRADING VOLUME
Thousand Shares

*7 YEAR PRICE SCORE 130.3   *12 MONTH PRICE SCORE 106.8
*NYSE COMPOSITE INDEX=100

INTERIM EARNINGS (Per Share):

Qtr.	Mar.	June	Sept.	Dec.
1998	0.27	0.28	0.29	0.30
1999	0.31	0.33	0.34	0.35
2000	0.35	0.36	0.36	0.37
2001	0.38	0.40	0.41	0.42

INTERIM DIVIDENDS (Per Share):

	Decl.	Ex.	Rec.	Pay.
0.14Q	4/18/01	5/23/01	5/25/01	7/02/01
0.14Q	7/18/01	8/29/01	8/31/01	10/01/01
0.14Q	10/17/01	11/28/01	11/30/01	1/02/02
0.17Q	1/16/02	2/20/02	2/22/02	4/01/02
0.17Q	4/17/02	5/29/02	5/31/02	7/01/02

Indicated div.: $0.68 (Div. Reinv. Plan)

CAPITALIZATION (12/31/01):

	($000)	(%)
Total Deposits	32,634,111	77.6
Long-Term Debt	5,484,485	13.0
Common & Surplus	3,962,375	9.4
Total	42,080,971	100.0

DIVIDEND ACHIEVER STATUS:

Rank: 84   10-Year Growth Rate: 13.15%
Total Years of Dividend Growth: 31

RECENT DEVELOPMENTS:

For the year ended 12/31/01, net income advanced 15.0% to $554.5 million from $482.3 million in the previous year. Net interest income increased 10.3% to $1.53 billion from $1.39 billion the year before. This improvement reflected the 16 basis-point increase in net interest margin and an increase in average earning assets. Provision for loan losses grew 27.4% to $118.3 million. Non-interest income rose 12.9% to $571.0 million, while non-interest expense increased 6.1% to $1.15 billion.

For the quarter ended 12/31/01, net income advanced 18.1% to $144.9 million from $122.8 million in the corresponding period of the prior year. Net interest income improved 21.5% to $416.4 million from $342.8 million the year before. Separately, the Company has worked to reduce its interest rate sensitivity in the future. As a result, more than 85.0% of SOTR's new and renewed commercial loans in 2001 were variable-rate loans. The Company will continue this loan policy throughout 2002 and 2003.

BUSINESS

SOUTHTRUST CORPORATION is a multibank holding company with headquarters in Birmingham, Alabama, that operates more than 700 banking and loan offices and 850 automatic teller machines in Alabama, Florida, Georgia, Mississippi, North Carolina, South Carolina, Tennessee, Texas and Virginia. Consolidated total assets as of 12/31/01 amounted to $48.75 billion. The Company has four reportable business segments: Commercial Banking, Regional Banking, Funds Management, and Other. The Commercial Banking segment derives its revenues from commercial, industrial and commercial real estate customers. This business segment also provides cash management, international and commercial leasing services. The Regional Banking segment generates revenues from retail lending, depository services, and regional commercial lending not underwritten by the Commercial Banking division. The Funds Management segment is responsible for the Company's asset and liability management. Other services segment include business segments such as non-bank subsidiaries and the Company's trust asset management division. These areas provide services such as mortgage banking, insurance, brokerage services and investment services.

ANNUAL FINANCIAL DATA

	12/31/01	12/31/00	12/31/99	12/31/98	12/31/97	12/31/96	12/31/95
Earnings Per Share	1.61	1.43	1.32	1.13	1.02	0.90	0.79
Tang. Book Val. Per Share	9.20	8.20	6.74	6.36	7.14	6.02	5.43
Dividends Per Share	0.55	0.48	0.42	0.37	0.32	0.29	0.26
Dividend Payout %	33.8	33.9	32.3	32.7	31.9	32.0	32.5
INCOME STATEMENT (IN MILLIONS):							
Total Interest Income	3,170.8	3,394.1	2,906.4	2,557.5	2,232.3	1,804.2	1,484.6
Total Interest Expense	1,642.7	2,008.4	1,539.5	1,386.3	1,186.1	938.2	791.4
Net Interest Income	1,528.1	Ⓘ1,385.7	1,366.9	1,171.2	1,046.2	866.0	693.2
Provision for Loan Losses	118.3	92.8	141.2	94.8	90.6	90.0	61.3
Non-Interest Income	571.0	505.7	443.6	386.1	270.5	254.8	208.7
Non-Interest Expense	1,153.4	1,087.2	1,010.5	914.4	748.2	643.3	536.5
Income Before Taxes	827.5	711.4	658.7	547.8	475.7	387.5	304.0
Net Income	554.5	482.3	443.2	368.9	306.7	254.7	199.0
Average Shs. Outstg. (000)	345,294	337,812	337,556	328,296	302,016	284,307	251,676
BALANCE SHEET (IN MILLIONS):							
Cash & Due from Banks	1,159.2	959.8	875.0	970.8	877.9	903.1	773.7
Securities Avail. for Sale	10,062.2	7,050.0	5,130.5	3,875.9	2,975.8	2,859.0	2,614.8
Total Loans & Leases	33,695.5	31,696.9	31,972.8	27,526.6	22,633.9	19,466.7	14,757.1
Allowance for Credit Losses	756.0	751.1	717.3	586.6	474.5	405.4	308.6
Net Loans & Leases	32,939.5	30,945.8	31,255.5	26,940.0	22,159.3	19,061.3	14,448.5
Total Assets	48,754.5	45,146.5	43,262.5	38,133.8	30,906.4	26,223.2	20,787.0
Total Deposits	32,634.1	30,702.5	27,739.3	24,839.9	19,586.6	17,305.5	14,575.1
Long-Term Obligations	5,484.5	4,178.1	4,655.8	3,935.3	3,888.8	2,727.4	1,187.3
Total Liabilities	44,792.2	41,794.1	40,335.1	35,395.5	28,711.8	24,488.3	19,356.2
Net Stockholders' Equity	3,962.4	3,352.5	2,927.4	2,738.3	2,194.6	1,734.9	1,430.9
Year-end Shs. Outstg. (000)	346,273	338,107	335,810	334,422	307,328	288,357	263,712
STATISTICAL RECORD:							
Return on Equity %	14.0	14.4	15.1	13.5	14.0	14.7	13.9
Return on Assets %	1.1	1.1	1.0	1.0	1.0	1.0	1.0
Equity/Assets %	8.1	7.4	6.8	7.2	7.1	6.6	6.9
Non-Int. Exp./Tot. Inc. %	54.9	57.5	55.8	58.7	56.8	57.4	59.5
Price Range	27.18-19.25	20.53-10.44	21.44-16.38	22.69-12.44	21.24-11.38	12.04-8.42	9.08-6.00
P/E Ratio	16.9-12.0	14.4-7.3	16.3-12.5	20.2-11.1	20.9-11.2	13.4-9.4	11.5-7.6
Average Yield %	2.3	3.1	2.2	2.1	2.0	2.8	3.4

Statistics are as originally reported. Adj. for stk. splits: 100% stk. div., 5/01; 3-for-2, 2/98
Ⓘ After a tax equivalent adjustment of $14.5 mill.

OFFICERS:
W. D. Malone Jr., Chmn., Pres., C.E.O.
A. E. Yother, Exec. V.P., Treas, Sec., Contr.

INVESTOR CONTACT: Bill Prater, Sr. V.P.,
(205) 254-5187

PRINCIPAL OFFICE: 420 North 20th Street,
Birmingham, AL 35203

TELEPHONE NUMBER: (205) 254-5530
FAX: (205) 254-5405
WEB: www.southtrust.com

NO. OF EMPLOYEES: 13,300 (approx.)

SHAREHOLDERS: 17,048 (approx. record)

ANNUAL MEETING: In April

INCORPORATED: DE, 1968

INSTITUTIONAL HOLDINGS:
No. of Institutions: 352
Shares Held: 170,641,360
% Held: 49.2

INDUSTRY: National commercial banks
(SIC: 6021)

TRANSFER AGENT(S): American Stock
Transfer & Trust Company, New York, NY

ST. PAUL COMPANIES, INC. (THE)

YIELD 2.5%
P/E RATIO ...

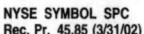
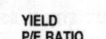

INTERIM EARNINGS (Per Share):

Qtr.	Mar.	June	Sept.	Dec.
1997	1.13	1.25	0.94	1.01
1998	0.76	d1.18	0.27	0.40
1999	0.68	0.90	0.56	0.93
2000	1.53	0.95	0.98	0.86
2001	0.90	0.41	d2.86	d3.49

INTERIM DIVIDENDS (Per Share):

Amt.	Decl.	Ex.	Rec.	Pay.
0.28Q	5/01/01	6/27/01	6/29/01	7/17/01
0.28Q	8/07/01	9/26/01	9/28/01	10/17/01
0.28Q	11/06/01	12/27/01	12/31/01	1/17/02
0.29Q	2/05/02	3/26/02	3/29/02	4/17/02

Indicated div.: $1.16 (Div. Reinv. Plan)

CAPITALIZATION (12/31/01):

	($000)	(%)
Long-Term Debt	2,130,000	29.4
Preferred Stock	58,000	0.8
Common & Surplus	5,056,000	69.8
Total	7,244,000	100.0

DIVIDEND ACHIEVER STATUS:
Rank: 223   10-Year Growth Rate: 5.70%
Total Years of Dividend Growth: 15

*7 YEAR PRICE SCORE 109.4   *12 MONTH PRICE SCORE 105.1
*NYSE COMPOSITE INDEX=100

RECENT DEVELOPMENTS: For the year ended 12/31/01, SPC reported a loss of $1.01 billion, before a loss from discontinued operations of $79.6 million, versus income of $970.0 million, before a gain from discontinued operations of $23.5 million, in the previous year. Results for 2001 included pre-tax restructuring and goodwill charges of $126.5 million, while results for 2000 included pre-tax credits of $4.0 million. Revenues increased 12.2% to $8.94 billion from $7.97 billion the year before.

PROSPECTS: Future prospects are positive as SPC's core businesses are performing well, buoyed by strong price increases. Meanwhile, SPC is on track to exit its health care business and a number of non-U.S. primary insurance markets. SPC is ahead of its expense reduction efforts and should exceed its expense savings goal set in December 2001. SPC has taken the necessary actions to eliminate $80.0 million in annual direct expenses and should secure an additional $50.0 million by the end of 2002.

BUSINESS

ST. PAUL COMPANIES, INC. is a management company principally engaged in two industry segments: commercial property-liability insurance and nonlife reinsurance products and services. The Company also has a presence in the asset management industry through its 77.0% majority ownership of The John Nuveen Company. As a management company, SPC oversees the operations of its subsidiaries and provides those subsidiaries with capital, management and administrative services. The primary business of the Company is underwriting, which produced 81.6% of consolidated revenues in 2001. The Company's investment banking-asset management operations accounted for 12.0% of consolidated revenues in 2001. In May 1997, the Company sold its insurance brokerage operation, The Minet Group. In April 1998, SPC acquired USF&G Corporation.

ANNUAL FINANCIAL DATA

	12/31/01	12/31/00	12/31/99	12/31/98	12/31/97	12/31/96	12/31/95
Earnings Per Share	④ d4.84	④ 4.32	③ 3.19	② 0.32	① 4.20	① 3.25	3.00
Tang. Book Val. Per Share	21.03	30.54	26.42	25.79	25.09	22.87	20.76
Dividends Per Share	1.11	1.07	1.03	0.98	0.93	0.86	0.79
Dividend Payout %	...	24.8	32.3	307.7	22.0	26.5	26.3
INCOME STATEMENT (IN MILLIONS):							
Total Premium Income	7,296.0	5,898.0	5,290.0	6,944.6	4,616.5	4,448.2	3,971.3
Net Investment Income	1,217.0	1,616.0	1,557.0	1,585.0	886.2	807.3	771.6
Other Income	430.0	1,094.0	722.0	578.8	716.6	478.6	666.7
Total Revenues	8,943.0	8,608.0	7,569.0	9,108.4	6,219.3	5,734.2	5,409.6
Policyholder Benefits	7,479.0	3,913.0	3,720.0	5,603.6	3,345.2	3,318.3	2,864.3
Income Before Income Taxes	d1,431.0	1,453.0	1,017.0	d46.3	1,018.7	699.1	656.2
Income Taxes	cr422.0	440.0	238.0	cr135.6	245.5	141.3	135.0
Net Income	④⑤d1,009.0	⑥1,013.0	③ 779.0	② 89.3	① 773.2	① 557.9	521.2
Average Shs. Outstg. (000)	212,000	233,000	246,000	238,682	184,522	168,838	170,798
BALANCE SHEET (IN MILLIONS):							
Cash & Cash Equivalents	2,304.0	1,347.0	1,583.0	1,209.2	552.9	470.6	1,223.6
Premiums Due	10,569.0	8,661.0	7,185.0	6,404.5	3,544.7	3,622.6	3,979.6
Invst. Assets: Fixed-term	15,911.0	20,470.0	19,329.0	21,056.3	12,449.8	11,944.1	10,372.9
Invst. Assets: Equities	1,410.0	1,466.0	1,618.0	1,258.5	1,033.9	808.3	711.5
Invst. Assets: Total	22,178.0	27,099.0	26,252.0	27,222.7	15,166.3	14,509.2	13,316.6
Total Assets	38,321.0	41,075.0	38,873.0	38,322.7	21,500.7	20,681.0	19,738.1
Long-Term Obligations	2,130.0	1,647.0	1,466.0	1,260.4	782.8	689.1	704.0
Net Stockholders' Equity	5,114.0	7,227.0	6,472.0	6,636.4	4,626.7	4,003.8	3,811.7
Year-end Shs. Outstg. (000)	207,624	218,308	224,830	233,750	167,456	167,032	167,952
STATISTICAL RECORD:							
Return on Revenues %	...	11.8	10.3	1.0	12.4	9.7	9.6
Return on Equity %	...	14.0	12.0	1.3	16.7	13.9	13.7
Return on Assets %	...	2.5	2.0	0.2	3.6	2.7	2.6
Price Range	54.44-34.00	57.00-21.31	37.06-25.38	47.19-28.06	42.75-28.81	30.38-25.06	29.69-21.75
P/E Ratio	...	13.2-4.9	11.6-8.0	147.4-87.7	10.2-6.9	9.4-7.7	9.9-7.3
Average Yield %	2.5	2.7	3.3	2.6	2.6	3.1	3.1

Statistics are as originally reported. Adj. for stk. split: 2-for-1, 5/98 ① Bef. disc. oper. loss $79.6 mill., 12/01; $19.3 mill., 12/00; $67.8 mill., 12/97; $107.8 mill., 12/96 ② Incl. nonrecurr. chrg. $221.0 mill. ③ Bef. acctg. change chrg. $29.9 mill. and excl. from disc. oper. $85.1 mill. ④ Incl. pre-tax restr. & goodwill chrgs. of $126.5 mill.

OFFICERS:
J. S. Fishman, Chmn., C.E.O.
T. A. Bradley, Sr. V.P., C.F.O.
B. A. Backberg, Sr. V.P., Sec.
J. A. MacColl, Exec. V.P., Gen. Couns.
INVESTOR CONTACT: Christine Hagen, Investor Relations, (651) 310-7788
PRINCIPAL OFFICE: 385 Washington Street, Saint Paul, MN 55102

TELEPHONE NUMBER: (651) 310-7911
FAX: (651) 310-3386
WEB: www.stpaul.com
NO. OF EMPLOYEES: 10,200 (approx.)
SHAREHOLDERS: 17,467
ANNUAL MEETING: In May
INCORPORATED: MN, May, 1853

INSTITUTIONAL HOLDINGS:
No. of Institutions: 379
Shares Held: 165,490,151
% Held: 79.7
INDUSTRY: Fire, marine, and casualty insurance (SIC: 6331)
TRANSFER AGENT(S): Wells Fargo Shareowner Services, South St. Paul, MN

STANLEY WORKS

NYSE SYMBOL SWK
Rec. Pr. 46.25 (3/31/02)

YIELD 2.1%
P/E RATIO 25.6

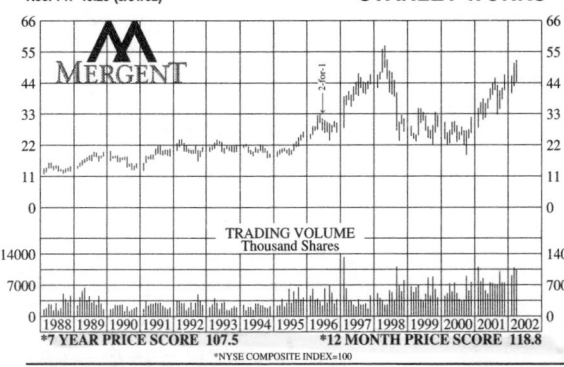

*7 YEAR PRICE SCORE 107.5   *12 MONTH PRICE SCORE 118.8

*NYSE COMPOSITE INDEX=100

INTERIM EARNINGS (Per Share):

Qtr.	Mar.	June	Sept.	Dec.
1997	0.41	d0.72	d0.46	0.29
1998	0.40	0.47	0.37	0.29
1999	0.34	0.28	0.56	0.49
2000	0.54	0.58	0.56	0.54
2001	0.54	0.58	0.62	0.07

INTERIM DIVIDENDS (Per Share):

Amt.	Decl.	Ex.	Rec.	Pay.
0.23Q	1/25/01	3/01/01	3/05/01	3/23/01
0.23Q	5/24/01	5/31/01	6/04/01	6/29/01
0.24Q	7/17/01	8/30/01	9/04/01	9/25/01
0.24Q	10/18/01	11/20/01	11/23/01	12/27/01
0.24Q	1/24/02	2/28/02	3/04/02	3/22/02

Indicated div.: $0.96 (Div. Reinv. Plan)

CAPITALIZATION (12/29/01):

	($000)	(%)
Long-Term Debt	196,800	19.1
Common & Surplus	832,300	80.9
Total	1,029,100	100.0

DIVIDEND ACHIEVER STATUS:
Rank: 244   10-Year Growth Rate: 4.42%
Total Years of Dividend Growth: 34

RECENT DEVELOPMENTS: For the year ended 12/29/01, net income decreased 18.6% to $158.3 million compared with $194.4 million in 2000. Results for 2001 included restructuring charges and asset write-offs of $72.4 million. Net sales were $2.62 billion, down 4.5% from $2.75 billion a year earlier. Tools segment net sales declined 5.6% to $2.02 billion, while Doors segment net sales slid 0.7% to $602.3 million.

PROSPECTS: The Company recently established additional measures to rationalize its cost structure, including facility closures and related workforce reductions. These activities are targeted for execution during the fourth quarter of 2001 and throughout 2002. Meanwhile, the Company expects to show greater working capital efficiency and further enhance cash generation during 2002 aided by significant inventory reductions.

BUSINESS

STANLEY WORKS is a worldwide producer of tools and door products for professional, industrial and consumer use. The Tools segment manufactures and markets carpenters', mechanics', pneumatic and hydraulic tools as well as tool sets. SWK markets its carpenters' tools under the STANLEY® INTELLITOOLS™, CONTRACTOR GRADE™, and GOLD BLATT® brands. The Doors segment manufactures and markets commercial and residential doors as well as closet doors and systems, home decor and door and consumer hardware. Products in the Doors segment include residential insulated steel, reinforced fiberglass and wood entrance door systems. Door products are marketed under the STANLEY®, MAGICDOOR®, Stanley-Acme-track™, MONARCH™ and ACME® brands. A substantial portion of SWK's products are sold through home centers and mass merchant distribution channels in the U.S.

ANNUAL FINANCIAL DATA

	12/29/01	12/30/00	1/1/00	1/2/99	1/3/98	12/28/96	12/30/95
Earnings Per Share	④ 1.81	2.22	③ 1.67	② 1.53	① d0.47	① 1.09	① 0.67
Cash Flow Per Share	2.76	3.17	2.62	2.41	0.34	1.93	1.58
Tang. Book Val. Per Share	7.04	6.58	6.19	5.32	5.67	7.68	6.79
Dividends Per Share	0.94	0.90	0.87	0.83	0.77	0.73	0.71
Dividend Payout %	51.9	40.5	52.1	54.2	...	67.0	106.8

INCOME STATEMENT (IN MILLIONS):

Total Revenues	2,624.4	2,748.9	2,751.8	2,729.1	2,669.5	2,670.8	2,624.3
Costs & Expenses	2,284.5	2,324.8	2,410.0	2,397.8	2,577.2	2,377.1	2,385.7
Depreciation & Amort.	82.9	83.3	85.6	79.7	72.4	74.7	81.2
Operating Income	257.0	340.8	256.2	251.6	19.9	219.0	157.4
Net Interest Inc./(Exp.)	d25.6	d27.1	d27.9	d23.1	d16.6	d22.5	d30.3
Income Before Income Taxes	236.7	293.7	230.8	215.4	d18.6	174.2	112.8
Income Taxes	78.4	99.3	80.8	77.6	23.3	77.3	53.7
Net Income	④ 158.3	194.4	③ 150.0	② 137.8	① d41.9	① 96.9	① 59.1
Cash Flow	241.2	277.7	235.6	217.5	30.5	171.6	140.3
Average Shs. Outstg. (000)	87,467	87,668	89,887	90,193	89,469	88,824	88,720

BALANCE SHEET (IN MILLIONS):

Cash & Cash Equivalents	115.2	93.6	88.0	110.1	152.2	84.0	75.4
Total Current Assets	1,141.4	1,094.3	1,091.0	1,086.4	1,005.3	910.9	915.1
Net Property	494.3	503.7	520.6	511.4	513.2	570.4	556.5
Total Assets	2,055.7	1,884.8	1,890.6	1,932.9	1,758.7	1,659.6	1,670.0
Total Current Liabilities	825.5	707.3	693.0	702.1	622.7	381.6	387.7
Long-Term Obligations	196.8	248.7	290.0	344.8	283.7	342.6	391.1
Net Stockholders' Equity	832.3	736.5	735.4	669.4	607.8	780.1	734.6
Net Working Capital	315.9	387.0	398.0	384.3	382.6	529.3	527.4
Year-end Shs. Outstg. (000)	84,659	85,188	88,945	88,772	88,788	88,720	88,758

STATISTICAL RECORD:

Operating Profit Margin %	9.8	12.4	9.3	9.2	0.7	8.2	6.0
Net Profit Margin %	6.0	7.1	5.5	5.0	...	3.6	2.3
Return on Equity %	19.0	26.4	20.4	20.6	...	12.4	8.0
Return on Assets %	7.7	10.3	7.9	7.1	...	5.8	3.5
Debt/Total Assets %	9.6	13.2	15.3	17.8	16.1	20.6	23.4
Price Range	46.97-28.06	31.88-18.44	35.00-22.00	57.25-23.50	47.38-28.00	32.81-23.63	26.69-17.81
P/E Ratio	25.9-15.5	14.4-8.3	21.0-13.2	37.4-15.4	...	30.1-21.7	40.1-26.8
Average Yield %	2.5	3.6	3.1	2.1	2.0	2.6	3.2

Statistics are as originally reported. Adj. for stk. split: 2-for-1, 6/96. ① Incl. pretax restruct chrgs. of $238.5 mill.; 1997: $47.8 mill., 1996; & $85.8 mill., 1995. ② Incl. restruct. chrg. of $27.8 mill. ③ Incl. restruct. credit of $21.3 mill. ④ Incl. restruct. chrg. and asset write-offs of $72.4 mill.

OFFICERS:
J. M. Trani, Chmn., C.E.O.
J. M. Loree, V.P., C.F.O.
B. H. Beatt, V.P., Gen. Couns., Sec.

INVESTOR CONTACT: Gerard J. Gould, Dir., Investor Relations, (860) 827-3833

PRINCIPAL OFFICE: 1000 Stanley Drive, P.O. Box 7000, New Britain, CT 06053

TELEPHONE NUMBER: (860) 225-5111
FAX: (860) 827-3895
WEB: www.stanleyworks.com

NO. OF EMPLOYEES: 14,400 (approx.)

SHAREHOLDERS: 15,290

ANNUAL MEETING: In Apr.

INCORPORATED: CT, July, 1852

INSTITUTIONAL HOLDINGS:
No. of Institutions: 243
Shares Held: 52,016,610
% Held: 61.1

INDUSTRY: Hand and edge tools, nec (SIC: 3423)

TRANSFER AGENT(S): EquiServe Limited Partnership, Boston, MA

STATE AUTO FINANCIAL CORP.

YIELD 0.9%
P/E RATIO 28.5

TRADING VOLUME
Thousand Shares

| 1988 | 1989 | 1990 | 1991 | 1992 | 1993 | 1994 | 1995 | 1996 | 1997 | 1998 | 1999 | 2000 | 2001 | 2002 |

*7 YEAR PRICE SCORE 114.9   *12 MONTH PRICE SCORE 99.3

*NYSE COMPOSITE INDEX=100

INTERIM EARNINGS (Per Share):

Qtr.	Mar.	June	Sept.	Dec.
1997	0.20	0.22	0.22	0.28
1998	0.27	0.06	0.25	0.29
1999	0.25	0.25	0.21	0.32
2000	0.35	0.32	0.20	0.34
2001	0.36	0.24	0.18	d0.27

INTERIM DIVIDENDS (Per Share):

Amt.	Decl.	Ex.	Rec.	Pay.
0.03Q	2/17/01	3/13/01	3/15/01	3/30/01
0.03Q	5/25/01	6/08/01	6/12/01	6/29/01
0.033Q	8/16/01	9/07/01	9/11/01	9/28/01
0.033Q	11/15/01	12/11/01	12/13/01	12/31/01
0.033Q	3/01/02	3/12/02	3/14/02	3/29/02

Indicated div.: $0.125 (Div. Reinv. Plan)

CAPITALIZATION (12/31/01):

	($000)	(%)
Common & Surplus	400,193	100.0
Total	400,193	100.0

DIVIDEND ACHIEVER STATUS:

Rank: 30   10-Year Growth Rate: 18.27%
Total Years of Dividend Growth: 10

RECENT DEVELOPMENTS: For the year ended 12/31/01, net income fell 56.8% to $20.6 million from $47.7 million in the previous year. Results were adversely affected by increased loss reserve adjustments on claims from the former Meridian Mutual business and a decrease in the Company's management and operations service fee income. Total revenue increased 34.7% to $623.3 million versus $462.8 million in the prior year. Revenues included net realized gains on investments of $2.0 million and $5.3

million, respectively. Earned premium revenues grew 39.5% to $555.2 million from $409.0 million in 2000. Net investment income rose 21.8% to $47.4 million, while management services income slipped 11.4% to $15.6 million. The Company's combined ratio was 107.0% on 12/31/01 compared with 98.4% on 12/31/00. Looking ahead, the Company anticipates improvement in earnings as a result of the implementation of its recent underwriting and pricing initiatives.

BUSINESS

STATE AUTO FINANCIAL CORP., through its principal insurance subsidiaries, State Auto Property and Casualty Insurance Company (State Auto P&C), Milbank Insurance Company, Farmers Casualty Insurance Company and State Auto Insurance Company (SAIC), provides personal and commercial insurance for the standard insurance market primarily in the central and eastern United States, excluding New York, New Jersey, and the New England states. The Company's principal lines of business include personal and commercial auto, homeowners, commercial multi-peril, workers' compensation, general liability and fire insurance. State Auto National Insurance Company and Mid-Plains Insurance Company write personal automobile insurance for risks in the nonstandard insurance market. Products of State Auto P&C, Milbank, Farmers Casualty, SAIC, National and Mid-Plains products are marketed through independent agents. STFC is a majority-owned subsidiary of State Automobile Mutual Insurance Company, an Ohio-domiciled property and casualty insurer.

ANNUAL FINANCIAL DATA

	12/31/01	12/31/00	12/31/99	12/31/98	12/31/97	12/31/96	12/31/95
Earnings Per Share	0.52	1.21	1.03	0.87	0.91	0.63	0.71
Tang. Book Val. Per Share	10.23	9.95	8.22	8.06	6.15	5.14	4.67
Dividends Per Share	0.125	0.115	0.105	0.095	0.085	0.077	0.070
Dividend Payout %	24.0	9.5	10.2	10.9	9.3	12.3	9.9
INCOME STATEMENT (IN THOUSANDS):							
Total Premium Income	555,207	397,967	392,058	356,210	254,682	240,345	232,524
Other Income	68,065	64,807	48,813	45,849	34,326	33,300	31,392
Total Revenues	623,272	462,774	440,871	402,059	289,008	273,645	263,916
Income Before Income Taxes	17,976	61,444	56,985	49,605	47,084	30,148	35,339
Income Taxes	cr2,639	13,730	14,169	12,108	13,125	7,546	9,797
Net Income	20,615	47,714	42,816	37,497	33,959	22,602	25,542
Average Shs. Outstg.	39,681	39,120	41,526	42,901	37,314	36,140	35,912
BALANCE SHEET (IN THOUSANDS):							
Cash & Cash Equivalents	30,016	21,305	24,560	32,605	23,918	12,868	11,227
Premiums Due	13,919	9,335	10,807	22,667	12,050	9,691	9,278
Invst. Assets: Fixed-term	1,078,811	692,558	571,787	537,770	399,599	384,307	369,847
Invst. Assets: Equities	59,845	58,312	55,518	42,196	4,580	. . .	. . .
Invst. Assets: Total	1,138,656	750,870	627,305	579,966	404,179	384,307	369,847
Total Assets	1,367,496	898,106	759,945	709,778	493,151	453,120	434,496
Net Stockholders' Equity	400,193	386,059	317,687	340,824	225,479	186,461	168,252
Year-end Shs. Outstg.	38,937	38,555	38,321	42,027	36,684	36,272	36,050
STATISTICAL RECORD:							
Return on Revenues %	3.3	10.3	9.7	9.3	11.8	8.3	9.7
Return on Equity %	5.2	12.4	13.5	11.0	15.1	12.1	15.2
Return on Assets %	1.5	5.3	5.6	5.3	6.9	5.0	5.9
Price Range	17.80-12.30	18.00-7.13	13.88-8.88	20.00-11.44	15.75-8.13	9.25-6.38	8.75-4.58
P/E Ratio	34.2-23.6	14.9-5.9	13.5-8.6	23.0-13.1	17.3-8.9	14.8-10.2	12.3-6.5
Average Yield %	0.8	0.9	0.9	0.6	0.7	1.0	1.0

Statistics are as originally reported. Adj. for stk. splits: 2-for-1, 7/98; 50% div., 7/96

OFFICERS:
R. H. Moone, Chmn., Pres., C.E.O.
S. J. Johnston, Sr. V.P., C.F.O., Treas.
J. R. Lowther, Sr. V.P., Sec., Gen. Couns.

INVESTOR CONTACT: James E. Duemey, Mgr., Inv. Rel., (614) 464-5373

PRINCIPAL OFFICE: 518 East Broad Street, Columbus, OH 43215-3976

TELEPHONE NUMBER: (614) 464-5000
FAX: (614) 464-5374
WEB: www.stauto.com

NO. OF EMPLOYEES: 2,042

SHAREHOLDERS: 948

ANNUAL MEETING: In May

INCORPORATED: OH, April, 1990

INSTITUTIONAL HOLDINGS:
No. of Institutions: 48
Shares Held: 5,980,282
% Held: 15.4

INDUSTRY: Fire, marine, and casualty insurance (SIC: 6331)

TRANSFER AGENT(S): National City Bank, Cleveland, OH

NYSE SYMBOL STT
Rec. Pr. 55.38 (3/31/02)

STATE STREET CORPORATION

YIELD 0.8%
P/E RATIO 29.1

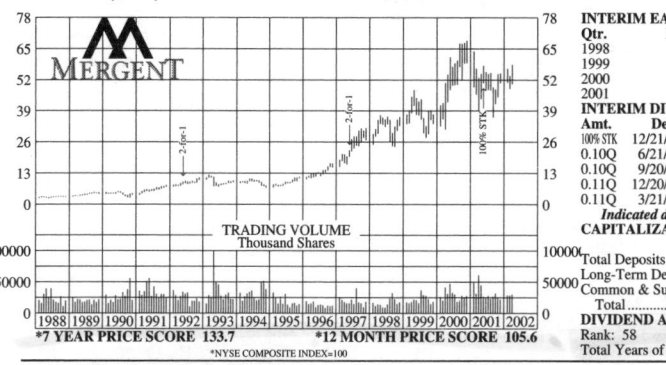

*7 YEAR PRICE SCORE 133.7 *12 MONTH PRICE SCORE 105.6
*NYSE COMPOSITE INDEX=100

TRADING VOLUME Thousand Shares

INTERIM EARNINGS (Per Share):

Qtr.	Mar.	June	Sept.	Dec.
1998	0.32	0.33	0.34	0.34
1999	0.37	0.38	0.39	0.76
2000	0.46	0.45	0.46	0.45
2001	0.37	0.50	0.52	

INTERIM DIVIDENDS (Per Share):

Amt.	Decl.	Ex.	Rec.	Pay.
100% STK	12/21/00	5/31/01	4/30/01	5/30/01
0.10Q	6/21/01	6/28/01	7/02/01	7/16/01
0.10Q	9/20/01	9/27/01	10/01/01	10/15/01
0.11Q	12/20/01	12/28/01	1/02/02	1/15/02
0.11Q	3/21/02	3/27/02	4/01/02	4/15/02

Indicated div.: $0.44 (Div. Reinv. Plan)

CAPITALIZATION (12/31/01):

	($000)	(%)
Total Deposits	38,559,000	88.4
Long-Term Debt	1,217,000	2.8
Common & Surplus	3,845,000	8.8
Total	43,621,000	100.0

DIVIDEND ACHIEVER STATUS:
Rank: 58   10-Year Growth Rate: 15.48%
Total Years of Dividend Growth: 21

RECENT DEVELOPMENTS: For the year ended 12/31/01, net income increased 5.5% to $628.0 million from $595.0 million in the prior year. Net interest income improved 14.7% to $1.03 billion. Total fee revenue grew 4.4% to $2.78 billion. Servicing fees rose 14.0% to $1.62 billion and processing fees climbed 2.6% to $279.0 million. Total revenue improved 7.0% to $3.80 billion. Results for 2001 included an after-tax investment write-off of $33.0 million.

PROSPECTS: The Company continues to perform well despite the slowdown in the economy. Servicing fees continue to increase, reflecting new business from existing and new clients, and strength in securities lending revenue resulting from effective use of collateral in a highly favorable U.S. interest-rate environment. This increase is being partially offset by continued declines in equity market values worldwide.

BUSINESS

STATE STREET CORPORATION (formerly State Street Boston Corporation) as of 12/31/01, is a bank holding company with $69.90 billion in assets that conducts business worldwide principally through its subsidiary, State Street Bank and Trust Company. The Company has two lines of business: services for institutional investors and investment management. Services for institutional investors are primarily accounting, custody and other services for large pools of assets. Investment management offers index and active equity strategies, short-term investment funds and fixed income products. As of 12/31/01, STT had $775.00 billion in assets under management. On 10/1/99, the Company sold its commercial lending business. On 2/8/01, STT acquired a majority interest in Bel Air Investment Advisors LLC. On 7/3/01, STT acquired DST Systems, Inc.'s portfolio accounting service business.

ANNUAL FINANCIAL DATA

	12/31/01	12/31/00	12/31/99	12/31/98	12/31/97	12/31/96	12/31/95
Earnings Per Share	1.90	1.82	① 1.89	1.33	1.16	0.90	0.75
Tang. Book Val. Per Share	11.88	10.09	8.31	7.19	5.97	5.47	4.82
Dividends Per Share	0.39	0.33	0.29	0.25	0.21	0.18	0.17
Dividend Payout %	20.5	18.2	15.3	18.8	18.1	20.6	22.1
INCOME STATEMENT (IN MILLIONS):							
Total Interest Income	2,855.0	3,256.0	2,437.0	2,237.0	1,755.0	1,443.0	1,336.6
Total Interest Expense	1,830.0	2,362.0	1,656.0	1,492.0	1,114.0	892.0	907.2
Net Interest Income	1,025.0	894.0	781.0	745.0	641.0	551.0	429.4
Provision for Loan Losses	10.0	9.0	14.0	17.0	16.0	8.0	8.0
Non-Interest Income	2,782.0	2,665.0	2,537.0	1,997.0	1,673.0	1,302.0	1,119.1
Non-Interest Expense	2,867.0	2,644.0	2,336.0	2,068.0	1,734.0	1,398.0	1,174.0
Income Before Taxes	930.0	906.0	968.0	657.0	564.0	447.0	366.5
Net Income	628.0	595.0	① 619.0	436.0	380.0	293.0	247.1
Average Shs. Outstg. (000)	330,492	328,088	327,502	327,854	327,578	326,532	332,232
BALANCE SHEET (IN MILLIONS):							
Cash & Due from Banks	1,651.0	1,618.0	2,930.0	1,365.0	2,411.0	1,623.0	1,421.9
Securities Avail. for Sale	21,775.0	14,744.0	15,489.0	10,072.0	10,580.0	9,642.0	6,039.2
Total Loans & Leases	5,341.0	5,273.0	4,293.0	6,309.0	5,562.0	4,713.0	3,986.1
Allowance for Credit Losses	58.0	57.0	48.0	84.0	83.0	73.0	63.5
Net Loans & Leases	5,283.0	5,216.0	4,245.0	6,225.0	5,479.0	4,640.0	3,922.7
Total Assets	69,896.0	69,298.0	60,896.0	47,082.0	37,975.0	31,524.0	25,785.2
Total Deposits	38,559.0	37,937.0	34,145.0	27,539.0	24,878.0	19,519.0	16,647.2
Long-Term Obligations	1,217.0	1,219.0	921.0	922.0	774.0	476.0	126.6
Total Liabilities	66,051.0	66,036.0	58,244.0	44,771.0	35,980.0	29,749.0	24,197.7
Net Stockholders' Equity	3,845.0	3,262.0	2,652.0	2,311.0	1,995.0	1,775.0	1,587.5
Year-end Shs. Outstg. (000)	323,670	323,422	319,180	321,390	334,446	324,616	329,552
STATISTICAL RECORD:							
Return on Equity %	16.3	18.2	23.3	18.9	19.0	16.5	15.6
Return on Assets %	0.9	0.9	1.0	0.9	1.0	0.9	1.0
Equity/Assets %	5.5	4.7	4.4	4.9	5.3	5.6	6.2
Non-Int. Exp./Tot. Inc. %	75.3	74.3	70.4	75.4	74.9	75.4	75.8
Price Range	63.93-36.25	68.40-31.22	47.63-27.75	37.16-23.94	31.84-15.66	17.13-10.44	11.56-7.00
P/E Ratio	33.6-19.1	37.7-17.2	25.2-14.7	27.9-18.0	27.4-13.5	19.1-11.6	15.5-9.4
Average Yield %	0.8	0.7	0.8	0.8	0.9	1.3	1.8

Statistics are as originally reported. Adj. for 2-for-1 stock splits, 5/01 & 5/97. ① Incl. pre-tax net gain on the sale of Co.'s commercial banking business of $282.0 mill.

OFFICERS:
D. A. Spina, Chmn., C.E.O
R. E. Logue, Pres., C.O.O.
R. L. O'Kelley, Exec. V.P., C.F.O., Treas.

INVESTOR CONTACT: Karen A. Warren, Inv. Rel., (617) 664-3477

PRINCIPAL OFFICE: 225 Franklin Street, Boston, MA 02110

TELEPHONE NUMBER: (617) 786-3000
FAX: (617) 985-8055
WEB: www.statestreet.com

NO. OF EMPLOYEES: 19,105 full-time; 648 part-time

SHAREHOLDERS: 5,648

ANNUAL MEETING: In April
INCORPORATED: MA, Oct., 1969

INSTITUTIONAL HOLDINGS:
No. of Institutions: 538
Shares Held: 235,671,856
% Held: 72.6

INDUSTRY: State commercial banks (SIC: 6022)

TRANSFER AGENT(S): State Street Bank and Trust Company, Boston, MA

STEPAN COMPANY

YIELD 2.7%
P/E RATIO 16.9

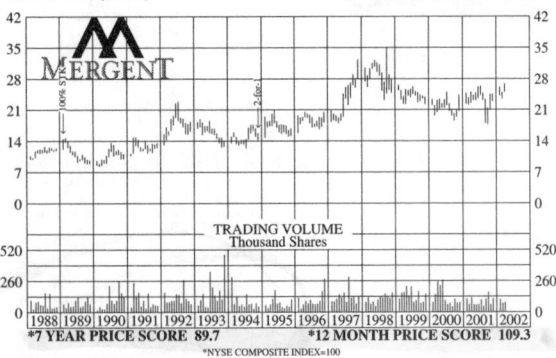

INTERIM EARNINGS (Per Share):

Qtr.	March	June	Sept.	Dec.
1998	0.52	0.64	0.45	0.51
1999	0.57	0.75	d0.02	0.76
2000	0.41	0.64	0.61	d0.25
2001	0.36	0.61	0.44	0.18

INTERIM DIVIDENDS (Per Share):

Amt.	Decl.	Ex.	Rec.	Pay.
0.175Q	2/20/01	2/26/01	2/28/01	3/15/01
0.175Q	5/01/01	5/29/01	5/31/01	6/15/01
0.175Q	8/07/01	8/29/01	8/31/01	9/14/01
0.182Q	11/01/01	11/28/01	11/30/01	12/14/01
0.182Q	2/12/02	2/26/02	2/28/02	3/15/02

Indicated div.: $0.73

CAPITALIZATION (12/31/01):

	($000)	(%)
Long-Term Debt	109,588	36.0
Deferred Income Tax	35,040	11.5
Preferred Stock	14,581	4.8
Common & Surplus	145,148	47.7
Total	304,357	100.0

TRADING VOLUME
Thousand Shares

*7 YEAR PRICE SCORE 89.7   ***12 MONTH PRICE SCORE 109.3**
NYSE COMPOSITE INDEX=100

DIVIDEND ACHIEVER STATUS:
Rank: 176   10-Year Growth Rate: 7.92%
Total Years of Dividend Growth: 35

RECENT DEVELOPMENTS: For the year ended 12/31/01, net income increased 7.6% to $16.2 million versus $15.0 million in the previous year. Net sales increased 1.8% to $711.5 million from $698.9 million a year earlier. Sales from the surfactants segment improved 4.1% to $558.9 million, while specialty products segment sales climbed 17.6% to $24.9 million. Sales from the polymers segment fell 9.3% to $127.7 million. Gross profit decreased 4.3% to $107.2 million from $112.0 million the year before.

PROSPECTS: During the fourth quarter of 2001, SCL acquired Manro Performance Chemicals Limited, a surfactant manufacturer that specializes in anionic surfactants, hydrotropes and acid catalysts, for $24.6 million. The acquisition is projected to contribute $0.20 to $0.25 per diluted share in 2002. Separately, SCL's enterprise resource planning system implementation should be completed in 2002 with additional charges of $0.20 to $0.25 per diluted share.

BUSINESS

THE STEPAN COMPANY is a producer of specialty and intermediate chemicals that are sold to other manufacturers for use in a variety of end products. The Company operates in three business segments: surfactants, polymers, and specialty products. Surfactants are a principal ingredient in consumer and industrial cleaning products such as detergents, shampoos, lotions, toothpastes and cosmetics. Other applications include lubricating ingredients and emulsifiers for agricultural products and plastics and composites. The polymers product group includes phthalic anhydride, polyurethane systems and polyurethane polyols. Polymer products are used in construction materials and components of automotive, boating and other consumer products. Polyurethane systems provide thermal insulation. Polyurethane polyols are used in manufacturing laminate board. Specialty products include chemicals used in food, flavoring and pharmaceutical applications. On 9/13/01, SCL acquired Manro Performance Chemicals Limited, a manufacturer of surfactants. Manro was renamed Stepan UK Limited.

ANNUAL FINANCIAL DATA

	12/31/01	12/31/00	12/31/99	12/31/98	12/31/97	12/31/96	12/31/95
Earnings Per Share	1.59	1.47	⑪ 2.08	2.12	1.86	1.80	1.51
Cash Flow Per Share	5.54	5.30	5.79	5.51	5.08	5.12	4.66
Tang. Book Val. Per Share	15.41	15.47	14.28	13.24	12.16	11.38	10.25
Dividends Per Share	0.71	0.66	0.61	0.56	0.51	0.48	0.45
Dividend Payout %	44.5	45.1	29.4	26.5	27.6	26.5	29.6
INCOME STATEMENT (IN THOUSANDS):							
Total Revenues	711,517	698,937	666,784	610,451	581,949	536,635	528,218
Costs & Expenses	640,320	627,632	585,554	527,681	502,298	464,111	465,214
Depreciation & Amort.	39,972	39,277	39,452	37,347	35,281	32,138	30,384
Operating Income	31,225	32,028	41,778	45,423	44,370	40,386	32,620
Net Interest Inc./(Exp.)	d7,168	d8,328	d8,376	d7,453	d7,595	d7,243	d7,865
Income Before Income Taxes	25,926	24,403	34,829	38,766	34,874	32,261	24,991
Income Taxes	9,774	9,395	12,700	15,312	14,464	13,194	8,872
Net Income	16,152	15,008	⑪ 22,129	23,454	20,410	19,067	16,119
Cash Flow	55,322	53,470	60,723	59,905	50,649	46,427	45,702
Average Shs. Outstg.	10,133	10,236	10,632	11,043	10,959	10,002	9,984
BALANCE SHEET (IN THOUSANDS):							
Cash & Cash Equivalents	4,224	3,536	3,969	983	5,507	4,778	3,148
Total Current Assets	185,194	177,213	166,660	149,758	146,482	153,698	150,154
Net Property	212,433	199,147	209,481	215,096	206,601	207,159	192,470
Total Assets	435,488	415,049	414,576	404,361	374,936	381,012	362,527
Total Current Liabilities	109,730	108,341	98,045	87,944	82,693	83,376	83,298
Long-Term Obligations	109,588	96,466	107,420	107,708	94,898	102,567	109,023
Net Stockholders' Equity	159,729	154,176	155,064	147,984	137,598	131,615	122,477
Net Working Capital	75,464	68,872	68,615	61,814	63,789	70,322	66,856
Year-end Shs. Outstg.	9,420	9,024	9,488	9,693	9,692	9,817	10,000
STATISTICAL RECORD:							
Operating Profit Margin %	4.4	4.6	6.3	7.4	7.6	7.5	6.2
Net Profit Margin %	2.3	2.1	3.3	3.8	3.5	3.6	3.1
Return on Equity %	10.1	9.7	14.3	15.8	14.8	14.5	13.2
Return on Assets %	3.7	3.6	5.3	5.8	5.4	5.0	4.4
Debt/Total Assets %	25.2	23.2	25.9	26.6	25.3	26.9	30.1
Price Range	26.38-17.65	25.00-18.50	26.69-22.19	35.13-23.13	32.38-18.00	20.50-15.75	20.88-14.75
P/E Ratio	16.6-11.1	17.0-12.6	12.8-10.7	16.6-10.9	17.4-9.7	11.4-8.7	13.8-9.8
Average Yield %	3.2	3.0	2.5	1.9	2.0	2.6	2.5

Statistics are as originally reported. ⑪ Incl. after-tax chrg. of $6.3 mill. related to a lawsuit settlement.

OFFICERS:
F. Q. Stepan, Chmn., C.E.O.
F. Q. Stepan Jr., Pres., C.O.O.
F. S. Eberts III, V.P., Gen Couns., Sec.

INVESTOR CONTACT: Walter J. Klein, V.P.-Finance, (847) 501-2340

PRINCIPAL OFFICE: Edens & Winnetka Roads, Northfield, IL 60093

TELEPHONE NUMBER: (847) 446-7500
FAX: (847) 446-2843
WEB: www.stepan.com
NO. OF EMPLOYEES: 1,491 (avg.)
SHAREHOLDERS: 1,231
ANNUAL MEETING: In April
INCORPORATED: IL, Jan., 1940; reincorp., DE, 1959

INSTITUTIONAL HOLDINGS:
No. of Institutions: 41
Shares Held: 2,694,676
% Held: 29.2

INDUSTRY: Surface active agents (SIC: 2843)

TRANSFER AGENT(S): Computershare Investor Services, Chicago, IL

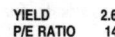

NYSE SYMBOL STI
Rec. Pr. 66.73 (3/31/02)

SUNTRUST BANKS, INC.

YIELD 2.6%
P/E RATIO 14.2

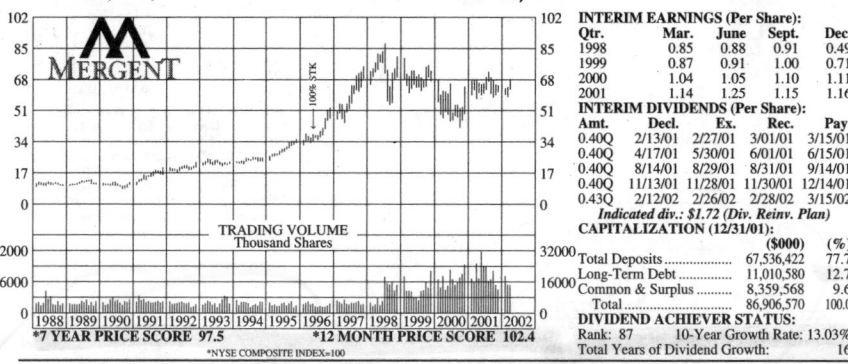

7 YEAR PRICE SCORE 97.5   **12 MONTH PRICE SCORE 102.4**
NYSE COMPOSITE INDEX=100

INTERIM EARNINGS (Per Share):

Qtr.	Mar.	June	Sept.	Dec.
1998	0.85	0.88	0.91	0.49
1999	0.87	0.91	1.00	0.71
2000	1.04	1.05	1.10	1.11
2001	1.14	1.25	1.15	1.16

INTERIM DIVIDENDS (Per Share):

Amt.	Decl.	Ex.	Rec.	Pay.
0.40Q	2/13/01	2/27/01	3/01/01	3/15/01
0.40Q	4/17/01	5/30/01	6/01/01	6/15/01
0.40Q	8/14/01	8/29/01	8/31/01	9/14/01
0.40Q	11/13/01	11/28/01	11/30/01	12/14/01
0.43Q	2/12/02	2/26/02	2/28/02	3/15/02

Indicated div.: $1.72 (Div. Reinv. Plan)

CAPITALIZATION (12/31/01):

	($000)	(%)
Total Deposits	67,536,422	77.7
Long-Term Debt	11,010,580	12.7
Common & Surplus	8,359,568	9.6
Total	86,906,570	100.0

DIVIDEND ACHIEVER STATUS:
Rank: 87   10-Year Growth Rate: 13.03%
Total Years of Dividend Growth: 16

RECENT DEVELOPMENTS: For the year ended 12/31/01, STI reported income of $1.37 billion, before an extraordinary gain of $6.3 million, versus net income of $1.29 billion in the previous year. Earnings for 2000 included pre-tax merger-related expenses of $42.4 million. Net interest income grew 4.6% to $3.25 billion from $3.11 billion in 2000. Provision for loan losses more than doubled to $275.2 million from $134.0 million a year earlier. Total non-interest income improved 21.5% to $2.16 billion, while total non-interest expense rose 10.1% to $3.11 billion.

PROSPECTS: On 2/15/02, STI announced that it has completed the acquisition of Huntington Bancshares, Inc.'s retail, small business, commercial, treasury managment and investment-related businesses in Florida. With the addition of 59 branches, deposits of about $4.50 billion and nearly 500,000 accounts, the acquisition significantly enhances STI's position in the high-growth Florida market. Separately, STI continues to expand its eBanking capabilities with the introduction of "My Solutions," a free, customizable Web portal on www.suntrust.com.

BUSINESS

SUNTRUST BANKS, INC., through its primary subsidiary, SunTrust Bank, provides deposit, credit, trust and investment services to a broad range of retail, business and institutional clients. Other subsidiaries provide mortgage banking, credit-related insurance, asset management, brokerage and capital market services. At 12/31/01, STI had total assets of $104.74 billion. The Company's more than 1,100 retail branches and 1,990 ATMs are located in Alabama, Florida, Georgia, Maryland, Tennessee, Virginia and the District of Columbia. In addition, STI provides customers with a full range of technology-based banking channels including Internet, personal computer and telephone banking.

ANNUAL FINANCIAL DATA

	12/31/01	12/31/00	12/31/99	12/31/98	12/31/97	12/31/96	12/31/95
Earnings Per Share	④ 4.70	③ 4.30	① ② 3.50	① 3.04	3.13	2.76	2.47
Tang. Book Val. Per Share	26.67	27.58	23.24	22.99	23.38	20.87	17.71
Dividends Per Share	1.60	1.48	1.38	1.00	0.93	0.82	0.74
Dividend Payout %	34.0	34.4	39.4	32.9	29.6	29.9	30.0
INCOME STATEMENT (IN MILLIONS):							
Total Interest Income	6,279.6	6,845.4	5,960.2	5,675.9	3,650.7	3,246.0	3,027.2
Total Interest Expense	3,027.0	3,737.0	2,814.8	2,746.8	1,756.4	1,461.8	1,350.8
Net Interest Income	3,252.6	3,108.4	3,145.5	2,929.1	1,894.4	1,784.2	1,676.4
Provision for Loan Losses	275.2	134.0	170.4	214.6	117.0	115.9	112.1
Non-Interest Income	2,155.8	1,773.6	1,660.0	1,716.2	934.2	818.0	713.1
Non-Interest Expense	3,113.5	2,828.5	2,939.4	2,932.4	1,685.6	1,583.1	1,451.5
Income Before Taxes	2,019.7	1,919.6	1,695.7	1,498.3	1,026.0	903.2	825.9
Net Income	④ 1,369.2	③ 1,294.1	① ② 1,124.0	① 971.0	667.3	616.6	565.5
Average Shs. Outstg. (000)	291,584	300,956	317,079	319,711	213,480	223,486	229,544
BALANCE SHEET (IN MILLIONS):							
Cash & Due from Banks	4,229.1	4,110.5	3,909.7	4,289.9	2,991.3	3,037.3	2,641.4
Securities Avail. for Sale	1,343.6	941.9	259.5	239.7	178.4	80.4	96.6
Total Loans & Leases	68,959.2	72,239.8	66,002.8	61,540.6	40,135.5	35,404.2	31,301.4
Allowance for Credit Losses	867.1	874.5	871.3	944.6	751.8	725.8	698.9
Net Loans & Leases	68,092.2	71,365.3	65,131.5	60,596.1	39,383.7	34,678.3	30,602.5
Total Assets	104,740.6	103,496.4	95,390.0	93,169.9	57,982.7	52,468.2	46,471.5
Total Deposits	67,536.4	69,533.3	60,100.5	59,033.3	38,197.5	36,890.4	33,183.2
Long-Term Obligations	11,010.6	7,895.4	4,967.3	4,757.9	3,171.8	1,565.3	1,002.4
Total Liabilities	96,381.1	95,257.2	87,763.1	84,991.3	52,783.4	47,588.3	42,201.9
Net Stockholders' Equity	8,359.6	8,239.2	7,626.9	8,178.6	5,199.4	4,880.0	4,269.6
Year-end Shs. Outstg. (000)	283,040	269,370	293,544	321,124	209,909	220,469	225,726
STATISTICAL RECORD:							
Return on Equity %	16.4	15.7	14.7	11.9	12.8	12.6	13.2
Return on Assets %	1.3	1.3	1.2	1.0	1.2	1.2	1.2
Equity/Assets %	8.0	8.0	8.0	8.8	9.0	9.3	9.2
Non-Int. Exp./Tot. Inc. %	57.6	57.9	61.2	63.1	59.6	60.8	60.7
Price Range	72.35-57.29	68.06-41.63	79.81-60.44	87.75-54.00	75.25-44.13	52.50-32.00	35.44-23.63
P/E Ratio	15.4-12.2	15.8-9.7	22.8-17.3	28.9-17.8	24.0-14.1	19.0-11.6	14.3-9.6
Average Yield %	2.5	2.7	2.0	1.4	1.5	2.0	2.5

Statistics are as originally reported. Adj. for 2-for-1 stk. split, 5/96. ① Incl. pre-tax merger-rel. chrg.: $45.6 mill., 1999; $119.4 mill., 1998. ② Bef. extraord. gain of $202.6 mill., 1999. ③ Incl. pre-tax merger-rel. chrgs. of $42.4 mill. ④ Bef. extraord. gain of $6.3 mill.

OFFICERS:
L. P. Humann, Chmn., Pres., C.E.O.
J. W. Spiegal, Vice-Chmn., C.F.O.
T. J. Hoepner, Vice-Chmn.

INVESTOR CONTACT: Gary Peacock, Jr., Dir., Inv. Rel., (404) 658-4879

PRINCIPAL OFFICE: 303 Peachtree Street N.E., Atlanta, GA 30308

TELEPHONE NUMBER: (404) 588-7711
FAX: (404) 827-6173
WEB: www.suntrust.com
NO. OF EMPLOYEES: 28,391
SHAREHOLDERS: 38,439
ANNUAL MEETING: In Apr.
INCORPORATED: GA, July, 1985

INSTITUTIONAL HOLDINGS:
No. of Institutions: 454
Shares Held: 128,735,937
% Held: 44.8

INDUSTRY: National commercial banks (SIC: 6021)

TRANSFER AGENT(S): SunTrust Bank, Atlanta, GA

NYSE SYMBOL SUP
Rec. Pr. 48.78 (3/31/02)

SUPERIOR INDUSTRIES INTERNATIONAL, INC.

YIELD 0.9%
P/E RATIO 23.1

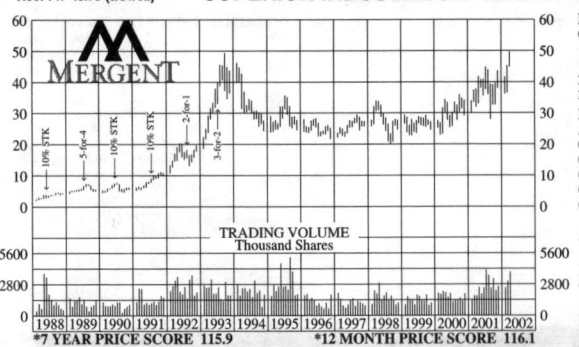

TRADING VOLUME
Thousand Shares

1988 1989 1990 1991 1992 1993 1994 1995 1996 1997 1998 1999 2000 2001 2002

*7 YEAR PRICE SCORE 115.9   *12 MONTH PRICE SCORE 116.1
*NYSE COMPOSITE INDEX=100

INTERIM EARNINGS (Per Share):

Qtr.	Mar.	June	Sept.	Dec.
1998	0.46	0.44	0.28	0.71
1999	0.57	0.71	0.54	0.81
2000	0.70	0.83	0.66	0.85
2001	0.61	0.51	0.41	0.58

INTERIM DIVIDENDS (Per Share):

Amt.	Decl.	Ex.	Rec.	Pay.
0.10Q	3/21/01	4/04/01	4/06/01	4/20/01
0.11Q	5/11/01	6/27/01	6/29/01	7/13/01
0.11Q	7/30/01	10/03/01	10/05/01	10/19/01
0.11Q	10/19/01	1/09/02	1/11/02	1/25/02
0.11Q	3/22/02	4/03/02	4/05/02	4/19/02

Indicated div.: $0.44 (Div. Reinv. Plan)

CAPITALIZATION (12/31/01):

	($000)	(%)
Deferred Income Tax	8,780	1.9
Common & Surplus	448,741	98.1
Total	457,521	100.0

DIVIDEND ACHIEVER STATUS:

Rank: 41   10-Year Growth Rate: 17.05%
Total Years of Dividend Growth: 16

RECENT DEVELOPMENTS: For the year ended 12/31/01, net income fell 30.8% to $55.4 million versus $79.9 million in 2000. Results for 2001 included the write-off of non-recurring start-up costs of $9.7 million related to the launch of SUP's aluminum suspension components business and its new, second aluminum wheel manufacturing facility in Chihuahua, Mexico. Net sales decreased slightly to $643.4 million from $644.9 million a year earlier. Operating income fell 37.4% to $76.1 million.

PROSPECTS: On 1/23/02, the Company announced the award of several new and replacement programs under a long-term supply agreement which has now been finalized and signed with General Motors Corporation. Separately, on 11/12/01, the Company announced it will be the aluminum road wheel supplier for the 2002 model year Chrysler PT Cruiser. Going forward, earnings should begin to benefit from the Company's new aluminum automotive suspension business.

BUSINESS

SUPERIOR INDUSTRIES INTERNATIONAL, INC. designs and manufactures automotive parts and accessories for original equipment manufacturers (OEMs) and for the automotive aftermarket. The OEM cast aluminum road wheels, the Company's primary product, are sold to General Motors, Ford, Daimler-Chrysler, BMW, Volkswagen, Audi, Land Rover, MG Rover Toyota, Mazda, Mitsubishi, Nissan and Isuzu, for factory installation as optional or standard equipment on selected vehicle models. In addition, the Company manufactures and distributes aftermarket accessories including bed mats, exhaust extensions, license frames, lug nuts, springs and suspension products, steering wheel covers and other miscellaneous accessories. The Company operates manufacturing facilities in the U.S., Mexico and Hungary.

ANNUAL FINANCIAL DATA

	12/31/01	12/31/00	12/31/99	12/31/98	12/31/97	12/31/96	12/31/95
Earnings Per Share	② 2.10	① 3.04	2.62	1.88	1.96	1.63	1.78
Cash Flow Per Share	3.18	4.07	3.67	2.84	2.92	2.58	2.70
Tang. Book Val. Per Share	17.30	15.45	13.35	11.42	10.30	8.87	7.89
Dividends Per Share	0.42	0.38	0.34	0.30	0.26	0.22	0.19
Dividend Payout %	20.0	12.5	13.0	16.0	13.3	13.5	10.7
INCOME STATEMENT (IN THOUSANDS):							
Total Revenues	643,395	644,899	571,782	539,431	549,131	504,241	521,997
Costs & Expenses	538,901	496,474	438,051	432,387	434,030	395,129	400,449
Depreciation & Amort.	28,388	26,920	28,523	26,698	26,917	27,330	27,716
Operating Income	76,106	121,505	105,208	80,346	88,184	81,782	93,832
Net Interest Inc./(Exp.)	4,048	7,323	5,451	4,287	2,170	d326	d2,182
Income Before Income Taxes	84,189	122,510	108,518	80,801	86,208	74,071	84,918
Income Taxes	28,835	42,573	37,710	28,482	30,819	27,221	31,854
Net Income	② 55,354	① 79,937	70,808	52,319	55,389	46,850	53,064
Cash Flow	83,742	106,857	99,331	79,017	82,306	74,180	80,780
Average Shs. Outstg.	26,361	26,255	27,056	27,818	28,221	28,798	29,895
BALANCE SHEET (IN THOUSANDS):							
Cash & Cash Equivalents	106,839	93,503	108,081	86,566	73,693	42,103	11,179
Total Current Assets	280,271	245,579	263,740	235,886	199,846	164,080	142,659
Net Property	228,181	218,713	163,113	158,194	147,989	161,670	177,538
Total Assets	540,838	491,664	460,468	427,430	382,679	357,590	341,770
Total Current Liabilities	71,137	75,022	86,847	91,111	65,415	76,369	81,746
Long-Term Obligations	…	…	340	673	1,344	1,940	5,814
Net Stockholders' Equity	448,741	399,319	353,086	312,034	287,416	251,111	229,153
Net Working Capital	209,134	170,557	176,893	144,775	134,431	87,711	60,913
Year-end Shs. Outstg.	25,933	25,840	26,454	27,312	27,902	28,324	29,029
STATISTICAL RECORD:							
Operating Profit Margin %	11.8	18.8	18.4	14.9	16.1	16.2	18.0
Net Profit Margin %	8.6	12.4	12.4	9.7	10.1	9.3	10.2
Return on Equity %	12.3	20.0	20.1	16.8	19.3	18.7	23.2
Return on Assets %	10.2	16.3	15.4	12.2	14.5	13.1	15.5
Debt/Total Assets %	…	…	0.1	0.2	0.4	0.5	1.7
Price Range	44.85-28.00	36.00-22.94	29.38-22.75	33.88-20.06	29.50-22.13	28.38-21.63	35.75-23.88
P/E Ratio	21.4-13.3	11.8-7.5	11.2-8.7	18.0-10.7	15.1-11.3	17.4-13.3	20.1-13.4
Average Yield %	1.2	1.3	1.3	1.1	1.0	0.9	0.6

Statistics are as originally reported. ① Incl. non-recurr. chrg. $2.5 mill. ② Incl. non-recurr. start-up chrg. of $9.7 mill.

OFFICERS:
L. L. Borick, Chmn., Pres.
R. J. Ornstein, V.P., C.F.O.
D. L. Levine, Corp. Sec., Treas.

INVESTOR CONTACT: Shareholder Relations, (818) 902-2701

PRINCIPAL OFFICE: 7800 Woodley Avenue, Van Nuys, CA 91406

TELEPHONE NUMBER: (818) 781-4973
FAX: (818) 780-3500
WEB: www.superiorindustries.com
NO. OF EMPLOYEES: 6,000 (approx.)
SHAREHOLDERS: 990 (approx.)
ANNUAL MEETING: In May
INCORPORATED: DE, June, 1969; reincorp., CA, June, 1994

INSTITUTIONAL HOLDINGS:
No. of Institutions: 152
Shares Held: 17,765,258
% Held: 68.6

INDUSTRY: Motor vehicle parts and accessories (SIC: 3714)

TRANSFER AGENT(S): Registrar and Transfer Company, Cranford, NJ

SUPERVALU INC.

YIELD 2.2%
P/E RATIO 16.8

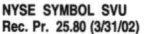

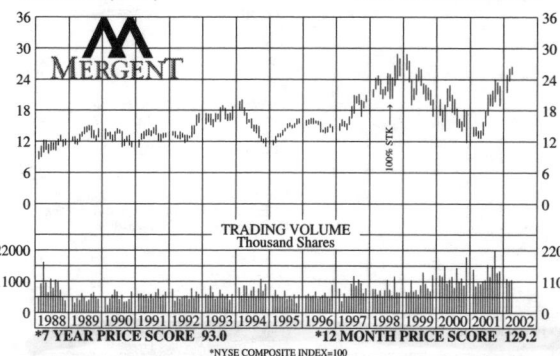

TRADING VOLUME
Thousand Shares

*7 YEAR PRICE SCORE 93.0   *12 MONTH PRICE SCORE 129.2
*NYSE COMPOSITE INDEX=100

INTERIM EARNINGS (Per Share):

Qtr.	May	Aug.	Nov.	Feb.
1998-99	0.43	0.33	0.37	0.45
1999-00	0.55	0.37	0.42	0.52
2000-01	0.53	0.43	0.36	d0.70
2001-02	0.45	0.39	0.44	0.26

INTERIM DIVIDENDS (Per Share):

Amt.	Decl.	Ex.	Rec.	Pay.
0.14Q	6/27/01	8/29/01	9/01/01	9/17/01
0.14Q	10/10/01	11/29/01	12/03/01	12/17/01
0.14Q	12/12/01	2/27/02	3/01/02	3/15/02
0.14Q	4/10/02	5/30/02	6/03/02	6/17/02

Indicated div.: $0.56 (Div. Reinv. Plan)

CAPITALIZATION (2/24/01):

	($000)	(%)
Long-Term Debt	1,444,376	37.7
Capital Lease Obligations..	564,098	14.7
Deferred Income Tax	29,656	0.8
Common & Surplus	1,793,495	46.8
Total	3,831,625	100.0

DIVIDEND ACHIEVER STATUS:
Rank: 235   10-Year Growth Rate: 4.87%
Total Years of Dividend Growth: 29

RECENT DEVELOPMENTS: For the fiscal year ended 2/23/02, net earnings totaled $205.5 million versus $82.0 million the year before. Results included after-tax restructuring and other charges of $35.2 million and $153.9 million in fiscal 2002 and fiscal 2001, respectively. Net sales declined 9.9% to $20.91 billion from $23.19 billion a year earlier. Food distribution net sales dropped 17.9% to $11.36 billion from $13.84 billion the previous year. Retail food net sales rose 2.1% to $9.55 billion from $9.35 billion in the prior year.

PROSPECTS: On 4/3/02, the Company announced that it has reached an agreement to acquire Deal$ - Nothing Over a Dollar, LLC, a 45-store general merchandise retailer with annual revenues of about $75.00 million. The acquisition, which is expected to be completed in May 2002, should help accelerate expansion of SVU's Save-A-Lot retail food operations. In fiscal 2003, the Company plans to open between 10 and 15 price superstores and approximately 150 new Save-A-Lot food stores, including licensed locations.

BUSINESS

SUPERVALU INC. is a major food retailer and distributor to independently-owned retail food stores. The Company operates three principal store formats at retail and sells food and non-food products at wholesale. As of 2/23/02, SVU operated 998 Save-A-Lot limited assortment stores, including 764 licensed Save-A-Lot locations, 202 price superstores under the Cub Foods, Shop 'n Save, Shoppers Food Warehouse, Metro and bigg's banners, and 60 other supermarkets, including Farm Fresh, Scott's Foods, and Hornbachers stores. Additionally, SVU is the primary supplier to approximately 2,750 supermarkets and mass merchandisers, as well as 31 of SVU's franchised Cub Foods locations, while serving as a secondary supplier to about 1,500 stores.

ANNUAL FINANCIAL DATA

	2/24/01	2/26/00	2/27/99	2/28/98	2/22/97	2/24/96	2/25/95
Earnings Per Share	④ 0.62	③ 1.87	1.57	② 1.83	1.30	1.22	① 0.31
Cash Flow Per Share	3.24	4.06	3.45	3.64	3.03	2.82	1.70
Tang. Book Val. Per Share	1.64	1.58	6.09	5.80	6.06	5.27	4.79
Dividends Per Share	0.55	0.54	0.53	0.51	0.49	0.48	0.46
Dividend Payout %	87.9	28.9	33.4	27.9	38.1	39.3	149.1

INCOME STATEMENT (IN MILLIONS):

Total Revenues	23,194.3	20,339.1	17,420.5	17,201.4	16,551.9	16,486.3	16,563.8
Costs & Expenses	22,500.3	19,470.9	16,772.7	16,565.9	15,939.3	15,900.5	16,255.2
Depreciation & Amort.	348.8	285.3	229.6	230.1	232.1	219.1	198.7
Operating Income	345.2	582.8	418.2	405.4	380.5	366.8	109.8
Net Interest Inc./(Exp.)	d190.8	d135.4	d101.9	d114.0	d120.7	d116.7	d111.3
Income Before Income Taxes	154.4	447.5	316.3	384.8	280.5	267.7	15.9
Income Taxes	72.4	204.5	124.9	154.0	105.5	101.3	cr27.4
Equity Earnings/Minority Int.	...	...	...	93.4	20.7	17.6	17.4
Net Income	④ 82.0	③ 242.9	191.3	② 230.8	175.0	166.4	① 43.3
Cash Flow	430.7	528.3	421.0	460.8	407.1	385.5	242.1
Average Shs. Outstg. (000)	132,829	130,090	121,961	126,550	134,510	136,554	142,776

BALANCE SHEET (IN MILLIONS):

Cash & Cash Equivalents	10.4	10.9	7.6	6.1	6.5	5.2	4.8
Total Current Assets	2,091.7	2,177.6	1,582.5	1,612.1	1,600.8	1,553.7	1,646.3
Net Property	2,232.8	2,168.2	1,699.0	1,589.6	1,648.5	1,600.2	1,571.3
Total Assets	6,407.2	6,495.4	4,265.9	4,093.0	4,283.3	4,183.5	4,305.1
Total Current Liabilities	2,341.2	2,509.6	1,521.9	1,457.2	1,369.1	1,326.7	1,447.1
Long-Term Obligations	2,008.5	1,953.7	1,246.3	1,260.7	1,420.6	1,445.6	1,459.8
Net Stockholders' Equity	1,793.5	1,821.5	1,305.6	1,201.9	1,307.4	1,216.2	1,193.2
Net Working Capital	d249.5	d332.0	60.6	154.9	231.7	227.0	199.2
Year-end Shs. Outstg. (000)	132,374	134,662	120,109	120,368	133,764	134,886	140,348

STATISTICAL RECORD:

Operating Profit Margin %	1.5	2.9	2.4	2.4	2.3	2.2	0.7
Net Profit Margin %	0.4	1.2	1.1	1.3	1.1	1.0	0.3
Return on Equity %	4.6	13.3	14.7	19.2	13.4	13.7	3.6
Return on Assets %	1.3	3.7	4.5	5.6	4.1	4.0	1.0
Debt/Total Assets %	31.3	30.1	29.2	30.8	33.2	34.6	33.9
Price Range	22.88-11.75	28.88-16.81	28.94-20.19	21.09-14.06	16.50-13.56	16.44-11.25	20.06-11.00
P/E Ratio	36.9-18.9	15.4-9.0	18.4-12.9	11.6-7.7	12.7-10.4	13.5-9.2	65.8-36.1
Average Yield %	3.1	2.3	2.1	2.9	3.3	3.5	2.9

Statistics are as originally reported. Adj. for 100% stk. div., 8/98. ① Incl. $244 mil total non-recur. chg. ② Incl. $53.7 mil ($0.43/sh.) non-recur net gain from sale of int. in ShopKo Stores, Inc. ③ Incl. $163.7 pre-tax gain on sale of Hazelwood Farms Bakeries & incl. $103.6 pre-tax restructuring chg. ④ Incl. $153.9 mil ($1.16/sh.) after-tax restr. & other chgs.

OFFICERS:
J. Noddle, Chmn., Pres., C.E.O.
P. K. Knous, Exec. V.P., C.F.O.

INVESTOR CONTACT: Yolanda Scharton, (952) 828-4540

PRINCIPAL OFFICE: 11840 Valley View Road, Eden Prairie, MN 55344

TELEPHONE NUMBER: (952) 828-4000
FAX: (952) 828-8998
WEB: www.supervalu.com
NO. OF EMPLOYEES: 57,800 (approx.)
SHAREHOLDERS: 7,265
ANNUAL MEETING: In May
INCORPORATED: DE, Dec., 1925

INSTITUTIONAL HOLDINGS:
No. of Institutions: 292
Shares Held: 101,135,067
% Held: 76.4
INDUSTRY: Groceries, general line (SIC: 5141)
TRANSFER AGENT(S): Wells Fargo Shareowner Services, St. Paul, MN

SUSQUEHANNA BANCSHARES, INC.

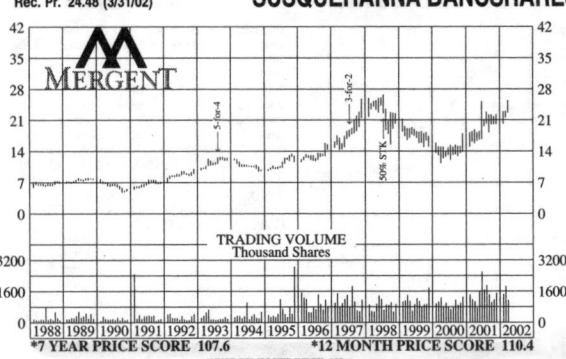

INTERIM EARNINGS (Per Share):

Qtr.	Mar.	June	Sept.	Dec.
1998	0.30	0.31	0.32	0.33
1999	0.32	0.33	0.40	0.12
2000	0.34	0.35	0.36	0.35
2001	0.32	0.36	0.36	0.37

INTERIM DIVIDENDS (Per Share):

Amt.	Decl.	Ex.	Rec.	Pay.
0.19Q	4/18/01	4/26/01	4/30/01	5/21/01
0.19Q	7/18/01	7/26/01	7/30/01	8/20/01
0.20Q	10/17/01	10/26/01	10/30/01	11/19/01
0.20Q	1/16/02	1/25/02	1/29/02	2/20/02
0.20Q	4/17/02	4/25/02	4/29/02	5/20/02

Indicated div.: $0.80 (Div. Reinv. Plan)

CAPITALIZATION (12/31/01):

	($000)	(%)
Total Deposits	3,484,331	85.3
Long-Term Debt	105,000	2.6
Common & Surplus	493,536	12.1
Total	4,082,867	100.0

TRADING VOLUME Thousand Shares

*7 YEAR PRICE SCORE 107.6   *12 MONTH PRICE SCORE 110.4

*NYSE COMPOSITE INDEX=100

DIVIDEND ACHIEVER STATUS:
Rank: 182   10-Year Growth Rate: 7.52%
Total Years of Dividend Growth: 31

RECENT DEVELOPMENTS: For the year ended 12/31/01, net income increased 1.4% to $55.7 million compared with $55.0 million the previous year. Results for 2000 included a pre-tax restructuring gain of $900,000. Net interest income improved 4.4% to $172.2 million from $165.0 million a year earlier. Net interest margin improved to 3.91% from $3.83% in 2000. Total interest income declined 3.4% to $341.3 million, while total interest expense decreased 10.3% to $169.1 million. Provision for loan and lease

losses grew 96.2% to $7.3 million. Non-interest income advanced 13.7% to $84.2 million, while non-interest expense rose 7.8% to $167.8 million. Looking ahead, diluted earnings per share are expected to range from $1.55 to $1.60 in 2002. Separately, during December 2001, SUSQ's subsidiary, Farmers & Merchants Bank and Trust, acquired four branches in West Virginia from F&M Bank-West Virginia, Inc., which included $54.0 million in loans and $69.0 million in deposits.

BUSINESS

SUSQUEHANNA BANCSHARES, INC. is a multi-state financial services holding company composed of nine banks, two leasing companies, a credit life reinsurance company, a trust and investment company, and an asset management company. The Company's banking subsidiaries provide financial services at 144 locations in the mid-Atlantic region. As of 12/31/01, the Company had assets of $5.05 billion, loans and leases of $3.52 billion and deposits of $3.48 billion. On 2/1/00, SUSQ acquired Boston Service Company, Inc., a provider of consumer automobile financing services. On 3/3/00, SUSQ acquired Valley Forge Asset Management Corp., an asset management company.

ANNUAL FINANCIAL DATA

	12/31/01	12/31/00	12/31/99	12/31/98	12/31/97	12/31/96	12/31/95
Earnings Per Share	1.41	1.40	1.17	1.26	1.20	1.01	0.99
Tang. Book Val. Per Share	12.54	11.56	10.92	10.91	10.25	9.87	9.38
Dividends Per Share	0.77	0.70	0.62	0.57	0.55	0.52	0.49
Dividend Payout %	54.6	50.0	53.0	45.2	45.6	51.3	49.3
INCOME STATEMENT (IN MILLIONS)							
Total Interest Income	341.3	353.4	299.8	292.8	264.1	231.8	189.8
Total Interest Expense	169.1	188.5	138.8	138.6	118.4	103.1	82.6
Net Interest Income	172.2	165.0	160.9	154.2	145.7	128.7	107.2
Provision for Loan Losses	7.3	3.7	7.2	5.2	4.6	4.6	5.0
Non-Interest Income	84.2	74.0	40.0	30.9	23.8	21.3	16.1
Non-Interest Expense	167.8	155.6	131.9	113.2	106.0	100.8	80.9
Income Before Taxes	81.3	79.7	61.8	66.7	58.8	44.6	37.4
Net Income	55.7	55.0	43.4	45.6	40.2	30.0	26.0
Average Shs. Outstg. (000)	39,593	39,365	37,137	36,179	33,495	29,612	26,267
BALANCE SHEET (IN MILLIONS)							
Cash & Due from Banks	149.2	129.1	144.5	105.3	97.3	98.5	87.1
Securities Avail. for Sale	88.6	59.0	17.7	76.0	41.9	96.1	92.1
Total Loans & Leases	3,519.5	3,433.6	2,995.2	2,773.6	2,569.6	2,173.1	1,713.0
Allowance for Credit Losses	37.7	37.2	37.2	35.2	34.6	31.9	27.6
Net Loans & Leases	3,481.8	3,396.4	2,957.9	2,738.4	2,535.1	2,141.1	1,685.4
Total Assets	5,051.1	4,792.9	4,310.6	4,064.8	3,524.9	3,038.5	2,586.2
Total Deposits	3,484.3	3,249.0	3,180.5	3,124.3	2,851.2	2,493.5	2,116.0
Long-Term Obligations	105.0	100.0	95.0	370.2	181.9	115.4	86.3
Total Liabilities	4,557.6	4,339.4	3,906.2	3,673.6	3,178.1	2,745.8	2,312.8
Net Stockholders' Equity	493.5	453.4	404.4	391.2	346.7	292.7	273.4
Year-end Shs. Outstg. (000)	39,344	39,221	37,022	35,857	33,833	29,657	29,135
STATISTICAL RECORD:							
Return on Equity %	11.3	12.1	10.7	11.6	11.6	10.2	9.5
Return on Assets %	1.1	1.1	1.0	1.1	1.1	1.0	1.0
Equity/Assets %	9.8	9.5	9.4	9.6	9.8	9.6	10.6
Non-Int. Exp./Tot. Inc. %	65.4	65.1	65.6	61.2	62.6	67.2	65.6
Price Range	37.99-15.00	17.98-11.25	21.25-14.88	26.75-15.50	25.83-14.33	15.89-11.56	13.45-9.56
P/E Ratio	26.9-10.6	12.8-8.0	18.2-12.7	21.2-12.3	21.5-11.9	15.7-11.4	13.6-9.6
Average Yield %	2.9	4.8	3.4	2.7	2.7	3.8	4.3

Statistics are as originally reported. Adj. for stk. splits: 50% div., 7/1/98; 3-for-2, 7/2/97
⊡ Incl. restructuring chrg. of $7.4 million, 12/99; gain of $900,000, 12/00

QUARTERLY DATA

(12/31/01)($000)	Rev.	Inc.
1st Quarter	86,393	12,496
2nd Quarter	84,833	14,208
3rd Quarter	86,683	14,337
4th Quarter	83,386	14,675

OFFICERS:
R. S. Bolinger, Chmn.
W. J. Reuter, Pres., C.E.O.
D. K. Hostetter, Exec. V.P., C.F.O., Treas.

INVESTOR CONTACT: Alison van Harskamp, (717) 625-6260

PRINCIPAL OFFICE: 26 North Cedar St., Lititz, PA 17543

TELEPHONE NUMBER: (717) 626-4721
FAX: (717) 626-1874
WEB: www.susqbanc.com
NO. OF EMPLOYEES: 1,635 full-time; 308 part-time
SHAREHOLDERS: 6,298 (record)
ANNUAL MEETING: In May
INCORPORATED: PA, Sept., 1982

INSTITUTIONAL HOLDINGS:
No. of Institutions: 111
Shares Held: 13,110,457
% Held: 33.3

INDUSTRY: National commercial banks
(SIC: 6021)

TRANSFER AGENT(S): The Bank of New York, New York, NY

SYNOVUS FINANCIAL CORPORATION

YIELD 1.9%
P/E RATIO 28.5

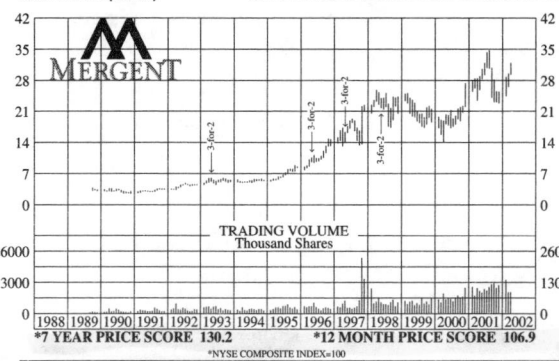

INTERIM EARNINGS (Per Share):

Qtr.	Mar.	June	Sept.	Dec.
1998	0.15	0.17	0.18	0.20
1999	0.18	0.19	0.21	0.22
2000	0.22	0.22	0.23	0.26
2001	0.25	0.26	0.27	0.29

INTERIM DIVIDENDS (Per Share):

Amt.	Decl.	Ex.	Rec.	Pay.
0.128Q	5/15/01	6/19/01	6/21/01	7/02/01
0.128Q	8/29/01	9/18/01	9/20/01	10/01/01
0.128Q	12/10/01	12/18/01	12/20/01	1/02/02
0.147Q	2/27/02	3/19/02	3/21/02	4/01/02

Indicated div.: $0.59 (Div. Reinv. Plan)

CAPITALIZATION (12/31/01):

	($000)	(%)
Total Deposits	12,146,198	81.0
Long-Term Debt	1,052,943	7.0
Minority Interest	98,638	0.7
Common & Surplus	1,694,946	11.3
Total	14,992,725	100.0

DIVIDEND ACHIEVER STATUS:
Rank: 25   10-Year Growth Rate: 20.39%
Total Years of Dividend Growth: 25

TRADING VOLUME
Thousand Shares

1988 1989 1990 1991 1992 1993 1994 1995 1996 1997 1998 1999 2000 2001 2002

*7 YEAR PRICE SCORE 130.2   ***12 MONTH PRICE SCORE 106.9**
*NYSE COMPOSITE INDEX=100

RECENT DEVELOPMENTS: For the year ended 12/31/01, net income increased 18.7% to $311.6 million from $262.6 million in the prior year. Net interest income rose 12.0% to $629.8 million from $562.3 million in 2000. Provision for losses on loans climbed 16.5% to $51.7 million the year before. Total non-interest income advanced 12.5% to $937.7 million from $833.5 million, while total non-interest expense grew 9.0% to $1.01 billion from $923.3 million.

PROSPECTS: Earnings per share growth for 2002 and 2003 is expected to be in the 15.0% to 18.0% range. Separately, on 12/14/01, the Company announced that it has completed the acquisition of FABP Bancshares, Inc., of Pensacola, Florida. FABP is a one-bank holding company that owns First American Bank of Pensacola, N.A., which has $305.0 million in assets. The acquisition has more than doubled the assets of SNV's Bank of Pensacola to $607.0 million.

BUSINESS

SYNOVUS FINANCIAL CORPO-RATION, with assets of $16.66 billion as of 12/31/01, is a registered bank holding company engaged in two principal business segments: banking, which encompasses commercial banking, trust services, mortgage banking, credit card banking and certain securities brokerage operations, and bankcard data processing. SNV has 38 wholly-owned subsidiaries located in Georgia, Alabama, Florida and South Carolina, offering a wide range of commercial banking services, including accepting customary types of demand and savings deposits; making individual, consumer, commercial, installment, first and second mortgage loans; and other fiduciary services. As of 12/31/01, SNV owned 81.1% of Total System Services, Inc.®, an electronic transaction processing company.

ANNUAL FINANCIAL DATA

	12/31/01	12/31/00	12/31/99	12/31/98	12/31/97	12/31/96	12/31/95
Earnings Per Share	1.05	0.92	0.80	0.70	0.62	0.53	0.45
Tang. Book Val. Per Share	5.75	4.98	4.35	3.96	3.44	2.99	2.66
Dividends Per Share	0.49	0.42	0.34	0.28	0.23	0.19	0.15
Dividend Payout %	46.9	45.6	42.9	40.0	36.9	35.0	34.4
INCOME STATEMENT (IN MILLIONS)							
Total Interest Income	1,130.9	1,097.8	888.0	769.2	725.7	663.3	615.8
Total Interest Expense	501.1	535.5	374.7	328.7	313.3	288.4	273.9
Net Interest Income	629.8	562.3	513.3	440.5	412.4	374.9	341.9
Provision for Loan Losses	51.7	44.3	34.0	26.7	32.3	31.8	25.8
Non-Interest Income	937.7	833.5	739.8	562.0	489.2	425.4	340.8
Non-Interest Expense	1,006.0	923.3	856.5	673.6	601.3	541.6	472.1
Income Before Taxes	490.0	411.7	349.3	291.6	258.9	219.3	179.5
Equity Earnings/Minority Int.	d19.9	d16.5	d13.2	d10.6	d9.1	d7.6	d5.3
Net Income	311.6	262.6	225.3	187.1	165.2	139.6	114.6
Average Shs. Outstg. (000)	295,850	286,882	283,355	269,151	265,665	261,299	258,647
BALANCE SHEET (IN MILLIONS)							
Cash & Due from Banks	648.2	558.1	466.5	348.4	388.1	405.0	...
Securities Avail. for Sale	2,088.3	1,807.0	1,716.7	1,514.1	1,325.0	1,276.1	1,106.3
Total Loans & Leases	12,439.6	10,768.3	9,077.5	7,420.5	6,615.6	6,075.5	5,528.8
Allowance for Credit Losses	192.5	164.3	136.8	119.4	108.8	104.9	96.2
Net Loans & Leases	12,247.1	10,604.0	8,940.7	7,301.2	6,506.8	5,970.5	5,432.6
Total Assets	16,657.9	14,908.1	12,547.0	10,498.0	9,260.3	8,612.3	7,545.8
Total Deposits	12,146.2	11,161.7	9,440.1	8,542.8	7,707.9	7,203.0	6,727.9
Long-Term Obligations	1,052.9	840.9	318.6	127.0	7.2	97.3	106.8
Total Liabilities	14,963.0	13,490.9	11,320.3	9,426.4	8,237.7	7,828.6	7,234.0
Net Stockholders' Equity	1,694.9	1,417.2	1,226.7	1,070.6	903.7	783.8	693.6
Year-end Shs. Outstg. (000)	294,674	284,643	282,014	270,218	262,808	261,779	260,665
STATISTICAL RECORD:							
Return on Equity %	18.4	18.5	18.4	17.5	18.3	17.8	16.5
Return on Assets %	1.9	1.8	1.8	1.8	1.8	1.6	1.5
Equity/Assets %	10.2	9.5	9.8	10.2	9.8	9.1	9.2
Non-Int. Exp./Tot. Inc. %	64.2	66.2	68.4	67.3	66.7	67.7	69.2
Price Range	34.74-22.75	27.38-14.00	25.13-17.25	25.92-17.25	22.42-13.11	14.83-7.78	8.89-5.26
P/E Ratio	33.1-21.7	29.8-15.2	31.4-21.6	37.0-24.6	36.2-21.1	27.8-14.6	20.0-11.8
Average Yield %	1.7	2.0	1.6	1.3	1.3	1.7	2.2

Statistics are as originally reported. Adj. for stk. splits: 3-for-2, 5/98; 4/97 & 4/96.

OFFICERS:
J. H. Blanchard, Chmn., C.E.O.
J. D. Yancey, Pres., C.O.O.
T. J. Prescott, Exec. V.P., C.F.O.

INVESTOR CONTACT: Patrick A. Reynolds, Dir. of Inv. Rel., (706) 649-5220

PRINCIPAL OFFICE: 901 Front Avenue, P.O. Box 120, Columbus, GA 31902

TELEPHONE NUMBER: (706) 649-2401
FAX: (706) 641-6555
WEB: www.synovus.com

NO. OF EMPLOYEES: 10,166

SHAREHOLDERS: 66,060 (approx.)

ANNUAL MEETING: In Apr.

INCORPORATED: GA, June, 1972

INSTITUTIONAL HOLDINGS:
No. of Institutions: 241
Shares Held: 112,328,637
% Held: 38.1

INDUSTRY: National commercial banks (SIC: 6021)

TRANSFER AGENT(S): State Street Bank and Trust Company, Boston, MA

SYSCO CORPORATION

	YIELD	1.2%
	P/E RATIO	31.4

INTERIM EARNINGS (Per Share):

Qtr.	Sept.	Dec.	Mar.	June
1997-98	0.12	0.13	0.10	0.15
1998-99	0.13	0.13	0.11	0.18
1999-00	0.16	0.16	0.16	0.22
2000-01	0.21	0.21	0.21	0.26
2001-02	0.24	0.24	...	...

INTERIM DIVIDENDS (Per Share):

Amt.	Decl.	Ex.	Rec.	Pay.
0.07Q	2/09/01	4/04/01	4/06/01	4/27/01
0.07Q	5/11/01	7/03/01	7/06/01	7/27/01
0.07Q	9/12/01	10/03/01	10/05/01	10/26/01
0.09Q	11/09/01	1/02/02	1/04/02	1/25/02
0.09Q	2/08/02	4/03/02	4/05/02	4/26/02

Indicated div.: $0.36 (Div. Reinv. Plan)

CAPITALIZATION (6/30/01):

	($000)	(%)
Long-Term Debt	961,421	28.5
Deferred Income Tax	269,685	8.0
Common & Surplus	2,147,520	63.6
Total	3,378,626	100.0

TRADING VOLUME
Thousand Shares

*7 YEAR PRICE SCORE 154.9   *12 MONTH PRICE SCORE 110.0

*NYSE COMPOSITE INDEX=100

DIVIDEND ACHIEVER STATUS:
Rank: 14   10-Year Growth Rate: 23.11%
Total Years of Dividend Growth: 25

RECENT DEVELOPMENTS: For the 13 weeks ended 12/29/01, net earnings totaled $158.5 million, up 13.7% compared with $139.4 million in the corresponding prior-year period. Sales climbed 5.7% to $5.59 billion from $5.29 billion a year earlier. Cost of sales was $4.48 billion, or 80.2% of total sales, versus $4.25 billion, or 80.4% of total sales, the year before. Earnings before income taxes advanced 13.7% to $256.7 million from $225.8 million the previous year.

PROSPECTS: On 12/5/01, the Company signed a definitive agreement to acquire the SERCA foodservice operations of Sobeys Inc. for approximately $278.0 million. Toronto, Ontario-based SERCA, which reported 2001 sales of $1.44 billion, supplies about 100,000 food products, as well as foodservice supplies and equipment, to about 80,000 customers throughout Canada. The transaction is expected to be completed by the end of fiscal 2002.

BUSINESS

SYSCO CORPORATION is a major marketer and distributor of foodservice products. Included among its customers are about 370,000 restaurants, hotels, hospitals, schools and other institutions. The Company distributes entree items, dry and canned foods, fresh produce, beverages, dairy products and certain nonfood products, including paper products and cleaning supplies. Through its SYGMA Network, Inc. subsidiary, the Company serves pizza, chicken, steak and hamburgers to fast-food chains and other limited menu chain restaurants. SYY has three Canadian facilities located in Vancouver, Edmonton and Toronto. In fiscal 2001, the foodservice sales breakdown was: 64% restaurants; 11% hospitals and nursing homes; 6% schools and colleges; 5% hotels and motels; and 14% other.

ANNUAL FINANCIAL DATA

	6/30/01	7/1/00	7/3/99	6/27/98	6/28/97	6/29/96	7/1/95
Earnings Per Share	0.88	① 0.68	0.54	① 0.48	0.43	0.38	0.35
Cash Flow Per Share	1.27	1.01	0.84	0.74	0.65	0.58	0.52
Tang. Book Val. Per Share	2.07	1.90	1.71	1.57	1.67	1.70	1.57
Dividends Per Share	0.28	0.24	0.20	0.18	0.15	0.13	0.11
Dividend Payout %	31.8	35.3	37.0	37.4	35.3	34.2	31.9
INCOME STATEMENT (IN MILLIONS):							
Total Revenues	21,784.5	19,303.3	17,422.8	15,327.5	14,454.6	13,395.1	12,118.0
Costs & Expenses	20,497.7	18,272.6	16,550.1	14,555.3	13,752.0	12,756.5	11,533.3
Depreciation & Amort.	248.2	220.7	205.0	181.2	160.3	144.7	130.8
Operating Income	1,038.5	810.0	667.7	591.0	542.3	494.0	454.0
Net Interest Inc./(Exp.)	d71.8	d70.8	d72.8	d58.4	d46.5	d41.0	d38.6
Income Before Income Taxes	966.7	737.6	593.9	532.5	496.0	453.9	417.6
Income Taxes	369.7	284.0	231.6	207.7	193.4	177.0	165.8
Net Income	596.9	① 453.6	362.3	① 324.8	302.5	276.9	251.8
Cash Flow	845.1	674.3	567.3	506.1	462.8	421.6	382.6
Average Shs. Outstg. (000)	667,949	669,556	673,594	686,880	708,940	730,396	731,120
BALANCE SHEET (IN MILLIONS):							
Cash & Cash Equivalents	135.7	159.1	149.3	110.3	117.7	107.8	133.9
Total Current Assets	2,984.9	2,733.2	2,408.8	2,180.1	1,964.4	1,922.3	1,789.4
Net Property	1,518.6	1,344.7	1,227.7	1,151.1	1,058.4	990.6	896.1
Total Assets	5,468.5	4,814.0	4,096.6	3,780.2	3,436.6	3,325.4	3,097.2
Total Current Liabilities	2,089.9	1,782.9	1,427.5	1,324.2	1,113.8	1,037.5	932.6
Long-Term Obligations	961.4	1,023.6	997.7	867.0	685.6	581.7	541.6
Net Stockholders' Equity	2,147.5	1,761.6	1,427.2	1,356.8	1,400.5	1,474.7	1,403.6
Net Working Capital	895.0	950.3	981.2	855.9	850.6	884.8	856.7
Year-end Shs. Outstg. (000)	665,138	662,970	659,344	670,018	689,752	721,652	731,460
STATISTICAL RECORD:							
Operating Profit Margin %	4.8	4.2	3.8	3.9	3.8	3.7	3.7
Net Profit Margin %	2.7	2.4	2.1	2.1	2.1	2.1	2.1
Return on Equity %	27.8	25.8	25.4	23.9	21.6	18.8	17.9
Return on Assets %	10.9	9.4	8.8	8.6	8.8	8.3	8.1
Debt/Total Assets %	17.6	21.3	24.4	22.9	20.0	17.5	17.5
Price Range	30.12-21.75	30.44-13.06	20.56-12.47	14.34-9.97	11.81-7.31	9.06-6.91	8.16-6.22
P/E Ratio	34.2-24.7	44.8-19.2	38.1-23.1	30.2-21.0	27.8-17.2	23.8-18.2	23.6-18.0
Average Yield %	1.1	1.1	1.2	1.5	1.6	1.6	1.5

Statistics are as originally reported. Adj. for 2-for-1 stk. split, 12/00 & 3/98. ① Bef. $8.0 mil ($0.01/sh) chg. for acctg. adj., 2000; $28.1 mil ($0.04/sh), 1998.

OFFICERS:
C. H. Cotros, Chmn., C.E.O.
R. J. Schnieders, Pres., C.O.O.
J. K. Stubblefield, Exec. V.P.-Fin. & Admin.

INVESTOR CONTACT: Diane Day Sanders, (281) 584-1390

PRINCIPAL OFFICE: 1390 Enclave Pkwy., Houston, TX 77077-2099

TELEPHONE NUMBER: (281) 584-1390
FAX: (281) 584-1734
WEB: www.sysco.com

NO. OF EMPLOYEES: 43,000 (approx.)

SHAREHOLDERS: 15,870

ANNUAL MEETING: In Nov.

INCORPORATED: DE, May, 1969

INSTITUTIONAL HOLDINGS:
No. of Institutions: 583
Shares Held: 445,483,166
% Held: 67.0

INDUSTRY: Groceries, general line (SIC: 5141)

TRANSFER AGENT(S): Fleet National Bank, Canton, MA

T. ROWE PRICE GROUP, INC.

YIELD 1.6%
P/E RATIO 25.6

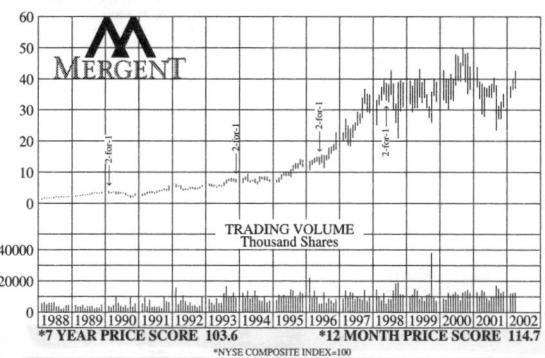

7 YEAR PRICE SCORE 103.6   **12 MONTH PRICE SCORE 114.7**

TRADING VOLUME
Thousand Shares

INTERIM EARNINGS (Per Share):

Qtr.	Mar.	June	Sept.	Dec.
1997	0.23	0.27	0.32	0.32
1998	0.32	0.34	0.33	0.35
1999	0.41	0.41	0.48	0.55
2000	0.58	0.54	0.53	0.43
2001	0.38	0.40	0.39	0.35

INTERIM DIVIDENDS (Per Share):

Amt.	Decl.	Ex.	Rec.	Pay.
0.15Q	3/12/01	3/23/01	3/27/01	4/06/01
0.15Q	6/07/01	6/20/01	6/22/01	7/06/01
0.15Q	9/06/01	9/19/01	9/21/01	10/05/01
0.16Q	12/13/01	12/24/01	12/27/01	1/11/02
0.16Q	3/08/02	3/19/02	3/21/02	4/05/02

Indicated div.: $0.64 (Div. Reinv. Plan)

CAPITALIZATION (12/31/01):

	($000)	(%)
Long-Term Debt	103,889	8.8
Common & Surplus	1,077,825	91.2
Total	1,181,714	100.0

DIVIDEND ACHIEVER STATUS:

Rank: 16   10-Year Growth Rate: 22.32%
Total Years of Dividend Growth: 15

RECENT DEVELOPMENTS: For the year ended 12/31/01, net income slid 27.2% to $195.9 million from $269.0 million in the prior year. Earnings included goodwill amortization of $28.9 million and $11.9 million in 2001 and 2000, respectively. Results for 2000 also included international investment research fees of $36.7 million. Total revenues fell 15.2% to $1.03 billion from $1.21 billion in 2000. Investment advisory fee income dropped 15.4% to $775.1 million. Administrative fee income slipped 7.3% to $219.6

million due to lower commissions from discount brokerage activities. Total operating expenses declined 7.6% to $696.9 million, reflecting the completion of several technology initiatives, cost-reduction actions initiated in 2001 and a reduction in advertising and promotion spending in this uncertain market environment. For the quarter ended 12/31/01, net income fell 18.9% to $45.0 million from $55.5 million in the corresponding prior-year period. Total revenues slipped 17.3% to $241.3 million.

BUSINESS

T. ROWE PRICE GROUP, INC. (formerly T. Rowe Price Associates, Inc.) and its subsidiaries serve as investment adviser to the T. Rowe Price Mutual Funds, other sponsored investment portfolios, and private accounts of other institutional and individual investors primarily located in the U.S., including defined benefit and defined contribution plans, endowments, foundations, trusts and other mutual funds. As of 12/28/00, T. Rowe Price Associates, Inc. shares were exchanged for shares of the Company effecting its structural change to a holding company. As of 12/31/01, total assets under management were $156.30 billion. TROW also provides investment advisory-related administrative services, including mutual fund transfer agent, accounting and shareholder services, participant recordkeeping and transfer agent services for defined contribution retirement plans, discount brokerage, and trust services.

REVENUES

(12/31/2001)	($000)	(%)
Investment Advisory Fees	775,074	75.4
Administrative Fees	219,628	21.4
Investment & Other	32,794	3.2
Total	1,027,496	100.0

ANNUAL FINANCIAL DATA

	12/31/01	12/31/00	12/31/99	12/31/98	12/31/97	12/31/96	12/31/95
Earnings Per Share	1.52	2.08	1.85	1.34	1.13	0.80	① 0.66
Cash Flow Per Share	2.14	2.49	2.11	1.59	1.35	0.94	0.79
Tang. Book Val. Per Share	3.35	2.42	6.41	5.11	4.12	3.00	2.39
Dividends Per Share	0.60	0.52	0.40	0.34	0.26	0.21	0.16
Dividend Payout %	39.5	25.0	21.6	25.4	23.0	26.4	24.2
INCOME STATEMENT (IN MILLIONS):							
Total Revenues	1,027.5	1,212.3	1,036.4	886.1	755.0	586.1	439.3
Costs & Expenses	616.4	700.4	589.0	540.7	461.2	380.5	282.3
Depreciation & Amort.	80.5	53.7	32.6	32.6	29.0	18.1	13.3
Operating Income	330.6	458.2	414.8	312.8	264.8	187.5	143.7
Income Before Income Taxes	330.6	458.2	414.8	312.8	264.8	187.5	143.7
Income Taxes	135.1	174.8	155.2	118.7	101.2	72.6	54.3
Equity Earnings/Minority Int.	0.4	d14.3	d20.2	d20.0	d19.2	d16.4	d12.9
Net Income	195.9	269.0	239.4	174.1	144.4	98.5	① 76.5
Cash Flow	276.4	322.7	272.0	206.8	173.4	116.5	89.7
Average Shs. Outstg. (000)	129,045	129,600	129,200	129,952	128,073	123,884	114,200
BALANCE SHEET (IN MILLIONS):							
Cash & Cash Equivalents	79.7	80.5	358.5	283.8	200.4	114.6	81.4
Total Current Assets	183.7	211.6	480.1	384.5	287.2	187.8	137.3
Net Property	241.8	255.7	210.3	166.6	142.5	101.2	60.2
Total Assets	1,313.1	1,469.5	998.0	796.8	646.1	478.8	365.3
Total Current Liabilities	106.0	154.8	149.9	128.9	109.6	95.0	69.5
Long-Term Obligations	103.9	312.3	17.7	...	...	...	...
Net Stockholders' Equity	1,077.8	991.1	770.2	614.3	486.7	345.7	274.2
Net Working Capital	77.8	56.7	330.2	254.7	177.6	92.8	67.8
Year-end Shs. Outstg. (000)	123,089	122,439	120,108	120,183	118,195	115,146	114,660
STATISTICAL RECORD:							
Operating Profit Margin %	32.2	37.8	40.0	35.3	35.1	32.0	32.7
Net Profit Margin %	19.1	22.2	23.1	19.7	19.1	16.8	17.4
Return on Equity %	18.2	27.1	31.1	28.3	29.7	28.5	27.9
Return on Assets %	14.9	18.3	24.0	21.9	22.4	20.6	20.9
Debt/Total Assets %	7.9	21.3	1.8	...	...	...	...
Price Range	43.94-23.44	49.94-30.06	43.25-25.88	42.88-20.88	36.88-18.25	22.81-10.66	14.19-6.75
P/E Ratio	28.9-15.4	24.0-14.5	23.4-14.0	32.0-15.6	32.6-16.1	28.7-13.4	21.5-10.2
Average Yield %	1.8	1.3	1.2	1.0	0.9	1.3	1.5

Statistics are as originally reported. Adj. for 2-for-1 stock splits: 4/98, 12/96. ① Bef. extraord. chrg. $1.0 mill.

OFFICERS:
G. A. Roche, Chmn., Pres.
J. S. Riepe, Vice-Chmn.
M. D. Testa, Vice-Chmn.
C. Wasiak, C.F.O.

INVESTOR CONTACT: Steve Norwitz, Investor Relations, (410) 345-2124

PRINCIPAL OFFICE: 100 East Pratt Street, Baltimore, MD 21202

TELEPHONE NUMBER: (410) 345-2000
FAX: (410) 752-3477
WEB: www.troweprice.com

NO. OF EMPLOYEES: 3,650 (approx.)

SHAREHOLDERS: 3,900 (approx.)

ANNUAL MEETING: In April

INCORPORATED: MD, Jan., 1947

INSTITUTIONAL HOLDINGS:
No. of Institutions: 265
Shares Held: 64,924,609
% Held: 52.5

INDUSTRY: Investment advice (SIC: 6282)

TRANSFER AGENT(S): Wells Fargo Shareowner Services, St. Paul, MN

TARGET CORPORATION

YIELD 0.6%
P/E RATIO 28.6

INTERIM EARNINGS (Per Share):

Qtr.	Apr.	July	Oct.	Jan.
1998-99	0.17	0.18	0.20	0.48
1999-00	0.21	0.25	0.26	0.53
2000-01	0.26	0.28	0.24	0.61
2001-02	0.28	0.30	0.20	0.73

INTERIM DIVIDENDS (Per Share):

Amt.	Decl.	Ex.	Rec.	Pay.
0.055Q	6/14/01	8/16/01	8/20/01	9/10/01
0.055Q	11/15/01	11/16/01	11/20/01	12/10/01
0.06Q	1/10/02	2/15/02	2/20/02	3/10/02
0.06Q	3/14/02	5/16/02	5/20/02	6/10/02

Indicated div.: $0.24 (Div. Reinv. Plan)

CAPITALIZATION (2/2/02):

	($000)	(%)
Long-Term Debt	8,088,000	50.7
Common & Surplus	7,860,000	49.3
Total	15,948,000	100.0

TRADING VOLUME
Thousand Shares

1988 1989 1990 1991 1992 1993 1994 1995 1996 1997 1998 1999 2000 2001 2002
*7 YEAR PRICE SCORE 145.4   *12 MONTH PRICE SCORE 117.1
*NYSE COMPOSITE INDEX=100

DIVIDEND ACHIEVER STATUS:
Rank: 207   10-Year Growth Rate: 6.25%
Total Years of Dividend Growth: 30

RECENT DEVELOPMENTS: For the 52 weeks ended 2/2/02, earnings totaled $1.37 billion, before a $6.0 million extraordinary charge for debt extinguishment, versus net earnings of $1.26 billion in the corresponding 53-week period the year before. Results for fiscal 2001 included a one-time pre-tax charge of $67.0 million related to restoring securitized accounts receivable to the financial statements. Total revenues climbed 8.1% to $39.89 billion, while comparable-store sales were up 2.7% year over year.

PROSPECTS: Strong sales and increased profitability at the Company's Target stores are more than offsetting sluggish sales at TGT's Mervyn's and Marshall Field's stores. Meanwhile, earnings growth from the Company's credit operations is being fueled by the national rollout of the Target Visa credit card. Looking ahead, TGT is projecting full-year 2002 earnings of $1.75 per share. The Company remains confident that it can deliver annual earnings per share growth of 15.0% over the long term.

BUSINESS

TARGET CORPORATION (formerly Dayton Hudson Corporation) is a diversified general merchandise retailer. As of 2/2/02, the Company operated 1,381 stores in 47 states including 1,053 Target stores, 264 Mervyn's stores and 64 Marshall Field's stores. Target is a national discount store chain offering low prices with stores selling hardlines and fashion softgoods; Mervyn's is a moderate-priced department store chain specializing in active and casual apparel and home softlines. Marshall Field's is a full-service, full-line department store chain offering moderate to better merchandise.

ANNUAL FINANCIAL DATA

	2/2/02	2/3/01	1/29/00	1/30/99	1/31/98	2/3/97	2/3/96
Earnings Per Share	[1] 1.51	1.38	[2] 1.27	[3] 1.02	[4] 0.85	[5] 0.52	0.33
Cash Flow Per Share	2.70	2.41	2.19	1.86	1.61	1.28	1.04
Tang. Book Val. Per Share	8.68	7.15	6.43	6.12	4.77	4.05	3.64
Dividends Per Share	0.22	0.21	0.20	0.18	0.17	0.15	0.14
Dividend Payout %	14.6	15.2	15.7	17.6	19.4	29.7	44.6

INCOME STATEMENT (IN MILLIONS):

Total Revenues	39,888.0	36,903.0	33,702.0	30,951.0	27,757.0	25,371.0	23,516.0
Costs & Expenses	36,129.0	33,485.0	30,519.0	28,217.0	25,322.0	23,496.0	21,979.0
Depreciation & Amort.	1,079.0	940.0	854.0	780.0	693.0	650.0	594.0
Operating Income	2,680.0	2,478.0	2,329.0	1,954.0	1,742.0	1,225.0	943.0
Net Interest Inc./(Exp.)	d464.0	d425.0	d393.0	d398.0	d416.0	d442.0	d442.0
Income Before Income Taxes	2,216.0	2,053.0	1,936.0	1,556.0	1,326.0	783.0	501.0
Income Taxes	842.0	789.0	751.0	594.0	524.0	309.0	190.0
Net Income	[1] 1,374.0	1,264.0	[2] 1,185.0	[3] 962.0	[4] 802.0	[5] 474.0	311.0
Cash Flow	2,453.0	2,204.0	2,039.0	1,742.0	1,495.0	1,124.0	905.0
Average Shs. Outstg. (000)	909,800	913,000	931,400	934,600	927,400	874,800	867,200

BALANCE SHEET (IN MILLIONS):

Cash & Cash Equivalents	499.0	356.0	220.0	255.0	211.0	201.0	175.0
Total Current Assets	9,648.0	7,304.0	6,483.0	6,005.0	5,561.0	5,440.0	4,955.0
Net Property	13,533.0	11,418.0	9,899.0	8,969.0	8,125.0	7,467.0	7,294.0
Total Assets	24,154.0	19,490.0	17,143.0	15,666.0	14,191.0	13,389.0	12,570.0
Total Current Liabilities	7,054.0	6,301.0	5,850.0	5,057.0	4,556.0	4,111.0	3,523.0
Long-Term Obligations	8,088.0	5,634.0	4,521.0	4,452.0	4,425.0	4,808.0	4,959.0
Net Stockholders' Equity	7,860.0	6,519.0	5,862.0	5,311.0	4,460.0	3,790.0	3,403.0
Net Working Capital	2,594.0	1,003.0	633.0	948.0	1,005.0	1,329.0	1,432.0
Year-end Shs. Outstg. (000)	905,200	911,683	911,682	823,618	875,600	868,000	864,000

STATISTICAL RECORD:

Operating Profit Margin %	6.7	6.7	6.9	6.3	6.3	4.8	4.0
Net Profit Margin %	3.4	3.4	3.5	3.1	2.9	1.9	1.3
Return on Equity %	17.5	19.4	20.2	18.1	18.0	12.5	9.1
Return on Assets %	5.7	6.5	6.9	6.1	5.7	3.5	2.5
Debt/Total Assets %	33.5	28.9	26.4	28.4	31.2	35.9	39.5
Price Range	41.74-26.00	39.19-21.63	38.50-25.03	27.13-15.72	18.50-8.97	10.16-5.76	6.71-5.27
P/E Ratio	27.6-17.2	28.4-15.7	30.3-19.7	26.6-15.4	21.8-10.6	19.6-11.1	20.6-16.2
Average Yield %	0.6	0.7	0.6	0.8	1.2	1.9	2.4

Statistics are as originally reported. Adj. for 2-for-1 stk. split, 7/00 & 4/98; 3-for-1 stk. split, 7/96. [1] Bef. $6 mil ($0.01/sh) extraord. chg. & incl. $67 mil pre-tax chg. [2] Bef. $41 mil ($0.05/sh) extraord. chg. [3] Bef. $27 mil ($0.03/sh) extraord. chg. [4] Bef. $51 mil ($0.06/sh) extraord. chg. & incl. $45 mil pre-tax gain. [5] Bef. $11 mil extraord. chg. & incl. $134 mil pretax chg.

OFFICERS:
R. J. Ulrich, Chmn., C.E.O.
G. L. Storch, Vice-Chmn.
D. A. Scovanner, Exec. V.P., C.F.O.
INVESTOR CONTACT: S.D. Kahn, V.P.-Inv. Rel., (612) 370-6736
PRINCIPAL OFFICE: 777 Nicollet Mall, Minneapolis, MN 55402-2055

TELEPHONE NUMBER: (612) 370-6948
FAX: (612) 370-5502
WEB: www.target.com
NO. OF EMPLOYEES: 252,000 (avg.)
SHAREHOLDERS: 15,773
ANNUAL MEETING: In May
INCORPORATED: MN, 1902

INSTITUTIONAL HOLDINGS:
No. of Institutions: 736
Shares Held: 758,103,336
% Held: 83.7

INDUSTRY: Variety stores (SIC: 5331)

TRANSFER AGENT(S): EquiServe, Jersey City, NJ

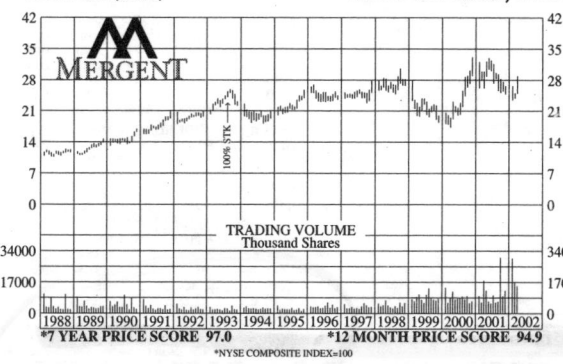

NYSE SYMBOL TE
Rec. Pr. 28.63 (3/31/02)

TECO ENERGY, INC.

YIELD	4.8%
P/E RATIO	12.8

INTERIM EARNINGS (Per Share):

Qtr.	Mar.	June	Sept.	Dec.
1998	0.23	0.44	0.54	0.31
1999	0.37	0.39	0.42	0.32
2000	0.42	0.46	0.65	0.44
2001	0.53	0.52	0.71	0.47

INTERIM DIVIDENDS (Per Share):

Amt.	Decl.	Ex.	Rec.	Pay.
0.335Q	1/18/01	1/30/01	2/01/01	2/15/01
0.345Q	4/18/01	4/27/01	5/01/01	5/15/01
0.345Q	7/18/01	7/30/01	8/01/01	8/15/01
0.345Q	10/17/01	10/30/01	11/01/01	11/15/01
0.345Q	1/16/02	1/30/02	2/01/02	2/15/02

Indicated div.: $1.38 (Div. Reinv. Plan)

CAPITALIZATION (12/31/01):

	($000)	(%)
Long-Term Debt	1,842,500	40.8
Deferred Income Tax	498,700	11.1
Redeemable Pfd. Stock	200,000	4.4
Common & Surplus	1,971,600	43.7
Total	4,512,800	100.0

DIVIDEND ACHIEVER STATUS:
Rank: 233   10-Year Growth Rate: 4.92%
Total Years of Dividend Growth: 42

TRADING VOLUME
Thousand Shares

*7 YEAR PRICE SCORE 97.0   *12 MONTH PRICE SCORE 94.9
*NYSE COMPOSITE INDEX=100

RECENT DEVELOPMENTS: For the year ended 12/31/01, net income advanced 21.0% to $303.7 million compared with $250.9 million in the previous year. Earnings for 2001 included an after-tax write-down of $6.1 million. Total income from regulated businesses improved 6.5% to $177.1 million, while total income from unregulated businesses jumped 49.6% to $126.6 million. Revenues increased 15.4% to $2.65 billion from $2.29 billion a year earlier. Income from operations increased 2.3% to $422.5 million from $413.1 million the year before.

PROSPECTS: For 2002, the Company is targeting earnings per share growth of at least 5.0%. The Company expects continued growth in its regulated electric and gas operations in Florida, where the service-based economy has only a small percentage of industrial load. TECO Coal should benefit from higher coal prices, while TECO Power Services anticipates higher earnings as a result of the escalation in capacity payments and lower interest expense at the San Jose Power Station.

BUSINESS

TECO ENERGY, INC. is a diversified, energy-related holding company. Tampa Electric, which accounted for 48.7% of TE's 2001 net income, generates, purchases, transmits, distributes and sells electric energy to West Central Florida. The Peoples Gas System division purchases, distributes and markets natural gas for residential, commercial, industrial and electric power generation customers in Florida. TECO Transport Corp. transports, stores and transfers coal and other bulk dry commodities. TECO Coal Corp. owns mineral rights, owns or operates surface and underground mines, coal processing and loading facilities in Kentucky, Tennessee and Virginia. TECO Power Services Corp. is a wholesale power supplier that owns and operates independent power projects. TECO Coalbed Methane, Inc. produces natural gas from coalbeds. TECO Solutions offers various services through Bosek, Gibson and Associates, Inc. and BCH Mechanical, Inc. TECO Propane Ventures represents the Company's 38.0% interest in US Propane.

ANNUAL FINANCIAL DATA

	12/31/01	12/31/00	12/31/99	12/31/98	12/31/97	12/31/96	12/31/95
Earnings Per Share	④2.24	③1.97	①②1.53	①②1.52	②1.61	1.71	1.60
Cash Flow Per Share	4.52	4.18	3.37	3.31	3.37	3.34	3.14
Tang. Book Val. Per Share	12.94	11.93	11.19	11.42	11.04	10.73	10.00
Dividends Per Share	1.37	1.33	1.28	1.23	1.17	1.10	1.05
Dividend Payout %	61.2	67.5	84.0	80.6	72.4	64.6	65.5
INCOME STATEMENT (IN MILLIONS):							
Total Revenues	2,648.6	2,295.1	1,983.0	1,958.1	1,862.3	1,473.0	1,392.3
Costs & Expenses	1,767.1	1,464.1	1,192.8	1,197.6	1,104.2	847.3	793.7
Depreciation & Amort.	307.7	277.4	241.3	236.1	231.3	190.6	179.6
Maintenance Exp.	151.3	140.0	125.3	128.9	114.2	92.2	101.3
Operating Income	422.5	413.6	423.6	395.5	412.6	342.9	317.7
Net Interest Inc./(Exp.)	d180.8	d166.9	d123.7	d104.3	d105.8	d86.9	d83.2
Income Taxes	cr10.1	18.5	87.0	81.0	94.7	71.4	59.1
Net Income	④303.7	③250.9	①②200.9	①②200.4	②211.4	200.7	186.1
Cash Flow	611.4	528.3	442.2	436.5	442.7	391.3	365.7
Average Shs. Outstg. (000)	135,400	126,300	131,200	131,700	131,200	117,200	116,500
BALANCE SHEET (IN MILLIONS):							
Gross Property	7,543.5	6,560.4	6,064.4	5,600.5	5,359.5	4,721.6	4,490.5
Accumulated Depreciation	2,705.2	2,590.3	2,436.6	2,292.9	2,123.0	1,765.0	1,616.2
Net Property	4,838.3	3,970.1	3,627.8	3,307.6	3,236.5	2,956.6	2,874.3
Total Assets	6,722.1	5,676.2	4,690.1	4,179.3	3,960.4	3,490.0	3,399.2
Long-Term Obligations	1,842.5	1,374.6	1,207.8	1,279.6	1,080.2	996.3	994.9
Net Stockholders' Equity	1,971.6	1,506.9	1,417.8	1,507.8	1,444.7	1,282.1	1,221.7
Year-end Shs. Outstg. (000)	139,600	126,300	126,700	132,000	130,900	117,600	116,700
STATISTICAL RECORD:							
Operating Profit Margin %	16.0	18.0	21.4	20.2	22.2	23.3	22.8
Net Profit Margin %	11.5	10.9	10.1	10.2	11.4	13.6	13.4
Net Inc./Net Property %	6.3	6.3	5.5	6.1	6.5	6.8	6.5
Net Inc./Tot. Capital %	6.7	7.1	6.4	6.1	7.1	7.6	7.3
Return on Equity %	15.4	16.7	14.2	13.3	14.6	15.7	15.2
Accum. Depr./Gross Prop. %	35.9	39.5	40.2	40.9	39.6	37.4	36.0
Price Range	32.97-24.75	33.19-17.25	28.00-18.38	30.63-24.75	28.00-22.75	27.00-23.00	25.75-20.00
P/E Ratio	14.7-11.0	16.8-8.8	18.3-12.0	20.1-16.3	17.4-14.1	15.8-13.4	16.1-12.5
Average Yield %	4.7	5.3	5.5	4.4	4.6	4.4	4.6

Statistics are as originally reported. ① Incl. non-recurr. chrg. $16.1 mill., 1999; $25.9 mill., 1998 ② Bef. disc. oper. loss $14.8 mill., 1999; gain $6.1 mill., 1998; loss $9.5 mill., 1997 ③ Incl. after-tax gain $8.3 mill. & nonrecurr. chrgs. $9.0 mill. ④ Incl. after-tax write-down of $6.1 mill.

OFFICERS:
R. D. Fagan, Chmn., Pres., C.E.O.
G. L. Gillette, Sr. V.P., Fin., C.F.O.

INVESTOR CONTACT: Mark N. Kane, Dir., Investor Relations, (813) 228-1772

PRINCIPAL OFFICE: 702 N. Franklin Street, Tampa, FL 33602

TELEPHONE NUMBER: (813) 228-4111
FAX: (813) 228-1670
WEB: www.tecoenergy.com
NO. OF EMPLOYEES: 6,315
SHAREHOLDERS: 22,989
ANNUAL MEETING: In April
INCORPORATED: FL, Jan., 1981

INSTITUTIONAL HOLDINGS:
No. of Institutions: 361
Shares Held: 59,058,962
% Held: 42.3

INDUSTRY: Electric services (SIC: 4911)

TRANSFER AGENT(S): EquiServe, LP, Providence, RI

TELEFLEX INC.

YIELD 1.2%
P/E RATIO 19.1

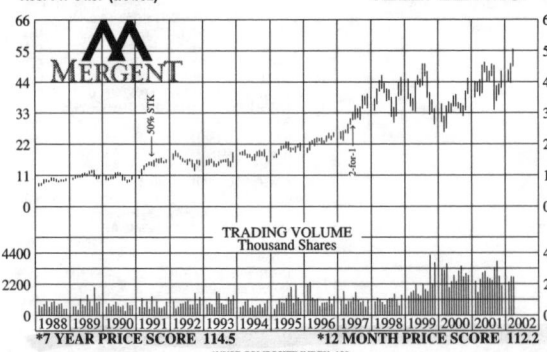

7 YEAR PRICE SCORE 114.5   **12 MONTH PRICE SCORE 112.2**
*NYSE COMPOSITE INDEX=100

INTERIM EARNINGS (Per Share):

Qtr.	Mar.	June	Sept.	Dec.
1997	0.45	0.49	0.36	0.56
1998	0.52	0.55	0.42	0.66
1999	0.60	0.67	0.49	0.71
2000	0.70	0.76	0.56	0.81
2001	0.77	0.79	0.56	0.74

INTERIM DIVIDENDS (Per Share):

Amt.	Decl.	Ex.	Rec.	Pay.
0.17Q	4/27/01	5/23/01	5/25/01	6/15/01
0.17Q	8/06/01	8/22/01	8/24/01	9/14/01
0.17Q	10/29/01	11/21/01	11/26/01	12/14/01
0.17Q	2/04/02	2/21/02	2/25/02	3/15/02

Indicated div.: $0.68 (Div. Reinv. Plan)

CAPITALIZATION (12/31/01):

	($000)	(%)
Long-Term Debt	228,180	22.7
Common & Surplus	778,143	77.3
Total	1,006,323	100.0

DIVIDEND ACHIEVER STATUS:

Rank: 89   10-Year Growth Rate: 12.97%
Total Years of Dividend Growth: 24

RECENT DEVELOPMENTS: For the year ended 12/31/01, net income climbed 2.8% to $112.3 million compared with $109.2 million in 2000. Revenues were $1.91 billion, up 8.0% from $1.76 billion in the prior year. Operating profit rose 5.1% to $188.2 million. Commercial products sales rose 5.6% to $908.2 million, while operating profit declined 3.6% to $83.8 million. Sales of aerospace products jumped 15.2% to $567.5 million, while medical products sales climbed 4.3% to $429.3 million.

PROSPECTS: On 1/21/02, TFX completed the acquisition of Autogastechniek Holland b.v., a manufacturer of alternative fuel systems and components for automobiles. The acquisition expands TFX's global presence in alternative fuel systems and related components. Separately, on 1/10/02, TFX acquired a 55.0% interest in Uniflex, Inc., a producer and seller of mechanical controls for the automobile industry in Japan. The new joint venture will be called Teleflex-NHK Automotive Co., Ltd.

BUSINESS

TELEFLEX INC. operates in three segments. Commercial Products (47.7% of 2001 sales and 40.5% of operating profit) designs and manufactures proprietary mechanical controls for the automotive market; mechanical, electrical and hydraulic controls, and electronics for the pleasure marine market; and proprietary products for fluid transfer and industrial applications. Medical Products (22.5%, 30.3%) manufactures and distributes a broad range of invasive disposable and reusable devices worldwide. Aerospace Products (29.8%, 29.2%) serves the aerospace and turbine engine markets. Its businesses design and manufacture precision controls and cargo systems for aviation; provide coating and repair services and manufactured components for users of both flight and land-based turbine engines.

ANNUAL FINANCIAL DATA

	12/31/01	12/31/00	12/26/99	12/27/98	12/28/97	12/29/96	12/31/95
Earnings Per Share	2.86	2.83	2.47	2.15	1.86	1.58	1.38
Cash Flow Per Share	5.21	4.83	4.22	3.71	3.13	2.65	2.43
Tang. Book Val. Per Share	19.99	18.01	15.85	14.21	12.49	11.30	10.28
Dividends Per Share	0.66	0.58	0.51	0.45	0.39	0.34	0.30
Dividend Payout %	23.1	20.5	20.4	20.7	20.8	21.5	21.8
INCOME STATEMENT (IN MILLIONS):							
Total Revenues	1,905.0	1,764.5	1,601.1	1,437.6	1,145.8	931.2	912.7
Costs & Expenses	1,624.4	1,508.1	1,373.2	1,235.7	977.0	791.8	782.7
Depreciation & Amort.	92.4	77.4	67.4	60.1	47.9	38.8	37.7
Operating Income	188.2	179.0	160.5	141.8	120.8	100.7	92.2
Net Interest Inc./(Exp.)	d28.5	d20.8	d17.7	d17.1	d14.4	d13.9	d18.6
Income Before Income Taxes	159.7	158.2	142.8	124.8	106.4	86.8	73.6
Income Taxes	47.4	49.0	47.5	42.2	36.3	29.6	24.7
Net Income	112.3	109.2	95.2	82.6	70.1	57.2	48.9
Cash Flow	204.7	186.6	162.6	142.7	118.0	95.9	86.6
Average Shs. Outstg. (000)	39,280	38,633	38,525	38,425	37,661	36,198	35,574
BALANCE SHEET (IN MILLIONS):							
Cash & Cash Equivalents	46.9	45.1	29.0	66.7	30.7	68.6	55.7
Total Current Assets	747.5	662.0	604.9	616.9	566.5	466.0	445.8
Net Property	565.7	489.5	465.9	431.8	364.0	291.8	271.8
Total Assets	1,635.0	1,401.3	1,263.4	1,215.9	1,079.2	857.9	785.2
Total Current Liabilities	495.4	383.9	329.4	311.5	294.9	196.7	193.2
Long-Term Obligations	228.2	220.6	246.2	275.6	237.6	195.9	196.8
Net Stockholders' Equity	778.1	690.4	602.6	534.5	463.8	409.2	355.4
Net Working Capital	252.1	278.2	275.5	305.5	271.6	269.4	252.7
Year-end Shs. Outstg. (000)	38,933	38,344	38,019	37,615	37,118	36,222	34,554
STATISTICAL RECORD:							
Operating Profit Margin %	9.9	10.1	10.0	9.9	10.5	10.8	10.1
Net Profit Margin %	5.9	6.2	5.9	5.7	6.1	6.1	5.4
Return on Equity %	14.4	15.8	15.8	15.4	15.1	14.0	13.8
Return on Assets %	6.9	7.8	7.5	6.8	6.5	6.7	6.2
Debt/Total Assets %	14.0	15.7	19.5	22.7	22.0	22.8	25.1
Price Range	50.99-34.00	45.38-26.13	50.44-28.88	46.38-29.50	39.75-23.19	26.13-18.94	22.88-17.19
P/E Ratio	17.8-11.9	16.0-9.2	20.4-11.7	21.6-13.7	21.4-12.5	16.5-12.0	16.6-12.5
Average Yield %	1.6	1.6	1.3	1.2	1.2	1.5	1.5

Statistics are as originally reported. Adj. for 2-for-1 split, 6/97.

OFFICERS:
L. K. Black, Chmn., C.E.O.
J. P. Black, Pres.
H. L. Zuber, Jr., V.P., C.F.O.
INVESTOR CONTACT: Janine Dusossoit, V.P., Investor Relations, (610) 834-6301
PRINCIPAL OFFICE: 630 West Germantown Pike, Suite 450, Plymouth Meeting, PA 19462

TELEPHONE NUMBER: (610) 834-6301
FAX: (610) 834-8228
WEB: www.teleflex.com
NO. OF EMPLOYEES: 17,600 (approx.)
SHAREHOLDERS: 1,300 (approx.)
ANNUAL MEETING: In Apr.
INCORPORATED: DE, June, 1943

INSTITUTIONAL HOLDINGS:
No. of Institutions: 221
Shares Held: 24,556,964
% Held: 62.9

INDUSTRY: Surgical and medical instruments (SIC: 3841)

TRANSFER AGENT(S): American Stock Transfer & Trust Company, New York, NY

TELEPHONE AND DATA SYSTEMS, INC.

YIELD 0.7%
P/E RATIO ...

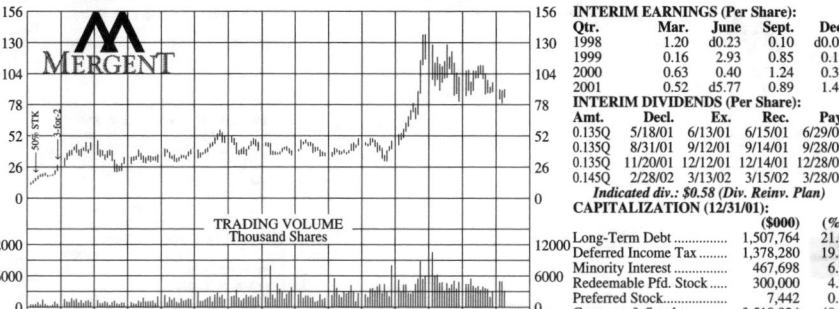

INTERIM EARNINGS (Per Share):

Qtr.	Mar.	June	Sept.	Dec.
1998	1.20	d0.23	0.10	d0.05
1999	0.16	2.93	0.85	0.18
2000	0.63	0.40	1.24	0.37
2001	0.52	d5.77	0.89	1.46

INTERIM DIVIDENDS (Per Share):

Amt.	Decl.	Ex.	Rec.	Pay.
0.135Q	5/18/01	6/13/01	6/15/01	6/29/01
0.135Q	8/31/01	9/12/01	9/14/01	9/28/01
0.135Q	11/20/01	12/12/01	12/14/01	12/28/01
0.145Q	2/28/02	3/13/02	3/15/02	3/28/02

Indicated div.: $0.58 (Div. Reinv. Plan)

CAPITALIZATION (12/31/01):

	($000)	(%)
Long-Term Debt	1,507,764	21.0
Deferred Income Tax	1,378,280	19.2
Minority Interest	467,698	6.5
Redeemable Pfd. Stock	300,000	4.2
Preferred Stock.................	7,442	0.1
Common & Surplus	3,518,924	49.0
Total	7,180,108	100.0

DIVIDEND ACHIEVER STATUS:
Rank: 212   10-Year Growth Rate: 6.05%
Total Years of Dividend Growth: 27

TRADING VOLUME
Thousand Shares

*7 YEAR PRICE SCORE 127.8   *12 MONTH PRICE SCORE 91.0
*NYSE COMPOSITE INDEX=100

RECENT DEVELOPMENTS: For the year ended 12/31/01, TDS posted a loss from continuing operations of $168.2 million versus income from continuing operations of $145.5 million a year earlier. Results for 2001 and 2000 included losses of $548.3 million and a gain of $15.7 million, respectively, on marketable securities and other investments. Total operating revenues rose 11.2% to $2.59 billion. U.S. Cellular revenues climbed 10.4% to $1.89 billion, while TDS Telecom revenues advanced 13.7% to $693.7 million. Separately, on 2/14/02, TDS announced that it has entered into a definitive agreement for the acquisition of Telecommunication Systems of New Hampshire, Inc. (TSNH). Through its Wilton and Hollis telephone companies, TSNH serves about 7,500 access lines in two exchanges, together with 1,400 Internet and digital subscriber line customers in south central New Hampshire.

BUSINESS

TELEPHONE AND DATA SYSTEMS, INC. is a diversified telecommunications service company with wireless telephone and wireline telephone operations. At 12/31/01, TDS served approximately 4.3 million customer units in 34 states, including 3.5 million wireless telephones and 847,900 telephone access lines. TDS also owns a portfolio of investments in publicly traded telecommunications companies. TDS conducts substantially all of its wireless operations through its 82.2%-owned subsidiary, United States Cellular Corporation. TDS conducts substantially all of its wireline telephone operations through its wholly-owned subsidiary, TDS Telecommunications Corporation. At 12/31/01, TDS Telecom operated 109 Incumbent Local Exchange Carrier telephone companies serving 650,700 access lines in 28 states. U.S. Cellular provided 73.2% of TDS's consolidated revenues and 72.7% of consolidated operating income in 2001. TDS Telecom provided 26.8% of consolidated revenues and 27.3% of consolidated operating income in 2001.

ANNUAL FINANCIAL DATA

	12/31/01	12/31/00	12/31/99	12/31/98	12/31/97	12/31/96	12/31/95
Earnings Per Share	④ d2.87	③ 2.39	② 5.02	1.03	① d0.19	② 2.08	1.74
Cash Flow Per Share	4.80	8.97	10.62	7.00	4.64	5.92	5.18
Tang. Book Val. Per Share	56.36	67.07	39.81	36.58	32.49	33.23	32.94
Dividends Per Share	0.54	0.50	0.46	0.44	0.42	0.40	0.38
Dividend Payout %	...	20.9	9.2	42.7	...	19.2	21.8
INCOME STATEMENT (IN MILLIONS):							
Total Revenues	2,588.5	2,326.9	1,963.1	1,805.7	1,471.5	1,214.6	954.4
Costs & Expenses	1,702.4	1,507.6	1,239.4	1,405.7	1,173.7	829.0	621.3
Depreciation & Amort.	450.0	399.1	353.3	409.5	301.6	231.6	201.1
Operating Income	436.2	420.1	370.4	d20.9	d3.7	154.1	132.0
Net Interest Inc./(Exp.)	d103.7	d100.6	d100.0	d126.4	d89.7	d42.9	d50.8
Income Before Income Taxes	d147.2	371.2	567.1	157.2	20.5	251.8	185.7
Income Taxes	cr44.9	149.5	228.2	69.3	28.6	123.6	81.0
Equity Earnings/Minority Int.	d66.0	d76.2	d89.9	d52.0	d5.3	26.7	25.9
Net Income	④ d168.2	③ 145.5	② 314.2	64.4	① d9.5	① 128.1	104.0
Cash Flow	281.3	544.2	666.3	426.6	279.5	359.7	302.5
Average Shs. Outstg. (000)	58,661	60,636	62,736	60,982	60,211	60,732	58,356
BALANCE SHEET (IN MILLIONS):							
Cash & Cash Equivalents	140.7	102.6	116.0	55.4	75.6	119.3	80.9
Total Current Assets	674.4	527.1	508.0	400.5	408.3	346.1	256.1
Net Property	2,558.0	2,180.6	2,095.9	2,672.6	2,465.7	1,828.9	2,471.8
Total Assets	8,046.8	8,634.6	5,375.8	5,527.5	4,971.6	4,200.0	3,469.1
Total Current Liabilities	816.2	984.4	369.7	623.4	905.9	509.3	427.7
Long-Term Obligations	1,507.8	1,173.0	1,279.9	1,553.1	1,264.2	982.2	858.9
Net Stockholders' Equity	3,526.4	3,943.9	2,492.1	2,263.9	1,999.1	2,060.9	1,714.1
Net Working Capital	d141.9	d457.3	138.3	d222.9	d497.6	d163.2	d171.6
Year-end Shs. Outstg. (000)	62,437	58,688	62,370	61,177	60,585	61,154	51,137
STATISTICAL RECORD:							
Operating Profit Margin %	16.8	18.1	18.9	...	...	12.7	13.8
Net Profit Margin %	...	6.3	16.0	3.6	...	10.5	10.9
Return on Equity %	...	3.7	12.6	2.8	...	6.2	6.1
Return on Assets %	...	1.7	5.8	1.2	...	3.1	3.0
Debt/Total Assets %	18.7	13.6	23.8	28.1	25.4	23.4	24.6
Price Range	111.25-85.16	128.50-80.60	137.00-44.13	50.13-36.63	49.94-34.50	48.88-34.75	46.38-35.63
P/E Ratio	...	53.8-33.7	27.3-8.8	48.7-29.7	...	23.5-16.7	26.7-20.5
Average Yield %	0.5	0.5	0.5	1.1	1.0	1.0	1.0

Statistics are as originally reported. ① Incls. non-recurr. credit 12/31/97: $41.4 mill.; credit 12/31/96: $138.7 mill. ② Incl. gain of $345.9 mill.; bef. disc. oper. loss of $142.3 mill. ③ Incl. gains on cellular & oth. invest. of $15.7 mill. ④ Incl. loss on marketable securities & oth. invest. of $548.3 mill.; bef. loss of $24.1 mill. on disp. of disc. ops.

OFFICERS:
L. T. Carlson, Chmn.
L. T. Carlson Jr., Pres., C.E.O.
S. L. Helton, Exec. V.P., C.F.O.
INVESTOR CONTACT: Julie Mathews, Investor Relations, (312) 630-1900
PRINCIPAL OFFICE: 30 North Lasalle Street, Suite 400, Chicago, IL 60602

TELEPHONE NUMBER: (312) 630-1900
FAX: (312) 630-1908
WEB: www.teldta.com
NO. OF EMPLOYEES: 8,560
SHAREHOLDERS: 2,386 (record)
ANNUAL MEETING: In May
INCORPORATED: IA, Mar., 1968; reincorp., DE, May, 1998

INSTITUTIONAL HOLDINGS:
No. of Institutions: 256
Shares Held: 41,819,604
% Held: 71.4
INDUSTRY: Radiotelephone communications (SIC: 4812)
TRANSFER AGENT(S): ComputerShare Investor Services, Chicago, IL

NYSE SYMBOL TNC
Rec. Pr. 41.92 (3/31/02)

TENNANT COMPANY

YIELD	1.9%
P/E RATIO	80.6

TRADING VOLUME
Thousand Shares

*7 YEAR PRICE SCORE 97.1 *12 MONTH PRICE SCORE 98.6
*NYSE COMPOSITE INDEX=100

INTERIM EARNINGS (Per Share):

Qtr.	Mar.	June	Sept.	Dec.
1997	0.44	0.64	0.60	0.75
1998	0.54	0.70	0.67	0.76
1999	0.53	0.66	0.35	0.61
2000	0.60	0.83	0.79	0.87
2001	0.02	0.14	0.32	0.04

INTERIM DIVIDENDS (Per Share):

Amt.	Decl.	Ex.	Rec.	Pay.
0.20Q	2/23/01	3/01/01	3/05/01	3/15/01
0.20Q	5/03/01	5/30/01	6/01/01	6/15/01
0.20Q	8/09/01	8/29/01	8/31/01	9/14/01
0.20Q	11/15/01	11/28/01	11/30/01	12/14/01
0.20Q	2/21/02	2/28/02	3/04/02	3/15/02

Indicated div.: $0.80 (Div. Reinv. Plan)

CAPITALIZATION (12/31/01):

	($000)	(%)
Long-Term Debt	10,000	6.1
Common & Surplus	154,328	93.9
Total	164,328	100.0

DIVIDEND ACHIEVER STATUS:

Rank: 264	10-Year Growth Rate: 2.92%
Total Years of Dividend Growth:	29

RECENT DEVELOPMENTS: For the year ended 12/31/01, net income plunged 83.0% to $4.8 million from $28.2 million in 2000. Results for 2001 included restructuring charges of $10.0 million and a pension settlement gain of $5.9 million. Net sales declined 6.8% to $423.0 million. North American segment net sales declined 7.9% to $302.1 million. European segment net sales were flat at $80.6 million. Other international segment net sales fell 11.3% to $40.3 million. Operating income decreased 69.2% to $13.4 million.

PROSPECTS: As part of its ongoing efforts to reduce costs and improve service, the Company is planning to consolidate its North American distribution operations from a current network of seven distribution centers into two new facilities that will be under the ownership and management of a third-party logistics services provider. Pre-tax restructuring charges of $3.2 million to $3.8 million are expected along with the elimination of up to 80 positions.

BUSINESS

TENNANT COMPANY specializes in the design, manufacture and marketing of products used primarily in the maintenance of non-residential floors. The equipment manufactured consists mainly of motorized cleaning equipment and related products, including floor cleaning and preservation products, and is sold through a direct sales organization and independent distributors in more than 40 countries throughout the world. The Company has manufacturing operations in Holland, Michigan, and Uden, The Netherlands. In January 1999, the Company acquired the business and assets of Paul Andra KG, a privately-owned manufacturer of commercial floor maintenance equipment in Germany.

ANNUAL FINANCIAL DATA

	12/31/01	12/31/00	12/31/99	12/31/98	12/31/97	12/31/96	12/31/95
Earnings Per Share	① 0.52	3.09	② 2.15	2.67	2.41	2.10	1.98
Cash Flow Per Share	2.53	5.11	4.20	4.51	4.15	3.73	3.40
Tang. Book Val. Per Share	15.18	15.16	13.06	12.68	12.00	11.15	9.57
Dividends Per Share	0.80	0.78	0.76	0.74	0.72	0.69	0.68
Dividend Payout %	153.8	25.2	35.3	27.7	29.9	32.9	34.3
INCOME STATEMENT (IN THOUSANDS):							
Total Revenues	422,970	454,044	429,407	389,388	372,428	344,433	325,368
Costs & Expenses	391,047	392,129	379,478	334,489	318,872	296,415	281,096
Depreciation & Amort.	18,507	18,391	18,667	17,550	17,468	16,387	14,090
Operating Income	13,416	43,524	31,262	37,349	36,088	31,631	30,182
Net Interest Inc./(Exp.)	340	807	d1,097	1,479	2,678	1,768	1,492
Income Before Income Taxes	13,749	44,044	30,586	39,092	37,630	32,329	29,435
Income Taxes	8,945	15,794	10,893	13,767	13,425	11,302	9,773
Net Income	① 4,804	28,250	② 19,693	25,325	24,205	21,027	19,662
Cash Flow	23,311	46,641	38,360	42,875	41,673	37,414	33,752
Average Shs. Outstg.	9,203	9,135	9,140	9,500	10,032	10,021	9,916
BALANCE SHEET (IN THOUSANDS):							
Cash & Cash Equivalents	23,783	21,512	14,928	17,693	16,279	9,881	4,247
Total Current Assets	152,387	176,628	165,093	150,868	143,105	126,481	123,508
Net Property	69,792	66,713	66,306	66,640	65,111	65,384	63,724
Total Assets	246,619	263,285	257,533	239,098	232,744	219,180	215,750
Total Current Liabilities	55,648	67,255	74,999	60,809	56,115	7,898	61,723
Long-Term Obligations	10,000	10,000	16,003	23,038	20,678	21,824	23,149
Net Stockholders' Equity	154,328	154,948	135,915	131,267	134,086	128,860	114,131
Net Working Capital	96,739	104,373	90,094	90,059	86,990	118,583	61,785
Year-end Shs. Outstg.	9,036	9,053	8,989	9,123	9,699	9,965	9,952
STATISTICAL RECORD:							
Operating Profit Margin %	3.2	9.6	7.3	9.6	9.7	9.2	9.3
Net Profit Margin %	1.1	6.2	4.6	6.5	6.5	6.1	6.0
Return on Equity %	3.1	18.2	14.5	19.3	18.1	16.3	17.2
Return on Assets %	1.9	10.7	7.6	10.6	10.3	9.2	9.1
Debt/Total Assets %	4.1	3.8	6.2	9.6	8.8	10.0	10.7
Price Range	49.56-32.80	53.38-28.25	45.00-31.44	45.75-33.00	39.63-26.13	27.50-21.25	29.00-22.25
P/E Ratio	95.3-63.1	17.3-9.1	20.9-14.6	17.1-12.4	16.4-10.8	13.1-10.1	14.6-11.2
Average Yield %	1.9	1.9	2.0	1.9	2.2	2.8	2.7

Statistics are as originally reported. ① Incl. non-recurr. chrg. $10.0 mill. and pension settlement gain of $5.9 mill. ② Incl. non-recurr. chrg. $6.7 mill.

OFFICERS:
J. M. Dolan, Pres., C.E.O.
A. T. Brausen, V.P., C.F.O., Treas.
J. J. Seifert, V.P., Sec., Gen. Couns.

INVESTOR CONTACT: Anthony T. Brausen, V.P., C.F.O. & Treas., (763) 540-1553

PRINCIPAL OFFICE: 701 North Lilac Drive, P.O. Box 1452, Minneapolis, MN 55440

TELEPHONE NUMBER: (763) 540-1208
FAX: (763) 540-1437
WEB: www.tennantco.com

NO. OF EMPLOYEES: 2,387 (avg.)

SHAREHOLDERS: 3,700 (approx.)

ANNUAL MEETING: In May

INCORPORATED: MN, Jan., 1909

INSTITUTIONAL HOLDINGS:
No. of Institutions: 61
Shares Held: 4,992,473
% Held: 55.4

INDUSTRY: Service industry machinery, nec (SIC: 3589)

TRANSFER AGENT(S): Wells Fargo Shareowners Services, St. Paul, MN

TOOTSIE ROLL INDUSTRIES, INC.

YIELD 0.6%
P/E RATIO 36.2

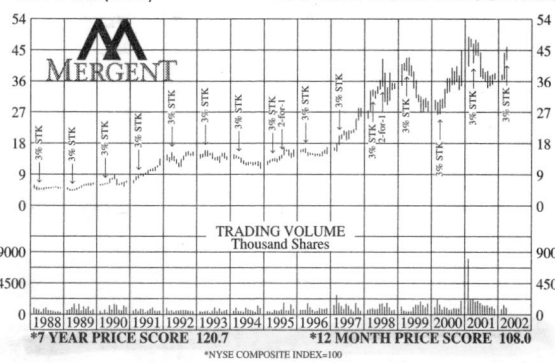

INTERIM EARNINGS (Per Share):

Qtr.	Mar.	June	Sept.	Dec.
1997	0.17	0.22	0.47	0.25
1998	0.20	0.26	0.50	0.28
1999	0.22	0.27	0.54	0.28
2000	0.24	0.30	0.60	0.30
2001	0.24	0.27	0.52	0.24

INTERIM DIVIDENDS (Per Share):

Amt.	Decl.	Ex.	Rec.	Pay.
0.07Q	5/30/01	6/14/01	6/18/01	7/09/01
0.07Q	9/17/01	9/26/01	9/28/01	10/09/01
0.07Q	12/04/01	12/13/01	12/17/01	1/04/02
0.07Q	2/19/02	3/01/02	3/05/02	4/04/02
3% STK	2/19/02	3/01/02	3/05/02	4/17/02

Indicated div.: $0.28

CAPITALIZATION (12/31/01):

	($000)	(%)
Long-Term Debt	7,500	1.4
Deferred Income Tax	16,792	3.2
Common & Surplus	508,461	95.4
Total	532,753	100.0

DIVIDEND ACHIEVER STATUS:
Rank: 26   10-Year Growth Rate: 19.90%
Total Years of Dividend Growth: 38

TRADING VOLUME
Thousand Shares

*7 YEAR PRICE SCORE 120.7   *12 MONTH PRICE SCORE 108.0
*NYSE COMPOSITE INDEX=100

RECENT DEVELOPMENTS: For the year ended 12/31/01, net earnings fell 13.3% to $65.7 million from $75.7 million in 2000. Results for 2001 included a nonrecurring charge of $2.6 million for the closing and consolidation of a small manufacturing plant, and for inventory adjustments. Earnings were negatively affected by lower gross profit margins, higher promotional expenses, and decreased investment income. Net sales decreased 0.8% to $423.5 million.

PROSPECTS: The Company is beginning to experience an increase in sales due to effective marketing and promotional programs, and an upturn in the economy. This is being partially offset by increased competitive pressures, and higher transportation and promotional expenses. Looking ahead, the Company aims to drive top-line growth through the leveraging of its broad product line, including product line extensions and new products.

BUSINESS

TOOTSIE ROLL INDUSTRIES, INC. is engaged in the manufacture and sale of candy. The majority of the Company's products are sold under the following registered trademarks: TOOTSIE ROLL, TOOTSIE ROLL POPS, CHILD'S PLAY, CARAMEL APPLE POPS, CHARMS, BLOW-POP and BLUE RAZZ. Other candy products include CELLA'S, MASON DOTS, MASON CROWS, JUNIOR MINTS, CHARLESTON CHEW, SUGAR DADDY and SUGAR BABIES, ANDES and FLUFFY STUFF cotton candy. In September 1988, TR acquired Charms Co. for approximately $65.0 million. On 5/12/00, TR acquired the assets of Andes Candies Inc. The Company has manufacturing facilities in Illinois, New York, Tennessee, Massachusetts, Wisconsin, Maryland, Mexico. TR celebrated its 100th anniversary in 1996.

ANNUAL FINANCIAL DATA

	12/31/01	12/31/00	12/31/99	12/31/98	12/31/97	12/31/96	12/31/95
Earnings Per Share	①1.30	1.49	1.38	1.29	1.15	0.89	0.76
Cash Flow Per Share	1.63	1.75	1.57	1.53	1.39	1.12	0.97
Tang. Book Val. Per Share	7.74	6.69	6.71	6.08	4.98	4.15	3.40
Dividends Per Share	0.27	0.25	0.21	0.16	0.13	0.11	0.09
Dividend Payout %	20.6	16.6	15.1	12.7	11.4	12.6	12.4
INCOME STATEMENT (IN THOUSANDS):							
Total Revenues	423,496	427,054	396,750	388,659	375,594	340,909	312,660
Costs & Expenses	312,852	303,011	282,252	274,587	272,688	257,309	240,463
Depreciation & Amort.	16,700	13,314	9,979	12,807	12,819	12,068	10,794
Operating Income	93,944	110,729	104,519	101,265	90,087	71,532	61,403
Net Interest Inc./(Exp.)	...	...	...	...	...	2,389	1,646
Income Before Income Taxes	100,787	117,808	111,447	106,063	95,361	75,098	64,038
Income Taxes	35,100	42,071	40,137	38,537	34,679	27,891	23,670
Net Income	①65,687	75,737	71,310	67,526	60,682	47,207	40,368
Cash Flow	82,387	89,051	81,289	80,333	73,501	59,275	51,162
Average Shs. Outstg.	50,451	50,917	51,924	52,495	52,753	52,934	52,934
BALANCE SHEET (IN THOUSANDS):							
Cash & Cash Equivalents	175,161	132,487	159,506	163,920	142,280	144,157	103,450
Total Current Assets	246,096	203,211	224,532	228,539	206,961	201,513	164,949
Net Property	132,575	131,118	95,897	83,024	78,364	81,687	81,999
Total Assets	618,676	562,442	529,416	487,423	436,742	391,456	353,816
Total Current Liabilities	57,846	57,446	56,109	53,384	53,606	48,184	55,306
Long-Term Obligations	7,500	7,500	7,500	7,500	7,500	7,500	7,500
Net Stockholders' Equity	508,461	458,696	430,646	396,457	351,163	312,881	272,186
Net Working Capital	188,250	145,765	168,423	175,155	153,355	153,329	109,643
Year-end Shs. Outstg.	50,525	50,460	51,458	50,749	52,299	52,934	51,803
STATISTICAL RECORD:							
Operating Profit Margin %	22.2	25.9	26.3	26.1	24.0	21.0	19.6
Net Profit Margin %	15.5	17.7	18.0	17.4	16.2	13.8	12.9
Return on Equity %	12.9	16.5	16.6	17.0	17.3	15.1	14.8
Return on Assets %	10.6	13.5	13.5	13.9	13.9	12.1	11.4
Debt/Total Assets %	1.2	1.3	1.4	1.5	1.7	1.9	2.1
Price Range	48.96-33.99	45.07-26.20	42.96-26.88	42.54-25.10	28.20-15.60	16.91-14.19	16.63-11.74
P/E Ratio	37.7-26.1	30.3-17.6	31.2-19.5	33.0-19.5	24.5-13.5	19.0-16.0	21.9-15.5
Average Yield %	0.6	0.7	0.6	0.6	0.6	0.7	0.7

Statistics are as originally reported. Adj. for all stk. splits and divs. through 4/02. ① Incl. a nonrecurr. chrg. of $2.6 mill. for the closing & consol. of a manufac. plant & for inventory adjustments.

OFFICERS:
M. J. Gordon, Chmn., C.E.O.
E. R. Gordon, Pres., C.O.O.
B. P. Bowen, Treas.

INVESTOR CONTACT: Barry P. Bowen, Treas., (773) 838-4834

PRINCIPAL OFFICE: 7401 South Cicero Avenue, Chicago, IL 60629

TELEPHONE NUMBER: (773) 838-3400
FAX: (773) 838-3534
WEB: www.tootsie.com

NO. OF EMPLOYEES: 1,950 (approx.)

SHAREHOLDERS: 6,000 (approx., common and class B common)

ANNUAL MEETING: In May
INCORPORATED: VA, June, 1919

INSTITUTIONAL HOLDINGS:
No. of Institutions: 145
Shares Held: 12,065,823
% Held: 23.7

INDUSTRY: Candy & other confectionery products (SIC: 2064)

TRANSFER AGENT(S): Mellon Investor Services, LLC, Ridgefield Park, NJ

NYSE SYMBOL **TRH**
Rec. Pr. 82.12 (3/31/02)

TRANSATLANTIC HOLDINGS, INC.

YIELD 0.5%
P/E RATIO 234.6

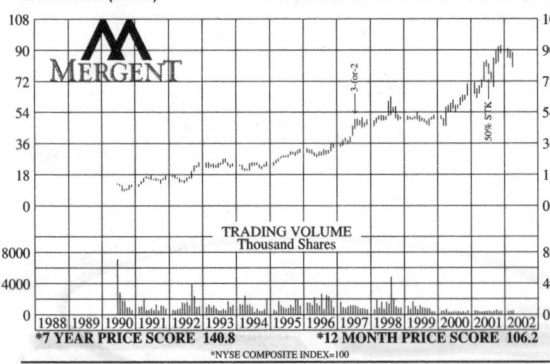

TRADING VOLUME
Thousand Shares

| 1988 | 1989 | 1990 | 1991 | 1992 | 1993 | 1994 | 1995 | 1996 | 1997 | 1998 | 1999 | 2000 | 2001 | 2002 |

*7 YEAR PRICE SCORE 140.8   ***12 MONTH PRICE SCORE 106.2**
*NYSE COMPOSITE INDEX=100

INTERIM EARNINGS (Per Share):

Qtr.	Mar.	June	Sept.	Dec.
1998	0.91	1.24	1.50	1.08
1999	1.42	1.13	0.69	0.34
2000	1.07	0.97	1.02	0.97
2001	0.96	0.76	d1.49	0.12

INTERIM DIVIDENDS (Per Share):

Amt.	Decl.	Ex.	Rec.	Pay.
50% STK	5/17/01	7/23/01	6/29/01	7/20/01
0.096Q	5/17/01	9/05/01	9/07/01	9/14/01
0.096Q	9/20/01	12/05/01	12/07/01	12/21/01
0.096Q	12/03/01	3/01/02	3/01/02	3/15/02
0.096Q	3/21/02	6/05/02	6/07/02	6/14/02

Indicated div.: $0.38

CAPITALIZATION (12/31/01):

	($000)	(%)
Common & Surplus	1,846,010	100.0
Total	1,846,010	100.0

DIVIDEND ACHIEVER STATUS:
Rank: 59   10-Year Growth Rate: 15.39%
Total Years of Dividend Growth: 11

RECENT DEVELOPMENTS: For the year ended 12/31/01, net income dropped 91.1% to $18.9 million versus $211.6 million in 2000. Earnings were adversely affected by $139.8 million in after-tax catastrophe losses, of which $130.0 million was associated with the events of 9/11/01, and $39.0 million for the reinsurance exposure related to Enron. Revenues increased 6.9% to $2.03 billion from $1.90 billion in the prior year. Net premiums earned rose 9.7% to $1.79 billion versus $1.63 billion a year earlier.

PROSPECTS: As a result of record industry catastrophe losses in 2001, demand for reinsurance products has risen, while the industry's capacity to provide those products has been strained. Due to this increased demand and clients seeking reinsurance from financially stronger companies, TRH's premium volume is growing substantially in an improved rate environment. Looking ahead, TRH believes it is well-positioned for growth by providing a broader range of products to a more diverse customer base.

BUSINESS

TRANSLANTIC HOLDINGS, INC., through its wholly-owned subsidiaries Transatlantic Reinsurance Company, Trans Re Zurich and Putnam Reinsurance Company, offers reinsurance capacity for a full range of property and casualty products on a treaty and facultative basis, directly and through brokers, to insurance and reinsurance companies, in both the domestic and international markets. The Company's principal lines of reinsurance include auto liability, other liability, accident and health, medical malpractice, marine and aviation, and surety and credit in the casualty lines, and fire and allied in the property lines. As of 12/31/01, the Company had operations based in Chicago, Toronto, Miami (serving Latin America and the Caribbean), Buenos Aires, Rio de Janeiro, London, Paris, Zurich, Warsaw, Johannesburg, Sydney, Hong Kong, Shanghai and Tokyo.

ANNUAL FINANCIAL DATA

	12/31/01	12/31/00	12/31/99	12/31/98	12/31/97	12/31/96	12/31/95
Earnings Per Share	① 0.36	4.03	3.58	4.73	3.56	4.49	3.83
Tang. Book Val. Per Share	35.33	35.59	31.53	30.96	26.17	32.95	28.71
Dividends Per Share	0.37	0.35	0.31	0.28	0.25	0.21	0.18
Dividend Payout %	103.3	8.6	8.8	5.9	7.1	4.7	4.6
INCOME STATEMENT (IN MILLIONS)							
Net Premium Income	1,790.3	1,631.5	1,484.6	1,380.6	1,259.3	1,130.6	981.2
Net Investment Income	240.1	234.5	230.7	222.0	207.6	192.6	172.9
Other Income	d0.2	...	...	...	...	...	...
Total Revenues	2,030.2	1,866.0	1,715.4	1,602.6	1,466.9	1,323.3	1,154.1
Income Before Income Taxes	d34.1	268.0	236.1	323.4	234.7	196.3	163.8
Income Taxes	cr53.0	56.3	48.7	75.8	49.2	41.5	31.9
Net Income	① 18.9	211.6	187.4	247.5	185.5	154.9	131.9
Average Shs. Outstg. (000)	52,736	52,476	52,323	52,298	52,127	34,475	34,409
BALANCE SHEET (IN MILLIONS):							
Cash & Cash Equivalents	559.5	157.3	110.0	95.6	87.5	136.7	60.7
Premiums Due	1,254.2	778.5	777.1	658.0	591.0	528.1	668.1
Invst. Assets: Fixed-term	3,653.9	3,427.8	3,462.1	3,533.5	3,440.9	3,060.8	2,666.1
Invst. Assets: Equities	512.6	545.7	537.1	511.4	458.2	386.7	255.1
Invst. Assets: Total	4,880.2	4,262.0	4,229.4	4,258.2	3,921.8	3,512.4	2,940.1
Total Assets	6,741.3	5,522.7	5,480.2	5,253.2	4,835.0	4,379.1	3,899.0
Net Stockholders' Equity	1,846.0	1,856.4	1,642.5	1,610.1	1,356.7	1,137.3	988.5
Year-end Shs. Outstg. (000)	52,256	52,160	52,092	52,000	51,845	34,520	34,425
STATISTICAL RECORD:							
Return on Revenues %	0.9	11.3	10.9	15.4	12.6	11.7	11.4
Return on Equity %	1.0	11.4	11.4	15.4	13.7	13.6	13.3
Return on Assets %	0.3	3.8	3.4	4.7	3.8	3.5	3.4
Price Range	92.75-62.00	70.59-45.84	53.67-46.04	63.00-45.84	51.04-33.89	36.11-27.72	32.83-23.22
P/E Ratio	257.6-172.2	17.5-11.4	15.0-12.9	13.3-9.7	14.3-9.5	8.0-6.2	8.6-6.1
Average Yield %	0.5	0.6	0.6	0.5	0.6	0.7	0.6

Statistics are as originally reported. Adj. for stk. splits: 50% div., 7/01; 3-for-2, 7/97 ①
Incl. after-tax catastrophe losses of $139.8 mill.

OFFICERS:
M. R. Greenberg, Chmn.
R. F. Orlich, Pres., C.E.O.
S. S. Skalicky, Exec. V.P., C.F.O.

INVESTOR CONTACT: Steven S. Skalicky, Exec. V.P., C.F.O., (212) 770-2040

PRINCIPAL OFFICE: 80 Pine Street, New York, NY 10005

TELEPHONE NUMBER: (212) 770-2000
FAX: (212) 785-7230
WEB: www.transre.com

NO. OF EMPLOYEES: 400 (approx.)

SHAREHOLDERS: 23,500 (approx.)

ANNUAL MEETING: In May

INCORPORATED: DE, 1986

TRUSTCO BANK CORP.

YIELD 4.6%
P/E RATIO 20.8

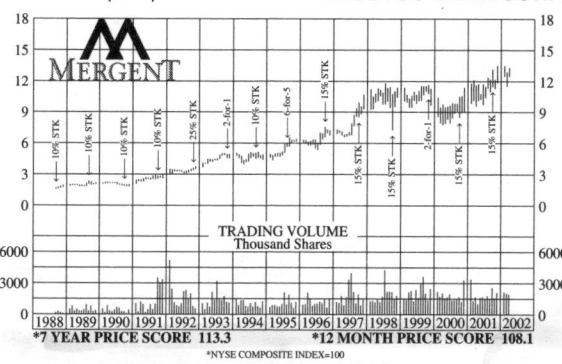

TRADING VOLUME
Thousand Shares

| 1988 | 1989 | 1990 | 1991 | 1992 | 1993 | 1994 | 1995 | 1996 | 1997 | 1998 | 1999 | 2000 | 2001 | 2002 |

*7 YEAR PRICE SCORE 113.3   *12 MONTH PRICE SCORE 108.1

*NYSE COMPOSITE INDEX=100

INTERIM EARNINGS (Per Share):

Qtr.	Mar.	June	Sept.	Dec.
1997	0.10	0.11	0.11	0.11
1998	0.11	0.12	0.13	0.12
1999	0.13	0.13	0.14	0.13
2000	0.14	0.15	0.15	0.14
2001	0.16	0.16	0.14	0.16

INTERIM DIVIDENDS (Per Share):

Amt.	Decl.	Ex.	Rec.	Pay.
0.15Q	5/15/01	6/06/01	6/08/01	7/02/01
0.15Q	8/21/01	9/05/01	9/07/01	10/01/01
15% STK	8/21/01	10/17/01	10/19/01	11/13/01
0.15Q	11/20/01	12/05/01	12/07/01	1/02/02
0.15Q	2/19/02	3/06/02	3/08/02	4/01/02

Indicated div.: $0.60 (Div. Reinv. Plan)

CAPITALIZATION (12/31/01):

	($000)	(%)
Total Deposits	2,092,906	91.0
Long-Term Debt	624	0.0
Common & Surplus	205,827	9.0
Total	2,299,357	100.0

DIVIDEND ACHIEVER STATUS:
Rank: 36   10-Year Growth Rate: 17.81%
Total Years of Dividend Growth: 25

RECENT DEVELOPMENTS: For the year ended 12/31/01, net income climbed 9.1% to $45.5 million compared with $41.7 million in the previous year. Results included a net gain of $4.5 million in 2001 and a net loss of $5.0 million in 2000 on securities transactions. Total interest income declined 2.9% to $168.7 million from $173.7 million in the prior year. Total interest expense decreased 3.8% to $72.8 million from $75.6 million a year earlier. Net interest income slipped 2.2% to $95.9 million from $98.1 million the year before. Provision for loan losses increased 20.1% to $4.9 million from $4.1 million in the previous year. Total noninterest income advanced 57.7% to $25.8 million from $16.4 million in 2000. Total noninterest expense rose 7.4% to $51.3 million from $47.8 million the year before.

BUSINESS

TRUSTCO BANK CORP. is a multi-bank holding company for Trustco Bank, N.A. and Trustco Savings Bank. As of 12/31/01, assets totaled $2.58 billion. Trustco Bank provides a range of both personal and business banking services to individuals, partnerships, corporations, municipalities and governments of New York. As of 12/31/01, the bank operated 55 banking offices and 49 automatic teller machines in Albany, Columbia, Greene, Rensselaer, Saratoga, Schenectady, Schoharie, Warren, and Washington counties of New York State. The largest part of such business consists of accepting deposits and making loans and investments. Trustco Savings Bank operates one branch and one ATM, serving communities in Montgomery County, New York. TRST also operates a non-bank subsidiary, ORE Subsidiary Corp., the manager of foreclosed properties acquired by the Bank.

ANNUAL FINANCIAL DATA

	12/31/01	12/31/00	12/31/99	12/31/98	12/31/97	12/31/96	12/31/95
Earnings Per Share	0.62	0.57	0.52	0.47	0.44	0.52	0.47
Tang. Book Val. Per Share	2.89	2.77	2.36	2.62	2.51	3.01	2.98
Dividends Per Share	0.52	0.45	0.42	0.36	0.31	0.27	0.24
Dividend Payout %	84.4	79.4	80.6	76.3	71.9	52.8	51.2
INCOME STATEMENT (IN MILLIONS):							
Total Interest Income	168.7	173.7	167.2	174.1	172.0	166.6	161.6
Total Interest Expense	72.8	75.6	74.0	88.3	86.5	82.3	80.2
Net Interest Income	95.9	98.1	93.2	85.7	85.5	84.3	81.4
Provision for Loan Losses	4.9	4.1	5.1	4.6	5.4	6.6	12.7
Non-Interest Income	25.8	16.4	15.4	22.1	17.2	10.3	14.1
Non-Interest Expense	51.3	47.8	45.6	48.8	46.2	42.0	44.4
Income Before Taxes	65.4	62.5	57.9	54.5	51.1	46.0	38.3
Net Income	45.5	41.7	38.2	35.0	32.2	28.7	25.5
Average Shs. Outstg. (000)	73,673	73,940	73,940	73,937	73,860	55,603	54,858
BALANCE SHEET (IN MILLIONS):							
Cash & Due from Banks	60.1	46.0	54.5	42.0	42.7	45.8	50.9
Securities Avail. for Sale	587.1	605.3	640.8	717.4	601.9	618.7	640.2
Total Loans & Leases	1,557.5	1,476.0	1,350.8	1,323.8	1,299.5	1,243.3	1,227.9
Allowance for Credit Losses	58.0	57.3	56.8	55.4	54.7	53.0	50.1
Net Loans & Leases	1,499.5	1,418.8	1,294.0	1,268.3	1,244.8	1,190.3	1,177.8
Total Assets	2,578.6	2,456.2	2,364.0	2,485.1	2,372.3	2,261.8	2,176.2
Total Deposits	2,092.9	2,011.0	1,994.9	2,107.4	2,021.9	1,953.1	1,930.6
Long-Term Obligations	0.6	0.9	...	...	...	...	...
Total Liabilities	2,372.8	2,260.4	2,197.7	2,299.2	2,193.4	2,099.4	2,016.1
Net Stockholders' Equity	205.8	195.8	166.4	185.8	178.8	162.4	160.1
Year-end Shs. Outstg. (000)	71,306	70,577	70,633	70,865	71,182	53,926	53,650
STATISTICAL RECORD:							
Return on Equity %	22.1	21.3	23.0	18.8	18.0	17.7	15.9
Return on Assets %	1.8	1.7	1.6	1.4	1.4	1.3	1.2
Equity/Assets %	8.0	8.0	7.0	7.5	7.5	7.2	7.4
Non-Int. Exp./Tot. Inc. %	43.8	40.0	40.0	45.6	44.9	42.4	46.7
Price Range	13.50-9.57	11.36-7.75	11.67-9.43	11.82-7.26	10.70-6.58	7.56-5.36	6.58-4.35
P/E Ratio	21.8-15.5	19.9-13.6	22.6-18.3	24.9-15.3	24.5-15.0	14.6-10.3	14.1-9.3
Average Yield %	4.5	4.7	3.9	3.8	3.6	4.2	4.4

Statistics are as originally reported. Adj. for stk. splits: 15% div., 11/01; 10/00; 2-for-1, 11/99; 15% div., 11/98; 15% div., 11/14/97; 15% div., 11/15/96; 6-for-5, 8/24/95.

OFFICERS:
R. A. McCormick, Chmn., Pres., C.E.O.
R. T. Cushing, V.P., C.F.O.
H. C. Collins, Sec.
W. M. McCartan, Asst. Sec.

INVESTOR CONTACT: Investor Relations, (518) 377-3311

PRINCIPAL OFFICE: 5 Sarnowski Drive, Glenville, NY 12302

TELEPHONE NUMBER: (518) 377-3311
FAX: (518) 381-3668

NO. OF EMPLOYEES: 465

SHAREHOLDERS: 13,085

ANNUAL MEETING: In May

INCORPORATED: NY, 1981

INSTITUTIONAL HOLDINGS:
No. of Institutions: 98
Shares Held: 17,085,287
% Held: 24.4

INDUSTRY: State commercial banks (SIC: 6022)

TRANSFER AGENT(S): Trustco Bank, Schenectady, NY

TRUSTMARK CORPORATION

YIELD 2.4%
P/E RATIO 14.7

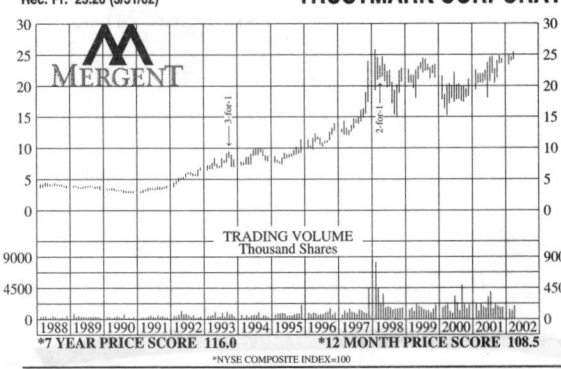

INTERIM EARNINGS (Per Share):

Qtr.	Mar.	June	Sept.	Dec.
1997	0.24	0.24	0.25	0.25
1998	0.27	0.28	0.29	0.30
1999	0.33	0.34	0.35	0.34
2000	0.40	0.39	0.37	0.37
2001	0.40	0.41	0.45	0.46

INTERIM DIVIDENDS (Per Share):

Amt.	Decl.	Ex.	Rec.	Pay.
0.135Q	5/08/01	5/30/01	6/01/01	6/15/01
0.135Q	7/10/01	8/29/01	9/01/01	9/15/01
0.15Q	11/13/01	11/28/01	12/01/01	12/15/01
0.15Q	2/12/02	2/27/02	3/01/02	3/15/02

Indicated div.: $0.60 (Div. Reinv. Plan)

CAPITALIZATION (12/31/01):

	($000)	(%)
Total Deposits	4,613,365	83.5
Long-Term Debt	225,000	4.1
Common & Surplus	685,444	12.4
Total	5,523,809	100.0

DIVIDEND ACHIEVER STATUS:
Rank: 95   10-Year Growth Rate: 12.37%
Total Years of Dividend Growth: 28

RECENT DEVELOPMENTS: For the year ended 12/31/01, TRMK reported net income of $111.3 million versus income of $104.2 million, before an accounting change charge of $2.5 million, in the prior year. Net interest income advanced 15.0% to $268.6 million from $233.6 million in 2000. Provision for loan losses grew 26.9% to $13.2 million. Total non-interest income rose 6.0% to $132.0 million, while total non-interest expense increased 14.0% to $215.9 million. Return on assets rose to 1.55% versus 1.51% in the prior year, while return on equity decreased to 16.23% from 16.55% in 2000. Separately, on 12/14/01, TRMK acquired Tennessee-based Nashoba Bancshares, Inc. in a cash transaction valued at $27.6 million. This acquisition expands TRMK's presence in the Memphis area to 22 locations.

BUSINESS

TRUSTMARK CORPORATION is the holding company for Trustmark National Bank, Trustmark Financial Services, Inc. and Trustmark Insurance Agency, Inc. Through these wholly-owned subsidiaries the Company provides banking, investment and insurance services to corporate, institutional and individual customers through over 150 offices in Mississippi and Tennessee. TRMK engages in business through three segments: Retail Banking, Commercial Banking and Financial Services. Retail Banking provides a full range of financial products and services to individuals and small business customers throughout Mississippi and Tennessee. Commercial Banking provides various financial products and services to corporate and middle market clients through the Company's commercial lending, commercial real estate, indirect lending and private banking groups. Financial Services includes trust and fiduciary services, discount brokerage services, insurance services, as well as credit card and mortgage services. Included in Financial Services is TRMK's proprietary mutual fund family, Performance Funds.

ANNUAL FINANCIAL DATA

	12/31/01	12/31/00	12/31/99	12/31/98	12/31/97	12/31/96	12/31/95
Earnings Per Share	1.72	☐ 1.53	1.36	1.14	0.98	0.93	0.86
Tang. Book Val. Per Share	8.93	8.70	8.39	8.29	7.61	6.95	6.32
Dividends Per Share	0.56	0.51	0.44	0.35	0.29	0.25	0.22
Dividend Payout %	32.3	33.3	32.4	30.9	29.8	26.9	25.9
INCOME STATEMENT (IN MILLIONS):							
Total Interest Income	477.8	488.8	448.5	420.1	376.9	358.1	348.3
Total Interest Expense	209.2	255.2	205.1	191.9	172.9	164.0	162.7
Net Interest Income	268.6	233.6	243.4	228.2	204.0	194.1	185.6
Provision for Loan Losses	13.2	10.4	9.1	7.8	4.7	5.8	2.4
Non-Interest Income	132.0	124.5	101.9	89.1	75.6	67.0	59.5
Non-Interest Expense	215.9	189.4	187.1	180.4	167.9	157.8	151.3
Income Before Taxes	171.4	158.3	149.2	129.1	107.0	97.4	91.3
Net Income	111.3	☐ 104.2	98.0	83.3	71.1	65.1	59.8
Average Shs. Outstg. (000)	64,877	67,929	71,921	72,946	72,786	69,822	69,822
BALANCE SHEET (IN MILLIONS):							
Cash & Due from Banks	328.8	298.7	280.0	312.5	292.6	337.1	299.0
Securities Avail. for Sale	1,061.5	1,120.6	783.2	776.0	610.6	528.0	488.9
Total Loans & Leases	4,524.4	4,143.9	4,014.9	3,702.3	2,983.7	2,634.6	2,580.2
Allowance for Credit Losses	75.5	65.9	65.9	66.2	64.1	63.0	70.1
Net Loans & Leases	4,448.8	4,078.1	3,949.1	3,636.2	2,919.6	2,571.6	2,510.1
Total Assets	7,180.3	6,887.0	6,743.4	6,355.2	5,545.2	5,193.7	4,992.6
Total Deposits	4,613.4	4,058.4	3,924.8	3,946.4	3,818.9	3,597.4	3,530.0
Long-Term Obligations	225.0	250.0	...	...	...	...	...
Total Liabilities	6,494.9	6,257.3	6,087.6	5,703.3	4,951.5	4,669.5	4,513.8
Net Stockholders' Equity	685.4	629.6	655.8	651.9	593.6	524.2	478.8
Year-end Shs. Outstg. (000)	63,706	64,755	70,424	72,532	72,740	69,822	69,822
STATISTICAL RECORD:							
Return on Equity %	16.2	16.5	14.9	12.8	12.0	12.4	12.5
Return on Assets %	1.5	1.5	1.5	1.3	1.3	1.3	1.2
Equity/Assets %	9.5	9.1	9.7	10.3	10.7	10.1	9.6
Non-Int. Exp./Tot. Inc. %	53.9	52.9	54.2	56.9	60.1	60.5	61.7
Price Range	24.82-18.00	22.25-15.25	24.50-18.00	25.88-15.13	24.00-12.00	14.00-9.75	11.38-7.38
P/E Ratio	14.4-10.5	14.5-10.0	18.0-13.2	22.7-13.3	24.5-12.2	15.1-10.5	13.3-8.6
Average Yield %	2.6	2.7	2.1	1.7	1.6	2.1	2.4

Statistics are as originally reported. Adj. for stk. splits: 2-for-1, 3/30/98 ☐ Bef. acctg. change chrg. $2.5 mill. ($0.03/sh.)

OFFICERS:
T. H. Kendall III, Chmn.
R. G. Hickson, Pres., C.E.O.
G. R. Host, Treas.

INVESTOR CONTACT: Joseph Rein, V.P.,
Investor Relations, (601) 949-6898

PRINCIPAL OFFICE: 248 East Capitol Street,
Jackson, MS 39201

TELEPHONE NUMBER: (601) 354-5111
FAX: (601) 949-2387
WEB: www.trustmark.com

NO. OF EMPLOYEES: 2,456 (approx.)

SHAREHOLDERS: 5,000 (approx.)

ANNUAL MEETING: In Mar.

INCORPORATED: MS, Aug., 1968

INSTITUTIONAL HOLDINGS:
No. of Institutions: 99
Shares Held: 11,190,651
% Held: 17.6

INDUSTRY: National commercial banks
(SIC: 6021)

TRANSFER AGENT(S): Trustmark National
Bank, Jackson, MS

UGI CORPORATION

YIELD 5.1%
P/E RATIO 17.6

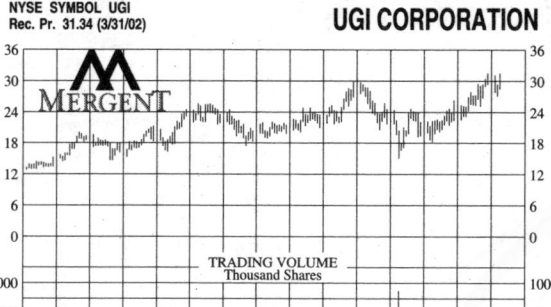

7 YEAR PRICE SCORE 103.0   **12 MONTH PRICE SCORE 105.5**
NYSE COMPOSITE INDEX=100

INTERIM EARNINGS (Per Share):

Qtr.	Dec.	Mar.	June	Sept.
1998-99	0.55	1.14	0.36	d0.31
1999-00	0.77	1.42	d0.17	d0.39
2000-01	1.00	1.67	d0.16	d0.60
2001-02	0.87	...	...	...

INTERIM DIVIDENDS (Per Share):

Amt.	Decl.	Ex.	Rec.	Pay.
0.40Q	4/24/01	5/29/01	5/31/01	7/01/01
0.40Q	7/31/01	8/29/01	8/31/01	10/01/01
0.40Q	10/30/01	11/28/01	11/30/01	1/01/02
0.40Q	1/29/02	2/26/02	2/28/02	4/01/02

Indicated div.: $1.60 (Div. Reinv. Plan)

CAPITALIZATION (9/30/01):

	($000)	(%)
Long-Term Debt	1,196,900	63.0
Deferred Income Tax	182,400	9.6
Minority Interest	246,200	13.0
Redeemable Pfd. Stock	20,000	1.1
Common & Surplus	255,600	13.4
Total	1,901,100	100.0

DIVIDEND ACHIEVER STATUS:

Rank: 268   10-Year Growth Rate: 2.67%
Total Years of Dividend Growth: 14

RECENT DEVELOPMENTS: For the quarter ended 12/31/01, net income was $24.1 million versus income of $27.1 million a year earlier, reflecting warmer-than-normal weather in UGI's domestic propane and utilities markets. However, more normal weather in Europe led to improved international results. Operating income from UGI's AmeriGas Propane, gas utility and electric utilities operations fell 26.6%, 18.6% and 3.6%, respectively, to $41.7 million, $24.9 million and $2.7 million.

PROSPECTS: UGI's long-term prospects are enhanced by its ongoing measured pursuit of international growth opportunities. For instance, UGI is working to expand the customer base at FLAGA, its Austrian-based propane company, and has stated that it is seeking additional acquisitions in the area. Also, UGI's March 2001 propane investment in Antargaz, which is one of the largest propane distributors in France, should provide a foundation for future European expansion.

BUSINESS

UGI CORPORATION is a holding company that operates propane distribution, gas and electric utility, energy marketing and related businesses through subsidiaries. The Company's majority-owned subsidiary AmeriGas Partners, L.P. conducts a retail propane distribution business. UGI Utilities, Inc. owns and operates a natural gas distribution utility in parts of eastern and southeastern Pennsylvania and an electricity distribution and electricity generation business in northeastern Pennsylvania. UGI Enterprises, Inc., conducts an energy marketing business. Enterprises owns and operates a propane distribution business in Austria, the Czech Republic, and Slovakia, and a heating, ventilation and air-conditioning service business in the Mid Atlantic states. Enterprises also participates in propane joint-venture businesses in France and in the Nantong region of China. Revenues in 2001 were derived: 57.4% propane, 20.3% gas utility, 3.4% electric utility, 15.0% energy services, 2.1% international propane, and 1.8% other enterprises.

ANNUAL FINANCIAL DATA

	9/30/01	9/30/00	9/30/99	9/30/98	9/30/97	9/30/96	9/30/95
Earnings Per Share	③1.90	1.64	②1.74	1.22	1.57	1.19	①0.24
Cash Flow Per Share	5.74	5.22	4.54	3.87	4.17	3.79	2.10
Dividends Per Share	1.57	1.52	1.47	1.45	1.43	1.41	1.39
Dividend Payout %	82.9	93.0	84.5	118.8	91.1	118.5	578.9
INCOME STATEMENT (IN MILLIONS)							
Total Revenues	2,468.1	1,761.7	1,383.6	1,439.7	1,642.0	1,557.6	877.6
Costs & Expenses	2,135.5	1,473.0	1,118.0	1,181.7	1,356.0	1,311.9	738.4
Depreciation & Amort.	105.2	97.5	89.7	87.8	86.1	86.0	60.9
Operating Income	227.4	191.2	175.9	170.2	199.9	159.7	78.3
Net Interest Inc./(Exp.)	d104.8	d98.5	d84.6	d84.4	d83.1	d79.5	d59.3
Income Before Income Taxes	121.0	91.1	109.6	83.6	114.0	77.4	16.2
Income Taxes	45.4	40.1	43.2	34.4	43.6	33.6	22.7
Equity Earnings/Minority Int.	d23.6	d6.3	d10.7	d8.9	d18.3	d4.3	14.4
Net Income	③52.0	44.7	②55.7	40.3	52.1	39.5	①7.9
Cash Flow	157.2	142.2	145.4	128.1	138.2	125.5	68.8
Average Shs. Outstg. (000)	27,373	27,255	32,016	33,123	33,132	33,142	32,710
BALANCE SHEET (IN MILLIONS)							
Cash & Cash Equivalents	91.1	101.7	55.6	148.4	129.4	97.1	132.7
Total Current Assets	458.9	426.1	290.9	350.6	403.9	381.6	367.3
Net Property	1,268.0	1,073.2	1,084.1	999.0	987.2	974.6	954.7
Total Assets	2,550.2	2,278.8	2,135.9	2,074.6	2,151.7	2,144.9	2,164.0
Total Current Liabilities	567.5	539.4	402.3	321.8	404.5	369.2	329.3
Long-Term Obligations	1,196.9	1,029.7	989.6	890.8	844.8	845.2	815.2
Net Stockholders' Equity	255.6	247.2	249.2	367.1	376.1	377.6	380.5
Net Working Capital	d108.6	d113.3	d111.4	28.8	d0.6	12.4	38.0
Year-end Shs. Outstg. (000)	27,296	26,994	27,270	32,823	33,199	33,136	32,917
STATISTICAL RECORD:							
Operating Profit Margin %	9.2	10.9	12.7	11.8	12.2	10.3	8.9
Net Profit Margin %	2.1	2.5	4.0	2.8	3.2	2.5	0.9
Return on Equity %	20.3	18.1	22.4	11.0	13.9	10.5	2.1
Return on Assets %	2.0	2.0	2.6	1.9	2.4	1.8	0.4
Debt/Total Assets %	46.9	45.2	46.3	42.9	39.3	39.4	37.7
Price Range	31.53-22.50	26.31-18.19	24.69-15.00	29.75-20.50	29.88-21.63	24.88-20.00	22.13-18.88
P/E Ratio	16.6-11.8	16.0-11.1	14.2-8.6	24.4-16.8	19.0-13.8	20.9-16.8	92.1-78.6
Average Yield %	5.8	6.9	7.4	5.8	5.6	6.3	6.8

Statistics are as originally reported. Incls. results of AP Propane on a consolidated basis for all yrs. shown. ① Incls. non-recurr. chrgs. totaling $24.9 mill. ② Incls. non-recurr. chrg. of $1.6 mill. ③ Incls. non-recurr. chrg. of $8.5 mill.; excl. acctg. chge. credit of $4.5 mill.

OFFICERS:
L. R. Greenberg, Chmn., Pres., C.E.O.
A. J. Mendicino, V.P., C.F.O.
B. P. Bovaird, V.P., Gen. Couns.

INVESTOR CONTACT: Robert W. Krick, Treas., (610) 337-1000

PRINCIPAL OFFICE: 460 North Gulph Road, King of Prussia, PA 19406

TELEPHONE NUMBER: (610) 337-1000
FAX: (610) 992-3254
WEB: www.ugicorp.com

NO. OF EMPLOYEES: 15,700 (approx.)

SHAREHOLDERS: 10,627 (record)

ANNUAL MEETING: In Feb.

INCORPORATED: PA, 1991

INSTITUTIONAL HOLDINGS:
No. of Institutions: 142
Shares Held: 14,223,812
% Held: 51.8

INDUSTRY: Gas and other services combined (SIC: 4932)

TRANSFER AGENT(S): Mellon Investor Services, LLC, Ridgefield Park, NJ

UNITED BANKSHARES, INC.

YIELD 3.1%
P/E RATIO 15.5

INTERIM EARNINGS (Per Share):

Qtr.	Mar.	June	Sept.	Dec.
1999	0.39	0.40	0.41	0.41
2000	0.42	0.43	0.44	0.11
2001	0.46	0.47	0.48	0.49

INTERIM DIVIDENDS (Per Share):

Amt.	Decl.	Ex.	Rec.	Pay.
0.22Q	2/26/01	3/07/01	3/09/01	4/02/01
0.23Q	5/22/01	6/06/01	6/08/01	7/02/01
0.23Q	8/27/01	9/12/01	9/14/01	10/01/01
0.23Q	11/19/01	12/12/01	12/14/01	1/02/02
0.23Q	2/25/02	3/06/02	3/08/02	4/01/02

Indicated div.: $0.92 (Div. Reinv. Plan)

CAPITALIZATION (12/31/01):

	($000)	(%)
Total Deposits	3,787,793	75.2
Long-Term Debt	736,455	14.6
Redeemable Pfd. Stock	8,800	0.2
Common & Surplus	506,529	10.1
Total	5,039,577	100.0

DIVIDEND ACHIEVER STATUS:
Rank: 165   10-Year Growth Rate: 8.46%
Total Years of Dividend Growth: 20

TRADING VOLUME
Thousand Shares

*7 YEAR PRICE SCORE 108.5   *12 MONTH PRICE SCORE 109.7
*NYSE COMPOSITE INDEX=100

RECENT DEVELOPMENTS: For the year ended 12/31/01, net income rose 35.6% to $80.0 million from $59.0 million in the prior year. Earnings for 2001 and 2000 included losses on security transactions of $518,000 and $13.9 million, respectively. Total interest income declined 4.6% to $360.6 million, while total interest expense fell 11.3% to $175.5 million. Net interest income grew 2.8% to $185.1 million from $180.1 million the year before. Provision for loan losses declined 18.5% to $12.8 million from $15.7 million a year earlier. Total non-interest income advanced to $62.2 million compared with $33.8 million in 2000. Total non-interest expense rose 4.8% to $115.7 million. Separately, UBSI acquired Century Bancshares, Inc. in a transaction valued at approximately $63.8 million. Century, with assets of about $414.0 million, expands UBSI's presence in Virginia, Washington, D.C., and Maryland with 11 offices.

BUSINESS

UNITED BANKSHARES, INC. is a bank holding company with assets of $5.63 billion as of 12/31/01. UBSI, through its subsidiaries, United National Bank and United Bank, engages primarily in community banking and mortgage banking and additionally offers most types of business permitted by law and regulation. Included among the banking services offered are the acceptance of deposits in checking, savings, time and money market accounts; the making of servicing of personal, commercial, floor plan and student loans; and the making of construction and real estate loans. UBSI also owns nonbank subsidiaries that engage in mortgage banking, asset management, investment banking and financial planning. As of 1/22/02, the Company operated 86 offices nationwide in West Virginia, Virginia, Maryland, Ohio, and Washington.

ANNUAL FINANCIAL DATA

	12/31/01	12/31/00	12/31/99	12/31/98	12/31/97	12/31/96	12/31/95
Earnings Per Share	1.90	1.40	1.61	1.02	1.35	1.00	1.18
Tang. Book Val. Per Share	11.80	10.32	9.32	9.75	9.32	8.57	8.37
Dividends Per Share	0.89	0.84	0.81	0.72	0.66	0.61	0.57
Dividend Payout %	46.8	60.0	50.3	70.6	48.9	61.0	48.5
INCOME STATEMENT (IN MILLIONS):							
Total Interest Income	360.6	377.8	354.7	325.6	190.3	172.4	136.5
Total Interest Expense	175.5	197.8	174.4	155.4	84.5	73.2	54.8
Net Interest Income	185.1	180.1	180.3	170.3	105.8	99.2	81.7
Provision for Loan Losses	12.8	15.7	8.8	12.2	3.1	2.6	2.1
Non-Interest Income	62.2	33.8	51.1	41.8	19.7	14.2	12.6
Non-Interest Expense	115.7	110.4	117.5	138.0	59.9	63.5	48.9
Income Before Taxes	118.7	87.7	105.0	61.9	62.4	47.2	43.4
Net Income	80.0	59.0	70.2	44.4	40.9	30.5	28.1
Average Shs. Outstg. (000)	42,065	42,260	43,722	43,461	30,272	30,506	23,858
BALANCE SHEET (IN MILLIONS):							
Cash & Due from Banks	156.1	142.8	131.1	124.6	80.4	86.3	78.9
Securities Avail. for Sale	1,147.3	865.3	1,207.4	565.2	273.9	161.6	196.7
Total Loans & Leases	3,505.4	3,197.5	3,177.4	2,659.3	2,060.5	1,851.3	1,378.0
Allowance for Credit Losses	50.5	45.5	46.9	46.1	31.8	27.4	24.0
Net Loans & Leases	3,454.9	3,152.0	3,130.5	2,613.2	2,028.7	1,823.8	1,354.0
Total Assets	5,631.8	4,904.5	5,069.2	4,567.9	2,699.8	2,326.9	1,815.4
Total Deposits	3,787.8	3,391.4	3,261.0	3,493.1	2,106.0	1,827.6	1,473.3
Long-Term Obligations	736.5	706.5	953.3	345.9	142.7	132.6	33.9
Total Liabilities	5,125.2	4,473.7	4,673.2	4,146.4	2,420.4	2,068.4	1,614.2
Net Stockholders' Equity	506.5	430.9	395.9	421.5	279.4	258.5	201.2
Year-end Shs. Outstg. (000)	42,927	41,765	42,487	43,256	29,968	30,180	24,032
STATISTICAL RECORD:							
Return on Equity %	15.8	13.7	17.7	10.5	14.7	11.8	14.0
Return on Assets %	1.4	1.2	1.4	1.0	1.5	1.3	1.5
Equity/Assets %	9.0	8.8	7.8	9.2	10.4	11.1	11.1
Non-Int. Exp./Tot. Inc. %	46.8	51.6	50.8	65.1	47.8	56.1	51.8
Price Range	29.50-19.44	24.44-16.38	27.69-22.63	34.19-20.75	24.38-16.13	16.50-13.13	15.50-11.63
P/E Ratio	15.5-10.2	17.5-11.7	17.2-14.1	33.5-20.3	18.1-11.9	16.5-13.1	13.2-9.9
Average Yield %	3.6	4.1	3.2	2.6	3.3	4.1	4.2

Statistics are as originally reported. Adj. for 2-for-1 stk. split, 3/98.

OFFICERS:
R. M. Adams, Chmn., C.E.O.
S. E. Wilson, Exec. V.P., C.F.O., Treas., Sec.

INVESTOR CONTACT: Investor Relations, (304) 424-8764

PRINCIPAL OFFICE: 300 United Center, 500 Virginia Street East, Charleston, WV 25301

TELEPHONE NUMBER: (304) 424-8704
FAX: (304) 424-8758
WEB: www.ubsi-wv.com

NO. OF EMPLOYEES: 1,361 (approx.)

SHAREHOLDERS: 11,474 (approx.)

ANNUAL MEETING: In May

INCORPORATED: WV, Mar., 1982

INSTITUTIONAL HOLDINGS:
No. of Institutions: 121
Shares Held: 13,591,606
% Held: 31.7

INDUSTRY: National commercial banks (SIC: 6021)

TRANSFER AGENT(S): Mellon Investor Services, LLC, Ridgefield Park, NJ

UNITED DOMINION REALTY TRUST, INC.

YIELD 7.0%
P/E RATIO 24.4

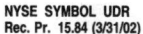

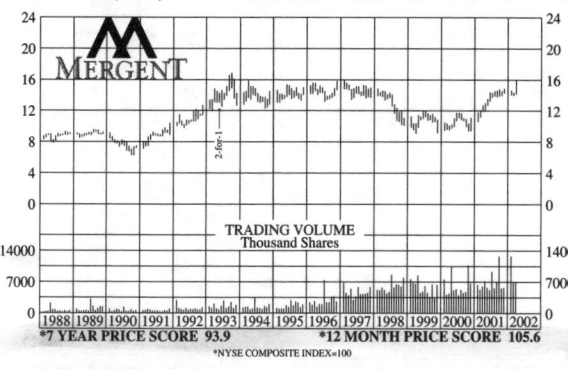

*7 YEAR PRICE SCORE 93.9 ***12 MONTH PRICE SCORE 105.6**

*NYSE COMPOSITE INDEX=100

TRADING VOLUME
Thousand Shares

INTERIM EARNINGS (Per Share):

Qtr.	Mar.	June	Sept.	Dec.
1997	0.20	0.17	0.26	0.17
1998	0.19	0.33	0.13	0.07
1999	0.19	0.39	0.19	0.12
2000	0.18	0.12	0.20	0.23
2001	0.06	0.32	0.14	0.13

INTERIM DIVIDENDS (Per Share):

Amt.	Decl.	Ex.	Rec.	Pay.
0.27Q	6/25/01	7/11/01	7/13/01	7/31/01
0.27Q	9/27/01	10/10/01	10/12/01	10/31/01
0.27Q	12/10/01	1/11/02	1/15/02	1/31/02
0.278Q	3/15/02	4/10/02	4/12/02	4/30/02

Indicated div.: $1.11 (Div. Reinv. Plan)

CAPITALIZATION (12/31/01):

	($000)	(%)
Long-Term Debt	2,109,075	65.3
Minority Interest	75,665	2.3
Preferred Stock	310,400	9.6
Common & Surplus	732,325	22.7
Total	3,227,465	100.0

DIVIDEND ACHIEVER STATUS:
Rank: 225   10-Year Growth Rate: 5.60%
Total Years of Dividend Growth: 16

RECENT DEVELOPMENTS: For the year ended 12/31/01, the Company reported income of $65.3 million, before an extraordinary loss of $3.5 million, versus income of $75.8 million, before an extraordinary gain of $831,000, in the previous year. Earnings for 2001 and 2000 included non-recurring charges of $10.8 million and $3.7 million, respectively. Earnings also included gains from the sale of real estate of $24.7 million in 2001 and $31.5 million in 2000. Total revenues declined 1.4% to $623.2 million.

PROSPECTS: Looking ahead, UDR is confident that it will continue to generate positive growth for 2002, meeting its expected funds from operations growth rate of 9.0% to 11.0%. Separately, UDR began 2001 with 2,426 apartment units under development of which 1,964 units have been delivered with a projected stabilized return on average of 10.5%. As of 12/31/01, the Company had three communities under construction containing a total of 462 apartment units, of which 254 units have previously been delivered.

BUSINESS

UNITED DOMINION REALTY TRUST, INC. is a self-administered equity real estate investment trust with activities related to the ownership, development, acquisition, renovation, management, marketing and strategic disposition of multifamily apartment communities nationwide. At 12/31/01, UDR's apartment portfolio included 274 communities located in 21 states, with a total of 77,567 completed apartment homes. In addition, the Company had 462 apartment homes under development at two additional phases of existing communities. The Company's apartment communities consist primarily of upper- and middle-income garden and townhouse communities that make up the broadest segment of the apartment market. UDR has regional offices in Richmond, Dallas and Atlanta.

ANNUAL FINANCIAL DATA

	12/31/01	12/31/00	12/31/99	12/31/98	12/31/97	12/31/96	12/31/95
Earnings Per Share	①②0.65	①0.73	①②0.89	①②0.72	①②0.80	①②0.66	0.63
Tang. Book Val. Per Share	7.10	7.91	8.59	9.11	9.01	9.09	7.30
Dividends Per Share	1.08	1.07	1.06	1.04	1.00	0.94	0.87
Dividend Payout %	165.8	146.2	118.8	144.4	124.7	143.2	138.1
INCOME STATEMENT (IN MILLIONS):							
Rental Income	618.6	616.8	618.7	478.7	386.7	242.1	195.2
Total Income	623.2	622.2	620.7	482.1	387.8	243.8	195.2
Costs & Expenses	278.7	260.0	280.4	225.3	172.2	110.5	86.5
Depreciation	155.3	157.4	126.2	103.2	78.8	48.7	40.0
Interest Expense	144.4	156.0	153.7	106.2	79.0	50.8	40.6
Income Before Income Taxes	69.5	80.2	98.4	74.0	70.5	38.1	33.1
Equity Earnings/Minority Int.	d4.2	d4.4	d5.7	d1.5	d0.3	d0.1	...
Net Income	①②65.3	①75.8	①②92.7	②72.5	①②70.2	①②38.0	33.1
Average Shs. Outstg. (000)	101,037	103,208	103,639	100,062	87,339	57,482	52,781
BALANCE SHEET (IN MILLIONS):							
Cash & Cash Equivalents	31.5	55.2	64.6	76.9	17.6	13.5	2.9
Total Real Estate Investments	3,212.2	3,252.1	3,204.7	3,362.6	2,080.9	1,834.3	1,001.6
Total Assets	3,348.1	3,454.0	3,688.3	3,762.9	2,313.7	1,966.9	1,080.6
Long-Term Obligations	2,109.1	2,040.9	2,176.1	2,167.5	1,192.9	1,044.8	530.3
Total Liabilities	2,305.4	2,235.1	2,378.1	2,388.8	1,255.4	1,116.5	564.2
Net Stockholders' Equity	1,042.7	1,218.9	1,310.2	1,374.1	1,058.4	850.4	516.4
Year-end Shs. Outstg. (000)	103,133	102,219	102,741	103,639	89,168	81,983	56,375
STATISTICAL RECORD:							
Net Inc.+Depr./Assets %	6.6	6.8	5.9	4.7	6.4	4.4	6.8
Return on Equity %	6.3	6.2	7.1	5.3	6.6	4.5	6.4
Return on Assets %	2.0	2.2	2.5	1.9	3.0	1.9	3.1
Price Range	14.85-10.56	11.75-9.38	12.06-9.06	14.81-10.06	16.00-13.38	15.81-13.13	15.38-13.00
P/E Ratio	55.0-39.1	28.7-22.9	22.3-16.8	30.2-20.5	26.7-22.3	32.3-26.8	30.7-26.0
Average Yield %	8.5	10.1	10.0	8.4	6.8	6.5	6.1

Statistics are as originally reported. ① Bef. extraord. chrg. $3.5 mill., 12/01; gain, $831,000, 12/00; gain $927,000, 12/99; chrg $138,000, 12/98; chrg. $50,000, 12/97; chrg. $23,000, 12/96 ② Incl. non-recurr. chrg. $10.8 mill., 12/01; $19.3 mill., 12/99; $15.6 mill., 12/98; $1.4 mill., 12/97; $290,000, 12/96

OFFICERS:
R. Larson, Chmn.
T. W. Toomey, Pres., C.E.O.
C. Genry, C.F.O.
INVESTOR CONTACT: Ella Neyland, Investor Relations, (804) 819-1879
PRINCIPAL OFFICE: 400 East Cary Street, Richmond, VA 23219-3802

TELEPHONE NUMBER: (804) 780-2691
FAX: (804) 343-1912
WEB: www.udrt.com
NO. OF EMPLOYEES: 1,985
SHAREHOLDERS: 7,943
ANNUAL MEETING: In May
INCORPORATED: VA, Dec., 1984

INSTITUTIONAL HOLDINGS:
No. of Institutions: 188
Shares Held: 41,254,857
% Held: 38.7
INDUSTRY: Real estate investment trusts (SIC: 6798)
TRANSFER AGENT(S): Mellon Investor Services, Pittsburgh, PA

UNITED FIRE & CASUALTY COMPANY

YIELD	2.2%
P/E RATIO	13.7

INTERIM EARNINGS (Per Share):

Qtr.	Mar.	June	Sept.	Dec.
1998	0.83	1.18	d0.19	0.41
1999	0.29	0.05	0.63	0.54
2000	0.34	0.09	0.71	0.41
2001	1.06	d0.02	0.15	1.21

INTERIM DIVIDENDS (Per Share):

Amt.	Decl.	Ex.	Rec.	Pay.
0.18Q	2/16/01	2/27/01	3/01/01	3/15/01
0.18Q	5/16/01	5/30/01	6/01/01	6/15/01
0.18Q	8/17/01	8/29/01	9/01/01	9/15/01
0.18Q	11/16/01	12/12/01	12/14/01	1/04/02
0.18Q	2/15/02	2/27/02	3/01/02	3/15/02
	Indicated div.: $0.72			

CAPITALIZATION (12/31/01):

	($000)	(%)
Deferred Income Tax	12,659	4.3
Common & Surplus	278,988	95.7
Total	291,647	100.0

DIVIDEND ACHIEVER STATUS:
Rank: 204   10-Year Growth Rate: 6.29%
Total Years of Dividend Growth: 16

7 YEAR PRICE SCORE 83.5   **12 MONTH PRICE SCORE 113.2**
*NYSE COMPOSITE INDEX=100

RECENT DEVELOPMENTS: For the year ended 12/31/01, net income advanced 55.2% to $24.1 million compared with $15.5 million in the previous year. Results for 2001 and 2000 included amortization of deferred policy acquisition costs of $67.5 million and $58.4 million, respectively. Results for 2001 also included a charge of $4.5 million related to the terrorist attacks from assumed property reinsurance claims. Total revenues increased 12.5% to $473.0 million from $420.6 million a year earlier, primarily due to an increase in premiums earned in the property and casualty segment and higher investment income from the life insurance segment. Revenues included investment losses of $84,000 and $1.8 million in 2001 and 2000, respectively. Net premiums earned climbed 11.6% to $372.0 million, while net investment income rose 13.9% to $98.9 million. Commission and policy fee income decreased 2.9% to $2.1 million. For the quarter ended 12/31/01, net income rocketed to $12.2 million versus $4.1 million in the corresponding prior-year quarter. Total revenues rose 10.5% to $122.8 million from $111.1 million the year before.

BUSINESS

UNITED FIRE & CASUALTY COMPANY and its insurance subsidiaries are engaged in the business of property and casualty and life insurance. The Company's property and casualty segment includes the following subsidiaries: Addison Insurance Company, a wholly-owned property and casualty insurer; Addison Insurance Agency, a wholly-owned general agency of Addison Insurance Company; Lafayette Insurance Company, a wholly-owned property and casualty insurer; Insurance Brokers & Managers Inc., a wholly-owned general agency of Lafayette Insurance Company; American Indemnity Financial Corporation, a wholly-owned holding company; American Indemnity Company, a wholly-owned property and casualty company of American Indemnity Financial Corporation and its subsidiaries: American Fire and Indemnity Company, Texas General Indemnity Company, American Computing Company, and the affiliate United Fire Lloyds, which is financially and operationally controlled by the Company. The Company's life insurance segment subsidiary is United Life Insurance Company, a wholly-owned life insurance company.

ANNUAL FINANCIAL DATA

	12/31/01	12/31/00	12/31/99	12/31/98	12/31/97	12/31/96	12/31/95
Earnings Per Share	② 2.40	1.55	1.53	2.28	2.68	2.04	2.66
Tang. Book Val. Per Share	27.48	25.01	22.84	25.31	25.74	21.12	19.13
Dividends Per Share	0.72	0.70	0.68	0.66	0.62	0.60	0.49
Dividend Payout %	30.0	45.2	44.4	28.9	23.1	29.4	18.4
INCOME STATEMENT (IN MILLIONS):							
Net Premium Income	372.0	333.4	273.1	245.7	244.9	234.8	207.5
Other Income	100.9	87.2	80.2	92.5	66.2	65.5	57.1
Total Revenues	473.0	420.6	353.2	338.3	311.1	300.3	264.6
Income Before Income Taxes	28.6	17.3	17.2	28.4	38.2	27.4	38.1
Income Taxes	4.5	1.8	1.8	4.7	9.4	5.4	9.2
Net Income	① 24.1	15.5	15.4	23.7	28.7	22.0	28.8
Average Shs. Outstg. (000)	10,036	10,047	10,080	10,393	10,727	10,774	10,830
BALANCE SHEET (IN MILLIONS):							
Cash & Cash Equivalents	48.2	58.3	29.9	34.0	21.6	43.7	28.5
Premiums Due	134.4	106.1	82.2	61.5	58.5	56.6	55.6
Invst. Assets: Equities	110.4	111.1	109.1	111.1	128.7	91.3	75.7
Invst. Assets: Loans	8.2	8.4	8.6	11.5	11.3	10.6	10.2
Invst. Assets: Total	176.7	190.7	151.3	170.9	171.6	141.2	116.0
Total Assets	467.6	450.1	388.3	337.4	333.6	305.8	268.7
Net Stockholders' Equity	279.0	257.4	237.8	256.3	277.2	227.9	208.8
Year-end Shs. Outstg. (000)	10,036	10,036	10,060	10,092	10,727	10,728	10,829
STATISTICAL RECORD:							
Return on Revenues %	5.1	3.7	4.4	7.0	9.2	7.3	10.9
Return on Equity %	8.6	6.0	6.5	9.2	10.4	9.6	13.8
Return on Assets %	5.2	3.4	4.0	7.0	8.6	7.2	10.7
Price Range	34.51-19.00	23.31-15.50	35.50-19.25	46.25-32.00	47.00-29.75	40.00-27.33	29.17-17.83
P/E Ratio	14.4-7.9	15.0-10.0	23.2-12.6	20.3-14.0	17.5-11.1	19.6-13.4	11.0-6.7
Average Yield %	2.7	3.6	2.5	1.7	1.6	1.8	2.1

Statistics are as originally reported. Adj. for stk. splits: 3-for-2, 1/5/96; 3-for-2, 1/5/95. ①
Incl. $4.5 mill. chrg. related to events of 9/11/01 from assumed property reinsurance claims.

OFFICERS:
S. McIntyre Jr., Chmn.
J. A. Rife, Pres., C.E.O.
K. G. Baker, V.P., C.F.O.
INVESTOR CONTACT: Investor Relations, (319) 399-5700
PRINCIPAL OFFICE: 118 Second Avenue, S.E., Cedar Rapids, IA 52407-3909

TELEPHONE NUMBER: (319) 399-5700
FAX: (319) 399-5499
WEB: www.unitedfiregroup.com
NO. OF EMPLOYEES: 719
SHAREHOLDERS: 891
ANNUAL MEETING: In May
INCORPORATED: IA, Jan., 1946

INSTITUTIONAL HOLDINGS:
No. of Institutions: 40
Shares Held: 3,054,688
% Held: 30.4
INDUSTRY: Fire, marine, and casualty insurance (SIC: 6331)
TRANSFER AGENT(S): Computershare Investor Services, Chicago, IL

UNITED MOBILE HOMES, INC.

YIELD 6.9%
P/E RATIO 16.8

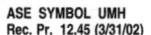

*7 YEAR PRICE SCORE 95.6 ***12 MONTH PRICE SCORE 107.7**
*NYSE COMPOSITE INDEX=100

INTERIM EARNINGS (Per Share):

Qtr.	Mar.	June	Sept.	Dec.
1997	0.16	0.15	0.13	0.19
1998	0.15	0.16	0.13	0.16
1999	0.15	0.15	0.15	0.18
2000	0.20	0.17	0.18	0.16
2001	0.19	0.22	0.23	0.10

INTERIM DIVIDENDS (Per Share):

Amt.	Decl.	Ex.	Rec.	Pay.
0.198Q	3/19/01	5/11/01	5/15/01	6/15/01
0.20Q	6/22/01	8/13/01	8/15/01	9/17/01
0.21Q	10/04/01	11/13/01	11/15/01	12/17/01
0.212Q	1/16/02	2/13/02	2/15/02	3/15/02
0.215Q	3/15/02	5/13/02	5/15/02	6/17/02

Indicated div.: $0.86 (Div. Reinv. Plan)

CAPITALIZATION (12/31/01):

	($000)	(%)
Long-Term Debt	38,652	58.0
Common & Surplus	27,965	42.0
Total	66,617	100.0

DIVIDEND ACHIEVER STATUS:
Rank: 63   10-Year Growth Rate: 14.91%
Total Years of Dividend Growth: 11

RECENT DEVELOPMENTS: For the year ended 12/31/01, net income advanced 7.0% to $5.6 million from $5.2 million in the previous year. Net income included losses on sales of investments and properties of $28,264 and $37,318 in 2001 and 2000, respectively. Total revenues jumped 30.2% to $26.9 million. Rental and related income rose 3.5% to $19.3 million, primarily due to the acquisition of a new community and rental increases to residents. Sales of manufactured homes was $4.8 million versus nil, while other

income was $105,845 versus nil a year earlier. Revenues included interest and dividend income of $2.2 million in 2001 and $1.7 million in 2000, as well as gains on the sale of securities of $530,324 and $257,142 in 2001 and 2000, respectively. The Company estimates that in 2002 it will purchase approximately 25 manufactured homes to be used as rentals for a total cost of $500,000. UMH anticipates these homes will generate approximately $300.00 per month in rental income in addition to lot rent.

BUSINESS

UNITED MOBILE HOMES, INC., a real estate investment trust, owns and operates 25 manufactured home communities containing 5,979 sites as of 12/31/01. The communities are located in New Jersey, New York, Ohio, Pennsylvania, and Tennessee. The Company's primary business is leasing manufactured home spaces on a month-to-month basis to private manufactured home owners. UMH also leases manufactured homes to residents.

QUARTERLY DATA

(12/31/2001)	REV	INC
1st Quarter................	5,251	1,396
2nd Quarter................	7,377	1,615
3rd Quarter	7,773	1,751
4th Quarter................	6,482	789

ANNUAL FINANCIAL DATA

	12/31/01	12/31/00	12/31/99	12/31/98	12/31/97	12/31/96	12/31/95
Earnings Per Share	① ② 0.74	① ② 0.71	① ② 0.63	0.60	0.63	0.61	0.44
Tang. Book Val. Per Share	3.71	3.09	2.93	3.20	3.03	2.55	1.76
Dividends Per Share	0.80	0.76	0.75	0.74	0.70	0.60	0.53
Dividend Payout %	108.4	106.7	119.0	122.9	111.1	98.3	119.3
INCOME STATEMENT (IN THOUSANDS):							
Total Income	26,882	20,645	18,807	17,193	15,664	14,627	13,399
Costs & Expenses	15,705	10,086	9,614	8,990	8,174	7,680	6,861
Depreciation	2,772	2,708	2,530	2,509	2,159	2,062	2,124
Interest Expense	2,826	2,625	2,106	1,506	1,123	1,435	1,676
Net Income	① ② 5,550	① ② 5,189	① ② 4,556	4,202	4,197	3,730	2,492
Average Shs. Outstg.	7,496	7,341	7,268	7,061	6,680	6,073	5,693
BALANCE SHEET (IN THOUSANDS):							
Cash & Cash Equivalents	27,486	16,894	13,519	8,585	3,739	2,636	2,043
Net Property	44,292	41,700	42,162	38,896	37,709	29,887	26,027
Total Real Estate Investments	40,681	38,418	39,193	36,252	35,293	27,724	24,173
Total Assets	80,335	62,946	58,575	50,047	43,599	35,875	29,758
Long-Term Obligations	38,652	32,056	30,419	21,412	20,111	17,351	17,708
Total Liabilities	52,370	40,106	37,184	26,834	22,769	19,449	19,468
Net Stockholders' Equity	27,965	22,839	21,391	23,213	20,831	16,426	10,290
Year-end Shs. Outstg.	7,542	7,394	7,313	7,247	6,865	6,434	5,851
STATISTICAL RECORD:							
Net Inc.+Depr./Assets %	10.4	12.5	12.1	13.4	14.6	16.0	14.7
Return on Equity %	19.8	22.7	21.3	18.1	20.1	22.7	24.2
Return on Assets %	6.9	8.2	7.8	8.4	9.6	10.4	8.4
Price Range	12.75-9.63	10.13-5.63	10.94-7.88	12.50-9.38	13.75-10.88	14.00-9.63	10.63-7.13
P/E Ratio	17.2-13.0	14.3-7.9	17.4-12.5	20.8-15.6	21.8-17.2	22.9-15.8	24.1-16.2
Average Yield %	7.2	9.6	8.0	6.7	5.7	5.1	5.9

Statistics are as originally reported. ① Incls. gains on the sale of securities of $530,324, 12/01; $257,142, 12/00; $53,473, 12/99 ② Incls. losses on the sale of assets of $28,264, 12/01; $37,318, 12/00; $1,964, 12/99

OFFICERS:
E. W. Landy, Chmn.
S. A. Landy, Pres.
A. T. Chew, V.P., C.F.O.
E. V. Bencivenga, Treas., Sec.

INVESTOR CONTACT: Investor Relations, (732) 577-9997

PRINCIPAL OFFICE: 3499 Route 9, Suite 3-C, Freehold, NJ 07728

TELEPHONE NUMBER: (732) 577-9997
FAX: (732) 577-9980
WEB: www.umh.com

NO. OF EMPLOYEES: 100 (approx.)

SHAREHOLDERS: 1,000 (approx. record)

ANNUAL MEETING: In May

INCORPORATED: NJ, 1968

INSTITUTIONAL HOLDINGS:
No. of Institutions: 12
Shares Held: 371,715
% Held: 5.0

INDUSTRY: Real estate investment trusts (SIC: 6798)

TRANSFER AGENT(S): Mellon Investor Services, New York, NY

NYSE SYMBOL UTR
Rec. Pr. 40.20 (3/31/02)

UNITRIN, INC.

YIELD 4.1%
P/E RATIO 7.2

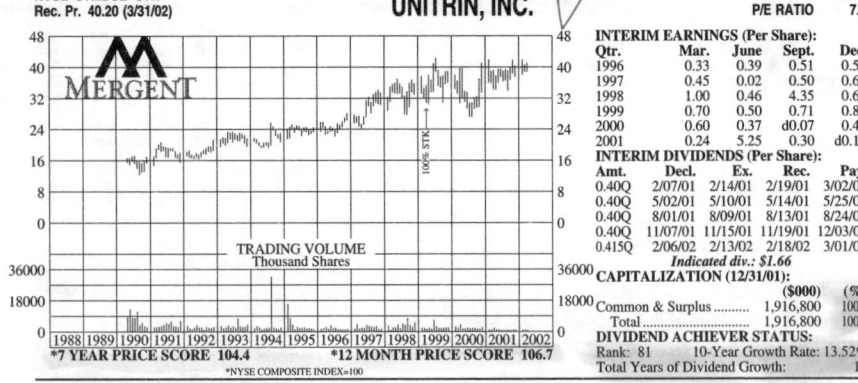

*7 YEAR PRICE SCORE 104.4   *12 MONTH PRICE SCORE 106.7
*NYSE COMPOSITE INDEX=100

INTERIM EARNINGS (Per Share):

Qtr.	Mar.	June	Sept.	Dec.
1996	0.33	0.39	0.51	0.53
1997	0.45	0.02	0.50	0.62
1998	1.00	0.46	4.35	0.60
1999	0.70	0.50	0.71	0.84
2000	0.60	0.37	d0.07	0.41
2001	0.24	5.25	0.30	0.18

INTERIM DIVIDENDS (Per Share):

Amt.	Decl.	Ex.	Rec.	Pay.
0.40Q	2/07/01	2/14/01	2/19/01	3/02/01
0.40Q	5/02/01	5/10/01	5/14/01	5/25/01
0.40Q	8/01/01	8/09/01	8/13/01	8/24/01
0.40Q	11/07/01	11/15/01	11/19/01	12/03/01
0.415Q	2/06/02	2/13/02	2/18/02	3/01/02

Indicated div.: $1.66

CAPITALIZATION (12/31/01):

	($000)	(%)
Common & Surplus	1,916,800	100.0
Total	1,916,800	100.0

DIVIDEND ACHIEVER STATUS:

Rank: 81   10-Year Growth Rate: 13.52%
Total Years of Dividend Growth: 11

RECENT DEVELOPMENTS: For the year ended 12/31/01, net income soared to $380.9 million from $91.0 million in the previous year. Total revenues grew 29.7% to $2.53 billion from $1.95 billion in 2000. Revenues for 2001 and 2000 included net gains on the sales of investments of $568.2 million and $140.5 million, respectively. Premiums revenue grew 8.3% to $1.57 billion. Consumer finance revenues rose 12.3% to $159.1 million, while net investment income rose 6.9% to $238.5 million.

PROSPECTS: UTR is continuing to implement certain premium rate increases in most product lines, subject to regulatory approvals. UTR is also continuing to review underwriting guidelines in certain markets and product lines and continues to implement certain underwriting changes as it writes and renews its business, including placing a moratorium on new business in certain markets where adequate rates cannot be obtained.

BUSINESS

UNITRIN, INC. is engaged, through its subsidiaries, in the property and casualty insurance, life and health insurance and consumer finance businesses. UTR conducts its operations through five operating segments: Multi Lines Insurance, which offers preferred and standard risk automobile, homeowners, fire, commercial liability and workers compensation; Specialty Lines Insurance, which offers automobile, motorcycle and watercraft insurance; Life and Health Insurance, which offers individual life, accident, health and hospitalization insurance products; Consumer Finance, which offers consumer loans primarily for the purchase of used automobiles as well as thrift products in the form of investment certificates and savings accounts; and Unitrin Direct, which offers personal automobile insurance marketed through direct mail, radio and television advertising and over the Internet. On 11/29/01, the Company completed the tax-free distribution to its shareholders of all class B common stock of Cutriss-Wright Corporation owned by UTR.

ANNUAL FINANCIAL DATA

	12/31/01	12/31/00	12/31/99	12/31/98	12/31/97	12/31/96	12/31/95
Earnings Per Share	5.60	1.32	2.74	6.51	1.56	1.76	1.87
Tang. Book Val. Per Share	23.27	19.93	18.98	20.06	17.24	16.77	16.81
Dividends Per Share	1.60	1.50	1.40	1.30	1.20	1.10	1.00
Dividend Payout %	28.6	113.6	51.1	20.0	77.2	62.7	53.6
INCOME STATEMENT (IN MILLIONS):							
Total Premium Income	1,568.0	1,447.9	1,373.3	1,228.3	1,222.0	1,220.3	1,099.1
Other Income	965.8	505.3	440.3	857.6	308.1	302.8	348.3
Total Revenues	2,533.8	1,953.2	1,813.6	2,085.9	1,530.1	1,523.1	1,447.4
Policyholder Benefits	1,217.1	1,039.6	889.1	781.8	780.1	799.7	717.5
Income Before Income Taxes	542.5	152.2	237.0	687.1	139.8	122.1	160.8
Income Taxes	190.3	54.4	77.9	238.6	47.1	40.2	55.3
Equity Earnings/Minority Int.	28.7	d6.8	41.9	62.3	25.2	50.6	45.1
Net Income	380.9	91.0	201.0	510.8	117.9	132.5	150.6
Average Shs. Outstg. (000)	67,900	68,800	73,100	78,200	75,200	75,442	80,800
BALANCE SHEET (IN MILLIONS):							
Cash & Cash Equivalents	27.9	23.3	24.1	8.6	14.5	17.0	9.1
Premiums Due	1,181.0	1,101.6	971.6	822.8	879.0	984.7	797.5
Invst. Assets: Fixed-term	2,926.4	2,733.2	2,651.8	2,557.3	2,315.4	2,207.4	2,457.1
Invst. Assets: Total	5,127.5	4,233.5	4,096.8	4,304.2	3,448.5	3,291.4	3,409.7
Total Assets	7,133.7	6,164.8	5,934.8	5,909.9	4,920.7	4,871.1	4,818.7
Net Stockholders' Equity	1,916.8	1,701.2	1,717.0	1,822.4	1,533.0	1,480.3	1,524.5
Year-end Shs. Outstg. (000)	67,547	67,648	70,993	76,000	75,170	74,682	76,980
STATISTICAL RECORD:							
Return on Revenues %	15.0	4.7	11.1	24.5	7.7	8.7	10.4
Return on Equity %	19.9	5.3	11.7	28.0	7.7	9.0	9.9
Return on Assets %	5.3	1.5	3.4	8.6	2.4	2.7	3.1
Price Range	41.95-33.90	41.13-27.19	42.38-30.50	37.06-27.78	34.25-24.25	28.19-22.13	25.25-21.50
P/E Ratio	7.5-6.1	31.2-20.6	15.5-11.1	5.7-4.3	22.0-15.6	16.1-12.6	13.5-11.5
Average Yield %	4.2	4.4	3.8	4.0	4.1	4.4	4.3

Statistics are as originally reported. Adj. for stk. split: 2-for-1, 3/26/99.

OFFICERS:
R. C. Vie, Chmn., C.E.O.
D. G. Southwell, Pres., C.O.O.
E. J. Draut, Exec. V.P., C.F.O.
S. Renwick, Sr. V.P., Sec., Gen. Couns.

INVESTOR CONTACT: Scott Renwick Sr. V.P., Sec., Gen. Couns., (312) 661-4930

PRINCIPAL OFFICE: One East Wacker Drive, Chicago, IL 60601

TELEPHONE NUMBER: (312) 661-4600
FAX: (312) 661-4690
WEB: www.unitrin.com

NO. OF EMPLOYEES: 7,700 (approx.)

SHAREHOLDERS: 7,700 (approx.)

ANNUAL MEETING: In May

INCORPORATED: DE, Feb., 1990

INSTITUTIONAL HOLDINGS:
No. of Institutions: 147
Shares Held: 14,613,046
% Held: 21.6

INDUSTRY: Fire, marine, and casualty insurance (SIC: 6331)

TRANSFER AGENT(S): First Union National Bank, Charlotte, NC

UNIVERSAL CORPORATION

YIELD 3.5%
P/E RATIO 9.1

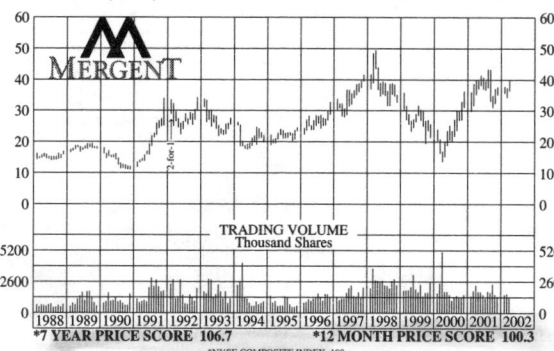

MERGENT

TRADING VOLUME
Thousand Shares

*7 YEAR PRICE SCORE 106.7   *12 MONTH PRICE SCORE 100.3

*NYSE COMPOSITE INDEX=100

INTERIM EARNINGS (Per Share):

Qtr.	Sept.	Dec.	Mar.	June
1997-98	0.63	1.08	1.18	1.10
1998-99	0.78	1.23	0.88	0.91
1999-00	0.93	0.85	1.29	0.69
2000-01	0.89	1.01	1.31	0.87
2001-02	1.04	1.09	...	...

INTERIM DIVIDENDS (Per Share):

Amt.	Decl.	Ex.	Rec.	Pay.
0.32Q	8/02/01	10/04/01	10/09/01	11/12/01
0.34Q	12/06/01	1/09/02	1/11/02	2/11/02
0.34Q	2/07/02	4/04/02	4/08/02	5/13/02

Indicated div.: $1.36 (Div. Reinv. Plan)

CAPITALIZATION (6/30/01):

	($000)	(%)
Long-Term Debt	515,349	46.8
Deferred Income Tax	6,380	0.6
Minority Interest	28,311	2.6
Common & Surplus	552,129	50.1
Total	1,102,169	100.0

DIVIDEND ACHIEVER STATUS:
Rank: 227   10-Year Growth Rate: 5.35%
Total Years of Dividend Growth: 31

RECENT DEVELOPMENTS: For the quarter ended 12/31/01, net income rose 4.4% to $29.1 million versus $27.9 million a year earlier, driven by strong shipments of tobacco and lower interest expense. Earnings for 2001 included a $4.7 million charge related to the re-denomination of value-added tax receivables in Argentina. Sales and other operating revenues fell 25.2% to $744.3 million, reflecting the growing trend among U.S. manufacturers of buying tobacco directly from farmers.

PROSPECTS: Higher costs associated with staffing both contract receiving stations and the auction system in the Company's U.S. tobacco operations tempers UVV's near-term outlook. The Company noted that the operating environment in the U.S. remains difficult as a result of reduced crops, uncompetitive leaf prices, and a high-cost marketing system. Meanwhile, small Brazilian and Zimbabwean crops have affected the quantities of tobacco handled in those origins.

BUSINESS

UNIVERSAL CORPORATION is an independent leaf tobacco merchant with additional operations in agri-products and the distribution of lumber and building products. UVV's tobacco business involves selecting, buying, shipping, processing, packing, storing and financing leaf tobacco in the U.S. and other tobacco growing countries for the account of, or for resale to, manufacturers of tobacco products throughout the world. The agri-products operations involve the selecting, buying, storing, financing, distribution, importing, and exporting of a number of products including tea, rubber, sunflower seeds, nuts, dried fruit, and canned and frozen foods. The lumber and building products operations involve distribution to the building and construction trade in the Netherlands and Belgium.

BUSINESS LINE ANALYSIS

(6/30/01)	Rev (%)	Inc (%)
Tobacco	68.3	85.9
Lumber & Building		
Product	16.5	9.2
Agri-products	15.2	4.9
Total	100.0	100.0

ANNUAL FINANCIAL DATA

	6/30/01	6/30/00	6/30/99	6/30/98	6/30/97	6/30/96	6/30/95
Earnings Per Share	4.08	④ 3.77	③ 3.80	3.99	2.88	② 2.04	① 0.73
Cash Flow Per Share	6.12	5.49	5.38	5.43	4.35	3.54	2.12
Tang. Book Val. Per Share	15.77	13.04	12.47	11.71	9.37	7.64	6.87
Dividends Per Share	1.28	1.24	1.20	1.12	1.06	1.02	1.00
Dividend Payout %	31.4	32.9	31.6	28.1	36.8	50.0	137.0
INCOME STATEMENT (IN MILLIONS)							
Total Revenues	3,017.6	3,402.0	4,004.9	4,287.2	4,112.7	3,570.2	3,280.9
Costs & Expenses	2,722.4	3,116.0	3,697.6	3,957.7	3,824.3	3,325.2	3,106.9
Depreciation & Amort.	56.4	52.0	52.8	51.1	51.6	52.5	48.6
Operating Income	238.8	233.9	254.6	278.4	236.8	192.5	124.5
Net Interest Inc./(Exp.)	d61.6	d56.9	d56.8	d64.0	d64.9	d68.8	d69.6
Income Before Income Taxes	187.4	189.6	211.8	248.0	171.9	123.7	55.8
Income Taxes	66.3	68.2	76.0	98.7	68.8	49.5	24.9
Equity Earnings/Minority Int.	1.8	5.0	5.5	8.8	d2.3	d2.9	d5.3
Net Income	112.7	④ 113.8	③ 127.3	141.3	100.9	② 71.4	① 25.6
Cash Flow	169.1	165.8	180.0	192.3	152.4	123.9	74.3
Average Shs. Outstg. (000)	27,645	30,205	33,477	35,388	35,076	35,038	35,014
BALANCE SHEET (IN MILLIONS)							
Cash & Cash Equivalents	109.5	61.4	92.8	79.8	109.1	214.8	158.1
Total Current Assets	1,132.6	1,088.2	1,170.3	1,430.3	1,431.2	1,329.0	1,262.4
Net Property	338.1	347.3	348.3	329.8	309.7	320.4	334.4
Total Assets	1,782.4	1,748.1	1,823.1	2,056.7	1,982.0	1,889.5	1,808.0
Total Current Liabilities	581.8	883.2	898.5	1,101.5	1,083.7	1,029.2	997.6
Long-Term Obligations	515.3	223.3	221.5	263.1	291.6	309.5	284.9
Net Stockholders' Equity	552.1	497.8	539.0	547.9	469.6	417.3	390.0
Net Working Capital	550.9	204.9	271.8	328.8	347.5	299.8	264.7
Year-end Shs. Outstg. (000)	27,185	28,147	32,091	34,866	35,139	35,056	35,030
STATISTICAL RECORD:							
Operating Profit Margin %	7.9	6.9	6.4	6.5	5.8	5.4	3.8
Net Profit Margin %	3.7	3.4	3.2	3.3	2.5	2.0	0.8
Return on Equity %	20.4	22.9	23.6	25.8	21.5	17.1	6.6
Return on Assets %	6.3	6.5	7.0	6.9	5.1	3.8	1.4
Debt/Total Assets %	28.9	12.8	12.2	12.8	14.7	16.4	15.8
Price Range	43.37-29.75	36.38-13.50	35.75-19.44	49.50-31.50	41.69-27.88	32.75-22.25	24.63-18.88
P/E Ratio	10.6-7.3	9.6-3.6	9.4-5.1	12.4-7.9	14.5-9.7	16.1-10.9	33.7-25.9
Average Yield %	3.5	5.0	4.3	2.8	3.0	3.7	4.6

Statistics are as originally reported. ① Incl. non-recurr. chrg. of $15.6 mill. ② Bef. extraord. gain of $900,000. ③ Incl. gain of $16.7 mill. fr. sale of invest. ④ Incl. after-tax restruct. chrg.: 2001, $6.0 mill.; 2000, $7.0 mill.

OFFICERS:
H. H. Harrell, Chmn., C.E.O.
A. B. King, Pres., C.O.O.
H. H. Roper, V.P., C.F.O.

INVESTOR CONTACT: Karen M. L. Whelan, V.P., Treas., (804) 254-8689

PRINCIPAL OFFICE: 1501 North Hamilton Street, Richmond, VA 23230

TELEPHONE NUMBER: (804) 359-9311
FAX: (804) 254-3594
WEB: www.universalcorp.com

NO. OF EMPLOYEES: 26,000 (approx.)

SHAREHOLDERS: 2,528

ANNUAL MEETING: In Oct.

INCORPORATED: VA, Jan., 1918

INSTITUTIONAL HOLDINGS:
No. of Institutions: 144
Shares Held: 18,196,752
% Held: 69.0

INDUSTRY: Farm-product raw materials, nec (SIC: 5159)

TRANSFER AGENT(S): Wells Fargo Shareowner Services, St. Paul, MN

UNIVERSAL HEALTH REALTY INCOME TRUST

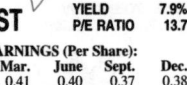

YIELD	7.9%
P/E RATIO	13.7

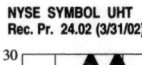

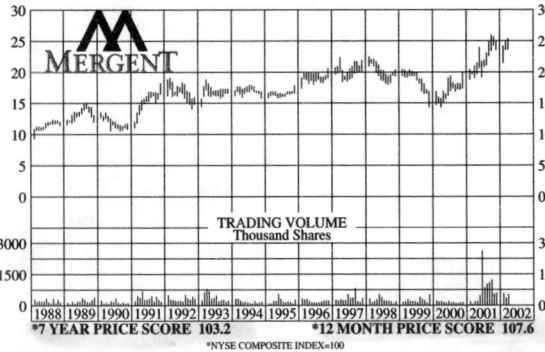

INTERIM EARNINGS (Per Share):

Qtr.	Mar.	June	Sept.	Dec.
1997	0.41	0.40	0.37	0.38
1998	0.40	0.39	0.39	0.42
1999	0.44	0.42	0.25	0.44
2000	0.44	0.42	0.43	0.52
2001	0.46	0.44	0.42	0.43

INTERIM DIVIDENDS (Per Share):

Amt.	Decl.	Ex.	Rec.	Pay.
0.465Q	3/01/01	3/14/01	3/16/01	3/30/01
0.465Q	6/01/01	6/13/01	6/15/01	6/29/01
0.47Q	9/04/01	9/17/01	9/14/01	9/28/01
0.475Q	12/03/01	12/13/01	12/17/01	12/31/01
0.475Q	3/08/02	3/14/02	3/18/02	3/29/02

Indicated div.: $1.90 (Div. Reinv. Plan)

CAPITALIZATION (12/31/01):

	($000)	(%)
Long-Term Debt	33,432	18.2
Minority Interest	43	0.0
Common & Surplus	150,034	81.8
Total	183,509	100.0

TRADING VOLUME
Thousand Shares

*7 YEAR PRICE SCORE 103.2   *12 MONTH PRICE SCORE 107.6
*NYSE COMPOSITE INDEX=100

DIVIDEND ACHIEVER STATUS:
Rank: 275   10-Year Growth Rate: 1.99%
Total Years of Dividend Growth: 14

RECENT DEVELOPMENTS: For the year ended 12/31/01, net income advanced 12.9% to $18.3 million versus $16.3 million in 2000. Results for 2001 included a gain on derivatives of $17,000. Results for 2000 included a gain of $1.9 million on the sale of real property to UHS. Total revenues inched up to $27.6 million from $27.3 million in 2000. Base rental revenues from non-related parties climbed 9.1% to $11.1 million, while base rental revenues from UHS facilities fell 7.6% to $13.0 million.

PROSPECTS: UNT's hospital facilities may continue to experience an improvement in revenues attributed to manage care payors. Also, pressures to control healthcare costs, as well as a shift away from traditional Medicare to Medicare managed plans should continue to reduce the number of patients whose healthcare coverage is provided under managed care plans. Meanwhile, UNT's facilities are likely to experience an increase in outpatient revenues due to advances in medical technologies.

BUSINESS

UNIVERSAL HEALTH REALTY INCOME TRUST is an organized Maryland real estate investment trust (REIT). As of 12/31/01, the Trust had investments in 42 facilities located in 15 states consisting of investments in healthcare and human service related facilities including acute care hospitals, behavioral healthcare facilities, rehabilitation hospitals, sub-acute care facilities, surgery centers, childcare centers and medical office buildings. Six of the Trust's hospital facilities and three medical office buildings are leased to subsidiaries of Universal Health Services, Inc. As of 12/31/01, Universal Health Services owned 6.6% of the Company's outstanding shares.

ANNUAL FINANCIAL DATA

	12/31/01	12/31/00	12/31/99	12/31/98	12/31/97	12/31/96	12/31/95
Earnings Per Share	④ 1.74	①⑤ 1.81	①② 1.56	1.60	1.56	1.58	1.52
Tang. Book Val. Per Share	12.85	11.05	11.09	11.32	11.47	11.62	11.74
Dividends Per Share	1.88	1.84	1.81	1.76	1.71	1.70	1.68
Dividend Payout %	107.8	101.7	116.0	109.7	109.3	107.3	110.5
INCOME STATEMENT (IN THOUSANDS):							
Rental Income	27,574	27,315	23,584	23,123	22,180	21,172	19,459
Interest Income	...	...	281	111	584	751	958
Total Income	27,574	27,315	23,865	23,234	22,764	21,923	20,417
Costs & Expenses	4,555	4,153	3,003	3,065	2,524	2,193	1,626
Depreciation	4,401	4,461	3,857	3,879	3,775	3,636	3,382
Interest Expense	3,896	6,114	4,004	3,490	2,943	2,565	1,825
Income Before Income Taxes	14,739	12,587	11,418	12,800	13,522	13,529	13,584
Equity Earnings/Minority Int.	3,610	1,774	2,554	1,537	445	629	...
Net Income	④ 18,349	①⑤ 16,256	①② 13,972	14,337	13,967	14,158	13,584
Average Shs. Outstg.	10,536	9,003	8,977	8,974	8,967	8,960	8,947
BALANCE SHEET (IN THOUSANDS):							
Cash & Cash Equivalents	629	294	852	572	1,238	137	139
Total Real Estate Investments	139,215	143,108	141,367	129,838	133,486	139,434	131,188
Total Assets	187,904	183,658	178,821	169,406	146,755	148,566	132,770
Long-Term Obligations	33,432	82,031	76,889	66,016	42,347	43,082	26,396
Total Liabilities	37,870	84,401	79,146	68,058	44,063	44,584	27,773
Net Stockholders' Equity	150,034	99,257	99,675	101,348	102,692	103,982	104,997
Year-end Shs. Outstg.	11,679	8,980	8,991	8,955	8,955	8,952	8,947
STATISTICAL RECORD:							
Net Inc.+Depr./Assets %	12.1	11.3	10.0	10.8	12.1	12.0	12.8
Return on Equity %	12.2	16.4	14.0	14.1	13.6	13.6	12.9
Return on Assets %	9.8	8.9	7.8	8.5	9.5	9.5	10.2
Price Range	26.00-18.75	19.88-14.25	20.50-14.25	22.50-17.94	22.38-18.38	20.63-17.38	17.88-15.75
P/E Ratio	14.9-10.8	11.0-7.9	13.1-9.1	14.1-11.2	14.3-11.8	13.1-11.0	11.8-10.4
Average Yield %	8.4	10.8	10.4	8.7	8.4	8.9	10.0

Statistics are as originally reported. ① Incl. a provision of $1.6 mill. for investment losses. ② Incl. pre-tax nonrecurr. chrgs. of $5.3 mill. ③ Incl. a gain of $1.9 mill. on the sale of real prop. to UHS. ④ Incl. a gain on derivatives of $17,000.

USA EDUCATION, INC.

YIELD 0.8%
P/E RATIO 42.9

INTERIM EARNINGS (Per Share):				
Qtr.	Mar.	June	Sept.	Dec.
1997	0.62	0.63	0.79	0.75
1998	0.80	0.84	0.64	0.66
1999	0.69	0.76	0.75	0.87
2000	0.93	0.73	0.55	0.56
2001	0.16	1.68	d1.25	1.69

INTERIM DIVIDENDS (Per Share):				
Amt.	Decl.	Ex.	Rec.	Pay.
0.175Q	5/10/01	5/30/01	6/01/01	6/15/01
0.175Q	7/26/01	9/05/01	9/07/01	9/21/01
0.20Q	10/26/01	12/05/01	12/07/01	12/21/01
0.20Q	1/25/02	2/27/02	3/01/02	3/15/02

Indicated div.: $0.80 (Div. Reinv. Plan)

CAPITALIZATION (12/31/01):

	($000)	(%)
Long-Term Debt	17,285,350	91.2
Preferred Stock	165,000	0.9
Common & Surplus	1,507,462	8.0
Total	18,957,812	100.0

TRADING VOLUME
Thousand Shares

*7 YEAR PRICE SCORE 165.1 ***12 MONTH PRICE SCORE 116.6**
*NYSE COMPOSITE INDEX=100

DIVIDEND ACHIEVER STATUS:
Rank: 108   10-Year Growth Rate: 11.55%
Total Years of Dividend Growth: 21

RECENT DEVELOPMENTS: For the year ended 12/31/01, net income declined 17.4% to $384.0 million from $465.0 million in the previous year. Results for 2001 included a derivative market value adjustment loss of $505.7 million, while results for 2000 included an integration charge of $53.0 million. Net interest income climbed 36.1% to $873.4 million from $641.8 million in the prior year. Provision for loan losses jumped 105.6% to $66.0 million.

PROSPECTS: In January 2002, the Company acquired Pioneer Credit General Recovery, Inc., a student loan collection service for the U.S. Department of Education, and agreed to acquire General Recovery, Inc., the nation's largest university-focused collection agency. Separately, on 4/9/02, the Company announced plans to change its name to SLM Corporation, effective 5/17/02.

BUSINESS

USA EDUCATION, INC. (formerly SLM Holding Corporation) is a state-chartered stockholder-owned corporation, created to provide liquidity, primarily through instituting a secondary market and warehousing facilities for insured student loans made under state-sponsored student loan programs. These programs include the Guaranteed Student Loan Program, which encompasses Stafford loans, "PLUS" loans and Supplemental Loans for Students loans, as well as the Health Education Assistance Loan Program. SLM provides financial services to financial institutions, educational institutions, state agencies, and students. The services include loan purchases, funding and operational support. On 7/7/00, the Company acquired Student Loan Funding Resources, Inc. On 7/31/00, the Company completed the purchase of USA Group's guarantee servicing, student loan servicing and secondary market operations for $770.0 million in cash and stock.

ANNUAL FINANCIAL DATA

	12/31/01	12/31/00	12/31/99	12/31/98	12/31/97	12/31/96	12/31/95
Earnings Per Share	④ 2.28	③ 2.76	3.06	2.95	② 2.80	② 2.13	①② 2.14
Tang. Book Val. Per Share	9.69	7.62	4.29	3.98	3.67	3.63	6.01
Dividends Per Share	0.73	0.66	0.61	0.57	0.52	0.47	0.43
Dividend Payout %	32.0	23.9	19.9	19.3	18.5	22.0	20.2
INCOME STATEMENT (IN MILLIONS):							
Total Interest Income	2,997.5	3,478.7	2,808.6	2,587.6	3,283.8	3,449.3	3,693.7
Total Interest Expense	2,124.1	2,836.9	2,114.8	1,925.0	2,526.2	2,582.9	3,020.6
Net Interest Income	873.4	641.8	693.8	662.7	757.7	866.4	673.0
Provision for Loan Losses	66.0	32.1	34.4	28.6	...	...	...
Non-Interest Income	517.6	687.6	450.8	477.0	500.9	146.9	...
Non-Interest Expense	707.7	585.7	358.6	360.9	493.8	405.7	160.6
Income Before Taxes	617.4	711.6	751.7	750.1	764.8	607.7	512.5
Equity Earnings/Minority Int.	d10.1	d10.7	d10.7	d10.7	d10.7	d10.7	...
Net Income	④ 384.0	③ 465.0	500.8	501.5	② 511.2	② 413.5	①② 371.2
Average Shs. Outstg. (000)	163,400	164,355	163,158	170,066	182,941	194,466	...
BALANCE SHEET (IN MILLIONS):							
Total Loans & Leases	42,769.0	39,485.8	35,879.3	31,005.6	32,764.3	38,016.3	39,513.5
Net Loans & Leases	42,769.0	39,485.8	35,879.3	31,005.6	32,764.3	38,016.3	39,513.5
Total Assets	52,874.0	48,791.8	44,024.8	37,210.0	39,908.8	47,629.9	50,001.7
Long-Term Obligations	17,285.4	14,910.9	4,496.3	8,810.6	14,541.3	22,606.2	30,082.6
Total Liabilities	51,201.5	47,376.5	43,183.9	36,556.4	39,234.2	46,795.9	48,920.5
Net Stockholders' Equity	1,672.5	1,415.3	840.9	653.6	674.6	833.9	1,081.2
Year-end Shs. Outstg. (000)	155,495	164,145	157,577	164,127	183,633	229,934	144,265
STATISTICAL RECORD:							
Return on Equity %	23.0	32.9	59.6	76.7	75.8	49.6	34.3
Return on Assets %	0.7	1.0	1.1	1.4	1.3	0.9	0.7
Equity/Assets %	3.2	2.9	1.9	1.8	1.7	1.8	2.2
Non-Int. Exp./Tot. Inc. %	50.9	44.1	31.3	31.7	39.2	40.0	23.9
Price Range	87.99-55.88	68.25-27.81	53.94-39.50	51.38-27.50	47.18-25.43	28.07-18.07	20.25-9.39
P/E Ratio	38.6-24.5	24.7-10.1	17.6-12.9	17.4-9.3	16.8-9.1	13.2-8.5	9.5-4.4
Average Yield %	1.0	1.4	1.3	1.4	1.4	2.0	2.9

Statistics are as originally reported. Adj. for stk split: 7-for-2, 1/98 ① Bef. acctg. change chrg. of $130.1 mill. ② Bef. chrgs. on debt extinguished, $3.3 mill., 1997; $4.8 mill., 1996; $4.9 mill., 1995 ③ Incl. one-time integration chrg. $53.0 mill ④ Incl. derivative mkt. value adjust. loss $505.7 mill.

OFFICERS:
E. A. Fox, Chmn.
A. L. Lord, Vice-Chmn., C.E.O.
T. J. Fitzpatrick, Pres., C.O.O.

INVESTOR CONTACT: Jefffrey R. Heinz, Asst. V.P., (703) 810-7743

PRINCIPAL OFFICE: 11600 Sallie Mae Drive, Reston, VA 20193

TELEPHONE NUMBER: (703) 810-3000
FAX: (703) 810-5074
WEB: www.salliemae.com

NO. OF EMPLOYEES: 6,011 (avg.)

SHAREHOLDERS: 554 (approx.)

ANNUAL MEETING: In May

INCORPORATED: DE, Feb., 1997

INSTITUTIONAL HOLDINGS:
No. of Institutions: 354
Shares Held: 139,781,824
% Held: 89.9

INDUSTRY: Personal credit institutions (SIC: 6141)

TRANSFER AGENT(S): Mellon Investor Services, New York, NY

NYSE SYMBOL VLY
Rec. Pr. 28.10 (Adj.; 3/31/02)

VALLEY NATIONAL BANCORP

YIELD 3.8%
P/E RATIO 20.2

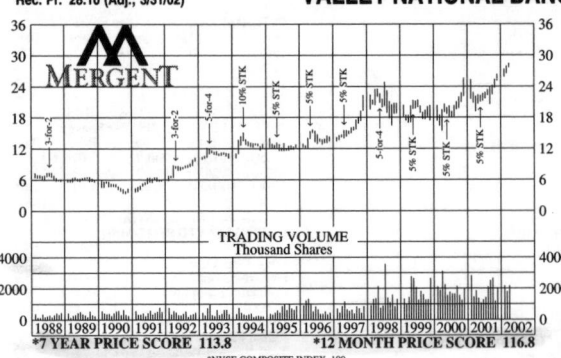

TRADING VOLUME
Thousand Shares

| 1988 | 1989 | 1990 | 1991 | 1992 | 1993 | 1994 | 1995 | 1996 | 1997 | 1998 | 1999 | 2000 | 2001 | 2002 |

*7 YEAR PRICE SCORE 113.8   *12 MONTH PRICE SCORE 116.8
*NYSE COMPOSITE INDEX=100

INTERIM EARNINGS (Per Share):

Qtr.	Mar.	June	Sept.	Dec.
1997	0.27	0.27	0.28	0.28
1998	0.30	0.31	0.31	0.30
1999	0.31	0.30	0.33	0.32
2000	0.33	0.34	0.34	0.34
2001	0.29	0.35	0.37	0.38

INTERIM DIVIDENDS (Per Share):

Amt.	Decl.	Ex.	Rec.	Pay.
0.265Q	5/07/01	6/04/01	6/06/01	7/02/01
0.265Q	8/21/01	9/05/01	9/07/01	10/01/01
0.265Q	11/22/01	12/05/01	12/07/01	1/02/02
0.265Q	2/27/02	3/06/02	3/08/02	4/01/02
5-for-4	4/10/02	5/20/02	5/03/02	5/17/02

Indicated div.: $0.85 (Adj.; Div. Reinv. Plan)

CAPITALIZATION (12/31/01):

	($000)	(%)
Total Deposits	6,306,974	79.2
Long-Term Debt	975,728	12.3
Common & Surplus	678,375	8.5
Total	7,961,077	100.0

DIVIDEND ACHIEVER STATUS:
Rank: 136   10-Year Growth Rate: 10.05%
Total Years of Dividend Growth: 10

RECENT DEVELOPMENTS: For the year ended 12/31/01, net income rose 6.7% to $135.2 million from $126.7 million in 2000. Results included net gains on the sale of loans of $10.6 million and $2.2 million in 2001 and 2000, respectively. Results for 2001 also included a gain of $2.1 million from bank-owned life insurance and merger charges of $9.0 million. Net interest income grew 6.1% to $334.8 million from $315.6 million the year before.

PROSPECTS: The Company continues to produce favorable returns as a result of strong loan volume, expense control and growth within its core market. Additionally, non-interest income continues to grow, due to increased service charges on deposit accounts, gains from securities transactions, and gains from loan sales. Also, the Company continues to benefit from its acquisition of Merchants New York Bancorp.

BUSINESS

VALLEY NATIONAL BANCORP, with over $8.58 billion in assets as of 12/31/01, is a bank holding company. The Company's principal subsidiary is Valley National Bank (VNB). VNB is a national banking association, which provides a full range of commercial and retail banking services through 126 branch offices located in 80 communities serving 10 counties throughout northern New Jersey and Manhattan. These services include the following: the acceptance of demand, savings and time deposits; extension of consumer, real estate, Small Business Administration and other commercial credits; title insurance; investment services; and full personal and corporate trust, as well as pension and fiduciary services. On 1/19/01, the Company acquired Merchants New York Bancorp, Inc. for $375.0 million.

ANNUAL FINANCIAL DATA

	12/31/01	12/31/00	12/31/99	12/31/98	12/31/97	12/31/96	12/31/95
Earnings Per Share	③1.38	②1.33	①1.26	①1.21	1.11	0.97	0.88
Tang. Book Val. Per Share	7.10	6.92	5.94	5.56	6.20	5.52	5.43
Dividends Per Share	0.82	0.77	0.72	0.65	0.57	0.51	0.49
Dividend Payout %	59.3	57.9	57.1	53.7	51.4	52.6	55.7
INCOME STATEMENT (IN MILLIONS):							
Total Interest Income	553.5	460.9	427.5	389.7	368.3	324.3	316.7
Total Interest Expense	218.7	202.8	169.2	160.1	156.0	145.5	143.3
Net Interest Income	334.8	258.1	258.4	229.6	212.3	178.8	173.4
Provision for Loan Losses	15.7	6.1	9.1	12.4	12.3	2.4	2.7
Non-Interest Income	68.5	50.9	47.3	43.1	42.3	26.3	21.0
Non-Interest Expense	188.2	141.0	137.9	134.8	123.2	101.2	90.2
Income Before Taxes	199.4	161.8	158.5	125.5	119.2	101.4	101.5
Net Income	③135.2	②106.8	①106.3	①97.3	85.0	67.5	62.6
Average Shs. Outstg. (000)	97,548	80,206	84,487	80,465	76,996	69,684	71,024
BALANCE SHEET (IN MILLIONS):							
Cash & Due from Banks	311.9	186.7	161.6	175.8	148.2	162.9	167.3
Securities Avail. for Sale	2,171.7	1,035.8	1,005.4	929.1	1,017.2	950.2	1,146.3
Total Loans & Leases	5,275.6	3,222.4	3,047.5	2,555.4	2,288.8	2,026.2	1,899.6
Allowance for Credit Losses	63.8	53.7	55.1	49.9	46.4	41.4	40.6
Net Loans & Leases	5,211.8	3,168.7	2,992.4	2,505.5	2,242.4	1,984.8	1,859.0
Total Assets	8,383.8	6,425.8	6,360.4	5,541.2	5,090.7	4,686.7	4,585.8
Total Deposits	6,307.0	5,123.7	5,051.3	4,674.7	4,403.0	4,176.2	4,083.9
Long-Term Obligations	975.7	591.8	564.9	...	...	...	...
Total Liabilities	7,705.4	5,880.8	5,806.9	4,985.4	4,615.3	4,290.1	4,185.6
Net Stockholders' Equity	678.4	545.1	553.5	555.8	475.4	396.5	400.2
Year-end Shs. Outstg. (000)	95,585	78,799	78,348	79,971	76,620	69,138	71,573
STATISTICAL RECORD:							
Return on Equity %	19.9	19.6	19.2	17.5	17.9	17.0	15.6
Return on Assets %	1.6	1.7	1.7	1.8	1.7	1.4	1.4
Equity/Assets %	8.1	8.5	8.7	10.0	9.3	8.5	8.7
Non-Int. Exp./Tot. Inc. %	46.7	45.6	45.1	49.4	48.4	49.3	46.4
Price Range	26.36-19.00	25.62-15.38	21.41-16.94	24.88-16.42	22.32-13.36	15.66-11.91	13.97-11.54
P/E Ratio	19.0-13.8	19.2-11.5	17.0-13.6	20.6-13.6	20.1-12.0	16.1-12.3	11.2-9.2
Average Yield %	3.6	3.8	3.8	3.1	3.2	3.7	3.8

Statistics are as originally reported. Adj. for 5% stk. spl., 5/01, 5/00, 5/99, 5/97, 5/96, 5/95; 5-for-4 stk. spl., 5/02, 5/98. ① Incl. merger-related chrg., 1999, $3.0 mill.; 1998, $4.5 mill. ② Incl. net gain on sale of loans of $2.0 mill. ③ Incl. a net gain on sales of loans of $10.6 mill., a gain of $2.1 mill. fr. bank-owned life insurance & merger-rel. chrgs. of $9.0 mill.

OFFICERS:
G. H. Lipkin, Chmn., Pres., C.E.O.
P. Southway, Vice-Chmn.
A. D. Eskow, Exec. V.P., C.F.O.

INVESTOR CONTACT: Investor Relations, (800) 522-4100 ext. 3380

PRINCIPAL OFFICE: 1455 Valley Road, Wayne, NJ 07470

TELEPHONE NUMBER: (973) 305-8800
FAX: (973) 305-1605
WEB: www.valleynationalbank.com

NO. OF EMPLOYEES: 2,129

SHAREHOLDERS: 9,359

ANNUAL MEETING: In Apr.

INCORPORATED: NJ, 1982

INSTITUTIONAL HOLDINGS:
No. of Institutions: 99
Shares Held: 14,350,435 (Adj.)
% Held: 15.1

INDUSTRY: National commercial banks (SIC: 6021)

TRANSFER AGENT(S): American Stock Transfer & Trust Company, New York, NY

VALSPAR CORPORATION (THE)

YIELD 1.2%
P/E RATIO 37.6

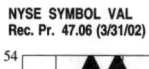

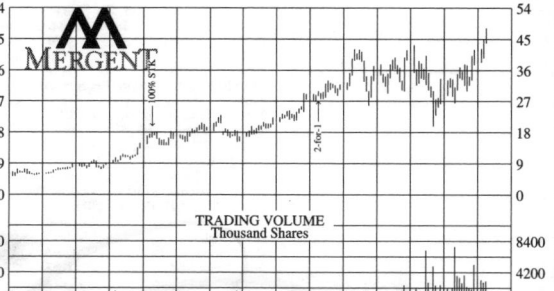

| | 1988 | 1989 | 1990 | 1991 | 1992 | 1993 | 1994 | 1995 | 1996 | 1997 | 1998 | 1999 | 2000 | 2001 | 2002 |

TRADING VOLUME
Thousand Shares

*7 YEAR PRICE SCORE 102.0   *12 MONTH PRICE SCORE 124.9

*NYSE COMPOSITE INDEX=100

INTERIM EARNINGS (Per Share):

Qtr.	Jan.	Apr.	July	Oct.
1998-99	0.22	0.51	0.59	0.55
1999-00	0.26	0.59	0.59	0.56
2000-01	0.10	0.44	0.51	0.05
2001-02	0.25	...	...	...

INTERIM DIVIDENDS (Per Share):

Amt.	Decl.	Ex.	Rec.	Pay.
0.135Q	2/28/01	3/29/01	4/02/01	4/16/01
0.135Q	6/13/01	6/28/01	7/02/01	7/13/01
0.135Q	8/15/01	9/27/01	10/01/01	10/15/01
0.14Q	12/12/01	12/27/01	12/31/01	1/15/02
0.14Q	2/27/02	3/27/02	4/01/02	4/15/02

Indicated div.: $0.56 (Div. Reinv. Plan)

CAPITALIZATION (10/26/01):

	($000)	(%)
Long-Term Debt	1,006,217	58.5
Deferred Income Tax	60,012	3.5
Common & Surplus	654,565	38.0
Total	1,720,794	100.0

DIVIDEND ACHIEVER STATUS:
Rank: 76   10-Year Growth Rate: 13.67%
Total Years of Dividend Growth: 23

RECENT DEVELOPMENTS: For the quarter ended 1/25/02, net income was $12.6 million compared with $4.5 million in the corresponding prior-year quarter. Net sales increased 27.9% to $431.0 million from $337.0 million a year earlier. The improvement in results was primarily attributed to cost-reduction initiatives, moderating raw material cost pressures, lower interest rates and the prescribed change in accounting for goodwill. Operating income surged 57.1% to $33.5 million.

PROSPECTS: VAL expects difficult market conditions for its industrial businesses to continue, partially offset by expected stronger sales from its architectural coatings business. Meanwhile, earnings should benefit from cost-reduction measures, lower debt levels and interest rates and other initiatives designed to improve operating performance. In addition, VAL is progressing with the integration of Lilly Industries, which it acquired on 12/20/00, and is realizing significant cost-reduction benefits.

BUSINESS

THE VALSPAR CORPORATION is a multinational paint and coatings manufacturer. The Company manufactures and distributes a broad portfolio of coatings products. The Industrial product line includes decorative and protective coatings for wood, metal, plastic and glass. The Packaging product line includes coatings and inks for rigid packaging containers. The Architectural, Automotive and Specialty product line includes interior and exterior decorative paints, stains, primers, varnishes and specialty decorative products, such as enamels, aerosols and faux finishes, automotive refinish and high performance floor coatings. The Other category includes specialty polymers and colorants, which are used internally and sold to other coatings manufacturers.

ANNUAL FINANCIAL DATA

	10/26/01	10/27/00	10/29/99	10/30/98	10/31/97	10/25/96	10/27/95
Earnings Per Share	[2]1.10	[3]2.00	[2]1.87	1.63	1.49	1.26	[1]1.08
Cash Flow Per Share	2.67	3.05	2.78	2.32	2.07	1.76	1.54
Tang. Book Val. Per Share	...	5.39	4.07	5.70	5.68	5.79	4.82
Dividends Per Share	0.54	0.52	0.46	0.42	0.36	0.33	0.30
Dividend Payout %	49.1	26.0	24.6	25.8	24.2	26.2	27.9
INCOME STATEMENT (IN MILLIONS):							
Total Revenues	1,921.0	1,483.3	1,387.7	1,155.1	1,017.3	859.8	790.2
Costs & Expenses	1,687.0	1,274.1	1,202.9	1,002.7	879.5	742.5	687.2
Depreciation & Amort.	73.1	45.2	39.8	30.7	25.8	22.3	20.3
Operating Income	160.9	163.9	145.0	121.7	112.0	95.0	82.7
Net Interest Inc./(Exp.)	d72.6	d22.0	d19.1	d10.7	d5.3	d3.0	d4.2
Income Before Income Taxes	91.2	141.7	135.1	118.8	109.2	93.0	79.2
Income Taxes	39.7	55.3	52.9	46.7	43.3	37.2	31.7
Net Income	[2]51.5	[3]86.5	[2]82.1	72.1	65.9	55.9	[1]47.5
Cash Flow	124.6	131.7	121.9	102.9	91.6	78.2	67.8
Average Shs. Outstg. (000)	46,658	43,196	43,836	44,320	44,233	44,402	44,182
BALANCE SHEET (IN MILLIONS):							
Cash & Cash Equivalents	20.1	20.9	33.2	15.0	11.1	7.1	4.9
Total Current Assets	661.5	533.9	514.9	426.1	356.8	275.2	236.9
Net Property	411.2	298.7	312.1	233.5	185.7	153.8	130.4
Total Assets	2,226.1	1,125.0	1,110.7	801.7	615.5	486.4	398.2
Total Current Liabilities	475.1	334.3	374.7	268.0	259.4	179.1	145.9
Long-Term Obligations	1,006.2	300.3	298.9	164.8	35.8	31.9	21.7
Net Stockholders' Equity	654.6	437.6	393.8	340.2	295.1	253.7	212.1
Net Working Capital	186.4	199.6	140.2	158.1	97.4	96.1	91.0
Year-end Shs. Outstg. (000)	49,482	42,481	42,983	43,418	43,678	43,854	43,978
STATISTICAL RECORD:							
Operating Profit Margin %	8.4	11.1	10.4	10.5	11.0	11.0	10.5
Net Profit Margin %	2.7	5.8	5.9	6.2	6.5	6.5	6.0
Return on Equity %	7.9	19.8	20.9	21.2	22.3	22.0	22.4
Return on Assets %	2.3	7.7	7.4	9.0	10.7	11.5	11.9
Debt/Total Assets %	45.2	26.7	26.9	20.6	5.8	6.6	5.4
Price Range	42.00-26.48	43.31-19.75	41.88-29.25	42.13-25.75	33.06-26.81	29.31-20.94	22.31-16.69
P/E Ratio	38.2-24.1	21.7-9.9	22.4-15.6	25.8-15.8	22.2-18.0	23.3-16.6	20.8-15.5
Average Yield %	1.6	1.6	1.3	1.2	1.2	1.3	1.5

Statistics are as originally reported. Adj. for stk. splits: 2-for-1, 3/97. [1] Reflects the acquisition of Sunbelt Coatings on a pooling-of-interests basis. [2] Incl. restruct. chrg. of $8.3 mill., 1999; $21.9 mill., 2001. [3] Incl. restr. credit of $1.2 mill.

OFFICERS:
R. M. Rompala, Chmn., C.E.O.
J. Ballach, Pres., C.O.O.
P. C. Reyelts, Sr. V.P., C.F.O.
R. Engh, Sr. V.P., Sec., Gen. Couns.

INVESTOR CONTACT: Rolf Engh, Sec., (612) 332-7371

PRINCIPAL OFFICE: 1101 Third Street South, Minneapolis, MN 55415

TELEPHONE NUMBER: (612) 332-7371
FAX: (612) 375-7723
WEB: www.valspar.com

NO. OF EMPLOYEES: 6,750 (approx.)

SHAREHOLDERS: 1,688

ANNUAL MEETING: In Feb.

INCORPORATED: DE, Dec., 1934

INSTITUTIONAL HOLDINGS:
No. of Institutions: 178
Shares Held: 31,658,596
% Held: 63.4

INDUSTRY: Paints and allied products (SIC: 2851)

TRANSFER AGENT(S): Mellon Investor Services, Ridgefield Park, NJ

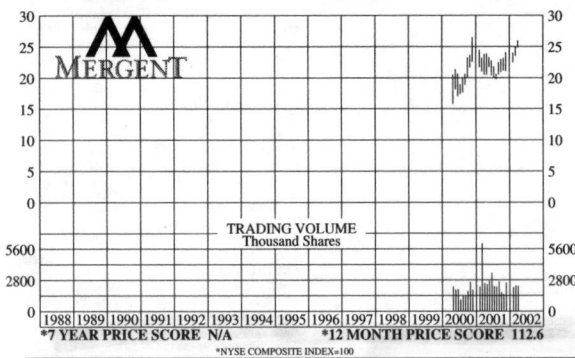

NYSE SYMBOL VVC
Rec. Pr. 25.69 (3/31/02)

VECTREN CORPORATION

YIELD 4.1%
P/E RATIO 25.4

7 YEAR PRICE SCORE N/A **12 MONTH PRICE SCORE 112.6**
*NYSE COMPOSITE INDEX=100

INTERIM EARNINGS (Per Share):

Qtr.	Mar.	June	Sept.	Dec.
1999	0.66	0.19	0.26	0.37
2000	0.36	0.13	0.25	0.43
2001	0.61	d0.15	0.07	0.48

INTERIM DIVIDENDS (Per Share):

Amt.	Decl.	Ex.	Rec.	Pay.
0.255Q	1/24/01	2/13/01	2/15/01	3/01/01
0.255Q	4/25/01	5/11/01	5/15/01	6/01/01
0.255Q	7/25/01	8/13/01	8/15/01	9/01/01
0.265Q	10/26/01	11/13/01	11/15/01	12/01/01
0.265Q	1/24/02	2/13/02	2/15/02	3/01/02

Indicated div.: $1.06 (Div. Reinv. Plan)

CAPITALIZATION (12/31/01):

	($000)	(%)
Long-Term Debt	1,014,000	49.0
Deferred Income Tax	206,700	10.0
Minority Interest	1,400	0.1
Common & Surplus	848,600	41.0
Total	2,070,700	100.0

DIVIDEND ACHIEVER STATUS:
Rank: 249   10-Year Growth Rate: 4.01%
Total Years of Dividend Growth: 26

RECENT DEVELOPMENTS: For the year ended 12/31/01, VVC reported income of $67.3 million versus net income of $72.0 million in 2000. Results for 2001 and 2000 included merger and integration costs of $2.8 million in 2001 and $41.1 million in 2000. Results for 2001 also included a $19.0 million restructuring charge. Earnings for 2001 were adversely affected by the warm weather, high gas prices early in the year and the general slowdown in the economy. Total revenues jumped 31.6% to $2.17 billion from $1.65 billion a year earlier.

PROSPECTS: VVC expects to grow earnings 6.0% to 8.0% on average over the next five years through average annual regulated earnings growth of 3.5% to 4.0% and non-regulated earnings growth of at least 15.0% per year. For 2002, the Company expects earnings per share in the range of $1.85 to $1.95. On 2/7/02, VVC announced the integration of two energy-marketing firms, Proliance Energy, LLC and Sigcorp Energy Services, LLC. During the first quarter, customer service, sales, account management activities, and billing, as well as other functions were consolidated.

BUSINESS

VECTREN CORPORATION was organized to reflect the merger on 3/31/00 of Indiana Energy, Inc. and SIGCORP, Inc., both of which were Dividend Achievers. VVC is an energy and applied technology holding company. The Company's energy delivery subsidiaries provide gas and/or electricity to nearly 1.0 million customers in adjoining service territories that cover nearly two-thirds of Indiana and west central Ohio. VVC's non-regulated subsidiaries and affiliates currently offer energy-related products and services. These include gas marketing and related services, coal production and sales, utility infrastructure services and broadband communications services.

ANNUAL FINANCIAL DATA

	12/31/01	12/31/00	12/31/99	12/31/98
Earnings Per Share	[2] 1.01	[1] 1.17	1.48	1.40
Cash Flow Per Share	2.86	2.90	2.89	2.73
Tang. Book Val. Per Share	9.68	8.69	11.58	...
Dividends Per Share	1.03	0.98	...	...
Dividend Payout %	102.0	83.8	...	...
INCOME STATEMENT (IN MILLIONS):				
Total Revenues	2,170.0	1,648.7	1,068.4	997.7
Costs & Expenses	1,906.7	1,412.1	820.6	767.6
Depreciation & Amort.	123.7	105.7	87.0	81.6
Operating Income	139.6	130.9	160.8	148.5
Net Interest Inc./(Exp.)	d82.6	d57.1	d42.9	d40.3
Income Taxes	18.6	34.2	45.7	42.3
Equity Earnings/Minority Int.	13.5	16.6	10.7	11.7
Net Income	[2] 67.4	[1] 72.0	90.7	86.6
Cash Flow	190.3	177.7	177.7	168.2
Average Shs. Outstg. (000)	66,900	61,380	61,430	61,578
BALANCE SHEET (IN MILLIONS):				
Gross Property	1,595.0	1,555.8	1,336.3	...
Net Property	1,776.7	1,659.2	1,400.8	...
Total Assets	2,856.6	2,909.2	1,980.5	...
Long-Term Obligations	1,014.0	632.0	486.7	...
Net Stockholders' Equity	848.6	748.6	729.0	...
Year-end Shs. Outstg. (000)	67,700	61,419	61,305	...
STATISTICAL RECORD:				
Operating Profit Margin %	6.4	7.9	15.0	14.9
Net Profit Margin %	3.1	4.4	8.5	8.7
Net Inc./Net Property %	3.8	4.3	6.5	...
Net Inc./Tot. Capital %	3.3	4.5	6.3	...
Return on Equity %	7.9	9.6	12.4	...
Price Range	24.44-19.76	26.50-15.75	...	...
P/E Ratio	24.2-19.6	22.6-13.5	...	...
Average Yield %	4.7	4.6	...	...

Statistics are as originally reported. [1] Incl. nonrecurr. merger & integration chrg., $41.1 mill. [2] Bef. extraord. loss of $7.7 mill. and acctg. change gain of $3.9 mill.; incl. pre-tax nonrecurr. chrgs. of $21.9 mill.

OFFICERS:
N. C. Ellerbrook, Chmn., C.E.O.
A. E. Goebel, Pres., C.O.O.
J. A. Benkert Jr., Exec. V.P., C.F.O.
INVESTOR CONTACT: Steven M. Schein, V.P., Investor Relations, (812) 491-4209
PRINCIPAL OFFICE: 20 N.W. Fourth Street, Evansville, IN 47708

TELEPHONE NUMBER: (812) 491-4000
FAX: (812) 491-4149
WEB: www.vectren.com
NO. OF EMPLOYEES: 1,986 (avg.)
SHAREHOLDERS: 14,151
ANNUAL MEETING: In March
INCORPORATED: IN, June, 1999

INSTITUTIONAL HOLDINGS:
No. of Institutions: 174
Shares Held: 25,826,958
% Held: 38.1
INDUSTRY: Gas and other services combined (SIC: 4932)
TRANSFER AGENT(S): National City Bank, Cleveland, OH

NYSE SYMBOL VFC
Rec. Pr. 43.25 (3/31/02)

VF CORPORATION

YIELD 2.2%
P/E RATIO 37.9

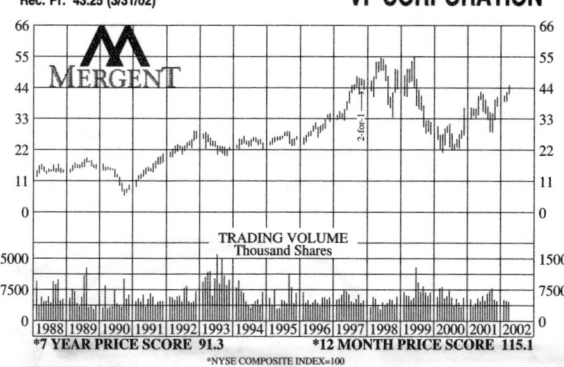

TRADING VOLUME
Thousand Shares

*7 YEAR PRICE SCORE 91.3   *12 MONTH PRICE SCORE 115.1
*NYSE COMPOSITE INDEX=100

INTERIM EARNINGS (Per Share):

Qtr.	Mar.	June	Sept.	Dec.
1998	0.62	0.69	0.96	0.84
1999	0.69	0.64	0.85	0.81
2000	0.66	0.64	0.88	0.08
2001	0.67	0.60	0.90	d1.03

INTERIM DIVIDENDS (Per Share):

Amt.	Decl.	Ex.	Rec.	Pay.
0.23Q	4/24/01	6/06/01	6/08/01	6/18/01
0.23Q	7/17/01	9/06/01	9/10/01	9/20/01
0.24Q	10/17/01	12/06/01	12/10/01	12/20/01
0.24Q	2/12/02	3/06/02	3/08/02	3/18/02

Indicated div.: $0.96 (Div. Reinv. Plan)

CAPITALIZATION (12/29/01):

	($000)	(%)
Long-Term Debt	904,035	30.0
Common & Surplus	2,112,796	70.0
Total	3,016,831	100.0

DIVIDEND ACHIEVER STATUS:
Rank: 210   10-Year Growth Rate: 6.19%
Total Years of Dividend Growth: 29

RECENT DEVELOPMENTS: For the year ended 12/31/01, net income fell 48.4% to $137.8 million from $267.1 million, before an accounting charge of $6.8 million, in 2000. Earnings for 2001 and 2000 included restructuring charges of $236.8 and $119.9 million, respectively. Results for 2001 also included a $0.06 per share gain on a reversal of charges. Net sales fell 4.0% to $5.52 billion from $5.75 billion in the previous year.

PROSPECTS: On 11/14/01, the Company announced a series of actions designed to improve profitability and spur future growth. In conjunction with these actions, VFC has decided to exit its private label knitwear business, swimwear and a small specialty workwear business, move additional production to lower cost manufacturing areas, and consolidate its domestic intimate apparel headquarters in one location.

BUSINESS

VF CORPORATION designs, manufactures and markets branded jeanswear, intimate apparel, children's playwear, occupational apparel, and daypacks. The Company's principal brands include: LEE, WRANGLER, VANITY FAIR®, VASSARETTE®, BESTFORM®, LILY OF FRANCE®, LEE SPORT® HEALTHTEX®, JANSPORT® EASTPAK® RED KAP® and THE NORTH FACE®. On 5/20/00, VFC acquired the Eastpak branded business and the CHIC jeans brand. On 8/16/00, VFC completed the acquisition of The North Face, Inc.

ANNUAL FINANCIAL DATA

	12/29/01	12/30/00	1/1/00	1/2/99	1/3/98	1/4/97	12/31/95
Earnings Per Share	② 1.19	① 2.27	2.99	3.10	2.70	2.32	1.21
Cash Flow Per Share	2.67	3.76	4.37	4.40	3.91	3.61	2.55
Tang. Book Val. Per Share	9.97	12.56	10.08	9.33	8.68	8.68	6.97
Dividends Per Share	0.93	0.89	0.85	0.81	0.77	0.73	0.69
Dividend Payout %	78.1	39.2	28.4	26.1	28.5	31.5	57.3
INCOME STATEMENT (IN MILLIONS):							
Total Revenues	5,518.8	5,747.9	5,551.6	5,478.8	5,222.2	5,137.2	5,062.3
Costs & Expenses	5,002.6	5,064.5	4,731.6	4,633.3	4,460.9	4,419.3	4,547.2
Depreciation & Amort.	169.0	173.4	167.4	161.4	156.3	160.6	167.7
Operating Income	347.2	510.0	652.6	684.2	605.1	557.3	347.4
Net Interest Inc./(Exp.)	d86.5	d81.0	d62.5	d55.9	d25.9	d49.4	d66.2
Income Before Income Taxes	262.8	431.5	595.6	631.6	585.9	508.4	284.1
Income Taxes	125.0	164.4	229.3	243.3	234.9	208.9	126.8
Net Income	② 137.8	① 267.1	366.2	388.3	350.9	299.5	157.3
Cash Flow	303.7	437.2	530.1	546.0	503.4	456.1	320.9
Average Shs. Outstg. (000)	114,764	117,218	122,258	124,995	129,720	127,292	127,486
BALANCE SHEET (IN MILLIONS):							
Cash & Cash Equivalents	332.0	118.9	79.9	63.2	124.1	270.6	84.1
Total Current Assets	2,031.4	2,110.1	1,877.4	1,848.2	1,601.5	1,706.3	1,667.6
Net Property	654.7	776.0	804.4	776.1	706.0	721.5	749.9
Total Assets	4,057.4	4,358.2	4,026.5	3,836.7	3,322.8	3,449.5	3,447.1
Total Current Liabilities	813.8	1,006.2	1,113.5	1,033.0	765.9	766.3	868.3
Long-Term Obligations	904.0	905.0	517.8	521.7	516.2	519.1	614.2
Net Stockholders' Equity	2,112.8	2,191.8	2,163.8	2,066.3	1,866.8	1,973.7	1,771.5
Net Working Capital	1,217.6	1,103.9	763.9	815.1	835.6	940.1	799.3
Year-end Shs. Outstg. (000)	109,998	86,807	116,205	119,466	121,225	127,816	126,878
STATISTICAL RECORD:							
Operating Profit Margin %	6.3	8.9	11.8	12.5	11.6	10.8	6.9
Net Profit Margin %	2.5	4.6	6.6	7.1	6.7	5.8	3.1
Return on Equity %	6.5	12.2	16.9	18.8	18.8	15.2	8.9
Return on Assets %	3.4	6.1	9.1	10.1	10.6	8.7	4.6
Debt/Total Assets %	22.3	20.8	12.9	13.6	15.5	15.0	17.8
Price Range	42.70-28.15	36.90-20.94	55.00-27.44	54.69-33.44	48.25-32.25	34.94-23.81	28.56-23.38
P/E Ratio	35.9-23.7	16.3-9.2	18.4-9.2	17.6-10.8	17.9-11.9	15.1-10.3	23.7-19.4
Average Yield %	2.6	3.1	2.1	1.8	1.9	2.5	2.7

Statistics are as originally reported. Adj. for stk. split: 2-for-1, 11/97. ① Incl. restruc. costs of $119.9 mill.; bef. acctg. chge. chrg. of $6.8 mill. ② Incl. restr. costs of $236.8 mill. & a $0.06 per sh. gain fr. reversal of charges.

OFFICERS:
M. J. McDonald, Chmn., Pres., C.E.O.
R. K. Shearer, V.P., Fin., C.F.O.
F. C. Pickard III, V.P., Treas.

INVESTOR CONTACT: Cindy Knoebel, Dir., Inv. Rel., (336) 547-6189

PRINCIPAL OFFICE: 628 Green Valley Road, Suite 500, Greensboro, NC 27408

TELEPHONE NUMBER: (336) 547-6000
FAX: (336) 547-7630
WEB: www.vfc.com

NO. OF EMPLOYEES: 71,000 (approx.)

SHAREHOLDERS: 6,279

ANNUAL MEETING: In Apr.

INCORPORATED: PA, Dec., 1889

INSTITUTIONAL HOLDINGS:
No. of Institutions: 242
Shares Held: 97,144,391
% Held: 88.1

INDUSTRY: Men's and boys' clothing, nec
(SIC: 2329)

TRANSFER AGENT(S): First Chicago Trust Company of New York, Jersey City, NJ

VIRCO MFG. CORPORATION

YIELD	0.8%
P/E RATIO	...

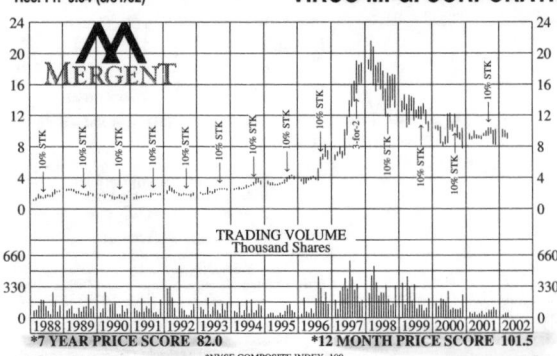

INTERIM EARNINGS (Per Share):

Qtr.	Apr.	July	Oct.	Jan.
1998-99	0.05	0.47	0.55	0.24
1999-00	d0.15	0.50	0.50	d0.06
2000-01	0.21	0.34	0.37	d0.58
2001-02	d0.30	0.36	0.32	d0.36

INTERIM DIVIDENDS (Per Share):

Amt.	Decl.	Ex.	Rec.	Pay.
0.02Q	6/14/01	6/27/01	6/29/01	7/31/01
10% STK	8/23/01	9/04/01	9/06/01	9/28/01
0.02Q	8/23/01	10/10/01	10/12/01	10/31/01
0.02Q	12/13/01	12/27/01	12/31/01	1/31/02
0.02Q	2/21/02	3/26/02	3/28/02	4/30/02

Indicated div.: $0.08

CAPITALIZATION (1/31/01):

	($000)	(%)
Long-Term Debt	43,741	30.7
Deferred Income Tax	4,533	3.2
Common & Surplus	94,141	66.1
Total	142,415	100.0

DIVIDEND ACHIEVER STATUS:
Rank: 23   10-Year Growth Rate: 20.76%
Total Years of Dividend Growth: 19

TRADING VOLUME
Thousand Shares

*7 YEAR PRICE SCORE 82.0   *12 MONTH PRICE SCORE 101.5
*NYSE COMPOSITE INDEX=100

RECENT DEVELOPMENTS: For the year ended 1/31/02, net income declined 94.3% to $246,000 compared with income of $4.3 million, before an accounting change charge of $297,000, in 2001. Results for 2002 included a loss of $86,000 on the sale of fixed assets. Results for 2001 included a one-time gain of $7.4 million from the sale of a warehouse in April and the settlement of a claim in October. Sales were $257.5 million, down 10.4% from $287.3 million a year earlier. In April 2002, the Company and

Furniture Focus, Inc. signed a letter of intent for VIR to acquire Furniture Focus, a reseller that offers complete package solutions for the Furniture, Fixtures and Equipment segments of bond-funded public school construction projects, primarily in the upper Midwest. Following the completion of due diligence, VIR will pay $2.4 million in cash for certain assets of the corporation, which are expected to contribute between $5.0 million to $7.0 million of additional revenue over the remainder of fiscal 2002.

BUSINESS

VIRCO MFG. CORPORATION is engaged in the design and production of furniture for contract and educational markets worldwide. The Company offers a broad product line of furniture for the K-12 market, as well as a variety of products for the pre-school markets, and has recently developed products that are targeted for college, university, and corporate learning center environments. These products include student and teacher desks, computer stations, chairs, activity tables, and folding and stacking chairs for cafeteria and auditorium seating. The Company also produces a variety of tables, chairs and storage equipment designed for the hospitality market, convention centers, churches, and corporate and government facilities. The Company's manufacturing and distribution facilities are located in California and Arkansas.

ANNUAL FINANCIAL DATA

	p1/31/02	1/31/01	1/31/00	1/31/99	1/31/98	1/31/97	1/31/96
Earnings Per Share	② 0.02	① 0.35	0.79	1.32	1.04	0.71	0.40
Cash Flow Per Share	...	1.40	1.57	1.85	1.57	1.20	0.81
Tang. Book Val. Per Share	...	7.59	7.51	6.93	5.94	4.93	4.28
Dividends Per Share	0.075	0.068	0.062	0.056	0.048	0.045	0.016
Dividend Payout %	375.0	19.6	7.8	4.2	4.6	6.4	4.2
INCOME STATEMENT (IN THOUSANDS):							
Total Revenues	257,462	287,342	266,641	273,620	258,194	236,277	224,349
Costs & Expenses	...	273,701	237,364	236,315	226,208	211,528	208,481
Depreciation & Amort.	...	13,412	9,993	7,132	7,110	6,541	5,364
Operating Income	...	229	19,284	30,173	24,876	18,208	10,504
Net Interest Inc./(Exp.)	...	d4,962	d2,385	d1,111	d1,794	d2,507	d3,130
Income Before Income Taxes	436	6,986	16,693	28,902	22,604	15,054	8,413
Income Taxes	190	2,673	6,527	11,272	8,752	5,728	3,204
Net Income	246	① 4,313	10,166	17,630	13,852	9,326	5,209
Cash Flow	...	17,725	20,159	24,762	20,962	15,867	10,573
Average Shs. Outstg.	12,432	12,623	12,806	13,369	13,370	13,188	13,122
BALANCE SHEET (IN THOUSANDS):							
Cash & Cash Equivalents	...	351	1,072	1,086	1,221	722	661
Total Current Assets	62,459	88,973	89,926	82,508	74,219	72,688	74,622
Net Property	...	94,645	87,937	59,320	39,369	37,478	36,955
Total Assets	161,372	199,549	190,863	151,380	122,015	118,020	119,225
Total Current Liabilities	27,995	45,800	38,503	35,103	30,187	27,545	23,302
Long-Term Obligations	43,154	43,741	46,027	21,344	9,459	21,513	35,909
Net Stockholders' Equity	90,223	94,141	93,834	88,923	77,325	63,965	55,461
Net Working Capital	34,464	43,173	51,423	47,405	44,032	45,143	51,320
Year-end Shs. Outstg.	...	12,411	12,500	12,836	13,011	12,970	12,970
STATISTICAL RECORD:							
Operating Profit Margin %	...	0.1	7.2	11.0	9.6	7.7	4.7
Net Profit Margin %	0.1	1.5	3.8	6.4	5.4	3.9	2.3
Return on Equity %	0.3	4.6	10.8	19.8	17.9	14.6	9.4
Return on Assets %	0.2	2.2	5.3	11.6	11.4	7.9	4.4
Debt/Total Assets %	...	21.9	24.1	14.1	7.8	18.2	30.1
Price Range	10.40-8.15	12.29-7.73	14.70-9.92	21.60-12.04	19.04-6.20	8.25-3.16	4.40-3.01
P/E Ratio	520.0-407.5	35.6-22.4	18.5-12.5	16.3-9.1	18.3-6.0	11.7-4.5	11.1-7.6
Average Yield %	0.8	0.7	0.5	0.3	0.4	0.8	0.4

Statistics are as originally reported. Adj. for all stk. splits and divs. thru 9/01. ① Bef. acctg. change chrg. $297,000 ② Incl. a loss of $86,000 on the sale of fixed assets.

OFFICERS:
R. A. Virtue, Chmn., Pres., C.E.O.
R. E. Dose, V.P., C.F.O., Treas., Sec.
D. A. Virtue, Exec. V.P.

INVESTOR CONTACT: Robert E. Dose, C.F.O., (310) 533-0474

PRINCIPAL OFFICE: 2027 Harpers Way, Torrance, CA 90501

TELEPHONE NUMBER: (310) 533-0474
FAX: (310) 538-0114
WEB: www.virco.com
NO. OF EMPLOYEES: 2,300 (approx.)
SHAREHOLDERS: 365 (approx.); 1,900 (approx. beneficial)
ANNUAL MEETING: In June
INCORPORATED: CA, Feb., 1950; reincorp., DE, Apr., 1984

INSTITUTIONAL HOLDINGS:
No. of Institutions: 11
Shares Held: 2,890,322
% Held: 23.5

INDUSTRY: Public building & related furniture (SIC: 2531)

TRANSFER AGENT(S): Mellon Investor Services, Ridgefield Park, NJ

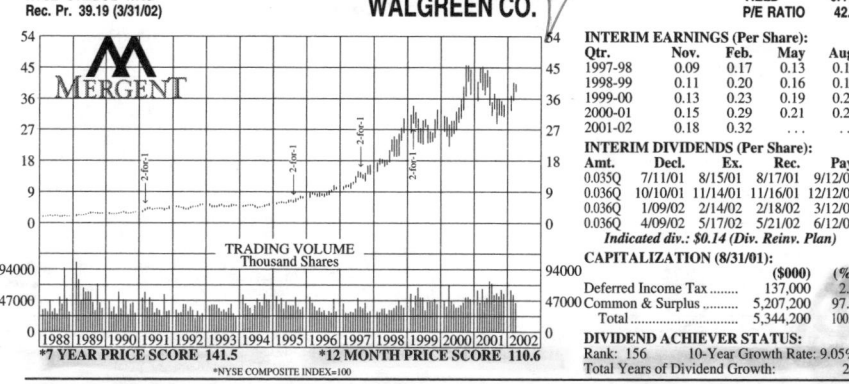

NYSE SYMBOL WAG
Rec. Pr. 39.19 (3/31/02)

WALGREEN CO.

YIELD 0.4%
P/E RATIO 42.6

INTERIM EARNINGS (Per Share):

Qtr.	Nov.	Feb.	May	Aug.
1997-98	0.09	0.17	0.13	0.15
1998-99	0.11	0.20	0.16	0.16
1999-00	0.13	0.23	0.19	0.21
2000-01	0.15	0.20	0.21	0.21
2001-02	0.18	0.32	...	...

INTERIM DIVIDENDS (Per Share):

Amt.	Decl.	Ex.	Rec.	Pay.
0.035Q	7/11/01	8/15/01	8/17/01	9/12/01
0.036Q	10/10/01	11/14/01	11/16/01	12/12/01
0.036Q	1/09/02	2/14/02	2/18/02	3/12/02
0.036Q	4/09/02	5/17/02	5/21/02	6/12/02
Indicated div.: $0.14 (Div. Reinv. Plan)				

CAPITALIZATION (8/31/01):

	($000)	(%)
Deferred Income Tax........	137,000	2.6
Common & Surplus	5,207,200	97.4
Total	5,344,200	100.0

TRADING VOLUME
Thousand Shares

*7 YEAR PRICE SCORE 141.5   *12 MONTH PRICE SCORE 110.6
*NYSE COMPOSITE INDEX=100

DIVIDEND ACHIEVER STATUS:
Rank: 156   10-Year Growth Rate: 9.05%
Total Years of Dividend Growth: 26

RECENT DEVELOPMENTS: For the quarter ended 2/28/02, net earnings advanced 10.0% to $326.6 million from $296.9 million the previous year. Results in the prior-year period included a $22.1 million pre-tax gain from a partial payment of the Company's share of the brand name prescription drug antitrust litigation settlement. Net sales climbed 16.5% to $7.49 billion from $6.43 billion the year before. Comparable-store sales increased 10.2% year over year.

PROSPECTS: Sales and earnings growth should benefit from the Company's aggressive store expansion program. WAG anticipates opening 475 new stores in fiscal 2002 and expects to operate more than 6,000 drugstores by 2010. Meanwhile, capital expenditures for fiscal 2002 are expected to reach $1.30 billion. In addition to new store construction, a significant portion of the expenditures will be used for technology upgrades and new distribution facilities.

BUSINESS

WALGREEN CO. operated 3,678 drugstores located in 43 states and Puerto Rico as of 2/28/02. The drugstores sell prescription and nonprescription drugs in addition to other products including general merchandise, cosmetics, toiletries, household items, food and beverages. Customer prescription purchases can be made at the drugstores as well as through the mail, telephone and the Internet. The Company's retail drugstore operations are supported by nine distribution centers and a mail service facility located in Beaverton, Oregon. Prescription drugs comprised 58% of fiscal 2001 total sales; general merchandise, 23%; nonprescription drugs, 12%; and cosmetics and toiletries, 7%.

ANNUAL FINANCIAL DATA

	8/31/01	8/31/00	8/31/99	8/31/98	8/31/97	8/31/96	8/31/95
Earnings Per Share	② 0.86	② 0.76	0.62	① 0.54	0.44	0.38	0.33
Cash Flow Per Share	1.12	0.99	0.82	0.72	0.60	0.52	0.46
Tang. Book Val. Per Share	5.11	4.19	3.47	2.86	2.40	2.08	1.82
Dividends Per Share	0.141	0.136	0.131	0.126	0.121	0.113	0.10
Dividend Payout %	16.4	17.9	21.1	23.3	27.5	29.7	30.3
INCOME STATEMENT (IN MILLIONS):							
Total Revenues	24,623.0	21,206.9	17,838.8	15,307.0	13,363.0	11,778.4	10,395.1
Costs & Expenses	22,955.5	19,752.7	16,613.3	14,283.0	12,491.0	11,027.0	9,743.5
Depreciation & Amort.	269.2	230.1	210.1	189.0	164.0	147.3	131.5
Operating Income	1,398.3	1,224.1	1,015.4	835.0	708.0	604.1	520.0
Net Interest Inc./(Exp.)	2.3	8.5	11.9	5.0	4.0	2.9	3.7
Income Before Income Taxes	1,422.7	1,263.3	1,027.3	877.0	712.0	606.9	523.7
Income Taxes	537.1	486.4	403.2	340.0	276.0	235.2	203.0
Net Income	② 885.6	② 776.9	624.1	① 537.0	436.0	371.7	320.8
Cash Flow	1,154.8	1,007.0	834.2	726.0	600.0	519.1	452.3
Average Shs. Outstg. (000)	1,028,947	1,019,889	1,014,282	1,005,692	996,670	993,744	990,108
BALANCE SHEET (IN MILLIONS):							
Cash & Cash Equivalents	16.9	12.8	141.8	144.0	73.0	8.8	22.2
Total Current Assets	4,393.9	3,550.1	3,221.7	2,623.0	2,326.0	2,019.0	1,812.9
Net Property	4,345.3	3,428.2	2,593.9	2,144.0	1,754.0	1,448.4	1,249.0
Total Assets	8,833.8	7,103.7	5,906.7	4,902.0	4,207.0	3,633.6	3,252.6
Total Current Liabilities	3,011.6	2,303.7	1,923.8	1,580.0	1,439.0	1,182.0	1,077.8
Long-Term Obligations	...	...	...	...	...	10.1	10.3
Net Stockholders' Equity	5,207.2	4,234.0	3,484.3	2,849.0	2,373.0	2,043.1	1,792.6
Net Working Capital	1,382.3	1,246.4	1,297.9	1,043.0	887.0	837.1	735.2
Year-end Shs. Outstg. (000)	1,019,425	1,010,819	1,004,022	996,488	987,580	984,564	984,564
STATISTICAL RECORD:							
Operating Profit Margin %	5.7	5.8	5.7	5.5	5.3	5.1	5.0
Net Profit Margin %	3.6	3.7	3.5	3.5	3.3	3.2	3.1
Return on Equity %	17.0	18.3	17.9	18.8	18.4	18.2	17.9
Return on Assets %	10.0	10.9	10.6	11.0	10.4	10.2	9.9
Debt/Total Assets %	...	...	...	...	...	0.3	0.3
Price Range	45.29-28.70	45.75-22.06	33.94-22.69	30.22-14.78	16.81-9.63	10.91-7.28	7.84-5.41
P/E Ratio	52.7-33.4	60.2-29.0	54.7-36.6	56.5-27.6	38.2-21.9	29.1-19.4	24.1-16.6
Average Yield %	0.4	0.4	0.5	0.6	0.9	1.2	1.5

Statistics are as originally reported. Adj. for 2-for-1 stk. split, 2/99 & 8/97. ① Bef. $26.4 mil ($0.03/sh) chg. for acctg. adj. & incl. $23.0 mil ($0.03/sh) after-tax gain. ② Incl. $22.1 mil ($0.01/sh) pre-tax gain from partial payment of a prescription-drug antitrust settlement, 2001; $33.5 mil ($0.02/sh), 2000.

OFFICERS:
L. D. Jorndt, Chmn.
D. W. Bernauer, Pres., C.E.O.
R. L. Polark, Sr. V.P., C.F.O.
M. A. Wagner, Treas.
INVESTOR CONTACT: John M. Palizza, Asst. Treas., (847) 940-2935
PRINCIPAL OFFICE: 200 Wilmot Road, Deerfield, IL 60015

TELEPHONE NUMBER: (847) 940-2500
FAX: (847) 914-2654
WEB: www.walgreens.com
NO. OF EMPLOYEES: 83,000 full-time (approx.); 46,000 part-time (approx.)
SHAREHOLDERS: 94,407
ANNUAL MEETING: In Jan.
INCORPORATED: IL, Feb., 1909

INSTITUTIONAL HOLDINGS:
No. of Institutions: 688
Shares Held: 596,097,704
% Held: 58.3
INDUSTRY: Drug stores and proprietary stores (SIC: 5912)
TRANSFER AGENT(S): Computershare Investor Services, Chicago, IL

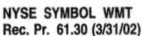

NYSE SYMBOL WMT
Rec. Pr. 61.30 (3/31/02)

WAL-MART STORES, INC.

YIELD 0.5%
P/E RATIO 41.1

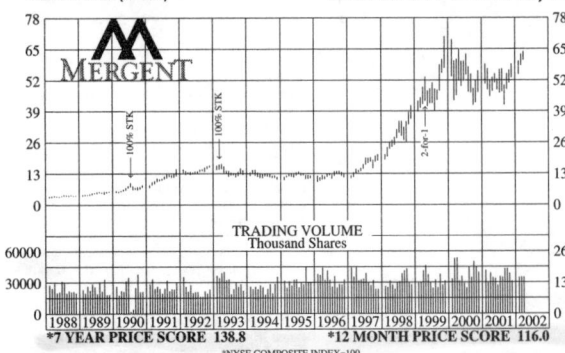

TRADING VOLUME
Thousand Shares

*7 YEAR PRICE SCORE 138.8 *12 MONTH PRICE SCORE 116.0
*NYSE COMPOSITE INDEX=100

INTERIM EARNINGS (Per Share):

Qtr.	Apr.	July	Oct.	Jan.
1998-99	0.19	0.23	0.23	0.35
1999-00	0.25	0.28	0.29	0.43
2000-01	0.30	0.36	0.31	0.45
2001-02	0.31	0.36	0.33	0.49

INTERIM DIVIDENDS (Per Share):

Amt.	Decl.	Ex.	Rec.	Pay.
0.07Q	5/31/01	6/20/01	6/22/01	7/09/01
0.07Q	8/16/01	9/19/01	9/21/01	10/09/01
0.07Q	11/19/01	12/19/01	12/21/01	1/07/02
0.075Q	3/08/02	3/20/02	3/22/02	4/18/02

Indicated div.: $0.30 (Div. Reinv. Plan)

CAPITALIZATION (1/31/02):

	($000)	(%)
Long-Term Debt	15,687,000	28.5
Capital Lease Obligations..	3,045,000	5.5
Minority Interest	1,207,000	2.2
Common & Surplus	35,102,000	63.8
Total	55,041,000	100.0

DIVIDEND ACHIEVER STATUS:
Rank: 22   10-Year Growth Rate: 20.85%
Total Years of Dividend Growth: 20

RECENT DEVELOPMENTS: For the year ended 1/31/02, net income rose 6.0% to $6.67 billion from $6.30 billion the year before. Total revenues climbed 13.7% to $219.81 billion. Net sales in the Wal-Mart Stores segment, including supercenters, increased 14.1% to $139.13 billion, while net sales in the Sam's Club segment grew 9.7% to $29.40 billion. International segment net sales were up 10.5% to $35.49 billion, while McLane's net sales jumped 30.8% to $13.79 billion, reflecting the acquisition of AmeriServe Food Distribution, Inc. Comparable-store sales rose 6.1% year over year.

PROSPECTS: The Company is projecting earnings per share of $1.74 to $1.76 during the current fiscal year. Results should benefit from increased market share related to the Chapter 11 bankruptcy filing on 1/22/02 by Kmart Corp. and the likely closing of between 500 and 700 Kmart stores. Meanwhile, the Company plans to accelerate its store expansion program in 2002. During 2001, WMT opened 178 new Supercenters, 33 discount department stores, 25 Sam's Club warehouses, and twelve Neighborhood Markets. In addition, WMT opened 107 new stores outside of the U.S.

BUSINESS

WAL-MART STORES, INC. operated 1,640 discount department stores, 1,077 Supercenters, 501 Sam's Clubs and 31 Neighborhood Markets in the United States as of 2/28/02. WMT also operated 555 Wal-Mart stores in Mexico, 251 in the United Kingdom, 196 in Canada, 95 in Germany, 22 in Brazil, 17 in Puerto Rico, 11 in Argentina, and nine in Korea. WMT also operated 19 stores in China via joint venture agreements. WMT's stores offer a wide assortment of merchandise to satisfy most of the clothing, home, recreational and convenience needs of the family. Supercenters combine food, general merchandise, and services including pharmacy, dry cleaning, portrait studios, photo finishing, hair salons, and optical shops. WMT also operates McLane Company, Inc., a specialty distributor serving over 50,000 convenience stores, mass merchandisers, quick-service restaurants and movie theaters.

ANNUAL FINANCIAL DATA

	1/31/02	1/31/01	1/31/00	1/31/99	1/31/98	1/31/97	1/31/96
Earnings Per Share	1.49	1.40	☐ 1.25	0.99	0.78	0.67	0.60
Cash Flow Per Share	2.22	2.04	1.78	1.41	1.14	0.99	0.88
Tang. Book Val. Per Share	5.95	4.99	3.69	4.18	4.13	3.75	3.22
Dividends Per Share	0.27	0.23	0.189	0.15	0.128	0.104	0.096
Dividend Payout %	18.1	16.4	15.1	15.2	16.4	15.5	16.0

INCOME STATEMENT (IN MILLIONS):

Total Revenues	219,812.0	193,295.0	166,809.0	139,208.0	119,299.0	106,146.0	94,749.0
Costs & Expenses	204,445.0	178,937.0	154,329.0	129,216.0	111,162.0	98,988.0	88,211.0
Depreciation & Amort.	3,290.0	2,868.0	2,375.0	1,872.0	1,634.0	1,463.0	1,304.0
Operating Income	12,077.0	11,490.0	10,105.0	8,120.0	6,503.0	5,695.0	5,234.0
Net Interest Inc./(Exp.)	d1,326.0	d1,374.0	d1,022.0	d797.0	d784.0	d845.0	d888.0
Income Before Income Taxes	10,751.0	10,116.0	9,083.0	7,323.0	5,719.0	4,850.0	4,346.0
Income Taxes	3,897.0	3,692.0	3,338.0	2,740.0	2,115.0	1,794.0	1,606.0
Equity Earnings/Minority Int.	d183.0	d129.0	d170.0	d153.0	d78.0	...	...
Net Income	6,671.0	6,295.0	☐ 5,575.0	4,430.0	3,526.0	3,056.0	2,740.0
Cash Flow	9,961.0	9,163.0	7,950.0	6,302.0	5,160.0	4,519.0	4,044.0
Average Shs. Outstg. (000)	4,481,000	4,484,000	4,474,000	4,485,000	4,533,000	4,592,000	4,598,000

BALANCE SHEET (IN MILLIONS):

Cash & Cash Equivalents	2,161.0	2,054.0	1,856.0	1,879.0	1,447.0	883.0	83.0
Total Current Assets	28,246.0	26,555.0	24,356.0	21,132.0	19,352.0	17,993.0	17,331.0
Net Property	45,750.0	40,934.0	35,969.0	25,973.0	23,606.0	20,324.0	18,894.0
Total Assets	83,451.0	78,130.0	70,349.0	49,996.0	45,384.0	39,604.0	37,541.0
Total Current Liabilities	27,282.0	28,949.0	25,803.0	16,762.0	14,460.0	10,957.0	11,454.0
Long-Term Obligations	18,732.0	15,655.0	16,674.0	9,607.0	9,674.0	10,016.0	10,600.0
Net Stockholders' Equity	35,102.0	31,343.0	25,834.0	21,112.0	18,503.0	17,143.0	14,756.0
Net Working Capital	964.0	d2,394.0	d1,447.0	4,370.0	4,892.0	7,036.0	5,877.0
Year-end Shs. Outstg. (000)	4,453,000	4,470,000	4,457,000	4,448,000	4,482,000	4,570,000	4,586,000

STATISTICAL RECORD:

Operating Profit Margin %	5.5	5.9	6.1	5.8	5.5	5.4	5.5
Net Profit Margin %	3.0	3.3	3.3	3.2	3.0	2.9	2.9
Return on Equity %	19.0	20.1	21.6	21.0	19.1	17.8	18.6
Return on Assets %	8.0	8.1	7.9	8.9	7.8	7.7	7.3
Debt/Total Assets %	22.4	20.0	23.7	19.2	21.3	25.3	28.2
Price Range	58.75-41.50	69.00-41.44	70.25-38.69	41.38-18.78	20.97-11.00	14.13-9.55	13.81-10.25
P/E Ratio	39.4-27.9	49.3-29.6	56.2-30.9	41.8-19.0	26.9-14.1	21.2-14.4	23.2-17.2
Average Yield %	0.5	0.4	0.3	0.4	0.8	0.9	0.8

Statistics are as originally reported. Adj. for 100% stk. div., 4/99. ☐ Bef. $198.0 mil ($0.04/sh) acctg. chg.

OFFICERS:
S. R. Walton, Chmn.
H. L. Scott, Jr., Pres., C.E.O.
T. M. Schoewe, Exec. V.P., C.F.O.
T. D. Hyde, Exec. V.P., Sr. Gen. Couns.

PRINCIPAL OFFICE: 702 Southwest 8th Street, Bentonville, AR 72716-8611

TELEPHONE NUMBER: (479) 273-4000
FAX: (479) 273-1986
WEB: www.wal-mart.com
NO. OF EMPLOYEES: 1,383,000 (avg.)
SHAREHOLDERS: 324,000
ANNUAL MEETING: In June
INCORPORATED: DE, Oct., 1969

INSTITUTIONAL HOLDINGS:
No. of Institutions: 1,085
Shares Held: 1,559,399,468
% Held: 35.0

INDUSTRY: Variety stores (SIC: 5331)
TRANSFER AGENT(S): EquiServe First Chicago Trust Company, Jersey City, NJ

NYSE SYMBOL WM
Rec. Pr. 33.13 (3/31/02)

WASHINGTON MUTUAL, INC.

YIELD 3.0%
P/E RATIO 10.6

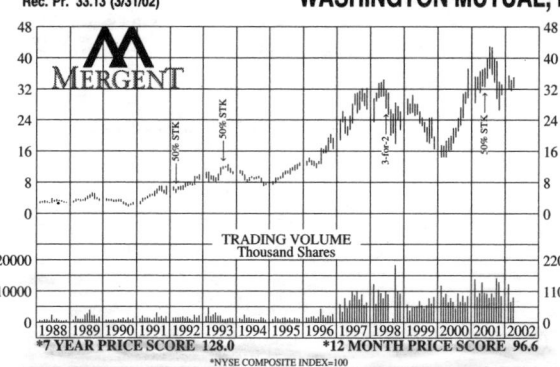

7 YEAR PRICE SCORE 128.0 **12 MONTH PRICE SCORE 96.6**
*NYSE COMPOSITE INDEX=100

TRADING VOLUME
Thousand Shares

INTERIM EARNINGS (Per Share):

Qtr.	Mar.	June	Sept.	Dec.
1998	0.45	0.47	0.49	0.19
1999	0.51	0.52	0.56	0.53
2000	0.56	0.61	0.57	0.63
2001	0.76	0.91	0.85	0.62

INTERIM DIVIDENDS (Per Share):

Amt.	Decl.	Ex.	Rec.	Pay.
50% STK	4/17/01	5/16/01	4/30/01	5/15/01
0.22Q	4/17/01	4/26/01	4/30/01	5/15/01
0.23Q	7/17/01	7/27/01	7/31/01	8/15/01
0.24Q	10/16/01	10/29/01	10/31/01	11/15/01
0.25Q	1/15/02	1/29/02	1/31/02	2/15/02

Indicated div.: $1.00 (Div. Reinv. Plan)

CAPITALIZATION (12/31/01):

	($000)	(%)
Total Deposits	107,182,000	55.0
Long-Term Debt	73,758,000	37.8
Common & Surplus	14,063,000	7.2
Total	195,003,000	100.0

DIVIDEND ACHIEVER STATUS:
Rank: 11   10-Year Growth Rate: 23.69%
Total Years of Dividend Growth: 12

RECENT DEVELOPMENTS: For the year ended 12/31/01, income was $2.73 billion, before an after-tax extraordinary gain of $382.0 million, compared with net income of $1.90 billion a year earlier. Earnings for 2001 and 2000 included pre-tax gains of $967.0 million and $262.0 million, respectively, from mortgage loans. Net interest income climbed 59.5% to $6.88 billion from $4.31 billion the year before. WM reported a gain of $861.0 million in 2001 and a loss of $1.0 million in 2000 from the sale of securities.

PROSPECTS: On 1/7/02, WM acquired Dime Bancorp, creating a platform in the greater New York metropolitan area. Separately, on 3/1/02, WM acquired certain operating assets of HomeSide Lending, Inc., the U.S. mortgage unit of the National Australia Bank Limited, in a transaction valued at about $2.10 billion. The acquisition included approximately $1.90 billion in performing warehoused prime residential mortgage loans. Additionally, WM will subservice HomeSide's $181.30 billion mortgage servicing portfolio, representing about 2.0 million customers.

BUSINESS

WASHINGTON MUTUAL, INC. is a holding company for both banking and nonbanking subsidiaries. The Company's primary banking subsidiaries are Washington Mutual Bank, FA (formerly Washington Mutual Savings Bank), Washington Mutual Bank and Washington Mutual Bank fsb. These organizations provide consumer banking, full-service securities brokerage, mutual fund management, and travel and insurance underwriting services. As of 12/31/01, WM and its subsidiaries had assets of $242.51 billion and operated more than 2,300 offices nationwide. On 7/1/97, WM acquired Great Western Financial Corp. On 10/1/98, WM acquired H.F. Ahmanson & Co. In February 2001, WM acquired the residential mortgage banking business of PNC Financial Services Group and Bank United Corp.

ANNUAL FINANCIAL DATA

	12/31/01	12/31/00	12/31/99	12/31/98	12/31/97	12/31/96	12/31/95
Earnings Per Share	①⑤3.15	⑤2.36	④2.11	③1.71	②0.83	②0.38	1.10
Tang. Book Val. Per Share	6.29	9.96	8.41	8.85	7.97	7.98	8.84
Dividends Per Share	0.90	0.76	0.65	0.55	0.47	0.40	0.34
Dividend Payout %	28.5	32.2	31.0	32.0	57.0	105.8	31.2

INCOME STATEMENT (IN MILLIONS):

Total Interest Income	15,065.0	13,783.0	12,062.2	11,225.5	6,811.0	3,149.2	2,916.1
Total Interest Expense	8,189.0	9,472.0	7,610.4	6,929.7	4,154.5	1,958.2	1,923.4
Net Interest Income	6,876.0	4,311.0	4,451.8	4,291.7	2,656.5	1,191.0	992.6
Provision for Loan Losses	575.0	185.0	167.1	162.0	207.1	201.5	75.0
Non-Interest Income	2,627.0	1,984.0	1,509.0	1,577.0	750.9	259.3	208.3
Non-Interest Expense	4,617.0	3,126.0	2,909.6	3,337.3	2,299.1	1,025.3	700.5
Income Before Taxes	4,311.0	2,984.0	2,884.2	2,369.5	901.1	223.5	425.5
Equity Earnings/Minority Int.	...	...	...	...	...	d13.6	d15.8
Net Income	①⑥2,732.0	⑤1,899.0	④1,817.1	③1,486.9	②481.8	②114.3	289.9
Average Shs. Outstg. (000)	864,700	804,695	861,830	867,843	555,852	253,933	247,374

BALANCE SHEET (IN MILLIONS):

Total Loans & Leases	132,991.0	119,626.0	113,745.7	107,612.2	67,124.9	30,694.2	24,428.1
Allowance for Credit Losses	1,404.0	1,014.0	1,041.9	1,067.8	670.5	590.8	319.0
Net Loans & Leases	131,587.0	118,612.0	112,703.7	106,544.4	66,454.4	30,103.4	24,109.1
Total Assets	242,506.0	194,716.0	186,513.6	165,493.9	96,981.3	44,551.9	42,026.6
Total Deposits	107,182.0	79,574.0	81,129.8	85,492.1	50,986.0	24,080.1	24,463.0
Long-Term Obligations	73,758.0	67,785.0	63,297.3	45,198.1	22,991.3	7,918.5	5,306.0
Total Liabilities	228,341.0	184,550.0	177,461.0	156,148.9	91,672.0	42,154.0	39,484.9
Net Stockholders' Equity	14,063.0	10,166.0	9,052.7	9,344.4	5,309.1	2,397.9	2,541.7
Year-end Shs. Outstg. (000)	873,089	809,784	857,384	890,112	579,510	283,820	269,298

STATISTICAL RECORD:

Return on Equity %	19.4	18.7	20.1	15.9	9.1	4.8	11.4
Return on Assets %	1.1	1.0	1.0	0.9	0.5	0.3	0.7
Equity/Assets %	5.8	5.2	4.9	5.6	5.5	5.4	6.0
Non-Int. Exp./Tot. Inc. %	48.6	49.7	48.8	56.9	67.5	70.7	58.3
Price Range	42.99-26.52	37.29-14.42	30.50-16.46	34.45-17.83	32.28-18.78	20.39-11.61	13.11-7.39
P/E Ratio	13.6-8.4	15.8-6.1	14.5-7.8	20.2-10.4	39.0-22.7	53.9-30.7	11.9-6.7
Average Yield %	2.6	2.9	2.8	2.1	1.8	2.4	3.3

Statistics are as originally reported. Results refl. the 7/1/97 acq'. of Great Western Financial Corp. & 10/1/98 acq. of H. F. Ahmanson & Co. Adj. for stk. 3-for-2 splits: 5/01, 6/98. ① Bef. extraord. gain of $382.0 mill. ② Incl. various pre-tax net exps. of $403.7 mill.; 1997; $256.7 mill., 1996 ③ Incl. net pre-tax non-recurr. gains of $316.0 mill. & write-down of $52.9 mill. ④ Incl. trans.-rel. exp. of $95.7 mill.; 2001; $261.6 mill., 2000. ⑤ Incl. pre-tax gain on sale of mtge. loans of $967.0 mill., 2001; $261.6 mill., 2000.

OFFICERS:
K. K. Killinger, Chmn., Pres., C.E.O.
W. A. Longbrake, C.F.O.
F. L. Chapman, Sr. Exec. V.P., Gen. Couns.
INVESTOR CONTACT: JoAnn DeGrande, First Vice-Pres., (206) 461-3186
PRINCIPAL OFFICE: 1201 Third Avenue, Seattle, WA 98101

TELEPHONE NUMBER: (206) 461-2000
FAX: (206) 554-2778
WEB: www.wamu.com
NO. OF EMPLOYEES: 39,465
SHAREHOLDERS: 42,399
ANNUAL MEETING: In Apr.
INCORPORATED: WA, Nov., 1994

INSTITUTIONAL HOLDINGS:
No. of Institutions: 684
Shares Held: 692,317,185
% Held: 71.3
INDUSTRY: Savings institutions, except federal (SIC: 6036)
TRANSFER AGENT(S): Mellon Investor Services, L.L.C., Ridgefield Park, NJ

WASHINGTON REAL ESTATE INVESTMENT TRUST

YIELD	4.6%
P/E RATIO	20.8

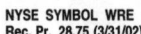

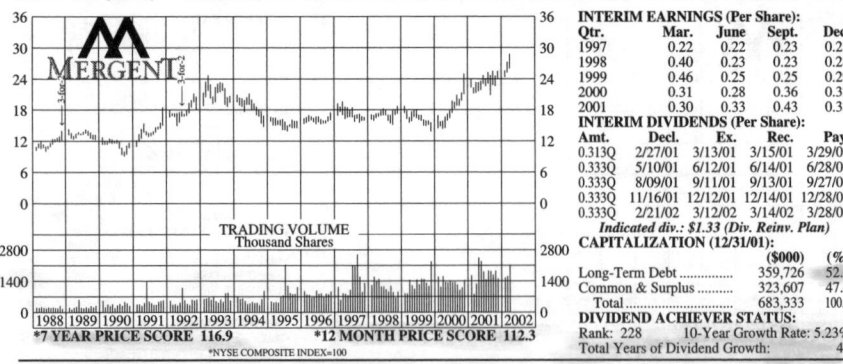

TRADING VOLUME	
Thousand Shares	

1988 1989 1990 1991 1992 1993 1994 1995 1996 1997 1998 1999 2000 2001 2002
*7 YEAR PRICE SCORE 116.9   ***12 MONTH PRICE SCORE 112.3**
*NYSE COMPOSITE INDEX=100

INTERIM EARNINGS (Per Share):

Qtr.	Mar.	June	Sept.	Dec.
1997	0.22	0.22	0.23	0.23
1998	0.40	0.23	0.23	0.28
1999	0.46	0.25	0.25	0.29
2000	0.31	0.28	0.36	0.32
2001	0.30	0.33	0.43	0.32

INTERIM DIVIDENDS (Per Share):

Amt.	Decl.	Ex.	Rec.	Pay.
0.313Q	2/27/01	3/13/01	3/15/01	3/29/01
0.333Q	5/10/01	6/12/01	6/14/01	6/28/01
0.333Q	8/09/01	9/11/01	9/13/01	9/27/01
0.333Q	11/16/01	12/12/01	12/14/01	12/28/01
0.333Q	2/21/02	3/12/02	3/14/02	3/28/02

Indicated div.: $1.33 (Div. Reinv. Plan)

CAPITALIZATION (12/31/01):

	($000)	(%)
Long-Term Debt	359,726	52.6
Common & Surplus	323,607	47.4
Total	683,333	100.0

DIVIDEND ACHIEVER STATUS:
Rank: 228   10-Year Growth Rate: 5.23%
Total Years of Dividend Growth: 40

RECENT DEVELOPMENTS: For the year ended 12/31/01, net income increased 16.0% to $52.4 million compared with $45.1 million in the previous year. Results for 2001 and 2000 included gains on the sale of real estate of $4.3 million and $3.6 million, respectively. Real estate rental revenue advanced 10.2% to $148.4 million from $134.7 million in the prior year. Operating income climbed 10.2% to $106.3 million from $96.4 million in 2000.

PROSPECTS: Long-term results should be favorably affected by the acquisition of Sullyfield Commercial Center, a two building industrial complex in Chantilly, Virginia for approximately $21.6 million. Separately, on 3/1/01, the Company announced that it sold a Washington, D.C. industrial property to an affiliate of U-Haul International for $6.2 million. The transaction resulted in a gain of approximately $4.5 million.

BUSINESS

WASHINGTON REAL ESTATE INVESTMENT TRUST is a self-administered qualified equity real estate investment trust. The trust's business consists of the ownership and operation of income-producing real estate properties principally in the Greater Washington, D.C.-Baltimore, MD area. Upon the purchase of a property, WRE begins a program of improving the real estate to increase the value and to improve the operations, with the goals of generating higher rental income and reducing expenses. As of 12/31/01, the trust owned a diversified portfolio consisting of 10 retail centers, 23 office buildings, nine multifamily buildings and 16 industrial properties. WRE's principal objective is to invest in high-quality real estate in prime locations and to monitor closely the management of these properties, which includes active leasing and ongoing capital improvement programs.

ANNUAL FINANCIAL DATA

	12/31/01	12/31/00	12/31/99	12/31/98	12/31/97	12/31/96	12/31/95
Earnings Per Share	①1.38	①1.26	①1.24	①1.15	0.90	0.88	0.88
Tang. Book Val. Per Share	8.33	7.24	7.20	7.11	7.07	6.15	6.29
Dividends Per Share	1.31	1.23	1.16	1.11	1.07	1.03	0.99
Dividend Payout %	94.9	97.6	93.3	96.5	118.9	117.0	112.5
INCOME STATEMENT (IN THOUSANDS):							
Total Income	148,424	134,732	118,975	103,597	79,429	65,541	52,597
Costs & Expenses	48,247	45,849	41,454	37,672	29,702	25,027	19,956
Depreciation	26,735	22,723	19,590	15,399	10,911	7,784	5,084
Interest Expense	27,011	25,531	22,271	17,106	9,691	5,474	2,170
Income Before Income Taxes	52,353	45,139	44,301	41,604	30,136	27,964	26,103
Net Income	①52,353	①45,139	①44,301	①41,064	30,136	27,964	26,103
Average Shs. Outstg.	37,951	35,872	35,700	35,700	33,400	31,800	29,787
BALANCE SHEET (IN THOUSANDS):							
Cash & Cash Equivalents	26,441	6,426	4,716	4,595	7,908	1,676	3,532
Total Real Estate Investments	651,961	597,607	578,296	530,573	448,300	306,739	232,375
Total Assets	707,935	632,047	608,480	558,707	468,571	318,488	241,784
Long-Term Obligations	359,726	351,260	297,038	238,912	107,461	107,590	7,706
Total Liabilities	382,717	371,833	349,769	303,447	216,483	122,865	42,049
Net Stockholders' Equity	323,607	258,656	257,189	253,733	252,088	195,623	199,735
Year-end Shs. Outstg.	38,829	35,740	35,721	35,692	35,678	31,803	31,752
STATISTICAL RECORD:							
Net Inc.+Depr./Assets %	11.2	10.7	10.5	10.1	8.8	11.2	12.9
Return on Equity %	16.2	17.5	17.2	16.2	12.0	14.3	13.1
Return on Assets %	7.4	7.1	7.3	7.3	6.4	8.8	10.8
Price Range	25.52-20.80	25.00-14.31	18.75-13.81	18.75-15.06	19.63-15.50	17.50-15.25	16.63-13.88
P/E Ratio	18.5-15.1	19.8-11.4	15.1-11.1	16.3-13.1	21.8-17.2	19.9-17.3	18.9-15.8
Average Yield %	5.7	6.3	7.1	6.6	6.1	6.3	6.5

Statistics are as originally reported. ① Incl. gain on sale of investment $4.3 mill., 2001; $3.6 mill., 2000; $7.9 mill., 1999; $6.8 mill., 1998.

OFFICERS:
E. B. Cronin Jr., Chmn., Pres., C.E.O.
L. M. Franklin, V.P., C.A.O., Sec.

INVESTOR CONTACT: Investor Relations,
(301) 984-9400

PRINCIPAL OFFICE: 6110 Executive
Boulevard, Suite 800, Rockville, MD
20852-3927

TELEPHONE NUMBER: (301) 984-9400
FAX: (301) 984-9610
WEB: www.writ.com

NO. OF EMPLOYEES: 263 (avg.)

SHAREHOLDERS: 37,000 (approx.)

ANNUAL MEETING: In May

INCORPORATED: DC, Nov., 1960; reincorp.,
MD, June, 1996

INSTITUTIONAL HOLDINGS:
No. of Institutions: 122
Shares Held: 10,275,892
% Held: 26.4

INDUSTRY: Real estate investment trusts
(SIC: 6798)

TRANSFER AGENT(S): American Stock &
Trust Company, New York, NY

WAUSAU-MOSINEE PAPER MILLS CORPORATION

YIELD 2.7%
P/E RATIO 67.2

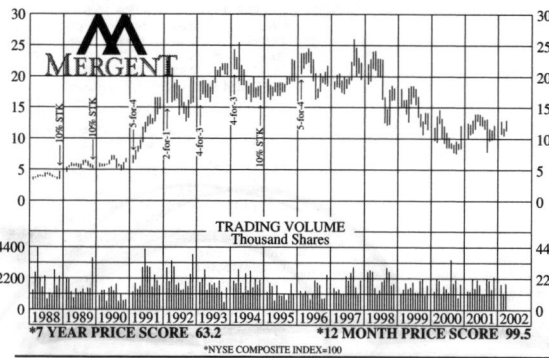

TRADING VOLUME
Thousand Shares

7 YEAR PRICE SCORE 63.2   **12 MONTH PRICE SCORE 99.5**
*NYSE COMPOSITE INDEX=100

INTERIM EARNINGS (Per Share):

Qtr.	Mar.	June	Sept.	Dec.
1998	d0.14	0.36	0.34	0.16
1999	0.26	0.19	0.22	0.14
2000	d0.25	0.15	0.09	0.02
2001	d0.09	0.05	0.14	0.09

INTERIM DIVIDENDS (Per Share):

Amt.	Decl.	Ex.	Rec.	Pay.
0.085Q	4/19/01	4/27/01	5/01/01	5/15/01
0.085Q	6/14/01	7/30/01	8/01/01	8/15/01
0.085Q	10/11/01	10/30/01	11/01/01	11/15/01
0.085Q	12/13/01	1/30/02	2/01/02	2/15/02

Indicated div.: $0.34 (Div. Reinv. Plan)

CAPITALIZATION (12/31/01):

	($000)	(%)
Long-Term Debt	192,264	29.0
Deferred Income Tax	105,638	15.9
Common & Surplus	364,855	55.1
Total	662,757	100.0

DIVIDEND ACHIEVER STATUS:

Rank: 125   10-Year Growth Rate: 10.61%
Total Years of Dividend Growth: 17

RECENT DEVELOPMENTS: For the year ended 12/31/01, net income amounted to $9.7 million from $718,000 in 2000. Results for 2000 included restructuring inventory charges of $599,000 and restructuring other charges of $21.7 million. Net sales declined 4.8% to $943.7 million from $990.9 million in 2000. Gross profit as a percentage of net sales was 10.3% compared with 10.5% in 2000. Operating income surged 59.2% to $30.6 million. Comparisons were made with restated prior-year figures.

PROSPECTS: Looking ahead, WMO does not expect market conditions to improve in the near term. Therefore, the Company will continue to focus on the internal initiatives begun in 2001 to improve operating efficiencies and cost-reduction measures. WMO is particularly focused on its Specialty Paper business, which has been most significantly affected by the economic downturn. Also, WMO will continue to emphasize product development and the identification of new, more profitable market niches.

BUSINESS

WAUSAU-MOSINEE PAPER MILLS CORPORATION (formerly Wausau Paper Mills Company) manufactures, converts and sells paper and paper products. The Company competes in different markets within the paper industry. Each of its operating groups serves distinct market niches. As of 12/31/01, the Company's ten operating facilities were organized into three operating groups: the Specialty Paper Group; the Printing & Writing Group; and the Towel & Tissue Group. The Specialty Paper Group combines the Company's Mosinee, Rhinelander, and Otis facilities to produce a wide variety of technical specialty papers. The Printing & Writing Group produces and converts two lines of paper products in five facilities. The Towel & Tissue Group produces a complete line of towel and tissue products which are marketed along with soap and dispensing system products for the industrial and commercial ''away-from-home'' market.

ANNUAL FINANCIAL DATA

	12/31/01	12/31/00	12/31/99	12/31/98	12/31/97	8/31/97	8/31/96
Earnings Per Share	0.19	①0.01	0.81	①0.73	①1.13	1.34	1.12
Cash Flow Per Share	1.37	1.16	1.86	1.63	1.95	2.07	1.75
Tang. Book Val. Per Share	7.08	0.01	7.66	7.46	7.61	7.82	7.25
Dividends Per Share	0.34	0.335	0.31	0.27	0.25	0.25	0.22
Dividend Payout %	178.9	N.M.	38.3	37.3	22.1	18.7	19.6
INCOME STATEMENT (IN THOUSANDS):							
Total Revenues	943,729	952,130	944,629	946,127	933,127	570,258	542,669
Costs & Expenses	852,174	874,046	810,061	824,157	765,040	462,152	450,006
Depreciation & Amort.	60,948	58,860	55,012	49,825	47,259	26,586	23,140
Operating Income	30,607	19,224	79,556	72,145	120,828	81,520	69,523
Net Interest Inc./(Exp.)	d14,154	d15,575	d11,593	d7,280	d8,008	d3,343	d2,224
Income Before Income Taxes	15,330	1,138	68,017	65,801	113,589	78,399	66,829
Income Taxes	5,670	420	25,600	25,000	48,191	29,500	25,600
Net Income	9,660	①718	42,327	①40,801	①65,398	48,899	41,229
Cash Flow	70,608	59,578	97,339	90,626	112,657	75,485	64,369
Average Shs. Outstg.	51,554	51,373	52,265	55,708	57,811	36,514	36,821
BALANCE SHEET (IN THOUSANDS):							
Cash & Cash Equivalents	12,010	10,579	5,397	2,495	2,584	5,297	2,372
Total Current Assets	223,035	256,412	252,311	242,126	234,929	149,419	119,240
Net Property	634,928	662,204	653,823	625,065	604,930	386,466	330,536
Total Assets	892,008	948,431	936,632	900,149	872,064	555,615	467,028
Total Current Liabilities	121,311	117,807	111,489	160,720	108,276	62,305	59,053
Long-Term Obligations	192,264	250,465	220,476	127,000	140,500	83,510	53,119
Net Stockholders' Equity	364,855	376,548	393,760	396,586	440,160	303,554	264,711
Net Working Capital	101,724	138,605	140,822	81,406	126,653	87,114	60,187
Year-end Shs. Outstg.	51,506	51,276	51,417	53,164	57,802	38,840	36,513
STATISTICAL RECORD:							
Operating Profit Margin %	3.2	2.0	8.4	7.6	12.9	14.3	12.8
Net Profit Margin %	1.0	0.1	4.5	4.3	7.0	8.6	7.6
Return on Equity %	2.6	0.2	10.7	10.3	14.9	16.1	15.6
Return on Assets %	1.1	0.1	4.5	4.5	7.5	8.8	8.8
Debt/Total Assets %	21.6	26.4	23.5	14.1	16.1	15.0	11.4
Price Range	14.00-7.85	14.63-7.56	18.44-10.63	24.13-12.13	26.00-17.13	26.00-17.13	24.50-16.25
P/E Ratio	73.6-41.3	N.M.	22.8-13.1	33.0-16.6	23.0-15.2	19.4-12.8	21.9-14.5
Average Yield %	3.1	3.0	2.1	1.5	1.2	1.2	1.1

Statistics are as originally reported. The data for 1997 reflects 12 months results for the periods of 12/31/97 and 8/31/97, respectively. Adj. for stk. splits: 5-for-4, 1/17/96; 10% div., 1/17/95. ① Incl. restruct. chrg. of $22.3 mill., 2000; $42.8 mill., 1998; $13.5 mill., 1997.

OFFICERS:
S. W. Orr, Jr., Chmn.
R. L. Radt, Vice-Chmn.
T. J. Howatt, Pres., C.E.O.
S. P. Doescher, Sr. V.P., C.F.O.
INVESTOR CONTACT: Investor Relations, (715) 693-4470
PRINCIPAL OFFICE: 1244 Kronenwetter Drive, Mosinee, WI 54455-9099

TELEPHONE NUMBER: (715) 693-4470
FAX: (715) 692-2082
WEB: www.wausaumosinee.com
NO. OF EMPLOYEES: 3,200 (approx.)
SHAREHOLDERS: 3,400 (approx. record); 6,900 (approx. beneficial)
ANNUAL MEETING: In Feb.
INCORPORATED: WI, June, 1899

INSTITUTIONAL HOLDINGS:
No. of Institutions: 125
Shares Held: 32,432,658
% Held: 63.0

INDUSTRY: Paper mills (SIC: 2621)

TRANSFER AGENT(S): Computershare Investor Services, Chicago, IL

WEINGARTEN REALTY INVESTORS

YIELD 6.5%
P/E RATIO 18.7

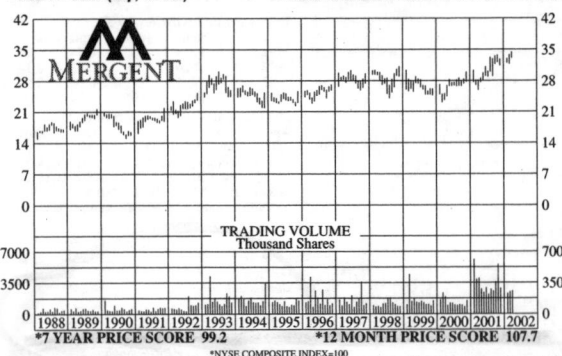

INTERIM EARNINGS (Per Share):

Qtr.	Mar.	June	Sept.	Dec.
1999	0.33	0.35	0.36	0.85
2000	0.36	0.37	0.37	0.36
2001	0.45	0.43	0.46	0.49

INTERIM DIVIDENDS (Per Share):

Amt.	Decl.	Ex.	Rec.	Pay.
0.79Q	4/19/01	5/16/01	5/18/01	6/15/01
0.79Q	7/31/01	8/22/01	8/24/01	9/14/01
0.79Q	10/25/01	11/29/01	12/03/01	12/14/01
0.833Q	2/26/02	3/06/02	3/08/02	3/15/02
50% STK	2/26/02	4/16/02	4/01/02	4/15/02

Indicated div.: $2.22 (Adj.; Div. Reinv. Plan)

CAPITALIZATION (12/31/01):

	($000)	(%)
Long-Term Debt	1,070,835	53.7
Minority Interest	3,886	0.2
Preferred Stock	263	0.0
Common & Surplus	920,809	46.1
Total	1,995,793	100.0

DIVIDEND ACHIEVER STATUS:
Rank: 231   10-Year Growth Rate: 5.11%
Total Years of Dividend Growth: 13

TRADING VOLUME
Thousand Shares

*7 YEAR PRICE SCORE 99.2   *12 MONTH PRICE SCORE 107.7
*NYSE COMPOSITE INDEX=100

RECENT DEVELOPMENTS: For the year ended 12/31/01, net income jumped 37.4% to $108.5 million compared with $79.0 million in 2000. Results for 2001 and 2000 included gains on sales of property of $8.3 million and $382,000, respectively. Total revenues increased 25.8% to $314.9 million from $250.2 million in 2000. Rentals revenues advanced 27.0% to $309.5 million. Comparisons were made with restated prior-year figures.

PROSPECTS: On 4/8/01, WRI completed the acquisition of seven supermarket-anchored shopping centers from Bob Hughes and Associates and related partnerships in the Raleigh-Durham market for approximately $94.9 million. WRI also acquired a supermarket-anchored shopping center in Plano, Texas. The sales price was not disclosed. Separately, WRI announced that it sold a portion of the Fondren Southwest Village Shopping Center in Houston, Texas.

BUSINESS

WEINGARTEN REALTY INVESTORS is a self-administered and self-managed real estate investment trust that acquires, develops and manages real estate, primarily anchored neighborhood and community shopping centers and, to a lesser extent, industrial properties. As of 12/31/01, the Company owned or operated under long-term leases interests in 287 developed income-producing real estate projects. WRI owned 228 shopping centers located in the Houston metropolitan area and in other parts of Texas and in California, Louisiana, Arizona, Nevada, Arkansas, New Mexico, Oklahoma, Tennessee, Kansas, Colorado, Missouri, Illinois, Florida North Carolina, Georgia, Mississippi and Maine. WRI also owned 57 industrial projects located in Tennessee, Nevada Georgia, Florida and Houston, Austin and Dallas, Texas. Also, WRI owned one multi-family residential project and one office building.

ANNUAL FINANCIAL DATA

	12/31/01	12/31/00	12/31/99	12/31/98	12/31/97	12/31/96	12/31/95
Earnings Per Share	② 1.84	② 1.46	①② 1.91	① 1.39	1.37	1.35	1.13
Tang. Book Val. Per Share	17.87	15.59	16.12	13.32	9.75	10.06	10.34
Dividends Per Share	2.11	2.00	1.89	1.79	1.71	1.65	1.60
Dividend Payout %	114.5	137.0	99.3	128.8	124.9	122.2	142.0
INCOME STATEMENT (IN MILLIONS):							
Rental Income	309.5	264.6	225.2	194.6	169.0	145.3	125.4
Interest Income	1.2	5.6	5.0	2.1	2.5	3.1	5.3
Total Income	314.9	273.4	230.3	198.1	174.5	151.1	134.2
Costs & Expenses	151.4	128.2	105.1	95.6	84.9	69.0	59.3
Depreciation	68.3	58.5	49.6	41.9	38.0	33.8	30.1
Income Before Income Taxes	103.5	87.0	96.1	61.4	55.0	53.9	44.8
Equity Earnings/Minority Int.	5.1	d8.0	0.2	0.3	...	...	...
Net Income	② 108.5	② 79.0	①② 96.3	① 61.8	55.0	53.9	44.8
Average Shs. Outstg. (000)	48,369	40,397	40,335	40,304	40,157	39,833	39,696
BALANCE SHEET (IN MILLIONS):							
Cash & Cash Equivalents	12.4	14.8	5.8	16.6	15.1	14.0	19.6
Total Assets	2,095.7	1,646.0	1,309.4	1,107.0	946.8	831.1	734.8
Long-Term Obligations	1,070.8	869.6	594.2	516.4	507.4	389.2	289.3
Total Liabilities	1,174.7	1,016.1	663.5	573.9	556.8	430.1	323.2
Net Stockholders' Equity	921.1	629.9	645.9	533.2	390.0	401.0	411.6
Year-end Shs. Outstg. (000)	51,521	40,382	40,043	40,010	39,990	39,864	39,819
STATISTICAL RECORD:							
Net Inc.+Depr./Assets %	8.4	8.4	11.1	9.4	9.8	10.6	10.2
Return on Equity %	11.8	12.5	14.9	11.6	14.1	13.5	10.9
Return on Assets %	5.2	4.8	7.4	5.6	5.8	6.5	6.1
Price Range	33.77-25.85	30.00-23.04	30.42-24.67	31.25-23.96	30.42-25.83	27.17-22.83	25.67-22.25
P/E Ratio	18.4-14.1	20.5-15.8	16.0-12.9	22.5-17.3	22.3-18.9	20.1-16.9	22.8-19.7
Average Yield %	7.1	7.5	6.9	6.5	6.1	6.6	6.7

Statistics are as originally reported. Adj. for 50.0% stk. split, 4/15/02. ① Bef. extraord. chrg., 1999, $190,000; 1998, $1.4 mill. ② Incl. gain on sales of prop. of $8.3 mill, 2001; $382,000, 2000; $20.6 mill., 1999.

OFFICERS:
S. Alexander, Chmn.
M. Debrovner, Vice-Chmn.
A. M. Alexander, Pres., C.E.O.
S. C. Richter, Sr. V.P., C.F.O.

INVESTOR CONTACT: Tracey Pursell, Dir.,
Inv. Rel., (713) 866-6050

PRINCIPAL OFFICE: 2600 Citadel Plaza
Drive, P.O. Box 924133, Houston, TX
77292-4133

TELEPHONE NUMBER: (713) 866-6000
FAX: (713) 866-6049
WEB: www.weingarten.com

NO. OF EMPLOYEES: 265

SHAREHOLDERS: 3,313 (record)

ANNUAL MEETING: In Apr.

INCORPORATED: TX, 1948

INSTITUTIONAL HOLDINGS:
No. of Institutions: 162
Shares Held: 18,604,197 (Adj.)
% Held: 36.1

INDUSTRY: Real estate investment trusts
(SIC: 6798)

TRANSFER AGENT(S): Mellon Investor
Services, Houston, TX

WEIS MARKETS, INC.

YIELD 3.6%
P/E RATIO 19.5

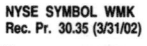

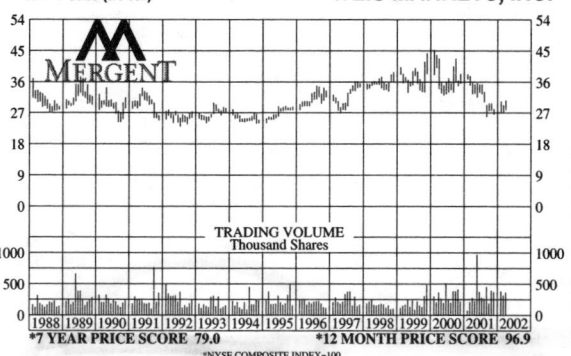

*7 YEAR PRICE SCORE 79.0   *12 MONTH PRICE SCORE 96.9
*NYSE COMPOSITE INDEX=100

TRADING VOLUME
Thousand Shares

INTERIM EARNINGS (Per Share):

Qtr.	Mar.	June	Sept.	Dec.
1997	0.43	0.46	0.46	0.52
1998	0.64	0.40	0.44	0.52
1999	0.51	0.46	0.46	0.48
2000	0.43	0.52	0.46	0.36
2001	0.41	0.26	0.43	0.46

INTERIM DIVIDENDS (Per Share):

Amt.	Decl.	Ex.	Rec.	Pay.
0.27Q	4/20/01	4/26/01	4/30/01	5/14/01
0.27Q	6/25/01	8/08/01	8/10/01	8/24/01
0.27Q	10/15/01	10/31/01	11/02/01	11/16/01
0.27Q	1/28/02	2/06/02	2/08/02	2/22/02
0.27Q	4/09/02	5/01/02	5/03/02	5/17/02

Indicated div.: $1.08 (Div. Reinv. Plan)

CAPITALIZATION (12/29/01):

	($000)	(%)
Long-Term Debt	25,000	4.4
Deferred Income Tax	16,051	2.8
Common & Surplus	525,364	92.8
Total	566,415	100.0

DIVIDEND ACHIEVER STATUS:
Rank: 226   10-Year Growth Rate: 5.37%
Total Years of Dividend Growth: 27

RECENT DEVELOPMENTS: For the 52 weeks ended 12/29/01, net income totaled $50.1 million, down 32.2% compared with $73.8 million in the corresponding 53-week period the year before. Net sales slipped 3.5% to $1.99 billion from $2.06 billion a year earlier. Results in 2000 included sales of $37.1 million from its food service division, which was sold in April 2000. Same-store sales, adjusted for the extra week in 2000, increased 0.5% year over year. Income before taxes dropped 29.9% to $81.8 million.

PROSPECTS: Operating profitability is being hampered by increased employee benefit costs, lower investment income and increased advertising and promotional spending. Meanwhile, the Company continues to focus on making technology upgrades in its existing stores. As of 1/19/02, the Company had installed self-scanning lanes in 50 of its stores. WMK opened a new superstore on 1/19/02 in Nanticoke, PA which will replace two smaller stores that were closed.

BUSINESS

WEIS MARKETS, INC. operates 163 supermarkets in Pennsylvania, New Jersey, New York, Maryland, Virginia and West Virginia as of 2/1/02. The Company supplies its retail stores from distribution centers in Sunbury, Northumberland, and Milton, PA. Many of WMK's private label products are supplied by the Company's ice cream manufacturing plant, fresh meat processing plant, and milk processing plant. The Company also owns SuperPetz, an operator of 33 pet supply stores in 11 states. On 4/8/00, the Company completed the sale of Weis Food Service, its regional food service division.

ANNUAL FINANCIAL DATA

	12/29/01	12/30/00	12/25/99	12/26/98	12/27/97	12/28/96	12/30/95
Earnings Per Share	1.55	①1.77	①1.91	①2.00	1.87	1.87	1.84
Cash Flow Per Share	3.13	2.99	3.02	3.11	2.91	2.77	2.61
Tang. Book Val. Per Share	19.31	22.74	22.03	21.33	20.28	19.47	18.61
Dividends Per Share	1.08	1.06	1.02	0.98	0.94	0.88	0.80
Dividend Payout %	69.7	59.9	53.4	49.0	50.3	47.1	43.5
INCOME STATEMENT (IN MILLIONS):							
Total Revenues	1,988.2	2,061.0	2,004.9	1,867.5	1,818.8	1,753.2	1,646.4
Costs & Expenses	1,874.3	1,930.0	1,865.6	1,744.8	1,690.2	1,624.5	1,527.1
Depreciation & Amort.	51.0	50.9	46.3	46.3	43.5	38.1	33.2
Operating Income	62.9	80.1	93.0	76.4	85.1	90.6	86.2
Income Before Income Taxes	81.8	116.8	124.0	134.5	118.6	120.7	121.7
Income Taxes	31.8	43.0	44.3	50.8	40.4	41.9	42.3
Net Income	50.1	②73.8	②79.7	②83.7	78.2	78.9	79.4
Cash Flow	101.0	124.7	126.0	130.0	121.7	117.0	112.6
Average Shs. Outstg. (000)	32,299	41,695	41,718	41,776	41,843	42,280	43,083
BALANCE SHEET (IN MILLIONS):							
Cash & Cash Equivalents	31.9	413.6	389.2	411.1	377.3	390.7	435.5
Total Current Assets	240.1	617.2	602.6	608.2	575.8	590.6	605.5
Net Property	440.0	441.8	439.4	398.4	365.2	343.9	286.0
Total Assets	704.2	1,085.9	1,058.2	1,029.2	971.8	966.3	923.2
Total Current Liabilities	137.8	120.3	120.8	118.7	104.3	127.4	115.3
Long-Term Obligations	25.0	...	...	...	...	...	...
Net Stockholders' Equity	525.4	947.9	918.5	890.6	847.3	815.5	791.6
Net Working Capital	102.3	496.9	481.7	489.5	471.6	463.3	491.1
Year-end Shs. Outstg. (000)	27,203	41,688	41,692	41,756	41,773	42,041	42,534
STATISTICAL RECORD:							
Operating Profit Margin %	3.2	3.9	4.6	4.1	4.7	5.2	5.2
Net Profit Margin %	2.5	3.6	4.0	4.5	4.3	4.5	4.8
Return on Equity %	9.5	7.8	8.7	9.4	9.2	9.6	10.0
Return on Assets %	7.1	6.8	7.5	8.1	8.0	8.2	8.6
Debt/Total Assets %	3.6	...	...	...	...	...	...
Price Range	38.25-25.80	45.25-32.00	44.31-32.88	38.88-33.25	36.25-26.88	34.88-27.75	29.00-24.00
P/E Ratio	24.7-16.6	25.6-18.1	23.2-17.2	19.4-16.6	19.4-14.4	18.6-14.8	15.8-13.0
Average Yield %	3.4	2.7	2.6	2.7	3.0	2.8	3.0

Statistics are as originally reported. ① Incl. $4.9 mil pre-tax litigation chg., 2000; $3.4 mil pre-tax gain fr. sale of asset, 1999; $8.3 mil ($0.20/sh) after-tax gain from sale of stk., 1998.

QUARTERLY DATA

(12/29/2001)($000)	REV	INC
1st Quarter	489,095	17,194
2nd Quarter	492,414	8,706
3nd Quarter	498,832	11,703
4rd Quarter	507,095	12,452

OFFICERS:
R. F. Weis, Chmn., Treas.
N. S. Rich, Pres.
W. R. Mills, V.P., Sec.

PRINCIPAL OFFICE: 1000 South Second Street, P.O. Box 471, Sunbury, PA 17801-0471

TELEPHONE NUMBER: (570) 286-4571
FAX: (570) 286-3286
WEB: www.weismarkets.com

NO. OF EMPLOYEES: 19,000 (approx.)

SHAREHOLDERS: 5,983 (approx.)

ANNUAL MEETING: In June

INCORPORATED: PA, Dec., 1924

INSTITUTIONAL HOLDINGS:
No. of Institutions: 64
Shares Held: 4,747,373
% Held: 17.5

INDUSTRY: Grocery stores (SIC: 5411)

TRANSFER AGENT(S): American Stock Transfer & Trust Company, New York, NY

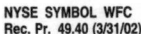

WELLS FARGO & COMPANY

YIELD	2.1%
P/E RATIO	24.9

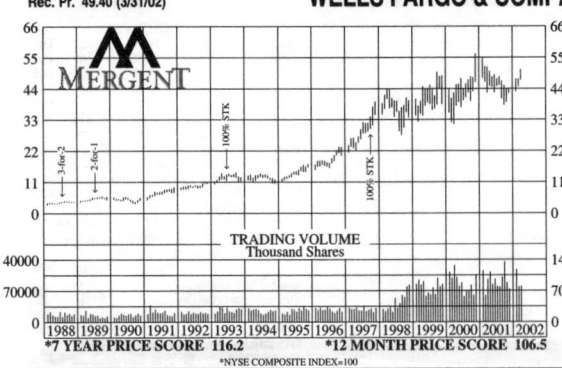

TRADING VOLUME
Thousand Shares

| 1988 | 1989 | 1990 | 1991 | 1992 | 1993 | 1994 | 1995 | 1996 | 1997 | 1998 | 1999 | 2000 | 2001 | 2002 |

*7 YEAR PRICE SCORE 116.2   ***12 MONTH PRICE SCORE 106.5**
*NYSE COMPOSITE INDEX=100

INTERIM EARNINGS (Per Share):

Qtr.	Mar.	June	Sept.	Dec.
1998	0.41	0.44	0.45	d0.12
1999	0.53	0.55	0.57	0.58
2000	0.61	0.63	0.64	0.65
2001	0.67	d0.05	0.67	0.69

INTERIM DIVIDENDS (Per Share):

Amt.	Decl.	Ex.	Rec.	Pay.
0.24Q	4/24/01	5/02/01	5/04/01	6/01/01
0.26Q	7/24/01	8/08/01	8/10/01	9/01/01
0.26Q	10/23/01	11/07/01	11/09/01	12/01/01
0.26Q	1/22/02	1/30/02	2/01/02	3/01/02

Indicated div.: $1.04 (Div. Reinv. Plan)

CAPITALIZATION (12/31/01):

	($000)	(%)
Total Deposits	187,266,000	74.7
Long-Term Debt	36,095,000	14.4
Preferred Stock	218,000	0.1
Common & Surplus	26,996,000	10.8
Total	250,575,000	100.0

DIVIDEND ACHIEVER STATUS:
Rank: 57   10-Year Growth Rate: 15.58%
Total Years of Dividend Growth: 14

RECENT DEVELOPMENTS: For the year ended 12/31/01, net income fell 15.0% to $3.42 billion. Results for 2001 and 2000 included a net venture capital loss of $1.63 billion and a gain of $1.94 billion, respectively. Results for 2001 and 2000 also included pre-tax net gains of $21.0 million and $58.0 million, respectively, from dispositions of premises and equipment. Net interest income rose 14.7% to $12.46 billion. Non-interest income slid 13.0% to $7.69 billion.

PROSPECTS: The Company continues to focus on maintaining credit quality as it benefits from a well-diversified portfolio, split nearly equally between consumer and commercial borrowers. Separately, WFC's Mexican border bank, which spans from San Diego to Brownsville, Texas, is attracting new banking households at a rate twice as fast as the rest of WFC's community banking franchise.

BUSINESS

WELLS FARGO & COMPANY (formerly Norwest Corporation), with $307.57 billion in assets as of 12/31/01, is a diversified financial services company providing banking, insurance, investments, mortgage and consumer finance through more than 5,400 financial services stores and the Internet across North America and elsewhere internationally. In early November 1998, the former Wells Fargo & Company merged with WFC Holdings, a subsidiary of Norwest Corp., with WFC Holdings as the surviving corporation. In connection with the merger, Norwest changed its name to Wells Fargo & Company. On 10/25/00, WFC acquired First Security, creating the largest banking franchise in the western region of the U.S.

ANNUAL FINANCIAL DATA

	12/31/01	12/31/00	12/31/99	12/31/98	12/31/97	12/31/96	12/31/95
Earnings Per Share	③④ 1.97	③ 2.33	③ 2.23	② 1.17	1.75	① 1.54	1.38
Tang. Book Val. Per Share	9.71	9.11	7.87	6.71	8.90	7.88	7.05
Dividends Per Share	1.00	0.90	0.79	0.70	0.61	0.53	0.45
Dividend Payout %	50.8	38.6	35.2	59.8	35.1	34.2	32.6
INCOME STATEMENT (IN MILLIONS)							
Total Interest Income	19,201.0	18,725.0	14,375.0	14,055.0	6,697.4	6,318.3	5,717.3
Total Interest Expense	6,741.0	7,860.0	5,020.0	5,065.0	2,664.0	2,617.0	2,448.0
Net Interest Income	12,460.0	10,865.0	9,355.0	8,990.0	4,033.4	3,701.3	3,269.3
Provision for Loan Losses	1,780.0	1,329.0	1,045.0	1,545.0	524.7	394.7	312.4
Non-Interest Income	7,690.0	8,843.0	7,420.0	6,427.0	2,963.2	2,564.6	1,865.0
Non-Interest Expense	12,891.0	11,830.0	9,782.0	10,579.0	4,421.3	4,089.7	3,399.1
Income Before Taxes	5,479.0	6,549.0	5,948.0	3,293.0	2,049.7	1,781.5	1,422.8
Net Income	③④ 3,423.0	③ 4,026.0	③ 3,747.0	② 1,950.0	1,351.0	① 1,153.9	956.0
Average Shs. Outstg. (000)	1,726,900	1,718,400	1,665,200	1,641,800	750,059	739,400	663,358
BALANCE SHEET (IN MILLIONS)							
Cash & Due from Banks	16,968.0	16,978.0	13,250.0	12,731.0	4,912.1	4,856.6	4,320.3
Securities Avail. for Sale	40,308.0	38,655.0	38,518.0	31,997.0	18,470.8	16,433.6	15,393.6
Total Loans & Leases	172,499.0	161,124.0	119,464.0	107,994.0	44,634.1	41,154.2	37,830.7
Allowance for Credit Losses	3,761.0	3,719.0	3,170.0	3,134.0	3,346.4	2,814.0	2,594.8
Net Loans & Leases	168,738.0	157,405.0	116,294.0	104,860.0	41,287.7	38,340.2	35,235.9
Total Assets	307,569.0	272,426.0	218,102.0	202,475.0	88,540.2	80,175.4	72,134.4
Total Deposits	187,266.0	169,559.0	132,708.0	136,788.0	55,457.1	50,130.2	42,028.8
Long-Term Obligations	36,095.0	32,046.0	23,375.0	19,709.0	12,766.7	13,082.2	13,676.8
Total Liabilities	280,355.0	245,938.0	195,971.0	181,716.0	81,518.0	74,111.2	66,822.3
Net Stockholders' Equity	27,214.0	26,488.0	22,131.0	20,759.0	7,022.2	6,064.2	5,312.1
Year-end Shs. Outstg. (000)	1,695,495	1,714,646	1,626,850	1,644,058	758,619	737,406	705,520
STATISTICAL RECORD:							
Return on Equity %	12.6	15.2	16.9	9.4	19.2	19.0	18.0
Return on Assets %	1.1	1.5	1.7	1.0	1.5	1.4	1.3
Equity/Assets %	8.8	9.7	10.1	10.3	7.9	7.6	7.4
Non-Int. Exp./Tot. Inc. %	64.0	60.0	58.3	68.6	63.2	65.3	66.2
Price Range	54.81-38.25	56.38-31.38	49.94-32.19	43.88-27.50	39.50-21.38	23.44-15.25	17.38-11.31
P/E Ratio	27.8-19.4	24.2-13.5	22.4-14.4	37.5-23.5	22.6-12.2	15.3-9.9	12.6-8.2
Average Yield %	2.1	2.1	1.9	2.0	2.0	2.7	3.1

Statistics are as originally reported. Reflects 11/98 merger with Norwest Corp. & subsequent name change to Wells Fargo & Co. Years prior to 12/31/98 represent the results of Norwest Corp. only. Adj. for 2-for-1 stock split, 10/97. ① Incl. one-time SAIF pre-tax chg. of $19.0 mill. ② Incl. $1.20 bill. in merger-related, a $320.0 mill. prov. for loan losses, & a pre-tax net loss of $325.0 mill. on the disposition of premises & equip. ③ Incl. pre-tax net gain on dispositions of premises & equip. of $21.0 mill., 2001; $58.0 mill., 2000; $16.0 mill., 1999. ④ Incl. net venture capital losses of $1.63 billion.

OFFICERS:
R. M. Kovacevich, Chmn., Pres., C.E.O.
L. S. Biller, Vice-Chmn. C.O.O.

INVESTOR CONTACT: Robert S. Strickland, Sr. V.P., (800) 411-4932

PRINCIPAL OFFICE: 420 Montgomery Street, San Francisco, CA 94163

TELEPHONE NUMBER: (800) 411-4932
FAX: (651) 450-4033
WEB: www.wellsfargo.com
NO. OF EMPLOYEES: 119,714
SHAREHOLDERS: 98,598
ANNUAL MEETING: In Apr.
INCORPORATED: DE, Jan., 1929

INSTITUTIONAL HOLDINGS:
No. of Institutions: 911
Shares Held: 1,084,316,131
% Held: 63.6

INDUSTRY: National commercial banks (SIC: 6021)

TRANSFER AGENT(S): Wells Fargo Shareowner Services, St. Paul, MN

WESBANCO, INC.

YIELD 3.8%
P/E RATIO 14.9

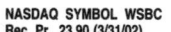

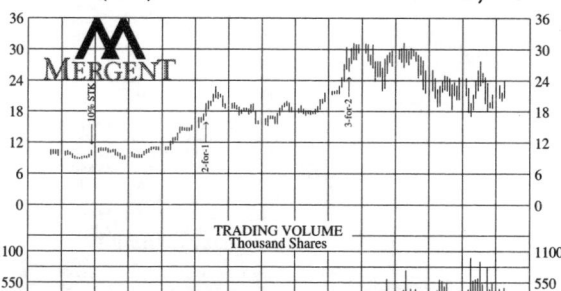

*7 YEAR PRICE SCORE 81.4   *12 MONTH PRICE SCORE 101.4
*NYSE COMPOSITE INDEX=100

INTERIM EARNINGS (Per Share):

Qtr.	Mar.	June	Sept.	Dec.
1997	0.35	0.36	0.37	0.32
1998	0.36	0.37	0.36	0.29
1999	0.33	0.40	0.30	0.34
2000	0.35	0.35	0.34	0.37
2001	0.40	0.40	0.39	0.41

INTERIM DIVIDENDS (Per Share):

Amt.	Decl.	Ex.	Rec.	Pay.
0.23Q	2/22/01	3/07/01	3/09/01	4/02/01
0.23Q	5/16/01	6/06/01	6/08/01	7/02/01
0.23Q	8/16/01	9/05/01	9/07/01	10/01/01
0.23Q	11/21/01	12/05/01	12/07/01	1/02/02
0.23Q	2/22/02	3/06/02	3/08/02	4/01/02

Indicated div.: $0.92 (Div. Rein. Plan)

CAPITALIZATION (12/31/01):

	($000)	(%)
Total Deposits	1,913,458	78.1
Long-Term Debt	279,131	11.4
Common & Surplus	258,201	10.5
Total	2,450,790	100.0

DIVIDEND ACHIEVER STATUS:
Rank: 183   10-Year Growth Rate: 7.46%
Total Years of Dividend Growth: 16

RECENT DEVELOPMENTS: For the year ended 12/31/01, net income climbed 7.7% to $29.0 million from $26.9 million in 2000. Net interest income rose 4.9% to $87.6 million from $83.5 million the year before. Provision for loan losses soared 85.9% to $6.0 million from $3.2 million the year before. Total non-interest income grew 5.2% to $24.6 million from $23.4 million a year earlier. Total non-interest expense rose slightly to $64.9 million from $64.5 million in

the previous year. Results benefited from increases in net interest income, deposit activity fees, and net securities gains, partially offset by a reduction in trust fee income and a rise in the provision for loan losses. Separately, on 3/1/02, the Company completed the acquisition of American Bancorporation and the merger of American's affiliate, Wheeling National Bank, with and into WSBC's affiliate, WesBanco Bank, Inc.

BUSINESS

WESBANCO, INC. is a bank holding company. The Company offers a range of financial services including retail banking, corporate banking, personal and corporate trust services, brokerage, mortgage banking and insurance. The Company's primary business function is the operation of a commercial bank through 59 offices located in West Virginia and Eastern Ohio. On 1/14/00, the Company restructured its banking and mortgage operations by merging all of its banking subsidiaries and its mortgage subsidiary into one state member banking corporation, WesBanco Bank, Inc. The Company also offers services through its non-banking affiliates. WesBanco Insurance Services, Inc. is a multi-line insurance agency specializing in property, casualty and life insurance for personal and commercial clients. WesBanco Securities, Inc. is a full service broker-dealer, which also offers discount brokerage services. WSBC also serves as investment adviser to a family of mutual funds under the name WesMark Funds, which include the WesMark Growth Fund, the WesMark Balanced Fund, the WesMark Bond Fund, the WesMark West Virginia Municipal Bond Fund, and the WesMark Small Company Growth Fund.

ANNUAL FINANCIAL DATA

	12/31/01	12/31/00	12/31/99	12/31/98	12/31/97	12/31/96	12/31/95
Earnings Per Share	1.60	1.41	1.37	1.36	1.40	1.39	1.42
Tang. Book Val. Per Share	14.46	12.31	13.63	14.35	15.58	14.42	13.34
Dividends Per Share	0.92	0.89	0.87	0.83	0.77	0.70	0.62
Dividend Payout %	57.2	63.1	63.5	61.0	55.2	50.5	43.7
INCOME STATEMENT (IN MILLIONS):							
Total Interest Income	163.9	163.1	155.9	162.7	124.5	112.9	97.9
Total Interest Expense	76.4	79.6	69.2	73.9	55.8	48.2	41.9
Net Interest Income	87.6	83.5	86.6	88.8	68.8	64.7	56.0
Provision for Loan Losses	6.0	3.2	4.3	4.4	4.3	4.3	2.8
Non-Interest Income	24.6	23.4	24.6	25.7	14.7	12.3	11.1
Non-Interest Expense	64.9	64.5	67.8	68.3	48.7	43.2	39.0
Income Before Taxes	41.3	39.2	39.1	41.8	30.4	29.5	25.4
Net Income	29.0	26.9	27.6	28.3	22.3	21.2	18.2
Average Shs. Outstg. (000)	18,124	19,093	20,230	20,867	15,868	15,254	12,705
BALANCE SHEET (IN MILLIONS):							
Cash & Due from Banks	81.6	72.8	67.2	63.0	56.4	58.8	49.0
Securities Avail. for Sale	517.5	350.3	354.7	465.7	342.5	276.2	172.1
Total Loans & Leases	1,534.2	1,588.3	1,513.7	1,363.7	1,021.3	1,026.4	858.4
Allowance for Credit Losses	20.8	20.0	19.8	19.1	15.5	15.5	20.6
Net Loans & Leases	1,513.4	1,568.3	1,493.9	1,344.6	1,005.7	1,010.8	837.8
Total Assets	2,474.5	2,310.1	2,269.7	2,242.7	1,789.3	1,677.8	1,371.8
Total Deposits	1,913.5	1,870.4	1,814.0	1,787.6	1,414.3	1,342.8	1,115.5
Long-Term Obligations	279.1	159.3	41.6	22.2	...	...	...
Total Liabilities	2,216.3	2,051.6	2,000.1	1,946.2	1,539.7	1,450.2	1,201.8
Net Stockholders' Equity	258.2	258.5	269.7	296.5	249.6	227.5	170.0
Year-end Shs. Outstg. (000)	17,854	20,997	19,790	20,660	16,016	15,783	12,744
STATISTICAL RECORD:							
Return on Equity %	11.2	10.4	10.2	9.5	8.9	9.3	10.7
Return on Assets %	1.2	1.2	1.2	1.3	1.2	1.3	1.3
Equity/Assets %	10.4	11.2	11.9	13.2	13.9	13.6	12.4
Non-Int. Exp./Tot. Inc. %	57.9	60.3	61.0	59.7	58.4	56.0	58.1
Price Range	27.75-17.00	26.06-18.31	31.25-21.50	31.13-22.00	31.25-21.17	21.67-17.17	20.00-15.17
P/E Ratio	17.3-10.6	18.5-13.0	22.8-15.7	22.9-16.2	22.3-15.1	15.6-12.4	14.1-10.7
Average Yield %	4.1	4.0	3.3	3.1	3.0	3.6	3.5

Statistics are as originally reported. Adj. for 3-for-2 stk. split 8/1/97.

OFFICERS:
J. C. Gardill, Chmn.
P. M. Limbert, Pres., C.E.O.
R. H. Young, Exec. V.P., C.F.O.

INVESTOR CONTACT: Investor Relations, (304) 234-9000

PRINCIPAL OFFICE: 1 Bank Plaza, Wheeling, WV 26003

TELEPHONE NUMBER: (304) 234-9000
FAX: (304) 232-3795
WEB: www.wesbanco.com

NO. OF EMPLOYEES: 1,003 (approx.)

SHAREHOLDERS: 5,139 (approx.)

ANNUAL MEETING: In Apr.

INCORPORATED: WV, 1977

INSTITUTIONAL HOLDINGS:
No. of Institutions: 49
Shares Held: 3,789,078
% Held: 21.1

INDUSTRY: National commercial banks (SIC: 6021)

TRANSFER AGENT(S): American Stock Transfer & Trust Company, New York, NY

WESCO FINANCIAL CORPORATION

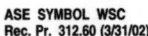

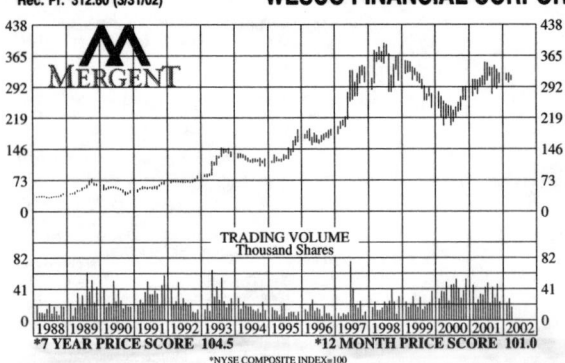

INTERIM EARNINGS (Per Share):

Qtr.	Mar.	June	Sept.	Dec.
1997	1.37	1.23	1.32	10.38
1998	1.24	6.65	1.32	0.87
1999	1.49	1.56	1.54	3.01
2000	18.64	41.87	62.24	6.81
2001	2.78	2.12	1.57	0.91

INTERIM DIVIDENDS (Per Share):

Amt.	Decl.	Ex.	Rec.	Pay.
0.315Q	3/22/01	5/07/01	5/09/01	6/06/01
0.315Q	7/17/01	8/06/01	8/08/01	9/06/01
0.315Q	9/19/01	11/05/01	11/07/01	12/05/01
0.325Q	1/17/02	2/04/02	2/06/02	3/06/02
0.325Q	3/21/02	5/06/02	5/08/02	6/05/02

Indicated div.: $1.30

CAPITALIZATION (12/31/01):

	($000)	(%)
Long-Term Debt	33,649	1.7
Common & Surplus	1,912,397	98.3
Total	1,946,046	100.0

DIVIDEND ACHIEVER STATUS:
Rank: 250   10-Year Growth Rate: 3.89%
Total Years of Dividend Growth: 30

TRADING VOLUME
Thousand Shares

*7 YEAR PRICE SCORE 104.5   *12 MONTH PRICE SCORE 101.0
*NYSE COMPOSITE INDEX=100

RECENT DEVELOPMENTS: For the year ended 12/31/01, net income plumeted 94.3% to $52.5 million from $922.5 million in the previous year. Total revenues dropped 69.2% to $561.1 million from $1.82 billion in the prior year. Revenues for 2000 included realized net securities gains of $1.31 billion. Sales and service revenues improved 4.1% to $443.6 million versus $426.1 million in 2000. Revenues from furniture rentals and sales decreased 5.5% to $395.4 million from $411.3 million a year earlier due to unfavora-

ble market conditions. Revenues from Precision Steel Warehouse declined 25.6% to $48.4 million due to lower demand. Revenues from insurance premiums earned surged 80.9% to $43.0 million reflecting its participation in a three-year arrangement for the reinsurance of certain property and casualty risk exposure ceded by a large, unaffiliated insurer. Dividend and interest income grew 18.8% to $71.0 million from $59.8 million a year earlier. Total costs and expenses increased 18.3% to $479.8 million.

BUSINESS

WESCO FINANCIAL CORPORATION is engaged in three principal businesses: the insurance business, through Wesco-Financial Insurance Company which engages in the property and casualty insurance business, and The Kansas Bankers Surety Company which provides specialized insurance coverages for banks; the furniture rental business, through CORT Business Services Corporation, a provider of rental furniture, accessories and related services in the rent-to-rent segment of the furniture industry; and the steel service center business, through Precision Steel Warehouse, Inc. The Company's operations also include, through MS Property Company, the ownership and management of commercial real estate property, and the development and liquidation of foreclosed real estate. Since 1973, the Company has been 80.1%-owned by Blue Chip Stamps, a wholly-owned subsidiary of Berkshire Hathaway Inc.

ANNUAL FINANCIAL DATA

	12/31/01	12/31/00	12/31/99	12/31/98	12/31/97	12/31/96	12/31/95
Earnings Per Share	7.38	ⓘ 129.56	7.60	10.08	14.30	4.30	4.85
Tang. Book Val. Per Share	231.46	241.16	262.20	308.20	243.56	171.36	134.50
Dividends Per Share	1.26	1.22	1.18	1.14	1.10	1.06	1.02
Dividend Payout %	17.1	0.9	15.5	11.3	7.7	24.7	21.0
INCOME STATEMENT (IN MILLIONS):							
Total Premium Income	43.0	23.8	17.7	15.9	11.5	10.1	9.3
Net Investment Income	71.0	59.8	49.7	40.5	36.6	33.3	30.3
Other Income	447.1	1,740.4	78.4	119.7	171.0	64.6	71.5
Total Revenues	561.1	1,824.0	145.7	176.2	219.1	108.0	111.1
Income Before Income Taxes	81.3	1,418.4	74.8	102.3	152.8	39.5	45.0
Income Taxes	28.8	495.9	20.7	30.5	51.0	8.9	10.5
Net Income	52.5	ⓘ 922.5	54.1	71.8	101.8	30.6	34.5
Average Shs. Outstg. (000)	7,120	7,120	7,120	7,120	7,120	7,120	7,120
BALANCE SHEET (IN MILLIONS):							
Cash & Cash Equivalents	120.8	153.8	66.3	320.0	10.7	23.0	88.0
Premiums Due	43.9	38.4	...	...	7.1	7.9	6.7
Invst. Assets: Fixed-term	924.2	839.7	310.0	66.6	279.7	176.9	119.6
Invst. Assets: Total	1,591.4	1,673.6	2,524.9	2,845.2	2,509.8	1,725.7	1,240.8
Total Assets	2,319.7	2,460.9	2,652.2	3,228.4	2,588.1	1,818.4	1,365.7
Long-Term Obligations	33.6	56.0	3.6	33.6	33.6	37.2	37.4
Net Stockholders' Equity	1,912.4	1,977.0	1,895.4	2,223.8	1,764.3	1,251.0	957.6
Year-end Shs. Outstg. (000)	7,120	7,120	7,120	7,120	7,120	7,120	7,120
STATISTICAL RECORD:							
Return on Revenues %	9.4	50.6	37.2	40.8	46.5	28.3	31.1
Return on Equity %	2.7	46.7	2.9	3.2	5.8	2.4	3.6
Return on Assets %	2.3	37.5	2.0	2.2	3.9	1.7	2.5
Price Range	350.00-270.00	294.00-200.00	354.00-241.50	395.00-280.00	343.00-180.00	194.00-155.00	192.00-113.00
P/E Ratio	47.4-36.6	2.3-1.5	46.6-31.8	39.2-27.8	24.0-12.6	45.1-36.0	39.6-23.3
Average Yield %	0.4	0.5	0.4	0.3	0.4	0.6	0.7

Statistics are as originally reported. ⓘ Incl. after-tax realized securities gains of $1.31 bill.

OFFICERS:
C. T. Munger, Chmn., C.E.O.
R. H. Bird, Pres.
J. L. Jacobson, V.P., C.F.O.
INVESTOR CONTACT: Investor Relations, (626) 585-6700
PRINCIPAL OFFICE: 301 East Colorado Boulevard, Suite 300, Pasadena, CA 91101-1901

TELEPHONE NUMBER: (626) 585-6700
FAX: (626) 449-1455
NO. OF EMPLOYEES: 2,970 (avg.)
SHAREHOLDERS: 600 (approx.)
ANNUAL MEETING: In May
INCORPORATED: DE, March, 1959

INSTITUTIONAL HOLDINGS:
No. of Institutions: 76
Shares Held: 6,151,778
% Held: 86.4
INDUSTRY: Metals service centers and offices (SIC: 5051)
TRANSFER AGENT(S): Mellon Investor Services, Los Angeles, CA

WESTAMERICA BANCORPORATION

YIELD 2.1%
P/E RATIO 18.1

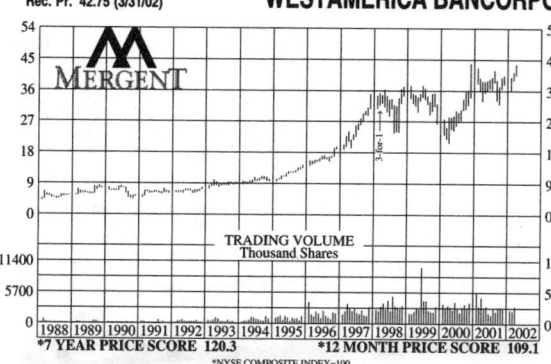

TRADING VOLUME
Thousand Shares

*7 YEAR PRICE SCORE 120.3   *12 MONTH PRICE SCORE 109.1
*NYSE COMPOSITE INDEX=100

INTERIM EARNINGS (Per Share):

Qtr.	Mar.	June	Sept.	Dec.
1997	0.21	0.07	0.40	0.42
1998	0.41	0.42	0.44	0.46
1999	0.46	0.47	0.50	0.51
2000	0.52	0.54	0.55	0.56
2001	0.56	0.58	0.60	0.62

INTERIM DIVIDENDS (Per Share):

Amt.	Decl.	Ex.	Rec.	Pay.
0.19Q	1/25/01	2/02/01	2/02/01	2/16/01
0.21Q	4/26/01	5/02/01	5/04/01	5/18/01
0.21Q	7/26/01	8/01/01	8/03/01	8/17/01
0.21Q	10/25/01	10/31/01	11/02/01	11/16/01
0.22Q	1/24/02	1/30/02	2/01/02	2/15/02

Indicated div.: $0.88

CAPITALIZATION (12/31/01):

	($000)	(%)
Total Deposits	3,234,635	90.4
Long-Term Debt	27,821	0.8
Common & Surplus	314,359	8.8
Total	3,576,815	100.0

DIVIDEND ACHIEVER STATUS:
Rank: 31   10-Year Growth Rate: 18.25%
Total Years of Dividend Growth: 12

RECENT DEVELOPMENTS: For the year ended 12/31/01, net income rose 5.6% to $84.3 million compared with $79.8 million in the previous year. Net interest income grew 4.0% to $188.2 million from $180.9 million in the prior year. Total interest income declined 4.6% to $257.1 million from $269.5 million a year earlier. The decrease was primarily due to lower interest income from loans outstanding and taxable investment sercurities available for sale. Total non-interest income climbed 3.7% to $42.7 million from $41.1 million, while total non-interest expense advanced 2.4% to $102.7 million from $100.2 million the year before. On 2/25/02, the Company and Kerman State Bank announced the signing of a definitive agreement under which WABC will acquire Kerman State Bank for approximately $15.8 million. The acquisition should be completed in the third quarter of 2002.

BUSINESS

WESTAMERICA BANCORPORA-TION, parent company of Westamerica Bank, Community Banker Services Corporation, Westamerica Commercial Credit, Inc., and Money Outlet, Inc., provides a full range of banking services to individual and corporate customers. The Company is a regional community bank with 90 branches in 23 Northern and Central California counties as 12/31/01. On 7/31/00, the Company opened three Money Outlet Inc., stores, a newly created subsidiary engaged in the business of selling checks, drafts, or money orders, or receiving money as agent of an obligor. On 8/17/00, WABC finalized the acquisition of First Counties Bank, a five-branch financial institution headquartered in Lake County, California. During the third quarter of 2000, the Company merged its subsidiary banks with and into Westamerica Bank.

QUARTERLY DATA

(12/31/2001)($000)	REV	INC
1st Quarter	81,042	20,424
2nd Quarter	79,759	20,758
3rd Quarter	78,233	21,325
4th Quarter	76,195	21,772

ANNUAL FINANCIAL DATA

	12/31/01	12/31/00	12/31/99	12/31/98	12/31/97	12/31/96	12/31/95
Earnings Per Share	2.36	2.16	1.94	1.73	1.10	1.31	1.06
Tang. Book Val. Per Share	9.19	9.32	8.10	9.25	9.51	8.44	7.62
Dividends Per Share	0.82	0.74	0.66	0.52	0.36	0.30	0.25
Dividend Payout %	34.7	34.3	34.0	30.1	32.7	22.6	23.3
INCOME STATEMENT (IN MILLIONS):							
Total Interest Income	257.1	269.5	257.7	266.8	270.7	174.3	174.4
Total Interest Expense	68.9	88.6	78.5	86.7	88.1	60.9	58.6
Net Interest Income	188.2	180.9	179.2	180.2	182.6	113.3	115.8
Provision for Loan Losses	3.6	3.7	4.8	5.2	7.6	4.6	5.6
Non-Interest Income	42.7	41.1	40.2	37.8	37.0	22.0	21.5
Non-Interest Expense	102.7	100.2	100.1	101.4	137.9	75.6	86.3
Income Before Taxes	124.6	118.2	114.5	111.4	74.1	55.2	45.4
Net Income	84.3	79.8	76.1	73.4	48.1	37.7	31.4
Average Shs. Outstg. (000)	35,748	36,936	39,194	42,524	43,827	28,839	29,631
BALANCE SHEET (IN MILLIONS):							
Cash & Due from Banks	...	...	...	...	...	149.4	182.1
Securities Avail. for Sale	949.5	921.5	982.6	987.9	1,003.5	696.9	620.6
Total Loans & Leases	2,485.3	2,484.5	2,325.0	2,304.2	2,270.2	1,453.8	1,399.5
Allowance for Credit Losses	52.9	54.6	55.7	57.6	58.9	44.5	45.8
Net Loans & Leases	2,432.4	2,429.9	2,269.3	2,246.6	2,211.3	1,409.3	1,353.7
Total Assets	3,928.0	4,031.4	3,893.2	3,844.3	3,848.4	2,548.5	2,490.9
Total Deposits	3,234.6	3,236.7	3,065.3	3,189.0	3,078.5	2,081.4	2,049.5
Long-Term Obligations	27.8	31.0	41.5	47.5	52.5	42.5	20.0
Total Liabilities	3,613.6	3,693.6	3,592.6	3,475.7	3,441.3	2,309.5	2,267.0
Net Stockholders' Equity	314.4	337.7	300.6	368.6	407.2	238.9	223.9
Year-end Shs. Outstg. (000)	34,220	36,251	37,125	39,828	42,799	28,305	29,594
STATISTICAL RECORD:							
Return on Equity %	26.8	23.6	25.3	19.9	11.8	15.8	14.0
Return on Assets %	2.1	2.0	2.0	1.9	1.3	1.5	1.3
Equity/Assets %	8.0	8.4	7.7	9.6	10.6	9.4	9.0
Non-Int. Exp./Tot. Inc. %	44.5	45.1	45.6	46.5	62.8	55.9	62.9
Price Range	42.64-31.92	43.94-20.75	37.50-26.38	37.25-23.63	35.00-18.83	19.75-14.17	14.42-9.67
P/E Ratio	18.1-13.5	20.3-9.6	19.3-13.6	21.5-13.7	31.8-17.1	15.1-10.8	13.6-9.1
Average Yield %	2.2	2.3	2.1	1.7	1.3	1.7	2.0

Statistics are as originally reported. Adj. for 3-for-1 stk. split, 2/25/98.

OFFICERS:
D. L. Payne, Chmn., Pres., C.E.O.
J. J. Finger, Sr. V.P., C.F.O.
E. J. Bowler, Sr. V.P., Treas.

INVESTOR CONTACT: E. Joseph Bowler,
(707) 863-6840

PRINCIPAL OFFICE: 1108 Fifth Ave., San Rafael, CA 94901

TELEPHONE NUMBER: (707) 863-8000
WEB: www.westamerica.com

NO. OF EMPLOYEES: 1,066

SHAREHOLDERS: 8,900 (approx. record)

ANNUAL MEETING: In Apr.

INCORPORATED: CA, Feb., 1972

INSTITUTIONAL HOLDINGS:
No. of Institutions: 130
Shares Held: 14,021,636
% Held: 41.3

INDUSTRY: National commercial banks
(SIC: 6021)

TRANSFER AGENT(S): Computershare
Investor Services, Chicago, IL

NASDAQ SYMBOL WEYS
Rec. Pr. 29.25 (3/31/02)

WEYCO GROUP, INC.

	YIELD	1.6%
	P/E RATIO	11.9

TRADING VOLUME
Thousand Shares

*7 YEAR PRICE SCORE 103.0   ***12 MONTH PRICE SCORE 117.7**
*NYSE COMPOSITE INDEX=100

INTERIM EARNINGS (Per Share):

Qtr.	Mar.	June	Sept.	Dec.
1997	0.50	0.37	0.59	0.42
1998	0.55	0.41	0.49	0.62
1999	0.61	0.48	0.57	0.89
2000	0.72	0.57	0.57	0.71
2001	0.59	0.42	0.62	0.83

INTERIM DIVIDENDS (Per Share):

Amt.	Decl.	Ex.	Rec.	Pay.
0.11Q	1/30/01	3/01/01	3/05/01	4/02/01
0.12Q	4/24/01	5/30/01	6/01/01	7/02/01
0.12Q	7/30/01	8/29/01	8/31/01	10/01/01
0.12Q	11/05/01	11/28/01	11/30/01	1/02/02
0.12Q	1/28/02	2/28/02	3/04/02	4/01/02

Indicated div.: $0.48

CAPITALIZATION (12/31/01):

	($000)	(%)
Deferred Income Tax	3,452	4.5
Common & Surplus	73,592	95.5
Total	77,044	100.0

DIVIDEND ACHIEVER STATUS:
Rank: 167   10-Year Growth Rate: 8.33%
Total Years of Dividend Growth: 21

RECENT DEVELOPMENTS: For the year ended 12/31/01, net earnings slid 10.6% to $9.5 million from $10.6 million in the previous year. Earnings were adversely affected by a difficult retail environment, partially offset by an improvement in WEYS' wholesale business in the second half of 2001, and benefits from cost-reduction initiatives. Net sales fell 11.1% to $131.7 million from $148.2 million in the prior year. Gross profit as a percent of net sales was 28.5%

versus 27.4% in 2000, primarily due to inbound freight cost-reductions. Operating earnings declined 16.4% to $13.4 million versus $16.0 million the year before. Separately, on 3/4/02, WEYS agreed to purchase the domestic wholesale business, related assets and certain retail stores from Florsheim Group, Inc. for $44.8 million in cash and the assumption of certain trade and lease liabilities.

BUSINESS

WEYCO GROUP, INC. is engaged in the manufacture, purchase and distribution of men's footwear. The Company's products consist of both mid-priced leather dress shoes and lower-priced casual footwear. These shoes are sold under various brand names. The principal brands of shoes sold are NUNN BUSH, NUNN BUSH NXXT, BRASS BOOT, STACY ADAMS and SAO BY STACY ADAMS. The Company's wholesale division, which generated approximately 96.0% of total sales in 2001, markets footwear through more than 8,000 shoe, clothing and department stores across the U.S. As of 12/31/00, the retail division consisted of nine Company-operated stores in the U.S.

ANNUAL FINANCIAL DATA

	12/31/01	12/31/00	12/31/99	12/31/98	12/31/97	12/31/96	12/31/95
Earnings Per Share	2.48	2.59	① 2.55	2.07	1.88	1.66	1.21
Cash Flow Per Share	2.88	2.95	2.84	2.20	2.05	1.87	1.41
Tang. Book Val. Per Share	19.63	17.96	16.28	14.73	13.96	12.41	11.34
Dividends Per Share	0.46	0.42	0.38	0.34	0.30	0.29	0.27
Dividend Payout %	18.5	16.2	14.9	16.4	16.1	17.3	22.6
INCOME STATEMENT (IN THOUSANDS):							
Total Revenues	131,693	148,155	133,498	127,074	127,029	129,314	120,643
Costs & Expenses	116,730	130,693	117,033	112,647	113,561	116,605	110,907
Depreciation & Amort.	1,609	1,490	1,242	626	821	1,045	1,134
Operating Income	13,354	15,972	15,223	13,801	12,646	11,664	8,602
Net Interest Inc./(Exp.)	726	479	831	1,419	1,475	. . .	. . .
Income Before Income Taxes	14,701	16,472	16,958	15,255	14,133	12,790	10,810
Income Taxes	5,200	5,850	5,900	5,450	5,065	4,718	4,003
Net Income	9,501	10,622	① 11,058	9,805	9,068	8,072	6,807
Cash Flow	11,110	12,112	12,300	10,431	9,890	9,117	7,941
Average Shs. Outstg.	3,862	4,108	4,339	4,731	4,825	4,871	5,641
BALANCE SHEET (IN THOUSANDS):							
Cash & Cash Equivalents	20,118	11,210	8,704	13,094	10,684	15,017	23,925
Total Current Assets	61,720	51,670	53,093	48,051	42,912	47,813	59,494
Net Property	15,337	16,272	16,594	13,801	2,313	2,653	3,513
Total Assets	97,954	91,943	95,919	92,782	82,204	73,077	79,328
Total Current Liabilities	20,911	17,758	26,253	26,387	24,643	13,973	13,498
Net Stockholders' Equity	73,592	71,345	67,751	65,148	66,677	59,104	64,083
Net Working Capital	40,810	33,912	26,840	21,664	28,269	33,840	45,997
Year-end Shs. Outstg.	3,749	3,973	4,161	4,424	4,775	4,762	5,652
STATISTICAL RECORD:							
Operating Profit Margin %	10.1	10.8	11.4	10.9	10.0	9.0	7.1
Net Profit Margin %	7.2	7.2	8.3	7.7	7.1	6.2	5.6
Return on Equity %	12.9	14.9	16.3	15.0	13.6	13.7	10.6
Return on Assets %	9.7	11.6	11.5	10.6	11.0	11.0	8.6
Price Range	26.00-22.90	26.63-22.50	27.00-21.63	29.00-21.00	34.00-13.42	14.33-12.50	13.67-11.00
P/E Ratio	10.5-9.2	10.3-8.7	10.6-8.5	14.0-10.1	18.1-7.1	8.6-7.5	11.3-9.1
Average Yield %	1.9	1.7	1.6	1.4	1.3	2.1	2.2

Statistics are as originally reported. Adj. for 3-for-1 stock split, 10/1/97. ① Incl. after-tax gain of $496,000 on the sale of assets.

OFFICERS:
T. W. Florsheim, Chmn.
T. W. Florsheim Jr., Pres., C.E.O.
J. F. Wittkowske, V.P., C.F.O., Sec.
J. W. Florsheim, Exec. V.P., C.O.O.

INVESTOR CONTACT: Investor Relations, (414) 908-1600

PRINCIPAL OFFICE: 333 West Estabrook Blvd., P.O. Box 1188, Milwaukee, WI 53212

TELEPHONE NUMBER: (414) 908-1600
FAX: (414) 908-1601
WEB: www.weycogroup.com

NO. OF EMPLOYEES: 295 (approx.)

SHAREHOLDERS: 307; 141 (cl. B)

ANNUAL MEETING: In April

INCORPORATED: WI, June, 1906

INSTITUTIONAL HOLDINGS:
No. of Institutions: 16
Shares Held: 681,791
% Held: 18.2

INDUSTRY: Men's footwear, except athletic (SIC: 3143)

TRANSFER AGENT(S): American Stock Transfer & Trust Company, New York, NY

WGL HOLDINGS, INC.

YIELD 4.7%
P/E RATIO 18.8

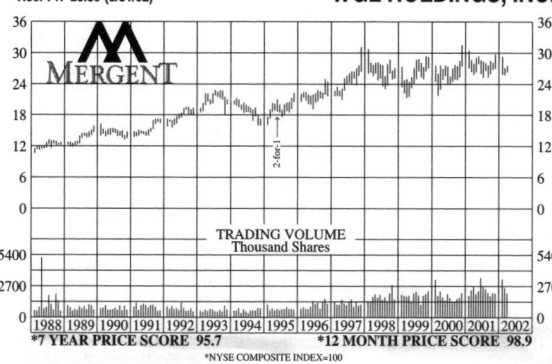

7 YEAR PRICE SCORE 95.7   **12 MONTH PRICE SCORE 98.9**
*NYSE COMPOSITE INDEX=100

INTERIM EARNINGS (Per Share):

Qtr.	Dec.	Mar.	June	Sept.
1997-98	0.87	1.22	d0.17	d0.38
1998-99	0.55	1.39	d0.15	d0.31
1999-00	0.85	1.39	d0.12	d0.33
2000-01	1.08	1.44	d0.15	d0.48
2001-02	0.62	...	...	...

INTERIM DIVIDENDS (Per Share):

Amt.	Decl.	Ex.	Rec.	Pay.
0.315Q	6/27/01	7/06/01	7/10/01	8/01/01
0.315Q	9/26/01	10/05/01	10/10/01	11/01/01
0.315Q	12/14/01	1/08/02	1/10/02	2/01/02
0.318Q	2/25/02	4/08/02	4/10/02	5/01/02

Indicated div.: $1.27 (Div. Reinv. Plan)

CAPITALIZATION (9/30/01):

	($000)	(%)
Long-Term Debt	584,370	36.3
Deferred Income Tax	209,292	13.0
Preferred Stock	28,173	1.7
Common & Surplus	788,253	49.0
Total	1,610,088	100.0

DIVIDEND ACHIEVER STATUS:
Rank: 276   10-Year Growth Rate: 1.87%
Total Years of Dividend Growth: 25

RECENT DEVELOPMENTS: For the quarter ended 12/31/01, net income dropped 40.0% to $30.2 million versus $50.4 million the year before. Results for 2001 included an impairment provision of $3.9 million for WGL's residential heating, ventilating and air conditioning investment, while results for 2000 included a gain of $346,000. Utility operating revenues fell 50.7% to $266.7 million. Net revenues decreased 22.0% to $132.3 million.

PROSPECTS: WGL's weather insurance policy is helping mitigate the effect of unusually warmer winter weather experienced in its utility's service territory. Meanwhile, the Company continues to develop its unregulated subsidiaries. For instance, WGL's energy marketing subsidiary has expanded its customer base by 43.0% in the last 12 months. Going forward, WGL expects recurring earnings per share to range from $1.45 to $1.55 for fiscal 2002.

BUSINESS

WGL HOLDINGS, INC., (formerly Washington Gas Light Company), through its subsidiaries, engages in the sale and distribution of natural gas and other energy-related products and services. Washington Gas Light Company is a regulated natural gas utility serving over 920,000 customers in Washington D.C., Virginia and Maryland. Hampshire Gas Company is a regulated natural gas storage business, serving Washington Gas Light Company. Washington Gas Energy Services, Inc. sells natural gas and electricity to the Washington D.C. area as well as Baltimore, Maryland and Richmond, Virginia. Washington Gas Energy Systems, Inc. designs cost-saving energy systems for the commercial and government markets. American Combustion Industries, Inc. is a contractor for the installation and service of heating, ventilating and air conditioning systems. Other nonregulated activities include consumer financing and land development. WGL owns a 50.0% interest in Primary Investors, LLC.

ANNUAL FINANCIAL DATA

	9/30/01	9/30/00	9/30/99	9/30/98	9/30/97	9/30/96	9/30/95
Earnings Per Share	⑤1.75	④1.79	③1.47	②1.54	1.85	①1.85	1.45
Cash Flow Per Share	3.29	3.27	2.88	2.90	3.13	3.09	2.65
Tang. Book Val. Per Share	16.24	15.31	14.72	13.83	13.48	12.79	11.95
Dividends Per Share	1.25	1.24	1.22	1.20	1.18	1.14	1.12
Dividend Payout %	71.7	69.0	82.6	77.6	63.8	61.3	77.1
INCOME STATEMENT (IN MILLIONS)							
Total Revenues	1,933.0	1,248.0	1,112.2	1,040.6	1,055.8	969.8	828.7
Costs & Expenses	1,624.4	969.6	861.1	802.8	799.8	720.7	616.4
Depreciation & Amort.	72.4	68.9	65.2	59.4	55.9	53.5	51.3
Maintenance Exp.	36.8	31.2	35.6	38.5	36.9	33.1	31.3
Operating Income	140.0	128.9	107.8	140.0	163.1	162.4	129.7
Net Interest Inc./(Exp.)	d50.0	d43.7	d37.0	d37.7	d34.1	d30.6	d31.9
Income Taxes	59.4	49.3	42.5	38.0	47.9	49.4	37.5
Net Income	⑤83.8	④84.6	③68.8	②68.6	82.0	①81.6	62.9
Cash Flow	154.8	152.2	132.6	126.7	136.6	133.8	112.9
Average Shs. Outstg. (000)	47,120	46,473	45,984	43,691	43,706	43,360	42,575
BALANCE SHEET (IN MILLIONS)							
Gross Property	2,340.4	2,225.3	2,114.1	1,992.8	1,846.5	1,722.0	1,608.5
Accumulated Depreciation	820.7	765.0	711.3	673.3	629.3	591.4	552.5
Net Property	1,519.7	1,460.3	1,402.7	1,319.5	1,217.1	1,130.6	1,056.1
Total Assets	2,081.1	1,939.8	1,766.7	1,682.4	1,552.0	1,464.6	1,360.1
Long-Term Obligations	584.4	559.6	506.1	428.6	431.6	353.9	329.1
Net Stockholders' Equity	816.4	739.7	712.5	636.2	617.5	587.2	541.5
Year-end Shs. Outstg. (000)	48,543	46,470	46,473	43,955	43,700	43,704	42,932
STATISTICAL RECORD:							
Operating Profit Margin %	7.2	10.3	9.7	13.5	15.5	16.8	15.7
Net Profit Margin %	4.3	6.8	6.2	6.6	7.8	8.4	7.6
Net Inc./Net Property %	5.5	5.8	4.9	5.2	6.7	7.2	6.0
Net Inc./Tot. Capital %	5.2	5.8	5.0	5.7	6.9	7.6	6.3
Return on Equity %	10.3	11.4	9.7	10.8	13.3	13.9	11.6
Accum. Depr./Gross Prop. %	35.1	34.4	33.6	33.8	34.1	34.3	34.3
Price Range	30.50-25.26	31.50-21.75	29.44-21.31	30.75-23.06	31.13-20.88	25.00-19.13	22.38-16.13
P/E Ratio	17.4-14.4	17.6-12.2	20.0-14.5	20.0-15.0	16.8-11.3	13.5-10.3	15.4-11.1
Average Yield %	4.5	4.6	4.8	4.4	4.5	5.1	5.8

Statistics are as originally reported. ① Incl. a nonrecurr. after-tax chg. of $3.8 mill. assoc. with the Company's reorganization. ② Incl. a net gain of $1.6 mill. from the sale of investments in venture capital funds. ③ Incl. a nonrecurr. gain of $3.0 mill. from the sale of non-utility assets and a nonrecurr. chrg. of $2.9 mill. fr. the sale of utility property. ④ Incl. a nonrecurr. gain of $711,000 mill. fr. the sale of assets. ⑤ Incl. impairment provision of $3.9 mill.

OFFICERS:
J. H. DeGraffenreidt Jr., Chmn., C.E.O.
T. D. McCallister, Pres., C.O.O.
F. M. Kline, V.P., C.F.O.
S. C. Jennings, Treas.

INVESTOR CONTACT: Melissa Adams, Dir. Inv. Rel., (703) 750-4440

PRINCIPAL OFFICE: 1100 H Street, N.W., Washington, DC 20080

TELEPHONE NUMBER: (703) 750-4440
FAX: (703) 624-2000
WEB: www.washgas.com

NO. OF EMPLOYEES: 2,190

SHAREHOLDERS: 20,029

ANNUAL MEETING: In Feb.

INCORPORATED: DC, Mar., 1957

INSTITUTIONAL HOLDINGS:
No. of Institutions: 150
Shares Held: 24,637,080
% Held: 50.7

INDUSTRY: Natural gas distribution (SIC: 4924)

TRANSFER AGENT(S): The Riggs National Bank, Washington, D.C.

WILMINGTON TRUST CORPORATION

	YIELD	2.9%
	P/E RATIO	17.9

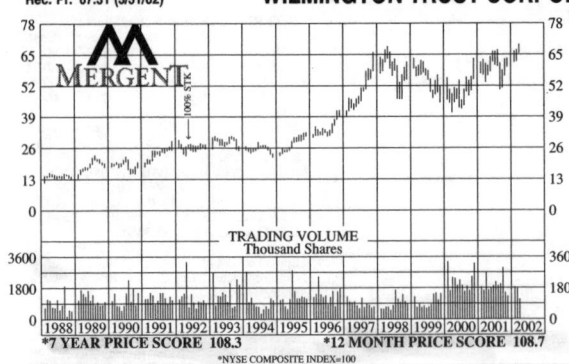

INTERIM EARNINGS (Per Share):

Qtr.	Mar.	June	Sept.	Dec.
1997	0.72	0.77	0.79	0.80
1998	0.79	0.82	0.86	0.87
1999	0.87	0.89	0.92	0.53
2000	0.94	0.94	0.95	0.87
2001	0.92	0.94	0.95	0.96

INTERIM DIVIDENDS (Per Share):

Amt.	Decl.	Ex.	Rec.	Pay.
0.48Q	4/19/01	4/27/01	5/01/01	5/15/01
0.48Q	7/19/01	7/30/01	8/01/01	8/15/01
0.48Q	10/18/01	10/30/01	11/01/01	11/15/01
0.48Q	1/17/02	1/30/02	2/01/02	2/15/02

Indicated div.: $1.92 (Div. Reinv. Plan)

CAPITALIZATION (12/31/01):

	($000)	(%)
Total Deposits	5,590,785	86.9
Long-Term Debt	160,500	2.5
Common & Surplus	682,530	10.6
Total	6,433,815	100.0

DIVIDEND ACHIEVER STATUS:

Rank: 157   10-Year Growth Rate: 9.05%
Total Years of Dividend Growth: 20

7 YEAR PRICE SCORE 108.3   **12 MONTH PRICE SCORE 108.7**
NYSE COMPOSITE INDEX=100

RECENT DEVELOPMENTS: For the year ended 12/31/01, the Company reported income of $124.0 million, before an after-tax accounting change charge of $1.1 million, compared with net income of $120.9 million in the prior year. Net interest income improved 1.4% to $258.8 million from $255.1 million a year earlier. Provision for loan losses decreased 9.4% to $19.9 million. Total other income improved 5.5% to $228.0 million, while total other expense grew 4.6% to $276.9 million.

PROSPECTS: On 1/7/02, WL announced that it has completed the acquisition of Balentine & Company, an investment counseling firm with over $1.00 billion in assets under management and more than $2.00 billion in institutional consulting relationships. The Balentine & Company name remains unchanged. Terms of the transaction were not disclosed. Separately, the Company continues to report strong growth in its regional banking, corporate financial services and private client advisory services.

BUSINESS

WILMINGTON TRUST CORPORA-TION and its subsidiaries, with assets of $7.52 billion as of 12/31/01, is a financial services company with offices in California, Delaware, Florida, Maryland, Nevada, New York, Pennsylvania, London, and the Cayman and Channel Islands. The Company provides wealth management, corporate trust, and commercial banking services to clients throughout the United States and in more than 50 other countries.

ANNUAL FINANCIAL DATA

	12/31/01	12/31/00	12/31/99	12/31/98	12/31/97	12/31/96	12/31/95
Earnings Per Share	☐ 3.77	3.70	3.21	3.34	3.08	2.83	2.56
Tang. Book Val. Per Share	14.50	12.96	10.34	12.14	15.03	13.71	13.09
Dividends Per Share	1.89	1.77	1.65	1.53	1.41	1.29	1.17
Dividend Payout %	50.1	47.8	51.4	45.8	45.8	45.6	45.7
INCOME STATEMENT (IN MILLIONS):							
Total Interest Income	468.8	530.5	462.2	456.9	430.6	402.9	377.3
Total Interest Expense	210.0	275.3	216.3	219.2	200.6	188.6	180.0
Net Interest Income	258.8	255.1	245.9	237.7	230.0	214.2	197.4
Provision for Loan Losses	19.9	21.9	17.5	20.0	21.5	16.0	12.3
Non-Interest Income	228.0	216.2	191.5	183.9	157.5	138.2	127.6
Non-Interest Expense	276.9	264.7	258.2	230.1	207.7	192.3	181.0
Income Before Taxes	190.0	184.8	161.7	171.5	158.4	144.1	131.7
Net Inome	☐ 124.0	120.9	72.5	88.7	79.6	74.6	70.6
Average Shs. Outstg. (000)	32,971	32,680	33,383	34,275	34,466	34,399	35,213
BALANCE SHEET (IN MILLIONS):							
Cash & Due from Banks	210.1	223.8	225.1	204.6	239.4	231.2	252.8
Securities Avail. for Sale	1,264.8	1,440.1	1,686.3	1,298.7	1,316.4	798.5	910.2
Total Loans & Leases	5,488.8	5,189.0	4,821.6	4,324.4	4,004.8	3,783.9	3,527.6
Allowance for Credit Losses	80.8	76.7	76.9	71.9	63.8	54.4	49.9
Net Loans & Leases	5,407.2	5,111.7	4,743.2	4,247.7	3,930.1	3,717.1	3,472.0
Total Assets	7,518.5	7,321.6	7,201.9	6,300.6	6,122.4	5,564.4	5,372.2
Total Deposits	5,590.8	5,286.0	5,369.5	4,536.8	4,169.0	3,913.7	3,587.6
Long-Term Obligations	160.5	168.0	168.0	168.0	43.0	43.0	28.0
Total Liabilities	6,835.9	6,729.7	6,703.7	5,754.4	5,619.3	5,099.7	4,912.8
Net Stockholders' Equity	682.5	591.9	498.2	546.2	503.0	464.7	459.4
Year-end Shs. Outstg. (000)	32,700	32,393	32,353	33,329	33,478	33,893	35,090
STATISTICAL RECORD:							
Return on Equity %	18.2	20.4	14.6	16.2	15.8	16.0	15.4
Return on Assets %	1.6	1.7	1.0	1.4	1.3	1.3	1.3
Equity/Assets %	9.1	8.1	6.9	8.7	8.2	8.4	8.6
Non-Int. Exp./Tot. Inc. %	57.6	56.8	64.3	59.1	57.5	58.5	59.7
Price Range	67.00-50.20	63.38-40.56	63.50-44.75	68.50-46.38	66.00-39.25	41.75-30.25	32.50-22.75
P/E Ratio	17.8-13.3	17.1-11.0	19.8-13.9	20.5-13.9	21.4-12.7	14.8-10.7	12.7-8.9
Average Yield %	3.2	3.4	3.0	2.7	2.7	3.6	4.2

Statistics are as originally reported. ☐ Bef. an after-tax acctg. change chrg. of $1.1 mill.

OFFICERS:
T. T. Cecala, Chmn., C.E.O.
R. V. Harra Jr., Pres., C.O.O., Treas.
D. R. Gibson, Sr. V.P., C.F.O.

INVESTOR CONTACT: Ellen Roberts, Media & Investor Relations, (302) 651-8069

PRINCIPAL OFFICE: Rodney Square North, 1100 North Market St., Wilmington, DE 19890-0001

TELEPHONE NUMBER: (302) 651-1000
FAX: (302) 651-8010
WEB: www.wilmingtontrust.com

NO. OF EMPLOYEES: 2,316 (avg.)

SHAREHOLDERS: 8,841 (record)

ANNUAL MEETING: In May

INCORPORATED: DE, Mar., 1901

INSTITUTIONAL HOLDINGS:
No. of Institutions: 202
Shares Held: 13,457,192
% Held: 41.5

INDUSTRY: State commercial banks (SIC: 6022)

TRANSFER AGENT(S): Wells Fargo Shareowner Services, St. Paul, MN

WORTHINGTON INDUSTRIES, INC.

YIELD 4.2%
P/E RATIO ...

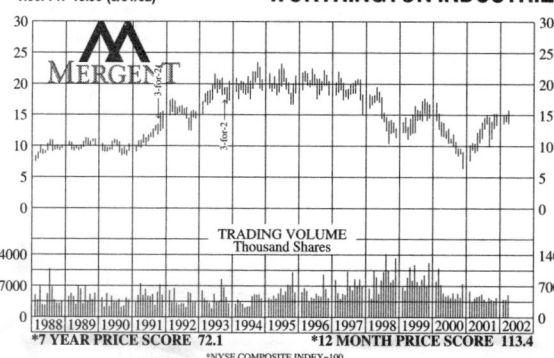

7 YEAR PRICE SCORE 72.1   **12 MONTH PRICE SCORE 113.4**
NYSE COMPOSITE INDEX=100

INTERIM EARNINGS (Per Share):

Qtr.	Aug.	Nov.	Feb.	May
1998-99	0.18	0.20	0.21	0.31
1999-00	0.27	0.28	0.26	0.25
2000-01	0.15	0.08	0.02	0.17
2001-02	0.17	0.13	d0.53	...

INTERIM DIVIDENDS (Per Share):

Amt.	Decl.	Ex.	Rec.	Pay.
0.16Q	2/22/01	3/13/01	3/15/01	3/29/01
0.16Q	5/19/01	6/13/01	6/15/01	6/29/01
0.16Q	8/23/01	9/17/01	9/15/01	9/29/01
0.16Q	11/29/01	12/12/01	12/15/01	12/29/01
0.16Q	2/21/02	3/13/02	3/15/02	3/29/02

Indicated div.: $0.64 (Div. Reinv. Plan)

CAPITALIZATION (5/31/01):

	($000)	(%)
Long-Term Debt	309,208	26.9
Deferred Income Tax	140,974	12.3
Minority Interest	49,536	4.3
Common & Surplus	649,665	56.5
Total	1,149,383	100.0

DIVIDEND ACHIEVER STATUS:
Rank: 164   10-Year Growth Rate: 8.53%
Total Years of Dividend Growth: 19

RECENT DEVELOPMENTS: For the quarter ended 2/28/02, the Company reported a net loss of $45.9 million compared with net income of $1.8 million in the equivalent 2001 quarter. Results for 2002 and 2001 included restructuring charges of $64.6 million and $6.5 million, respectively. Results for 2002 also included a pre-tax reserve of $21.2 million for the potential impairment of certain assets. Total net sales declined 3.1% to $405.7 million.

PROSPECTS: On 1/24/02, the Company announced that it will implement a consolidation plan designed to improve profitability and better utilize assets. The consolidation plan will directly affect eight facilities and more than 500 employees. Once fully implemented, the consolidation of facilities and elimination of overhead costs is expected to improve operating profitability by approximately $10.0 million annually.

BUSINESS

WORTHINGTON INDUSTRIES, INC. is a diversified metal processing company that focuses on steel processing and metals-related businesses. The Company manufactures metal products such as automotive aftermarket stampings, pressure cylinders, metal framing, metal ceiling grid systems and laser welded blanks. As of 3/20/02, WOR operated 59 facilities in 10 countries. The Company is involved in three business segments: Processed Steel Products, Metal Framing and Pressure Cylinders. The Processed Steel Products segment includes The Worthington Steel Company business unit and The Gerstenslager Company business unit. The Metal Framing segment is made up of Dietrich Industries, Inc. and the Pressure Cylinders segment consists of Worthington Cylinder Corporation. In addition, the Company holds an equity position in seven joint ventures as of 4/3/02.

ANNUAL FINANCIAL DATA

	5/31/01	5/31/00	5/31/99	5/31/98	5/31/97	5/31/96	5/31/95
Earnings Per Share	④ 0.42	1.06	①②0.90	①③0.85	0.97	1.01	1.29
Cash Flow Per Share	1.24	1.86	1.74	1.48	1.50	1.44	1.66
Tang. Book Val. Per Share	6.67	6.92	6.74	7.08	6.38	6.32	6.50
Dividends Per Share	0.63	0.59	0.55	0.51	0.47	0.43	0.39
Dividend Payout %	150.0	55.7	61.1	60.0	48.4	42.6	30.2
INCOME STATEMENT (IN MILLIONS):							
Total Revenues	1,826.1	1,962.6	1,763.1	1,624.4	1,911.7	1,477.8	1,483.6
Costs & Expenses	1,690.3	1,722.1	1,538.4	1,427.5	1,706.1	1,312.5	1,295.6
Depreciation & Amort.	70.6	71.0	78.5	61.5	51.4	39.2	34.1
Operating Income	65.2	169.5	146.2	135.5	154.2	126.1	153.8
Net Interest Inc./(Exp.)	d33.4	d39.8	d43.1	d25.6	d18.4	d8.3	d6.0
Income Before Income Taxes	56.0	150.6	132.8	130.6	150.5	147.8	186.7
Income Taxes	20.4	56.5	49.1	48.3	57.2	56.5	70.0
Equity Earnings/Minority Int.	25.2	26.8	24.5	19.3	13.8	29.1	38.3
Net Income	④ 35.6	94.2	①②83.6	①③82.3	93.3	91.3	116.7
Cash Flow	106.1	165.1	162.1	143.8	144.7	130.6	150.8
Average Shs. Outstg. (000)	85,623	88,598	93,106	96,949	96,557	90,812	90,730
BALANCE SHEET (IN MILLIONS):							
Cash & Cash Equivalents	0.2	0.5	7.6	3.8	7.2	19.0	2.0
Total Current Assets	449.7	624.2	624.3	643.0	594.1	476.0	451.9
Net Property	836.7	862.5	871.3	933.2	691.0	512.3	334.9
Total Assets	1,475.9	1,673.9	1,687.0	1,842.3	1,561.2	1,220.1	917.0
Total Current Liabilities	306.6	433.3	427.7	410.0	246.8	151.3	179.2
Long-Term Obligations	309.2	362.2	365.8	439.6	450.4	298.7	53.5
Net Stockholders' Equity	649.7	673.4	689.6	780.3	715.5	639.5	590.3
Net Working Capital	143.1	191.0	196.5	233.0	347.3	324.8	272.7
Year-end Shs. Outstg. (000)	85,375	85,755	89,949	96,657	96,711	90,830	90,840
STATISTICAL RECORD:							
Operating Profit Margin %	3.6	8.6	8.3	8.3	8.1	8.5	10.4
Net Profit Margin %	1.9	4.8	4.7	5.1	4.9	6.2	7.9
Return on Equity %	5.5	14.0	12.1	10.5	13.0	14.3	19.8
Return on Assets %	2.4	5.6	5.0	4.5	6.0	7.5	12.7
Debt/Total Assets %	21.0	21.6	21.7	23.9	28.8	24.5	5.8
Price Range	17.00-6.38	17.69-11.06	19.56-10.38	22.00-15.13	22.50-17.50	23.25-16.63	23.50-17.50
P/E Ratio	40.5-15.2	16.7-10.4	21.7-11.5	25.9-17.8	23.2-18.0	23.0-16.5	18.2-13.6
Average Yield %	5.4	4.1	3.7	2.7	2.4	2.2	1.9

Statistics are as originally reported. ① Bef. disc. oper. loss 5/31/99: $20.9 mill.; gain 5/31/98: $17.3 mill. ② Bef. acctg. change chrg. $7.8 mill. ③ Bef. extraord. credit $18.8 mill. ④ Incl. restruct. chrg. of $6.5 mill.

OFFICERS:
J. P. McConnell, Chmn., C.E.O.
J. S. Christie, Pres., C.O.O.
J. T. Baldwin, V.P., C.F.O.

INVESTOR CONTACT: Investor Relations, (614) 438-3210

PRINCIPAL OFFICE: 1205 Dearborn Drive, Columbus, OH 43085

TELEPHONE NUMBER: (614) 438-3210
FAX: (614) 438-3256
WEB: www.worthingtonindustries.com

NO. OF EMPLOYEES: 7,500 (approx.)

SHAREHOLDERS: 10,848 (approx.)

ANNUAL MEETING: in Sept.

INCORPORATED: DE, Dec., 1996; reincorp., OH, Sept., 1998

INSTITUTIONAL HOLDINGS:
No. of Institutions: 191
Shares Held: 34,981,503
% Held: 41.0

INDUSTRY: Cold finishing of steel shapes (SIC: 3316)

TRANSFER AGENT(S): Fleet National Bank, Boston, MA

NYSE SYMBOL WPS
Rec. Pr. 39.44 (3/31/02)

WPS RESOURCES CORPORATION

YIELD 5.3%
P/E RATIO 14.3

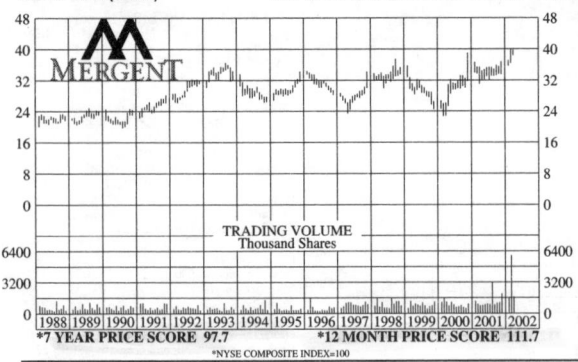

TRADING VOLUME
Thousand Shares

*7 YEAR PRICE SCORE 97.7   *12 MONTH PRICE SCORE 111.7
*NYSE COMPOSITE INDEX=100

INTERIM EARNINGS (Per Share):

Qtr.	Mar.	June	Sept.	Dec.
1998	0.72	0.41	0.45	0.24
1999	0.86	0.38	0.52	0.48
2000	1.10	0.43	0.49	0.51
2001	0.89	0.41	0.41	0.70

INTERIM DIVIDENDS (Per Share):

Amt.	Decl.	Ex.	Rec.	Pay.
0.525Q	7/12/01	8/29/01	8/31/01	9/20/01
0.525Q	10/11/01	11/28/01	11/30/01	12/20/01
0.525Q	2/14/02	2/26/02	2/28/02	3/20/02
0.525Q	4/11/02	5/29/02	5/31/02	6/20/02

Indicated div.: $2.10 (Div. Reinv. Plan)

CAPITALIZATION (12/31/01):

	($000)	(%)
Long-Term Debt	727,800	45.1
Deferred Income Tax	69,500	4.3
Preferred Stock	101,100	6.3
Common & Surplus	715,900	44.3
Total	1,614,300	100.0

DIVIDEND ACHIEVER STATUS:
Rank: 274   10-Year Growth Rate: 2.16%
Total Years of Dividend Growth: 43

RECENT DEVELOPMENTS: For the year ended 12/31/01, net income increased 15.8% to $77.6 million compared with $67.0 million in the previous year. Earnings growth was primarily attributed to increased profitability in the Company's nonregulated segments, offset by lower earnings at the electric and gas utility segments. Operating revenues jumped 37.3% to $2.68 billion from $1.95 billion the year before.

PROSPECTS: On 12/26/01, WPS Power Development, Inc., a subsidiary of WPS, announced that it has agreed to purchase three upstate New York power plants and other assets from CH Resources, Inc. for about $61.0 million. The three plants have a combined capacity of 257 megawatts and are located in Beaver Falls, Niagara Falls and Syracuse. Going forward, WPS will continue to invest in generation assets at both WPS Power Development and Wisonsin Public Service.

BUSINESS

WPS RESOURCES CORPORATION (formerly Wisconsin Public Service Corp.) operates as a holding company with both regulated utility and non-regulated business units. The Company's principal wholly-owned subsidiaries are: Wisconsin Public Service Corporation (WPSC), a regulated electric and gas utility in Wisconsin and Michigan; Upper Peninsula Power Company, a regulated electric utility in Michigan; and WPS Energy Services, Inc. and WPS Power Development, Inc., both non-regulated subsidiaries. As of 12/31/01, WPSC served 400,862 electric retail and 290,353 gas retail customers.

ANNUAL FINANCIAL DATA

	12/31/01	12/31/00	12/31/99	12/31/98	12/31/97	12/31/96	12/31/95
Earnings Per Share	2.74	2.53	2.24	1.76	2.25	2.00	2.32
Cash Flow Per Share	6.38	7.05	5.94	5.63	6.11	5.94	6.47
Tang. Book Val. Per Share	22.73	20.21	19.97	19.48	20.00	19.56	19.39
Dividends Per Share	2.08	2.04	2.00	1.96	1.92	1.88	1.84
Dividend Payout %	75.9	80.6	89.3	111.4	85.3	94.0	79.3
INCOME STATEMENT (IN MILLIONS):							
Total Revenues	2,675.5	1,951.6	1,098.5	1,063.7	878.3	858.3	719.8
Costs & Expenses	2,466.1	1,646.1	819.5	808.3	644.4	617.2	461.6
Depreciation & Amort.	102.1	119.6	98.7	102.5	92.2	93.9	99.1
Maintenance Exp.	...	73.0	60.6	52.8	41.7	48.8	50.8
Operating Income	107.3	112.8	119.7	100.0	100.1	98.3	108.4
Net Interest Inc./(Exp.)	d55.8	d50.8	d32.8	d28.6	d26.4	d25.3	d25.5
Income Taxes	4.8	6.0	29.7	23.4	29.3	24.4	30.8
Equity Earnings/Minority Int.	...	...	...	0.6	0.8	0.3	...
Net Income	77.6	67.0	59.6	46.6	53.7	47.8	55.3
Cash Flow	179.7	186.6	158.3	149.2	145.9	141.7	154.4
Average Shs. Outstg. (000)	28,200	26,463	26,644	26,511	23,873	23,891	23,897
BALANCE SHEET (IN MILLIONS):							
Gross Property	2,954.0	2,547.7	2,429.2	2,197.6	1,899.4	1,825.8	1,760.0
Accumulated Depreciation	1,515.3	1,365.4	1,293.4	1,206.1	1,032.1	952.3	905.4
Net Property	1,463.6	1,198.3	1,150.9	1,010.2	886.4	892.9	868.9
Total Assets	2,870.0	2,816.1	1,816.5	1,510.4	1,299.6	1,330.7	1,266.7
Long-Term Obligations	727.8	660.0	584.5	343.0	304.0	611.6	613.2
Net Stockholders' Equity	817.0	593.9	587.5	568.4	529.0	518.7	514.6
Year-end Shs. Outstg. (000)	31,496	26,851	26,851	26,551	23,897	23,897	23,897
STATISTICAL RECORD:							
Operating Profit Margin %	4.0	5.8	10.9	9.4	11.4	11.5	15.1
Net Profit Margin %	2.9	3.4	5.4	4.4	6.1	5.6	7.7
Net Inc./Net Property %	5.3	5.6	5.2	4.6	6.1	5.0	6.4
Net Inc./Tot. Capital %	4.8	4.8	4.5	4.3	5.6	3.8	4.4
Return on Equity %	9.5	11.3	10.1	8.2	10.2	9.2	10.7
Accum. Depr./Gross Prop. %	51.3	53.6	53.2	54.9	54.3	52.2	51.4
Price Range	36.80-31.00	39.00-22.63	35.75-24.44	37.50-29.94	34.25-23.38	34.38-28.25	34.25-26.75
P/E Ratio	13.4-11.3	15.4-8.9	16.0-10.9	21.3-17.0	15.2-10.4	17.2-14.1	14.8-11.5
Average Yield %	6.1	6.6	6.6	5.8	6.7	6.0	6.0

Statistics are as originally reported.

NYSE SYMBOL WWY
Rec. Pr. 53.31 (3/31/02)

WRIGLEY (WM.) JR. COMPANY

YIELD 1.5%
P/E RATIO 33.1

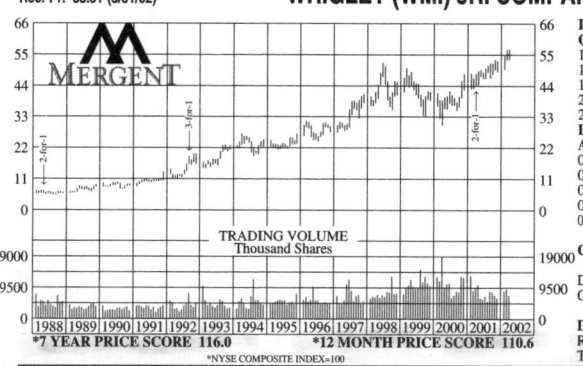

TRADING VOLUME
Thousand Shares

| 1988 | 1989 | 1990 | 1991 | 1992 | 1993 | 1994 | 1995 | 1996 | 1997 | 1998 | 1999 | 2000 | 2001 | 2002 |

*7 YEAR PRICE SCORE 116.0   *12 MONTH PRICE SCORE 110.6
*NYSE COMPOSITE INDEX=100

INTERIM EARNINGS (Per Share):

Qtr.	Mar.	June	Sept.	Dec.
1997	0.27	0.33	0.30	0.27
1998	0.33	0.37	0.32	0.31
1999	0.30	0.38	0.34	0.32
2000	0.33	0.41	0.37	0.35
2001	0.36	0.44	0.41	0.40

INTERIM DIVIDENDS (Per Share):

Amt.	Decl.	Ex.	Rec.	Pay.
0.19Q	1/23/01	4/10/01	4/13/01	5/01/01
0.19Q	5/24/01	7/11/01	7/13/01	8/01/01
0.19Q	8/15/01	10/11/01	10/15/01	11/01/01
0.19Q	10/24/01	1/11/02	1/15/02	2/01/02
0.205Q	1/23/02	4/11/02	4/15/02	5/01/02

Indicated div.: $0.82 (Div. Reinv. Plan)

CAPITALIZATION (12/31/01):

	($000)	(%)
Deferred Income Tax	43,206	3.3
Common & Surplus	1,276,197	96.7
Total	1,319,403	100.0

DIVIDEND ACHIEVER STATUS:
Rank: 126   10-Year Growth Rate: 10.48%
Total Years of Dividend Growth: 21

RECENT DEVELOPMENTS: For the twelve months ended 12/31/01, net earnings increased 10.3% to $363.0 million compared with $328.9 million in the corresponding year-earlier period. Net sales advanced 13.2% to $2.43 billion from $2.15 billion the year before. Gross profit grew 15.4% to $1.43 billion, or 59.0% of net sales, compared with $1.24 billion, or 57.9% of net sales, the previous year. Operating income was $513.4 million, up 10.8% from $463.2 million the year before.

PROSPECTS: WWY's outlook is favorable, reflecting recent selective selling price increases, higher sales of premium-priced products and cost controls that are leading to improved profit margins. In addition to strong sales of the Company's core brands, WWY's bottom line results are benefiting from an accelerated pace of new product introductions, especially in the U.S. Meanwhile, WWY should continue to benefit from its investment in brand building through advertising and merchandising efforts.

BUSINESS

WM. WRIGLEY JR. COMPANY is the world's largest chewing gum producer. Main brands are WRIGLEY'S SPEARMINT, DOUBLEMINT, JUICY FRUIT, WINTERFRESH, BIG RED, EXTRA, FREEDENT, ECLIPSE, and HUBBA BUBBA bubble gum. Additional brands manufactured and marketed internationally include ORBIT, AIRWAVES, ICEWHITE, EXCEL, ARROWMINT, COOL CRUNCH, DULCE 16, P.K. and COOL AIR. Through its Amurol Confections Company subsidiary, the Company also manufactures and markets various non-gum items, such as a line of suckers, dextrose candy, liquid gel candy and hard roll candies. As of 12/31/01, Wrigley brands were produced in 15 factories, including four plants in the U.S. plus 11 others outside the U.S. Sales for 2001 were derived from North America, 41.8%; Europe, 41.8%; Asia, 12.4%; Pacific, 3.0%; other, 1.0%. WWY's largest non-U.S. markets by shipments were Australia, Canada, China, France, Germany, Philippines, Poland, Russia, Taiwan and the United Kingdom.

ANNUAL FINANCIAL DATA

	12/31/01	12/31/00	12/31/99	12/31/98	12/31/97	12/31/96	12/31/95
Earnings Per Share	1.61	1.45	1.33	2️⃣ 1.32	1️⃣ 1.17	1️⃣ 1.00	0.97
Cash Flow Per Share	1.91	1.70	1.59	1.55	1.39	1.20	1.15
Tang. Book Val. Per Share	5.67	4.87	4.97	4.98	4.25	3.87	3.43
Dividends Per Share	0.74	0.70	0.67	0.65	0.58	0.51	0.48
Dividend Payout %	46.3	48.3	50.0	49.4	50.0	51.3	49.7
INCOME STATEMENT (IN MILLIONS):							
Total Revenues	2,429.6	2,145.7	2,079.2	2,023.4	1,954.2	1,850.6	1,769.7
Costs & Expenses	1,848.0	1,624.6	1,572.9	1,526.1	1,508.5	1,443.1	1,373.8
Depreciation & Amort.	68.3	57.9	61.2	55.8	50.4	47.3	43.8
Operating Income	513.4	463.2	445.1	441.5	395.2	360.2	352.2
Net Interest Inc./(Exp.)	...	...	d0.7	d0.6	d1.0	d1.1	d2.0
Income Before Income Taxes	527.4	479.3	444.4	440.9	394.2	359.1	350.2
Income Taxes	164.4	150.4	136.2	136.4	122.6	128.8	126.5
Net Income	363.0	328.9	308.2	2️⃣ 304.5	1️⃣ 271.6	1️⃣ 230.3	223.7
Cash Flow	431.3	386.8	369.4	360.3	322.1	277.6	267.5
Average Shs. Outstg. (000)	225,349	227,036	231,722	231,928	231,928	231,966	232,132
BALANCE SHEET (IN MILLIONS):							
Cash & Cash Equivalents	333.2	329.9	306.9	351.7	327.4	300.6	231.7
Total Current Assets	913.8	828.7	803.7	843.2	797.7	729.4	672.1
Net Property	684.4	607.0	559.1	520.1	430.5	388.1	347.5
Total Assets	1,765.6	1,574.7	1,547.7	1,520.9	1,343.1	1,233.5	1,099.2
Total Current Liabilities	332.3	288.2	251.8	218.6	225.8	218.2	213.4
Net Stockholders' Equity	1,276.2	1,132.9	1,138.8	1,157.0	985.4	897.4	796.9
Net Working Capital	581.5	540.5	551.9	624.5	571.9	511.3	458.7
Year-end Shs. Outstg. (000)	224,950	232,442	228,992	232,220	231,938	231,940	232,004
STATISTICAL RECORD:							
Operating Profit Margin %	21.1	21.6	21.4	21.8	20.2	19.5	19.9
Net Profit Margin %	14.9	15.3	14.8	15.0	13.9	12.4	12.6
Return on Equity %	28.4	29.0	27.1	26.3	27.6	25.7	28.1
Return on Assets %	20.6	20.9	19.9	20.0	20.2	18.7	20.4
Price Range	53.30-42.94	48.31-29.94	50.31-33.25	52.16-35.47	41.03-27.28	31.44-24.19	27.00-21.44
P/E Ratio	33.1-26.7	33.3-20.6	37.8-25.0	39.7-27.0	35.1-23.3	31.6-24.3	28.0-22.2
Average Yield %	1.5	1.8	1.6	1.5	1.7	1.8	2.0

Statistics are as originally reported. Adj. for 2-for-1 stk. split, 2/01. 1️⃣ Incls. non-recurring net chrg. 12/31/97: $3.3 mill.; chrg. 12/31/96: $13.0 mill. 2️⃣ Incls. one-time gain of $10.4 mill.

OFFICERS:
W. Wrigley, Jr., Pres., C.E.O.
R. V. Waters, Sr. V.P., C.F.O.
A. J. Schneider, Treas.
H. Malovany, V.P., Sec., Gen. Couns.

INVESTOR CONTACT: Christopher Perille, Sr. Dir., Corp. Comm. (312) 645-4077

PRINCIPAL OFFICE: 410 North Michigan Avenue, Chicago, IL 60611

TELEPHONE NUMBER: (312) 644-2121
FAX: (312) 645-4083
WEB: www.wrigley.com

NO. OF EMPLOYEES: 10,800 (approx.)

SHAREHOLDERS: 38,100; 3,215 (cl. B)

ANNUAL MEETING: In March

INCORPORATED: DE, Oct., 1927

INSTITUTIONAL HOLDINGS:
No. of Institutions: 373
Shares Held: 82,936,806
% Held: 36.8

INDUSTRY: Chewing gum (SIC: 2067)

TRANSFER AGENT(S): EquiServe Trust Company, Jersey City, NJ

NYSE SYMBOL XEL
Rec. Pr. 25.35 (3/31/02)

XCEL ENERGY, INC.

YIELD 5.9%
P/E RATIO 11.1

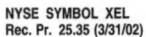
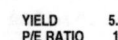
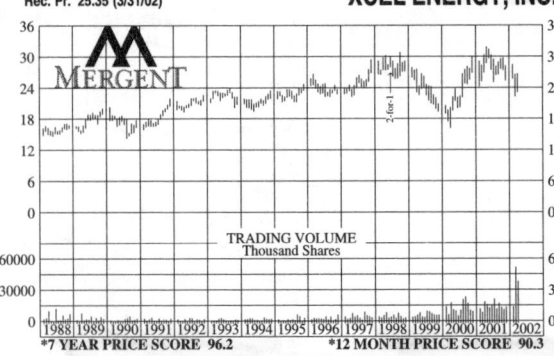

TRADING VOLUME
Thousand Shares

*7 YEAR PRICE SCORE 96.2   *12 MONTH PRICE SCORE 90.3
*NYSE COMPOSITE INDEX=100

INTERIM EARNINGS (Per Share):

Qtr.	Mar.	June	Sept.	Dec.
1998	0.37	0.23	0.67	0.58
1999	0.34	0.06	0.72	0.32
2000	0.30	0.39	0.29	0.40
2001	0.61	0.49	0.79	0.39

INTERIM DIVIDENDS (Per Share):

Amt.	Decl.	Ex.	Rec.	Pay.
0.375Q	6/27/01	7/05/01	7/09/01	7/20/01
0.375Q	8/22/01	9/28/01	10/02/01	10/20/01
0.375Q	12/12/01	12/28/01	1/02/02	1/20/02
0.375Q	3/27/02	4/04/02	4/08/02	4/20/02

Indicated div.: $1.50 (Div. Reinv. Plan)

CAPITALIZATION (12/31/01):

	($000)	(%)
Long-Term Debt	12,117,516	55.4
Deferred Income Tax	2,289,550	10.5
Minority Interest	654,670	3.0
Redeemable Pfd. Stock	494,000	2.3
Preferred Stock..............	105,320	0.5
Common & Surplus	6,194,477	28.3
Total..........................	21,855,533	100.0

DIVIDEND ACHIEVER STATUS:
Rank: 272   10-Year Growth Rate: 2.39%
Total Years of Dividend Growth: 26

RECENT DEVELOPMENTS: For the year ended 12/31/01, income climbed 43.8% to $784.7 million, before an extraordinary gain of $10.3 million, from $545.8 million, before an extraordinary loss of $19.0 million, in the previous year. Results for 2001 and 2000 included special charges of $62.2 million and $241.0 million, respectively. Total operating revenues climbed 29.6% to $15.03 billion.

PROSPECTS: On 2/15/02, the Company announced that its board of directors approved plans to acquire all of the outstanding publicly-held shares of its subsidiary, NRG Energy, Inc. Under the agreement, NRG shareholders will receive 0.50 shares of Xcel Energy common stock for each share held. Looking ahead, XEL expects earnings per share to range between $2.40 to $2.50 in 2002.

BUSINESS

XCEL ENERGY, INC. (formerly Northern States Power Company) is a public utility holding company formed on 8/18/00 upon the merger of New Century Energies and Northern States Power Company. As of 12/31/01, the Company provided a portfolio of energy-related products and services to 3.2 million electricity customers and 1.7 million natural gas customers. The Company, with operations in 12 Western and Midwestern states, has six public utility subsidiaries: Southwestern Public Service Company, Public Service Company of Colorado, Cheyenne Light, Fuel and Power Company, Northern States Power Company Minnesota, Northern States Power Company Wisconsin, and Black Mountain Gas Company. The Company operates numerous non-utility subsidiaries and owns 74.0% of NRG Energy, Inc., as of 2/15/02.

ANNUAL FINANCIAL DATA

	12/31/01	12/31/00	12/31/99	12/31/98	12/31/97	12/31/96	12/31/95
Earnings Per Share	④ 2.27	③ 1.60	② 1.43	1.84	① 1.61	1.91	1.96
Cash Flow Per Share	5.11	4.14	7.24	7.70	7.81	8.12	8.63
Tang. Book Val. Per Share	17.91	16.32	15.97	15.62	15.27	14.71	14.24
Dividends Per Share	1.50	1.47	1.44	1.42	1.40	1.36	1.33
Dividend Payout %	66.1	91.8	100.7	77.2	86.6	71.5	68.1
INCOME STATEMENT (IN MILLIONS):							
Total Revenues	15,028.2	11,591.8	3,188.2	3,130.5	3,043.7	2,955.4	2,894.2
Costs & Expenses	12,110.6	9,162.6	1,553.9	1,539.2	1,498.5	1,449.8	1,366.8
Depreciation & Amort.	974.6	858.1	473.9	423.2	398.9	381.4	372.1
Maintenance Exp.	...	...	178.6	181.1	164.5	155.8	158.2
Operating Income	1,942.9	1,571.1	343.5	364.3	361.8	366.0	345.9
Net Interest Inc./(Exp.)	d710.2	d641.2	d220.5	d162.7	d144.7	d130.7	d122.9
Income Taxes	336.7	304.9	cr61.0	cr40.6	cr48.1	cr14.6	5.1
Equity Earnings/Minority Int.	d72.5	d40.5	...	...	...	31.0	29.2
Net Income	④ 784.7	③ 545.8	② 642.3	742.4	① 712.6	746.2	804.2
Cash Flow	1,755.1	1,399.6	1,110.8	1,160.0	1,100.5	1,115.4	1,163.8
Average Shs. Outstg. (000)	343,742	338,111	153,443	150,743	140,870	137,358	134,832
BALANCE SHEET (IN MILLIONS):							
Gross Property	30,759.9	24,032.2	9,783.9	9,424.2	9,062.3	8,741.3	8,406.9
Accumulated Depreciation	9,594.8	8,759.3	5,332.5	5,028.9	4,701.0	4,403.4	4,096.6
Net Property	21,165.1	15,272.9	4,451.5	4,395.2	4,361.3	4,337.9	4,310.3
Total Assets	28,735.1	21,768.8	9,767.7	7,396.3	7,144.1	6,636.9	6,228.6
Long-Term Obligations	12,117.5	7,583.4	3,453.4	1,851.1	1,878.9	1,592.6	1,542.3
Net Stockholders' Equity	6,299.8	5,667.4	2,662.9	2,586.6	2,572.1	2,376.3	2,267.9
Year-end Shs. Outstg. (000)	345,801	340,834	153,041	152,697	149,236	138,126	136,352
STATISTICAL RECORD:							
Operating Profit Margin %	12.9	13.6	10.8	11.6	11.9	12.4	12.0
Net Profit Margin %	5.2	4.7	20.1	23.7	23.4	25.3	27.8
Net Inc./Net Property %	3.7	3.6	14.4	16.9	16.3	17.2	18.7
Net Inc./Tot. Capital %	3.6	3.5	9.0	13.6	13.1	15.6	17.3
Return on Equity %	12.5	9.6	24.1	28.7	27.7	31.4	35.5
Accum. Depr./Gross Prop. %	31.2	36.4	54.5	53.4	51.9	50.4	48.7
Price Range	31.85-24.19	30.00-16.13	27.94-19.31	30.81-25.69	29.44-22.25	26.69-22.25	24.75-21.25
P/E Ratio	14.0-10.7	18.7-10.1	19.5-13.5	16.7-14.0	18.3-13.8	14.0-11.6	12.6-10.8
Average Yield %	5.4	6.4	6.1	5.0	5.4	5.6	5.8

Statistics are as originally reported. Results for 1999 and earlier are for Northern States Power Co. Adj. for stk. split: 2-for-1, 6/1/98 ① Incl. non-recurr. chrg. $29.0 mill. fr. termination of merger. ② Incl. spec. chrgs. of $31.1 mill. ③ Incl. spec. chrgs. rel. to merger of $241.0 mill, excl. extraord. item of $19.0 mill. ④ Incl. spec. chrgs. of $62.2 mill.; excl. extraord. gain $10.3 mill.

OFFICERS:
J. J. Howard, Chmn.
W. H. Brunetti, Pres., C.E.O.
E. J. McIntyre, V.P., C.F.O.

INVESTOR CONTACT: Richard J. Kolkmann, Dir. Investor Relations, (612) 215-4559

PRINCIPAL OFFICE: 8000 Nicollet Mall, Minneapolis, MN 55402

TELEPHONE NUMBER: (612) 330-5500
FAX: (612) 330-5688
WEB: www.xcelenergy.com

NO. OF EMPLOYEES: 16,595 (avg.)

SHAREHOLDERS: 134,410

ANNUAL MEETING: In April

INCORPORATED: MN, June, 1909

INSTITUTIONAL HOLDINGS:
No. of Institutions: 371
Shares Held: 153,611,163
% Held: 41.5

INDUSTRY: Electric and other services combined (SIC: 4931)

TRANSFER AGENT(S): Wells Fargo Shareowner Services, South St. Paul, MN

COMMERCE BANCORP, INC.

YIELD 1.3%
P/E RATIO 29.7

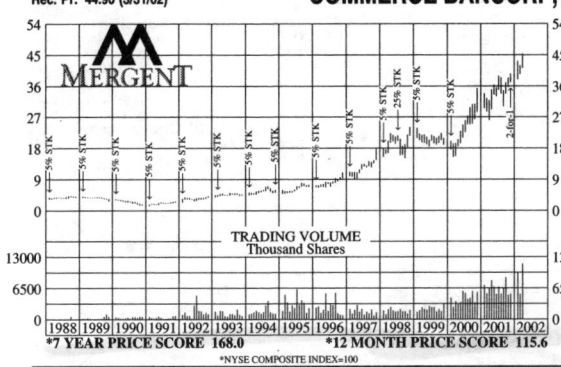

7 YEAR PRICE SCORE 168.0   **12 MONTH PRICE SCORE 115.6**
*NYSE COMPOSITE INDEX=100

INTERIM EARNINGS (Per Share):

Qtr.	Mar.	June	Sept.	Dec.
1998	----	0.94	----	
1999	----	1.09	----	
2000	0.29	0.31	0.32	0.33
2001	0.35	0.37	0.38	0.41

INTERIM DIVIDENDS (Per Share):

Amt.	Decl.	Ex.	Rec.	Pay.
0.275Q	6/19/01	7/03/01	7/06/01	7/20/01
0.275Q	9/19/01	10/03/01	10/05/01	10/19/01
2-for-1	11/21/01	12/19/01	12/03/01	12/18/01
0.15Q	12/18/01	1/02/02	1/04/02	1/18/02
0.15Q	3/19/02	4/03/02	4/05/02	4/19/02

Indicated div.: $0.60

CAPITALIZATION (12/31/01):

	($000)	(%)
Total Deposits	10,185,594	93.4
Long-Term Debt	80,500	0.7
Common & Surplus	636,570	5.8
Total	10,902,664	100.0

DIVIDEND ACHIEVER STATUS:
Rank: 43   10-Year Growth Rate: 16.94%
Total Years of Dividend Growth: 10

RECENT DEVELOPMENTS: For the year ended 12/31/01, net income increased 28.7% to $103.0 million compared with $80.0 million in the previous year. Net interest income advanced 35.2% to $401.3 million from $296.9 million the year before. Net interest margin was 4.76% versus 4.62% in 2000, reflecting the Company's low-cost core deposit base. Provision for loan losses grew 89.4% to $26.4 million from $13.9 million a year earlier.

PROSPECTS: The Company expects revenue growth of 25.0%, net income growth of 20.0% to 25.0%, and earnings per share growth of 15.0% to 20.0% in 2002. Separately, during the fourth quarter of 2001, the Company opened 17 new branch offices, increasing the total offices opened to 184, as it successfully implemented its plan to open 30 to 35 new branches during 2001. The Company intends to open approximately 40 branch offices during 2002.

BUSINESS

COMMERCE BANCORP, INC. is a bank holding company headquartered in Cherry Hill, New Jersey. CBH, as of 12/31/01, had assets of $11.36 billion and total deposits of $10.19 billion. CBH provides a full range of retail and commercial banking services for consumers and small and mid-sized companies. Lending services are focused on commercial real estate and commercial and consumer loans to local borrowers. As of 12/31/01, CBH had over 180 full-service retail branch offices located in New Jersey, Pennsylvania, Delaware and New York.

ANNUAL FINANCIAL DATA

	12/31/01	12/31/00	12/31/99	12/31/98	12/31/97	12/31/96	12/31/95
Earnings Per Share	1.51	1.25	1.09	0.94	0.81	0.76	0.70
Tang. Book Val. Per Share	9.67	7.75	5.98	5.97	5.28	4.93	4.99
Dividends Per Share	0.55	0.48	0.41	0.44	0.28	0.23	0.20
Dividend Payout %	36.4	38.9	38.2	46.3	34.3	30.1	28.9
INCOME STATEMENT (IN MILLIONS):							
Total Interest Income	604.4	505.3	386.4	289.3	244.2	179.4	165.5
Total Interest Expense	203.0	208.4	142.1	115.6	97.0	70.9	70.2
Net Interest Income	401.3	296.9	244.4	173.7	147.1	108.5	95.3
Provision for Loan Losses	26.4	13.9	9.2	5.9	4.7	3.0	2.2
Non-Interest Income	196.8	150.8	114.6	88.9	57.4	30.0	21.5
Non-Interest Expense	420.0	315.4	252.5	182.0	137.9	94.1	77.7
Income Before Taxes	151.7	118.4	97.3	74.8	61.9	41.5	36.9
Net Income	103.0	80.0	66.0	49.3	40.3	26.6	23.5
Average Shs. Outstg. (000)	68,102	64,222	60,930	52,397	49,951	34,594	32,808
BALANCE SHEET (IN MILLIONS):							
Cash & Due from Banks	557.7	443.9	317.6	245.4	167.9	159.6	147.5
Securities Avail. for Sale	4,435.5	2,130.6	1,782.1	1,368.9	1,323.0	741.2	529.2
Total Loans & Leases	4,583.4	3,687.3	2,961.1	1,931.4	1,411.3	1,096.2	907.5
Allowance for Credit Losses	67.0	48.7	38.4	26.4	21.3	14.3	13.3
Net Loans & Leases	4,516.4	3,638.6	2,922.7	1,905.0	1,390.0	1,081.8	894.2
Total Assets	11,363.7	8,295.5	6,635.8	4,894.1	3,939.0	2,862.0	2,415.9
Total Deposits	10,185.6	7,387.6	5,608.9	4,435.1	3,369.4	2,573.4	2,225.1
Long-Term Obligations	80.5	80.5	80.5	80.5	80.5	23.0	23.0
Total Liabilities	10,727.1	7,804.3	6,279.0	4,593.3	3,688.2	2,680.6	2,253.9
Net Stockholders' Equity	636.6	492.2	356.8	300.7	250.8	181.4	162.0
Year-end Shs. Outstg. (000)	65,833	63,523	59,689	50,411	46,029	35,261	30,975
STATISTICAL RECORD:							
Return on Equity %	16.2	16.3	18.5	16.4	16.1	14.7	14.5
Return on Assets %	0.9	1.0	1.0	1.0	1.0	0.9	1.0
Equity/Assets %	5.6	5.9	5.4	6.1	6.4	6.3	6.7
Non-Int. Exp./Tot. Inc. %	70.2	70.4	70.3	69.3	67.4	67.9	66.5
Price Range	39.60-26.00	35.41-15.44	23.81-18.45	24.04-15.05	17.95-9.03	10.94-6.62	8.03-4.86
P/E Ratio	26.2-17.2	28.4-12.4	21.9-17.0	25.5-16.0	22.3-11.2	14.5-8.8	11.5-7.0
Average Yield %	1.7	1.9	2.0	2.2	2.0	2.6	3.1

Statistics are as originally reported. Adjusted for stk. splits: 2-for-1, 12/01; 5%, 1/96, 1/97, 1/98, 1/99, 1/00; 25%, 7/98.

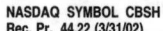

COMMERCE BANCSHARES, INC.

YIELD 1.5%
P/E RATIO 16.2

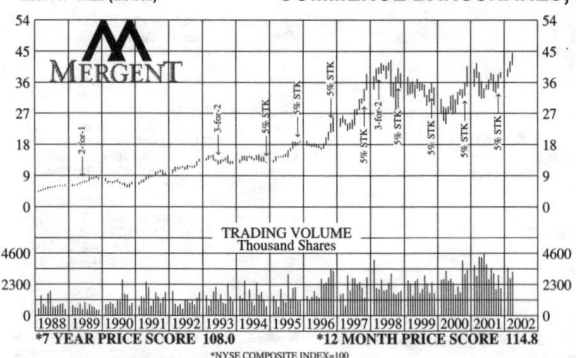

TRADING VOLUME
Thousand Shares

| 1988 | 1989 | 1990 | 1991 | 1992 | 1993 | 1994 | 1995 | 1996 | 1997 | 1998 | 1999 | 2000 | 2001 | 2002 |

*7 YEAR PRICE SCORE 108.0   *12 MONTH PRICE SCORE 114.8
*NYSE COMPOSITE INDEX=100

INTERIM EARNINGS (Per Share):

Qtr.	Mar.	June	Sept.	Dec.
1997	0.43	0.48	0.50	0.53
1998	0.50	0.54	0.58	0.60
1999	0.56	0.62	0.62	0.64
2000	0.60	0.67	0.67	0.69
2001	0.66	0.68	0.68	0.71

INTERIM DIVIDENDS (Per Share):

Amt.	Decl.	Ex.	Rec.	Pay.
0.16Q	7/27/01	9/12/01	9/14/01	9/28/01
0.16Q	10/26/01	11/28/01	11/30/01	12/14/01
5% STK	10/26/01	11/28/01	11/30/01	12/14/01
0.163Q	2/01/02	3/06/02	3/08/02	3/28/02
0.163Q	4/17/02	6/05/02	6/07/02	6/27/02

Indicated div.: $0.65 (Div. Reinv. Plan)

CAPITALIZATION (12/31/01):

	($000)	(%)
Total Deposits	10,031,966	85.8
Long-Term Debt	392,586	3.4
Common & Surplus	1,272,483	10.9
Total	11,697,035	100.0

DIVIDEND ACHIEVER STATUS:
Rank: 128   10-Year Growth Rate: 10.45%
Total Years of Dividend Growth: 33

RECENT DEVELOPMENTS: For the year ended 12/31/01, net income increased 1.9% to $182.0 million compared with $178.6 million in the prior year, primarily due to solid growth in non-interest income and expense control. Total interest income declined 7.5% to $751.0 million from $812.2 million in the previous year. Net interest income amounted to $467.9 million, down 2.7% from $480.7 mil-

lion a year earlier. Average loan balances declined slightly from the prior-year quarter, while average interest-bearing deposits grew by 9.9%. Provision for loan losses grew 3.6% to $36.4 million. Total non-interest income rose 9.8% to $277.5 million, while total non-interest expense increased 2.2% to $439.6 million.

BUSINESS

COMMERCE BANCSHARES, INC., with assets of $12.90 billion as of 12/31/01, is a bank holding company that owns or controls substantially all of the outstanding capital stock of one national banking association located in Missouri, one national banking association located in Illinois, three national banking associations located in Kansas, and a credit card bank located in Nebraska. In addition, the Company directly owns several non-banking subsidiaries that are engaged in owning real estate. These real estate subsidiaries are engaged in leasing to the Company's banking subsidiaries, underwriting credit life and credit accident and health insurance, selling property and casualty insurance, providing venture capital through a small business investment corporation as well as a venture capital limited partnership, and mortgage banking.

ANNUAL FINANCIAL DATA

	12/31/01	12/31/00	12/31/99	12/31/98	12/31/97	12/31/96	12/31/95
Earnings Per Share	2.73	2.63	2.35	2.09	① 1.84	1.63	1.42
Tang. Book Val. Per Share	18.67	16.52	14.71	14.18	12.71	11.69	10.61
Dividends Per Share	0.61	0.56	0.52	0.48	0.43	0.38	0.34
Dividend Payout %	22.3	21.4	22.1	22.8	23.2	23.3	24.1
INCOME STATEMENT (IN MILLIONS):							
Total Interest Income	751.0	812.2	750.6	728.5	682.9	647.6	631.0
Total Interest Expense	283.1	331.5	284.6	300.7	285.1	281.9	275.3
Net Interest Income	467.9	480.7	466.0	427.7	397.8	365.7	355.7
Provision for Loan Losses	36.4	35.2	35.3	36.9	31.4	24.5	14.6
Non-Interest Income	277.5	252.8	236.2	214.0	180.1	159.2	133.2
Non-Interest Expense	439.6	430.4	419.0	379.3	344.4	318.0	305.5
Income Before Taxes	269.4	267.9	247.9	225.6	202.1	182.4	168.8
Net Income	182.0	178.6	166.2	150.1	① 132.7	119.5	107.6
Average Shs. Outstg. (000)	66,722	67,888	69,950	71,893	72,061	73,610	75,989
BALANCE SHEET (IN MILLIONS):							
Cash & Due from Banks	824.2	616.7	685.2	738.7	978.2	833.3	774.9
Securities Avail. for Sale	3,667.2	1,885.7	2,475.4	3,002.4	2,620.5	2,681.7	2,561.6
Total Loans & Leases	7,638.5	7,906.7	7,576.9	7,046.9	6,224.4	5,472.3	5,317.8
Allowance for Credit Losses	130.0	128.4	123.0	117.1	105.9	98.2	98.5
Net Loans & Leases	7,508.5	7,778.2	7,453.9	6,929.8	6,118.5	5,374.1	5,219.3
Total Assets	12,902.8	11,115.1	11,400.9	11,402.0	10,306.9	9,698.2	9,574.0
Total Deposits	10,032.0	9,081.7	9,164.1	9,530.2	8,700.6	8,166.4	8,193.1
Long-Term Obligations	392.6	224.7	25.7	27.1	7.2	14.1	14.6
Total Liabilities	11,630.3	9,971.4	10,321.1	10,321.2	9,326.2	8,773.9	8,690.2
Net Stockholders' Equity	1,272.5	1,143.8	1,079.8	1,080.8	980.8	924.3	883.8
Year-end Shs. Outstg. (000)	65,437	65,706	68,768	70,800	70,464	71,555	73,778
STATISTICAL RECORD:							
Return on Equity %	14.3	15.6	15.4	13.9	13.5	12.9	12.2
Return on Assets %	1.4	1.6	1.5	1.3	1.3	1.2	1.1
Equity/Assets %	9.9	10.3	9.5	9.5	9.5	9.5	9.2
Non-Int. Exp./Tot. Inc. %	59.0	58.7	59.7	59.1	59.6	60.6	62.5
Price Range	41.55-31.35	40.72-23.92	37.69-29.21	42.48-27.97	38.53-21.94	25.86-16.54	19.03-12.79
P/E Ratio	15.2-11.5	15.5-9.1	16.0-12.4	20.3-13.4	20.9-11.9	15.9-10.2	13.4-9.0
Average Yield %	1.7	1.7	1.5	1.4	1.4	1.8	2.1

Statistics are as originally reported. Adj. for stk. splits: 5% div., 12/14/01; 5% div., 12/15/00; 5% div., 12/18/98; 3-for-2, 3/30/98; 5% div., 12/12/97; 5% div., 12/13/96; 5% div., 12/15/95. ① Incl. non-recurr. credit $3.3 mill.

OFFICERS:
D. W. Kemper, Chmn., Pres., C.E.O.
J. M. Kemper, Vice-Chmn.
W. A. Sullins, Jr., Vice Chmn.
A. B. Clark, Exec. V.P., C.F.O., Treas.

INVESTOR CONTACT: Jeffrey Aberdeen, Controller, (816) 234-2081

PRINCIPAL OFFICE: 1000 Walnut, Kansas City, MO 64106

TELEPHONE NUMBER: (816) 234-2000
FAX: (816) 234-2369
WEB: www.commercebank.com

NO. OF EMPLOYEES: 4,502 full-time; 800 part-time

SHAREHOLDERS: 5,363

ANNUAL MEETING: In Apr.

INCORPORATED: MO, Aug., 1966

INDUSTRY: State commercial banks (SIC: 6022)

TRANSFER AGENT(S): First Chicago Trust Company of New York, Jersey City, NJ

COMMERCIAL NET LEASE REALTY, INC.

YIELD 9.0%
P/E RATIO 14.7

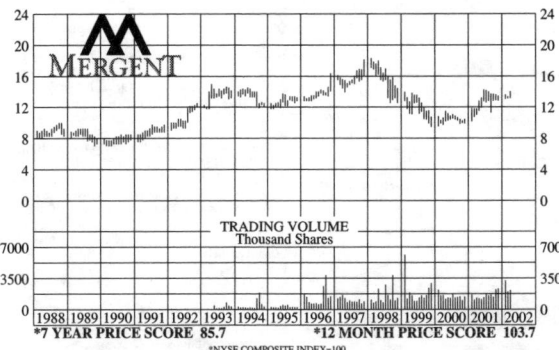

*7 YEAR PRICE SCORE 85.7   *12 MONTH PRICE SCORE 103.7
*NYSE COMPOSITE INDEX=100

TRADING VOLUME
Thousand Shares

INTERIM EARNINGS (Per Share):

Qtr.	Mar.	June	Sept.	Dec.
1997	0.31	0.31	0.32	0.32
1998	0.15	0.32	0.34	0.29
1999	0.32	0.23	0.29	0.31
2000	0.28	0.28	0.28	0.41
2001	0.38	0.34	0.24	d0.01

INTERIM DIVIDENDS (Per Share):

Amt.	Decl.	Ex.	Rec.	Pay.
0.315Q	4/19/01	4/26/01	4/30/01	5/15/01
0.315Q	7/17/01	7/27/01	7/31/01	8/15/01
0.315Q	10/15/01	10/29/01	10/31/01	11/15/01
0.315Q	1/15/02	1/29/02	1/31/02	2/15/02
0.315Q	4/15/02	4/26/02	4/30/02	5/15/02

Indicated div.: $1.26 (Div. Reinv. Plan)

CAPITALIZATION (12/31/01):

	($000)	(%)
Long-Term Debt	435,333	43.5
Preferred Stock	50,000	5.0
Common & Surplus	514,640	51.5
Total	999,973	100.0

DIVIDEND ACHIEVER STATUS:
Rank: 278   10-Year Growth Rate: 1.74%
Total Years of Dividend Growth: 12

RECENT DEVELOPMENTS: For the year ended 12/31/01, net earnings were $29.0 million versus income of $38.6 million, before an accounting change charge of $367,000, the year before. Results for 2001 and 2000 included gains on the disposition of real estate of $4.6 million and $4.1 million, respectively. Total revenue slipped to $80.5 million from $80.9 million in 2000. Rental and earned income fell 5.3% to $69.9 million, while interest and other income advanced 50.0% to $10.7 million.

PROSPECTS: During the fourth quarter, the Company announced that it disposed of six properties generating net proceeds of $9.5 million. These properties were leased to Golden Corral (2), OfficeMax, Heilig-Meyers, Steak & Ale and Applebee's. Separately, the Company noted that operations in its real estate investment trust subsidiary have improved to a profitable level. Going forward, NNN should benefit from its acquisition of Captec Net Lease Realty, Inc., effective on 12/1/01.

BUSINESS

COMMERCIAL NET LEASE REALTY, INC. is a fully integrated, self-administered real estate investment trust that acquires, owns, manages and indirectly develops a diversified portfolio of freestanding properties. The Company invests in single-tenant, freestanding retail properties that are located in intensive commercial corridors with purchase prices up to $8.0 million. As of 1/30/02, the Company owned 360 properties that are generally leased to major retail businesses under long-term commercial net leases. These businesses include Barnes & Noble, Best Buy, Eckerd and Office Max. On 12/1/01, NNN acquired Captec Net Lease Realty, Inc.

ANNUAL FINANCIAL DATA

	12/31/01	12/31/00	12/31/99	12/31/98	12/31/97	12/31/96	12/31/95
Earnings Per Share	1 0.91	1 2 1.27	1 1.16	1 1.10	1 1.25	1 1.18	1.09
Tang. Book Val. Per Share	12.68	12.93	12.94	13.00	12.96	15.04	11.65
Dividends Per Share	1.26	1.25	1.24	1.23	1.20	1.18	1.16
Dividend Payout %	138.4	98.0	106.9	111.8	96.0	100.0	106.4
INCOME STATEMENT (IN THOUSANDS):							
Rental Income	58,092	60,591	58,417	48,935	38,143	25,140	15,200
Interest Income	20,550	19,147	16,243	13,476	11,992	8,229	5,380
Total Income	80,526	80,891	76,543	64,773	50,135	33,369	20,580
Costs & Expenses	20,573	6,768	16,436	13,835	3,723	2,844	1,981
Depreciation	9,211	9,088	8,634	6,759	5,302	3,553	2,058
Interest Expense	24,952	26,528	21,920	13,460	11,478	7,206	3,834
Income Before Income Taxes	30,438	42,598	36,277	32,074	30,283	19,839	12,707
Equity Earnings/Minority Int.	d1,475	d3,980	d966	367	102	...	...
Net Income	1 28,963	1 2 38,618	1 35,311	1 32,441	1 30,385	1 19,839	12,707
Average Shs. Outstg.	31,717	30,440	30,408	29,397	24,221	16,799	11,664
BALANCE SHEET (IN THOUSANDS):							
Cash & Cash Equivalents	6,974	2,190	3,329	1,442	2,160	1,410	301
Total Real Estate Investments	706,280	514,962	546,193	519,948	400,977	269,031	155,957
Total Assets	1,006,628	761,611	749,789	685,595	537,014	370,953	219,257
Long-Term Obligations	435,333	360,381	350,971	292,907	171,836	116,956	82,600
Total Liabilities	441,988	367,710	358,427	301,705	174,870	118,379	83,415
Net Stockholders' Equity	564,640	393,901	391,362	383,890	362,144	252,574	135,842
Year-end Shs. Outstg.	40,599	30,457	30,256	29,521	27,954	16,799	11,664
STATISTICAL RECORD:							
Net Inc.+Depr./Assets %	3.8	6.3	5.9	5.7	6.6	6.3	6.7
Return on Equity %	5.1	9.8	9.0	8.5	8.4	7.9	9.4
Return on Assets %	2.9	5.1	4.7	4.7	5.7	5.3	5.8
Price Range	14.25-10.13	11.50-9.50	13.94-9.44	18.31-12.50	18.13-13.88	16.38-12.75	13.75-11.75
P/E Ratio	15.7-11.1	9.1-7.5	12.0-8.1	16.6-11.4	14.5-11.1	13.9-10.8	12.6-10.8
Average Yield %	10.3	11.9	10.6	8.0	7.5	8.1	9.1

Statistics are as originally reported. 1 Incl. gain on sale of investment $4.6 mill., 2001; $4.1 mill., 2000; $6.7 mill., 1999; $1.4 mill., 1998; $651,000, 1997; $73,000, 1996. 2 Excl. acctg. chg. of $367,000.

OFFICERS:
J. M. Seneff Jr., Chmn., C.E.O.
R. A. Bourne, Vice-Chmn.
G. M. Ralston, Pres., C.O.O.

INVESTOR CONTACT: Kevin B. Habicht, Investor Relations, (407) 265-7348

PRINCIPAL OFFICE: 450 South Orange Avenue, Suite 900, Orlando, FL 32801

TELEPHONE NUMBER: (407) 265-7348
FAX: (407) 423-2894
WEB: www.cnlreit.com
NO. OF EMPLOYEES: 35
SHAREHOLDERS: 1,303
ANNUAL MEETING: In May
INCORPORATED: DE, June, 1984; reincorp., MD, June, 1994

INSTITUTIONAL HOLDINGS:
No. of Institutions: 93
Shares Held: 7,689,128
% Held: 18.9

INDUSTRY: Real estate investment trusts (SIC: 6798)

TRANSFER AGENT(S): First Union National Bank, Charlotte, NC

COMMUNITY BANK SYSTEM, INC.

YIELD 3.6%
P/E RATIO 18.6

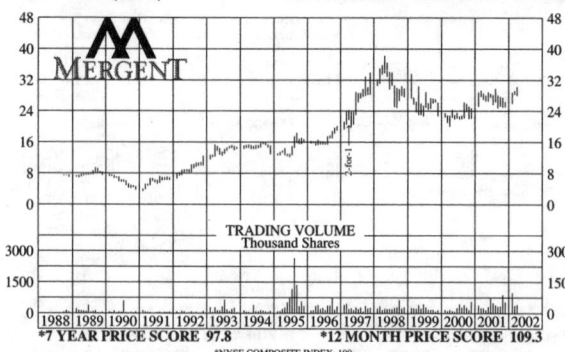

TRADING VOLUME
Thousand Shares

| 1988 | 1989 | 1990 | 1991 | 1992 | 1993 | 1994 | 1995 | 1996 | 1997 | 1998 | 1999 | 2000 | 2001 | 2002 |

*7 YEAR PRICE SCORE 97.8   ***12 MONTH PRICE SCORE 109.3**
*NYSE COMPOSITE INDEX=100

INTERIM EARNINGS (Per Share):

Qtr.	Mar.	June	Sept.	Dec.
1998	0.48	0.50	0.56	0.51
1999	0.50	0.55	0.68	0.69
2000	0.70	0.72	0.72	0.70
2001	0.50	0.18	0.55	0.39

INTERIM DIVIDENDS (Per Share):

Amt.	Decl.	Ex.	Rec.	Pay.
0.27Q	5/18/01	6/13/01	6/15/01	7/10/01
0.27Q	8/17/01	9/17/01	9/14/01	10/10/01
0.27Q	11/15/01	12/12/01	12/14/01	1/10/02
0.27Q	2/21/02	3/13/02	3/15/02	4/10/02

Indicated div.: $1.08 (Div. Reinv. Plan)

CAPITALIZATION (12/31/01):

	($000)	(%)
Total Deposits	2,545,970	80.7
Long-Term Debt	263,100	8.3
Redeemable Pfd. Stock	77,819	2.5
Common & Surplus	267,980	8.5
Total	3,154,869	100.0

DIVIDEND ACHIEVER STATUS:

Rank: 117   10-Year Growth Rate: 11.01%
Total Years of Dividend Growth: 10

RECENT DEVELOPMENTS: For the year ended 12/31/01, income was $20.7 million, before an extraordinary loss of $1.6 million, versus net income of $24.9 million a year earlier. Results for 2001 and 2000 included acquisition and unusual expenses of $8.2 million and $400,000, respectively. Net interest income rose 6.9% to $96.7 million, due to an increase in average earning assets. Total other income grew 25.8% to $29.1 million from $23.1 million last year, and included investment security gains of $2.5 million in 2001 and investment security losses of $159,000 in 2000.

PROSPECTS: CBU continues to move forward integrating acquisitions made in 2001 that added $1.20 billion in assets and increased the Company's branch network by 70.0% to 119 locations. Meanwhile, for the year ended 12/31/01, nonperforming loans, defined by CBU as nonaccruing loans plus accruing loans 90 days or more past due, rose 22.9% to $9.1 million, primarily due to increases in commercial and residential mortgage loan nonaccruals. The ratio of nonperforming loans to total loans rose slightly to 0.53% versus 0.49% the year before.

BUSINESS

COMMUNITY BANK SYSTEM, INC. is a community retail bank. As of 12/31/01, CBU provided banking services through its two regional offices, as well as through 119 customer facilities in the 22 counties of New York State and in two counties in Northern Pennsylvania. At 12/31/01, the Company had total assets of $3.21 billion. CBU account services include checking accounts, interest-checking accounts, money market accounts, savings accounts, time deposit accounts, and individual retirement accounts. The Company also offers a range of other financial services, including pension administration and consulting, estate settlement services and various financial and insurance products including mutual funds, annuities, long-term health care and other selected insurance products.

ANNUAL FINANCIAL DATA

	12/31/01	12/31/00	12/31/99	12/31/98	12/31/97	12/31/96	12/31/95
Earnings Per Share	② 1.62	2.85	2.42	① 2.05	2.02	1.84	1.71
Tang. Book Val. Per Share	9.74	12.64	8.09	9.01	7.82	9.85	8.37
Dividends Per Share	1.08	1.02	0.94	0.83	0.74	0.68	0.60
Dividend Payout %	66.7	35.8	38.8	40.5	36.6	36.8	35.2
INCOME STATEMENT (IN MILLIONS):							
Total Interest Income	197.9	145.2	123.9	122.9	117.6	97.7	83.4
Total Interest Expense	101.2	74.0	55.9	58.5	54.8	42.4	36.3
Net Interest Income	96.7	71.2	67.9	64.4	62.9	55.3	47.1
Provision for Loan Losses	7.1	7.2	5.1	5.1	4.5	2.9	1.8
Non-Interest Income	29.1	21.0	15.5	17.0	11.8	8.9	6.6
Non-Interest Expense	89.0	56.0	52.7	51.9	45.8	37.4	33.0
Income Before Taxes	29.6	29.0	25.6	24.4	24.4	23.8	18.9
Net Income	② 20.7	20.3	17.6	① 15.5	15.6	14.1	11.5
Average Shs. Outstg. (000)	11,825	7,136	7,295	7,671	7,676	6,943	6,522
BALANCE SHEET (IN MILLIONS):							
Cash & Due from Banks	106.6	59.3	76.5	. . .	82.1	52.5	56.9
Total Loans & Leases	1,733.1	1,093.8	1,006.1	916.0	845.0	658.4	573.6
Allowance for Credit Losses	24.1	9.7	10.3	11.3	14.2	14.0	20.4
Net Loans & Leases	1,709.0	1,084.1	995.8	904.8	830.8	644.3	553.2
Total Assets	3,210.8	2,022.6	1,840.7	1,680.7	1,633.7	1,343.9	1,152.0
Total Deposits	2,546.0	1,457.7	1,360.3	1,378.1	1,345.7	1,027.2	1,016.9
Long-Term Obligations	263.1	331.1	324.0	. . .	. . .	. . .	. . .
Total Liabilities	2,942.9	1,883.3	1,732.2	1,560.5	1,515.7	1,234.5	1,052.0
Net Stockholders' Equity	268.0	139.4	108.5	120.2	118.0	109.4	100.1
Year-end Shs. Outstg. (000)	12,903	6,993	7,296	7,296	7,587	7,474	7,359
STATISTICAL RECORD:							
Return on Equity %	7.7	14.6	16.3	12.9	13.2	12.9	11.5
Return on Assets %	0.6	1.0	1.0	0.9	1.0	1.1	1.0
Equity/Assets %	8.3	6.9	5.9	7.1	7.2	8.1	8.7
Non-Int. Exp./Tot. Inc. %	70.8	60.7	63.2	63.7	61.3	58.4	61.6
Price Range	29.85-24.75	26.25-20.00	33.63-22.63	38.25-24.81	34.00-19.25	20.13-15.13	18.38-12.13
P/E Ratio	18.4-15.3	9.2-7.0	13.9-9.3	18.7-12.1	16.8-9.5	11.0-8.2	10.8-7.1
Average Yield %	4.0	4.4	3.3	2.6	2.8	3.8	3.9

Statistics are as originally reported. Adj. for 2-for-1 stk. split, 3/97. ① Bef. acctg. chg. credit of $193,860. ② Incl. acquisition & unusual exp. of $8.2 mill.; bef. extraord. loss of $1.6 mill.

QUARTERLY DATA

(12/31/2001)($000)	REV	INC
1st Quarter	29,166	5,749
2nd Quarter	29,710	2,110
3rd Quarter	30,779	6,443
4th Quarter	33,537	4,827

OFFICERS:

J. A. Gabriel, Chmn.
S. A. Belden, Pres., C.E.O.
D. G. Wallace, Treas.
INVESTOR CONTACT: David G. Wallace, Treas., (315) 445-2282
PRINCIPAL OFFICE: 5790 Widewaters Parkway, DeWitt, NY 13214-1883

TELEPHONE NUMBER: (315) 445-2282
FAX: (315) 445-2997
WEB: www.communitybankna.com
NO. OF EMPLOYEES: 1,115
SHAREHOLDERS: 9,000 (approx. record)
ANNUAL MEETING: In May
INCORPORATED: DE, Apr., 1983

INSTITUTIONAL HOLDINGS:
No. of Institutions: 66
Shares Held: 3,123,750
% Held: 24.2
INDUSTRY: National commercial banks
(SIC: 6021)
TRANSFER AGENT(S): American Stock Transfer & Trust Company, New York, NY

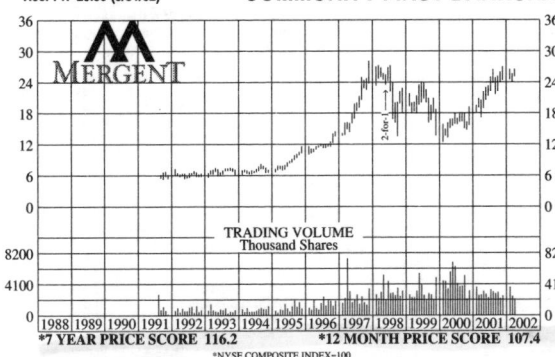

NASDAQ SYMBOL CFBX
Rec. Pr. 25.86 (3/31/02)

COMMUNITY FIRST BANKSHARES, INC.

YIELD 2.9%
P/E RATIO 16.4

INTERIM EARNINGS (Per Share):

Qtr.	Mar.	June	Sept.	Dec.
1998	0.35	0.21	0.88	0.14
1999	0.36	0.38	0.39	0.35
2000	0.37	0.38	0.40	0.40
2001	0.24	0.43	0.45	0.46

INTERIM DIVIDENDS (Per Share):

Amt.	Decl.	Ex.	Rec.	Pay.
0.16Q	4/26/01	5/30/01	6/01/01	6/15/01
0.18Q	8/07/01	8/29/01	9/01/01	9/15/01
0.18Q	10/29/01	11/28/01	12/01/01	12/15/01
0.19Q	2/06/02	2/27/02	3/01/02	3/15/02

Indicated div.: $0.76

CAPITALIZATION (12/31/01):

	($000)	(%)
Total Deposits	4,750,813	90.6
Long-Term Debt	136,841	2.6
Common & Surplus	356,705	6.8
Total	5,244,359	100.0

TRADING VOLUME
Thousand Shares

*7 YEAR PRICE SCORE 116.2   ***12 MONTH PRICE SCORE 107.4**
NYSE COMPOSITE INDEX=100

DIVIDEND ACHIEVER STATUS:
Rank: 3   10-Year Growth Rate: 32.75%
Total Years of Dividend Growth: 10

RECENT DEVELOPMENTS: For the year ended 12/31/01, net income declined 9.2% to $65.1 million compared with $71.6 million in 2000. Results for 2001 included a non-recurring restructuring charge of $7.7 million. Net interest income grew 1.7% to $271.8 million versus $267.3 million the year before. Interest income amounted to $434.0 million, down 9.1% from $477.6 million in the prior year.

Interest expense decreased 22.9% to $162.2 million the year before. Provision for loan losses rose 11.0% to $17.5 million from $15.8 million a year earlier. Total non-interest income climbed 2.0% to $76.7 million versus $75.2 million in 2000. Total non-interest expense was $232.4 million, up 6.0% from $219.3 million in the previous year.

BUSINESS

COMMUNITY FIRST BANK-SHARES, INC. is a bank holding company that as of 12/31/01 operated through one bank subsidiary with banking offices in 138 communities in Arizona, California, Colorado, Iowa, Minnesota, Nebraska, New Mexico, North Dakota, South Dakota, Utah, Wisconsin and Wyoming. The banks are community banks that provide a range of commercial and consumer banking services primarily to individuals and businesses in small and medium-sized communities and surrounding market areas. The Company provides the banks with access to lines of financial services including trust products and administration, insurance and investment services, data processing services, credit policy formulation and review, investment management and specialized staff support. The Company continues to seek opportunities to acquire banks and bank branches in communities, which generally have a population of between 3,000 and 50,000 and are located in CFBX's key target acquisition states.

QUARTERLY DATA

(12/31/2001)($000)	REV	INC
1st Quarter	133,983	10,228
2nd Quarter	130,924	17,733
3rd Quarter	126,906	18,440
4th Quarter	118,081	18,658

ANNUAL FINANCIAL DATA

	12/31/01	12/31/00	12/31/99	12/31/98	12/31/97	12/31/96	12/31/95
Earnings Per Share	① 1.57	1.54	1.48	② 0.98	③ 1.20	④ 0.90	④ 0.88
Tang. Book Val. Per Share	6.44	5.50	5.96	5.77	5.95	5.32	5.83
Dividends Per Share	0.68	0.60	0.56	0.44	0.35	0.29	0.24
Dividend Payout %	43.3	39.0	37.8	44.9	29.2	32.2	27.3
INCOME STATEMENT (IN MILLIONS):							
Total Interest Income	434.0	477.6	465.2	449.2	278.6	229.4	162.1
Total Interest Expense	162.2	210.3	185.8	188.5	117.3	95.2	73.9
Net Interest Income	271.8	267.3	279.4	260.8	161.3	134.2	88.1
Provision for Loan Losses	17.5	15.8	20.2	22.5	5.4	6.8	2.4
Non-Interest Income	76.7	75.2	72.5	60.3	36.6	27.4	17.8
Non-Interest Expense	232.4	219.3	218.2	230.1	125.2	104.3	68.0
Income Before Taxes	98.5	107.4	113.5	68.4	67.4	50.5	35.5
Net Income	① 65.1	71.6	74.9	② 47.0	③ 45.9	④ 32.5	④ 22.8
Average Shs. Outstg. (000)	41,471	46,579	50,671	47,882	38,138	33,398	22,968
BALANCE SHEET (IN MILLIONS):							
Cash & Due from Banks	248.3	256.1	247.1	251.0	222.1	175.7	106.9
Securities Avail. for Sale	1,437.1	1,714.5	1,937.5	1,980.5	1,498.9	506.9	405.1
Total Loans & Leases	3,736.7	3,738.2	3,690.4	3,386.1	2,637.1	2,064.1	1,495.5
Allowance for Credit Losses	55.0	52.2	48.9	50.2	36.2	26.2	19.5
Net Loans & Leases	3,681.7	3,686.0	3,641.5	3,336.0	2,600.9	2,037.9	1,475.9
Total Assets	5,772.3	6,089.7	6,302.2	6,003.0	4,855.5	3,116.4	2,326.8
Total Deposits	4,750.8	5,019.9	4,909.9	4,884.7	3,619.3	2,537.4	1,989.9
Long-Term Obligations	136.8	124.0	75.6	93.5	116.5	46.8	69.8
Total Liabilities	5,295.6	5,624.3	5,775.0	5,477.7	4,396.2	2,870.5	2,169.8
Net Stockholders' Equity	356.7	345.4	407.3	405.2	339.3	244.6	156.1
Year-end Shs. Outstg. (000)	40,246	41,867	47,118	47,119	40,646	34,304	22,818
STATISTICAL RECORD:							
Return on Equity %	18.2	20.7	18.4	11.6	13.5	13.3	14.6
Return on Assets %	1.1	1.2	1.2	0.8	0.9	1.0	1.0
Equity/Assets %	6.2	5.7	6.5	6.7	7.0	7.8	6.7
Non-Int. Exp./Tot. Inc. %	66.7	64.0	62.0	71.7	63.3	64.5	64.2
Price Range	27.00-17.13	19.19-12.38	24.06-13.63	27.25-13.50	28.13-13.63	14.50-10.00	11.63-6.63
P/E Ratio	17.2-10.9	12.5-8.0	16.3-9.2	27.8-13.8	23.4-11.4	15.7-10.8	12.6-7.2
Average Yield %	3.1	3.8	3.0	2.2	1.7	2.4	2.6

Statistics are as originally reported. ① Incl. non-recur. restr. chg. of $7.7 mill. ② Bef. loss of $4.9 mill. fr. disc. ops.; incl. one-time chg. of $3.7 mill. ③ Bef. extraord. loss of $265,000; incl. one-time chg. of $398,000. ④ Incl. one-time chg. of $2.9 mill., 12/96; chg. of $768,000, 12/95 for acq., integration & conforming exp.

OFFICERS:
D. R. Mengedoth, Chmn.
R. K. Strand, Vice-Chmn., C.O.O.
M. A. Anderson, Pres., C.E.O.

INVESTOR CONTACT: Weber Shandwick Worldwide, (888) 292-2378

PRINCIPAL OFFICE: 520 Main Avenue, Fargo, ND 58124-0001

TELEPHONE NUMBER: (701) 298-5600
FAX: (701) 237-4517
WEB: www.communityfirst.com

NO. OF EMPLOYEES: 1,999 full-time; 518 part-time

SHAREHOLDERS: 2,215 (record); 9,000 (beneficial)

ANNUAL MEETING: In Apr.

INCORPORATED: DE, 1989

INSTITUTIONAL HOLDINGS:
No. of Institutions: 141
Shares Held: 22,738,104
% Held: 57.0

INDUSTRY: State commercial banks (SIC: 6022)

TRANSFER AGENT(S): Wells Fargo Shareowner Services, South St. Paul, MN

COMMUNITY TRUST BANCORP, INC.

YIELD 3.3%
P/E RATIO 13.3

TRADING VOLUME
Thousand Shares

*7 YEAR PRICE SCORE 99.7   *12 MONTH PRICE SCORE 110.7

*NYSE COMPOSITE INDEX=100

INTERIM EARNINGS (Per Share):

Qtr.	Mar.	June	Sept.	Dec.
1997	0.44	0.45	0.44	0.25
1998	0.38	0.38	0.06	0.44
1999	0.46	0.49	0.50	0.51
2000	0.42	0.48	0.48	0.49
2001	0.45	0.51	0.46	0.51

INTERIM DIVIDENDS (Per Share):

Amt.	Decl.	Ex.	Rec.	Pay.
0.20Q	1/23/01	3/13/01	3/15/01	4/01/01
0.20Q	4/24/01	6/13/01	6/15/01	7/01/01
0.20Q	7/24/01	9/12/01	9/15/01	10/01/01
0.21Q	10/23/01	12/12/01	12/15/01	1/01/02
0.21Q	1/29/02	3/13/02	3/15/02	4/01/02

Indicated div.: $0.84 (Div. Reinv. Plan)

CAPITALIZATION (12/31/01):

	($000)	(%)
Total Deposits	2,155,772	90.9
Long-Term Debt	22,969	1.0
Common & Surplus	191,606	8.1
Total	2,370,347	100.0

DIVIDEND ACHIEVER STATUS:
Rank: 170   10-Year Growth Rate: 8.30%
Total Years of Dividend Growth: 13

RECENT DEVELOPMENTS: For the twelve months ended 12/31/01, net income totaled $22.3 million, essentially unchanged compared with the same period a year earlier. Net interest income slipped 1.3% to $83.1 million from $84.2 million the previous year. Total interest income was $176.8 million, up 0.6% versus $175.7 million the year before. Noninterest income increased 21.8% to $23.8 million from $19.5 million a year earlier. Noninterest expense grew 4.9% to $64.9 million from $61.9 million in 2000. Total interest expense climbed 2.4% to $93.7 million from $91.5 million in the prior year. Provision for loan losses amounted to $9.2 million, the same as a year earlier. Separately, on 1/3/02, the Company announced it has completed its acquisition of Citizens National Bank & Trust Company of Hazard, Kentucky. The acquisition increases CTBI's assets by $136.0 million.

BUSINESS

COMMUNITY TRUST BANCORP, INC. is a bank holding company with assets of $2.50 billion as of 12/31/01 that currently owns all the capital stock of two commercial banks and one trust company, serving small and mid-sized communities in eastern, central, south central Kentucky, and southern West Virginia. The commercial banks are Community Trust Bank, NA, Pikeville and Citizens National Bank & Trust, Hazard. The trust company, Trust Company of Kentucky, NA, Lexington, purchased the trust operations of its subsidiary banks and has additional offices in Pikeville, Ashland, Middlesboro and Versailles, Kentucky. On 12/29/00, the Company merged its thrift subsidiary, Community Trust Bank, FSB, into the Bank. On 1/26/01, Community Trust Bank, NA, acquired the deposits, loans, and fixed assets of The Bank of Mt. Vernon, Inc.

ANNUAL FINANCIAL DATA

	12/31/01	12/31/00	12/31/99	12/31/98	12/31/97	12/31/96	12/31/95
Earnings Per Share	1.93	1.87	1.97	1.25	①1.44	1.55	0.91
Tang. Book Val. Per Share	11.12	10.73	10.23	9.24	11.52	10.28	9.36
Dividends Per Share	0.80	0.74	0.71	0.66	0.60	0.54	0.48
Dividend Payout %	41.4	39.8	36.1	52.9	41.6	34.9	52.8
INCOME STATEMENT (IN MILLIONS):							
Total Interest Income	176.8	175.7	163.5	160.6	150.6	144.4	131.0
Total Interest Expense	93.7	91.5	79.7	84.0	74.1	69.1	65.0
Net Interest Income	83.1	84.2	83.8	76.6	76.5	75.4	66.0
Provision for Loan Losses	9.2	9.2	9.1	16.0	11.2	7.3	5.9
Non-Interest Income	23.8	19.5	21.0	19.5	18.4	14.4	11.1
Non-Interest Expense	64.9	61.9	64.4	62.2	59.9	55.2	55.9
Income Before Taxes	32.8	32.6	31.3	17.9	23.9	27.3	15.4
Net Income	22.3	22.3	21.8	14.0	①16.0	18.8	10.8
Average Shs. Outstg. (000)	11,568	11,955	11,089	11,069	11,132	12,163	11,926
BALANCE SHEET (IN MILLIONS):							
Cash & Due from Banks	96.2	72.7	99.8	98.1	61.4	63.9	67.5
Securities Avail. for Sale	367.2	236.6	270.3	301.1	165.6	230.0	279.7
Total Loans & Leases	1,711.1	1,694.5	1,619.5	1,502.4	1,428.4	1,309.6	1,115.1
Allowance for Credit Losses	23.6	25.9	25.1	26.1	20.5	18.8	16.1
Net Loans & Leases	1,687.4	1,668.6	1,594.4	1,476.3	1,408.0	1,290.8	1,099.0
Total Assets	2,503.9	2,262.0	2,176.1	2,248.0	1,852.7	1,840.0	1,730.2
Total Deposits	2,155.8	1,943.9	1,877.3	1,921.1	1,465.0	1,480.8	1,467.4
Long-Term Obligations	23.0	61.4	70.6	105.2	155.3	130.1	91.5
Total Liabilities	2,312.3	2,080.1	2,003.7	2,083.2	1,694.6	1,695.3	1,596.4
Net Stockholders' Equity	191.6	181.9	172.4	164.8	158.0	144.8	133.8
Year-end Shs. Outstg. (000)	11,426	11,701	11,043	11,072	12,176	12,151	12,144
STATISTICAL RECORD:							
Return on Equity %	11.6	12.3	12.7	8.5	10.1	13.0	8.1
Return on Assets %	0.9	1.0	1.0	0.6	0.9	1.0	0.6
Equity/Assets %	7.7	8.0	7.9	7.3	8.5	7.9	7.7
Non-Int. Exp./Tot. Inc. %	60.8	59.7	61.4	64.7	63.1	61.5	72.4
Price Range	28.50-15.00	19.77-13.13	22.16-17.95	27.84-17.56	26.34-18.41	19.53-13.90	19.16-14.28
P/E Ratio	14.8-7.8	10.6-7.0	11.2-9.1	22.3-14.0	18.3-12.8	12.6-9.0	21.1-15.7
Average Yield %	3.7	4.5	3.5	2.9	2.7	3.2	2.9

Statistics are as originally reported. Adj. for 10% stk. splits, 4/15/00, 4/15/99 & 4/15/97.
① Bef. extraord. gain of $3.1 mill.

OFFICERS:
B. Coleman, Chmn.
J. R. Hale, Pres., C.E.O.
M. Gooch, Exec. V.P., Treas.
W. Hickman, III, Exec. V.P., Sec.

INVESTOR CONTACT: Investor Relations, (606) 432-1414

PRINCIPAL OFFICE: 346 North Mayo Trail, Pikeville, KY 41501

TELEPHONE NUMBER: (606) 432-1414
FAX: (606) 437-3345
WEB: www.ctbi.com

NO. OF EMPLOYEES: 883

SHAREHOLDERS: 1,668 (approx.)

ANNUAL MEETING: In Apr.

INCORPORATED: KY, Aug., 1980

INSTITUTIONAL HOLDINGS:
No. of Institutions: 46
Shares Held: 2,656,089
% Held: 23.3

INDUSTRY: National commercial banks (SIC: 6021)

TRANSFER AGENT(S): Community Trust Bank, NA, Versailles, KY

NASDAQ SYMBOL CBSS
Rec. Pr. 30.87 (3/31/02)

COMPASS BANCSHARES INC.

YIELD 3.2%
P/E RATIO 14.6

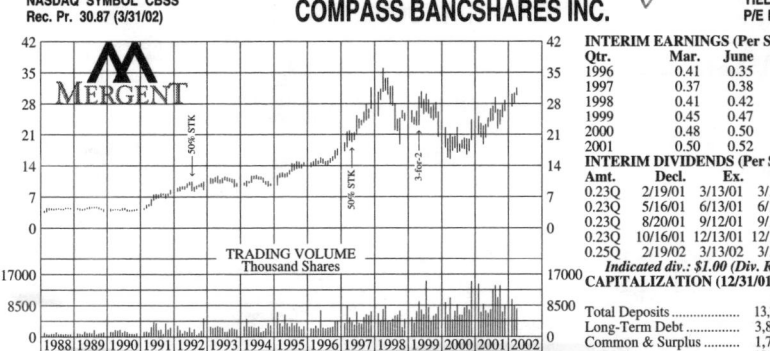

TRADING VOLUME
Thousand Shares

*7 YEAR PRICE SCORE 104.5   *12 MONTH PRICE SCORE 115.3
*NYSE COMPOSITE INDEX=100

INTERIM EARNINGS (Per Share):

Qtr.	Mar.	June	Sept.	Dec.
1996	0.41	0.35	0.29	0.37
1997	0.37	0.38	0.39	0.42
1998	0.41	0.42	0.43	0.34
1999	0.45	0.47	0.48	0.48
2000	0.48	0.50	0.52	0.50
2001	0.50	0.52	0.53	0.56

INTERIM DIVIDENDS (Per Share):

Amt.	Decl.	Ex.	Rec.	Pay.
0.23Q	2/19/01	3/13/01	3/15/01	4/02/01
0.23Q	5/16/01	6/13/01	6/15/01	7/02/01
0.23Q	8/20/01	9/12/01	9/14/01	10/01/01
0.23Q	10/16/01	12/13/01	12/17/01	1/02/02
0.25Q	2/19/02	3/13/02	3/15/02	4/01/02

Indicated div.: $1.00 (Div. Reinv. Plan)

CAPITALIZATION (12/31/01):

	($000)	(%)
Total Deposits	13,735,245	71.2
Long-Term Debt	3,837,450	19.9
Common & Surplus	1,715,641	8.9
Total	19,288,336	100.0

DIVIDEND ACHIEVER STATUS:

Rank: 83   10-Year Growth Rate: 13.44%
Total Years of Dividend Growth: 20

RECENT DEVELOPMENTS: For the year ended 12/31/01, net income increased 11.9% to $270.4 million from $241.6 million in the previous year. Results for 2000 included a gain of $16.7 million from branch sales. Net interest income advanced 14.9% to $825.9 million. Provision for loan losses grew 62.0% to $106.2 million. Total non-interest income improved 30.5% to $376.4 million, while total non-interest expense advanced 14.4% to $685.8 million.

Non-interest bearing deposits grew 13.0% year over year and accounted for 25.0% of total deposits. For the quarter ended 12/31/01, net income grew 32.6% to $72.2 million, while net interest income rose 24.3% to $227.7 million. Separately, on 1/9/02, CBSS acquired Horizons Insurance Group, Inc., a Dallas, Texas-based full-line general insurance brokerage firm with revenues of more than $4.0 million.

BUSINESS

COMPASS BANCSHARES INC. (formerly Central Bancshares of the South, Inc.) is a bank holding company headquartered in Birmingham, Alabama, with total assets of $22.77 billion as of 12/31/01. Principal subsidiaries include Compass Bank; Compass Banks of Texas, Inc., a Delaware bank holding company, which owns Compass Bank, a Texas state bank headquartered in Houston, Texas; Central Bank of the South, an Alabama banking corporation headquartered in Anniston, Alabama; Arizona Bank; and Western Bancshares, Inc., in Albuquerque, New Mexico. In fiscal 2000, the Company expanded into New Mexico and Colorado with the acquisitions of Albuquerque-based Western Bancshares, Inc. and Denver-based MegaBank Financial Corp., Inc. In January 2001, the Company expanded into Nebraska with the acquisition of FirsTier Corporation. As of 12/31/01, Compass Bank conducted general commercial banking and trust services at 341 full-service bank offices, including 118 in Texas, 87 in Alabama, 60 in Arizona, 41 in Florida, 24 in Colorado, nine in New Mexico and two in Nebraska.

ANNUAL FINANCIAL DATA

	12/31/01	12/31/00	12/31/99	12/31/98	12/31/97	12/31/96	12/31/95
Earnings Per Share	2.11	① 2.00	① 1.88	1.57	1.56	1.42	1.28
Tang. Book Val. Per Share	13.53	12.24	10.52	10.30	9.70	8.81	8.23
Dividends Per Share	0.91	0.86	0.78	0.68	0.62	0.55	0.48
Dividend Payout %	43.1	43.0	41.2	43.6	39.5	38.9	37.1
INCOME STATEMENT (IN MILLIONS):							
Total Interest Income	1,517.7	1,432.8	1,247.6	1,134.5	949.0	820.4	726.9
Total Interest Expense	691.9	752.0	608.4	555.2	473.9	417.9	377.3
Net Interest Income	825.9	680.8	639.2	579.4	475.2	402.4	349.7
Provision for Loan Losses	106.2	53.5	31.1	38.4	22.4	17.6	10.2
Non-Interest Income	376.4	298.9	241.1	222.5	181.5	154.7	122.1
Non-Interest Expense	685.8	569.6	517.9	491.0	395.7	337.5	290.0
Income Before Taxes	410.2	356.6	331.2	272.4	238.5	202.1	171.5
Net Income	270.4	241.6	① 217.0	180.9	155.6	128.9	110.3
Average Shs. Outstg. (000)	129,138	120,454	114,441	113,745	99,771	90,835	86,265
BALANCE SHEET (IN MILLIONS):							
Cash & Due from Banks	716.0	719.5	684.5	831.6	693.7	670.4	530.9
Securities Avail. for Sale	6,585.0	5,049.5	4,243.8	3,773.4	2,422.2	2,132.6	2,119.7
Total Loans & Leases	15,926.4	11,494.5	10,789.5	10,103.2	8,677.0	7,459.8	6,361.4
Allowance for Credit Losses	2,410.5	153.6	143.6	138.6	127.4	121.2	108.6
Net Loans & Leases	13,515.9	11,340.9	10,645.8	9,964.6	8,549.5	7,338.7	6,252.7
Total Assets	23,015.0	19,992.2	18,150.8	17,288.9	13,459.6	11,814.2	10,262.2
Total Deposits	13,735.2	14,033.2	12,808.9	12,013.4	9,632.5	9,220.6	7,729.1
Long-Term Obligations	3,837.5	2,529.3	2,564.3	2,046.0	1,387.1	701.5	584.9
Total Liabilities	21,299.4	18,511.8	16,954.5	16,092.8	12,499.5	11,011.2	9,555.6
Net Stockholders' Equity	1,715.6	1,480.5	1,196.2	1,196.1	960.0	803.1	706.7
Year-end Shs. Outstg. (000)	126,801	120,972	113,709	113,351	98,987	91,181	85,842
STATISTICAL RECORD:							
Return on Equity %	15.8	16.3	18.1	15.1	16.2	16.1	15.6
Return on Assets %	1.2	1.2	1.2	1.0	1.2	1.1	1.1
Equity/Assets %	7.5	7.4	6.6	6.9	7.1	6.8	6.9
Non-Int. Exp./Tot. Inc. %	57.0	58.1	58.8	61.2	60.3	60.6	61.5
Price Range	29.46-18.75	24.44-15.50	30.75-20.50	36.00-18.75	31.67-17.22	17.83-13.67	15.00-9.56
P/E Ratio	14.0-8.9	12.2-7.7	16.4-10.9	23.0-12.0	20.3-11.0	12.6-9.6	11.7-7.5
Average Yield %	3.8	4.3	3.0	2.5	2.5	3.5	3.9

Statistics are as originally reported. Adj. for stk. splits: 3-for-2, 4/2/99 & 4/2/97. ① Incl. merger-related chrg. $8.9 mill., 12/00; $5.1 mill., 12/99.

NYSE SYMBOL CAG
Rec. Pr. 24.25 (3/31/02)

CONAGRA FOODS, INC.

YIELD 3.9%
P/E RATIO 18.1

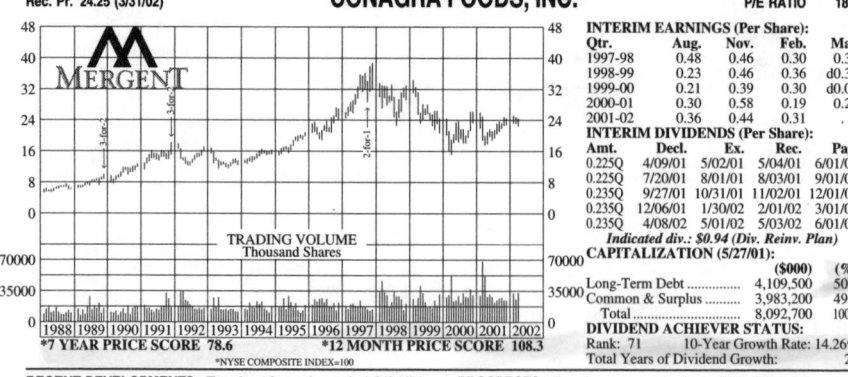

7 YEAR PRICE SCORE 78.6   **12 MONTH PRICE SCORE 108.3**
*NYSE COMPOSITE INDEX=100

INTERIM EARNINGS (Per Share):

Qtr.	Aug.	Nov.	Feb.	May
1997-98	0.48	0.46	0.30	0.36
1998-99	0.23	0.46	0.36	d0.30
1999-00	0.21	0.39	0.30	d0.04
2000-01	0.30	0.58	0.19	0.23
2001-02	0.36	0.44	0.31	...

INTERIM DIVIDENDS (Per Share):

Amt.	Decl.	Ex.	Rec.	Pay.
0.225Q	4/09/01	5/02/01	5/04/01	6/01/01
0.225Q	7/20/01	8/01/01	8/03/01	9/01/01
0.235Q	9/27/01	10/31/01	11/02/01	12/01/01
0.235Q	12/06/01	1/30/02	2/01/02	3/01/02
0.235Q	4/08/02	5/01/02	5/03/02	6/01/02

Indicated div.: $0.94 (Div. Reinv. Plan)

CAPITALIZATION (5/27/01):

	($000)	(%)
Long-Term Debt	4,109,500	50.8
Common & Surplus	3,983,200	49.2
Total	8,092,700	100.0

DIVIDEND ACHIEVER STATUS:
Rank: 71   10-Year Growth Rate: 14.26%
Total Years of Dividend Growth: 24

RECENT DEVELOPMENTS: For the 13 weeks ended 2/24/02, net income jumped 47.5% to $170.8 million from $115.8 million a year earlier. Net sales slid 2.1% to $6.24 billion from $6.38 billion the year before. Higher sales in the Packaged Foods and Agricultural Products segments were more than offset by lower sales in the Meat Processing and Food Ingredients segments. Operating profit grew 30.1% to $462.9 million from $355.7 million in the previous year. Comparisons were made with restated prior-year figures.

PROSPECTS: Earnings growth is being driven by new product introductions, product improvements and marketing investments made in prior periods. In addition, operating profitability is benefiting from higher prices and increased operating efficiencies stemming from plant closings. However, sales are being negatively affected by volume changes stemming from the Company's efforts to improve product and customer mix.

BUSINESS

CONAGRA FOODS, INC. (formerly ConAgra, Inc.) operates in four industry segments: Packaged Foods (43.6% of sales and 75.6% of operating profit as of 2/24/02) includes branded shelf-stable, frozen and refrigerated products for retail and foodservice markets. Meat Processing (35.6%, 13.2%) includes the Company's fresh beef, pork and poultry operations. Food Ingredients (6.0%, 8.6%) includes spices, grain milling and ingredients for food products. Agricultural Products (14.8%, 2.6%) includes CAG's crop inputs distribution business and its agricultural merchandising operations. The Company's major brands include: HEALTHY CHOICE, BANQUET, CHEF BOYARDEE, WESSON, HUNT'S, ORVILLE REDENBACHER'S, SLIM JIM, PETER PAN, PARKAY, VAN CAMP'S, PAM, SWISS MISS, EGG BEATERS, REDDI-WIP, ACT II, FLEISCHMANN'S, BUTTERBALL, ARMOUR and BUMBLE BEE.

ANNUAL FINANCIAL DATA

	5/27/01	5/28/00	5/30/99	5/31/98	5/25/97	5/26/96	5/28/95
Earnings Per Share	① 1.33	② 0.86	② 0.75	① 1.36	1.34	② 0.40	1.03
Cash Flow Per Share	2.48	1.98	1.80	2.33	2.24	1.28	1.85
Tang. Book Val. Per Share	...	1.22	1.02	0.85	0.08	...	0.15
Dividends Per Share	0.84	0.74	0.65	0.56	0.49	0.43	0.37
Dividend Payout %	62.8	85.9	86.3	41.5	36.8	108.8	36.3
INCOME STATEMENT (IN MILLIONS):							
Total Revenues	27,194.2	25,385.8	24,594.3	23,840.5	24,002.1	24,821.6	24,108.9
Costs & Expenses	25,073.9	23,557.6	22,654.8	22,073.8	22,293.4	23,192.4	22,632.5
Depreciation & Amort.	592.9	536.5	499.8	446.3	413.8	407.9	375.8
Operating Income	1,527.4	1,291.7	1,439.7	1,320.4	1,294.9	1,221.3	1,100.6
Net Interest Inc./(Exp.)	d423.3	d303.4	d316.6	d299.3	d277.2	d304.9	d278.1
Income Before Income Taxes	1,104.1	666.1	682.3	1,021.1	1,017.5	408.6	825.9
Income Taxes	421.6	253.1	323.9	393.1	402.7	219.7	330.3
Equity Earnings/Minority Int.	...	...	...	...	...	...	3.4
Net Income	① 682.5	② 413.0	② 358.4	① 628.0	615.0	② 188.9	495.6
Cash Flow	1,275.4	949.5	858.2	1,074.3	1,028.8	588.2	847.4
Average Shs. Outstg. (000)	514,300	478,600	476,700	461,300	459,000	459,000	458,000
BALANCE SHEET (IN MILLIONS):							
Cash & Cash Equivalents	198.1	157.6	62.8	95.2	105.8	113.7	60.0
Total Current Assets	7,362.6	5,966.5	5,656.1	5,487.4	5,205.0	5,566.9	5,140.2
Net Property	3,884.7	3,584.0	3,614.2	3,395.8	3,242.5	2,820.5	2,796.0
Total Assets	16,480.8	12,295.8	12,146.1	11,702.8	11,277.1	11,196.6	10,801.0
Total Current Liabilities	6,935.6	5,489.2	5,386.4	5,070.2	4,989.6	5,193.7	3,964.9
Long-Term Obligations	4,109.5	2,566.8	2,543.1	2,487.4	2,355.7	2,262.9	2,520.0
Net Stockholders' Equity	3,983.2	2,964.1	2,908.8	2,778.9	2,471.7	2,255.5	2,495.4
Net Working Capital	427.0	477.3	269.7	417.2	215.4	373.2	1,175.3
Year-end Shs. Outstg. (000)	537,067	492,212	488,173	459,076	476,126	486,312	491,394
STATISTICAL RECORD:							
Operating Profit Margin %	5.6	5.1	5.9	5.5	5.4	4.9	4.6
Net Profit Margin %	2.5	1.6	1.5	2.6	2.6	0.8	2.1
Return on Equity %	17.1	13.9	12.3	22.6	24.9	8.4	19.9
Return on Assets %	4.1	3.4	3.0	5.4	5.5	1.7	4.6
Debt/Total Assets %	24.9	20.9	20.9	21.3	20.9	20.2	23.3
Price Range	26.19-15.06	34.38-20.63	33.63-22.56	38.75-24.50	27.38-18.81	20.88-14.88	16.56-12.75
P/E Ratio	19.7-11.3	40.0-24.0	44.8-30.1	28.5-18.0	20.4-14.0	52.8-37.6	16.1-12.4
Average Yield %	4.1	2.7	2.3	1.8	2.1	2.4	2.6

Statistics are as originally reported. Adj. for 2-for-1 stk. split, 10/97. ① Bef. $43.9 mil acctg. chg., 2001; $14.8 mil, 1998. ② Incl. $621.4 mil pre-tax, non-recur. chg., 2000; $337.0 mil after-tax, non-recur. chg., 1999; & $356.3 mil after-tax, non-recur. chg., 1996.

OFFICERS:
B. C. Rohde, Chmn., Pres., C.E.O.
J. P. O'Donnell, Exec. V.P., C.F.O., Sec.
K. W. Gerhardt, Sr. V.P., Chief Info. Off.

INVESTOR CONTACT: Shareholder Services, (800) 214-0349

PRINCIPAL OFFICE: One ConAgra Drive, Omaha, NE 68102-5001

TELEPHONE NUMBER: (402) 595-4000
FAX: (402) 595-4707
WEB: www.conagra.com
NO. OF EMPLOYEES: 89,000 (approx.)
SHAREHOLDERS: 34,000 (record); 190,000 (approx. beneficial)
ANNUAL MEETING: In Sept.
INCORPORATED: NE, Sept., 1919; reincorp., DE, Dec., 1975

INSTITUTIONAL HOLDINGS:
No. of Institutions: 432
Shares Held: 320,307,640
% Held: 59.6

INDUSTRY: Meat packing plants (SIC: 2011)

TRANSFER AGENT(S): Wells Fargo Shareowner Services, St. Paul, MN

CONNECTICUT WATER SERVICE, INC.

YIELD	3.0%
P/E RATIO	22.6

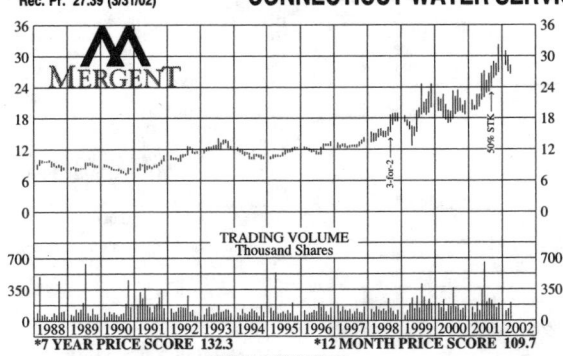

TRADING VOLUME
Thousand Shares

*7 YEAR PRICE SCORE 132.3 *12 MONTH PRICE SCORE 109.7
*NYSE COMPOSITE INDEX=100

INTERIM EARNINGS (Per Share):

Qtr.	Mar.	June	Sept.	Dec.
1997	0.21	0.17	0.39	0.22
1998	0.21	0.21	0.38	0.22
1999	0.21	0.25	0.37	0.20
2000	0.21	0.25	0.37	0.25
2001	0.30	0.37	0.38	0.16

INTERIM DIVIDENDS (Per Share):

Amt.	Decl.	Ex.	Rec.	Pay.
0.30Q	5/09/01	5/30/01	6/01/01	6/15/01
50% STK	8/15/01	9/10/01	8/27/01	9/07/01
0.20Q	8/15/01	8/30/01	9/04/01	9/17/01
0.20Q	11/14/01	11/29/01	12/03/01	12/17/01
0.20Q	1/09/02	2/27/02	3/01/02	3/15/02

Indicated div.: $0.81 (Div. Reinv. Plan)

CAPITALIZATION (12/31/01):

	($000)	(%)
Long-Term Debt	63,953	39.5
Deferred Income Tax	27,125	16.8
Common & Surplus	70,783	43.7
Total	161,861	100.0

DIVIDEND ACHIEVER STATUS:
Rank: 282   10-Year Growth Rate: 1.24%
Total Years of Dividend Growth: 26

RECENT DEVELOPMENTS: For the twelve months ended 12/31/01, net income grew 6.9% to $8.4 million from $7.9 million in 2000. The improvement in earnings was primarily attributed to greater tax benefits, higher revenues from increased customer water consumption and increased non-water sales earnings. Results for 2001 and 2000 included gain on property transactions of $1.1 million and $532,000 and merger costs of $352,000 and $408,000, respectively. Operating revenues increased 3.2% to $45.4 million. Com-

parisons were made with restated 2000 results. On 2/26/02, the Company announced that it signed a definitive agreement with Unionville Water Company to combine their respective water utility operations in a stock-for-stock transaction valued at approximately $6.3 million. Unionville Water Company serves over 5,400 customers, or a population of more than 14,000 people, and produces annual revenues of approximately $2.4 million.

BUSINESS

CONNECTICUT WATER SERVICE, INC. is the parent company of three regulated water companies, which supply water to customers for residential, commercial, industrial and municipal purposes in 40 towns in Connecticut and Massachusetts. The Company and its subsidiaries represent the largest domestic investor-owned water system in the state of Connecticut in terms of operating revenues and utility plant investment. The area served has an estimated population of 290,000. Water supply sources vary among the regions, but from the systems as a whole, about 45.0% of the total dependable yield comes from reservoirs and 55.0% from wells. The remainder comes from interconnections with other systems.

ANNUAL FINANCIAL DATA

	12/31/01	12/31/00	12/31/99	12/31/98	12/31/97	12/31/96	12/31/95
Earnings Per Share	①1.10	②1.09	②1.03	②1.02	②1.00	0.97	0.97
Cash Flow Per Share	1.75	1.72	1.65	1.60	1.53	1.48	1.46
Tang. Book Val. Per Share	9.25	8.92	8.61	8.52	8.26	8.03	7.76
Dividends Per Share	0.804	0.80	0.79	0.78	0.77	0.76	0.75
Dividend Payout %	73.1	73.2	76.6	76.2	77.2	77.6	77.4
INCOME STATEMENT (IN THOUSANDS):							
Total Revenues	45,392	41,512	42,624	37,924	38,501	38,592	39,350
Costs & Expenses	29,072	25,687	26,883	21,584	22,591	23,380	24,020
Depreciation & Amort.	5,006	4,666	4,514	3,981	3,624	3,420	3,282
Maintenance Exp.	...	...	...	2,055	1,952	1,664	2,026
Operating Income	11,314	11,159	11,227	10,304	10,334	10,128	10,022
Net Interest Inc./(Exp.)	d4,632	d4,541	d4,391	d4,177	d4,182	d3,788	d3,790
Income Taxes	...	...	57	262	215	21	33
Net Income	①8,439	②7,963	②7,494	②6,965	②6,804	6,603	6,363
Cash Flow	13,407	12,591	11,970	10,908	10,390	9,985	9,607
Average Shs. Outstg.	7,662	7,308	7,272	6,803	6,786	6,743	6,566
BALANCE SHEET (IN THOUSANDS):							
Gross Property	279,027	254,612	244,653	223,661	216,103	202,957	192,100
Accumulated Depreciation	76,697	67,641	63,311	56,335	52,346	49,059	45,564
Net Property	202,330	186,971	181,342	167,326	163,757	153,898	146,536
Total Assets	230,867	214,627	210,113	193,814	188,505	183,868	175,687
Long-Term Obligations	63,953	64,658	65,399	62,501	54,532	54,430	54,460
Net Stockholders' Equity	70,783	65,678	63,267	58,717	56,841	55,167	52,560
Year-end Shs. Outstg.	7,649	7,279	7,258	6,804	6,791	6,777	6,676
STATISTICAL RECORD:							
Operating Profit Margin %	24.9	26.9	26.3	27.2	26.8	26.2	25.5
Net Profit Margin %	18.6	19.2	17.6	18.4	17.7	17.1	16.2
Net Inc./Net Property %	4.2	4.3	4.1	4.2	4.2	4.3	4.3
Net Inc./Tot. Capital %	5.2	5.1	4.9	4.8	5.1	5.1	5.0
Return on Equity %	11.9	12.1	11.8	11.9	12.0	12.0	12.1
Accum. Depr./Gross Prop. %	27.5	26.6	25.9	25.2	24.2	24.2	23.7
Price Range	32.21-19.50	23.50-17.00	24.67-12.67	19.00-13.33	14.33-12.22	13.56-11.00	12.56-10.11
P/E Ratio	29.3-17.7	21.6-15.6	24.0-12.3	18.6-13.1	14.4-12.3	13.9-11.3	13.0-10.5
Average Yield %	3.1	3.9	4.2	4.8	5.8	6.2	6.6

Statistics are as originally reported. Adj. for stk. split: 3-for-2, 9/7/01; 3-for-2, 9/15/98 ① Incls. gain of $1.1 mill. from prop. transaction & merger costs of $352,000. ② Incls. gain on prop. trans. of $534,000, 12/00; $161,000, 12/99; $475,000, 12/98; $183,000, 12/97.

OFFICERS:
M. T. Chiaraluce, Chmn., Pres., C.E.O.
D. C. Benoit, V.P., C.F.O. Treas.
P. J. Bancroft, Asst. Treas., Contr.

INVESTOR CONTACT: David C. Benoit, (860) 669-8630 ext. 3030

PRINCIPAL OFFICE: 93 West Main Street, Clinton, CT 06413-1600

TELEPHONE NUMBER: (860) 669-8636
FAX: (860) 669-9326
WEB: www.ctwater.com

NO. OF EMPLOYEES: 181 (avg.)

SHAREHOLDERS: 5,000 (approx.)

ANNUAL MEETING: In Mar.

INCORPORATED: CT, Feb., 1956

INSTITUTIONAL HOLDINGS:
No. of Institutions: 45
Shares Held: 1,103,713
% Held: 14.5

INDUSTRY: Water supply (SIC: 4941)

TRANSFER AGENT(S): Registrar and Transfer Co., Cranford, NJ

CONSOLIDATED EDISON, INC.

7 YEAR PRICE SCORE 94.5   **12 MONTH PRICE SCORE 104.8**

*NYSE COMPOSITE INDEX=100

INTERIM EARNINGS (Per Share):

Qtr.	Mar.	June	Sept.	Dec.
1998	0.73	0.26	1.49	0.56
1999	0.76	0.30	1.50	0.57
2000	0.88	0.33	1.32	0.30
2001	0.84	0.48	1.30	0.59

INTERIM DIVIDENDS (Per Share):

Amt.	Decl.	Ex.	Rec.	Pay.
0.55Q	7/19/01	8/13/01	8/15/01	9/15/01
0.55Q	10/18/01	11/09/01	11/14/01	12/15/01
0.555Q	1/17/02	2/11/02	2/13/02	3/15/02
0.555Q	4/18/02	5/13/02	5/15/02	6/15/02

Indicated div.: $2.22 (Div. Reinv. Plan)

CAPITALIZATION (12/31/01):

	($000)	(%)
Long-Term Debt	5,501,217	40.2
Capital Lease Obligations..	41,088	0.3
Deferred Income Tax	2,235,295	16.3
Redeemable Pfd. Stock	37,050	0.2
Preferred Stock	212,563	1.6
Common & Surplus	5,666,268	41.4
Total	13,693,481	100.0

DIVIDEND ACHIEVER STATUS:
Rank: 279   10-Year Growth Rate: 1.69%
Total Years of Dividend Growth: 27

RECENT DEVELOPMENTS: For the year ended 12/31/01, net income rose 16.7% to $695.8 million compared with $596.4 million in 2000. Total operating revenues climbed 2.1% to $9.63 billion from $9.43 billion in the prior year. Electric operating revenues declined 0.7% to $6.89 billion. However, gas operating revenues increased 16.2% to $1.47 billion. Operating income increased 11.0% to $1.13 billion from $1.02 billion a year earlier.

PROSPECTS: The Company expects to incur approximately $400.0 million in costs for emergency response to the terrorist attacks on the World Trade Center on 9/11/01. These costs included temporary and permanent restoration of electric, gas and steam transmission and distribution facilities damaged in the attack. In addition, ED expects its insurers to cover about $65.0 million of the costs and will seek federal reimbursement for the remaining costs.

BUSINESS

CONSOLIDATED EDISON, INC. (formerly Consolidated Edison Company of New York) provides a range of energy-related products and services through six subsidiaries. Consolidated Edison Company of New York is a regulated utility providing electric, gas and steam service to New York City and Westchester County, New York. Orange and Rockland Utilities, Inc. is a regulated utility serving customers in southeastern New York state and adjacent sections of New Jersey and northeastern Pennsylvania. Con Edison Solutions is a retail energy services company and Con Edison Energy is a wholesale energy supply company. Con Edison Development is an infrastructure development company and Con Edison Communications is a telecommunications infrastructure company. Sales for 2001 were derived: electric, 71.5%; gas, 15.2%; steam, 5.2%; and non-utility, 8.1%.

ANNUAL FINANCIAL DATA

	12/31/01	12/31/00	12/31/99	12/31/98	12/31/97	12/31/96	12/31/95
Earnings Per Share	3.21	①2.74	3.13	3.04	2.95	2.93	2.93
Cash Flow Per Share	5.68	5.51	5.49	5.25	5.09	5.04	4.87
Tang. Book Val. Per Share	30.66	26.39	25.90	25.88	25.18	24.37	23.51
Dividends Per Share	2.20	2.18	2.14	2.12	2.10	2.08	2.04
Dividend Payout %	68.5	79.6	68.4	69.7	71.2	71.0	69.6
INCOME STATEMENT (IN MILLIONS):							
Total Revenues	9,634.0	9,431.4	7,491.3	7,093.0	7,121.3	6,959.7	6,536.9
Costs & Expenses	7,550.0	7,370.6	5,507.4	5,043.8	5,098.3	4,991.1	4,527.6
Depreciation & Amort.	526.2	586.4	526.2	518.5	502.8	496.4	455.8
Maintenance Exp.	430.3	458.0	438.0	477.4	474.8	458.6	512.1
Operating Income	1,127.5	1,016.1	1,019.8	1,053.3	1,045.4	1,013.6	1,041.4
Net Interest Inc./(Exp.)	d430.9	d407.4	d337.6	d325.8	d333.1	d323.5	d329.0
Income Taxes	cr21.9	cr10.6	cr26.9	cr2.2	cr3.2	cr1.0	1.1
Net Income	695.8	①596.4	714.2	729.7	712.8	694.1	723.9
Cash Flow	1,208.5	1,169.2	1,226.8	1,231.3	1,197.3	1,184.6	1,144.1
Average Shs. Outstg. (000)	212,920	212,186	223,442	234,308	235,082	234,977	234,930
BALANCE SHEET (IN MILLIONS):							
Gross Property	16,317.9	17,020.5	16,002.8	16,033.9	15,557.2	15,251.6	14,766.1
Accumulated Depreciation	4,473.0	5,234.7	4,733.6	4,726.2	4,392.4	4,285.7	4,037.0
Net Property	12,248.4	11,893.4	11,353.8	11,406.5	11,267.1	11,067.3	10,814.4
Total Assets	16,996.1	16,767.2	15,531.5	14,381.4	14,722.5	14,057.2	13,949.9
Long-Term Obligations	5,542.3	5,446.9	4,559.1	4,087.4	4,228.8	4,281.3	3,962.5
Net Stockholders' Equity	5,878.8	5,685.0	5,624.6	6,238.2	6,163.5	5,965.7	6,062.7
Year-end Shs. Outstg. (000)	188,916	188,816	192,452	232,833	235,490	234,994	234,956
STATISTICAL RECORD:							
Operating Profit Margin %	11.7	10.8	13.6	14.9	14.7	14.6	15.9
Net Profit Margin %	7.2	6.3	9.5	10.3	10.0	10.0	11.1
Net Inc./Net Property %	5.7	5.0	6.3	6.4	6.3	6.3	6.7
Net Inc./Tot. Capital %	5.1	4.4	5.7	5.7	5.6	5.5	5.8
Return on Equity %	11.8	10.5	12.7	11.7	11.6	11.6	11.9
Accum. Depr./Gross Prop. %	27.4	30.8	29.6	29.5	28.2	28.1	27.3
Price Range	43.37-31.44	39.50-26.19	53.44-33.56	56.13-39.06	41.50-27.00	34.75-25.88	32.25-25.50
P/E Ratio	13.5-9.8	14.4-9.6	17.1-10.7	18.5-12.8	14.1-9.2	11.9-8.8	11.0-8.7
Average Yield %	5.9	6.6	4.9	4.5	6.1	6.9	7.1

Statistics are as originally reported. ① Incl. approx. $84.9 mill. chg. fr. replacement power costs.

OFFICERS:
E. R. McGrath, Chmn., Pres., C.E.O.
J. S. Freilich, Exec. V.P., C.F.O.
J. McMahon, Sr. V.P., Gen. Couns.

INVESTOR CONTACT: Jan C. Childress, Dir. of Inv. Rel., (212) 460-6611

PRINCIPAL OFFICE: 4 Irving Place, New York, NY 10003

TELEPHONE NUMBER: (212) 460-4600
FAX: (212) 475-0734
WEB: www.conedison.com

NO. OF EMPLOYEES: 14,463

SHAREHOLDERS: 108,999

ANNUAL MEETING: In May

INCORPORATED: NY, Nov., 1884

INSTITUTIONAL HOLDINGS:
No. of Institutions: 324
Shares Held: 81,203,605
% Held: 38.3

INDUSTRY: Electric and other services combined (SIC: 4931)

TRANSFER AGENT(S): The Bank of New York, New York, NY

CORUS BANKSHARES, INC.

YIELD 1.3%
P/E RATIO 12.6

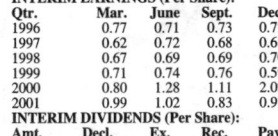

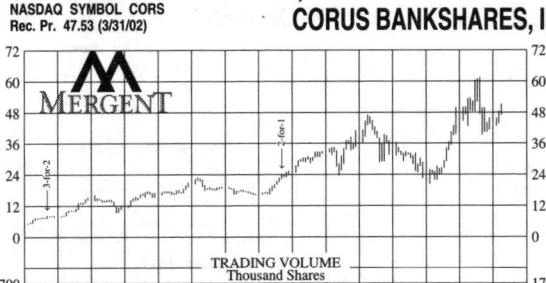

TRADING VOLUME
Thousand Shares

7 YEAR PRICE SCORE 123.2   *12 MONTH PRICE SCORE 99.6*

*NYSE COMPOSITE INDEX=100

INTERIM EARNINGS (Per Share):

Qtr.	Mar.	June	Sept.	Dec.
1996	0.77	0.71	0.73	0.72
1997	0.62	0.72	0.68	0.61
1998	0.67	0.69	0.69	0.70
1999	0.71	0.74	0.76	0.59
2000	0.80	1.28	1.11	2.02
2001	0.99	1.02	0.93	

INTERIM DIVIDENDS (Per Share):

Amt.	Decl.	Ex.	Rec.	Pay.
0.15Q	2/15/01	3/23/01	3/27/01	4/10/01
0.155Q	4/23/01	6/25/01	6/27/01	7/10/01
0.155Q	8/16/01	9/25/01	9/27/01	10/10/01
0.155Q	11/13/01	12/24/01	12/27/01	1/10/02
0.155Q	2/13/02	3/25/02	3/27/02	4/10/02

Indicated div.: $0.62

CAPITALIZATION (12/31/01):

	($000)	(%)
Total Deposits	2,121,456	80.7
Long-Term Debt	55,816	2.1
Common & Surplus	450,886	17.2
Total	2,628,158	100.0

DIVIDEND ACHIEVER STATUS:

Rank: 66   10-Year Growth Rate: 14.68%
Total Years of Dividend Growth: 15

RECENT DEVELOPMENTS: For the year ended 12/31/01, net income decreased 27.5% to $54.2 million compared with $74.8 million in the prior year. Results were negatively affected by lower interest rates. Earnings for the prior year included various nonrecurring items that resulted in a net pre-tax charge of $3.0 million. Net interest income declined 11.0% to $107.7 million from $121.1 million the year before. Total noninterest income fell 45.6% to $25.7 million from $47.3 million a year earlier. Total noninterest expense decreased 6.5% to $51.1 million from $54.7 million in 2000. Provision for loan losses amounted to nil in 2001 and 2000. Total deposits grew to $2.12 billion from $2.11 billion in the previous year. Net loans decreased 5.1% to $1.43 billion from $1.51 billion the year before.

BUSINESS

CORUS BANKSHARES, INC. is a bank holding company with total assets of $2.66 billion as of 12/31/01. CORS provides consumer and corporate banking products and services through its wholly-owned banking subsidiary, Corus Bank, N.A. The bank has eleven branches in the Chicago metropolitan area and offers general banking services such as checking, savings, money market and time deposit accounts as well as safe deposit boxes and a variety of additional services. The bank also provides clearing, depository and credit services to more than 525 currency exchanges in the Chicago area and an additional 20 in Milwaukee, Wisconsin. On 12/31/00, the Company's subsidiary, Bancorp operations Company merged with CORS.

ANNUAL FINANCIAL DATA

	12/31/01	12/31/00	12/31/99	12/31/98	12/31/97	12/31/96	12/31/95
Earnings Per Share	3.79	☐ 5.23	2.82	2.75	2.63	2.93	2.37
Tang. Book Val. Per Share	31.52	28.06	22.19	21.15	19.25	15.07	12.14
Dividends Per Share	0.61	0.59	0.57	0.55	0.52	0.45	0.34
Dividend Payout %	16.1	11.3	20.2	20.0	19.8	15.4	14.2
INCOME STATEMENT (IN MILLIONS):							
Total Interest Income	188.6	223.7	196.6	187.5	183.9	191.0	171.1
Total Interest Expense	80.9	102.6	90.4	89.3	82.7	79.6	72.6
Net Interest Income	107.7	121.1	106.1	98.2	101.3	111.3	98.5
Provision for Loan Losses	...	...	...	10.0	16.0	16.0	5.8
Non-Interest Income	25.7	47.3	18.9	25.7	26.9	22.8	14.1
Non-Interest Expense	51.1	54.7	63.1	51.9	51.7	50.2	51.6
Income Before Taxes	82.3	113.7	62.0	62.0	60.5	67.9	55.2
Net Income	54.2	☐ 74.8	40.7	40.6	39.4	43.9	35.8
Average Shs. Outstg. (000)	14,309	14,302	14,464	14,773	14,966	14,994	15,241
BALANCE SHEET (IN MILLIONS):							
Cash & Due from Banks	58.5	111.1	72.3	72.1	62.2	57.5	104.8
Securities Avail. for Sale	300.1	442.0	487.2	897.7	531.9	379.0	364.4
Total Loans & Leases	1,475.2	1,551.9	1,727.4	1,551.6	1,546.0	1,623.1	1,558.8
Allowance for Credit Losses	40.5	39.6	32.1	35.8	30.7	32.7	25.6
Net Loans & Leases	1,434.8	1,512.3	1,695.3	1,515.8	1,515.3	1,590.5	1,533.1
Total Assets	2,659.3	2,598.5	2,388.2	2,589.4	2,251.9	2,218.5	2,125.1
Total Deposits	2,121.5	2,107.6	1,964.4	2,154.7	1,863.1	1,900.7	1,898.5
Short-Term Obligations	55.8	...	...	...	...	...	...
Long-Term Obligations	...	40.0	40.0	40.0	40.0	40.0	...
Total Liabilities	2,208.4	2,196.1	2,060.4	2,271.3	1,960.3	1,982.9	1,930.4
Net Stockholders' Equity	450.9	402.4	327.8	318.1	291.6	235.6	194.7
Year-end Shs. Outstg. (000)	14,160	14,143	14,369	14,551	14,681	14,820	15,027
STATISTICAL RECORD:							
Return on Equity %	12.0	18.6	12.4	12.8	13.5	18.6	18.4
Return on Assets %	2.0	2.9	1.7	1.6	1.7	2.0	1.7
Equity/Assets %	17.0	15.5	13.7	12.3	13.0	10.6	9.2
Non-Int. Exp./Tot. Inc. %	40.7	33.6	49.9	43.7	42.0	38.4	45.3
Price Range	61.50-39.20	50.00-20.25	36.44-22.50	47.13-28.63	41.00-23.50	33.00-24.75	25.50-16.38
P/E Ratio	16.2-10.3	9.6-3.9	12.9-8.0	17.1-10.4	15.6-8.9	11.3-8.4	10.8-6.9
Average Yield %	1.2	1.7	1.9	1.5	1.6	1.6	1.6

Statistics are as originally reported. Adj. for stk. split: 2-for-1, 10/95 ☐ Incl. a $22.5 mill. gain on sale of student loans.

OFFICERS:
J. C. Glickman, Chmn.
R. J. Glickman, Pres., C.E.O.
T. H. Taylor, Exec. V.P., C.F.O.

INVESTOR CONTACT: Investor Relations,
(773) 832-3088

PRINCIPAL OFFICE: 3959 N. Lincoln Ave.,
Chicago, IL 60613-2431

TELEPHONE NUMBER: (773) 832-3088
FAX: (773) 549-0734
WEB: www.corusbank.com

NO. OF EMPLOYEES: 506

SHAREHOLDERS: 2,500 (approx.)

ANNUAL MEETING: In April

INCORPORATED: MN, 1958

INSTITUTIONAL HOLDINGS:
No. of Institutions: 86
Shares Held: 4,527,228
% Held: 32.0

INDUSTRY: State commercial banks (SIC: 6022)

TRANSFER AGENT(S): Mellon Investor Services, LLC, Ridgefield Park, NJ

COUSINS PROPERTIES INCORPORATED

YIELD 5.7%
P/E RATIO 18.5

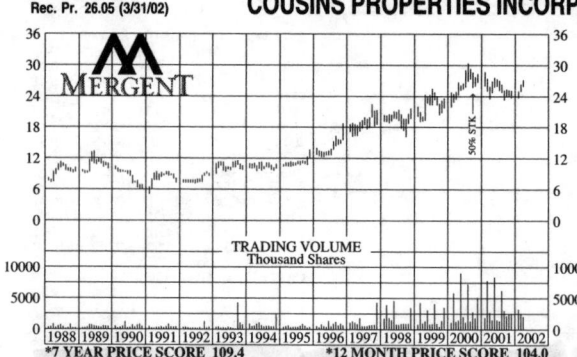

TRADING VOLUME
Thousand Shares

| 1988 | 1989 | 1990 | 1991 | 1992 | 1993 | 1994 | 1995 | 1996 | 1997 | 1998 | 1999 | 2000 | 2001 | 2002 |

*7 YEAR PRICE SCORE 109.4   ***12 MONTH PRICE SCORE 104.0**

*NYSE COMPOSITE INDEX=100

INTERIM EARNINGS (Per Share):

Qtr.	Mar.	June	Sept.	Dec.
1998	0.23	0.25	0.22	0.24
1999	0.31	1.29	0.26	0.26
2000	0.43	0.27	0.27	0.29
2001	0.62	0.25	0.27	0.27

INTERIM DIVIDENDS (Per Share):

Amt.	Decl.	Ex.	Rec.	Pay.
0.34Q	5/01/01	5/16/01	5/18/01	5/30/01
0.34Q	7/27/01	8/08/01	8/10/01	8/24/01
0.37Q	11/13/01	12/05/01	12/07/01	12/21/01
0.37Q	1/25/02	2/06/02	2/08/02	2/22/02

Indicated div.: $1.48 (Div. Reinv. Plan)

CAPITALIZATION (12/31/01):

	($000)	(%)
Long-Term Debt	585,275	55.8
Common & Surplus	462,673	44.2
Total	1,047,948	100.0

DIVIDEND ACHIEVER STATUS:
Rank: 65   10-Year Growth Rate: 14.69%
Total Years of Dividend Growth: 10

RECENT DEVELOPMENTS: For the year ended 12/31/01, net income was $70.8 million compared with income of $62.6 million, before an accounting charge of $566,000, in the prior year. Results for 2001 and 2000 included gains of $23.5 million and $11.9 million, respectively. Total revenues increased 22.9% to $177.7 million from $144.6 million the year before. Rental property revenues advanced 27.6% to $145.5 million from $114.0 million in 2000.

PROSPECTS: The Company has been awarded the development manager contract from the City of Irvin, Texas to assist in the development of the $100.0 million Irving convention center. Separately, the Company announced that it has signed a 14,000 square-foot lease with Laureate Medical Group, a privately-owned internal medicine practice in Atlanta, Georgia, to move into the new Emory Crawford Long Medical Office Tower.

BUSINESS

COUSINS PROPERTIES INCORPORATED is a fully-integrated, self-administered equity real estate investment trust. The Company is engaged in the acquisition, financing, development, management and leasing of properties. The Company's portfolio consists of interests in 13.3 million square feet of office space, 3.1 million square feet of retail space and 900,000 square feet of medical office space, and more than 300 acres of strategically located land for future commercial development. CUZ also provides leasing and management services to third-party investors. Its client-services portfolio comprises 7.8 million square feet of Class A office space. In the Dallas area, the Company leases and manages The Towers at Williams Square, 1700 Pacific, Millennium Center, Spectrum Center, Beal Bank, 6565 MacArthur at Sierra, 122 West Carpenter and O'Connor Ridge. CUZ serves as development manager for Las Colinas, planning managing and marketing this prestigious 12,000 acre master-planned business and residential community, and represents more than 1,400 acres of land on behalf of its largest landowner.

ANNUAL FINANCIAL DATA

	12/31/01	12/31/00	12/31/99	12/31/98	12/31/97	12/31/96	12/31/95
Earnings Per Share	③ 1.41	② 1.26	① 2.12	① 0.94	① 0.84	① 0.96	① 0.63
Tang. Book Val. Per Share	9.36	9.24	9.07	7.94	7.85	6.90	6.56
Dividends Per Share	1.05	0.83	0.75	0.66	0.57	0.50	0.44
Dividend Payout %	74.5	65.6	35.2	70.4	68.2	51.8	70.2
INCOME STATEMENT (IN MILLIONS):							
Rental Income	145.5	114.0	62.5	67.7	62.3	33.1	19.3
Total Income	177.7	144.6	97.8	98.3	86.0	58.5	41.0
Costs & Expenses	77.2	64.1	49.9	47.5	40.8	33.9	23.0
Depreciation	44.7	32.8	16.9	15.2	14.0	7.2	4.5
Interest Expense	27.6	13.6	0.6	11.6	14.1	6.5	0.7
Income Before Income Taxes	23.9	30.1	28.1	22.8	14.3	9.3	11.1
Income Taxes	cr0.6	cr1.1	2.4	cr0.1	cr1.5	cr1.7	0.7
Equity Earnings/Minority Int.	46.4	31.4	78.4	22.4	21.4	30.0	16.0
Net Income	③ 70.8	② 62.6	① 104.1	① 45.3	① 37.3	① 41.0	① 26.3
Average Shs. Outstg. (000)	50,280	49,731	49,031	48,060	44,540	42,780	41,975
BALANCE SHEET (IN MILLIONS):							
Cash & Cash Equivalents	10.6	1.7	1.5	1.3	32.7	1.6	1.6
Total Real Estate Investments	939.8	884.4	732.9	438.7	416.0	357.3	219.9
Total Assets	1,077.5	973.3	785.7	752.9	617.7	556.6	418.0
Long-Term Obligations	585.3	485.1	312.3	198.9	226.3	231.8	113.4
Total Liabilities	614.8	518.8	347.9	373.0	247.1	257.5	140.3
Net Stockholders' Equity	462.7	454.5	437.7	379.9	370.7	299.2	277.7
Year-end Shs. Outstg. (000)	49,425	49,211	48,262	47,831	47,208	43,380	42,335
STATISTICAL RECORD:							
Net Inc.+Depr./Assets %	10.7	9.8	15.4	8.0	8.3	8.7	7.4
Return on Equity %	15.3	13.8	23.8	11.9	10.1	13.7	9.5
Return on Assets %	6.6	6.4	13.2	6.0	6.0	7.4	6.3
Price Range	28.75-23.30	30.42-21.92	25.50-19.04	21.71-16.13	22.50-16.17	18.75-12.25	13.67-10.38
P/E Ratio	20.4-16.5	24.1-17.4	12.0-9.0	23.1-17.2	26.8-19.2	19.5-12.8	21.8-16.5
Average Yield %	4.0	3.2	3.4	3.5	3.0	3.2	3.7

Statistics are as originally reported. Adj. for 3-for-2 stk. split, 10/00. ① Incl. gains on sales of properties of $6.4 mill., 1994; $1.9 mill., 1995; $12.8 mill., 1996; $6.0 mill., 1997; $3.9 mill., 1998; $58.8 mill., 1999. ② Bef. acctg. chng. chrg. of $566,000; incl. gain of $11.9 mill. on sale of prop. ③ Incl. gain of $23.5 mill. on the sale of prop.

OFFICERS:
T. G. Cousins, Chmn.
T. D. Bell, Jr., Pres., C.E.O.
T. G. Charlesworth, Sr. V.P., Sec., Gen. Couns.

INVESTOR CONTACT: Carl Y. Dickson, Dir., Inv. Rel., (770) 857-2391

PRINCIPAL OFFICE: 2500 Windy Ridge Pkwy., Suite 1600, Atlanta, GA 30339-5683

TELEPHONE NUMBER: (770) 955-2200
FAX: (770) 857-2360
WEB: www.cousinsproperties.com

NO. OF EMPLOYEES: 431 (avg.)

SHAREHOLDERS: 1,114

ANNUAL MEETING: In May

INCORPORATED: GA, Nov., 1961; reincorp., GA, June, 1972

INSTITUTIONAL HOLDINGS:
No. of Institutions: 113
Shares Held: 19,915,176
% Held: 39.9

INDUSTRY: Real estate investment trusts (SIC: 6798)

TRANSFER AGENT(S): First Union National Bank, Charlotte, NC

CRAWFORD & COMPANY

YIELD	4.1%
P/E RATIO	22.2

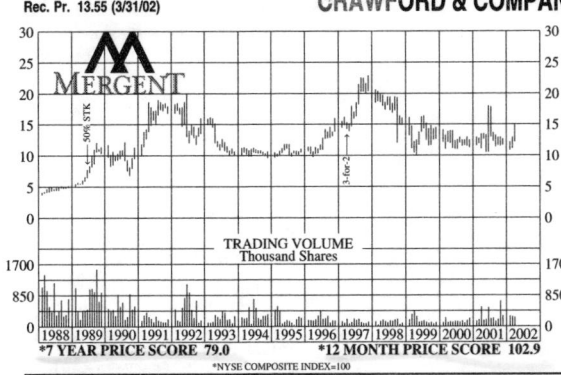

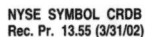

TRADING VOLUME
Thousand Shares

1988|1989|1990|1991|1992|1993|1994|1995|1996|1997|1998|1999|2000|2001|2002

*7 YEAR PRICE SCORE 79.0   ***12 MONTH PRICE SCORE 102.9**
*NYSE COMPOSITE INDEX=100

INTERIM EARNINGS (Per Share):

Qtr.	Mar.	June	Sept.	Dec.
1997	0.12	0.27	0.29	0.25
1998	0.23	0.24	d0.04	0.21
1999	0.20	0.21	0.16	0.21
2000	0.21	0.22	0.20	d0.11
2001	0.17	0.18	0.14	0.12

INTERIM DIVIDENDS (Per Share):

Amt.	Decl.	Ex.	Rec.	Pay.
0.14Q	4/24/01	5/02/01	5/04/01	4/18/01
0.14Q	7/24/01	8/03/01	8/07/01	8/17/01
0.14Q	10/30/01	11/07/01	11/09/01	11/20/01
0.14Q	1/29/02	2/07/02	2/11/02	2/22/02

Indicated div.: $0.56

CAPITALIZATION (12/31/01):

	($000)	(%)
Long-Term Debt	36,378	16.2
Common & Surplus	188,300	83.8
Total	224,678	100.0

DIVIDEND ACHIEVER STATUS:
Rank: 153   10-Year Growth Rate: 9.15%
Total Years of Dividend Growth: 21

RECENT DEVELOPMENTS: For the year ended 12/31/01, net income grew 16.2% to $29.4 million from $25.3 million in the previous year. Earnings for 2000 included a software write-down charge of $16.7 million. Revenues increased 1.9% to $725.5 million from $712.2 million in the prior year. Domestic revenues improved 3.0% to $534.7 million, while international revenues declined 1.1% to $190.9 million.

PROSPECTS: Looking ahead, earnings should benefit from the award of several new programs with self-insured clients and the favorable premium rate environment in the domestic insurance market. Meanwhile, CRD expects its international operations will continue to grow after experiencing a return to growth in the most recent quarter due to strong growth in its Canadian operations and weakening of the U.S. dollar compared with third quarter 2001 levels.

BUSINESS

CRAWFORD & COMPANY is a diversified services firm organized into three business units: Risk Management Services (RMS), Healthcare Management (HCM) and Claims Services. RMS primarily fulfills corporate market needs by providing risk management and claims adjusting services including risk management information systems and services through the subsidiary, Crawford Risk Sciences Group. HCM offers a full range of managed care services for both the corporate and insurance markets. Claims Service is responsible for handling claims support to the insurance industry through the complete investigation, evaluation, disposition and management of losses. As of 12/31/01, the Company operated over 700 offices in 65 countries. In 1999, the Company acquired the Garden City Group, which manages class action litigation settlements.

ANNUAL FINANCIAL DATA

	12/31/01	12/31/00	12/31/99	12/31/98	12/31/97	12/31/96	12/31/95
Earnings Per Share	0.61	① 0.52	0.78	① 0.54	① 0.93	0.84	0.69
Cash Flow Per Share	1.03	0.93	1.11	0.83	1.23	1.15	1.01
Tang. Book Val. Per Share	2.10	2.79	3.35	3.46	3.30	3.38	3.19
Dividends Per Share	0.56	0.55	0.52	0.50	0.44	0.39	0.36
Dividend Payout %	91.8	105.7	66.7	92.6	47.3	46.0	52.2
INCOME STATEMENT (IN THOUSANDS):							
Total Revenues	725,539	712,174	701,926	667,271	692,322	633,625	607,577
Costs & Expenses	652,333	646,399	621,154	609,790	604,715	545,939	530,332
Depreciation & Amort.	20,626	20,149	17,028	14,798	15,423	15,716	16,865
Operating Income	52,580	45,626	63,744	42,683	72,184	71,970	60,380
Net Interest Inc./(Exp.)	d4,779	d4,476	...	...	...	...	...
Income Before Income Taxes	47,801	41,150	63,744	42,683	72,184	71,970	60,380
Income Taxes	18,356	15,802	24,480	16,395	27,697	29,160	24,360
Equity Earnings/Minority Int.	...	...	...	1,177	2,502	...	...
Net Income	29,445	① 25,348	39,264	① 27,465	① 46,989	42,810	36,020
Cash Flow	50,071	45,497	56,292	42,263	62,412	58,526	52,885
Average Shs. Outstg.	48,559	48,933	50,498	50,938	50,687	51,032	52,277
BALANCE SHEET (IN THOUSANDS):							
Cash & Cash Equivalents	21,966	22,136	17,716	8,423	55,380	55,485	46,398
Total Current Assets	261,635	263,725	267,836	251,146	278,814	246,896	234,380
Net Property	39,264	42,797	48,891	42,943	39,192	33,163	36,448
Total Assets	431,415	458,351	474,028	433,269	428,866	378,085	366,983
Total Current Liabilities	156,307	157,639	157,990	140,574	124,569	110,652	95,054
Long-Term Obligations	36,378	36,662	16,053	1,854	731	376	9,412
Net Stockholders' Equity	188,300	217,767	250,279	240,051	215,005	221,536	220,860
Net Working Capital	105,328	106,086	109,846	110,572	154,245	136,244	139,326
Year-end Shs. Outstg.	48,540	48,451	50,718	50,903	49,393	50,111	51,792
STATISTICAL RECORD:							
Operating Profit Margin %	7.2	6.4	9.1	6.4	10.4	11.4	9.9
Net Profit Margin %	4.1	3.6	5.6	4.1	6.8	6.8	5.9
Return on Equity %	15.6	11.6	15.7	11.4	21.9	19.3	16.3
Return on Assets %	6.8	5.5	8.3	6.3	11.0	11.3	9.8
Debt/Total Assets %	8.4	8.0	3.4	0.4	0.2	0.1	2.6
Price Range	18.00-10.50	14.13-11.00	16.38-10.13	20.63-12.00	22.88-13.88	16.00-9.75	11.83-9.67
P/E Ratio	29.5-17.2	27.2-21.1	21.0-13.0	38.2-22.2	24.6-14.9	19.0-11.6	17.1-14.0
Average Yield %	3.9	4.4	3.9	3.1	2.4	3.0	3.3

Statistics are as originally reported. Adj. for stk. split: 3-for-2, 3/97 ① Incl. non-recurr. chrg. $16.7 mill., 12/00; $3.0 mill., 12/98; $13.0 mill., 12/97.

OFFICERS:
A. L. Meyers Jr., Chmn., C.E.O.
G. L. Davis, Pres., C.E.O., C.O.O.
J. F. Giblin, Exec. V.P., C.F.O.

INVESTOR CONTACT: Investor Relations, (404) 847-4571

PRINCIPAL OFFICE: 5620 Glenridge Dr., N.E., Atlanta, GA 30342

TELEPHONE NUMBER: (404) 256-0830
FAX: (404) 847-4359
WEB: www.crawfordandcompany.com

NO. OF EMPLOYEES: 8,569

SHAREHOLDERS: 1,897 (approx. class A); 830 (approx. class B)

ANNUAL MEETING: In April
INCORPORATED: GA, May, 1943

INSTITUTIONAL HOLDINGS:
No. of Institutions: 42
Shares Held: 21,005,981
% Held: 43.3

INDUSTRY: Insurance agents, brokers, & service (SIC: 6411)

TRANSFER AGENT(S): SunTrust Bank, Atlanta, GA

CVB FINANCIAL CORPORATION

YIELD 2.8%
P/E RATIO 18.0

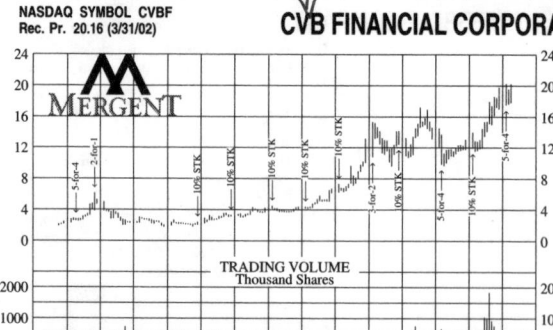

7 YEAR PRICE SCORE 135.5 **12 MONTH PRICE SCORE 115.8**

*NYSE COMPOSITE INDEX=100

INTERIM EARNINGS (Per Share):

Qtr.	Mar.	June	Sept.	Dec.
1997	0.14	0.16	0.20	0.23
1998	0.20	0.21	0.23	0.24
1999	0.23	0.26	0.27	0.17
2000	0.28	0.30	0.32	0.33
2001	0.25	0.27	0.30	0.30

INTERIM DIVIDENDS (Per Share):

Amt.	Decl.	Ex.	Rec.	Pay.
0.14Q	6/20/01	7/02/01	7/05/01	7/19/01
0.15Q	9/19/01	10/01/01	10/03/01	10/18/01
5-for-4	12/19/01	1/22/02	1/04/02	1/18/02
0.13Q	12/19/01	1/03/02	1/07/02	1/21/02
0.14Q	3/20/02	4/01/02	4/03/02	4/17/02

Indicated div.: $0.56 (Div. Reinv. Plan)

CAPITALIZATION (12/31/01):

	($000)	(%)
Total Deposits	1,876,959	77.2
Long-Term Debt	334,999	13.8
Common & Surplus	220,748	9.1
Total	2,432,706	100.0

DIVIDEND ACHIEVER STATUS:
Rank: 18   10-Year Growth Rate: 21.78%
Total Years of Dividend Growth: 11

RECENT DEVELOPMENTS: For the year ended 12/31/01, net income advanced 15.5% to $40.1 million versus $34.7 million in 2000. Results for 2001 and 2000 included a gain of $60,000 and a loss of $218,000, respectively, on the sale of securities. Results for 2001 and 2000 also included gains of $126,000 and $223,000, respectively, on the sale of other real estate owned. Net interest income climbed 10.9% to 9.5% to $103.1 million from $94.1 million in 2000.

PROSPECTS: On 1/18/02, CVBF announced that it's principal subsidiary, Citizens Business Bank, executed a definitive agreement and plan to acquire Western Security Bancorp's principal subsidiary, Western Security Bank, NA. The acquisition should expand Citizens Business Bank's presence in the San Fernando Valley of California. The transaction is subject to shareholder and regulatory approval and is expected to close in the second quarter of 2002.

BUSINESS

CVB FINANCIAL CORPORATION is a bank holding company, with assets, as of 12/31/01, totaling $2.51 billion. The Company's largest subsidiary, Citizens Business Bank, operates 31 banking offices located in the Inland Empire, Orange County, San Gabriel Valley and Kern County areas of California. The Company provides a full complement of all business banking products and services; including asset management services. CVB owns 100% of Community Trust Deed Services, which prepares and files notices of default, reconveyances and related documents and acts as a trustee under deeds of trust. The Company also owns 100% of CVB Ventures Inc., which charges fees and collects commissions for acting as an intermediary for emerging growth companies in obtaining capital, loans, leases and other financing vehicles. On 10/4/99, the Company acquired Orange National Bancorporation and its subsidiary, Orange National Bank, which had deposits of approximately $250.4 million and net loans of approximately $152.0 million.

ANNUAL FINANCIAL DATA

	12/31/01	12/31/00	12/31/99	12/31/98	12/31/97	12/31/96	12/31/95
Earnings Per Share	1.13	0.98	①0.74	0.70	0.59	②0.69	0.65
Tang. Book Val. Per Share	6.16	5.24	3.89	3.73	3.55	4.10	4.13
Dividends Per Share	0.44	0.35	0.28	0.21	0.14	0.10	0.09
Dividend Payout %	38.9	35.5	37.6	30.0	23.4	14.6	14.1
INCOME STATEMENT (IN THOUSANDS):							
Total Interest Income	155,877	150,867	128,478	96,840	84,656	74,894	64,695
Total Interest Expense	52,806	56,760	38,466	31,248	24,976	21,466	16,555
Net Interest Income	103,071	94,107	90,012	65,592	59,680	53,428	48,141
Provision for Loan Losses	1,750	2,800	2,700	2,500	2,670	2,888	2,575
Non-Interest Income	22,192	19,023	18,630	14,976	13,823	14,279	9,090
Non-Interest Expense	60,155	56,345	64,737	45,024	42,890	41,909	35,053
Income Before Taxes	63,358	53,985	41,205	33,043	27,943	22,910	19,603
Net Income	40,058	34,683	①25,960	20,787	17,370	②13,333	11,457
Average Shs. Outstg.	35,415	35,208	35,016	29,598	29,473	19,434	17,626
BALANCE SHEET (IN THOUSANDS):							
Cash & Due from Banks	82,651	130,315	118,360	100,033	107,725	142,502	104,886
Securities Avail. for Sale	1,181,503	1,070,074	877,332	676,162	434,106	333,348	260,374
Total Loans & Leases	1,190,922	1,054,800	956,118	691,353	619,589	592,204	508,537
Allowance for Credit Losses	23,851	22,459	20,327	15,685	14,106	15,518	12,088
Net Loans & Leases	1,167,071	1,032,341	935,791	675,668	605,484	576,687	496,449
Total Assets	2,514,102	2,307,996	2,010,757	1,555,207	1,258,769	1,160,421	936,927
Total Deposits	1,876,959	1,595,030	1,501,073	1,215,305	1,075,695	990,597	803,574
Long-Term Obligations	334,999	11,234	16,951	95	7,922	12,610	6,738
Total Liabilities	2,293,354	2,119,366	1,869,987	1,439,500	1,156,684	1,071,334	858,680
Net Stockholders' Equity	220,748	188,630	140,770	115,707	102,085	89,087	78,260
Year-end Shs. Outstg.	34,782	34,574	33,986	28,415	25,738	18,855	16,877
STATISTICAL RECORD:							
Return on Equity %	18.1	18.4	18.4	18.0	17.0	15.0	14.6
Return on Assets %	1.6	1.5	1.3	1.3	1.4	1.1	1.2
Equity/Assets %	8.8	8.2	7.0	7.4	8.1	7.7	8.4
Non-Int. Exp./Tot. Inc. %	48.0	49.8	59.6	55.9	54.4	61.9	61.2
Price Range	19.79-11.50	14.55-9.64	17.24-10.69	15.34-9.59	13.18-6.22	6.73-4.09	4.52-3.68
P/E Ratio	17.5-10.2	14.8-9.8	23.2-14.4	21.8-13.6	22.4-10.6	9.8-5.9	7.0-5.7
Average Yield %	2.8	2.9	2.0	1.7	1.4	1.9	2.2

Statistics are as originally reported. Adj. for stk. splits: 5-for-4, 12/01; 10% div., 1/01; 5-for-4, 1/00; 10% div., 1/99; 3-for-2, 1/98; 10% div., 1/97, 1/96 & 1/95. ① Incl. acquisition-related costs of $4.9 mill. ② Incl. litigation settlement gain $2.1 mill.

OFFICERS:
G. A. Borba, Chmn.
D. L. Wiley, Pres., C.E.O.
E. J. Biebrich Jr., Exec. V.P., C.F.O.

INVESTOR CONTACT: D. Lynn Wiley, Pres. & C.E.O., (909) 980-4030

PRINCIPAL OFFICE: 701 North Haven Avenue, Suite 350, Ontario, CA 91764

TELEPHONE NUMBER: (909) 980-4030
FAX: (909) 481-2130
WEB: www.cbbank.com
NO. OF EMPLOYEES: 355 full-time; 220 part-time
SHAREHOLDERS: 1,401 (approx.)
ANNUAL MEETING: In May
INCORPORATED: CA, Apr., 1981

INSTITUTIONAL HOLDINGS:
No. of Institutions: 57
Shares Held: 5,354,921
% Held: 15.4

INDUSTRY: State commercial banks (SIC: 6022)

TRANSFER AGENT(S): U.S. Stock Transfer Corporation, Glendale, CA

DIEBOLD, INC.

YIELD	1.6%
P/E RATIO	43.3

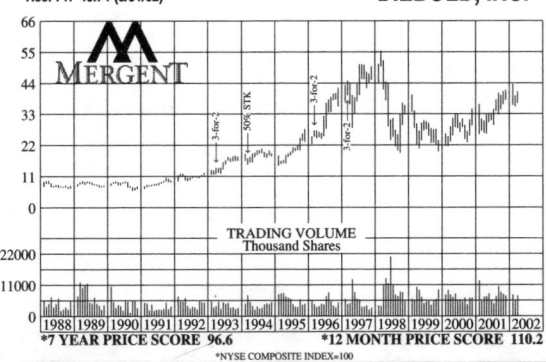

TRADING VOLUME
Thousand Shares

1988 1989 1990 1991 1992 1993 1994 1995 1996 1997 1998 1999 2000 2001 2002

*7 YEAR PRICE SCORE 96.6   ***12 MONTH PRICE SCORE 110.2**

*NYSE COMPOSITE INDEX=100

INTERIM EARNINGS (Per Share):

Qtr.	Mar.	June	Sept.	Dec.
1998	0.39	d0.21	0.43	0.50
1999	0.42	0.46	0.47	0.50
2000	0.44	0.50	0.49	0.49
2001	0.11	0.39	0.20	0.24

INTERIM DIVIDENDS (Per Share):

Amt.	Decl.	Ex.	Rec.	Pay.
0.16Q	4/26/01	5/16/01	5/18/01	6/08/01
0.16Q	8/07/01	8/15/01	8/17/01	9/07/01
0.16Q	10/09/01	11/14/01	11/16/01	12/07/01
0.165Q	2/06/02	2/13/02	2/15/02	3/08/02

Indicated div.: $0.66 (Div. Reinv. Plan)

CAPITALIZATION (12/31/01):

	($000)	(%)
Long-Term Debt	20,800	2.2
Minority Interest	9,382	1.0
Common & Surplus	903,110	96.8
Total	933,292	100.0

DIVIDEND ACHIEVER STATUS:
Rank: 185   10-Year Growth Rate: 7.31%
Total Years of Dividend Growth: 48

RECENT DEVELOPMENTS: For the year ended 12/31/01, net income was $66.9 million versus $136.9 million the year before. Results for 2001 included one-time pre-tax realignment charges of $42.3 million and other pre-tax special charges totaling $31.4 million. Total net sales rose 1.0% to $1.76 billion from $1.74 billion a year earlier. Gross profit was $524.1 million, or 29.8% of net sales, compared with $564.1 million, or 32.4% of net sales, the previous year.

PROSPECTS: Results in the second half of 2002 are expected to benefit from the integration of Global Election Systems Inc., a manufacturer and distributor of computerized voting systems acquired on 1/22/02, as well as the service outsourcing businesses of Bank of America and Mosler, Inc., which were acquired in late 2001. DBD is targeting full-year 2002 revenue growth of 6.0% to 8.0%, along with earnings of between $2.15 and $2.25 per share.

BUSINESS

DIEBOLD, INC. provides card-based transaction systems, security products, and customer service solutions to the financial, education, and healthcare industries. The Company develops, manufactures, sells and services the following products: automated teller machines, electronic and physical security systems, bank facility equipment, software and integrated systems for global financial and commercial markets. The products segment accounted for 52.5% of revenues, while the services segment accounted for 47.5% for the year ended 12/31/01.

ANNUAL FINANCIAL DATA

	12/31/01	12/31/00	12/31/99	12/31/98	12/31/97	12/31/96	12/31/95
Earnings Per Share	⑪0.93	1.92	⑪1.85	⑪1.10	1.76	1.42	1.11
Cash Flow Per Share	1.57	2.42	2.35	1.47	2.03	1.72	1.32
Tang. Book Val. Per Share	8.79	8.94	9.63	9.87	9.69	8.36	7.37
Dividends Per Share	0.64	0.62	0.60	0.56	0.50	0.45	0.43
Dividend Payout %	68.8	32.3	32.4	50.9	28.4	31.9	38.3
INCOME STATEMENT (IN MILLIONS):							
Total Revenues	1,760.1	1,743.6	1,259.2	1,185.7	1,226.9	1,030.2	863.4
Costs & Expenses	1,575.9	1,478.8	1,038.3	1,053.8	1,024.4	868.8	742.4
Depreciation & Amort.	45.5	35.9	34.7	25.6	18.7	21.0	14.2
Operating Income	138.9	229.0	186.1	106.2	183.9	140.4	106.8
Net Interest Inc./(Exp.)	d12.7	d17.7	. . .	. . .	. . .	. . .	. . .
Income Before Income Taxes	99.8	204.4	201.3	119.8	185.7	146.5	113.2
Income Taxes	32.9	67.4	72.5	43.7	63.1	49.1	37.0
Net Income	⑪66.9	136.9	⑪128.9	⑪76.1	122.5	97.4	76.2
Cash Flow	112.3	172.8	163.6	101.8	141.2	118.4	90.4
Average Shs. Outstg. (000)	71,783	71,479	69,562	69,310	69,490	68,796	68,649
BALANCE SHEET (IN MILLIONS):							
Cash & Cash Equivalents	125.7	126.5	84.6	80.0	56.8	65.1	46.7
Total Current Assets	952.4	804.4	647.9	543.5	549.8	479.6	376.2
Net Property	190.2	174.9	160.7	147.1	143.9	95.9	84.1
Total Assets	1,651.9	1,585.4	1,298.8	1,004.2	991.1	859.1	745.2
Total Current Liabilities	658.0	566.8	382.4	235.5	242.1	228.2	186.0
Long-Term Obligations	20.8	20.8	20.8	20.8	20.8	. . .	. . .
Net Stockholders' Equity	903.1	936.1	844.4	699.1	668.6	575.6	506.2
Net Working Capital	294.4	237.6	265.5	308.0	307.8	251.4	190.2
Year-end Shs. Outstg. (000)	71,357	71,547	71,096	68,881	69,005	68,841	68,712
STATISTICAL RECORD:							
Operating Profit Margin %	7.9	13.1	14.8	9.0	15.0	13.6	12.4
Net Profit Margin %	3.8	7.9	10.2	6.4	10.0	9.5	8.8
Return on Equity %	7.4	14.6	15.3	10.9	18.3	16.9	15.1
Return on Assets %	4.0	8.6	9.9	7.6	12.4	11.3	10.2
Debt/Total Assets %	1.3	1.3	1.6	2.1	2.1	. . .	. . .
Price Range	41.50-25.75	34.75-21.50	39.88-19.69	55.31-19.13	50.63-28.00	42.33-22.45	27.61-14.67
P/E Ratio	44.6-27.7	18.1-11.2	21.6-10.6	50.3-17.4	28.8-15.9	29.8-15.8	24.8-13.2
Average Yield %	1.9	2.2	2.0	1.5	1.3	1.4	2.0

Statistics are as originally reported. Adj. for 3-for-2 stk. split, 2/97 & 2/96. ⑪ Incl. $73.7 mil pre-tax chg. for realignment and other special charges, 2001; $1.2 mil one-time pre-tax chg., 1999; $41.9 mil ($0.60/sh) after-tax chg. for realignment program, 1998.

OFFICERS:
W. W. O'Dell, Chmn., Pres., C.E.O.
W. B. Vance, C.O.O.
G. T. Geswein, Sr. V.P., C.F.O.

INVESTOR CONTACT: Sandy K. Upperman, Mgr., Inv. Rel., (800) 766-5859

PRINCIPAL OFFICE: 5995 Mayfair Road, P.O. Box 3077, North Canton, OH 44720-8077

TELEPHONE NUMBER: (330) 490-4000
FAX: (330) 588-3794
WEB: www.diebold.com

NO. OF EMPLOYEES: 12,674

SHAREHOLDERS: 82,001 (approx.)

ANNUAL MEETING: In Apr.

INCORPORATED: OH, Aug., 1876

INSTITUTIONAL HOLDINGS:
No. of Institutions: 285
Shares Held: 47,973,363
% Held: 66.7

INDUSTRY: Calculating and accounting equipment (SIC: 3578)

TRANSFER AGENT(S): The Bank of New York, New York, NY

DOLLAR GENERAL CORPORATION

YIELD	0.8%
P/E RATIO	26.3

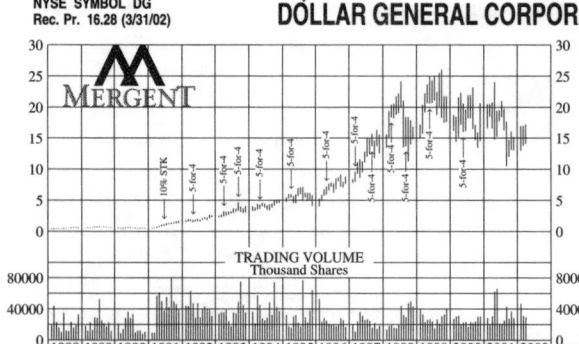

TRADING VOLUME
Thousand Shares

*7 YEAR PRICE SCORE 97.1   *12 MONTH PRICE SCORE 98.3
*NYSE COMPOSITE INDEX=100

INTERIM EARNINGS (Per Share):

Qtr.	Apr.	July	Oct.	Jan.
1998-99	0.09	0.10	0.12	0.23
1999-00	0.11	0.12	0.15	0.27
2000-01	0.14	0.12	0.15	0.21
2001-02	0.11	0.08	0.14	0.29

INTERIM DIVIDENDS (Per Share):

Amt.	Decl.	Ex.	Rec.	Pay.
0.032Q	3/01/01	3/08/01	3/12/01	3/26/01
0.032Q	4/23/01	5/03/01	5/07/01	5/21/01
0.032Q	8/13/01	8/23/01	8/27/01	9/10/01
0.032Q	11/13/01	11/21/01	11/26/01	12/10/01
0.032Q	3/18/02	3/27/02	4/01/02	4/15/02

Indicated div.: $0.13 (Div. Reinv. Plan)

CAPITALIZATION (2/1/02):

	($000)	(%)
Long-Term Debt	339,470	23.9
Deferred Income Tax	37,646	2.7
Common & Surplus	1,041,718	73.4
Total	1,418,834	100.0

DIVIDEND ACHIEVER STATUS:
Rank: 9   10-Year Growth Rate: 25.58%
Total Years of Dividend Growth: 11

RECENT DEVELOPMENTS: For the 52 weeks ended 2/1/02, net income totaled $207.5 million compared with $70.6 million in the corresponding 53-week period the year before. Results in the prior-year period included a $162.0 million charge for a litigation settlement. Sales climbed 17.0% to $5.32 billion from $4.55 billion a year earlier. Sales growth was fueled by the operation of 540 net new stores and a 7.3% increase in same-store sales. Gross profit was $1.51 billion, or 28.4% of sales, versus $1.25 billion, or 27.5% of sales, the previous year.

PROSPECTS: In 2002, DG plans to open about 600 new stores, close between 60 and 80 existing locations, and remodel or relocate approximately 100 stores. The Company is targeting sales growth of between 14.0% and 16.0%, same-store sales growth in the 5.0% to 7.0% range, and earnings growth of between 13.0% and 15.0% in fiscal 2002. During the year, DG expects to increase its selection of highly consumable and seasonal merchandise, as well as expand its assortment of perishable items, such as milk and bread, into more than 1,000 stores.

BUSINESS

DOLLAR GENERAL CORPORA-TION sells general merchandise at everyday low prices through a chain of 5,620 stores in 27 states as of 3/15/02. The Company also operates distribution centers in Florida, Kentucky, Mississippi, Missouri, Ohio, Oklahoma and Virginia. The Company offers hard goods, including health and beauty aids, cleaning supplies, housewares, stationery, and seasonal goods. DG also markets soft goods, including apparel for the whole family, shoes, and domestics. In addition to its regular hard good and soft goods inventory, the Company also sells manufacturers' overruns, closeouts, and "irregulars" at a discount from regular prices. DG emphasizes even-dollar pricing of its merchandise, most of which is priced at $1 or in increments of $1.

ANNUAL FINANCIAL DATA

	2/1/02	2/2/01	1/28/00	1/29/99	1/30/98	1/31/97	1/31/96
Earnings Per Share	0.62	⊡ 0.21	0.65	0.54	0.43	0.34	0.26
Cash Flow Per Share	0.99	0.55	0.84	0.70	0.55	0.43	0.34
Tang. Book Val. Per Share	3.13	2.60	2.80	2.61	1.70	1.78	1.52
Dividends Per Share	0.13	0.12	0.10	0.08	0.07	0.05	0.04
Dividend Payout %	20.6	57.9	15.0	15.1	16.2	14.6	15.2
INCOME STATEMENT (IN MILLIONS):							
Total Revenues	5,322.9	4,550.6	3,888.0	3,221.0	2,627.3	2,134.4	1,764.2
Costs & Expenses	4,826.1	4,285.2	3,474.7	2,878.6	2,353.0	1,913.8	1,590.0
Depreciation & Amort.	123.0	111.4	63.9	53.1	38.7	31.0	25.2
Operating Income	373.6	154.0	349.3	289.3	235.5	189.7	148.9
Net Interest Inc./(Exp.)	d45.8	d45.4	d5.2	d8.3	d3.8	d4.7	d7.4
Income Before Income Taxes	327.8	108.6	344.1	280.9	231.8	185.0	141.5
Income Taxes	120.3	38.0	124.7	98.9	87.2	69.9	53.7
Net Income	207.5	⊡ 70.6	219.4	182.0	144.6	115.1	87.8
Cash Flow	330.5	182.0	282.2	231.6	180.1	143.7	111.1
Average Shs. Outstg. (000)	335,017	333,858	336,963	335,499	334,943	337,582	334,888
BALANCE SHEET (IN MILLIONS):							
Cash & Cash Equivalents	261.5	162.3	58.8	22.3	7.1	6.6	4.3
Total Current Assets	1,556.0	1,124.9	1,095.5	878.9	666.7	504.6	516.2
Net Property	988.9	973.1	346.5	326.4	241.4	208.5	158.6
Total Assets	2,552.4	2,282.5	1,450.9	1,211.8	914.8	718.1	680.0
Total Current Liabilities	1,133.6	537.9	472.3	455.1	307.7	224.5	253.7
Long-Term Obligations	339.5	720.8	1.2	0.8	1.3	2.6	3.3
Net Stockholders' Equity	1,041.7	861.8	925.9	725.8	583.9	485.5	420.0
Net Working Capital	422.5	587.0	623.2	423.8	359.0	280.1	262.5
Year-end Shs. Outstg. (000)	332,606	331,198	330,865	277,370	343,926	272,995	275,116
STATISTICAL RECORD:							
Operating Profit Margin %	7.0	3.4	9.0	9.0	9.0	8.9	8.4
Net Profit Margin %	3.9	1.6	5.6	5.7	5.5	5.4	5.0
Return on Equity %	19.9	8.2	23.7	25.1	24.8	23.7	20.9
Return on Assets %	8.1	3.1	15.1	15.0	15.8	16.0	12.9
Debt/Total Assets %	13.3	31.6	0.1	0.1	0.1	0.4	0.5
Price Range	24.05-10.50	23.19-13.44	26.10-15.08	24.19-11.26	16.38-7.80	9.14-4.04	7.13-4.09
P/E Ratio	38.8-16.9	110.4-64.0	40.3-23.3	44.5-20.7	38.2-18.2	26.8-11.8	27.2-15.6
Average Yield %	0.8	0.7	0.5	0.5	0.6	0.8	0.7

Statistics are as originally reported. Adj. for all stk. splits & divs. through 5/00. ⊡ Incl. $162.0 mil. pre-tax litigation chrg.

OFFICERS:
C. Turner, Jr., Chmn., C.E.O.
D. S. Shaffer, Pres., C.O.O.
J. J. Hagan, Exec. V.P., C.F.O.
INVESTOR CONTACT: Kiley Fleming, Dir., Inv. Rel., (615) 855-5525
PRINCIPAL OFFICE: 100 Mission Ridge, Goodlettsville, TN 37072

TELEPHONE NUMBER: (615) 855-4000
FAX: (615) 855-5527
WEB: www.dollargeneral.com
NO. OF EMPLOYEES: 48,000 (approx.)
SHAREHOLDERS: 16,039 (approx.)
ANNUAL MEETING: In June
INCORPORATED: KY, 1955; reincorp., TN, June, 1998

INSTITUTIONAL HOLDINGS:
No. of Institutions: 263
Shares Held: 204,767,900
% Held: 61.6

INDUSTRY: Variety stores (SIC: 5331)

TRANSFER AGENT(S): Registrar and Transfer Company, Cranford, NJ

DONEGAL GROUP INC.

YIELD 4.3%
P/E RATIO 14.7

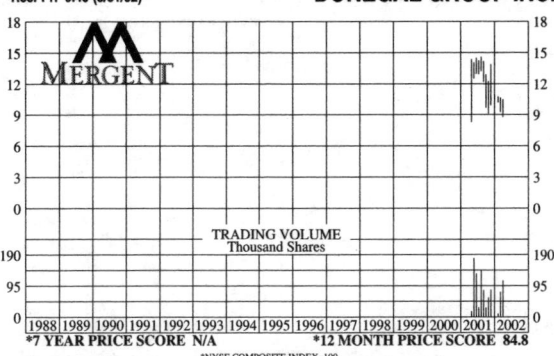

INTERIM EARNINGS (Per Share):

Qtr.	Mar.	June	Sept.	Dec.
1998	0.40	0.22	0.01	0.46
1999	0.26	0.16	d0.29	0.67
2000	0.15	0.28	0.30	0.29
2001	0.33	0.30	0.11	d0.10

INTERIM DIVIDENDS (Per Share):

Amt.	Decl.	Ex.	Rec.	Pay.
0.10Q	4/19/01	5/11/01	5/15/01	5/30/01
0.10Q	7/20/01	7/30/01	8/01/01	8/15/01
0.10Q	10/18/01	10/30/01	11/01/01	11/15/01
0.10Q	12/20/01	1/30/02	2/01/02	2/15/02
0.10Q	4/19/02	4/29/02	5/01/02	5/15/02

Indicated div.: $0.40 (Div. Reinv. Plan)

CAPITALIZATION (12/31/01):

	($000)	(%)
Long-Term Debt	27,600	18.6
Common & Surplus	120,928	81.4
Total	148,528	100.0

TRADING VOLUME
Thousand Shares

7 YEAR PRICE SCORE N/A *12 MONTH PRICE SCORE 84.8*
NYSE COMPOSITE INDEX=100

DIVIDEND ACHIEVER STATUS:
Rank: 131   10-Year Growth Rate: 10.30%
Total Years of Dividend Growth: 12

RECENT DEVELOPMENTS: For the year ended 12/31/01, net income fell 34.2% to $5.8 million from $8.8 million in the previous year. Results for 2001 included reserve strengthening of $4.2 million and charges related to guaranty fund assessments of approximately $543,000 resulting from the insolvency of Reliance Insurance Company. Total revenues grew 8.5% to $185.2 million from $170.6 million in the prior year. Net premiums earned amounted to $167.8 million, up 10.7% from $151.6 million the year before. During

the fourth quarter of 2001, DGICA announced a variety of actions designed to improve its underwriting results and return it to underwriting profitability. These actions include additional rate increases effective for 2002 renewals in personal lines which will average approximately 8.0% and increases averaging 15.0% to 20.0% in commercial lines for 2002 renewals. The Company has taken steps to reduce operating expenses and simplify its corporate structure through the merging of certain smaller subsidiaries.

BUSINESS

DONEGAL GROUP INC. is an insurance holding company, which through its subsidiaries, engages in the property and casualty insurance business in 15 mid-Atlantic and southeastern states. DGIC and its subsidiaries underwrite a full lines of personal, farm and commercial products including businessowners, commercial multiperil, automobile, homeowners, boatowners, farmowners, workers' compensation and other coverages. The Company has three reportable segments, which consist of the investment function, the personal lines of insurance and the commercial lines of insurance. DGIC's subsidiaries include Atlantic States Insurance Company, Southern Heritage Insurance Company, Southern Insurance Company of Virginia, Pioneer Insurance Company; and through a pooling agreement with its parent, Donegal Mutual Insurance Company, which owned 63.5% and 62.1% of the Company's class A and class B common shares, respectively, as of 3/12/02. On 4/19/01, DGIC's common stock was divided 66.7% class A shares and 33.3% class B shares.

ANNUAL FINANCIAL DATA

	12/31/01	12/31/00	12/31/99	12/31/98	12/31/97	12/31/96	12/31/95
Earnings Per Share	0.64	1.02	0.80	1.09	1.32	1.10	1.30
Cash Flow Per Share	0.78	1.11	0.91	1.16	1.37	1.17	1.35
Tang. Book Val. Per Share	13.44	12.84	12.24	12.27	15.19	13.64	9.54
Dividends Per Share	0.39	0.36	0.35	0.33	0.28	0.24	0.22
Dividend Payout %	60.9	35.3	43.8	30.3	21.2	21.8	16.9
INCOME STATEMENT (IN THOUSANDS):							
Total Revenues	185,164	168,223	159,711	130,586	121,328	112,519	97,885
Costs & Expenses	174,697	152,276	153,610	117,096	105,853	100,662	84,851
Depreciation & Amort.	1,128	839	936	521	391	236	380
Operating Income	9,339	15,108	5,164	12,970	15,084	11,622	12,653
Net Interest Inc./(Exp.)	d2,247	d3,285	d1,535	d1,293	d910	d375	d8
Income Before Income Taxes	7,092	11,823	3,629	11,677	14,174	11,246	12,646
Income Taxes	1,274	2,936	cr3,028	2,659	3,532	2,350	2,788
Net Income	5,818	8,887	6,657	9,018	10,641	8,896	9,858
Cash Flow	6,946	9,726	7,593	9,539	11,032	9,132	10,238
Average Shs. Outstg.	9,078	8,737	8,327	8,250	8,036	7,815	7,594
BALANCE SHEET (IN THOUSANDS):							
Cash & Cash Equivalents	201,868	135,760	119,961	129,275	83,857	73,708	67,893
Total Current Assets	297,973	224,778	195,423	201,161	139,309	123,958	113,532
Net Property	4,569	5,017	5,517	5,920	4,939	2,161	2,283
Total Assets	456,632	439,101	399,733	385,232	304,105	273,129	235,704
Total Current Liabilities	12,910	8,842	10,963	10,084	12,245	7,144	6,310
Long-Term Obligations	27,600	40,000	37,000	37,500	10,500	8,500	5,000
Net Stockholders' Equity	120,928	113,745	103,415	100,631	91,597	81,277	72,283
Net Working Capital	285,063	215,936	184,461	191,076	127,065	116,814	107,222
Year-end Shs. Outstg.	8,997	8,859	8,452	8,203	6,031	5,961	7,574
STATISTICAL RECORD:							
Operating Profit Margin %	5.0	9.0	3.2	9.9	12.4	10.3	12.9
Net Profit Margin %	3.1	5.3	4.2	6.9	8.8	7.9	10.1
Return on Equity %	4.8	7.8	6.4	9.0	11.6	10.9	13.6
Return on Assets %	1.3	2.0	1.7	2.3	3.5	3.3	4.2
Debt/Total Assets %	6.0	9.1	9.3	9.7	3.5	3.1	2.1
Price Range	13.10-8.50	13.94-5.75	16.25-5.75	22.79-12.63	16.88-11.26	11.68-9.15	10.83-7.84
P/E Ratio	61.4-39.8	13.7-5.6	20.3-7.2	20.9-11.6	12.8-8.5	10.6-8.3	8.3-6.0
Average Yield %	3.7	3.2	1.9	2.0	2.3	2.4	2.4

Statistics are as originally reported. Adj. for 1-for-3 stk. split & 200% stk. div., 4/20/01. Share and per share amounts reflect B shares prior to 4/20/01.

OFFICERS:
D. H. Nikolaus, Pres., C.E.O.
R. G. Spontak, Sr. V.P., C.F.O., Sec.
D. J. Wagner, Treas.

INVESTOR CONTACT: Ralph G. Spontak, Sr.
V.P. & C.F.O., (717) 426-1931

PRINCIPAL OFFICE: 1195 River Road, P.O.
Box 302, Marietta, PA 17547-0302

TELEPHONE NUMBER: (717) 426-1931
FAX: (717) 426-7009
WEB: www.donegalgroup.com

NO. OF EMPLOYEES: 437 (avg.)

SHAREHOLDERS: 586 (approx.)

ANNUAL MEETING: In Apr.

INCORPORATED: DE, Aug., 1986

INSTITUTIONAL HOLDINGS:
No. of Institutions: 10
Shares Held: 1,247,413
% Held: 0.0

INDUSTRY: Fire, marine, and casualty insurance (SIC: 6331)

TRANSFER AGENT(S): EquiServe Trust
Company, Jersey City, NJ

DONNELLEY (R.R.) & SONS CO.

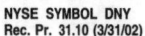

	YIELD	3.1%
	P/E RATIO	155.5

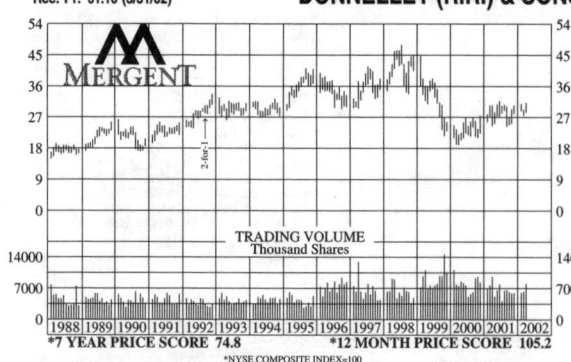

*7 YEAR PRICE SCORE 74.8   *12 MONTH PRICE SCORE 105.2
*NYSE COMPOSITE INDEX=100

INTERIM EARNINGS (Per Share):

Qtr.	Mar.	June	Sept.	Dec.
1997	0.24	0.31	0.56	0.31
1998	0.30	0.61	0.71	0.67
1999	0.33	0.40	0.67	1.01
2000	0.38	0.46	0.75	0.58
2001	0.12	0.05	0.36	d0.33

INTERIM DIVIDENDS (Per Share):

Amt.	Decl.	Ex.	Rec.	Pay.
0.24Q	7/26/01	8/08/01	8/10/01	9/01/01
0.24Q	9/20/01	11/07/01	11/09/01	12/01/01
0.24Q	1/24/02	2/04/02	2/06/02	3/01/02
0.24Q	3/28/02	5/08/02	5/10/02	6/01/02

Indicated div.: $0.96 (Div. Reinv. Plan)

CAPITALIZATION (12/31/01):

	($000)	(%)
Long-Term Debt	881,318	44.5
Deferred Income Tax	212,099	10.7
Common & Surplus	888,407	44.8
Total	1,981,824	100.0

DIVIDEND ACHIEVER STATUS:
Rank: 198   10-Year Growth Rate: 6.52%
Total Years of Dividend Growth: 32

RECENT DEVELOPMENTS: For the year ended 12/31/01, net income dropped 90.6% to $25.0 million compared with $266.9 million in 2000. Results for 2001 included restructuring and impairment charges totaling $195.5 million. Net sales were $5.30 billion, down 8.1% from $5.77 billion in the prior year. Gross profit decreased 17.1% to $910.5 million from $1.10 billion in the previous year. Earnings from operations fell 70.6% to $147.3 million.

PROSPECTS: On 1/31/02, the Company announced a partnership with Shanghai Press and Publications Administration. Under the agreement, the companies will build a $30.0 million print manufacturing facility in Shanghai. DNY will maintain 100.0% control over the operations. The new plant is expected to open by the end of the year. Looking ahead, the Company expects earnings per share for 2002 to be between $1.50 and $1.65.

BUSINESS

DONNELLEY (R.R.) & SONS CO. is engaged in distributing, managing and reproducing print and digital information for the publishing, retailing, merchandising and information technology markets worldwide. Services provided to customers include presswork and binding, including on-demand customized publications; conventional and digital preproduction operations; software manufacturing, marketing and support services (through Stream International Holdings); design and related creative services (through Coris Inc.); electronic communication networks for simultaneous worldwide product releases; digital services to publishers; and the planning for and fulfillment of truck, rail, mail and air distribution for products of DNY and its customers. Sales for 2001 industry segment data were derived: commercial print, 85.2%; logistics services, 14.6%; and other, 0.2%.

ANNUAL FINANCIAL DATA

	12/31/01	12/31/00	12/31/99	12/31/98	12/31/97	12/31/96	12/31/95
Earnings Per Share	⑥ 0.21	⑤ 2.17	④ 2.40	③ 2.08	② 1.40	① d1.04	1.95
Cash Flow Per Share	3.41	5.34	5.29	4.67	3.91	1.53	4.54
Tang. Book Val. Per Share	3.15	5.88	6.01	6.85	8.31	7.49	7.46
Dividends Per Share	0.94	0.90	0.86	0.82	0.78	0.74	0.68
Dividend Payout %	447.4	41.5	35.8	39.4	55.7	...	34.9
INCOME STATEMENT (IN MILLIONS):							
Total Revenues	5,297.8	5,764.3	5,183.4	5,018.4	4,850.0	6,599.0	6,511.8
Costs & Expenses	4,771.8	4,872.9	4,278.6	4,242.3	4,110.8	6,345.8	5,554.2
Depreciation & Amort.	378.7	390.4	374.4	367.8	370.4	389.1	398.2
Operating Income	147.3	501.0	530.4	408.4	368.8	d136.0	559.4
Net Interest Inc./(Exp.)	d71.2	d89.6	d88.2	d78.2	d90.8	d95.5	d109.8
Income Before Income Taxes	74.9	434.0	506.5	509.3	303.8	d110.5	439.5
Income Taxes	49.9	167.1	195.0	214.7	97.2	47.1	140.7
Net Income	⑥ 25.0	⑤ 266.9	④ 311.5	③ 294.6	② 206.5	① d157.6	298.8
Cash Flow	403.7	657.3	685.9	662.4	577.0	231.5	697.0
Average Shs. Outstg. (000)	118,498	123,093	129,566	141,865	147,508	151,800	153,500
BALANCE SHEET (IN MILLIONS):							
Cash & Cash Equivalents	48.6	60.9	41.9	66.2	47.8	31.1	33.1
Total Current Assets	940.2	1,206.4	1,229.9	1,145.0	1,146.6	1,752.9	1,908.0
Net Property	1,490.1	1,620.6	1,710.7	1,700.9	1,788.1	1,944.7	2,009.0
Total Assets	3,400.0	3,914.2	3,853.5	3,787.8	4,134.2	4,849.0	5,384.8
Total Current Liabilities	984.3	1,190.6	1,203.5	898.3	812.6	1,147.5	1,130.4
Long-Term Obligations	881.3	739.2	748.5	999.0	1,153.2	1,430.7	1,561.0
Net Stockholders' Equity	888.4	1,232.5	1,138.3	1,300.9	1,591.5	1,631.3	2,173.2
Net Working Capital	d44.1	15.9	26.4	246.7	333.9	605.3	777.6
Year-end Shs. Outstg. (000)	140,889	121,055	123,237	134,322	145,118	145,554	153,953
STATISTICAL RECORD:							
Operating Profit Margin %	2.8	8.7	10.2	8.1	7.6	...	8.6
Net Profit Margin %	0.5	4.6	6.0	5.9	4.3	...	4.6
Return on Equity %	2.8	21.7	27.4	22.6	13.0	...	13.7
Return on Assets %	0.7	6.8	8.1	7.8	5.0	...	5.5
Debt/Total Assets %	25.9	18.9	19.4	26.4	27.9	29.5	29.0
Price Range	31.90-24.30	27.50-19.00	44.75-21.50	48.00-33.75	41.75-29.50	39.88-29.38	41.25-28.88
P/E Ratio	151.8-115.7	12.7-8.8	18.6-9.0	23.1-16.2	29.8-21.1	...	21.2-14.8
Average Yield %	3.3	4.0	2.6	2.0	2.2	2.1	1.9

Statistics are as originally reported. ① Incl. $560.6 mill. pre-tax restr. chg. & $80.0 mill. gains from IPO's. ② Bef. loss fr. disc. ops. of $76.9 mill. ($0.51/sh) & incl. $70.7 mill. pre-tax restr. chg. ③ Incl. $168.9 mill. gain fr. sale of subsidiaries & $80.1 mill. loss fr. businesses held for sale. ④ Incl. $42.8 mill. gain fr. sale of bus. & excl. $3.2 mill. loss fr. disc. ops. ⑤ Excl. $13.0 mill. pre-tax gain fr. sale of shares. ⑥ Incl. $195.5 mill. restr. & impair. chgs.

OFFICERS:
W. L. Davis, Chmn., Pres., C.E.O.
J. R. Donnelley, Vice-Chmn.
G. A. Stoklosa, Exec. V.P., C.F.O.

INVESTOR CONTACT: Sara Gopal, Director, Investor Relations, (312) 326-7754

PRINCIPAL OFFICE: 77 West Wacker Drive, Chicago, IL 60601

TELEPHONE NUMBER: (312) 326-8000
FAX: (312) 326-8543
WEB: www.rrdonnelley.com

NO. OF EMPLOYEES: 33,000 (approx.)

SHAREHOLDERS: 8,786

ANNUAL MEETING: In Mar.

INCORPORATED: DE, May, 1956

INSTITUTIONAL HOLDINGS:
No. of Institutions: 282
Shares Held: 87,445,063
% Held: 77.4

INDUSTRY: Commercial printing, lithographic (SIC: 2752)

TRANSFER AGENT(S): First Chicago Trust Company of New York, Jersey City, NJ

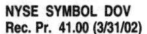

DOVER CORPORATION

YIELD 1.3%
P/E RATIO 50.0

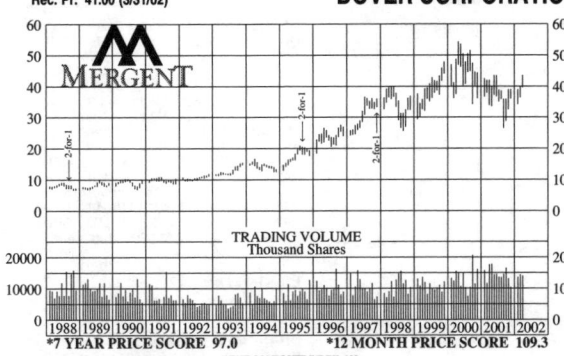

TRADING VOLUME
Thousand Shares

| 1988 | 1989 | 1990 | 1991 | 1992 | 1993 | 1994 | 1995 | 1996 | 1997 | 1998 | 1999 | 2000 | 2001 | 2002 |

*7 YEAR PRICE SCORE 97.0   *12 MONTH PRICE SCORE 109.3

*NYSE COMPOSITE INDEX=100

INTERIM EARNINGS (Per Share):

Qtr.	Mar.	June	Sept.	Dec.
1996	0.34	0.39	0.64	0.36
1997	0.35	0.56	0.46	0.44
1998	0.40	0.45	0.42	0.36
1999	0.32	0.44	0.58	0.58
2000	0.57	0.67	0.71	0.66
2001	0.38	0.24	0.02	0.18

INTERIM DIVIDENDS (Per Share):

Amt.	Decl.	Ex.	Rec.	Pay.
0.125Q	5/03/01	5/29/01	5/31/01	6/15/01
0.135Q	8/02/01	8/29/01	8/31/01	9/14/01
0.135Q	11/01/01	11/28/01	11/30/01	12/14/01
0.135Q	2/14/02	2/26/02	2/28/02	3/15/02

Indicated div.: $0.54 (Div. Reinv. Plan)

CAPITALIZATION (12/31/01):

	($000)	(%)
Long-Term Debt	1,033,243	28.3
Deferred Income Tax	102,853	2.8
Common & Surplus	2,519,539	68.9
Total	3,655,635	100.0

DIVIDEND ACHIEVER STATUS:
Rank: 144   10-Year Growth Rate: 9.76%
Total Years of Dividend Growth: 46

RECENT DEVELOPMENTS: For the year ended 12/31/01, earnings from continuing operations slid 67.7% to $166.8 million versus earnings from continuing operations of $516.8 million in 2000. Results for 2000 included a nonrecurring gain of $10.5 million. Sales fell 14.1% to $4.46 billion. Sales were hurt by the decline in the electronics industry, which affected DOV's circuit board assembly and test and specialized electronic components businesses.

PROSPECTS: DOV's near-term prospects remain uninspiring, due to the weak capital spending outlook for the Company's datacom/telecom/networking customers and the recessionary environment in the manufacturing sector of the U.S. economy. However, DOV's long-term outlook looks appealing, supported by favorable growth prospects in the markets the Company serves.

BUSINESS

DOVER CORPORATION is a diversified industrial manufacturing corporation encompassing over 50 operating companies. Dover Diversified (24.7% of 2001 revenues), builds packaging and printing machinery, heat transfer equipment, food refrigeration and display cases, specialized bearings and compressors, construction and agricultural cabs, as well as products for use in the defense, aerospace and automotive industries. Dover Industries (26.0%) makes products for use in the waste handling, bulk transport, automotive service, commercial food service and packaging, welding, cash dispenser and construction industries. Dover Resources Inc. (21.1%), manufactures products primarily for the automotive, fluid handling, petroleum, winch and chemical equipment industries. Dover Technologies (28.2%) builds automated assembly and testing equipment for the electronics industry, industrial printers for coding and marking, and specialized electronic components. On 1/5/99, the Company sold Dover Elevator for $1.16 billion.

ANNUAL FINANCIAL DATA

	12/31/01	12/31/00	12/31/99	12/31/98	12/31/97	12/31/96	12/31/95
Earnings Per Share	⑤0.82	④2.61	③1.92	①1.45	②1.79	②1.73	②1.23
Cash Flow Per Share	1.90	3.60	2.79	2.20	2.54	2.27	1.70
Tang. Book Val. Per Share	1.97	1.79	1.07	2.11	2.66	2.29	1.79
Dividends Per Share	0.52	0.48	0.44	0.40	0.36	0.32	0.28
Dividend Payout %	63.4	18.4	22.9	27.6	20.1	18.5	22.9
INCOME STATEMENT (IN MILLIONS):							
Total Revenues	4,459.7	5,400.7	4,446.4	3,977.7	4,547.7	4,076.3	3,745.9
Costs & Expenses	3,940.7	4,354.1	3,627.8	3,278.0	3,764.3	3,412.5	3,199.6
Depreciation & Amort.	220.0	203.4	183.2	167.7	170.7	125.1	107.8
Operating Income	299.0	843.2	635.4	532.0	612.7	538.7	438.4
Net Interest Inc./(Exp.)	d75.3	d88.5	d34.9	d46.4	d37.0	d23.5	d20.1
Income Before Income Taxes	238.4	772.3	615.0	488.6	616.8	588.7	417.1
Income Taxes	71.6	239.1	210.0	162.2	211.4	198.5	138.8
Net Income	⑤166.8	④533.2	③405.1	①326.4	②405.4	②390.2	②278.3
Cash Flow	386.8	736.6	588.3	494.1	576.1	515.3	386.1
Average Shs. Outstg. (000)	204,013	204,677	210,679	224,386	226,815	226,524	226,906
BALANCE SHEET (IN MILLIONS):							
Cash & Cash Equivalents	176.9	186.7	138.0	96.8	146.7	217.8	148.8
Total Current Assets	1,654.9	1,974.8	1,611.6	1,304.5	1,591.3	1,489.8	1,384.4
Net Property	761.4	755.5	646.5	572.0	570.6	494.9	423.9
Total Assets	4,602.2	4,892.1	4,131.9	3,627.3	3,277.5	2,993.4	2,666.7
Total Current Liabilities	819.2	1,604.6	1,334.9	989.7	1,196.6	1,139.1	1,081.0
Long-Term Obligations	1,033.2	631.8	608.0	610.1	262.6	253.0	255.6
Net Stockholders' Equity	2,519.5	2,441.6	2,038.8	1,910.9	1,703.6	1,489.7	1,227.7
Net Working Capital	835.8	370.2	276.7	314.8	394.8	350.7	303.3
Year-end Shs. Outstg. (000)	202,579	203,184	204,629	220,407	234,507	225,060	227,340
STATISTICAL RECORD:							
Operating Profit Margin %	6.7	15.6	14.3	13.4	13.5	13.2	11.7
Net Profit Margin %	3.7	9.9	9.1	8.2	8.9	9.6	7.4
Return on Equity %	6.6	21.8	19.9	17.1	23.8	26.2	22.7
Return on Assets %	3.6	10.9	9.8	9.0	12.4	13.0	10.4
Debt/Total Assets %	22.5	12.9	14.7	16.8	8.0	8.5	9.6
Price Range	43.55-26.40	54.38-34.13	47.94-29.31	39.94-25.50	36.69-24.13	27.56-18.31	20.84-12.91
P/E Ratio	53.1-32.2	20.8-13.1	25.0-15.3	27.5-17.6	20.5-13.5	16.0-10.6	17.0-10.5
Average Yield %	1.5	1.1	1.1	1.2	1.2	1.4	1.7

Statistics are as originally reported. Adj. for 2-for-1 stk. split, 12/97; 100% stk. div., 9/95. ① Bef. inc. fr. disc. ops. of $52.4 mill. ② Incl. pre-tax cr. 12/31/97: $32.2 mill.; cr. 12/31/96: $75.1 mill.; chrg. 12/31/95: $31.9 mill. ③ Incl. non-recurr. gain of $10.3 mill.; bef. gain fr. disc. ops. of $523.9 mill. ④ Incl. non-recurr. gain of $10.5 mill.; bef. loss fr. disc. ops. of $13.6 mill. ($0.07/sh.) ⑤ Bef. inc. fr. disc. ops. of $81.7 mill. ($0.40/sh.)

OFFICERS:
T. L. Reece, Chmn., Pres., C.E.O.
D. S. Smith, V.P., C.F.O.
R. G. Kuhbach, V.P., Sec., Gen. Couns.

INVESTOR CONTACT: David S. Smith, V.P., C.F.O., (212) 922-1640

PRINCIPAL OFFICE: 280 Park Avenue, New York, NY 10017-1292

TELEPHONE NUMBER: (212) 922-1640
FAX: (212) 922-1656
WEB: www.dovercorporation.com

NO. OF EMPLOYEES: 26,600 (approx.)

SHAREHOLDERS: 16,000 (approx.)

ANNUAL MEETING: In Apr.

INCORPORATED: DE, 1947

INSTITUTIONAL HOLDINGS:
No. of Institutions: 390
Shares Held: 152,054,407
% Held: 75.0

INDUSTRY: Construction machinery (SIC: 3531)

TRANSFER AGENT(S): Mellon Investor Services, Ridgefield Park, NJ

DQE, INC.

YIELD 7.9%
P/E RATIO ...

TRADING VOLUME
Thousand Shares

| 1988|1989|1990|1991|1992|1993|1994|1995|1996|1997|1998|1999|2000|2001|2002 |

*7 YEAR PRICE SCORE 57.3   *12 MONTH PRICE SCORE 101.0
*NYSE COMPOSITE INDEX=100

INTERIM EARNINGS (Per Share):

Qtr.	Mar.	June	Sept.	Dec.
1997	0.58	0.61	0.75	0.55
1998	0.58	0.51	0.78	0.62
1999	0.61	0.53	0.63	0.84
2000	0.62	0.23	1.02	0.44
2001	0.22	d2.17	0.40	d1.19

INTERIM DIVIDENDS (Per Share):

Amt.	Decl.	Ex.	Rec.	Pay.
0.42Q	1/25/01	3/07/01	3/09/01	4/01/01
0.42Q	5/24/01	6/06/01	6/08/01	7/01/01
0.42Q	7/26/01	9/06/01	9/10/01	10/01/01
0.42Q	11/14/01	12/06/01	12/10/01	1/01/02
0.42Q	2/28/02	3/07/02	3/11/02	4/01/02

Indicated div.: $1.68 (Div. Reinv. Plan)

CAPITALIZATION (12/31/01):

	($000)	(%)
Long-Term Debt	1,198,759	51.7
Deferred Income Tax	611,429	26.4
Common & Surplus	508,461	21.9
Total	2,318,649	100.0

DIVIDEND ACHIEVER STATUS:
Rank: 221   10-Year Growth Rate: 5.76%
Total Years of Dividend Growth: 12

RECENT DEVELOPMENTS: For the year ended 12/31/01, DQE reported a net loss of $153.4 million versus income of $138.1 million, before an accounting gain of $15.5 million, in 2000. Results for the current year included one-time charges of $216.8 million. Earnings in 2001 and 2000 included investment income of $83.0 million and $227.7 million, respectively. Total operating revenues fell 2.6% to $1.30 billion from $1.33 billion the year before.

PROSPECTS: During 2002, DQE will focus on seeking growth through a disciplined investment and management approach. DQE is exploring opportunities to sell certain of its non-complementary assets. Furthermore, cost reductions as a result of DQE's restructuring are expected to enhance profitability at Duquesne Light. Meanwhile, DQE expects earnings per share to be $1.68 and $1.80 for 2002 and 2003, respectively.

BUSINESS

DQE, INC. is a multi-utility delivery and services company providing electricity, water and communications to more than one million customers throughout the U.S. DQE's expanded business lines include propane distribution, communication systems, and financing and insurance services for DQE and various affiliates. DQE's subsidiaries are Duquesne Power, Inc., Duquesne Light Company, AquaSource, Inc., DQE Capital Corp., DQE Energy Services, Inc., DQE Energy Partners, Inc, DQE Enterprises, Inc., DQE Financial Corp., DQE Communications, Inc., ProAm, Inc. and Cherrington Insurance Ltd.

ANNUAL FINANCIAL DATA

	12/31/01	12/31/00	12/31/99	12/31/98	12/31/97	12/31/96	12/31/95
Earnings Per Share	③ d2.75	② 2.39	2.62	① 2.48	2.54	2.32	2.20
Cash Flow Per Share	3.90	7.40	5.10	5.32	5.70	5.20	4.80
Tang. Book Val. Per Share	9.09	14.02	18.78	19.18	19.30	18.01	17.13
Dividends Per Share	1.68	1.60	1.52	1.44	1.36	1.28	1.19
Dividend Payout %	...	66.9	58.0	58.1	53.5	55.2	53.9
INCOME STATEMENT (IN MILLIONS):							
Total Revenues	1,296.1	1,327.6	1,341.2	1,269.6	1,230.2	1,225.2	1,220.2
Costs & Expenses	1,018.2	829.5	750.6	705.7	623.7	621.9	613.6
Depreciation & Amort.	370.9	343.2	196.3	217.2	242.8	222.9	202.6
Maintenance Exp.	23.7	50.6	75.4	74.9	82.9	78.4	81.5
Operating Income	d116.8	104.3	318.8	271.9	280.7	302.0	322.5
Net Interest Inc./(Exp.)	d104.4	d123.6	d158.7	d110.2	d115.6	d110.3	d107.6
Income Taxes	cr56.1	70.4	110.7	101.0	95.8	87.4	96.7
Net Income	③ d153.4	② 138.1	201.4	① 196.7	199.1	179.1	170.6
Cash Flow	218.1	481.3	396.2	413.0	441.9	402.1	373.1
Average Shs. Outstg. (000)	55,888	65,002	77,676	77,683	77,492	77,349	77,674
BALANCE SHEET (IN MILLIONS):							
Gross Property	2,448.1	2,411.3	4,369.3	4,884.1	4,625.1	4,787.5	4,746.1
Accumulated Depreciation	759.7	704.2	2,541.2	3,167.3	1,962.8	1,969.9	1,685.9
Net Property	1,688.3	1,707.1	1,828.1	1,716.8	2,662.3	2,817.5	3,060.2
Total Assets	2,979.7	3,618.0	5,325.9	4,969.8	4,450.0	4,396.4	4,365.6
Long-Term Obligations	1,198.8	1,349.3	1,649.9	1,401.5	1,413.7	1,468.2	1,435.5
Net Stockholders' Equity	508.5	783.7	1,347.9	1,484.0	1,499.2	1,391.9	1,328.7
Year-end Shs. Outstg. (000)	55,908	55,886	71,766	77,373	77,680	77,273	77,556
STATISTICAL RECORD:							
Operating Profit Margin %	...	7.9	23.8	21.4	22.8	24.6	26.4
Net Profit Margin %	...	10.4	15.0	15.5	16.2	14.6	14.0
Net Inc./Net Property %	...	8.1	11.0	11.5	7.5	6.4	5.6
Net Inc./Tot. Capital %	...	4.6	5.0	5.4	5.6	4.9	4.8
Return on Equity %	...	17.6	14.9	13.3	13.3	12.9	12.8
Accum. Depr./Gross Prop. %	31.0	29.2	58.2	64.8	42.4	41.1	35.5
Price Range	33.70-16.55	53.00-30.75	44.25-33.63	44.13-31.56	34.63-26.50	31.50-25.75	30.75-15.83
P/E Ratio	...	22.2-12.9	16.9-12.8	17.8-12.7	13.6-10.4	13.6-11.1	14.0-7.2
Average Yield %	6.7	3.8	3.9	3.8	4.4	4.5	5.1

Statistics are as originally reported. Adj. for stk. splits: 3-for-2, 5/95 ① Bef. extraordinary item of $82.5 mill. ② Excl. acct. chng. credit of $15.9 mill. ③ Incl. one-time chrgs. of $216.8 mill.

OFFICERS:
M. K. O'Brien, Pres., C.E.O.
Exec. V.P.
F. C. Cordisco, V.P., Treas.
D. High, V.P., Gen. Couns.

INVESTOR CONTACT: Investor Relations, (412) 393-1238

PRINCIPAL OFFICE: 411 Seventh Avenue, Pittsburgh, PA 15219

TELEPHONE NUMBER: (412) 393-6000
FAX: (412) 393-6065
WEB: www.dqe.com

NO. OF EMPLOYEES: 2,538

SHAREHOLDERS: 56,000 (approx.)

ANNUAL MEETING: In June

INCORPORATED: PA, 1989

INSTITUTIONAL HOLDINGS:
No. of Institutions: 139
Shares Held: 14,976,865
% Held: 26.8

INDUSTRY: Electric services (SIC: 4911)

TRANSFER AGENT(S): BankBoston, N.A., Boston, MA

EATON VANCE CORPORATION

YIELD	0.7%
P/E RATIO	24.5

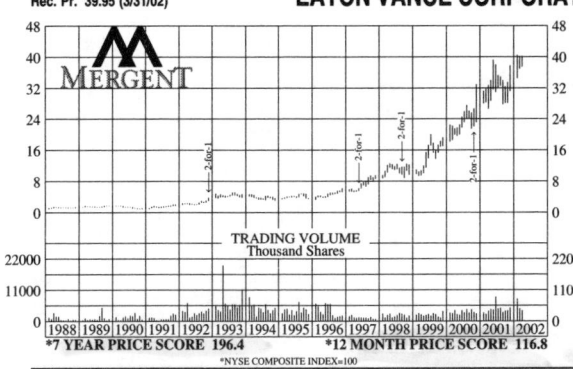

TRADING VOLUME
Thousand Shares

*7 YEAR PRICE SCORE 196.4 *12 MONTH PRICE SCORE 116.8
*NYSE COMPOSITE INDEX=100

INTERIM EARNINGS (Per Share):

Qtr.	Jan.	Apr.	July	Oct.
1998-99	d0.14	0.14	0.35	0.35
1999-00	0.39	0.40	0.38	0.42
2000-01	0.44	0.29	0.44	0.44
2001-02	0.46	...	...	...

INTERIM DIVIDENDS (Per Share):

Amt.	Decl.	Ex.	Rec.	Pay.
0.06Q	7/11/01	7/27/01	7/31/01	8/13/01
0.072Q	10/17/01	10/29/01	10/31/01	11/12/01
0.072Q	1/16/02	1/29/02	1/31/02	2/11/02
0.072Q	4/17/02	4/26/02	4/30/02	5/13/02

Indicated div.: $0.29

CAPITALIZATION (10/31/01):

	($000)	(%)
Long-Term Debt	215,488	36.4
Deferred Income Tax	73,878	12.5
Minority Interest	965	0.2
Common & Surplus	301,126	50.9
Total	591,457	100.0

DIVIDEND ACHIEVER STATUS:
Rank: 20   10-Year Growth Rate: 21.42%
Total Years of Dividend Growth: 20

RECENT DEVELOPMENTS: For the quarter ended 1/31/02, net income rose 3.6% to $33.2 million from $32.0 million the previous year. Earnings included a pre-tax gain of $1.4 million in 2002 and a pre-tax loss of $255,000 in 2001 from the sale of investments. Total revenue grew 8.8% to $130.7 million. Revenues from investment adviser and administration fees rose 17.6% to $71.9 million, while distribution and underwriter fees revenue fell 7.3% to $36.5 million.

PROSPECTS: Asset growth benefited from the acquisitions of Atlanta Capital Management Company, LLC and Fox Asset Management, LLC, which added $7.90 billion of assets on 9/30/01. Beginning in 2005, EV will have the right to acquire the remaining 30.0% of Atlanta Capital over a five-year period. Meanwhile, beginning in 2007, EV will have the right to acquire the remaining 20.0% of Fox Management over a five-year period.

BUSINESS

EATON VANCE CORPORATION creates, markets and manages mutual funds and provides management and counseling services to institutions and individuals. The Company conducts its investment management and counseling business through two wholly-owned subsidiaries, Eaton Vance Management and Boston Management and Research. As of 10/31/01, the Company provides investment advice and administration services to 157 funds and to 1,193 separately managed individual and institutional accounts. EV's funds consist of money markets, equities, bank loans, and taxable and non-taxable fixed income. As of 1/31/02, assets under management totaled $59.27 billion.

REVENUES

(10/31/2001)	($000)	(%)
Investment Advisor		
Fees	252,332	52.0
Distribution Income	149,614	31.0
Income from Real Estate	82,868	16.9
Other income	1,558	0.1
Total	486,372	100.0

ANNUAL FINANCIAL DATA

	10/31/01	10/31/00	10/31/99	10/31/98	10/31/97	10/31/96	10/31/95
Earnings Per Share	⑤⑥1.60	⑤1.58	③⑤0.71	④0.41	0.52	①0.47	②0.36
Cash Flow Per Share	2.67	2.74	1.58	1.29	1.26	1.19	1.07
Tang. Book Val. Per Share	2.81	3.65	2.73	2.94	3.03	2.77	2.59
Dividends Per Share	0.25	0.20	0.16	0.13	0.10	0.09	0.08
Dividend Payout %	15.8	12.8	22.7	31.5	20.2	19.0	22.4
INCOME STATEMENT (IN THOUSANDS):							
Total Revenues	486,372	429,566	348,950	249,987	200,910	181,361	167,922
Costs & Expenses	218,533	161,959	205,380	134,591	79,941	67,335	68,175
Depreciation & Amort.	76,946	84,943	65,666	66,744	57,064	55,005	52,563
Operating Income	190,893	182,664	77,904	48,652	63,905	59,021	47,184
Net Interest Inc./(Exp.)	4,556	3,652	671	1,791	d380	d7	d2,061
Income Before Income Taxes	178,666	187,179	85,910	50,038	67,470	59,922	43,741
Income Taxes	62,469	71,128	33,505	19,515	27,236	24,088	16,773
Equity Earnings/Minority Int.	790	384	10	105	384	1,639	...
Net Income	⑧⑥116,020	⑥116,051	⑧⑤52,405	④30,523	40,234	①35,834	②26,968
Cash Flow	192,966	200,994	118,071	97,267	97,298	90,839	79,531
Average Shs. Outstg.	72,300	73,222	74,494	75,514	77,396	76,616	74,312
BALANCE SHEET (IN THOUSANDS):							
Cash & Cash Equivalents	210,709	102,479	77,395	96,435	140,520	116,375	79,121
Total Current Assets	237,480	120,242	90,488	130,433	164,168	130,072	98,602
Net Property	14,938	13,161	12,459	2,696	2,537	2,828	2,855
Total Assets	675,301	432,989	358,229	380,260	387,375	360,262	357,586
Total Current Liabilities	83,844	61,793	48,890	48,957	39,968	24,081	24,727
Long-Term Obligations	215,488	21,429	28,571	35,714	50,964	54,549	56,102
Net Stockholders' Equity	301,126	254,950	194,268	211,809	226,280	210,780	194,520
Net Working Capital	153,636	58,449	41,598	81,476	124,200	105,991	73,875
Year-end Shs. Outstg.	68,617	69,544	70,520	71,332	73,876	75,072	74,528
STATISTICAL RECORD:							
Operating Profit Margin %	39.2	42.5	22.3	19.5	31.8	32.5	28.1
Net Profit Margin %	23.9	27.0	15.0	12.2	20.0	19.8	16.1
Return on Equity %	38.5	45.5	27.0	14.4	17.8	17.0	13.9
Return on Assets %	17.2	26.8	14.6	8.0	10.4	9.9	7.5
Debt/Total Assets %	31.9	4.9	8.0	9.4	13.2	15.1	15.7
Price Range	39.22-26.50	32.94-18.13	20.00-9.34	12.55-8.72	9.50-5.22	6.22-3.25	4.91-3.41
P/E Ratio	24.5-16.6	20.8-11.5	28.4-13.3	31.0-21.5	18.3-10.0	13.3-6.9	13.6-9.4
Average Yield %	0.8	0.9	1.1	1.2	1.4	1.9	2.0

Statistics are as originally reported. Adj. for 2-for-1 stk. splits: 11/00, 8/98, & 5/97. ① Bef. extraord. cr. of $1.6 mill. ② Bef. disc. oper. gain of $3.4 mill. ③ Bef. acctg. chrg. of $36.6 mill. ④ Incl. real estate impair. loss of $2.6 mill. & invest. gain of $2.1 mill. ⑤ Incl. invest. loss of $2.6 mill., 10/31/01; gain of $226,000, 10/31/00; gain of $7.3 mill., 10/31/99. ⑥ Incl. impair. loss of $15.1 mill.

OFFICERS:
J. B. Hawkes, Chmn., Pres., C.E.O.
W. M. Steul, V.P., C.F.O., Treas.
A. R. Dynner, V.P., Sec.

INVESTOR CONTACT: William M. Steul, V.P. & C.F.O., (617) 482-8260

PRINCIPAL OFFICE: 255 State Street, Boston, MA 02109

TELEPHONE NUMBER: (617) 482-8260
FAX: (617) 482-2396
WEB: www.eatonvance.com
NO. OF EMPLOYEES: 562
SHAREHOLDERS: 970 (approx.)
ANNUAL MEETING: In May
INCORPORATED: MD, May, 1959; reincorp., MD, Feb., 1981

INSTITUTIONAL HOLDINGS:
No. of Institutions: 189
Shares Held: 33,856,007
% Held: 48.6

INDUSTRY: Investment advice (SIC: 6282)

TRANSFER AGENT(S): EquiServe, L.P., Boston, MA

EMERSON ELECTRIC CO. ✓

YIELD 2.7%
P/E RATIO 26.3

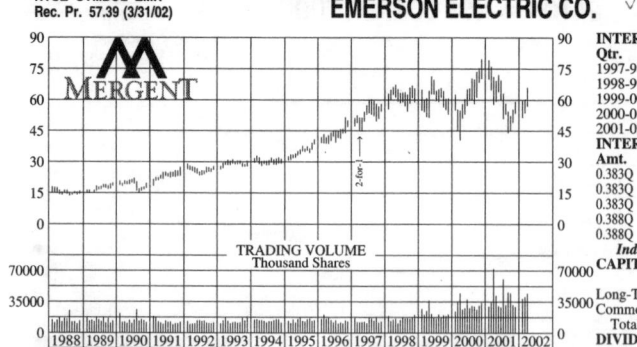

MERGENT

TRADING VOLUME
Thousand Shares

| 1988 | 1989 | 1990 | 1991 | 1992 | 1993 | 1994 | 1995 | 1996 | 1997 | 1998 | 1999 | 2000 | 2001 | 2002 |

*7 YEAR PRICE SCORE 90.7   *12 MONTH PRICE SCORE 106.1
*NYSE COMPOSITE INDEX=100

INTERIM EARNINGS (Per Share):

Qtr.	Dec.	Mar.	June	Sept.
1997-98	0.64	0.69	0.73	0.71
1998-99	0.69	0.74	0.79	0.78
1999-00	0.75	0.82	0.87	0.86
2000-01	0.83	0.83	0.77	d0.03
2001-02	0.61	...	...	...

INTERIM DIVIDENDS (Per Share):

Amt.	Decl.	Ex.	Rec.	Pay.
0.383Q	2/06/01	2/14/01	2/16/01	3/09/01
0.383Q	5/01/01	5/09/01	5/11/01	6/11/01
0.383Q	8/07/01	8/15/01	8/17/01	9/10/01
0.388Q	11/06/01	11/14/01	11/16/01	12/10/01
0.388Q	2/05/02	2/13/02	2/15/02	3/11/02

Indicated div.: $1.55 (Div. Reinv. Plan)

CAPITALIZATION (9/30/01):

	($000)	(%)
Long-Term Debt	2,255,600	26.9
Common & Surplus	6,114,000	73.1
Total	8,369,600	100.0

DIVIDEND ACHIEVER STATUS:
Rank: 161   10-Year Growth Rate: 8.68%
Total Years of Dividend Growth: 45

RECENT DEVELOPMENTS: For the first quarter ended 12/31/01, net earnings fell 28.7% to $254.7 million versus $357.4 million in the equivalent 2000 quarter. Results for 2001 were adversely affected by weak economic conditions and customers acting to reduce inventories and production. Net sales decreased 15.9% to $3.29 billion from $3.92 billion a year earlier. Industrial automation sales declined 12.8% to $656.4 million, while electronics and telecom sales fell 41.6% to $634.5 million.

PROSPECTS: The Company is optimistic in regard to its future market environment and expects steady improvement in business conditions as the year progresses. Important early indicators reflect solid results since early December. Going forward, EMR will continue to focus on restructuring actions. EMR is reducing salaried headcount, closing and consolidating facilities, and discontinuing certain product areas that have not met growth and profitability expectations.

BUSINESS

EMERSON ELECTRIC CO. is a global manufacturer of a broad range of electrical, electromechanical and electronic products and systems sold through independent distributors and to original equipment manufacturers. The process control segment provides measurement and fluid flow instrumentation, valves and control systems as well as services for process and industrial applications. The industrial automation segment provides industrial motors, drives, controls and equipment. The electronics and telecommunications segment provides power supplies and power distribution, protection and conversion equipment, and fiber optic conduits. The heating, ventilating and air conditioning segment provides a broad range of components and systems for refrigeration and comfort control markets. The appliance and tools segment provides motors, controls and other components for appliances, refrigeration and comfort control applications as well as disposers, tools and storage products.

ANNUAL FINANCIAL DATA

	9/30/01	9/30/00	9/30/99	9/30/98	9/30/97	9/30/96	9/30/95
Earnings Per Share	① 2.40	3.30	3.00	2.77	2.52	2.27	2.03
Cash Flow Per Share	4.05	4.87	4.45	4.03	3.67	3.31	2.99
Tang. Book Val. Per Share	2.22	2.53	4.43	4.79	5.23	5.75	5.55
Dividends Per Share	1.54	1.46	1.33	1.21	1.10	1.00	0.92
Dividend Payout %	64.0	44.1	44.4	43.7	43.8	44.3	45.3

INCOME STATEMENT (IN MILLIONS):

	9/30/01	9/30/00	9/30/99	9/30/98	9/30/97	9/30/96	9/30/95
Total Revenues	15,479.6	15,544.8	14,269.5	13,447.2	12,298.6	11,149.9	10,012.9
Costs & Expenses	12,878.2	12,400.4	11,421.4	10,809.5	9,882.5	8,949.4	8,067.8
Depreciation & Amort.	708.5	678.5	637.5	562.5	511.6	464.6	408.9
Operating Income	1,892.9	2,465.9	2,210.6	2,075.2	1,904.5	1,735.9	1,536.2
Net Interest Inc./(Exp.)	d304.3	d287.6	d189.7	d151.7	d120.9	d126.9	d110.6
Income Before Income Taxes	1,588.6	2,178.3	2,020.9	1,923.5	1,783.6	1,609.0	1,459.9
Income Taxes	556.8	755.9	707.3	694.9	661.7	590.5	530.9
Net Income	① 1,031.8	1,422.4	1,313.6	1,228.6	1,121.9	1,018.5	929.0
Cash Flow	1,740.3	2,100.9	1,951.1	1,791.1	1,633.5	1,483.1	1,337.9
Average Shs. Outstg. (000)	429,500	431,400	438,400	444,100	445,000	448,096	447,506

BALANCE SHEET (IN MILLIONS):

	9/30/01	9/30/00	9/30/99	9/30/98	9/30/97	9/30/96	9/30/95
Cash & Cash Equivalents	355.7	280.8	266.1	209.7	221.1	149.0	117.3
Total Current Assets	5,320.1	5,482.7	5,124.4	5,001.3	4,716.8	4,187.2	3,784.1
Net Property	3,288.0	3,243.4	3,154.4	3,011.6	2,735.4	2,450.8	2,134.9
Total Assets	15,046.4	15,164.3	13,623.5	12,659.8	11,463.3	10,481.0	9,399.0
Total Current Liabilities	5,379.1	5,218.8	4,590.4	4,021.7	3,842.4	3,021.1	3,280.7
Long-Term Obligations	2,255.6	2,247.7	1,317.1	1,056.6	570.7	772.6	208.6
Net Stockholders' Equity	6,114.0	6,402.8	6,180.5	5,803.3	5,420.7	5,353.4	4,870.8
Net Working Capital	d59.0	263.9	534.0	979.6	874.4	1,166.1	503.4
Year-end Shs. Outstg. (000)	419,626	427,477	433,044	438,224	440,804	447,440	447,898

STATISTICAL RECORD:

	9/30/01	9/30/00	9/30/99	9/30/98	9/30/97	9/30/96	9/30/95
Operating Profit Margin %	12.2	15.9	15.5	15.4	15.5	15.6	15.3
Net Profit Margin %	6.7	9.2	9.2	9.1	9.1	9.1	9.3
Return on Equity %	16.9	22.2	21.3	21.2	20.7	19.0	19.1
Return on Assets %	6.9	9.4	9.6	9.7	9.8	9.7	9.9
Debt/Total Assets %	15.0	14.8	9.7	8.3	5.0	7.4	2.2
Price Range	79.25-44.04	79.75-40.50	71.44-51.44	67.44-54.50	60.38-45.00	51.75-38.75	40.88-30.75
P/E Ratio	33.0-18.3	24.2-12.3	23.8-17.1	24.3-19.7	24.0-17.9	22.8-17.1	20.1-15.1
Average Yield %	2.5	2.4	2.2	2.0	2.1	2.2	2.6

Statistics are as originally reported. Adjusted for 2-for-1 stock split 11/96. ① Incl. pre-tax rationalization chrg. of $377.0 mill.

OFFICERS:
C. F. Knight, Chmn.
J. G. Berges, Pres.
D. N. Farr, C.E.O.
INVESTOR CONTACT: Robert T. Sharp, Dir., Investor Relations, (314) 553-2197
PRINCIPAL OFFICE: 8000 West Florissant Avenue, P.O. Box 4100, St. Louis, MO 63136

TELEPHONE NUMBER: (314) 553-2000
FAX: (314) 553-3527
WEB: www.gotoemerson.com
NO. OF EMPLOYEES: 124,500 (approx.)
SHAREHOLDERS: 33,700 (approx.)
ANNUAL MEETING: In Feb.
INCORPORATED: MO, Sept., 1890

INSTITUTIONAL HOLDINGS:
No. of Institutions: 814
Shares Held: 281,616,606
% Held: 66.9

INDUSTRY: Process control instruments (SIC: 3823)

TRANSFER AGENT(S): Mellon Investor Services, LLC, South Hackensack, NJ

ENERGEN CORPORATION

YIELD 2.6%
P/E RATIO 14.1

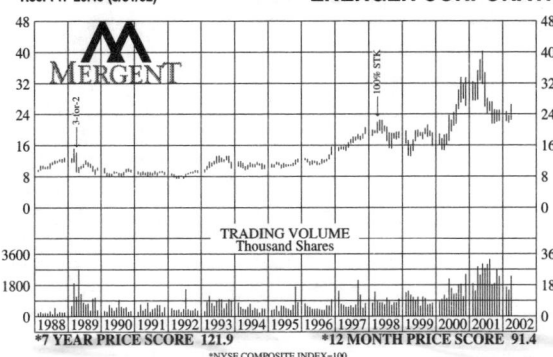

INTERIM EARNINGS (Per Share):

Qtr.	Dec.	Mar.	June	Sept.
1997-98	0.21	1.37	Nil	d0.34
1998-99	0.13	1.42	0.12	d0.28
1999-00	0.30	1.36	0.15	d0.06
2000-01	0.44	1.52	0.33	d0.10

Qtr.	Mar.	June	Sept.	Dec.
2001				0.12

INTERIM DIVIDENDS (Per Share):

Amt.	Decl.	Ex.	Rec.	Pay.
0.17Q	1/24/01	2/13/01	2/15/01	3/01/01
0.17Q	4/25/01	5/11/01	5/15/01	6/01/01
0.175Q	7/25/01	8/13/01	8/15/01	9/04/01
0.175Q	10/24/01	11/13/01	11/15/01	12/03/01
0.175Q	1/30/02	2/13/02	2/15/02	3/01/02

Indicated div.: $0.70 (Div. Reinv. Plan)

CAPITALIZATION (9/30/01):

	($000)	(%)
Long-Term Debt	544,110	53.1
Common & Surplus	480,767	46.9
Total	1,024,877	100.0

TRADING VOLUME
Thousand Shares

1988 1989 1990 1991 1992 1993 1994 1995 1996 1997 1998 1999 2000 2001 2002
*7 YEAR PRICE SCORE 121.9   *12 MONTH PRICE SCORE 91.4
*NYSE COMPOSITE INDEX=100

DIVIDEND ACHIEVER STATUS:
Rank: 257   10-Year Growth Rate: 3.59%
Total Years of Dividend Growth: 19

RECENT DEVELOPMENTS: EGN changed its fiscal year end to December 31 beginning in 2002. For the quarter ended 12/31/01, net income dropped 73.3% to $3.7 million versus $13.7 million in the equivalent 2000 period. Results for 2001 included a $5.5 million non-cash, Enron-related charge. Total revenues declined 16.2% to $147.3 million from $175.9 million in 2000. Natural gas distribution revenues fell 18.8% to $96.7 million, while oil and gas operations revenues decreased 10.8% to $50.7 million.

PROSPECTS: For calendar 2002, EGN expects earnings in the range of $1.85 to $1.95 per diluted share. On 4/8/02, EGN's subsidiary, Energen Resources Corporation, acquired approximately 43.0 million barrels of oil equivalent reserves in the Permian Basin in west Texas from First Permian, LLC. Under the agreement, Energen Resources paid $120.0 million in cash and about $70.0 million in EGN common shares.

BUSINESS

ENERGEN CORPORATION is a diversified energy holding company engaged in the business of natural gas distribution and oil and gas exploration and production. EGN provides natural gas to residential, commercial and industrial customers located in Alabama. Alagasco, EGN's principal subsidiary, is the largest natural gas distribution utility in the State of Alabama. EGN's utility operations are subject to regulation by the Alabama Public Service Commission. The oil and gas exploration and production arm of Energen is Energen Resources, which conducts its activities in the Gulf of Mexico. In fiscal 2001, revenues were derived: 70.6% natural gas distribution and 29.4% oil and gas production activities.

ANNUAL FINANCIAL DATA

	9/30/01	9/30/00	9/30/99	9/30/98	9/30/97	9/30/96	9/30/95
Earnings Per Share	2.18	① 1.75	1.38	1.23	1.16	0.98	0.89
Cash Flow Per Share	4.98	4.61	4.35	3.98	3.53	2.84	2.24
Tang. Book Val. Per Share	15.61	13.21	12.09	11.23	13.49	8.44	7.96
Dividends Per Share	0.69	0.67	0.65	0.63	0.61	0.59	0.57
Dividend Payout %	31.6	38.3	47.1	51.2	52.8	60.5	64.4

INCOME STATEMENT (IN THOUSANDS):

	9/30/01	9/30/00	9/30/99	9/30/98	9/30/97	9/30/96	9/30/95
Total Revenues	784,973	555,595	497,517	502,627	448,230	399,442	321,204
Costs & Expenses	573,989	372,721	331,519	360,143	325,444	308,449	249,369
Depreciation & Amort.	86,975	87,073	88,615	80,999	59,688	41,118	29,577
Maintenance Exp.	...	...	...	...	11,112	11,078	9,849
Operating Income	124,009	95,801	77,383	61,485	51,986	38,797	32,409
Net Interest Inc./(Exp.)	d42,070	d37,769	d37,173	d30,001	d22,906	d13,920	d11,818
Income Taxes	15,976	6,789	135	cr2,221	3,097	5,048	3,681
Net Income	67,896	① 53,018	41,410	36,249	28,997	21,541	19,308
Cash Flow	154,871	140,091	130,025	117,248	88,685	62,659	48,885
Average Shs. Outstg.	31,084	30,359	29,921	29,438	25,126	22,046	21,812

BALANCE SHEET (IN THOUSANDS):

	9/30/01	9/30/00	9/30/99	9/30/98	9/30/97	9/30/96	9/30/95
Gross Property	1,581,330	1,422,770	1,315,581	1,148,205	1,037,840	769,112	621,710
Accumulated Depreciation	587,669	519,444	458,614	395,794	375,303	328,262	299,096
Net Property	998,334	907,829	861,107	756,344	667,003	444,916	327,264
Total Assets	1,223,879	1,203,041	1,184,895	993,455	919,797	570,971	459,084
Long-Term Obligations	544,110	353,932	371,824	372,782	279,602	195,545	131,600
Net Stockholders' Equity	480,767	400,860	361,504	329,249	301,143	188,405	173,924
Year-end Shs. Outstg.	30,799	30,351	29,904	29,327	22,326	22,326	21,844

STATISTICAL RECORD:

	9/30/01	9/30/00	9/30/99	9/30/98	9/30/97	9/30/96	9/30/95
Operating Profit Margin %	15.8	17.2	15.6	12.2	11.6	9.7	10.1
Net Profit Margin %	8.6	9.5	8.3	7.2	6.5	5.4	6.0
Net Inc./Net Property %	6.8	5.8	4.8	4.8	4.3	4.8	5.9
Net Inc./Tot. Capital %	6.6	7.0	5.6	5.2	5.0	5.6	6.3
Return on Equity %	14.1	13.2	11.5	11.0	9.6	11.4	11.1
Accum. Depr./Gross Prop. %	37.2	36.5	34.9	34.5	36.2	42.7	48.1
Price Range	40.25-21.50	33.56-14.69	21.25-13.13	22.50-15.13	20.63-14.50	15.63-10.88	12.56-10.06
P/E Ratio	18.5-9.9	19.2-8.4	15.4-9.5	18.3-12.3	17.9-12.6	16.0-11.2	14.2-11.4
Average Yield %	2.2	2.8	3.8	3.3	3.5	4.5	5.0

Statistics are as originally reported. Adjusted for 2-for-1 stock split, 3/98. ① Incl. an after-tax gain of $1.9 mill. on the sale of offshore properties.

OFFICERS:
W. M. Warren Jr., Chmn., Pres., C.E.O.
G. C. Ketcham, Exec. V.P., C.F.O., Treas.

INVESTOR CONTACT: Julie S. Ryland, Asst. V.P., Inv. Rel., (800) 654-3206

PRINCIPAL OFFICE: 605 Richard Arrington Jr. Blvd. North, Birmingham, AL 35203-2707

TELEPHONE NUMBER: (205) 326-2700
FAX: (205) 326-2704
WEB: www.energen.com

NO. OF EMPLOYEES: 1,485

SHAREHOLDERS: 8,400 (approx.)

ANNUAL MEETING: In Jan.

INCORPORATED: AL, Jan., 1978

INSTITUTIONAL HOLDINGS:
No. of Institutions: 155
Shares Held: 16,545,290
% Held: 53.0

INDUSTRY: Natural gas distribution (SIC: 4924)

TRANSFER AGENT(S): EquiServe, First Chicago Trust Division, Jersey City, NJ

ENERGY WEST INCORPORATED

YIELD 5.0%
P/E RATIO 7.8

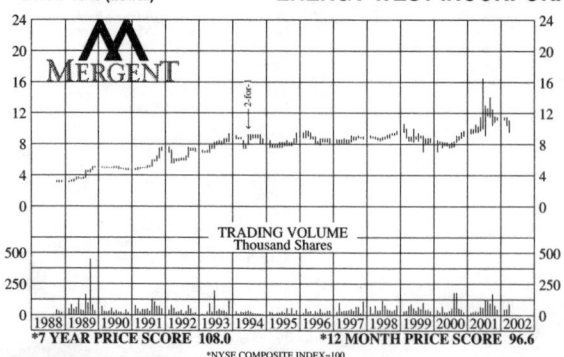

INTERIM EARNINGS (Per Share):

Qtr.	Sept.	Dec.	Mar.	June
1998-99	d0.28	0.31	0.53	0.10
1999-00	d0.27	0.20	0.59	0.01
2000-01	d0.24	0.52	1.04	0.22
2001-02	d0.17	0.25	...	...

INTERIM DIVIDENDS (Per Share):

Amt.	Decl.	Ex.	Rec.	Pay.
0.125Q	2/23/01	3/14/01	3/16/01	3/30/01
0.13Q	6/07/01	6/13/01	6/15/01	6/29/01
0.13Q	9/13/01	9/19/01	9/21/01	9/28/01
0.13Q	11/15/01	12/19/01	12/21/01	1/04/02
0.13Q	2/22/02	3/13/02	3/15/02	3/29/02

Indicated div.: $0.52 (Div. Reinv. Plan)

CAPITALIZATION (6/30/01):

	($000)	(%)
Long-Term Debt	15,881	23.8
Deferred Income Tax	3,836	5.7
Common & Surplus	47,108	70.5
Total	66,824	100.0

DIVIDEND ACHIEVER STATUS:
Rank: 219   10-Year Growth Rate: 5.78%
Total Years of Dividend Growth: 15

TRADING VOLUME
Thousand Shares

*7 YEAR PRICE SCORE 108.0   *12 MONTH PRICE SCORE 96.6
*NYSE COMPOSITE INDEX=100

RECENT DEVELOPMENTS: For the quarter ended 12/31/01, net income dropped 52.9% to $622,544 compared with $1.3 million in the corresponding prior-year quarter. Earnings primarily reflected reduced margins related to the remarketing of electricity in EWST's marketing and wholesales operation as market prices have stabilized. Total revenue decreased 13.6% to $24.8 million from $28.7 million a year earlier. Revenues from natural gas operations declined 5.5% to $12.2 million from $12.9 million in 2000. Revenues from propane operations fell 40.2% to $2.8 million from $4.6 million the year before. Energy marketing and wholesale revenues decreased 12.0% to $9.9 million from $11.2 million in the previous year. Operating income fell 49.5% to $1.2 million from $2.3 million in the year-earlier quarter. Total interest charges declined 15.3% to $503,339, primarily due to lower short-term interest rates.

BUSINESS

ENERGY WEST INCORPORATED is a regulated public utility, with certain non-utility operations conducted through its subsidiaries. The Company's regulated utility operations involve the distribution and sale of natural gas to the public in the Great Falls and West Yellowstone, Montana and Cody, Wyoming areas and sale of propane to the public through underground propane vapor systems in the Payson, Arizona and Cascade, Montana areas. The Company also distributes natural gas through an underground system in West Yellowstone, Montana that is supplied by liquefied natural gas. EWST conducts certain non-utility operations through its three wholly-owned subsidiaries, Energy West Propane, Inc. (EWP), Energy West Resources, Inc. (EWR) and Energy West Development, Inc. (EWD). EWP is engaged in the distribution of retail and wholesale bulk propane in Wyoming, Arizona and Montana. EWR is involved in the marketing of gas and electricity and gas storage in Montana and Wyoming. EWD owns one real estate property in Great Falls, Montana.

ANNUAL FINANCIAL DATA

	6/30/01	6/30/00	6/30/99	6/30/98	6/30/97	6/30/96	6/30/95
Earnings Per Share	1.10	0.53	⊡ 0.66	0.64	0.55	0.61	0.68
Cash Flow Per Share	2.05	1.41	1.46	1.47	1.35	1.41	1.47
Tang. Book Val. Per Share	18.74	17.90	18.04	17.85	14.29	14.27	13.97
Dividends Per Share	0.51	0.49	0.47	0.45	0.43	0.41	0.39
Dividend Payout %	46.4	92.4	71.2	70.3	78.2	67.2	57.3
INCOME STATEMENT (IN THOUSANDS):							
Total Revenues	119,940	72,196	53,461	43,064	38,215	31,318	30,548
Costs & Expenses	111,559	66,886	48,272	37,324	33,127	26,520	25,679
Depreciation & Amort.	2,379	2,170	1,948	1,986	1,893	1,834	1,778
Operating Income	6,002	3,140	3,240	3,753	3,195	2,965	3,092
Net Interest Inc./(Exp.)	d2,097	d1,674	d1,093	d1,583	d1,525	d1,243	d939
Income Before Income Taxes	4,341	2,047	2,564	2,312	1,996	2,173	2,329
Income Taxes	1,575	750	977	792	703	766	816
Net Income	2,765	1,297	⊡ 1,587	1,520	1,293	1,407	1,513
Cash Flow	5,144	3,466	3,536	3,506	3,186	3,241	3,290
Average Shs. Outstg.	2,510	2,457	2,419	2,391	2,357	2,299	2,235
BALANCE SHEET (IN THOUSANDS):							
Cash & Cash Equivalents	221	112	226	58	149	893	567
Total Current Assets	26,621	16,287	11,429	12,326	12,398	9,092	6,263
Net Property	32,999	31,804	29,372	27,572	27,398	26,090	23,550
Total Assets	62,278	51,547	44,201	43,335	42,885	37,495	32,375
Total Current Liabilities	24,416	14,841	7,230	6,745	15,317	11,088	6,786
Long-Term Obligations	15,881	16,395	16,840	17,278	9,684	10,046	10,435
Net Stockholders' Equity	47,108	44,318	43,904	42,901	33,678	33,126	31,500
Net Working Capital	2,205	1,446	4,199	5,581	d2,919	d1,995	d523
Year-end Shs. Outstg.	2,513	2,475	2,434	2,403	2,357	2,321	2,254
STATISTICAL RECORD:							
Operating Profit Margin %	5.0	4.3	6.1	8.7	8.4	9.5	10.1
Net Profit Margin %	2.3	1.8	3.0	3.5	3.4	4.5	5.0
Return on Equity %	5.9	2.9	3.6	3.5	3.8	4.2	4.8
Return on Assets %	4.4	2.5	3.6	3.5	3.0	3.8	4.7
Debt/Total Assets %	25.5	31.8	38.1	39.9	22.6	26.8	32.2
Price Range	16.50-9.05	9.75-7.00	10.63-7.00	9.75-8.38	9.13-8.13	9.75-7.88	9.50-7.50
P/E Ratio	15.0-8.2	18.4-13.2	16.1-10.6	15.2-13.1	16.6-14.8	16.0-12.9	14.0-11.0
Average Yield %	4.0	5.9	5.3	5.0	5.0	4.7	4.6

Statistics are as originally reported. ⊡ Incls. gain of $236,291 from sales of assets.

OFFICERS:
E. J. Bernica, Pres., C.E.O.
J. S. Hogan, Asst. V.P., Treas.
J. C. Allen, V.P., Sec., Gen. Couns.

INVESTOR CONTACT: JoAnn Hogan, Treas., (406) 791-7555

PRINCIPAL OFFICE: 1 First Avenue South, Great Falls, MT 59401

TELEPHONE NUMBER: (406) 791-7500
FAX: (406) 791-7560
WEB: www.ewst.com

NO. OF EMPLOYEES: 138 (avg.)

SHAREHOLDERS: N/A

ANNUAL MEETING: In Nov.

INCORPORATED: MT, 1909

ENERGYSOUTH, INC.

YIELD 4.0%
P/E RATIO 15.1

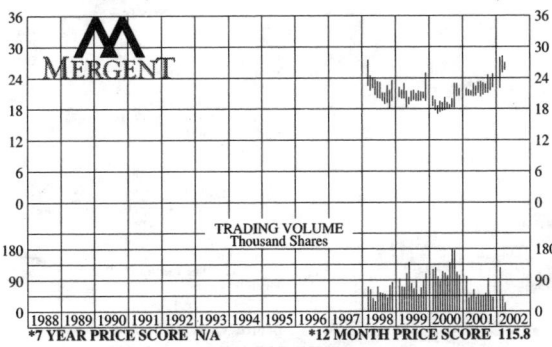

*7 YEAR PRICE SCORE N/A   *12 MONTH PRICE SCORE 115.8
*NYSE COMPOSITE INDEX=100

TRADING VOLUME
Thousand Shares

INTERIM EARNINGS (Per Share):

Qtr.	Dec.	Mar.	June	Sept.
1997-98	0.40	0.97	0.23	0.10
1998-99	0.59	0.76	0.22	0.18
1999-00	0.54	0.84	0.21	0.18
2000-01	0.55	0.73	0.10	0.14
2001-02	0.75	...	...	...

INTERIM DIVIDENDS (Per Share):

Amt.	Decl.	Ex.	Rec.	Pay.
0.26Q	4/27/01	6/13/01	6/15/01	7/01/01
0.26Q	7/27/01	9/12/01	9/14/01	10/01/01
0.26Q	10/19/01	12/21/01	12/17/01	1/01/02
0.26Q	1/25/02	3/13/02	3/15/02	4/01/02

Indicated div.: $1.04 (Div. Reinv. Plan)

CAPITALIZATION (9/30/01):

	($000)	(%)
Long-Term Debt	90,592	51.0
Deferred Income Tax	13,660	7.7
Minority Interest	3,270	1.8
Common & Surplus	70,124	39.5
Total	177,646	100.0

DIVIDEND ACHIEVER STATUS:
Rank: 216   10-Year Growth Rate: 5.94%
Total Years of Dividend Growth: 24

RECENT DEVELOPMENTS: For the first quarter ended 12/31/01, the Company reported net income of $3.8 million compared with income of $2.7 million, before an extraordinary loss of $1.4 million in the previous year. Earnings for 2001 were positively affected by a general rate increase at Mobile Gas Service Corporation effective 10/2/01. Total revenues decreased 29.3% to $24.2 million from $34.1 million a year earlier. Gas revenues fell 30.5% to $22.8 million due to lower gas costs that were passed through to customers, which more than offset general revenues received from rate increases. Merchandise sales inched up to $982,000 from $981,000 in 2000, while other revenues rose 6.9% to $372,000. Cost of gas dropped 65.1% to $6.3 million from $17.9 million the year before. In November 2001, Bay Gas Storage Company, Ltd. began transporting gas under a long-term contract with the completion of a new 24-inch, 18-mile pipeline connecting Bay Gas to Gulf South Pipeline Company's high pressure pipeline.

BUSINESS

ENERGYSOUTH, INC. is the holding Company for Mobile Gas Service Corporation (MGS), a natural gas utility, and its subsidiaries. MGS is engaged in the purchase, distribution, sale and transportation of natural gas to over 100,000 residential, commercial and industrial customers in Southwest Alabama with a service territory covering approximately 300 square miles. MGS also sells natural gas appliances. EnergySouth Services, Inc. provides consulting work for utilities and industrial customers, and limited gas transportation services through its 51.0% interest in Southern Gas Transmission Company. As of 9/30/01, MGS Storage Services, Inc. held a general partnership interest of 90.9% in Bay Gas Storage Company, Ltd., which operates an underground gas storage cavern and related pipeline facilities for the storage and delivery of natural gas for MGS and other customers. The Company also owns MGS Marketing Services, Inc, which assists existing and potential customers in the purchase of natural gas.

ANNUAL FINANCIAL DATA

	9/30/01	9/30/00	9/30/99	9/30/98	9/30/97	9/30/96	9/30/95
Earnings Per Share	②1.52	1.78	①1.75	1.71	1.67	1.79	0.84
Cash Flow Per Share	3.06	3.21	3.13	2.84	2.74	2.94	1.89
Tang. Book Val. Per Share	14.20	13.95	13.11	12.29	11.36	10.43	9.36
Dividends Per Share	1.02	0.97	0.91	0.84	0.77	0.73	0.71
Dividend Payout %	67.1	54.5	52.0	49.1	46.1	40.8	84.5
INCOME STATEMENT (IN THOUSANDS):							
Total Revenues	107,759	74,097	68,060	74,022	72,670	71,378	59,111
Costs & Expenses	61,483	27,546	40,698	47,743	47,410	45,562	41,043
Depreciation & Amort.	7,696	7,079	6,795	6,596	5,740	5,406	5,055
Maintenance Exp.	20,981	20,218	1,579	1,533	1,542	1,945	1,419
Operating Income	17,599	19,254	18,988	18,150	17,978	18,465	11,594
Net Interest Inc./(Exp.)	d4,783	d4,424	d4,850	d4,240	d4,624	d4,390	d4,990
Income Taxes	4,604	5,270	5,003	4,967	4,712	5,013	2,264
Equity Earnings/Minority Int.	d651	d768	d511	d526	d516	d431	d312
Net Income	②7,561	8,792	①8,624	8,417	8,126	8,631	4,028
Cash Flow	15,257	15,871	15,419	15,013	13,866	14,037	9,083
Average Shs. Outstg.	4,987	4,944	4,933	4,926	4,883	4,838	4,812
BALANCE SHEET (IN THOUSANDS):							
Gross Property	231,445	189,162	179,531	172,000	166,154	155,579	146,777
Accumulated Depreciation	60,853	54,811	49,855	44,872	40,289	36,099	31,853
Net Property	170,592	134,351	129,676	127,128	125,865	119,480	114,924
Total Assets	218,852	167,380	173,635	166,541	161,867	152,118	136,567
Long-Term Obligations	90,592	55,222	58,017	58,979	63,580	54,509	57,328
Net Stockholders' Equity	70,124	68,544	64,154	59,895	55,177	50,400	45,063
Year-end Shs. Outstg.	4,937	4,912	4,894	4,872	4,856	4,833	4,817
STATISTICAL RECORD:							
Operating Profit Margin %	16.3	26.0	27.9	24.5	24.7	25.9	19.6
Net Profit Margin %	7.0	11.9	12.7	11.4	11.2	12.1	6.8
Net Inc./Net Property %	4.4	6.5	6.7	6.6	6.5	7.2	3.5
Net Inc./Tot. Capital %	4.3	6.3	6.3	6.3	6.2	7.4	3.6
Return on Equity %	10.8	12.8	13.4	14.1	14.7	17.1	8.9
Accum. Depr./Gross Prop. %	26.3	29.0	27.8	26.1	24.2	23.2	21.7
Price Range	24.86-20.36	23.00-17.00	25.00-18.25	27.50-18.00	...	...	...
P/E Ratio	16.4-13.4	12.9-9.6	14.3-10.4	16.1-10.5	...	...	...
Average Yield %	4.5	4.8	4.2	3.7	...	...	...

Statistics are as originally reported. Adj. to reflect 3-for-2 conversion of stock from Mobile Gas Service Corp. to EnergySouth, Inc. on 1/30/98. ① Bef. net acctg. chng. chrg. of $349,000. ② Bef. extraord. loss of $1.4 million.

OFFICERS:
J. C. Hope III, Chmn.
W. L. Hovell, Vice-Chmn.
J. S. Davis, Pres., C.E.O.

INVESTOR CONTACT: Charles P. Huffman, Sr. V.P., C.F.O., (251) 476-2720

PRINCIPAL OFFICE: 2828 Dauphin Street, Mobile, AL 36606

TELEPHONE NUMBER: (251) 450-4774
FAX: (251) 478-5817
WEB: www.energysouth.com
NO. OF EMPLOYEES: 294
SHAREHOLDERS: 1,438
ANNUAL MEETING: In Jan.
INCORPORATED: AL, May, 1933

INSTITUTIONAL HOLDINGS:
No. of Institutions: 25
Shares Held: 962,980
% Held: 19.4

INDUSTRY: Natural gas distribution (SIC: 4924)

TRANSFER AGENT(S): BankBoston, NA c/o EquiServe, Boston, MA

EXXON MOBIL CORPORATION

YIELD 2.1%
P/E RATIO 19.8

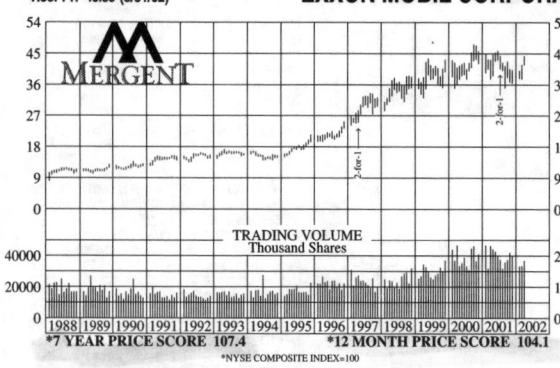

TRADING VOLUME
Thousand Shares

	1988	1989	1990	1991	1992	1993	1994	1995	1996	1997	1998	1999	2000	2001	2002

*7 YEAR PRICE SCORE 107.4   *12 MONTH PRICE SCORE 104.1
*NYSE COMPOSITE INDEX=100

INTERIM EARNINGS (Per Share):

Qtr.	Mar.	June	Sept.	Dec.
1997	0.44	0.40	0.37	0.50
1998	0.38	0.33	0.29	0.31
1999	0.21	0.25	0.31	0.33
2000	0.44	0.58	0.59	0.71
2001	0.71	0.65	0.46	0.39

INTERIM DIVIDENDS (Per Share):

Amt.	Decl.	Ex.	Rec.	Pay.
2-for-1	5/30/01	7/19/01	6/20/01	7/18/01
0.23Q	7/25/01	8/09/01	8/13/01	9/10/01
0.23Q	10/31/01	11/07/01	11/09/01	12/10/01
0.23Q	1/30/02	2/07/02	2/11/02	3/11/02

Indicated div.: $0.92 (Div. Reinv. Plan)

CAPITALIZATION (12/31/01):

	($000)	(%)
Long-Term Debt	7,099,000	7.1
Deferred Income Tax	16,359,000	16.5
Minority Interest	2,825,000	2.8
Common & Surplus	73,161,000	73.6
Total	99,444,000	100.0

DIVIDEND ACHIEVER STATUS:

Rank: 262	10-Year Growth Rate: 3.00%
Total Years of Dividend Growth:	19

RECENT DEVELOPMENTS: For the year ended 12/31/01, net income was $15.11 billion, before an extraordinary gain of $215.0 million, compared with $15.99 billion, before an extraordinary gain of $1.73 billion, the previous year. Results for 2001 and 2000 included merger expenses of $748.0 million and $1.41 billion, respectively. Total revenues declined 8.3% to $213.49 billion from $232.75 billion a year earlier.

PROSPECTS: The Company's near-term outlook remains lackluster, reflecting significantly lower year-over-year crude oil realizations and the sharp drop in North America natural gas prices that are pressuring the Company's upstream operations. In addition, XOM's downstream operations are experiencing weaker refining margins. The chemicals segment outlook is also uncertain, as a result of weak market conditions and lower volumes.

BUSINESS

EXXON MOBIL CORPORATION'S principal business is energy, involving exploration for, and production of, crude oil and natural gas, manufacturing of petroleum products and transportation and sale of crude oil, natural gas and petroleum products. Exxon Mobil is a major manufacturer and marketer of basic petrochemicals, including olefins, aromatics, polyethylene and polypropylene plastics and a wide variety of specialty products. Exxon Mobil is engaged in exploration for, and mining and sale of coal, copper and other minerals. Exxon Mobil also has interests in electric power generation facilities. As of 12/31/01, XOM owned 69.6% of Imperial Oil Limited. In 2001, worldwide proved reserves were: crude oil and natural gas liquids, 11,491 million barrels; and natural gas, 55,946 billion cubic feet. On 11/30/99, Exxon Corp. acquired Mobil Corporation in a transaction valued at $81.00 billion.

ANNUAL FINANCIAL DATA

	12/31/01 ⑧	12/31/00	12/31/99	12/31/98	12/31/97	12/31/96	12/31/95
Earnings Per Share	⑧ 2.18	⑧ 2.28	① 1.13	① 1.31	① 1.69	① 1.51	1.30
Cash Flow Per Share	3.32	3.43	2.35	2.43	2.78	2.58	2.39
Tang. Book Val. Per Share	10.74	10.21	9.12	8.99	8.85	8.70	8.05
Dividends Per Share	0.91	0.88	0.83	0.82	0.81	0.78	0.75
Dividend Payout %	41.7	38.7	74.2	62.8	48.2	51.8	57.9
INCOME STATEMENT (IN MILLIONS):							
Total Revenues	213,488.0	232,748.0	185,527.0	117,772.0	137,242.0	134,249.0	123,920.0
Costs & Expenses	181,132.0	196,948.0	165,378.0	103,276.0	118,555.0	116,540.0	107,607.0
Depreciation & Amort.	7,944.0	8,130.0	8,304.0	5,340.0	5,474.0	5,329.0	5,386.0
Operating Income	24,412.0	27,670.0	11,845.0	9,156.0	13,213.0	12,380.0	10,927.0
Net Interest Inc./(Exp.)	d293.0	d589.0	d695.0	d1000.0	d415.0	d464.0	d485.0
Income Before Income Taxes	24,119.0	27,081.0	11,150.0	9,056.0	12,798.0	11,916.0	10,442.0
Income Taxes	9,014.0	11,091.0	3,240.0	2,616.0	4,338.0	4,406.0	3,972.0
Net Income	⑧ 15,105.0	⑧ 15,990.0	① 7,910.0	① 6,440.0	② 8,460.0	② 7,510.0	6,470.0
Cash Flow	23,049.0	24,120.0	16,214.0	11,780.0	13,934.0	12,839.0	11,856.0
Average Shs. Outstg. (000)	6,941,000	7,034,000	6,906,000	4,856,000	5,010,000	4,968,000	4,968,000
BALANCE SHEET (IN MILLIONS):							
Cash & Cash Equivalents	6,547.0	7,081.0	1,761.0	1,461.0	4,062.0	2,969.0	1,789.0
Total Current Assets	35,681.0	40,399.0	31,141.0	17,593.0	21,192.0	19,910.0	17,318.0
Net Property	89,602.0	89,829.0	94,043.0	65,199.0	66,414.0	66,607.0	65,446.0
Total Assets	143,174.0	149,000.0	144,521.0	92,630.0	96,064.0	95,527.0	91,296.0
Total Current Liabilities	30,114.0	38,191.0	38,733.0	19,412.0	19,654.0	19,505.0	18,736.0
Long-Term Obligations	7,099.0	7,280.0	8,402.0	4,530.0	7,050.0	7,236.0	7,778.0
Net Stockholders' Equity	73,161.0	70,757.0	63,466.0	43,750.0	43,660.0	43,542.0	40,436.0
Net Working Capital	5,567.0	2,208.0	d7,592.0	d1,819.0	1,538.0	405.0	d1,418.0
Year-end Shs. Outstg. (000)	6,809,000	6,930,000	6,959,784	4,856,000	4,914,000	4,968,000	4,968,000
STATISTICAL RECORD:							
Operating Profit Margin %	11.4	11.9	6.4	7.8	9.6	9.2	8.8
Net Profit Margin %	7.1	6.9	4.3	5.5	6.2	5.6	5.2
Return on Equity %	20.6	22.6	12.5	14.7	19.4	17.2	16.0
Return on Assets %	10.6	10.7	5.5	7.0	8.8	7.9	7.1
Debt/Total Assets %	5.0	4.9	5.8	4.9	7.3	7.6	8.5
Price Range	45.84-35.01	47.72-34.94	43.63-32.16	38.66-28.31	33.63-24.13	25.31-19.47	21.50-15.03
P/E Ratio	21.0-16.1	21.0-15.4	38.8-28.6	29.6-21.7	20.0-14.3	16.8-12.9	16.6-11.6
Average Yield %	2.3	2.1	2.2	2.4	2.8	3.5	4.1

Statistics are as originally reported. Adj. for stk. splits: 2-for-1, 4/97 & 7/01. ① Bef. acctg. chrg. of $70.0 mill. ② Incl. non-recurr. credit 12/31/97: $305.0 mill.; credit 12/31/96: $90.0 mill. ③ Incl. non-recurr. chrg. of $625.0 mill. ④ Incl. merger rel. exp. of $1.41 bill.; bef. extraord. gain fr. required asset divest. of $1.73 bill. ($0.50/sh.) ⑧ Incl. results of Mobil Corporation. ⑧ Bef. extraord. gain of $215.0 mill.; incl. merger rel. exp. of $748.0 mill.

OFFICERS:
L. R. Raymond, Chmn.
R. Dahan, Exec. V.P.
H. J. Longwell, Exec. V.P.

INVESTOR CONTACT: Media Relations,
(972) 444-1109

PRINCIPAL OFFICE: 5959 Las Colinas Blvd.,
Irving, TX 75039-2298

TELEPHONE NUMBER: (972) 444-1000
FAX: (972) 444-1348
WEB: www.exxon.mobil.com

NO. OF EMPLOYEES: 97,900 (approx.)

SHAREHOLDERS: 697,972

ANNUAL MEETING: In May

INCORPORATED: NJ, Aug., 1882

INSTITUTIONAL HOLDINGS:
No. of Institutions: 1,251
Shares Held: 3,343,219,000
% Held: 49.1

INDUSTRY: Petroleum refining (SIC: 2911)

TRANSFER AGENT(S): ExxonMobil
Shareholder Services c/o EquiServe Trust
Company, NA, Boston, MA

F.N.B. CORPORATION

YIELD 2.7%
P/E RATIO 17.4

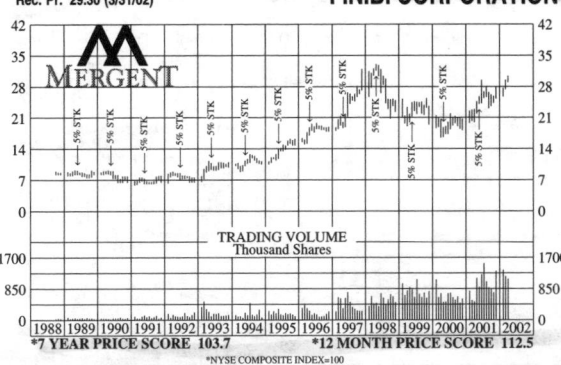

*7 YEAR PRICE SCORE 103.7   *12 MONTH PRICE SCORE 112.5
*NYSE COMPOSITE INDEX=100

INTERIM EARNINGS (Per Share,):

Qtr.	Mar.	June	Sept.	Dec.
1998	0.35	0.33	0.34	0.33
1999	0.37	0.41	0.43	0.43
2000	0.42	0.44	0.46	0.48
2001	0.24	0.41	0.51	0.52

INTERIM DIVIDENDS (Per Share):

Amt.	Decl.	Ex.	Rec.	Pay.
5% STK	4/23/01	5/01/01	5/03/01	5/31/01
0.18Q	5/23/01	5/30/01	6/02/01	6/15/01
0.20Q	8/22/01	8/29/01	9/01/01	9/15/01
0.20Q	11/15/01	11/28/01	11/30/01	12/15/01
0.20Q	2/15/02	2/28/02	3/04/02	3/15/02

Indicated div.: $0.80 (Div. Reinv. Plan)

CAPITALIZATION (12/31/01):

	($000)	(%)
Total Deposits	3,292,392	87.5
Long-Term Debt	103,013	2.7
Preferred Stock	1	0.0
Common & Surplus	369,196	9.8
Total	3,764,602	100.0

DIVIDEND ACHIEVER STATUS:

Rank: 49   10-Year Growth Rate: 16.03%
Total Years of Dividend Growth: 17

RECENT DEVELOPMENTS: For the year ended 12/31/01, net income increased 1.3% to $44.6 million versus $44.0 million in 2000. Results for 2001 and 2000 included amortization of intangibles of $2.5 million and $2.1 million, respectively. Results for 2001 also included one-time charges totaling $11.0 million. Net interest income advanced 5.9% to $171.0 million from $161.5 million a year earlier. Total interest income slipped 1.7% to $296.7 million, while total interest expense declined 10.5% to $125.7 million. Non-

interest income jumped 30.6% to $82.8 million, while non-interest expense rose 17.7% to $174.8 million. Comparisons were made with restated prior-year results. On 1/18/02, FBAN announced the acquisition of Promistar Financial Corporation through a pooling-of-interests transaction valued at $436.0 million. On 1/31/02, FBAN completed the acquisition of Central Bank Shares Inc., the parent of Bank of Central Florida. The acquisition should be immediately accretive to earnings.

BUSINESS

F.N.B. CORPORATION is a financial holding company that provides, through its subsidiaries, a full range of financial services to consumers and small- to medium-size businesses in its market areas. The bank subsidiaries offer traditional full-service commercial banking services, including commercial and individual demand and time deposit accounts and commercial, mortgage and individual installment loans. In addition, the bank subsidiaries offer various alternative investment products, including mutual funds and annuities. The consumer finance subsidiary offers personal installment loans to individuals and purchase installment sales finance contracts from retail merchants. As of 12/31/01, the Company owned and operated three community banks and one consumer finance company in Pennsylvania, southwestern Florida, northern and central Tennessee and eastern Ohio. FBAN also owns two insurance agencies, one in Florida and one in Pennsylvania.

ANNUAL FINANCIAL DATA

	12/31/01	12/31/00	12/31/99	12/31/98	12/31/97	12/31/96	12/31/95
Earnings Per Share	③ 1.68	② 1.79	1.70	① 1.45	① 1.88	① 1.59	1.65
Tang. Book Val. Per Share	14.36	13.79	12.52	12.97	13.44	13.52	13.35
Dividends Per Share	0.75	0.68	0.65	0.61	0.52	0.50	0.27
Dividend Payout %	44.7	37.8	38.0	42.3	27.6	31.2	16.6
INCOME STATEMENT (IN MILLIONS):							
Total Interest Income	296.7	290.9	254.9	236.0	195.5	139.0	135.4
Total Interest Expense	125.7	135.3	106.5	103.4	84.5	58.2	58.1
Net Interest Income	171.0	155.6	148.4	132.6	111.0	80.7	77.3
Provision for Loan Losses	12.9	10.9	9.2	7.3	10.6	6.1	5.7
Non-Interest Income	82.8	55.6	46.9	31.7	23.1	15.3	15.0
Non-Interest Expense	174.8	137.5	129.7	109.2	88.2	62.8	60.0
Income Before Taxes	66.1	62.9	56.5	47.9	35.4	27.1	26.7
Net Income	③ 44.6	② 42.8	39.3	① 31.9	① 24.3	① 18.4	18.1
Average Shs. Outstg. (000)	26,586	23,115	24,007	22,010	17,555	11,047	10,448
BALANCE SHEET (IN MILLIONS):							
Cash & Due from Banks	155.9	141.8	171.2	128.9	87.9	70.3	59.8
Total Loans & Leases	3,246.9	3,024.8	2,865.8	2,360.7	1,905.8	1,327.1	1,239.4
Allowance for Credit Losses	40.8	38.7	36.3	31.0	27.3	22.4	21.6
Net Loans & Leases	3,161.7	2,923.3	2,767.5	2,298.8	1,858.2	1,281.4	1,191.2
Total Assets	4,129.1	3,886.5	3,706.2	3,250.7	2,649.5	1,726.7	1,707.0
Total Deposits	3,292.4	3,102.9	2,909.4	2,708.6	2,192.7	1,429.7	1,442.1
Long-Term Obligations	103.0	116.1	117.6	69.5	67.2	34.2	39.8
Total Liabilities	3,759.9	3,565.3	3,415.9	2,978.5	2,418.9	1,572.0	1,563.1
Net Stockholders' Equity	369.2	321.2	290.3	272.2	230.6	154.8	143.9
Year-end Shs. Outstg. (000)	25,711	23,166	23,025	20,797	16,942	11,184	10,440
STATISTICAL RECORD:							
Return on Equity %	12.1	13.3	13.5	11.7	10.5	11.9	12.6
Return on Assets %	1.1	1.1	1.1	1.0	0.9	1.1	1.1
Equity/Assets %	8.9	8.3	7.8	8.4	8.7	9.0	8.4
Non-Int. Exp./Tot. Inc. %	68.9	65.1	66.4	66.4	65.8	65.4	64.9
Price Range	29.50-19.76	21.91-16.44	25.40-19.01	33.04-20.73	31.98-18.02	19.79-14.93	16.23-10.48
P/E Ratio	17.6-11.8	12.2-9.2	15.6-11.6	22.8-14.3	17.0-9.6	12.5-9.4	9.9-6.4
Average Yield %	3.1	3.5	2.9	2.3	2.1	2.9	2.0

Statistics are as originally reported. Adj. for stk. splits: 5% div., 5/96, 5/97, 5/98, 5/99, 5/00, 5/01. ① Incl. non-recurr. chg. $1.8 mill., 1999; $5.5 mill., 1998; $13.4 mill., 1997, $1.9 mill., 1996. ② Incl. chg. of $2.1 mill. from amort. of intang. ③ Incl. one-time legal expense chrg. of $4.0 mill., merger-related chrg. of $3.8 mill. and restr. chrg. of $3.2 mill.

OFFICERS:	TELEPHONE NUMBER: (941) 262-7600	INSTITUTIONAL HOLDINGS:
P. Mortensen, Chmn.	WEB: www.fnbcorporation.com	No. of Institutions: 83
S. J. Gurgovits, Vice-Chmn.	NO. OF EMPLOYEES: 2,586 full-time; 599 part-time	Shares Held: 8,095,754
G. L. Tice, Pres., C.E.O.		% Held: 19.4
INVESTOR CONTACT: Clay W. Cone, V.P.-Corp. Affairs, (941) 436-1676	SHAREHOLDERS: 12,386	INDUSTRY: National commercial banks (SIC: 6021)
	ANNUAL MEETING: In May	
PRINCIPAL OFFICE: 2150 Goodlette Road North, Naples, FL 34102	INCORPORATED: PA, June, 1974; reincorp., FL, June, 2001	TRANSFER AGENT(S): F.N.B. Shareholder Services, Naples, FL

FAMILY DOLLAR STORES, INC.

YIELD 0.8%
P/E RATIO 28.6

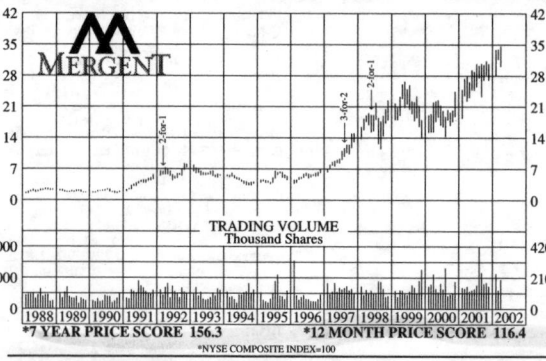

INTERIM EARNINGS (Per Share):

Qtr.	Nov.	Feb.	May	Aug.
1997-98	0.14	0.16	0.18	0.12
1998-99	0.17	0.24	0.24	0.16
1999-00	0.21	0.32	0.29	0.18
2000-01	0.24	0.35	0.31	0.20
2001-02	0.29	0.37	...	...

INTERIM DIVIDENDS (Per Share):

Amt.	Decl.	Ex.	Rec.	Pay.
0.06Q	1/18/01	3/13/01	3/15/01	4/16/01
0.06Q	5/15/01	6/13/01	6/15/01	7/16/01
0.06Q	8/23/01	9/17/01	9/14/01	10/15/01
0.06Q	11/07/01	12/12/01	12/14/01	1/15/02
0.065Q	1/17/02	3/13/02	3/15/02	4/15/02

Indicated div.: $0.26

CAPITALIZATION (9/1/01):

	($000)	(%)
Deferred Income Tax	50,436	5.0
Common & Surplus	959,015	95.0
Total	1,009,451	100.0

DIVIDEND ACHIEVER STATUS:
Rank: 93   10-Year Growth Rate: 12.60%
Total Years of Dividend Growth: 25

TRADING VOLUME
Thousand Shares

1988|1989|1990|1991|1992|1993|1994|1995|1996|1997|1998|1999|2000|2001|2002

*7 YEAR PRICE SCORE 156.3   ***12 MONTH PRICE SCORE 116.4**

*NYSE COMPOSITE INDEX=100

RECENT DEVELOPMENTS: For the 13 weeks ended 3/2/02, net income rose 5.5% to $63.8 million from $60.5 million in the corresponding 14-week period a year earlier. Net sales totaled $1.11 billion, up 6.5% versus $1.04 billion the previous year. Results in the recent period benefited from an 8.0% increase in existing-store sales and sales from new stores opened as part of FDO's store expansion program. Gross profit was $364.7 million, or 33.0% of net sales, versus $338.5 million, or 32.6% of net sales, in 2001.

PROSPECTS: Results are benefiting from strong demand for FDO's basic merchandise, as well as for its apparel and seasonal products. Going forward, revenue and earnings growth should continue to be driven by the Company's aggressive store expansion program and improving economic conditions. During the current fiscal year, FDO plans to open about 525 new stores and close 50 stores. The Company is targeting long-term earnings growth of approximately 20.0% on an annual basis.

BUSINESS

FAMILY DOLLAR STORES, INC. operated 4,303 discount stores as of 3/19/02. The stores are located in a contiguous 39-state area ranging as far northwest as South Dakota, northeast to Maine, southeast to Florida and southwest to Arizona. The stores' relatively small size, generally 6,000 to 8,000 square feet, gives FDO flexibility to open them in various markets from small rural towns to large urban centers. The stores are located in strip shopping centers or as freestanding buildings convenient to FDO's low- and middle-income customer base. The merchandise, which is generally priced under $10.00, is sold in a no-frills, low overhead, self-service environment.

ANNUAL FINANCIAL DATA

	9/1/01	8/26/00	8/28/99	8/29/98	8/31/97	8/31/96	8/31/95
Earnings Per Share	1.10	1.00	0.81	0.60	0.44	0.35	0.34
Cash Flow Per Share	1.49	1.31	1.07	0.80	0.61	0.50	0.47
Tang. Book Val. Per Share	5.57	4.66	4.00	3.36	2.75	2.61	2.40
Dividends Per Share	0.23	0.21	0.20	0.17	0.16	0.14	0.13
Dividend Payout %	21.4	21.5	24.1	29.2	36.0	40.9	37.4
INCOME STATEMENT (IN MILLIONS):							
Total Revenues	3,665.4	3,132.6	2,751.2	2,361.9	1,995.0	1,714.6	1,546.9
Costs & Expenses	3,299.3	2,807.2	2,484.7	2,161.1	1,844.4	1,591.2	1,430.3
Depreciation & Amort.	67.7	54.5	43.8	34.8	29.1	24.6	22.2
Operating Income	298.4	270.9	222.7	166.0	121.5	98.8	94.4
Income Before Income Taxes	298.4	270.9	222.7	166.0	121.5	98.8	94.4
Income Taxes	108.9	98.9	82.6	62.7	46.8	38.2	36.3
Net Income	189.5	172.0	140.1	103.3	74.7	60.6	58.1
Cash Flow	257.2	226.5	183.9	138.1	103.8	85.2	80.3
Average Shs. Outstg. (000)	172,774	172,649	172,511	173,224	171,187	170,441	170,055
BALANCE SHEET (IN MILLIONS):							
Cash & Cash Equivalents	21.8	43.6	95.3	134.2	42.5	18.8	8.9
Total Current Assets	807.3	750.7	720.0	646.6	544.7	507.9	475.0
Net Property	580.9	487.6	371.1	291.8	231.2	184.6	156.6
Total Assets	1,399.7	1,243.7	1,095.3	942.2	780.3	696.8	632.2
Total Current Liabilities	390.3	412.0	378.5	343.3	261.2	234.2	210.4
Net Stockholders' Equity	959.0	798.0	690.7	578.2	500.2	445.0	407.8
Net Working Capital	417.0	338.7	341.4	303.4	283.5	273.7	264.7
Year-end Shs. Outstg. (000)	172,036	171,132	172,751	172,204	182,063	170,606	170,232
STATISTICAL RECORD:							
Operating Profit Margin %	8.1	8.6	8.1	7.0	6.1	5.8	6.1
Net Profit Margin %	5.2	5.5	5.1	4.4	3.7	3.5	3.8
Return on Equity %	19.8	21.6	20.3	17.9	14.9	13.6	14.3
Return on Assets %	13.5	13.8	12.8	11.0	9.6	8.7	9.1
Price Range	31.35-18.38	24.50-14.25	26.75-14.00	22.44-11.50	15.06-6.25	7.00-3.67	6.58-3.63
P/E Ratio	28.5-16.7	24.5-14.2	33.0-17.3	37.4-19.2	34.6-14.4	20.0-10.5	19.2-10.6
Average Yield %	0.9	1.1	1.0	1.0	1.5	2.7	2.5

Statistics are as originally reported. Adj. for 2-for-1 stk. split, 4/98 & 3-for-2 stk. split, 7/97.

QUARTERLY DATA

(9/1/01)($000)	Rev	Inc
1st Quarter	820,148	41,461
2nd Quarter	1,037,368	60,455
3rd Quarter	887,037	53,489
4th Quarter	920,809	34,100

OFFICERS:
L. Levine, Chmn.
R. J. Kelly, Vice-Chmn., C.F.O.
H. R. Levine, Pres., C.E.O.
R. D. Alexander, Exec. V.P., C.O.O.
INVESTOR CONTACT: George R. Mahoney, Jr., Exec. V.P., (704) 814-3252
PRINCIPAL OFFICE: 10401 Old Monroe Road, P.O. Box 1017, Charlotte, NC 28101

TELEPHONE NUMBER: (704) 847-6961
FAX: (704) 847-5534
WEB: www.familydollar.com
NO. OF EMPLOYEES: 18,000 full-time (approx.); 18,000 part-time (approx.)
SHAREHOLDERS: 1,985 (approx.)
ANNUAL MEETING: In Nov.
INCORPORATED: DE, Nov., 1969

INSTITUTIONAL HOLDINGS:
No. of Institutions: 299
Shares Held: 140,919,150
% Held: 81.7

INDUSTRY: Variety stores (SIC: 5331)

TRANSFER AGENT(S): Mellon Investor Services, Ridgefield Park, NJ

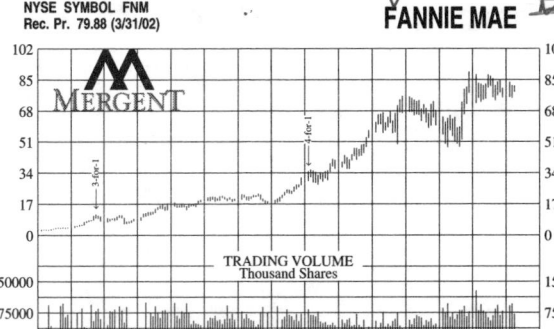

NYSE SYMBOL **FNM**
Rec. Pr. 79.88 (3/31/02)

FANNIE MAE

YIELD 1.7%
P/E RATIO 13.6

7 YEAR PRICE SCORE 124.6   **12 MONTH PRICE SCORE 100.4**

NYSE COMPOSITE INDEX=100

TRADING VOLUME
Thousand Shares

INTERIM EARNINGS (Per Share):

Qtr.	Mar.	June	Sept.	Dec.
1997	0.67	0.69	0.72	0.75
1998	0.78	0.80	0.82	0.85
1999	0.88	0.91	0.94	0.99
2000	1.02	1.02	1.09	1.13
2001	1.14	1.45	1.32	1.98

INTERIM DIVIDENDS (Per Share):

Amt.	Decl.	Ex.	Rec.	Pay.
0.30Q	7/17/01	7/27/01	7/31/01	8/25/01
0.30Q	10/16/01	10/29/01	10/31/01	11/25/01
0.33Q	1/15/02	1/29/02	1/31/02	2/25/02
0.33Q	4/16/02	4/26/02	4/30/02	5/25/02

Indicated div.: $1.32 (Div. Reinv. Plan)

CAPITALIZATION (12/31/01):

	($000)	(%)
Long-Term Debt	419,975,000	95.9
Preferred Stock	2,303,000	0.5
Common & Surplus	15,815,000	3.6
Total	438,093,000	100.0

DIVIDEND ACHIEVER STATUS:
Rank: 45   10-Year Growth Rate: 16.53%
Total Years of Dividend Growth: 16

RECENT DEVELOPMENTS: For the year ended 12/31/01, FNM reported income of $6.07 billion versus income of $4.42 billion in the previous year. Results for 2001 excluded an extraordinary loss of $340.5 million and an accounting gain of $167.9 million, while results for 2000 excluded an extraordinary gain of $31.5 million. Net interest income grew 42.6% to $8.09 billion from $5.67 billion in 2000. Total other income rose 24.9% to $1.63 billion versus $1.31 billion the year before.

PROSPECTS: Going forward, FNM should continue to benefit from strong loan growth as consumers are expected to take advantage of the low interest rate environment. In addition, FNM expects high levels of business activity during the second half of 2001 to have beneficial carryover effects in 2002. Meanwhile, FNM has begun disclosing extensive detail regarding its use of and exposure from off-balance-sheet derivatives instruments, including interest rate swaps and caps.

BUSINESS

FANNIE MAE (formerly Federal National Mortgage Association) is the largest investor in home mortgage loans in the U.S. The Company was established in 1938 as a U.S. government agency to provide supplemental liquidity to the mortgage market and was transformed into a stockholder-owned and privately-managed company by legislation enacted in 1968. FNM provides funds to the mortgage market by purchasing mortgage loans from lenders, thereby replenishing their funds for additional lending. FNM also issues mortgage-backed securities (MBS), primarily in exchange for pools of mortgage loans from lenders, which also increase the liquidity of residential mortgage loans. Fannie Mae receives guaranty fees for its guaranty of timely payment of principal and interest on MBS certificates.

ANNUAL FINANCIAL DATA

	12/31/01	12/31/00	12/31/99	12/31/98	12/31/97	12/31/96	12/31/95
Earnings Per Share	①② 5.92	① 4.26	① 3.73	① 3.26	① 2.84	① 2.50	① 1.96
Tang. Book Val. Per Share	15.86	18.58	16.02	13.95	12.34	11.10	10.04
Dividends Per Share	1.20	1.12	1.08	0.96	0.84	0.76	0.68
Dividend Payout %	20.3	26.3	29.0	29.4	29.6	30.4	34.7

INCOME STATEMENT (IN MILLIONS):

Total Interest Income	49,170.0	42,781.0	35,495.0	29,995.0	26,378.0	23,772.0	21,071.0
Total Interest Expense	41,080.0	37,107.0	30,601.0	25,885.0	22,429.0	20,180.0	18,024.0
Net Interest Income	8,090.0	5,674.0	4,894.0	4,110.0	3,949.0	3,592.0	3,047.0
Provision for Loan Losses	cr115.0	cr120.0	cr120.0	cr50.0	100.0	195.0	140.0
Non-Interest Income	1,633.0	1,307.0	1,473.0	1,504.0	1,399.0	1,282.0	1,179.0
Non-Interest Expense	1,547.0	1,119.0	1,047.0	1,019.0	911.0	774.0	1,091.0
Income Before Taxes	8,291.0	5,982.0	5,440.0	4,645.0	4,337.0	3,905.0	2,995.0
Net Income	②③ 6,067.0	① 4,416.0	① 3,921.0	① 3,444.0	① 3,068.0	① 2,754.0	① 2,155.0
Average Shs. Outstg. (000)	1,006,000	1,009,000	1,031,000	1,037,000	1,056,000	1,083,000	1,102,000

BALANCE SHEET (IN MILLIONS):

Securities Avail. for Sale	35,883.0	21,136.0	18,091.0	16,216.0	5,906.0	3,500.0	57,273.0
Total Loans & Leases	707,476.0	610,122.0	523,941.0	414,515.0	316,678.0	286,259.0	252,588.0
Allowance for Credit Losses	2,309.0	2,723.0	1,161.0	cr708.0	362.0	...	...
Net Loans & Leases	705,167.0	607,399.0	522,780.0	415,223.0	316,316.0	286,259.0	252,588.0
Total Assets	799,791.0	675,072.0	575,167.0	485,014.0	391,673.0	351,041.0	316,550.0
Long-Term Obligations	419,975.0	362,360.0	321,037.0	254,878.0	194,374.0	171,370.0	153,021.0
Total Liabilities	781,673.0	654,234.0	557,538.0	469,561.0	377,880.0	338,268.0	305,591.0
Net Stockholders' Equity	18,118.0	20,838.0	17,629.0	15,453.0	13,793.0	12,773.0	10,959.0
Year-end Shs. Outstg. (000)	997,000	999,000	1,019,000	1,025,000	1,037,000	1,061,000	1,092,000

STATISTICAL RECORD:

Return on Equity %	33.5	21.2	22.2	22.3	22.2	21.6	19.7
Return on Assets %	0.8	0.7	0.7	0.7	0.8	0.8	0.7
Equity/Assets %	2.3	3.1	3.1	3.2	3.5	3.6	3.5
Non-Int. Exp./Tot. Inc. %	15.9	16.0	16.4	18.2	17.0	15.9	25.8
Price Range	87.94-72.08	89.38-47.88	75.88-58.56	76.19-49.56	57.31-36.13	41.63-27.50	31.50-17.19
P/E Ratio	14.9-12.2	21.0-11.2	20.3-15.7	23.4-15.2	20.2-12.7	16.6-11.0	16.1-8.8
Average Yield %	1.5	1.6	1.6	1.5	1.8	2.2	2.8

Statistics are as originally reported. Adj. for stk. split: 4-for-1, 1/96. ① Bef. extraord. chrg. $340.5 mill.; 12/01; gain $31.5 mill., 12/00; chrg., $9.2 mill.,12/99; $10.7 mill., 12/98; $12.8 mill., 12/97; $29.0 mill., 12/96; $11.4 mill., 12/95; ② Bef. acctg. gain. of $167.9 mill.

OFFICERS:
F. D. Raines, Chmn., C.E.O.
D. H. Mudd, Vice-Chmn., C.O.O.
J. T. Howard, Exec. V.P., C.F.O.
L. K. Knight, Sr. V.P., Treas.
INVESTOR CONTACT: Investor Relations, (202) 752-7115
PRINCIPAL OFFICE: 3900 Wisconsin Ave., N.W., Washington, DC 20016-2892

TELEPHONE NUMBER: (202) 752-7000
FAX: (202) 752-4934
WEB: www.fanniemae.com
NO. OF EMPLOYEES: 4,500 (approx.)
SHAREHOLDERS: 26,000 (approx.)
ANNUAL MEETING: In May
INCORPORATED: 1938

INSTITUTIONAL HOLDINGS:
No. of Institutions: 1,051
Shares Held: 826,278,045
% Held: 82.6
INDUSTRY: Federal & fed.-sponsored credit (SIC: 6111)
TRANSFER AGENT(S): First Chicago Trust Company of New York, Jersey City, NJ

FEDERAL REALTY INVESTMENT TRUST

YIELD 7.5%
P/E RATIO 17.0

INTERIM EARNINGS (Per Share):				
Qtr.	Mar.	June	Sept.	Dec.
1998	0.27	0.26	0.14	0.27
1999	0.29	0.12	0.30	0.30
2000	0.31	0.51	0.32	0.31
2001	0.32	0.51	0.33	0.35

INTERIM DIVIDENDS (Per Share):				
Amt.	Decl.	Ex.	Rec.	Pay.
0.47Q	5/07/01	6/21/01	6/25/01	7/16/01
0.48Q	9/21/01	10/03/01	10/05/01	10/15/01
0.48Q	11/07/01	12/28/01	1/02/02	1/15/02
0.48Q	2/28/02	3/21/02	3/25/02	4/15/02

Indicated div.: $1.92 (Div. Reinv. Plan)

CAPITALIZATION (12/31/01):	($mill.)	(%)
Long-Term Debt	835.3	53.5
Capital Lease Obligations..	100.3	6.4
Minority Interest	33.0	2.1
Preferred Stock	235.0	15.1
Common & Surplus	357.4	22.9
Total	1,561.0	100.0

DIVIDEND ACHIEVER STATUS:
Rank: 271   10-Year Growth Rate: 2.41%
Total Years of Dividend Growth: 34

TRADING VOLUME
Thousand Shares

7 YEAR PRICE SCORE 85.0   **12 MONTH PRICE SCORE 116.6**
NYSE COMPOSITE INDEX=100

RECENT DEVELOPMENTS: For the year ended 12/31/01, net income grew 13.6% to $68.8 million from $60.5 million in the previous year. Results for 2001 and 2000 included a gain on the sale of real estate of $9.2 million and $3.7 million, respectively. Total revenues increased 7.6% to $300.5 million versus $279.3 million in the prior year. Revenues were enhanced by solid growth in rental income due to lease rollovers and incremental rent increases from developments and redevelopments.

PROSPECTS: On 3/11/02, FRT announced the adoption of a new business plan and management changes designed to renew the Company's primary focus to its traditional business of acquiring and redeveloping neighborhood shopping centers. Consistent with this plan, FRT will pursue the acquisition of income producing shopping centers in and around existing core markets. Meanwhile, FRT will continue to operate its existing operating main street retail properties to maximize their growth and asset value.

BUSINESS

FEDERAL REALTY INVESTMENT TRUST is an equity real estate investment trust specializing in the ownership, management, development and redevelopment of prime retail and mixed-use properties. As of 12/31/01, the Trust owned or had an interest in 58 community and neighborhood shopping centers comprising over 12.0 million square feet, primarily located in densely populated and affluent communities throughout the northeast and mid-Atlantic United States. In addition, FRT owned 62 retail and urban mixed-use properties comprising over 2.0 million square feet located in strategic markets across the United States and one apartment complex.

ANNUAL FINANCIAL DATA

	12/31/01	12/31/00	12/31/99	12/31/98	12/31/97	12/31/96	12/31/95
Earnings Per Share	1.52	1.35	1.02	0.94	1.14	0.86	0.72
Tang. Book Val. Per Share	8.92	9.31	10.00	10.73	11.59	10.84	10.18
Dividends Per Share	1.89	1.82	1.77	1.73	1.69	1.65	1.59
Dividend Payout %	124.3	134.8	173.5	184.0	148.2	191.8	221.5
INCOME STATEMENT (IN MILLIONS):							
Rental Income	279.9	260.7	245.8	222.2	188.5	164.9	142.8
Interest Income	6.6	7.5	7.6	5.9	6.0	4.4	4.1
Total Income	300.5	279.3	264.7	238.5	204.3	179.1	154.4
Costs & Expenses	106.5	96.2	93.8	89.2	74.1	66.2	56.9
Depreciation	59.9	53.3	50.0	46.0	41.4	38.2	34.9
Interest Expense	69.3	66.4	61.5	55.1	47.3	45.6	39.3
Income Before Income Taxes	73.9	67.1	52.3	48.1	47.8	29.1	22.8
Equity Earnings/Minority Int.	d5.2	d6.5	d3.9	d3.1	d1.3	d0.4	0.3
Net Income	68.8	60.5	48.4	45.0	46.5	28.7	23.1
Average Shs. Outstg. (000)	40,266	39,910	40,638	40,080	38,988	33,573	31,860
BALANCE SHEET (IN MILLIONS):							
Cash & Cash Equivalents	17.6	11.4	11.7	17.2	17.0	11.0	10.5
Total Real Estate Investments	1,708.5	1,503.7	1,403.5	1,356.1	1,206.1	924.3	818.9
Total Assets	1,838.0	1,621.1	1,534.0	1,484.3	1,316.6	1,035.3	886.2
Long-Term Obligations	935.6	809.2	757.9	583.8	551.9	519.5	462.6
Total Liabilities	1,245.6	1,153.4	1,032.2	954.4	762.8	646.4	558.7
Net Stockholders' Equity	592.4	467.7	501.8	529.9	553.8	388.9	327.5
Year-end Shs. Outstg. (000)	40,071	39,469	40,201	40,080	39,148	35,886	32,160
STATISTICAL RECORD:							
Net Inc.+Depr./Assets %	7.0	7.0	6.4	6.1	6.7	6.5	6.5
Return on Equity %	11.6	12.9	9.7	8.5	8.4	7.4	7.1
Return on Assets %	3.7	3.7	3.2	3.0	3.5	2.8	2.6
Price Range	23.96-18.97	22.31-17.75	24.88-16.38	25.94-19.38	28.75-24.50	28.75-20.25	23.63-19.75
P/E Ratio	15.8-12.5	16.5-13.1	24.4-16.1	27.6-20.6	25.2-21.5	33.4-23.5	32.8-27.4
Average Yield %	8.8	9.1	6.4	7.6	6.3	6.7	7.4

Statistics are as originally reported.

OFFICERS:
S. J. Guttman, Chmn., C.E.O.
D. C. Wood, Pres., C.O.O.
L. E. Finger, Sr. V.P., C.F.O., Treas.

INVESTOR CONTACT: Andrew Blocher,
V.P., Investor Relations, (301) 998-8166

PRINCIPAL OFFICE: 1626 East Jefferson
Street, Rockville, MD 20852-4041

TELEPHONE NUMBER: (301) 998-8100
FAX: (301) 998-3700
WEB: www.federalrealty.com
NO. OF EMPLOYEES: 243
SHAREHOLDERS: 5,932
ANNUAL MEETING: In May
INCORPORATED: DC, 1962; reincorp., MD,
June, 1999

INSTITUTIONAL HOLDINGS:
No. of Institutions: 127
Shares Held: 21,764,990
% Held: 54.1

INDUSTRY: Real estate investment trusts
(SIC: 6798)

TRANSFER AGENT(S): American Stock
Transfer & Trust Company, New York, NY

FEDERAL SIGNAL CORP.

YIELD	3.4%
P/E RATIO	22.8

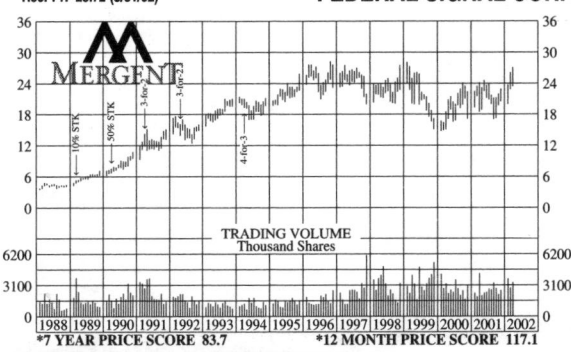

TRADING VOLUME
Thousand Shares

*7 YEAR PRICE SCORE 83.7   ***12 MONTH PRICE SCORE 117.1**
*NYSE COMPOSITE INDEX=100

INTERIM EARNINGS (Per Share):

Qtr.	Mar.	June	Sept.	Dec.
1997	0.30	0.35	0.35	0.29
1998	0.24	0.35	0.36	0.36
1999	0.29	0.30	0.30	0.37
2000	0.30	0.36	0.32	0.29
2001	0.26	0.37	0.20	0.21

INTERIM DIVIDENDS (Per Share):

Amt.	Decl.	Ex.	Rec.	Pay.
0.195Q	2/01/01	3/13/01	3/15/01	4/03/01
0.195Q	4/19/01	6/12/01	6/14/01	7/05/01
0.195Q	7/19/01	9/11/01	9/13/01	10/02/01
0.195Q	10/18/01	12/12/01	12/14/01	1/03/02
0.20Q	2/07/02	3/12/02	3/14/02	4/02/02

Indicated div.: $0.80 (Div. Reinv. Plan)

CAPITALIZATION (12/31/01):

	($000)	(%)
Long-Term Debt	446,595	53.5
Deferred Income Tax	29,280	3.5
Common & Surplus	359,436	43.0
Total	835,311	100.0

DIVIDEND ACHIEVER STATUS:
Rank: 104   10-Year Growth Rate: 11.65%
Total Years of Dividend Growth: 14

RECENT DEVELOPMENTS: For the year ended 12/31/01, income from continuing operations declined 19.2% to $46.6 million versus income of $57.7 million, before an accounting change charge of $844,000, in 2000. Results for both years included after-tax restructuring charges of $2.3 million. Results for 2001 and 2000 excluded gains of $983,000 and $726,000, respectively, from discontinued operations. Net sales fell 3.0% to $1.07 billion.

PROSPECTS: In the near term, FSS will attempt to improve operational efficiencies, which should result in increased operating margin and strong cash generation. FSS anticipates demand for public safety and security products to grow as a result of the terrorist attacks on 9/11/01. FSS also expects results for its municipal product offering to remain fairly stable in 2002, while results in various industrial markets will likely show little improvement.

BUSINESS

FEDERAL SIGNAL CORP. is a manufacturer and worldwide supplier of public safety, signaling and communications equipment, fire trucks, emergency and street sweeping vehicles, parking control equipment, custom on-premise signage, carbide cutting tools, precision punches and related die components. The Safety Products Group provides warning, signal and communication products while the Sign Group produces identification signs and communication displays. Standard and special die components and precision parts are manufactured by the Tool Group. The Vehicle Group makes commercial fire apparatus and rescue vehicles. Revenues for 2001 were derived: safety products, 23.9%; tool group, 15.1%; environmental products, 26.2%; and fire rescue, 34.8%.

ANNUAL FINANCIAL DATA

	12/31/01	12/31/00	12/31/99	12/31/98	12/31/97	12/31/96	12/31/95
Earnings Per Share	④ 1.03	③ 1.27	1.25	1.30	1.29	② 1.35	① 1.13
Cash Flow Per Share	1.69	1.90	1.84	1.81	1.73	1.75	1.47
Tang. Book Val. Per Share	1.74	1.82	1.67	1.98	2.45	2.36	2.24
Dividends Per Share	0.78	0.76	0.73	0.70	0.65	0.56	0.48
Dividend Payout %	75.2	59.4	58.6	53.8	50.2	41.5	42.5
INCOME STATEMENT (IN MILLIONS):							
Total Revenues	1,072.2	1,106.1	1,061.9	1,002.8	924.9	896.4	816.1
Costs & Expenses	949.9	960.4	928.2	877.5	804.7	775.1	704.3
Depreciation & Amort.	30.3	29.1	27.2	23.6	20.5	18.4	15.9
Operating Income	92.0	116.7	106.5	101.8	99.7	102.9	95.9
Net Interest Inc./(Exp.)	d26.4	d31.4	d23.3	d19.3	d17.2	d15.4	d13.3
Income Before Income Taxes	64.5	84.4	84.4	86.2	84.8	93.4	77.3
Income Taxes	17.9	26.8	26.9	26.8	25.9	31.4	25.7
Net Income	④ 46.6	③ 57.7	57.5	59.4	59.0	② 62.0	① 51.6
Cash Flow	76.8	86.7	84.8	83.0	79.5	80.4	67.5
Average Shs. Outstg. (000)	45,443	45,521	45,958	45,846	45,840	45,952	45,859
BALANCE SHEET (IN MILLIONS):							
Cash & Cash Equivalents	16.9	13.6	8.8	15.3	10.7	12.4	9.4
Total Current Assets	342.3	348.9	346.1	311.2	268.6	267.0	235.5
Net Property	113.7	112.6	115.4	97.4	84.7	82.8	78.5
Total Assets	1,014.7	991.1	961.0	836.0	727.9	703.9	620.0
Total Current Liabilities	179.4	288.9	269.5	195.2	227.0	374.6	314.4
Long-Term Obligations	446.6	316.9	307.0	288.8	177.5	34.3	39.7
Net Stockholders' Equity	359.4	357.4	354.0	321.8	299.8	272.8	248.1
Net Working Capital	162.9	60.0	76.7	116.0	41.6	d107.6	d78.9
Year-end Shs. Outstg. (000)	45,129	45,304	46,114	45,329	45,606	45,318	45,290
STATISTICAL RECORD:							
Operating Profit Margin %	8.6	10.5	10.0	10.1	10.8	11.5	11.8
Net Profit Margin %	4.3	5.2	5.4	5.9	6.4	6.9	6.3
Return on Equity %	13.0	16.1	16.3	18.5	19.7	22.7	20.8
Return on Assets %	4.6	5.8	6.0	7.1	8.1	8.8	8.3
Debt/Total Assets %	44.0	32.0	31.9	34.5	24.4	4.9	6.4
Price Range	24.63-17.00	24.13-14.75	28.13-15.06	27.50-20.06	27.50-19.88	28.25-20.88	25.88-19.63
P/E Ratio	23.9-16.5	19.0-11.6	22.5-12.0	21.2-15.4	21.3-15.4	20.9-15.5	22.9-17.4
Average Yield %	3.7	3.9	3.4	2.9	2.7	2.3	2.1

Statistics are as originally reported. ① Incl. $4.2 mill. ($0.09/sh) chg. for litigation. ② Incl. $2.8 mill. after-tax gain on sale of assets. ③ Bef. inc. from disc. opers. of $726,000 and accts. change chrg. of $844,000 & incl. pre-tax restruct. chrg. of $3.7 mill. ④ Bef. income from disc. oper. of $983,000 & incl. pre-tax restruct. chrg. of $2.3 mill.

OFFICERS:
J. J. Ross, Chmn., C.E.O.
A. E. Graves, Pres., C.O.O.
S. K. Kushner, V.P., C.F.O.

INVESTOR CONTACT: Stephanie K. Kushner, V.P., C.F.O., (630) 954-2020

PRINCIPAL OFFICE: 1415 West 22nd Street, Oak Brook, IL 60523-2004

TELEPHONE NUMBER: (630) 954-2000
FAX: (630) 954-2030
WEB: www.federalsignal.com

NO. OF EMPLOYEES: 6,631 (avg.)

SHAREHOLDERS: 3,872

ANNUAL MEETING: In Apr.

INCORPORATED: IL, Mar., 1901; reincorp., DE, Mar., 1969

INSTITUTIONAL HOLDINGS:
No. of Institutions: 156
Shares Held: 27,820,271
% Held: 61.6

INDUSTRY: Motor vehicles and car bodies (SIC: 3711)

TRANSFER AGENT(S): EquiServe Trust Company, Jersey City, NJ

NYSE SYMBOL FNF
Rec. Pr. 26.37 (3/31/02)

FIDELITY NATIONAL FINANCIAL, INC.

YIELD 1.5%
P/E RATIO 7.5

*7 YEAR PRICE SCORE 118.1   ***12 MONTH PRICE SCORE 112.4**
NYSE COMPOSITE INDEX=100

TRADING VOLUME
Thousand Shares

INTERIM EARNINGS (Per Share):

Qtr.	Mar.	June	Sept.	Dec.
1997	0.15	0.40	0.65	0.51
1998	0.51	0.89	0.75	0.79
1999	0.55	0.68	0.55	0.27
2000	0.05	0.42	0.49	0.48
2001	0.52	1.02	0.95	1.04

INTERIM DIVIDENDS (Per Share):

Amt.	Decl.	Ex.	Rec.	Pay.
0.10Q	4/25/01	7/11/01	7/13/01	7/27/01
10% STK	7/25/01	8/07/01	8/09/01	8/23/01
0.10Q	7/25/01	10/10/01	10/12/01	10/26/01
0.10Q	10/24/01	1/09/02	1/11/02	1/25/02
0.10Q	1/23/02	4/10/02	4/12/02	4/26/02

Indicated div.: $0.40 (Div. Reinv. Plan)

CAPITALIZATION (12/31/01):

	($000)	(%)
Long-Term Debt	565,690	25.5
Deferred Income Tax	14,074	0.6
Common & Surplus	1,638,870	73.9
Total	2,218,634	100.0

DIVIDEND ACHIEVER STATUS:

Rank: 48   10-Year Growth Rate: 16.04%
Total Years of Dividend Growth: 14

RECENT DEVELOPMENTS: For the year ended 12/31/01, net income soared to $311.2 million, before an accounting change charge of $5.7 million, from net income of $108.3 million in the previous year. Results were driven by low interest rates, which fueled strong new home purchase volumes. Earnings for 2001 and 2000 included after-tax non-recurring charges of $10.0 million and $13.4 million, respectively. Total title premiums climbed 38.5% to $2.69 billion from $1.95 billion a year earlier.

PROSPECTS: On 1/27/02, FNF announced that it has launched a new company designed to improve the speed and efficiency of real property title insurance underwriting by creating a nationwide capability for standardizing and automating title research. Based in Santa Barbara, CA, Property Insight will combine all of the automated title plants and plant operations from Fidelity Title, Chicago Title, Ticor Title and Security Union.

BUSINESS

FIDELITY NATIONAL FINANCIAL, INC., through its principal subsidiaries, is a major title insurance and diversified real estate-related services business. The Company's title insurance underwriters are Fidelity National Title, Chicago Title, Ticor Title, Security Union Title and Alamo Title. The Company provides title insurance in 49 states, the District of Columbia, Guam, Mexico, Puerto Rico, the U.S. Virgin Islands and Canada. In addition, the Company performs other real estate-related services such as escrow, appraisal services, collection and trust activities, real estate information and technology services, trustee's sale guarantees, credit reporting, attorney services, flood certifications, real estate tax services, reconveyances, recording, foreclosure publishing and posting services and exchange intermediary services in connection with real estate transactions. On 3/20/00, FNF acquired Chicago Title Corporation.

ANNUAL FINANCIAL DATA

	12/31/01	12/31/00	12/31/99	12/31/98	12/31/97	12/31/96	12/31/95
Earnings Per Share	④ 3.54	1.62	2.06	③ 2.94	② 1.72	1.29	① 0.40
Tang. Book Val. Per Share	19.13	15.92	14.46	12.48	9.01	5.95	4.34
Dividends Per Share	0.37	0.36	0.25	0.23	0.21	0.19	0.16
Dividend Payout %	10.5	22.4	12.3	7.9	12.2	14.9	40.7
INCOME STATEMENT (IN MILLIONS):							
Total Premium Income	2,694.5	1,946.2	939.5	910.3	533.2	476.0	285.6
Other Income	1,179.6	795.8	412.8	378.2	213.5	161.0	124.3
Total Revenues	3,874.1	2,742.0	1,352.2	1,288.5	746.7	636.9	409.8
Policyholder Benefits	134.7	97.3	52.7	59.3	38.7	33.3	19.0
Income Before Income Taxes	518.6	194.1	117.8	175.1	73.4	40.6	9.5
Income Taxes	207.5	85.8	47.0	69.4	32.0	16.2	1.8
Net Income	④ 311.2	108.3	70.9	③ 105.7	② 41.5	24.3	① 7.6
Average Shs. Outstg. (000)	88,059	67,030	34,470	36,821	25,994	18,987	18,989
BALANCE SHEET (IN MILLIONS):							
Cash & Cash Equivalents	542.6	263.0	38.6	51.3	54.0	64.0	47.4
Premiums Due	992.7	936.4	79.1	86.7	61.5	73.3	58.2
Invst. Assets: Fixed-term	1,216.2	1,188.7	347.1	330.1	217.0	166.3	129.2
Invst. Assets: Total	1,803.8	1,685.3	506.9	510.5	326.3	227.7	180.1
Total Assets	4,416.0	3,834.0	1,029.2	969.5	600.6	509.3	405.1
Long-Term Obligations	565.7	791.4	226.4	214.6	123.0	148.9	136.0
Net Stockholders' Equity	1,638.9	1,106.7	432.5	396.7	196.3	110.3	77.9
Year-end Shs. Outstg. (000)	85,681	69,499	29,907	31,785	21,797	18,529	17,965
STATISTICAL RECORD:							
Return on Revenues %	8.0	4.0	5.2	8.2	5.6	3.8	1.9
Return on Equity %	19.0	9.8	16.4	26.6	21.1	22.1	9.8
Return on Assets %	7.0	2.8	6.9	10.9	6.9	4.8	1.9
Price Range	34.66-17.91	35.80-10.57	27.95-12.22	36.05-18.96	25.98-8.64	12.29-8.20	11.80-6.13
P/E Ratio	9.8-5.1	22.1-6.5	13.5-5.9	12.3-6.5	15.1-5.0	9.6-6.4	29.6-15.4
Average Yield %	1.4	1.6	1.3	0.8	1.2	1.9	1.8

Statistics are as originally reported. Adj. for 10.0% stk. div., 8/01, 12/98, 12/97 & 12/96. ① Excl. extraord. gain of $813,000. ② Excl. net extraord. loss of $1.7 mill. ③ Incl. $7.3 mil in pre-tax merger-related expenses. ④ Excl. acctg. chrg. $5.7 mill.; Incl. after-tax non-recurr. chrgs. $10.0 mill.

OFFICERS:
W. P. Foley, II, Chmn., C.E.O.
P. F. Stone, C.O.O.
A. L. Stinson, Exec. V.P., C.F.O.

INVESTOR CONTACT: Dan Murphy, Dir., Inv. Rel., (949) 622-4333

PRINCIPAL OFFICE: 17911 Von Karman Avenue, Suite 300, Irvine, CA 92614

TELEPHONE NUMBER: (949) 622-4333
FAX: (949) 622-4153
WEB: www.fnf.com

NO. OF EMPLOYEES: 17,600 (approx.)

SHAREHOLDERS: 1,797 (approx.)

ANNUAL MEETING: In June

INCORPORATED: DE, Nov., 1984

INSTITUTIONAL HOLDINGS:
No. of Institutions: 237
Shares Held: 58,900,391
% Held: 68.1

INDUSTRY: Title insurance (SIC: 6361)

REGISTRAR(S): Continental Stock Transfer and Trust Co., New York, NY

FIFTH THIRD BANCORP

	YIELD	1.4%
	P/E RATIO	36.5

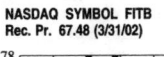

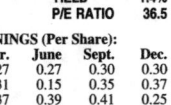

INTERIM EARNINGS (Per Share):

Qtr.	Mar.	June	Sept.	Dec.
1997	0.27	0.27	0.30	0.30
1998	0.31	0.15	0.35	0.37
1999	0.37	0.39	0.41	0.25
2000	0.44	0.41	0.48	0.50
2001	0.51	0.22	0.47	0.65

INTERIM DIVIDENDS (Per Share):

Amt.	Decl.	Ex.	Rec.	Pay.
0.20Q	6/19/01	6/27/01	6/29/01	7/16/01
0.20Q	9/18/01	9/26/01	9/28/01	10/16/01
0.23Q	12/18/01	12/27/01	12/31/01	1/15/02
0.23Q	3/19/02	3/26/02	3/29/02	4/16/02

Indicated div.: $0.92 (Div. Reinv. Plan)

CAPITALIZATION (12/31/01):

	($000)	(%)
Total Deposits	45,854,000	75.2
Long-Term Debt	7,030,000	11.5
Minority Interest	421,000	0.7
Preferred Stock	9,000	0.0
Common & Surplus	7,630,000	12.5
Total	60,944,000	100.0

DIVIDEND ACHIEVER STATUS:
Rank: 34   10-Year Growth Rate: 17.91%
Total Years of Dividend Growth: 29

7 YEAR PRICE SCORE 142.8   **12 MONTH PRICE SCORE 109.8**

*NYSE COMPOSITE INDEX=100

TRADING VOLUME
Thousand Shares

RECENT DEVELOPMENTS: For the year ended 12/31/01, FITB reported income of $1.10 billion, before an after-tax accounting change charge of $6.8 million, versus net income of $1.14 billion a year earlier. Results for 2001 and 2000 included pre-tax merger-related charges of $348.6 million and $87.0 million, respectively. Total interest income fell 4.8% to $4.71 billion. Interest and fees on loans and leases decreased 4.7% to $3.42 billion, while total

interest on securities slipped 4.5% to $1.21 billion. Net interest income rose 7.9% to $2.43 billion from $2.25 billion the year before. Provision for credit losses totaled $236.1 million versus $137.7 million in 2000. For the quarter ended 12/31/01, net income increased 20.8% to $385.7 million from $319.3 million in the corresponding prior-year period. Net interest income grew 10.0% to $629.0 million. Comparisons were made with restated 2000 figures.

BUSINESS

FIFTH THIRD BANCORP is a bank holding company headquartered in Cincinnati, Ohio. As of 1/5/02, the Company had about $70.12 billion in assets and operated 16 affiliates with 933 full-service banking centers, including 142 Bank Mart® locations open seven days a week inside select grocery stores and 1,847 Jeanie® ATMs in Ohio, Kentucky, Indiana, Florida, Michigan, Illinois and West Virginia. The Company operates in four main businesses: Retail, Commercial, Investment Advisors and Midwest Payment Systems, the bank's data processing subsidiary. On 3/9/01, FITB acquired Capital Holdings, Inc. On 4/2/01, FITB acquired Old Kent Financial Corporation for about $5.50 billion. On 10/31/01, FITB acquired USB, Inc., a provider of payment processing services.

ANNUAL FINANCIAL DATA

	12/31/01	12/31/00	12/31/99	12/31/98	12/31/97	12/31/96	12/31/95
Earnings Per Share	②1.86	①1.83	①1.43	①1.17	1.13	①0.95	0.86
Tang. Book Val. Per Share	13.09	10.50	8.80	7.94	6.52	6.00	5.09
Dividends Per Share	0.78	0.68	0.56	0.44	0.37	0.32	0.27
Dividend Payout %	41.9	37.2	39.1	37.3	32.5	33.2	31.2

INCOME STATEMENT (IN MILLIONS)

Total Interest Income	4,709.0	3,263.0	2,738.0	2,018.7	1,478.4	1,385.1	1,173.2
Total Interest Expense	2,276.0	1,793.0	1,333.0	1,015.9	733.4	695.9	609.7
Net Interest Income	2,433.0	1,470.0	1,405.0	1,002.8	745.0	689.2	563.4
Provision for Loan Losses	236.0	89.0	134.0	109.2	80.3	64.0	43.0
Non-Interest Income	1,797.0	1,013.0	877.0	636.2	445.5	368.4	305.7
Non-Interest Expense	2,341.0	1,119.0	1,122.0	803.6	506.2	493.3	395.6
Income Before Taxes	1,653.0	1,275.0	1,026.0	726.3	603.9	500.3	430.6
Net Income	②1,101.0	①863.0	①668.0	①476.1	401.2	①335.1	287.7
Average Shs. Outstg. (000)	591,316	475,978	471,855	398,007	354,789	350,980	333,717

BALANCE SHEET (IN MILLIONS)

Cash & Due from Banks	2,301.0	985.0	1,213.0	819.9	720.1	808.9	628.5
Securities Avail. for Sale	20,507.0	15,602.0	12,688.0	8,334.6	6,397.1	6,223.9	4,151.2
Total Loans & Leases	42,459.0	26,936.0	25,887.0	18,468.2	13,985.8	12,963.0	12,016.7
Allowance for Credit Losses	1,535.0	1,367.0	1,290.0	956.1	748.1	635.4	503.4
Net Loans & Leases	40,924.0	25,569.0	24,597.0	17,512.2	13,237.8	12,327.5	11,513.3
Total Assets	71,026.0	45,857.0	41,589.0	28,921.8	21,375.1	20,549.0	17,052.9
Total Deposits	45,854.0	30,948.0	26,083.0	18,780.4	14,914.1	14,374.7	12,485.8
Long-Term Obligations	7,030.0	4,034.0	1,977.0	2,288.2	457.9	277.7	425.4
Total Liabilities	62,966.0	40,966.0	37,512.0	25,743.3	19,097.6	18,404.9	15,328.3
Net Stockholders' Equity	7,639.0	4,891.0	4,077.0	3,178.5	2,277.4	2,144.1	1,724.6
Year-end Shs. Outstg. (000)	582,675	465,652	463,330	400,377	349,256	357,389	338,928

STATISTICAL RECORD:

Return on Equity %	14.4	17.6	16.4	15.0	17.6	15.6	16.7
Return on Assets %	1.6	1.9	1.6	1.6	1.9	1.6	1.7
Equity/Assets %	10.8	10.7	9.8	11.0	10.7	10.4	10.1
Non-Int. Exp./Tot. Inc. %	55.3	45.1	49.2	49.0	42.5	46.6	45.5
Price Range	64.77-45.69	60.88-29.33	50.29-38.59	49.42-31.67	37.11-18.00	22.00-12.89	15.11-9.28
P/E Ratio	34.8-24.6	33.3-16.0	35.1-26.9	42.1-27.0	32.9-15.9	23.1-13.5	17.5-10.8
Average Yield %	1.4	1.5	1.3	1.1	1.3	1.8	2.2

Statistics are as originally reported. Adj. for stk. splits: 50% div., 7/14/00; 4/15/98; 7/15/97; 1/12/96. ① Incl. non-recurr. chrg. $34.0 mill., 12/00; $82.0 mill., 12/99; $89.7 mill., 12/98; $16.6 mill., 12/96. ② Bef. acctg. chrg. of $6.8 mill.; incl. pre-tax merger-related chrg. of $348.6 mill.

OFFICERS:
G. A. Schaefer Jr., Pres., C.E.O.
N. E. Arnold, Exec. V.P., C.F.O.
P. L. Reynolds, Exec. V.P., Gen. Couns.
R. M. Graf, Treas.
INVESTOR CONTACT: Neal E. Arnold, Exec. V.P. & C.F.O., (513) 579-4356
PRINCIPAL OFFICE: Fifth Third Center, Cincinnati, OH 45263

TELEPHONE NUMBER: (513) 579-5300
FAX: (513) 579-6246
WEB: www.53.com
NO. OF EMPLOYEES: 18,373 (avg.)
SHAREHOLDERS: 58,203
ANNUAL MEETING: In Mar.
INCORPORATED: OH, 1974

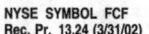

FIRST COMMONWEALTH FINANCIAL CORP.

YIELD 4.5%
P/E RATIO 15.2

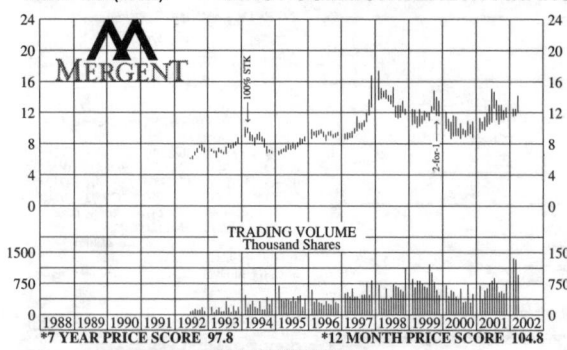

100% STK
2-for-1

TRADING VOLUME
Thousand Shares

1988 1989 1990 1991 1992 1993 1994 1995 1996 1997 1998 1999 2000 2001 2002

*7 YEAR PRICE SCORE 97.8   *12 MONTH PRICE SCORE 104.8
*NYSE COMPOSITE INDEX=100

INTERIM EARNINGS (Per Share):

Qtr.	Mar.	June	Sept.	Dec.
1998	0.16	0.17	0.19	0.03
1999	0.20	0.24	0.22	0.21
2000	0.20	0.23	0.20	0.19
2001	0.21	0.21	0.22	0.23

INTERIM DIVIDENDS (Per Share):

Amt.	Decl.	Ex.	Rec.	Pay.
0.145Q	6/12/01	6/27/01	6/29/01	7/13/01
0.145Q	9/11/01	9/26/01	9/28/01	10/15/01
0.15Q	12/11/01	12/27/01	12/31/01	1/15/02
0.15Q	3/12/02	3/26/02	3/29/02	4/15/02

Indicated div.: $0.60 (Div. Reinv. Plan)

CAPITALIZATION (12/31/01):

	($000)	(%)
Total Deposits	3,093,150	74.9
Long-Term Debt	629,220	15.2
Redeemable Pfd. Stock	35,000	0.8
Common & Surplus	370,066	9.0
Total	4,127,436	100.0

DIVIDEND ACHIEVER STATUS:
Rank: 102   10-Year Growth Rate: 11.81%
Total Years of Dividend Growth: 14

RECENT DEVELOPMENTS: For the year ended 12/31/01, net income rose 6.2% to $50.2 million compared with $47.2 million a year earlier. Results for 2001 and 2000 included securities gains of $3.3 million and $1.7 million, respectively. Net interest income advanced 3.2% to $141.7 million from $137.3 million the previous year. Provision for credit losses rose 14.6% to $11.5 million. Non-interest income declined 3.0% to $32.4 million, while non-interest expense rose 5.6% to $105.0 million.

PROSPECTS: The Company's revenues are benefiting from higher fee income. For instance, service charges on deposits increased 5.7% to $11.2 million and included increases in insufficient funds fees and bank club fees. FCF noted that standardization of service charge routines achieved during conversion of the Company's deposit system during 2001 also generated additional fee revenue. Furthermore, the new deposit processing system implemented during the third quarter of 2001 is expected to increase deposit fees in future periods.

BUSINESS

FIRST COMMONWEALTH FINANCIAL CORPORATION is a financial services holding company with $4.58 billion in assets, as of 12/31/01. The Company operates through two state-chartered banks in 17 counties in western and central Pennsylvania: First Commonwealth Bank, headquartered in Indiana, PA, and Southwest Bank, headquartered in Greensburg, PA. First Commonwealth Bank operates through divisions doing business under the following names: NBOC Bank, Deposit Bank, Cenwest Bank, First Bank of Leechburg, Peoples Bank, Central Bank, Peoples Bank of Western Pennsylvania, Unitas Bank, and Reliable Bank. Southwest Bank was obtained through the Company's 12/31/98 merger with Southwest National Corp. In addition to its bank operations, FCF provides financial services and insurance products through First Commonwealth Trust Company and First Commonwealth Insurance Agency. Also, the Company operates Commonwealth Systems Corporation, a data processing subsidiary, and First Commonwealth Professional Resources Inc., a subsidiary providing professional services to affiliated organizations.

ANNUAL FINANCIAL DATA

	12/31/01	12/31/00	12/31/99	12/31/98	12/31/97	12/31/96	12/31/95
Earnings Per Share	0.86	0.82	0.88	0.55	0.70	0.63	0.58
Tang. Book Val. Per Share	6.33	5.74	4.93	5.74	6.17	5.89	5.64
Dividends Per Share	0.58	0.56	0.49	0.44	0.40	0.36	0.32
Dividend Payout %	67.4	68.3	55.7	80.0	57.5	57.1	55.2
INCOME STATEMENT (IN MILLIONS)							
Total Interest Income	308.9	311.9	297.5	283.4	199.8	182.3	175.7
Total Interest Expense	167.2	174.5	152.7	148.3	102.8	88.3	82.4
Net Interest Income	141.7	137.3	144.9	135.1	97.1	94.0	93.3
Provision for Loan Losses	11.5	10.0	9.5	15.0	6.9	4.5	4.1
Non-Interest Income	32.4	33.4	25.9	26.3	19.8	13.7	10.4
Non-Interest Expense	105.0	99.5	93.6	100.2	65.9	63.6	62.1
Income Before Taxes	65.4	61.5	72.6	46.2	44.1	39.7	37.5
Net Income	50.2	47.2	53.0	34.0	30.5	27.6	25.5
Average Shs. Outstg. (000)	58,118	57,619	60,569	61,666	43,932	43,908	44,010
BALANCE SHEET (IN MILLIONS)							
Cash & Due from Banks	98.1	90.7	92.7	96.6	60.1	69.4	62.4
Securities Avail. for Sale	1,469.1	1,238.2	1,144.0	1,042.6	396.6	244.4	244.2
Total Loans & Leases	2,569.2	2,492.9	2,503.7	2,382.2	1,937.7	1,778.1	1,531.2
Allowance for Credit Losses	35.5	35.6	37.2	39.7	36.6	50.1	61.8
Net Loans & Leases	2,533.8	2,457.2	2,466.5	2,342.5	1,901.1	1,728.0	1,469.4
Total Assets	4,583.5	4,372.3	4,340.8	4,096.8	2,929.3	2,584.6	2,364.3
Total Deposits	3,093.2	3,064.1	2,948.8	2,931.1	2,242.5	2,104.8	1,962.8
Long-Term Obligations	629.2	621.9	603.4	630.9	193.1	40.9	5.3
Total Liabilities	4,213.5	4,038.2	4,054.2	3,741.4	2,657.5	2,323.3	2,112.0
Net Stockholders' Equity	370.1	334.2	286.7	355.4	271.8	261.4	252.3
Year-end Shs. Outstg. (000)	58,452	58,195	58,143	61,876	44,092	44,388	44,744
STATISTICAL RECORD:							
Return on Equity %	13.6	14.1	18.5	9.6	11.2	10.6	10.1
Return on Assets %	1.1	1.1	1.2	0.8	1.0	1.1	1.1
Equity/Assets %	8.1	7.6	6.6	8.7	9.3	10.1	10.7
Non-Int. Exp./Tot. Inc. %	60.3	58.2	54.8	62.1	56.4	59.0	59.9
Price Range	15.10-9.44	12.13-8.63	14.88-10.06	17.41-11.25	16.81-8.56	9.88-8.38	8.94-6.56
P/E Ratio	17.6-11.0	14.8-10.5	16.9-11.4	31.6-20.5	24.2-12.3	15.7-13.3	15.4-11.3
Average Yield %	4.7	5.4	3.9	3.1	3.2	3.9	4.1

Statistics are as originally reported. Adj. for 100% stk. div., 10/99.

OFFICERS:
E. J. Trimarchi, Chmn.
D. S. Dahlman, Vice-Chmn.
J. E. O'Dell, Pres., C.E.O.

INVESTOR CONTACT: Shareholder Relations, (800) 331-4107

PRINCIPAL OFFICE: 22 North Sixth St., P.O. Box 400, Indiana, PA 15701

TELEPHONE NUMBER: (724) 349-7220
FAX: (724) 349-6427
WEB: www.fcfbank.com

NO. OF EMPLOYEES: 1,465

SHAREHOLDERS: 13,000 (approx.)

ANNUAL MEETING: In Apr.

INCORPORATED: PA, Nov., 1983

INSTITUTIONAL HOLDINGS:
No. of Institutions: 59
Shares Held: 8,551,901
% Held: 14.6

INDUSTRY: National commercial banks (SIC: 6021)

TRANSFER AGENT(S): The Bank of New York, New York, NY

FIRST FEDERAL CAPITAL CORP.

YIELD 2.5%
P/E RATIO 12.5

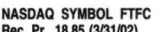

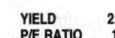

INTERIM EARNINGS (Per Share):

Qtr.	Mar.	June	Sept.	Dec.
1998	0.24	0.24	0.24	0.26
1999	0.26	0.32	0.29	0.30
2000	0.29	0.30	0.32	0.34
2001	0.32	0.34	0.36	0.49

INTERIM DIVIDENDS (Per Share):

Amt.	Decl.	Ex.	Rec.	Pay.
0.12Q	4/24/01	5/15/01	5/17/01	6/07/01
0.12Q	7/26/01	8/14/01	8/16/01	9/06/01
0.12Q	10/25/01	11/13/01	11/15/01	12/06/01
0.12Q	1/24/02	2/12/02	2/14/02	3/07/02

Indicated div.: $0.48 (Div. Reinv. Plan)

CAPITALIZATION (12/31/01):

	($000)	(%)
Total Deposits	2,029,254	75.5
Long-Term Debt	467,415	17.4
Common & Surplus	192,398	7.2
Total	2,689,067	100.0

TRADING VOLUME
Thousand Shares

DIVIDEND ACHIEVER STATUS:
Rank: 2   10-Year Growth Rate: 40.30%
Total Years of Dividend Growth: 10

*7 YEAR PRICE SCORE 111.5   *12 MONTH PRICE SCORE 110.7
*NYSE COMPOSITE INDEX=100

RECENT DEVELOPMENTS: For the year ended 12/31/01, net income was $28.4 million versus $23.1 million a year earlier. Results for 2001 included a gain on the sale of investments of $13,199, while results for 2000 included a gain on the sale of real estate investments of $1.2 million. Net interest income rose 6.2% to $63.2 million. Provision for loan losses climbed 74.8% to $1.8 million, reflecting additional provisions that were recorded to maintain FTFC's allowance for loan losses at a level deemed appropriate by management. Total non-interest income, which included the previously mentioned gains, advanced 39.0% to $49.5 million from $35.6 million the previous year. Total non-interest expense rose 15.2% to $67.1 million. On 1/17/02, FTFC announced the signing of a definitive agreement with Marquette Bank, N.A. to purchase three Marquette Bank offices in Rochester, Minnesota. Also, on 3/13/02, FTFC announced the signing of a definitive agreement with Commercial Federal Bank of Omaha, Nebraska. to purchase four supermarket banking offices located in the Minnesota cities of Rochester, Albert Lea, Austin and Mankato.

BUSINESS

FIRST FEDERAL CAPITAL CORP., through its First Federal Savings Bank La Crosse - Madison subsidiary, is a savings bank with assets of $2.72 billion, as of 12/31/01. FTFC's primary business is community banking, which includes attracting deposits from and making loans to the general public, businesses, government, and professional customers. The Company's primary market areas include communities located in the western, south-central, and eastern portions of Wisconsin and the northern portion of Illinois, as well as contiguous counties in Iowa and Minnesota. As of 3/13/02, FTFC maintained 80 banking offices and 41 in-store supermarket banking locations throughout its market areas.

ANNUAL FINANCIAL DATA

	12/31/01	12/31/00	12/31/99	12/31/98	12/31/97	12/31/96	12/31/95
Earnings Per Share	③ 1.51	② 1.25	1.17	0.98	0.89	① 0.50	① 0.57
Tang. Book Val. Per Share	6.81	6.09	5.06	4.80	4.74	4.26	4.21
Dividends Per Share	0.47	0.42	0.34	0.27	0.23	0.21	0.18
Dividend Payout %	31.1	33.6	29.1	27.5	26.4	41.1	32.0
INCOME STATEMENT (IN MILLIONS):							
Total Interest Income	171.5	161.4	130.1	118.7	115.0	104.0	88.9
Total Interest Expense	108.3	101.9	76.0	71.5	70.3	63.7	55.0
Net Interest Income	63.2	59.5	54.1	47.2	44.7	40.3	33.9
Provision for Loan Losses	1.8	1.0	0.4	0.3	0.5	…	…
Non-Interest Income	49.5	35.6	35.2	31.4	24.3	19.8	17.1
Non-Interest Expense	67.1	58.3	54.3	47.6	40.2	44.2	34.4
Income Before Taxes	43.8	35.9	34.6	30.7	28.3	15.9	16.6
Net Income	③ 28.4	② 23.1	22.4	19.4	17.4	① 10.1	① 10.6
Average Shs. Outstg. (000)	18,871	18,472	19,138	19,864	19,691	20,043	18,616
BALANCE SHEET (IN MILLIONS):							
Cash & Due from Banks	70.8	25.4	65.6	43.6	29.9	24.6	30.4
Securities Avail. for Sale	35.5	0.8	0.9	…	21.4	74.0	80.3
Total Loans & Leases	1,857.1	1,778.5	1,545.0	1,183.6	1,201.6	1,138.8	962.3
Allowance for Credit Losses	5.8	6.0	6.4	6.1	7.7	32.8	30.2
Net Loans & Leases	1,851.3	1,772.5	1,538.6	1,177.5	1,193.9	1,106.0	932.1
Total Assets	2,717.7	2,352.7	2,084.6	1,786.5	779.8	844.4	1,402.5
Total Deposits	2,029.3	1,699.3	1,471.3	1,460.1	382.0	353.0	969.4
Long-Term Obligations	467.4	368.2	469.6	189.8	275.8	383.6	322.3
Total Liabilities	2,525.3	2,206.2	1,957.3	1,663.8	670.4	748.9	1,303.5
Net Stockholders' Equity	192.4	146.5	127.3	122.7	109.4	95.4	98.9
Year-end Shs. Outstg. (000)	20,201	18,345	18,403	18,361	18,381	18,381	19,694
STATISTICAL RECORD:							
Return on Equity %	14.8	15.8	17.6	15.8	15.9	10.6	10.8
Return on Assets %	1.0	1.0	1.1	1.1	2.2	1.2	0.8
Equity/Assets %	7.1	6.2	6.1	6.9	14.0	11.3	7.1
Non-Int. Exp./Tot. Inc. %	59.5	61.2	60.8	60.6	58.3	73.6	67.4
Price Range	16.81-12.50	14.88-10.13	18.38-10.50	18.75-10.88	17.00-7.83	8.17-6.00	6.58-4.67
P/E Ratio	11.1-8.3	11.9-8.1	15.7-9.0	19.1-11.1	19.2-8.9	16.2-11.9	11.5-8.1
Average Yield %	3.2	3.4	2.4	1.8	1.9	2.9	3.3

Statistics are as originally reported. Adj. for stk. splits: 2-for-1, 6/98; 3-for-2, 6/97. ① Incl. loss on sale of invest. securities: $311,151, 1996; $28,580, 1995. ② Incl. gain on sale of real estate invests. of $1.2 mill. ③ Incl. gain on sale of invest. securities of $13,199.

OFFICERS:
T. W. Schini, Chmn.
D. A. Nordeen, Vice-Chmn.
J. C. Rusch, Pres., C.E.O., C.O.O.
INVESTOR CONTACT: Michael Dosland, Sr. V.P., C.F.O., (608) 784-8000
PRINCIPAL OFFICE: 605 State Street, Box 1868, La Crosse, WI 54602-1868

TELEPHONE NUMBER: (608) 784-8000
FAX: (608) 784-6627
WEB: www.firstfed.com
NO. OF EMPLOYEES: 1,033
SHAREHOLDERS: 1,448 (record)
ANNUAL MEETING: In Apr.
INCORPORATED: WI, July, 1989

INSTITUTIONAL HOLDINGS:
No. of Institutions: 53
Shares Held: 4,469,321
% Held: 22.3
INDUSTRY: Federal savings institutions (SIC: 6035)
TRANSFER AGENT(S): Wells Fargo Shareowner Services, St. Paul, MN

FIRST FINANCIAL BANCORP

YIELD 3.8%
P/E RATIO 17.1

TRADING VOLUME
Thousand Shares

| 1988 | 1989 | 1990 | 1991 | 1992 | 1993 | 1994 | 1995 | 1996 | 1997 | 1998 | 1999 | 2000 | 2001 | 2002 |

*7 YEAR PRICE SCORE 86.0   ***12 MONTH PRICE SCORE 102.1**

*NYSE COMPOSITE INDEX=100

INTERIM EARNINGS (Per Share):

Qtr.	Mar.	June	Sept.	Dec.
1997	0.23	0.24	0.24	0.25
1998	0.24	0.26	0.27	0.28
1999	0.27	0.18	0.30	0.29
2000	0.29	0.30	0.31	0.30
2001	0.29	0.21	0.26	0.16

INTERIM DIVIDENDS (Per Share):

Amt.	Decl.	Ex.	Rec.	Pay.
0.15Q	2/28/01	3/07/01	3/09/01	4/02/01
0.15Q	5/22/01	5/30/01	6/01/01	7/02/01
0.15Q	8/28/01	9/05/01	9/07/01	10/01/01
0.15Q	11/27/01	12/05/01	12/07/01	1/02/02
0.15Q	2/26/02	3/06/02	3/08/02	4/01/02

Indicated div.: $0.60 (Div. Reinv. Plan)

CAPITALIZATION (12/31/01):

	($000)	(%)
Total Deposits	3,085,093	82.7
Long-Term Debt	260,345	7.0
Deferred Income Tax	1,388	0.0
Common & Surplus	384,543	10.3
Total	3,731,369	100.0

DIVIDEND ACHIEVER STATUS:
Rank: 122   10-Year Growth Rate: 10.79%
Total Years of Dividend Growth: 18

RECENT DEVELOPMENTS: For the twelve months ended 12/31/01, net earnings dropped 25.6% to $43.3 million compared with $58.2 million in the prior year. Results for 2001 and 2000 included amortization of intangibles of $2.7 million and $3.3 million, respectively. Results for 2000 also included a restructuring credit of $353,000. Net interest income declined 2.9% to $163.0 million from $167.9 million in the previous year. Provision for loan losses more than doubled to $26.8 million compared with $11.3 million in the prior year. Total non-interest income advanced 12.1% to $54.2 million from $48.4 million the year before. Total non-interest expenses grew 5.9% to $125.0 million from $118.0 million a year earlier. Total interest income decreased 7.5% to $289.7 million. Results were hampered by the decline in interest rates and a slowing economy. Comparisons were made with restated prior-year figures.

BUSINESS

FIRST FINANCIAL BANCORP is a financial holding company that engages in the business of commercial banking and other financial activities through 13 wholly-owned subsidiaries, including First National Bank of Southwestern Ohio, Bright National Bank and National Bank of Hastings, all national banking associations in Ohio. The range of banking services provided by FFBC's subsidiaries to their customers include commercial lending, real estate lending, consumer credit, credit card, and other personal loan financing. In addition, the institutions offer deposit services that include interest-bearing and noninterest-bearing deposit accounts and time deposits. Most subsidiaries provide safe deposit facilities. Trust and asset management services are provided by FFBC's subsidiaries, excluding the savings banks, the finance company, the insurance agency, and the service corporation.

ANNUAL FINANCIAL DATA

	12/31/01	12/31/00	12/31/99	12/31/98	12/31/97	12/31/96	12/31/95
Earnings Per Share	0.91	② 1.19	① 1.02	1.05	0.96	0.91	0.91
Tang. Book Val. Per Share	7.47	7.40	6.75	6.20	6.80	6.92	7.08
Dividends Per Share	0.59	0.57	0.52	0.47	0.43	0.39	0.36
Dividend Payout %	65.1	47.9	51.0	45.1	44.9	42.7	39.4
INCOME STATEMENT (IN MILLIONS):							
Total Interest Income	289.7	315.5	282.4	219.5	192.2	171.3	153.9
Total Interest Expense	126.8	145.4	117.2	88.4	76.8	69.7	63.5
Net Interest Income	163.0	170.1	165.2	131.1	115.4	101.6	90.3
Provision for Loan Losses	26.8	11.3	9.2	6.1	4.7	3.4	2.1
Non-Interest Income	54.2	45.0	41.3	34.3	27.0	22.1	20.6
Non-Interest Expense	125.0	116.8	120.7	92.7	77.7	71.3	63.3
Income Before Taxes	65.4	82.0	76.6	66.6	59.9	49.0	45.4
Net Income	43.3	② 58.2	① 50.3	44.1	40.3	33.9	31.8
Average Shs. Outstg. (000)	47,479	48,863	49,335	42,014	42,196	37,127	34,905
BALANCE SHEET (IN MILLIONS):							
Cash & Due from Banks	211.1	182.1	225.8	136.5	142.3	110.8	108.7
Securities Avail. for Sale	595.6	564.8	490.1	313.2	332.6	290.7	294.1
Total Loans & Leases	2,874.4	3,012.1	3,040.5	2,269.5	1,978.6	1,701.7	1,532.6
Allowance for Credit Losses	48.8	43.4	43.5	32.3	29.1	24.1	21.0
Net Loans & Leases	2,825.5	2,968.7	2,997.0	2,237.2	1,949.5	1,677.6	1,511.6
Total Assets	3,854.8	3,932.5	3,940.7	2,836.2	2,577.8	2,182.8	2,009.9
Total Deposits	3,085.1	3,151.4	2,991.2	2,326.6	2,230.2	1,880.0	1,785.6
Long-Term Obligations	260.3	205.2	161.8	105.3	41.1	6.5	2.8
Total Liabilities	3,470.3	3,537.4	3,568.2	2,569.2	2,349.9	2,003.2	1,869.2
Net Stockholders' Equity	384.5	395.1	372.5	301.9	286.3	258.5	234.2
Year-end Shs. Outstg. (000)	46,600	48,286	49,213	41,813	42,071	37,358	33,066
STATISTICAL RECORD:							
Return on Equity %	11.3	14.7	13.5	14.6	14.1	13.1	13.6
Return on Assets %	1.1	1.5	1.3	1.6	1.6	1.6	1.6
Equity/Assets %	10.0	10.0	9.5	10.6	11.1	11.8	11.7
Non-Int. Exp./Tot. Inc. %	57.5	54.3	58.4	56.1	54.6	57.6	57.1
Price Range	18.25-14.17	20.12-13.33	26.41-17.32	27.17-18.89	19.97-10.91	11.63-10.25	11.55-10.57
P/E Ratio	20.1-15.6	16.9-9.9	25.9-17.0	25.9-18.0	20.9-11.4	12.7-11.2	12.7-11.6
Average Yield %	3.7	3.4	2.4	2.1	2.8	3.6	3.2

Statistics are as originally reported. Adj. for stk. splits: 6/1/98, 2-for-1; 10% div., 1/3/00, 10/1/97 & 11/1/96; 5%, 4/2/01. ① Incl. restr. chrg. of $6.9 mill. ② Incl. restr. credit of $353,000.

OFFICERS:
S. N. Pontius, Pres., C.E.O.
C. D. Lefferson, Sr. V.P., C.F.O.

INVESTOR CONTACT: Richard E. Weinman, Sr. V.P., (513) 425-7548

PRINCIPAL OFFICE: 300 High Street, Hamilton, OH 45011

TELEPHONE NUMBER: (513) 867-4700
FAX: (513) 867-4515
WEB: www.ffbh-oh.com

NO. OF EMPLOYEES: 1,832 (avg.)
SHAREHOLDERS: 4,700 (record)
ANNUAL MEETING: In Apr.
INCORPORATED: OH, Aug., 1982

INSTITUTIONAL HOLDINGS:
No. of Institutions: 62
Shares Held: 16,755,997
% Held: 36.0

INDUSTRY: National commercial banks (SIC: 6021)

TRANSFER AGENT(S): Registrar and Transfer Company, Cranford, NJ

FIRST INDIANA CORPORATION

YIELD 3.3%
P/E RATIO 15.6

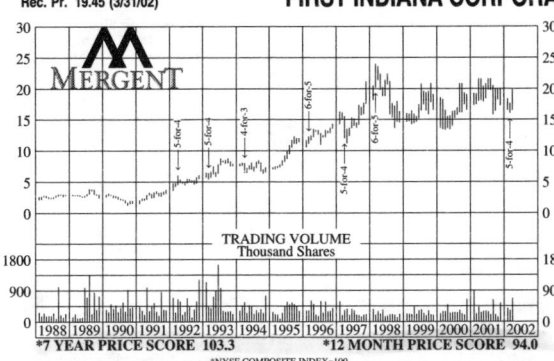

7 YEAR PRICE SCORE 103.3 | **12 MONTH PRICE SCORE 94.0**
*NYSE COMPOSITE INDEX=100

INTERIM EARNINGS (Per Share):

Qtr.	Mar.	June	Sept.	Dec.
1998	0.26	0.28	0.30	0.31
1999	0.29	0.31	0.42	0.40
2000	0.34	0.38	0.40	0.43
2001	0.42	0.42	0.43	d0.02

INTERIM DIVIDENDS (Per Share):

Amt.	Decl.	Ex.	Rec.	Pay.
0.16Q	4/18/01	6/04/01	6/06/01	6/19/01
0.16Q	7/18/01	9/04/01	9/06/01	9/18/01
0.16Q	10/17/01	12/04/01	12/06/01	12/18/01
5-for-4	1/16/02	2/28/02	2/13/02	2/27/02
0.16Q	1/16/02	3/01/02	3/05/02	3/15/02

Indicated div.: $0.64

CAPITALIZATION (12/31/01):

	($000)	(%)
Total Deposits	1,379,478	73.2
Long-Term Debt	296,647	15.7
Common & Surplus	209,031	11.1
Total	1,885,156	100.0

DIVIDEND ACHIEVER STATUS:
Rank: 10   10-Year Growth Rate: 23.97%
Total Years of Dividend Growth: 10

RECENT DEVELOPMENTS: For the year ended 12/31/01, net earnings decreased 19.4% to $20.0 million from $24.8 million in the previous year. Net interest income declined 4.8% to $74.0 million from $77.8 million in the prior year. This decrease was mainly due to lower interest rates, partially offset by an increase in lower-cost demand and savings deposits on average. Net interest margin was 3.69% compared with 3.88% a year earlier. Provision for loan losses increased 56.1% to $15.2 million from $9.8 million

the year before. Total non-interest income grew 71.5% to $44.0 million from $25.6 million a year earlier, fueled by expanded customer relationships, the Company's merger with The Somerset Group in September 2000 and asset sales. Total non-interest expense rose 31.2% to $70.5 million from $53.7 million in the previous year. FINB's efficiency ratio was 59.74% compared with 51.96% in 2000. Total deposits slid 1.5% to $1.38 billion, while total loans slipped 1.6% to $1.76 billion.

BUSINESS

FIRST INDIANA CORPORATION is a full-service financial services company offering comprehensive financial solutions to businesses and individuals. FINB is the holding company for First Indiana Bank, N.A., a national bank headquartered in Indianapolis, and Somerset Financial Services, an accounting and consulting firm. As of 12/31/01, First Indiana Bank has $2.00 billion in assets and owns 26 offices in Central Indiana, plus construction and consumer loan offices in Indiana, Arizona, Florida, Illinois, North Carolina, Oregon, and Ohio. The Company also originates consumer loans in 46 states through a national independent agent network. Through Somerset Financial Services and FirstTrust Indiana, a division of First Indiana Bank, the Company offers a full array of tax planning, accounting, consulting, wealth management, and investment advisory and trust services.

ANNUAL FINANCIAL DATA

	12/31/01	12/31/00	12/31/99	12/31/98	12/31/97	12/31/96	12/31/95
Earnings Per Share	1.25	1.55	1.42	1.15	1.09	① 0.85	1.07
Tang. Book Val. Per Share	12.69	11.87	11.31	10.45	9.66	8.43	8.34
Dividends Per Share	0.51	0.45	0.42	0.38	0.32	0.30	0.25
Dividend Payout %	41.0	28.9	29.4	33.3	29.4	35.3	23.3
INCOME STATEMENT (IN MILLIONS):							
Total Interest Income	157.1	172.8	146.0	135.8	127.3	125.5	124.1
Total Interest Expense	83.1	95.0	75.6	73.1	64.4	63.8	66.0
Net Interest Income	74.0	77.8	70.4	62.8	63.0	61.7	58.0
Provision for Loan Losses	15.2	9.8	9.4	9.8	10.7	10.8	7.9
Non-Interest Income	44.0	25.6	27.0	23.8	18.0	17.8	16.3
Non-Interest Expense	70.5	53.7	52.3	45.8	41.1	47.3	38.6
Income Before Taxes	32.3	39.9	35.6	31.0	29.2	21.5	27.7
Net Income	20.0	24.8	22.3	19.1	17.7	① 13.7	17.3
Average Shs. Outstg. (000)	15,999	15,997	16,050	16,571	16,314	16,146	16,076
BALANCE SHEET (IN MILLIONS):							
Securities Avail. for Sale	147.9	158.8	103.2	113.3	106.1	101.4	96.8
Total Loans & Leases	1,756.5	1,972.1	1,896.9	1,741.2	1,479.4	1,317.0	1,214.2
Allowance for Credit Losses	37.1	221.2	223.4	222.6	130.8	101.4	16.2
Net Loans & Leases	1,719.4	1,750.8	1,673.4	1,518.5	1,348.5	1,215.6	1,198.0
Total Assets	2,046.7	2,085.9	1,979.8	1,796.0	1,613.4	1,496.4	1,523.9
Total Deposits	1,379.5	1,400.0	1,312.1	1,227.9	1,107.6	1,095.5	1,119.1
Long-Term Obligations	296.6	336.8	366.9	327.2	257.5	215.5	214.8
Total Liabilities	1,837.6	1,887.1	1,802.7	1,626.2	1,460.4	1,357.8	1,394.7
Net Stockholders' Equity	209.0	198.8	177.1	166.0	153.0	138.7	129.3
Year-end Shs. Outstg. (000)	15,443	15,574	15,654	15,879	15,835	16,451	15,510
STATISTICAL RECORD:							
Return on Equity %	9.6	12.5	12.6	11.5	11.6	9.9	13.4
Return on Assets %	1.0	1.2	1.1	1.1	1.1	0.9	1.1
Equity/Assets %	10.2	9.5	8.9	9.3	9.5	9.3	8.5
Non-Int. Exp./Tot. Inc. %	59.7	52.0	53.7	52.9	50.8	59.4	52.0
Price Range	21.60-15.74	20.85-13.30	20.90-14.20	24.00-13.60	21.17-11.17	14.33-10.56	12.28-7.00
P/E Ratio	17.3-12.6	13.4-8.6	14.8-10.0	20.8-11.8	19.5-10.3	16.9-12.5	11.5-6.6
Average Yield %	2.7	2.6	2.4	2.0	2.0	2.4	2.6

Statistics are as originally reported. Adj. for stk. splits: 5-for-4, 2/02 & 2/97; 6-for-5, 3/98 & 1/96. ① Incl. gain of $1.2 mill. on the sale of subsidiary.

OFFICERS:
R. H. McKinney, Chmn.
M. M. McKinney, Vice-Chmn., C.E.O.
O. B. Melton Jr., Pres., C.O.O.
W. J. Brunner, V.P., Treas.

INVESTOR CONTACT: Investor Relations,
(317) 472-2184

PRINCIPAL OFFICE: 135 North Pennsylvania Street, Indianapolis, IN 46204

TELEPHONE NUMBER: (317) 269-1200
FAX: (317) 269-1341
WEB: www.firstindiana.com

NO. OF EMPLOYEES: 738 (avg.)

SHAREHOLDERS: 1,814 (approx. record)

ANNUAL MEETING: In Mar.

INCORPORATED: IN, 1986

INSTITUTIONAL HOLDINGS:
No. of Institutions: 44
Shares Held: 3,309,154
% Held: 21.4

INDUSTRY: Federal savings institutions
(SIC: 6035)

TRANSFER AGENT(S): Computershare
Investor Services, Chicago, IL

1ST SOURCE CORPORATION

YIELD 1.5%
P/E RATIO 13.0

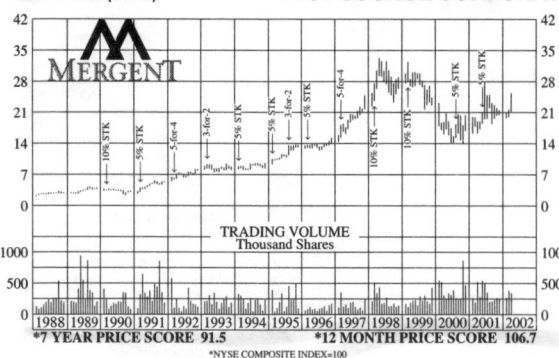

7 YEAR PRICE SCORE 91.5   **12 MONTH PRICE SCORE 106.7**

*NYSE COMPOSITE INDEX=100

INTERIM EARNINGS (Per Share):

Qtr.	Mar.	June	Sept.	Dec.
1997	0.29	0.30	0.30	0.34
1998	0.32	0.34	0.37	0.41
1999	0.40	0.37	0.41	0.50
2000	0.41	0.43	0.44	0.51
2001	0.65	0.44	0.29	0.44

INTERIM DIVIDENDS (Per Share):

Amt.	Decl.	Ex.	Rec.	Pay.
0.09Q	4/24/01	5/02/01	5/04/01	5/15/01
5% STK	4/24/01	5/02/01	5/04/01	5/15/01
0.09Q	7/17/01	8/01/01	8/03/01	8/15/01
0.09Q	10/23/01	11/01/01	11/05/01	11/15/01
0.09Q	1/14/02	2/01/02	2/05/02	2/15/02

Indicated div.: $0.36

CAPITALIZATION (12/31/01):

	($000)	(%)
Total Deposits	2,882,806	90.1
Long-Term Debt	11,939	0.4
Common & Surplus	306,190	9.6
Total	3,200,935	100.0

DIVIDEND ACHIEVER STATUS:
Rank: 78   10-Year Growth Rate: 13.58%
Total Years of Dividend Growth: 14

RECENT DEVELOPMENTS: For the year ended 12/31/01, net income climbed 1.8% to $40.7 million from $40.0 million in the previous year. Net interest income advanced 13.2% to $118.8 million from $105.0 million the year before. Total interest income increased 2.9% to $242.2 million from $235.4 million in the prior year. Total interest expense declined 5.4% to $123.4 million from $130.4 million in the previous year. Total non-interest income rose 25.6% to $92.8 million from $73.9 million a year earlier.

SRCE increased its provision for loan losses by 92.4% to $28.6 million from $14.89 million in 2000, reflecting the continued softening of the economy, which has led to a rise in loan losses and non-performing loans. Total non-interest expense increased 16.6% to $121.2 million from $104.0 million the year before. During the fourth quarter, SRCE acquired $222.0 million in deposits, along with facilities in Fort Wayne, New Haven, Bluffton, Auburn, Columbia City and Huntington, Indiana.

BUSINESS

1ST SOURCE CORPORATION is a registered bank holding company, with $3.56 billion in assets as of 12/31/01. Through its subsidiary, 1st Source Bank, it provides consumer and commercial banking services to individual and business customers through 64 banking locations, as of 1/14/02, in 17 counties in Indiana and Michigan, eight Trustcorp Mortgage offices in Indiana, Ohio, Michigan and North Carolina, and 28 locations nationwide for the 1st Source Bank Specialty Finance Group. 1st Source Bank also competes for business nationwide by offering specialized financing services for used private aircraft, automobiles for leasing and rental agencies, heavy duty trucks, construction and environmental equipment.

REVENUES

(12/31/2001)	($000)	(%)
Loans	211,801	87.5
Invest Securities, taxable	22,695	9.4
Invest Securities, tax-exempt	6,867	2.8
Other Interest & Fee Income	820	0.3
Total	242,183	100.0

ANNUAL FINANCIAL DATA

	12/31/01	12/31/00	12/31/99	12/31/98	12/31/97	12/31/96	12/31/95
Earnings Per Share	1.82	1.79	1.69	1.45	1.23	1.20	1.08
Tang. Book Val. Per Share	14.58	12.97	11.38	11.32	10.14	11.25	10.51
Dividends Per Share	0.35	0.33	0.28	0.25	0.23	0.20	0.17
Dividend Payout %	19.3	18.7	16.8	17.4	18.4	16.6	15.8
INCOME STATEMENT (IN MILLIONS):							
Total Interest Income	242.2	235.4	200.4	196.1	173.3	148.8	135.1
Total Interest Expense	123.4	130.4	100.7	102.2	87.3	73.4	64.9
Net Interest Income	118.8	105.0	99.7	93.9	86.0	75.4	70.2
Provision for Loan Losses	28.6	14.9	7.4	9.2	6.1	4.6	2.8
Non-Interest Income	92.8	73.9	63.3	51.5	35.7	25.5	19.5
Non-Interest Expense	121.2	104.0	99.0	85.5	73.0	60.6	54.9
Income Before Taxes	61.8	60.0	56.5	50.8	42.6	35.6	32.0
Net Income	40.7	40.0	38.0	33.2	28.2	23.2	21.0
Average Shs. Outstg. (000)	21,170	20,982	21,211	21,357	21,546	19,402	19,445
BALANCE SHEET (IN MILLIONS):							
Cash & Due from Banks	129.4	118.1	101.9	132.5	90.9	137.6	94.5
Securities Avail. for Sale	640.5	503.9	470.0	443.7	299.9	302.6	270.3
Total Loans & Leases	2,535.4	2,309.1	2,063.2	1,881.7	1,796.8	1,455.6	1,259.4
Allowance for Credit Losses	57.6	44.6	40.2	40.9	35.4	29.5	27.5
Net Loans & Leases	2,477.7	2,264.4	2,023.0	1,840.8	1,761.4	1,426.0	1,231.9
Total Assets	3,562.7	3,182.2	2,872.9	2,732.0	2,418.2	2,079.8	1,799.3
Total Deposits	2,882.8	2,462.7	2,127.5	2,177.1	1,891.8	1,634.0	1,441.7
Long-Term Obligations	11.9	12.1	12.2	13.2	16.7	18.6	21.8
Total Liabilities	3,211.8	2,866.9	2,589.4	2,471.4	2,178.5	1,907.9	1,646.7
Net Stockholders' Equity	306.2	270.6	238.8	215.9	195.0	171.8	152.6
Year-end Shs. Outstg. (000)	20,995	20,856	20,990	19,063	19,232	15,269	14,520
STATISTICAL RECORD:							
Return on Equity %	13.3	13.9	15.0	14.4	13.6	13.5	13.8
Return on Assets %	1.1	1.3	1.3	1.2	1.2	1.1	1.2
Equity/Assets %	8.6	8.5	8.3	7.9	8.1	8.3	8.5
Non-Int. Exp./Tot. Inc. %	57.4	58.9	60.8	58.5	59.8	60.2	61.3
Price Range	28.07-16.31	23.13-13.93	32.43-21.66	33.30-22.30	24.92-14.39	15.30-12.45	13.70-9.33
P/E Ratio	15.4-9.0	12.3-7.4	18.3-12.2	21.8-14.6	19.2-11.1	12.2-9.9	12.1-8.2
Average Yield %	1.6	1.9	1.1	1.0	1.2	1.5	1.6

Statistics are as originally reported. Adj. for stk. splits: 10% div., 2/12/99 & 2/13/98; 5-for-4, 2/14/97; 5% div., 5/15/01, 8/15/00, 2/15/96, 2/15/95 & 2/15/94; 3-for-2, 8/18/95.

OFFICERS:
C. J. Murphy, III, Chmn., Pres., C.E.O.
L. E. Lentych, Sr. V.P., C.F.O., Treas.
J. B. Griffith, Sr. V.P., Gen. Couns., Sec.

INVESTOR CONTACT: Larry E. Lentych, C.F.O., (219) 235-2702

PRINCIPAL OFFICE: 100 N. Michigan St., South Bend, IN 46601

TELEPHONE NUMBER: (219) 235-2000
FAX: (219) 235-2912
WEB: www.1stsource.com

NO. OF EMPLOYEES: 1,260 (approx.)

SHAREHOLDERS: 1,119

ANNUAL MEETING: In Apr.

INCORPORATED: IN, Jan., 1922

INSTITUTIONAL HOLDINGS:
No. of Institutions: 56
Shares Held: 13,090,788
% Held: 62.2

INDUSTRY: State commercial banks (SIC: 6022)

TRANSFER AGENT(S): 1st Source Bank, South Bend, IN

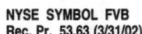

NYSE SYMBOL FVB
Rec. Pr. 53.63 (3/31/02)

FIRST VIRGINIA BANKS, INC.

YIELD 3.0%
P/E RATIO 15.4

7 YEAR PRICE SCORE 101.0   *NYSE COMPOSITE INDEX=100   **12 MONTH PRICE SCORE 112.2**

INTERIM EARNINGS (Per Share):

Qtr.	Mar.	June	Sept.	Dec.
1998	0.61	0.62	0.62	0.68
1999	0.88	0.68	0.75	0.70
2000	0.70	0.73	0.76	0.82
2001	0.87	0.81	0.96	0.84

INTERIM DIVIDENDS (Per Share):

Amt.	Decl.	Ex.	Rec.	Pay.
0.39Q	5/23/01	6/27/01	6/29/01	7/16/01
0.39Q	8/22/01	9/26/01	9/28/01	10/15/01
0.40Q	11/28/01	12/27/01	12/31/01	1/14/02
0.40Q	2/27/02	3/26/02	3/28/02	4/15/02

Indicated div.: $1.60 (Div. Reinv. Plan)

CAPITALIZATION (12/31/01):

	($000)	(%)
Total Deposits	8,649,636	88.1
Long-Term Debt	19,526	0.2
Preferred Stock	421	0.0
Common & Surplus	1,152,065	11.7
Total	9,821,648	100.0

DIVIDEND ACHIEVER STATUS:
Rank: 140   10-Year Growth Rate: 9.97%
Total Years of Dividend Growth: 24

RECENT DEVELOPMENTS: For the year ended 12/31/01, net income increased 15.8% to $164.5 million from $142.0 million in the prior year. Net interest income improved 3.8% to $440.6 million. Provision for loan losses declined 28.4% to $6.8 million. Total non-interest income advanced 27.1% to $150.0 million from $118.0 million the year before. Net loans grew 2.3% to $6.44 billion compared with $6.30 billion a year earlier.

PROSPECTS: As nonperforming assets continue to decline, the Company continues to report increased earnings while maintaining its high asset quality despite the sluggish economy and an increasing number of borrowers defaulting on their loans nationwide. Separately, the Company successfully completed its integration of Suffolk, Virginia-based James River Bankshares, Inc.

BUSINESS

FIRST VIRGINIA BANKS, INC., with assets of approximately $10.62 billion as of 12/31/01, provides retail, commercial, international, and mortgage banking; insurance; trust and asset management services; and personal investment services through its subsidiaries. There are eight banks in the First Virginia group with 310 offices in Virginia, 56 offices in Maryland and 13 offices in East Tennessee. In addition, FVB operates a full-service insurance agency, First Virginia Insurance Services, Inc. On 7/2/01, FVB acquired James River Bankshares, Inc.

QUARTERLY DATA

(12/31/2001)	REV	INC
1st Quarter	163,816	40,284
2nd Quarter	168,086	46,520
3rd Quarter	160,287	37,385
4th Quarter	161,134	40,262

ANNUAL FINANCIAL DATA

	12/31/01	12/31/00	12/31/99	12/31/98	12/31/97	12/31/96	12/31/95
Earnings Per Share	3.48	3.01	③ 3.00	2.53	② 2.45	① 2.33	2.19
Tang. Book Val. Per Share	19.91	18.08	17.49	16.07	16.13	15.97	15.19
Dividends Per Share	1.54	1.46	1.32	1.16	1.02	0.95	0.89
Dividend Payout %	44.3	48.5	44.0	45.8	41.6	40.6	40.8
INCOME STATEMENT (IN MILLIONS)							
Total Interest Income	653.3	643.8	640.6	663.6	631.1	587.2	573.6
Total Interest Expense	212.8	219.3	206.9	234.3	222.9	212.3	215.5
Net Interest Income	440.6	424.5	433.7	429.3	408.2	374.9	358.1
Provision for Loan Losses	6.8	9.4	14.2	20.8	17.2	17.7	8.3
Non-Interest Income	150.0	118.0	136.6	116.8	103.6	98.5	89.9
Non-Interest Expense	332.7	322.1	327.3	325.7	303.2	279.3	271.4
Income Before Taxes	251.1	211.0	228.8	199.6	191.3	176.3	168.3
Net Income	164.5	142.0	③ 150.9	130.2	② 124.8	① 116.3	111.6
Average Shs. Outstg. (000)	47,317	47,257	50,238	51,529	50,880	49,905	51,084
BALANCE SHEET (IN MILLIONS)							
Cash & Due from Banks	386.2	323.0	441.8	377.4	386.8	378.2	397.9
Securities Avail. for Sale	1,553.6	301.4	227.0	286.1	243.2	323.6	299.5
Total Loans & Leases	6,510.6	6,366.5	6,385.4	6,093.2	5,938.0	5,364.8	5,038.1
Allowance for Credit Losses	71.9	70.3	70.1	70.3	68.1	62.8	57.9
Net Loans & Leases	6,438.6	6,296.2	6,315.3	6,022.9	5,869.9	5,302.0	4,980.2
Total Assets	10,623.0	9,516.5	9,451.8	9,564.7	9,011.6	8,236.1	8,221.5
Total Deposits	8,649.6	7,825.8	7,863.9	8,055.1	7,619.8	7,042.7	7,056.1
Long-Term Obligations	19.5	1.1	2.2	3.2	2.8	3.9	2.7
Total Liabilities	9,470.5	8,523.8	8,421.3	8,574.4	8,000.5	7,364.8	7,351.9
Net Stockholders' Equity	1,152.5	992.7	1,030.5	990.3	1,011.2	871.3	869.6
Year-end Shs. Outstg. (000)	47,827	46,163	49,162	50,094	51,817	48,612	50,927
STATISTICAL RECORD:							
Return on Equity %	14.3	14.3	14.6	13.1	12.3	13.4	12.8
Return on Assets %	1.5	1.5	1.6	1.4	1.4	1.4	1.4
Equity/Assets %	10.8	10.4	10.9	10.4	11.2	10.6	10.6
Non-Int. Exp./Tot. Inc. %	56.8	56.8	59.4	59.3	59.8	59.3	59.2	60.6
Price Range	52.15-38.54	48.94-29.00	52.63-40.50	59.44-39.69	53.38-30.83	32.67-25.50	29.33-21.33
P/E Ratio	15.0-11.1	16.3-9.6	17.5-13.5	23.5-15.7	21.8-12.6	14.0-10.9	13.4-9.8
Average Yield %	3.4	3.7	2.8	2.3	2.4	3.3	3.5

Statistics are as originally reported. Adj. for 3-for-2 split, 9/97. ① Incl. one-time pre-tax SAIF chg. of $1.1 mill. ② Incl. $2.1 mill. gain fr. the sale of seven offices. ③ Incl. a pre-tax gain of $17.9 million fr. the sale of the Co.'s credit card portfolio.

OFFICERS:
B. J. Fitzpatrick, Chmn., Pres., C.E.O.
R. F. Bowman, Exec. V.P., C.F.O., Treas.
T. P. Jennings, Sr. V.P., Gen. Couns.

INVESTOR CONTACT: Barbara J. Chapman, V.P., Sec., (800) 995-9416

PRINCIPAL OFFICE: 6400 Arlington Boulevard, Falls Church, VA 22042-2336

TELEPHONE NUMBER: (703) 241-4000
FAX: (703) 241-3360
WEB: www.firstvirginia.com

NO. OF EMPLOYEES: 4,913

SHAREHOLDERS: 19,886 (record); 547 (preferred)

ANNUAL MEETING: In May

INCORPORATED: VA, Oct., 1949

INSTITUTIONAL HOLDINGS:
No. of Institutions: 175
Shares Held: 13,823,221
% Held: 28.9

INDUSTRY: State commercial banks (SIC: 6022)

TRANSFER AGENT(S): Registrar and Transfer Company, Cranford, NJ

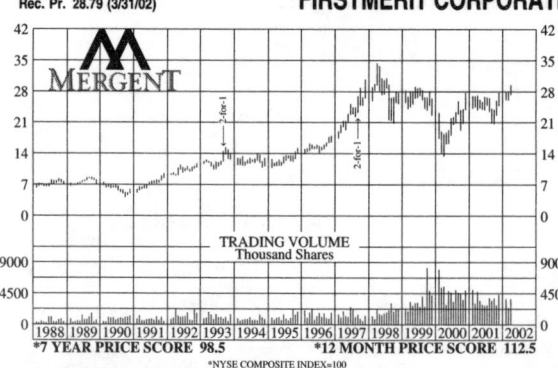

NASDAQ SYMBOL FMER
Rec. Pr. 28.79 (3/31/02)

FIRSTMERIT CORPORATION

YIELD 3.3%
P/E RATIO 20.3

INTERIM EARNINGS (Per Share):

Qtr.	Mar.	June	Sept.	Dec
1998	0.35	0.38	0.38	0.23
1999	Nil	0.41	0.44	0.46
2000	0.45	0.45	0.45	0.45
2001	0.45	0.46	0.49	0.02

INTERIM DIVIDENDS (Per Share):

Amt.	Decl.	Ex.	Rec.	Pay.
0.23Q	2/15/01	2/22/01	2/26/01	3/19/01
0.23Q	5/17/01	5/24/01	5/29/01	6/18/01
0.23Q	8/16/01	8/23/01	8/27/01	9/17/01
0.24Q	11/15/01	11/21/01	11/26/01	12/17/01
0.24Q	2/21/02	2/28/02	3/04/02	3/18/02

Indicated div.: $0.96 (Div. Reinv. Plan)

CAPITALIZATION (12/31/01):

	($000)	(%)
Total Deposits	7,539,400	89.2
Preferred Stock	1,209	0.0
Common & Surplus	909,598	10.8
Total	8,450,207	100.0

DIVIDEND ACHIEVER STATUS:
Rank: 159   10-Year Growth Rate: 8.77%
Total Years of Dividend Growth: 19

TRADING VOLUME
Thousand Shares

*7 YEAR PRICE SCORE 98.5   *12 MONTH PRICE SCORE 112.5
*NYSE COMPOSITE INDEX=100

RECENT DEVELOPMENTS: For the year ended 12/31/01, the Company reported income of $122.6 million, before an after-tax accounting change charge of $6.3 million, compared with net income of $159.8 million in the prior year. Results for 2001 included a one-time after-tax charge of $41.1 million related to the Company's exit of the manufactured housing finance business. Net interest income increased 4.1% to $391.5 million from $376.2 million a year earlier. Provision for loan losses advanced 89.0% to

$61.8 million from $32.7 million the year before. Total other income grew 11.3% to $182.4 million compared with $163.9 million in the prior year. Total other expenses rose 19.4% to $328.6 million from $275.2 million a year earlier. For the quarter ended 12/31/01, net income dropped 95.4% to $1.8 million from $40.0 million in the corresponding period of the previous year. Results for 2001 included the aforementioned charge. Net interest income improved 13.7% to $105.8 million.

BUSINESS

FIRSTMERIT CORPORATION is a multi-bank holding company with $10.19 billion in assets as of 12/31/01. The Company, through its affiliates, operates principally as a regional banking organization, providing banking, fiduciary, financial, insurance and investment services to corporate, institutional and individual customers throughout northeastern and Central Ohio and Western Pennsylvania counties. FirstMerit Bank, N.A., the Company's largest subsidiary, is comprised of nine supercommunity banks in Ohio and one in Western Pennsylvania. At 12/31/01, FirstMerit Bank, N.A. operated 157 full-service banking offices in 22 Ohio and western Pennsylvania counties. On 2/12/99, the Company acquired Signal Corp. On 10/31/01, FMER exited the manufactured housing lending business.

ANNUAL FINANCIAL DATA

	12/31/01	12/31/00	12/31/99	12/31/98	12/31/97	12/31/96	12/31/95
Earnings Per Share	③ 1.42	1.80	② 1.31	1.34	1.36	1.09	① 0.39
Tang. Book Val. Per Share	9.06	10.48	9.39	10.39	8.56	8.19	8.10
Dividends Per Share	0.93	0.86	0.76	0.66	0.61	0.55	0.51
Dividend Payout %	65.5	47.8	58.0	49.3	44.8	50.5	132.4

INCOME STATEMENT (IN MILLIONS):

Total Interest Income	726.9	791.5	684.9	503.1	407.8	411.7	416.6
Total Interest Expense	335.4	415.3	300.9	197.7	152.4	160.8	180.9
Net Interest Income	391.5	376.2	384.0	305.4	255.5	251.0	235.7
Provision for Loan Losses	61.8	32.7	37.4	28.4	21.6	17.8	19.8
Non-Interest Income	182.4	163.9	154.7	110.5	83.6	82.5	68.5
Non-Interest Expense	328.6	275.2	316.5	242.7	191.1	209.7	227.8
Income Before Taxes	183.5	232.2	184.8	144.8	126.4	106.0	56.7
Net Income	③ 122.6	159.8	② 125.7	97.5	86.4	70.9	① 25.7
Average Shs. Outstg. (000)	86,289	88,861	91,523	72,703	63,537	65,216	66,908

BALANCE SHEET (IN MILLIONS):

Cash & Due from Banks	190.0	235.9	215.1	246.0	166.7	222.2	287.7
Total Loans & Leases	7,387.3	7,237.1	7,014.2	4,997.4	3,834.9	3,656.0	3,770.4
Allowance for Credit Losses	125.2	108.3	104.9	78.9	53.8	49.3	46.8
Net Loans & Leases	7,262.1	7,128.8	6,909.3	4,918.4	3,781.1	3,606.7	3,723.5
Total Assets	10,193.4	10,215.2	10,115.5	7,127.4	5,307.5	5,228.0	5,596.5
Total Deposits	7,539.4	7,614.9	6,860.1	5,461.6	4,255.2	4,204.9	4,501.9
Total Liabilities	9,282.6	9,300.3	9,281.9	6,358.7	4,777.1	4,704.3	5,053.6
Net Stockholders' Equity	910.8	914.9	833.6	768.6	530.3	523.7	542.9
Year-end Shs. Outstg. (000)	84,991	87,032	88,375	74,009	61,967	63,912	66,996

STATISTICAL RECORD:

Return on Equity %	· 13.5	17.5	15.1	12.7	16.3	13.5	4.7
Return on Assets %	1.2	1.6	1.2	1.4	1.6	1.4	0.5
Equity/Assets %	8.9	9.0	8.2	10.8	10.0	10.0	9.7
Non-Int. Exp./Tot. Inc. %	57.3	50.9	58.8	58.4	56.4	62.9	74.9
Price Range	28.00-20.66	27.75-13.38	29.13-22.56	34.38-20.75	30.75-17.38	18.00-13.88	15.25-10.72
P/E Ratio	19.7-14.5	15.4-7.4	22.2-17.2	25.7-15.5	22.6-12.8	16.5-12.7	39.6-27.8
Average Yield %	3.8	4.2	2.9	2.4	2.5	3.5	3.9

Statistics are as originally reported. Adj. for stk. splits: 2-for-1, 9/29/97. ① Bef. extraord. credit $5.6 mill. ($0.09/sh.) ② Bef. extraord. chrg. of $5.8 mill. ③ Bef. acctg. change chrg. of $6.3 mill., incl. one-time after-tax chrg. of $41.1 mill.

OFFICERS:
J. R. Cochran, Chmn., C.E.O.
S. A. Bostic, Pres., C.O.O.
T. E. Bichsel, Exec. V.P., C.F.O.

INVESTOR CONTACT: Terry E. Patton, Secretary, (330) 996-6300

PRINCIPAL OFFICE: III Cascade Plaza, 7th Floor, Akron, OH 44308-1103

TELEPHONE NUMBER: (330) 996-6300
FAX: (330) 384-7321
WEB: www.fmer.com

NO. OF EMPLOYEES: 2,300 (approx.)

SHAREHOLDERS: 10,188 (approx.)

ANNUAL MEETING: In April

INCORPORATED: OH, Nov., 1981

INSTITUTIONAL HOLDINGS:
No. of Institutions: 162
Shares Held: 25,671,765
% Held: 30.3

INDUSTRY: State commercial banks (SIC: 6022)

TRANSFER AGENT(S): FirstMerit Bank, N.A., Akron, OH

FLORIDA PUBLIC UTILITIES COMPANY

YIELD 3.9%
P/E RATIO 17.6

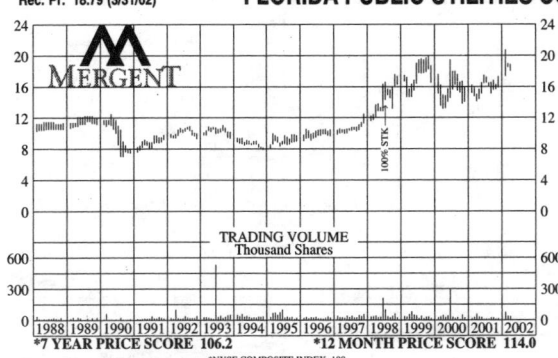

TRADING VOLUME
Thousand Shares

1988|1989|1990|1991|1992|1993|1994|1995|1996|1997|1998|1999|2000|2001|2002
*7 YEAR PRICE SCORE 106.2   *12 MONTH PRICE SCORE 114.0
*NYSE COMPOSITE INDEX=100

INTERIM EARNINGS (Per Share):

Qtr.	Mar.	June	Sept.	Dec.
1997	0.35	0.18	0.31	0.24
1998	0.47	0.19	0.15	0.21
1999	0.48	0.24	0.18	0.27
2000	0.50	0.19	0.17	0.30
2001	0.53	0.17	0.19	0.18

INTERIM DIVIDENDS (Per Share):

Amt.	Decl.	Ex.	Rec.	Pay.
0.18Q	3/06/01	3/14/01	3/16/01	4/02/01
0.185Q	5/31/01	6/13/01	6/15/01	7/02/01
0.185Q	8/28/01	9/05/01	9/07/01	10/01/01
0.185Q	12/04/01	12/12/01	12/14/01	1/02/02
0.185Q	3/05/02	3/13/02	3/15/02	4/01/02

Indicated div.: $0.74 (Div. Reinv. Plan)

CAPITALIZATION (12/31/01):

	($000)	(%)
Long-Term Debt	52,500	58.9
Deferred Income Tax	7,308	8.2
Common & Surplus	29,329	32.9
Total	89,137	100.0

DIVIDEND ACHIEVER STATUS:
Rank: 251   10-Year Growth Rate: 3.86%
Total Years of Dividend Growth: 33

RECENT DEVELOPMENTS: For the year ended 12/31/01, net income declined 7.2% to $3.1 million compared with $3.3 million in the corresponding year-earlier period. The Company attributed the lower earnings primarily to mild weather, decreased tourism in the quarter ended 12/31/01, higher general and operating expenses, and increased interest expense. Results for 2001 included a gain of $15,000 from the sale of non-utility property. Total revenues rose 8.7% to $92.1 million from $84.8 million the previous year, reflecting increased fuel costs, customer growth and new late fee charges. Operating income slipped 4.0% to $6.3 million. Separately, in December 2001, FPU acquired certain net assets of Atlantic Utilities, the Florida operation of Southern Union Company, in a cash transaction valued at approximately $10.0 million. Atlantic Utilities served about 4,400 natural gas customers in New Smyrna Beach and about 1,900 propane customers in central and south Florida.

BUSINESS

FLORIDA PUBLIC UTILITIES COMPANY is regulated by the Florida Public Service Commission (except for propane gas service) and provides natural and propane gas service, electric service and water service to consumers in Florida. The Company is comprised of the following four divisions as of 12/31/01: the South Florida division serves natural gas to 29,498 customers and propane gas to 5,939 customers; the Central Florida division serves 15,944 natural gas customers and 2,876 propane customers; the Northwest Florida division provides electricity to 12,181 customers; and the Northeast Florida division serves 13,811 electric customers and 6,966 water customers and 1,323 propane customers.

ANNUAL FINANCIAL DATA

	12/31/01	12/31/00	12/31/99	12/31/98	12/31/97	12/31/96	12/31/95
Earnings Per Share	③ 1.06	1.16	② 1.17	1.02	① 1.07	0.93	0.83
Cash Flow Per Share	2.76	2.82	2.90	2.44	2.42	2.25	2.10
Tang. Book Val. Per Share	8.12	9.73	9.23	9.21	8.79	8.31	7.98
Dividends Per Share	0.73	0.70	0.66	0.62	0.60	0.59	0.58
Dividend Payout %	68.9	60.3	56.4	60.8	56.3	64.3	69.9
INCOME STATEMENT (IN THOUSANDS):							
Total Revenues	92,143	84,759	74,098	76,192	78,134	78,810	72,027
Costs & Expenses	77,872	70,520	60,608	63,220	66,075	66,780	60,760
Depreciation & Amort.	4,839	4,698	4,557	4,269	4,029	3,876	3,694
Maintenance Exp.	3,165	3,013	2,763	2,807	2,512	2,526	2,409
Operating Income	6,267	6,528	6,170	5,896	5,518	5,628	5,164
Net Interest Inc./(Exp.)	d3,591	d3,487	d2,968	d2,840	d2,895	d2,858	d2,767
Net Income	③ 3,052	3,288	② 3,529	3,068	① 3,191	2,751	2,438
Cash Flow	7,862	7,957	8,057	7,308	7,191	6,598	6,103
Average Shs. Outstg.	2,851	2,820	2,996	2,993	2,968	2,938	2,908
BALANCE SHEET (IN THOUSANDS):							
Gross Property	151,656	132,903	123,898	117,656	112,356	106,684	100,658
Accumulated Depreciation	54,327	48,703	45,626	42,429	39,632	36,808	34,380
Net Property	97,329	84,200	78,272	75,227	72,724	69,876	66,278
Total Assets	139,989	108,588	96,807	92,406	88,622	90,994	85,240
Long-Term Obligations	52,500	23,500	23,500	23,500	23,500	23,500	23,500
Net Stockholders' Equity	29,329	27,510	25,866	27,622	26,189	24,511	23,302
Year-end Shs. Outstg.	2,886	2,828	2,802	3,000	2,978	2,948	2,920
STATISTICAL RECORD:							
Operating Profit Margin %	6.8	7.7	8.3	7.7	7.1	7.1	7.2
Net Profit Margin %	3.3	3.9	4.8	4.0	4.1	3.5	3.4
Net Inc./Net Property %	3.1	3.9	4.5	4.1	4.4	3.9	3.7
Net Inc./Tot. Capital %	3.4	5.6	6.2	5.3	5.7	5.4	4.8
Return on Equity %	10.4	12.0	13.6	11.1	12.2	11.2	10.5
Accum. Depr./Gross Prop. %	35.8	36.6	36.8	36.1	35.3	34.5	34.2
Price Range	17.49-14.05	19.50-13.13	20.00-14.63	17.63-11.56	12.50-9.81	10.56-9.00	10.00-8.00
P/E Ratio	16.5-13.3	16.8-11.3	17.1-12.5	17.3-11.3	11.7-9.2	11.4-9.7	12.0-9.6
Average Yield %	4.6	4.3	3.8	4.2	5.4	6.1	6.4

Statistics are as originally reported. Adj. for 2-for-1 stk. split, 7/98. ① Incl. non-recurr. credit $837,000 ② Incl. non-recurr. credit of $134,000 ③ Incl. gain fr. sale of non-utility prop. of $15,000.

OFFICERS:
J. T. English, Pres., C.E.O.
C. L. Stein, Sr. V.P., C.O.O.
G. M. Bachman, C.F.O., Treas.

INVESTOR CONTACT: Jack R. Brown, V.P., Corp. Sec., (561) 838-1729

PRINCIPAL OFFICE: 401 South Dixie Highway, West Palm Beach, FL 33401

TELEPHONE NUMBER: (561) 838-1729
WEB: www.fpuc.com

NO. OF EMPLOYEES: 358 (avg.)

SHAREHOLDERS: 2,674 (approx.)

ANNUAL MEETING: In May

INCORPORATED: FL, Mar., 1924

INSTITUTIONAL HOLDINGS:
No. of Institutions: 13
Shares Held: 808,830
% Held: 28.3

INDUSTRY: Electric and other services combined (SIC: 4931)

TRANSFER AGENT(S): American Stock Transfer & Trust Company, New York, NY

NYSE SYMBOL BEN
Rec. Pr. 41.92 (3/31/02)

FRANKLIN RESOURCES, INC.

YIELD 0.7%
P/E RATIO 23.7

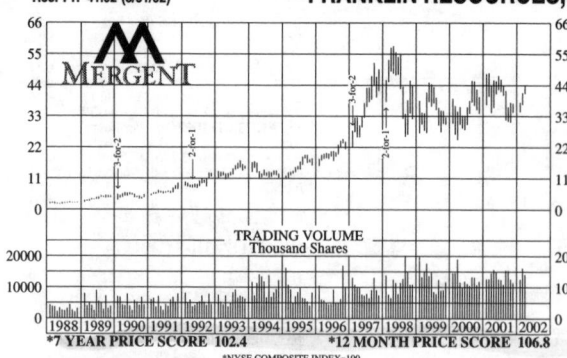

7 YEAR PRICE SCORE 102.4   **12 MONTH PRICE SCORE 106.8**
*NYSE COMPOSITE INDEX=100

INTERIM EARNINGS (Per Share):

Qtr.	Dec.	Mar.	June	Sept.
1997-98	0.52	0.50	0.52	0.44
1998-99	0.27	0.41	0.49	0.52
1999-00	0.55	0.58	0.58	0.58
2000-01	0.61	0.54	0.46	0.32
2001-02	0.45	...	...	...

INTERIM DIVIDENDS (Per Share):

Amt.	Decl.	Ex.	Rec.	Pay.
0.065Q	3/22/01	3/29/01	4/02/01	4/16/01
0.065Q	6/25/01	7/02/01	7/05/01	7/13/01
0.065Q	9/27/01	10/03/01	10/08/01	10/16/01
0.07Q	12/14/01	12/27/01	12/31/01	1/14/02
0.07Q	3/13/02	3/26/02	3/29/02	4/16/02

Indicated div.: $0.28 (Div. Reinv. Plan)

CAPITALIZATION (9/30/01):

	($000)	(%)
Long-Term Debt	566,013	12.5
Common & Surplus	3,977,896	87.5
Total	4,543,909	100.0

DIVIDEND ACHIEVER STATUS:
Rank: 88   10-Year Growth Rate: 12.99%
Total Years of Dividend Growth: 12

RECENT DEVELOPMENTS: For the quarter ended 12/31/01, net income declined 20.7% to $118.5 million from $149.5 million in the prior-year period. Total operating revenues rose 9.6% to $618.2 million from $564.1 million in the previous year. Investment management fees grew 3.2% to $356.8 million from $345.8 million a year earlier. Underwriting and distribution fees increased 16.8% to $192.0 million versus $164.4 million in the prior year. Shareholder servicing fees fell 1.8% to $47.3 million.

PROSPECTS: The Company plans to continue to implement cost-control measures and should continue to see high investment performance across all asset classes. Separately, as of 12/31/01, fixed income assets comprised 30.0% of total assets under management versus 29.0% a year earlier. Moreover, hybrid assets, or assets that are invested in stocks, bonds and money market securities, jumped to 14.5% from 4.5% in 2000.

BUSINESS

FRANKLIN RESOURCES, INC., operating as Franklin Templeton Investments, is engaged in providing investment management, marketing, distribution, transfer agency and other administrative services to the open-end investment companies of the Franklin Templeton Group and to U.S. and international managed and institutional accounts. The Company also provides investment management and related services to a number of closed-end investment companies. In addition, the Company provides investment management, marketing and distribution services to certain sponsored investment companies organized in the Grand Duchy of Luxembourg. In addition, the Company also provides advisory services, variable annuity products, and sponsors and manages public and private real estate programs. As of 12/31/01, BEN's subsidiaries had approximately $266.30 billion in assets under management. On 4/10/01, BEN acquired Fiduciary Trust Company International for approximately $775.0 million.

ANNUAL FINANCIAL DATA

	9/30/01	9/30/00	9/30/99	9/30/98	9/30/97	9/30/96	9/30/95
Earnings Per Share	② 1.91	2.28	① 1.69	1.98	1.72	1.26	1.08
Cash Flow Per Share	2.79	3.09	2.48	2.74	2.20	1.42	1.27
Tang. Book Val. Per Share	7.63	7.37	5.79	4.08	2.50	3.15	2.06
Dividends Per Share	0.26	0.24	0.22	0.20	0.17	0.15	0.13
Dividend Payout %	13.6	10.5	13.0	10.1	9.9	11.6	12.3
INCOME STATEMENT (IN MILLIONS)							
Total Revenues	2,354.8	2,340.1	2,262.5	2,577.3	2,163.3	1,522.6	845.8
Costs & Expenses	1,531.1	1,394.9	1,445.2	1,653.3	1,361.3	1,065.0	436.7
Depreciation & Amort.	223.8	199.6	200.0	191.4	123.9	40.5	40.9
Operating Income	512.0	663.4	539.1	642.1	591.5	417.1	368.1
Net Interest Inc./(Exp.)	d10.6	d14.0	d21.0	d22.5	d25.3	d11.3	d11.2
Income Before Income Taxes	637.8	739.6	574.1	676.3	615.7	456.2	386.7
Income Taxes	153.1	177.5	147.4	175.8	181.7	141.5	117.7
Net Income	② 484.7	562.1	① 426.7	500.5	434.1	314.7	268.9
Cash Flow	708.6	761.7	626.7	691.8	558.0	355.2	309.9
Average Shs. Outstg. (000)	253,663	246,624	252,757	252,941	253,430	249,939	243,729
BALANCE SHEET (IN MILLIONS)							
Cash & Cash Equivalents	2,081.2	1,408.7	1,231.8	1,048.0	656.6	701.7	493.8
Total Current Assets	3,159.5	1,955.9	1,703.7	1,470.8	1,210.5	1,249.9	1,107.3
Net Property	449.6	444.7	416.4	349.2	...	...	...
Total Assets	6,265.7	4,042.4	3,666.8	3,480.0	2,878.1	2,212.6	2,126.1
Total Current Liabilities	1,528.1	728.5	662.9	655.5	709.9	551.7	686.8
Long-Term Obligations	566.0	294.1	294.3	494.5	493.2	399.5	382.4
Net Stockholders' Equity	3,977.9	2,965.5	2,657.0	2,280.8	1,854.2	1,400.6	1,161.0
Net Working Capital	1,631.4	1,227.3	1,040.8	815.3	500.6	698.2	420.5
Year-end Shs. Outstg. (000)	260,798	243,730	251,007	251,742	252,064	240,816	242,820
STATISTICAL RECORD							
Operating Profit Margin %	21.7	28.4	23.8	24.9	27.3	27.4	43.5
Net Profit Margin %	20.6	24.0	18.9	19.4	20.1	20.7	31.8
Return on Equity %	12.2	19.0	16.1	21.9	23.4	22.5	23.2
Return on Assets %	7.7	13.9	11.6	14.4	15.1	14.2	12.6
Debt/Total Assets %	9.0	7.3	8.0	14.2	17.1	18.1	18.0
Price Range	48.30-30.85	45.63-24.63	45.00-27.00	57.88-25.75	51.91-22.08	24.92-15.46	19.33-11.00
P/E Ratio	25.3-16.2	20.0-10.8	26.6-16.0	29.2-13.0	30.3-12.9	19.8-12.3	17.9-10.2
Average Yield %	0.7	0.7	0.6	0.5	0.5	0.7	0.9

Statistics are as originally reported. Adj. for stk. splits: 3-for-2, 12/96; 2-for-1, 12/97 ① Incl. restr. chrg. $58.5 mill. ② Incl. one-time chrg. of $7.6 mill.

OFFICERS:
C. B. Johnson, Chmn., C.E.O.
H. E. Burns, Vice-Chmn.
R. H. Johnson Jr., Vice-Chmn.
M. L. Flanagan, Pres., C.F.O.

INVESTOR CONTACT: Alan Weinfeld, Investor Relations, (650) 525-8900

PRINCIPAL OFFICE: One Franklin Parkway, San Mateo, CA 94403

TELEPHONE NUMBER: (650) 312-2000
FAX: (650) 312-3655
WEB: www.frk.com

NO. OF EMPLOYEES: 6,800 (approx.)

SHAREHOLDERS: 5,050 (approx.)

ANNUAL MEETING: In Jan.

INCORPORATED: DE, Nov., 1969

INSTITUTIONAL HOLDINGS:
No. of Institutions: 331
Shares Held: 103,894,217
% Held: 39.7

INDUSTRY: Investment advice (SIC: 6282)

TRANSFER AGENT(S): Bank of New York, New York, NY

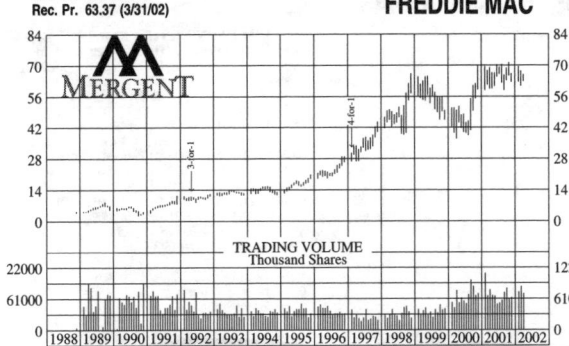

NYSE SYMBOL FRE			
Rec. Pr. 63.37 (3/31/02)	**FREDDIE MAC**	YIELD	1.4%
		P/E RATIO	10.6

INTERIM EARNINGS (Per Share):

Qtr.	Mar.	June	Sept.	Dec.
1997	0.44	0.46	0.49	0.51
1998	0.54	0.56	0.58	0.62
1999	0.68	0.74	0.74	0.78
2000	0.81	0.83	0.86	0.89
2001	1.12	1.29	1.49	2.06

INTERIM DIVIDENDS (Per Share):

Amt.	Decl.	Ex.	Rec.	Pay.
0.20Q	3/02/01	3/08/01	3/12/01	3/30/01
0.20Q	6/01/01	6/07/01	6/11/01	6/29/01
0.20Q	9/07/01	9/17/01	9/17/01	9/28/01
0.20Q	12/07/01	12/13/01	12/17/01	12/31/01
0.22Q	3/01/02	3/07/02	3/11/02	3/29/02

Indicated div.: $0.88 (Div. Reinv. Plan)

TRADING VOLUME
Thousand Shares

CAPITALIZATION (12/31/01):

	($000)	(%)
Long-Term Debt	314,733,000	95.3
Preferred Stock................	4,596,000	1.4
Common & Surplus	10,777,000	3.3
Total	330,106,000	100.0

*7 YEAR PRICE SCORE 130.4   ***12 MONTH PRICE SCORE 99.8**
*NYSE COMPOSITE INDEX=100

DIVIDEND ACHIEVER STATUS:
Rank: 42   10-Year Growth Rate: 16.98%
Total Years of Dividend Growth: 11

RECENT DEVELOPMENTS: For the year ended 12/31/01, income was $4.37 billion, before an extraordinary charge of $231.0 million and an accounting gain of $5.0 million, versus $2.54 billion, before an extraordinary gain of $8.0 million, in the previous year. Results were fueled by record portfolio growth, strong revenue gains and continued low credit costs. Total revenues climbed 65.2% to $7.37 billion from $4.46 billion in the prior year. Net interest income on earning assets leapt 93.1% to $5.48 billion.

PROSPECTS: The Company is benefiting from a strong housing market as homeowners are continuing to take advantage of low interest rates to refinance their mortgages and apply for new mortgages. The Company's total mortgage portfolio grew 18.0% in 2001 to $1.138 trillion. Looking ahead, the Company expects 2002 operating earnings to be driven by growth in the mortgage market as well as continued expansion from its retained portfolio and securitization businesses.

BUSINESS

FREDDIE MAC (formerly The Federal Home Loan Mortgage Corporation) is a federally chartered and stockholder-owned corporation. FRE purchases conventional residential mortgages from mortgage lending institutions and finances most of its purchases with sales of guaranteed mortgage securities called Mortgage Participation Certificates for which FRE ultimately assumes the risk of borrower default. FRE also maintains an investment portfolio that consists principally of federal funds sold, reverse repurchase agreements and tax-advantaged and other short-term investments. FRE's financial performance is driven primarily by the growth of its total servicing portfolio, the mix of sold versus retained portfolios, the spreads earned on the sold and retained portfolios and mortgage default costs.

ANNUAL FINANCIAL DATA

	12/31/01	12/31/00	12/31/99	12/31/98	12/31/97	12/31/96	12/31/95
Earnings Per Share	①②5.96	③3.39	③2.95	2.31	1.88	①1.67	1.42
Tang. Book Val. Per Share	15.50	16.81	11.98	11.55	8.74	9.62	8.14
Dividends Per Share	0.80	0.68	0.60	0.48	0.40	0.35	0.30
Dividend Payout %	13.4	20.1	20.3	20.8	21.3	21.0	21.1

INCOME STATEMENT (IN MILLIONS):

Total Interest Income	34,288.0	28,350.0	22,753.0	16,638.0	13,001.0	10,783.0	8,393.0
Total Interest Expense	28,808.0	25,512.0	20,213.0	14,711.0	11,370.0	9,241.0	6,997.0
Net Interest Income	5,480.0	2,838.0	2,540.0	1,927.0	1,631.0	1,542.0	1,396.0
Provision for Loan Losses	45.0	40.0	60.0	190.0	310.0	320.0	255.0
Non-Interest Income	1,639.0	1,489.0	1,405.0	1,307.0	1,298.0	1,249.0	1,087.0
Non-Interest Expense	1,020.0	883.0	834.0	791.0	755.0	758.0	681.0
Income Before Taxes	6,300.0	3,534.0	3,161.0	2,356.0	1,964.0	1,797.0	1,586.0
Net Income	①②4,373.0	③2,539.0	③2,218.0	1,700.0	1,395.0	①1,258.0	1,091.0
Average Shs. Outstg. (000)	696,876	696,448	700,211	684,658	692,000	710,000	720,000

BALANCE SHEET (IN MILLIONS):

Total Loans & Leases	494,585.0	385,451.0	322,914.0	255,670.0	164,543.0	137,826.0	107,706.0
Allowance for Credit Losses	326.0	334.0	345.0	322.0	293.0	306.0	295.0
Net Loans & Leases	494,259.0	385,117.0	322,569.0	255,348.0	164,250.0	137,520.0	107,411.0
Total Assets	617,340.0	459,297.0	386,684.0	321,421.0	194,597.0	173,866.0	137,181.0
Long-Term Obligations	314,733.0	243,323.0	185,186.0	93,525.0	87,714.0	76,876.0	57,820.0
Total Liabilities	601,967.0	444,460.0	375,159.0	310,586.0	187,076.0	167,135.0	131,318.0
Net Stockholders' Equity	15,373.0	14,837.0	11,525.0	10,835.0	7,521.0	6,731.0	5,863.0
Year-end Shs. Outstg. (000)	695,304	692,584	695,091	695,179	679,000	695,000	716,000

STATISTICAL RECORD:

Return on Equity %	28.4	17.1	19.2	15.7	18.5	18.7	18.6
Return on Assets %	0.7	0.6	0.6	0.5	0.7	0.7	0.8
Equity/Assets %	2.5	3.2	3.0	3.4	3.9	3.9	4.3
Non-Int. Exp./Tot. Inc. %	14.3	20.4	21.1	24.5	25.8	27.2	27.4
Price Range	71.25-58.75	70.13-36.88	65.25-45.38	66.38-38.69	44.56-26.69	29.00-19.06	20.91-12.47
P/E Ratio	12.0-9.9	20.7-10.9	22.1-15.4	28.7-16.7	23.7-14.2	17.4-11.4	14.7-8.8
Average Yield %	1.2	1.3	1.1	0.9	1.1	1.5	1.8

Statistics are as originally reported. Adj. for stk. split: 4-for-1, 1/97. ① Bef. extraord. chrg. $231.0 mill., 12/01; $15.0 mill., 12/96 ② Bef. acctg. change credit $5.0 mill., 12/01 ③ Bef. extraord. gain $8.0 mill., 12/00; $5.0 mill., 12/99

OFFICERS:
L. C. Brendsel, Chmn., C.E.O.
D. W. Glenn, Vice-Chmn., Pres.
V. A. Clarke, Exec. V.P., C.F.O.

INVESTOR CONTACT: Shareholder Relations, (800) 373-3343

PRINCIPAL OFFICE: 8200 Jones Branch Drive, McLean, VA 22102-3110

TELEPHONE NUMBER: (703) 903-2000
FAX: (703) 903-2759
WEB: www.freddiemac.com

NO. OF EMPLOYEES: 3,500 (approx.)

SHAREHOLDERS: 5,627 (approx.)

ANNUAL MEETING: In May

INCORPORATED: July, 1970

INSTITUTIONAL HOLDINGS:
No. of Institutions: 776
Shares Held: 609,274,495
% Held: 87.7

INDUSTRY: Federal & fed.-sponsored credit (SIC: 6111)

TRANSFER AGENT(S): First Chicago Trust Company of New York, Jersey City, NJ

FRISCH'S RESTAURANTS, INC.

YIELD 1.8%
P/E RATIO 12.3

INTERIM EARNINGS (Per Share):

Qtr.	Sept.	Dec.	Feb.	May
1998-99	0.23	0.12	0.16	0.23
1999-00	0.30	0.25	0.22	0.31
2000-01	0.45	0.38	0.24	0.42
2001-02	0.39	0.42	0.37	...

INTERIM DIVIDENDS (Per Share):

Amt.	Decl.	Ex.	Rec.	Pay.
0.08Q	3/13/01	3/28/01	3/30/01	4/10/01
0.08Q	6/12/01	6/22/01	6/26/01	7/10/01
0.09Q	9/04/01	9/24/01	9/26/01	10/10/01
0.09Q	11/27/01	12/26/01	12/28/01	1/10/02
0.09Q	3/19/02	3/26/02	3/29/02	4/10/02

Indicated div.: $0.36

CAPITALIZATION (6/3/01):

	($000)	(%)
Long-Term Debt	26,643	30.4
Capital Lease Obligations..	4,504	5.1
Common & Surplus	56,446	64.4
Total	87,593	100.0

DIVIDEND ACHIEVER STATUS:
Rank: 224   10-Year Growth Rate: 5.69%
Total Years of Dividend Growth: 18

TRADING VOLUME
Thousand Shares

1988 1989 1990 1991 1992 1993 1994 1995 1996 1997 1998 1999 2000 2001 2002
*7 YEAR PRICE SCORE 108.5   *12 MONTH PRICE SCORE 133.2
*NYSE COMPOSITE INDEX=100

RECENT DEVELOPMENTS: For the twelve weeks ended 3/10/02, net earnings advanced 41.6% to $1.9 million compared with earnings from continuing operations of $1.3 million, in the corresponding prior-year period. Earnings for 2001 excluded a $53,000 loss from discontinued operations. Also, results for 2001 included a $1.1 million charge for the impairment of long-lived assets. Total revenue increased 14.1% to $48.1 million from $42.1 million a year earlier. Sales jumped 17.4% to $47.8 million, while other revenue fell 79.5% to $293,000. Total cost of sales climbed 16.1% to $42.0 million, or 87.4% of total revenue, from $36.2 million, or 85.9% of total revenue, in the previous year. Big Boy same-store sales, which were aided by the very mild winter weather in the third quarter, improved 7.3%. In addition, FRS' Golden Corral sales remain strong, backed by expanded advertising. Looking ahead, the Company has plans to develop an additional 26 Golden Corral restaurants through 2007, including three restaurants scheduled to open in April, June and July of 2002.

BUSINESS

FRISCH'S RESTAURANTS, INC. operates 88 family restaurants under the name of Frisch's Big Boy in Indiana, Kentucky and Ohio, and licenses another 36 restaurants to other Big Boy operators at 4/8/02. In addition, the Company owns and operates 15 Golden Corral restaurants in greater Cincinnati and Dayton, Ohio and Louisville, Kentucky with plans to develop 26 more through 2007 in the Cincinnati, Dayton, Louisville, Cleveland and Toledo markets. Trademarks that the Company has the right to use include "Frisch's," "Big Boy," and "Golden Corral." In November 2000, the Company sold its Clarion Hotel Riverview for $12.0 million. In May 2001, FRS sold its Quality Hotel Central for $3.9 million.

ANNUAL FINANCIAL DATA

	6/3/01	5/28/00	5/30/99	5/31/98	6/1/97	6/2/96	5/28/95
Earnings Per Share	③ 1.27	② 1.08	① 0.74	0.73	0.17	0.32	0.33
Cash Flow Per Share	2.95	2.77	2.41	2.21	1.63	1.77	1.70
Tang. Book Val. Per Share	11.12	9.99	9.24	6.68	8.94	9.02	8.92
Dividends Per Share	0.32	0.29	0.28	0.24	0.23	0.22	0.21
Dividend Payout %	25.2	26.8	37.8	32.9	135.7	69.3	64.6

INCOME STATEMENT (IN THOUSANDS):

Total Revenues	190,030	167,200	159,551	152,222	165,931	166,945	163,059
Costs & Expenses	168,832	145,742	140,221	133,077	151,344	150,766	148,184
Depreciation & Amort.	8,599	9,621	9,937	9,256	10,486	10,350	9,821
Operating Income	12,599	11,837	9,394	9,889	4,101	5,829	5,054
Net Interest Inc./(Exp.)	d2,607	d2,410	d2,437	d3,076	d2,373	d2,411	d1,961
Income Before Income Taxes	9,992	9,426	6,957	6,813	1,728	3,417	3,093
Income Taxes	3,435	3,351	2,539	2,268	541	1,108	735
Net Income	③6,557	②6,075	①4,418	4,545	1,187	2,310	2,358
Cash Flow	15,156	15,696	14,355	13,801	11,673	12,660	12,179
Average Shs. Outstg.	5,144	5,658	5,967	6,238	7,151	7,157	7,157

BALANCE SHEET (IN THOUSANDS):

Cash & Cash Equivalents	280	565	200	84	231	135	220
Total Current Assets	6,965	20,778	6,924	6,508	6,882	8,564	8,141
Net Property	88,419	73,901	84,369	82,196	80,764	99,240	98,058
Total Assets	108,310	107,779	103,426	106,724	111,260	118,396	115,548
Total Current Liabilities	17,932	17,722	16,534	14,958	15,699	18,458	18,224
Long-Term Obligations	31,147	33,766	29,415	39,135	28,082	32,207	30,489
Net Stockholders' Equity	56,446	54,167	55,288	49,910	64,684	65,307	64,627
Net Working Capital	d10,967	3,056	d9,610	d8,450	d8,816	d9,894	d10,084
Year-end Shs. Outstg.	5,012	5,345	5,901	7,362	7,148	7,158	7,158

STATISTICAL RECORD:

Operating Profit Margin %	6.6	7.1	5.9	6.5	2.5	3.5	3.1
Net Profit Margin %	3.5	3.6	2.8	3.0	0.7	1.4	1.4
Return on Equity %	11.6	11.2	8.0	9.1	1.8	3.5	3.6
Return on Assets %	6.1	5.6	4.3	4.3	1.1	2.0	2.0
Debt/Total Assets %	28.8	31.3	28.4	36.7	25.2	27.2	26.4
Price Range	15.13-8.50	11.25-8.25	13.88-7.13	17.38-10.50	16.00-7.39	9.94-7.63	13.67-8.50
P/E Ratio	11.9-6.7	10.4-7.6	...	23.8-14.4	94.1-43.5	31.0-23.8	41.4-24.5
Average Yield %	2.7	3.0	2.7	1.7	2.0	2.5	2.0

Statistics are as originally reported. Adj. for stk. splits: 4% div., 12/27/96; 4% div., 12/27/95. ① Bef. extraord. gain of $3.7 mill. ② Bef. inc. from discont. opers. of $70,400. ③ Bef. inc. from discont. opers. of $1.1 mill.; incl. impairment chrg. of $1.5 mill.

OFFICERS:
J. C. Maier, Chmn.
C. F. Maier, Pres., C.E.O.
D. H. Walker, V.P., C.F.O., Treas.

INVESTOR CONTACT: Donald H. Walker,
V.P., C.F.O. & Treas., (513) 559-5184

PRINCIPAL OFFICE: 2800 Gilbert Avenue,
Cincinnati, OH 45206

TELEPHONE NUMBER: (513) 961-2660
FAX: (513) 559-5160
WEB: www.frischs.com
NO. OF EMPLOYEES: 4,000 full-time
(approx.); 2,700 part-time (approx.)
SHAREHOLDERS: 2,600 (approx.)
ANNUAL MEETING: In Oct.
INCORPORATED: OH, Oct., 1947

INSTITUTIONAL HOLDINGS:
No. of Institutions: 23
Shares Held: 1,579,200
% Held: 32.3

INDUSTRY: Eating places (SIC: 5812)

TRANSFER AGENT(S): Continental Stock
Transfer & Trust Company, New York, NY

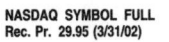

FULLER (H.B.) COMPANY

YIELD	1.4%
P/E RATIO	21.1

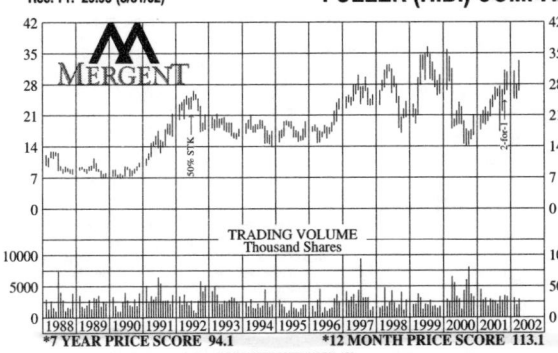

TRADING VOLUME
Thousand Shares

*7 YEAR PRICE SCORE 94.1   *12 MONTH PRICE SCORE 113.1

*NYSE COMPOSITE INDEX=100

INTERIM EARNINGS (Per Share):

Qtr.	Feb.	May	Aug.	Nov.
1998	0.22	0.41	d0.37	0.33
1999	0.28	0.36	0.43	0.51
2000	0.35	0.63	0.26	0.51
2001	0.20	0.42	0.52	0.46
2002	0.02	...	...	...

INTERIM DIVIDENDS (Per Share):

Amt.	Decl.	Ex.	Rec.	Pay.
0.215Q	4/19/01	4/26/01	4/30/01	5/11/01
0.215Q	6/28/01	7/18/01	7/20/01	8/10/01
0.215Q	9/14/01	10/17/01	10/19/01	11/09/01
2-for-1	10/15/01	11/19/01	10/26/01	11/16/01
0.107Q	1/22/02	1/25/02	1/29/02	2/12/02

Indicated div.: $0.43 (Div. Reinv. Plan)

CAPITALIZATION (12/1/01):

	($000)	(%)
Long-Term Debt	203,001	30.9
Minority Interest	19,558	3.0
Preferred Stock	306	0.0
Common & Surplus	433,720	66.1
Total	656,585	100.0

DIVIDEND ACHIEVER STATUS:
Rank: 179   10-Year Growth Rate: 7.63%
Total Years of Dividend Growth: 34

RECENT DEVELOPMENTS: For the thirteen weeks ended 3/2/02, the Company reported net income of $666,000 compared with income of $5.0 million, before an accounting change charge of $501,000, in the corresponding period of the prior year. Earnings for 2002 included a charge of $4.9 million related to asset impairments, severance and other restructuring costs. Net sales slid 4.5% to $293.2 million from $306.9 million a year earlier, reflecting lower

sales volumes and the negative effects of a strong dollar against other currencies. Global adhesive sales decreased by 4.5%, while specialty group sales declined 4.4% over the prior year. Softened demand resulted in volume declines of 3.0% and 1.9% in the adhesives and specialty groups, respectively. Gross profit slipped 9.0% to $75.2 million, or 25.6% of net sales, from $82.6 million, or 26.9% of net sales, the year before.

BUSINESS

H.B. FULLER COMPANY and its subsidiaries are principally engaged in the manufacture and distribution of industrial adhesives, coatings, sealants, paints and other specialty chemical products worldwide. The Company's subsidiary, Kativo Chemical Industries, S.A., and its subsidiaries manufacture and distribute paints, adhesives, plastics, printing inks and related chemical products in Central America, Panama, Mexico and South America. The Company has manufacturing operations in North America, Europe, Latin America and the Asia/Pacific region. As of 12/1/01, FULL had manufacturing operations in 43 countries in North and Latin America, Europe and the Asia/Pacific region.

ANNUAL FINANCIAL DATA

	12/1/01	12/2/00	11/27/99	11/28/98	11/29/97	11/30/96	11/30/95
Earnings Per Share	[1] 1.59	1.74	[2] 1.58	[2] 0.58	[1] 1.43	1.61	[1] 1.11
Cash Flow Per Share	3.51	3.59	3.39	2.37	3.09	3.27	2.57
Tang. Book Val. Per Share	12.37	11.07	9.88	8.51	10.51	10.06	8.71
Dividends Per Share	0.43	0.42	0.41	0.39	0.36	0.33	0.31
Dividend Payout %	26.9	24.0	25.9	68.2	25.2	20.3	28.2
INCOME STATEMENT (IN MILLIONS):							
Total Revenues	1,274.1	1,352.6	1,364.5	1,347.2	1,306.8	1,275.7	1,243.8
Costs & Expenses	1,131.6	1,197.9	1,209.9	1,236.5	1,172.8	1,148.0	1,132.9
Depreciation & Amort.	54.4	52.2	50.8	49.5	46.8	47.0	41.2
Operating Income	88.1	102.5	103.7	61.2	87.3	80.8	69.8
Net Interest Inc./(Exp.)	d21.2	d23.8	d26.8	d27.0	d19.8	d18.9	d18.1
Income Before Income Taxes	63.5	76.9	74.4	32.8	65.3	76.6	50.4
Income Taxes	19.8	28.5	31.8	18.8	26.7	31.2	19.1
Equity Earnings/Minority Int.	1.3	0.7	1.5	2.0	1.6	0.1	d0.1
Net Income	[1] 44.9	49.2	[2] 44.1	[2] 16.0	[1] 40.3	45.4	[1] 31.2
Cash Flow	99.3	101.3	94.9	65.5	87.1	92.4	72.4
Average Shs. Outstg. (000)	28,330	28,206	27,956	27,688	28,200	28,228	28,118
BALANCE SHEET (IN MILLIONS):							
Cash & Cash Equivalents	11.5	10.5	5.8	4.6	2.7	3.5	9.1
Total Current Assets	403.9	435.1	440.1	457.9	409.2	388.2	387.6
Net Property	371.1	394.7	412.5	414.5	398.6	391.2	355.1
Total Assets	966.2	1,010.4	1,025.6	1,046.2	917.6	869.3	828.9
Total Current Liabilities	204.2	226.7	265.9	285.2	237.5	246.6	245.6
Long-Term Obligations	203.0	250.5	263.7	300.1	230.0	172.8	166.5
Net Stockholders' Equity	434.0	404.7	376.4	341.4	339.1	334.7	299.4
Net Working Capital	199.7	208.3	174.2	172.7	171.6	141.6	142.1
Year-end Shs. Outstg. (000)	28,281	28,240	28,080	27,965	27,682	28,132	28,014
STATISTICAL RECORD:							
Operating Profit Margin %	6.9	7.6	7.6	4.5	6.7	6.3	5.6
Net Profit Margin %	3.5	3.6	3.2	1.2	3.1	3.6	2.5
Return on Equity %	10.4	12.1	11.7	4.7	11.9	13.6	10.4
Return on Assets %	4.7	4.9	4.3	1.5	4.4	5.2	3.8
Debt/Total Assets %	21.0	24.8	25.7	28.7	25.1	19.9	20.1
Price Range	31.19-17.25	35.88-14.06	36.44-19.06	32.50-17.00	30.13-22.50	24.81-14.75	19.88-14.88
P/E Ratio	19.6-10.8	20.6-8.1	23.1-12.1	56.5-29.6	21.1-15.7	15.4-9.2	17.9-13.4
Average Yield %	1.8	1.7	1.5	1.6	1.4	1.7	1.8

Statistics are as originally reported. Adj. for 2-for-1 stk. split, 11/16/01. [1] Bef. acctg. chrg.: 12/1/01, $501,000; 11/29/97, $3.4 mill.; 11/30/95, $2.5 mill. [2] Incl. non-recurr. chrg. 11/27/99: $17.2 mill.; 11/28/98: $26.7 mill.

OFFICERS:
A. P. Stroucken, Chmn., Pres., C.E.O.
R. A. Tucker, Sr. V.P., C.F.O., Treas.
W. L. Gacki, V.P., Treas.

INVESTOR CONTACT: Scott Dvorak, Dir. of Investor Relations, (651) 236-5150

PRINCIPAL OFFICE: 1200 Willow Lake Boulevard, St. Paul, MN 55110-5101

TELEPHONE NUMBER: (651) 236-5900
WEB: www.hbfuller.com

NO. OF EMPLOYEES: 4,900 (approx.)

SHAREHOLDERS: 3,606

ANNUAL MEETING: In April

INCORPORATED: MN, Dec., 1915

INSTITUTIONAL HOLDINGS:
No. of Institutions: 141
Shares Held: 18,158,864
% Held: 64.2

INDUSTRY: Adhesives and sealants (SIC: 2891)

TRANSFER AGENT(S): Wells Fargo Shareowner Services, Minnesota, MN

FULTON FINANCIAL CORPORATION

YIELD 2.7%
P/E RATIO 18.4

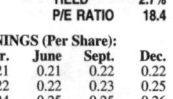

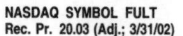

TRADING VOLUME
Thousand Shares

| 1988 | 1989 | 1990 | 1991 | 1992 | 1993 | 1994 | 1995 | 1996 | 1997 | 1998 | 1999 | 2000 | 2001 | 2002 |

*7 YEAR PRICE SCORE 109.0   *12 MONTH PRICE SCORE 110.7
*NYSE COMPOSITE INDEX=100

INTERIM EARNINGS (Per Share):

Qtr.	Mar.	June	Sept.	Dec.
1997	0.21	0.21	0.22	0.22
1998	0.22	0.22	0.23	0.25
1999	0.24	0.25	0.25	0.26
2000	0.26	0.28	0.28	0.28
2001	0.27	0.29	0.23	0.30

INTERIM DIVIDENDS (Per Share):

Amt.	Decl.	Ex.	Rec.	Pay.
0.17Q	7/17/01	9/19/01	9/21/01	10/15/01
0.17Q	10/16/01	12/19/01	12/21/01	1/15/02
0.17Q	1/15/02	3/13/02	3/15/02	4/15/02
25% STK	3/19/02	5/21/02	4/24/02	5/20/02

Indicated div.: $0.54 (Adj.; Div. Reinv. Plan)

CAPITALIZATION (12/31/01):

	($000)	(%)
Total Deposits	5,986,804	88.1
Common & Surplus	811,454	11.9
Total	6,798,258	100.0

DIVIDEND ACHIEVER STATUS:
Rank: 150   10-Year Growth Rate: 9.42%
Total Years of Dividend Growth: 28

RECENT DEVELOPMENTS: For the year ended 12/31/01, net income was $113.6 million compared with $106.8 million the previous year. Results for 2001 included merger-related expenses of $7.1 million. Net interest income totaled $290.2 million, up 5.2% from $275.8 million in 2000, driven by the effect of acquisitions. Provision for loan losses declined 2.9% to $14.6 million versus $15.0 million the year before. Total other income climbed 34.7% to $101.0 million, reflecting investment securities gains,

investment management and trust services income due to the January 2001 acquisition of Dearden, Maguire, Weaver and Barrett, LLC, and mortgage sales gains due to significant refinance activity resulting from lower mortgage interest rates. Comparisons were made with restated prior-year results to reflect the 7/1/01 acquisition of Drovers Bancshares Corporation, which was accounted for on a pooling-of-interests basis.

BUSINESS

FULTON FINANCIAL CORPORATION, with $7.77 billion in assets at 12/31/01, is the financial holding company for 100.0% of the stock of eleven community banks, three financial services companies and five non-bank entities. The Company's eleven wholly-owned subsidiary banks are located primarily in suburban or semi-rural geographical markets throughout Pennsylvania, Maryland, New Jersey and Delaware. The Company's 100.0%-owned five non-bank subsidiaries are Fulton Life Insurance Company, Fulton Financial Realty Company, Central Pennsylvania Financial Corp., FFC Management, Inc., and Drovers Capital Trust I. In January 2001, FULT acquired investment management and advisory company Dearden, Maguire, Weaver and Barrett, LLC. On 7/1/01, FULT acquired Drovers Bancshares Corporation.

QUARTERLY DATA

(12/31/2001)($000)	REV	INC
1st Quarter	133,253	28,251
2nd Quarter	130,472	30,327
3rd Quarter	130,009	24,162
4th Quarter	124,444	30,849

ANNUAL FINANCIAL DATA

	12/31/01	12/31/00	12/31/99	12/31/98	12/31/97	12/31/96	12/31/95
Earnings Per Share	☐ 1.10	1.10	1.02	0.92	0.85	0.76	0.70
Tang. Book Val. Per Share	7.15	7.20	6.51	6.37	6.18	5.60	5.25
Dividends Per Share	0.52	0.46	0.42	0.38	0.34	0.31	0.28
Dividend Payout %	47.1	41.8	40.9	40.9	40.6	41.1	39.8
INCOME STATEMENT (IN MILLIONS):							
Total Interest Income	518.2	462.6	418.9	409.3	319.6	268.7	235.9
Total Interest Expense	228.0	210.5	174.8	177.8	137.0	113.8	102.1
Net Interest Income	290.2	252.1	244.1	231.5	182.6	154.9	133.8
Provision for Loan Losses	14.6	8.6	8.2	5.6	7.7	4.2	2.0
Non-Interest Income	101.0	69.6	62.8	60.6	41.1	32.8	29.0
Non-Interest Expense	216.7	165.0	161.0	158.2	122.3	110.2	100.0
Income Before Taxes	160.0	148.0	137.7	128.3	93.6	73.3	60.7
Net Income	☐ 113.6	103.8	97.2	88.5	65.2	52.0	45.6
Average Shs. Outstg. (000)	103,939	94,046	95,588	95,759	85,190	68,690	59,191
BALANCE SHEET (IN MILLIONS):							
Cash & Due from Banks	356.5	267.2	245.6	247.6	172.4	165.0	140.1
Securities Avail. for Sale	1,687.8	1,140.6	1,137.8	1,206.1	597.4	317.1	222.3
Total Loans & Leases	5,373.0	4,879.7	4,432.0	4,040.5	3,317.2	2,783.6	2,364.8
Allowance for Credit Losses	71.9	73.2	67.3	67.5	56.6	48.2	44.0
Net Loans & Leases	5,301.1	4,806.5	4,364.8	3,973.0	3,260.6	2,735.4	2,320.8
Total Assets	7,770.7	6,571.2	6,070.0	5,838.7	4,460.8	3,769.4	3,334.7
Total Deposits	5,986.8	4,934.4	4,546.8	4,593.0	3,621.6	3,054.2	2,730.4
Long-Term Obligations	...	442.0	328.3	296.0	47.7	49.2	34.7
Total Liabilities	6,959.3	5,891.8	5,455.7	5,230.3	3,985.5	3,383.7	2,994.8
Net Stockholders' Equity	811.5	679.3	614.3	608.3	475.3	385.7	339.9
Year-end Shs. Outstg. (000)	103,250	94,369	94,332	95,483	84,631	68,834	59,049
STATISTICAL RECORD:							
Return on Equity %	14.0	15.3	15.8	14.5	13.7	13.5	13.4
Return on Assets %	1.5	1.6	1.6	1.5	1.5	1.4	1.4
Equity/Assets %	10.4	10.3	10.1	10.4	10.7	10.2	10.2
Non-Int. Exp./Tot. Inc. %	55.4	51.3	52.5	54.2	54.7	58.7	61.5
Price Range	18.40-14.62	18.19-11.43	16.33-12.34	19.86-11.21	17.15-9.84	10.53-8.72	9.92-7.34
P/E Ratio	16.8-13.3	16.5-10.3	16.1-12.1	21.5-12.1	20.2-11.6	13.9-11.5	14.1-10.4
Average Yield %	3.1	3.1	2.9	2.4	2.5	3.2	3.3

Statistics are as originally reported. Adj. for all stock splits through 5/02. ☐ Incl. merger-related expenses of $7.1 mill.

OFFICERS:
R. A. Fulton, Jr., Chmn., C.E.O.
R. S. Smith, Jr., Pres., C.O.O.
C. J. Nugent, Sr. Exec. V.P., C.F.O.

INVESTOR CONTACT: Corp. Comm. Dept., (717) 291-2739

PRINCIPAL OFFICE: One Penn Square, P.O. Box 4887, Lancaster, PA 17604

TELEPHONE NUMBER: (717) 291-2411
FAX: (717) 291-2695
WEB: www.fult.com

NO. OF EMPLOYEES: 2,818

SHAREHOLDERS: 17,145

ANNUAL MEETING: In Apr.

INCORPORATED: PA, 1982

INSTITUTIONAL HOLDINGS:
No. of Institutions: 109
Shares Held: 22,891,124 (Adj.)
% Held: 22.2

INDUSTRY: National commercial banks (SIC: 6021)

TRANSFER AGENT(S): Stock Transfer Department, Lancaster, PA

GALLAGHER (ARTHUR J.) & COMPANY

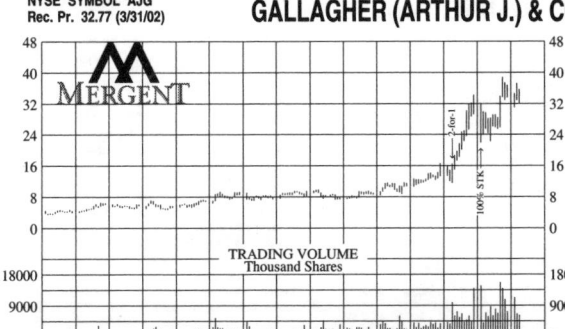

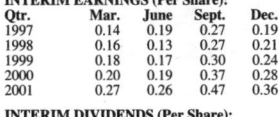

INTERIM EARNINGS (Per Share):

Qtr.	Mar.	June	Sept.	Dec.
1997	0.14	0.19	0.27	0.19
1998	0.16	0.13	0.27	0.21
1999	0.18	0.17	0.30	0.24
2000	0.20	0.19	0.37	0.28
2001	0.27	0.26	0.47	0.36

INTERIM DIVIDENDS (Per Share):

Amt.	Decl.	Ex.	Rec.	Pay.
0.13Q	5/22/01	6/27/01	6/29/01	7/13/01
0.13Q	9/17/01	9/26/01	9/28/01	10/15/01
0.13Q	11/15/01	12/27/01	12/31/01	1/15/02
0.15Q	1/24/02	3/26/02	3/29/02	4/15/02

Indicated div.: $0.60

CAPITALIZATION (12/31/01):

	($000)	(%)
Common & Surplus	371,613	100.0
Total	371,613	100.0

DIVIDEND ACHIEVER STATUS:
Rank: 96   10-Year Growth Rate: 12.36%
Total Years of Dividend Growth: 17

TRADING VOLUME
Thousand Shares

1988 1989 1990 1991 1992 1993 1994 1995 1996 1997 1998 1999 2000 2001 2002
*7 YEAR PRICE SCORE 177.2   *12 MONTH PRICE SCORE 112.9
*NYSE COMPOSITE INDEX=100

RECENT DEVELOPMENTS: For the year ended 12/31/01, net income climbed 34.8% to $125.3 million from $93.0 million in the previous year. Revenues grew 14.4% to $910.0 million from $795.3 million in the prior year. Revenues from commissions rose 13.7% to $534.5 million from $470.2 million in 2000. Revenues from fees improved 15.5% to $324.9 million versus $281.2 million the year before. Comparisons were made with restated prior-year results.

PROSPECTS: The Company is experiencing an improvement in the renewal base of insurance coverages across all lines of its business due to the effect of higher pricing conditions existing throughout the industry. Meanwhile, earnings are being positively affected by continuing new business development as well as the monetization of the Company's limited partnership interests in its synthetic fuel facilities.

BUSINESS

ARTHUR J. GALLAGHER & COMPANY is engaged in providing insurance brokerage, risk management, employee benefit and other related services to clients in the United States and abroad. The Company's principal activity is the negotiation and placement of insurance for its clients. In addition, AJG specializes in furnishing risk management services that include assisting clients in analyzing risks and determining whether proper protection is best obtained through the purchase of insurance or through retention of those risks and the adoption of corporate risk management policies and cost-effective loss control and prevention programs. Risk management also includes claims management, loss control consulting and property appraisals. As of 12/31/01, the Company had offices in nine countries and does business in more than 100 countries around the world through a network of correspondent brokers and consultants.

ANNUAL FINANCIAL DATA

	12/31/01	12/31/00	12/31/99	12/31/98	12/31/97	12/31/96	12/31/95
Earnings Per Share	1.39	1.05	0.88	0.78	0.78	0.66	0.64
Tang. Book Val. Per Share	3.60	3.75	3.14	2.69	2.31	1.89	1.79
Dividends Per Share	0.51	0.45	0.39	0.34	0.30	0.28	0.24
Dividend Payout %	36.3	42.4	44.0	43.9	38.9	42.5	38.2

INCOME STATEMENT (IN MILLIONS):

Total Revenues	910.0	740.6	605.8	540.7	488.0	456.7	412.0
Income Before Income Taxes	141.9	125.4	104.2	84.5	80.8	69.4	62.9
Income Taxes	16.6	37.6	36.5	28.0	27.5	23.6	21.4
Net Income	125.3	87.8	67.8	56.5	53.3	45.8	41.5
Average Shs. Outstg. (000)	90,127	83,924	77,132	72,824	68,152	71,100	65,260

BALANCE SHEET (IN MILLIONS):

Cash & Cash Equivalents	306.8	258.1	170.0	148.1	148.3	144.2	121.3
Premiums Due	555.3	405.2	364.9	288.3	217.6	237.6	193.7
Invst. Assets: Total	70.9	83.3	84.1	77.5	101.9	90.3	87.8
Total Assets	1,471.8	1,062.3	884.1	746.0	641.8	590.4	495.8
Net Stockholders' Equity	371.6	314.4	242.5	202.5	163.9	134.5	118.1
Year-end Shs. Outstg. (000)	85,111	79,497	73,680	70,580	66,364	65,172	61,704

STATISTICAL RECORD:

Return on Revenues %	13.8	11.9	11.2	10.5	10.9	10.0	10.1
Return on Equity %	33.7	27.9	27.9	27.9	32.5	34.0	35.1
Return on Assets %	8.5	8.3	7.7	7.6	8.3	7.8	8.4
Price Range	38.82-21.88	34.25-11.53	16.56-10.56	11.69-8.39	9.56-7.44	9.88-7.28	9.50-7.53
P/E Ratio	27.9-15.7	32.6-11.0	18.8-12.0	15.1-10.8	12.2-9.5	15.0-11.1	15.0-11.9
Average Yield %	1.7	1.9	2.9	3.4	3.6	3.3	2.8

Statistics are as originally reported. Adjusted for 2-for-1 stock split: 1/01 & 3/00.

OFFICERS:
R. E. Gallagher, Chmn.
J. P. Gallagher, Jr., Pres., C.E.O.
M. J. Cloherty, Exec. V.P., C.F.O.

INVESTOR CONTACT: Marsha J. Akin,
Investor Relations, (630) 773-3800

PRINCIPAL OFFICE: Two Pierce Place,
Itasca, IL 60143-3141

TELEPHONE NUMBER: (630) 773-3800
FAX: (630) 285-4000
WEB: www.ajg.com

NO. OF EMPLOYEES: 6,500 (approx.)

SHAREHOLDERS: 700 (approx.)

ANNUAL MEETING: In May

INCORPORATED: IL, 1960; reincorp., DE, 1972

GANNETT CO., INC.

YIELD 1.2%
P/E RATIO 24.3

TRADING VOLUME
Thousand Shares

1988	1989	1990	1991	1992	1993	1994	1995	1996	1997	1998	1999	2000	2001	2002

*7 YEAR PRICE SCORE 104.7 ***12 MONTH PRICE SCORE 115.1**
*NYSE COMPOSITE INDEX=100

INTERIM EARNINGS (Per Share):

Qtr.	Mar.	June	Sept.	Dec.
1998	1.20	0.78	0.62	0.92
1999	0.64	0.98	0.74	1.01
2000	0.74	1.00	0.79	1.12
2001	0.66	0.88	0.66	0.93

INTERIM DIVIDENDS (Per Share):

Amt.	Decl.	Ex.	Rec.	Pay.
0.22Q	5/08/01	6/06/01	6/08/01	7/02/01
0.23Q	8/28/01	9/17/01	9/14/01	10/01/01
0.23Q	10/23/01	12/12/01	12/14/01	1/02/02
0.23Q	2/19/02	3/06/02	3/08/02	4/01/02

Indicated div.: $0.92 (Div. Reinv. Plan)

CAPITALIZATION (12/30/01):

	($000)	(%)
Long-Term Debt	5,080,025	44.9
Deferred Income Tax	503,397	4.4
Common & Surplus	5,735,922	50.7
Total	11,319,344	100.0

DIVIDEND ACHIEVER STATUS:
Rank: 255   10-Year Growth Rate: 3.68%
Total Years of Dividend Growth: 30

RECENT DEVELOPMENTS: For the year ended 12/30/01, net income declined 14.5% to $831.2 million versus income from continuing operations of $971.9 million in 2000. Results for 2001 and 2000 included amortization of intangible assets of $241.3 million and $180.5 million, respectively. Results for 2000 excluded a gain of $2.4 million from discontinued operation and a gain of $744.7 million on the sale of cable business. Total operating revenues were $6.34 billion, up 2.0% from $6.22 billion in 2000.

PROSPECTS: Results may continue to be hampered by the effects of the terrorist attacks of 9/11/01, softness in newspaper and television advertising revenue, and higher newsprint costs. However, GCI's efforts to reduce operating costs and lower interest expenses should help to mitigate the effects of weak advertising conditions. GCI expects to be well-positioned to take advantage of market opportunities as economic conditions begin to improve.

BUSINESS

GANNETT CO., INC. is a diversified news and information company that publishes newspapers and operates broadcasting stations, and a television entertainment programming unit. GCI is also engaged in marketing, commercial printing, a newswire data service, data services, news programming and alarm services. As of 12/30/01, GCI had operations in 43 states, the District of Columbia, Canada, Guam, and the U.S. Virgin Islands. GCI is the largest U.S. newspaper group in terms of circulation, with 95 daily newspapers, including USA TODAY, more than 300 non-daily publications and USA WEEK END, a weekly newspaper magazine. In the U.K., GCI subsidiary Newsquest plc publishes nearly 300 titles, including 15 daily newspapers. GCI owns and operates 22 television stations in major markets. On 1/31/00, Gannett sold its cable business, Multimedia Cablevision, Inc.

ANNUAL FINANCIAL DATA

	12/30/01	12/31/00	12/26/99	12/27/98	12/28/97	12/31/96	12/31/95
Earnings Per Share	[5] 3.12	[4] 3.63	[3] 3.26	[2] 3.50	2.50	[1] 2.22	1.71
Cash Flow Per Share	4.78	5.03	4.26	4.59	3.55	3.23	2.45
Tang. Book Val. Per Share	...	...	...	0.66	...	...	...
Dividends Per Share	0.89	0.85	0.81	0.80	0.73	0.70	0.69
Dividend Payout %	28.5	23.4	24.8	22.9	29.2	31.8	40.2
INCOME STATEMENT (IN MILLIONS):							
Total Revenues	6,344.2	6,222.3	5,260.2	5,121.3	4,729.5	4,421.1	4,006.7
Costs & Expenses	4,310.6	4,029.1	3,417.0	3,367.6	3,112.2	3,067.3	2,944.9
Depreciation & Amort.	443.8	375.9	280.1	310.2	301.1	287.4	210.0
Operating Income	1,589.8	1,817.3	1,563.1	1,443.5	1,316.3	1,066.4	851.9
Net Interest Inc./(Exp.)	d217.2	d192.0	d88.9	d60.1	d91.7	d128.8	d44.7
Income Before Income Taxes	1,370.6	1,608.8	1,527.2	1,669.4	1,209.0	1,086.7	803.5
Income Taxes	539.4	636.9	607.8	669.5	496.3	462.7	326.2
Net Income	[5] 831.2	[4] 971.9	[3] 919.4	[2] 999.9	712.7	[1] 624.0	477.3
Cash Flow	1,275.0	1,347.9	1,199.5	1,310.1	1,013.8	911.3	687.2
Average Shs. Outstg. (000)	266,833	268,118	281,608	285,711	285,610	281,782	280,312
BALANCE SHEET (IN MILLIONS):							
Cash & Cash Equivalents	140.6	193.2	46.2	66.2	52.8	31.2	47.0
Total Current Assets	1,178.2	1,302.3	1,075.2	906.4	884.6	766.6	854.1
Net Property	2,465.5	2,461.4	2,223.9	2,063.8	2,192.0	1,994.1	2,070.7
Total Assets	13,096.1	12,980.4	9,006.4	6,979.5	6,890.4	6,349.6	6,503.8
Total Current Liabilities	1,127.7	1,174.0	883.8	728.0	767.5	719.0	812.8
Long-Term Obligations	5,080.0	5,747.9	2,463.5	1,306.9	1,740.5	1,880.3	2,767.9
Net Stockholders' Equity	5,735.9	5,103.4	4,629.6	3,979.8	3,479.7	2,930.8	2,145.6
Net Working Capital	50.5	128.3	191.4	178.4	117.1	47.6	41.3
Year-end Shs. Outstg. (000)	265,797	264,272	277,926	279,001	283,874	282,636	281,130
STATISTICAL RECORD:							
Operating Profit Margin %	25.1	29.2	29.7	28.2	27.8	24.1	21.3
Net Profit Margin %	13.1	15.6	17.5	19.5	15.1	14.1	11.9
Return on Equity %	14.5	19.0	19.9	25.1	20.5	21.3	22.2
Return on Assets %	6.3	7.5	10.2	14.3	10.3	9.8	7.3
Debt/Total Assets %	38.8	44.3	27.3	18.7	25.3	29.6	42.6
Price Range	71.14-53.00	81.56-48.38	83.63-60.63	75.13-47.63	61.69-35.69	39.38-29.50	32.44-24.75
P/E Ratio	22.8-17.0	22.5-13.3	25.7-18.6	21.5-13.6	24.7-14.3	17.8-13.3	19.0-14.5
Average Yield %	1.4	1.3	1.1	1.3	1.5	2.0	2.4

Statistics are as originally reported. Adj. for 2-for-1 spl., 10/97. [1] Excl. $294.6 mill. aft-tx gain & $24.5 mill. inco. fr. disc. ops; incl. $93.0 mill. aft-tax gain. [2] Incl. $184.0 mill. aft-tax gain fr. disp. of 5 radio stations & alarm security bus. [3] Incl. $33.0 mill. net gain fr. exchange of TV stations & excl. $38.5 mill. gain fr. disc. ops. [4] Excl. $2.4 mill. net income fr. disc. ops. & $744.7 mill. net gain fr. sale of bus. [5] Incl. $241.3 mill. amort. of intang.

OFFICERS:
D. H. McCorkindale, Chmn., Pres., C.E.O.
L. Miller, Exec. V.P., C.F.O.

INVESTOR CONTACT: Gracia Martore, Investor Relations, (703) 854-6918

PRINCIPAL OFFICE: 7950 Jones Branch Drive, McLean, VA 22107-0910

TELEPHONE NUMBER: (703) 854-6000
FAX: (703) 364-0855
WEB: www.gannett.com
NO. OF EMPLOYEES: 51,500 (approx.)
SHAREHOLDERS: 13,700 (approx.)
ANNUAL MEETING: In May
INCORPORATED: NY, Dec., 1923; reincorp., DE, May, 1972

INSTITUTIONAL HOLDINGS:
No. of Institutions: 596
Shares Held: 202,790,458
% Held: 76.1

INDUSTRY: Newspapers (SIC: 2711)

TRANSFER AGENT(S): Wells Fargo Shareowner Services, St. Paul, MN

GATX CORPORATION

YIELD 4.0%
P/E RATIO 212.0

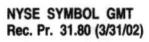

TRADING VOLUME
Thousand Shares

14000
7000
0

1988 1989 1990 1991 1992 1993 1994 1995 1996 1997 1998 1999 2000 2001 2002
*7 YEAR PRICE SCORE 91.2   *12 MONTH PRICE SCORE 90.4
*NYSE COMPOSITE INDEX=100

INTERIM EARNINGS (Per Share):

Qtr.	Mar.	June	Sept.	Dec.
1998	0.74	0.61	0.76	0.51
1999	0.78	0.75	0.83	0.64
2000	0.76	0.67	0.78	d1.60
2001	0.09	0.46	d0.15	d0.25

INTERIM DIVIDENDS (Per Share):

Amt.	Decl.	Ex.	Rec.	Pay.
0.31Q	4/27/01	6/13/01	6/15/01	6/30/01
0.31Q	7/27/01	9/17/01	9/14/01	9/30/01
0.31Q	10/12/01	12/12/01	12/14/01	12/31/01
0.32Q	2/08/02	3/06/02	3/08/02	3/31/02

Indicated div.: $1.28 (Div. Reinv. Plan)

CAPITALIZATION (12/31/01):

	($000)	(%)
Long-Term Debt	3,625,500	70.6
Capital Lease Obligations..	163,000	3.2
Deferred Income Tax	464,500	9.0
Common & Surplus	881,800	17.2
Total	5,134,800	100.0

DIVIDEND ACHIEVER STATUS:
Rank: 181   10-Year Growth Rate: 7.53%
Total Years of Dividend Growth: 16

RECENT DEVELOPMENTS: For the year ended 12/31/01, income from continuing operations was $7.5 million versus income from continuing operations of $30.8 million the previous year. Results for 2001 and 2000 included provisions of $98.4 million and $17.7 million for possible losses, and asset impairment charges of $85.2 million and $5.0 million, respectively. Results for 2001 and 2000 also included net non-recurring charges of $800,000 and $160.5 million, respectively. Revenues rose 13.5% to $1.49 billion.

PROSPECTS: Continued economic weakness, particularly within the telecommunications sector, coupled with uncertainty regarding GMT's air business in the wake of September 11th, cloud the Company's near-term outlook. Accordingly, GMT expects full-year 2002 earnings to be in the range of $2.00 to $2.25 per share. Meanwhile, lower inventories and reduced new car orders have set the stage for future rail growth, brightening GMT's long-term outlook.

BUSINESS

GATX CORP. operates in two industry segments. The Financial Services segment provides financing for equipment and other capital assets on a worldwide basis and consists of four business units: Air, Technology, Venture Finance and Specialty Finance. The GATX Rail segment is principally engaged in leasing rail equipment, including tank cars, freight cars and locomotives. As of 12/31/01, GMT owned or had an interest in about 129,000 railcars in North America, comprised of 71,000 tank cars and 58,000 specialized freight cars. GMT also owns or has an interest in about 900 locomotives. In March 2001, GMT purchased Dyrekcja Eksploatacji Cystern, Poland's national tank car fleet. GATX Rail also owns a 49.5% interest in KVG Kesselwagen Vermietgesellschaft mbH, a German and Austrian-based tank car and specialty railcar leasing company, and a 37.5% interest in Switzerland-based AAE Cargo. As of 12/31/01, GMT had substantially completed the sale of its Integrated Solution Group, which included GATX Terminals Corporation and GATX Logistics, Inc.

ANNUAL FINANCIAL DATA

	12/31/01	12/31/00	12/31/99	12/31/98	12/31/97	12/31/96	12/31/95
Earnings Per Share	⅗ 0.15	② 0.63	3.01	2.62	① d1.27	2.19	2.15
Cash Flow Per Share	8.61	7.51	9.14	7.92	4.32	7.13	6.37
Tang. Book Val. Per Share	18.09	16.25	17.20	14.87	13.39	16.73	15.60
Dividends Per Share	1.24	1.20	1.10	1.00	0.92	0.86	0.80
Dividend Payout %	826.1	190.4	36.5	38.2	...	39.4	37.2
INCOME STATEMENT (IN MILLIONS):							
Total Revenues	1,488.6	1,311.8	1,773.0	1,763.1	1,701.9	1,414.4	1,246.4
Costs & Expenses	830.3	520.4	1,064.6	1,098.1	1,314.5	880.5	787.7
Depreciation & Amort.	415.9	334.8	308.2	267.5	252.3	202.4	171.6
Operating Income	242.4	377.6	400.2	397.5	135.1	331.5	287.1
Net Interest Inc./(Exp.)	d249.9	d242.6	d232.2	d234.9	d222.4	d202.8	d170.1
Income Before Income Taxes	5.6	53.5	253.9	162.6	d87.3	128.7	117.0
Income Taxes	cr1.9	22.7	102.6	74.3	cr5.5	54.4	47.6
Equity Earnings/Minority Int.	...	...	...	43.6	30.9	28.4	31.4
Net Income	③ 7.5	② 30.8	151.3	131.9	① d50.9	102.7	100.8
Cash Flow	423.4	365.4	459.5	399.3	194.7	291.9	259.2
Average Shs. Outstg. (000)	49,202	48,753	50,301	50,426	45,084	40,966	40,718
BALANCE SHEET (IN MILLIONS):							
Cash & Cash Equivalents	347.3	173.6	102.5	94.5	77.8	46.2	34.8
Total Current Assets	1,823.0	1,684.5	1,144.1	1,032.4	1,168.5	1,039.1	963.9
Net Property	2,983.9	2,654.1	3,282.0	2,790.1	2,710.5	2,846.4	2,369.1
Total Assets	6,109.7	6,263.7	5,866.8	4,939.3	4,947.8	4,750.2	4,042.9
Total Current Liabilities	658.9	1,016.2	815.5	707.0	805.2	608.1	611.7
Long-Term Obligations	3,788.5	3,752.3	3,432.6	2,821.7	2,819.4	2,664.1	2,092.5
Net Stockholders' Equity	881.8	789.5	836.0	732.9	655.4	774.9	717.8
Net Working Capital	1,164.1	668.3	328.6	325.4	363.3	431.0	352.2
Year-end Shs. Outstg. (000)	48,756	48,599	48,599	49,284	48,942	46,128	45,792
STATISTICAL RECORD:							
Operating Profit Margin %	16.3	28.8	22.6	22.5	7.9	23.4	23.0
Net Profit Margin %	0.5	2.3	8.5	7.5	...	7.3	8.1
Return on Equity %	0.9	3.9	18.1	18.0	...	13.3	14.0
Return on Assets %	0.1	0.5	2.6	2.7	...	2.2	2.5
Debt/Total Assets %	62.0	59.9	58.5	57.1	57.0	56.1	51.8
Price Range	49.94-23.65	50.50-28.38	40.88-28.06	47.56-26.25	36.00-23.75	25.63-21.50	27.13-20.19
P/E Ratio	332.7-157.6	80.1-45.0	13.6-9.3	18.2-10.0	...	11.7-9.8	12.6-9.4
Average Yield %	3.4	3.0	3.2	2.7	3.1	3.6	3.4

Statistics are as originally reported. Adj. for 2-for-1 stk. split, 6/98. ① Incl. non-recurr. chrg. of $163.0 mill. ② Excl. inc. fr. disc. ops. of $35.8 mill. ($0.74/sh.) ③ Bef. income of $165.4 mill. from disc. ops.; incl. net pre-tax chrgs. totaling $184.4 mill., related primarily to possible losses and asset impairments.

OFFICERS:
R. H. Zech, Chmn., Pres., C.E.O.
B. A. Kenney, V.P., C.F.O.
R. J. Cinancio, V.P., Sec., Gen. Couns.

INVESTOR CONTACT: Irma Dominguez, Inv. Rel. Coord., (312) 612-8799

PRINCIPAL OFFICE: 500 West Monroe Street, Chicago, IL 60661-3676

TELEPHONE NUMBER: (312) 621-6200
FAX: (312) 621-6665
WEB: www.gatx.com

NO. OF EMPLOYEES: 1,900 (approx.)

SHAREHOLDERS: 3,618 (approx.)

ANNUAL MEETING: In Apr.

INCORPORATED: NY, July, 1916

INSTITUTIONAL HOLDINGS:
No. of Institutions: 200
Shares Held: 43,811,729
% Held: 89.8

INDUSTRY: Rental of railroad cars (SIC: 4741)

TRANSFER AGENT(S): Mellon Investor Services, Ridgefield Park, NJ

GENERAL DYNAMICS CORPORATION

YIELD 1.3%
P/E RATIO 20.2

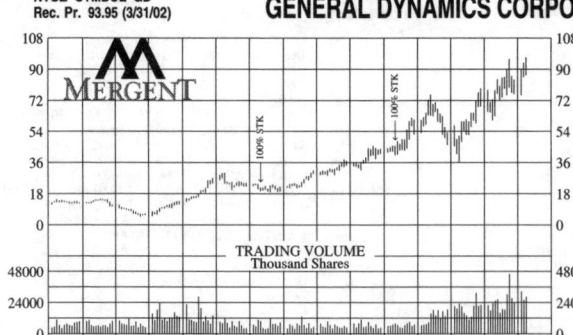

INTERIM EARNINGS (Per Share):

Qtr.	Mar.	June	Sept.	Dec.
1998	0.65	0.72	0.74	0.75
1999	2.07	0.81	0.91	0.98
2000	0.91	1.01	1.47	1.09
2001	1.19	1.21	1.13	1.21

INTERIM DIVIDENDS (Per Share):

Amt.	Decl.	Ex.	Rec.	Pay.
0.28Q	3/07/01	4/10/01	4/13/01	5/11/01
0.28Q	6/06/01	7/11/01	7/13/01	8/10/01
0.28Q	8/01/01	10/03/01	10/05/01	11/09/01
0.28Q	12/05/01	1/16/02	1/18/02	2/08/02
0.30Q	3/06/02	4/10/02	4/12/02	5/10/02

Indicated div.: $1.20 (Div. Reinv. Plan)

CAPITALIZATION (12/31/01):

	($000)	(%)
Long-Term Debt	724,000	13.8
Common & Surplus	4,528,000	86.2
Total	5,252,000	100.0

TRADING VOLUME
Thousand Shares

1988 1989 1990 1991 1992 1993 1994 1995 1996 1997 1998 1999 2000 2001 2002
*7 YEAR PRICE SCORE 138.4   *12 MONTH PRICE SCORE 114.0
*NYSE COMPOSITE INDEX=100

DIVIDEND ACHIEVER STATUS:
Rank: 51   10-Year Growth Rate: 15.97%
Total Years of Dividend Growth: 10

RECENT DEVELOPMENTS: For the year ended 12/31/01, net income increased 4.7% to $943.0 million compared with $901.0 million in the prior year. Earnings for 2001 and 2000 included income tax credits of $28.0 million and $90.0 million, respectively. Net sales advanced 17.4% to $12.16 billion. Marine Systems segment sales grew 5.8% to $3.61 billion, while Aerospace segment sales rose 7.8% to $3.27 billion. Information Systems and Technology segment sales improved 17.3% to $2.80 billion, and Combat Systems segment sales advanced 73.6% to $2.21 billion.

PROSPECTS: For 2002, the Company expects double-digit growth in earnings and revenues with strong cash generation stemming from a large and growing backlog. At the end of 2001, backlog totaled approximately $30.00 billion, an increase of nearly 50.0% versus the end of 2000. Meanwhile, the Company formed Eagle Enterprise Inc. under its Combat Systems group. Eagle Enterprise will be responsible for the design, development and transition to production of network-centric combat systems and architectures.

BUSINESS

GENERAL DYNAMICS CORPO-
RATION is a major defense contractor operating in four business segments. The Marine Systems segment designs, engineers, constructs, overhauls, and supports nuclear submarines. Combat Systems designs, engineers and manufactures armored vehicles and defense electronic equipment. Information Systems and Technology, created as a result of the acquisitions of Computing Devices International and Advanced Technology Systems, provides GD with broader and deeper capabilities in electronics and systems integration and information management. Other consists of coal mining, ship management, and ship financing services. On 9/1/99, GD acquired GTE Government Systems Corporation. On 1/26/01, GD acquired Primex Technologies, Inc.

ANNUAL FINANCIAL DATA

	12/31/01	12/31/00	12/31/99	12/31/98	12/31/97	12/31/96	12/31/95
Earnings Per Share	② 4.65	② 4.48	4.36	2.86	2.50	2.14	① 1.96
Cash Flow Per Share	5.98	5.60	5.35	3.86	3.20	2.67	2.26
Tang. Book Val. Per Share	3.84	6.43	3.27	5.46	5.64	13.60	12.44
Dividends Per Share	1.10	1.02	0.94	0.86	0.82	0.80	0.74
Dividend Payout %	23.7	22.8	21.6	30.2	32.8	37.6	37.6
INCOME STATEMENT (IN MILLIONS):							
Total Revenues	12,163.0	10,356.0	8,959.0	4,970.0	4,062.0	3,581.0	3,067.0
Costs & Expenses	10,407.0	8,801.0	7,556.0	4,302.0	3,525.0	3,161.0	2,714.0
Depreciation & Amort.	271.0	226.0	200.0	126.0	91.0	67.0	38.0
Operating Income	1,485.0	1,329.0	1,203.0	542.0	446.0	353.0	315.0
Net Interest Inc./(Exp.)	d56.0	d60.0	d34.0	4.0	36.0	55.0	55.0
Income Before Income Taxes	1,424.0	1,262.0	1,126.0	549.0	479.0	409.0	375.0
Income Taxes	481.0	361.0	246.0	185.0	163.0	139.0	128.0
Net Income	② 943.0	② 901.0	880.0	364.0	316.0	270.0	① 247.0
Cash Flow	1,214.0	1,127.0	1,080.0	490.0	407.0	337.0	285.0
Average Shs. Outstg. (000)	202,907	201,262	202,057	127,000	127,000	126,000	126,000
BALANCE SHEET (IN MILLIONS):							
Cash & Cash Equivalents	442.0	177.0	270.0	220.0	441.0	894.0	1,095.0
Total Current Assets	4,893.0	3,551.0	3,491.0	1,873.0	1,689.0	1,858.0	2,013.0
Net Property	1,768.0	1,294.0	1,169.0	698.0	592.0	441.0	398.0
Total Assets	11,069.0	7,987.0	7,774.0	4,572.0	4,091.0	3,299.0	3,164.0
Total Current Liabilities	4,579.0	2,901.0	3,453.0	1,461.0	1,291.0	833.0	859.0
Long-Term Obligations	724.0	162.0	169.0	249.0	257.0	156.0	170.0
Net Stockholders' Equity	4,528.0	3,820.0	3,171.0	2,219.0	1,915.0	1,714.0	1,567.0
Net Working Capital	314.0	650.0	38.0	412.0	398.0	1,025.0	1,154.0
Year-end Shs. Outstg. (000)	200,746	200,502	201,013	127,000	126,000	126,000	126,000
STATISTICAL RECORD:							
Operating Profit Margin %	12.2	12.8	13.4	10.9	11.0	9.9	10.3
Net Profit Margin %	7.8	8.7	9.8	7.3	7.8	7.5	8.1
Return on Equity %	20.8	23.6	27.8	16.4	16.5	15.8	15.8
Return on Assets %	8.5	11.3	11.3	8.0	7.7	8.2	7.8
Debt/Total Assets %	6.5	2.0	2.2	5.4	6.3	4.7	5.4
Price Range	96.00-60.50	79.00-36.25	75.44-46.19	62.00-40.25	45.75-31.56	37.75-28.50	31.50-21.19
P/E Ratio	20.6-13.0	17.6-8.1	17.3-10.6	21.7-14.1	18.3-12.6	17.7-13.3	16.1-10.8
Average Yield %	1.4	1.8	1.5	1.7	2.1	2.4	2.8

Statistics are as originally reported. Adj. for 100% stk. div., 4/98. ① Bef. gain on disp. of $74.0 mill. ② Incl. research & dev. tax credit of $28.0 mill., 2001; $90.0 mill., 2000.

OFFICERS:
N. D. Chabraja, Chmn., C.E.O.
M. J. Mancuso, Sr. V.P., C.F.O.
D. H. Fogg, V.P., Treas.

INVESTOR CONTACT: R. Lewis, Investor Relations, (703) 876-3195

PRINCIPAL OFFICE: 3190 Fairview Park Drive, Falls Church, VA 22042-4523

TELEPHONE NUMBER: (703) 876-3000
FAX: (703) 876-3125
WEB: www.generaldynamics.com
NO. OF EMPLOYEES: 51,700 (approx.)
SHAREHOLDERS: 17,900 (approx.)
ANNUAL MEETING: In May
INCORPORATED: DE, Feb., 1952

GENERAL ELECTRIC COMPANY

YIELD 1.9%
P/E RATIO 26.6

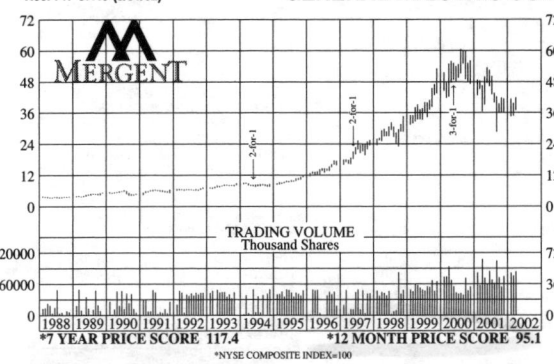

7 YEAR PRICE SCORE 117.4   *NYSE COMPOSITE INDEX=100*   **12 MONTH PRICE SCORE 95.1**

INTERIM EARNINGS (Per Share):

Qtr.	Mar.	June	Sept.	Dec.
1998	0.19	0.25	0.23	0.27
1999	0.22	0.29	0.27	0.31
2000	0.26	0.34	0.32	0.36
2001	0.30	0.39	0.39	0.39

INTERIM DIVIDENDS (Per Share):

Amt.	Decl.	Ex.	Rec.	Pay.
0.16Q	2/09/01	3/05/01	3/07/01	4/25/01
0.16Q	6/22/01	7/05/01	7/09/01	7/25/01
0.16Q	9/07/01	9/26/01	9/28/01	10/25/01
0.18Q	12/14/01	12/27/01	12/31/01	1/25/02
0.18Q	2/15/02	2/27/02	3/01/02	4/25/02

Indicated div.: $0.72 (Div. Reinv. Plan)

CAPITALIZATION (12/31/01):

	($000)	(%)
Long-Term Debt	79,806,000	53.6
Deferred Income Tax	9,130,000	6.1
Minority Interest	5,215,000	3.5
Common & Surplus	54,824,000	36.8
Total	148,975,000	100.0

DIVIDEND ACHIEVER STATUS:
Rank: 72   10-Year Growth Rate: 14.18%
Total Years of Dividend Growth: 26

RECENT DEVELOPMENTS: For the year ended 12/31/01, income was $14.13 billion, before an accounting change, versus net income of $12.74 billion in 2000. Revenues fell 3.0% to $125.91 billion. Materials revenues declined 11.9% to $7.07 billion, while GE Capital Services segment revenues fell 11.8% to $58.35 billion. Revenues from aircraft engines rose 5.7% to $11.39 billion, and Power Systems segment revenues jumped 36.0% to $20.21 billion.

PROSPECTS: For 2002, GE expects ongoing earnings in the range of $1.65 to $1.67 per share, before accounting changes. On 1/24/02, the Company's subsidiary, GE Capital Corporation, announced its agreement to acquire DaimlerChrysler Capital Services' Commercial Real Estate and Asset Based Lending portfolios for about $1.20 billion in cash. Also, GE recently acquired the Honeywell Tensor operation and Honeywell Advanced Composites, Inc.

BUSINESS

GENERAL ELECTRIC COMPANY'S businesses and their contributions to 2001 revenues are as follows: Financial Services (45.1%) are provided by GE Capital Services through General Electric Capital Corporation and GE Global Insurance Holding Corporation. Power Systems (15.6%) provides electricity generating products, services and energy management systems. The Industrial Products and Systems segment (9.0%) includes lighting, transportation systems, industrial systems, and GE Supply. Aircraft Engines (8.8%) develops and manufactures engines for commercial aircraft. Technical Products and Services (7.0%) is a provider of medical and transportation systems, information services and business-to-business e-commerce networks. Materials (5.5%) consists of plastics and specialty materials, including silicones, polymer additives and industrial and gem quality diamonds. Appliances (4.5%) is a supplier of major appliances. Broadcasting (4.5%) operations are conducted through NBC.

ANNUAL FINANCIAL DATA

	12/31/01	12/31/00	12/31/99	12/31/98	12/31/97	12/31/96	12/31/95
Earnings Per Share	② 1.41	1.27	1.07	0.93	① 0.82	0.73	0.65
Cash Flow Per Share	2.11	2.04	1.77	1.52	1.34	1.11	1.01
Tang. Book Val. Per Share	2.33	2.32	1.68	1.55	1.56	1.53	1.63
Dividends Per Share	0.64	0.55	0.47	0.40	0.35	0.31	0.27
Dividend Payout %	45.4	43.0	42.8	42.9	42.3	41.8	42.0
INCOME STATEMENT (IN MILLIONS):							
Total Revenues	125,913.0	129,853.0	111,630.0	100,469.0	90,840.0	79,179.0	70,028.0
Costs & Expenses	57,070.0	58,486.0	50,295.0	46,028.0	43,097.0	35,764.0	32,661.0
Depreciation & Amort.	7,089.0	7,736.0	6,691.0	5,860.0	5,269.0	3,785.0	3,594.0
Operating Income	61,754.0	63,631.0	54,644.0	48,581.0	42,474.0	39,630.0	33,773.0
Net Interest Inc./(Exp.)	d11,062.0	d11,720.0	d10,013.0	d9,753.0	d8,384.0	d7,904.0	d7,286.0
Income Before Income Taxes	19,701.0	18,446.0	15,577.0	13,477.0	11,179.0	10,806.0	9,737.0
Income Taxes	5,573.0	5,711.0	4,860.0	4,181.0	2,976.0	3,526.0	3,164.0
Equity Earnings/Minority Int.	d348.0	d427.0	d365.0	d265.0	d240.0	d269.0	d204.0
Net Income	② 14,128.0	12,735.0	10,717.0	9,296.0	① 8,203.0	7,280.0	6,573.0
Cash Flow	21,217.0	20,471.0	17,408.0	15,156.0	13,472.0	11,065.0	10,167.0
Average Shs. Outstg. (000)	10,052,000	10,057,000	9,834,000	9,990,000	10,035,000	9,924,000	10,104,000
BALANCE SHEET (IN MILLIONS):							
Cash & Cash Equivalents	110,099.0	99,534.0	90,312.0	83,034.0	76,482.0	64,080.0	43,890.0
Total Current Assets	128,254.0	116,848.0	105,850.0	97,307.0	91,301.0	77,257.0	57,020.0
Net Property	42,140.0	40,015.0	41,022.0	35,730.0	32,316.0	28,795.0	25,679.0
Total Assets	495,023.0	437,006.0	405,200.0	355,935.0	304,012.0	272,402.0	228,035.0
Total Current Liabilities	198,904.0	156,112.0	161,216.0	141,579.0	120,668.0	100,507.0	82,600.0
Long-Term Obligations	79,806.0	82,132.0	71,427.0	59,663.0	46,603.0	49,246.0	51,027.0
Net Stockholders' Equity	54,824.0	50,492.0	42,557.0	38,880.0	34,438.0	31,125.0	29,609.0
Net Working Capital	d70,650.0	d39,264.0	d55,366.0	d44,272.0	d29,367.0	d23,250.0	d24,981.0
Year-end Shs. Outstg. (000)	9,925,938	9,932,006	9,854,529	9,813,000	9,795,000	9,870,000	10,002,000
STATISTICAL RECORD:							
Operating Profit Margin %	49.0	49.0	49.0	48.4	46.8	50.1	48.2
Net Profit Margin %	11.2	9.8	9.6	9.3	9.0	9.2	9.4
Return on Equity %	25.8	25.2	25.2	23.9	23.8	23.4	22.2
Return on Assets %	2.9	2.9	2.6	2.6	2.7	2.7	2.9
Debt/Total Assets %	16.1	18.8	17.6	16.8	15.3	18.1	22.4
Price Range	53.55-28.50	60.50-41.64	53.16-31.35	34.64-23.00	25.52-15.98	17.69-11.58	12.19-8.31
P/E Ratio	38.0-20.2	47.6-32.8	48.8-28.8	37.1-24.6	31.1-19.5	24.1-15.8	18.7-12.8
Average Yield %	1.6	1.1	1.1	1.4	1.7	2.1	2.7

Statistics are as originally reported. Adj. for 3-for-1 stock split, 2/00; 2-for-1, 5/97. ① Incl. an after-tax gain of $1.50 bill. from the exchange of Lockheed Martin pfd. stk. & after-tax charges of $1.50 bill. for restruct. & oth. spec. matters. ② Bef. acctg. chng. chrg. of $444.0 mill.

OFFICERS:
J. R. Immelt, Chmn., C.E.O.
D. D. Dammerman, Vice-Chmn.
R. C. Wright, Vice-Chmn.
G. Rogers, Vice-Chmn.

INVESTOR CONTACT: David Frail, Shareholder Relations, (203) 373-3387

PRINCIPAL OFFICE: 3135 Easton Turnpike, Fairfield, CT 06431-0001

TELEPHONE NUMBER: (203) 373-2211
FAX: (203) 373-3131
WEB: www.ge.com

NO. OF EMPLOYEES: 310,000 (avg.)

SHAREHOLDERS: 634,000 (approx.)

ANNUAL MEETING: In April

INCORPORATED: NY, April, 1892

INSTITUTIONAL HOLDINGS:
No. of Institutions: 1,338
Shares Held: 732,861,796
% Held: 50.6

INDUSTRY: Electric lamps (SIC: 3641)

TRANSFER AGENT(S): GE Shareowner Services, c/o The Bank of New York, New York, NY

GENUINE PARTS COMPANY

YIELD 3.2%
P/E RATIO 21.4

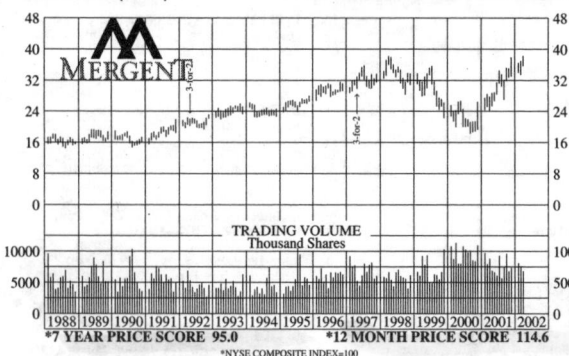

INTERIM EARNINGS (Per Share):

Qtr.	Mar.	June	Sept.	Dec.
1998	0.45	0.48	0.48	0.58
1999	0.48	0.52	0.51	0.61
2000	0.52	0.55	0.53	0.61
2001	0.52	0.55	0.54	0.14

INTERIM DIVIDENDS (Per Share):

Amt.	Decl.	Ex.	Rec.	Pay.
0.285Q	2/19/01	3/07/01	3/09/01	4/02/01
0.285Q	4/17/01	6/06/01	6/08/01	7/02/01
0.285Q	8/21/01	9/05/01	9/07/01	10/01/01
0.285Q	11/19/01	12/05/01	12/07/01	1/02/02
0.29Q	2/18/02	3/06/02	3/08/02	4/01/02

Indicated div.: $1.16 (Div. Reinv. Plan)

CAPITALIZATION (12/31/01):

	($000)	(%)
Long-Term Debt	835,580	25.4
Deferred Income Tax	60,985	1.9
Minority Interest	45,777	1.4
Common & Surplus	2,345,123	71.3
Total	3,287,465	100.0

DIVIDEND ACHIEVER STATUS:
Rank: 217   10-Year Growth Rate: 5.91%
Total Years of Dividend Growth: 45

TRADING VOLUME
Thousand Shares

*7 YEAR PRICE SCORE 95.0   *12 MONTH PRICE SCORE 114.6
*NYSE COMPOSITE INDEX=100

RECENT DEVELOPMENTS: For the year ended 12/31/01, net income fell 22.9% to $297.1 million versus $385.3 million in 2000. Results for 2001 included after-tax consolidation and impairment charges of $64.4 million. Total net sales slipped 1.8% to $8.22 billion from $8.37 billion a year earlier. Industrial sales decreased 4.6% to $2.23 billion, while electrical/electronic materials sales fell 30.5% to $387.8 million. Automotive sales rose 2.1% to $4.25 billion, and office products sales grew 3.2% to $1.38 billion.

PROSPECTS: Due to the weak economy, GPC is taking actions to align its costs with current business conditions. These actions should have a positive effect on results going forward. GPC continues to work on increasing efficiencies, strengthening its competitive position, improving return on invested capital and maintaining levels of customer service. Accordingly, GPC expects earnings per share in the range of $2.10 to $2.15, excluding the effect of a new accounting rule, for 2002.

BUSINESS

GENUINE PARTS COMPANY is a service organization engaged in the distribution of automotive replacement parts, industrial replacement parts, office products and electrical and electronic materials. GPC's largest division is its Automotive Parts Group, which distributes automotive replacement parts and accessory items to NAPA auto parts stores. The Industrial Parts Group distributes replacement parts, equipment and related supplies throughout the United States, Canada and Mexico. The Office Products Group distributes products including information processing, supplies, furniture and machines. The Electrical and Electronic Materials Group distributes materials for the manufacture and repair of electrical and electronic apparatus. In January 2000, GPC purchased a 15.0% ownership interest in Mitchell Repair Information Company, LLC.

ANNUAL FINANCIAL DATA

	12/31/01	12/31/00	12/31/99	12/31/98	12/31/97	12/31/96	12/31/95
Earnings Per Share	⚊1.71	2.20	2.11	1.98	1.90	1.82	1.68
Cash Flow Per Share	2.21	2.72	2.61	2.36	2.23	2.10	1.92
Tang. Book Val. Per Share	10.97	10.50	9.80	9.52	10.39	9.62	9.03
Dividends Per Share	1.13	1.08	1.03	0.99	0.94	0.88	0.82
Dividend Payout %	66.1	49.3	48.8	50.0	49.6	48.3	48.9
INCOME STATEMENT (IN MILLIONS):							
Total Revenues	8,220.7	8,369.9	7,981.7	6,614.0	6,005.2	5,720.5	5,261.9
Costs & Expenses	7,638.9	7,630.8	7,263.7	5,955.6	5,380.8	5,124.8	4,707.9
Depreciation & Amort.	85.8	92.3	90.0	69.3	58.9	50.4	43.2
Operating Income	496.0	646.8	628.1	589.1	565.6	545.2	510.8
Income Before Income Taxes	496.0	646.8	628.1	589.1	565.6	545.2	510.8
Income Taxes	198.9	261.4	250.4	233.3	223.2	215.2	201.6
Net Income	⚊297.1	385.3	377.6	355.8	342.4	330.1	309.2
Cash Flow	382.9	477.6	467.6	425.1	401.3	380.5	352.4
Average Shs. Outstg. (000)	173,633	175,327	179,238	180,081	180,165	181,568	183,923
BALANCE SHEET (IN MILLIONS):							
Cash & Cash Equivalents	85.8	27.7	45.7	85.0	72.8	67.4	44.3
Total Current Assets	3,146.2	3,019.5	2,895.2	2,683.4	2,093.6	1,937.6	1,764.0
Net Property	345.1	395.3	413.5	404.0	372.5	346.0	303.2
Total Assets	4,206.6	4,142.1	3,929.7	3,600.4	2,754.4	2,521.6	2,274.1
Total Current Liabilities	919.2	988.3	916.0	818.4	556.9	568.4	475.5
Long-Term Obligations	835.6	770.6	702.4	588.6	209.5	110.2	60.6
Net Stockholders' Equity	2,345.1	2,260.8	2,177.5	2,053.3	1,859.5	1,732.1	1,650.9
Net Working Capital	2,227.0	2,031.2	1,979.2	1,864.9	1,536.6	1,369.3	1,288.4
Year-end Shs. Outstg. (000)	173,474	172,390	177,276	179,505	178,948	180,048	182,870
STATISTICAL RECORD:							
Operating Profit Margin %	6.0	7.7	7.9	8.9	9.4	9.5	9.7
Net Profit Margin %	3.6	4.6	4.7	5.4	5.7	5.8	5.9
Return on Equity %	12.7	17.0	17.3	17.3	18.4	19.1	18.7
Return on Assets %	7.1	9.3	9.6	9.9	12.4	13.1	13.6
Debt/Total Assets %	19.9	18.6	17.9	16.3	7.6	4.4	2.7
Price Range	37.94-23.91	26.69-18.25	35.75-22.25	38.25-28.25	35.88-28.67	31.67-26.67	28.00-23.67
P/E Ratio	22.2-14.0	12.1-8.3	16.9-10.5	19.3-14.3	18.9-15.1	17.4-14.7	16.7-14.1
Average Yield %	3.7	4.8	3.6	3.0	2.9	3.0	3.2

Statistics are as originally reported. Adj. for stk. splits: 3-for-2, 4/97 ⚊Incl. after-tax non-recurr. chrg. of $64.4 mill.

OFFICERS:
L. L. Prince, Chmn., C.E.O.
T. C. Gallagher, Pres., C.O.O.
J. W. Nix, Exec. V.P., C.F.O.

INVESTOR CONTACT: Jerry Nix, Exec. V.P., C.F.O., (770) 612-2048

PRINCIPAL OFFICE: 2999 Circle 75 Parkway, Atlanta, GA 30339

TELEPHONE NUMBER: (770) 953-1700
FAX: (770) 956-2211
WEB: www.genpt.com

NO. OF EMPLOYEES: 31,000 (approx.)

SHAREHOLDERS: 7,930

ANNUAL MEETING: In April

INCORPORATED: GA, May, 1928

INSTITUTIONAL HOLDINGS:
No. of Institutions: 329
Shares Held: 120,051,354
% Held: 69.1

INDUSTRY: Motor vehicle supplies and new parts (SIC: 5013)

TRANSFER AGENT(S): Sun Trust Bank, Atlanta, GA

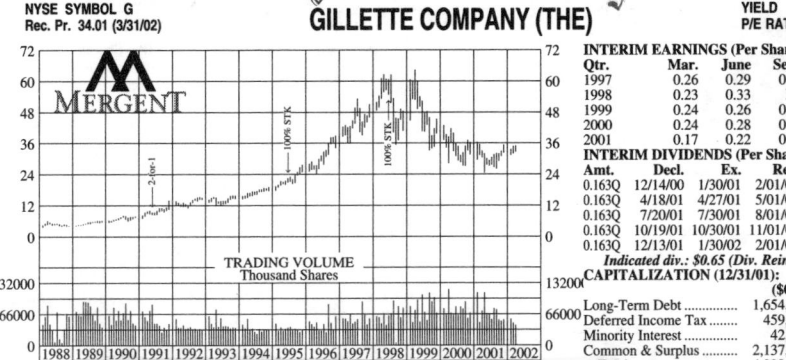

NYSE SYMBOL G
Rec. Pr. 34.01 (3/31/02)

GILLETTE COMPANY (THE)

YIELD		1.9%
P/E RATIO		39.5

*7 YEAR PRICE SCORE 70.2   ***12 MONTH PRICE SCORE 112.7**
*NYSE COMPOSITE INDEX=100

INTERIM EARNINGS (Per Share):

Qtr.	Mar.	June	Sept.	Dec.
1997	0.26	0.29	0.32	0.41
1998	0.23	0.33	Nil	0.39
1999	0.24	0.26	0.32	0.32
2000	0.24	0.28	0.33	d0.08
2001	0.17	0.22	0.28	0.19

INTERIM DIVIDENDS (Per Share):

Amt.	Decl.	Ex.	Rec.	Pay.
0.163Q	12/14/00	1/30/01	2/01/01	3/05/01
0.163Q	4/18/01	4/27/01	5/01/01	6/05/01
0.163Q	7/20/01	7/30/01	8/01/01	9/05/01
0.163Q	10/19/01	10/30/01	11/01/01	12/05/01
0.163Q	12/13/01	1/30/02	2/01/02	3/05/02

Indicated div.: $0.65 (Div. Reinv. Plan)

CAPITALIZATION (12/31/01):

	($000)	(%)
Long-Term Debt	1,654,000	38.5
Deferred Income Tax	459,000	10.7
Minority Interest	42,000	1.0
Common & Surplus	2,137,000	49.8
Total	4,292,000	100.0

DIVIDEND ACHIEVER STATUS:

Rank: 55   10-Year Growth Rate: 15.79%
Total Years of Dividend Growth: 24

RECENT DEVELOPMENTS: For the year ended 12/31/01, net income was $910.0 million versus income of $821.0 million, before a loss from discontinued operations of $429.0 million, in the prior year. Results for 2001 and 2000 included after-tax restructuring and asset impairment charges of $172.0 million and $572.0 million, respectively. Net sales declined 2.9% to $8.96 billion from $9.23 billion the year before. Prior-year revenues were restated.

PROSPECTS: Results are being negatively affected by lower sales volume as G continues to recover from its year-long effort to cut excess inventory. Meanwhile, the Company is beginning to benefit from significantly increased marketing support, which is helping to halt recent market share declines. Separately, the Company expects its restructuring program will result in about $135.0 million in pre-tax savings in 2002.

BUSINESS

THE GILLETTE COMPANY manufactures and sells a wide variety of consumer products throughout the world. The Company's five primary businesses are: Blades and Razors (38.1% of 2001 sales), which include male shaving systems sold under the MACH3, SENSOREXCEL, SENSOR, ATRA, TRAC II, CUSTOM PLUS and GOOD NEWS brands, and female shaving systems sold under the GILLETTE FOR WOMEN VENUS, SENSOR EXCEL FOR WOMEN, SENSOR FOR WOMEN, and AGILITY brands; Personal Care (9.8%), which offers shave preparations, after-shave products and deodorants and antiperspirants sold under the GILLETTE SERIES, SATIN CARE, RIGHT GUARD, SOFT & DRI and DRY IDEA brands; Duracell (26.4%), which include the DURACELL ULTRA and COPPERTOP alkaline batteries, and DURACELL primary lithium, zinc air and rechargeable nickel-metal hydride batteries; Oral Care (14.2%), which offers manual and power toothbrushes sold under the BRAUN and ORAL-B brands; and Braun (11.5%), which sells electric shavers under the BRAUN brand and hair epilators under the SILK EPIL brand.

ANNUAL FINANCIAL DATA

	12/31/01	12/31/00	12/31/99	12/31/98	12/31/97	12/31/96	12/31/95
Earnings Per Share	① 0.86	①② 0.77	1.14	① 0.95	1.25	① 0.86	0.93
Cash Flow Per Share	1.34	1.28	1.58	1.35	1.61	1.20	1.20
Tang. Book Val. Per Share	0.74	0.33	0.58	1.81	2.07	1.56	1.34
Dividends Per Share	0.65	0.64	0.57	0.49	0.41	0.34	0.29
Dividend Payout %	75.6	82.5	50.0	51.3	33.1	40.3	31.1
INCOME STATEMENT (IN MILLIONS):							
Total Revenues	8,961.0	9,295.0	9,897.0	10,056.0	10,062.0	9,697.7	6,794.7
Costs & Expenses	6,954.0	7,248.0	7,292.0	7,808.0	7,316.0	7,680.3	5,175.0
Depreciation & Amort.	509.0	535.0	500.0	459.0	422.0	381.1	248.4
Operating Income	1,498.0	1,512.0	2,105.0	1,789.0	2,324.0	1,636.3	1,371.3
Net Interest Inc./(Exp.)	d141.0	d218.0	d129.0	d86.0	d69.0	d66.9	d49.1
Income Before Income Taxes	1,342.0	1,288.0	1,930.0	1,669.0	2,221.0	1,525.0	1,296.9
Income Taxes	432.0	467.0	670.0	588.0	794.0	576.3	473.4
Net Income	① 910.0	①② 821.0	1,260.0	① 1,081.0	1,427.0	① 948.7	823.5
Cash Flow	1,419.0	1,356.0	1,760.0	1,540.0	1,849.0	1,325.2	1,067.2
Average Shs. Outstg. (000)	1,058,000	1,063,000	1,111,000	1,144,000	1,148,000	1,107,000	887,000
BALANCE SHEET (IN MILLIONS):							
Cash & Cash Equivalents	947.0	62.0	80.0	102.0	105.0	83.9	49.5
Total Current Assets	4,455.0	4,682.0	5,132.0	5,440.0	4,690.0	4,753.2	3,104.5
Net Property	3,548.0	3,550.0	3,667.0	3,472.0	3,104.0	2,565.8	1,636.9
Total Assets	9,969.0	10,402.0	11,786.0	11,902.0	10,864.0	10,435.3	6,340.3
Total Current Liabilities	4,838.0	5,471.0	4,180.0	3,478.0	2,641.0	2,934.7	2,124.0
Long-Term Obligations	1,654.0	1,650.0	2,931.0	2,256.0	1,476.0	1,490.4	691.1
Net Stockholders' Equity	2,137.0	1,924.0	3,060.0	4,543.0	4,841.0	4,490.9	2,513.3
Net Working Capital	d383.0	d789.0	952.0	1,962.0	2,049.0	1,818.5	980.5
Year-end Shs. Outstg. (000)	1,056,000	1,053,000	1,065,000	1,105,000	1,120,938	1,132,156	888,928
STATISTICAL RECORD:							
Operating Profit Margin %	16.7	16.3	21.3	17.8	23.1	16.9	20.2
Net Profit Margin %	10.2	8.8	12.7	10.7	14.2	9.8	12.1
Return on Equity %	42.6	42.7	41.2	23.8	29.5	21.1	32.8
Return on Assets %	9.1	7.9	10.7	9.1	13.1	9.1	13.0
Debt/Total Assets %	16.6	15.9	24.9	19.0	13.6	14.3	10.9
Price Range	36.38-24.50	43.00-27.13	64.38-33.06	62.66-35.31	53.19-36.00	38.88-24.13	27.69-17.69
P/E Ratio	42.3-28.5	55.8-35.2	56.5-29.0	65.9-37.2	42.7-28.9	45.5-28.2	29.9-19.1
Average Yield %	2.1	1.8	1.2	1.0	0.9	1.1	1.3

Statistics are as originally reported. Adj. for stk. splits: 2-for-1, 6/98 & 6/95. ① Incl. non-recurr. chrgs. $172.0 mill., 12/01; $572.0 mill., 12/00; $535.0 mill., 12/98; $413.0 mill., 12/96 ② Bef. loss from disc. opers., $429.0 mill.

OFFICERS:
J. Kilts, Chmn., C.E.O.
E. F. DeGraan, Pres., C.O.O.
C. W. Cramb Jr., Sr. V.P., C.F.O.

INVESTOR CONTACT: Skip Loper, V.P., Investor Relations, (617) 421-7968

PRINCIPAL OFFICE: Prudential Tower Building, Boston, MA 02199

TELEPHONE NUMBER: (617) 421-7000
FAX: (617) 421-7123
WEB: www.gillette.com

NO. OF EMPLOYEES: 31,500 (approx.)

SHAREHOLDERS: 46,787

ANNUAL MEETING: In May

INCORPORATED: DE, Sept., 1917

INSTITUTIONAL HOLDINGS:
No. of Institutions: 743
Shares Held: 725,770,077
% Held: 68.8

INDUSTRY: Hand and edge tools, nec (SIC: 3423)

TRANSFER AGENT(S): Boston Equiserve, Boston, MA

NYSE SYMBOL GDW
Rec. Pr. 63.50 (3/31/02)

GOLDEN WEST FINANCIAL CORPORATION

YIELD 0.5%
P/E RATIO 12.4

INTERIM EARNINGS (Per Share):

Qtr.	Mar.	June	Sept.	Dec.
1998	0.64	0.68	0.62	0.66
1999	0.70	0.72	0.72	0.73
2000	0.78	0.84	0.86	0.93
2001	1.10	1.30	1.28	1.44

INTERIM DIVIDENDS (Per Share):

Amt.	Decl.	Ex.	Rec.	Pay.
0.063Q	10/31/00	2/13/01	2/15/01	3/12/01
0.063Q	5/02/01	5/11/01	5/15/01	6/11/01
0.063Q	7/27/01	8/13/01	8/15/01	9/10/01
0.072Q	10/31/01	11/13/01	11/15/01	12/10/01
0.072Q	1/24/02	2/13/02	2/15/02	3/11/02

Indicated div.: $0.29

CAPITALIZATION (12/31/01):

	($000)	(%)
Total Deposits	34,472,585	59.9
Long-Term Debt	18,835,235	32.7
Common & Surplus	4,284,190	7.4
Total	57,592,010	100.0

DIVIDEND ACHIEVER STATUS:
Rank: 60   10-Year Growth Rate: 15.17%
Total Years of Dividend Growth: 18

7 YEAR PRICE SCORE 151.4   12 MONTH PRICE SCORE 109.6
*NYSE COMPOSITE INDEX=100

RECENT DEVELOPMENTS: For the year ended 12/31/01, the Company reported income of $818.8 million, before an after-tax accounting change charge of $6.1 million, compared with net income of $545.8 million in the prior year. Results for 2001 included a pre-tax loss of $9.7 million from changes in the fair value of derivatives. Net interest income advanced 41.7% to $1.63 billion from $1.15 billion a year earlier.

PROSPECTS: Net interest income benefited from the decline in short-term interest rates over the past twelve months. However, the same declining interest rates also negatively affected demand for adjustable rate mortgages. Many of the Company's existing borrowers are replacing their home loans with new fixed-rate mortgages. During the fourth quarter of 2001, adjustable rate mortgages comprised 79.2% of GDW's new loan volume.

BUSINESS

GOLDEN WEST FINANCIAL CORPORATION, with assets of $58.59 billion as of 12/31/01, is a savings and loan holding company. The Company's principal subsidiary is World Savings Bank, FSB (formerly World Savings Bank, FSB and World Savings & Loan Association). As of 12/31/01, the Company operated 121 savings branch offices in California, 44 in Florida, 36 in Colorado, 23 in Texas, 15 in Arizona, 11 in New Jersey, eight in Kansas, five in Illinois and two in Nevada. As of 12/31/01, GDW operated 462 offices in 38 states under the World name. The Company operates as a financial intermediary attracting deposits (primarily in the form of savings accounts) and investing funds in loans and securities backed by residential real estate.

QUARTERLY DATA

(12/31/2001)($000)	REV	INC
1st Quarter	1,117,506	170,061
2nd Quarter	1,164,572	208,929
3rd Quarter	1,084,504	205,840
4th Quarter	1,019,769	227,975

ANNUAL FINANCIAL DATA

	12/31/01	12/31/00	12/31/99	12/31/98	12/31/97	12/31/96	12/31/95
Earnings Per Share	③ 5.11	3.41	2.87	② 2.58	2.04	① 2.11	1.33
Tang. Book Val. Per Share	27.55	23.28	19.80	18.32	15.76	13.66	12.12
Dividends Per Share	0.26	0.22	0.19	0.17	0.15	0.13	0.12
Dividend Payout %	5.1	6.5	6.7	6.7	7.4	6.2	8.8
INCOME STATEMENT (IN MILLIONS):							
Total Interest Income	4,209.6	3,796.5	2,825.8	2,962.6	2,832.5	2,581.6	2,427.4
Total Interest Expense	2,578.3	2,645.4	1,822.4	1,995.2	1,942.0	1,750.6	1,704.6
Net Interest Income	1,631.3	1,151.2	1,003.5	967.3	890.5	831.0	722.8
Provision for Loan Losses	22.3	9.2	cr2.1	11.3	57.6	84.3	61.2
Non-Interest Income	236.7	160.8	143.3	137.6	81.3	74.9	42.5
Non-Interest Expense	513.8	424.8	386.1	354.5	327.0	453.4	319.0
Income Before Taxes	1,332.0	877.9	762.7	739.2	587.2	368.2	385.2
Net Income	③ 818.8	545.8	480.0	② 447.1	354.1	① 369.9	234.5
Average Shs. Outstg. (000)	160,358	160,278	166,951	173,462	173,319	173,967	175,971
BALANCE SHEET (IN MILLIONS):							
Securities Avail. for Sale	856.1	462.8	398.5	490.6	765.9	1,008.8	1,184.7
Total Loans & Leases	41,139.6	33,860.3	28,090.1	25,991.6	33,553.5	30,397.2	28,181.4
Allowance for Credit Losses	74.3	97.7	170.3	270.3	292.8	283.8	253.8
Net Loans & Leases	41,065.4	33,762.6	27,919.8	25,721.3	33,260.7	30,113.4	28,181.4
Total Assets	58,586.3	55,704.0	42,142.2	38,468.7	39,421.3	37,730.6	35,118.2
Total Deposits	34,472.6	30,047.9	27,714.9	26,219.1	24,109.7	22,099.9	20,847.9
Long-Term Obligations	18,835.2	20,330.6	9,728.2	7,075.2	9,627.1	10,122.4	7,769.6
Total Liabilities	54,302.1	52,016.7	38,947.4	35,344.4	36,892.2	35,380.1	32,839.8
Net Stockholders' Equity	4,284.2	3,687.3	3,194.9	3,124.3	2,698.0	2,350.5	2,278.4
Year-end Shs. Outstg. (000)	155,532	158,410	161,358	170,583	171,207	172,026	176,613
STATISTICAL RECORD:							
Return on Equity %	19.1	14.8	15.0	14.3	13.1	15.7	10.3
Return on Assets %	1.4	1.0	1.1	1.2	0.9	1.0	0.7
Equity/Assets %	7.3	6.6	7.6	8.1	6.8	6.2	6.5
Non-Int. Exp./Tot. Inc. %	27.5	32.4	33.7	32.1	33.6	50.1	41.7
Price Range	70.90-45.02	70.50-26.88	38.41-28.91	38.16-23.27	32.33-19.62	22.91-16.33	19.16-11.58
P/E Ratio	13.9-8.8	20.7-7.9	13.4-10.1	14.8-9.0	15.8-9.6	10.9-7.7	14.4-8.7
Average Yield %	0.4	0.5	0.6	0.6	0.6	0.7	0.8

Statistics are as originally reported. Adj. for stk. split: 3-for-1, 12/10/99. ① Bef. acct. chrg. of $205.2 mill. & incl. one-time SAIF chg. of $133.0 mill. & a tax benefit of $139.5 mill. ② Bef. extraord. loss of $12.5 mill. ③ Bef. acctg. chrg. of $6.1 mill.; incl. a pre-tax loss of $9.7 mill. fr. changes in the fair value of derivatives.

OFFICERS:
H. M. Sandler, Co-Chmn., Co-C.E.O.
M. O. Sandler, Co-Chmn., Co-C.E.O.
R. W. Kettell, Pres., C.F.O., Treas.
M. Roster, Exec. V.P., Sec., Gen. Couns.

INVESTOR CONTACT: William C. Nunan, Sr. Vice-Pres., (510) 446-3614

PRINCIPAL OFFICE: 1901 Harrison Street, Oakland, CA 94612

TELEPHONE NUMBER: (510) 446-3420
FAX: (510) 446-3072
WEB: www.worldsavingsjobs.com

NO. OF EMPLOYEES: 6,113 full-time; 1,025 part-time

SHAREHOLDERS: 1,241 (record)

ANNUAL MEETING: In May

INCORPORATED: DE, May, 1959

INSTITUTIONAL HOLDINGS:
No. of Institutions: 319
Shares Held: 107,087,191
% Held: 69.0

INDUSTRY: Federal savings institutions (SIC: 6035)

TRANSFER AGENT(S): Mellon Investor Services, LLC, San Francisco, CA

GORMAN-RUPP COMPANY

YIELD 2.4%
P/E RATIO 15.7

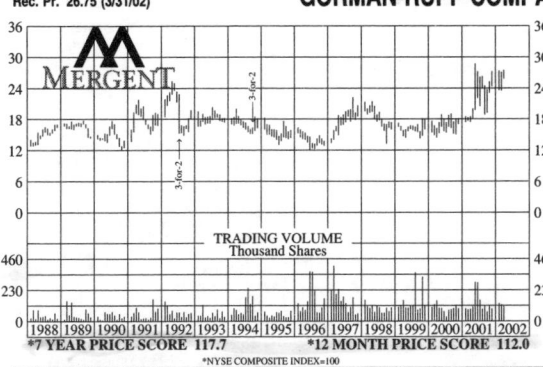

INTERIM EARNINGS (Per Share):

Qtr.	Mar.	June	Sept.	Dec.
1997	0.32	0.32	0.35	0.24
1998	0.38	0.35	0.39	0.25
1999	0.33	0.40	0.45	0.34
2000	0.48	0.42	0.37	0.34
2001	0.42	0.47	0.34	0.39

INTERIM DIVIDENDS (Per Share):

Amt.	Decl.	Ex.	Rec.	Pay.
0.16Q	1/25/01	2/13/01	2/15/01	3/09/01
0.16Q	4/26/01	5/11/01	5/15/01	6/08/01
0.16Q	7/26/01	8/13/01	8/15/01	9/10/01
0.16Q	10/25/01	11/13/01	11/15/01	12/10/01
0.16Q	1/24/02	2/13/02	2/15/02	3/08/02

Indicated div.: $0.64 (Div. Reinv. Plan)

CAPITALIZATION (12/31/01):

	($000)	(%)
Common & Surplus	107,910	100.0
Total	107,910	100.0

DIVIDEND ACHIEVER STATUS:
Rank: 254   10-Year Growth Rate: 3.71%
Total Years of Dividend Growth: 29

TRADING VOLUME
Thousand Shares

1988|1989|1990|1991|1992|1993|1994|1995|1996|1997|1998|1999|2000|2001|2002
*7 YEAR PRICE SCORE 117.7   ***12 MONTH PRICE SCORE 112.0**
*NYSE COMPOSITE INDEX=100

RECENT DEVELOPMENTS: For the year ended 12/31/01, net income was $14.6 million compared with $13.8 million the previous year. Results for 2000 included pre-tax net plant relocation expense of $1.1 million. Total revenues advanced 6.4% to $203.8 million from $191.5 million the previous year. GRC attributed the improved results, in part, to increases in orders for pumps and fabricated components used in the power generation industry. Separately, on 2/26/02, GRC acquired American Machine & Tool Co. (AMT) for a cash purchase price of approximately $16.0

million. AMT, which had revenues of about $14.9 million for the fiscal year ended 10/31/01, is a developer and manufacturer of standard centrifugal pumps for industrial and commercial fluid-handling applications. Also, on 3/1/02, GRC acquired Flo-Pak, Inc. for a cash purchase price of approximately $6.5 million. Flo-Pak, which had revenues of about $11.0 million for the year ended 12/31/01, is a manufacturer of designed pumping systems for the heating, ventilation and air-conditioning market.

BUSINESS

THE GORMAN-RUPP COMPANY designs, manufactures and sells pumps and related equipment, such as pump and motor controls, for use in water, wastewater, construction, industrial, petroleum, original equipment, agricultural, fire protection, military and other liquid-handling applications.

ANNUAL FINANCIAL DATA

	12/31/01	12/31/00	12/31/99	12/31/98	12/31/97	12/31/96	12/31/95
Earnings Per Share	1.70	①1.61	1.52	1.37	1.23	1.15	1.10
Cash Flow Per Share	2.54	2.41	2.28	2.10	1.92	1.81	1.70
Tang. Book Val. Per Share	12.64	11.67	10.74	9.75	9.07	8.44	7.81
Dividends Per Share	0.64	0.62	0.60	0.58	0.56	0.53	0.52
Dividend Payout %	37.6	38.5	39.5	42.3	45.5	46.1	47.3
INCOME STATEMENT (IN THOUSANDS)							
Total Revenues	203,813	191,484	180,165	172,246	165,568	155,678	150,793
Costs & Expenses	173,650	162,425	152,135	146,764	142,657	134,340	130,569
Depreciation & Amort.	7,128	6,863	6,489	6,330	5,959	5,675	5,173
Operating Income	23,035	22,196	21,541	19,152	16,952	15,663	15,051
Income Before Income Taxes	23,035	22,196	21,541	19,152	16,952	15,663	15,051
Income Taxes	8,450	8,400	8,460	7,400	6,340	5,735	5,590
Net Income	14,585	①13,796	13,081	11,752	10,612	9,928	9,461
Cash Flow	21,713	20,659	19,570	18,082	16,571	15,603	14,634
Average Shs. Outstg.	8,556	8,583	8,586	8,600	8,609	8,617	8,587
BALANCE SHEET (IN THOUSANDS):							
Cash & Cash Equivalents	20,583	7,630	7,339	8,665	7,737	4,284	3,250
Total Current Assets	89,119	82,289	78,185	78,556	81,695	71,926	71,401
Net Property	53,895	57,885	53,609	43,916	40,919	40,549	42,163
Total Assets	148,113	145,881	136,875	127,477	127,865	117,650	119,816
Total Current Liabilities	18,103	19,079	17,439	17,431	17,036	15,199	19,727
Long-Term Obligations	...	3,413	3,107	783	6,689	3,796	7,188
Net Stockholders' Equity	107,910	99,999	92,295	83,706	78,060	72,737	67,240
Net Working Capital	71,016	63,210	60,746	61,125	64,659	56,727	51,674
Year-end Shs. Outstg.	8,538	8,566	8,592	8,581	8,609	8,618	8,607
STATISTICAL RECORD:							
Operating Profit Margin %	11.3	11.6	12.0	11.1	10.2	10.1	10.0
Net Profit Margin %	7.2	7.2	7.3	6.8	6.4	6.4	6.3
Return on Equity %	13.5	13.8	14.2	14.0	13.6	13.6	14.1
Return on Assets %	9.8	9.5	9.6	9.2	8.3	8.4	7.9
Debt/Total Assets %	...	2.3	2.3	0.6	5.2	3.2	6.0
Price Range	28.75-17.38	19.00-14.38	18.13-14.27	21.50-13.25	22.25-13.38	16.38-12.00	18.25-13.00
P/E Ratio	16.9-10.2	11.8-8.9	11.9-9.4	15.7-9.7	18.1-10.9	14.2-10.4	16.6-11.8
Average Yield %	2.8	3.7	3.7	3.3	3.1	3.7	3.3

Statistics are as originally reported. ① Incl. non-recurr. chrg., $1.1 mill.

OFFICERS:
J. C. Gorman, Chmn.
J. S. Gorman, Pres., C.E.O.
K. E. Dudley, C.F.O.
INVESTOR CONTACT: Robert E. Kirkendall, Corp. Sec., (419) 755-1294
PRINCIPAL OFFICE: 305 Bowman St., Mansfield, OH 44903

TELEPHONE NUMBER: (419) 755-1011
FAX: (419) 755-1233
WEB: www.gormanrupp.com
NO. OF EMPLOYEES: 1,055
SHAREHOLDERS: 1,344
ANNUAL MEETING: In Apr.
INCORPORATED: OH, Apr., 1934

INSTITUTIONAL HOLDINGS:
No. of Institutions: 43
Shares Held: 3,856,123
% Held: 45.1
INDUSTRY: Pumps and pumping equipment (SIC: 3561)
TRANSFER AGENT(S): National City Bank, Cleveland, OH

GRAINGER (W.W.), INC.

YIELD 1.2%
P/E RATIO 30.6

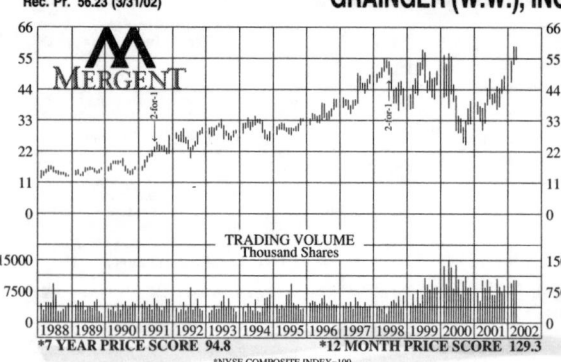

TRADING VOLUME
Thousand Shares

| 1988 | 1989 | 1990 | 1991 | 1992 | 1993 | 1994 | 1995 | 1996 | 1997 | 1998 | 1999 | 2000 | 2001 | 2002 |

*7 YEAR PRICE SCORE 94.8   ***12 MONTH PRICE SCORE 129.3**

*NYSE COMPOSITE INDEX=100

INTERIM EARNINGS (Per Share):

Qtr.	Mar.	June	Sept.	Dec.
1997	0.52	0.57	0.56	0.63
1998	0.58	0.60	0.57	0.69
1999	0.60	0.53	0.49	0.30
2000	0.44	0.59	0.51	0.51
2001	0.45	0.15	0.59	0.65

INTERIM DIVIDENDS (Per Share):

Amt.	Decl.	Ex.	Rec.	Pay.
0.175Q	4/25/01	5/03/01	5/07/01	6/01/01
0.175Q	8/01/01	8/09/01	8/13/01	9/01/01
0.175Q	10/31/01	11/07/01	11/12/01	12/01/01
0.175Q	1/30/02	2/07/02	2/11/02	3/01/02

Indicated div.: $0.70

CAPITALIZATION (12/31/01):

	($000)	(%)
Long-Term Debt	118,219	6.9
Deferred Income Tax	1,239	0.1
Minority Interest	139	0.0
Common & Surplus	1,603,189	93.1
Total	1,722,786	100.0

DIVIDEND ACHIEVER STATUS:

Rank: 163	10-Year Growth Rate: 8.58%
Total Years of Dividend Growth:	30

RECENT DEVELOPMENTS: For the twelve months ended 12/31/01, net earnings slipped 9.5% to $174.5 million from $192.9 million the previous year. Results for 2001 included a $39.1 million pre-tax restructuring charge, a $20.1 million charge from the liquidation of equity in an unconsolidated entity and a $138,000 gain on the sale of an investment. Results for 2000 included a $30.0 million gain on the sale of an investment. Net sales slid 4.5% to $4.75 billion from $4.98 billion a year earlier.

PROSPECTS: Continued weak economic conditions in North America and sluggish sales of seasonal products are being partially offset by increased sales processed through the Company's Internet sites. Meanwhile, profitability from GWW's lab safety supply segment is being hurt by weakness in the industrial markets and higher operating expenses stemming from the expanded use of specialty catalogs. GWW is targeting earnings of $2.30 to $2.65 per share in 2002.

BUSINESS

W.W. GRAINGER, INC. is a nationwide distributor of equipment, components, and supplies to the commercial, industrial, contractor and institutional markets. Products include motors, fans, blowers, pumps, compressors, air and power tools, heating and air conditioning equipment, as well as other items offered in its Grainger Industrial Supply Catalog and through its Grainger.com Web site. The Company serves its customers through its network of branches in the U.S., Canada and Mexico, and has regional distribution facilities located in Chicago, IL, Kansas City, MO, and Greenville County, SC.

ANNUAL FINANCIAL DATA

	12/31/01	12/31/00	12/31/99	12/31/98	12/31/97	12/31/96	12/31/95
Earnings Per Share	② 1.84	① 2.05	1.92	2.44	2.27	2.02	1.82
Cash Flow Per Share	2.93	3.18	2.96	3.24	3.05	2.74	2.51
Tang. Book Val. Per Share	15.09	14.08	13.47	11.39	11.13	11.65	10.87
Dividends Per Share	0.70	0.67	0.63	0.58	0.53	0.49	0.45
Dividend Payout %	38.0	32.7	32.8	24.0	23.3	24.3	24.4
INCOME STATEMENT (IN MILLIONS):							
Total Revenues	4,754.3	4,977.0	4,533.9	4,341.3	4,136.6	3,537.2	3,276.9
Costs & Expenses	4,312.5	4,535.0	4,118.4	3,854.4	3,663.8	3,117.4	2,889.8
Depreciation & Amort.	103.2	106.9	98.2	78.9	79.7	74.3	70.9
Operating Income	338.6	335.1	317.2	408.0	393.2	345.5	316.3
Net Interest Inc./(Exp.)	d7.8	d22.5	d14.0	d5.1	d2.6	3.3	d4.1
Income Before Income Taxes	297.3	331.6	303.8	400.8	389.6	348.9	312.1
Income Taxes	122.8	138.7	123.0	162.3	157.8	140.4	125.5
Net Income	② 174.5	① 192.9	180.7	238.5	231.8	208.5	186.7
Cash Flow	277.7	299.8	279.0	317.4	311.5	282.8	257.5
Average Shs. Outstg. (000)	94,728	94,224	94,315	97,847	102,178	103,272	102,482
BALANCE SHEET (IN MILLIONS):							
Cash & Cash Equivalents	168.8	63.4	62.7	43.1	46.9	126.9	11.5
Total Current Assets	1,392.6	1,483.0	1,471.1	1,206.4	1,183.0	1,320.2	1,062.7
Net Property	689.7	676.4	697.8	660.5	592.9	551.0	518.4
Total Assets	2,331.2	2,459.6	2,564.8	2,103.9	1,997.8	2,119.0	1,669.2
Total Current Liabilities	553.8	747.3	870.5	664.5	533.9	616.1	444.1
Long-Term Obligations	118.2	125.3	124.9	122.9	131.2	6.2	8.7
Net Stockholders' Equity	1,603.2	1,537.4	1,480.5	1,278.7	1,294.7	1,462.7	1,179.1
Net Working Capital	838.8	735.7	600.6	541.9	649.1	704.2	618.5
Year-end Shs. Outstg. (000)	93,345	93,933	93,382	93,505	97,722	105,856	101,790
STATISTICAL RECORD:							
Operating Profit Margin %	7.1	6.7	7.0	9.4	9.5	9.8	9.7
Net Profit Margin %	3.7	3.9	4.0	5.5	5.6	5.9	5.7
Return on Equity %	10.9	12.5	12.2	18.7	17.9	14.3	15.8
Return on Assets %	7.5	7.8	7.0	11.3	11.6	9.8	11.2
Debt/Total Assets %	5.1	5.1	4.9	5.8	6.6	0.3	0.5
Price Range	48.99-29.51	56.88-24.31	58.13-36.88	54.72-36.44	49.88-35.25	40.75-31.31	33.81-27.75
P/E Ratio	26.6-16.0	27.7-11.9	30.3-19.2	22.4-14.9	22.0-15.5	20.2-15.5	18.6-15.2
Average Yield %	1.8	1.7	1.3	1.3	1.2	1.4	1.4

Statistics are as originally reported. Adj. for 2-for-1 stk. split, 6/98. ① Incl. $29.8 mil ($0.19/sh) one-time gain from the sale of an investment security. ② Incl. $39.1 mil restr. chg., a $20.1 mil loss fr. liquidation of equity in unconsol. subsid. and a $138,000 gain on invest. sale.

OFFICERS:
R. L. Keyser, Chmn., C.E.O.
W. M. Clark, Pres., C.O.O.
P. O. Loux, Sr. V.P., C.F.O.

INVESTOR CONTACT: William D. Chapman, Dir., Inv. Rel., (847) 535-0881

PRINCIPAL OFFICE: 100 Grainger Parkway, Lake Forest, IL 60045-5201

TELEPHONE NUMBER: (847) 535-1000
FAX: (847) 535-0878
WEB: www.grainger.com
NO. OF EMPLOYEES: 13,342 full-time; 2,043 part-time
SHAREHOLDERS: 1,700 (approx.)
ANNUAL MEETING: In Apr.
INCORPORATED: IL, Dec., 1928

INSTITUTIONAL HOLDINGS:
No. of Institutions: 316
Shares Held: 54,479,871
% Held: 58.2

INDUSTRY: Electrical apparatus and equipment (SIC: 5063)

TRANSFER AGENT(S): BankBoston, N.A., Boston, MA

HARLEYSVILLE GROUP INC.

YIELD 2.3%
P/E RATIO 18.1

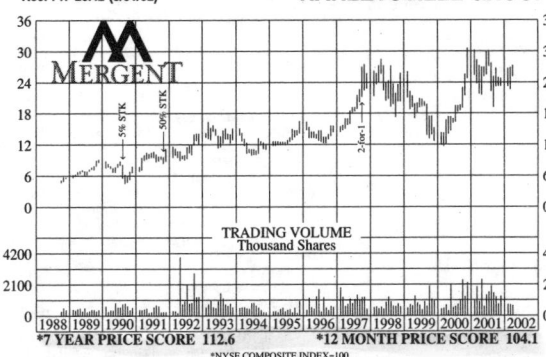

INTERIM EARNINGS (Per Share):

Qtr.	Mar.	June	Sept.	Dec.
1997	0.38	0.46	0.55	0.49
1998	0.47	0.56	0.48	0.64
1999	0.50	0.52	d0.01	0.44
2000	0.25	0.37	0.45	0.60
2001	0.33	0.37	0.26	0.50

INTERIM DIVIDENDS (Per Share):

Amt.	Decl.	Ex.	Rec.	Pay.
0.14Q	2/28/01	3/13/01	3/15/01	3/30/01
0.14Q	5/23/01	6/13/01	6/15/01	6/29/01
0.15Q	8/22/01	9/12/01	9/14/01	9/28/01
0.15Q	11/28/01	12/12/01	12/14/01	12/31/01
0.15Q	2/27/02	3/13/02	3/15/02	3/29/02

Indicated div.: $0.60

CAPITALIZATION (12/31/01):

	($000)	(%)
Long-Term Debt	96,055	14.0
Common & Surplus	590,298	86.0
Total	686,353	100.0

DIVIDEND ACHIEVER STATUS:
Rank: 143   10-Year Growth Rate: 9.85%
Total Years of Dividend Growth: 15

RECENT DEVELOPMENTS: For the year ended 12/31/01, net income declined 10.7% to $43.5 million from $48.7 million in the previous year. Earnings for 2001 included a charge of $2.6 million in the fourth quarter associated with a guaranty fund and other assessments resulting from the liquidation of Reliance Insurance Company. Total revenues grew 3.1% to $827.8 million from $802.6 million in the prior year. Revenues included a realized investment loss of $3.1 million in 2001 and a realized investment gain of $9.8 million in 2000. Premiums earned grew 6.0% to $729.9 million from $688.3 million a year earlier, primarily due to an increase in premiums earned for commercial lines. Net investment income slipped 1.5% to $85.5 million from $86.8 million the year before. Toal expenses were $776.0 million, up 4.2% from $744.9 million in the previous year.

BUSINESS

HARLEYSVILLE GROUP INC. is a regional insurance holding company headquartered in Pennsylvania engaged, through its subsidiaries, in the property and casualty insurance business. As of 12/31/01, the Company was approximately 56.0% owned by Harleysville Mutual Insurance Company. HGIC and Harleysville Mutual Insurance Company operate together as a network of regional insurance companies that underwrite personal and commercial coverages. These insurance coverages are marketed in 32 Eastern and Midwestern states through approximately 1,900 local independent agencies. The companies include: Harleysville-Atlantic Insurance Company; Harleysville Insurance Company of New Jersey; Harleysville Insurance Company of New York; Harleysville Insurance Company of Ohio; Harleysville Lake States Insurance Company; Harleysville Preferred Insurance Company; Harleysville Worcester Insurance Company; and Mid-America Insurance Company. Additionally, the company operates two limited partnerships: Harleysville Asset Management L.P. and Insurance Management Resources L.P.

ANNUAL FINANCIAL DATA

	12/31/01	12/31/00	12/31/99	12/31/98	12/31/97	12/31/96	12/31/95
Earnings Per Share	② 1.46	1.67	① 1.45	2.15	1.86	1.03	1.53
Tang. Book Val. Per Share	20.05	19.54	18.29	18.17	15.49	13.09	12.58
Dividends Per Share	0.58	0.55	0.52	0.48	0.44	0.40	0.39
Dividend Payout %	39.7	32.9	35.9	22.3	23.7	38.8	25.2
INCOME STATEMENT (IN MILLIONS):							
Total Premium Income	729.9	688.3	707.2	664.6	624.9	615.2	477.0
Net Investment Income	85.5	86.8	85.9	86.0	81.8	78.0	68.4
Other Income	12.3	27.4	31.7	28.7	17.5	14.2	13.1
Total Revenues	827.8	802.6	824.8	779.3	724.2	707.4	558.5
Income Before Income Taxes	51.8	57.7	47.8	80.4	67.3	31.4	52.6
Income Taxes	8.3	9.0	4.9	17.0	13.2	2.7	11.3
Net Income	② 43.5	48.7	① 42.8	63.4	54.1	28.7	41.3
Average Shs. Outstg. (000)	29,819	29,136	29,565	29,520	29,032	27,844	27,064
BALANCE SHEET (IN MILLIONS):							
Cash & Cash Equivalents	38.5	52.3	79.5	18.8	29.8	37.3	47.4
Premiums Due	226.0	201.7	196.3	197.6	184.0	173.7	149.1
Invst. Assets: Equities	150.7	193.8	198.2	174.9	121.8	69.9	34.6
Invst. Assets: Total	1,611.1	1,599.1	1,604.0	1,579.6	1,451.6	1,291.3	1,085.2
Total Assets	2,045.3	2,021.9	2,020.1	1,934.5	1,801.2	1,622.6	1,378.3
Long-Term Obligations	96.1	96.5	96.8	97.1	97.4	97.7	98.0
Net Stockholders' Equity	590.3	566.6	526.9	529.7	446.5	370.2	345.0
Year-end Shs. Outstg. (000)	29,445	29,002	28,812	29,151	28,822	28,278	27,436
STATISTICAL RECORD:							
Return on Revenues %	5.3	6.1	5.2	8.1	7.5	4.1	7.4
Return on Equity %	7.4	8.6	8.1	12.0	12.1	7.7	12.0
Return on Assets %	2.1	2.4	2.1	3.3	3.0	1.8	3.0
Price Range	30.25-19.11	30.63-11.63	26.13-12.63	28.50-17.25	27.50-14.38	16.38-12.25	16.50-11.75
P/E Ratio	20.7-13.1	18.3-7.0	18.0-8.7	13.3-8.0	14.8-7.7	15.9-11.9	10.8-7.7
Average Yield %	2.4	2.6	2.7	2.1	2.1	2.8	2.7

Statistics are as originally reported. Adj. for stk. split: 2-for-1, 10/6/97 ① Bef. acctg. change chrg. $2.9 mill. ② Incl. non-recurr. chrg. $2.6 mill.

OFFICERS:
W. R. Bateman II, Chmn., Pres., C.E.O.
B. J. Magee, Sr. V.P., C.F.O.
M. R. Cummins, Exec. V.P., Chief Invest. Officer, Treas.

INVESTOR CONTACT: Investor Relations, (215) 256-5020

PRINCIPAL OFFICE: 355 Maple Avenue, Harleysville, PA 19438-2297

TELEPHONE NUMBER: (215) 256-5000
FAX: (215) 256-5340
WEB: www.harleysvillegroup.com

NO. OF EMPLOYEES: 2,450 (avg.)

SHAREHOLDERS: 2,161 (approx.)

ANNUAL MEETING: In April

INCORPORATED: DE, May, 1986

INSTITUTIONAL HOLDINGS:
No. of Institutions: 78
Shares Held: 8,892,863
% Held: 30.2

INDUSTRY: Fire, marine, and casualty insurance (SIC: 6331)

TRANSFER AGENT(S): Mellon Investor Services, New York, NY

HAVERTY FURNITURE COMPANIES, INC.

YIELD 1.2%
P/E RATIO 16.2

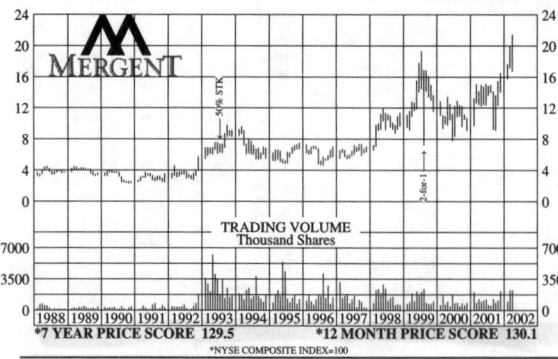

7 YEAR PRICE SCORE 129.5 **12 MONTH PRICE SCORE 130.1** *NYSE COMPOSITE INDEX=100

TRADING VOLUME
Thousand Shares

INTERIM EARNINGS (Per Share):

Qtr.	Mar.	June	Sept.	Dec.
1998	0.14	0.09	0.21	0.30
1999	0.28	0.22	0.31	0.40
2000	0.30	0.28	0.35	0.39
2001	0.21	0.12	0.26	0.47

INTERIM DIVIDENDS (Per Share):

Amt.	Decl.	Ex.	Rec.	Pay.
0.052Q	2/07/01	2/08/01	2/12/01	2/23/01
0.052Q	5/10/01	5/17/01	5/21/01	5/31/01
0.052Q	7/26/01	8/07/01	8/09/01	8/24/01
0.052Q	11/05/01	11/14/01	11/16/01	11/30/01
0.052Q	2/01/02	2/07/02	2/11/02	2/22/02

Indicated div.: $0.21

CAPITALIZATION (12/31/01):

	($000)	(%)
Long-Term Debt	131,599	39.5
Common & Surplus	201,398	60.5
Total	332,997	100.0

DIVIDEND ACHIEVER STATUS:

Rank: 230   10-Year Growth Rate: 5.17%
Total Years of Dividend Growth: 31

RECENT DEVELOPMENTS: For the year ended 12/31/01, net income declined 18.5% to $22.7 million compared with income of $27.9 million, before an accounting change charge of $3.4 million, in 2000. Sales, including credit service charges, declined 0.6% to $689.2 million from $693.6 million a year earlier. Gross profit as a percentage of net sales was 47.7% versus 47.5% in 2000. Selling, general and administrative expenses increased 2.4% to $284.0 million from $277.4 million the year before.

PROSPECTS: Looking ahead, in 2002, the Company will remodel and open eight former HOMELIFE stores. In addition, there are ten store openings planned for 2002, three of which will be replacements, for a net total of seven additional stores. As a result, net selling square footage is expected to increase 267,000 square feet, or 7.6%. Meanwhile, the Company will continue to emphasize margin improvement and efficient operations.

BUSINESS

HAVERTY FURNITURE COMPANIES, INC. is a full-service home furnishings retailer with 104 stores in 14 central and southern states as of 2/8/02. The Company's stores, primarily targeted at middle and upper-middle income families, offers a wide selection of well-known, brand-name furniture including BROYHILL, THOMASVILLE, LANE/ACTION, LA-Z-BOY, BERNHARDT, and CLAYTON MARCUS. HVT has regional warehouses located in Charlotte, North Carolina, Jackson, Mississippi and Ocala, Florida serving all of the Company's local markets except for Dallas, Texas, and Atlanta, Georgia, which each have a metropolitan area warehouse.

QUARTERLY DATA

(12/31/2001)	Rev	Inc
1st Quarter	167,599	4,307
2nd Quarter	152,116	2,563
3rd Quarter	170,645	2,611
4th Quarter	187,753	10,229

ANNUAL FINANCIAL DATA

	12/31/01	12/31/00	12/31/99	12/31/98	12/31/97	12/31/96	12/31/95
Earnings Per Share	1.06	☐1.31	1.19	0.72	0.57	0.53	0.53
Cash Flow Per Share	1.81	2.06	1.84	1.36	1.16	1.06	0.99
Tang. Book Val. Per Share	9.45	8.64	7.81	7.08	6.79	6.42	6.06
Dividends Per Share	0.21	0.20	0.19	0.17	0.16	0.153	0.15
Dividend Payout %	19.8	15.5	16.0	22.9	28.1	29.0	28.6
INCOME STATEMENT (IN THOUSANDS):							
Total Revenues	689,178	693,575	633,721	557,258	506,118	470,250	407,846
Costs & Expenses	622,276	619,117	560,744	496,428	449,650	419,777	365,880
Depreciation & Amort.	16,239	15,738	14,844	14,272	13,792	12,644	10,634
Operating Income	50,663	58,720	58,133	46,558	42,676	37,829	31,332
Net Interest Inc./(Exp.)	d10,581	d11,707	d11,402	d13,183	d14,330	d14,463	d11,158
Income Before Income Taxes	36,340	43,861	42,870	26,295	20,787	19,132	19,444
Income Taxes	13,630	16,010	15,470	9,460	7,400	6,885	7,261
Net Income	22,710	☐27,851	27,400	16,835	13,387	12,247	12,183
Cash Flow	38,949	43,589	42,244	31,107	27,179	24,891	22,817
Average Shs. Outstg.	21,502	21,203	22,982	22,912	23,340	23,388	23,110
BALANCE SHEET (IN THOUSANDS):							
Cash & Cash Equivalents	727	3,256	1,762	1,874	390	414	2,146
Total Current Assets	305,755	295,992	271,678	278,177	289,629	283,130	257,410
Net Property	146,399	144,525	126,997	111,333	114,618	114,350	112,405
Total Assets	460,905	448,163	404,648	392,901	406,514	399,875	371,778
Total Current Liabilities	123,903	95,520	98,434	70,467	132,908	125,440	97,473
Long-Term Obligations	131,599	170,369	134,687	161,778	111,489	120,434	129,233
Net Stockholders' Equity	201,398	179,375	168,793	158,058	159,554	150,916	140,955
Net Working Capital	181,852	200,472	173,244	207,710	156,721	157,690	159,937
Year-end Shs. Outstg.	21,302	20,773	21,610	22,330	23,482	23,510	23,248
STATISTICAL RECORD:							
Operating Profit Margin %	7.4	8.5	9.2	8.4	8.4	8.0	7.7
Net Profit Margin %	3.3	4.0	4.3	3.0	2.6	2.6	3.0
Return on Equity %	11.3	15.5	16.2	10.7	8.4	8.1	8.6
Return on Assets %	4.9	6.2	6.8	4.3	3.3	3.1	3.3
Debt/Total Assets %	28.6	38.0	33.3	41.2	27.4	30.1	34.8
Price Range	16.55-9.10	13.44-7.75	19.33-7.19	12.00-6.50	7.38-5.44	7.31-4.63	7.50-4.81
P/E Ratio	15.6-8.6	10.3-5.9	16.2-6.0	16.7-9.0	12.9-9.5	13.9-8.8	14.3-9.2
Average Yield %	1.6	1.9	1.4	1.8	2.5	2.6	2.4

Statistics are as originally reported. Adj. for stk. split: 2-for-1, 8/25/99. ☐ Bef. $3.4 mil. ($0.16/sh) acctg. change chrg.

OFFICERS:
C. H. Ridley, Chmn.
J. E. Slater, Jr., Pres., C.E.O.
D. L. Fink, Exec. V.P., C.F.O.

INVESTOR CONTACT: Dennis L. Fink, Exec. V.P., C.F.O., (404) 443-2900

PRINCIPAL OFFICE: 780 Johnson Ferry Road, Suite 800, Atlanta, GA 30342

TELEPHONE NUMBER: (404) 443-2900
FAX: (404) 443-4180
WEB: www.havertys.com
NO. OF EMPLOYEES: 3,720 (approx.)
SHAREHOLDERS: 3,400 (approx., common); 200 (class A)
ANNUAL MEETING: In Mar.
INCORPORATED: MD, Sept., 1929

INSTITUTIONAL HOLDINGS:
No. of Institutions: 78
Shares Held: 11,213,581
% Held: 52.9

INDUSTRY: Furniture stores (SIC: 5712)

TRANSFER AGENT(S): SunTrust Bank, Atlanta, GA

HEALTH CARE PROPERTY INVESTORS, INC.

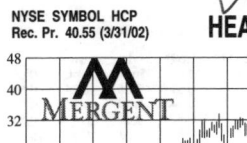

		YIELD	7.9%
		P/E RATIO	22.8

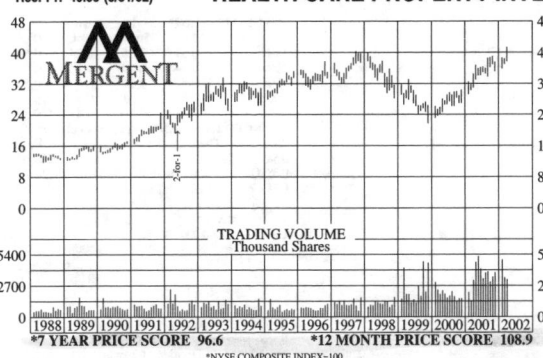

TRADING VOLUME
Thousand Shares

1988 | 1989 | 1990 | 1991 | 1992 | 1993 | 1994 | 1995 | 1996 | 1997 | 1998 | 1999 | 2000 | 2001 | 2002

*7 YEAR PRICE SCORE 96.6   *12 MONTH PRICE SCORE 108.9

*NYSE COMPOSITE INDEX=100

INTERIM EARNINGS (Per Share):

Qtr.	Mar.	June	Sept.	Dec.
1997	0.60	0.54	0.54	0.53
1998	0.54	0.53	0.72	0.73
1999	0.49	0.49	0.80	0.49
2000	0.52	0.55	0.46	0.60
2001	0.39	0.54	0.32	0.53

INTERIM DIVIDENDS (Per Share):

Amt.	Decl.	Ex.	Rec.	Pay.
0.76Q	1/25/01	2/01/01	2/05/01	2/20/01
0.77Q	4/23/01	5/01/01	5/03/01	5/18/01
0.78Q	7/23/01	8/01/01	8/03/01	8/20/01
0.79Q	10/22/01	10/31/01	11/02/01	11/20/01
0.80Q	1/23/02	1/31/02	2/04/02	2/20/02

Indicated div.: $3.20 (Div. Reinv. Plan)

CAPITALIZATION (12/31/01):

	($000)	(%)
Long-Term Debt	949,252	41.9
Minority Interest	69,968	3.1
Preferred Stock	274,487	12.1
Common & Surplus	972,237	42.9
Total	2,265,944	100.0

DIVIDEND ACHIEVER STATUS:
Rank: 194   10-Year Growth Rate: 6.72%
Total Years of Dividend Growth: 16

RECENT DEVELOPMENTS: For the year ended 12/31/01, net income was $121.2 million compared with income of $133.5 million, before an extraordinary gain of $274,000, in the prior year. Results for 2001 and 2000 included gain on the sale of real estate properties of $1.2 million and $11.8 million, respectively. Results for 2000 included a charge of $2.0 million for the write-off of an equity investment. Total revenues increased slightly to $332.5 million.

PROSPECTS: The Company announced that $240.0 million of new health care real estate investments, including new construction, were completed during 2001. Meanwhile, the Company is well-positioned to pursue other investments without the need to raise new equity capital. Going forward, the Company must execute its $400.0 million investment plan to achieve its goal for 2002.

BUSINESS

HEALTH CARE PROPERTY INVESTORS, INC. is a real estate investment trust that invests in health-care-related facilities throughout the United States, including long-term care facilities, congregate care and assisted living facilities, acute care and rehabilitation hospitals, medical office buildings and physician group practice clinics. The Company's investment portfolio as of 12/31/01 included 429 facilities in 42 states. The Company's investments include 176 long-term care facilities, nine freestanding rehabilitation hospitals, 94 congregate care and assisted living centers, 21 acute care hospitals, 86 medical office buildings, 37 physician group practice clinics and six health care laboratory and biotech research facilities. On 11/4/99, HCP acquired American Health Properties, Inc., in a stock-for-stock transaction, and its 72 healthcare properties in 22 states.

ANNUAL FINANCIAL DATA

	12/31/01	12/31/00	12/31/99	12/31/98	12/31/97	12/31/96	12/31/95
Earnings Per Share	① 1.78	① ② 2.13	① 2.25	① 2.54	① 2.19	2.12	① 2.83
Tang. Book Val. Per Share	17.24	17.10	17.99	13.15	12.72	11.74	11.88
Dividends Per Share	3.10	2.94	2.78	2.62	2.46	2.30	2.14
Dividend Payout %	174.1	138.0	123.6	103.1	112.3	108.5	75.6
INCOME STATEMENT (IN THOUSANDS):							
Rental Income	310,602	306,830	199,570	138,439	113,920	104,627	86,795
Total Income	332,460	329,807	224,793	161,549	128,503	120,393	105,696
Costs & Expenses	121,833	129,751	85,535	50,372	36,401	33,227	26,093
Depreciation	84,098	72,590	47,860	32,523	25,656	23,149	19,208
Income Before Income Taxes	127,761	139,222	101,701	92,707	68,493	64,017	83,945
Equity Earnings/Minority Int.	d6,595	d5,729	d5,476	d5,540	d3,704	d3,376	d3,679
Net Income	121,166	①② 133,493	① 96,225	① 87,167	① 64,789	60,641	① 80,266
Average Shs. Outstg.	53,975	51,100	34,861	33,664	28,994	28,652	28,348
BALANCE SHEET (IN THOUSANDS):							
Cash & Cash Equivalents	8,408	58,623	7,696	4,504	4,084	2,811	9,045
Total Real Estate Investments	2,194,556	2,100,509	2,192,988	1,131,119	786,502	623,734	527,994
Total Assets	2,431,153	2,398,703	2,469,390	1,356,612	940,964	753,653	667,831
Long-Term Obligations	949,252	954,428	964,007	621,045	385,958	379,504	267,384
Total Liabilities	1,184,429	1,254,148	1,269,133	761,193	498,695	416,847	328,371
Net Stockholders' Equity	1,246,724	1,144,555	1,200,257	595,419	442,269	336,806	339,460
Year-end Shs. Outstg.	56,387	50,874	51,421	30,987	30,216	28,678	28,574
STATISTICAL RECORD:							
Net Inc.+Depr./Assets %	8.4	8.6	5.8	8.8	9.6	11.1	14.9
Return on Equity %	9.7	11.7	8.0	14.6	14.6	18.0	23.6
Return on Assets %	5.0	5.6	3.9	6.4	6.9	8.0	12.0
Price Range	39.03-29.25	30.44-23.06	33.13-21.69	40.00-28.25	40.38-31.88	37.75-30.50	35.25-28.00
P/E Ratio	21.9-16.4	14.3-10.8	14.7-9.6	15.7-11.1	18.4-14.6	17.8-14.4	12.5-9.9
Average Yield %	9.1	11.0	10.1	7.7	6.8	6.7	6.8

Statistics are as originally reported. ① Incl non-recurr. credit 12/31/01: $1.2 mill.; 12/31/00: $11.8 mill. ($0.23/sh.); 12/31/99: $10.3 mill. ($0.27/sh.); 12/31/98: $14.1 mill.; 12/31/97: $2.0 mill.; 12/31/95: $23.6 mill. ② Incls. one-time chrg. of $2.0 mill.; bef. extraord. gain of $274,000.

QUARTERLY DATA

12/31/2001 ($000)	REV	INC
1st Quarter	78,365	19,799
2nd Quarter	84,450	28,675
3rd Quarter	84,137	17,848
4th Quarter	85,508	29,944

OFFICERS:
K. B. Roath, Chmn., Pres., C.E.O.
J. G. Reynolds, Exec. V.P., C.F.O.
D. Ghose, Sr. V.P., Treas.

INVESTOR CONTACT: Kenneth B. Roath, Chmn., Pres. & C.E.O., (949) 221-0600

PRINCIPAL OFFICE: 4675 MacArthur Court, Suite 900, Newport Beach, CA 92660

TELEPHONE NUMBER: (949) 221-0600
FAX: (949) 221-0607
WEB: www.hcpi.com
NO. OF EMPLOYEES: N/A
SHAREHOLDERS: 4,800 (approx., record); 70,000 (approx., beneficial)
ANNUAL MEETING: In May
INCORPORATED: MD, Mar., 1985

INSTITUTIONAL HOLDINGS:
No. of Institutions: 183
Shares Held: 23,405,396
% Held: 41.1
INDUSTRY: Real estate investment trusts
(SIC: 6798)

TRANSFER AGENT(S): The Bank of New York, New York, NY

HEALTH CARE REIT, INC.

YIELD 8.4%
P/E RATIO 18.4

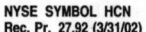

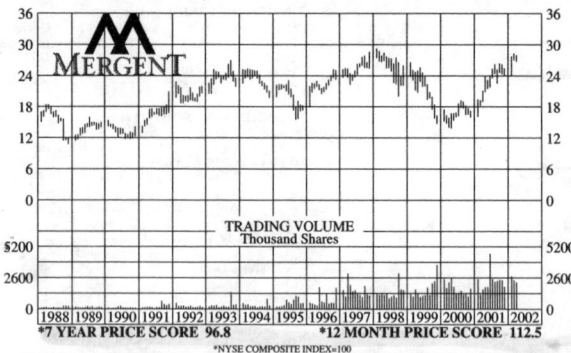

TRADING VOLUME
Thousand Shares

*7 YEAR PRICE SCORE 96.8   ***12 MONTH PRICE SCORE 112.5**
NYSE COMPOSITE INDEX=100

INTERIM EARNINGS (Per Share):

Qtr.	Mar.	June	Sept.	Dec.
1997	0.51	0.55	0.54	0.54
1998	0.54	0.54	0.56	0.60
1999	0.57	0.56	0.57	0.51
2000	0.52	0.51	0.48	0.40
2001	0.41	0.40	0.41	0.30

INTERIM DIVIDENDS (Per Share):

Amt.	Decl.	Ex.	Rec.	Pay.
0.585Q	7/17/01	7/27/01	7/31/01	8/20/01
0.585Q	10/16/01	10/29/01	10/31/01	11/20/01
0.585Q	1/17/02	1/29/02	1/31/02	2/20/02
0.585Q	4/16/02	4/26/02	4/30/02	5/20/02

Indicated div.: $2.34 (Div. Reinv. Plan)

CAPITALIZATION (12/31/01):

	($000)	(%)
Long-Term Debt	491,216	39.3
Preferred Stock	150,000	12.0
Common & Surplus	607,870	48.7
Total	1,249,086	100.0

DIVIDEND ACHIEVER STATUS:

Rank: 265   10-Year Growth Rate: 2.83%
Total Years of Dividend Growth: 12

RECENT DEVELOPMENTS: For the year ended 12/31/01, income was $60.8 million, before an extraordinary loss of $213,000, versus net income of $68.1 million in 2000. Results for 2001 and 2000 included a loss of $1.3 million and a gain of $1.7 million, respectively, from the sale of properties. The 2000 results also included a loss on investment of $2.0 million. Total revenues slipped to $135.1 million from $135.3 million in 2000.

PROSPECTS: HCN continues to meet its financial and operational expectations. During 2001, HCN completed equity and debt offerings and invested enough proceeds to surpass its new investments goal of $100.0 million to $125.0 million in the second half of the year. The funds from operations produced from these new investments and anticipated investments in 2002 are expected to return HCN's dividend payout ratio to the mid-80.0% range by the end of 2002.

BUSINESS

HEALTH CARE REIT, INC. is a self-administered real estate investment trust that invests in health care facilities, primarily nursing homes and assisted living facilities. The Company also invests in specialty care facilities. As of 12/31/01, the Company had $1.23 billion of real estate investments in 214 facilities located in 33 states and managed by 38 different operators. Long-term care facilities, which include nursing homes and assisted living facilities, comprised approximately 93.0% of the Company's investment portfolio.

ANNUAL FINANCIAL DATA

	12/31/01	12/31/00	12/31/99	12/31/98	12/31/97	12/31/96	12/31/95
Earnings Per Share	② 1.52	① 1.91	2.21	2.24	2.12	2.18	1.16
Tang. Book Val. Per Share	18.57	19.04	19.52	19.79	19.31	17.77	15.59
Dividends Per Share	2.34	2.33	2.27	2.19	2.11	2.08	2.075
Dividend Payout %	153.9	122.2	102.7	97.8	99.5	95.4	178.9
INCOME STATEMENT (IN THOUSANDS):							
Rental Income	98,988	88,312	72,700	41,953	22,178	10,003	6,352
Interest Income	31,294	41,064	48,076	47,515	45,999	36,734	30,837
Total Income	135,120	135,270	128,604	97,992	73,308	54,402	44,596
Costs & Expenses	9,078	10,405	7,959	6,714	5,458	5,856	10,084
Depreciation	30,227	22,706	17,885	10,254	5,287	2,427	1,580
Interest Expense	32,018	34,622	26,916	18,030	15,365	14,635	12,752
Net Income	② 60,762	① 68,056	75,638	62,309	46,478	30,676	13,635
Average Shs. Outstg.	31,027	28,643	28,384	25,954	21,929	14,093	11,710
BALANCE SHEET (IN THOUSANDS):							
Cash & Cash Equivalents	9,826	2,844	2,129	1,269	1,381	1,350	1,706
Total Real Estate Investments	956,851	803,987	826,779	619,989	297,275	…	…
Total Assets	1,269,843	1,156,904	1,271,171	1,073,424	734,327	519,831	358,092
Long-Term Obligations	491,216	319,852	361,342	247,429	170,670	92,270	56,060
Total Liabilities	511,973	458,297	564,175	439,665	264,403	194,295	170,494
Net Stockholders' Equity	757,870	698,607	706,996	633,759	469,924	325,536	187,598
Year-end Shs. Outstg.	32,740	28,806	28,532	28,240	24,341	18,320	12,034
STATISTICAL RECORD:							
Net Inc.+Depr./Assets %	7.2	7.8	7.4	6.8	7.0	6.4	4.2
Return on Equity %	8.0	9.7	10.7	9.8	9.9	9.4	7.3
Return on Assets %	4.8	5.9	6.0	5.8	6.3	5.9	3.8
Price Range	26.40-16.06	19.25-13.81	26.63-14.69	29.25-20.00	28.63-22.25	25.25-17.88	23.13-15.50
P/E Ratio	17.4-10.6	10.1-7.2	12.0-6.6	13.1-8.9	13.5-10.5	11.6-8.2	19.9-13.4
Average Yield %	11.0	14.1	11.0	8.9	8.3	9.6	10.7

Statistics are as originally reported. ① Incls. gain of $1.7 mill. from the sale of prop. & loss on invest. of $2.0 mill. ② Bef. extraord. loss of $213,000, incl. loss of $1.3 mill. from sale of prop.

QUARTERLY DATA

(12/31/2001)($000)	REV	INC
1st Quarter	32,577	11,827
2nd Quarter	32,765	11,747
3rd Quarter	34,834	13,591
4th Quarter	34,944	9,879

OFFICERS:
G. L. Chapman, Chmn., Pres., C.E.O.
R. W. Braun, Exec. V.P., C.F.O., C.O.O.
M. A. Crabtree, Treas., Contr.

INVESTOR CONTACT: Ray Braun, Exec.
V.P., C.F.O., C.O.O., (419) 247-2800

PRINCIPAL OFFICE: One SeaGate, Suite 1500, Toledo, OH 43604

TELEPHONE NUMBER: (419) 247-2800
FAX: (419) 247-2826
WEB: www.hcreit.com

NO. OF EMPLOYEES: 24

SHAREHOLDERS: 4,691 (record)

ANNUAL MEETING: In May

INCORPORATED: DE, Apr., 1985

INSTITUTIONAL HOLDINGS:
No. of Institutions: 109
Shares Held: 6,694,539
% Held: 19.7

INDUSTRY: Real estate investment trusts
(SIC: 6798)

TRANSFER AGENT(S): Mellon Investor
Serices, LLC, Ridgefield Park, NJ

HEINZ (H.J.) COMPANY

YIELD 3.9%
P/E RATIO 33.5

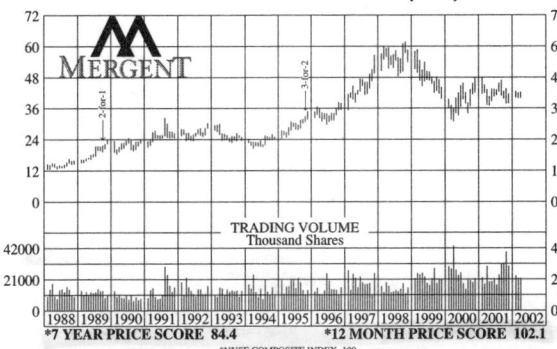

MERGENT

TRADING VOLUME
Thousand Shares

| | 1988 | 1989 | 1990 | 1991 | 1992 | 1993 | 1994 | 1995 | 1996 | 1997 | 1998 | 1999 | 2000 | 2001 | 2002 |

*7 YEAR PRICE SCORE 84.4   ***12 MONTH PRICE SCORE 102.1**

NYSE COMPOSITE INDEX=100

INTERIM EARNINGS (Per Share):

Qtr.	July	Oct.	Jan.	Apr.
1998-99	0.58	0.63	0.33	0.25
1999-00	0.57	1.14	0.47	0.27
2000-01	0.57	0.54	0.77	d0.49
2001-02	0.57	0.59	0.57	

INTERIM DIVIDENDS (Per Share):

Amt.	Decl.	Ex.	Rec.	Pay.
0.393Q	6/13/01	6/21/01	6/25/01	7/10/01
0.405Q	9/17/01	9/25/01	9/27/01	10/10/01
0.405Q	12/12/01	12/20/01	12/24/01	1/10/02
0.405Q	3/13/02	3/21/02	3/25/02	4/10/02

Indicated div.: $1.62 (Div. Reinv. Plan)

CAPITALIZATION (5/2/01):

	($000)	(%)
Long-Term Debt	3,014,853	64.9
Deferred Income Tax	253,690	5.5
Preferred Stock	126	0.0
Common & Surplus	1,373,601	29.6
Total	4,642,270	100.0

DIVIDEND ACHIEVER STATUS:

Rank: 154   10-Year Growth Rate: 9.14%
Total Years of Dividend Growth: 38

RECENT DEVELOPMENTS: For the quarter ended 1/30/02, net income was $201.7 million, down 25.5% versus $270.5 million the year before. Results in the prior-year period included after-tax restructuring charges of $50.1 million and a $93.2 million Italian tax gain. Sales climbed 12.4% to $2.55 billion from $2.27 billion the previous year. Gross profit was $1.00 billion, or 39.2% of sales, versus $884.1 million, or 39.0% of sales, a year earlier.

PROSPECTS: Sales growth is being fueled by recent acquisitions in HNZ's core businesses of ketchup, condiments and sauces, convenience meals, frozen foods, and infant and nutritional foods. Going forward, the Company plans to sharpen its mareting focus on higher-margin products in an effort to increase operating profitability. In addition, HNZ is taking steps to reduce expenses by 1.0% to 2.0% per year by phasing out underperforming products.

BUSINESS

H.J. HEINZ COMPANY manufactures and markets an extensive line of processed food products throughout the world, including ketchup and other sauces/condiments, frozen dinners, pet food, baby food, frozen potato products and canned soups, vegetables and fruits. Major U.S. brands include HEINZ, WEIGHT WATCHERS, ORE-IDA, SMART ONES, STARKIST, 9-LIVES, POUNCE, BOSTON MARKET, KIBBLES 'N BITS, and BAGEL BITES. Overseas, well-known brands include PLASMON, PUDLISZKI, ABC, ORLANDO, WATTIE'S, OLIVINE, FARLEY'S, and JURAN. Fiscal 2001 sales were derived: Ketchup, Condiments & Sauces, 26.9%; Frozen Foods, 20.8%; Soups, Beans & Pasta Meals, 12.9%; Pet Products, 12.2%; Tuna, 11.0%; Infant/Nutritional Foods, 10.3%; and Other, 5.9%.

ANNUAL FINANCIAL DATA

	5/2/01	5/3/00	4/28/99	4/29/98	4/30/97	5/1/96	5/3/95
Earnings Per Share	② 1.41	⑤ 2.47	① 1.29	① 2.15	① 0.80	1.74	1.59
Cash Flow Per Share	2.28	3.32	2.11	2.99	1.72	2.66	2.43
Tang. Book Val. Per Share	...	...	...	...	0.03	0.87	0.34
Dividends Per Share	1.50	1.40	1.29	1.19	1.08	0.98	0.90
Dividend Payout %	106.0	56.5	99.8	55.1	135.6	56.6	56.6
INCOME STATEMENT (IN MILLIONS):							
Total Revenues	9,430.4	9,407.9	9,299.6	9,209.3	9,357.0	9,112.3	8,086.8
Costs & Expenses	8,148.4	7,833.0	7,888.1	7,375.3	8,260.2	7,480.9	6,615.7
Depreciation & Amort.	299.2	306.5	302.2	313.6	340.5	343.8	315.3
Operating Income	982.4	1,733.1	1,109.3	1,520.3	756.3	1,287.6	1,155.8
Net Interest Inc./(Exp.)	d310.3	d244.4	d233.7	d226.0	d235.4	d232.6	d174.0
Income Before Income Taxes	673.1	1,463.7	835.1	1,255.0	479.1	1,023.7	938.0
Income Taxes	178.1	573.1	360.8	453.4	177.2	364.3	347.0
Net Income	② 494.9	③ 890.6	④ 474.3	⑥ 801.6	⑦ 301.9	659.3	591.0
Cash Flow	794.1	1,197.0	776.5	1,115.2	642.3	1,003.1	906.2
Average Shs. Outstg. (000)	347,758	360,095	367,830	372,953	373,703	377,156	372,807
BALANCE SHEET (IN MILLIONS):							
Cash & Cash Equivalents	144.2	154.1	123.1	99.4	188.4	108.4	207.0
Total Current Assets	3,116.8	3,169.9	2,886.8	2,686.5	3,013.1	3,046.7	2,823.0
Net Property	2,168.4	2,358.8	2,171.0	2,394.7	2,479.2	2,616.8	2,534.4
Total Assets	9,035.2	8,850.7	8,053.6	8,023.4	8,437.8	8,623.7	8,247.2
Total Current Liabilities	3,655.1	2,126.1	2,786.3	2,164.3	2,880.4	2,715.1	2,564.1
Long-Term Obligations	3,014.9	3,935.8	2,472.2	2,768.3	2,284.0	2,281.7	2,326.8
Net Stockholders' Equity	1,373.7	1,595.9	1,803.0	2,216.5	2,440.4	2,706.8	2,472.9
Net Working Capital	d538.3	1,043.9	100.5	522.2	132.7	331.6	259.0
Year-end Shs. Outstg. (000)	348,949	347,443	359,128	363,418	367,184	368,598	365,514
STATISTICAL RECORD:							
Operating Profit Margin %	10.4	18.4	11.9	16.5	8.1	14.1	14.3
Net Profit Margin %	5.2	9.5	5.1	8.7	3.2	7.2	7.3
Return on Equity %	36.0	55.8	26.3	36.2	12.4	24.4	23.9
Return on Assets %	5.5	10.1	5.9	10.0	3.6	7.6	7.2
Debt/Total Assets %	33.4	44.5	30.7	34.5	27.1	26.5	28.2
Price Range	48.00-30.81	58.81-39.50	61.75-48.50	56.69-35.25	38.38-29.75	34.88-24.25	26.00-20.50
P/E Ratio	34.0-21.9	23.8-16.0	47.9-37.6	26.4-16.4	48.0-37.2	20.0-13.9	16.4-12.9
Average Yield %	3.8	2.8	2.3	2.6	3.2	3.3	3.9

Statistics are as originally reported. Adj. for 3-for-2 stk. split, 9/95. ① Incl. $34.7 mil ($0.10/sh) net chg., 2000; $408.2 mil ($1.11/sh) net chg., 1999; $12.5 mil net gain, 1998; $664.6 mil net chg., 1996. ② Bef. $16.9 mil ($0.05/sh) acctg. chg. & incl. $494.6 mil ($1.41/sh) net special chg. and $93.2 mil ($0.27/sh) tax gain.

OFFICERS:

W. R. Johnson, Chmn., Pres., C.E.O.
A. Winkleblack, Exec. V.P., C.F.O.
L. F. Stein, Sr. V.P., Gen. Couns.

INVESTOR CONTACT: Jack Runkel, V.P., Investor Relations, (412) 456-6034

PRINCIPAL OFFICE: 600 Grant Street, Pittsburgh, PA 15219

TELEPHONE NUMBER: (412) 456-5700
FAX: (412) 456-6128
WEB: www.heinz.com

NO. OF EMPLOYEES: 45,800 (approx.)

SHAREHOLDERS: 55,400 (approx.)

ANNUAL MEETING: In Sept.

INCORPORATED: PA, July, 1900

INSTITUTIONAL HOLDINGS:
No. of Institutions: 508
Shares Held: 217,489,484
% Held: 62.1

INDUSTRY: Food preparations, nec (SIC 2099)

TRANSFER AGENT(S): Mellon Investor Services, Ridgefield Park, NJ

HERSHEY FOODS CORPORATION

YIELD 1.8%
P/E RATIO 45.7

INTERIM EARNINGS (Per Share):

Qtr.	Mar.	June	Sept.	Dec.
1998	0.52	0.33	0.74	0.76
1999	1.57	0.35	0.62	0.70
2000	0.51	0.29	0.78	0.84
2001	0.57	0.38	0.88	d0.33

INTERIM DIVIDENDS (Per Share):

Amt.	Decl.	Ex.	Rec.	Pay.
0.28Q	2/07/01	2/21/01	2/23/01	3/15/01
0.28Q	4/24/01	5/23/01	5/25/01	6/15/01
0.302Q	8/07/01	8/22/01	8/24/01	9/14/01
0.302Q	10/02/01	11/20/01	11/23/01	12/14/01
0.302Q	2/13/02	2/21/02	2/25/02	3/15/02

Indicated div.: $1.21 (Div. Reinv. Plan)

CAPITALIZATION (12/31/01):

	($000)	(%)
Long-Term Debt	876,972	38.5
Deferred Income Tax	255,769	11.2
Common & Surplus	1,147,204	50.3
Total	2,279,945	100.0

DIVIDEND ACHIEVER STATUS:
Rank: 147   10-Year Growth Rate: 9.50%
Total Years of Dividend Growth: 27

TRADING VOLUME
Thousand Shares

*7 YEAR PRICE SCORE 106.6   *12 MONTH PRICE SCORE 109.4
*NYSE COMPOSITE INDEX=100

RECENT DEVELOPMENTS: For the year ended 12/31/01, net income was $207.2 million compared with $334.5 million in the corresponding year-earlier period. Results for 2001 included a pre-tax charge of $228.3 million related to a business realignment and asset impairments. Results for 2001 also included a pre-tax gain of $19.2 million on the sale of the Company's Luden's throat drops business. Net sales advanced 8.0% to $4.56 billion.

PROSPECTS: Results going forward should benefit from recent business realignment actions, including a voluntary workforce reduction program, HSY has initiated to enhance the future performance of the Company. HSY projects savings from its business realignment program will total about $75.0 million to $80.0 million per year once fully implemented, with the ongoing savings being largely reinvested in enhanced brand building and selling capabilities.

BUSINESS

HERSHEY FOODS CORPORATION and its subsidiaries are engaged in the manufacture, distribution and sale of consumer food products including: chocolate and non-chocolate confectionery products sold in the form of bar goods, bagged items and boxed items; and grocery products sold in the form of baking ingredients, chocolate drink mixes, peanut butter, dessert toppings and beverages. HSY's products are marketed in over 90 countries worldwide under more than 50 brands. Principal brands include: HERSHEY'S, REESE'S, MR. GOODBAR, JOLLY RANCHER, KIT KAT, MILK DUDS, WHOPPERS, YORK, TWIZZLERS, and SUPER BUBBLE. In January 1999, HSY sold a 94.0% majority interest in its former U.S. pasta business to New World, LLC. On 12/15/00, HSY acquired Nabisco, Inc.'s mints and gum businesses for $135.0 million. Acquired brands include ICE BREAKERS and BREATH SAVERS COOL BLASTS intense mints, BREATH SAVERS mints, and ICE BREAKERS, CARE*FREE, STICK*FREE, BUBBLE YUM, and FRUIT STRIPE gums. In July 2001, HSY acquired the chocolate and confectionery business of Visagis. In September 2001, HSY sold its LUDEN'S throat drop business to Pharmacia Consumer Healthcare.

ANNUAL FINANCIAL DATA

	12/31/01	12/31/00	12/31/99	12/31/98	12/31/97	12/31/96	12/31/95
Earnings Per Share	② 1.50	2.42	① 3.26	2.34	2.23	1.77	1.70
Cash Flow Per Share	2.89	3.69	4.41	3.43	3.24	2.64	2.50
Tang. Book Val. Per Share	3.99	5.14	4.68	3.58	2.11	3.89	4.23
Dividends Per Share	1.17	1.08	1.00	0.92	0.84	0.76	0.69
Dividend Payout %	77.7	44.6	30.7	39.3	37.7	42.9	40.3
INCOME STATEMENT (IN MILLIONS):							
Total Revenues	4,557.2	4,221.0	3,970.9	4,435.6	4,302.2	3,989.3	3,690.7
Costs & Expenses	3,973.4	3,422.4	3,249.3	3,634.8	3,519.3	3,292.7	3,046.0
Depreciation & Amort.	190.5	176.0	163.3	158.2	152.8	133.5	133.9
Operating Income	393.4	622.7	558.4	642.7	630.2	563.1	510.8
Net Interest Inc./(Exp.)	d69.1	d76.0	d74.3	d85.7	d76.3	d48.0	d44.8
Income Before Income Taxes	343.5	546.6	727.9	557.0	554.0	479.7	466.0
Income Taxes	136.4	212.1	267.6	216.1	217.7	206.6	184.0
Net Income	② 207.2	334.5	① 460.3	340.9	336.3	273.2	281.9
Cash Flow	397.7	510.5	623.6	499.0	489.0	406.7	415.8
Average Shs. Outstg. (000)	137,696	138,365	141,300	145,563	151,016	153,995	166,036
BALANCE SHEET (IN MILLIONS):							
Cash & Cash Equivalents	134.1	32.0	118.1	39.0	54.2	61.4	32.3
Total Current Assets	1,167.5	1,295.3	1,280.0	1,134.0	1,034.8	986.2	922.3
Net Property	1,534.9	1,585.4	1,510.5	1,648.1	1,648.2	1,601.9	1,436.0
Total Assets	3,247.4	3,447.8	3,346.7	3,404.1	3,291.2	3,184.8	2,830.6
Total Current Liabilities	606.4	766.9	712.8	814.8	795.7	817.3	864.4
Long-Term Obligations	877.0	877.7	878.2	879.1	1,029.1	655.3	357.0
Net Stockholders' Equity	1,147.2	1,175.0	1,098.6	1,042.3	852.8	1,161.0	1,083.0
Net Working Capital	561.1	528.4	567.2	319.1	239.1	169.0	58.0
Year-end Shs. Outstg. (000)	179,951	136,282	138,460	143,147	142,932	152,942	154,532
STATISTICAL RECORD:							
Operating Profit Margin %	8.6	14.8	14.1	14.5	14.6	14.1	13.8
Net Profit Margin %	4.5	7.9	11.6	7.7	7.8	6.8	7.6
Return on Equity %	18.1	28.5	41.9	32.7	39.4	23.5	26.0
Return on Assets %	6.4	9.7	13.8	10.0	10.2	8.6	10.0
Debt/Total Assets %	27.0	25.5	26.2	25.8	31.3	20.6	12.6
Price Range	70.15-55.13	66.44-37.75	64.88-45.75	76.38-59.69	63.88-42.13	51.75-31.94	33.94-24.00
P/E Ratio	46.8-36.7	27.5-15.6	19.9-14.0	32.6-25.5	28.6-18.9	29.2-18.0	20.0-14.1
Average Yield %	1.9	2.1	1.8	1.4	1.6	1.8	2.4

Statistics are as originally reported. Adj. for 2-for-1 stk. split, 9/96. ① Incl. non-recurr. credit of $165.0 mill. ② Incl. pre-tax chrg. of $228.3 mill. for business realign. & asset impairmnts. and pre-tax gain of $19.2 mill. on sale of Luden's business.

OFFICERS:
R. H. Lenny, Chmn., Pres., C.E.O.
F. Cerminara, Sr. V.P., C.F.O.

INVESTOR CONTACT: James A. Edris, Director, Investor Relations, (717) 534-7556

PRINCIPAL OFFICE: 100 Crystal A Drive, Hershey, PA 17033

TELEPHONE NUMBER: (717) 534-6799
FAX: (717) 531-6161
WEB: www.hersheys.com

NO. OF EMPLOYEES: 14,400 full-time (approx.); 1,600 part-time (approx.)

SHAREHOLDERS: 40,311 (class B)

ANNUAL MEETING: In April

INCORPORATED: DE, Oct., 1927

INSTITUTIONAL HOLDINGS:
No. of Institutions: 391
Shares Held: 52,133,100
% Held: 38.1

INDUSTRY: Chocolate and cocoa products (SIC: 2066)

TRANSFER AGENT(S): Mellon Investor Services, Ridgefield Park, NJ

HILB, ROGAL & HAMILTON COMPANY

YIELD 1.1%
P/E RATIO 31.8

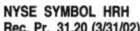
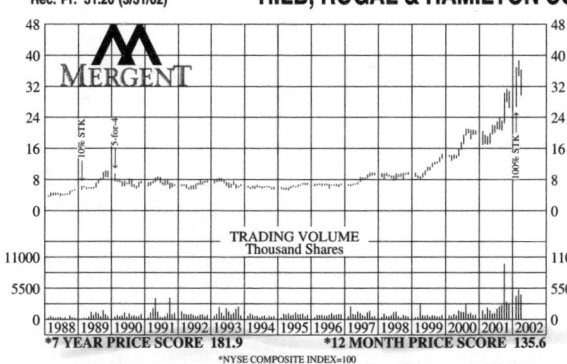

TRADING VOLUME
Thousand Shares

1988 | 1989 | 1990 | 1991 | 1992 | 1993 | 1994 | 1995 | 1996 | 1997 | 1998 | 1999 | 2000 | 2001 | 2002

*7 YEAR PRICE SCORE 181.9   *12 MONTH PRICE SCORE 135.6
*NYSE COMPOSITE INDEX=100

INTERIM EARNINGS (Per Share):

Qtr.	Mar.	June	Sept.	Dec.
1997	0.21	0.14	0.10	0.05
1998	0.23	0.18	0.13	0.06
1999	0.30	0.12	0.21	0.12
2000	0.24	0.18	0.22	0.15
2001	0.27	0.27	0.32	0.12

INTERIM DIVIDENDS (Per Share):

Amt.	Decl.	Ex.	Rec.	Pay.
0.175Q	5/01/01	6/13/01	6/15/01	6/29/01
0.175Q	7/30/01	9/17/01	9/14/01	9/28/01
0.175Q	11/08/01	12/12/01	12/14/01	12/28/01
100% STK	11/08/01	1/02/02	12/14/01	12/31/01
0.087Q	2/12/02	3/13/02	3/15/02	3/29/02

Indicated div.: $0.35

CAPITALIZATION (12/31/01):

	($000)	(%)
Long-Term Debt	114,443	44.5
Common & Surplus	142,801	55.5
Total	257,245	100.0

DIVIDEND ACHIEVER STATUS:
Rank: 200   10-Year Growth Rate: 6.51%
Total Years of Dividend Growth: 15

RECENT DEVELOPMENTS: For the year ended 12/31/01, net income jumped 46.2% to $32.3 million versus income of $22.1 million, before an accounting change charge of $325,000, in 2000. Results for 2001 and 2000 included amortization of intangibles of $13.9 million and $12.2 million, respectively. Total revenues rose 26.0% to $330.3 million from $262.1 million in the previous year. Commissions and fees increased 26.0% to $323.1 million versus $256.4 million the year before.

PROSPECTS: Looking ahead, the Company plans to invest in its sales, service and placement capabilities through training and new recruiting efforts. In addition, HRH set a long-term goal of increasing earnings per share, before non-recurring items, by at least 15.0% annually. Separately, on 3/15/02, the Company acquired substantially all of the assets of LFC Insurance Agents & Brokers, Inc., a provider of property and casualty insurance and risk management services. Terms of the transaction were not disclosed.

BUSINESS

HILB, ROGAL & HAMILTON COMPANY places various types of insurance, including property/casualty, marine, aviation and employee benefits, with insurance underwriters on behalf of its clients through the network of its wholly-owned subsidiary insurance agencies. The agencies operate 80 offices in 23 states. The client base consists mainly of middle market commercial and industrial accounts. Insurance commissions accounted for approximately 91.0% of the Company's total revenues in 2001. HRH also advises clients on risk management and employee benefits and provides claims administration and loss control consulting services to clients, which contributed approximately 7.0% in revenues in 2001. On 5/3/99, the Company acquired all of the outstanding common stock of American Phoenix Corporation.

ANNUAL FINANCIAL DATA

	12/31/01	12/31/00	12/31/99	12/31/98	12/31/97	12/31/96	12/31/95
Earnings Per Share	0.98	② 0.78	① 0.72	0.59	0.49	0.43	0.41
Cash Flow Per Share	1.91	1.34	1.24	1.04	0.93	0.83	0.75
Dividends Per Share	0.35	0.34	0.33	0.32	0.31	0.30	0.29
Dividend Payout %	35.7	43.6	45.8	54.2	63.3	69.8	70.7
INCOME STATEMENT (IN THOUSANDS):							
Total Revenues	330,267	262,119	227,226	175,364	173,709	158,243	148,147
Costs & Expenses	244,492	196,607	170,576	136,174	138,159	127,098	118,234
Depreciation & Amort.	19,984	17,596	15,191	11,509	11,667	10,856	9,757
Operating Income	65,792	47,917	41,458	27,681	23,882	20,290	20,156
Net Interest Inc./(Exp.)	d9,062	d8,179	d6,490	d2,317	d2,037	d1,245	d560
Income Before Income Taxes	56,730	39,737	33,069	25,364	21,845	19,045	19,597
Income Taxes	24,381	17,610	13,583	10,418	9,055	7,638	7,768
Net Income	32,349	② 22,127	① 19,486	14,945	12,790	11,406	11,829
Cash Flow	52,332	39,723	34,677	26,454	24,457	22,262	21,586
Average Shs. Outstg.	27,411	29,784	28,014	25,418	26,430	26,986	28,940
BALANCE SHEET (IN THOUSANDS):							
Cash & Cash Equivalents	55,080	31,008	25,276	22,779	26,207	24,862	28,175
Total Current Assets	197,408	131,478	111,201	78,202	76,833	76,256	78,615
Net Property	19,485	16,495	15,413	12,387	11,762	16,092	13,700
Total Assets	499,301	353,371	317,981	188,066	181,607	181,475	163,249
Total Current Liabilities	225,045	151,001	124,307	88,505	88,273	89,112	87,340
Long-Term Obligations	114,443	103,113	111,826	43,658	32,458	27,196	11,750
Net Stockholders' Equity	142,801	88,222	71,176	45,710	51,339	55,298	56,646
Net Working Capital	d27,637	d19,523	d13,106	d10,303	d11,440	d12,856	d8,724
Year-end Shs. Outstg.	28,311	26,560	26,118	24,234	25,626	26,642	29,358
STATISTICAL RECORD:							
Operating Profit Margin %	19.9	18.3	18.2	15.8	13.7	12.8	13.6
Net Profit Margin %	9.8	8.4	8.6	8.5	7.4	7.2	8.0
Return on Equity %	22.7	25.1	27.4	32.7	24.9	20.6	20.9
Return on Assets %	6.5	6.3	6.1	7.9	4.2	3.8	4.4
Debt/Total Assets %	22.9	29.2	35.2	23.2	10.8	9.0	4.4
Price Range	31.38-16.88	21.06-12.81	14.56-7.78	9.94-7.69	9.81-6.25	7.00-5.69	7.19-5.25
P/E Ratio	64.0-34.4	54.0-32.8	40.4-21.6	33.6-26.0	40.4-25.8	33.0-26.8	35.0-25.6
Average Yield %	0.7	1.0	1.5	1.8	2.0	2.4	2.3

Statistics are as originally reported. Adj. for 100% stk. div., 12/01. ① Incl. $1.9 mill. integration chg. & $4.9 mill. non-recur. gain. ② Excl. $325,000 cumulative effect of an acctg. chg.

OFFICERS:
A. L. Rogal, Chmn., C.E.O.
M. L. Vaughan III, Pres., C.O.O.
C. Jones, Sr. V.P., C.F.O., Treas.
W. L. Smith, Sr. V.P., General Couns., Sec.

INVESTOR CONTACT: Carolyn Jones, Sr. V.P., Gen. Couns. & Sec., (804) 747-6500

PRINCIPAL OFFICE: 4951 Lake Brook Drive, Suite 500, Glen Allen, VA 23060

TELEPHONE NUMBER: (804) 747-6500
FAX: (804) 747-6046
WEB: www.hrh.com

NO. OF EMPLOYEES: 2,600 (approx.)

SHAREHOLDERS: 594

ANNUAL MEETING: In May

INCORPORATED: VA, 1982

INSTITUTIONAL HOLDINGS:
No. of Institutions: 140
Shares Held: 21,794,544
% Held: 77.1

INDUSTRY: Insurance agents, brokers, & service (SIC: 6411)

TRANSFER AGENT(S): Mellon Investor Services, LLC, Ridgefield Park, NJ

HILLENBRAND INDUSTRIES, INC.

YIELD 1.5%
P/E RATIO 22.7

INTERIM EARNINGS (Per Share):

Qtr.	Feb.	May	Aug.	Nov.
1998-99	0.67	0.53	0.35	0.58
1999-00	0.58	0.56	0.54	0.76
2000-01	0.40	0.65	0.65	1.01
Qtr.	Dec.	Mar.	June	Sept.
2001-02	1.00	...	...	...

INTERIM DIVIDENDS (Per Share):

Amt.	Decl.	Ex.	Rec.	Pay.
0.21Q	7/10/01	7/25/01	7/27/01	8/31/01
0.21Q	10/09/01	10/24/01	10/26/01	11/30/01
0.23Q	1/15/02	2/06/02	2/08/02	2/22/02
0.077E	1/15/02	2/27/02	3/01/02	3/29/02

Indicated div.: $0.92 (Div. Reinv. Plan)

CAPITALIZATION (12/1/01):

	($000)	(%)
Long-Term Debt	305,000	22.8
Deferred Income Tax	8,000	0.6
Common & Surplus	1,026,000	76.6
Total	1,339,000	100.0

TRADING VOLUME
Thousand Shares

*7 YEAR PRICE SCORE 109.7   *12 MONTH PRICE SCORE 110.7
*NYSE COMPOSITE INDEX=100

DIVIDEND ACHIEVER STATUS:
Rank: 112   10-Year Growth Rate: 11.22%
Total Years of Dividend Growth: 31

RECENT DEVELOPMENTS: For the 52 weeks ended 12/01/01, net income increased 10.4% to $170.0 million versus $154.0 million in the prior 53-week year. Results included net unusual charges of $32.0 million in 2001 and $3.0 million in 2000. Total revenues increased slightly to $2.11 billion from $2.10 billion a year earlier. Health care sales increased 1.1% to $809.0 million, while health care therapy rental revenues climbed 8.7% to $339.0 million. Insurance revenues fell 5.7% to $346.0 million.

PROSPECTS: Beginning in 2002 the Company's fiscal year will end on September 30. The Company reported results for its first quarter ended 12/31/01 on 2/5/02. For fiscal 2002, the Company anticipates revenues between $2.20 and $2.25 billion. For the full-year ending 9/30/02, earnings should be in the range of $3.36 to $3.41 per share. Gross margins are expected to improve to between 41.0% and 42.0% of total revenues.

BUSINESS

HILLENBRAND INDUSTRIES, INC. is organized into two business segments. The Health Care Group consists of Hill-Rom, Inc., a manufacturer of equipment for the health care market and provider of wound care and pulmonary/trauma management services. Hill-Rom produces adjustable hospital beds, infant incubators, radiant warmers, hospital procedural stretchers, hospital patient room furniture, medical gas and vacuum systems and architectural systems designed to meet the needs of medical-surgical critical care, long-term care, home-care and perinatal providers. The Funeral Services Group consists of Batesville Casket Company, Inc., a manufacturer of caskets and other products for the funeral industry, and Forethought Financial Services, Inc., a provider of funeral planning financial products.

ANNUAL FINANCIAL DATA

	12/1/01	12/2/00	11/27/99	11/28/98	11/29/97	11/30/96	12/2/95
Earnings Per Share	[4] 2.71	[3] 2.44	[2] 1.87	[1] 2.73	2.28	2.02	1.27
Cash Flow Per Share	4.30	3.86	3.35	4.93	3.76	3.44	3.07
Tang. Book Val. Per Share	13.24	10.42	10.17	11.29	11.09	9.28	8.30
Dividends Per Share	0.84	0.80	0.78	0.72	0.66	0.62	0.60
Dividend Payout %	31.0	32.8	41.7	26.4	28.9	30.7	47.2
INCOME STATEMENT (IN MILLIONS):							
Total Revenues	2,107.0	2,096.0	2,047.0	2,001.0	1,776.0	1,684.0	1,624.9
Costs & Expenses	1,771.0	1,763.0	1,738.0	1,624.0	1,410.0	1,349.0	1,317.8
Depreciation & Amort.	100.0	89.0	98.0	149.0	102.0	99.0	127.6
Operating Income	236.0	244.0	211.0	228.0	264.0	236.0	179.5
Net Interest Inc./(Exp.)	d23.0	d27.0	d27.0	d27.0	d21.0	d22.0	d20.3
Income Before Income Taxes	223.0	240.0	195.0	293.0	259.0	233.0	169.8
Income Taxes	53.0	86.0	71.0	109.0	102.0	93.0	79.9
Net Income	[4] 170.0	[3] 154.0	[2] 124.0	[1] 184.0	157.0	140.0	89.9
Cash Flow	270.0	243.0	222.0	333.0	259.0	239.0	217.5
Average Shs. Outstg. (000)	62,814	62,913	66,296	67,578	68,796	69,474	70,758
BALANCE SHEET (IN MILLIONS):							
Cash & Cash Equivalents	284.0	132.0	170.0	297.0	364.0	266.0	171.3
Total Current Assets	868.0	724.0	782.0	858.0	821.0	694.0	640.2
Net Property	266.0	272.0	267.0	302.0	329.0	346.0	367.1
Total Assets	5,049.0	4,597.0	4,433.0	4,280.0	3,828.0	3,396.0	3,070.3
Total Current Liabilities	320.0	286.0	371.0	375.0	359.0	320.0	300.7
Long-Term Obligations	305.0	302.0	302.0	303.0	203.0	204.0	206.8
Net Stockholders' Equity	1,026.0	831.0	838.0	952.0	886.0	787.0	745.8
Net Working Capital	548.0	442.0	411.0	483.0	462.0	374.0	339.4
Year-end Shs. Outstg. (000)	62,467	62,404	63,547	66,759	68,511	68,786	70,177
STATISTICAL RECORD:							
Operating Profit Margin %	11.2	11.6	10.3	11.4	14.9	14.0	11.0
Net Profit Margin %	8.1	7.3	6.1	9.2	8.8	8.3	5.5
Return on Equity %	16.6	18.5	14.8	19.3	17.7	17.8	12.0
Return on Assets %	3.4	3.4	2.8	4.3	4.1	4.1	2.9
Debt/Total Assets %	6.0	6.6	6.8	7.1	5.3	6.0	6.7
Price Range	58.51-41.56	56.38-28.75	56.81-26.13	64.69-44.38	50.88-35.50	40.25-31.88	34.13-27.00
P/E Ratio	21.6-15.3	23.1-11.8	30.4-14.0	23.7-16.3	22.3-15.6	19.9-15.8	26.9-21.3
Average Yield %	1.7	1.9	1.9	1.3	1.5	1.7	2.0

Statistics are as originally reported. [1] Incl. non-recurr. chrg. $66.0 mill. [2] Incl. unusual chrg. $38.0 mill. [3] Incl. non-recurr. chrgs. of $3.0 mill. [4] Incl. non-recurr. chrg. of $32.0 mill.

OFFICERS:
R. J. Hillenbrand, Chmn.
F. W. Rockwood, Pres., C.E.O.
S. K. Sorensen, V.P., C.F.O.
M. R. Lanning, V.P., Treas.
INVESTOR CONTACT: Mark R. Lanning, VP & Treasurer, (812) 934-8400
PRINCIPAL OFFICE: 700 State Route 46 East, Batesville, IN 47006-8835

TELEPHONE NUMBER: (812) 934-7000
FAX: (812) 934-7364
WEB: www.hillenbrand.com
NO. OF EMPLOYEES: 10,200 (approx.)
SHAREHOLDERS: 19,100 (approx. record)
ANNUAL MEETING: In Apr.
INCORPORATED: IN, Aug., 1969

INSTITUTIONAL HOLDINGS:
No. of Institutions: 203
Shares Held: 24,809,605
% Held: 39.6
INDUSTRY: Burial caskets (SIC: 3995)
TRANSFER AGENT(S): Computershare Investor Services, Chicago, IL

HOME DEPOT (THE), INC.

YIELD 0.4%
P/E RATIO 37.7

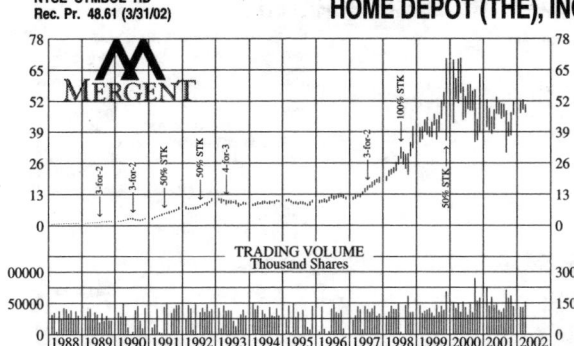

TRADING VOLUME
Thousand Shares

*7 YEAR PRICE SCORE 132.6 *12 MONTH PRICE SCORE 108.2
*NYSE COMPOSITE INDEX=100

INTERIM EARNINGS (Per Share):

Qtr.	Apr.	July	Oct.	Jan.
1998-99	0.15	0.21	0.17	0.18
1999-00	0.21	0.29	0.25	0.25
2000-01	0.27	0.36	0.28	0.20
2001-02	0.27	0.39	0.33	0.30

INTERIM DIVIDENDS (Per Share):

Amt.	Decl.	Ex.	Rec.	Pay.
0.04Q	2/22/01	3/06/01	3/08/01	3/22/01
0.04Q	5/30/01	6/12/01	6/14/01	6/28/01
0.04Q	8/16/01	8/28/01	8/30/01	9/13/01
0.05Q	11/15/01	11/28/01	11/30/01	12/13/01
0.05Q	3/01/02	3/12/02	3/14/02	3/28/02

Indicated div.: $0.20 (Div. Reinv. Plan)

CAPITALIZATION (1/28/01):

	($000)	(%)
Long-Term Debt	1,545,000	9.2
Deferred Income Tax	195,000	1.2
Minority Interest	11,000	0.1
Common & Surplus	15,004,000	89.5
Total	16,755,000	100.0

DIVIDEND ACHIEVER STATUS:

Rank: 5   10-Year Growth Rate: 30.13%
Total Years of Dividend Growth: 14

RECENT DEVELOPMENTS: For the 53 weeks ended 2/3/02, net earnings grew 17.9% to $3.04 billion from $2.58 billion in the corresponding 52-week period the previous year. Net sales rose 17.1% to $53.55 billion from $45.74 billion a year earlier. Comparable-store sales were flat year-over-year. Gross profit totaled $16.15 billion, or 30.2% of net sales, compared with $13.68 billion, or 29.9% of net sales, the year before. Operating income increased 17.7% to $4.93 billion from $4.19 billion in the prior year.

PROSPECTS: On 3/20/02, HD announced that it has signed an agreement to acquire Del Norte, a four-store chain of home improvement stores in Juarez, Mexico. Terms of the transaction, which are subject to approval by the Mexican government, were not disclosed. The Company is projecting annual revenue growth of between 15.0% and 18.0%, along with earnings growth of 18.0% to 20.0%, from 2002 through 2004, driven by gross margin expansion, cost-control initiatives and new product and service offerings.

BUSINESS

THE HOME DEPOT, INC. operated 1,359 retail warehouse stores as of 3/20/02 in the United States, Canada, Mexico and Puerto Rico that offer a wide assortment of building materials and home improvement products. The average Home Depot store has about 108,000 square feet of interior floor space and is stocked with approximately 40,000 to 50,000 separate items. Most stores have about 24,000 square feet of additional outdoor selling area for landscaping supplies. HD also operates 41 EXPO Design Center stores that sell products and services primarily for design and renovation projects, four Villager's Hardware stores, and one Home Depot Floor Store outlet.

ANNUAL FINANCIAL DATA

	p2/3/02	1/28/01	1/30/00	1/31/99	2/1/98	2/2/97	1/28/96
Earnings Per Share	1.29	1.10	1.00	0.71	①0.52	0.43	0.34
Cash Flow Per Share	1.62	1.35	1.19	0.86	0.63	0.53	0.42
Tang. Book Val. Per Share	...	6.32	5.22	3.83	3.17	2.71	2.28
Dividends Per Share	0.17	0.16	0.11	0.08	0.06	0.05	0.04
Dividend Payout %	13.2	14.5	11.3	10.8	12.2	11.9	12.3

INCOME STATEMENT (IN MILLIONS):

Total Revenues	53,553.0	45,738.0	38,434.0	30,219.0	24,156.0	19,535.5	15,470.4
Costs & Expenses	...	40,946.0	34,176.0	27,185.0	21,961.0	17,769.5	14,109.3
Depreciation & Amort.	764.0	601.0	463.0	373.0	283.0	232.3	181.2
Operating Income	4,932.0	4,191.0	3,795.0	2,661.0	1,912.0	1,533.7	1,179.8
Net Interest Inc./(Exp.)	25.0	26.0	9.0	d7.0	2.0	9.5	15.4
Income Before Income Taxes	4,957.0	4,217.0	3,804.0	2,654.0	1,898.0	1,534.8	1,195.3
Income Taxes	1,913.0	1,636.0	1,484.0	1,040.0	738.0	597.0	463.8
Equity Earnings/Minority Int.	...	...	...	...	d16.0	d8.4	...
Net Income	3,044.0	2,581.0	2,320.0	1,614.0	①1,160.0	937.7	731.5
Cash Flow	3,808.0	3,182.0	2,783.0	1,987.0	1,443.0	1,170.1	912.7
Average Shs. Outstg. (000)	2,353,000	2,352,000	2,342,000	2,320,000	2,286,000	2,194,884	2,150,897

BALANCE SHEET (IN MILLIONS):

Cash & Cash Equivalents	2,546.0	177.0	170.0	62.0	174.0	558.4	108.0
Total Current Assets	10,361.0	7,777.0	6,390.0	4,933.0	4,460.0	3,709.4	2,672.0
Net Property	15,375.0	13,068.0	10,227.0	8,160.0	6,509.0	5,437.0	4,461.0
Total Assets	26,394.0	21,385.0	17,081.0	13,465.0	11,229.0	9,341.7	7,354.0
Total Current Liabilities	6,501.0	4,385.0	3,656.0	2,857.0	2,456.0	1,842.1	1,416.5
Long-Term Obligations	1,250.0	1,545.0	750.0	1,566.0	1,303.0	1,246.6	720.1
Net Stockholders' Equity	18,082.0	15,004.0	12,341.0	8,740.0	7,098.0	5,955.2	4,987.8
Net Working Capital	3,860.0	3,392.0	2,734.0	2,076.0	2,004.0	1,867.2	1,255.5
Year-end Shs. Outstg. (000)	...	2,323,747	2,304,317	2,213,178	2,196,324	2,162,318	2,146,977

STATISTICAL RECORD:

Operating Profit Margin %	9.2	9.2	9.9	8.8	7.9	7.9	7.6
Net Profit Margin %	5.7	5.6	6.0	5.3	4.8	4.8	4.7
Return on Equity %	16.8	17.2	18.8	18.5	16.3	15.7	14.7
Return on Assets %	11.5	12.1	13.6	12.0	10.3	10.0	9.9
Debt/Total Assets %	4.7	7.2	4.4	11.6	11.6	13.3	9.8
Price Range	53.73-30.30	70.00-34.69	69.75-34.59	41.34-18.44	20.17-10.61	13.22-9.22	11.11-8.14
P/E Ratio	41.7-23.5	63.6-31.5	69.7-34.6	58.2-26.0	39.0-20.5	30.7-21.4	32.5-23.8
Average Yield %	0.4	0.3	0.2	0.3	0.4	0.5	0.4

Statistics are as originally reported. Adj. for 3-for-2 stk. split, 12/99; 100% stk. div., 7/98 & 3-for-2 stk. split, 7/97. ① Incl. $104 mil pre-tax, non-recur. chg.

OFFICERS:
R. L. Nardelli, Chmn. Pres., C.E.O.
C. Tome, Exec. V.P., C.F.O.

INVESTOR CONTACT: Investor Relations, (770) 384-2666

PRINCIPAL OFFICE: 2455 Paces Ferry Road N.W., Atlanta, GA 30339-4024

TELEPHONE NUMBER: (770) 433-8211
FAX: (770) 431-2707
WEB: www.homedepot.com
NO. OF EMPLOYEES: 250,000 (approx.)
SHAREHOLDERS: 212,010
ANNUAL MEETING: In May
INCORPORATED: DE, June, 1978

INSTITUTIONAL HOLDINGS:
No. of Institutions: 1,087
Shares Held: 1,415,680,399
% Held: 60.4

INDUSTRY: Lumber and other building materials (SIC: 5211)

TRANSFER AGENT(S): Fleet National Bank, Boston, MA

HON INDUSTRIES INCORPORATED

YIELD 1.8%
P/E RATIO 22.5

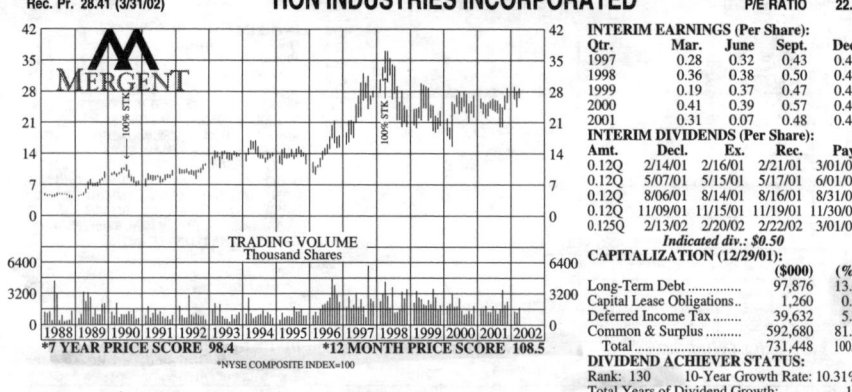

INTERIM EARNINGS (Per Share):

Qtr.	Mar.	June	Sept.	Dec.
1997	0.28	0.32	0.43	0.42
1998	0.36	0.38	0.50	0.48
1999	0.19	0.37	0.47	0.41
2000	0.41	0.39	0.57	0.40
2001	0.31	0.07	0.48	0.40

INTERIM DIVIDENDS (Per Share):

Amt.	Decl.	Ex.	Rec.	Pay.
0.12Q	2/14/01	2/16/01	2/21/01	3/01/01
0.12Q	5/07/01	5/15/01	5/17/01	6/01/01
0.12Q	8/06/01	8/14/01	8/16/01	8/31/01
0.12Q	11/09/01	11/15/01	11/19/01	11/30/01
0.125Q	2/13/02	2/20/02	2/22/02	3/01/02

Indicated div.: $0.50

CAPITALIZATION (12/29/01):

	($000)	(%)
Long-Term Debt	97,876	13.4
Capital Lease Obligations..	1,260	0.2
Deferred Income Tax	39,632	5.4
Common & Surplus	592,680	81.0
Total	731,448	100.0

DIVIDEND ACHIEVER STATUS:
Rank: 130   10-Year Growth Rate: 10.31%
Total Years of Dividend Growth: 13

TRADING VOLUME
Thousand Shares

*7 YEAR PRICE SCORE 98.4   *12 MONTH PRICE SCORE 108.5
*NYSE COMPOSITE INDEX=100

RECENT DEVELOPMENTS: For the year ended 12/29/01, net income declined 29.9% to $74.4 million compared with $106.2 million in 2000. Results for 2001 included restructuring and impairment charges of $24.0 million. Net sales decreased 12.4% to $1.79 billion from $2.05 billion a year earlier. Net sales for the office furniture segment fell 17.1% to $1.37 billion, while net sales for the health products segment rose 7.5% to $426.1 million.

PROSPECTS: HNI expects current weak economic conditions to continue to challenge sales growth and profitability in the first half of 2002. Meanwhile, HNI will continue to focus on new product development and streamlining processes and operations through simplification and rapid continuous improvement. HNI will continue to make investments in innovative new products, technology, brand building and increased distribution.

BUSINESS

HON INDUSTRIES INCORPO-RATED manufactures and markets office furniture and hearth products. Office products include filing cabinets, seating, including task chairs, executive desk chairs and side chairs, desks, tables, bookcases and credenzas. The office products are sold through mass merchandisers, warehouse clubs, a national system of dealers, retail superstores, end-user customers, and federal and state governments. The Hearth Technologies operating company products are comprised of wood-burning, pellet-burning, and gas-burning factory-built fireplaces, fireplace inserts, gas logs, and stoves. The hearth products are sold through wholesalers, a national system of dealers and large regional contractors. The Company has locations in the United States and Canada.

ANNUAL FINANCIAL DATA

	12/29/01	12/30/00	1/1/00	1/2/99	1/3/98	12/28/96	12/31/95
Earnings Per Share	⊡1.26	1.77	⊡1.44	1.72	1.45	⊡1.13	0.67
Cash Flow Per Share	2.64	3.08	2.51	2.58	2.05	1.44	1.02
Tang. Book Val. Per Share	6.45	5.97	6.45	5.77	4.59	3.39	3.54
Dividends Per Share	0.48	0.44	0.38	0.32	0.28	0.25	0.24
Dividend Payout %	38.1	24.9	26.4	18.6	19.3	22.1	35.8
INCOME STATEMENT (IN MILLIONS):							
Total Revenues	1,792.4	2,046.3	1,789.3	1,696.4	1,362.7	998.1	893.1
Costs & Expenses	1,588.0	1,789.2	1,577.4	1,464.3	1,181.9	873.1	805.0
Depreciation & Amort.	81.4	79.0	65.5	53.0	35.6	25.3	21.4
Operating Income	123.1	178.0	146.4	179.2	145.2	106.2	66.7
Net Interest Inc./(Exp.)	d6.8	d12.1	d8.9	d9.1	d6.0	d0.9	d1.2
Income Before Income Taxes	116.3	166.0	137.6	170.1	139.1	105.3	65.5
Income Taxes	41.9	59.7	50.2	63.8	52.2	37.2	24.4
Net Income	⊡74.4	106.2	⊡87.4	106.3	87.0	⊡61.7	41.1
Cash Flow	155.8	185.3	152.8	159.3	122.6	86.9	62.5
Average Shs. Outstg. (000)	59,088	60,140	60,855	61,650	59,780	60,228	60,991
BALANCE SHEET (IN MILLIONS):							
Cash & Cash Equivalents	78.8	3.2	22.2	17.7	46.3	32.7	46.9
Total Current Assets	319.7	330.1	316.6	290.3	295.2	205.5	194.2
Net Property	405.0	454.3	455.6	444.2	341.0	234.6	210.0
Total Assets	961.9	1,022.5	906.7	864.5	754.7	513.5	409.5
Total Current Liabilities	230.4	264.9	225.1	217.4	200.8	152.6	128.9
Long-Term Obligations	99.1	147.0	142.2	153.6	153.1	97.8	53.6
Net Stockholders' Equity	592.7	573.3	501.3	462.0	381.7	252.4	216.2
Net Working Capital	89.2	65.3	91.4	72.9	94.4	53.0	65.3
Year-end Shs. Outstg. (000)	58,673	59,797	60,172	61,290	61,659	59,426	60,789
STATISTICAL RECORD:							
Operating Profit Margin %	6.9	8.7	8.2	10.6	10.7	10.6	7.5
Net Profit Margin %	4.2	5.2	4.9	6.3	6.4	6.2	4.6
Return on Equity %	12.6	18.5	17.4	23.0	22.8	24.4	19.0
Return on Assets %	7.7	10.4	9.6	12.3	11.5	12.0	10.0
Debt/Total Assets %	10.3	14.4	15.7	17.8	20.3	19.0	13.1
Price Range	28.85-19.96	27.88-15.56	29.88-18.75	37.19-20.00	32.13-16.00	21.38-9.25	15.63-11.50
P/E Ratio	22.9-15.8	15.7-8.8	20.7-13.0	21.6-11.6	22.2-11.0	18.9-8.2	23.3-17.2
Average Yield %	2.0	2.0	1.6	1.1	1.2	1.6	1.8

Statistics are as originally reported. Adj. for stk. split: 2-for-1, 3/27/98. ⊡ Incl. non-recurr. credit $3.2 mill., 1996; net chrg. $12.5 mill., 1999; $24.0 mill., 2001.

OFFICERS:
J. D. Michaels, Chmn., Pres., C.E.O.
D. C. Stuebe, V.P., C.F.O.
J. I. Johnson, V.P., Sec., Gen. Couns.
INVESTOR CONTACT: Melinda C. Ellsworth, V.P., Treas., Investor Relations, (563) 264-7400
PRINCIPAL OFFICE: 414 East Third Street, P.O. Box 1109, Muscatine, IA 52761-7109

TELEPHONE NUMBER: (563) 264-7400
FAX: (563) 264-7217
WEB: www.honi.com
NO. OF EMPLOYEES: 8,800 full-time (approx.); 200 part-time (approx.)
SHAREHOLDERS: 6,694
ANNUAL MEETING: In May
INCORPORATED: IA, Jan., 1944

INSTITUTIONAL HOLDINGS:
No. of Institutions: 144
Shares Held: 26,934,333
% Held: 45.9

INDUSTRY: Office furniture, except wood (SIC: 2522)

TRANSFER AGENT(S): Computershare Investor Services, LLC, Chicago, IL

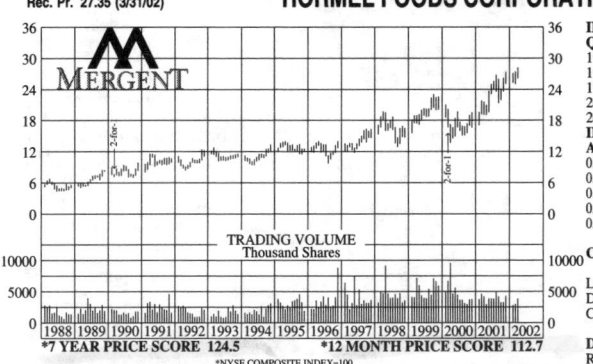

NYSE SYMBOL HRL
Rec. Pr. 27.35 (3/31/02)

HORMEL FOODS CORPORATION

YIELD 1.4%
P/E RATIO 20.0

INTERIM EARNINGS (Per Share):

Qtr.	Jan.	Apr.	July	Oct.
1997-98	0.31	0.17	0.14	0.31
1998-99	0.29	0.22	0.20	0.41
1999-00	0.30	0.26	0.21	0.44
2000-01	0.30	0.28	0.24	0.49
2001-02	0.36	...	...	...

INTERIM DIVIDENDS (Per Share):

Amt.	Decl.	Ex.	Rec.	Pay.
0.092Q	3/26/01	4/18/01	4/21/01	5/15/01
0.092Q	5/22/01	7/18/01	7/21/01	8/15/01
0.092Q	9/25/01	10/17/01	10/20/01	11/15/01
0.098Q	11/21/01	1/16/02	1/19/02	2/14/02
0.098Q	3/25/02	4/17/02	4/20/02	5/15/02

Indicated div.: $0.39 (Div. Reinv. Plan)

CAPITALIZATION (10/27/01):

	($000)	(%)
Long-Term Debt	462,407	31.7
Deferred Income Tax	460	0.0
Common & Surplus	995,881	68.3
Total	1,458,748	100.0

DIVIDEND ACHIEVER STATUS:
Rank: 149   10-Year Growth Rate: 9.45%
Total Years of Dividend Growth: 34

TRADING VOLUME
Thousand Shares

*7 YEAR PRICE SCORE 124.5   *12 MONTH PRICE SCORE 112.7
*NYSE COMPOSITE INDEX=100

RECENT DEVELOPMENTS: For the 13 weeks ended 1/26/02, net earnings totaled $50.4 million, up 21.2% compared with $41.5 million a year earlier. Net sales climbed 10.3% to $983.0 million from $891.2 million the previous year. Gross profit was $246.3 million, or 25.1% of net sales, versus $210.8 million, or 23.6% of net sales, the year before. Operating income advanced 28.9% to $84.6 million from $65.6 million in the prior year.

PROSPECTS: Results are being positively affected by strong sales of HORMEL brand products and successful new product launches. Looking ahead, the Company's aggressive advertising and promotional spending should help drive revenue growth, while recently-completed initiatives focused on streamlining HRL's Jennie-O turkey processing operations are expected to reduce production costs going forward.

BUSINESS

HORMEL FOODS CORPORATION (formerly Geo. A. Hormel & Co.) and its subsidiaries produce and market a variety of processed, packaged food products. The Company's main products include: meat and meat products, including hams, sausages, wieners, sliced bacon, luncheon meats, stews, chilies, hash and meat spreads. The products are sold fresh, frozen, cured, smoked, cooked or canned. The majority of its products are sold under the HORMEL name. Other trade names include: SPAM, LIGHT & LEAN, FARM FRESH, DINTY MOORE, BLACK LABEL, TOPSHELF, MARY KITCHEN, KID'S KITCHEN and OLD SMOKE HOUSE. Through its wholly-owned subsidiary, Jennie-O Foods, Inc., the Company is a producer and marketer of whole and processed turkey products.

ANNUAL FINANCIAL DATA

	10/27/01	10/28/00	10/30/99	10/31/98	10/25/97	10/26/96	10/28/95
Earnings Per Share	1.30	1.20	①1.11	①0.93	0.72	①0.52	0.79
Cash Flow Per Share	1.95	1.67	1.55	1.33	1.06	0.80	1.03
Tang. Book Val. Per Share	4.45	5.64	5.20	4.82	4.55	4.27	4.24
Dividends Per Share	0.37	0.35	0.33	0.32	0.31	0.30	0.29
Dividend Payout %	28.5	29.2	29.7	34.6	43.4	57.7	36.9
INCOME STATEMENT (IN MILLIONS):							
Total Revenues	4,124.1	3,675.1	3,357.8	3,261.0	3,256.6	3,098.7	3,046.2
Costs & Expenses	3,733.6	3,346.6	3,052.2	2,988.9	3,030.3	2,943.0	2,825.5
Depreciation & Amort.	90.2	65.9	64.7	60.3	52.9	42.7	37.2
Operating Income	300.3	262.6	240.9	211.9	173.3	113.0	183.4
Net Interest Inc./(Exp.)	d18.2	1.3	3.6	d13.7	d15.0	d1.6	d1.5
Income Before Income Taxes	285.0	264.4	251.5	217.3	170.9	125.5	194.7
Income Taxes	102.6	94.2	88.0	78.0	61.4	46.1	74.2
Net Income	182.4	170.2	①163.4	①139.3	109.5	①79.4	120.4
Cash Flow	272.6	236.1	228.1	199.6	162.4	122.1	157.7
Average Shs. Outstg. (000)	140,125	141,523	147,010	150,406	152,990	153,018	153,378
BALANCE SHEET (IN MILLIONS):							
Cash & Cash Equivalents	186.3	106.6	248.6	238.0	152.4	203.1	198.0
Total Current Assets	883.3	711.1	800.1	717.4	671.4	723.3	659.3
Net Property	679.9	541.5	505.6	486.9	488.7	421.5	333.1
Total Assets	2,162.7	1,641.9	1,685.6	1,555.9	1,528.5	1,436.1	1,223.9
Total Current Liabilities	420.2	342.6	385.4	267.7	260.6	266.4	217.8
Long-Term Obligations	462.4	145.9	184.7	204.9	198.2	127.0	17.0
Net Stockholders' Equity	995.9	873.9	841.1	813.3	802.2	785.6	732.0
Net Working Capital	463.1	368.5	414.7	449.7	410.8	456.9	441.5
Year-end Shs. Outstg. (000)	138,663	138,569	142,725	146,992	151,552	155,020	153,404
STATISTICAL RECORD:							
Operating Profit Margin %	7.3	7.1	7.2	6.5	5.3	3.6	6.0
Net Profit Margin %	4.4	4.6	4.9	4.3	3.4	2.6	4.0
Return on Equity %	18.3	19.5	19.4	17.1	13.6	10.1	16.5
Return on Assets %	8.4	10.4	9.7	9.0	7.2	5.5	9.8
Debt/Total Assets %	21.4	8.9	11.0	13.2	13.0	8.8	1.4
Price Range	27.35-17.00	20.97-13.63	23.09-15.50	19.69-12.84	16.38-11.75	14.00-9.69	14.00-11.44
P/E Ratio	21.0-13.1	17.5-11.4	20.8-14.0	21.3-13.9	22.9-16.4	26.9-18.6	17.8-14.6
Average Yield %	1.7	2.0	1.7	2.0	2.2	2.5	2.3

Statistics are as originally reported. Adj. for 2-for-1 stk. split, 2/15/00. ① Incl. $3.8 mil ($0.03/sh) gain, 1999; $17.4 mil ($0.12/sh) after-tax gain, 1998; $5.4 mil ($0.04/sh) non-recur. chg., 1996.

OFFICERS:
J. W. Johnson, Chmn., Pres., C.E.O.
M. J. McCoy, Exec. V.P., C.F.O.
G. J. Ray, Exec. V.P.

INVESTOR CONTACT: Fred Halvin, Investor Relations, (507) 437-5007

PRINCIPAL OFFICE: 1 Hormel Place, Austin, MN 55912-3680

TELEPHONE NUMBER: (507) 437-5611
FAX: (507) 437-5489
WEB: www.hormel.com

NO. OF EMPLOYEES: 15,600 (avg.)

SHAREHOLDERS: 11,200 (approx.)

ANNUAL MEETING: In Jan.

INCORPORATED: DE, Sept., 1928

INSTITUTIONAL HOLDINGS:
No. of Institutions: 166
Shares Held: 37,028,017
% Held: 26.7

INDUSTRY: Meat packing plants (SIC: 2011)

TRANSFER AGENT(S): Wells Fargo Shareowner Services, South St. Paul, MN

NYSE SYMBOL HI
Rec. Pr. 56.80 (3/31/02)

HOUSEHOLD INTERNATIONAL INC.

YIELD 1.5%
P/E RATIO 13.9

*7 YEAR PRICE SCORE 128.0   *12 MONTH PRICE SCORE 91.7
*NYSE COMPOSITE INDEX=100

INTERIM EARNINGS (Per Share):

Qtr.	Mar.	June	Sept.	Dec.
1997	0.43	0.49	0.57	0.66
1998	0.51	d1.03	0.63	0.71
1999	0.65	0.67	0.83	0.92
2000	0.78	0.80	0.94	1.03
2001	0.91	0.93	1.07	1.17

INTERIM DIVIDENDS (Per Share):

Amt.	Decl.	Ex.	Rec.	Pay.
0.22Q	5/09/01	6/27/01	6/29/01	7/15/01
0.22Q	9/17/01	9/26/01	9/28/01	10/15/01
0.22Q	11/12/01	12/27/01	12/31/01	1/15/02
0.22Q	3/13/02	3/26/02	3/28/02	4/15/02

Indicated div.: $0.88 (Div. Reinv. Plan)

CAPITALIZATION (12/31/01):

	($000)	(%)
Long-Term Debt	56,823,600	87.4
Common & Surplus	8,202,800	12.6
Total	65,026,400	100.0

DIVIDEND ACHIEVER STATUS:
Rank: 169   10-Year Growth Rate: 8.31%
Total Years of Dividend Growth: 49

RECENT DEVELOPMENTS: For the year ended 12/31/01, net income grew 13.1% to $1.92 billion from $1.70 billion in the previous year. Net interest income increased 22.7% to $5.85 billion from $4.77 billion in 2000. Provision for credit losses climbed 37.6% to $2.91 billion versus $2.12 billion a year earlier. Securitization revenue rose 20.2% to $1.76 billion. Insurance revenue grew 18.0% to $662.4 million, while investment income declined 3.7% to $167.7 million. Fee income improved 17.1% to $966.9 million. Other income increased 41.0% to $322.5 million.

PROSPECTS: The Company continues to benefit from strong growth in receivables and revenues. HI's managed portfolio, which grew 15.1% to $100.80 billion from $87.61 billion at 12/31/00, was fueled by growth in its real estate secured portfolio, which makes up over 44.0% of total managed receivables. Meanwhile, the Company's managed revenues are being driven by a strong net interest margin, which widened to 8.85% from 8.01% a year earlier due to lower funding costs.

BUSINESS

HOUSEHOLD INTERNATIONAL INC., through its subsidiaries, provides middle-market consumers with real estate secured loans, auto finance loans, MasterCard® and Visa® credit cards, private label credit cards and personal non-credit card loans. The Company also offers tax refund anticipation loans in the United States and credit and specialty insurance products in the United States, United Kingdom and Canada. The Company's operations are divided into three reportable segments: Consumer, Credit Card Services and International. HI's Consumer segment consists of its consumer lending, mortgage services, retail services and auto finance businesses. The Company's Credit Card Services segment includes its domestic MasterCard and Visa credit card business. The Company's International segment includes its foreign operations in the United Kingdom and Canada. Net income for 2001 was derived: Consumer, 64.0%; Credit Card Services, 17.7%; International, 9.9%; and Other, 8.4%. In June 1997, HI acquired the consumer finance subsidiary of Transamerica Corp. In June 1998, HI acquired Beneficial Corporation.

ANNUAL FINANCIAL DATA

	12/31/01	12/31/00	12/31/99	12/31/98	12/31/97	12/31/96	12/31/95
Earnings Per Share	4.08	3.55	☐3.07	1.03	2.17	1.77	1.44
Cash Flow Per Share	4.73	4.19	3.67	1.65	2.99	2.58	2.32
Tang. Book Val. Per Share	14.54	13.26	10.39	9.36	8.59	6.77	7.25
Dividends Per Share	0.82	0.72	0.66	0.59	0.53	0.47	0.43
Dividend Payout %	20.1	20.3	21.5	57.3	24.5	26.6	29.8
INCOME STATEMENT (IN MILLIONS):							
Total Revenues	13,915.7	11,960.9	9,499.1	8,897.0	5,503.1	5,058.8	5,144.4
Costs & Expenses	10,668.9	9,048.7	6,986.3	7,636.2	4,217.2	3,996.0	4,127.0
Depreciation & Amort.	308.3	301.7	292.1	308.1	256.7	240.5	263.7
Operating Income	2,938.5	2,610.5	2,220.7	952.7	1,029.2	822.3	753.7
Income Before Income Taxes	2,938.5	2,610.5	2,220.7	952.7	1,029.2	822.3	753.7
Income Taxes	1,015.0	909.8	734.3	428.6	342.6	283.7	300.5
Net Income	1,923.5	1,700.7	☐1,486.4	524.1	686.6	538.6	453.2
Cash Flow	2,216.3	1,993.2	1,769.3	817.2	931.5	762.4	690.5
Average Shs. Outstg. (000)	468,100	476,200	481,800	496,400	311,400	295,500	297,900
BALANCE SHEET (IN MILLIONS):							
Cash & Cash Equivalents	543.6	490.2	270.6	457.4	280.4	239.2	270.4
Total Current Assets	79,807.1	67,651.9	52,429.0	44,405.5	24,143.1	24,484.0	22,114.5
Net Property	531.1	517.6	476.4	472.1	309.4	353.1	391.7
Total Assets	89,416.0	76,706.3	60,749.4	52,892.7	30,302.6	29,594.5	29,218.8
Total Current Liabilities	18,586.6	19,464.8	15,757.8	12,022.9	7,869.9	8,793.2	11,368.2
Long-Term Obligations	56,823.6	45,053.0	34,887.3	30,438.6	14,849.0	14,802.0	11,227.9
Net Stockholders' Equity	8,202.8	7,951.2	6,450.9	6,221.4	4,516.2	2,941.2	2,690.9
Net Working Capital	61,220.5	48,187.1	36,671.2	32,382.6	16,273.2	15,690.8	10,746.3
Year-end Shs. Outstg. (000)	457,124	471,020	467,911	483,100	321,474	291,195	291,486
STATISTICAL RECORD:							
Operating Profit Margin %	21.1	21.8	23.4	10.7	18.7	16.3	14.7
Net Profit Margin %	13.8	14.2	15.6	5.9	12.5	10.6	8.8
Return on Equity %	23.4	21.4	23.0	8.4	15.2	18.3	16.8
Return on Assets %	2.2	2.2	2.4	1.0	2.3	1.8	1.6
Debt/Total Assets %	63.5	58.7	57.4	57.5	49.0	50.0	38.4
Price Range	69.98-48.00	57.44-29.50	52.31-32.19	53.69-23.00	43.33-26.21	32.71-17.33	22.79-11.96
P/E Ratio	17.2-11.8	16.2-8.3	17.0-10.5	52.1-22.3	20.0-12.1	18.5-9.8	15.9-8.3
Average Yield %	1.4	1.7	1.6	1.5	1.5	1.9	2.5

Statistics are as originally reported. Adj. for stk. split: 200% div., 6/98 ☐ Incl. chrg. of $1.00 bill. for merger costs & gain of $189.4 mill. for sale of Beneficial Canada.

OFFICERS:
W. F. Aldinger, Chmn., C.E.O.
L. N. Bangs, Vice-Chmn.
D. A. Schoenholz, C.F.O.

INVESTOR CONTACT: Celeste Murphy, Dir. Inv. Rel., (847) 564-7568

PRINCIPAL OFFICE: 2700 Sanders Road, Prospect Heights, IL 60070

TELEPHONE NUMBER: (847) 564-5000
FAX: (847) 205-7490
WEB: www.household.com

NO. OF EMPLOYEES: 32,000 (approx.)

SHAREHOLDERS: 19,089

ANNUAL MEETING: In May

INCORPORATED: DE, Feb., 1981

INSTITUTIONAL HOLDINGS:
No. of Institutions: 541
Shares Held: 377,122,162
% Held: 82.6

INDUSTRY: Personal credit institutions (SIC: 6141)

TRANSFER AGENT(S): Computershare Investor Services, Chicago, IL

HUBBELL, INC.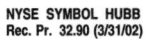

YIELD 4.0%
P/E RATIO 40.1

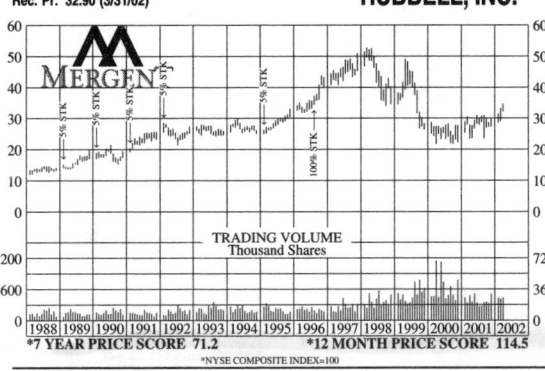

INTERIM EARNINGS (Per Share):

Qtr.	Mar.	June	Sept.	Dec.
1997	0.53	0.60	0.60	0.16
1998	0.58	0.67	0.64	0.63
1999	0.60	0.65	0.54	0.42
2000	0.55	0.67	0.55	0.48
2001	0.36	0.37	0.33	d0.24

INTERIM DIVIDENDS (Per Share):

Amt.	Decl.	Ex.	Rec.	Pay.
0.33Q	3/05/01	3/15/01	3/19/01	4/11/01
0.33Q	6/07/01	6/14/01	6/18/01	7/11/01
0.33Q	9/13/01	9/20/01	9/24/01	10/11/01
0.33Q	12/05/01	12/13/01	12/17/01	1/11/02
0.33Q	3/05/02	3/20/02	3/22/02	4/11/02

Indicated div.: $1.32 (Div. Reinv. Plan)

CAPITALIZATION (12/31/01):

	($000)	(%)
Long-Term Debt	99,800	11.9
Common & Surplus	736,500	88.1
Total	836,300	100.0

DIVIDEND ACHIEVER STATUS:
Rank: 192   10-Year Growth Rate: 6.84%
Total Years of Dividend Growth: 41

TRADING VOLUME
Thousand Shares

*7 YEAR PRICE SCORE 71.2   *12 MONTH PRICE SCORE 114.5
*NYSE COMPOSITE INDEX=100

RECENT DEVELOPMENTS: For the year ended 12/31/01, net income dropped 65.1% to $48.3 million compared with $138.2 million in 2000. Results for 2001 included a one-time charge of $40.0 million, while results for 2000 included a credit of $100,000. Also, results for 2001 and 2000 included gains on the sale of businesses of $4.7 million and $36.2 million, respectively. Net sales decreased 7.9% to $1.31 billion from $1.42 billion a year earlier.

PROSPECTS: On 3/20/02, the Company signed a definitive agreement to acquire LCA Group Inc., the domestic lighting division of U.S. Industries, Inc., for approximately $250.0 million. The transaction is expected to be completed in the second quarter of 2002. Separately, HUBB announced the acquisition of Hawke International, a supplier of a range of products used in harsh and hazardous locations worldwide.

BUSINESS

HUBBELL, INC. specializes in the engineering, manufacture, and sale of electrical and electronic products for the commercial, industrial, utility, and telecommunications markets. These products may be classified into three segments: electrical, power systems and industrial technology. The Company operates manufacturing facilities in North America, Switzerland, Puerto Rico, Italy, Mexico, and the United Kingdom and maintains sales offices in Hong Kong, the People's Republic of China, South Korea, and the Middle East. Hubbell participates in joint ventures with partners in Taiwan.

QUARTERLY DATA

(12/31/01) ($000)	Rev	Inc
1st Quarter	344,100	21,100
2nd Quarter	341,200	21,800
3rd Quarter	325,700	19,500
4th Quarter	301,200	(14,100)

ANNUAL FINANCIAL DATA

	12/31/01	12/31/00	12/31/99	12/31/98	12/31/97	12/31/96	12/31/95
Earnings Per Share	④ 0.82	③ 2.25	② 2.21	2.50	① 1.89	2.10	1.83
Cash Flow Per Share	1.72	3.15	3.01	3.21	2.52	2.74	2.37
Tang. Book Val. Per Share	7.98	8.64	9.56	9.27	9.54	8.79	8.04
Dividends Per Share	1.32	1.30	1.26	1.20	1.10	0.99	0.89
Dividend Payout %	161.0	57.8	57.0	48.0	58.2	47.1	48.8
INCOME STATEMENT (IN MILLIONS):							
Total Revenues	1,312.2	1,424.1	1,451.8	1,424.6	1,378.8	1,297.4	1,143.1
Costs & Expenses	1,207.4	1,220.9	1,213.4	1,150.4	1,164.0	1,060.6	941.9
Depreciation & Amort.	53.0	54.9	52.8	48.1	43.2	39.3	36.2
Operating Income	56.5	184.5	194.4	226.1	171.6	197.5	165.0
Net Interest Inc./(Exp.)	d15.5	d19.7	d15.9	d9.9	d7.3	d8.4	d8.5
Income Before Income Taxes	55.8	184.3	197.0	230.5	180.2	199.3	167.0
Income Taxes	7.5	46.1	51.2	61.1	49.9	57.8	45.1
Net Income	④ 48.3	③ 138.2	② 145.8	169.4	① 130.3	141.5	121.9
Cash Flow	101.3	193.1	198.6	217.5	173.5	180.8	158.2
Average Shs. Outstg. (000)	58,900	61,300	65,900	67,700	68,843	65,938	66,744
BALANCE SHEET (IN MILLIONS):							
Cash & Cash Equivalents	76.5	74.8	24.0	30.1	75.2	134.4	87.0
Total Current Assets	508.3	620.0	552.8	564.8	596.2	591.2	500.1
Net Property	264.2	305.3	308.9	310.1	251.9	217.9	204.2
Total Assets	1,205.4	1,454.5	1,399.2	1,390.4	1,284.8	1,186.4	1,057.2
Total Current Liabilities	283.9	489.4	343.4	345.0	256.3	255.4	194.9
Long-Term Obligations	99.8	99.7	99.6	99.6	99.5	99.5	102.1
Net Stockholders' Equity	736.5	769.5	855.8	840.6	830.3	743.1	667.3
Net Working Capital	224.4	130.6	209.4	219.8	339.9	335.8	305.2
Year-end Shs. Outstg. (000)	58,719	58,758	64,252	65,600	67,027	66,059	65,852
STATISTICAL RECORD:							
Operating Profit Margin %	4.3	15.0	13.4	15.9	12.4	15.2	14.4
Net Profit Margin %	3.7	9.7	10.0	11.9	9.5	10.9	10.7
Return on Equity %	6.6	18.0	17.0	20.2	15.7	19.0	18.3
Return on Assets %	4.0	9.5	10.4	12.2	10.1	11.9	11.5
Debt/Total Assets %	8.3	6.9	7.1	7.2	7.7	8.4	9.7
Price Range	30.98-23.30	28.81-21.63	49.19-26.25	52.75-33.88	50.94-40.75	43.88-31.75	33.06-24.82
P/E Ratio	37.8-28.4	12.8-9.6	22.3-11.9	21.1-13.5	26.9-21.6	20.9-15.1	18.1-13.6
Average Yield %	4.9	5.2	3.3	2.8	2.4	2.6	3.1

Statistics are as originally reported. Adj. for 5% stock dividend, 2/95; 2-for-1 stock split, 8/96. ① Incl. after-tax chrg. of $32.2 mill. for consolidation & reorganization. ② Incl. a one-time gain of $8.8 mill. fr. the sale of The Kerite Company. ③ Incl. after-tax spec. and nonrecurr. chrgs. of $23.7 mill. & a one-time gain of $36.2 mill. fr. the sale of WavePacer DSL assets. ④ Incl. a chrg. of $40.0 mill. and a $4.7 mill. gain on the sale of a business.

OFFICERS:
G. J. Ratcliffe, Chmn.
T. H. Powers, Pres., C.E.O.
W. T. Tolley, Sr. V.P., C.F.O.
J. H. Biggart Jr., V.P., Treas.

INVESTOR CONTACT: Thomas R. Conlin, Investor Relations, (203) 799-4100

PRINCIPAL OFFICE: 584 Derby-Milford Road, Orange, CT 06477-4024

TELEPHONE NUMBER: (203) 799-4100
FAX: (203) 799-4333
WEB: www.hubbell.com

NO. OF EMPLOYEES: 8,771 (approx.)

SHAREHOLDERS: 916 (Class A); 4,174 (Class B)

ANNUAL MEETING: In May
INCORPORATED: CT, May, 1905

INSTITUTIONAL HOLDINGS:
No. of Institutions: 202
Shares Held: 34,034,123
% Held: 57.7

INDUSTRY: Commercial lighting fixtures (SIC: 3646)

TRANSFER AGENT(S): Mellon Investor Services, Ridgefield Park, NJ

HUDSON UNITED BANCORP

YIELD 3.3%
P/E RATIO 15.9

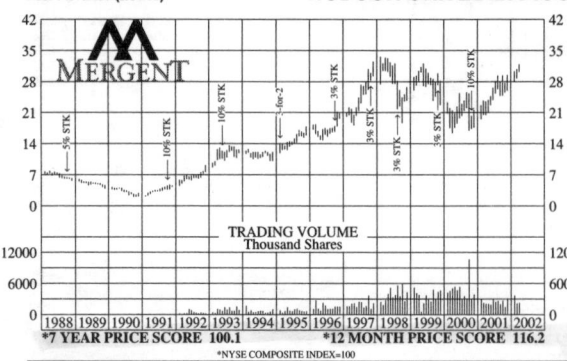

	42
42	42
35	35
28	28
21	21
14	14
7	7
0	0

TRADING VOLUME
Thousand Shares

12000 — 12000
6000 — 6000

1988 1989 1990 1991 1992 1993 1994 1995 1996 1997 1998 1999 2000 2001 2002

*7 YEAR PRICE SCORE 100.1   ***12 MONTH PRICE SCORE 116.2**
*NYSE COMPOSITE INDEX=100

INTERIM EARNINGS (Per Share):

Qtr.	Mar.	June	Sept.	Dec.
1998	0.31	0.10	d0.44	0.51
1999	0.48	0.49	0.50	d0.31
2000	0.53	d0.22	0.45	0.17
2001	0.46	0.49	0.51	0.54

INTERIM DIVIDENDS (Per Share):

Amt.	Decl.	Ex.	Rec.	Pay.
0.25Q	4/25/01	5/16/01	5/18/01	6/01/01
0.25Q	7/24/01	8/15/01	8/17/01	9/04/01
0.26Q	10/24/01	11/20/01	11/23/01	12/03/01
0.26Q	1/24/02	2/13/02	2/15/02	3/01/02

Indicated div.: $1.04 (Div. Reinv. Plan)

CAPITALIZATION (12/31/01):

	($000)	(%)
Total Deposits	5,983,545	90.4
Long-Term Debt	123,000	1.9
Redeemable Pfd. Stock	125,300	1.9
Common & Surplus	383,904	5.8
Total	6,615,749	100.0

DIVIDEND ACHIEVER STATUS:
Rank: 29   10-Year Growth Rate: 18.66%
Total Years of Dividend Growth: 11

RECENT DEVELOPMENTS: For the year ended 12/31/01, net income was $94.5 million versus $49.8 million a year earlier. Earnings for 2001 included trading asset gains of $10.2 million, while results for 2000 included merger-related and restructuring charges of $15.0 million. Net interest income fell 10.8% to $285.4 million. Provision for loan losses jumped 42.3% to $34.1 million. Non-interest income more than tripled to $109.4 million from $31.1 million in 2000. Non-interest expense decreased 9.1% to $227.2 million.

PROSPECTS: The Company's noninterest income is benefiting from continuing increases in credit card fees, as a result of growth in its private-label credit card business, higher retail service fees, and the Company's investment in bank-owned life insurance in June of 2001. Looking ahead, the Company has expressed comfort with full-year 2002 earnings estimates of approximately $2.26 per share, excluding non-recurring items.

BUSINESS

HUDSON UNITED BANCORP (formerly HUBCO, Inc.) is a bank holding company for Hudson United Bank. a full-service commercial bank that operates over 200 branches throughout New Jersey, Connecticut, lower New York state, and southeastern Pennsylvania. The Company directly owns Hudson United Bank and four additional subsidiaries, which are HUBCO Capital Trust I, HUBCO Capital Trust II, JBI Capital Trust I and Jefferson Delaware Inc. The Company is also the indirect owner, through Hudson United Bank, of 9 subsidiaries. At 12/31/01, HU, through its subsidiaries, had total deposits of $5.98 billion, total loans and leases of $4.44 billion and total assets of $7.00 billion.

QUARTERLY DATA

(12/31/2001)($000)	REV	INC
1st Quarter	70,428	22,043
2nd Quarter	71,960	23,284
3rd Quarter	70,647	23,915
4th Quarter	72,331	25,219

ANNUAL FINANCIAL DATA

	12/31/01	12/31/00	12/31/99	12/31/98	12/31/97	12/31/96	12/31/95
Earnings Per Share	② 2.00	① 0.92	① 1.18	① 0.49	① 1.80	① 0.77	1.47
Tang. Book Val. Per Share	6.50	5.58	7.07	8.25	6.32	6.51	7.77
Dividends Per Share	1.01	0.93	0.88	0.78	0.65	0.57	0.48
Dividend Payout %	50.5	101.3	74.7	157.4	35.9	73.6	32.0
INCOME STATEMENT (IN MILLIONS):							
Total Interest Income	470.4	608.3	644.6	468.5	218.0	204.2	120.7
Total Interest Expense	185.0	288.6	301.5	214.4	77.8	72.8	39.6
Net Interest Income	285.4	319.7	343.1	254.2	140.2	131.4	81.1
Provision for Loan Losses	34.1	24.0	52.2	14.4	7.3	12.3	4.2
Non-Interest Income	109.4	31.1	88.7	33.3	41.1	30.3	17.8
Non-Interest Expense	227.2	250.0	271.3	232.1	93.6	116.2	60.2
Income Before Taxes	133.4	76.8	108.3	41.0	80.4	33.1	34.5
Net Income	② 94.5	① 49.8	① 69.3	① 23.2	① 49.3	① 21.5	23.7
Average Shs. Outstg. (000)	47,160	54,186	58,566	47,242	27,358	27,953	15,317
BALANCE SHEET (IN MILLIONS):							
Cash & Due from Banks	231.6	276.8	277.6	218.0	167.1	128.9	85.7
Securities Avail. for Sale	1,302.4	422.7	2,804.3	2,260.6	550.5	655.5	300.7
Total Loans & Leases	4,444.6	5,277.5	5,670.5	3,386.8	1,773.8	1,884.4	854.0
Allowance for Credit Losses	70.0	95.2	98.7	53.5	37.2	35.2	17.0
Net Loans & Leases	4,374.6	5,182.3	5,571.8	3,333.3	1,736.6	1,849.2	837.0
Total Assets	6,999.5	6,817.2	9,686.3	6,778.7	3,046.5	3,115.7	1,613.2
Total Deposits	5,983.5	5,813.3	6,455.3	5,051.4	2,314.4	2,592.1	1,425.0
Long-Term Obligations	123.0	123.0	132.0	100.0	100.0	100.0	25.0
Total Liabilities	6,615.6	6,448.8	9,167.1	6,321.8	2,860.4	2,909.4	1,483.2
Net Stockholders' Equity	383.9	368.5	519.2	456.8	186.1	206.3	130.0
Year-end Shs. Outstg. (000)	45,814	47,965	57,086	45,787	25,571	26,585	15,753
STATISTICAL RECORD:							
Return on Equity %	24.6	13.5	13.4	5.1	26.5	10.4	18.2
Return on Assets %	1.3	0.7	0.7	0.3	1.6	0.7	1.5
Equity/Assets %	5.5	5.4	5.4	6.7	6.1	6.6	8.1
Non-Int. Exp./Tot. Inc. %	57.6	71.3	62.8	80.7	51.6	71.9	60.8
Price Range	29.50-19.50	25.63-16.36	32.11-22.67	33.63-18.65	32.56-18.10	21.21-14.74	17.87-11.85
P/E Ratio	14.7-9.7	27.9-17.8	27.2-19.2	68.1-37.7	18.1-10.1	27.4-19.0	11.8-7.8
Average Yield %	4.1	4.4	3.2	3.0	2.5	3.2	3.3

Statistics are as originally reported. Adj. for all stk. splits thru 12/00. ① Incl. merger-rel. & restruct. costs of $15.0 mill. 2000; $32.0 mill. 1999; $66.4 mill. 1998; $270,000, 1997; $22.0 mill. 1996. ② Incl. trading asset gains of $10.2 mill.

OFFICERS:
K. T. Neilson, Chmn., Pres., C.E.O.
W. A. Houlihan, Exec. V.P., C.F.O.
D. L. Van Borkulo-Nuzzo, Exec. V.P., Sec.

INVESTOR CONTACT: William Houlihan, Exec. V.P., C.F.O., (201) 236-2803

PRINCIPAL OFFICE: 1000 MacArthur Blvd., Mahwah, NJ 07430

TELEPHONE NUMBER: (201) 236-2600
FAX: (201) 236-2649
WEB: www.hudsonunitedbank.com
NO. OF EMPLOYEES: 1,777
SHAREHOLDERS: 7,670 (approx.)
ANNUAL MEETING: In Apr.
INCORPORATED: NJ, June, 1982

INSTITUTIONAL HOLDINGS:
No. of Institutions: 152
Shares Held: 22,539,934
% Held: 48.8

INDUSTRY: State commercial banks (SIC: 6022)

TRANSFER AGENT(S): American Stock Transfer Company, New York, NY

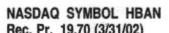

HUNTINGTON BANCSHARES, INC. ✓

	YIELD	3.2%
	P/E RATIO	27.7

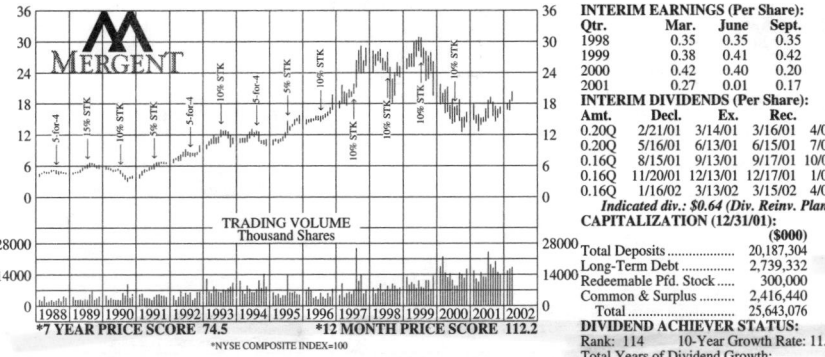

INTERIM EARNINGS (Per Share):

Qtr.	Mar.	June	Sept.	Dec.
1998	0.35	0.35	0.35	0.13
1999	0.38	0.41	0.42	0.45
2000	0.42	0.40	0.20	0.30
2001	0.27	0.01	0.17	0.26

INTERIM DIVIDENDS (Per Share):

Amt.	Decl.	Ex.	Rec.	Pay.
0.20Q	2/21/01	3/14/01	3/16/01	4/02/01
0.20Q	5/16/01	6/13/01	6/15/01	7/02/01
0.16Q	8/15/01	9/13/01	9/17/01	10/01/01
0.16Q	11/20/01	12/13/01	12/17/01	1/02/02
0.16Q	1/16/02	3/13/02	3/15/02	4/01/02

Indicated div.: $0.64 (Div. Reinv. Plan)

CAPITALIZATION (12/31/01):

	($000)	(%)
Total Deposits	20,187,304	78.7
Long-Term Debt	2,739,332	10.7
Redeemable Pfd. Stock	300,000	1.2
Common & Surplus	2,416,440	9.4
Total	25,643,076	100.0

TRADING VOLUME
Thousand Shares

*7 YEAR PRICE SCORE 74.5 ***12 MONTH PRICE SCORE 112.2**

*NYSE COMPOSITE INDEX=100

DIVIDEND ACHIEVER STATUS:
Rank: 114   10-Year Growth Rate: 11.09%
Total Years of Dividend Growth: 35

RECENT DEVELOPMENTS: For the year ended 12/31/01, net income decreased 45.6% to $178.5 million from $328.4 million in the prior year. Earnings for 2001 and 2000 included pre-tax special charges of $100.0 million and $50.0 million, respectively. Net interest income increased 5.7% to $996.2 million from $942.4 million a year earlier. Provision for loan losses more than tripled to $308.8 million from $90.5 million in 2000. Non-interest income rose 3.2% to $509.5 million, while non-interest expense jumped

15.6% to $1.02 billion. Separately, earnings per share for 2002 are expected to range from $1.32 to $1.36, excluding restructuring charges and a gain from the sale of operations. Meanwhile, on 2/15/02, HBAN sold its retail and corporate banking operations in Florida. On 2/21/02, HBAN signed a definitive agreement to acquire Haberer Registered Investment Advisor, Inc., which had $500.0 million in assets under management as of 12/31/01.

BUSINESS

HUNTINGTON BANCSHARES, INC. was incorporated in Maryland in 1966. The Company is a multi-state bank holding company, headquartered in Columbus, Ohio, with assets of $28.50 billion at 12/31/01. The Company's subsidiaries are engaged in full-service commercial and consumer banking, mortgage banking, lease financing, trust services, discount brokerage services, underwriting credit life and disability insurance, issuing commercial paper guaranteed by Huntington, and selling other insurance and financial products and services. HBAN's subsidiaries operate 332 offices domestically in Indiana, Kentucky, Michigan, Ohio and West Virginia. International offices are located in the Cayman Islands and Hong Kong. The Company has more than 900 ATMs. HBAN also owns The Huntington Mortgage Company. On 2/15/02, HBAN sold its retail and corporate banking operations in Florida.

ANNUAL FINANCIAL DATA

	12/31/01	12/31/00	12/31/99	12/31/98	12/31/97	12/31/96	12/31/95
Earnings Per Share	⚀ 0.71	⚀ 1.32	⚀ 1.66	⚀ 1.17	⚀ 1.14	1.35	1.22
Tang. Book Val. Per Share	6.77	9.43	8.90	8.37	7.94	7.96	7.80
Dividends Per Share	0.76	0.75	0.68	0.62	0.56	0.51	0.48
Dividend Payout %	107.0	56.5	40.9	52.9	49.0	37.7	39.4

INCOME STATEMENT (IN MILLIONS):

Total Interest Income	1,939.5	2,108.5	2,026.0	1,999.4	1,981.5	1,510.5	1,461.9
Total Interest Expense	943.3	1,166.1	984.2	978.3	954.2	751.6	737.3
Net Interest Income	996.2	942.4	1,041.8	1,021.1	1,027.2	758.8	724.6
Provision for Loan Losses	308.8	90.5	88.4	105.2	107.8	65.1	28.7
Non-Interest Income	509.5	493.6	573.6	438.2	342.8	273.0	243.0
Non-Interest Expense	1,023.6	885.6	912.1	913.9	803.1	567.9	560.4
Income Before Taxes	173.3	459.9	614.8	440.1	459.2	398.8	378.4
Net Income	⚀ 178.5	⚀ 328.4	⚀ 422.1	⚀ 301.8	⚀ 292.7	262.1	244.5
Average Shs. Outstg. (000)	251,716	249,570	255,647	258,279	257,061	194,269	201,493

BALANCE SHEET (IN MILLIONS):

Cash & Due from Banks	1,138.4	1,322.7	1,208.0	1,215.8	1,142.5	915.6	861.0
Securities Avail. for Sale	25.7	21.1	26.7	28.8	40.1	62.3	80.5
Total Loans & Leases	21,601.9	20,610.2	20,668.4	19,454.6	17,738.2	14,260.7	13,261.7
Allowance for Credit Losses	410.6	297.9	299.3	290.9	258.2	199.1	194.5
Net Loans & Leases	21,191.3	20,312.3	20,369.1	19,163.6	17,480.1	14,061.7	13,067.2
Total Assets	28,500.2	28,594.4	29,037.0	28,296.3	26,730.5	20,851.5	20,254.6
Total Deposits	20,187.3	19,777.2	19,792.6	19,722.8	17,983.7	13,385.9	12,636.6
Long-Term Obligations	2,739.3	3,338.1	3,951.8	3,247.3	2,686.0	1,556.3	2,103.0
Total Liabilities	26,083.7	26,233.3	26,854.6	26,147.5	24,705.1	19,340.0	18,735.7
Net Stockholders' Equity	2,416.4	2,366.0	2,182.4	2,134.6	2,025.4	1,511.5	1,518.9
Year-end Shs. Outstg. (000)	251,194	250,859	245,340	255,003	255,201	189,799	194,800

STATISTICAL RECORD:

Return on Equity %	7.4	13.9	19.3	14.1	14.4	17.3	16.1
Return on Assets %	0.6	1.1	1.5	1.1	1.1	1.3	1.2
Equity/Assets %	8.5	8.3	7.5	7.5	7.6	7.2	7.5
Non-Int. Exp./Tot. Inc. %	68.0	63.3	61.1	64.4	59.8	56.7	59.0
Price Range	19.28-12.63	21.82-12.52	30.89-19.49	28.55-18.18	29.21-17.08	19.72-13.97	15.76-9.98
P/E Ratio	27.2-17.8	16.5-9.5	18.7-11.8	24.5-15.6	25.6-15.0	14.6-10.3	12.9-8.2
Average Yield %	4.8	4.3	2.7	2.6	2.4	3.0	3.7

Statistics are as originally reported. Adj. for 10% stock div., 7/00, 7/99, 7/98, 7/97 & 7/96. ⚀ Incl. special chrg. of $100.0 mill., 2001; $50.0 mill., 2000; $96.8 mill., 1999; $90.0 mill., 1998; $47.2 mill., 1997.

OFFICERS:
T. E. Hoaglin, Chmn., Pres., C.E.O.
M. J. McMennamin, Vice-Chmn., C.F.O., Treas.

INVESTOR CONTACT: Laurie Counsel, Investor Relations Director, (614) 480-3878

PRINCIPAL OFFICE: Huntington Center, 41 South High Street, Columbus, OH 43287

TELEPHONE NUMBER: (614) 480-8300
FAX: (614) 480-3761
WEB: www.huntington.com

NO. OF EMPLOYEES: 8,552

SHAREHOLDERS: 30,744

ANNUAL MEETING: In April

INCORPORATED: MD, April, 1966

INSTITUTIONAL HOLDINGS:
No. of Institutions: 247
Shares Held: 75,714,489
% Held: 30.1

INDUSTRY: National commercial banks (SIC: 6021)

TRANSFER AGENT(S): Computershare Investor Services, Chicago, IL

ILLINOIS TOOL WORKS, INCORPORATED

YIELD 1.2%
P/E RATIO 27.6

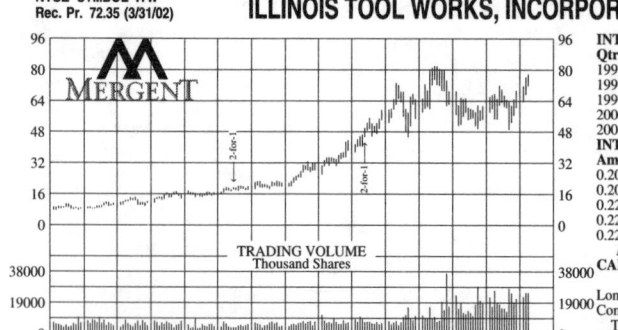

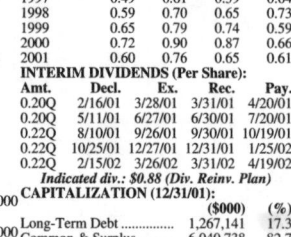

INTERIM EARNINGS (Per Share):

Qtr.	Mar.	June	Sept.	Dec.
1997	0.49	0.61	0.59	0.64
1998	0.59	0.70	0.65	0.73
1999	0.65	0.79	0.74	0.59
2000	0.72	0.90	0.87	0.66
2001	0.60	0.76	0.65	0.61

INTERIM DIVIDENDS (Per Share):

Amt.	Decl.	Ex.	Rec.	Pay.
0.20Q	2/16/01	3/28/01	3/31/01	4/20/01
0.20Q	5/11/01	6/27/01	6/30/01	7/20/01
0.22Q	8/10/01	9/26/01	9/30/01	10/19/01
0.22Q	10/25/01	12/27/01	12/31/01	1/25/02
0.22Q	2/15/02	3/26/02	3/31/02	4/19/02

Indicated div.: $0.88 (Div. Reinv. Plan)

CAPITALIZATION (12/31/01):

	($000)	(%)
Long-Term Debt	1,267,141	17.3
Common & Surplus	6,040,738	82.7
Total	7,307,879	100.0

DIVIDEND ACHIEVER STATUS:
Rank: 61   10-Year Growth Rate: 15.15%
Total Years of Dividend Growth: 39

TRADING VOLUME
Thousand Shares

*7 YEAR PRICE SCORE 103.9   *12 MONTH PRICE SCORE 117.2
*NYSE COMPOSITE INDEX=100

RECENT DEVELOPMENTS: For the year ended 12/31/01, income decreased 17.2% to $802.4 million. Results for 2001 and 2000 excluded income of $3.2 million and a loss of $11.5 million, respectively, from discontinued operations. Operating revenues slid 2.3% to $9.29 billion, reflecting weakness in many of ITW's North American and international end markets. Operating income decreased 17.2% to $1.31 billion. Results have been restated to reflect the pending divestiture of the Consumer Products segment.

PROSPECTS: On 12/14/01, the Company's directors authorized the divestiture of ITW's Consumer Products businesses. The Company feels that the consumer businesses are not a good fit for ITW. During the fourth quarter of 2001, ITW invested nearly $8.0 million in restructuring projects in order to reap the benefits of improving market conditions, which is expected to occur in the second half of 2002. Accordingly, ITW expects earnings for 2002 to be in the range of $2.95 to $3.25 per diluted share.

BUSINESS

ILLINOIS TOOL WORKS, INCORPORATED manufactures and markets a variety of products and systems. As of 12/14/01, ITW had more than 600 operations in 43 countries. The Engineered Products-North America segment (30.8% of net sales for 2001) and the Engineered Products-International segment (15.3%) manufacture short lead-time components and fasteners, and specialty products. The Specialty Systems-North America segment (35.1%) produces longer lead-time machinery and related consumables, and specialty equipment for applications. The Specialty Systems-International segment (17.3%) manufacture longer lead-time machinery and related consumables, and specialty equipment for industrial spray coating and other applications. The Leasing and Investment segment (1.5%) makes investments in mortgage-related assets, leveraged and direct financing leases of equipment, properties and property developments, and affordable housing. ITW acquired Premark International, Inc. in November 1999 for $3.40 billion.

ANNUAL FINANCIAL DATA

	12/31/01	12/31/00	12/31/99	12/31/98	12/31/97	12/31/96	12/31/95
Earnings Per Share	②2.62	3.15	①2.76	2.67	2.33	1.97	1.65
Cash Flow Per Share	3.88	4.50	3.89	3.50	3.07	2.68	2.29
Tang. Book Val. Per Share	10.82	9.64	9.27	8.59	8.14	6.80	5.94
Dividends Per Share	0.82	0.74	0.63	0.51	0.43	0.35	0.31
Dividend Payout %	31.3	23.5	22.8	19.1	18.5	17.8	18.8
INCOME STATEMENT (IN MILLIONS):							
Total Revenues	9,292.8	9,983.6	9,333.2	5,647.9	5,220.4	4,996.7	4,152.2
Costs & Expenses	7,600.4	8,006.8	7,584.5	4,356.8	4,107.8	4,017.9	3,373.7
Depreciation & Amort.	386.3	413.4	343.3	211.8	185.4	178.2	151.9
Operating Income	1,306.1	1,563.4	1,405.4	1,079.3	927.2	800.6	626.5
Net Interest Inc./(Exp.)	d68.1	d72.4	d67.5	d14.2	d19.4	d27.8	d31.6
Income Before Income Taxes	1,230.8	1,478.2	1,352.7	1,059.6	924.4	770.3	623.7
Income Taxes	428.4	520.2	511.6	386.8	337.4	284.0	236.1
Net Income	②802.4	958.0	①841.1	672.8	587.0	486.3	387.6
Cash Flow	1,188.8	1,371.4	1,184.4	884.6	772.3	664.5	539.5
Average Shs. Outstg. (000)	306,306	304,414	304,649	252,443	251,760	247,556	235,978
BALANCE SHEET (IN MILLIONS):							
Cash & Cash Equivalents	282.2	151.3	233.0	93.5	185.9	137.7	116.6
Total Current Assets	3,163.2	3,329.1	3,272.9	1,834.5	1,858.6	1,701.1	1,532.5
Net Property	1,633.7	1,722.5	1,633.9	987.5	884.1	808.3	694.9
Total Assets	9,822.3	9,603.5	9,060.3	6,118.2	5,394.8	4,806.2	3,613.1
Total Current Liabilities	1,518.2	1,817.6	2,045.4	1,222.0	1,157.9	1,219.3	850.9
Long-Term Obligations	1,267.1	1,549.0	1,360.7	947.0	854.3	818.9	615.6
Net Stockholders' Equity	6,040.7	5,401.0	4,815.4	3,338.0	2,806.5	2,396.0	1,924.2
Net Working Capital	1,645.1	1,371.4	1,227.6	612.5	700.8	481.8	681.6
Year-end Shs. Outstg. (000)	305,169	302,449	300,569	250,128	249,598	247,772	236,466
STATISTICAL RECORD:							
Operating Profit Margin %	14.1	15.7	15.1	19.1	17.8	16.0	15.1
Net Profit Margin %	8.6	9.6	9.0	11.9	11.2	9.7	9.3
Return on Equity %	13.3	17.7	17.5	20.2	20.9	20.3	20.1
Return on Assets %	8.2	10.0	9.3	11.0	10.9	10.1	10.7
Debt/Total Assets %	12.9	16.1	15.0	15.5	15.8	17.0	17.0
Price Range	71.99-49.15	69.00-49.50	82.00-58.13	73.19-45.19	59.50-37.38	43.63-25.94	32.75-19.88
P/E Ratio	27.5-18.8	21.9-15.7	29.7-21.1	27.4-16.9	25.5-16.0	22.2-13.2	19.9-12.1
Average Yield %	1.4	1.2	0.9	0.9	0.9	1.0	1.2

Statistics are as originally reported. Adj. for stk. splits: 2-for-1, 5/97. ① Incl. Premark International, Inc. merger-related costs of $81.0 mill. ② Excl. discont. oper. of $3.2 mill.

OFFICERS:
W. J. Farrell, Chmn., C.E.O.
F. S. Ptak, Vice-Chmn.
J. C. Kinney, Sr. V.P., C.F.O.
S. S. Hudnut, Sr. V.P., Sec., Gen. Couns.

INVESTOR CONTACT: Investor Relations, (847) 724-7500

PRINCIPAL OFFICE: 3600 West Lake Avenue, Glenview, IL 60025-5811

TELEPHONE NUMBER: (847) 724-7500
FAX: (847) 657-4261
WEB: www.itw.com

NO. OF EMPLOYEES: 52,000 (approx.)

SHAREHOLDERS: 15,330 (approx.)

ANNUAL MEETING: In May

INCORPORATED: DE, June, 1961

INSTITUTIONAL HOLDINGS:
No. of Institutions: 551
Shares Held: 233,528,145
% Held: 76.3

INDUSTRY: Plastics products, nec (SIC: 3089)

TRANSFER AGENT(S): Computershare Investor Service, L.L.C., Chicago, IL

COMERICA, INC.

	YIELD	3.1%
	P/E RATIO	16.1

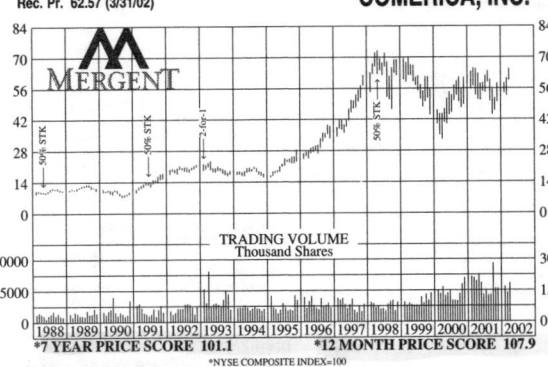

7 YEAR PRICE SCORE 101.1   **12 MONTH PRICE SCORE 107.9**
*NYSE COMPOSITE INDEX=100

INTERIM EARNINGS (Per Share):

Qtr.	Mar.	June	Sept.	Dec.
1997	0.73	0.77	0.82	0.85
1998	0.88	0.92	0.95	0.97
1999	0.98	1.03	1.05	1.08
2000	1.10	1.15	1.18	1.20
2001	0.50	1.13	1.14	1.11

INTERIM DIVIDENDS (Per Share):

Amt.	Decl.	Ex.	Rec.	Pay.
0.44Q	1/23/01	3/13/01	3/15/01	4/01/01
0.44Q	5/22/01	6/13/01	6/15/01	7/01/01
0.44Q	7/24/01	9/17/01	9/15/01	10/01/01
0.44Q	11/27/01	12/12/01	12/15/01	1/01/02
0.48Q	1/22/02	3/13/02	3/15/02	4/01/02

Indicated div.: $1.92 (Div. Reinv. Plan)

CAPITALIZATION (12/31/01):

	($000)	(%)
Total Deposits	37,570,379	78.5
Long-Term Debt	5,502,511	11.5
Common & Surplus	4,807,464	10.0
Total	47,880,354	100.0

DIVIDEND ACHIEVER STATUS:
Rank: 115   10-Year Growth Rate: 11.07%
Total Years of Dividend Growth: 18

RECENT DEVELOPMENTS: For the year ended 12/31/01, net income decreased 10.3% to $709.6 million from $790.7 million in the prior year. Earnings included a pre-tax net loss of $11.8 million in 2001 and a pre-tax net gain of $64.3 million in 2000 related to various items. Earnings for 2001 also included a pre-tax restructuring charge of $151.7 million. Net interest income grew 4.9% to $2.10 billion.

PROSPECTS: For 2002, earnings per share are expected to range from $4.90 to $5.05, including the benefit from a change in accounting for goodwill of $0.16. Non-performing assets are anticipated to be in the range of 1.50% to 1.80% of loans and other real estate. Net charge-offs are expected to be 0.50% to 0.60% of loans in the first half of 2002 and 0.40% to 0.50% of loans for the full year.

BUSINESS

COMERICA, INC. is a bank holding company headquartered in Detroit, Michigan. The Company, as of 12/31/01, had assets of $50.73 billion and total deposits of $37.57 billion. CMA operates banking subsidiaries in Michigan, Texas and California, banking operations in Florida, and businesses in several other states. CMA is a diversified financial services provider, offering a broad range of financial products and services for businesses and individuals. CMA has an investment services affiliate, Munder Capital Management, and operates banking subsidiaries in Canada and Mexico. On 1/30/01, CMA acquired Imperial Bancorp in a transaction valued at $1.30 billion.

ANNUAL FINANCIAL DATA

	12/31/01	12/31/00	12/31/99	12/31/98	12/31/97	12/31/96	12/31/95
Earnings Per Share	② ③ 3.88	② 4.63	4.14	① 3.72	3.19	① 2.37	2.36
Tang. Book Val. Per Share	27.15	23.94	20.60	17.94	16.02	14.77	15.17
Dividends Per Share	1.72	1.56	1.40	1.25	1.12	0.99	0.89
Dividend Payout %	44.3	33.7	33.8	33.5	35.1	41.7	37.9
INCOME STATEMENT (IN MILLIONS):							
Total Interest Income	3,393.5	3,261.6	2,672.7	2,616.8	2,647.4	2,562.8	2,613.9
Total Interest Expense	1,291.2	1,602.8	1,125.6	1,155.5	1,204.6	1,150.5	1,314.0
Net Interest Income	2,102.3	1,658.9	1,547.1	1,461.3	1,442.8	1,412.3	1,299.9
Provision for Loan Losses	236.0	145.0	114.0	113.0	146.0	114.0	86.5
Non-Interest Income	803.3	825.9	716.9	603.1	528.0	507.0	498.7
Non-Interest Expense	1,559.0	1,188.4	1,117.0	1,020.0	1,008.0	1,159.0	1,086.4
Income Before Taxes	1,110.6	1,151.4	1,033.1	931.4	816.7	646.2	625.7
Net Income	② ③ 709.6	② 749.3	672.6	① 607.1	530.5	① 417.2	413.4
Average Shs. Outstg. (000)	177,665	156,398	158,397	158,757	161,040	172,281	175,341
BALANCE SHEET (IN MILLIONS):							
Cash & Due from Banks	1,925.3	1,496.7	1,202.0	1,773.1	1,927.1	1,901.8	2,028.4
Securities Avail. for Sale	5,369.5	2,843.1	3,352.4	2,821.8	4,208.9	4,800.0	6,870.0
Total Loans & Leases	41,196.3	36,060.3	32,693.3	30,604.9	28,895.0	26,206.7	24,442.3
Allowance for Credit Losses	655.1	538.1	476.5	452.4	424.1	367.2	341.3
Net Loans & Leases	40,541.2	35,522.2	32,216.8	30,152.5	28,470.9	25,839.5	24,100.9
Total Assets	50,732.0	41,985.2	38,653.3	36,600.8	36,292.4	34,102.5	35,469.9
Total Deposits	37,570.4	27,168.0	23,291.4	24,313.1	22,586.3	22,367.2	23,167.2
Long-Term Obligations	5,502.5	8,088.7	8,579.9	5,282.3	7,286.4	4,241.8	4,644.4
Total Liabilities	45,924.5	37,977.9	35,178.7	33,554.2	33,530.6	31,950.5	32,862.1
Net Stockholders' Equity	4,807.5	4,007.3	3,474.6	3,046.6	2,761.8	2,615.6	2,607.7
Year-end Shs. Outstg. (000)	177,075	156,944	156,518	155,881	156,815	160,211	171,906
STATISTICAL RECORD:							
Return on Equity %	14.8	18.7	19.4	19.9	19.2	15.9	15.9
Return on Assets %	1.4	1.8	1.7	1.7	1.5	1.2	1.2
Equity/Assets %	9.5	9.5	9.0	8.3	7.6	7.7	7.4
Non-Int. Exp./Tot. Inc. %	53.7	47.8	49.3	49.4	51.1	60.4	60.4
Price Range	65.15-44.02	61.13-32.94	70.00-44.00	73.00-46.50	61.88-34.17	39.58-24.17	28.50-16.08
P/E Ratio	16.8-11.3	13.2-7.1	16.9-10.6	19.6-12.5	19.4-10.7	16.7-10.2	12.1-6.8
Average Yield %	3.2	3.3	2.5	2.1	2.3	3.1	4.0

Statistics are as originally reported. Adj. for 50% stk. div., 4/98. ① Incl. merger-related or restructuring charges: $6.8 mill., 1998; $90.0 mill., 1996; $22.0 mill. ② Incl. a pre-tax net gain on the sales of businesses of $31.2 mill., 2001; $47.6 mill., 2000. ③ Incl. pre-tax restr. chrg. of $151.7 mill.

OFFICERS:
E. A. Miller, Chmn.
R. W. Babb Jr., Vice-Chmn., Pres., C.E.O.,
C.F.O.

INVESTOR CONTACT: Judith S. Love,
Investor Relations, (313) 222-2840

PRINCIPAL OFFICE: Comerica Tower at
Detroit Center, Detroit, MI 48226-3509

TELEPHONE NUMBER: (313) 222-9743
FAX: (313) 222-6091
WEB: www.comerica.com

NO. OF EMPLOYEES: 10,307 full-time; 1,485
part-time

SHAREHOLDERS: 16,915 (approx.)

ANNUAL MEETING: In May

INCORPORATED: DE, 1973

INSTITUTIONAL HOLDINGS:
No. of Institutions: 382
Shares Held: 107,964,333
% Held: 61.0

INDUSTRY: National commercial banks
(SIC: 6021)

TRANSFER AGENT(S): Wells Fargo
Shareowner Services, South St. Paul, MN

COLGATE-PALMOLIVE COMPANY

YIELD	1.3%
P/E RATIO	31.1

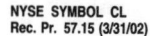

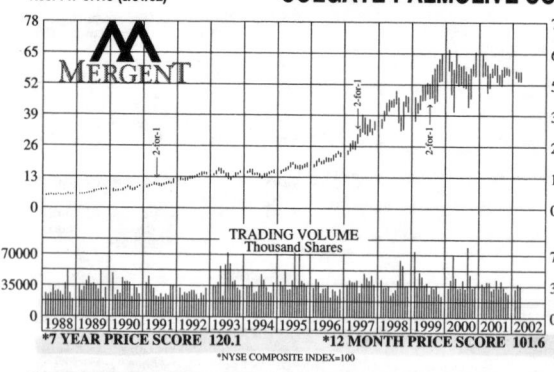

TRADING VOLUME
Thousand Shares

| 1988 | 1989 | 1990 | 1991 | 1992 | 1993 | 1994 | 1995 | 1996 | 1997 | 1998 | 1999 | 2000 | 2001 | 2002 |

*7 YEAR PRICE SCORE 120.1 ***12 MONTH PRICE SCORE 101.6**
*NYSE COMPOSITE INDEX=100

INTERIM EARNINGS (Per Share):

Qtr.	Mar.	June	Sept.	Dec.
1997	0.28	0.29	0.31	0.32
1998	0.30	0.31	0.33	0.37
1999	0.33	0.36	0.38	0.41
2000	0.38	0.42	0.44	0.46
2001	0.44	0.42	0.49	0.49

INTERIM DIVIDENDS (Per Share):

Amt.	Decl.	Ex.	Rec.	Pay.
0.18Q	7/12/01	7/24/01	7/26/01	8/15/01
0.18Q	10/11/01	10/24/01	10/26/01	11/15/01
0.18Q	1/10/02	1/23/02	1/25/02	2/15/02
0.18Q	3/14/02	4/24/02	4/26/02	5/15/02

Indicated div.: $0.72 (Div. Reinv. Plan)

CAPITALIZATION (12/31/01):

	($000)	(%)
Long-Term Debt	2,812,000	67.9
Deferred Income Tax	480,600	11.6
Preferred Stock...............	341,300	8.2
Common & Surplus	505,100	12.2
Total	4,139,000	100.0

DIVIDEND ACHIEVER STATUS:
Rank: 132 10-Year Growth Rate: 10.22%
Total Years of Dividend Growth: 39

RECENT DEVELOPMENTS: For the year ended 12/31/01, net income rose 7.8% to $1.15 billion from $1.06 billion in the previous year. Earnings for 2001 included charges of $15.0 million related to the Kmart bankruptcy and a write-down of assets in Argentina. Net sales inched up 0.7% to $9.43 billion from $9.36 billion in the previous year. Sales benefited from strong unit volume growth, partially offset by unfavorable currency translation.

PROSPECTS: Looking ahead, the Company expects strong volume growth along with gross profit margin increases to fuel projects and double-digit earnings per share growth in 2002. Future results should benefit from global market share increases across key categories including toothpaste, toothbrushes, dishwashing liquid, deodorants, bar and liquid soap, body wash, all-purpose cleaners, fabric softeners and pet nutrition.

BUSINESS

COLGATE-PALMOLIVE COMPANY is a consumer products company that markets its products in over 200 countries. The Company operates in two distinct product segments. Oral, Personal and Household Care accounted for 87.0% of 2001 revenues and consists of tooth pastes, toothbrushes, soaps, shampoos, baby products, deodorants, detergents, cleaners, shave products and other similar items under brand names including COLGATE, PALMOLIVE, MENNEN, SOFT SOAP, IRISH SPRINGS, PROTEX, SORRISO, KOLYNOS, AJAX, AXION, SOUPLINE, SUAVITEL and FAB. Pet Nutrition, 13.0%, consists of pet food products manufactured and marketed by Hill's Pet Nutrition. Hill's markets pet foods primarily under SCIENCE DIET, which is sold by authorized pet supply retailers, breeders and veterinarians for every day nutritional needs, and PRESCRIPTION DIET for dogs and cats with disease conditions.

ANNUAL FINANCIAL DATA

	12/31/01	12/31/00	12/31/99	12/31/98	12/31/97	12/31/96	12/31/95
Earnings Per Share	① 1.89	1.70	1.47	1.31	1.14	1.05	① 0.26
Cash Flow Per Share	2.44	2.23	2.00	1.82	1.63	1.62	0.81
Dividends Per Share	0.68	0.63	0.59	0.55	0.53	0.47	0.44
Dividend Payout %	35.7	37.1	40.1	42.1	46.7	44.8	169.2
INCOME STATEMENT (IN MILLIONS):							
Total Revenues	9,427.8	9,357.9	9,118.2	8,971.6	9,056.7	8,749.0	8,358.2
Costs & Expenses	7,162.3	7,227.3	7,138.2	7,157.1	7,378.6	7,186.9	7,392.9
Depreciation & Amort.	336.2	337.8	340.2	330.3	319.9	316.3	300.3
Operating Income	1,929.3	1,792.8	1,639.8	1,484.2	1,358.2	1,245.8	665.0
Net Interest Inc./(Exp.)	d166.1	d173.3	d171.6	d172.9	d183.5	d197.4	d205.4
Income Before Income Taxes	1,668.7	1,567.2	1,394.6	1,250.1	1,102.3	954.6	363.5
Income Taxes	522.1	503.4	457.3	401.5	361.9	319.6	191.5
Net Income	① 1,146.6	1,063.8	937.3	848.6	740.4	635.0	① 172.0
Cash Flow	1,461.1	1,380.9	1,256.5	1,158.0	1,039.2	929.9	450.7
Average Shs. Outstg. (000)	607,700	627,300	638,800	648,400	650,200	586,400	580,800
BALANCE SHEET (IN MILLIONS):							
Cash & Cash Equivalents	172.7	212.5	235.2	194.5	205.3	307.8	256.6
Total Current Assets	2,203.4	2,347.2	2,354.8	2,244.9	2,196.5	2,372.3	2,360.2
Net Property	2,513.5	2,528.3	2,551.1	2,589.2	2,441.0	2,428.9	2,155.2
Total Assets	6,984.8	7,252.3	7,423.1	7,685.2	7,538.7	7,901.5	7,642.3
Total Current Liabilities	2,123.5	2,244.1	2,273.5	2,114.4	1,959.5	1,904.3	1,753.1
Long-Term Obligations	2,812.0	2,536.9	2,243.3	2,300.6	2,340.3	2,786.8	2,992.0
Net Stockholders' Equity	846.4	1,468.1	1,833.7	2,085.6	2,178.6	2,034.1	1,679.8
Net Working Capital	79.9	103.1	81.3	130.5	237.0	468.0	607.1
Year-end Shs. Outstg. (000)	550,700	566,656	578,863	585,420	591,280	588,536	583,200
STATISTICAL RECORD:							
Operating Profit Margin %	20.5	19.2	18.0	16.5	15.0	14.2	8.0
Net Profit Margin %	12.2	11.4	10.3	9.5	8.2	7.3	2.1
Return on Equity %	135.5	72.5	51.1	40.7	34.0	31.2	10.2
Return on Assets %	16.4	14.7	12.6	11.0	9.8	8.0	2.3
Debt/Total Assets %	40.3	35.0	30.2	29.9	31.0	35.3	39.2
Price Range	64.75-48.50	66.75-40.50	65.00-36.56	49.44-32.53	39.34-22.50	24.13-17.22	19.34-14.50
P/E Ratio	34.3-25.7	39.3-23.8	44.2-24.9	37.9-24.9	34.7-19.8	23.0-16.4	74.4-55.7
Average Yield %	1.2	1.2	1.2	1.3	1.7	2.3	2.6

Statistics are as originally reported. Adj. for stk. splits: 2-for-1, 6/99 & 5/97 ① Incl. non-recurr. chrg. $15.0 mill., 12/01; $369.2 mill., 12/95; $5.2 mill.

OFFICERS:
R. Mark, Chmn., C.E.O.
W. S. Shanahan, Pres., C.O.O.

INVESTOR CONTACT: Bina Thompson, Inv. Rel., (212) 310-3072

PRINCIPAL OFFICE: 300 Park Ave., New York, NY 10022-7499

TELEPHONE NUMBER: (212) 310-2000
FAX: (212) 310-3284
WEB: www.colgate.com

NO. OF EMPLOYEES: 38,500 (avg.)

SHAREHOLDERS: 40,900 (com.); 224 (pfd.)

ANNUAL MEETING: In May

INCORPORATED: DE, July, 1923

INSTITUTIONAL HOLDINGS:
No. of Institutions: 718
Shares Held: 374,362,658
% Held: 67.9

INDUSTRY: Toilet preparations (SIC: 2844)

TRANSFER AGENT(S): First Chicago Trust Company of New York, Jersey City, NJ

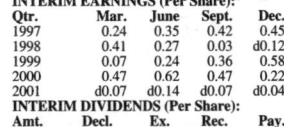

NASDAQ SYMBOL COHU
Rec. Pr. 28.49 (3/31/02)

COHU, INC.

YIELD 0.7%
P/E RATIO ...

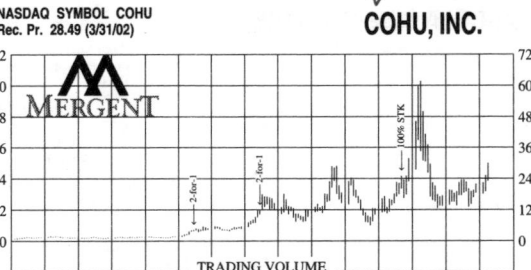

TRADING VOLUME
Thousand Shares

| 1988 | 1989 | 1990 | 1991 | 1992 | 1993 | 1994 | 1995 | 1996 | 1997 | 1998 | 1999 | 2000 | 2001 | 2002 |

*7 YEAR PRICE SCORE 98.1   ***12 MONTH PRICE SCORE 123.7**

*NYSE COMPOSITE INDEX=100

INTERIM EARNINGS (Per Share):

Qtr.	Mar.	June	Sept.	Dec.
1997	0.24	0.35	0.42	0.45
1998	0.41	0.27	0.03	d0.12
1999	0.07	0.24	0.36	0.58
2000	0.47	0.62	0.47	0.22
2001	d0.07	d0.14	d0.07	d0.04

INTERIM DIVIDENDS (Per Share):

Amt.	Decl.	Ex.	Rec.	Pay.
0.05Q	2/01/01	3/15/01	3/19/01	4/27/01
0.05Q	5/15/01	6/20/01	6/22/01	8/03/01
0.05Q	7/25/01	9/12/01	9/14/01	11/02/01
0.05Q	10/25/01	12/05/01	12/07/01	1/11/02
0.05Q	1/30/02	3/14/02	3/18/02	4/30/02

Indicated div.: $0.20

CAPITALIZATION (12/31/01):

	($000)	(%)
Deferred Income Tax	4,300	2.2
Common & Surplus	190,531	97.8
Total	194,831	100.0

DIVIDEND ACHIEVER STATUS:
Rank: 39   10-Year Growth Rate: 17.46%
Total Years of Dividend Growth: 14

RECENT DEVELOPMENTS: For the year ended 12/31/01, the Company reported a net loss of $6.5 million compared with income of $37.0 million, before an after-tax accounting charge of $3.3 million, in 2000. Results for 2001 included a gain of $7.7 million for the sale of facilities and an acquired in-process research and development charge of $2.1 million. Net sales fell 56.3% to $126.6 million versus $289.6 million in the prior year. Sales for 2001 included 75.0% from semiconductor test handling equipment, 17.0% from

television cameras and 8.0% from metal detection and microwave communications equipment. Loss from operations was $16.0 million compared with operating income of $50.3 million a year earlier. New orders for 2001 were $113.9 million compared to $258.6 million in 2000. The Company's backlog at 12/31/01 was $38.2 million. Overall results were negatively affected by the steep decline in semiconductor equipment spending.

BUSINESS

COHU, INC. operates through two chief business segments. The semiconductor equipment segment, operated under the Company's wholly-owned subsidiary Delta Design, Inc., designs, manufactures and sells semiconductor test handling equipment to semiconductor manufacturers throughout the world. The television camera segment (the Electronics Division) designs, manufactures and sells closed circuit television cameras and systems to original equipment manufacturers, contractors and government agencies. The Company's other operating segments include Fisher Research Laboratory, Inc., a metal detection business, and Broadcast Microwave Services, Inc., a microwave radio equipment company. Revenues for 2001 were derived: semiconductor equipment, 75.0%; television cameras, 17.0%; and other, 8.0%.

ANNUAL FINANCIAL DATA

	12/31/01	12/31/00	12/31/99	12/31/98	12/31/97	12/31/96	12/31/95
Earnings Per Share	d0.32	1.76	1.26	0.58	1.47	1.25	1.23
Cash Flow Per Share	d0.09	1.93	1.43	0.72	1.57	1.34	1.33
Tang. Book Val. Per Share	8.83	9.71	8.10	6.97	6.49	5.02	3.82
Dividends Per Share	0.20	0.195	0.17	0.15	0.12	0.10	0.07
Dividend Payout %	...	11.1	13.9	25.9	7.8	7.6	5.9
INCOME STATEMENT (IN THOUSANDS):							
Total Revenues	126,550	289,564	208,780	171,511	187,756	159,353	178,759
Costs & Expenses	137,921	235,672	170,831	156,135	142,720	120,821	138,645
Depreciation & Amort.	4,623	3,585	3,294	2,799	2,148	1,653	1,884
Operating Income	d15,994	50,307	34,655	12,577	42,888	36,879	38,230
Net Interest Inc./(Exp.)	4,427	5,731	4,271	3,469	2,999	1,960	692
Income Before Income Taxes	d11,567	56,038	38,926	16,046	45,887	38,839	38,922
Income Taxes	cr5,100	19,000	13,000	4,400	16,700	14,600	15,300
Net Income	d6,467	37,038	25,926	11,646	29,187	24,239	23,622
Cash Flow	d1,844	40,623	29,220	14,445	31,335	25,892	25,506
Average Shs. Outstg.	20,434	21,048	20,502	19,940	19,900	19,354	19,168
BALANCE SHEET (IN THOUSANDS):							
Cash & Cash Equivalents	89,967	92,587	81,600	86,703	53,550	52,986	28,874
Total Current Assets	176,423	192,716	202,769	143,398	141,530	98,585	88,076
Net Property	35,849	38,117	17,016	17,613	18,949	16,811	13,171
Total Assets	221,559	231,495	220,733	162,231	162,892	117,926	103,934
Total Current Liabilities	25,619	32,133	56,719	23,255	35,329	20,582	30,848
Net Stockholders' Equity	190,531	197,840	162,356	137,463	126,211	96,272	72,029
Net Working Capital	150,804	160,583	146,050	120,143	106,201	78,003	57,228
Year-end Shs. Outstg.	20,543	20,313	19,938	19,558	19,098	18,682	18,184
STATISTICAL RECORD:							
Operating Profit Margin %	...	17.4	16.6	7.3	22.8	23.1	21.4
Net Profit Margin %	...	12.8	12.4	6.8	15.5	15.2	13.2
Return on Equity %	...	18.7	16.0	8.5	23.1	25.2	32.8
Return on Assets %	...	16.0	11.7	7.2	17.9	20.6	22.7
Price Range	23.55-13.05	61.75-12.63	31.75-10.56	24.31-6.00	28.88-10.75	18.13-7.38	18.00-5.44
P/E Ratio	...	35.1-7.2	25.2-8.4	41.9-10.3	19.7-7.3	14.5-5.9	14.6-4.4
Average Yield %	1.1	0.5	0.8	1.0	0.6	0.7	0.6

Statistics are as originally reported. Adj. for stk. splits: 2-for-1, 9/99; 6/95.

OFFICERS:
C. A. Schwan, Chmn.
J. A. Donahue, Pres., C.E.O.
J. H. Allen, V.P. Fin., C.F.O., Sec.

INVESTOR CONTACT: John H. Allen, V.P.--Fin., C.F.O. and Sec., (858) 541-5194

PRINCIPAL OFFICE: 12367 Crothwaite Circle, Poway, CA 92064-6817

TELEPHONE NUMBER: (858) 848-8100
FAX: (858) 277-0221
WEB: www.cohu.com

NO. OF EMPLOYEES: 930 (approx.)

SHAREHOLDERS: 1,096

ANNUAL MEETING: N/A

INCORPORATED: DE, Jan., 1957

INSTITUTIONAL HOLDINGS:
No. of Institutions: 83
Shares Held: 10,496,848
% Held: 51.0

INDUSTRY: Instruments to measure electricity (SIC: 3825)

TRANSFER AGENT(S): Mellon Investor Services, Ridgefield Park, NJ

NYSE SYMBOL KO
Rec. Pr. 52.26 (3/31/02)

COCA-COLA COMPANY (THE)

YIELD 1.5%
P/E RATIO 32.7

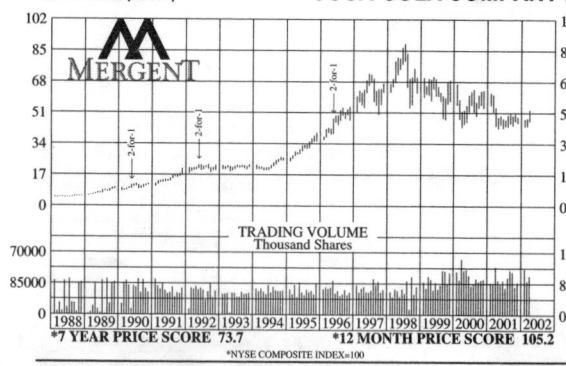

*7 YEAR PRICE SCORE 73.7   *12 MONTH PRICE SCORE 105.2
*NYSE COMPOSITE INDEX=100

INTERIM EARNINGS (Per Share):

Qtr.	Mar.	June	Sept.	Dec.
1997	0.40	0.53	0.41	0.33
1998	0.35	0.48	0.36	0.24
1999	0.30	0.38	0.32	d0.02
2000	d0.02	0.37	0.43	0.10
2001	0.35	0.45	0.43	0.37

INTERIM DIVIDENDS (Per Share):

Amt.	Decl.	Ex.	Rec.	Pay.
0.18Q	7/19/01	9/17/01	9/15/01	10/01/01
0.18Q	10/17/01	11/28/01	12/01/01	12/15/01
0.20Q	2/21/02	3/13/02	3/15/02	4/01/02
0.20Q	4/17/02	6/12/02	6/15/02	7/01/02

Indicated div.: $0.80 (Div. Reinv. Plan)

CAPITALIZATION (12/31/01):

	($000)	(%)
Long-Term Debt	1,219,000	9.4
Deferred Income Tax	442,000	3.4
Common & Surplus	11,366,000	87.2
Total	13,027,000	100.0

DIVIDEND ACHIEVER STATUS:
Rank: 105   10-Year Growth Rate: 11.61%
Total Years of Dividend Growth: 39

RECENT DEVELOPMENTS: For the year ended 12/31/01, income was $3.98 billion, before an accounting change charge of $10.0 million, versus net income of $2.18 billion the previous year. Results for 2001 included a non-recurring pre-tax gain of $91.0 million. Results for 2000 included pre-tax charges of $850.0 million for an organizational realignment, $188.0 million related to a lawsuit settlement, and $405.0 million primarily for asset writedowns. Net operating revenues rose 1.0% to $20.09 billion.

PROSPECTS: During 2002, KO will continue to implement its strategic priorities, which include accelerating carbonated soft drink growth, led by Coca-Cola; selectively broadening KO's beverage portfolio to generate profitable growth; and increasing system profitability and capability to grow together with the Company's bottling partners. One key challenge for KO in 2002 will be its ability to sustain the torrid 2001 growth rates of 62.0%, 18.0% and 13.0% that were experienced in waters, juices and juice drinks, and sports drinks, respectively.

BUSINESS

THE COCA-COLA COMPANY is engaged in the manufacturing, distributing and marketing of soft drink concentrates and syrups. Principal beverage products are: COCA-COLA, COCA-COLA CLASSIC, DIET COKE, CHERRY COKE, FANTA, SPRITE, MR. PIBB, MELLO YELLOW, BARQ'S ROOT BEER, POWERADE, FRUITOPIA, DASANI plus other assorted diet and caffeine-free versions. The Minute Maid Company produces, juice and juice-drink products. Brands include MINUTE MAID, FIVE ALIVE, BRIGHT & EARLY, BACARDI brand tropical fruit mixers and HI-C. Coca-Cola Nestle Refreshments, KO's joint venture with Nestle S.A., markets ready-to-drink teas and coffees in certain countries. In 2001, sales were derived: North America, 37.4%; Europe, Eurasia & Middle East, 22.4%; Asia, 24.9%; Latin America, 11.3%; Africa, 3.1%; and corporate, 0.9%. As of 12/31/01, KO held an approximate 38.0% interest in Coca-Cola Enterprises, Inc.

ANNUAL FINANCIAL DATA

	12/31/01	12/31/00	12/31/99	12/31/98	12/31/97	12/31/96	12/31/95
Earnings Per Share	④ 1.60	③ 0.88	② 0.98	1.42	① 1.64	1.40	1.18
Cash Flow Per Share	1.92	1.19	1.30	1.67	1.89	1.59	1.36
Tang. Book Val. Per Share	3.53	2.98	3.06	3.19	2.66	2.18	1.78
Dividends Per Share	0.72	0.68	0.64	0.60	0.56	0.50	0.44
Dividend Payout %	45.0	77.3	65.3	42.3	34.1	35.7	37.3

INCOME STATEMENT (IN MILLIONS):

	12/31/01	12/31/00	12/31/99	12/31/98	12/31/97	12/31/96	12/31/95
Total Revenues	20,092.0	20,458.0	19,805.0	18,813.0	18,868.0	18,546.0	18,018.0
Costs & Expenses	13,937.0	15,994.0	15,031.0	13,201.0	13,241.0	14,152.0	13,538.0
Depreciation & Amort.	803.0	773.0	792.0	645.0	626.0	479.0	454.0
Operating Income	5,352.0	3,691.0	3,982.0	4,967.0	⑤ 5,001.0	3,915.0	4,026.0
Net Interest Inc./(Exp.)	36.0	d102.0	d77.0	d58.0	d47.0	d48.0	d27.0
Income Before Income Taxes	5,670.0	3,399.0	3,819.0	5,198.0	6,055.0	4,596.0	4,328.0
Income Taxes	1,691.0	1,222.0	1,388.0	1,665.0	1,926.0	1,104.0	1,342.0
Net Income	④ 3,979.0	③ 2,177.0	② 2,431.0	3,533.0	① 4,129.0	3,492.0	2,986.0
Cash Flow	4,782.0	2,950.0	3,223.0	4,178.0	4,755.0	3,971.0	3,440.0
Average Shs. Outstg. (000)	2,487,000	2,487,000	2,487,000	2,496,000	2,515,000	2,494,000	2,524,000

BALANCE SHEET (IN MILLIONS):

	12/31/01	12/31/00	12/31/99	12/31/98	12/31/97	12/31/96	12/31/95
Cash & Cash Equivalents	1,934.0	1,892.0	1,812.0	1,807.0	1,843.0	1,658.0	1,315.0
Total Current Assets	7,171.0	6,620.0	6,480.0	6,380.0	5,969.0	5,910.0	5,450.0
Net Property	4,453.0	4,168.0	4,267.0	3,669.0	3,743.0	3,550.0	4,336.0
Total Assets	22,417.0	20,834.0	21,623.0	19,145.0	16,940.0	16,161.0	15,041.0
Total Current Liabilities	8,429.0	9,321.0	9,856.0	8,640.0	7,379.0	7,406.0	7,348.0
Long-Term Obligations	1,219.0	835.0	854.0	687.0	801.0	1,116.0	1,141.0
Net Stockholders' Equity	11,366.0	9,316.0	9,513.0	8,403.0	7,311.0	6,156.0	5,392.0
Net Working Capital	d1,258.0	d2,701.0	d3,376.0	d2,260.0	d1,410.0	d1,496.0	d1,898.0
Year-end Shs. Outstg. (000)	2,486,227	2,484,761	2,471,575	2,466,000	2,471,000	2,481,000	2,504,589

STATISTICAL RECORD:

	12/31/01	12/31/00	12/31/99	12/31/98	12/31/97	12/31/96	12/31/95
Operating Profit Margin %	26.6	18.0	20.1	26.4	26.5	21.1	22.3
Net Profit Margin %	19.8	10.6	12.3	18.8	21.9	18.8	16.6
Return on Equity %	35.0	23.4	25.6	42.0	56.5	56.7	55.4
Return on Assets %	17.7	10.4	11.2	18.5	24.4	21.6	19.9
Debt/Total Assets %	5.4	4.0	3.9	3.6	4.7	6.9	7.6
Price Range	62.19-42.37	66.88-42.88	70.88-47.31	88.94-53.63	72.63-50.00	54.25-36.06	40.19-24.38
P/E Ratio	38.9-26.5	76.0-48.7	72.3-48.3	62.6-37.8	44.3-30.5	38.7-25.8	34.1-20.7
Average Yield %	1.4	1.2	1.1	0.8	0.9	1.1	1.4

Statistics are as originally reported. Adj. for 2-for-1 stk. split, 5/96. ① Incl. non-recurr. pre-tax net gain of $290.0 mill. ② Incl. non-recurr. chrg. of $813.0 mill. ③ Incl. non-recurr. chrgs. of $1.04 bill. ($0.29/sh.) & asset writedown of $405.0 mill. ($0.16/sh.) ④ Incl. non-recurr. pre-tax gain of $91.0 mill.; bef. acctg. chge. chrg. of $10.0 mill.

OFFICERS:
D. N. Daft, Chmn., C.E.O.
B. G. Dyson, Vice-Chmn., C.O.O.
G. P. Fayard, Sr. V.P., C.F.O.

INVESTOR CONTACT: Institutional Investor Inquires, (404) 676-5766

PRINCIPAL OFFICE: One Coca-Cola Plaza, Atlanta, GA 30313

TELEPHONE NUMBER: (404) 676-2121
FAX: (404) 676-6792
WEB: www.coca-cola.com

NO. OF EMPLOYEES: 38,000 (approx.)

SHAREHOLDERS: 371,794 (record)

ANNUAL MEETING: In Apr.

INCORPORATED: DE, Sept., 1919

INSTITUTIONAL HOLDINGS:
No. of Institutions: 982
Shares Held: 1,360,220,740
% Held: 54.7

INDUSTRY: Bottled and canned soft drinks (SIC: 2086)

TRANSFER AGENT(S): EquiServe, Jersey City, NJ

CLOROX COMPANY (THE)

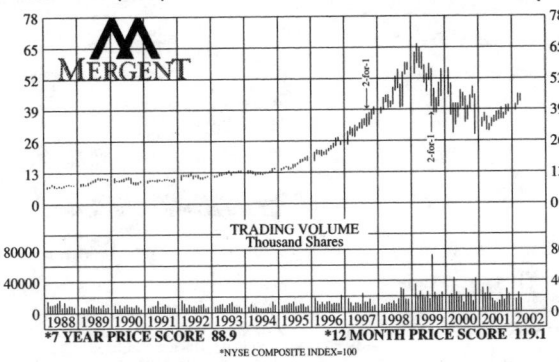

TRADING VOLUME
Thousand Shares

*7 YEAR PRICE SCORE 88.9   *12 MONTH PRICE SCORE 119.1
*NYSE COMPOSITE INDEX=100

INTERIM EARNINGS (Per Share):

Qtr.	Sept.	Dec.	Mar.	June
1997-98	0.36	0.24	0.36	0.47
1998-99	0.41	0.28	0.09	0.21
1999-00	0.36	0.32	0.44	0.52
2000-01	0.42	0.27	0.33	0.34
2001-02	0.45	0.22	...	...

INTERIM DIVIDENDS (Per Share):

Amt.	Decl.	Ex.	Rec.	Pay.
0.21Q	3/21/01	4/26/01	4/30/01	5/15/01
0.21Q	7/18/01	7/30/01	8/01/01	8/15/01
0.21Q	9/19/01	10/29/01	10/31/01	11/15/01
0.21Q	1/16/02	1/29/02	1/31/02	2/15/02
0.21Q	3/20/02	4/26/02	4/30/02	5/15/02

Indicated div.: $0.84 (Div. Reinv. Plan)

CAPITALIZATION (6/30/01):

	($000)	(%)
Long-Term Debt	685,000	25.1
Deferred Income Tax	147,000	5.4
Common & Surplus	1,900,000	69.5
Total	2,732,000	100.0

DIVIDEND ACHIEVER STATUS:
Rank: 172   10-Year Growth Rate: 8.18%
Total Years of Dividend Growth: 25

RECENT DEVELOPMENTS: For the quarter ended 12/31/01, net earnings dropped 20.3% to $51.0 million from $64.0 million in the prior-year period. Earnings for 2001 included restructuring and asset impairment charges of $66.0 million. Net sales rose 2.9% to $901.0 million from $876.0 million in 2000. North American household product sales improved 3.0%, while specialty product sales increased 5.0%. Latin America and other household product sales inched up 1.0%, while pre-tax profit plummeted 184.0%.

PROSPECTS: CLX is benefiting from gross margin improvements and recent cost-saving projects. Earnings are also being boosted by continued strength in the Company's GLAD and cat litter businesses and record second-quarter KINGSFORD charcoal and ARMOR ALL auto care shipments. Looking ahead, CLX expects fiscal-year sales and volume growth in the low- to mid-single digits, while earnings before one-time items are expected to be $1.84 to $1.87 a share.

BUSINESS

THE CLOROX COMPANY is a manufacturer and marketer of household products, both domestic and international, and products for institutional markets. CLX operates in four business segments: U.S. Home Care and Cleaning, U.S. Specialty Products, U.S. Food, Food Preparation and Storage, and International. The U.S. Home Care and Cleaning segment include products such as SOFT SCRUB, CLOROX TUFFY FORMULA 409, LIQUID PLUMR, PINE-SOL, TILEX, and SOS. The U.S. Specialty Products segment include brand names such as ARMOR ALL, STP and KINGSFORD CHARCOAL. Products in the U.S. Food, Food Preparation and Storage segment include HIDDEN VALLEY dressings, BRITA, GLAD, and GLADWARE businesses and SCOOP AWAY, JONNY CAT and FRESH STEP cat litters. The International segment, which includes CLX's overseas operations, exports and Puerto Rico, primarily focuses on the laundry, household cleaning and insecticide categories. On 1/29/99, the Company acquired First Brands Corp. for $2.00 billion.

ANNUAL FINANCIAL DATA

	6/30/01	6/30/00	6/30/99	6/30/98	6/30/97	6/30/96	6/30/95
Earnings Per Share	①②1.36	②1.64	②1.03	1.41	1.21	1.07	0.95
Cash Flow Per Share	2.30	2.48	1.87	2.06	1.82	1.63	1.43
Tang. Book Val. Per Share	1.38	1.10	0.31	...	...	1.11	1.68
Dividends Per Share	0.84	0.82	0.76	0.68	0.61	0.56	0.51
Dividend Payout %	61.8	50.0	73.8	48.2	50.6	51.9	53.4

INCOME STATEMENT (IN MILLIONS):

Total Revenues	3,903.0	4,083.0	4,003.0	2,741.3	2,532.7	2,217.8	1,984.2
Costs & Expenses	3,067.0	3,138.0	3,250.0	2,065.6	1,939.9	1,686.3	1,521.2
Depreciation & Amort.	225.0	201.0	202.0	137.6	126.4	116.5	103.9
Operating Income	611.0	744.0	551.0	538.1	466.4	415.0	359.1
Net Interest Inc./(Exp.)	d88.0	d98.0	d97.0	d69.7	d55.6	d38.3	d25.1
Income Before Income Taxes	487.0	622.0	430.0	471.9	416.0	370.4	337.9
Income Taxes	162.0	228.0	184.0	174.0	166.6	148.3	137.1
Net Income	①②325.0	②394.0	②246.0	298.0	249.4	222.1	200.8
Cash Flow	550.0	595.0	448.0	435.5	375.8	338.6	304.7
Average Shs. Outstg. (000)	239,483	239,614	240,002	211,270	206,584	207,740	212,588

BALANCE SHEET (IN MILLIONS):

Cash & Cash Equivalents	251.0	245.0	132.0	89.7	101.0	90.8	137.3
Total Current Assets	1,103.0	1,454.0	1,116.0	798.7	673.5	573.8	600.3
Net Property	1,046.0	1,079.0	1,054.0	596.3	570.6	551.4	525.0
Total Assets	3,995.0	4,353.0	4,132.0	3,030.0	2,778.0	2,178.9	1,906.7
Total Current Liabilities	1,069.0	1,541.0	1,368.0	1,225.1	892.7	623.9	479.3
Long-Term Obligations	685.0	590.0	702.0	316.3	565.9	356.3	253.1
Net Stockholders' Equity	1,900.0	1,794.0	1,570.0	1,085.2	1,036.0	932.8	943.9
Net Working Capital	34.0	d87.0	d252.0	d426.4	d219.2	d50.0	121.0
Year-end Shs. Outstg. (000)	236,691	235,361	235,311	207,370	206,390	205,032	209,608

STATISTICAL RECORD:

Operating Profit Margin %	15.7	18.2	13.8	19.6	18.4	18.7	18.1
Net Profit Margin %	8.3	9.6	6.1	10.9	9.8	10.0	10.1
Return on Equity %	17.1	22.0	15.7	27.5	24.1	23.8	21.3
Return on Assets %	8.1	9.1	6.0	9.8	9.0	10.2	10.5
Debt/Total Assets %	17.1	13.6	17.0	10.4	20.4	16.4	13.3
Price Range	40.85-29.95	56.38-28.38	66.47-37.50	58.75-37.19	40.19-24.31	27.56-17.50	19.81-13.81
P/E Ratio	30.0-22.0	34.4-17.3	64.5-36.4	41.7-26.4	33.3-20.2	25.8-16.4	21.0-14.6
Average Yield %	2.4	1.9	1.5	1.4	1.9	2.5	3.0

Statistics are as originally reported. Results for 1999 and subsequent years include First Brands Corp. Adj. for stk. splits: 2-for-1, 8/99 and 9/97. ① Bef. acctg. change chrg. $2.0 mill. ② Incl. one-time chrgs. $98.0 mill., 6/01; $21.0 mill., 6/00; $180.0 mill., 6/99.

OFFICERS:
G. C. Sullivan, Chmn., C.E.O.
G. E. Johnston, Pres., C.O.O.
K. M. Rose, V.P., C.F.O.

INVESTOR CONTACT: Steve Silberblatt, Investor Relations, (510) 271-7291

PRINCIPAL OFFICE: 1221 Broadway, Oakland, CA 94612-1888

TELEPHONE NUMBER: (510) 271-7000
FAX: (510) 832-1463
WEB: www.clorox.com

NO. OF EMPLOYEES: 11,000 (approx.)
SHAREHOLDERS: 15,365 (approx.)
ANNUAL MEETING: In Nov.
INCORPORATED: DE, 1986

INSTITUTIONAL HOLDINGS:
No. of Institutions: 409
Shares Held: 123,237,677
% Held: 52.9

INDUSTRY: Polishes and sanitation goods (SIC: 2842)

TRANSFER AGENT(S): First Chicago Trust Company of New York, Jersey City, NJ

CLECO CORPORATION

YIELD 3.7%
P/E RATIO 15.8

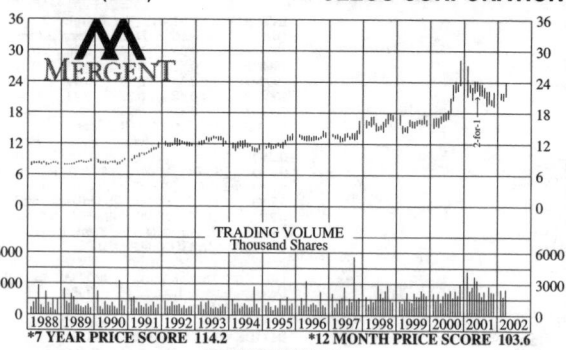

INTERIM EARNINGS (Per Share):

Qtr.	Mar.	June	Sept.	Dec.
1998	0.15	0.32	0.48	0.19
1999	0.18	0.30	0.54	0.18
2000	0.22	0.36	0.63	0.18
2001	0.25	0.29	0.65	0.32

INTERIM DIVIDENDS (Per Share):

Amt.	Decl.	Ex.	Rec.	Pay.
0.435Q	4/27/01	5/03/01	5/07/01	5/15/01
2-for-1	2/26/01	5/22/01	5/07/01	5/21/01
0.22Q	7/27/01	8/02/01	8/06/01	8/15/01
0.22Q	10/26/01	11/01/01	11/05/01	11/15/01
0.22Q	1/25/02	1/31/02	2/04/02	2/15/02

Indicated div.: $0.88 (Div. Reinv. Plan)

CAPITALIZATION (12/31/01):

	($000)	(%)
Long-Term Debt	626,777	46.7
Deferred Income Tax	208,522	15.5
Preferred Stock	15,988	1.2
Common & Surplus	491,966	36.6
Total	1,343,253	100.0

DIVIDEND ACHIEVER STATUS:
Rank: 266   10-Year Growth Rate: 2.82%
Total Years of Dividend Growth: 20

RECENT DEVELOPMENTS: For the year ended 12/31/01, income from continuing operations amounted to $72.3 million versus $69.3 million in 2000. Earnings for 2001 and 2000 excluded losses from discontinued operations of $2.0 million and $6.9 million, respectively. Total revenues jumped 29.1% to $1.06 billion, primarily due to energy marketing and tolling operations, which soared 117.6% to $435.8 million. Total operating expenses as a percentage of revenues climbed to 85.9% from 82.0% the year before.

PROSPECTS: On 3/25/02, the Company announced that it will acquire Mirant's 50.0% equity interest in the 725-megawatt power plant the two companies are building in northeast Louisiana. Under the agreement, CNL will assume Mirant's $19.5 million future equity commitment to the project and pay $48.0 million to retire Mirant's project debt. Mirant will continue to control output of the plant under a 20-year power sales agreement, while CNL will operate and maintain the plant.

BUSINESS

CLECO CORPORATION, under an energy services holding structure, is the parent company of Cleco Power LLC and Cleco Midstream Resources LLC. Cleco Power LLC is a regulated electric utility company that, as of 12/31/01, provides electricity to approximately 250,000 customers in Lousiana. Cleco Midstream Resources LLC is a nonregulated regional energy services group that develops and operates electric power generation facilities; invests in and develops natural gas pipelines and other gas-related assets; and provides energy services to organizations that operate electric utility systems. The other segment consists of a shared services subsidiary, an investment subsidiary, a retail subsidiary, Utility Construction and Technology Solutions, LLC.

QUARTERLY DATA

(12/31/01)($000)	REV	INC
1st Quarter	253,111	30,128
2nd Quarter	303,700	33,689
3rd Quarter	306,969	59,396
4th Quarter	194,839	26,327

ANNUAL FINANCIAL DATA

	12/31/01	12/31/00	12/31/99	12/31/98	12/31/97	12/31/96	12/31/95
Earnings Per Share	②1.51	①1.46	1.19	1.12	1.09	1.12	1.04
Cash Flow Per Share	2.73	2.57	2.19	2.11	2.02	2.07	1.94
Tang. Book Val. Per Share	10.94	10.33	9.77	9.45	9.10	8.76	8.41
Dividends Per Share	0.87	0.84	0.83	0.81	0.79	0.77	0.75
Dividend Payout %	57.6	57.5	69.7	72.3	72.5	68.8	72.1
INCOME STATEMENT (IN MILLIONS):							
Total Revenues	1,058.6	820.0	768.2	515.2	456.2	435.4	394.4
Costs & Expenses	813.3	582.3	576.2	328.9	280.5	264.6	231.3
Depreciation & Amort.	60.0	55.2	49.5	49.1	45.9	42.7	40.6
Maintenance Exp.	30.7	35.3	29.9	30.3	23.3	23.5	22.6
Operating Income	149.5	147.2	112.5	80.3	78.8	78.4	74.7
Net Interest Inc./(Exp.)	d40.0	d42.7	d27.9	d27.0	d28.2	d27.8	d28.0
Income Taxes	38.4	35.0	27.2	26.7	27.7	26.2	25.2
Net Income	②72.3	①69.3	56.8	53.8	52.5	52.1	48.7
Cash Flow	130.4	122.7	104.3	100.7	96.3	92.8	87.2
Average Shs. Outstg. (000)	47,764	47,655	47,697	47,734	47,728	44,906	44,862
BALANCE SHEET (IN MILLIONS):							
Gross Property	1,880.4	1,836.9	1,767.3	1,641.5	1,544.2	1,428.1	1,371.2
Accumulated Depreciation	655.8	604.1	555.7	551.7	518.7	475.2	441.7
Net Property	1,224.7	1,232.8	1,211.6	1,089.8	1,025.6	952.9	929.5
Total Assets	1,768.1	1,845.7	1,704.7	1,429.0	1,361.0	1,321.8	1,266.0
Long-Term Obligations	626.8	659.1	579.6	343.0	365.9	340.9	360.8
Net Stockholders' Equity	508.0	480.0	452.5	437.5	420.1	402.9	385.1
Year-end Shs. Outstg. (000)	44,961	44,991	44,884	44,962	44,926	44,906	44,854
STATISTICAL RECORD:							
Operating Profit Margin %	14.1	18.0	14.6	15.6	17.3	18.0	18.9
Net Profit Margin %	6.8	8.5	7.4	10.4	11.5	12.0	12.3
Net Inc./Net Property %	5.9	5.6	4.7	4.9	5.1	5.5	5.2
Net Inc./Tot. Capital %	5.4	4.8	3.9	4.7	4.6	4.8	4.4
Return on Equity %	14.2	14.4	12.5	12.3	12.5	12.9	12.6
Accum. Depr./Gross Prop. %	34.9	32.9	31.4	33.6	33.6	33.3	32.2
Price Range	27.25-19.25	28.25-15.06	17.75-14.13	18.06-14.31	16.56-12.38	14.63-12.56	14.06-11.00
P/E Ratio	18.0-12.7	19.4-10.4	15.0-11.9	16.1-12.8	15.2-11.4	13.1-11.3	13.5-10.6
Average Yield %	3.7	3.9	5.2	5.0	5.5	5.7	6.0

Statistics are as originally reported. Adj. for 2-for-1 stock split 5/21/01. ① Bef. extraord. gain of $2.5 mill. & disc. opers. loss $6.9 mill. ② Bef. a loss from discont. opers. of $2.0 mill.

OFFICERS:
D. M. Eppler, Pres., C.E.O.
D. Samil, Sr. V.P., C.F.O.
M. P. Prudhomme, Sec.

INVESTOR CONTACT: Kenneth Nolley, (318) 484-7715

PRINCIPAL OFFICE: 2030 Donahue Ferry Road, Pineville, LA 71360-5226

TELEPHONE NUMBER: (318) 484-7400
FAX: (318) 484-7465
WEB: www.cleco.com

NO. OF EMPLOYEES: 1,392

SHAREHOLDERS: 8,990

ANNUAL MEETING: In April
INCORPORATED: LA, Dec., 1932

INSTITUTIONAL HOLDINGS:
No. of Institutions: 150
Shares Held: 24,075,604
% Held: 53.5

INDUSTRY: Electric services (SIC: 4911)

TRANSFER AGENT(S): EquiServe Trust Company, N.A., Jersey City, NJ

NYSE SYMBOL CLC
Rec. Pr. 32.00 (3/31/02)

CLARCOR INC.

YIELD 1.5%
P/E RATIO 20.0

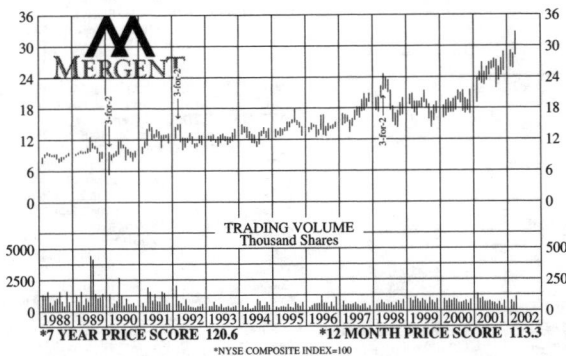

*7 YEAR PRICE SCORE 120.6   *12 MONTH PRICE SCORE 113.3
*NYSE COMPOSITE INDEX=100

INTERIM EARNINGS (Per Share):

Qtr.	Feb.	May	Aug.	Nov.
1998	0.22	0.32	0.35	0.41
1999	0.25	0.36	0.40	0.45
2000	0.29	0.41	0.41	0.53
2001	0.40	0.36	0.41	0.51
2002	0.32	...	...	...

INTERIM DIVIDENDS (Per Share):

Amt.	Decl.	Ex.	Rec.	Pay.
0.117Q	6/25/01	7/11/01	7/13/01	7/27/01
0.12Q	9/24/01	10/10/01	10/12/01	10/26/01
0.12Q	12/17/01	1/09/02	1/11/02	1/25/02
0.12Q	3/19/02	4/10/02	4/12/02	4/26/02

Indicated div.: $0.48 (Div. Reinv. Plan)

CAPITALIZATION (11/30/01):

	($000)	(%)
Long-Term Debt	135,203	31.8
Deferred Income Tax	15,114	3.6
Minority Interest	434	0.1
Common & Surplus	274,261	64.5
Total	425,012	100.0

DIVIDEND ACHIEVER STATUS:
Rank: 270   10-Year Growth Rate: 2.56%
Total Years of Dividend Growth: 21

RECENT DEVELOPMENTS: For the first quarter ended 3/2/02, net earnings declined 18.4% to $8.0 million compared with $9.8 million in the corresponding prior-year quarter. Net sales increased 1.3% to $158.3 million from $156.2 million a year earlier. Industrial/Environmental Filtration segment sales climbed 10.8% to $86.0 million. Engine/Mobile Filtration segment sales slipped 1.6% to $57.8 million, while Packaging segment sales fell 27.1% to $14.5 milllion.

PROSPECTS: CLC recently signed several new total filtration contracts with large manufacturing companies, each of which are expected to add at least $4.0 million in annual sales once fully implemented over the next few years. Also, CLC plans to expand the capabilities of Total Filtration Systems in 2002 with investments in its distribution and technology infrastructure. Separately, CLC expects earnings in the range of $1.73 to $1.80 per share in fiscal 2002.

BUSINESS

CLARCOR INC. is a diversified marketer and manufacturer of mobile, industrial and environmental filtration products and consumer and industrial packaging products sold in domestic and international markets. The Engine/Mobile Filtration segment (2001 operating profit and net sales contribution was 68.3% and 37.6%, respectively) markets a full line of oil, air, fuel, coolant and hydraulic fluid filters. The filters are used in a wide variety of applications and in processes where filter efficiency, reliability and durability are essential. The Industrial/Environmental Filtration segment (22.1%, 51.9%) includes products used primarily for commercial, residential and industrial applications. The segment markets commercial and industrial air filters and systems, electrostatic contamination control equipment and electrostatic high precision spraying equipment. The Packaging segment (9.6%, 10.5%) includes a variety of custom styled containers and packaging items used primarily by the food, confectionery, spice, drug, toiletries and chemical specialties industries. In June 2001, CLC acquired Total Filtration Systems, Inc. for $33.3 million in cash.

ANNUAL FINANCIAL DATA

	11/30/01	11/30/00	11/27/99	11/28/98	11/29/97	11/30/96	11/30/95
Earnings Per Share	1.68	1.64	1.46	1.30	①② 1.11	1.12	0.99
Cash Flow Per Share	2.56	2.50	2.09	1.80	1.60	1.56	1.36
Tang. Book Val. Per Share	6.40	5.75	4.98	6.90	6.41	5.87	5.23
Dividends Per Share	0.47	0.46	0.45	0.44	0.437	0.43	0.42
Dividend Payout %	28.0	28.2	31.0	34.0	39.1	38.2	42.7
INCOME STATEMENT (IN THOUSANDS):							
Total Revenues	666,964	652,148	477,869	426,773	394,264	333,388	290,194
Costs & Expenses	569,304	555,082	406,420	362,730	335,268	283,073	246,585
Depreciation & Amort.	21,850	21,079	15,372	12,380	11,600	9,785	8,244
Operating Income	75,810	75,987	56,077	51,663	47,396	40,530	35,365
Net Interest Inc./(Exp.)	d9,616	d10,836	d2,282	d1,053	d2,759	d3,243	d1,863
Income Before Income Taxes	65,734	63,487	55,615	51,347	44,192	40,019	33,961
Income Taxes	23,804	23,201	20,137	19,262	17,164	14,896	12,182
Equity Earnings/Minority Int.	d37	d49	d66	d6	d110	d145	175
Net Income	41,893	40,237	35,412	32,079	①② 26,918	24,978	21,954
Cash Flow	63,743	61,316	50,784	44,459	38,518	34,763	30,198
Average Shs. Outstg.	24,892	24,506	24,314	24,649	24,134	22,289	22,202
BALANCE SHEET (IN THOUSANDS):							
Cash & Cash Equivalents	7,418	10,864	14,745	33,321	30,324	17,372	18,769
Total Current Assets	244,350	230,479	227,670	168,173	160,527	124,379	117,570
Net Property	137,316	140,121	126,026	86,389	82,905	78,586	67,036
Total Assets	530,617	501,930	472,991	305,766	282,519	243,964	223,262
Total Current Liabilities	94,931	97,826	97,475	61,183	54,237	45,156	42,460
Long-Term Obligations	135,203	141,486	145,981	36,419	37,656	35,522	34,417
Net Stockholders' Equity	274,261	242,093	210,718	186,807	171,162	146,059	130,815
Net Working Capital	149,419	132,653	130,195	106,990	106,290	79,223	75,110
Year-end Shs. Outstg.	24,626	24,381	24,020	23,949	24,243	22,313	22,173
STATISTICAL RECORD:							
Operating Profit Margin %	11.4	11.7	11.7	12.1	12.0	12.2	12.2
Net Profit Margin %	6.3	6.2	7.4	7.5	6.8	7.5	7.6
Return on Equity %	15.3	16.6	16.8	17.2	15.7	17.1	16.8
Return on Assets %	7.9	8.0	7.5	10.5	9.5	10.2	9.8
Debt/Total Assets %	25.5	28.2	30.9	11.9	13.3	14.6	15.4
Price Range	28.88-19.00	21.50-16.06	21.38-14.25	24.67-14.25	20.83-13.33	16.75-12.42	18.00-12.42
P/E Ratio	17.1-8.11.3.0	13.1-9.8	14.6-9.8	19.0-11.0	18.7-12.0	15.0-11.1	18.2-12.6
Average Yield %	2.0	2.5	2.5	2.3	2.5	2.9	2.8

Statistics are as originally reported. Adj. for stk. splits: 3-for-2, 4/98 ① Incl. non-recurr. credit of $1.7 mill. ② Incl. non-recurr chrg. $3.0 mill.

OFFICERS:
N. E. Johnson, Chmn., Pres., C.E.O.
B. A. Klein, V.P., C.F.O.
D. J. Boyd, V.P., Sec., Gen. Couns.

INVESTOR CONTACT: Bruce A. Klein, V.P., C.F.O., (815) 962-8867

PRINCIPAL OFFICE: 2323 Sixth St, P.O. Box 7007, Rockford, IL 61125

TELEPHONE NUMBER: (815) 962-8867
FAX: (815) 962-0417
WEB: www.clarcor.com
NO. OF EMPLOYEES: 4,545 (approx.)
SHAREHOLDERS: 1,500 (of record); 6,000 (beneficial)
ANNUAL MEETING: In March
INCORPORATED: IL, 1904; reincorp., DE, 1969

INSTITUTIONAL HOLDINGS:
No. of Institutions: 127
Shares Held: 16,830,226
% Held: 68.3

INDUSTRY: Motor vehicle parts and accessories (SIC: 3714)

TRANSFER AGENT(S): EquiServe, First Chicago Trust Division, Jersey City, NJ

CITIZENS BANKING CORP.

YIELD 3.5%
P/E RATIO 14.4

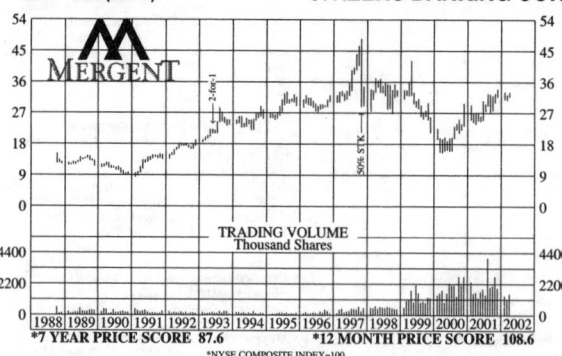

7 YEAR PRICE SCORE 87.6 **12 MONTH PRICE SCORE 108.6**
*NYSE COMPOSITE INDEX=100

INTERIM EARNINGS (Per Share):

Qtr.	Mar.	June	Sept.	Dec.
1997	0.50	d0.18	0.40	0.39
1998	0.48	0.49	0.52	0.53
1999	0.47	0.50	0.49	d0.19
2000	0.46	0.47	0.54	0.44
2001	0.51	0.59	0.60	0.56

INTERIM DIVIDENDS (Per Share):

Amt.	Decl.	Ex.	Rec.	Pay.
0.275Q	4/17/01	4/25/01	4/27/01	5/09/01
0.275Q	7/20/01	7/25/01	7/27/01	8/08/01
0.275Q	10/19/01	10/24/01	10/26/01	11/14/01
0.275Q	1/18/02	1/23/02	1/25/02	2/06/02
0.285Q	4/16/02	4/24/02	4/26/02	5/08/02

Indicated div.: $1.14 (Div. Reinv. Plan)

CAPITALIZATION (12/31/01):

	($000)	(%)
Total Deposits	5,965,126	81.8
Long-Term Debt	629,099	8.6
Common & Surplus	697,464	9.6
Total	7,291,689	100.0

DIVIDEND ACHIEVER STATUS:

Rank: 145	10-Year Growth Rate: 9.70%
Total Years of Dividend Growth:	18

RECENT DEVELOPMENTS: For the year ended 12/31/01, net income increased 15.4% to $104.7 million compared with $90.7 million in 2000. Earnings for 2001 included a gain of $6.2 million on investment securities, a gain of $11.0 million on the sale of NYCE stock, a gain of $2.6 million on the sale of credit card assets, and a gain of $793,000 on the sale of a bank. Results for 2000 included a special charge of $15.5 million. Net interest income declined 2.2% to $308.0 million from $314.9 million in the previous year.

Provision for loan losses increased 25.8% to $26.4 million from $21.0 million in 2000. Total non-interest income climbed 30.0% to $117.5 million versus $90.3 million the year before. Return on average assets advanced to 1.32% from 1.12%, while return on average shareholders' equity rose to 14.90% from 13.94% in the prior year. Total deposits slid 4.5% to $5.97 billion, while total loans decreased 7.8% to $5.92 billion.

BUSINESS

CITIZENS BANKING CORP. is a multibank holding company, which directly or indirectly owns five banking subsidiaries and eight nonbanking subsidiaries, with total assets of $7.68 billion as of 12/31/01. The Corporation's subsidiary banks are full service commercial banks offering a variety of financial services to corporate, commercial, correspondent and individual bank customers. These services include commercial, mortgage and consumer lending, demand and time deposits, trust services, investment services, retirement planning, asset management, insurance services, safe deposit facilities, and other financial products and services. Citizens operates 201 banking offices located in the four midwestern states of Michigan, Wisconsin, Iowa, and Illinois.

ANNUAL FINANCIAL DATA

	12/31/01	12/31/00	12/31/99	12/31/98	12/31/97	12/31/96	12/31/95
Earnings Per Share	③ 2.25	② 1.91	① 1.28	1.98	① 1.11	1.28	1.16
Tang. Book Val. Per Share	13.70	12.67	11.28	13.76	12.47	8.73	7.91
Dividends Per Share	1.08	1.01	0.92	0.82	0.74	0.67	0.60
Dividend Payout %	48.2	53.1	71.5	41.4	67.0	52.8	51.9
INCOME STATEMENT (IN MILLIONS):							
Total Interest Income	573.6	622.0	542.4	339.9	335.9	255.9	240.6
Total Interest Expense	265.6	307.1	231.9	142.0	144.0	109.8	103.1
Net Interest Income	308.0	314.9	310.5	197.8	191.8	146.1	137.5
Provision for Loan Losses	26.4	21.0	24.7	14.1	15.3	8.3	6.4
Non-Interest Income	117.5	90.3	79.8	56.3	46.7	40.5	36.4
Non-Interest Expense	251.2	242.2	236.8	158.3	153.4	126.0	121.1
Income Before Taxes	147.9	126.5	90.0	81.7	46.0	52.3	46.4
Net Income	③ 104.7	② 90.7	① 62.0	56.8	① 31.5	37.4	33.6
Average Shs. Outstg. (000)	46,590	47,543	48,617	28,743	28,420	29,332	29,150
BALANCE SHEET (IN MILLIONS):							
Cash & Due from Banks	224.4	318.1	250.7	140.5	168.4	137.9	172.8
Securities Avail. for Sale	38.2	...	...	...	...	...	...
Total Loans & Leases	5,922.4	6,422.8	5,917.5	3,584.5	3,541.6	2,620.7	2,428.5
Allowance for Credit Losses	80.3	80.1	76.4	46.4	45.9	36.0	34.8
Net Loans & Leases	5,842.1	6,342.7	5,841.1	3,538.1	3,495.7	2,584.7	2,393.7
Total Assets	7,678.9	8,405.1	7,899.4	4,501.4	4,439.3	3,483.9	3,463.9
Total Deposits	5,965.1	6,244.1	6,129.0	3,764.4	3,694.3	2,864.8	2,864.7
Long-Term Obligations	629.1	471.1	127.1	130.9	108.2	84.1	105.4
Total Liabilities	6,981.4	7,725.1	7,265.7	4,060.3	4,029.4	3,168.6	3,166.7
Net Stockholders' Equity	697.5	680.0	633.7	441.1	409.8	315.2	297.2
Year-end Shs. Outstg. (000)	45,098	46,510	47,568	28,100	28,048	28,680	28,668
STATISTICAL RECORD:							
Return on Equity %	15.0	13.3	9.8	12.9	7.7	11.9	11.3
Return on Assets %	1.4	1.1	0.8	1.3	0.7	1.1	1.0
Equity/Assets %	9.1	8.1	8.0	9.8	9.2	9.0	8.6
Non-Int. Exp./Tot. Inc. %	59.0	59.8	60.7	62.3	64.3	67.5	69.6
Price Range	34.02-23.69	29.81-15.50	42.25-21.25	37.13-26.75	48.50-28.75	32.25-27.25	33.25-24.94
P/E Ratio	15.1-10.5	15.6-8.1	33.0-16.6	18.7-13.5	43.7-25.9	25.3-21.4	28.8-21.6
Average Yield %	3.8	4.5	2.9	2.6	1.9	2.3	2.1

Statistics are as originally reported. Adj. for stk. splits: 50% div., 11/18/97. ① Incl. after-tax chrg. $9.5 mill., 12/00; $28.4 mill., 12/99; $17.3 mill., 12/97. ② Incl. special chrg. of $15.5 mill. ③ Incl. gain of $6.2 mill. on investment securities, gain of $11.0 mill. on sale of NYCE stock, gain of $2.6 mill. on sale of credit card assets, gain of $793,000 on sale of bank.

OFFICERS:
R. J. Vitito, Chmn.
J. W. Ennest, Vice-Chmn., C.F.O., Treas.
W. R. Hartman, Pres., C.E.O.

INVESTOR CONTACT: Linda M. Manson, (810) 766-7733

PRINCIPAL OFFICE: 328 S. Saginaw Street, Flint, MI 48502

TELEPHONE NUMBER: (810) 766-7500
FAX: (810) 766-7503
WEB: www.cbclientsfirst.com
NO. OF EMPLOYEES: 2,776
SHAREHOLDERS: 16,400 (approx.)
ANNUAL MEETING: In Apr.
INCORPORATED: MI, Jan., 1982

INSTITUTIONAL HOLDINGS:
No. of Institutions: 102
Shares Held: 11,714,997
% Held: 25.8

INDUSTRY: National commercial banks (SIC: 6021)

TRANSFER AGENT(S): Computershare Investor Services, Chicago, IL

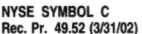

NYSE SYMBOL C
Rec. Pr. 49.52 (3/31/02)

CITIGROUP INC.

YIELD 1.5%
P/E RATIO 17.9

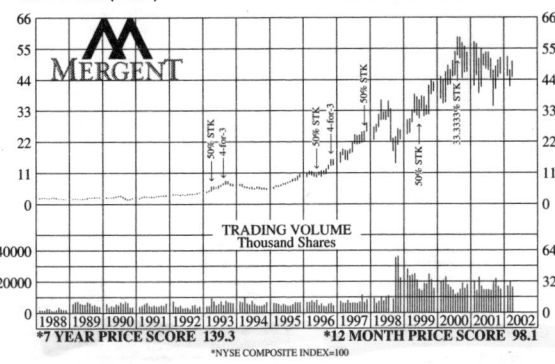

TRADING VOLUME
Thousand Shares

1988 | 1989 | 1990 | 1991 | 1992 | 1993 | 1994 | 1995 | 1996 | 1997 | 1998 | 1999 | 2000 | 2001 | 2002

*7 YEAR PRICE SCORE 139.3   *12 MONTH PRICE SCORE 98.1
*NYSE COMPOSITE INDEX=100

INTERIM EARNINGS (Per Share):

Qtr.	Mar.	June	Sept.	Dec.
1997	0.34	0.37	0.43	0.15
1998	0.46	0.47	0.11	0.14
1999	0.52	0.53	0.53	0.56
2000	0.78	0.65	0.67	0.55
2001	0.70	0.71	0.61	0.74

INTERIM DIVIDENDS (Per Share):

Amt.	Decl.	Ex.	Rec.	Pay.
0.16Q	7/16/01	8/02/01	8/06/01	8/24/01
0.16Q	10/16/01	11/01/01	11/05/01	11/21/01
0.16Q	1/15/02	1/31/02	2/04/02	2/22/02
0.18Q	4/16/02	5/02/02	5/06/02	5/24/02

Indicated div.: $0.72 (Div. Reinv. Plan)

CAPITALIZATION (12/31/01):

	($000)	(%)
Long-Term Debt	121,631,000	57.9
Redeemable Pfd. Stock	7,125,000	3.4
Preferred Stock	1,525,000	0.7
Common & Surplus	79,722,000	38.0
Total	210,003,000	100.0

DIVIDEND ACHIEVER STATUS:
Rank: 10-Year Growth Rate: 31.95%
Total Years of Dividend Growth: 15

RECENT DEVELOPMENTS: For the year ended 12/31/01, income was $14.28 billion, before an accounting change charge of $158.0 million, versus net income of $13.52 billion in 2000. Results for 2001 and 2000 included after-tax restructuring and merger-related charges of $285.0 million and $621.0 million, respectively. Results for 2001 also included pre-tax charges totaling $698.0 million related to and the turmoil in Argentina. Total revenues, net of interest expenses, increased 6.5% to $80.06 billion.

PROSPECTS: On 3/22/02, the Company sold a 21.0% stake of its Travelers Property Casualty Corp. through an initial public offering. Net proceeds from the offering are expected to be about $3.70 billion. C also plans to spin off its remaining majority interest in Travelers to Company shareholders in a tax-free transaction by year-end 2002 with the Company retaining approximately 9.9% ownership.

BUSINESS

CITIGROUP INC., (formerly Travelers Group Inc.) was formed on 10/8/98 by the merger of Travelers Group and Citicorp. The Company consists of businesses that produce a broad range of financial services -- asset management, banking and consumer finance, credit and charge cards, insurance, investments, investment banking and trading -- and use diverse channels to make them available to consumer and corporate customers around the world. Among its businesses are Citibank, Commercial Credit, Primerica Financial Services, Salomon Smith Barney, Salomon Smith Barney Asset Management, Banamex, Travelers Life & Annuity, and Travelers Property Casualty. On 11/28/97, the Company acquired Salomon Inc. On 1/18/00, the Company acquired Shroders PLC. On 11/30/00, the Company acquired Associates First Capital Corporation. On 8/6/01, the Company acquired Grupo Financiero Banamex-Accival for approximately $12.48 billion.

ANNUAL FINANCIAL DATA

	12/31/01	12/31/00	12/31/99	12/31/98	12/31/97	12/31/96	12/31/95
Earnings Per Share	[7] 2.75	[6] 2.62	[5] 2.15	[4] 1.22	[3] 1.27	[2] 1.15	[1] 0.81
Tang. Book Val. Per Share	15.57	12.84	10.64	8.94	6.99	4.95	4.74
Dividends Per Share	0.60	0.52	0.41	0.28	0.20	0.15	0.13
Dividend Payout %	21.8	19.8	18.9	22.8	15.7	13.0	16.5
INCOME STATEMENT (IN MILLIONS):							
Total Premium Income	13,460.0	12,429.0	10,441.0	9,850.0	8,995.0	7,633.0	4,977.0
Net Investment Income	66,565.0	64,939.0	44,900.0	46,239.0	17,618.0	6,712.0	5,474.0
Other Income	31,997.0	34,458.0	26,664.0	20,342.0	10,996.0	7,000.0	6,132.0
Total Revenues	112,022.0	111,826.0	82,005.0	76,431.0	37,609.0	21,345.0	16,583.0
Policyholder Benefits	11,759.0	10,147.0	8,671.0	8,365.0	7,714.0	7,366.0	5,017.0
Income Before Income Taxes	21,897.0	21,143.0	15,948.0	9,269.0	5,012.0	3,398.0	2,521.0
Income Taxes	7,526.0	7,525.0	5,703.0	3,234.0	1,696.0	1,051.0	893.0
Equity Earnings/Minority Int.	d87.0	d99.0	d251.0	d228.0	d212.0	d47.0	...
Net Income	[7] 14,284.0	[8] 13,519.0	[9] 9,994.0	[10] 5,807.0	[3] 3,104.0	[2] 2,320.0	[1] 1,628.0
Average Shs. Outstg. (000)	5,147,000	5,122,200	4,591,332	4,630,399	2,359,799	1,916,400	1,904,400
BALANCE SHEET (IN MILLIONS):							
Cash & Cash Equivalents	298,228.0	253,011.0	235,968.0	228,513.0	253,499.0	83,611.0	61,163.0
Premiums Due	47,528.0	36,237.0	32,677.0	30,905.0	30,939.0	22,408.0	16,584.0
Securities Avail. for Sale	144,904.0	132,513.0	109,155.0	119,845.0	139,732.0	56,463.0	39,696.0
Invst. Assets: Loans	391,933.0	367,022.0	244,206.0	221,958.0	10,816.0	8,071.0	7,238.0
Total Assets	1,051,450.0	902,210.0	716,937.0	668,641.0	386,555.0	151,067.0	114,475.0
Total Deposits	374,525.0	300,586.0	261,091.0	228,649.0	...	...	...
Long-Term Obligations	121,631.0	111,778.0	47,092.0	48,671.0	28,352.0	11,327.0	9,190.0
Net Stockholders' Equity	81,247.0	66,206.0	49,686.0	42,708.0	20,893.0	13,085.0	11,710.0
Year-end Shs. Outstg. (000)	5,118,689	5,022,222	4,490,032	4,515,999	2,889,999	1,912,800	1,895,999
STATISTICAL RECORD:							
Return on Revenues %	12.8	12.1	12.2	7.6	8.3	10.8	9.8
Return on Equity %	17.6	20.4	20.1	13.6	14.9	17.6	13.9
Return on Assets %	1.4	1.5	1.4	0.9	0.8	1.3	1.4
Price Range	57.38-34.51	59.13-35.34	43.69-24.50	36.75-14.58	28.69-14.58	15.83-9.42	10.65-5.40
P/E Ratio	20.9-12.5	22.6-13.5	20.4-11.4	30.2-11.7	22.6-11.5	13.8-8.2	13.1-6.7
Average Yield %	1.3	1.1	1.2	1.1	0.9	1.2	1.7

Statistics are as originally reported. Results prior to fourth quarter of 1998 are for Travelers Group. Adj. for stk. splits: 33.3% stk. div., 8/25/00; 3-for-2, 5/99; 11/97; 4-for-3, 8/00, 11/96; 3-for-2, 5/96 [1] Bef. gain fr. disc. ops. of $206.0 mil. [2] Bef. gain fr. disc. ops. of $31.0 mil.; incl. non-recur. credit of $397.0 mil. [3] Incl. non-recur. chrg. of $255.4 mil. [4] Incl. non-recur. chrg. of $795.0 mil. [5] Bef. acctg. chrg. of $127.0 mil.; incl. non-recur. credit of $47.0 mil. [6] Incl. restr. & merger-rel. chg. of $621.0 mil. [7] Bef. acctg. chrg. of $158.0 mil.; incl. restr. & merger-rel. chg. of $285.0 mil., and non-recur. chrg. of $698.0 mil.

OFFICERS:
S. I. Weill, Chmn., C.E.O.
D. C. Maughan, Vice-Chmn.
W. R. Rhodes, Vice-Chmn.
P. J. Collins, Vice-Chmn.
R. Druskin, C.O.O., Chief Tech. Off.

PRINCIPAL OFFICE: 399 Park Avenue, New York, NY 10043

TELEPHONE NUMBER: (212) 559-1000
FAX: (212) 816-8913
WEB: www.citigroup.com
NO. OF EMPLOYEES: 272,000 (approx.)
SHAREHOLDERS: 221,400 (approx.)
ANNUAL MEETING: In April
INCORPORATED: DE, Dec., 1993

INSTITUTIONAL HOLDINGS:
No. of Institutions: 1,307
Shares Held: -1,029,267,107
% Held: 63.7
INDUSTRY: National commercial banks (SIC: 6021)
TRANSFER AGENT(S): Citibank Shareholder Services, Jersey City, NJ

CINTAS CORPORATION

YIELD 0.5%
P/E RATIO 37.2

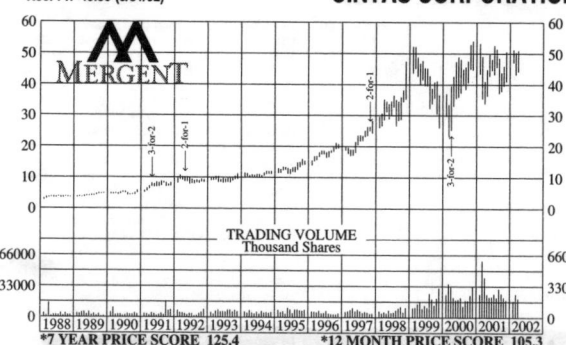

INTERIM EARNINGS (Per Share):

Qtr.	Aug.	Nov.	Feb.	May
1996-97	0.14	0.16	0.16	0.18
1997-98	0.17	0.19	0.18	0.20
1998-99	0.21	0.25	0.23	0.11
1999-00	0.25	0.29	0.29	0.31
2000-01	0.30	0.33	0.32	0.35
2001-02	0.33	0.34	0.32	...

INTERIM DIVIDENDS (Per Share):

Amt.	Decl.	Ex.	Rec.	Pay.
0.22A	1/16/01	1/31/01	2/02/01	3/26/01
0.25A	1/31/02	2/13/02	2/15/02	4/08/02

Indicated div.: $0.25

CAPITALIZATION (5/31/01):

	($mill.)	(%)
Long-Term Debt	220.9	14.7
Deferred Income Tax	49.1	3.3
Common & Surplus	1,231.3	82.0
Total	1,501.3	100.0

DIVIDEND ACHIEVER STATUS:
Rank: 21   10-Year Growth Rate: 21.38%
Total Years of Dividend Growth: 19

TRADING VOLUME
Thousand Shares

66000
33000
0

| 1988 | 1989 | 1990 | 1991 | 1992 | 1993 | 1994 | 1995 | 1996 | 1997 | 1998 | 1999 | 2000 | 2001 | 2002 |

7 YEAR PRICE SCORE 125.4   **12 MONTH PRICE SCORE 105.3**
*NYSE COMPOSITE INDEX=100

RECENT DEVELOPMENTS: For the quarter ended 2/28/02, net income rose 1.2% to $55.6 million from $54.9 million in the equivalent prior-year period. Earnings benefited from productivity improvements and cost-control efforts. Total revenue increased 1.6% to $545.5 million from $536.7 million a year earlier, reflecting the addition of new customers, partially offset by a decline in uniform sales to hospitality and transportation clients since the events of 9/11/01. Rentals revenue rose 6.3% to $425.3 million, while other services revenue fell 12.1% to $120.2 million. On 3/18/02, CTAS agreed to acquire Omni Services, Inc., a U.S. wholly-owned subsidiary of Filuxel SA. Omni Services, a uniform rental company, has annual revenues of about $320.0 million and has more than 90,000 customers.

BUSINESS

CINTAS CORPORATION rents and sells uniforms. CTAS provides services to businesses of all types, from small service and manufacturing companies to major corporations. The Company classifies its businesses into two operating segments: Rentals and Other Services. The Rental operating segment (74.5% of 2001 revenues) designs and manufactures corporate identity uniforms, which it rents, along with other items, to its customers. The Other Services operating segment (25.5%) involves the design, manufacture and direct sale of uniforms to its customers as well as the sale of ancillary services including sanitation supplies, first aid products and services and cleanroom supplies. As of 5/31/01, the Company operated seven distribution facilities and fifteen wholly-owned manufacturing facilities, which provide for a substantial amount of its standard uniform needs. Additional products are purchased from several outside suppliers. In March 1999, CTAS acquired Unitog Company, based in Kansas City, Missouri. In April 1999, the Company acquired Chicago based Uniforms To You.

ANNUAL FINANCIAL DATA

	5/31/01	5/31/00	5/31/99	5/31/98	5/31/97	5/31/96	5/31/95
Earnings Per Share	1.30	1.14	☐ 0.82	☐ 0.79	0.64	0.53	0.45
Cash Flow Per Share	1.95	1.72	1.35	1.16	0.97	0.84	0.71
Tang. Book Val. Per Share	7.27	6.20	5.24	4.17	2.83	2.29	1.84
Dividends Per Share	0.19	0.15	0.12	0.10	0.08	0.07	0.06
Dividend Payout %	14.4	12.9	14.6	12.6	13.1	12.5	12.7
INCOME STATEMENT (IN MILLIONS):							
Total Revenues	2,160.7	1,902.0	1,751.6	1,198.3	839.9	730.1	615.1
Costs & Expenses	1,680.7	1,478.7	1,380.1	940.2	641.8	558.2	471.2
Depreciation & Amort.	112.1	99.5	90.2	57.2	47.7	43.1	37.7
Operating Income	367.9	323.8	281.3	200.9	150.4	128.8	106.2
Net Interest Inc./(Exp.)	d10.7	d11.2	d11.8	d4.4	d3.8	d6.6	d5.2
Income Before Income Taxes	356.5	311.8	224.9	179.4	146.6	122.2	101.0
Income Taxes	134.0	118.4	85.1	56.6	55.8	47.0	38.2
Net Income	222.5	193.4	☐ 138.9	☐ 122.9	90.8	75.2	62.7
Cash Flow	334.5	292.9	229.2	180.1	138.6	118.3	100.4
Average Shs. Outstg. (000)	171,629	169,987	169,341	155,435	142,893	141,297	140,673
BALANCE SHEET (IN MILLIONS):							
Cash & Cash Equivalents	110.2	109.8	88.1	100.9	102.9	82.5	45.5
Total Current Assets	819.7	721.5	634.5	508.6	356.0	297.5	241.4
Net Property	702.1	642.5	573.1	367.1	287.4	252.6	228.0
Total Assets	1,752.2	1,581.3	1,407.8	1,017.8	761.8	668.8	596.2
Total Current Liabilities	250.9	235.4	212.1	159.0	116.1	102.6	95.0
Long-Term Obligations	220.9	254.4	283.6	180.0	111.5	117.9	120.3
Net Stockholders' Equity	1,231.3	1,042.9	871.4	654.5	512.4	429.5	364.3
Net Working Capital	568.8	486.1	422.4	349.6	239.8	194.9	146.4
Year-end Shs. Outstg. (000)	169,371	168,282	166,424	156,917	144,801	141,597	141,015
STATISTICAL RECORD:							
Operating Profit Margin %	17.0	17.0	16.1	16.8	17.9	17.6	17.3
Net Profit Margin %	10.3	10.2	7.9	10.3	10.8	10.3	10.2
Return on Equity %	18.1	18.5	15.9	18.8	17.7	17.5	17.2
Return on Assets %	12.7	12.2	9.9	12.1	11.9	11.2	10.5
Debt/Total Assets %	12.6	16.1	20.1	17.7	14.6	17.6	20.2
Price Range	54.00-23.17	52.25-26.00	47.50-26.00	28.33-17.00	21.17-13.92	16.00-11.17	12.08-9.92
P/E Ratio	41.5-17.8	45.8-22.8	57.9-31.7	35.7-21.4	33.2-21.8	30.0-20.9	27.0-22.2
Average Yield %	0.5	0.4	0.3	0.4	0.5	0.5	0.5

Statistics are as originally reported. Adj. for stk. splits: 3-for-2, 3/7/00; 2-for-1, 11/18/97.
☐ Incl. non-recur. chrg. $11.3 mill., 5/99; credit $17.1 mill., 5/98.

OFFICERS:
R. T. Farmer, Chmn.
R. J. Kohlhepp, C.E.O.
S. D. Farmer, Pres., C.O.O.

INVESTOR CONTACT: William C. Gale, V.P., C.F.O., (513) 459-1200

PRINCIPAL OFFICE: 6800 Cintas Blvd., P.O. Box 625737, Cincinnati, OH 45262-5737

TELEPHONE NUMBER: (513) 459-1200
FAX: (513) 573-4030
WEB: www.cintas.com

NO. OF EMPLOYEES: 24,193 (approx.)

SHAREHOLDERS: 2,200 (approx. of record); 31,000 (approx. beneficial)

ANNUAL MEETING: In Oct.

INCORPORATED: OH, 1968; reincorp., WA, Dec., 1986.

INSTITUTIONAL HOLDINGS:
No. of Institutions: 333
Shares Held: 94,188,703
% Held: 55.5

INDUSTRY: Men's and boys' work clothing
(SIC: 2326)

TRANSFER AGENT(S): The Fifth Third Bank, Cincinnati, OH

NASDAQ SYMBOL CINF
Rec. Pr. 43.66 (3/31/02)

CINCINNATI FINANCIAL CORPORATION

YIELD 2.0%
P/E RATIO 37.0

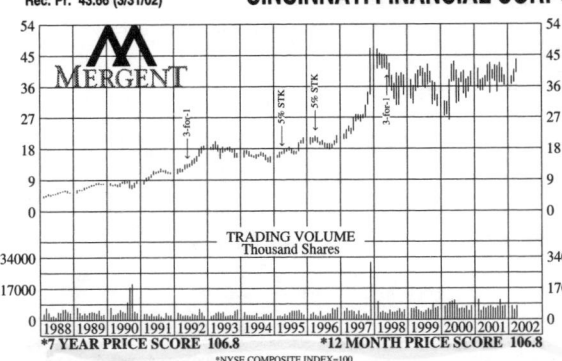

INTERIM EARNINGS (Per Share):

Qtr.	Mar.	June	Sept.	Dec.
1998	0.49	0.35	0.31	0.27
1999	0.38	0.52	0.34	0.28
2000	0.48	0.45	0.03	d0.26
2001	0.44	0.30	0.22	0.22

INTERIM DIVIDENDS (Per Share):

Amt.	Decl.	Ex.	Rec.	Pay.
0.21Q	5/25/01	6/20/01	6/22/01	7/16/01
0.21Q	8/17/01	9/19/01	9/21/01	10/15/01
0.21Q	11/16/01	12/19/01	12/21/01	1/15/02
0.223Q	2/02/02	3/20/02	3/22/02	4/15/02

Indicated div.: $0.89 (Div. Reinv. Plan)

CAPITALIZATION (12/31/01):

	($000)	(%)
Long-Term Debt	426,000	5.1
Deferred Income Tax	2,001,000	23.8
Common & Surplus	5,998,000	71.2
Total	8,425,000	100.0

DIVIDEND ACHIEVER STATUS:
Rank: 101   10-Year Growth Rate: 11.87%
Total Years of Dividend Growth: 41

TRADING VOLUME
Thousand Shares

*7 YEAR PRICE SCORE 106.8   *12 MONTH PRICE SCORE 106.8
*NYSE COMPOSITE INDEX=100

RECENT DEVELOPMENTS: For the year ended 12/31/01, net income jumped to $193.0 million from $118.0 million in the previous year. Results for 2000 included an after-tax asset impairment charge of $25.0 million. Total revenues increased 9.9% to $2.56 billion from $2.33 billion in the prior year, reflecting higher premium rates on new and renewal commercial business and higher investment income. Net earned premiums grew 12.8% to $2.15 billion

from $1.91 billion the previous year. Property casualty premiums grew 13.4% to $2.07 billion, while life and accidental health premiums remained at prior-year levels. Net investment income rose 1.4% to $421.0 million, while realized losses on investments for 2001 and 2000 were $25.0 million and $2.0 million, respectively. Other income climbed 18.2% to $13.0 million.

BUSINESS

CINCINNATI FINANCIAL CORPORATION, through four insurance subsidiaries, sells insurance, primarily in the Midwest and Southeast regions of the U.S. through a network of local independent agents. Insurance products include fire, automobile, casualty, bonds and all related forms of property casualty insurance as well as life insurance, long-term care, disability income policies and annuities. The Cincinnati Insurance Company is licensed for the sale of life insurance and accident and health insurance in 48 states and the District of Columbia. The Cincinnati Casualty Company is licensed in the fire and casualty insurance business on both a direct and agency billing basis in 40 states. The Cincinnati Indemnity Company is engaged in the writing of nonstandard personal and casualty lines of insurance in 31 states. CFC-I owns certain real estate in the Greater Cincinnati area and is in the business of leasing or financing various items, principally automobiles, trucks, computer equipment, machine tools, construction equipment, and office equipment. CinFin offers investment management services to corporations, insurance agencies and companies, institutions, pension plans, and high net worth individuals.

ANNUAL FINANCIAL DATA

	12/31/01	12/31/00	12/31/99	12/31/98	12/31/97	12/31/96	12/31/95
Earnings Per Share	1.19	①0.73	1.52	1.41	1.77	1.31	1.33
Tang. Book Val. Per Share	37.02	37.26	33.46	33.72	28.35	18.95	15.90
Dividends Per Share	0.82	0.74	0.66	0.60	0.53	0.47	0.42
Dividend Payout %	68.9	101.4	43.6	42.3	30.1	36.1	31.2
INCOME STATEMENT (IN MILLIONS):							
Total Premium Income	2,152.0	1,906.9	1,732.0	1,612.7	1,516.4	1,422.9	1,314.1
Net Investment Income	421.0	415.3	386.8	368.0	348.6	327.3	300.0
Other Income	d12.0	8.8	9.5	73.6	77.4	58.5	41.5
Total Revenues	2,561.0	2,331.0	2,128.2	2,054.3	1,942.4	1,808.7	1,655.7
Policyholder Benefits	1,663.0	1,581.1	1,254.4	1,221.1	1,054.9	1,087.1	964.2
Income Before Income Taxes	221.0	108.7	321.6	307.1	394.6	282.4	295.2
Income Taxes	28.0	cr9.7	66.9	65.5	95.2	58.7	67.8
Net Income	193.0	①118.4	254.7	241.6	299.4	223.8	227.4
Average Shs. Outstg. (000)	162,000	163,921	168,615	172,078	170,795	173,349	173,058
BALANCE SHEET (IN MILLIONS):							
Cash & Cash Equivalents	93.0	60.3	339.6	58.6	80.2	59.9	20.0
Premiums Due	1,274.0	897.6	358.7	332.5	299.4	304.8	285.1
Invst. Assets: Fixed-term	3,010.0	2,721.3	2,617.4	2,812.2	2,751.2	2,561.8	2,447.0
Invst. Assets: Equities	8,495.0	8,526.0	7,510.9	7,454.8	5,999.3	3,740.2	3,041.8
Invst. Assets: Total	11,571.0	11,315.8	10,194.2	10,325.0	8,797.1	6,355.0	5,528.6
Total Assets	13,959.0	13,287.1	11,380.2	11,086.5	9,493.4	7,045.5	6,109.3
Long-Term Obligations	426.0	449.2	456.4	471.5	58.4	79.8	80.0
Net Stockholders' Equity	5,998.0	5,995.0	5,421.3	5,620.9	4,717.0	3,162.9	2,658.0
Year-end Shs. Outstg. (000)	162,000	160,891	162,021	166,681	166,356	166,908	167,130
STATISTICAL RECORD:							
Return on Revenues %	7.5	5.1	12.0	11.8	15.4	12.4	13.7
Return on Equity %	3.2	2.0	4.7	4.3	6.3	7.1	8.6
Return on Assets %	1.4	0.9	2.2	2.2	3.2	3.2	3.7
Price Range	42.93-34.00	43.31-26.19	42.50-30.13	46.92-30.50	47.08-20.67	21.83-17.75	21.19-15.34
P/E Ratio	36.1-28.6	59.3-35.9	28.0-19.8	33.3-21.6	26.6-11.7	16.7-13.6	15.9-11.5
Average Yield %	2.1	2.1	1.8	1.5	1.6	2.4	2.3

Statistics are as originally reported. Adj. for 3-for-1 stk. split, 5/15/98; 5% div., 4/30/96; 5% div., 4/28/95. ① Incl. one-time asset impair. chrg. of $39.1 mill.

J. J. Schiff, Jr., Chmn., Pres., C.E.O.
J. E. Benoski, Vice-Chmn., Sr. V.P.
K. W. Stecher, Sr. V.P., C.F.O., Treas., Sec.

INVESTOR CONTACT: Kenneth W. Stecher, Sr. V.P., C.F.O., Treas. Sec., (513) 870-2639

PRINCIPAL OFFICE: 6200 S. Gilmore Road, Fairfield, OH 45014-5141

TELEPHONE NUMBER: (513) 870-2000
FAX: (513) 870-2066
WEB: www.cinfin.com

NO. OF EMPLOYEES: 3,299 (avg.)

SHAREHOLDERS: 11,325 (approx.)

ANNUAL MEETING: In Apr.

INCORPORATED: OH, Sept., 1968

INSTITUTIONAL HOLDINGS:
No. of Institutions: 264
Shares Held: 69,564,960
% Held: 43.1

INDUSTRY: Fire, marine, and casualty insurance (SIC: 6331)

TRANSFER AGENT(S): Cincinnati Financial Corporation, Cincinnati, OH

CHUBB CORPORATION (THE)

YIELD 1.9%
P/E RATIO 130.5

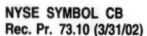

TRADING VOLUME
Thousand Shares

| 1988 | 1989 | 1990 | 1991 | 1992 | 1993 | 1994 | 1995 | 1996 | 1997 | 1998 | 1999 | 2000 | 2001 | 2002 |

*7 YEAR PRICE SCORE 97.0   ***12 MONTH PRICE SCORE 105.6**

*NYSE COMPOSITE INDEX=100

INTERIM EARNINGS (Per Share):

Qtr.	Mar.	June	Sept.	Dec.
1997	1.09	1.09	1.12	1.13
1998	1.12	1.08	1.04	0.95
1999	1.14	1.18	0.44	0.93
2000	0.87	1.02	1.17	0.95
2001	0.97	0.83	d1.40	0.16

INTERIM DIVIDENDS (Per Share):

Amt.	Decl.	Ex.	Rec.	Pay.
0.34Q	6/01/01	6/13/01	6/15/01	7/03/01
0.34Q	9/07/01	9/19/01	9/21/01	10/09/01
0.34Q	12/07/01	12/19/01	12/21/01	1/08/02
0.35Q	3/08/02	3/20/02	3/22/02	4/09/02

Indicated div.: $1.40 (Div. Reinv. Plan)

CAPITALIZATION (12/31/01):

	($000)	(%)
Long-Term Debt	1,351,000	17.2
Common & Surplus	6,525,300	82.8
Total	7,876,300	100.0

DIVIDEND ACHIEVER STATUS:
Rank: 201   10-Year Growth Rate: 6.49%
Total Years of Dividend Growth: 37

RECENT DEVELOPMENTS: For the year ended 12/31/01, net income fell 84.4% to $111.5 million from $714.6 million in the previous year. Results for 2001 included an after-tax charge of $143.0 million from surety bond losses related to Enron and after-tax costs of $420.0 million related to the events on 9/11/01. Net premiums earned improved 8.3% to $6.66 billion from $6.15 billion in 2000. Net investment income rose 2.7% to $982.8 million, while real estate and other revenues climbed 17.6% to $114.0 million.

PROSPECTS: Going forward, CB should benefit from improved rates across nearly all lines, as the higher cost of reinsurance, the losses from September 11th and reduced investment income and capital gains have put intense pressure on CB's competitors to earn an underwriting profit. In addition, CB should benefit from better terms and conditions and the ability to be more selective in assuming risks. Moreover, CB should benefit from its strong balance sheet, conservative loss reserves and ample liquidity.

BUSINESS

THE CHUBB CORPORATION is a holding company with subsidiaries principally engaged in the property and casualty insurance business. The property and casualty insurance subsidiaries provide insurance coverages principally in North America, Europe, Latin America, Asia and Australia. CB also has investments in high quality bonds, U.S. Treasury, government agency, mortgage-backed securities and corporate issues as well as equity securities. CB has a real estate group that is composed of Bellemead Development Corporation and its subsidiaries. The group's activities involve commercial development primarily in New Jersey and residential development activities primarily in central Florida. In 2001, the combined loss and expense ratio after policyholder's dividends was 113.4%.

ANNUAL FINANCIAL DATA

	12/31/01	12/31/00	12/31/99	12/31/98	12/31/97	12/31/96	12/31/95
Earnings Per Share	② 0.63	4.01	3.66	4.19	4.4	① 2.75	3.93
Tang. Book Val. Per Share	35.62	37.13	32.85	34.78	32.11	31.24	30.14
Dividends Per Share	1.35	1.31	1.27	1.22	1.14	1.05	0.96
Dividend Payout %	214.3	32.7	34.8	29.1	26.0	38.4	24.6
INCOME STATEMENT (IN MILLIONS):							
Total Premium Income	6,656.4	6,145.9	5,652.0	5,303.8	5,157.4	4,569.3	4,770.1
Other Income	1,097.6	1,105.6	1,077.6	1,046.0	1,506.6	1,111.3	1,319.1
Total Revenues	7,754.0	7,251.5	6,729.6	6,349.8	6,664.0	5,680.5	6,089.2
Policyholder Benefits	5,357.4	4,127.7	3,942.0	3,493.7	3,307.0	3,010.8	3,219.2
Income Before Income Taxes	d66.0	851.0	710.1	849.7	974.1	546.9	900.1
Income Taxes	cr177.5	136.4	89.0	142.7	204.6	60.7	203.4
Net Income	② 111.5	714.6	621.1	707.0	769.5	① 486.2	696.6
Average Shs. Outstg. (000)	175,800	178,300	169,800	168,600	176,200	174,402	179,884
BALANCE SHEET (IN MILLIONS):							
Cash & Cash Equivalents	1,400.1	1,079.1	1,223.3	352.5	736.6	280.6	496.4
Premiums Due	1,692.8	1,409.8	1,234.7	1,199.3	1,144.4	984.9	872.9
Invst. Assets: Fixed-term	16,116.7	15,564.4	14,519.1	13,318.9	12,453.4	11,158.8	12,602.8
Invst. Assets: Equities	710.4	830.6	769.2	1,092.2	871.1	646.3	587.8
Invst. Assets: Loans	...	...	...	...	...	...	212.3
Invst. Assets: Total	19,234.2	18,128.8	17,188.3	15,501.3	14,839.6	13,685.0	15,630.0
Total Assets	29,449.0	25,026.7	23,537.0	20,746.0	19,615.6	19,938.9	22,996.5
Long-Term Obligations	1,351.0	753.8	759.2	607.5	398.6	1,070.5	1,156.0
Net Stockholders' Equity	6,525.3	6,981.7	6,271.8	5,644.1	5,657.1	5,462.9	5,262.7
Year-end Shs. Outstg. (000)	170,071	174,919	175,490	162,267	176,200	174,861	174,602
STATISTICAL RECORD:							
Return on Revenues %	1.4	9.9	9.2	11.1	11.5	8.6	11.4
Return on Equity %	1.7	10.2	9.9	12.5	13.6	8.9	13.2
Return on Assets %	0.4	2.9	2.6	3.4	3.9	2.4	3.0
Price Range	86.63-55.54	90.25-43.25	76.38-44.00	88.81-55.38	78.50-51.13	56.25-40.88	50.31-38.06
P/E Ratio	137.5-88.1	22.5-10.8	20.9-12.0	21.2-13.2	17.9-11.6	20.5-14.9	12.8-9.7
Average Yield %	1.9	2.0	2.1	1.7	1.8	2.2	2.2

Statistics are as originally reported. Adj. for stk. split: 2-for-1, 5/96 ① Bef. disc. oper. gain $26.5 mill. ② Incl. after-tax chrg. of $143.0 mill. fr. 9/11/01 attacks & after-tax chrgs. of $143.0 mill. from Enron.

CHEVRONTEXACO CORP.

YIELD 3.1%
P/E RATIO 24.4

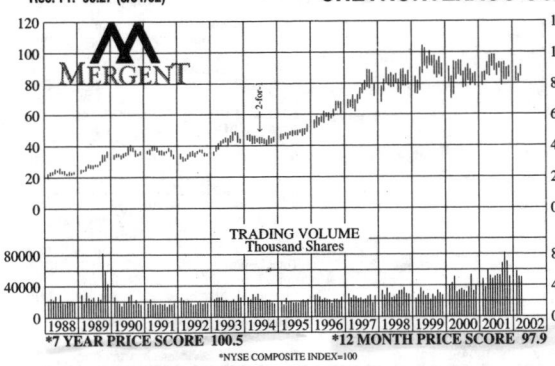

TRADING VOLUME
Thousand Shares

*7 YEAR PRICE SCORE 100.5   *12 MONTH PRICE SCORE 97.9
*NYSE COMPOSITE INDEX=100

INTERIM EARNINGS (Per Share):

Qtr.	Mar.	June	Sept.	Dec.
1998	0.76	0.88	0.70	0.66
1999	0.50	0.53	0.88	1.23
2000	1.59	1.71	2.35	2.32
2001	2.29	1.99	1.66	d2.24

INTERIM DIVIDENDS (Per Share):

Amt.	Decl.	Ex.	Rec.	Pay.
0.65Q	4/25/01	5/16/01	5/18/01	6/11/01
0.65Q	7/25/01	8/15/01	8/17/01	9/10/01
0.70Q	10/31/01	11/14/01	11/16/01	12/10/01
0.70Q	1/30/02	2/13/02	2/15/02	3/11/02

Indicated div.: $2.80 (Div. Reinv. Plan)

CAPITALIZATION (12/31/01):

	($000)	(%)
Long-Term Debt	8,704,000	17.6
Capital Lease Obligations..	285,000	0.6
Deferred Income Tax	6,132,000	12.4
Minority Interest	283,000	0.6
Common & Surplus	33,958,000	68.8
Total	49,362,000	100.0

DIVIDEND ACHIEVER STATUS:
Rank: 232   10-Year Growth Rate: 5.01%
Total Years of Dividend Growth: 14

RECENT DEVELOPMENTS: For the year ended 12/31/01, income was $3.93 billion versus net income of $7.73 billion in 2000. Results for 2001 and 2000 included special charges of $1.74 billion and $378.0 million, respectively, primarily for asset write-offs and revaluations. 2001 results also included merger-related charges of $1.78 billion. Total revenues and other income fell 10.8% to $106.25 billion. Comparisons were made with restated prior-year figures.

PROSPECTS: On 2/6/02, the Company announced a $9.40 billion capital and exploratory spending program for 2002, including $1.60 billion in non-cash affiliates' expenditures. The 2002 program is 21.7% lower than the previous year; however, the Company noted that after adjusting for major acquisitions, divestitures and lease buy-backs, underlying spending in 2002 is about 9.0% lower year over year.

BUSINESS

CHEVRONTEXACO CORP. (formerly Chevron Corp.) is a global energy company engaged in the exploration and production, refining, marketing and transportation of crude oil, natural gas and natural gas liquids. CVX is also engaged in chemicals manufacturing and sales, and holds investments in power generation and gasification businesses. Formed as a result of the acquisition by Chevron Corporation of Texaco Inc. on 10/9/01, CVX operates in the U.S. and approximately 180 other countries. As of 12/31/01, net proved reserves of crude oil, condensate and natural gas liquids totaled 8,524 million barrels, while net proved reserves of natural gas totaled 19,410 billion cubic feet. In addition, CVX operates more than 8,000 service stations and 650 convenience stores in more than 30 countries.

ANNUAL FINANCIAL DATA

	12/31/01	12/31/00	12/31/99	12/31/98	12/31/97	12/31/96	12/31/95
Earnings Per Share	④ 3.70	③ 7.97	② 3.14	2.04	4.95	① 3.99	① 1.43
Cash Flow Per Share	10.34	12.34	7.48	5.57	8.44	7.39	6.61
Tang. Book Val. Per Share	31.82	31.08	27.04	25.81	26.64	23.82	22.02
Dividends Per Share	2.65	2.60	2.48	2.44	2.28	2.08	1.93
Dividend Payout %	71.6	32.6	79.0	119.6	46.1	52.1	134.6
INCOME STATEMENT (IN MILLIONS):							
Total Revenues	106,245.0	52,129.0	36,586.0	30,557.0	41,950.0	43,893.0	37,082.0
Costs & Expenses	89,941.0	39,551.0	29,600.0	25,998.0	33,836.0	36,573.0	31,511.0
Depreciation & Amort.	7,059.0	2,848.0	2,866.0	2,320.0	2,300.0	2,216.0	3,381.0
Operating Income	9,245.0	9,730.0	4,120.0	2,239.0	5,814.0	5,104.0	2,190.0
Net Interest Inc./(Exp.)	d833.0	d460.0	d472.0	d405.0	d312.0	d364.0	d401.0
Income Before Income Taxes	8,291.0	9,270.0	3,648.0	1,834.0	5,502.0	4,740.0	1,789.0
Income Taxes	4,360.0	4,085.0	1,578.0	495.0	2,246.0	2,133.0	859.0
Net Income	④ 3,931.0	③ 5,185.0	② 2,070.0	1,339.0	3,256.0	① 2,607.0	① 930.0
Cash Flow	10,984.0	8,033.0	4,936.0	3,659.0	5,556.0	4,823.0	4,311.0
Average Shs. Outstg. (000)	1,062,900	651,100	659,500	657,100	658,400	653,000	652,000
BALANCE SHEET (IN MILLIONS):							
Cash & Cash Equivalents	3,150.0	2,630.0	2,032.0	1,413.0	1,670.0	1,637.0	1,394.0
Total Current Assets	18,327.0	8,213.0	8,297.0	6,297.0	7,006.0	7,942.0	7,867.0
Net Property	43,233.0	22,894.0	25,317.0	23,729.0	22,671.0	21,496.0	21,696.0
Total Assets	77,572.0	41,264.0	40,668.0	36,540.0	35,473.0	34,854.0	34,330.0
Total Current Liabilities	20,654.0	7,674.0	8,889.0	7,166.0	6,946.0	8,907.0	9,445.0
Long-Term Obligations	8,989.0	5,153.0	5,485.0	4,393.0	4,431.0	3,988.0	4,521.0
Net Stockholders' Equity	33,958.0	19,925.0	17,749.0	17,034.0	17,472.0	15,623.0	14,355.0
Net Working Capital	d2,327.0	539.0	d592.0	d869.0	60.0	d965.0	d1,578.0
Year-end Shs. Outstg. (000)	1,067,221	641,060	656,346	660,000	655,900	656,000	652,000
STATISTICAL RECORD:							
Operating Profit Margin %	8.7	18.7	11.3	7.3	13.9	11.6	5.9
Net Profit Margin %	3.7	9.9	5.7	4.4	7.8	5.9	2.5
Return on Equity %	11.6	26.0	11.7	7.9	18.6	16.7	6.5
Return on Assets %	5.1	12.6	5.1	3.7	9.2	7.5	2.7
Debt/Total Assets %	11.6	12.5	13.5	12.0	12.5	11.4	13.2
Price Range	98.49-78.44	94.88-69.94	104.44-73.13	90.19-67.75	89.19-61.75	68.38-51.00	53.63-43.38
P/E Ratio	26.6-21.2	11.9-8.8	33.3-23.3	44.2-33.2	18.0-12.5	17.1-12.8	37.5-30.3
Average Yield %	3.0	3.2	2.8	3.1	3.0	3.5	4.0

Statistics are as originally reported. Results for 2001 refl. acq. of Texaco Inc. The financial data for 12/31/00 & prior yrs. refl. the former opers. of Chevron Corporation only. ① Incl. nonrecurr. chrg. 12/31/96: $44.0 mill.; chrgs. 12/31/95: $1.03 bill. ② Incl. spec. chrgs. of $216.0 mill. ③ Incl. spec. chrgs. of $252.0 mill. ④ Incl. spec. chrgs. of $1.74 bill. & merger-rel. chrgs. of $1.78 bill.; bef. extraord. loss of $643.0 mill.

OFFICERS:
D. J. O'Reilly, Chmn., C.E.O.
P. J. Robertson, Vice-Chmn., V.P.
G. F. Tilton, Vice-Chmn.

INVESTOR CONTACT: Peter Trueblood, Mgr., Investor Relations, (415) 894-5690

PRINCIPAL OFFICE: 575 Market Street, San Francisco, CA 94105-2586

TELEPHONE NUMBER: (415) 894-7700
FAX: (415) 894-6017
WEB: www.chevrontexaco.com

NO. OF EMPLOYEES: 55,763 (avg.)

SHAREHOLDERS: 250,000 (approx.)

ANNUAL MEETING: In Apr.

INCORPORATED: DE, Jan., 1926

INSTITUTIONAL HOLDINGS:
No. of Institutions: 1,058
Shares Held: 614,447,293
% Held: 57.6

INDUSTRY: Petroleum refining (SIC: 2911)

TRANSFER AGENT(S): Mellon Investor Services, Ridgefield Park, NJ

CHEMICAL FINANCIAL CORPORATION

YIELD 3.2%
P/E RATIO 15.9

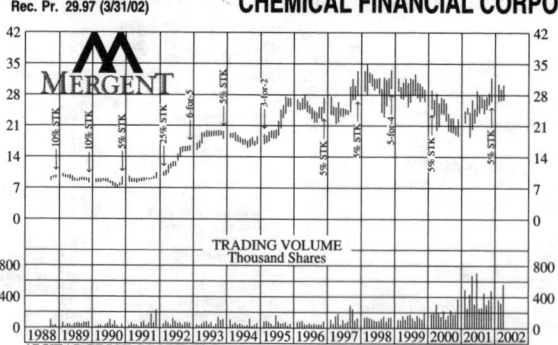

TRADING VOLUME
Thousand Shares

1988 1989 1990 1991 1992 1993 1994 1995 1996 1997 1998 1999 2000 2001 2002

*7 YEAR PRICE SCORE 88.5   ***12 MONTH PRICE SCORE 108.2**
*NYSE COMPOSITE INDEX=100

INTERIM EARNINGS (Per Share):

Qtr.	Mar.	June	Sept.	Dec.
1998	0.38	0.42	0.44	0.50
1999	0.43	0.45	0.47	0.50
2000	0.46	0.49	0.49	0.53
2001	0.17	0.53	0.58	0.61

INTERIM DIVIDENDS (Per Share):

Amt.	Decl.	Ex.	Rec.	Pay.
0.24Q	7/16/01	9/05/01	9/07/01	9/21/01
0.24Q	10/15/01	11/14/01	11/16/01	12/07/01
5% STK	10/15/01	12/05/01	12/07/01	12/21/01
0.24Q	1/22/02	2/27/02	3/01/02	3/15/02
0.24Q	4/15/02	6/05/02	6/07/02	6/21/02

Indicated div.: $0.96 (Div. Reinv. Plan)

CAPITALIZATION (12/31/01):

	($000)	(%)
Total Deposits	2,789,524	83.3
Long-Term Debt	167,893	5.0
Common & Surplus	389,456	11.6
Total	3,346,873	100.0

DIVIDEND ACHIEVER STATUS:
Rank: 98   10-Year Growth Rate: 12.18%
Total Years of Dividend Growth: 26

RECENT DEVELOPMENTS: For the twelve months ended 12/31/01, net income rose 4.7% to $42.7 million from $40.8 million in the same period a year earlier. Results for 2001 included a $7.1 million after-tax charge related to the acquisition of Shoreline Financial Corporation and internal bank consolidations. Net interest income climbed 13.2% to $130.1 million from $114.9 million the prior year. Total interest income grew 4.0% to $219.3 million from $210.9 million the year before, while total interest expense

declined 7.1% to $89.2 million from $96.0 million the previous year. Total noninterest income advanced 25.0% to $31.9 million from $25.5 million in 2000, fueled by sharply higher income from the Company's mortgage banking operations. Total assets amounted to $3.49 billion, up 14.5% from $3.05 billion in 2000. Total loans rose 18.1% to $2.18 billion, while total deposits increased 14.2% to $2.79 billion. Comparisons were made with restated prior-year figures.

BUSINESS

CHEMICAL FINANCIAL CORPORATION is a bank holding company headquartered in Midland, Michigan, with total assets of $3.49 billion as of 12/31/01. The Company's three subsidiary banks, Chemical Bank and Trust Company, Chemical Bank Shoreline and Chemical Bank West, operate 128 "Chemical Bank" offices and two loan production offices throughout 33 counties in the lower peninsula of Michigan. Non-bank subsidiaries include CFC Data Corp., a provider of data processing services, CFC Financial Services, an insurance company operating under the Chemical Financial Insurance Agency and CFC Investment Center names, and CFC Title Services, an issuer of title insurance to buyers and sellers of residential and commercial mortgage properties.

ANNUAL FINANCIAL DATA

	12/31/01	12/31/00	12/31/99	12/31/98	12/31/97	12/31/96	12/31/95
Earnings Per Share	① 1.89	1.96	1.85	1.73	1.60	1.47	1.47
Tang. Book Val. Per Share	15.41	19.19	17.71	17.07	15.11	14.03	13.95
Dividends Per Share	0.91	0.84	0.76	0.70	0.61	0.53	0.45
Dividend Payout %	48.4	42.7	41.2	40.2	38.1	35.8	30.5
INCOME STATEMENT (IN MILLIONS):							
Total Interest Income	219.3	131.1	121.6	121.6	117.3	113.3	105.6
Total Interest Expense	89.2	54.0	47.1	49.1	48.3	46.2	44.2
Net Interest Income	130.1	77.0	74.8	72.5	69.0	67.1	61.4
Provision for Loan Losses	2.0	0.5	0.5	1.0	1.0	1.1	1.1
Non-Interest Income	31.9	17.4	16.0	15.6	13.1	12.2	11.7
Non-Interest Expense	94.6	50.9	49.0	48.3	45.7	45.1	42.6
Income Before Taxes	65.3	43.1	41.4	38.8	35.4	33.0	29.4
Net Income	① 42.7	29.0	27.7	26.0	23.9	22.0	19.7
Average Shs. Outstg. (000)	22,564	14,787	14,974	15,034	14,979	14,974	13,478
BALANCE SHEET (IN MILLIONS):							
Cash & Due from Banks	150.5	95.0	98.8	98.5	95.8	89.5	88.1
Securities Avail. for Sale	731.4	433.3	428.0	489.0	494.2	441.8	341.7
Total Loans & Leases	2,182.5	1,085.9	1,009.0	898.3	845.6	807.7	738.7
Allowance for Credit Losses	31.0	18.2	18.2	18.1	17.4	16.6	15.7
Net Loans & Leases	2,151.5	1,067.6	990.8	880.2	828.2	791.0	723.0
Total Assets	3,488.3	1,973.4	1,890.4	1,872.6	1,765.1	1,698.8	1,643.9
Total Deposits	2,789.5	1,606.2	1,561.7	1,554.3	1,475.8	1,429.9	1,397.3
Long-Term Obligations	167.9	0.2	0.2	8.0	9.0	10.0	12.1
Total Liabilities	3,098.9	1,704.7	1,640.8	1,630.8	1,541.2	1,491.5	1,458.3
Net Stockholders' Equity	389.5	268.7	249.6	241.8	223.9	207.3	185.5
Year-end Shs. Outstg. (000)	22,514	14,004	14,095	14,171	14,819	14,774	13,304
STATISTICAL RECORD:							
Return on Equity %	11.0	10.8	11.1	10.8	10.7	10.6	10.6
Return on Assets %	1.2	1.5	1.5	1.4	1.4	1.3	1.2
Equity/Assets %	11.2	13.6	13.2	12.9	12.7	12.2	11.3
Non-Int. Exp./Tot. Inc. %	58.4	54.0	54.4	55.8	55.8	57.0	58.7
Price Range	31.85-18.39	29.03-18.63	32.65-25.28	34.83-22.86	33.38-21.42	27.97-21.72	27.64-16.78
P/E Ratio	16.9-9.7	14.8-9.5	17.7-13.7	20.1-13.2	20.9-13.4	19.0-14.8	18.9-11.5
Average Yield %	3.6	3.5	2.6	2.4	2.2	2.1	2.0

Statistics are as originally reported. Adj for stk. splits: 5% div., 12/01, 1/00, 12/97, 12/96 & 5-for-4, 12/98. ① Incl. $7.1 mill. after-tax merger and restructuring charge.

OFFICERS:
A. W. Ott, Chmn.
D. B. Ramaker, Pres., C.E.O.
L. A. Gwizdala, Sr. V.P., C.F.O., Treas.

INVESTOR CONTACT: Lori A. Gwizdala, C.F.O., (989) 839-5350

PRINCIPAL OFFICE: 333 East Main Street, Midland, MI 48640-0569

TELEPHONE NUMBER: (989) 839-5350
FAX: (989) 839-5255
WEB: www.chemicalbankmi.com

NO. OF EMPLOYEES: 1,427

SHAREHOLDERS: 10,000 (approx.)

ANNUAL MEETING: In Apr.

INCORPORATED: MI, Aug., 1974

INSTITUTIONAL HOLDINGS:
No. of Institutions: 54
Shares Held: 4,337,573
% Held: 19.3

INDUSTRY: State commercial banks (SIC: 6022)

TRANSFER AGENT(S): Computershare Investor Services, Chicago, IL

NYSE SYMBOL CF
Rec. Pr. 31.22 (3/31/02)

CHARTER ONE FINANCIAL, INC.

YIELD 2.6%
P/E RATIO 13.9

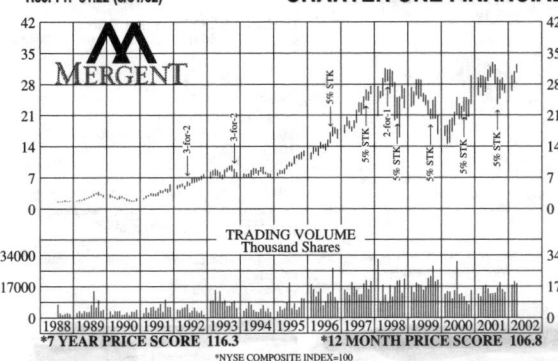

TRADING VOLUME
Thousand Shares

*7 YEAR PRICE SCORE 116.3   *12 MONTH PRICE SCORE 106.8
*NYSE COMPOSITE INDEX=100

INTERIM EARNINGS (Per Share):

Qtr.	Mar.	June	Sept.	Dec.
1998	0.37	0.40	0.41	0.23
1999	0.43	0.45	0.44	0.09
2000	0.48	0.45	0.49	0.50
2001	0.51	0.57	0.57	0.59

INTERIM DIVIDENDS (Per Share):

Amt.	Decl.	Ex.	Rec.	Pay.
0.20Q	4/18/01	5/03/01	5/07/01	5/21/01
0.20Q	7/18/01	8/02/01	8/06/01	8/20/01
5% STK	7/18/01	9/17/01	9/14/01	9/28/01
0.20Q	10/24/01	11/02/01	11/06/01	11/20/01
0.20Q	1/22/02	2/04/02	2/06/02	2/20/02

Indicated div.: $0.80 (Div. Reinv. Plan)

CAPITALIZATION (12/31/01):

	($000)	(%)
Total Deposits	25,123,309	68.4
Long-Term Debt	8,657,238	23.6
Common & Surplus	2,928,500	8.0
Total	36,709,047	100.0

DIVIDEND ACHIEVER STATUS:
Rank: 17   10-Year Growth Rate: 21.83%
Total Years of Dividend Growth: 13

RECENT DEVELOPMENTS: For the year ended 12/31/01, net income increased 15.4% to $500.7 million from $434.0 million in the prior year. Earnings for 2001 and 2000 included pre-tax non-recurring net gains of $114.3 million and $9.3 million, respectively. Earnings for 2000 also included pre-tax merger expenses of $29.5 million. Net interest income improved 9.7% to $990.4 million from $903.0 million the year before.

PROSPECTS: On 1/11/02, the Company announced that it entered into a definitive agreement to acquire Charter National Bancorp, Inc. in a cash-out merger. Charter Bank, the principal subsidiary of Charter National, is a state-chartered commercial bank with nearly $300.0 million in assets, $250.0 million in deposits and eight branch offices in Michigan. The acquisition is expected to close in the second quarter of 2002.

BUSINESS

CHARTER ONE FINANCIAL, INC. is a bank holding company whose principal line of business is consumer banking, which includes retail banking, mortgage banking and other related financial services. As of 12/31/01, CF had $38.17 billion in total assets. CF has 456 branch locations in Ohio, Michigan, Illinois, New York, Massachusetts and Vermont, and operates 919 automated teller machines at various banking offices. Additionally, Charter One Mortgage Corp., CF's mortgage banking subsidiary, operates 29 loan production offices across 10 states. On 10/1/99, CF acquired St. Paul Bancorp, Inc. On 11/5/99, CF acquired fourteen Vermont National Bank offices from Chittenden Corporation. On 7/2/01, CF acquired Alliance Bancorp.

REVENUES

12/31/2001	($000)	(%)
Loans & Leases	1,872,270	65.7
Mortgage-Backed Securities	453,427	15.9
Investment Securities	11,589	0.4
Other Interest-Earning Assets	40,960	1.4
Noninterest Income	473,624	16.6
Total	2,851,870	100.0

ANNUAL FINANCIAL DATA

	12/31/01	12/31/00	12/31/99	12/31/98	12/31/97	12/31/96	12/31/95
Earnings Per Share	④ 2.21	③ 1.91	①② 1.39	①② 1.40	①② 0.96	1.10	① 0.29
Tang. Book Val. Per Share	11.49	10.45	9.57	8.96	8.15	7.65	7.26
Dividends Per Share	0.75	0.64	0.54	0.45	0.39	0.34	0.28
Dividend Payout %	34.0	33.8	39.1	32.5	40.5	30.6	95.8
INCOME STATEMENT (IN MILLIONS)							
Total Interest Income	2,378.2	2,247.1	2,128.5	1,760.4	1,377.7	1,004.5	1,087.4
Total Interest Expense	1,387.8	1,344.1	1,194.4	1,031.3	850.7	621.1	769.6
Net Interest Income	990.4	903.0	934.1	729.1	527.0	383.4	317.8
Provision for Loan Losses	100.8	54.2	35.2	29.5	40.9	4.0	1.0
Non-Interest Income	473.6	392.9	230.6	211.6	110.8	57.1	d47.8
Non-Interest Expense	629.7	604.0	633.3	492.5	373.9	244.0	215.7
Income Before Taxes	733.6	637.7	496.1	418.7	223.0	192.5	53.2
Net Income	④ 500.7	③ 434.0	①② 335.5	①② 277.0	①② 151.1	127.7	① 34.0
Average Shs. Outstg. (000)	227,032	228,471	240,175	197,651	157,420	116,484	117,058
BALANCE SHEET (IN MILLIONS)							
Cash & Due from Banks	...	530.8	689.1	334.1	214.7	152.3	163.1
Securities Avail. for Sale	8,030.5	4,087.2	4,193.1	2,299.2	1,070.2	265.4	1,843.0
Total Loans & Leases	25,842.1	24,297.4	22,545.8	17,688.0	12,360.1	8,295.0	6,842.9
Allowance for Credit Losses	446.0	347.3	268.9	185.3	...	194.6	168.6
Net Loans & Leases	25,396.1	23,950.2	22,276.9	17,502.7	12,360.1	8,100.3	6,674.3
Total Assets	38,174.5	32,971.4	31,464.8	24,467.3	19,760.3	13,904.6	13,578.9
Total Deposits	25,123.3	19,605.7	19,074.0	15,165.1	10,219.2	7,841.2	7,012.5
Long-Term Obligations	8,657.2	9,636.3	9,226.2	6,186.1	5,370.5	3,194.3	3,163.1
Total Liabilities	35,246.0	30,515.2	29,421.4	22,592.1	18,383.4	12,975.9	12,734.5
Net Stockholders' Equity	2,928.5	2,456.2	2,397.7	1,875.1	1,376.9	928.7	844.4
Year-end Shs. Outstg. (000)	224,340	218,640	230,707	191,470	157,914	112,904	114,911
STATISTICAL RECORD:							
Return on Equity %	17.1	17.7	14.0	14.8	11.0	13.8	4.0
Return on Assets %	1.3	1.3	1.1	1.1	0.8	0.9	0.3
Equity/Assets %	7.7	7.4	7.6	7.7	7.0	6.7	6.2
Non-Int. Exp./Tot. Inc. %	43.0	46.6	54.4	52.4	58.6	55.4	79.9
Price Range	32.98-23.40	30.00-14.52	29.14-16.67	31.64-15.99	27.64-16.92	18.41-11.07	13.08-7.93
P/E Ratio	14.9-10.6	15.7-7.6	21.0-12.0	22.6-11.4	28.8-17.6	16.8-10.1	44.8-25.3
Average Yield %	2.7	2.9	2.4	1.9	1.7	2.3	2.7

Statistics are as originally reported. Adj. for stk. splits: 5% stk. div., 9/01, 9/00, 9/99; 9/98; 2-for-1, 5/98; 5% stk. div., 10/97; 5% stk. div., 9/96. ① Incl. non-recurr. chrg. $37.5 mill., 1995; $60.6 mill., 1997; $55.7 mill., 1998; $63.5 mill., 1999. ② Bef. extraord. chrg.: $2.7 mill., 1997; $61.7 mill., 1998; $1.6 mill., 1999. ③ Incl. pre-tax merger expenses of $29.5 mill. & non-recurr. net gains of $9.3 mill. ④ Incl. pre-tax nonrecurr. net gains of $114.3 mill.

OFFICERS:
C. J. Koch, Chmn., Pres., C.E.O.
H. G. Chorbajian, Vice-Chmn.
J. L. Schostak, Vice-Chmn.
R. W. Neu, Exec. V.P., C.F.O.

INVESTOR CONTACT: Ellen L. Batkie, Senior V.P., (800) 262-6301

PRINCIPAL OFFICE: 1215 Superior Avenue, Cleveland, OH 44114

TELEPHONE NUMBER: (216) 566-5300
FAX: (216) 566-1465
WEB: www.charterone.com

NO. OF EMPLOYEES: 6,850

SHAREHOLDERS: 20,000 (approx.)

ANNUAL MEETING: In April

INCORPORATED: DE, 1987

INSTITUTIONAL HOLDINGS:
No. of Institutions: 310
Shares Held: 137,252,101
% Held: 62.6

INDUSTRY: Federal savings institutions (SIC: 6035)

TRANSFER AGENT(S): EquiServe, Providence, RI

CENTURYTEL, INC.

YIELD	0.6%
P/E RATIO	14.0

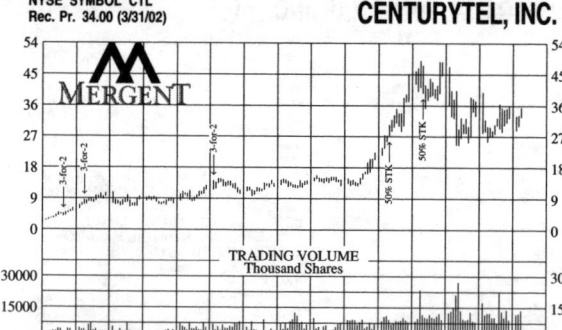

7 YEAR PRICE SCORE 102.2   **12 MONTH PRICE SCORE 107.6**
*NYSE COMPOSITE INDEX=100

INTERIM EARNINGS (Per Share):

Qtr.	Mar.	June	Sept.	Dec.
1998	0.41	0.46	0.39	0.37
1999	0.43	0.38	0.46	0.43
2000	0.35	0.41	0.47	0.40
2001	0.33	1.09	0.65	0.35

INTERIM DIVIDENDS (Per Share):

Amt.	Decl.	Ex.	Rec.	Pay.
0.05Q	5/22/01	5/30/01	6/01/01	6/15/01
0.05Q	8/21/01	8/29/01	8/31/01	9/14/01
0.05Q	11/15/01	11/28/01	11/30/01	12/14/01
0.052Q	2/26/02	3/07/02	3/11/02	3/22/02

Indicated div.: $0.21 (Div. Reinv. Plan)

CAPITALIZATION (12/31/01):

	($000)	(%)
Long-Term Debt	2,087,500	47.2
Preferred Stock	7,975	0.2
Common & Surplus	2,329,405	52.6
Total	4,424,880	100.0

DIVIDEND ACHIEVER STATUS:
Rank: 241   10-Year Growth Rate: 4.62%
Total Years of Dividend Growth: 28

RECENT DEVELOPMENTS: For the year ended 12/31/01, net income was $343.0 million compared with $231.5 million a year earlier. Earnings for 2001 and 2000 included pre-tax non-recurring gains of $200.0 million and $20.6 million, respectively. Total revenues rose 14.7% to $2.12 billion from $1.85 billion the previous year, primarily due to the Verizon access lines acquired on 7/31/00. Operating income advanced 6.2% to $557.9 million versus $525.4 million the year before.

PROSPECTS: On 3/19/02, CTL announced a definitive stock purchase agreement with ALLTEL Corporation to sell its wireless business and related licenses for $1.65 billion in cash. The cellular licenses and operations include about 7.8 million population equivalents in markets consolidated by the Company. The CTL consolidated markets service almost 800,000 cellular subscribers in portions of Arkansas, Louisiana, Michigan, Mississippi, Texas and Wisconsin. The transaction is expected to close by 9/30/02.

BUSINESS

CENTURYTEL, INC. (formerly Century Telephone Enterprises, Inc.) is a regional diversified telecommunications company that is primarily engaged in providing integrated communications services including local exchange, wireless, long distance, Internet access and security monitoring services. As of 1/31/02, Century's telephone subsidiaries provided service to nearly 3.0 million customers in 21 states. Century Cellunet, Inc. provides mobile communications services. Century Business Communications, Inc. offers mailing, direct marketing and creative services, database management, workflow analysis and systems consultation. Century Telecommunications, Inc. provides long-distance service and operator services on a regional basis. Interactive Communications, Inc. provides interactive information services. On 7/31/00, CTL acquired certain assets from Verizon Communications for approximately $1.10 billion.

ANNUAL FINANCIAL DATA

	12/31/01	12/31/00	12/31/99	12/31/98	12/31/97	12/31/96	12/31/95
Earnings Per Share	[4] 2.41	[3] 1.63	[3] 1.70	[1] 1.64	[2] 1.87	[2] 0.96	0.88
Cash Flow Per Share	5.63	4.37	4.16	3.98	3.02	1.94	1.75
Tang. Book Val. Per Share	...	...	1.45	...	...	3.61	2.95
Dividends Per Share	0.20	0.19	0.18	0.17	0.165	0.16	0.15
Dividend Payout %	8.3	11.7	10.6	10.6	8.8	16.7	16.8
INCOME STATEMENT (IN MILLIONS):							
Total Revenues	2,117.5	1,845.9	1,676.7	1,577.1	901.5	749.7	644.8
Costs & Expenses	1,086.2	932.5	819.8	768.7	474.3	394.4	328.2
Depreciation & Amort.	473.4	388.1	348.8	328.6	159.5	132.0	113.8
Operating Income	557.9	525.4	508.1	479.8	267.8	223.3	202.9
Net Interest Inc./(Exp.)	d225.5	d183.3	d150.6	d167.6	d56.5	d44.7	d43.6
Income Before Income Taxes	553.1	386.2	429.3	387.5	408.3	203.6	183.1
Income Taxes	210.0	154.7	189.5	158.7	152.4	74.6	68.3
Equity Earnings/Minority Int.	15.6	16.8	d0.2	20.1	22.3	20.3	12.0
Net Income	[4] 343.0	[3] 231.5	[3] 239.8	[1] 228.8	[2] 256.0	[2] 129.1	114.8
Cash Flow	816.2	619.6	588.2	556.9	415.0	260.7	228.4
Average Shs. Outstg. (000)	142,307	141,864	141,432	140,105	137,142	134,829	130,806
BALANCE SHEET (IN MILLIONS):							
Cash & Cash Equivalents	13.4	19.0	56.6	5.7	26.0	8.4	8.5
Total Current Assets	300.3	376.5	286.1	226.2	283.5	109.2	95.3
Net Property	2,999.6	2,959.3	2,256.5	2,351.5	2,258.4	1,149.0	1,047.8
Total Assets	6,318.7	6,393.3	4,705.4	4,935.5	4,709.2	2,028.5	1,862.4
Total Current Liabilities	1,294.0	743.4	309.2	304.8	322.1	144.1	139.9
Long-Term Obligations	2,087.5	3,050.3	2,078.3	2,558.0	2,609.5	625.9	622.9
Net Stockholders' Equity	2,337.4	2,032.1	1,848.0	1,531.5	1,300.3	1,028.2	888.4
Net Working Capital	d993.7	d366.9	d23.1	d78.6	d38.6	d34.9	d44.6
Year-end Shs. Outstg. (000)	141,233	140,667	139,946	138,083	136,656	134,683	133,007
STATISTICAL RECORD:							
Operating Profit Margin %	26.3	28.5	30.3	30.4	29.7	29.8	31.5
Net Profit Margin %	16.2	12.5	14.3	14.5	28.4	17.2	17.8
Return on Equity %	14.7	11.4	13.0	14.9	19.7	12.6	12.9
Return on Assets %	5.4	3.6	5.1	4.6	5.4	6.4	6.2
Debt/Total Assets %	33.0	47.7	44.2	51.8	55.4	30.9	33.4
Price Range	39.88-25.45	47.31-24.44	49.00-35.19	45.17-21.56	22.42-12.67	15.78-12.67	14.72-12.00
P/E Ratio	16.5-10.6	29.0-15.0	28.8-20.7	27.5-13.1	12.0-6.8	16.5-13.2	16.8-13.7
Average Yield %	0.6	0.5	0.4	0.5	0.9	1.1	1.1

Statistics are as originally reported. Adj. for 50% stk. div., 3/99 & 3/98. [1] Incl. non-recurr. pre-tax credit of $49.9 mill. [2] Incl. pre-tax credit 12/31/97: $169.9 mill.; credit 12/31/96, $815,000. [3] Incl. pre-tax gain on sales of assets of $20.6 mill., 2000; $62.8 mill., 1999. [4] Incl. pre-tax non-recurr. gain of $200.0 mill.

OFFICERS:
C. M. Williams, Chmn.
G. F. Post III, Vice-Chmn., Pres., C.E.O.
R. S. Ewing, Jr., Exec. V.P., C.F.O.

INVESTOR CONTACT: Jeffrey S. Glover, V.P., Inv. Rel., (318) 388-9000

PRINCIPAL OFFICE: 100 CenturyTel Drive, Monroe, LA 71203

TELEPHONE NUMBER: (318) 388-9000
FAX: (318) 789-8656
WEB: www.centurytel.com
NO. OF EMPLOYEES: 6,900 (approx.)
SHAREHOLDERS: 5,300 (approx.)
ANNUAL MEETING: In May
INCORPORATED: LA, Apr., 1968

INSTITUTIONAL HOLDINGS:
No. of Institutions: 316
Shares Held: 100,511,038
% Held: 71.2

INDUSTRY: Telephone communications, exc. radio (SIC: 4813)

TRANSFER AGENT(S): Computershare Investor Services, LLC, Chicago, IL

CEDAR FAIR, L.P.

YIELD 6.9%
P/E RATIO 21.0

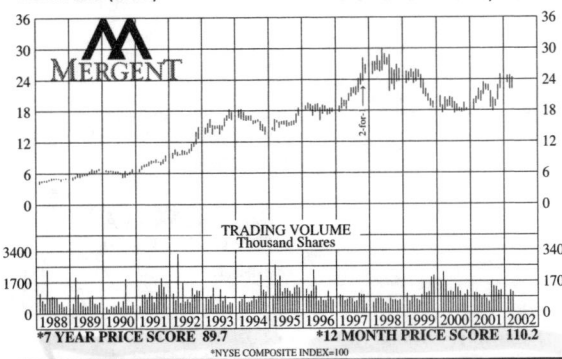

*7 YEAR PRICE SCORE 89.7   *12 MONTH PRICE SCORE 110.2
*NYSE COMPOSITE INDEX=100

INTERIM EARNINGS (Per Share):

Qtr.	Mar.	June	Sept.	Dec.
1997	d0.37	0.31	1.81	d0.28
1998	d0.44	0.37	1.79	d0.14
1999	d0.41	0.37	1.83	d0.15
2000	d0.51	0.36	1.83	d0.17
2001	d0.60	0.13	2.10	d0.50

INTERIM DIVIDENDS (Per Share):

Amt.	Decl.	Ex.	Rec.	Pay.
0.39Q	3/09/01	4/02/01	4/04/01	5/15/01
0.39Q	6/15/01	7/02/01	7/05/01	8/15/01
0.41Q	9/20/01	10/01/01	10/03/01	11/15/01
0.41Q	12/20/01	1/02/02	1/04/02	2/15/02
0.41Q	3/11/02	4/01/02	4/03/02	5/15/02

Indicated div.: $1.64 (Div. Reinv. Plan)

CAPITALIZATION (12/31/01):

	($000)	(%)
Long-Term Debt	373,000	54.8
Common & Surplus	308,250	45.2
Total	681,250	100.0

DIVIDEND ACHIEVER STATUS:
Rank: 177   10-Year Growth Rate: 7.83%
Total Years of Dividend Growth: 14

RECENT DEVELOPMENTS: For the year ended 12/31/01, net income declined 25.6% to $57.9 million compared with $77.8 million in 2000, reflecting a decline in combined in-park guest per capita spending, a modest capital program and the overall weakness in the economy. Results for 2001 included a non-cash unit option expense of $11.7 million, while results for 2000 included a non-recurring charge to terminate general partner fees of $7.8 million. Net revenues increased 0.9% to $477.3 million.

PROSPECTS: The Company plans to invest $42.0 million in capital improvements at its eleven properties. The Company expects that increasing returns from its newest parks will contribute to at least 3.0% to 5.0% internal growth in net revenues in the upcoming season. This improvement is expected to be driven by increases in attendance at both Cedar Point and Knott's Berry Farm and increased guest per capita spending across all eleven properties.

BUSINESS

CEDAR FAIR, L.P. is a limited partnership managed by Cedar Fair Management Company. The partnership owns and operates six amusement parks: Cedar Point, located on Lake Erie in Sandusky, OH; Knott's Berry Farm, located in Buena Park, CA; Dorney Park & Wildwater Kingdom, near Allentown, PA; Valleyfair, located in near Minneapolis, MN. Worlds of Fun and Oceans of Fun, located in Kansas City, MO; and Michigan's Adventure, located near Muskegon, MI. The partnership's water parks are located in Chula Vista and Palm Springs, CA and adjacent to Cedar Point, Knott's Berry Farm and Worlds of Fun. The parks are family-oriented, with recreational facilities for people of all ages, and provide rides and entertainment. All principal rides and attractions are owned and operated by the partnership. The Company has two hotels: Breakers Tower at Cedar Point and the Buena Park Hotel. FUN also operates Knott's Camp Snoopy at the Mall of America in Bloomington, MN under a management contract.

ANNUAL FINANCIAL DATA

	12/31/01	12/31/00	12/31/99	12/31/98	12/31/97	12/31/96	12/31/95
Earnings Per Share	② 1.13	① 1.50	1.63	1.58	1.47	1.59	1.45
Cash Flow Per Share	1.96	2.27	2.31	2.20	1.95	2.02	1.83
Tang. Book Val. Per Share	5.88	6.31	6.56	6.38	5.24	3.47	3.06
Dividends Per Share	1.58	1.50	1.39	1.28	1.26	1.18	1.13
Dividend Payout %	139.8	100.2	85.1	81.3	85.5	73.9	78.0

INCOME STATEMENT (IN THOUSANDS):

Total Revenues	477,256	472,920	438,001	419,500	264,137	250,523	218,197
Costs & Expenses	336,213	317,832	286,194	274,827	166,306	150,330	128,442
Depreciation & Amort.	42,486	39,572	35,082	32,065	21,528	19,072	16,742
Operating Income	98,557	115,516	116,755	112,608	76,303	81,121	73,013
Net Interest Inc./(Exp.)	d24,143	d21,357	d15,371	d14,660	d7,845	d6,942	d6,877
Income Before Income Taxes	74,414	94,159	101,384	97,948	68,458	74,179	66,136
Income Taxes	16,520	16,353	15,580	14,507	...	...	...
Net Income	② 57,894	① 77,806	85,794	83,441	68,458	74,179	66,136
Cash Flow	100,380	117,378	120,856	115,506	89,986	93,251	82,878
Average Shs. Outstg.	51,113	51,679	52,390	52,414	46,265	46,116	45,214

BALANCE SHEET (IN THOUSANDS):

Cash & Cash Equivalents	2,280	2,392	638	1,137	2,520	1,279	111
Total Current Assets	26,868	25,278	24,184	20,967	21,954	11,730	9,805
Net Property	771,918	728,919	674,640	600,044	567,137	281,638	253,840
Total Assets	810,231	764,143	708,961	631,325	599,619	304,104	274,717
Total Current Liabilities	96,700	114,024	86,559	77,231	62,426	39,241	37,648
Long-Term Obligations	373,000	300,000	261,200	200,350	189,750	87,600	80,000
Net Stockholders' Equity	308,250	330,589	349,986	341,991	285,381	169,994	151,476
Net Working Capital	d69,832	d88,646	d62,375	d56,264	d40,472	d27,511	d27,843
Year-end Shs. Outstg.	50,514	50,813	51,798	51,980	52,403	45,920	45,920

STATISTICAL RECORD:

Operating Profit Margin %	20.7	24.4	26.7	26.8	28.9	32.4	33.5
Net Profit Margin %	12.1	16.5	19.6	19.9	25.9	29.6	30.3
Return on Equity %	18.8	23.5	24.5	24.4	24.0	43.6	43.7
Return on Assets %	7.1	10.2	12.1	13.2	11.4	24.4	24.1
Debt/Total Assets %	46.0	39.3	36.8	31.7	31.6	28.8	29.1
Price Range	25.00-17.80	20.88-17.44	26.00-18.44	30.13-21.75	28.25-17.69	19.50-16.13	18.56-14.06
P/E Ratio	22.1-15.8	13.9-11.6	15.9-11.3	19.1-13.8	19.2-12.0	12.3-10.1	12.8-9.7
Average Yield %	7.4	7.8	6.2	5.0	5.5	6.6	6.9

Statistics are as originally reported. Adj. for stk. split: 2-for-1, 11/7/97. ① Incl. nonrecurr. chrg. of $7.8 mill. to terminate general partner fees. ② Incl. non-cash unit option exp. of $11.7 mill.

OFFICERS:
R. L. Kinzel, Pres., C.E.O.
B. A. Jackson, Corp. V.P., C.F.O.
T. W. Salamone, Treas.

INVESTOR CONTACT: Brian C. Witherow, Corporate Director - Investor Relations, (419) 627-2233

PRINCIPAL OFFICE: One Cedar Point Drive, Sandusky, OH 44870-5259

TELEPHONE NUMBER: (419) 626-0830
FAX: (419) 627-2260
WEB: www.cedarfair.com
NO. OF EMPLOYEES: 1,400 (approx.)
SHAREHOLDERS: 10,000 (approx.)
ANNUAL MEETING: N/A
INCORPORATED: MN, 1983; reincorp., DE, 1987

INSTITUTIONAL HOLDINGS:
No. of Institutions: 106
Shares Held: 10,301,447
% Held: 20.4

INDUSTRY: Amusement parks (SIC: 7996)

TRANSFER AGENT(S): American Stock Transfer & Trust Company, New York, NY

NYSE SYMBOL CSL
Rec. Pr. 43.72 (3/31/02)

CARLISLE COMPANIES INCORPORATED

YIELD 1.9%
P/E RATIO 53.3

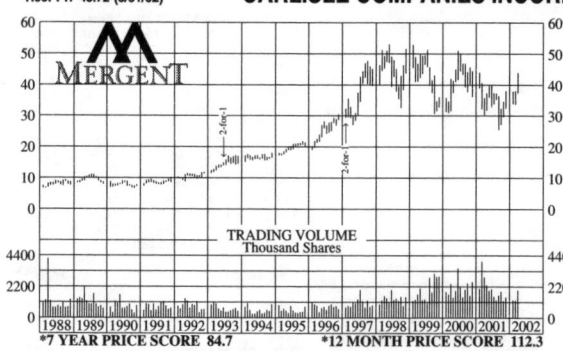

TRADING VOLUME
Thousand Shares

1988|1989|1990|1991|1992|1993|1994|1995|1996|1997|1998|1999|2000|2001|2002

7 YEAR PRICE SCORE 84.7 | **12 MONTH PRICE SCORE 112.3**
*NYSE COMPOSITE INDEX=100

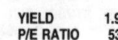

INTERIM EARNINGS (Per Share):

Qtr.	Mar.	June	Sept.	Dec.
1998	0.62	0.80	0.73	0.62
1999	0.71	0.91	0.81	0.70
2000	0.83	1.04	0.92	0.35
2001	d0.33	0.54	0.36	0.25

INTERIM DIVIDENDS (Per Share):

Amt.	Decl.	Ex.	Rec.	Pay.
0.20Q	2/07/01	2/14/01	2/16/01	3/01/01
0.20Q	5/02/01	5/15/01	5/17/01	6/01/01
0.21Q	8/01/01	8/15/01	8/17/01	9/01/01
0.21Q	11/07/01	11/14/01	11/16/01	12/01/01
0.21Q	2/06/02	2/13/02	2/18/02	3/01/02

Indicated div.: $0.84 (Div. Reinv. Plan)

CAPITALIZATION (12/31/01):

	($000)	(%)
Long-Term Debt	461,744	46.1
Common & Surplus	540,284	53.9
Total	1,002,028	100.0

DIVIDEND ACHIEVER STATUS:
Rank: 138   10-Year Growth Rate: 10.04%
Total Years of Dividend Growth: 25

RECENT DEVELOPMENTS: For the year ended 12/31/01, net earnings declined 74.2% to $24.8 million versus $96.2 million in 2000. Results for 2001 included an after-tax restructuring charge of $21.5 million. Net sales increased 4.4% to $1.85 billion from $1.77 billion a year earlier. Construction Materials segment sales jumped 14.2% to $464.9 million, while Industrial Components segment sales grew 5.8% to $679.0 million. General Industry segment sales improved 8.0% to $453.6 million, while Automotive Components segment sales fell 16.7% to $252.0 million.

PROSPECTS: The Company is responding to recessionary economic conditions by reducing production levels and costs, cutting inventory and increasing its cash flow. Also, the Company believes that aggressive actions taken in 2001 to close less efficient facilities and to realign and consolidate other plants will provide a foundation for growth going forward. Meanwhile, results in the Automotive Components segment continue to be negatively affected by reductions in North American vehicle production.

BUSINESS

CARLISLE COMPANIES INCORPORATED produces and sells a diverse line of products in six industry segments. The Industrial Components segment (25.8% of 2001 revenue) manufactures and distributes tire and wheel assemblies and high-performance wire/cable and cable assemblies.

The Construction Materials segment (25.1%) manufactures membranes and accessories for rubber and plastic roofing systems for non-residential flat roofs. The Automotive Components segment (13.6%) manufactures highly engineered plastic and rubber components for the automotive industry. The Transportation Products segment (6.5%) produces specialty and high-payload trailers and dump bodies. The Specialty Products segment (6.3%) manufactures heavy-duty friction and braking systems for trucks and off-highway equipment. The General Industry segment (22.7%) consists of several businesses with products, including stainless steel in-plant processing equipment, food service products and cheesemaking systems. In January 1999, CSL divested its perishable cargo business.

ANNUAL FINANCIAL DATA

	12/31/01	12/31/00	12/31/99	12/31/98	12/31/97	12/31/96	12/31/95
Earnings Per Share	② 0.82	3.14	① 3.13	2.77	2.28	1.80	1.41
Cash Flow Per Share	2.92	5.09	4.67	4.24	3.53	2.76	2.15
Tang. Book Val. Per Share	6.72	9.79	10.63	8.85	7.48	6.55	7.71
Dividends Per Share	0.82	0.76	0.68	0.60	0.53	0.47	0.42
Dividend Payout %	100.0	24.2	21.7	21.7	23.0	25.8	29.8
INCOME STATEMENT (IN MILLIONS):							
Total Revenues	1,849.5	1,771.1	1,611.3	1,517.5	1,260.6	1,017.5	822.5
Costs & Expenses	1,720.9	1,536.1	1,396.0	1,320.7	1,094.4	890.6	723.2
Depreciation & Amort.	64.0	59.5	47.4	45.2	38.8	29.8	23.2
Operating Income	64.6	175.4	167.9	151.6	127.4	97.1	76.1
Net Interest Inc./(Exp.)	d29.1	d28.0	d19.2	d22.7	d16.5	d9.1	d6.1
Income Before Income Taxes	37.9	150.9	155.5	140.3	116.8	92.0	72.9
Income Taxes	13.1	54.7	59.7	55.4	46.1	36.4	28.8
Net Income	② 24.8	96.2	① 95.8	84.9	70.7	55.7	44.1
Cash Flow	88.8	155.7	143.2	130.1	109.4	85.4	67.3
Average Shs. Outstg. (000)	30,450	30,599	30,635	30,674	31,025	30,953	31,266
BALANCE SHEET (IN MILLIONS):							
Cash & Cash Equivalents	15.6	9.0	10.4	3.9	1.7	8.3	3.2
Total Current Assets	553.3	576.5	541.0	478.5	417.5	345.9	281.9
Net Property	447.7	402.6	349.5	354.8	294.2	264.2	193.1
Total Assets	1,398.0	1,305.7	1,080.7	1,022.9	861.2	742.5	542.4
Total Current Liabilities	273.8	399.9	240.4	255.3	226.1	170.6	128.2
Long-Term Obligations	461.7	281.9	281.7	273.5	209.6	315.5	72.7
Net Stockholders' Equity	540.3	547.9	478.1	406.9	348.8	307.5	273.3
Net Working Capital	279.5	176.5	300.7	223.2	191.4	175.3	153.7
Year-end Shs. Outstg. (000)	30,263	30,251	30,128	30,179	30,351	30,351	30,638
STATISTICAL RECORD:							
Operating Profit Margin %	3.5	9.9	10.4	10.0	10.1	9.5	9.3
Net Profit Margin %	1.3	5.4	5.9	5.6	5.6	5.5	5.4
Return on Equity %	4.6	17.6	20.0	20.9	20.3	18.1	16.1
Return on Assets %	1.8	7.4	8.9	8.3	8.2	7.5	8.1
Debt/Total Assets %	33.0	21.6	26.1	26.7	24.3	42.5	13.4
Price Range	44.00-25.50	51.00-30.94	52.94-30.63	53.06-32.56	47.75-27.00	30.50-19.00	21.81-17.25
P/E Ratio	53.7-31.1	16.2-9.9	16.9-9.8	19.2-11.8	20.9-11.8	16.9-10.6	15.5-12.2
Average Yield %	2.4	1.9	1.6	1.4	1.4	1.9	2.2

Statistics are as originally reported. Adj. for stk. split: 2-for-1, 1/97 ① Incl. non-recurr. gain of $685,000. ② Incl. after-tax restructuring chrg. of $21.5 mill.

OFFICERS:
S. P. Munn, Chmn.
R. D. McKinnish, Pres., C.E.O.

INVESTOR CONTACT: Investor Relations, (704) 501-1100

PRINCIPAL OFFICE: 13925 Ballantyne Corporate Place, Suite 400, Charlotte, NC 28277

TELEPHONE NUMBER: (704) 501-1100
FAX: (704) 501-1190
WEB: www.carlisle.com
NO. OF EMPLOYEES: 11,710 (approx.)
SHAREHOLDERS: 2,257 (record)
ANNUAL MEETING: In April
INCORPORATED: DE, Sept., 1917; reincorp., DE, May, 1986

INSTITUTIONAL HOLDINGS:
No. of Institutions: 131
Shares Held: 16,084,376
% Held: 53.2

INDUSTRY: Tires and inner tubes (SIC: 3011)

TRANSFER AGENT(S): Computershare Investor Services, Chicago, IL

CALIFORNIA WATER SERVICE GROUP

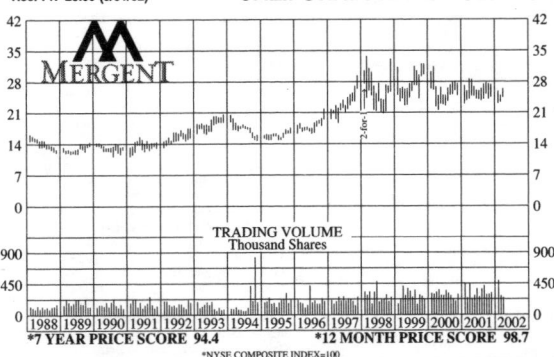

INTERIM EARNINGS (Per Share):

Qtr.	Mar.	June	Sept.	Dec.
1998	0.12	0.28	0.72	0.33
1999	0.20	0.44	0.62	0.30
2000	0.09	0.38	0.60	0.23
2001	0.01	0.37	0.39	0.20

INTERIM DIVIDENDS (Per Share):

Amt.	Decl.	Ex.	Rec.	Pay.
0.279Q	1/24/01	1/30/01	2/01/01	2/15/01
0.279Q	4/18/01	4/27/01	5/01/01	5/15/01
0.279Q	7/25/01	7/30/01	8/01/01	8/15/01
0.279Q	10/24/01	10/30/01	11/01/01	11/15/01
0.28Q	1/30/02	2/06/02	2/08/02	2/22/02

Indicated div.: $1.12 (Div. Reinv. Plan)

CAPITALIZATION (12/31/01):

	($000)	(%)
Long-Term Debt	202,600	47.0
Deferred Income Tax	28,816	6.7
Preferred Stock	3,475	0.8
Common & Surplus	196,619	45.6
Total	431,510	100.0

DIVIDEND ACHIEVER STATUS:
Rank: 273   10-Year Growth Rate: 2.17%
Total Years of Dividend Growth: 34

*7 YEAR PRICE SCORE 94.4   *12 MONTH PRICE SCORE 98.7
*NYSE COMPOSITE INDEX=100

RECENT DEVELOPMENTS: For the year ended 12/31/01, net income decreased 25.0% to $15.0 million compared with $20.0 million in 2000. The decrease in earnings was due to lower water sales to existing customers due to weather conditions, significantly higher purchased power costs and delays in regulatory rate relief. Operating revenues advanced slightly to $246.8 million versus $244.8 million in the previous year. Net operating income fell 24.2% to $25.2 million from $33.2 million a year earlier.

PROSPECTS: In 2002, the Company will seek to expand the non-regulated side of the business by pursuing non-regulated service contracts, maximizing the value of its excess real estate and leasing portions of its properties to partners like cellular telephone service providers. In addition, the Company plans to invest more in its infrastructure in 2002. Much of the capital investment planned for 2002 is needed to enable CWT to meet increasingly strict water quality standards.

BUSINESS

CALIFORNIA WATER SERVICE GROUP is a public utility water company that provides regulated and non-regulated water utility services to more than 2.0 million customers in 98 communities in California, Washington and New Mexico as of 1/30/02. CWT is the parent company of California Water Service Co., CWS Utility Services, New Mexico Water Service Co. and Washington Water Service Co. The sole business of the Company consists of the production, purchase, storage, purification, distribution and sale of water for domestic, industrial, public, and irrigation uses, and for fire protection. Annual water production totaled nearly 127 billion gallons for 2001, with 51.6% from wells and surface supplies and 48.4% from purchased water.

REVENUES

12/31/2001	($000)	(%)
Residential	173,823	70.4
Business	44,944	18.2
Industrial	9,907	4.0
Public Authorities	11,860	4.8
Other	6,286	2.6
Total	246,820	100.0

ANNUAL FINANCIAL DATA

	12/31/01	12/31/00	12/31/99	12/31/98	12/31/97	12/31/96	12/31/95
Earnings Per Share	0.97	1.31	1.53	1.45	1.83	1.51	1.17
Cash Flow Per Share	2.24	2.53	2.76	2.61	2.93	2.52	2.09
Tang. Book Val. Per Share	12.95	13.13	13.70	13.38	13.00	12.22	11.72
Dividends Per Share	1.11	1.10	1.08	1.07	1.05	1.04	1.02
Dividend Payout %	114.9	84.0	70.9	73.8	57.6	69.1	87.5
INCOME STATEMENT (IN THOUSANDS):							
Total Revenues	246,820	244,806	206,440	186,273	195,324	182,764	165,086
Costs & Expenses	180,584	170,079	138,669	122,056	124,036	119,265	110,686
Depreciation & Amort.	19,226	18,368	15,802	14,563	13,570	12,665	11,436
Maintenance Exp.	12,131	11,592	9,183	9,030	9,319	8,317	7,722
Operating Income	25,151	33,196	30,610	30,074	34,349	30,367	25,392
Net Interest Inc./(Exp.)	d16,029	d14,646	d13,201	d12,446	d11,902	d11,907	d11,462
Income Taxes	9,728	11,571	12,176	10,550	13,950	12,150	9,850
Net Income	14,965	19,963	19,919	18,395	23,305	19,067	14,698
Cash Flow	34,038	38,179	35,568	32,805	36,822	31,579	25,981
Average Shs. Outstg.	15,285	15,173	12,936	12,619	12,619	12,580	12,506
BALANCE SHEET (IN THOUSANDS):							
Gross Property	909,658	851,281	737,352	680,690	647,648	618,432	584,392
Accumulated Depreciation	285,316	269,273	221,998	202,385	187,241	174,844	162,217
Net Property	624,342	582,008	515,354	478,305	460,407	443,588	422,175
Total Assets	710,214	666,605	587,618	548,499	531,297	512,390	484,883
Long-Term Obligations	202,600	187,098	156,572	136,345	139,205	142,153	145,540
Net Stockholders' Equity	200,094	202,309	180,657	172,279	167,540	157,701	150,424
Year-end Shs. Outstg.	15,182	15,146	13,208	12,936	12,619	12,619	12,538
STATISTICAL RECORD:							
Operating Profit Margin %	10.2	13.6	14.8	16.1	17.6	16.6	15.4
Net Profit Margin %	6.1	8.2	9.6	9.9	11.9	10.4	8.9
Net Inc./Net Property %	2.4	3.4	3.9	3.8	5.1	4.3	3.5
Net Inc./Tot. Capital %	3.5	4.8	5.6	5.5	7.0	5.9	4.7
Return on Equity %	7.5	9.9	11.0	10.7	13.9	12.1	9.8
Accum. Depr./Gross Prop. %	31.4	31.6	30.1	29.7	28.9	28.3	27.8
Price Range	28.60-22.88	31.38-21.50	32.00-22.56	33.75-20.75	29.38-18.63	21.88-16.25	17.63-14.81
P/E Ratio	29.5-23.6	23.9-16.4	20.9-14.7	23.3-14.3	16.1-10.2	14.5-10.8	15.1-12.7
Average Yield %	4.3	4.2	4.0	3.9	4.4	4.5	6.3

Statistics are as originally reported. Adj. for stk. split: 2-for-1, 1/98

OFFICERS:
R. W. Foy, Chmn.
P. C. Nelson, Pres., C.E.O.
G. F. Feeney, V.P., C.F.O., Treas.

INVESTOR CONTACT: Gerald F. Feeney,
(408) 367-8216

PRINCIPAL OFFICE: 1720 North First Street,
San Jose, CA 95112

TELEPHONE NUMBER: (408) 367-8200
FAX: (408) 437-9185
WEB: www.calwater.com

NO. OF EMPLOYEES: 783 (avg.)

SHAREHOLDERS: 11,000 (approx.)

ANNUAL MEETING: In Apr.

INCORPORATED: CA, Dec., 1926

INSTITUTIONAL HOLDINGS:
No. of Institutions: 63
Shares Held: 2,547,720
% Held: 16.8

INDUSTRY: Water supply (SIC: 4941)

TRANSFER AGENT(S): Fleet National Bank
c/o EquiServe L.P., Providence, R.I.

BROWN-FORMAN CORPORATION

YIELD 1.9%
P/E RATIO 21.6

INTERIM EARNINGS (Per Share):

Qtr.	July	Oct.	Jan.	Apr.
1998-99	0.54	0.97	0.72	0.70
1999-00	0.56	1.06	0.80	0.76
2000-01	0.62	1.17	0.80	0.79
2001-02	0.57	1.17	0.84	...

INTERIM DIVIDENDS (Per Share):

Amt.	Decl.	Ex.	Rec.	Pay.
0.33Q	1/25/01	3/06/01	3/08/01	4/01/01
0.33Q	5/24/01	6/05/01	6/07/01	7/01/01
0.33Q	7/26/01	8/29/01	9/03/01	10/01/01
0.35Q	11/15/01	12/03/01	12/05/01	1/01/02
0.35Q	1/24/02	3/01/02	3/05/02	4/01/02

Indicated div.: $1.40 (Div. Reinv. Plan)

CAPITALIZATION (4/30/01):

	($000)	(%)
Long-Term Debt	40,000	3.1
Deferred Income Tax	62,000	4.8
Common & Surplus	1,187,000	92.1
Total	1,289,000	100.0

DIVIDEND ACHIEVER STATUS:
Rank: 218   10-Year Growth Rate: 5.86%
Total Years of Dividend Growth: 17

TRADING VOLUME Thousand Shares

1988|1989|1990|1991|1992|1993|1994|1995|1996|1997|1998|1999|2000|2001|2002

*7 YEAR PRICE SCORE 103.4   *12 MONTH PRICE SCORE 108.6

*NYSE COMPOSITE INDEX=100

RECENT DEVELOPMENTS: For the quarter ended 1/31/02, net income increased 1.8% to $57.3 million compared with $56.3 million in the corresponding period of the previous year. Net sales grew 2.0% to $570.5 million from $559.4 million the year before. Sales for the wine and spirits segment increased 1.6% to $400.5 million, while sales for the consumer durables segment improved 2.8% to $170.0 million. Operating income fell 2.8% to $88.3 million.

PROSPECTS: The Company continues to focus on its business initiatives that are aimed at strengthening production practices and reducing inventories. The total cost of this program is expected to lower net income by $20.0 million over fiscal years 2002 and 2003. These investments should significantly improve the Company's long-term cash flow and earnings. Meanwhile, the Company expects solid earnings growth for fiscal 2002 and beyond.

BUSINESS

BROWN-FORMAN CORPORATION, with assets as of 1/31/02 of $1.94 billion, operates in two business segments: wines and spirits and consumer durables. The wines and spirits segment includes the production, importing and marketing of wines and distilled spirits under brand names of JACK DANIEL's, SOUTHERN COMFORT, CANADIAN MIST, KORBEL CALIFORNIA CHAMPAGNES, and FETZER VINEYARDS CALIFORNIA WINES. The consumer durables segment includes tableware and flatware sold under the LENOX, GORHAM, DANSK, and KIRK STEFF brand names, as well as HARTMANN luggage. In fiscal 2001, sales (operating income) were as follows: 72.2% (87.4%), wine and spirits; and 27.8% (12.6%), consumer durables.

ANNUAL FINANCIAL DATA

	4/30/01	4/30/00	4/30/99	4/30/98	4/30/97	4/30/96	4/30/95
Earnings Per Share	3.40	3.18	2.93	2.67	2.45	2.31	2.15
Cash Flow Per Share	4.33	4.08	3.74	3.42	3.17	2.99	2.78
Tang. Book Val. Per Share	13.50	11.36	9.53	8.04	6.73	5.26	3.94
Dividends Per Share	1.24	1.18	1.12	1.08	1.04	0.99	0.95
Dividend Payout %	36.5	37.1	38.2	40.4	42.4	42.9	44.0
INCOME STATEMENT (IN MILLIONS):							
Total Revenues	2,180.0	2,134.0	2,030.0	1,924.0	1,841.0	1,807.0	1,679.6
Costs & Expenses	1,742.0	1,724.0	1,653.0	1,566.0	1,504.0	1,487.0	1,368.4
Depreciation & Amort.	64.0	62.0	55.0	51.0	50.0	46.0	43.5
Operating Income	374.0	348.0	322.0	307.0	287.0	274.0	267.8
Net Interest Inc./(Exp.)	d8.0	d5.0	d4.0	d11.0	d14.0	d17.0	d20.7
Income Before Income Taxes	366.0	343.0	318.0	296.0	273.0	257.0	247.1
Income Taxes	133.0	125.0	116.0	111.0	104.0	97.0	98.4
Net Income	233.0	218.0	202.0	185.0	169.0	160.0	148.6
Cash Flow	297.0	280.0	257.0	235.0	218.0	205.0	191.7
Average Shs. Outstg. (000)	68,600	68,600	68,700	69,000	69,014	68,996	68,996
BALANCE SHEET (IN MILLIONS):							
Cash & Cash Equivalents	86.0	180.0	171.0	78.0	58.0	54.0	62.5
Total Current Assets	994.0	1,020.0	999.0	869.0	802.0	768.0	697.9
Net Property	424.0	376.0	348.0	281.0	292.0	281.0	252.2
Total Assets	1,939.0	1,802.0	1,735.0	1,494.0	1,428.0	1,381.0	1,285.6
Total Current Liabilities	538.0	522.0	517.0	382.0	399.0	303.0	285.6
Long-Term Obligations	40.0	41.0	53.0	50.0	63.0	211.0	246.8
Net Stockholders' Equity	1,187.0	1,048.0	917.0	817.0	730.0	634.0	545.8
Net Working Capital	456.0	498.0	482.0	487.0	403.0	465.0	412.3
Year-end Shs. Outstg. (000)	68,459	68,512	68,506	68,996	68,996	68,996	68,996
STATISTICAL RECORD:							
Operating Profit Margin %	17.2	16.3	15.9	16.0	15.6	15.2	15.9
Net Profit Margin %	10.7	10.2	10.0	9.6	9.2	8.9	8.8
Return on Equity %	19.6	20.8	22.0	22.6	23.2	25.2	27.2
Return on Assets %	12.0	12.1	11.6	12.4	11.8	11.6	11.6
Debt/Total Assets %	2.1	2.3	3.1	3.3	4.4	15.3	19.2
Price Range	69.25-41.88	77.25-54.94	76.88-51.75	55.38-42.00	47.50-35.25	40.75-29.38	32.50-26.13
P/E Ratio	20.4-12.3	24.3-17.3	26.2-17.7	20.7-15.7	19.4-14.4	17.6-12.7	15.1-12.2
Average Yield %	2.2	1.8	1.7	2.2	2.5	2.8	3.2

Statistics are as originally reported.

OFFICERS:
O. Brown II, Chmn., C.E.O.
W. M. Street, Pres.
P. A. Wood, Exec. V.P., C.F.O.
M. B. Crutcher, Sr. V.P., Sec., Gen. Couns.

INVESTOR CONTACT: John Bridendall, Sr.
V.P.-Corp. Dev., (502) 774-7290

PRINCIPAL OFFICE: 850 Dixie Highway, Louisville, KY 40210

TELEPHONE NUMBER: (502) 585-1100
FAX: (502) 774-7876
WEB: www.brown-forman.com
NO. OF EMPLOYEES: 5,700 full-time (approx.); 1,700 part-time (approx.)
SHAREHOLDERS: 3,765 (Class A common); 4,486 (Class B common)
ANNUAL MEETING: In July
INCORPORATED: KY, 1901; reincorp., DE, 1933

INSTITUTIONAL HOLDINGS:
No. of Institutions: 183
Shares Held: 28,183,688
% Held: 41.3

INDUSTRY: Wines, brandy, and brandy spirits (SIC: 2084)

TRANSFER AGENT(S): First Chicago Trust Company of New York, New York City

BRISTOL-MYERS SQUIBB COMPANY

YIELD 2.8%
P/E RATIO 31.6

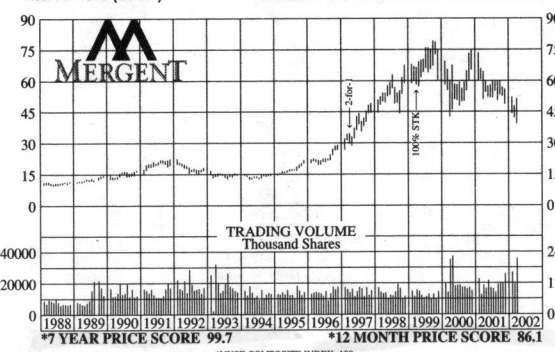

TRADING VOLUME
Thousand Shares

7 YEAR PRICE SCORE 99.7   *12 MONTH PRICE SCORE 86.1*
NYSE COMPOSITE INDEX=100

INTERIM EARNINGS (Per Share):

Qtr.	Mar.	June	Sept.	Dec.
1997	0.41	0.37	0.43	0.39
1998	0.46	0.41	0.48	0.21
1999	0.53	0.47	0.54	0.52
2000	0.56	0.50	0.45	0.54
2001	0.63	0.56	0.63	d0.54

INTERIM DIVIDENDS (Per Share):

Amt.	Decl.	Ex.	Rec.	Pay.
0.275Q	3/06/01	4/04/01	4/06/01	5/01/01
0.275Q	6/05/01	7/03/01	7/06/01	8/01/01
0.275Q	9/17/01	10/03/01	10/05/01	11/01/01
0.28Q	12/13/01	1/02/02	1/04/02	2/01/02
0.28Q	3/05/02	4/03/02	4/05/02	5/01/02

Indicated div.: $1.12 (Div. Reinv. Plan)

CAPITALIZATION (12/31/01):

	($000)	(%)
Long-Term Debt	6,237,000	36.7
Common & Surplus	10,736,000	63.3
Total	16,973,000	100.0

DIVIDEND ACHIEVER STATUS:

Rank: 207   10-Year Growth Rate: 6.25%
Total Years of Dividend Growth: 29

RECENT DEVELOPMENTS: For the year ended 12/31/01, income from continuing operations dropped 38.3% to $2.53 billion versus income from continuing operations of $4.10 billion in 2000. The 2001 results included a pre-tax acquired in-process research and development charge of $2.74 billion. Also, results for 2001 and 2000 included pre-tax net non-recurring charges of $389.0 million and $348.0 million, respectively. Net sales climbed 6.6% to $19.42 billion.

PROSPECTS: The Company continues to invest in a growing pipeline of new pharmaceutical products, including a number of compounds with significant potential that BMY expects to submit for filing by the end of 2002. Furthermore, BMY will look to build external alliances and enhance productivity. For the full year 2002, the Company expects diluted earnings per share to range from $2.25 to $2.35.

BUSINESS

BRISTOL-MYERS SQUIBB COMPANY, through its divisions and subsidiaries, is a major producer and distributor of medicines. Major products include PRAVACHOL (11.2% of 2001 sales), a cholesterol-lowering agent; GLUCOPHAGE (10.5%), an oral medication for treatment of non-insulin dependent (type 2) diabetes; PLAVIX (7.0%), a platelet aggregation inhibitor and TAXOL (6.2%), an anticancer agent. The Company also produces and distributes infant formulas, ostomy products and wound care products. In August 2001, BMY completed the tax-free spin-off of its Zimmer business. On 11/15/01, the Company sold its Clairol beauty care subsidiary for $4.95 billion.

ANNUAL FINANCIAL DATA

	12/31/01	12/31/00	12/31/99	12/31/98	12/31/97	12/31/96	12/31/95
Earnings Per Share	[5] 1.29	[4] 2.05	2.06	[3] 1.55	[2] 1.57	1.42	[1] 0.90
Cash Flow Per Share	1.68	2.42	2.39	1.85	1.86	1.68	1.12
Tang. Book Val. Per Share	1.70	3.96	3.61	3.01	2.82	2.53	2.28
Dividends Per Share	1.10	0.98	0.86	0.78	0.76	0.75	0.74
Dividend Payout %	85.3	47.8	41.7	50.3	48.4	52.8	82.7
INCOME STATEMENT (IN MILLIONS):							
Total Revenues	19,423.0	18,216.0	20,222.0	18,284.0	16,701.0	15,065.0	13,767.0
Costs & Expenses	15,914.0	11,992.0	13,691.0	12,337.0	11,897.0	10,593.0	10,014.0
Depreciation & Amort.	781.0	746.0	678.0	625.0	591.0	519.0	448.0
Operating Income	2,728.0	5,478.0	5,853.0	5,322.0	4,213.0	3,953.0	3,305.0
Net Interest Inc./(Exp.)	...	...	...	d67.0	d12.0	17.0	42.0
Income Before Income Taxes	2,986.0	5,478.0	5,767.0	4,268.0	4,812.0	4,013.0	2,402.0
Income Taxes	459.0	1,382.0	1,600.0	1,127.0	1,279.0	1,163.0	590.0
Net Income	[5] 2,527.0	[4] 4,096.0	4,167.0	[3] 3,141.0	[2] 3,205.0	2,850.0	[1] 1,812.0
Cash Flow	3,308.0	4,842.0	4,845.0	3,766.0	3,796.0	3,369.0	2,260.0
Average Shs. Outstg. (000)	1,965,000	1,997,000	2,027,000	2,031,000	2,042,000	2,008,000	2,024,000
BALANCE SHEET (IN MILLIONS):							
Cash & Cash Equivalents	5,654.0	3,385.0	2,957.0	2,529.0	1,794.0	2,185.0	2,178.0
Total Current Assets	12,349.0	9,824.0	9,267.0	8,782.0	7,736.0	7,528.0	7,018.0
Net Property	4,879.0	4,548.0	4,621.0	4,429.0	4,156.0	3,964.0	3,760.0
Total Assets	27,057.0	17,578.0	17,114.0	16,272.0	14,977.0	14,685.0	13,930.0
Total Current Liabilities	8,826.0	5,632.0	5,537.0	5,791.0	5,032.0	5,050.0	4,806.0
Long-Term Obligations	6,237.0	1,336.0	1,342.0	1,364.0	1,279.0	966.0	635.0
Net Stockholders' Equity	10,736.0	9,180.0	8,645.0	7,576.0	7,219.0	6,570.0	5,823.0
Net Working Capital	3,523.0	4,192.0	3,730.0	2,991.0	2,704.0	2,478.0	2,212.0
Year-end Shs. Outstg. (000)	1,935,621	1,953,535	1,980,806	1,988,000	1,986,000	2,002,000	2,020,000
STATISTICAL RECORD:							
Operating Profit Margin %	14.0	30.1	28.9	29.1	25.2	26.2	24.0
Net Profit Margin %	13.0	22.5	20.6	17.2	19.2	18.9	13.2
Return on Equity %	23.5	44.6	48.2	41.5	44.4	43.4	31.1
Return on Assets %	9.3	23.3	24.3	19.3	21.4	19.4	13.0
Debt/Total Assets %	23.1	7.6	7.8	8.4	8.5	6.6	4.6
Price Range	73.50-48.50	74.88-42.44	79.25-57.25	67.63-44.16	49.09-26.63	29.09-19.50	21.78-14.44
P/E Ratio	57.0-37.6	36.5-20.7	38.5-27.8	43.6-28.5	31.3-17.0	20.5-13.7	24.3-16.1
Average Yield %	1.8	1.7	1.4	2.0	3.1	4.1	

Statistics are as originally reported. Adj. for 2-for-1 stk. split, 2/97 & 2/99. [1] Incl. spec. after-tax chg. of $590.0 mill. & $98.0 mill. prov. for litig. [2] Incl. pre-tax prov. of $225.0 mill. for restr. & $225.0 mill. gain on sale of a bus. [3] Incl. spec. chg. of $800.0 mill. [4] Bef. gain fr. disc. ops. of $615.0 mill.; incl. pre-tax chrgs. of $226.0 mill. [5] Bef. gain fr. disc. ops. of $2.72 bill.; incl. net pre-tax chrgs. of $3.13 bill.

OFFICERS:
P. R. Dolan, Chmn., Pres., C.E.O.
F. Schiff, Sr. V.P., C.F.O.

INVESTOR CONTACT: Timothy Cost, Investor Relations, (212) 546-4103

PRINCIPAL OFFICE: 345 Park Avenue, New York, NY 10154-0037

TELEPHONE NUMBER: (212) 546-4000
FAX: (212) 546-4020
WEB: www.bms.com
NO. OF EMPLOYEES: 46,000 (approx.)
SHAREHOLDERS: 107,626 (approx.)
ANNUAL MEETING: In May
INCORPORATED: DE, Aug., 1933

INSTITUTIONAL HOLDINGS:
No. of Institutions: 1,169
Shares Held: 1,192,855,815
% Held: 61.7
INDUSTRY: Pharmaceutical preparations (SIC: 2834)
TRANSFER AGENT(S): Mellon Investor Services, Ridgefield Park, NJ

BRIGGS & STRATTON CORPORATION

YIELD 2.8%
P/E RATIO 51.7

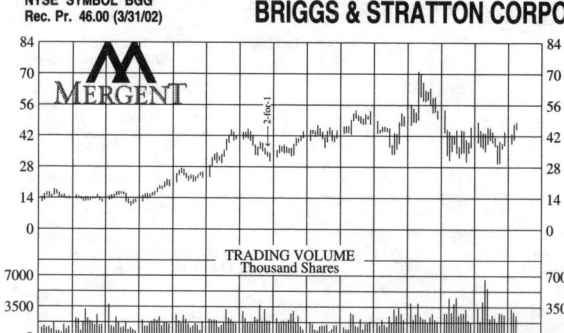

MERGENT

TRADING VOLUME
Thousand Shares

*7 YEAR PRICE SCORE 79.0   *12 MONTH PRICE SCORE 114.1
*NYSE COMPOSITE INDEX=100

INTERIM EARNINGS (Per Share):

Qtr.	Sept.	Dec.	Mar.	June
1997-98	d0.10	0.41	1.45	1.13
1998-99	0.19	1.05	1.79	1.51
1999-00	1.10	1.77	1.84	1.24
2000-01	d0.29	0.92	1.38	0.21
2001-02	d0.81	0.11	...	...

INTERIM DIVIDENDS (Per Share):

Amt.	Decl.	Ex.	Rec.	Pay.
0.31Q	8/01/01	8/21/01	8/23/01	10/01/01
0.31Q	10/17/01	11/29/01	12/03/01	1/02/02
0.32Q	1/16/02	2/27/02	3/01/02	4/01/02
0.32Q	4/17/02	5/30/02	6/03/02	6/28/02

Indicated div.: $1.28 (Div. Reinv. Plan)

CAPITALIZATION (7/1/01):

	($000)	(%)
Long-Term Debt	508,134	53.5
Deferred Income Tax	18,351	1.9
Common & Surplus	422,752	44.5
Total	949,237	100.0

DIVIDEND ACHIEVER STATUS:
Rank: 243   10-Year Growth Rate: 4.48%
Total Years of Dividend Growth: 10

RECENT DEVELOPMENTS: For the quarter ended 12/31/01, net income was $2.4 million compared with $19.9 million in the same period a year earlier. Results for 2001 included after-tax expenses of $5.2 million representing the cost of an early retirement incentive program. Net sales declined 8.9% to $335.3 million. Engines sales fell 16.5% to $307.5 million, primarily due to a 12.0% decrease in unit sales and a sales mix weighted toward small horsepower engines. Generac Portable Products, which was acquired in May 2001, posted sales of $39.6 million.

PROSPECTS: BGG's near-term outlook is mixed. On the positive side, the Company anticipates engine sales and production levels will improve over the second half of fiscal 2002, reflecting original equipment manufacturers' efforts to move the assembly of lawn and garden equipment closer to the spring retail selling season. However, BGG's Generac business is experiencing softening business conditions for both the generator and pressure washer product lines. Consequently, BGG's net income is now projected to range from $56.0 million to $60.0 million.

BUSINESS

BRIGGS & STRATTON CORPO-RATION is a producer of air-cooled gasoline engines for outdoor power equipment. The Company designs, manufactures, markets and services these products for original equipment manufacturers (OEMs) worldwide. These engines are primarily aluminum alloy gasoline engines ranging from 3 through 25 horsepower. BGG's engines are used primarily by the lawn and garden equipment industry. Major lawn and garden equipment applications include walk-behind lawn mowers, riding lawn mowers and garden tillers. Briggs & Stratton engines are marketed under various brand names including CLASSIC™, SPRINT™, QUATTRO™, QUANTUM®, INTEK™, I/C®, INDUSTRIAL PLUS™ and VANGUARD™. On 5/15/01, BGG acquired Generac Portable Products for net cash of $267.0 million. Dividends have been paid since 1929.

QUARTERLY DATA

(7/1/01)($000)	Rev	Inc
First Quarter	181,251	(6,304)
Second Quarter	368,207	19,928
Third Quarter	430,683	29,889
Fourth Quarter	332,305	4,500

ANNUAL FINANCIAL DATA

	7/1/01	7/2/00	6/27/99	6/28/98	6/29/97	6/30/96	7/2/95
Earnings Per Share	2.21	⑤ 5.97	4.52	2.85	2.16	3.19	3.62
Cash Flow Per Share	4.90	8.22	6.64	4.78	3.68	4.68	5.16
Tang. Book Val. Per Share	11.53	18.51	15.45	12.87	13.40	17.17	15.19
Dividends Per Share	1.24	1.21	1.17	1.13	1.10	1.06	1.01
Dividend Payout %	56.1	20.3	25.9	39.6	50.9	33.2	27.9
INCOME STATEMENT (IN MILLIONS)							
Total Revenues	1,312.4	1,590.6	1,501.7	1,327.6	1,316.4	1,287.0	1,339.7
Costs & Expenses	1,153.6	1,334.0	1,272.0	1,155.2	1,169.3	1,090.6	1,125.5
Depreciation & Amort.	59.7	51.4	49.6	47.7	43.4	43.0	44.4
Operating Income	99.1	205.2	180.1	124.7	103.7	153.4	169.8
Net Interest Inc./(Exp.)	d30.7	d21.3	d17.0	d19.4	d9.9	d10.1	d8.6
Income Before Income Taxes	71.9	216.6	169.8	113.1	99.3	149.1	170.4
Income Taxes	23.9	80.2	63.7	42.5	37.7	56.6	65.6
Net Income	48.0	⑤ 136.5	106.1	70.6	61.6	92.4	104.8
Cash Flow	107.7	187.8	155.7	118.4	104.9	135.4	149.3
Average Shs. Outstg. (000)	21,966	22,842	23,459	24,775	28,551	28,927	28,927
BALANCE SHEET (IN MILLIONS)							
Cash & Cash Equivalents	88.7	17.0	60.8	84.5	112.9	150.6	170.6
Total Current Assets	613.4	472.0	459.1	382.0	418.4	452.7	453.3
Net Property	416.4	395.6	404.5	391.9	396.3	374.2	343.3
Total Assets	1,296.2	930.2	875.9	793.4	842.2	838.2	798.5
Total Current Liabilities	242.2	312.8	282.5	222.9	214.0	190.2	197.3
Long-Term Obligations	508.1	98.5	113.3	128.1	142.9	60.0	75.0
Net Stockholders' Equity	422.8	409.5	365.9	316.5	351.1	500.5	439.5
Net Working Capital	371.2	159.2	176.6	159.1	204.4	262.5	256.1
Year-end Shs. Outstg. (000)	21,599	21,746	23,200	23,824	25,414	28,927	28,927
STATISTICAL RECORD:							
Operating Profit Margin %	7.6	12.9	12.0	9.4	7.9	11.9	12.7
Net Profit Margin %	3.7	8.6	7.1	5.3	4.7	7.2	7.8
Return on Equity %	11.4	33.3	29.0	22.3	17.5	18.5	23.8
Return on Assets %	3.7	14.7	12.1	8.9	7.3	11.0	13.1
Debt/Total Assets %	39.2	10.6	12.9	16.1	17.0	7.2	9.4
Price Range	48.38-29.65	53.88-30.38	71.13-46.69	52.44-33.63	53.63-42.63	46.88-36.50	44.13-32.25
P/E Ratio	21.9-13.4	9.0-5.1	15.7-10.3	18.4-11.8	24.8-19.7	14.7-11.4	12.2-8.9
Average Yield %	3.2	2.9	2.0	2.6	2.3	2.5	2.6

Statistics are as originally reported. ⑤ Incl. non-recurr. gain $16.5 mill.

OFFICERS:
F. P. Stratton, Jr., Chmn.
J. S. Shiely, Pres., C.E.O.
J. E. Brenn, Sr. V.P., C.F.O.
INVESTOR CONTACT: G. R. Thompson, V.P., Corp. Comm., (414) 259-5312
PRINCIPAL OFFICE: 12301 West Wirth Street, Wauwatosa, WI 53222

TELEPHONE NUMBER: (414) 259-5333
FAX: (414) 259-9594
WEB: www.briggsandstratton.com
NO. OF EMPLOYEES: 6,974
SHAREHOLDERS: 4,101
ANNUAL MEETING: In Oct.
INCORPORATED: DE, June, 1924; reincorp., WI, Oct., 1992

INSTITUTIONAL HOLDINGS:
No. of Institutions: 146
Shares Held: 18,060,977
% Held: 83.5
INDUSTRY: Internal combustion engines, nec (SIC: 3519)
TRANSFER AGENT(S): Firstar Trust Company, Milwaukee, WI

BRADY CORPORATION

YIELD 2.1%
P/E RATIO 39.5

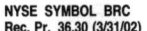

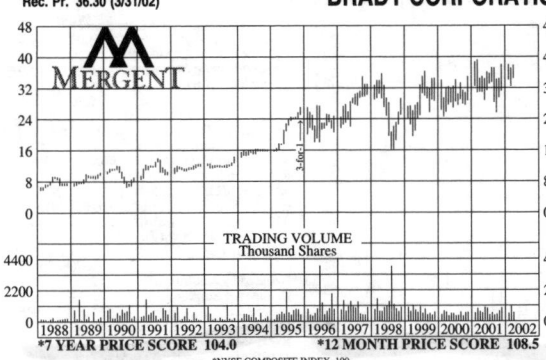

TRADING VOLUME
Thousand Shares

7 YEAR PRICE SCORE 104.0 *NYSE COMPOSITE INDEX=100 **12 MONTH PRICE SCORE 108.5**

INTERIM EARNINGS (Per Share):

Qtr.	Oct.	Jan.	Apr.	July
1998-99	0.38	0.35	0.57	0.43
1999-00	0.54	0.43	0.51	0.57
2000-01	0.49	0.37	0.44	d0.12
2001-02	0.34	0.26	...	...

INTERIM DIVIDENDS (Per Share):

Amt.	Decl.	Ex.	Rec.	Pay.
0.18Q	2/20/01	4/06/01	4/10/01	4/30/01
0.18Q	5/15/01	7/09/01	7/11/01	7/31/01
0.19Q	9/17/01	10/05/01	10/10/01	10/31/01
0.19Q	11/15/01	1/09/02	1/11/02	1/31/02
0.19Q	2/19/02	4/08/02	4/10/02	4/30/02

Indicated div.: $0.76 (Div. Reinv. Plan)

CAPITALIZATION (7/31/01):

	($000)	(%)
Long-Term Debt	4,144	1.4
Preferred Stock	2,855	0.9
Common & Surplus	299,724	97.7
Total	306,723	100.0

DIVIDEND ACHIEVER STATUS:
Rank: 52   10-Year Growth Rate: 15.92%
Total Years of Dividend Growth: 17

RECENT DEVELOPMENTS: For the quarter ended 1/31/02, net income totaled $6.1 million, down 28.8% compared with $8.6 million in the equivalent period of the prior year. Net sales declined 11.3% to $120.6 million from $136.0 million a year earlier. Identification Solutions and Specialty Tapes group sales fell 19.2% to $53.7 million, while Graphics and Workplace Solutions group sales decreased 3.8% to $66.9 million. Operating income dropped 32.5% to $9.4 million from $14.1 million the year before.

PROSPECTS: BRC is targeting sales of $520.0 million to $530.0 million during the current fiscal year, along with net income of $33.0 million to $35.0 million. Going forward, BRC will continue to invest in long-term strategic growth initiatives including process improvement, acquisitions, and new product development. On 11/9/01, BRC announced that it has acquired StrandWare, Inc., a developer and marketer of bar-code, label-design and data-collection software with annual sales of about $3.0 million.

BUSINESS

BRADY CORPORATION (formerly W.H. Brady Co.) is an international manufacturer and marketer of identification products and specialty coated materials, which are designed to help companies improve safety, security, productivity and performance. BRC's array of labels are used in applications ranging from marking wires and cables in facilities, electrical, telecommunication and transportation equipment to marking electronic components and printed circuit boards that require identification for purposes such as maintenance, work-in-process or asset tracking. Offerings ranging from signs, pipemakers, lockout/tagout devices, labels and tags to services including consulting, product installation and training enable companies to comply with safety and environmental regulations.

ANNUAL FINANCIAL DATA

	7/31/01	7/31/00	7/31/99	7/31/98	7/31/97	7/31/96	7/31/95
Earnings Per Share	[1] 1.18	2.05	[1] 1.73	[1] 1.23	1.44	1.27	1.28
Cash Flow Per Share	2.17	2.84	2.41	1.83	1.05	0.88	1.71
Tang. Book Val. Per Share	8.89	8.25	8.17	7.87	7.64	6.96	7.69
Dividends Per Share	0.73	0.69	0.65	0.61	0.54	0.43	0.30
Dividend Payout %	61.9	33.7	37.6	49.6	37.5	33.9	23.5
INCOME STATEMENT (IN THOUSANDS):							
Total Revenues	545,944	541,077	470,862	455,150	426,081	359,542	314,362
Costs & Expenses	478,776	453,953	391,941	395,932	361,562	307,775	264,618
Depreciation & Amort.	22,646	17,833	15,149	13,288	14,151	10,602	9,159
Operating Income	44,522	69,291	63,772	45,930	50,368	41,165	40,585
Net Interest Inc./(Exp.)	d418	d578	d445	d403	d256	d302	d555
Income Before Income Taxes	44,790	76,131	64,782	46,165	51,271	45,433	44,639
Income Taxes	17,244	28,930	25,198	18,129	19,564	17,406	16,728
Net Income	[1] 27,546	47,201	[1] 39,584	[1] 28,036	31,707	28,027	27,911
Cash Flow	49,933	64,775	54,474	41,065	45,599	38,370	36,811
Average Shs. Outstg.	23,107	22,933	22,683	22,602	43,816	43,694	21,681
BALANCE SHEET (IN THOUSANDS):							
Cash & Cash Equivalents	62,811	60,784	75,466	65,609	65,329	49,281	89,067
Total Current Assets	194,993	203,183	203,169	184,053	187,969	156,111	164,472
Net Property	84,533	80,660	66,984	67,165	62,442	65,649	58,573
Total Assets	392,476	398,134	351,210	311,824	291,662	261,835	230,005
Total Current Liabilities	71,163	87,099	73,285	58,667	57,245	46,423	34,534
Long-Term Obligations	4,144	4,157	1,402	3,716	3,890	1,809	1,903
Net Stockholders' Equity	302,579	291,224	260,564	233,373	206,547	189,263	170,823
Net Working Capital	123,830	116,084	129,884	125,386	130,724	109,688	129,938
Year-end Shs. Outstg.	22,914	22,731	22,605	22,496	21,941	21,863	21,831
STATISTICAL RECORD:							
Operating Profit Margin %	8.2	12.8	13.5	10.1	11.8	11.4	12.9
Net Profit Margin %	5.0	8.7	8.4	6.2	7.4	7.8	8.9
Return on Equity %	9.1	16.2	15.2	12.0	15.4	14.8	16.3
Return on Assets %	7.0	11.9	11.3	9.0	10.9	10.7	12.1
Debt/Total Assets %	1.1	1.0	0.4	1.2	1.3	0.7	0.8
Price Range	39.24-25.55	34.94-24.50	36.31-19.50	35.75-16.25	35.00-21.63	27.50-18.00	27.00-15.67
P/E Ratio	33.3-21.7	17.0-12.0	21.0-11.3	29.1-13.2	24.3-15.0	21.7-14.2	21.1-12.3
Average Yield %	2.3	2.3	2.3	2.3	1.9	1.9	1.4

Statistics are as originally reported. Adj. for stk. splits: 3-for-1, 12/95. [1] Incl. $9.6 mil non-recur. pre-tax chrg., 2001; $611,000 gain, 1999; $5.4 mil chrg., 1998.

OFFICERS:
K. M. Hudson, Pres., C.E.O.
D. W. Schroeder, Sr. V.P., C.F.O.
D. Rearic, Sr. V.P., Treas., Asst. Sec.

INVESTOR CONTACT: Laurie Spiegelberg Bernardy, V.P., Corp. Comm., (414) 438-6880

PRINCIPAL OFFICE: 6555 West Good Hope Road, Milwaukee, WI 53223-0571

TELEPHONE NUMBER: (414) 358-6600
FAX: (414) 438-6910
WEB: www.bradycorp.com

NO. OF EMPLOYEES: 3,200 (avg.)

SHAREHOLDERS: 362 (class A); 3 (class B)

ANNUAL MEETING: In Nov.

INCORPORATED: WI, 1939

INSTITUTIONAL HOLDINGS:
No. of Institutions: 104
Shares Held: 15,287,706
% Held: 66.4

INDUSTRY: Signs and advertising specialities (SIC: 3993)

TRANSFER AGENT(S): Firstar Bank, N.A., Milwaukee, WI

BOWL AMERICA INC.

YIELD 3.8%
P/E RATIO 18.2

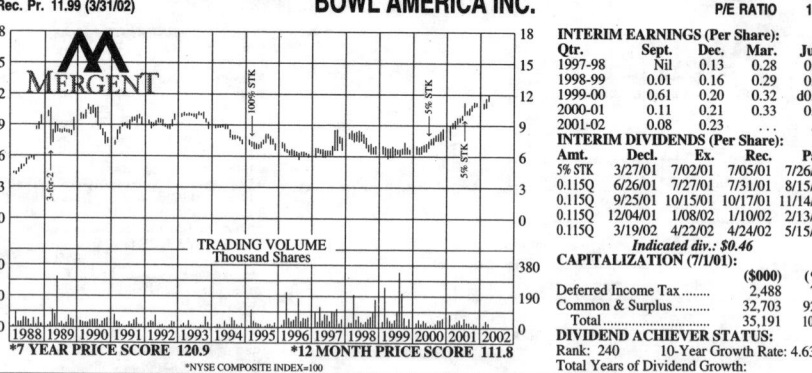

*7 YEAR PRICE SCORE 120.9   *12 MONTH PRICE SCORE 111.8
*NYSE COMPOSITE INDEX=100

INTERIM EARNINGS (Per Share):

Qtr.	Sept.	Dec.	Mar.	June
1997-98	Nil	0.13	0.28	0.08
1998-99	0.01	0.16	0.29	0.09
1999-00	0.61	0.20	0.32	d0.38
2000-01	0.11	0.21	0.33	0.02
2001-02	0.08	0.23	...	...

INTERIM DIVIDENDS (Per Share):

Amt.	Decl.	Ex.	Rec.	Pay.
5% STK	3/27/01	7/02/01	7/05/01	7/26/01
0.115Q	6/26/01	7/27/01	7/31/01	8/15/01
0.115Q	9/25/01	10/15/01	10/17/01	11/14/01
0.115Q	12/04/01	1/08/02	1/10/02	2/13/02
0.115Q	3/19/02	4/22/02	4/24/02	5/15/02

Indicated div.: $0.46

CAPITALIZATION (7/1/01):

	($000)	(%)
Deferred Income Tax	2,488	7.1
Common & Surplus	32,703	92.9
Total	35,191	100.0

DIVIDEND ACHIEVER STATUS:
Rank: 240   10-Year Growth Rate: 4.63%
Total Years of Dividend Growth: 29

RECENT DEVELOPMENTS: For the thirteen weeks ended 12/30/01, net earnings remained flat at $1.2 million compared with the corresponding 2000 quarter. Operating revenues climbed 3.9% to $7.9 million from $7.6 million in the prior-year quarter. Bowling and other revenues rose 3.6% to $5.5 million from $5.4 million the year before, reflecting increased open play linage and a higher average game rate. Food, beverage and merchandise sales rose 4.5% to $2.3

million from $2.2 million a year earlier. Operating income increased 3.9% to $1.7 million versus $1.6 million a year earlier. For the 26 weeks ended 12/30/01, net earnings dropped 11.0% to $1.6 million compared with $1.8 million in the prior year. Total operating revenues advanced 2.4% to $14.3 million from $14.0 million in the previous year. Operating income was unchanged at $2.2 million.

BUSINESS

BOWL AMERICA INC. as of 9/1/01 operated 12 bowling centers in Washington, D.C., two bowling centers in Baltimore, Maryland, one bowling center in Orlando, Florida, three bowling centers in Jacksonville, Florida, and three bowling centers in Richmond, Virginia. These 21 bowling centers contain a total of 820 lanes and are fully air-conditioned with facilities for the service of food and beverages, game rooms, rental lockers and playroom facilities. All centers provide shoes for rental and bowling balls are provided free. In addition, each center retails bowling accessories.

REVENUES

(7/1/01)	($000)	(%)
Bowling & Other	20,807	70.8
Food, Beverage & Merchandise	8,594	29.2
Total	29,401	100.0

ANNUAL FINANCIAL DATA

	7/1/01	7/2/00	6/27/99	6/28/98	6/29/97	6/30/96	7/2/95
Earnings Per Share	0.67	0.68	0.50	0.45	0.36	0.37	0.47
Cash Flow Per Share	1.01	1.03	0.85	0.78	0.67	0.67	0.75
Tang. Book Val. Per Share	6.06	6.17	5.57	5.14	4.86	4.77	4.66
Dividends Per Share	0.45	0.41	0.38	0.363	0.358	0.345	0.335
Dividend Payout %	66.7	59.8	75.8	81.4	98.7	92.9	71.4
INCOME STATEMENT (IN THOUSANDS):							
Total Revenues	29,401	28,902	27,547	27,087	26,995	27,327	29,494
Costs & Expenses	22,568	21,051	20,727	20,661	21,475	21,795	23,026
Depreciation & Amort.	1,940	2,100	2,268	2,323	2,111	2,035	1,942
Operating Income	4,893	5,751	4,552	4,103	3,410	3,497	4,526
Net Interest Inc./(Exp.)	1,036	823	685	675	633	664	593
Income Before Income Taxes	5,928	6,574	5,237	4,778	4,042	4,161	5,119
Income Taxes	2,060	2,361	1,902	1,716	1,552	1,567	1,849
Net Income	3,868	4,213	3,335	3,062	2,490	2,594	3,270
Cash Flow	5,809	6,313	5,603	5,385	4,601	4,629	5,212
Average Shs. Outstg.	5,745	6,147	6,629	6,864	6,889	6,947	6,971
BALANCE SHEET (IN THOUSANDS):							
Cash & Cash Equivalents	7,575	10,397	9,248	9,986	8,173	8,881	7,635
Total Current Assets	9,613	11,445	10,453	11,194	9,366	10,508	9,259
Net Property	21,079	19,368	20,909	22,223	23,455	22,681	23,399
Total Assets	37,598	40,711	41,748	40,435	38,003	37,901	36,585
Total Current Liabilities	2,407	2,165	2,064	1,968	2,286	2,855	2,254
Net Stockholders' Equity	32,703	34,868	35,477	35,292	33,382	32,904	32,444
Net Working Capital	7,206	9,330	8,389	9,226	7,080	7,653	7,004
Year-end Shs. Outstg.	5,399	5,654	6,373	6,860	6,867	6,867	6,883
STATISTICAL RECORD:							
Operating Profit Margin %	16.6	19.9	16.5	15.1	12.6	12.8	15.3
Net Profit Margin %	13.2	14.6	12.1	11.3	9.2	9.5	11.1
Return on Equity %	11.8	12.1	9.4	8.7	7.5	7.9	10.1
Return on Assets %	10.3	10.3	8.0	7.6	6.6	6.8	8.9
Price Range	11.30-7.62	8.69-6.24	7.37-5.78	8.50-6.24	8.62-5.90	7.37-5.67	8.16-6.58
P/E Ratio	16.8-11.3	12.7-9.1	14.7-11.5	19.1-14.0	23.8-16.3	19.9-15.3	17.4-14.0
Average Yield %	4.7	5.5	5.8	4.9	4.9	5.3	4.6

Statistics are as originally reported. Adj. for 5.0% stk. split 7/26/00, 7/26/01.

OFFICERS:
L. H. Goldberg, Pres., C.E.O., C.O.O.
R. E. Macklin, Sr. V.P., Treas.
C. A. Dragoo, Contr., Asst. Treas.
A. J. Levy, Sr. V.P., Sec.

INVESTOR CONTACT: Investor Relations, (703) 941-6300

PRINCIPAL OFFICE: 6446 Edsall Road, Alexandria, VA 22312

TELEPHONE NUMBER: (703) 941-6300

FAX: (703) 256-2430

NO. OF EMPLOYEES: 750 (approx.)

SHAREHOLDERS: 468 (approx. class A com.); 32 (approx. class B com.)

ANNUAL MEETING: In Dec.

INCORPORATED: MD, July, 1958

INSTITUTIONAL HOLDINGS:
No. of Institutions: 8
Shares Held: 352,569
% Held: 6.8

INDUSTRY: Bowling centers (SIC: 7933)

TRANSFER AGENT(S): American Stock Transfer & Trust Co., New York, NY

BLACK HILLS CORPORATION

YIELD 3.5%
P/E RATIO 9.6

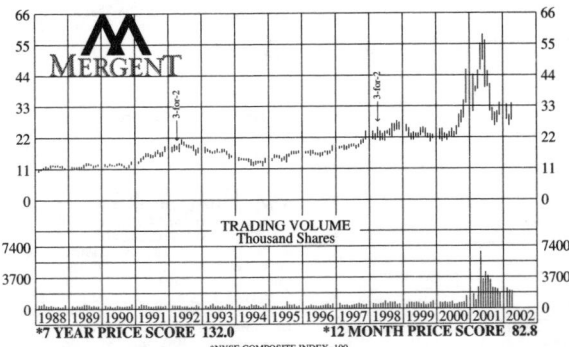

*7 YEAR PRICE SCORE 132.0   *12 MONTH PRICE SCORE 82.8

*NYSE COMPOSITE INDEX=100

INTERIM EARNINGS (Per Share):

Qtr.	Mar.	June	Sept.	Dec.
1998	0.39	0.35	0.44	0.01
1999	0.42	0.36	0.45	0.50
2000	0.42	0.38	0.71	0.83
2001	1.37	1.34	0.61	0.18

INTERIM DIVIDENDS (Per Share):

Amt.	Decl.	Ex.	Rec.	Pay.
0.28Q	4/24/01	5/16/01	5/18/01	6/01/01
0.28Q	7/24/01	8/14/01	8/16/01	9/01/01
0.28Q	11/06/01	11/15/01	11/19/01	12/01/01
0.29Q	1/31/02	2/13/02	2/15/02	3/01/02

Indicated div.: $1.16 (Div. Reinv. Plan)

CAPITALIZATION (12/31/01):

	($000)	(%)
Long-Term Debt	415,798	40.5
Deferred Income Tax	75,398	7.3
Minority Interest	19,533	1.9
Preferred Stock	5,549	0.5
Common & Surplus	509,615	49.7
Total	1,025,893	100.0

DIVIDEND ACHIEVER STATUS:
Rank: 256   10-Year Growth Rate: 3.65%
Total Years of Dividend Growth: 21

RECENT DEVELOPMENTS: For the year ended 12/31/01, net income advanced 66.7% to $88.1 million versus $52.8 million in the previous year. Operating revenues decreased 4.0% to $1.56 billion from $1.62 billion a year earlier. Total operating expenses declined 8.0% to $1.39 billion, or 89.1% of revenues, from $1.51 billion, or 92.9% of revenues, the year before. Operating income jumped 48.3% to $170.2 million from $114.8 million in 2000. Other net expense climbed 35.0% to $27.4 million.

PROSPECTS: On 3/14/02, Black Hills Energy Inc. announced the purchase from Equilon Pipeline Company, LLC of an interest in Millenium Pipeline Company, L.P. and Millenium Terminal Company, L.P., giving BKH 100.0% ownership of the Millenium companies (MCs). MCs own and operate a pipeline with a capacity of about 65,000 barrels per day which transports crude oil from its 1.1 million barrel storage facility in Beaumont to a transfer point to connecting carriers in Longview, Texas.

BUSINESS

BLACK HILLS CORPORATION is an energy and communications company with three business groups. Black Hills Energy, Inc. (BHE) (63.9% and 85.0% of 2001 net income and revenues, respectively) produces and markets electric power and fuel. It produces and sells electricity in several markets with a strong emphasis in the western United States. BHE produces coal natural gas and crude oil primarily in the Rocky Mountain region, which it sells nationwide. Black Hills Power, Inc. (49.5%, 13.7%) is an electric utility serving approximately 59,200 customers in western South Dakota, northeastern Wyoming and southeastern Montana as of 12/31/01. Black Hills FiberCom, LLC (d13.4%, 1.3%) provides broadband communications to residential and business customers in Rapid City and the northern Black Hills region of South Dakota. Broadband offerings include bundled telephone, high speed internet and cable entertainment services.

ANNUAL FINANCIAL DATA

	12/31/01	12/31/00	12/31/99	12/31/98	12/31/97	12/31/96	12/31/95
Earnings Per Share	3.42	2.37	1.73	☐1.19	1.49	1.40	1.19
Cash Flow Per Share	5.49	3.84	2.89	2.30	2.52	2.45	2.09
Tang. Book Val. Per Share	18.95	12.14	10.14	9.52	9.46	8.91	8.43
Dividends Per Share	1.12	1.08	1.04	1.00	0.95	0.92	0.89
Dividend Payout %	32.7	45.6	60.1	84.0	63.5	65.7	75.3
INCOME STATEMENT (IN MILLIONS):							
Total Revenues	1,558.6	1,623.8	791.9	679.3	313.7	162.6	149.8
Costs & Expenses	1,334.3	1,476.2	704.9	606.0	232.4	85.5	88.0
Depreciation & Amort.	54.1	32.9	25.1	24.0	22.3	22.8	19.7
Operating Income	170.2	114.8	61.9	49.2	58.9	54.3	42.2
Net Interest Inc./(Exp.)	d37.2	d23.3	d11.8	d11.8	d11.8	d12.2	d7.0
Income Taxes	50.5	30.4	15.8	11.7	14.3	13.6	10.7
Equity Earnings/Minority Int.	d4.2	d11.3	...	...	...	...	...
Net Income	88.1	52.8	37.1	☐25.8	32.4	30.3	25.6
Cash Flow	141.6	85.6	62.1	49.8	54.7	53.0	45.3
Average Shs. Outstg. (000)	25,771	22,281	21,482	21,665	21,706	21,660	21,614
BALANCE SHEET (IN MILLIONS):							
Gross Property	737.9	961.6	659.9	619.5	598.3	581.5	557.6
Accumulated Depreciation	328.4	277.8	246.3	229.9	197.2	181.1	164.4
Net Property	539.2	794.3	464.2	389.6	401.1	400.4	393.3
Total Assets	1,658.8	1,320.3	674.8	559.4	508.7	467.4	448.8
Long-Term Obligations	415.8	307.1	160.7	162.0	163.4	164.7	166.1
Net Stockholders' Equity	515.2	282.3	216.6	206.7	205.4	193.2	182.3
Year-end Shs. Outstg. (000)	26,891	22,921	21,372	21,719	21,705	21,675	21,638
STATISTICAL RECORD:							
Operating Profit Margin %	10.9	7.1	7.8	7.2	18.8	33.4	28.1
Net Profit Margin %	5.7	3.3	4.7	3.8	10.3	18.6	17.1
Net Inc./Net Property %	16.3	6.7	8.0	6.6	8.1	7.6	6.5
Net Inc./Tot. Capital %	8.6	7.7	8.5	6.1	7.7	7.4	6.5
Return on Equity %	17.1	18.7	17.1	12.5	15.8	15.7	14.0
Accum. Depr./Gross Prop. %	44.5	28.9	37.3	37.1	33.0	31.1	29.5
Price Range	58.50-26.00	46.06-20.44	26.50-20.31	27.94-20.69	24.29-17.50	19.17-15.17	17.42-13.17
P/E Ratio	17.1-7.6	19.4-8.6	15.3-11.7	23.5-17.4	16.3-11.7	13.7-10.8	14.7-11.1
Average Yield %	2.7	3.2	4.4	4.1	4.5	5.4	5.8

Statistics are as originally reported. Adj. for 3-for-2 stk. split, 3/98 ☐ Inc. non-recurr. chrg. $8.8 mill.

OFFICERS:
D. P. Landguth, Chmn., C.E.O.
E. E. Hoyt, Pres., C.O.O.
M. T. Thies, Sr. V.P., C.F.O.

INVESTOR CONTACT: Dale T. Jahr, Dir., Investor Relations, (605) 721-2326

PRINCIPAL OFFICE: 625 Ninth Street, Rapid City, SD 57701

TELEPHONE NUMBER: (605) 721-1700
FAX: (605) 721-2599
WEB: www.blackhillscorp.com

NO. OF EMPLOYEES: 785

SHAREHOLDERS: 5,509 (record)

ANNUAL MEETING: In May

INCORPORATED: SD, Aug., 1941

INSTITUTIONAL HOLDINGS:
No. of Institutions: 147
Shares Held: 12,035,987
% Held: 45.4

INDUSTRY: Electric services (SIC: 4911)

TRANSFER AGENT(S): Wells Fargo Shareowner Services, South St. Paul, MN

BEMIS COMPANY, INC.

YIELD 1.9%
P/E RATIO 20.6

INTERIM EARNINGS (Per Share):

Qtr.	Mar.	June	Sept.	Dec.
1997	0.37	0.52	0.47	0.64
1998	0.41	0.56	0.52	0.60
1999	0.35	0.60	0.59	0.63
2000	0.55	0.66	0.60	0.63
2001	0.56	0.67	0.68	0.73

INTERIM DIVIDENDS (Per Share):

Amt.	Decl.	Ex.	Rec.	Pay.
0.25Q	2/01/01	2/14/01	2/16/01	3/01/01
0.25Q	5/03/01	5/16/01	5/18/01	6/01/01
0.25Q	8/02/01	8/13/01	8/15/01	9/04/01
0.25Q	10/25/01	11/14/01	11/16/01	12/03/01
0.26Q	1/31/02	2/13/02	2/15/02	3/01/02

Indicated div.: $1.04 (Div. Reinv. Plan)

CAPITALIZATION (12/31/01):

	($000)	(%)
Long-Term Debt Ⓣ............	595,249	37.1
Deferred Income Tax........	121,979	7.6
Common & Surplus..........	886,148	55.3
Total........................	1,603,376	100.0

DIVIDEND ACHIEVER STATUS:
Rank: 155   10-Year Growth Rate: 9.06%
Total Years of Dividend Growth: 18

RECENT DEVELOPMENTS: For the year ended 12/31/01, net income increased 7.1% to $140.3 million compared with $130.6 million in 2000. Net sales were $2.29 billion, up 5.9% from $2.16 billion a year earlier. Flexible packaging segment net sales advanced 8.6% to $1.80 billion, primarily due to recent acquisitions. Net sales from the pressure-sensitive materials segment decreased 2.9% to $491.0 million, reflecting the weakened economy and overcapacity in the industry.

PROSPECTS: The flexible packaging segment is benefiting from an improved plastic packaging sales mix, an ongoing focus on cost control, and performance improvement in the paper packaging division. However, the pressure sensitive materials segment is being negatively affected by general overcapacity in the industry it serves. Nevertheless, this segment should benefit from manufacturing improvements, which should lead to improved results in 2002.

BUSINESS

BEMIS COMPANY, INC. is a manufacturer of flexible packaging products and pressure-sensitive materials, selling to customers throughout the United States, Canada, and Europe, with a growing presence in Asia Pacific, South America, and Mexico. Flexible packaging products include a broad range of consumer and industrial packaging consisting of high-barrier products that include advanced multi-layer coextruded, coated and laminated film structures; polyethylene products; and paper products. Pressure-Sensitive Materials include roll label products, graphics and distribution products, and technical and industrial products. In 2001, sales were as follows: flexible packaging, 79%, and pressure-sensitive materials, 21%.

ANNUAL FINANCIAL DATA

	12/31/01	12/31/00	12/31/99	12/31/98	12/31/97	12/31/96	12/31/95
Earnings Per Share	2.64	2.44	2.18	2.09	2.00	1.90	1.63
Cash Flow Per Share	4.98	4.46	4.04	3.76	3.46	3.14	2.74
Tang. Book Val. Per Share	8.78	9.52	13.91	12.83	12.08	10.83	9.76
Dividends Per Share	1.00	0.96	0.92	0.88	0.80	0.72	0.64
Dividend Payout %	37.9	39.3	42.2	42.1	40.0	37.9	39.3
INCOME STATEMENT (IN MILLIONS):							
Total Revenues	2,293.1	2,164.6	1,918.0	1,848.0	1,877.2	1,655.4	1,523.4
Costs & Expenses	1,908.8	1,811.5	1,602.1	1,550.5	1,603.1	1,413.9	1,317.1
Depreciation & Amort.	124.1	108.1	97.7	88.9	78.9	66.2	58.0
Operating Income	260.2	245.0	218.2	208.5	195.3	175.4	148.3
Net Interest Inc./(Exp.)	d30.3	d31.6	d21.2	d21.9	d18.9	d13.4	d11.5
Income Before Income Taxes	227.4	211.5	185.9	181.9	175.0	162.8	136.1
Income Taxes	87.1	80.9	71.1	70.5	67.4	61.7	50.9
Equity Earnings/Minority Int.	d0.6	d0.5	d4.2	d4.4	d5.4	d4.7	d3.8
Net Income	140.3	130.6	114.8	111.4	107.6	101.1	85.2
Cash Flow	264.5	238.7	212.5	200.3	186.4	167.3	143.2
Average Shs. Outstg. (000)	53,122	53,553	52,657	53,324	53,880	53,252	52,311
BALANCE SHEET (IN MILLIONS):							
Cash & Cash Equivalents	35.1	28.9	18.2	23.7	13.8	10.2	22.0
Total Current Assets	586.9	640.0	583.6	517.9	516.4	466.9	442.3
Net Property	852.7	825.8	776.2	740.1	685.2	583.5	534.6
Total Assets	1,923.0	1,888.6	1,532.1	1,453.1	1,362.6	1,168.8	1,030.6
Total Current Liabilities	238.2	495.1	253.3	242.8	251.2	214.4	219.2
Long-Term Obligations	595.2	438.0	372.3	371.4	316.8	241.1	166.4
Net Stockholders' Equity	886.1	798.8	725.9	670.8	639.9	567.1	512.8
Net Working Capital	348.7	144.9	330.3	275.2	265.2	252.5	223.1
Year-end Shs. Outstg. (000)	52,870	52,602	52,189	52,269	52,968	52,361	52,567
STATISTICAL RECORD:							
Operating Profit Margin %	11.3	11.3	11.4	11.3	10.4	10.6	9.7
Net Profit Margin %	6.1	6.0	6.0	6.0	5.7	6.1	5.6
Return on Equity %	15.8	16.4	15.8	16.6	16.8	17.8	16.6
Return on Assets %	7.3	6.9	7.5	7.7	7.9	8.6	8.3
Debt/Total Assets %	31.0	23.2	24.3	25.6	23.2	20.6	16.1
Price Range	52.47-28.69	39.31-22.94	40.38-30.19	46.94-33.50	47.94-33.63	37.63-25.63	30.00-23.00
P/E Ratio	19.9-10.9	16.1-9.4	18.5-13.8	22.5-16.0	24.0-16.8	19.8-13.5	18.4-14.1
Average Yield %	2.5	3.1	2.6	2.2	2.0	2.3	2.4

Statistics are as originally reported. Ⓣ Incl. capital lease obligations.

OFFICERS:
J. H. Roe, Chmn.
J. H. Curler, Pres., C.E.O.
B. R. Field, III, Sr. V.P., C.F.O., Treas.

INVESTOR CONTACT: Melanie E. R. Miller, Investor Relations, (612) 376-3030

PRINCIPAL OFFICE: 222 South 9th Street, Suite 2300, Minneapolis, MN 55402-4099

TELEPHONE NUMBER: (612) 376-3000
FAX: (612) 340-6174
WEB: www.bemis.com
NO. OF EMPLOYEES: 11,012 (avg.)
SHAREHOLDERS: 4,747
ANNUAL MEETING: In May
INCORPORATED: MO, May, 1885

INSTITUTIONAL HOLDINGS:
No. of Institutions: 230
Shares Held: 31,621,086
% Held: 59.7

INDUSTRY: Paper coated & laminated, packaging (SIC: 2671)

TRANSFER AGENT(S): Wells Fargo Shareowner Services, South St. Paul, MN

BELO CORPORATION

YIELD 1.3%
P/E RATIO ...

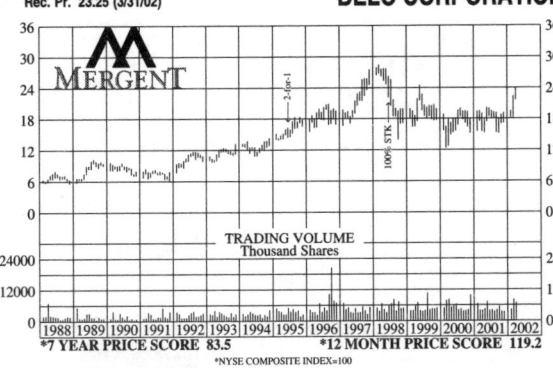

TRADING VOLUME
Thousand Shares

| 1988 | 1989 | 1990 | 1991 | 1992 | 1993 | 1994 | 1995 | 1996 | 1997 | 1998 | 1999 | 2000 | 2001 | 2002 |

*7 YEAR PRICE SCORE 83.5 ***12 MONTH PRICE SCORE 119.2**
*NYSE COMPOSITE INDEX=100

INTERIM EARNINGS (Per Share):

Qtr.	Mar.	June	Sept.	Dec.
1996	0.17	0.30	0.21	0.39
1997	0.19	0.21	0.12	0.19
1998	0.11	0.24	0.08	0.10
1999	0.11	0.67	0.14	0.58
2000	0.13	0.27	0.15	0.76
2001	0.01	Nil	Nil	d0.02

INTERIM DIVIDENDS (Per Share):

Amt.	Decl.	Ex.	Rec.	Pay.
0.075Q	7/27/01	8/15/01	8/17/01	9/07/01
0.075Q	9/28/01	11/14/01	11/16/01	12/07/01
0.075Q	11/30/01	2/06/02	2/08/02	3/01/02
0.075Q	2/08/02	5/15/02	5/17/02	6/07/02

Indicated div.: $0.30

CAPITALIZATION (12/31/01):

	($000)	(%)
Long-Term Debt	1,696,900	49.4
Deferred Income Tax	416,500	12.1
Common & Surplus	1,320,745	38.5
Total	3,434,145	100.0

DIVIDEND ACHIEVER STATUS:

Rank: 160   10-Year Growth Rate: 8.72%
Total Years of Dividend Growth: 14

RECENT DEVELOPMENTS: For the year ended 12/31/01, net loss amounted to $2.7 million compared with net income of $150.8 million in 2000. Results for 2000 included a gain of $104.6 million for the sale of subsidiaries and investments. Total net operating revenues declined 14.1% to $1.36 billion from $1.59 billion in the previous year. Operating earnings fell 46.0% to $163.6 million compared with $302.7 million in the prior year.

PROSPECTS: In the near-term, BLC may continue to experience lower revenues as a result of poor economic conditions and the weak advertising environment. However, on the expense side, BLC should benefit from cost-reduction measures implemented during 2001. Meanwhile, BLC will continue to focus on growing market share. Separately, on 3/14/02, BLC acquired KTTU-TV, the UPN affiliate in Tucson, Arizona, for $18.0 million in cash.

BUSINESS

BELO CORPORATION is a media company with a diversified group of television broadcasting, newspaper publishing, interactive media and cable news operations in several markets and regions, including Texas, the Pacific Northwest, the Southwest, Rhode Island, and the mid-Atlantic region. The Company owns and operates 19 network-affiliated television stations; four daily newspapers, including The Dallas Morning News, The Providence Journal and The Press-Enterprise in Riverside, California; and six local or regional cable news channels. The Company also manages one television station through a local marketing agreement. Six of the Company's stations are in the top 16 U.S. television markets. The Company's television group reaches 13.9% of all U.S. television households. Revenues for 2001 were derived: newspaper publishing, 54.0%; television, 43.8%; interactive media, 1.0%; and other, 1.2%.

ANNUAL FINANCIAL DATA

	12/31/01	12/31/00	12/31/99	12/31/98	12/31/97	12/31/96	12/31/95
Earnings Per Share	d0.02	⊡ 1.29	⊡ 1.50	0.52	0.71	1.06	0.84
Cash Flow Per Share	1.64	2.87	2.91	1.80	1.86	1.84	1.59
Dividends Per Share	0.30	0.28	0.26	0.24	0.22	0.20	0.16
Dividend Payout %	...	21.7	17.3	46.1	31.0	19.4	18.7
INCOME STATEMENT (IN MILLIONS):							
Total Revenues	1,364.6	1,588.8	1,434.0	1,407.3	1,248.4	824.3	735.3
Costs & Expenses	1,018.0	1,101.1	1,000.5	1,014.8	872.6	593.5	539.3
Depreciation & Amort.	183.0	185.0	169.0	159.4	135.0	65.2	59.4
Operating Income	163.6	302.7	264.5	233.1	240.8	165.6	136.6
Net Interest Inc./(Exp.)	d112.7	d132.8	d110.6	d107.6	d90.8	d27.6	d30.0
Income Before Income Taxes	21.8	266.8	276.5	130.5	154.1	144.0	111.0
Income Taxes	24.4	116.0	98.1	65.6	71.2	56.5	44.4
Net Income	d2.7	⊡ 150.8	⊡ 178.3	64.9	83.0	87.5	66.6
Cash Flow	180.3	335.8	347.3	224.3	218.0	152.7	126.0
Average Shs. Outstg. (000)	109,816	117,198	119,177	124,836	117,122	83,020	79,292
BALANCE SHEET (IN MILLIONS):							
Cash & Cash Equivalents	35.9	87.7	45.6	19.5	11.9	13.8	12.8
Total Current Assets	332.2	421.0	352.0	275.8	277.0	171.9	165.3
Net Property	597.1	637.6	655.0	626.8	608.3	370.8	361.8
Total Assets	3,672.2	3,893.3	3,976.3	3,539.1	3,623.0	1,224.1	1,154.0
Total Current Liabilities	185.4	302.7	259.8	180.7	214.5	89.3	81.7
Long-Term Obligations	1,696.9	1,789.6	1,849.5	1,634.0	1,614.0	631.9	557.4
Net Stockholders' Equity	1,320.7	1,349.4	1,389.8	1,248.1	1,326.0	370.5	388.5
Net Working Capital	146.8	118.3	92.1	95.0	62.5	82.6	83.6
Year-end Shs. Outstg. (000)	109,816	109,854	118,656	118,925	124,694	72,520	76,484
STATISTICAL RECORD:							
Operating Profit Margin %	12.0	19.1	18.4	16.6	19.3	20.1	18.6
Net Profit Margin %	...	9.5	12.4	4.6	6.6	10.6	9.1
Return on Equity %	...	11.2	12.8	5.2	6.3	23.6	17.1
Return on Assets %	...	3.9	4.5	1.8	2.3	7.1	5.8
Debt/Total Assets %	46.2	46.0	46.5	46.2	44.6	51.6	48.3
Price Range	20.10-15.15	20.00-12.31	24.50-16.38	28.47-13.94	27.56-16.63	20.88-15.50	18.38-13.91
P/E Ratio	...	15.5-9.5	16.3-10.9	54.7-26.8	38.8-23.4	19.8-14.7	21.9-16.6
Average Yield %	1.7	1.7	1.3	1.1	1.0	1.1	1.0

Statistics are as originally reported. Adj. for stk. splits: 2-for-1, 6/98 and 5/95. ⊡ Incl. gain on sale of subsidaires & invest., 2000, $104.6 mill.; 1999, $117.8 mill.

OFFICERS:
R. W. Decherd, Chmn., Pres., C.E.O.
D. A. Shive, Exec. V.P., C.F.O.

INVESTOR CONTACT: Carey P. Hendrickson, V.P., Investor Relations, (214) 977-6626

PRINCIPAL OFFICE: 400 South Record Street, Dallas, TX 75265-5237

TELEPHONE NUMBER: (214) 977-6606
FAX: (214) 977-6603
WEB: www.belo.com
NO. OF EMPLOYEES: 7,820 (approx.)
SHAREHOLDERS: 9,985 (approx. series A); 540 (approx. series B)
ANNUAL MEETING: In May
INCORPORATED: DE, May, 1987

INSTITUTIONAL HOLDINGS:
No. of Institutions: 177
Shares Held: 61,812,155
% Held: 55.6

INDUSTRY: Newspapers (SIC: 2711)

TRANSFER AGENT(S): BankBoston, NA., Boston, MA

BECTON, DICKINSON AND COMPANY

YIELD 1.0%
P/E RATIO 21.4

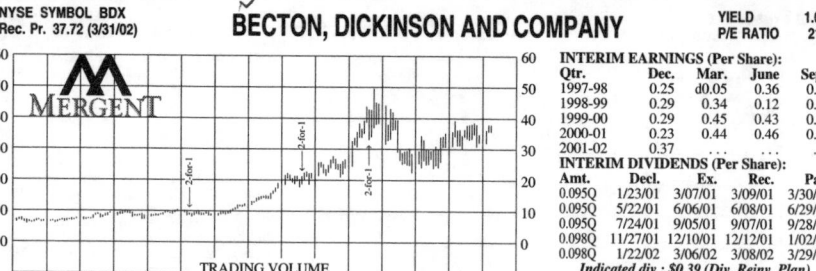

TRADING VOLUME
Thousand Shares

1988|1989|1990|1991|1992|1993|1994|1995|1996|1997|1998|1999|2000|2001|2002
*7 YEAR PRICE SCORE 106.4   *12 MONTH PRICE SCORE 108.4
*NYSE COMPOSITE INDEX=100

INTERIM EARNINGS (Per Share):

Qtr.	Dec.	Mar.	June	Sept.
1997-98	0.25	d0.05	0.36	0.34
1998-99	0.29	0.34	0.12	0.29
1999-00	0.29	0.45	0.43	0.32
2000-01	0.23	0.44	0.46	0.49
2001-02	0.37	...	...	...

INTERIM DIVIDENDS (Per Share):

Amt.	Decl.	Ex.	Rec.	Pay.
0.095Q	1/23/01	3/07/01	3/09/01	3/30/01
0.095Q	5/22/01	6/06/01	6/08/01	6/29/01
0.095Q	7/24/01	9/05/01	9/07/01	9/28/01
0.098Q	11/27/01	12/10/01	12/12/01	1/02/02
0.098Q	1/22/02	3/06/02	3/08/02	3/29/02

Indicated div.: $0.39 (Div. Reinv. Plan)

CAPITALIZATION (9/30/01):

	($000)	(%)
Long-Term Debt	782,996	24.5
Deferred Income Tax	90,117	2.8
Preferred Stock	40,528	1.3
Common & Surplus	2,288,239	71.5
Total	3,201,880	100.0

DIVIDEND ACHIEVER STATUS:
Rank: 135   10-Year Growth Rate: 10.11%
Total Years of Dividend Growth: 29

RECENT DEVELOPMENTS: For the quarter ended 12/31/01, net income was $99.7 million compared with income of $73.7 million, before an accounting charge, in the prior year. Revenues climbed 9.3% to $944.9 million. Revenues in the medical systems segment increased 9.3% to $503.0 million, while revenues in the clinical laboratory solutions segment rose 7.3% to $294.7 million. Revenues in the biosciences segment increased 13.7% to $147.2 million.

PROSPECTS: Revenues continue to be boosted primarily by safety-engineered devices, prefillable drug delivery devices and the Company's biosciences products. Separately, BDX expects diluted earnings per share for fiscal 2002 to be approximately $1.90, which includes a gain from an accounting change and excludes restructuring items and possible divestures.

BUSINESS

BECTON, DICKINSON AND COMPANY is principally engaged in the manufacture and sale of a broad line of medical supplies and devices and diagnostic systems used by healthcare professionals, medical research institutions and the general public. BDX's operations consist of three worldwide business segments: Medical Systems (53.5% of revenues), Clinical Laboratory Solutions (30.8% of revenues) and Biosciences (15.7% of revenues). Major products in the Medical Systems segment are hypodermic products, specially designed devices for diabetes care, prefillable drug delivery systems, infusion therapy products, elastic support products and thermometers. Major products in the Clinical Laboratory Solutions segment are specimen collection products and services. Major products in the Biosciences segment are clinical and industrial microbiology products, sample collection products, cellular analysis systems, and hematology instruments.

ANNUAL FINANCIAL DATA

	9/30/01	9/30/00	9/30/99	9/30/98	9/30/97	9/30/96	9/30/95
Earnings Per Share	1.63	③ 1.49	1.04	① ② 0.90	1.21	1.10	0.90
Cash Flow Per Share	2.76	2.59	2.02	1.78	2.08	1.91	1.66
Tang. Book Val. Per Share	5.35	3.80	2.74	3.30	4.11	4.43	4.46
Dividends Per Share	0.38	0.37	0.34	0.29	0.26	0.23	0.20
Dividend Payout %	23.3	24.8	32.7	32.2	21.5	20.9	22.9

INCOME STATEMENT (IN MILLIONS):

Total Revenues	3,754.3	3,618.3	3,418.4	3,116.9	2,810.5	2,769.8	2,712.5
Costs & Expenses	2,802.7	2,815.3	2,714.3	2,482.7	2,150.2	2,138.0	2,108.1
Depreciation & Amort.	305.7	288.3	258.9	228.7	209.8	200.5	207.8
Operating Income	645.9	514.8	445.2	405.4	450.5	431.2	396.7
Net Interest Inc./(Exp.)	d55.4	d74.2	d72.1	d56.3	d39.4	d37.4	d42.8
Income Before Income Taxes	576.8	519.9	372.7	340.9	422.6	393.7	349.6
Income Taxes	138.3	127.0	96.9	104.3	122.6	110.2	97.9
Net Income	438.4	③ 392.9	275.7	① ② 236.6	300.1	283.4	251.7
Cash Flow	741.4	678.7	532.0	462.7	507.2	481.3	456.8
Average Shs. Outstg. (000)	268,833	263,239	264,580	262,128	245,230	253,418	276,804

BALANCE SHEET (IN MILLIONS):

Cash & Cash Equivalents	86.7	54.8	64.6	90.6	141.0	165.1	240.0
Total Current Assets	1,762.9	1,660.7	1,683.7	1,542.8	1,312.6	1,276.8	1,327.5
Net Property	1,716.0	1,576.1	1,431.1	1,302.7	1,250.7	1,244.1	1,281.0
Total Assets	4,802.3	4,505.1	4,437.0	3,846.0	3,080.3	2,889.8	2,999.5
Total Current Liabilities	1,264.7	1,353.5	1,329.3	1,091.9	678.2	766.1	720.0
Long-Term Obligations	783.0	779.6	954.2	765.2	665.4	468.2	557.6
Net Stockholders' Equity	2,328.8	1,956.0	1,768.7	1,613.8	1,385.4	1,325.2	1,398.4
Net Working Capital	498.3	307.1	354.4	450.8	634.4	510.7	607.5
Year-end Shs. Outstg. (000)	259,237	253,496	250,798	247,843	244,168	247,220	260,300

STATISTICAL RECORD:

Operating Profit Margin %	17.2	14.2	13.0	13.0	16.0	15.6	14.6
Net Profit Margin %	11.7	10.9	8.1	7.6	10.7	10.2	9.3
Return on Equity %	18.8	20.1	15.6	14.7	21.7	21.4	18.0
Return on Assets %	9.1	8.7	6.2	6.2	9.7	9.8	8.4
Debt/Total Assets %	16.3	17.3	21.5	19.9	21.6	16.2	18.6
Price Range	39.25-29.96	35.31-23.75	44.19-22.38	49.63-24.38	27.81-20.94	22.75-17.69	19.00-12.00
P/E Ratio	24.1-18.4	23.7-15.9	42.5-21.5	55.1-27.1	23.0-17.3	20.7-16.1	21.2-13.4
Average Yield %	1.1	1.3	1.0	0.8	1.1	1.1	1.3

Statistics are as originally reported. Adj. for 2-for-1 stock split, 2/93, 8/96, 8/98. ① Incl. a one-time chg. of $7.0 mill. for in-proc. res. & dev. rel. to two recent acqs. & incl. a spec. pre-tax chg. of $90.9 mill. ② Incl. a one-time gain of $7.0 mill. from a favorable tax judge. in Brazil; a pre-tax chgs. of $103.0 mill. ③ Incl. a one-time pre-tax spec. chrg. of $57.5 mill. and net gains on invest. of $76.2 mill.

OFFICERS:
E. J. Ludwig, Chmn., Pres. C.E.O.
J. R. Considine, Exec. V.P., C.F.O.
B. M. Healy, V.P., Gen. Couns., Sec.
INVESTOR CONTACT: Dean J. Paranicas, Inv. Rel., (201) 847-7102
PRINCIPAL OFFICE: 1 Becton Drive, Franklin Lakes, NJ 07417-1880

TELEPHONE NUMBER: (201) 847-6800
FAX: (201) 847-6475
WEB: www.bd.com
NO. OF EMPLOYEES: 24,800 (approx.)
SHAREHOLDERS: 10,330 (approx. record)
ANNUAL MEETING: In Feb.
INCORPORATED: NJ, Nov., 1906

INSTITUTIONAL HOLDINGS:
No. of Institutions: 419
Shares Held: 207,617,539
% Held: 80.3
INDUSTRY: Surgical and medical instruments (SIC: 3841)
TRANSFER AGENT(S): First Chicago Trust Company of New York, Jersey City, NJ

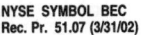

NYSE SYMBOL BEC		
Rec. Pr. 51.07 (3/31/02)		

BECKMAN COULTER, INC.

YIELD	0.7%
P/E RATIO	23.0

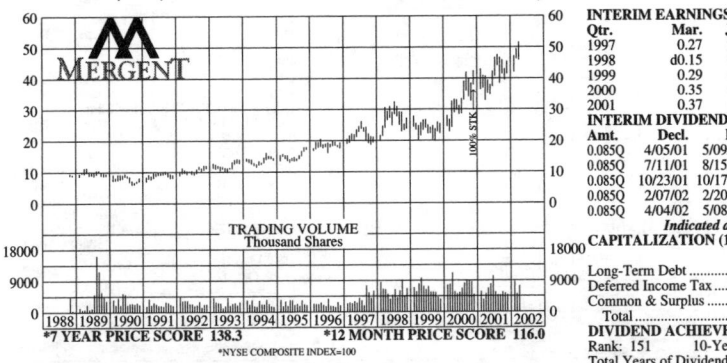

TRADING VOLUME
Thousand Shares

| 1988 | 1989 | 1990 | 1991 | 1992 | 1993 | 1994 | 1995 | 1996 | 1997 | 1998 | 1999 | 2000 | 2001 | 2002 |

*7 YEAR PRICE SCORE 138.3   *12 MONTH PRICE SCORE 116.0
*NYSE COMPOSITE INDEX=100

INTERIM EARNINGS (Per Share):

Qtr.	Mar.	June	Sept.	Dec.
1997	0.27	0.36	0.34	d5.82
1998	d0.15	0.16	0.24	0.32
1999	0.29	0.44	0.41	0.65
2000	0.35	0.53	0.47	0.69
2001	0.37	0.58	0.52	0.75

INTERIM DIVIDENDS (Per Share):

Amt.	Decl.	Ex.	Rec.	Pay.
0.085Q	4/05/01	5/09/01	5/11/01	5/31/01
0.085Q	7/11/01	8/15/01	8/17/01	9/06/01
0.085Q	10/23/01	10/17/01	10/19/01	11/08/01
0.085Q	2/07/02	2/20/02	2/22/02	3/14/02
0.085Q	4/04/02	5/08/02	5/10/02	5/30/02

Indicated div.: $0.34

CAPITALIZATION (12/31/01):

	($000)	(%)
Long-Term Debt	760,300	56.3
Deferred Income Tax	72,300	5.4
Common & Surplus	518,200	38.4
Total	1,350,800	100.0

DIVIDEND ACHIEVER STATUS:

Rank: 151   10-Year Growth Rate: 9.28%
Total Years of Dividend Growth: 10

RECENT DEVELOPMENTS: For the year ended 12/31/01, earnings increased 12.7% to $141.5 million, before an accounting charge of $3.1 million, compared with net earnings of $125.5 million in the previous year. Results for 2001 and 2000 included pre-tax restructuring credits of $500,000 and $2.4 million, respectively. Sales climbed 5.1% to $1.98 billion from $1.89 billion in the prior year. Clinical diagnostics sales rose 3.6% to $1.53 billion

PROSPECTS: The Company signed 14 integrated health network (IHN) agreements valued at approximately $103.5 million in the fourth quarter ended 12/31/01. BEC expects to generate $196.5 million in revenue over the next five years from the total number of IHN contracts signed in 2001. Meanwhile, BEC should continue to benefit from the introduction of new instrument systems in three product lines of clinical diagnostics.

BUSINESS

BECKMAN COULTER, INC. (formerly Beckman Instruments Inc.) designs, manufactures, sells, and services laboratory systems for biological analysis and investigation into life processes. The Company targets three markets: the life sciences laboratory market, specialty testing and the hospital and clinical diagnostic laboratory market. Customers such as universities, research institutions, pharmaceutical companies, hospitals and clinical laboratories use BEC's products across the entire spectrum of biologically-based endeavors, from basic scientific research to daily analysis of blood samples. Beckman Coulter markets its products in approximately 130 countries. BEC's products are used in all phases of the battle against disease to improve methodologies for biological discovery and diagnosis.

ANNUAL FINANCIAL DATA

	12/31/01	12/31/00	12/31/99	12/31/98	12/31/97	12/31/96	12/31/95
Earnings Per Share	⑤ 2.21	④ 2.03	④ 1.79	③ 0.57	② d4.79	1.29	① 0.85
Cash Flow Per Share	4.19	4.23	4.20	3.17	d2.81	2.81	2.22
Tang. Book Val. Per Share	...	...	...	...	...	7.13	5.97
Dividends Per Share	0.34	0.33	0.32	0.31	0.30	0.26	0.22
Dividend Payout %	15.4	16.0	17.9	53.5	...	20.2	25.9
INCOME STATEMENT (IN MILLIONS):							
Total Revenues	1,984.0	1,886.9	1,808.7	1,718.2	1,198.0	1,028.0	930.1
Costs & Expenses	1,618.0	1,518.2	1,448.5	1,451.0	1,325.9	817.7	767.9
Depreciation & Amort.	126.4	136.1	143.7	152.4	109.1	87.8	79.1
Operating Income	239.6	232.6	216.5	114.8	d237.0	122.5	83.1
Net Interest Inc./(Exp.)	d46.9	d65.6	d66.0	d74.4	d23.3	d12.3	d8.1
Income Before Income Taxes	205.0	181.9	154.7	46.6	d251.9	111.5	72.4
Income Taxes	63.5	56.4	48.7	13.1	12.5	36.8	23.5
Net Income	⑤ 141.5	④ 125.5	④ 106.0	③ 33.5	② d264.4	74.7	① 48.9
Cash Flow	267.9	261.6	249.7	185.9	d155.3	162.5	128.0
Average Shs. Outstg. (000)	64,011	61,800	59,400	58,600	55,200	57,800	57,614
BALANCE SHEET (IN MILLIONS):							
Cash & Cash Equivalents	36.0	29.6	34.4	24.7	33.5	42.7	34.4
Total Current Assets	1,035.6	927.8	966.4	956.6	976.7	579.4	533.3
Net Property	347.4	298.2	305.9	309.4	410.9	263.5	252.1
Total Assets	2,178.0	2,018.2	2,110.8	2,133.3	2,331.0	960.1	907.8
Total Current Liabilities	509.9	501.1	575.9	719.3	894.9	279.3	251.2
Long-Term Obligations	760.3	862.8	980.7	982.2	1,181.3	176.6	162.7
Net Stockholders' Equity	518.2	343.9	227.9	126.9	81.8	398.9	347.9
Net Working Capital	525.7	426.7	390.5	237.3	81.8	300.1	282.1
Year-end Shs. Outstg. (000)	61,200	59,700	58,000	56,800	55,200	55,952	58,248
STATISTICAL RECORD:							
Operating Profit Margin %	12.1	12.3	12.0	6.7	...	11.9	8.9
Net Profit Margin %	7.1	6.7	5.9	1.9	...	7.3	5.3
Return on Equity %	27.3	36.5	46.5	26.4	...	18.7	14.1
Return on Assets %	6.5	6.2	5.0	1.6	...	7.8	5.4
Debt/Total Assets %	34.9	42.8	46.5	46.0	50.7	18.4	17.9
Price Range	47.60-32.80	42.44-22.78	27.88-19.75	32.47-20.03	26.16-18.69	20.56-16.00	17.94-13.00
P/E Ratio	21.5-14.8	20.9-11.2	15.6-11.1	57.0-35.1	...	15.9-12.4	21.1-15.3
Average Yield %	0.8	1.0	1.3	1.3	1.4	1.4	1.4

Statistics are as originally reported. Adj. for 2-for-1 stk. split., 12/00. ① Incl. pre-tax restruct. chgs. of $27.7 mill. ② Incl. a $0.05 per sh. dil. for exps. assoc./w the acq. of the Access® immunoassay product line & incl. after-tax chgs. totaling $318.4 mill. ③ Incl. after-tax chrgs. of $110.9 mill. ④ Incl. a pre-tax restruct. gain of $2.4 mill., 2000; $200,001, 1999. ⑤ Bef. acctg. chrg. of $3.1 mill.; incl. restruct. credit of $500,000.

OFFICERS:
J. P. Wareham, Chmn., Pres., C.E.O.
A. I. Khalifa, V.P., C.F.O.
J. T. Glover, V.P., Treas.

INVESTOR CONTACT: Jeanie Herbert, Investor Relations, (714) 773-7620

PRINCIPAL OFFICE: 4300 N. Harbor Boulevard, Fullerton, CA 92835

TELEPHONE NUMBER: (714) 871-4848
FAX: (714) 773-8283
WEB: www.beckmancoulter.com
NO. OF EMPLOYEES: 10,094 (approx.)
SHAREHOLDERS: 6,239 (approx.)
ANNUAL MEETING: In Apr.
INCORPORATED: DE, July, 1988

INSTITUTIONAL HOLDINGS:
No. of Institutions: 240
Shares Held: 49,367,131
% Held: 80.5

INDUSTRY: Analytical instruments (SIC: 3826)

TRANSFER AGENT(S): First Chicago Trust Company of New York, Jersey City, NJ

BB&T CORPORATION

YIELD 2.7%
P/E RATIO 17.6

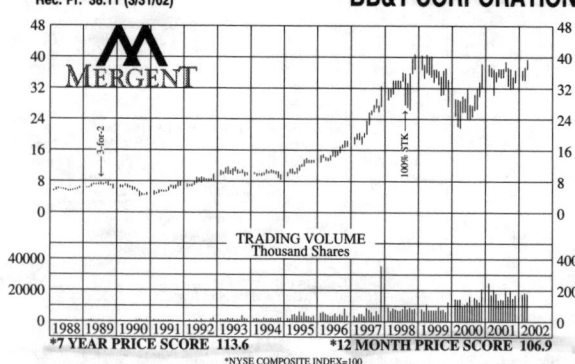

INTERIM EARNINGS (Per Share):

Qtr.	Mar.	June	Sept.	Dec.
1998	0.39	0.42	0.44	0.46
1999	0.44	0.49	0.44	0.47
2000	0.46	0.48	0.12	0.56
2001	0.53	0.54	0.48	0.61

INTERIM DIVIDENDS (Per Share):

Amt.	Decl.	Ex.	Rec.	Pay.
0.23Q	2/27/01	4/10/01	4/13/01	5/01/01
0.26Q	6/16/01	7/11/01	7/13/01	8/01/01
0.26Q	8/28/01	10/10/01	10/12/01	11/01/01
0.26Q	12/18/01	1/16/02	1/18/02	2/04/02
0.26Q	2/26/02	4/10/02	4/12/02	5/01/02

Indicated div.: $1.04 (Div. Reinv. Plan)

CAPITALIZATION (12/31/01):

	($000)	(%)
Total Deposits	44,733,275	71.5
Long-Term Debt	11,721,076	18.7
Common & Surplus	6,150,209	9.8
Total	62,604,560	100.0

DIVIDEND ACHIEVER STATUS:
Rank: 56   10-Year Growth Rate: 15.60%
Total Years of Dividend Growth: 30

TRADING VOLUME
Thousand Shares

*7 YEAR PRICE SCORE 113.6   *12 MONTH PRICE SCORE 106.9
*NYSE COMPOSITE INDEX=100

RECENT DEVELOPMENTS: For the year ended 12/31/01, net income increased 39.4% to $973.6 million from $698.5 million in the prior year. Results for 2001 included after-tax net non-recurring merger-related charges of $126.5 million. Net interest income rose 5.2% to $2.43 billion from $2.31 billion in the prior year. Provision for loan and lease losses grew 52.4% to $224.3 million. Non-interest income advanced 62.8% to $1.38 billion, while non-interest expense increased 11.4% to $2.23 billion.

PROSPECTS: On 3/21/02, the Company completed its acquisition of AREA Bancshares Corporation, the largest independent bank holding company in Kentucky, for $513.3 million in stock. AREA, with $29.9 billion in assets, operates 71 banking offices in 31 communities. AREA also operates a trust company and retail brokerage. Separately, on 3/11/02, the Company completed the acquisition of MidAmerica Bancorp for $418.5 million.

BUSINESS

BB&T CORPORATION, a multi-bank holding company with assets of $70.87 billion as of 12/31/01, owns 1,081 banking offices in the Carolinas, Virginia, West Virginia, Tennessee, Kentucky, Georgia, Maryland, Alabama and Washington, D.C. BBT's largest subsidiary is Branch Banking and Trust Company (BB&T-NC). BB&T-NC's subsidiaries include BB&T Leasing Corp., BB&T Investment Services, and BB&T Insurance Services. BBT's other subsidiaries include Branch Banking and Trust Co. of South Carolina, Branch Banking and Trust Co. of Virginia, and Fidelity Service Corporation. On 3/26/99, BBT acquired Scott & Stringfellow Financial, Inc. On 1/13/00, BBT acquired Premier Bancshares, Inc. On 7/7/00, BBT acquired One Valley Bancorp Inc.

QUARTERLY DATA

(12/31/2001)($000)	REV	INC
1st Quarter	893,749	236,500
2nd Quarter	977,966	237,229
3rd Quarter	1,001,133	221,966
4th Quarter	1,008,980	277,943

ANNUAL FINANCIAL DATA

	12/31/01	12/31/00	12/31/99	12/31/98	12/31/97	12/31/96	12/31/95
Earnings Per Share	②2.12	⑥1.55	⑤1.83	④1.71	③1.30	②1.28	①0.83
Tang. Book Val. Per Share	13.50	11.92	9.66	9.51	8.22	7.91	8.08
Dividends Per Share	0.98	0.86	0.75	0.66	0.58	0.50	0.43
Dividend Payout %	46.2	55.5	41.0	38.6	44.6	39.1	51.8
INCOME STATEMENT (IN MILLIONS):							
Total Interest Income	4,849.5	4,339.7	3,115.8	2,481.2	2,122.9	1,606.6	1,548.2
Total Interest Expense	2,415.1	2,322.0	1,534.1	1,233.8	1,023.4	778.1	806.6
Net Interest Income	2,434.5	2,017.6	1,581.7	1,247.4	1,099.5	828.5	741.5
Provision for Loan Losses	224.3	127.4	92.1	80.3	89.9	53.7	31.4
Non-Interest Income	1,378.7	777.0	761.4	528.0	474.9	297.4	226.4
Non-Interest Expense	2,228.4	1,761.5	1,346.9	961.4	937.1	654.1	672.3
Income Before Taxes	1,360.4	905.7	904.1	733.7	547.4	418.2	264.2
Net Income	⑥973.6	⑥626.4	⑤612.8	④501.8	③359.9	②283.7	①178.1
Average Shs. Outstg. (000)	459,269	398,916	335,298	293,571	276,440	220,972	207,964
BALANCE SHEET (IN MILLIONS):							
Cash & Due from Banks	1,871.4	1,471.0	1,138.8	938.8	839.6	638.7	582.6
Securities Avail. for Sale	16,719.4	13,878.6	10,575.3	8,031.8	6,549.4	5,136.8	5,201.3
Total Loans & Leases	48,404.6	41,933.8	30,152.2	23,375.2	20,012.0	14,524.6	13,636.2
Allowance for Credit Losses	3,513.3	3,001.5	1,627.8	1,024.6	495.2	344.0	241.1
Net Loans & Leases	44,891.3	38,932.4	28,524.5	22,350.7	19,516.9	14,180.7	13,395.0
Total Assets	70,869.9	59,340.2	43,481.0	34,427.2	29,177.6	21,246.6	20,492.9
Total Deposits	44,733.3	38,014.5	27,251.1	23,046.9	20,210.1	14,953.9	14,684.1
Long-Term Obligations	11,721.1	8,354.7	5,491.7	4,736.9	3,283.0	2,051.8	1,383.9
Total Liabilities	64,719.7	54,554.3	40,281.8	31,668.7	26,940.0	19,517.4	18,818.9
Net Stockholders' Equity	6,150.2	4,785.9	3,199.2	2,758.5	2,237.6	1,729.2	1,674.1
Year-end Shs. Outstg. (000)	455,683	401,649	331,170	290,211	272,104	218,594	206,714
STATISTICAL RECORD:							
Return on Equity %	15.8	13.1	19.2	18.2	16.1	16.4	10.6
Return on Assets %	1.4	1.1	1.4	1.5	1.2	1.3	0.9
Equity/Assets %	8.7	8.1	7.4	8.0	7.7	8.1	8.2
Non-Int. Exp./Tot. Inc. %	60.4	58.5	57.4	54.4	59.6	58.3	68.2
Price Range	38.84-30.24	38.25-21.69	40.63-27.19	40.75-26.25	32.50-17.50	18.50-12.88	14.00-9.38
P/E Ratio	18.3-14.3	24.7-14.0	22.2-14.9	23.8-15.3	25.0-13.5	14.5-10.1	16.9-11.3
Average Yield %	2.8	2.9	2.2	2.0	2.3	3.2	3.7

Statistics are as originally reported. Adj. for 100% stock div., 8/98. ① Incl. $108.0 pre-tax merger-rel. chgs., $19.8 mill. in sec. losses, & $12.3 mill. gain on the sale of divest. deposits. ② Incl. one-time after-tax SAIF chg. of $21.3 mill. ③ Incl. $42.7 mill. in after-tax UCB merger-rel. chgs. ④ Incl. after-tax merger costs of $10.9 mill. ⑤ Incl. non-recur. chrg. of $46.2 mill. ⑥ Incl. aft.-tax nonrecur. chrgs. of $126.5 mill., 12/01; $248.6 mill., 12/00.

OFFICERS:
J. A. Allison IV, Chmn., C.E.O.
K. S. King, Pres.
S. E. Reed, Sr. Exec. V.P., C.F.O.

INVESTOR CONTACT: Thomas A. Nicholson Jr., Sr. V.P., (336) 733-3058

PRINCIPAL OFFICE: 200 West Second Street, Winston-Salem, NC 27102-1250

TELEPHONE NUMBER: (336) 733-2000
FAX: (336) 721-3499
WEB: www.bbandt.com
NO. OF EMPLOYEES: 20,400 (approx.)
SHAREHOLDERS: 114,461
ANNUAL MEETING: In Apr.
INCORPORATED: NC, 1897; reincorp., NC, 1968

BARD (C.R.), INC.

YIELD 1.4%
P/E RATIO 21.5

TRADING VOLUME
Thousand Shares

| 1988 | 1989 | 1990 | 1991 | 1992 | 1993 | 1994 | 1995 | 1996 | 1997 | 1998 | 1999 | 2000 | 2001 | 2002 |

7 YEAR PRICE SCORE 115.3   **12 MONTH PRICE SCORE 102.4**
*NYSE COMPOSITE INDEX=100

INTERIM EARNINGS (Per Share):

Qtr.	Mar.	June	Sept.	Dec.
1997	0.46	0.46	d0.07	0.42
1998	0.44	0.71	0.42	3.03
1999	0.51	0.55	0.58	0.64
2000	0.62	0.65	0.66	0.16
2001	0.65	0.68	0.68	0.74

INTERIM DIVIDENDS (Per Share):

Amt.	Decl.	Ex.	Rec.	Pay.
0.21Q	12/13/00	1/18/01	1/22/01	2/02/01
0.21Q	4/18/01	4/26/01	4/30/01	5/11/01
0.21Q	7/11/01	7/19/01	7/23/01	8/03/01
0.21Q	10/10/01	10/18/01	10/22/01	11/02/01
0.21Q	12/12/01	1/16/02	1/21/02	2/01/02

Indicated div.: $0.84 (Div. Reinv. Plan)

CAPITALIZATION (12/31/01):

	($000)	(%)
Long-Term Debt	156,400	16.5
Common & Surplus	788,700	83.5
Total	945,100	100.0

DIVIDEND ACHIEVER STATUS:
Rank: 209   10-Year Growth Rate: 6.21%
Total Years of Dividend Growth: 30

RECENT DEVELOPMENTS:
For the year ended 12/31/01, net income jumped 34.0% to $143.2 million compared with $106.9 million in the previous year. Results for 2000 included a gain from dispositions of cardiology businesses of $15.4 million. Net sales climbed 7.5% to $1.18 billion. Vascular net sales rose 4.0% to $250.9 million, while urology net sales increased 8.0% to $390.1 million. Oncology net sales grew 8.5% to $274.6 million and surgery net sales jumped 12.4% to $205.2 million.

PROSPECTS:
On 2/6/02, BCR and Tyco International Ltd. mutually terminated their merger agreement. Each party will bear their own costs and expenses and no break up fee will be paid. Going forward, BCR has targeted 8.0% revenue growth for full-year 2002. BCR also anticipates earnings per share to be between $3.27 and $3.31 for 2002, including a $0.24 per share for an accounting change and excluding a charge associated with the termination of BCR's merger agreement with Tyco International Ltd.

BUSINESS

BARD (C.R.), INC. is a multinational developer, manufacturer and marketer of health care products. The Company engages in the design, manufacture, packaging, distribution and sale of medical, surgical, diagnostic and patient-care devices. Bard holds strong positions in cardiovascular, urological, surgical and general health care products. BCR products are marketed worldwide to hospitals, individual health care professionals, extended care facilities, alternate site facilities and the home, employing a combination of direct delivery and medical specialty distributors. Hospitals, physicians and nursing homes purchase approximately 90.0% of the Company's products as of 12/31/01. The Vascular Group accounted for 21.2% of 2001 sales; Urology, 33.0%; Oncology, 23.3%; Surgery, 17.4%; and other, 5.1%.

ANNUAL FINANCIAL DATA

	12/31/01	12/31/00	12/31/99	12/31/98	12/31/97	12/31/96	12/31/95
Earnings Per Share	2.75	② 2.09	⑤ 2.28	④ 4.51	③ 1.26	② 1.62	① 1.53
Cash Flow Per Share	3.78	3.06	3.22	5.56	2.26	2.63	2.42
Tang. Book Val. Per Share	7.94	5.06	4.67	4.05	2.62	2.71	4.36
Dividends Per Share	0.84	0.82	0.78	0.74	0.70	0.66	0.62
Dividend Payout %	30.5	39.2	34.2	16.4	55.6	40.7	40.5
INCOME STATEMENT (IN MILLIONS):							
Total Revenues	1,181.3	1,098.8	1,036.5	1,164.7	1,213.5	1,194.4	1,137.8
Costs & Expenses	914.9	854.9	797.5	947.3	991.8	976.0	947.3
Depreciation & Amort.	53.2	49.6	49.1	58.7	57.3	57.4	50.6
Operating Income	213.2	194.3	189.9	158.7	164.4	161.0	139.9
Net Interest Inc./(Exp.)	d14.2	d19.3	d19.3	d26.4	d32.9	d26.4	d24.2
Income Before Income Taxes	204.9	154.0	173.3	464.4	104.9	102.7	123.5
Income Taxes	61.7	47.1	55.2	212.1	32.6	10.2	36.7
Net Income	143.2	⑥ 106.9	⑤ 118.1	④ 252.3	③ 72.3	② 92.5	① 86.8
Cash Flow	196.4	156.5	167.2	311.0	129.6	149.9	137.4
Average Shs. Outstg. (000)	52,001	51,222	51,882	55,970	57,273	57,090	56,731
BALANCE SHEET (IN MILLIONS):							
Cash & Cash Equivalents	271.0	119.7	95.9	42.4	60.7	78.0	51.3
Total Current Assets	647.4	526.6	529.1	488.5	563.5	576.9	503.9
Net Property	157.9	155.5	169.7	172.7	206.4	226.1	214.2
Total Assets	1,231.1	1,089.2	1,126.4	1,079.8	1,279.3	1,332.5	1,091.0
Total Current Liabilities	234.5	224.5	352.5	302.8	310.6	336.2	273.3
Long-Term Obligations	156.4	204.3	158.4	160.0	340.7	342.8	198.4
Net Stockholders' Equity	788.7	613.9	574.3	567.6	573.1	601.5	564.6
Net Working Capital	412.9	302.1	176.6	185.7	252.9	240.7	230.6
Year-end Shs. Outstg. (000)	52,384	50,909	50,782	51,498	56,785	56,986	57,101
STATISTICAL RECORD:							
Operating Profit Margin %	18.0	17.7	18.3	13.6	13.5	13.5	12.3
Net Profit Margin %	12.1	9.7	11.4	21.7	6.0	7.7	7.6
Return on Equity %	18.2	17.4	20.6	44.5	12.6	15.4	15.4
Return on Assets %	11.6	9.8	10.5	23.4	5.7	6.9	8.0
Debt/Total Assets %	12.7	18.8	14.1	14.8	26.6	25.7	18.2
Price Range	64.95-40.86	54.94-35.00	59.88-41.69	50.25-28.50	39.00-26.38	37.38-25.88	32.25-25.50
P/E Ratio	23.6-14.9	26.3-16.7	26.3-18.3	11.1-6.3	30.9-20.9	23.1-16.0	21.1-16.7
Average Yield %	1.6	1.8	1.5	1.9	2.1	2.1	2.1

Statistics are as originally reported. ① Incl. one-time chg. of $17.7 mill. ② Incl. net nonrecurr. chgs. of $12.9 mill. ③ Incl. pre-tax restruct chg. of $44.1 mill. & a nonrecurr. net gain of $3.9 mill. ④ Incl. net gain of $163.8 mill. fr. the sale of cardiology bus. & several nonrecur. chgs. total. $25.9 mill. ⑤ Incl. gain of $9.2 mill. fr. the sale cardiology bus. ⑥ Incl. gain of $15.4 mill. fr. the sale cardiology bus.

OFFICERS:
W. H. Longfield, Chmn., C.E.O.
C. P. Slacik, Sr. V.P., C.F.O.
N. C. Adler, V.P., Gen. Couns., Sec.
INVESTOR CONTACT: Todd C. Schermerhorn, Inv. Rel., (908) 277-8139
PRINCIPAL OFFICE: 730 Central Avenue, Murray Hill, NJ 07974

TELEPHONE NUMBER: (908) 277-8000
FAX: (908) 277-8278
WEB: www.crbard.com
NO. OF EMPLOYEES: 7,700 (approx.)
SHAREHOLDERS: 5,859
ANNUAL MEETING: In Apr.
INCORPORATED: NJ, Feb., 1923

INSTITUTIONAL HOLDINGS:
No. of Institutions: 242
Shares Held: 31,643,675
% Held: 60.2
INDUSTRY: Surgical and medical instruments (SIC: 3841)
TRANSFER AGENT(S): EquiServe, Jersey City, NJ

BANTA CORPORATION

YIELD 1.8%
P/E RATIO 17.8

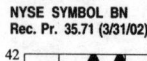
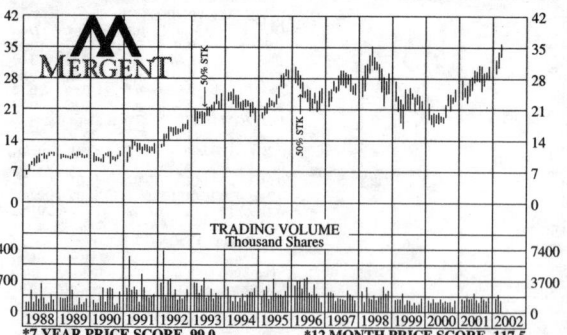

TRADING VOLUME
Thousand Shares

*7 YEAR PRICE SCORE 99.0 *12 MONTH PRICE SCORE 117.5
*NYSE COMPOSITE INDEX=100

INTERIM EARNINGS (Per Share):

Qtr.	Mar.	June	Sept.	Dec.
1997	0.33	0.42	0.19	0.50
1998	0.37	0.45	0.55	0.43
1999	0.35	d0.97	0.65	0.59
2000	0.39	0.50	0.78	0.69
2001	0.11	0.50	0.75	0.65

INTERIM DIVIDENDS (Per Share):

Amt.	Decl.	Ex.	Rec.	Pay.
0.15Q	1/30/01	4/10/01	4/13/01	5/01/01
0.15Q	4/24/01	7/11/01	7/13/01	8/01/01
0.16Q	7/31/01	10/17/01	10/19/01	11/01/01
0.16Q	12/06/01	1/16/02	1/18/02	2/01/02
0.16Q	1/29/02	4/10/02	4/12/02	5/01/02

Indicated div.: $0.64 (Div. Reinv. Plan)

CAPITALIZATION (12/29/01):

	($000)	(%)
Long-Term Debt	130,981	23.4
Deferred Income Tax	21,080	3.8
Common & Surplus	407,278	72.8
Total	559,339	100.0

DIVIDEND ACHIEVER STATUS:
Rank: 152   10-Year Growth Rate: 9.19%
Total Years of Dividend Growth: 23

RECENT DEVELOPMENTS: For the year ended 12/29/01, net income decreased 14.9% to $50.0 million versus $58.7 million in 2000. Results for 2001 included a write-off of $12.5 million related to an investment. Net sales were $1.46 billion, down 5.2% from $1.54 billion in the prior year. Gross profit slipped 4.0% to $298.1 million from $310.5 million the year before. Operating earnings declined 5.6% to $108.4 million versus $114.8 million in the previous year.

PROSPECTS: The Company anticipates adverse market conditions will continue through the first half of 2002. Consequently, earnings for the first six months of the year are anticipated to be comparable to the same period in 2001, before last year's one-time write-off. Meanwhile, BN expects sales and earnings to grow in the mid-single digits for the full-year 2002. Meanwhile, the Company will continue to focus on cost containment.

BUSINESS

BANTA CORPORATION is a North American provider of a broad range of printing and digital imaging services. BN operates in three business segments: print, turnkey services, and healthcare. The print segment provides products and services to publishers of educational and general books and special interest magazines. The print segment also supplies direct marketing materials and consumer and business catalogs. The turnkey services segment provides supply-chain management, product assembly, fulfillment and product localization services to technology companies. The healthcare products segment is primarily engaged in the production of disposable products used in outpatient clinics, dental offices and hospitals. Sales (and operating income) for 2001 were derived: printing and digital imaging, 69.5% (73.3%); supply-chain management, 23.8% (19.2%); and healthcare, 6.7% (7.5%).

ANNUAL FINANCIAL DATA

	12/29/01	12/30/00	1/1/00	1/2/99	1/3/98	12/28/96	12/31/95
Earnings Per Share	② 2.01	2.35	① 0.59	1.80	① 1.44	1.63	1.75
Cash Flow Per Share	5.04	5.38	3.10	4.06	3.50	3.49	3.42
Tang. Book Val. Per Share	13.89	12.41	12.31	11.83	11.80	12.29	16.83
Dividends Per Share	0.61	0.60	0.56	0.51	0.47	0.44	0.37
Dividend Payout %	30.3	25.5	94.9	28.3	32.6	26.8	21.3
INCOME STATEMENT (IN MILLIONS):							
Total Revenues	1,457.9	1,537.7	1,278.3	1,335.8	1,202.5	1,083.8	1,022.7
Costs & Expenses	1,274.1	1,347.2	1,161.7	1,171.4	1,060.8	933.3	873.7
Depreciation & Amort.	75.4	75.7	68.2	66.9	62.1	58.3	51.1
Operating Income	108.4	114.8	48.4	97.5	79.5	92.2	97.9
Net Interest Inc./(Exp.)	d13.7	d16.8	d12.4	d10.8	d11.1	d10.2	d9.9
Income Before Income Taxes	82.2	96.6	34.6	86.1	70.8	84.2	89.1
Income Taxes	32.2	37.9	18.6	33.2	27.5	33.3	35.5
Net Income	② 50.0	58.7	① 16.0	52.9	① 43.3	50.9	53.6
Cash Flow	125.4	134.5	84.2	119.8	105.4	109.2	104.6
Average Shs. Outstg. (000)	24,857	24,980	27,177	29,475	30,113	31,249	30,624
BALANCE SHEET (IN MILLIONS):							
Cash & Cash Equivalents	66.0	27.7	27.7	26.6	16.4	57.4	27.1
Total Current Assets	357.5	406.7	355.9	354.6	365.7	347.5	310.8
Net Property	325.0	344.3	327.4	318.6	338.4	319.9	313.7
Total Assets	788.0	854.5	773.3	770.0	781.2	719.2	678.8
Total Current Liabilities	184.8	240.3	245.4	196.5	200.4	127.8	122.9
Long-Term Obligations	131.0	179.2	113.5	120.6	130.1	133.7	135.0
Net Stockholders' Equity	407.3	370.9	353.8	409.9	414.1	420.6	387.1
Net Working Capital	172.7	166.4	110.5	158.1	165.3	219.6	188.0
Year-end Shs. Outstg. (000)	24,730	24,567	23,943	28,261	29,793	30,969	20,560
STATISTICAL RECORD:							
Operating Profit Margin %	7.4	7.5	3.8	7.3	6.6	8.5	9.6
Net Profit Margin %	3.4	3.8	1.3	4.0	3.6	4.7	5.2
Return on Equity %	12.3	15.8	4.5	12.9	10.5	12.1	13.8
Return on Assets %	6.3	6.9	2.1	6.9	5.5	7.1	7.9
Debt/Total Assets %	16.6	21.0	14.7	15.7	16.6	18.6	19.9
Price Range	31.04-22.49	25.70-17.19	27.38-16.75	35.25-21.81	29.88-21.63	30.67-20.50	30.08-19.00
P/E Ratio	15.4-11.2	10.9-7.3	46.4-28.4	19.6-12.1	20.7-15.0	18.8-12.6	17.2-10.9
Average Yield %	2.3	2.8	2.5	1.8	1.8	1.7	1.5

Statistics are as originally reported. Adj. for 50% stk. div., 3/1/96. ① Incl. restr. charges of $55.0 mill., 1/00; $13.5 mill., 1/98. ② Incl. $12.5 mill. write-down of invest.

OFFICERS:
D. D. Belcher, Chmn., C.E.O.
S. A. Streeter, Pres., C.O.O.
D. W. Kiener, V.P., C.F.O.

INVESTOR CONTACT: Investor Relations, (920) 751-7777

PRINCIPAL OFFICE: 225 Main Street, Menasha, WI 54952-8003

TELEPHONE NUMBER: (920) 751-7777
FAX: (920) 751-7790
WEB: www.banta.com

NO. OF EMPLOYEES: 8,000 (approx.)

SHAREHOLDERS: 1,898 (record)

ANNUAL MEETING: In Apr.

INCORPORATED: WI, 1901

INSTITUTIONAL HOLDINGS:
No. of Institutions: 147
Shares Held: 19,467,496
% Held: 77.8

INDUSTRY: Commercial printing, nec (SIC: 2759)

TRANSFER AGENT(S): Firstar Bank, N.A., Milwaukee, WI

BANK OF AMERICA CORPORATION

YIELD 3.5%
P/E RATIO 16.3

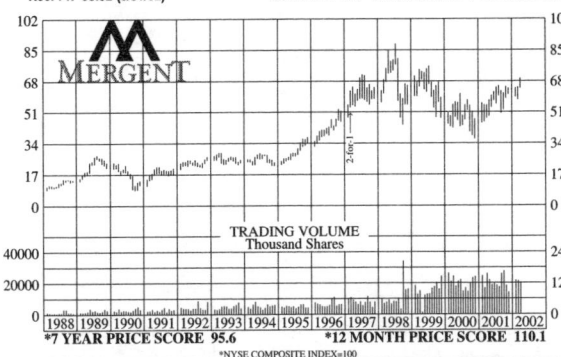

*7 YEAR PRICE SCORE 95.6 ***12 MONTH PRICE SCORE 110.1**

*NYSE COMPOSITE INDEX=100

INTERIM EARNINGS (Per Share):

Qtr.	Mar.	June	Sept.	Dec.
1998	0.51	1.43	0.21	0.66
1999	1.08	1.07	1.23	1.10
2000	1.33	1.23	1.10	0.85
2001	1.15	1.24	0.51	1.28

INTERIM DIVIDENDS (Per Share):

Amt.	Decl.	Ex.	Rec.	Pay.
0.56Q	4/25/01	5/30/01	6/01/01	6/22/01
0.56Q	7/25/01	9/05/01	9/07/01	9/28/01
0.60Q	10/24/01	12/05/01	12/07/01	12/28/01
0.60Q	1/23/02	2/27/02	3/01/02	3/22/02

Indicated div.: $2.40 (Div. Reinv. Plan)

CAPITALIZATION (12/31/01):

	($000)	(%)
Total Deposits	373,495,000	77.1
Long-Term Debt	62,496,000	12.9
Preferred Stock	65,000	0.0
Common & Surplus	48,455,000	10.0
Total	484,511,000	100.0

DIVIDEND ACHIEVER STATUS:
Rank: 100   10-Year Growth Rate: 11.91%
Total Years of Dividend Growth: 24

RECENT DEVELOPMENTS: For the year ended 12/31/01, net income declined 9.6% to $6.79 billion from $7.52 billion in the previous year. Results for 2001 included a charge of $1.31 billion for business exit costs, while results for 2000 included a merger charge of $550.0 million. Net interest income increased 10.6% to $20.29 billion from $18.35 billion in the prior year. Provision for credit losses grew 69.1% to $4.29 billion. Non-interest income decreased 1.6% to $14.35 billion.

PROSPECTS: The Company will continue to focus on its strategy of realigning its business units in a cost-efficient manner and replacing its old product- and geography-based management structure. Near-term results should continue to reflect the solid performance in BAC's three major business lines, consumer and commercial banking, asset management and global corporate and investment banking. Moreover, BAC should benefit from its strong reserves and capital, despite the sluggish economy.

BUSINESS

BANK OF AMERICA CORPORATION (formerly NationsBank Corporation) is a bank holding company with $621.76 billion in total assets as of 12/31/01. The Company was formed on 9/30/98 as a result of the former BankAmerica's merging into NationsBank. The Company adopted its present name on 4/29/99. BAC provides financial products and services to households and businesses, and provides international corporate financial services for business transactions. The Company maintains full-service operations in 21 states and the District of Columbia, and oversees, through its network of 4,251 banking centers, 13,113 ATMs, telephone and Internet channels.

ANNUAL FINANCIAL DATA

	12/31/01	12/31/00	12/31/99	12/31/98	12/31/97	12/31/96	12/31/95
Earnings Per Share	③ 4.18	② 4.52	② 4.48	② 2.90	4.17	① 4.00	3.56
Tang. Book Val. Per Share	20.79	19.00	15.66	16.68	14.86	18.43	19.08
Dividends Per Share	2.28	2.06	1.85	1.59	1.37	1.20	1.04
Dividend Payout %	54.5	45.6	41.3	54.8	32.9	30.0	29.2
INCOME STATEMENT (IN MILLIONS):							
Total Interest Income	38,293.0	43,258.0	37,323.0	38,588.0	16,579.0	13,796.0	13,220.0
Total Interest Expense	18,003.0	24,816.0	19,086.0	20,290.0	8,681.0	7,467.0	7,773.0
Net Interest Income	20,290.0	18,442.0	18,237.0	18,298.0	7,898.0	6,329.0	5,447.0
Provision for Loan Losses	4,287.0	2,535.0	1,820.0	2,920.0	800.0	605.0	382.0
Non-Interest Income	14,348.0	14,514.0	14,309.0	13,206.0	5,155.0	3,713.0	3,107.0
Non-Interest Expense	24,521.0	18,633.0	18,511.0	20,536.0	7,457.0	5,803.0	5,136.0
Income Before Taxes	10,117.0	11,788.0	12,215.0	8,048.0	4,796.0	3,634.0	3,036.0
Net Income	③ 6,792.0	② 7,517.0	② 7,882.0	② 5,165.0	3,077.0	① 2,375.0	1,995.0
Average Shs. Outstg. (000)	1,625,654	1,664,929	1,760,058	1,775,760	737,791	590,216	544,959
BALANCE SHEET (IN MILLIONS):							
Securities Avail. for Sale	137,726.0	113,140.0	124,945.0	124,942.0	72,120.0	32,809.0	39,578.0
Total Loans & Leases	329,153.0	392,193.0	370,662.0	357,328.0	146,417.0	125,031.0	119,020.0
Allowance for Credit Losses	6,875.0	6,838.0	6,828.0	7,122.0	5,407.0	4,716.0	4,150.0
Net Loans & Leases	322,278.0	385,355.0	363,834.0	350,206.0	141,010.0	120,315.0	114,870.0
Total Assets	621,764.0	642,191.0	632,574.0	617,679.0	264,562.0	185,794.0	187,298.0
Total Deposits	373,495.0	364,244.0	347,273.0	357,260.0	138,194.0	106,498.0	100,691.0
Long-Term Obligations	62,496.0	67,547.0	55,486.0	45,888.0	27,204.0	22,985.0	17,775.0
Total Liabilities	573,244.0	594,563.0	588,142.0	571,741.0	243,225.0	172,085.0	174,497.0
Net Stockholders' Equity	48,520.0	47,628.0	44,432.0	45,938.0	21,337.0	13,709.0	12,801.0
Year-end Shs. Outstg. (000)	1,559,297	1,613,632	1,677,273	1,724,484	712,188	573,000	549,000
STATISTICAL RECORD:							
Return on Equity %	14.0	15.8	17.7	11.2	14.4	17.3	15.6
Return on Assets %	1.1	1.2	1.2	0.8	1.2	1.3	1.1
Equity/Assets %	7.8	7.4	7.0	7.4	8.1	7.4	6.8
Non-Int. Exp./Tot. Inc. %	70.8	56.5	56.9	65.2	57.1	57.8	60.0
Price Range	65.54-45.00	61.00-36.31	76.38-47.63	88.44-44.00	71.69-48.00	52.63-32.19	37.38-22.31
P/E Ratio	15.7-10.8	13.5-8.0	17.0-10.6	30.5-15.2	17.2-11.5	13.2-8.0	10.5-6.3
Average Yield %	4.1	4.2	3.0	2.4	2.3	2.8	3.5

Statistics are as originally reported. Results for 1998 and subsequent years refl. merger of NationsBank Corp. & BankAmerica Corp. on 9/30/98. Adj. for 2-for-1 stk. split, 2/97. ① Incl. aft.-tax merger-rel. chgs. of $77.0 mill. ② Incl. merg.-rel. & restr. chgs. of $346.0 mill., 2000; $358.0 mill., 1999; $1.80 bill., 1998. ③ Incl. a loss of $1.31 bill. rel. to the exit of certain consumer finance businesses.

OFFICERS:
K. D. Lewis, Chmn., Pres., C.E.O.
J. H. Hance Jr., Vice-Chmn., C.F.O.

INVESTOR CONTACT: Jane Smith, Manager, Shareholder Relations, (704) 386-5681

PRINCIPAL OFFICE: Bank of America Corporate Center, Charlotte, NC 28255

TELEPHONE NUMBER: (704) 386-6500
FAX: (704) 388-9278
WEB: www.bankofamerica.com
NO. OF EMPLOYEES: 142,670
SHAREHOLDERS: 244,009
ANNUAL MEETING: In April
INCORPORATED: NC, July, 1968; reincorp., DE, Sept., 1998

INSTITUTIONAL HOLDINGS:
No. of Institutions: 893
Shares Held: 1,011,444,039
% Held: 65.6

INDUSTRY: National commercial banks (SIC: 6021)

TRANSFER AGENT(S): Mellon Investor Services LLC, South Hackensack, NJ

BANDAG, INC.

YIELD 3.3%
P/E RATIO 17.8

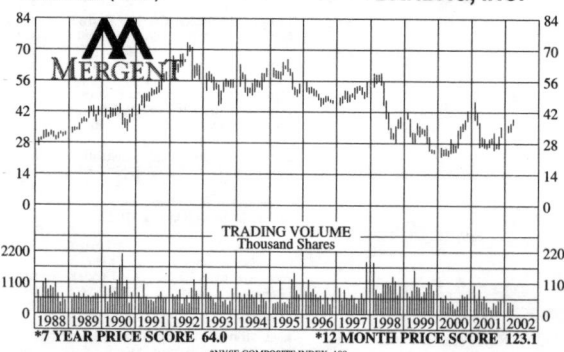

*7 YEAR PRICE SCORE 64.0   *12 MONTH PRICE SCORE 123.1
*NYSE COMPOSITE INDEX=100

INTERIM EARNINGS (Per Share):

Qtr.	Mar.	June	Sept.	Dec.
1998	0.40	0.62	0.77	0.84
1999	0.46	0.73	0.82	0.38
2000	0.48	0.85	0.86	0.71
2001	0.11	0.46	0.71	0.84

INTERIM DIVIDENDS (Per Share):

Amt.	Decl.	Ex.	Rec.	Pay.
0.305Q	3/13/01	3/15/01	3/19/01	4/20/01
0.305Q	5/15/01	6/15/01	6/19/01	7/20/01
0.305Q	8/28/01	9/18/01	9/20/01	10/19/01
0.315Q	11/13/01	12/18/01	12/20/01	1/18/02
0.315Q	3/12/02	3/20/02	3/22/02	4/19/02

Indicated div.: $1.26 (Div. Reinv. Plan)

CAPITALIZATION (12/31/01):

	($000)	(%)
Long-Term Debt	40,921	7.7
Deferred Income Tax	2,580	0.5
Common & Surplus	488,996	91.8
Total	532,497	100.0

DIVIDEND ACHIEVER STATUS:

Rank: 171   10-Year Growth Rate: 8.29%
Total Years of Dividend Growth: 25

RECENT DEVELOPMENTS:

For the year ended 12/31/01, net earnings fell 27.3% to $43.8 million versus $60.3 million in 2000. Results for 2001 included net after-tax non-recurring charges of $2.0 million. Total revenues decreased 3.1% to $982.2 million from $1.01 billion a year earlier. Net sales declined 3.1% to $964.9 million as weakness in several sectors of the economy affected the transportation industry. Interest income slipped 3.3% to $7.3 million, while other income increased 2.2% to $10.1 million.

PROSPECTS:

The recent oversupply of new replacement tires appears to be working its way through the distribution channel. New-tire producers are announcing price increases, indicating reduced supply, and the Company is seeing lower casing prices, which may indicate a coming influx of casings readily available for retreading. BDG expects business and the economy to begin to recover in the second half of 2002.

BUSINESS

BANDAG, INC. is engaged in the manufacture of precured tread rubber, equipment, and supplies primarily for the retreading of truck and bus tires by a patented cold-bonding reaction. The Company also does some custom processing of rubber compounds. As of 12/31/01, revenues are generated by 1,151 franchised dealers in the U.S. and abroad who are licensed to produce and market cold process retreads utilizing the Bandag process. BDG's wholly-owned subsidiary, Tire Management Solutions, Inc., provides tire management systems outsourcing for commercial truck fleets. Tire Distribution Systems, Inc., also a wholly-owned subsidiary, sells and services new and retread tires.

ANNUAL FINANCIAL DATA

	12/31/01	12/31/00	12/31/99	12/31/98	12/31/97	12/31/96	12/31/95
Earnings Per Share	②2.12	2.90	②2.40	②2.63	①5.33	3.44	3.82
Cash Flow Per Share	4.35	5.33	4.87	4.91	6.93	4.89	5.18
Tang. Book Val. Per Share	21.22	20.03	18.62	19.14	17.00	17.85	16.60
Dividends Per Share	1.22	1.18	1.14	1.10	1.00	0.90	0.80
Dividend Payout %	57.5	40.7	47.5	41.8	18.8	26.2	20.9
INCOME STATEMENT (IN MILLIONS):							
Total Revenues	982.2	1,013.4	1,027.9	1,079.5	931.7	769.0	755.3
Costs & Expenses	862.2	854.9	872.3	917.8	688.6	602.4	563.6
Depreciation & Amort.	46.2	50.5	53.8	51.4	36.9	34.6	34.6
Operating Income	73.9	108.1	101.8	110.3	206.3	132.0	157.1
Net Interest Inc./(Exp.)	d7.4	d8.7	d9.7	d10.8	d3.3	d1.2	d2.0
Income Before Income Taxes	66.5	99.4	92.1	99.5	202.9	130.8	155.1
Income Taxes	22.7	39.0	39.8	40.2	80.9	49.2	58.1
Net Income	②43.8	60.3	②52.3	②59.3	①122.0	81.6	97.0
Cash Flow	90.0	110.8	106.1	110.7	158.9	116.2	131.6
Average Shs. Outstg. (000)	20,686	20,778	21,764	22,559	22,908	23,746	25,420
BALANCE SHEET (IN MILLIONS):							
Cash & Cash Equivalents	155.0	93.4	60.1	47.6	198.0	33.5	40.8
Total Current Assets	450.2	427.2	428.1	439.1	599.0	341.7	328.5
Net Property	158.0	177.2	198.0	213.0	197.6	145.1	144.9
Total Assets	718.6	714.5	722.4	784.2	899.9	588.3	554.2
Total Current Liabilities	186.1	132.7	154.1	174.9	306.5	139.2	122.0
Long-Term Obligations	40.9	105.2	111.2	108.8	123.2	10.1	11.9
Net Stockholders' Equity	489.0	474.2	454.1	495.7	463.4	410.9	404.1
Net Working Capital	264.1	294.4	274.1	264.2	292.5	202.5	206.4
Year-end Shs. Outstg. (000)	20,642	20,562	20,771	21,955	22,813	22,923	24,178
STATISTICAL RECORD:							
Operating Profit Margin %	7.5	10.7	9.9	10.2	22.1	17.2	20.8
Net Profit Margin %	4.5	6.0	5.1	5.5	13.1	10.6	12.8
Return on Equity %	9.0	12.7	11.5	12.0	26.3	19.9	24.0
Return on Assets %	6.1	8.4	7.2	7.6	13.6	13.9	17.5
Debt/Total Assets %	5.7	14.7	15.4	14.5	13.7	1.7	2.1
Price Range	46.75-25.01	42.63-21.88	41.63-23.50	59.75-28.31	55.75-45.00	55.88-44.50	65.88-49.00
P/E Ratio	22.1-11.8	14.7-7.5	17.3-9.8	22.7-10.8	10.5-8.4	16.2-12.9	17.2-12.8
Average Yield %	3.4	3.7	3.5	2.5	2.0	1.8	1.4

Statistics are as originally reported. ① Incl. nonrecurr. gain of $78.6 mill. on sale of secur. ② Incl. nonrecurr. chrg. of $2.0 mill., 2001; $13.5 mill., 1999; $4.2 mill., 1998.

QUARTERLY DATA

(12/31/2001)($000)	Rev	Inc
1st Quarter	209,242	2,328
2nd Quarter	244,758	9,512
3rd Quarter	261,712	14,614
4th Quarter	249,156	17,378

OFFICERS:
M. G. Carver, Chmn., Pres., C.E.O.
W. W. Heidbreder, V.P., C.F.O., Sec.
L. A. Carver, Treas.

INVESTOR CONTACT: Warren W. Heidbreder, V.P., C.F.O., Sec., (563) 262-1260

PRINCIPAL OFFICE: 2905 North Highway 61, Muscatine, IA 52761-5886

TELEPHONE NUMBER: (563) 262-1400
FAX: (563) 262-1069
WEB: www.bandag.com
NO. OF EMPLOYEES: 4,014 (approx.)
SHAREHOLDERS: 1,879 (com.); 1,070 (cl. A); 210 (cl. B)
ANNUAL MEETING: In May
INCORPORATED: IA, Dec., 1957

INSTITUTIONAL HOLDINGS:
No. of Institutions: 91
Shares Held: 5,409,911
% Held: 26.2

INDUSTRY: Tires and inner tubes (SIC: 3011)

TRANSFER AGENT(S): BankBoston c/o EquiServe, Boston, MA

BANCORPSOUTH, INC.

YIELD 3.0%
P/E RATIO 16.6

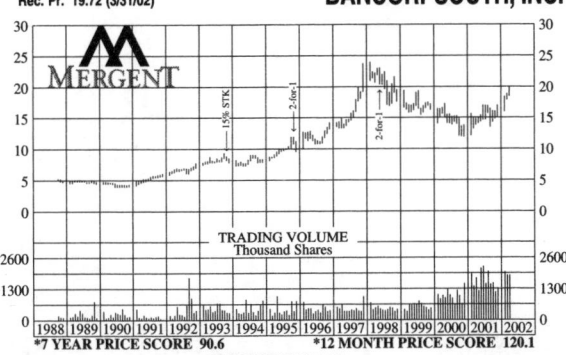

TRADING VOLUME
Thousand Shares

| 1988 | 1989 | 1990 | 1991 | 1992 | 1993 | 1994 | 1995 | 1996 | 1997 | 1998 | 1999 | 2000 | 2001 | 2002 |

*7 YEAR PRICE SCORE 90.6   ***12 MONTH PRICE SCORE 120.1**
*NYSE COMPOSITE INDEX=100

INTERIM EARNINGS (Per Share):

Qtr.	Mar.	June	Sept.	Dec.
1998	0.27	0.28	0.25	0.21
1999	0.29	0.29	0.31	0.31
2000	0.31	0.31	0.11	0.15
2001	0.27	0.28	0.26	0.38

INTERIM DIVIDENDS (Per Share):

Amt.	Decl.	Ex.	Rec.	Pay.
0.14Q	1/24/01	3/13/01	3/15/01	4/02/01
0.14Q	4/27/01	6/13/01	6/15/01	7/02/01
0.14Q	7/25/01	9/17/01	9/14/01	10/01/01
0.15Q	10/24/01	12/12/01	12/14/01	1/02/02
0.15Q	1/23/02	3/13/02	3/15/02	4/01/02

Indicated div.: $0.60 (Div. Reinv. Plan)

CAPITALIZATION (12/31/01):

	($000)	(%)
Total Deposits	7,856,840	89.3
Long-Term Debt	140,939	1.6
Common & Surplus	805,403	9.1
Total	8,803,182	100.0

DIVIDEND ACHIEVER STATUS:

Rank: 119   10-Year Growth Rate: 10.84%
Total Years of Dividend Growth: 15

RECENT DEVELOPMENTS: For the year ended 12/31/01, net income climbed 32.3% to $98.5 million compared with $74.4 million in the previous year. Earnings for 2000 included after-tax merger-related charges of $22.5 million. Net interest revenue increased 2.3% to $334.7 million. Provision for credit losses declined 14.9% to $22.3 million from $26.2 million in 2000. Non-interest revenue jumped 50.3% to $128.6 million, while non-interest expense rose 7.7% to $295.3 million.

PROSPECTS: On 2/28/02, BXS completed its acquisition of Pinnacle Bancshares, Inc., which operates two full-service banks in Arkansas through its Pinnacle Bank subsidiary. The acquisition strengthens the Company's operations in Arkansas by providing its first locations in Little Rock. Meanwhile, earnings are being positively affected by strong mortgage refinancing market conditions, gains from the sale of investment securities and increased net interest margin.

BUSINESS

BANCORPSOUTH, INC. is a bank holding company with, as of 12/31/01, total assets of approximately $9.40 billion. The Company operates approximately 250 commercial banking, insurance, trust, broker/dealer and consumer finance locations in Alabama, Arkansas, Louisiana, Mississippi, Tennessee and Texas. The Company, through its subsidiaries, provides a range of financial services and products to individuals and small-to-medium size businesses. In addition, the Bank operates investment services, consumer finance, credit life insurance and insurance agency subsidiaries. Its principal subsidiary is BancorpSouth Bank. On 8/31/00, the Company completed the acquisition of First United Bancshares, Inc.

ANNUAL FINANCIAL DATA

	12/31/01	12/31/00	12/31/99	12/31/98	12/31/97	12/31/96	12/31/95
Earnings Per Share	1.19	① 0.88	1.20	1.01	1.02	1.01	0.85
Tang. Book Val. Per Share	9.92	9.39	8.68	8.48	8.09	7.50	6.86
Dividends Per Share	0.56	0.52	0.48	0.44	0.38	0.34	0.30
Dividend Payout %	47.1	59.1	40.0	43.6	37.4	33.7	35.5
INCOME STATEMENT (IN MILLIONS):							
Total Interest Income	665.8	674.0	414.2	383.5	307.1	277.9	252.4
Total Interest Expense	331.1	346.9	196.7	187.4	144.1	126.5	114.5
Net Interest Income	334.7	327.2	217.5	196.1	163.0	151.4	138.0
Provision for Loan Losses	22.3	26.2	14.7	15.0	9.0	8.8	6.2
Non-Interest Income	128.6	85.6	79.3	53.0	43.7	40.7	31.2
Non-Interest Expense	295.3	274.2	183.0	152.1	132.0	118.5	111.8
Income Before Taxes	145.8	112.3	99.1	82.0	65.7	64.9	51.3
Net Income	98.5	① 74.4	69.0	54.5	45.4	42.9	35.5
Average Shs. Outstg. (000)	82,979	84,811	57,524	53,871	44,788	42,426	42,030
BALANCE SHEET (IN MILLIONS):							
Cash & Due from Banks	341.5	314.9	217.3	175.4	286.3	153.1	149.9
Securities Avail. for Sale	1,083.2	857.4	345.3	549.8	406.2	230.7	239.8
Total Loans & Leases	6,127.0	6,161.1	4,131.4	3,561.4	2,852.9	2,554.1	2,371.7
Allowance for Credit Losses	137.0	147.5	133.4	142.3	133.7	122.1	111.2
Net Loans & Leases	5,990.1	6,013.6	3,998.0	3,419.1	2,719.2	2,432.1	2,260.5
Total Assets	9,395.4	9,044.0	5,776.9	5,203.7	4,180.1	3,617.2	3,306.2
Total Deposits	7,856.8	7,480.9	4,815.4	4,441.9	3,540.3	3,161.4	2,863.6
Long-Term Obligations	140.9	152.0	138.6	178.3	47.5	55.8	73.6
Total Liabilities	8,590.0	8,254.5	5,279.5	4,747.4	3,819.7	3,301.9	3,018.1
Net Stockholders' Equity	805.4	789.6	497.4	456.4	360.4	315.3	288.1
Year-end Shs. Outstg. (000)	81,226	84,043	57,304	53,833	44,542	42,026	41,994
STATISTICAL RECORD:							
Return on Equity %	12.2	9.4	13.9	11.9	12.6	13.6	12.3
Return on Assets %	1.0	0.8	1.2	1.0	1.1	1.2	1.1
Equity/Assets %	8.6	8.7	8.6	8.8	8.6	8.7	8.7
Non-Int. Exp./Tot. Inc. %	65.2	64.0	62.5	61.3	64.2	61.7	65.7
Price Range	17.00-12.06	17.25-11.88	19.44-15.38	24.00-16.81	23.78-13.25	14.25-10.06	11.94-8.06
P/E Ratio	14.3-10.1	19.6-13.5	16.2-12.8	23.8-16.6	23.4-13.1	14.1-10.0	14.1-9.5
Average Yield %	3.9	3.6	2.8	2.2	2.1	2.8	3.0

Statistics are as originally reported. Adj. for 2-for-1 split, 5/98. ① Incl. after-tax merger-related charges of $22.5 mill.

OFFICERS:
A. B. Patterson, Chmn., C.E.O.
J. V. Kelley, Pres., C.O.O.
L. N. Allen, Jr., C.F.O., Treas.

INVESTOR CONTACT: Nash Allen, Jr., (662) 680-2330

PRINCIPAL OFFICE: One Mississippi Plaza, Tupelo, MS 38804

TELEPHONE NUMBER: (662) 680-2000
FAX: (662) 680-2570
WEB: www.bancorpsouth.com

NO. OF EMPLOYEES: 3,920

SHAREHOLDERS: 10,178

ANNUAL MEETING: In Apr.

INCORPORATED: MS, July, 1982

INSTITUTIONAL HOLDINGS:
No. of Institutions: 77
Shares Held: 10,994,976
% Held: 13.5

INDUSTRY: State commercial banks (SIC: 6022)

TRANSFER AGENT(S): SunTrust Bank, Atlanta, GA

BALDOR ELECTRIC COMPANY

YIELD 2.3%
P/E RATIO 34.2

*7 YEAR PRICE SCORE 93.2   *12 MONTH PRICE SCORE 107.6
*NYSE COMPOSITE INDEX=100

TRADING VOLUME
Thousand Shares

INTERIM EARNINGS (Per Share):

Qtr.	Mar.	June	Sept.	Dec.
1998	0.31	0.30	0.29	0.27
1999	0.29	0.30	0.30	0.30
2000	0.35	0.36	0.33	0.29
2001	0.21	0.19	0.16	0.10

INTERIM DIVIDENDS (Per Share):

Amt.	Decl.	Ex.	Rec.	Pay.
0.13Q	2/05/01	3/07/01	3/09/01	3/30/01
0.13Q	4/28/01	6/06/01	6/08/01	6/29/01
0.13Q	8/14/01	9/05/01	9/07/01	9/28/01
0.13Q	11/14/01	12/10/01	12/12/01	1/02/02
0.13Q	2/11/02	3/05/02	3/07/02	3/28/02

Indicated div.: $0.52 (Div. Reinv. Plan)

CAPITALIZATION (12/29/01):

	($000)	(%)
Long-Term Debt	98,673	26.0
Deferred Income Tax	18,726	4.9
Common & Surplus	262,485	69.1
Total	379,884	100.0

DIVIDEND ACHIEVER STATUS:
Rank: 68   10-Year Growth Rate: 14.55%
Total Years of Dividend Growth: 18

RECENT DEVELOPMENTS: For the year ended 12/29/01, net income dropped 51.6% to $22.4 million compared with $46.3 million in the previous year. The decline in earnings was due to consolidation of three plants, continued investments in product availability and productivity improvement and the lower absorption of fixed costs due to lower sales. Net sales decreased 10.3% to $557.5 million from $621.2 million in the prior year. Gross profit fell 21.0% to $156.0 million from $197.4 million in 2000.

PROSPECTS: In 2002, the Company will continue to focus on investing in product facilities, expanding its product lines, improving its sales force and maintaining its product availability. Meanwhile, BEZ is benefiting from an increase in incoming orders, which grew 5.0% in January 2002 versus the prior-year period. Moreover, favorable sales of the Company's SUPER-E® motors and drives reflect growing customer acceptance of BEZ's high-efficiency motors.

BUSINESS

BALDOR ELECTRIC COMPANY designs, manufactures and markets a line of electric motors, adjustable speed drives and soft starters that are used with electric motors. The alternating current motor product and controls line ranges in size from $1/50$ horsepower (HP) up to 1500 HP. The direct current (DC) motor product line ranges from $1/50$ HP to 800 HP. The adjustable speed controls product line ranges from $1/50$ HP to 700 HP. The Company's industrial control products include servo products, DC controls, position controls and inverter and vector drives. BEZ's motors and drives are designed, manufactured and marketed for general purposes and individual customer requirements and specifications. In addition, BEZ sells power generators, drives, speed reducers, industrial grinders, buffers, polishing lathes, stampings, castings and repair parts.

QUARTERLY DATA

(12/29/01)($000)	REV	INC
1st Quarter	150,155	7,167
2nd Quarter	146,668	6,449
3rd Quarter	138,125	5,423
4th Quarter	122,511	3,346

ANNUAL FINANCIAL DATA

	12/29/01	12/30/00	1/1/00	1/2/99	1/3/98	12/28/96	12/30/95
Earnings Per Share	0.65	1.34	1.19	1.17	1.09	0.97	0.84
Cash Flow Per Share	1.25	1.91	1.79	1.71	1.61	1.45	1.24
Tang. Book Val. Per Share	6.05	7.72	7.48	7.21	6.76	5.73	5.69
Dividends Per Share	0.52	0.49	0.43	0.40	0.35	0.29	0.25
Dividend Payout %	80.0	36.6	36.1	34.2	31.7	29.5	29.5
INCOME STATEMENT (IN THOUSANDS):							
Total Revenues	558,298	623,080	579,262	591,425	559,783	505,372	475,699
Costs & Expenses	492,045	515,634	475,737	487,802	463,829	420,590	398,742
Depreciation & Amort.	20,679	19,838	20,767	20,511	19,337	17,277	15,583
Operating Income	45,574	87,608	82,758	83,112	76,617	67,505	61,374
Income Before Income Taxes	35,532	74,021	70,523	71,952	65,635	57,192	52,946
Income Taxes	13,147	27,758	26,800	27,342	25,270	22,019	20,641
Net Income	22,385	46,263	43,723	44,610	40,365	35,173	32,305
Cash Flow	43,064	66,101	64,490	65,121	59,702	52,450	47,888
Average Shs. Outstg.	34,506	34,570	36,077	38,067	37,063	36,291	38,521
BALANCE SHEET (IN THOUSANDS):							
Cash & Cash Equivalents	16,616	15,005	42,908	38,789	21,475	25,842	34,809
Total Current Assets	251,281	262,421	272,330	256,488	219,440	218,157	212,093
Net Property	142,115	138,820	124,802	123,137	104,097	95,364	89,071
Total Assets	457,527	464,978	423,941	411,926	355,889	325,486	313,462
Total Current Liabilities	77,643	87,618	88,374	80,362	78,172	71,182	67,026
Long-Term Obligations	98,673	99,832	56,305	57,015	27,929	45,027	25,255
Net Stockholders' Equity	262,485	260,845	266,109	264,292	243,434	200,325	211,377
Net Working Capital	173,638	174,803	183,956	176,126	141,268	146,975	145,069
Year-end Shs. Outstg.	33,918	33,769	35,592	36,677	36,029	34,935	37,160
STATISTICAL RECORD:							
Operating Profit Margin %	8.2	14.1	14.3	14.1	13.7	13.4	12.9
Net Profit Margin %	4.0	7.4	7.5	7.5	7.2	7.0	6.8
Return on Equity %	8.5	17.7	16.4	16.9	16.6	17.6	15.3
Return on Assets %	4.9	9.9	10.3	10.8	11.3	10.8	10.3
Debt/Total Assets %	21.6	21.5	13.3	13.8	7.8	13.8	8.1
Price Range	25.15-18.00	22.50-14.88	21.69-17.00	27.19-19.06	23.82-18.19	18.76-13.88	19.88-12.94
P/E Ratio	38.7-27.7	16.8-11.1	18.2-14.3	23.2-16.3	21.8-16.7	19.4-14.3	23.7-15.4
Average Yield %	2.4	2.6	2.2	1.7	1.6	1.8	1.5

Statistics are as originally reported. Adj. for a 3-for-2 stock split 9/95; 4-for-3, 12/97.

OFFICERS:
R. S. Boreham Jr., Chmn.
J. A. McFarland, Pres., C.E.O.
R. E. Tucker, C.F.O., Treas.

INVESTOR CONTACT: Lloyd G. Davis, Exec. V.P., C.O.O., Sec., (479) 646-4711

PRINCIPAL OFFICE: 5711 R. S. Boreham, Jr. Street, Ft. Smith, AR 72901

TELEPHONE NUMBER: (479) 646-4711
FAX: (479) 648-5792
WEB: www.baldor.com

NO. OF EMPLOYEES: 3,684
SHAREHOLDERS: 4,456
ANNUAL MEETING: In April
INCORPORATED: MO, March, 1920

INSTITUTIONAL HOLDINGS:
No. of Institutions: 106
Shares Held: 12,108,128
% Held: 35.6

INDUSTRY: Motors and generators (SIC: 3621)

TRANSFER AGENT(S): Continental Stock Transfer & Trust Company, New York, NY

AVON PRODUCTS, INC.

YIELD	1.5%
P/E RATIO	19.5

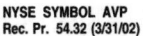

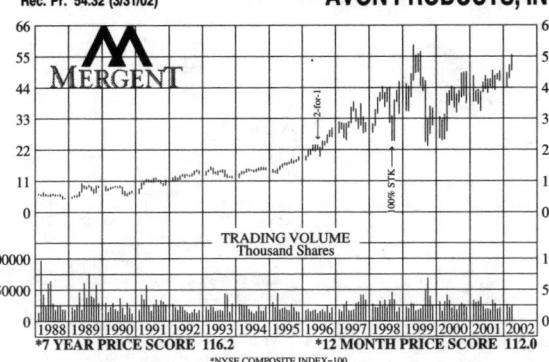

TRADING VOLUME
Thousand Shares

1988 1989 1990 1991 1992 1993 1994 1995 1996 1997 1998 1999 2000 2001 2002
*7 YEAR PRICE SCORE 116.2   *12 MONTH PRICE SCORE 112.0
*NYSE COMPOSITE INDEX=100

INTERIM EARNINGS (Per Share):

Qtr.	Mar.	June	Sept.	Dec.
1997	0.16	0.36	0.26	0.51
1998	d0.12	0.42	0.16	0.56
1999	d0.19	0.46	0.34	0.58
2000	0.31	0.52	0.39	0.81
2001	0.34	0.57	0.42	0.46

INTERIM DIVIDENDS (Per Share):

Amt.	Decl.	Ex.	Rec.	Pay.
0.19Q	2/01/01	2/13/01	2/15/01	3/01/01
0.19Q	5/03/01	5/14/01	5/16/01	6/01/01
0.19Q	8/01/01	8/14/01	8/16/01	9/04/01
0.19Q	11/01/01	11/13/01	11/15/01	12/03/01
0.20Q	1/31/02	2/13/02	2/15/02	3/01/02

Indicated div.: $0.80 (Div. Reinv. Plan)

CAPITALIZATION (12/31/01):

	($000)	(%)
Long-Term Debt	1,236,300	103.7
Deferred Income Tax	30,600	2.6
Common & Surplus	d74,600	-6.3
Total	1,192,300	100.0

DIVIDEND ACHIEVER STATUS:
Rank: 174   10-Year Growth Rate: 8.06%
Total Years of Dividend Growth: 11

RECENT DEVELOPMENTS: For the year ended 12/31/01, income was $430.3 million, before an accounting charge of $300,000, versus income of $485.1 million, before an accounting charge of $6.7 million, in 2000. Results for 2001 included a net after-tax gain of $13.1 million, a non-cash, after-tax asset impairment charge of $14.5 million, and after-tax charges of $71.1 million. Total revenue rose 4.9% to $5.99 billion from $5.71 billion.

PROSPECTS: AVP benefited from robust holiday gift sales in the U.S., strength of its Wellness line, and the LITTLE BLACK DRESS fragrance launch, as well as sales from its "Heart of America" lapel pin. However, sales and operating profits in Latin America are being adversely affected by the economic turmoil and the devaluation of the peso in Argentina. In 2002, AVP expects to see increasing sequential growth in earnings as the year progresses.

BUSINESS

AVON PRODUCTS, INC. is a global manufacturer and marketer of beauty and related products. AVP's products fall into three product categories: Beauty, which consists of cosmetics, fragrance and toiletries; Beauty Plus, which consists of jewelry, watches and apparel and accessories; and Beyond Beauty, which consists of home products gift and decorative and candles. In 2001, the Company introduced a new global product category of women's health and wellness. The Company's business primarily is comprised of direct selling, which is conducted in North America, Latin America, the Pacific and Europe. As of 12/31/01, the Company has operations in 58 countries, including the U.S., and its products are distributed in 85 more for coverage in 143 countries. Sales are made principally through a combination of direct selling and marketing by approximately 3.5 million independent Avon Representative, about 451,000 of whom are in the U.S.

ANNUAL FINANCIAL DATA

	12/31/01	12/31/00	12/31/99	12/31/98	12/31/97	12/31/96	12/31/95
Earnings Per Share	1.79	③2.02	④1.17	②1.02	1.27	1.19	①1.05
Cash Flow Per Share	2.25	2.40	1.49	1.29	1.54	1.43	1.26
Tang. Book Val. Per Share	...	...	...	1.09	1.08	0.91	0.71
Dividends Per Share	0.76	0.74	0.72	0.68	0.63	0.58	0.53
Dividend Payout %	42.5	36.6	61.5	66.7	49.6	48.7	50.0
INCOME STATEMENT (IN MILLIONS)							
Total Revenues	5,994.5	5,714.6	5,289.1	5,212.7	5,079.4	4,814.2	4,492.1
Costs & Expenses	5,002.3	4,828.8	4,656.7	4,667.5	4,469.5	4,204.9	3,926.3
Depreciation & Amort.	124.0	97.1	83.0	72.0	72.1	64.5	58.3
Operating Income	749.4	788.7	549.4	473.2	537.8	544.8	507.5
Net Interest Inc./(Exp.)	d56.7	d76.2	d32.1	d18.8	d18.8	d25.5	d21.9
Income Before Income Taxes	665.7	691.0	506.6	455.9	534.9	510.4	465.0
Income Taxes	230.9	201.7	204.2	190.8	197.9	191.4	176.4
Equity Earnings/Minority Int.	d4.5	d4.2	...	4.9	1.8	d1.1	d2.5
Net Income	430.3	③485.1	④302.4	②270.0	338.8	317.9	①286.1
Cash Flow	554.3	582.2	385.4	342.0	410.9	382.4	344.4
Average Shs. Outstg. (000)	246,050	242,950	259,370	265,950	267,000	267,400	272,960
BALANCE SHEET (IN MILLIONS)							
Cash & Cash Equivalents	508.5	122.7	117.4	105.6	141.9	184.5	151.4
Total Current Assets	1,889.1	1,545.7	1,337.8	1,341.4	1,344.0	1,349.6	1,215.0
Net Property	774.9	768.4	734.8	669.9	611.0	566.6	537.8
Total Assets	3,193.1	2,826.4	2,528.6	2,433.5	2,272.9	2,222.4	2,052.8
Total Current Liabilities	1,461.0	1,359.3	1,712.8	1,329.5	1,355.9	1,391.3	1,245.3
Long-Term Obligations	1,236.3	1,108.2	701.4	201.0	102.2	104.5	114.2
Net Stockholders' Equity	d74.6	d215.8	d406.1	285.1	285.0	241.7	192.7
Net Working Capital	428.1	186.4	d375.0	11.9	d11.9	d41.7	d30.3
Year-end Shs. Outstg. (000)	236,681	354,536	237,895	262,520	263,628	265,640	270,468
STATISTICAL RECORD:							
Operating Profit Margin %	12.5	13.8	10.4	9.1	10.6	11.3	11.3
Net Profit Margin %	7.2	8.5	5.7	5.2	6.7	6.6	6.4
Return on Equity %	...	...	...	94.7	118.9	131.5	148.5
Return on Assets %	13.5	17.2	12.0	11.1	14.9	14.3	13.9
Debt/Total Assets %	38.7	39.2	27.7	8.3	4.5	4.7	5.6
Price Range	50.12-35.55	49.75-25.25	59.13-23.31	46.25-25.00	39.00-25.31	29.75-18.16	19.59-13.50
P/E Ratio	28.0-19.9	24.6-12.5	50.5-19.9	45.3-24.5	30.7-19.9	25.0-15.3	18.7-12.9
Average Yield %	1.8	2.0	1.7	1.9	2.0	2.4	3.2

Statistics are as originally reported. Adj. for stk. splits: 2-for-1, 9/98; 6/96. ① Bef. disc. oper. loss 1995, $29.6 mill. ② Incl. non-recur. chrg. of $70.5 mill. ③ Bef. acctg. change chrg. of $6.7 mill. ④ Incl. pre-tax special chrg. of $105.2 mill.

OFFICERS:
A. Jung, Chmn., C.E.O.
S. J. Kropf, Pres., C.O.O.
R. J. Corti, Exec. V.P., C.F.O.

INVESTOR CONTACT: Marilyn Reynolds,
Shareholder Relations, (212) 282-5619

PRINCIPAL OFFICE: 1345 Avenue of the
Americas, New York, NY 10105-0196

TELEPHONE NUMBER: (212) 282-5000
FAX: (212) 282-6035
WEB: www.avon.com

NO. OF EMPLOYEES: 43,800 (avg.)

SHAREHOLDERS: 21,393

ANNUAL MEETING: In May

INCORPORATED: NY, Jan., 1916

INSTITUTIONAL HOLDINGS:
No. of Institutions: 413
Shares Held: 197,265,929
% Held: 83.5

INDUSTRY: Toilet preparations (SIC: 2844)

TRANSFER AGENT(S): EquiServe, Jersey
City, NJ

AVERY DENNISON CORPORATION

YIELD 2.2%
P/E RATIO 24.6

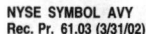

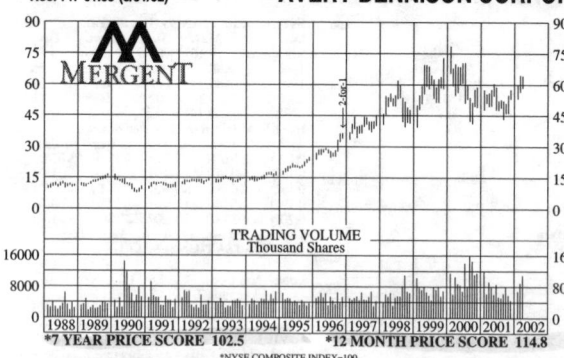

TRADING VOLUME
Thousand Shares

16000
8000
0

1988|1989|1990|1991|1992|1993|1994|1995|1996|1997|1998|1999|2000|2001|2002

*7 YEAR PRICE SCORE 102.5   *12 MONTH PRICE SCORE 114.8
*NYSE COMPOSITE INDEX=100

INTERIM EARNINGS (Per Share):

Qtr.	Mar.	June	Sept.	Dec.
1997	0.47	0.48	0.51	0.52
1998	0.52	0.55	0.54	0.54
1999	0.18	0.63	0.65	0.67
2000	0.70	0.73	0.73	0.69
2001	0.65	0.61	0.63	0.59

INTERIM DIVIDENDS (Per Share):

Amt.	Decl.	Ex.	Rec.	Pay.
0.30Q	1/25/01	3/05/01	3/07/01	3/21/01
0.30Q	4/26/01	6/04/01	6/06/01	6/20/01
0.30Q	7/26/01	8/31/01	9/05/01	9/19/01
0.33Q	10/25/01	12/03/01	12/05/01	12/19/01
0.33Q	1/24/02	3/04/02	3/06/02	3/20/02

Indicated div.: $1.32 (Div. Reinv. Plan)

CAPITALIZATION (12/29/01):

	($000)	(%)
Long-Term Debt	626,700	38.0
Deferred Income Tax	91,100	5.5
Common & Surplus	929,400	56.4
Total	1,647,200	100.0

DIVIDEND ACHIEVER STATUS:
Rank: 94   10-Year Growth Rate: 12.46%
Total Years of Dividend Growth: 26

RECENT DEVELOPMENTS: For the year ended 12/29/01, income fell 14.1% to $243.4 million, before an accounting change charge of $200,000, compared with net income of $283.5 million in 2000. Results for 2001 included a charge for the recent currency devaluation in Argentina. Net sales were $3.80 billion, down 2.3% from $3.89 billion. Sales for the pressure-sensitive adhesives and materials segment climbed 4.0% to $2.16 billion, while consumer and converted segment sales fell 5.3% to $1.77 billion.

PROSPECTS: On 1/9/02, the Company announced that its acquisition of Jackstadt GmbH will be delayed due to further review by the German Federal Cartel Office. The timing and outcome of this final regulatory approval is unknown, but both companies will attempt to complete the transaction within the next few months. Meanwhile, the Company is cautious about near-term earnings due to the uncertainty of current market conditions.

BUSINESS

AVERY DENNISON CORPORA-TION is a worldwide manufacturer of pressure-sensitive adhesives and materials, office products and converted products. A portion of self-adhesive material is converted into labels and other products through embossing, printing, stamping and die-cutting, and some are sold in unconverted form as base materials, tapes and reflective sheeting. AVY also manufactures and sells a variety of office products and other items not involving pressure-sensitive components, such as notebooks, three-ring binders, organization systems, felt-tip markers, glues, fasteners, business forms, tickets, tags, and imprinting equipment. Sales for 2001 were derived: pressure-sensitive adhesives and materials, 54.9%; and consumer and converted products, 45.1%.

ANNUAL FINANCIAL DATA

	12/29/01	12/30/00	1/1/00	1/2/99	12/27/97	12/28/96	12/30/95
Earnings Per Share	③ 2.47	2.84	② 2.13	2.15	1.93	① 1.68	① 1.35
Cash Flow Per Share	4.05	4.41	3.61	3.37	3.03	2.76	2.36
Tang. Book Val. Per Share	4.70	4.35	4.18	6.88	6.87	6.72	8.91
Dividends Per Share	1.23	1.11	0.99	0.87	0.72	0.62	0.56
Dividend Payout %	49.8	39.1	46.5	40.5	37.3	36.9	41.1
INCOME STATEMENT (IN MILLIONS):							
Total Revenues	3,803.3	3,893.5	3,768.2	3,459.9	3,345.7	3,222.5	3,113.9
Costs & Expenses	3,237.6	3,255.7	3,244.0	2,961.4	2,886.0	2,801.1	2,737.0
Depreciation & Amort.	156.0	156.9	150.4	127.2	116.8	113.4	107.9
Operating Income	409.7	480.9	373.8	371.3	342.9	308.0	269.0
Net Interest Inc./(Exp.)	d50.2	d54.6	d43.4	d34.6	d31.7	d37.4	d44.3
Income Before Income Taxes	359.8	426.3	330.4	336.7	311.2	270.6	224.7
Income Taxes	116.4	142.8	115.0	113.4	106.4	94.7	81.0
Net Income	③ 243.4	283.5	② 215.4	223.3	205.3	① 175.9	① 143.7
Cash Flow	399.4	440.4	365.8	350.5	321.6	289.3	251.6
Average Shs. Outstg. (000)	98,600	99,800	101,300	104,100	106,100	105,000	106,500
BALANCE SHEET (IN MILLIONS):							
Cash & Cash Equivalents	19.1	11.4	6.9	18.5	3.3	3.8	27.0
Total Current Assets	982.5	982.4	956.0	802.0	793.5	804.5	800.1
Net Property	1,074.6	1,079.0	1,043.5	1,035.6	985.3	962.7	907.4
Total Assets	2,819.2	2,699.1	2,592.5	2,142.6	2,046.5	2,036.7	1,963.6
Total Current Liabilities	951.3	800.7	850.4	664.3	629.9	693.9	672.5
Long-Term Obligations	626.7	772.9	617.5	465.9	404.1	370.7	334.0
Net Stockholders' Equity	929.4	828.1	809.9	833.3	837.2	832.0	1,069.4
Net Working Capital	31.2	181.7	105.6	137.7	163.6	110.6	127.6
Year-end Shs. Outstg. (000)	109,891	110,245	98,800	100,000	102,400	103,600	106,100
STATISTICAL RECORD:							
Operating Profit Margin %	10.8	12.4	9.9	10.7	10.2	9.6	8.6
Net Profit Margin %	6.4	7.3	5.7	6.5	6.1	5.5	4.6
Return on Equity %	26.2	34.2	26.6	26.8	24.5	21.1	17.6
Return on Assets %	8.6	10.5	8.3	10.4	10.0	8.6	7.3
Debt/Total Assets %	22.2	28.6	23.8	21.7	19.7	18.2	17.0
Price Range	60.50-43.25	78.50-41.13	73.00-39.38	62.06-39.44	45.31-33.38	36.50-23.75	25.06-16.56
P/E Ratio	24.5-17.5	27.6-14.5	34.3-18.5	28.9-18.3	23.5-17.3	21.7-14.1	18.6-12.3
Average Yield %	2.4	1.9	1.8	1.7	1.8	2.1	2.7

Statistics are as originally reported. Adj. for 2-for-1 split, 12/96. ① Incl. non-recur. chgs. of $2.1 mill., 1996; $1.5 mill., 1995. ② Incl. $65.0 mill. one-time restr. chg. ③ Excl. $200,000 acct. chg.

OFFICERS:
P. M. Neal, Chmn., C.E.O.
D. A. Scarborough, Pres., C.O.O.
D. R. O'Bryant, Sr. V.P., C.F.O

INVESTOR CONTACT: Cynthia S. Guenther, V.P., Investor Relations, (626) 304-2000

PRINCIPAL OFFICE: 150 North Orange Grove Boulevard, Pasadena, CA 91103

TELEPHONE NUMBER: (626) 304-2000
FAX: (626) 792-7312
WEB: www.averydennison.com

NO. OF EMPLOYEES: 17,300 (avg.)

SHAREHOLDERS: 12,368

ANNUAL MEETING: In Apr.

INCORPORATED: DE, Sept., 1946

INSTITUTIONAL HOLDINGS:
No. of Institutions: 353
Shares Held: 79,203,824
% Held: 72.1

INDUSTRY: Paper coated and laminated, nec (SIC: 2672)

TRANSFER AGENT(S): First Chicago Trust Company of New York, Jersey City, NJ

AUTOMATIC DATA PROCESSING, INC.

| YIELD | 0.8% |
| P/E RATIO | 36.9 |

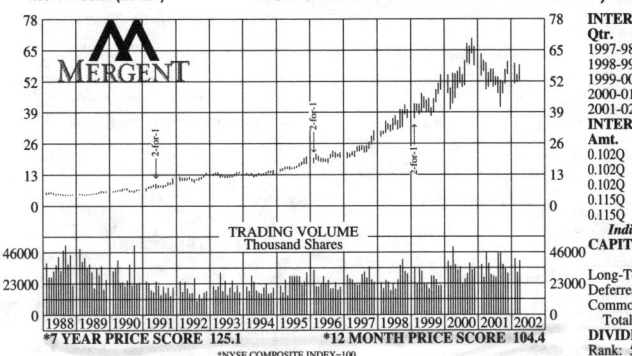

TRADING VOLUME
Thousand Shares

1988 1989 1990 1991 1992 1993 1994 1995 1996 1997 1998 1999 2000 2001 2002

*7 YEAR PRICE SCORE 125.1   *12 MONTH PRICE SCORE 104.4
*NYSE COMPOSITE INDEX=100

INTERIM EARNINGS (Per Share):

Qtr.	Sept.	Dec.	Mar.	June
1997-98	0.18	0.25	0.31	0.26
1998-99	0.20	0.27	0.36	0.30
1999-00	0.23	0.31	0.42	0.35
2000-01	0.27	0.32	0.45	0.40
2001-02	0.31	0.42	...	...

INTERIM DIVIDENDS (Per Share):

Amt.	Decl.	Ex.	Rec.	Pay.
0.102Q	1/23/01	3/07/01	3/09/01	4/01/01
0.102Q	5/15/01	6/06/01	6/08/01	7/01/01
0.102Q	8/13/01	9/17/01	9/14/01	10/01/01
0.115Q	11/13/01	12/12/01	12/14/01	1/01/02
0.115Q	1/16/02	3/13/02	3/15/02	4/01/02

Indicated div.: $0.46 (Div. Reinv. Plan)

CAPITALIZATION (6/30/01):

	($000)	(%)
Long-Term Debt	110,227	2.2
Deferred Income Tax	207,928	4.1
Common & Surplus	4,700,997	93.7
Total	5,019,152	100.0

DIVIDEND ACHIEVER STATUS:
Rank: 53   10-Year Growth Rate: 15.91%
Total Years of Dividend Growth: 26

RECENT DEVELOPMENTS: For the three months ended 12/31/01, net earnings rose 20.7% to $264.6 million compared with $219.2 million in the equivalent quarter of 2000. Total revenues were $1.68 billion, up 2.5% from $1.64 billion in the prior-year period. Revenues continue to be negatively affected by lower interest rates. However, cost controls efforts are helping to maintain margins. Comparisons were made with restated prior-year results.

PROSPECTS: The Company expects revenue growth to improve slightly in the second half of fiscal 2002. However, later in the year, ADP anticipates a decline in interest income due to its high average client balances and the reinvestment of maturing investments in its portfolio at lower yields. Separately, on 1/16/02, the Company completed the acquisition of the AutoVista™ claims line of business from ComputerLogic®.

BUSINESS

AUTOMATIC DATA PROCESSING, INC. is an independent computer services firm with over 500,000 clients. AUD's Employer Services group (57.3% of 2001 revenues) provides employers with payroll, human resources, tax deposit and reporting services. Brokerage Services (25.0% of revenues) provides securities transaction processing, investor support tools, market data services, and investor communications-related services to the financial community worldwide. ADP Dealer Services (9.8% of revenues) is a major provider of computing, data and professional services to auto and truck dealers in the U.S., Canada, Europe, Asia and Latin America. Other Service groups (7.9% of revenues) include claims services and ADP International.

ANNUAL FINANCIAL DATA

	6/30/01	6/30/00	6/30/99	6/30/98	6/30/97	6/30/96	6/30/95
Earnings Per Share	③ 1.44	1.31	② 1.10	0.99	① 0.88	0.79	0.69
Cash Flow Per Share	1.93	1.74	1.52	1.37	1.27	1.14	0.99
Tang. Book Val. Per Share	4.97	4.71	3.97	2.90	2.30	1.86	2.41
Dividends Per Share	0.41	0.35	0.30	0.27	0.23	0.20	0.16
Dividend Payout %	28.5	26.7	27.7	26.8	26.1	25.5	23.4
INCOME STATEMENT (IN MILLIONS)							
Total Revenues	7,017.6	6,287.5	5,540.1	4,798.1	4,112.2	3,566.6	2,893.7
Costs & Expenses	5,079.9	4,668.1	4,163.7	3,645.2	3,136.9	2,699.8	2,162.6
Depreciation & Amort.	320.9	284.3	272.8	244.6	223.4	201.6	172.5
Operating Income	1,616.9	1,335.1	1,103.6	908.2	751.8	665.1	558.6
Net Interest Inc./(Exp.)	d14.3	d13.1	d19.1	d24.0	d27.8	d29.7	d24.3
Income Before Income Taxes	1,525.0	1,289.6	1,084.5	884.2	724.0	635.4	534.3
Income Taxes	600.3	448.8	387.7	278.9	210.5	180.7	139.5
Net Income	③ 924.7	840.8	② 696.8	605.3	① 513.5	454.7	394.8
Cash Flow	1,245.6	1,125.1	969.6	849.9	736.9	656.3	567.4
Average Shs. Outstg. (000)	645,989	646,098	636,892	620,822	581,980	577,934	570,224
BALANCE SHEET (IN MILLIONS)							
Cash & Cash Equivalents	1,790.6	1,824.4	1,092.5	897.2	1,024.9	636.2	697.6
Total Current Assets	3,083.5	3,064.5	2,194.3	1,829.3	1,805.3	1,454.3	1,211.1
Net Property	614.7	597.3	579.3	583.7	519.3	468.3	416.0
Total Assets	17,889.1	16,850.8	5,824.8	5,175.4	4,382.8	3,839.9	3,201.1
Total Current Liabilities	1,336.3	1,296.7	1,286.4	1,221.0	1,019.9	835.6	543.2
Long-Term Obligations	110.2	132.0	145.8	192.1	401.2	403.7	390.2
Net Stockholders' Equity	4,701.0	4,582.8	4,007.9	3,406.5	2,660.6	2,315.3	2,096.6
Net Working Capital	1,747.2	1,767.8	907.9	608.3	785.5	618.7	667.9
Year-end Shs. Outstg. (000)	623,936	628,746	623,627	604,212	585,698	575,242	576,336
STATISTICAL RECORD:							
Operating Profit Margin %	23.0	21.2	19.9	18.9	18.3	18.6	19.3
Net Profit Margin %	13.2	13.4	12.6	12.6	12.5	12.7	13.6
Return on Equity %	19.7	18.3	17.4	17.8	19.3	19.6	18.8
Return on Assets %	5.2	5.0	12.0	11.7	11.7	11.8	12.3
Debt/Total Assets %	0.6	0.8	2.5	3.7	9.2	10.5	12.2
Price Range	63.56-41.00	69.94-40.00	54.81-36.25	42.16-28.78	31.34-19.75	22.88-17.81	20.59-14.38
P/E Ratio	44.1-28.5	53.4-30.5	49.8-33.0	42.6-29.1	35.6-22.4	29.1-22.7	29.7-20.7
Average Yield %	0.8	0.6	0.7	0.7	0.9	1.0	0.9

Statistics are as originally reported. Adj. for 2-for-1 stk. split, 1/99 & 1/96. ① Incl. non-recur. chg. of $11.7 mill. ② Incl. about $37.0 pre-tax gain, $40.0 mill. provision for taxes, & $14.0 mill. net non-recur. adjustment. ③ Incl. $54.0 mill. non-cash, non-recur. write-off of investment.

OFFICERS:
A. F. Weinbach, Chmn., C.E.O.
G. C. Butler, Pres., C.O.O.
K. E. Dykstra, V.P., Fin.

INVESTOR CONTACT: Karen E. Dykstra,
V.P., Fin., (973) 974-5000

PRINCIPAL OFFICE: One ADP Boulevard,
Roseland, NJ 07068

TELEPHONE NUMBER: (973) 974-5000
FAX: (973) 974-5000
WEB: www.adp.com

NO. OF EMPLOYEES: 41,000 (approx.)

SHAREHOLDERS: 34,000 (approx.)

ANNUAL MEETING: In Nov.

INCORPORATED: DE, June, 1961

INSTITUTIONAL HOLDINGS:
No. of Institutions: 795
Shares Held: 449,377,872
% Held: 72.4

INDUSTRY: Data processing and preparation
(SIC: 7374)

TRANSFER AGENT(S): Mellon Investor
Services, Ridgefield Park, NJ

ATMOS ENERGY CORPORATION

YIELD 5.0%
P/E RATIO 17.4

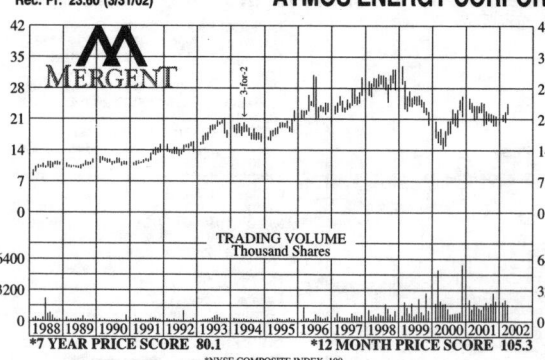

INTERIM EARNINGS (Per Share):

Qtr.	Dec.	Mar.	June	Sept.
1997-98	0.68	1.25	0.06	d0.13
1998-99	0.50	0.94	d0.17	d0.68
1999-00	0.46	0.94	d0.14	d0.11
2000-01	0.70	1.13	d0.08	d0.19
2001-02	0.50	...	...	...

INTERIM DIVIDENDS (Per Share):

Amt.	Decl.	Ex.	Rec.	Pay.
0.29Q	2/14/01	2/22/01	2/26/01	3/12/01
0.29Q	5/09/01	5/23/01	5/25/01	6/11/01
0.29Q	8/08/01	8/22/01	8/24/01	9/10/01
0.295Q	11/07/01	11/21/01	11/26/01	12/10/01
0.295Q	2/13/02	2/21/02	2/25/02	3/11/02

Indicated div.: $1.18 (Div. Reinv. Plan)

CAPITALIZATION (9/30/01):

	($000)	(%)
Long-Term Debt	692,399	48.9
Deferred Income Tax	138,934	9.8
Common & Surplus	583,864	41.3
Total	1,415,197	100.0

TRADING VOLUME
Thousand Shares

*7 YEAR PRICE SCORE 80.1   *12 MONTH PRICE SCORE 105.3
*NYSE COMPOSITE INDEX=100

DIVIDEND ACHIEVER STATUS:
Rank: 253   10-Year Growth Rate: 3.74%
Total Years of Dividend Growth: 14

RECENT DEVELOPMENTS: For the first quarter ended 12/31/01, net income declined 10.2% to $20.6 million compared with $23.0 million in the corresponding 2000 quarter. Earnings were adversely affected by a decrease in natural gas sales volumes resulting from weather that was 29.0% warmer year-over-year. Operating revenues dropped 38.7% to $271.3 million from $442.8 million a year earlier. Gross profit as a percentage of net sales climbed to 40.3% from 24.8% in the previous year.

PROSPECTS: On 4/1/02, ATO announced the selection of its subsidiary, Atmos Power Systems, Inc., to build for lease a 21 megawatt natural-gas-fired power plant for an industrial customer in Tennessee. On 1/15/02, ATO's Woodward Marketing subsidiary acquired natural gas sales contracts for about $1.0 million from Duke Energy Trading and Marketing. Separately, the proposed $150.0 million acquisition of Mississippi Valley Gas Company should be complete by the end of fiscal 2002.

BUSINESS

ATMOS ENERGY CORPORATION distributes natural gas to about 1.4 million residential, commercial, industrial and agricultural customers in eleven states as of 12/31/01. ATO's Louisiana distribution system is operated through Trans Louisiana Gas Company and the Kentucky distribution system is operated through Western Kentucky Gas Company. The Texas distribution system is operated through the Energas Company. The Colorado, Kansas, and Missouri distribution systems are operated through Greeley Gas Company. United Cities Gas Company is a natural gas utility company engaged in the distribution and sale of natural gas to customers in Tennessee, Illinois, Virginia, Kansas, Missouri, Georgia, and Iowa. In addition, the Company owns a 19.0% interest in U.S. Propane, L.P.

ANNUAL FINANCIAL DATA

	9/30/01	9/30/00	9/30/99	9/30/98	② 9/30/97	9/30/96	9/30/95
Earnings Per Share	1.47	1.14	0.58	1.84	① 0.81	1.51	1.22
Cash Flow Per Share	3.31	3.25	2.58	3.62	2.25	3.04	2.80
Tang. Book Val. Per Share	12.43	12.28	12.09	12.21	11.04	10.75	10.20
Dividends Per Share	1.17	1.15	1.11	1.07	1.02	0.97	0.93
Dividend Payout %	79.2	100.4	191.3	58.1	125.9	64.2	76.2
INCOME STATEMENT (IN THOUSANDS):							
Total Revenues	1,442,275	850,152	690,196	848,208	906,835	483,744	435,820
Costs & Expenses	1,235,644	690,268	565,142	671,635	786,045	402,862	365,260
Depreciation & Amort.	70,470	66,920	61,674	53,416	42,207	24,417	24,333
Maintenance Exp.	6,368	7,648	9,141	10,278	11,974	4,212	4,276
Operating Income	130,281	85,316	54,239	112,879	66,609	52,253	41,951
Net Interest Inc./(Exp.)	d47,011	d43,823	d36,298	d30,149	d28,185	d14,585	d13,262
Income Taxes	33,368	20,319	9,555	31,806	14,298	13,310	9,574
Net Income	56,090	35,918	17,744	55,265	① 23,838	23,949	18,873
Cash Flow	126,560	102,838	79,418	108,681	66,045	48,366	43,206
Average Shs. Outstg.	38,247	31,594	30,819	30,031	29,409	15,892	15,416
BALANCE SHEET (IN THOUSANDS):							
Gross Property	2,109,867	1,579,803	1,549,258	1,446,420	1,332,672	666,438	595,359
Accumulated Depreciation	774,469	597,457	583,476	528,560	483,545	252,871	232,107
Net Property	1,335,398	982,346	965,782	917,860	849,127	413,567	363,252
Total Assets	2,036,180	1,348,758	1,230,537	1,141,390	1,088,311	501,861	445,783
Long-Term Obligations	692,399	363,198	377,483	398,548	302,981	122,303	131,303
Net Stockholders' Equity	583,864	392,466	377,663	371,158	327,260	172,298	158,278
Year-end Shs. Outstg.	40,792	31,952	31,248	30,398	29,642	16,021	15,519
STATISTICAL RECORD:							
Operating Profit Margin %	9.0	10.0	7.9	13.3	7.3	10.8	9.6
Net Profit Margin %	3.9	4.2	2.6	6.5	2.6	5.0	4.3
Net Inc./Net Property %	4.2	3.7	1.8	6.0	2.8	5.8	5.2
Net Inc./Tot. Capital %	4.0	4.0	2.0	6.5	3.3	7.2	5.8
Return on Equity %	9.6	9.2	4.7	14.9	7.3	13.9	11.9
Accum. Depr./Gross Prop. %	36.7	37.8	37.7	36.5	36.3	37.9	39.0
Price Range	25.75-19.45	26.25-14.25	33.00-19.63	32.25-24.75	30.50-22.13	31.00-20.88	23.00-16.13
P/E Ratio	17.5-13.2	23.0-12.5	56.9-33.8	17.5-13.5	37.6-27.3	20.5-13.8	18.9-13.2
Average Yield %	5.2	5.7	4.2	3.8	3.9	3.7	4.8

Statistics are as originally reported. ① Incl. a non-recurr. after-tax chg. of $2.8 mill. related to mgmt. changes & an after-tax charge of $12.6 mill. for merger & integration exps. ② Incl. results of United Cities Gas Company

OFFICERS:
R. W. Best, Chmn., Pres., C.E.O.
J. P. Reddy, Sr. V.P., C.F.O.

INVESTOR CONTACT: Susan C. Kappes,
V.P. Investor Relations, (972) 855-3729

PRINCIPAL OFFICE: Three Lincoln Centre,
Suite 1800, 5430 LBJ Freeway, Dallas, TX
75240

TELEPHONE NUMBER: (972) 934-9227
FAX: (972) 855-3040
WEB: www.atmosenergy.com

NO. OF EMPLOYEES: 2,361 (avg.)

SHAREHOLDERS: 30,524

ANNUAL MEETING: In Feb.

INCORPORATED: TX, Oct., 1983

INSTITUTIONAL HOLDINGS:
No. of Institutions: 132
Shares Held: 17,899,941
% Held: 43.6

INDUSTRY: Natural gas transmission (SIC: 4922)

TRANSFER AGENT(S): EquiServe Trust
Company, N.A., Providence, RI

ASSOCIATED BANC-CORP.

YIELD 3.3%
P/E RATIO 14.1

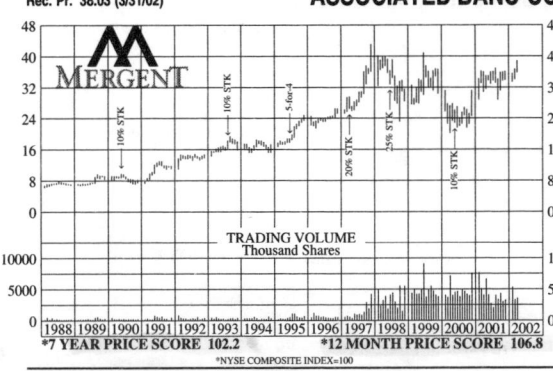

7 YEAR PRICE SCORE 102.2   *12 MONTH PRICE SCORE 106.8*

*NYSE COMPOSITE INDEX=100

INTERIM EARNINGS (Per Share):

Qtr.	Mar.	June	Sept.	Dec.
1997	0.49	0.52	0.53	d0.77
1998	0.56	0.58	0.55	0.55
1999	0.55	0.56	0.59	0.63
2000	0.62	0.63	0.61	0.60
2001	0.63	0.69	0.68	0.70

INTERIM DIVIDENDS (Per Share):

Amt.	Decl.	Ex.	Rec.	Pay.
0.31Q	4/25/01	4/27/01	5/01/01	5/15/01
0.31Q	7/25/01	7/30/01	8/01/01	8/15/01
0.31Q	10/24/01	10/30/01	11/01/01	11/15/01
0.31Q	1/23/02	1/30/02	2/01/02	2/15/02

Indicated div.: $1.24 (Div. Reinv. Plan)

CAPITALIZATION (12/31/01):

	($000)	(%)
Total Deposits	8,612,611	79.8
Long-Term Debt	1,103,395	10.2
Common & Surplus	1,070,416	9.9
Total	10,786,422	100.0

DIVIDEND ACHIEVER STATUS:
Rank: 82   10-Year Growth Rate: 13.50%
Total Years of Dividend Growth: 28

RECENT DEVELOPMENTS: For the year ended 12/31/01, net income rose 6.9% to $179.5 million versus $168.0 million a year earlier. Earnings for 2001 and 2000 included pre-tax asset sale gains of $2.0 million and $24.4 million, respectively. Total interest income decreased 5.4% to $880.6 million from $931.2 million in the previous year. Total interest expense declined 16.2% to $458.6 million from $547.6 million in the prior year. Net interest income grew 10.0% to $422.0 million from $383.6 million in 2000. Provision for loan losses climbed 39.6% to $28.2 million from $20.2 million a year earlier. Total noninterest income advanced 6.2% to $195.6 million from $184.2 million in the previous year. Looking ahead, diluted earnings per share are expected to increase 10.0% to 12.0% in 2002. Moreover, ASBC anticipates continued commercial loan growth, improved core deposit growth, and a steady net interest margin. Separately, on 2/28/02, ASBC completed its acquisition of Minneapolis-based Signal Financial Corp.

BUSINESS

ASSOCIATED BANC-CORP. is a multi-bank holding company headquartered in Green Bay, Wisconsin.

ASBC provides advice and specialized services to its affiliates in banking policy and operations, including auditing, data processing, marketing/advertising, investing, legal/compliance, personnel services, trust services, risk management, facilities management, security, corporate-wide purchasing, treasury, finance, accounting, and other financial services functionally related to banking. Through its affiliates, ASBC provides a wide range of banking services to individuals and small- to medium-sized businesses. As of 12/31/01, ASBC had total assets of $13.60 billion and more than 200 banking offices serving over 150 communities in Wisconsin, Illinois and Minnesota.

On 12/19/98, ASBC acquired Citizens Bankshares Inc.

ANNUAL FINANCIAL DATA

	12/31/01	12/31/00	12/31/99	12/31/98	12/31/97	12/31/96	12/31/95
Earnings Per Share	2.70	2.46	2.34	2.24	①0.74	1.89	1.72
Tang. Book Val. Per Share	16.38	14.65	13.09	12.70	11.75	12.98	11.95
Dividends Per Share	1.22	1.11	1.05	0.95	0.81	0.69	0.59
Dividend Payout %	45.2	45.1	44.9	42.4	109.5	36.5	34.3
INCOME STATEMENT (IN MILLIONS):							
Total Interest Income	880.6	931.2	814.5	785.8	787.2	311.7	264.4
Total Interest Expense	458.6	547.6	418.8	411.0	411.6	142.5	117.8
Net Interest Income	422.0	383.6	395.7	374.7	375.6	169.3	146.6
Provision for Loan Losses	28.2	20.2	19.2	14.7	31.7	4.7	3.2
Non-Interest Income	195.6	184.2	165.9	168.0	96.0	65.1	53.0
Non-Interest Expense	338.4	317.7	305.1	295.0	323.6	140.4	123.1
Income Before Taxes	251.0	229.8	237.3	233.0	116.3	89.3	73.4
Net Income	179.5	168.0	164.9	157.0	①52.4	57.2	46.7
Average Shs. Outstg. (000)	66,516	68,410	70,467	70,168	70,329	30,298	27,233
BALANCE SHEET (IN MILLIONS):							
Cash & Due from Banks	588.0	368.2	284.7	331.5	288.0	236.3	206.5
Securities Avail. for Sale	3,197.0	2,891.6	2,841.5	2,357.0	2,167.7	437.4	359.0
Total Loans & Leases	9,019.9	8,913.4	8,357.9	7,272.7	7,076.6	3,159.9	2,611.2
Allowance for Credit Losses	128.2	120.2	113.2	99.7	92.7	47.4	39.1
Net Loans & Leases	8,891.7	8,793.1	8,244.8	7,173.0	6,983.8	3,112.4	2,572.2
Total Assets	13,604.4	13,128.4	12,519.9	11,250.7	10,691.4	4,419.1	3,697.8
Total Deposits	8,612.6	9,291.6	8,691.8	8,557.8	8,364.1	3,508.0	2,973.1
Long-Term Obligations	1,103.4	122.4	24.3	26.0	15.3	21.1	18.1
Total Liabilities	12,534.0	12,159.7	11,610.1	10,371.9	9,877.7	4,025.9	3,372.2
Net Stockholders' Equity	1,070.4	968.7	909.8	878.7	813.7	393.1	325.6
Year-end Shs. Outstg. (000)	65,335	66,116	69,520	69,176	69,267	30,295	27,250
STATISTICAL RECORD:							
Return on Equity %	16.8	17.3	18.1	17.9	6.4	14.6	14.3
Return on Assets %	1.3	1.3	1.3	1.4	0.5	1.3	1.3
Equity/Assets %	7.9	7.4	7.3	7.8	7.6	8.9	8.8
Non-Int. Exp./Tot. Inc. %	54.9	55.2	54.6	55.0	64.2	60.1	61.8
Price Range	36.97-28.75	31.25-20.11	40.91-27.44	40.18-23.07	43.09-25.15	26.51-21.36	24.85-16.61
P/E Ratio	13.7-10.6	12.7-8.2	17.5-11.7	18.0-10.3	58.1-33.9	14.0-11.3	14.5-9.7
Average Yield %	3.7	4.3	3.1	3.0	2.4	2.9	2.8

Statistics are as originally reported. Adj. for stk. splits: 10% div., 6/00; 25% div., 6/12/98; 20% div., 3/17/97; 5-for-4, 6/15/95. ① Incl. non-recurr. chrg. $103.7 mill.

OFFICERS:
H. B. Conlon, Chmn.
J. C. Seramur, Vice-Chmn.
R. C. Gallagher, Pres., C.E.O.

INVESTOR CONTACT: Joe Selner, Investor Relations, (920) 491-7120

PRINCIPAL OFFICE: 1200 Hansen Road, Green Bay, WI 54304

TELEPHONE NUMBER: (920) 491-7000
FAX: (920) 433-3261
WEB: www.associatedbank.com

NO. OF EMPLOYEES: 3,845

SHAREHOLDERS: 9,651 (approx.); 20,700 (approx. beneficial)

ANNUAL MEETING: In Apr.

INCORPORATED: WI, 1964

INSTITUTIONAL HOLDINGS:
No. of Institutions: 177
Shares Held: 25,115,112
% Held: 36.5

INDUSTRY: State commercial banks (SIC: 6022)

TRANSFER AGENT(S): First Chicago Trust Company of New York, Jersey City, NJ

ARCHER DANIELS MIDLAND COMPANY

YIELD	1.4%
P/E RATIO	21.1

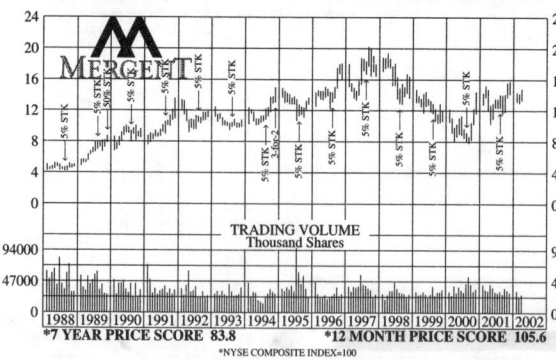

TRADING VOLUME
Thousand Shares

1988 1989 1990 1991 1992 1993 1994 1995 1996 1997 1998 1999 2000 2001 2002
*7 YEAR PRICE SCORE 83.8   *12 MONTH PRICE SCORE 105.6
*NYSE COMPOSITE INDEX=100

INTERIM EARNINGS (Per Share):

Qtr.	Sept.	Dec.	Mar.	June
1997-98	0.19	0.21	0.10	0.10
1998-99	0.17	0.16	0.02	0.07
1999-00	0.06	0.15	0.15	0.10
2000-01	0.16	0.19	0.14	0.09
2001-02	0.20	0.23	...	...

INTERIM DIVIDENDS (Per Share):

Amt.	Decl.	Ex.	Rec.	Pay.
0.05Q	5/03/01	5/09/01	5/11/01	6/04/01
0.05Q	8/02/01	8/09/01	8/13/01	9/04/01
5% STK	8/02/01	8/30/01	9/04/01	9/24/01
0.05Q	11/01/01	11/07/01	11/12/01	12/04/01
0.05Q	1/29/02	2/06/02	2/08/02	3/05/02

Indicated div.: $0.20

CAPITALIZATION (6/30/01):

	($000)	(%)
Long-Term Debt	3,351,067	32.4
Deferred Income Tax	644,295	6.2
Common & Surplus	6,331,683	61.3
Total	10,327,045	100.0

DIVIDEND ACHIEVER STATUS:
Rank: 40   10-Year Growth Rate: 17.20%
Total Years of Dividend Growth: 27

RECENT DEVELOPMENTS: For the quarter ended 12/31/01, net earnings climbed 20.4% to $150.0 million from $124.6 million a year earlier. Results for 2001 included a $20.0 million loss from securities transactions, while results for 2000 included a $562,000 gain from securities transactions. Net sales and other operating income increased 12.4% to $5.55 billion from $4.94 billion the year before. Operating profit advanced 27.8% to $341.3 million.

PROSPECTS: Increased demand for livestock feed is helping boost operating profitability from ADM's soybean-processing operations. Separately, sharply lower prices for ethanol, a fuel additive made from corn, due to excess supplies and reduced fuel demand is negatively affecting the Company's profit from its corn milling operations. On 1/10/02, ADM ceased milling operations at its Des Moines, Iowa flour mill due to excess industry capacity.

BUSINESS

ARCHER DANIELS MIDLAND COMPANY is engaged in the business of processing and merchandising agricultural commodities. ADM is one of the largest domestic processors of oil seeds and vegetable oil, and one of the largest flour millers and corn refiners in the U.S. ADM's corn wet milling operations produce corn syrups, high fructose syrups, glucose, corn starches and ethyl alcohol (ethanol). Other operations include storage of grain, shelling of peanuts, production of consumer food products and formula feeds, production of malt products and refining of sugar. ADM Investor Services provides the Company and other commercial firms with commodity hedging services and is a futures commission merchant.

ANNUAL FINANCIAL DATA

	6/30/01	6/30/00	6/30/99	6/30/98	6/30/97	6/30/96	6/30/95
Earnings Per Share	⑤ 0.58	④ 0.45	③ 0.41	② 0.59	② 0.54	① 0.99	1.10
Cash Flow Per Share	1.51	1.42	1.32	1.40	1.24	1.59	1.66
Tang. Book Val. Per Share	9.64	9.39	9.13	9.47	8.92	8.82	8.34
Dividends Per Share	0.193	0.184	0.175	0.167	0.159	0.151	0.095
Dividend Payout %	33.3	40.9	42.7	28.3	29.4	15.3	8.6
INCOME STATEMENT (IN MILLIONS):							
Total Revenues	⑧ 20,051.4	12,876.8	14,283.3	16,108.6	13,853.3	13,314.0	12,671.9
Costs & Expenses	18,728.7	11,739.0	13,130.2	14,828.3	12,752.3	11,980.4	11,052.0
Depreciation & Amort.	622.0	647.6	632.0	560.1	475.5	419.2	406.8
Operating Income	700.8	490.2	531.0	720.3	625.4	914.4	1,213.1
Income Before Income Taxes	521.9	353.2	419.8	610.0	644.4	1,054.4	1,181.5
Income Taxes	138.6	52.3	138.5	206.4	267.1	358.5	385.6
Net Income	⑤ 383.3	④ 300.9	③ 281.3	② 403.6	② 377.3	① 695.9	795.9
Cash Flow	1,005.3	948.5	903.5	963.7	852.8	1,115.1	1,202.7
Average Shs. Outstg. (000)	664,507	669,279	685,328	686,047	690,352	702,012	725,345
BALANCE SHEET (IN MILLIONS):							
Cash & Cash Equivalents	817.8	931.4	903.6	725.5	728.0	1,354.8	1,119.3
Total Current Assets	6,150.3	6,162.4	5,789.6	5,451.7	4,284.3	4,384.7	3,712.6
Net Property	4,920.4	5,277.1	5,567.2	5,322.7	4,708.6	4,114.3	3,762.3
Total Assets	14,339.9	14,423.1	14,029.9	13,833.5	11,354.4	10,449.9	9,756.9
Total Current Liabilities	3,867.0	4,332.9	3,840.3	3,717.3	2,248.8	1,633.6	1,172.4
Long-Term Obligations	3,351.1	3,277.2	3,191.9	2,847.1	2,344.9	2,003.0	2,070.1
Net Stockholders' Equity	6,331.7	6,110.2	6,240.6	6,504.9	6,050.1	6,144.8	5,854.2
Net Working Capital	2,283.3	1,829.4	1,949.3	1,734.4	2,035.6	2,751.1	2,540.3
Year-end Shs. Outstg. (000)	656,853	650,683	683,341	686,612	677,955	696,621	702,177
STATISTICAL RECORD:							
Operating Profit Margin %	3.5	3.8	3.7	4.5	4.5	6.9	9.6
Net Profit Margin %	1.9	2.3	2.0	2.5	2.7	5.2	6.3
Return on Equity %	6.1	4.9	4.5	6.2	6.2	11.3	13.6
Return on Assets %	2.7	2.1	2.0	2.9	3.3	6.7	8.2
Debt/Total Assets %	23.4	22.7	22.8	20.6	20.7	19.2	21.2
Price Range	15.80-10.24	14.47-7.80	14.74-10.38	19.44-12.80	20.26-13.32	18.12-12.22	14.93-10.66
P/E Ratio	27.2-17.6	32.3-17.4	36.1-25.4	32.9-21.7	37.3-24.5	18.4-12.4	13.6-9.7
Average Yield %	1.5	1.7	1.4	1.0	0.9	1.0	0.7

Statistics are as originally reported. Adj. for all stk. divs. & splits through 9/01. ① Incl. $0.04/sh net chg. ② Incl. $48 mil. chg. for fines & litig. costs & $0.04/sh. gain fr. secs. transactions, 1998; & $0.18/sh net chg., 1997. ③ Excl. $15.3 mil. extraord. chg. & incl. $63.0 mil. gain fr. secs. trans. ④ Incl. $72.0 mil. chg. for plant closings, $0.00 mil. tax credit & $6.0 mil. after-tax gain fr. secs. trans. ⑤ Incl. $0.09/sh. gain fr. secs. trans. & $0.03/sh. loss fr. invests. ⑧ Reflects the adoption of new accounting standards related to recognizing sales.

OFFICERS:
G. A. Andreas, Chmn., C.E.O.
P. B. Mulhollem, Pres., C.O.O.
D. J. Schmalz, Sr. V.P., C.F.O.

INVESTOR CONTACT: Dwight Grimestad, V.P., Inv. Rel., (217) 424-4586

PRINCIPAL OFFICE: 4666 Faries Parkway, Box 1470, Decatur, IL 62525

TELEPHONE NUMBER: (217) 424-5200
FAX: (217) 424-5381
WEB: www.admworld.com
NO. OF EMPLOYEES: 22,834 (avg.)
SHAREHOLDERS: 27,918
ANNUAL MEETING: In Nov.
INCORPORATED: DE, May, 1923

INSTITUTIONAL HOLDINGS:
No. of Institutions: 374
Shares Held: 396,862,071
% Held: 60.6

INDUSTRY: Soybean oil mills (SIC: 2075)

TRANSFER AGENT(S): Hickory Point Bank & Trust, Decatur, IL

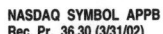

APPLEBEE'S INTERNATIONAL, INC.

YIELD 0.2%
P/E RATIO 21.0

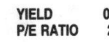

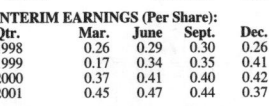

7 YEAR PRICE SCORE 137.2   **12 MONTH PRICE SCORE 117.4**
*NYSE COMPOSITE INDEX=100

TRADING VOLUME
Thousand Shares

INTERIM EARNINGS (Per Share):

Qtr.	Mar.	June	Sept.	Dec.
1998	0.26	0.29	0.30	0.26
1999	0.17	0.34	0.35	0.41
2000	0.37	0.41	0.40	0.42
2001	0.45	0.47	0.44	0.37

INTERIM DIVIDENDS (Per Share):

Amt.	Decl.	Ex.	Rec.	Pay.
0.11A	12/15/00	12/27/00	12/29/00	1/29/01
50% STK	5/10/01	6/13/01	5/25/01	6/12/01
0.08A	12/14/01	12/21/01	12/26/01	1/29/02

Indicated div.: $0.08

CAPITALIZATION (12/30/01):

	($000)	(%)
Long-Term Debt	74,525	18.6
Deferred Income Tax	1,442	0.4
Common & Surplus	325,183	81.1
Total	401,150	100.0

DIVIDEND ACHIEVER STATUS:
Rank: 12   10-Year Growth Rate: 23.49%
Total Years of Dividend Growth: 10

RECENT DEVELOPMENTS:
For the year ended 12/30/01, the Company reported earnings of $65.7 million, before an extraordinary charge of $1.2 million, versus net earnings of $63.2 million in the 53-week period a year earlier. Results included losses on asset dispositions of $1.5 million and $1.3 million in 2001 and 2000, respectively. Total operating revenues increased 7.9% to $744.3 million from $690.2 million in 2000. Company restaurant sales advanced 7.5%

to $651.1 million from $605.4 million in 2000, reflecting new restaurant openings and a 2.5% increase in comparable restaurant sales. Franchise income rose 10.0% to $93.2 million from $84.7 million the year before, due to new restaurant openings and a 3.0% comparable restaurant increase. For 2002, APPB expects more than 100 new restaurant openings including approximately 25 Company-owned units and between 80 and 90 franchised units.

BUSINESS

APPLEBEE'S INTERNATIONAL, INC. develops, franchises and operates a national chain of casual dining restaurants under the trademark of "Applebee's Neighborhood Grill & Bar." Each of the restaurants is designed as a neighborhood establishment featuring a selection of moderately-priced food and beverage items with full service luncheon and evening dining. As of 2/27/02, there were 1,398 Applebee's restaurants in 49 states and eight countries. On 4/13/99, the Company completed the sale of its Rio Bravo International division, comprised of 40 Company and 25 franchised restaurants, to Chevys Inc.

ANNUAL FINANCIAL DATA

	12/30/01	12/31/00	12/26/99	12/27/98	12/28/97	12/29/96	12/31/95
Earnings Per Share	[1][3] 1.73	[3] 1.60	[3] 1.26	[1] 1.11	0.95	0.81	[2] 0.63
Cash Flow Per Share	2.74	2.54	2.09	1.88	1.46	1.20	0.95
Tang. Book Val. Per Share	6.58	5.17	4.05	4.34	5.03	4.62	3.71
Dividends Per Share	0.073	0.067	0.060	0.053	0.047	0.040	0.03
Dividend Payout %	4.2	4.2	4.8	4.8	4.9	4.9	5.3

INCOME STATEMENT (IN THOUSANDS):

Total Revenues	744,344	690,152	669,584	647,562	515,820	413,131	343,563
Costs & Expenses	593,638	546,069	539,069	523,850	420,352	336,353	283,582
Depreciation & Amort.	38,279	36,876	35,605	35,150	24,185	17,945	14,269
Operating Income	112,427	107,207	94,910	88,562	71,283	58,833	45,712
Net Interest Inc./(Exp.)	d7,456	d9,304	d10,814	d9,922	d1,705	d1,571	d2,507
Income Before Income Taxes	103,877	99,938	85,735	80,409	71,801	60,725	45,326
Income Taxes	38,227	36,777	31,537	29,753	26,710	22,711	17,833
Net Income	[1][3] 65,650	[3] 63,161	[3] 54,198	[1] 50,656	45,091	38,014	[2] 27,493
Cash Flow	103,929	100,037	89,803	85,806	69,276	55,959	41,762
Average Shs. Outstg.	37,918	39,447	42,902	45,578	47,460	46,782	43,979

BALANCE SHEET (IN THOUSANDS):

Cash & Cash Equivalents	22,747	12,075	3,982	6,646	19,814	57,410	52,024
Total Current Assets	67,999	53,181	34,211	34,909	43,954	83,992	74,557
Net Property	330,924	314,216	300,140	364,058	276,082	196,950	159,832
Total Assets	500,411	471,707	442,216	510,904	377,474	314,111	270,680
Total Current Liabilities	97,746	93,835	77,662	65,951	62,488	41,843	38,475
Long-Term Obligations	74,525	90,461	106,293	145,522	22,579	24,435	25,832
Net Stockholders' Equity	325,183	281,718	253,873	296,053	290,443	244,792	203,993
Net Working Capital	d29,747	d40,654	d43,451	d31,042	d18,534	42,149	36,082
Year-end Shs. Outstg.	37,211	37,830	39,896	44,310	47,223	46,949	46,524

STATISTICAL RECORD:

Operating Profit Margin %	15.1	15.5	14.2	13.7	13.8	14.2	13.3
Net Profit Margin %	8.8	9.2	8.1	7.8	8.7	9.2	8.0
Return on Equity %	20.2	22.4	21.3	17.1	15.5	15.5	13.5
Return on Assets %	13.1	13.4	12.3	9.9	11.9	12.1	10.2
Debt/Total Assets %	14.9	19.2	24.0	28.5	6.0	7.8	9.5
Price Range	36.89-18.92	25.04-13.63	23.33-13.42	17.33-10.75	20.75-12.00	22.83-11.83	21.17-8.92
P/E Ratio	21.3-10.9	15.7-8.5	18.5-10.6	15.6-9.7	21.8-12.6	28.1-14.6	33.8-14.2
Average Yield %	0.3	0.3	0.3	0.4	0.3	0.2	0.2

Statistics are as originally reported. Adj. for stk. splits: 50%, 6/01 [1] Bef. extraord. chrg. $1.2 mill., 12/01; $641,000, 12/98. [2] Incl. non-recurr. chrg. $1.8 mill., 12/95. [3] Incl. loss on disposition of restaurant & equipment: $1.5 mill., 12/01; $1.3 mill., 12/00; 5.6 mill., 12/99.

OFFICERS:
L. L. Hill, Chmn., Pres., C.E.O.
G. D. Shadid, Exec. V.P., C.O.O.
S. K. Lumpkin, Exec. V.P., C.F.O., Treas.

INVESTOR CONTACT: Carol DiRaimo, (913) 967-4109

PRINCIPAL OFFICE: 4551 W. 107th Street, Suite 100, Overland Park, KS 66207

TELEPHONE NUMBER: (913) 967-4000
FAX: (913) 341-1694
WEB: www.applebees.com

NO. OF EMPLOYEES: 20,900

SHAREHOLDERS: 941 (record)

ANNUAL MEETING: In May

INCORPORATED: DE, 1983

INSTITUTIONAL HOLDINGS:
No. of Institutions: 176
Shares Held: 32,004,340
% Held: 86.4

INDUSTRY: Eating places (SIC: 5812)

TRANSFER AGENT(S): American Stock Transfer & Trust Company, New York, NY

AON CORPORATION

YIELD 2.6%
P/E RATIO 47.3

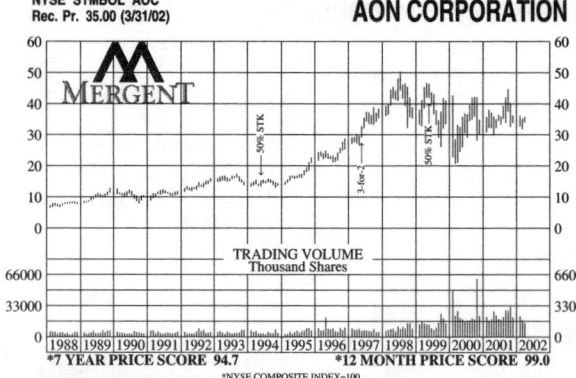

INTERIM EARNINGS (Per Share):

Qtr.	Mar.	June	Sept.	Dec.
1998	0.53	0.54	0.47	0.53
1999	0.13	0.57	0.52	0.05
2000	0.47	0.49	0.53	0.33
2001	0.07	0.11	0.26	0.30

INTERIM DIVIDENDS (Per Share):

Amt.	Decl.	Ex.	Rec.	Pay.
0.225Q	4/20/01	5/01/01	5/03/01	5/16/01
0.225Q	7/13/01	7/31/01	8/02/01	8/15/01
0.225Q	10/12/01	10/30/01	11/01/01	11/14/01
0.225Q	1/18/02	2/08/02	2/12/02	2/25/02

Indicated div.: $0.90 (Div. Reinv. Plan)

CAPITALIZATION (12/31/01):

	($000)	(%)
Long-Term Debt	1,694,000	32.5
Common & Surplus	3,521,000	67.5
Total	5,215,000	100.0

DIVIDEND ACHIEVER STATUS:
Rank: 195   10-Year Growth Rate: 6.69%
Total Years of Dividend Growth: 50

RECENT DEVELOPMENTS: For the year ended 12/31/01, net income dropped to $203.0 million versus income of $481.0 million, before an accounting change charge of $7.0 million, in the previous year. Results for 2001 included unusual charges of $68.0 million related to the 9/11/01 terrorist attacks. In addition, results for 2001 and 2000 included special charges of $218.0 million and $82.0 million, respectively. Total revenue increased 4.1% to $7.68 billion from $7.38 billion in the prior year.

PROSPECTS: In 2001, Aon announced plans to spin off its underwriting operations to stockholders through a new company to be named Combined Specialty Group, Inc. The spin-off is scheduled for the second quarter of 2002. Meanwhile, AON's U.S. retail brokerage operations are experiencing challenges in implementing parts of its restructuring plan. The destruction of the World Trade Center, the location of Aon's largest retail brokerage office, occurred as the Company was in transition to a new operating model.

BUSINESS

AON CORPORATION is a holding company whose subsidiaries operate in three distinct segments: Insurance Brokerage and Other Services, Consulting, and Insurance Underwriting. The Insurance Brokerage and Other Services segment (59.3% of 2001 operating revenues) consists principally of Aon's retail, reinsurance, specialty and wholesale brokerage operations. The Consulting segment (12.0% of 2001 operating revenues) provides a full range of employee benefits, human resources, compensation, and change management services. The Insurance Underwriting segment (28.7% of 2001 operating revenues) is comprised of direct sales of life and accident and health, warranty, specialty and other insurance products.

ANNUAL FINANCIAL DATA

	12/31/01	12/31/00	12/31/99	12/31/98	12/31/97	12/31/96	12/31/95
Earnings Per Share	⑤ 0.73	④ 1.82	③ 1.33	2.07	1.12	① 1.10	① 1.14
Tang. Book Val. Per Share	...	...	...	...	...	4.93	4.38
Dividends Per Share	0.90	0.87	0.81	0.73	0.68	0.63	0.60
Dividend Payout %	122.6	47.8	61.1	35.4	60.7	57.3	52.1
INCOME STATEMENT (IN MILLIONS):							
Total Premium Income	2,027.0	1,921.0	1,854.0	1,706.0	1,608.9	1,526.7	1,426.5
Other Income	5,649.0	5,454.0	5,216.0	4,787.0	4,141.7	2,361.5	2,039.2
Total Revenues	7,676.0	7,375.0	7,070.0	6,493.0	5,750.6	3,888.2	3,465.7
Policyholder Benefits	1,111.0	1,037.0	973.0	896.0	842.3	789.5	698.5
Income Before Income Taxes	399.0	854.0	635.0	931.0	541.6	445.6	458.0
Income Taxes	156.0	333.0	243.0	349.0	203.1	153.8	154.0
Equity Earnings/Minority Int.	d40.0	d40.0	d40.0	d41.0	d39.7	...	...
Net Income	⑤ 203.0	④ 481.0	③ 352.0	541.0	298.8	① 291.8	① 303.7
Average Shs. Outstg. (000)	272,000	263,000	262,700	259,350	255,750	247,950	244,575
BALANCE SHEET (IN MILLIONS):							
Cash & Cash Equivalents	3,414.0	3,443.0	3,199.0	2,944.0	2,782.4	1,676.4	1,053.6
Premiums Due	7,986.0	8,230.0	7,346.0	6,543.0	6,183.1	4,555.2	2,844.3
Invst. Assets: Fixed-term	2,149.0	2,337.0	2,497.0	3,103.0	3,143.6	2,826.1	7,687.1
Invst. Assets: Loans	...	...	...	...	...	87.2	858.3
Invst. Assets: Total	6,146.0	6,019.0	6,184.0	6,452.0	5,922.1	5,212.8	10,639.1
Total Assets	22,386.0	22,251.0	21,132.0	19,688.0	18,691.2	13,722.7	19,735.8
Long-Term Obligations	1,694.0	1,798.0	1,011.0	580.0	637.1	521.2	554.3
Net Stockholders' Equity	3,521.0	3,388.0	3,051.0	3,017.0	2,822.1	2,832.9	2,673.7
Year-end Shs. Outstg. (000)	247,700	256,100	253,753	256,191	251,957	249,525	243,675
STATISTICAL RECORD:							
Return on Revenues %	2.6	6.5	5.0	8.3	5.2	7.5	8.8
Return on Equity %	5.8	14.2	11.5	17.9	10.6	10.3	11.4
Return on Assets %	0.9	2.2	1.7	2.7	1.6	2.1	1.5
Price Range	44.80-29.75	42.75-20.69	46.67-26.06	50.38-32.17	38.96-26.78	28.78-21.11	22.61-13.95
P/E Ratio	61.4-40.7	23.5-11.4	35.1-19.6	24.3-15.5	34.8-23.9	26.1-19.2	19.8-12.2
Average Yield %	2.4	2.7	2.2	1.8	2.1	2.5	3.3

Statistics are as originally reported. Adj. for stk. splits: 3-for-2, 5/99 & 5/97 ① Bef. disc. oper. gain 1996, $43.4 mill.; 1995, $99.1 mill. ② Bef. acctg. change chrg. $79.6 mill. ③ Incl. non-recurr. chrg. $313.0 mill. ④ Bef. acctg. change chrg. of $7.0 mill., but incl. special chrgs. of $82.0 mill. ⑤ Incl. unusual chrgs. $68.0 mill. & special chrgs. of $218.0 mill.

OFFICERS:
P. G. Ryan, Chmn., C.E.O.
M. D. O'Halleran, Pres., C.O.O.
H. N. Medvin, Exec. V.P., C.F.O.

INVESTOR CONTACT: Sean P. O'Neill, V.P., Fin. Rel., (312) 701-3983

PRINCIPAL OFFICE: 123 North Wacker Drive, Chicago, IL 60606

TELEPHONE NUMBER: (312) 701-3000
FAX: (312) 701-3080
WEB: www.aon.com

NO. OF EMPLOYEES: 53,000 (approx.)

SHAREHOLDERS: 11,912 (approx.)

ANNUAL MEETING: In April

INCORPORATED: DE, 1979

INSTITUTIONAL HOLDINGS:
No. of Institutions: 335
Shares Held: 158,874,257
% Held: 58.5

INDUSTRY: Accident and health insurance
(SIC: 6321)

TRANSFER AGENT(S): First Chicago Trust Company of New York, Jersey City, NJ

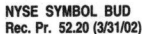

NYSE SYMBOL BUD
Rec. Pr. 52.20 (3/31/02)

ANHEUSER-BUSCH COMPANIES, INC.

YIELD 1.4%
P/E RATIO 27.6

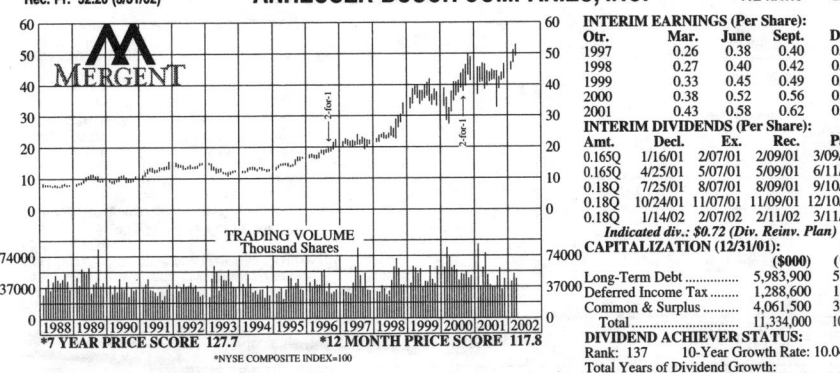

TRADING VOLUME
Thousand Shares

*7 YEAR PRICE SCORE 127.7   ***12 MONTH PRICE SCORE 117.8**

*NYSE COMPOSITE INDEX=100

INTERIM EARNINGS (Per Share):

Qtr.	Mar.	June	Sept.	Dec.
1997	0.26	0.38	0.40	0.15
1998	0.27	0.40	0.42	0.18
1999	0.33	0.45	0.49	0.21
2000	0.38	0.52	0.56	0.23
2001	0.43	0.58	0.62	0.26

INTERIM DIVIDENDS (Per Share):

Amt.	Decl.	Ex.	Rec.	Pay.
0.165Q	1/16/01	2/07/01	2/09/01	3/09/01
0.165Q	4/25/01	5/07/01	5/09/01	6/11/01
0.18Q	7/25/01	8/07/01	8/09/01	9/10/01
0.18Q	10/24/01	11/07/01	11/09/01	12/10/01
0.18Q	1/14/02	2/07/02	2/11/02	3/11/02

Indicated div.: $0.72 (Div. Reinv. Plan)

CAPITALIZATION (12/31/01):

	($000)	(%)
Long-Term Debt	5,983,900	52.8
Deferred Income Tax	1,288,600	11.4
Common & Surplus	4,061,500	35.8
Total	11,334,000	100.0

DIVIDEND ACHIEVER STATUS:
Rank: 137   10-Year Growth Rate: 10.04%
Total Years of Dividend Growth: 27

RECENT DEVELOPMENTS: For the year ended 12/31/01, net income increased 9.9% to $1.70 billion from $1.55 billion in the previous year. Results for 2001 included a pre-tax gain on the sale of SeaWorld Cleveland of $17.8 million. Net sales rose 3.3% to $12.91 billion from $12.50 billion the year before. Gross profit as a percentage of net sales was 38.4% versus 37.4% in 2000. Operating income improved 9.2% to $2.72 billion.

PROSPECTS: On 2/6/02, the Company announced the introduction of its premium flavored malt beverage, BACARDI SILVER, which is composed of Bacardi rum and citrus flavors. BUD will produce, market and exclusively distribute BACARDI SILVER. Separately, earnings per share growth is anticipated to range from 10.0% to 12.0% in 2002. BUD also expects to achieve double-digit earnings per share growth over the long-term.

BUSINESS

ANHEUSER-BUSCH COMPANIES, INC. is a diversified corporation whose chief subsidiary is Anheuser-Busch, Inc., the world's largest brewer. Beer is sold under brand names including BUDWEISER, MICHELOB, BUSCH, and NATURAL LIGHT. Additionally, theme park operations are conducted through BUD's subsidiary, Busch Entertainment Corporation, which owns nine theme parks as of 12/31/01. BUD also engages in packaging, malt and rice production, international beer, non-beer beverages, real estate development, marketing communications, and transportation services. As of 12/31/01, BUD owns approximately 50.2% of Grupo Modelo, S.A. de C.V., a Mexican brewer.

ANNUAL FINANCIAL DATA

	12/31/01	12/31/00	12/31/99	12/31/98	12/31/97	12/31/96	12/31/95
Earnings Per Share	[4] 1.89	1.69	1.47	1.27	[1] 1.18	[2] 1.14	[3] 0.86
Cash Flow Per Share	2.82	2.56	2.29	2.02	1.86	1.73	1.41
Tang. Book Val. Per Share	4.62	4.11	4.25	4.42	4.15	4.05	4.36
Dividends Per Share	0.69	0.63	0.58	0.54	0.50	0.46	0.42
Dividend Payout %	36.5	37.3	39.5	42.7	42.4	40.3	48.8
INCOME STATEMENT (IN MILLIONS):							
Total Revenues	12,911.5	12,261.8	11,703.7	11,245.8	11,066.2	10,883.7	10,340.5
Costs & Expenses	9,371.8	8,963.6	8,624.4	8,382.1	8,329.5	8,260.7	7,982.0
Depreciation & Amort.	834.5	803.5	777.0	738.4	683.7	593.9	565.6
Operating Income	2,705.2	2,494.7	2,302.3	2,125.3	2,053.0	2,029.1	1,792.9
Net Interest Inc./(Exp.)	d333.2	d313.8	d285.3	d259.7	d211.2	d187.9	d191.7
Income Before Income Taxes	2,359.8	2,179.9	2,007.6	1,852.6	1,832.5	1,892.9	1,461.7
Income Taxes	913.2	828.3	762.9	704.3	703.6	736.8	575.1
Equity Earnings/Minority Int.	240.1	200.0	157.5	85.0	50.3	...	...
Net Income	[4] 1,704.5	1,551.6	1,402.2	1,233.3	[1] 1,179.2	[2] 1,156.1	[3] 886.6
Cash Flow	2,539.0	2,355.1	2,179.2	1,971.7	1,862.9	1,750.0	1,452.2
Average Shs. Outstg. (000)	901,600	919,700	953,600	975,000	999,400	1,011,600	1,031,600
BALANCE SHEET (IN MILLIONS):							
Cash & Cash Equivalents	162.6	159.9	152.1	224.8	147.3	93.6	93.6
Total Current Assets	1,550.4	1,547.9	1,600.6	1,640.4	1,583.9	1,465.8	1,510.6
Net Property	8,390.0	8,243.8	7,964.6	7,849.0	7,750.6	7,208.2	6,763.0
Total Assets	13,862.0	13,084.5	12,640.4	12,484.3	11,727.1	10,463.6	10,590.9
Total Current Liabilities	1,732.3	1,675.7	1,987.2	1,730.3	1,500.7	1,430.9	1,242.0
Long-Term Obligations	5,983.9	5,374.5	4,880.6	4,718.6	4,365.6	3,270.9	3,270.1
Net Stockholders' Equity	4,061.5	4,128.9	3,921.5	4,216.0	4,041.8	4,029.1	4,433.9
Net Working Capital	d181.9	d127.8	d386.6	d89.9	83.2	34.9	268.6
Year-end Shs. Outstg. (000)	879,100	903,600	922,200	953,200	974,040	994,714	1,015,904
STATISTICAL RECORD:							
Operating Profit Margin %	21.0	20.3	19.7	18.9	18.6	18.6	17.3
Net Profit Margin %	13.1	12.7	12.0	11.0	10.7	10.6	8.6
Return on Equity %	42.0	37.6	35.8	29.3	29.2	28.7	20.0
Return on Assets %	12.3	11.9	11.1	9.9	10.1	11.0	8.4
Debt/Total Assets %	43.2	41.1	38.6	37.8	37.2	31.3	30.9
Price Range	46.95-32.60	49.88-27.31	42.00-32.22	34.13-21.47	24.13-19.25	22.50-16.19	17.00-12.69
P/E Ratio	24.8-17.2	29.5-16.2	28.6-21.9	27.0-17.0	20.4-16.3	19.7-14.2	19.8-14.8
Average Yield %	1.7	1.6	1.6	1.9	2.3	2.4	2.8

Statistics are as originally reported. Adj. for 2-for-1 stk. split, 9/00 & 9/96. [1] Bef. acctg. change chrge. of $10.0 mill. [2] Incl. $54.7 mill. gain fr. the sale of the St. Louis Cardinals & bef. disc. oper. gain of $33.8 mill. [3] Incl. $160.0 mill. pre-tax write off & excl. disc. oper. loss of $244.3 mill. [4] Incl. pre-tax gain of $17.8 mill.

OFFICERS:
A. A. Busch III, Chmn., Pres.
W. R. Baker, V.P., C.F.O.
J. Jacobs, Exec. V.P., C.O.O.

INVESTOR CONTACT: Carlos Ramirez, Investor Relations, (314) 577-9629

PRINCIPAL OFFICE: One Busch Place, St. Louis, MO 63118

TELEPHONE NUMBER: (314) 577-2000
FAX: (314) 577-2900
WEB: www.anheuser-busch.com
NO. OF EMPLOYEES: 23,432
SHAREHOLDERS: 57,347
ANNUAL MEETING: In April
INCORPORATED: DE, April, 1979

INSTITUTIONAL HOLDINGS:
No. of Institutions: 702
Shares Held: 525,198,743
% Held: 59.7

INDUSTRY: Malt beverages (SIC: 2082)

TRANSFER AGENT(S): Mellon Investor Services, LLC, Ridgefield Park, NJ

AMSOUTH BANCORPORATION

YIELD 4.0%
P/E RATIO 15.2

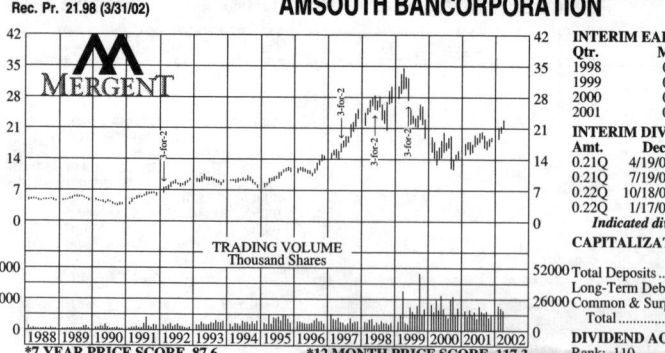

INTERIM EARNINGS (Per Share):

Qtr.	Mar.	June	Sept.	Dec.
1998	0.34	0.36	0.37	0.38
1999	0.39	0.42	0.44	d0.16
2000	0.35	0.26	d0.10	0.34
2001	0.34	0.36	0.37	0.38

INTERIM DIVIDENDS (Per Share):

Amt.	Decl.	Ex.	Rec.	Pay.
0.21Q	4/19/01	6/14/01	6/18/01	7/02/01
0.21Q	7/19/01	9/17/01	9/17/01	10/01/01
0.22Q	10/18/01	12/17/01	12/19/01	1/02/02
0.22Q	1/17/02	3/14/02	3/18/02	4/01/02

Indicated div.: $0.88 (Div. Reinv. Plan)

CAPITALIZATION (12/31/01):

	($000)	(%)
Total Deposits	26,167,017	74.3
Long-Term Debt	6,102,255	17.3
Common & Surplus	2,955,099	8.4
Total	35,224,371	100.0

TRADING VOLUME
Thousand Shares

*7 YEAR PRICE SCORE 87.6
*NYSE COMPOSITE INDEX=100
*12 MONTH PRICE SCORE 117.3

DIVIDEND ACHIEVER STATUS:
Rank: 110   10-Year Growth Rate: 11.44%
Total Years of Dividend Growth: 31

RECENT DEVELOPMENTS: For the year ended 12/31/01, net income advanced 63.0% to $536.3 million compared with $329.1 million in the previous year. Earnings for 2000 included merger-related costs of $110.2 million. Net interest income rose 1.1% to $1.39 billion. Provision for loan losses dropped 17.8% to $187.1 million. Non-interest revenues grew 11.8% to $748.2 million from $669.5 million in the previous year. Non-interest expense, excluding merger-related costs, declined 5.6% to $1.19 billion.

PROSPECTS: The Company should continue to perform well, supported by a wider net interest margin, improved credit quality, and growing low-cost deposits and home equity loans. Separately, on 12/19/01, the Company completed the upgrade of its Internet Banking software. More than 322,000 new users have signed up since the end of February 2001, when the bank began offering free Internet Banking for life, bringing the Company's total number of on-line customers to more than 450,000.

BUSINESS

AMSOUTH BANCORPORATION is a regional bank holding company headquartered in Birmingham, Alabama. As of 12/31/01, ASO had assets of $38.60 billion and operated 600 branch banking offices and more than 1,200 ATMs in the following southeastern states: Alabama, Florida, Tennessee, Mississippi, Georgia, and Louisiana. ASO's affiliates, AmSouth N.A., AmSouth Bank of Florida, AmSouth Bank of Tennessee, AmSouth Bank of Georgia and AmSouth Bank of Alabama, AmSouth Investment Services and AmSouth Leasing Corporation, provide a full line of traditional and non-traditional financial services including consumer and commercial banking, mortgage lending, trust services and investment management. On 10/1/99, ASO acquired First American Corporation.

ANNUAL FINANCIAL DATA

	12/31/01	12/31/00	12/31/99	12/31/98	12/31/97	12/31/96	12/31/95
Earnings Per Share	1.45	⑤ 0.86	④ 0.86	③ 1.45	1.21	② 0.96	① 0.89
Tang. Book Val. Per Share	8.14	7.53	7.56	8.05	7.64	7.38	7.16
Dividends Per Share	0.84	0.80	0.67	0.53	0.50	0.47	0.45
Dividend Payout %	57.9	93.0	78.3	36.9	41.0	49.5	50.7
INCOME STATEMENT (IN MILLIONS):							
Total Interest Income	2,634.5	3,070.4	2,932.8	1,462.5	1,377.8	1,353.8	1,275.1
Total Interest Expense	1,239.7	1,691.3	1,424.8	763.6	701.5	701.4	679.4
Net Interest Income	1,394.9	1,379.1	1,507.9	699.0	676.3	652.4	595.7
Provision for Loan Losses	187.1	227.6	165.6	58.1	67.4	65.2	40.1
Non-Interest Income	748.2	669.5	847.6	346.6	266.0	235.3	231.8
Non-Interest Expense	1,185.4	1,366.4	1,648.5	582.1	526.2	534.2	512.1
Income Before Taxes	770.6	454.6	541.4	405.3	348.7	288.3	275.2
Net Income	536.3	⑤ 329.1	④ 340.5	③ 262.7	226.2	② 182.7	① 175.0
Average Shs. Outstg. (000)	370,948	384,677	396,515	181,922	186,179	191,042	196,634
BALANCE SHEET (IN MILLIONS):							
Cash & Due from Banks	1,441.6	1,278.7	1,563.3	619.6	658.5	648.5	651.6
Securities Avail. for Sale	4,842.5	1,920.9	6,016.7	3,033.5	2,509.1	2,294.4	2,482.8
Total Loans & Leases	25,852.2	25,088.2	26,436.4	12,869.9	12,342.8	12,168.6	11,819.8
Allowance for Credit Losses	1,091.3	852.2	533.1	283.7	284.4	267.4	255.5
Net Loans & Leases	24,760.9	24,236.0	25,903.3	12,586.2	12,058.5	11,901.2	11,564.8
Total Assets	38,600.4	38,936.0	43,406.6	19,794.1	18,622.3	18,407.3	17,738.8
Total Deposits	26,167.0	26,623.3	27,912.4	13,283.8	12,945.2	12,467.6	13,408.8
Long-Term Obligations	6,102.3	5,883.4	5,603.5	3,239.8	1,633.2	1,435.7	447.8
Total Liabilities	35,645.3	36,122.6	40,447.3	18,474.1	17,237.0	17,011.4	16,355.3
Net Stockholders' Equity	2,955.1	2,813.4	2,959.2	1,427.6	1,385.2	1,395.8	1,383.5
Year-end Shs. Outstg. (000)	363,035	373,807	391,374	177,377	181,208	189,081	193,269
STATISTICAL RECORD:							
Return on Equity %	18.1	11.7	11.5	18.4	16.3	13.1	12.6
Return on Assets %	1.4	0.8	0.8	1.3	1.2	1.0	1.0
Equity/Assets %	7.7	7.0	6.8	7.2	7.4	7.6	7.8
Non-Int. Exp./Tot. Inc. %	55.3	66.7	70.0	55.7	55.8	66.0	61.9
Price Range	20.24-15.00	20.06-11.69	34.59-18.75	30.42-20.46	25.36-14.00	15.07-10.19	12.26-7.63
P/E Ratio	14.0-10.3	23.3-13.6	40.2-21.8	21.0-14.1	20.9-11.5	15.8-10.6	13.8-8.6
Average Yield %	4.8	5.0	2.5	2.1	2.5	3.8	4.3

Statistics are as originally reported. Adj. for 3-for-2 splits 5/99, 4/98, 4/97. ① Incl. pre-tax gain on the sale of 3rd party mtg. servicing portfolio to G.E. Capital Services, Inc. & $22.0 mill. in add'l. exps. rel. to consol. & workforce reduction. ② Incl. SAIF pre-tax chrg. of $24.2 mill. ③ Incl. $28.0 mill. gain fr. sale of assets. ④ Incl. net gain fr. sale of businesses of $8.6 mill. & merger-rel. chrgs. of $301.4 mill. ⑤ Incl. pre-tax merger-rel. costs of $110.2 mill. & a gain of $538,000 on the sale of businesses.

OFFICERS:
C. D. Ritter, Chmn., Pres., C.E.O.
S. D. Gibson, Vice-Chmn., C.F.O.
S. A. Yoder, Exec. V.P., Gen. Couns., Sec.
INVESTOR CONTACT: M. List Underwood, Jr., Exec. V.P.-Corp. Fin., (205) 801-0265
PRINCIPAL OFFICE: 1900 Fifth Avenue North, Birmingham, AL 35203

TELEPHONE NUMBER: (205) 320-7151
FAX: (205) 326-4072
WEB: www.amsouth.com
NO. OF EMPLOYEES: 11,900 (approx.)
SHAREHOLDERS: 34,632 (approx.)
ANNUAL MEETING: In Apr.
INCORPORATED: DE, Nov., 1970

INSTITUTIONAL HOLDINGS:
No. of Institutions: 310
Shares Held: 126,847,984
% Held: 35.0
INDUSTRY: State commercial banks (SIC: 6022)
TRANSFER AGENT(S): The Bank of New York, New York, NY

AMERICAN WATER WORKS COMPANY, INC.

YIELD 2.2%
P/E RATIO 26.9

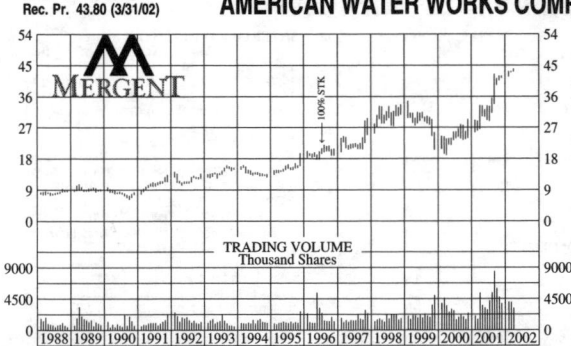

TRADING VOLUME
Thousand Shares

*7 YEAR PRICE SCORE 124.8   *12 MONTH PRICE SCORE 117.5

*NYSE COMPOSITE INDEX=100

INTERIM EARNINGS (Per Share):

Qtr.	Mar.	June	Sept.	Dec.
1998	0.26	0.42	0.57	0.33
1999	0.23	0.33	0.54	0.33
2000	0.27	0.45	0.51	0.38
2001	0.24	0.50	0.56	0.33

INTERIM DIVIDENDS (Per Share):

Amt.	Decl.	Ex.	Rec.	Pay.
0.235Q	7/03/01	7/25/01	7/27/01	8/15/01
0.235Q	10/04/01	10/24/01	10/26/01	11/15/01
0.245Q	1/03/02	1/23/02	1/25/02	2/15/02
0.245Q	4/04/02	4/24/02	4/26/02	5/15/02

Indicated div.: $0.98 (Div. Reinv. Plan)

CAPITALIZATION (12/31/01):

	($000)	(%)
Long-Term Debt	2,550,019	51.7
Deferred Income Tax	624,449	12.7
Common & Surplus	1,758,018	35.6
Total	4,932,486	100.0

DIVIDEND ACHIEVER STATUS:
Rank: 173   10-Year Growth Rate: 8.13%
Total Years of Dividend Growth: 26

RECENT DEVELOPMENTS: For the year ended 12/31/01, net income increased slightly to $161.5 million compared with $161.1 million in 2000. Results for 2001 included a $10.0 million charge associated with AWK's proposed acquisition by RWE AG, and a $4.8 million gain on the sale of water assets serving the City of Salisbury, MA. Operating revenues advanced 6.5% to $1.44 billion versus $1.35 billion a year earlier.

PROSPECTS: Completion of the terms of the RWE AG acquisition agreement, which was approved by AWK's shareholders on 1/17/02, is anticipated in 2003. Also in January, AWK completed the six-state acquisition of the water and wastewater assets of Citizens Communication Company, which was formerly known as Citizens Utility Company. The acquisition adds 300,000 more customers and $140.0 million in additional annual revenue.

BUSINESS

AMERICAN WATER WORKS COMPANY, INC., through its regulated and unregulated subsidiaries provides water and wastewater service in 28 states and three Canadian Provinces. As public utilities, the regulated subsidiaries function under rules and regulations prescribed by state regulatory commissions. AWK provides water and wastewater management services through its unregulated subsidiary, American Water Services. In addition, American Water Resources is a wholly-owned subsidiary whose function is to primarily invest in water and wastewater related products and services. As of 12/31/01, AWK maintained 2.6 million water customers and 44,000 wastewater customers.

ANNUAL FINANCIAL DATA

	12/31/01	12/31/00	12/31/99	12/31/98	12/31/97	12/31/96	12/31/95
Earnings Per Share	③ 1.61	1.61	② 1.40	1.58	1.45	1.31	① 1.32
Cash Flow Per Share	3.64	3.41	3.11	2.88	2.68	2.62	
Tang. Book Val. Per Share	16.19	16.92	15.85	15.32	14.28	13.49	12.07
Dividends Per Share	0.94	0.90	0.86	0.82	0.76	0.70	0.64
Dividend Payout %	58.4	55.9	61.4	51.9	52.4	53.4	48.5
INCOME STATEMENT (IN MILLIONS):							
Total Revenues	1,438.9	1,350.6	1,260.9	1,017.8	954.2	894.6	802.8
Costs & Expenses	778.1	717.9	675.6	528.1	507.8	498.7	471.6
Depreciation & Amort.	201.2	176.6	165.6	129.8	112.5	101.9	87.0
Operating Income	459.6	456.2	419.6	359.9	333.9	294.0	244.3
Net Interest Inc./(Exp.)	d191.2	d188.7	d170.4	d150.5	d142.7	d133.1	d108.7
Income Taxes	110.3	105.3	91.4	83.3	74.7	63.8	
Net Income	③ 161.5	161.1	② 138.9	131.0	119.1	101.7	① 92.1
Cash Flow	362.1	333.9	300.6	256.8	227.7	199.6	175.0
Average Shs. Outstg. (000)	99,465	97,988	96,544	80,298	79,144	74,609	66,764
BALANCE SHEET (IN MILLIONS):							
Gross Property	6,945.9	6,554.5	6,143.7	4,945.0	4,527.7	4,188.9	3,510.6
Accumulated Depreciation	1,418.1	1,276.4	1,152.6	848.5	755.4	682.8	590.8
Net Property	5,642.7	5,371.5	5,084.5	4,153.2	3,828.1	3,560.1	2,962.6
Total Assets	6,607.1	6,134.8	5,952.2	4,708.3	4,314.3	4,032.2	3,403.1
Long-Term Obligations	2,550.0	2,271.2	2,393.1	2,106.0	1,870.8	1,716.4	1,384.6
Net Stockholders' Equity	1,758.0	1,669.7	1,542.3	1,239.2	1,142.4	1,057.9	818.9
Year-end Shs. Outstg. (000)	100,014	98,691	97,304	80,895	79,993	78,421	67,826
STATISTICAL RECORD:							
Operating Profit Margin %	31.9	33.8	33.3	35.4	35.0	32.9	30.4
Net Profit Margin %	11.2	11.9	11.0	12.9	12.5	11.4	11.5
Net Inc./Net Property %	2.9	3.0	2.7	3.2	3.1	2.9	3.1
Net Inc./Tot. Capital %	3.3	3.5	3.0	3.4	3.4	3.1	3.5
Return on Equity %	9.2	9.5	8.9	10.4	10.3	9.5	11.0
Accum. Depr./Gross Prop. %	20.4	19.5	18.8	17.2	16.7	16.3	16.8
Price Range	42.50-25.50	29.38-18.94	34.75-20.50	33.75-25.25	29.69-19.88	22.00-17.75	19.63-13.38
P/E Ratio	26.4-15.8	18.2-11.8	24.8-14.6	21.4-16.0	20.5-13.7	16.8-13.5	14.9-10.1
Average Yield %	2.8	3.7	3.1	2.8	3.1	3.5	3.9

Statistics are as originally reported. Adj. for stk. split: 2-for-1, 8/96 ① Incl. non-recurr. cr. of $3.9 mill. ($0.06/sh.) ② Incl. after-tax nonrecurr. chrg. of $20.5 mill. ③ Incl. acquisition exp. of $10.0 mill. and a gain of $4.8 mill. on the sale of Salisbury.

OFFICERS:
M. Ware, Chmn.
A. P. Terracciano, Vice-Chmn.
J. J. Barr, Pres., C.E.O.
E. C. Wolf, V.P., C.F.O.

INVESTOR CONTACT: James E. Harrison, VP, Investor Relations, (856) 346-8207

PRINCIPAL OFFICE: 1025 Laurel Oak Rd., Voorhees, NJ 08043

TELEPHONE NUMBER: (856) 346-8200
FAX: (856) 346-8300
WEB: www.amwater.com

NO. OF EMPLOYEES: 6,400

SHAREHOLDERS: 38,665

ANNUAL MEETING: In May

INCORPORATED: DE, Aug., 1936

INSTITUTIONAL HOLDINGS:
No. of Institutions: 224
Shares Held: 35,144,101
% Held: 35.1

INDUSTRY: Water supply (SIC: 4941)

TRANSFER AGENT(S): BankBoston N.A., Boston, MA

AMERICAN STATES WATER COMPANY

YIELD 3.7%
P/E RATIO 17.6

INTERIM EARNINGS (Per Share):

	Mar.	June	Sept.	Dec.
1997	0.14	0.34	0.67	0.41
1998	0.20	0.31	0.71	0.40
1999	0.33	0.49	0.74	0.23
2000	0.32	0.43	0.86	0.30
2001	0.30	0.49	0.93	0.28

INTERIM DIVIDENDS (Per Share):

Amt.	Decl.	Ex.	Rec.	Pay.
0.325Q	4/23/01	5/04/01	5/08/01	6/01/01
0.325Q	7/27/01	8/03/01	8/07/01	9/01/01
0.325Q	10/30/01	11/02/01	11/06/01	12/01/01
0.325Q	2/05/02	2/06/02	2/08/02	3/01/02

Indicated div.: $1.30 (Div. Reinv. Plan)

CAPITALIZATION (12/31/01):

	($000)	(%)
Long-Term Debt	245,692	25.9
Deferred Income Tax	55,217	5.8
Redeemable Pfd. Stock	280	0.0
Preferred Stock	1,600	0.2
Common & Surplus	647,536	68.1
Total	950,325	100.0

DIVIDEND ACHIEVER STATUS:
Rank: 280   10-Year Growth Rate: 1.68%
Total Years of Dividend Growth: 48

TRADING VOLUME
Thousand Shares

*7 YEAR PRICE SCORE 111.3   *12 MONTH PRICE SCORE 104.4

*NYSE COMPOSITE INDEX=100

RECENT DEVELOPMENTS: For the year ended 12/31/01, net income increased 13.1% to $20.5 million compared with $18.1 million in 2000. Operating revenues advanced 7.4% to $197.5 million from $184.0 million a year earlier, reflecting various rate increases effective during the year at its SCW unit that were partially offset by a 3.4% decline in water sales, and the inclusion in consolidated results of the acquisition of Chaparral City Water Company in Arizona.

PROSPECTS: Looking ahead, AWR will attempt to renegotiate its existing power supply contracts to lower its costs further. The Company should benefit from a 2/4/02 ruling by the California Supreme Court regarding the various water quality-related lawsuits in which it is involved, as the court judged that water that meets state and federal standards should not form the basis of claims against state-regulated water utilities.

BUSINESS

AMERICAN STATES WATER CO. is a public utility engaged principally in the purchase, production, distribution, and sale of water, and distribution of electricity through its primary subsidiary Southern California Water Company (SCW). SCW is organized into three water service regions and one electric customer service area operating within 75 communities in 10 counties in the State of California and provides water service in 21 customer service areas. As of 12/31/01, SCW served 246,799 water customers and 21,747 electric customers. Through its American States Utility Services (ASUS) subsidiary, the Company contracts to lease, operate and maintain government-owned water and wastewater systems and to provide other services to local governments to assist them in the operation and maintenance of their water and wastewater systems. ASUS has approximately 90,000 accounts under contract. Through its Chaparral City Water Company, the Company serves approximately 11,353 customers in the town of Fountain Hills, Arizona and a portion of the City of Scottsdale, Arizona.

ANNUAL FINANCIAL DATA

	12/31/01	12/31/00	12/31/99	12/31/98	12/31/97	12/31/96	12/31/95
Earnings Per Share	2.00	1.91	1.79	1.62	1.56	1.69	1.54
Cash Flow Per Share	3.77	3.54	3.39	3.06	2.83	3.01	2.69
Tang. Book Val. Per Share	64.24	55.96	54.37	48.16	46.82	45.33	44.96
Dividends Per Share	1.30	1.285	1.28	1.26	1.25	1.23	1.21
Dividend Payout %	65.0	67.3	71.5	77.8	79.8	72.5	78.2
INCOME STATEMENT (IN THOUSANDS):							
Total Revenues	197,514	183,960	173,421	148,060	153,755	151,529	129,813
Costs & Expenses	142,871	136,314	130,543	110,120	118,910	117,711	99,392
Depreciation & Amort.	17,951	15,339	14,364	12,929	11,387	10,389	9,033
Operating Income	36,692	32,307	28,514	25,061	23,458	23,429	21,388
Net Interest Inc./(Exp.)	d15,735	d14,122	d12,945	d11,207	d10,157	d10,500	d9,559
Income Before Income Taxes	20,447	18,086	16,101	14,573	14,059	13,460	12,165
Net Income	20,447	18,086	16,101	14,573	14,059	13,460	12,165
Cash Flow	38,314	33,339	30,377	27,412	25,354	23,755	21,102
Average Shs. Outstg.	10,171	9,411	8,958	8,958	8,957	7,891	7,845
BALANCE SHEET (IN THOUSANDS):							
Cash & Cash Equivalents	30,496	5,808	2,189	620	4,186	3,783	343
Total Current Assets	87,789	52,480	44,340	39,288	44,494	43,762	42,970
Net Property	539,842	509,096	449,595	414,753	383,623	357,776	334,968
Total Assets	683,764	616,646	533,181	484,671	457,074	430,922	406,255
Total Current Liabilities	63,636	80,217	54,965	63,768	56,180	44,688	46,541
Long-Term Obligations	245,692	176,452	167,363	120,809	115,286	107,190	107,455
Net Stockholders' Equity	649,136	565,418	488,615	433,007	421,032	404,402	354,327
Net Working Capital	24,153	d27,737	d10,625	d24,480	d11,686	d926	d3,571
Year-end Shs. Outstg.	10,080	10,076	8,958	8,958	8,958	8,886	7,845
STATISTICAL RECORD:							
Operating Profit Margin %	18.6	17.6	16.4	16.9	15.3	15.5	16.5
Net Profit Margin %	10.4	9.8	9.3	9.8	9.1	8.9	9.4
Return on Equity %	3.1	3.2	3.3	3.4	3.3	3.3	3.4
Return on Assets %	3.0	2.9	3.0	3.0	3.1	3.1	3.0
Debt/Total Assets %	35.9	28.6	31.4	24.9	25.2	24.9	26.5
Price Range	39.60-28.50	37.94-25.00	39.75-22.19	29.25-21.13	25.63-20.25	24.13-18.75	21.00-15.75
P/E Ratio	19.8-14.2	19.9-13.1	22.2-12.4	18.1-13.0	16.4-13.0	14.3-11.1	13.6-10.2
Average Yield %	3.8	4.1	4.1	5.0	5.4	5.7	6.6

Statistics are as originally reported.

OFFICERS:
L. E. Ross, Chmn.
F. E. Wicks, Pres., C.E.O.
M. Harris III, V.P., C.F.O., Treas., Sec.

INVESTOR CONTACT: McClellan Harris, III, (909) 394-3600 ext. 705

PRINCIPAL OFFICE: 630 East Foothill Blvd., San Dimas, CA 91773-9016

TELEPHONE NUMBER: (909) 394-3600
FAX: (909) 394-0711
WEB: www.aswater.com
NO. OF EMPLOYEES: 492 (avg.)
SHAREHOLDERS: 3,404 (approx.)
ANNUAL MEETING: In Apr.
INCORPORATED: CA, Dec., 1929

INSTITUTIONAL HOLDINGS:
No. of Institutions: 96
Shares Held: 3,992,375
% Held: 39.6

INDUSTRY: Water supply (SIC: 4941)

TRANSFER AGENT(S): Mellon Investor Services, L.L.C., Ridgefield Park, NJ

AMERICAN NATIONAL INSURANCE COMPANY

YIELD	3.1%
P/E RATIO	38.6

TRADING VOLUME
Thousand Shares

1988 1989 1990 1991 1992 1993 1994 1995 1996 1997 1998 1999 2000 2001 2002

*7 YEAR PRICE SCORE 92.4   ***12 MONTH PRICE SCORE 112.3**

*NYSE COMPOSITE INDEX=100

INTERIM EARNINGS (Per Share):

Qtr.	Mar.	June	Sept.	Dec.
1997	2.37	1.66	2.10	3.25
1998	2.50	1.78	1.54	1.63
1999	4.20	1.55	1.73	2.60
2000	2.36	1.56	1.45	d0.08
2001	1.39	1.56	d0.17	d0.33

INTERIM DIVIDENDS (Per Share):

Amt.	Decl.	Ex.	Rec.	Pay.
0.73Q	2/22/01	2/28/01	3/02/01	3/16/01
0.73Q	4/27/01	5/30/01	6/01/01	6/15/01
0.73Q	7/26/01	9/05/01	9/07/01	9/21/01
0.74Q	10/25/01	12/05/01	12/07/01	12/21/01
0.74Q	12/14/01	2/27/02	3/01/02	3/15/02

Indicated div.: $2.96 (Div. Reinv. Plan)

CAPITALIZATION (12/31/00):

	($000)	(%)
Deferred Income Tax	148,691	4.7
Common & Surplus	3,023,657	95.3
Total	3,172,348	100.0

DIVIDEND ACHIEVER STATUS:
Rank: 229   10-Year Growth Rate: 5.23%
Total Years of Dividend Growth: 28

RECENT DEVELOPMENTS: For the year ended 12/31/01, net income fell 53.7% to $64.9 million from $140.2 million in the previous year. Earnings for 2001 were negatively affected by a reserve of $21.1 million, net of reinsurance, for potential claims associated with the terrorist attacks on 9/11/01, premium deficiency reserves of $23.4 million on long term care products and certain individual medical insurance products, continued start-up costs of the Mexican operations of $6.5 million and losses in the property and casualty business of $6.4 million. Earnings for 2001 and

2000 included realized investment gains of $4.2 million and $15.0 million, respectively. Revenues increased 16.3% to $2.13 billion from $1.83 billion in the prior year. The property and casualty operations are operating at a loss; however, the corrective actions implemented in the health division are beginning to positively affect earnings. Meanwhile, ANAT's measure for life and annuity weighted premium sales increased 24.5% year-over-year versus its target increase of 23.3%.

BUSINESS

AMERICAN NATIONAL INSUR-ANCE COMPANY serves more than 3.3 million policy holders in 49 states, the District of Columbia, Mexico, Puerto Rico, Guam, American Samoa and Western Europe. ANAT offers a broad line of insurance coverages including: life, health, disability and annuities; group life and health; personal lines property and casualty and credit insurance. ANAT also offers investment and advisory services through its subsidiary broker-dealer, Securities Management and Research, Inc. ANAT's major insurance subsidiary companies include American National Life Insurance Co. of Texas, American National Property and Casualty Co., American National de Mexico, Garden State Life Insurance Co., Farm Family Life Insurance Co., Farm Family Casualty Insurance Co., United Farm Family Insurance Co. and Standard Life and Accident Insurance Co.

ANNUAL FINANCIAL DATA

	p12/31/01	12/31/00	12/31/99	12/31/98	12/31/97	12/31/96	12/31/95
Earnings Per Share	① 2.45	5.29	10.07	7.45	9.38	8.14	7.79
Tang. Book Val. Per Share	...	114.19	115.68	110.07	102.17	93.43	87.66
Dividends Per Share	2.93	2.86	2.78	2.70	2.62	2.54	2.40
Dividend Payout %	119.6	54.1	27.6	36.2	27.9	31.2	30.8
INCOME STATEMENT (IN MILLIONS):							
Total Premium Income	...	1,292.0	1,230.9	1,193.7	1,140.5	1,034.9	981.1
Net Investment Income	...	479.1	473.9	475.2	472.9	435.7	386.9
Other Income	...	63.4	184.7	75.7	126.5	79.4	102.9
Total Revenues	2,134.4	1,834.5	1,889.6	1,744.7	1,739.9	1,550.0	1,471.0
Policyholder Benefits	...	963.5	866.1	828.6	895.9	831.1	749.0
Income Before Income Taxes	...	206.9	388.7	273.9	373.0	305.5	306.3
Income Taxes	...	66.8	122.1	76.5	124.7	89.9	99.9
Net Income	① 64.9	140.2	266.6	197.4	248.4	215.6	206.4
Average Shs. Outstg. (000)	26,479	26,479	26,479	26,479	26,479	26,479	26,479
BALANCE SHEET (IN MILLIONS):							
Cash & Cash Equivalents	...	1,046.6	947.9	833.4	732.6	547.3	511.7
Premiums Due	...	572.2	395.9	328.3	274.9	223.6	197.1
Invst. Assets: Fixed-term	...	3,534.5	3,636.8	3,566.0	3,605.9	3,430.7	2,966.9
Invst. Assets: Equities	...	844.9	963.3	1,051.9	882.9	754.0	710.7
Invst. Assets: Loans	...	1,318.6	1,326.6	1,321.8	1,403.9	1,401.9	1,227.2
Invst. Assets: Total	...	7,148.2	7,372.9	7,263.6	7,082.8	6,661.8	5,919.8
Total Assets	...	9,270.4	9,090.5	8,815.7	8,483.0	7,988.5	7,140.0
Net Stockholders' Equity	...	3,023.7	3,063.1	2,914.6	2,705.4	2,473.9	2,321.1
Year-end Shs. Outstg. (000)	...	26,479	26,479	26,479	26,479	26,479	26,479
STATISTICAL RECORD:							
Return on Revenues %	3.0	7.6	14.1	11.3	14.3	13.9	14.0
Return on Equity %	...	4.6	8.7	6.8	9.2	8.7	8.9
Return on Assets %	...	1.5	2.9	2.2	2.9	2.7	2.9
Price Range	84.10-64.50	73.50-49.00	89.38-60.63	100.88-73.00	105.00-73.00	75.50-63.00	66.75-45.50
P/E Ratio	34.3-26.3	13.9-9.3	8.9-6.0	14.7-9.8	11.2-7.8	9.3-7.7	8.6-5.8
Average Yield %	3.9	4.7	3.7	3.0	2.9	3.7	4.3

Statistics are as originally reported. ① Incl. chrgs. of $21.1 mill. related to terrorist attacks on 9/11/01 & start-up costs of $6.5 mill.

OFFICERS:
R. L. Moody, Chmn., C.E.O.
G. R. Ferdinandtsen, Pres., C.O.O.
V. E. Soier Jr., V.P., Sec., Treas.

INVESTOR CONTACT: Vince Soler, (409) 766-6447

PRINCIPAL OFFICE: One Moody Plaza, Galveston, TX 77550-7999

TELEPHONE NUMBER: (409) 763-4661
FAX: (409) 766-6502
WEB: www.anico.com
NO. OF EMPLOYEES: 1,500
SHAREHOLDERS: 1,557 (approx.)
ANNUAL MEETING: In April
INCORPORATED: TX, March, 1905

INSTITUTIONAL HOLDINGS:
No. of Institutions: 85
Shares Held: 4,578,521
% Held: 17.3

INDUSTRY: Life insurance (SIC: 6311)

TRANSFER AGENT(S): Mellon Investor Services, South Hackensack, NJ

AMERICAN INTERNATIONAL GROUP, INC.

YIELD 0.2%
P/E RATIO 35.2

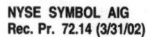

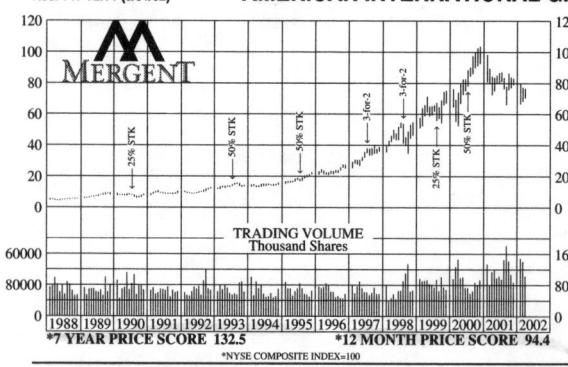

TRADING VOLUME
Thousand Shares

| 1988 | 1989 | 1990 | 1991 | 1992 | 1993 | 1994 | 1995 | 1996 | 1997 | 1998 | 1999 | 2000 | 2001 | 2002 |

*7 YEAR PRICE SCORE 132.5   ***12 MONTH PRICE SCORE 94.4**
*NYSE COMPOSITE INDEX=100

INTERIM EARNINGS (Per Share):

Qtr.	Mar.	June	Sept.	Dec.
1998	0.36	0.38	0.38	0.41
1999	0.41	0.67	0.54	0.56
2000	0.57	0.90	0.60	0.64
2001	0.70	0.50	0.15	0.70

INTERIM DIVIDENDS (Per Share):

Amt.	Decl.	Ex.	Rec.	Pay.
0.042Q	5/16/01	8/07/01	8/09/01	9/14/01
0.042Q	9/19/01	12/05/01	12/07/01	12/21/01
0.042Q	11/14/01	2/27/02	3/01/02	3/15/02
0.042Q	3/13/02	6/05/02	6/07/02	6/14/02

Indicated div.: $0.17

CAPITALIZATION (12/31/01):

	($000)	(%)
Long-Term Debt	37,447,000	40.1
Minority Interest	1,509,000	1.6
Redeemable Pfd. Stock	2,202,000	2.4
Common & Surplus	52,150,000	55.9
Total	93,308,000	100.0

DIVIDEND ACHIEVER STATUS:
Rank: 97   10-Year Growth Rate: 12.30%
Total Years of Dividend Growth: 16

RECENT DEVELOPMENTS: For the year ended 12/31/01, earnings were $5.50 billion, before an accounting charge of $136.2 million, versus $6.64 billion in 2001. Results for 2001 and 2000 included after-tax acquisition and related charges of $1.38 billion and $207.0 million, respectively, and realized capital losses of $541.7 million in 2001 and $214.4 million in 2000. Results for 2001 also included after-tax losses of $533.0 million resulting from the events of 9/11/01. Total revenues rose 9.9% to $55.46 billion. Comparisons were made with restated prior-year results.

PROSPECTS: Earnings are benefiting from continued international growth and the integration of recently acquired American General Corporation. Meanwhile, during the fourth quarter of 2001, the Company announced that the Chinese government will allow the Company to establish, operate and own insurance operations in four cities: Beijing, Suzhou, Dongguan, and Jiangmen. Separately, on 1/20/02, the Company announced the termination of its proposed investment in three affiliates of the Hyundai Group of Korea.

BUSINESS

AMERICAN INTERNATIONAL GROUP, INC. is a U.S.-based international insurance and financial services organization and an underwriter of commercial and industrial insurance in the United States. AIG's global businesses also include financial services and asset management, including aircraft leasing, financial products, trading and market making, consumer finance, institutional, retail and direct investment fund asset management, real estate investment management, and retirement savings products. Major insurance subsidiaries are: American Home Assurance Co., National Union Fire Insurance Co. of Pittsburgh, PA., and New Hampshire Insurance Co. On 1/1/99, AIG acquired SunAmerica Inc. for $18.00 billion. On 8/28/01, the Company acquired American General Corporation for approximately $23.00 billion.

ANNUAL FINANCIAL DATA

	12/31/01	12/31/00	12/31/99	12/31/98	12/31/97	12/31/96	12/31/95
Earnings Per Share	☐ 2.07	2.41	2.15	1.90	1.68	1.46	1.26
Tang. Book Val. Per Share	19.94	16.98	14.33	13.78	12.20	11.13	9.91
Dividends Per Share	0.16	0.14	0.13	0.11	0.10	0.09	0.08
Dividend Payout %	7.6	5.8	5.9	5.9	6.0	6.0	6.1
INCOME STATEMENT (IN MILLIONS)							
Total Premium Income	38,608.0	31,017.0	27,486.0	24,345.0	22,346.7	20,833.1	19,443.9
Other Income	16,851.0	11,423.0	10,265.0	6,507.0	5,600.7	5,041.2	4,386.1
Total Revenues	55,459.0	42,440.0	37,751.0	30,852.0	27,947.4	25,874.3	23,829.9
Policyholder Benefits	13,863.0	7,186.0	6,919.0	6,036.0	5,607.0	5,451.1	4,936.7
Income Before Income Taxes	8,139.0	8,349.0	7,512.0	5,472.0	4,617.2	3,957.1	3,420.5
Income Taxes	2,339.0	2,458.0	2,219.0	1,594.0	1,366.6	1,116.0	955.5
Equity Earnings/Minority Int.	d301.0	d255.0	d238.0	d112.0	81.7	56.1	45.4
Net Income	☐ 5,499.0	5,636.0	5,055.0	3,766.0	3,332.3	2,897.3	2,510.4
Average Shs. Outstg. (000)	2,650,000	2,343,000	2,350,500	1,978,125	1,982,768	1,987,221	1,999,780
BALANCE SHEET (IN MILLIONS)							
Cash & Cash Equivalents	65,150.0	53,692.0	43,995.0	36,784.0	28,972.3	22,963.9	19,285.6
Premiums Due	60,594.0	42,012.0	37,898.0	35,652.0	33,109.0	29,937.1	29,610.3
Invst. Assets: Fixed-term	200,616.0	102,010.0	90,142.0	61,906.0	51,326.7	48,148.0	42,441.1
Invst. Assets: Equities	6,188.0	6,125.0	6,002.0	5,565.0	5,209.3	5,989.6	5,294.9
Invst. Assets: Loans	18,092.0	12,243.0	12,134.0	8,247.0	7,919.8	7,876.8	7,860.5
Invst. Assets: Total	297,855.0	173,524.0	152,204.0	114,526.0	94,970.6	87,696.9	76,934.5
Total Assets	492,982.0	306,577.0	268,238.0	194,398.0	163,970.7	148,431.0	134,136.4
Long-Term Obligations	37,447.0	20,672.0	2,344.0	1,620.0	13,885.4	13,299.3	9,915.3
Net Stockholders' Equity	52,150.0	39,619.0	33,306.0	27,131.0	24,001.1	22,044.2	19,827.1
Year-end Shs. Outstg. (000)	2,615,432	2,332,713	2,323,692	1,968,750	1,967,394	1,980,454	2,000,464
STATISTICAL RECORD:							
Return on Revenues %	9.9	13.3	13.4	12.2	11.9	11.2	10.5
Return on Equity %	10.5	14.2	15.2	13.9	13.9	13.1	12.7
Return on Assets %	1.1	1.8	1.9	1.9	2.0	2.0	1.9
Price Range	98.3-66.00	103.75-52.38	75.25-51.00	54.74-34.60	40.02-25.25	27.59-20.89	22.14-15.19
P/E Ratio	47.5-31.9	43.0-21.7	35.0-23.7	28.7-18.2	23.8-15.0	18.9-14.3	18.0-12.1
Average Yield %	0.2	0.2	0.2	0.3	0.3	0.4	0.4

Statistics are as originally reported. Adj. for stk. splits: 25% div., 7/30/99; 3-for-2, 7/98, 7/97 ☐ Bef. acctg. change chrg. $136.2 mill.; Incl. after-tax acquisition chrgs. $1.38 bill.; a realized capital loss $541.7 mill. & after-tax loss of $533.0 mill. related to the terrorist attacks on 9/11/01.

OFFICERS:
M. R. Greenberg, Chmn., C.E.O.
T. R. Tizzio, Sr. Vice-Chmn.
E. E. Matthews, Vice-Chmn.
INVESTOR CONTACT: Investor Relations, (212) 770-7000
PRINCIPAL OFFICE: 70 Pine Street, New York, NY 10270

TELEPHONE NUMBER: (212) 770-7000
FAX: (212) 344-6828
WEB: www.aig.com
NO. OF EMPLOYEES: 81,000 (approx.)
SHAREHOLDERS: 59,000 (approx.)
ANNUAL MEETING: In May
INCORPORATED: DE, June, 1967

INSTITUTIONAL HOLDINGS:
No. of Institutions: 1,222
Shares Held: 1,531,738,125
% Held: 58.6
INDUSTRY: Fire, marine, and casualty insurance (SIC: 6331)
TRANSFER AGENT(S): First Chicago Trust Company of New York, Jersey City, NJ

ALLTEL CORPORATION

YIELD 2.4%
P/E RATIO 16.6

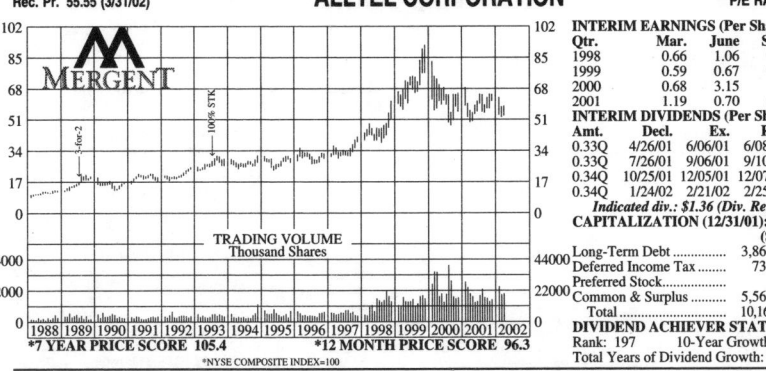

*7 YEAR PRICE SCORE 105.4   *12 MONTH PRICE SCORE 96.3
*NYSE COMPOSITE INDEX=100

INTERIM EARNINGS (Per Share):

Qtr.	Mar.	June	Sept.	Dec.
1998	0.66	1.06	0.57	0.55
1999	0.59	0.67	0.47	0.73
2000	0.68	3.15	1.53	0.83
2001	1.19	0.70	0.71	0.74

INTERIM DIVIDENDS (Per Share):

Amt.	Decl.	Ex.	Rec.	Pay.
0.33Q	4/26/01	6/06/01	6/08/01	7/03/01
0.33Q	7/26/01	9/06/01	9/10/01	10/03/01
0.34Q	10/25/01	12/05/01	12/07/01	1/03/02
0.34Q	1/24/02	2/21/02	2/25/02	4/03/02

Indicated div.: $1.36 (Div. Reinv. Plan)

CAPITALIZATION (12/31/01):

	($000)	(%)
Long-Term Debt	3,861,500	38.0
Deferred Income Tax	738,000	7.3
Preferred Stock	400	0.0
Common & Surplus	5,565,400	54.7
Total	10,165,300	100.0

DIVIDEND ACHIEVER STATUS:
Rank: 197   10-Year Growth Rate: 6.55%
Total Years of Dividend Growth: 41

RECENT DEVELOPMENTS: For the year ended 12/31/01, income was $1.05 billion compared with income of $1.97 billion in 2000. Earnings for 2001 and 2000 included pretax merger and integration expenses and other charges of $92.2 million and $25.4 million, as well as pre-tax gains on the disposal of assets and other items of $357.6 million and $1.93 billion, respectively. Total revenues and sales rose 4.8% to $7.60 billion.

PROSPECTS: On 3/19/02, AT announced an agreement to purchase all the wireless properties owned by CenturyTel Inc. for $1.65 billion in cash. The proposed acquisition would add more than 700,000 customers and expand the Company's wireless footprint into complementary new markets across Arkansas, Louisiana, Michigan, Mississippi, Texas and Wisconsin. The transaction is expected to close by 9/30/02.

BUSINESS

ALLTEL CORPORATION, with more than 10.0 million communication customers in 24 states as of 1/24/02, provides wireless and wireline local, long-distance, network access and Internet services, wide-area paging service and information processing management services and advanced application software. Telecommunications products are warehoused and sold by the Company's distribution subsidiary. A subsidiary also publishes telephone directories for affiliates and other independent telephone companies. In July 1998, AT completed its merger with 360(degree) Communications Company. On 7/2/99, AT acquired Aliant Communications Inc. for $1.80 billion. On 10/3/00, AT purchased certain wireless properties from SBC Communications, Inc. for $387.6 million in cash.

ANNUAL FINANCIAL DATA

	12/31/01	12/31/00	12/31/99	12/31/98	12/31/97	12/31/96	12/31/95
Earnings Per Share	⑤⑥ 3.34	④⑥ 6.20	③ 2.47	① 1.89	② 2.70	① 1.53	1.86
Cash Flow Per Share	7.07	9.31	5.19	4.44	5.10	3.75	4.02
Tang. Book Val. Per Share	6.87	5.92	7.03	5.82	8.67	8.88	7.64
Dividends Per Share	1.32	1.28	1.2	1.16	1.10	1.04	0.96
Dividend Payout %	39.5	20.6	49.4	61.4	40.7	68.0	51.6

INCOME STATEMENT (IN MILLIONS):

Total Revenues	7,598.9	7,067.0	6,302.3	5,194.0	3,263.6	3,192.4	3,109.7
Costs & Expenses	4,766.5	4,411.1	3,915.0	3,597.9	2,065.8	2,176.7	2,015.9
Depreciation & Amort.	1,167.7	988.4	862.2	707.1	450.8	424.1	409.8
Operating Income	1,664.7	1,667.5	1,525.1	889.0	747.0	591.6	684.0
Net Interest Inc./(Exp.)	d288.9	d310.8	d280.2	d263.7	d130.2	d130.8	d138.2
Income Before Income Taxes	1,751.8	3,350.7	1,330.9	972.3	828.7	461.4	571.8
Income Taxes	704.3	1,385.3	547.2	446.9	320.8	169.7	217.2
Equity Earnings/Minority Int.	d14.8	23.3	d11.6	12.7	...	...	d8.7
Net Income	⑤⑥ 1,047.5	④⑥ 1,965.4	③ 783.6	① 525.5	② 507.9	① 291.7	354.6
Cash Flow	2,215.1	2,953.7	1,644.9	1,231.7	957.6	714.8	763.3
Average Shs. Outstg. (000)	313,500	317,200	316,814	277,276	187,689	190,370	190,072

BALANCE SHEET (IN MILLIONS):

Cash & Cash Equivalents	85.3	67.2	17.6	55.5	16.2	13.9	21.4
Total Current Assets	1,767.8	1,780.7	1,167.2	980.8	665.8	709.5	731.2
Net Property	6,781.3	6,549.0	5,734.5	4,828.1	3,190.5	3,041.5	2,972.8
Total Assets	12,609.0	12,182.0	10,774.2	9,374.2	5,633.4	5,359.2	5,073.1
Total Current Liabilities	1,285.1	1,515.9	1,194.0	1,206.5	637.3	590.7	569.3
Long-Term Obligations	3,861.5	4,611.7	3,750.4	3,491.8	1,874.2	1,756.1	1,761.6
Net Stockholders' Equity	5,565.8	5,095.4	4,205.7	3,270.9	2,208.5	2,097.1	1,935.6
Net Working Capital	482.7	264.8	d26.8	d225.7	28.6	118.8	162.0
Year-end Shs. Outstg. (000)	310,530	312,984	314,258	281,198	183,673	187,200	189,268

STATISTICAL RECORD:

Operating Profit Margin %	21.9	23.6	24.2	17.1	22.9	18.5	22.0
Net Profit Margin %	13.8	27.8	12.4	10.1	15.6	9.1	11.4
Return on Equity %	18.8	38.6	18.6	16.1	23.0	13.9	18.3
Return on Assets %	8.3	16.1	7.3	5.6	9.0	5.4	7.0
Debt/Total Assets %	30.6	37.9	34.8	37.2	33.3	32.8	34.7
Price Range	68.69-49.43	82.94-47.75	91.81-56.31	61.38-38.25	41.63-29.75	35.63-26.63	31.13-23.25
P/E Ratio	20.6-14.8	13.4-7.7	37.2-22.8	32.5-20.2	15.4-11.0	23.3-17.4	16.7-12.5
Average Yield %	2.2	2.0	1.6	2.3	3.1	3.3	3.5

Statistics are as originally reported. ① Incl. pre-tax net chrg. of $10.8 mill. ② Incl. non-recurr. credit 12/31/97: $189.7 mill.; chrg. 12/31/96: $74.2 mill. ③ Incl. chrgs. of $90.5 mill. ④ Incl. pre-tax chrgs. of $25.4 mill. & pre-tax gain on disp. of assets & non-recurr. items of $1.93 bill. ⑤ Incl. pre-tax chrgs. of $92.2 mill. & pre-tax gain on disp. of assets & non-recurr. items of $357.6 mill. ⑥ Bef. acctg. chge. credit 12/31/01: $19.5 mill.; chrg. 12/31/00: $36.6 mill.

OFFICERS:
J. T. Ford, Chmn., C.E.O.
S. T. Ford, Pres., C.O.O.
J. R. Gardner, Sr. V.P., C.F.O.

INVESTOR CONTACT: Kerry Brooks, V.P., Inv. Rel., (501) 905-8991

PRINCIPAL OFFICE: One Allied Drive, Little Rock, AR 72202

TELEPHONE NUMBER: (501) 905-8000
FAX: (501) 905-0962
WEB: www.alltel.com
NO. OF EMPLOYEES: 23,955 (avg.)
SHAREHOLDERS: 256,759 (approx.)
ANNUAL MEETING: In Apr.
INCORPORATED: OH, June, 1960; reincorp., DE, 1990

INSTITUTIONAL HOLDINGS:
No. of Institutions: 529
Shares Held: 179,969,005
% Held: 57.9

INDUSTRY: Telephone communications, exc. radio (SIC: 4813)

TRANSFER AGENT(S): First Union National Bank of North Carolina, Charlotte, NC

ALFA CORPORATION

YIELD 2.1%
P/E RATIO 15.9

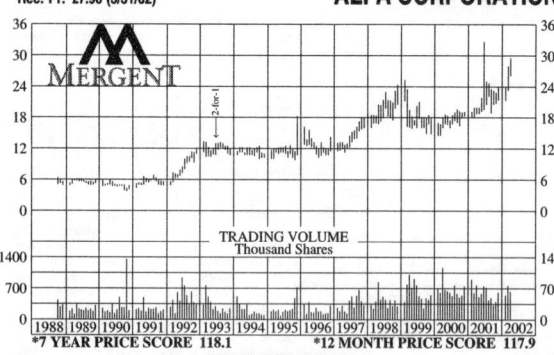

7 YEAR PRICE SCORE 118.1 **12 MONTH PRICE SCORE 117.9**
*NYSE COMPOSITE INDEX=100

TRADING VOLUME
Thousand Shares

INTERIM EARNINGS (Per Share):

Qtr.	Mar.	June	Sept.	Dec.
1997	0.32	0.34	0.32	0.30
1998	0.39	0.29	0.37	0.33
1999	0.40	0.40	0.41	0.39
2000	0.41	0.53	0.35	0.40
2001	0.36	0.44	0.47	0.49

INTERIM DIVIDENDS (Per Share):

Amt.	Decl.	Ex.	Rec.	Pay.
0.13Q	1/22/01	2/13/01	2/15/01	3/01/01
0.145Q	4/26/01	5/11/01	5/15/01	6/01/01
0.145Q	7/23/01	8/13/01	8/15/01	8/31/01
0.145Q	10/22/01	11/13/01	11/15/01	11/30/01
0.145Q	1/28/02	2/13/02	2/15/02	3/01/02

Indicated div.: $0.58 (Div. Reinv. Plan)

CAPITALIZATION (12/31/01):

	($000)	(%)
Deferred Income Tax	41,313	7.5
Common & Surplus	509,112	92.5
Total	550,425	100.0

DIVIDEND ACHIEVER STATUS:
Rank: 134   10-Year Growth Rate: 10.14%
Total Years of Dividend Growth: 16

RECENT DEVELOPMENTS: For the year ended 12/31/01, income improved to $70.0 million, before an accounting charge of $456,328, from net income of $66.8 million in the prior year. Earnings benefited from an increase in the number of new homeowner policies written and higher investment income. Total revenues increased 7.1% to $546.3 million from $510.3 million in the previous year. Revenues included realized investment gains of $6.4 million and $5.3 million for 2001 and 2000, respectively. Pre-

miums from property and casualty insurance grew 5.5% to $396.9 million from $376.1 million in 2000. Premiums and policy charges from life insurance rose 5.5% to $56.0 million from $53.1 million a year earlier. Net investment income climbed 16.2% to $84.7 million, while other income declined 23.4% to $2.3 million. Total expenses amounted to $448.2 million, up 7.9% from $415.6 million the year before.

BUSINESS

ALFA CORPORATION is a financial services holding company with total investments of $1.49 billion as of 12/31/01. The Company and its subsidiaries together with Alfa Mutual Companies comprise the Alfa Group. Alfa's primary business is personal lines of property and casualty insurance and life insurance. Alfa's subsidiaries write life insurance in Alabama, Georgia and Mississippi and casualty insurance in Georgia and Mississippi. The Company's noninsurance subsidiaries are engaged in consumer financing, leasing, real estate investments, residential and commercial construction and real estate sales.

ANNUAL FINANCIAL DATA

	12/31/01	12/31/00	12/31/99	12/31/98	12/31/97	12/31/96	12/31/95
Earnings Per Share	① 1.77	1.70	1.60	1.38	1.29	0.79	0.55
Tang. Book Val. Per Share	12.99	12.10	10.33	10.63	9.65	7.93	7.57
Dividends Per Share	0.56	0.51	0.47	0.44	0.40	0.39	0.38
Dividend Payout %	31.9	30.0	29.5	31.7	30.8	49.0	68.2
INCOME STATEMENT (IN MILLIONS):							
Total Premium Income	452.9	429.2	405.3	391.8	371.0	337.2	308.1
Net Investment Income	84.7	72.9	67.8	62.5	57.5	54.2	50.9
Other Income	8.7	8.2	9.1	6.6	5.5	5.0	3.8
Total Revenues	546.3	510.3	482.3	461.0	434.0	396.3	362.8
Policyholder Benefits	312.9	295.9	281.7	277.9	266.1	267.3	249.6
Income Before Income Taxes	98.1	94.7	92.1	83.3	76.8	45.9	31.0
Income Taxes	28.1	27.9	27.5	26.5	24.0	13.7	8.7
Net Income	① 70.0	66.8	64.6	56.7	52.8	32.2	22.3
Average Shs. Outstg. (000)	39,482	39,407	40,236	41,148	40,931	40,787	40,786
BALANCE SHEET (IN MILLIONS):							
Cash & Cash Equivalents	160.5	60.4	60.0	60.6	30.9	44.6	34.3
Premiums Due	19.8	13.9	13.0	23.4	11.5	9.5	13.8
Invst. Assets: Fixed-term	960.9	946.9	813.9	775.8	733.6	613.1	576.1
Invst. Assets: Equities	74.7	114.6	113.2	103.1	116.1	96.0	89.0
Invst. Assets: Loans	138.6	116.6	43.1	39.0	35.5	32.5	30.1
Invst. Assets: Total	1,491.2	1,355.0	1,155.2	1,084.1	1,027.7	886.0	841.1
Total Assets	1,697.6	1,546.3	1,335.3	1,246.7	1,170.1	1,019.3	965.4
Net Stockholders' Equity	509.1	473.6	408.7	423.6	382.9	323.3	308.6
Year-end Shs. Outstg. (000)	39,180	39,149	39,542	39,868	39,688	40,787	40,786
STATISTICAL RECORD:							
Return on Revenues %	12.8	13.1	13.4	12.3	12.2	8.1	6.2
Return on Equity %	13.7	14.1	15.8	13.4	13.8	10.0	7.2
Return on Assets %	4.1	4.3	4.8	4.5	4.5	3.2	2.3
Price Range	32.69-18.13	19.63-14.50	25.38-14.81	24.38-16.00	18.13-11.25	16.25-10.25	18.25-9.75
P/E Ratio	18.5-10.2	11.5-8.5	15.9-9.3	17.7-11.6	14.0-8.7	20.6-13.0	33.2-17.7
Average Yield %	2.2	3.0	2.4	2.2	2.7	2.9	2.7

Statistics are as originally reported. ① Bef. acctg. loss of $456,328

OFFICERS:
J. A. Newby, Chmn., Pres., C.E.O.
S. G. Rutledge, Sr. V.P., C.F.O.
A. Scott, Sr. V.P., Sec., Gen. Couns.

INVESTOR CONTACT: Steve Rutledge, Sr.
V.P., (334) 288-3900

PRINCIPAL OFFICE: 2108 East South Blvd.,
P.O. Box 11000, Montgomery, AL 36191

TELEPHONE NUMBER: (334) 288-3900
FAX: (334) 288-0905
WEB: www.alfains.com

NO. OF EMPLOYEES: 613 (avg.)

SHAREHOLDERS: 2,800 (approx.)

ANNUAL MEETING: In April

INCORPORATED: DE, 1974

INSTITUTIONAL HOLDINGS:
No. of Institutions: 59
Shares Held: 4,073,406
% Held: 10.4

INDUSTRY: Fire, marine, and casualty
insurance (SIC: 6331)

REGISTRAR(S): American Stock Transfer
and Trust Company, New York, NY

ALBERTSON'S, INC.

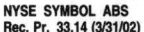

YIELD 2.3%
P/E RATIO 26.9

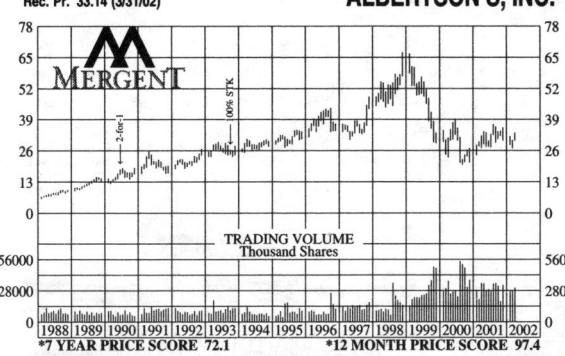

7 YEAR PRICE SCORE 72.1   *12 MONTH PRICE SCORE 97.4*
*NYSE COMPOSITE INDEX=100

INTERIM EARNINGS (Per Share):

Qtr.	Apr.	July	Oct.	Jan.
1998-99	0.45	0.52	0.56	0.77
1999-00	0.56	d0.49	0.31	0.62
2000-01	0.42	0.46	0.41	0.54
2001-02	0.46	d0.37	0.43	0.71

INTERIM DIVIDENDS (Per Share):

Amt.	Decl.	Ex.	Rec.	Pay.
0.19Q	6/13/01	7/12/01	7/16/01	8/10/01
0.19Q	9/05/01	10/11/01	10/15/01	11/10/01
0.19Q	12/03/01	1/11/02	1/15/02	2/10/02
0.19Q	3/13/02	4/11/02	4/15/02	5/10/02

Indicated div.: $0.76 (Div. Reinv. Plan)

CAPITALIZATION (1/31/02):

	($000)	(%)
Long-Term Debt	5,060,000	44.7
Capital Lease Obligations..	276,000	2.4
Deferred Income Tax	71,000	0.6
Common & Surplus	5,915,000	52.2
Total	11,322,000	100.0

DIVIDEND ACHIEVER STATUS:
Rank: 118   10-Year Growth Rate: 10.90%
Total Years of Dividend Growth: 30

RECENT DEVELOPMENTS: For the 52 weeks ended 1/31/02, net earnings totaled $501.0 million, down 34.5% versus $765.0 million the year before. Results for 2001 included a one-time pre-tax charge of $468.0 million, primarily related to restructuring, a $54.0 million gain from the sale of 80 Osco drugstores, and a $15.0 million merger-related credit. Results for 2000 included a one-time merger-related charge of $24.0 million. Sales rose 3.2% to $37.93 billion.

PROSPECTS: In fiscal 2002, ABS is targeting comparable-store sales growth of 2.0% and earnings per share of $2.15, excluding one-time charges. The Company plans to exit several under-performing markets, including Houston, San Antonio, Memphis and Nashville. The Company expects these initiatives will generate cost savings of $250.0 million by the end of the second quarter in 2002, increasing to more than $500.0 million annually by mid-2003.

BUSINESS

ALBERTSON'S, INC. is one of the largest retail food-drug chains in the United States. As of 3/13/02, ABS operated more than 2,400 stores in 33 states under three different formats: combination food-drug, conventional, and warehouse. Combination food-drug units, ranging between 35,000 sq. ft. and 107,000 sq. ft., consist of grocery, general merchandise, and meat and produce departments, along with pharmacy, lobby/video, floral, and bakery service departments. The Company's stores are operated under the Albertson's, Albertson's-Osco, Albertson's-Sav-on, Jewel-Osco, Acme, Sav-on Drugs, Osco Drug, Max Foods, Super Saver and Seessel's by Albertson's banners. On 6/23/99, ABS acquired American Stores Company.

QUARTERLY DATA

(1/31/2002)($000)	REV	INC
1st Quarter	9,331,000	186,000
2nd Quarter	9,577,000	(151,000)
3rd Quarter	9,363,000	176,000
4th Quarter	9,660,000	290,000

ANNUAL FINANCIAL DATA

	1/31/02	2/1/01	2/3/00	1/28/99	1/29/98	1/30/97	2/1/96
Earnings Per Share	⑤1.23	④1.83	③2.00	②2.30	2.08	1.96	1.84
Cash Flow Per Share	3.74	4.22	3.17	3.82	3.40	3.13	2.83
Tang. Book Val. Per Share	10.51	9.85	9.72	10.84	9.85	8.96	7.75
Dividends Per Share	0.76	0.75	0.71	0.67	0.63	0.58	0.50
Dividend Payout %	61.8	41.0	71.0	29.1	30.3	29.6	27.2
INCOME STATEMENT (IN MILLIONS):							
Total Revenues	37,931.0	36,762.0	37,478.0	16,005.1	14,689.5	13,776.7	12,585.0
Costs & Expenses	35,592.0	34,099.0	35,326.0	14,656.6	13,469.1	12,632.8	11,526.4
Depreciation & Amort.	1,026.0	1,001.0	912.0	375.4	328.8	294.3	251.5
Operating Income	1,313.0	1,662.0	1,240.0	973.2	891.7	849.6	807.2
Net Interest Inc./(Exp.)	d432.0	d385.0	d353.0	d77.1	d82.6	d64.6	d55.6
Income Before Income Taxes	873.0	1,274.0	899.0	894.8	826.9	794.8	758.5
Income Taxes	372.0	509.0	472.0	327.7	310.1	301.1	293.5
Net Income	⑤501.0	④765.0	②427.0	①367.2	516.8	493.8	465.0
Cash Flow	1,527.0	1,766.0	1,339.0	942.5	845.6	788.1	716.4
Average Shs. Outstg. (000)	408,000	418,000	423,000	246,808	248,497	251,710	253,080
BALANCE SHEET (IN MILLIONS):							
Cash & Cash Equivalents	85.0	57.0	231.0	80.6	108.1	90.9	69.1
Total Current Assets	4,609.0	4,300.0	4,582.0	1,833.9	1,627.9	1,475.9	1,283.0
Net Property	9,282.0	9,622.0	8,913.0	3,974.0	3,383.4	3,054.6	2,697.5
Total Assets	15,967.0	16,078.0	15,701.0	6,234.0	5,218.6	4,714.6	4,135.9
Total Current Liabilities	3,582.0	3,395.0	4,055.0	1,378.8	1,275.5	1,055.1	1,088.5
Long-Term Obligations	5,336.0	5,942.0	4,992.0	1,684.5	1,130.6	1,051.8	732.3
Net Stockholders' Equity	5,915.0	5,694.0	5,702.0	2,810.5	2,419.5	2,247.0	1,952.5
Net Working Capital	1,027.0	905.0	527.0	455.1	352.3	420.8	194.5
Year-end Shs. Outstg. (000)	407,000	405,000	424,000	245,697	245,736	250,690	251,919
STATISTICAL RECORD:							
Operating Profit Margin %	3.5	4.5	3.3	6.1	6.1	6.2	6.4
Net Profit Margin %	1.3	2.1	1.1	3.5	3.5	3.6	3.7
Return on Equity %	8.5	13.4	7.5	20.2	21.4	22.0	23.8
Return on Assets %	3.1	4.8	2.7	9.1	9.9	10.5	11.2
Debt/Total Assets %	33.4	37.0	31.8	27.0	21.7	22.3	17.7
Price Range	36.99-24.00	39.25-20.06	66.63-29.00	67.13-44.00	48.63-30.50	43.75-31.50	34.63-27.25
P/E Ratio	30.1-19.5	21.4-11.0	66.6-29.0	29.2-19.1	23.4-14.7	22.3-16.1	18.8-14.8
Average Yield %	2.5	2.5	1.5	1.2	1.6	1.5	1.6

Statistics are as originally reported. ① Incl. $24.4 mil pre-tax impairment chg. for store closures. ② Bef. $23.3 mil ($0.05/sh) extraord. chg. & incl. one-time pre-tax chgs. totaling $689.0 mil related to the acq. of American Stores Company and a litigation settlement. ③ Refl. acquis. of American Stores Co. in 6/99. ④ Incl. $105.0 mil ($0.25/sh) one-time after-tax chg. ⑤ Incl. $468.0 mil pre-tax restr. chg., $54.0 mil gain fr. sale of 80 Osco drugstores and a $15.0 mil merger-related credit.

OFFICERS:
L. R. Johnston, Chmn., C.E.O.
P. L. Lynch, Pres., C.O.O.
F. D. Thorton, Exec. V.P., C.F.O.

INVESTOR CONTACT: Renee Bergquist, (208) 395-6622

PRINCIPAL OFFICE: 250 Parkcenter Blvd., P.O. Box 20, Boise, ID 83726

TELEPHONE NUMBER: (208) 395-6200
FAX: (208) 395-6777
WEB: www.albertsons.com
NO. OF EMPLOYEES: 220,000 (approx.)
SHAREHOLDERS: 30,400 (approx.)
ANNUAL MEETING: In June
INCORPORATED: DE, Apr., 1969

INSTITUTIONAL HOLDINGS:
No. of Institutions: 420
Shares Held: 256,535,702
% Held: 63.0

INDUSTRY: Grocery stores (SIC: 5411)

TRANSFER AGENT(S): Mellon Investor Services, Ridgefield Park, NJ

ALBERTO-CULVER COMPANY

YIELD 0.7%
P/E RATIO 27.0

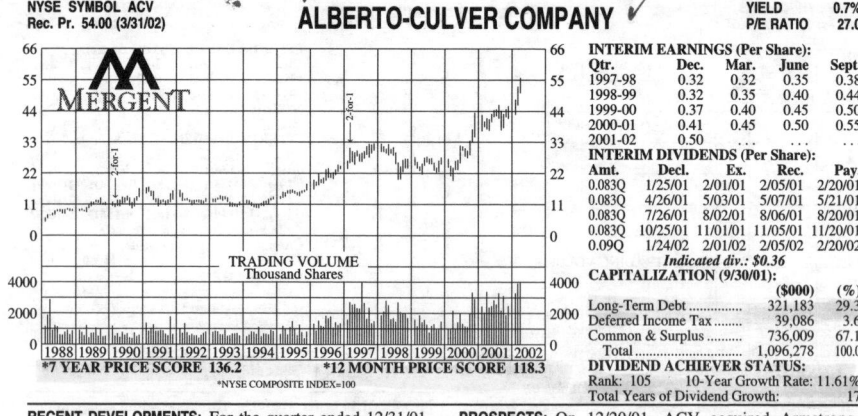

*7 YEAR PRICE SCORE 136.2 *12 MONTH PRICE SCORE 118.3

*NYSE COMPOSITE INDEX=100

TRADING VOLUME
Thousand Shares

INTERIM EARNINGS (Per Share):

Qtr.	Dec.	Mar.	June	Sept.
1997-98	0.32	0.32	0.35	0.38
1998-99	0.32	0.35	0.40	0.44
1999-00	0.37	0.40	0.45	0.50
2000-01	0.41	0.45	0.50	0.55
2001-02	0.50	...	...	...

INTERIM DIVIDENDS (Per Share):

Amt.	Decl.	Ex.	Rec.	Pay.
0.083Q	1/25/01	2/01/01	2/05/01	2/20/01
0.083Q	4/26/01	5/03/01	5/07/01	5/21/01
0.083Q	7/26/01	8/02/01	8/06/01	8/20/01
0.083Q	10/25/01	11/01/01	11/05/01	11/20/01
0.09Q	1/24/02	2/01/02	2/05/02	2/20/02

Indicated div.: $0.36

CAPITALIZATION (9/30/01):

	($000)	(%)
Long-Term Debt	321,183	29.3
Deferred Income Tax	39,086	3.6
Common & Surplus	736,009	67.1
Total	1,096,278	100.0

DIVIDEND ACHIEVER STATUS:

Rank: 105   10-Year Growth Rate: 11.61%
Total Years of Dividend Growth: 17

RECENT DEVELOPMENTS: For the quarter ended 12/31/01, net earnings increased 24.0% to $29.3 million from $23.6 million in the equivalent prior-year quarter. Earnings benefited from stronger sales of the Company's value-priced consumer packaged goods and from Sally Beauty businesses. Net sales increased 8.9% to $614.3 million from $563.9 million in the previous year. Gross profit as a percentage of sales amounted to 48.9% versus 47.8% a year earlier. Operating income grew 22.9% to $50.4 million.

PROSPECTS: On 12/20/01, ACV acquired Armstrong-McCall, a Texas-based full-service beauty products distributor and franchisor, for an undisclosed amount. This acquisition will extend the reach of the Company's beauty systems group throughout the South and Southwest U.S. and into Mexico and should contribute about $75.0 million in sales in the last three quarters of fiscal 2002 and be slightly accretive to earnings per share through the balance of the year.

BUSINESS

ALBERTO-CULVER COMPANY is engaged in developing, manufacturing, distributing and marketing branded consumer products worldwide. Alberto-Culver North America includes ACV's consumer products in the U.S. and Canada, while Alberto-Culver International sells consumer products in more than 120 other countries. ACV's third segment, Specialty Distribution - Sally, consists of Sally Beauty Company, a specialty distributor of professional beauty supplies with 2,131 stores as of 12/31/01, in the U.S., Germany, the United Kingdom, Canada, Japan and Mexico, and its Beauty Systems Group, which sells professional beauty products through 344 Company-owned stores and 130 franchised stores, and through over 600 professional distributor sales consultants. Brands sold by ACV include ALBERTO VO5, ST. IVES SWISS FORMULA and TRESEMME hair and skin beauty care products.

ANNUAL FINANCIAL DATA

	9/30/01	9/30/00	9/30/99	9/30/98	9/30/97	9/30/96	9/30/95
Earnings Per Share	1.91	① 1.83	1.51	1.37	① 1.49	① 1.11	0.95
Cash Flow Per Share	2.80	2.71	2.25	1.94	2.17	1.70	1.39
Tang. Book Val. Per Share	6.90	5.16	5.81	5.75	5.57	4.33	5.08
Dividends Per Share	0.33	0.30	0.26	0.24	0.20	0.18	0.16
Dividend Payout %	17.3	16.4	17.2	17.5	13.4	16.2	16.9
INCOME STATEMENT (IN MILLIONS)							
Total Revenues	2,494.2	2,247.2	1,975.9	1,834.7	1,775.3	1,590.4	1,358.2
Costs & Expenses	2,253.7	2,024.0	1,787.3	1,655.6	1,592.0	1,445.4	1,242.8
Depreciation & Amort.	51.4	49.6	42.2	38.1	38.9	32.9	24.7
Operating Income	189.1	173.5	146.5	141.0	144.4	112.1	90.8
Net Interest Inc./(Exp.)	d21.8	d19.2	d12.7	d8.6	d8.2	d12.1	d6.5
Income Before Income Taxes	167.2	154.3	133.8	132.4	136.1	100.0	84.2
Income Taxes	56.9	51.1	47.5	49.3	50.7	37.3	31.6
Net Income	110.4	① 103.2	86.3	83.1	① 85.4	① 62.7	52.7
Cash Flow	161.8	152.8	128.5	121.2	124.4	95.7	77.3
Average Shs. Outstg. (000)	57,838	56,410	57,162	62,420	57,202	56,426	55,698
BALANCE SHEET (IN MILLIONS)							
Cash & Cash Equivalents	202.8	115.0	57.8	73.3	87.6	71.6	147.0
Total Current Assets	876.9	740.5	645.6	591.6	580.3	512.7	536.5
Net Property	235.8	240.1	238.8	223.5	191.0	175.9	157.8
Total Assets	1,516.5	1,389.8	1,184.5	1,068.2	1,000.1	909.3	815.1
Total Current Liabilities	390.3	340.8	336.4	313.6	311.3	286.6	234.8
Long-Term Obligations	321.2	340.9	225.2	171.8	149.4	161.5	183.1
Net Stockholders' Equity	736.0	636.5	568.8	534.0	497.0	425.1	370.9
Net Working Capital	486.6	399.7	309.2	277.9	269.0	226.1	301.7
Year-end Shs. Outstg. (000)	56,828	55,939	55,726	57,210	56,142	55,630	55,458
STATISTICAL RECORD:							
Operating Profit Margin %	7.6	7.7	7.4	7.7	8.1	7.0	6.7
Net Profit Margin %	4.4	4.6	4.4	4.5	4.8	3.9	3.9
Return on Equity %	15.0	16.2	15.2	15.6	17.2	14.8	14.2
Return on Assets %	7.3	7.4	7.3	7.8	8.5	6.9	6.5
Debt/Total Assets %	21.2	24.5	19.0	16.1	14.9	17.8	22.5
Price Range	46.26-36.88	43.50-19.38	27.88-21.56	32.44-19.75	32.56-23.56	25.00-16.25	18.25-12.94
P/E Ratio	24.2-19.3	23.8-10.6	18.5-14.3	23.7-14.4	21.9-15.8	22.5-14.6	19.3-13.7
Average Yield %	0.8	1.0	1.1	0.9	0.7	0.9	1.0

Statistics are as originally reported. Adj. for stk. splits: 2-for-1, 2/97. ① Incl. non-recurr. gain 2000, $6.0 mill.; credit 1997, $15.6 mill., 1996, $9.8 mill. ② Incl. special div. of $0.02.

OFFICERS:
L. H. Lavin, Chmn.
B. E. Lavin, Vice-Chmn., Treas., Sec.
H. B. Bernick, Pres., C.E.O.

INVESTOR CONTACT: Wesley C. Davidson, V.P., Invest. Rel., (708) 450-3145

PRINCIPAL OFFICE: 2525 Armitage Avenue, Melrose Park, IL 60160

TELEPHONE NUMBER: (708) 450-3000
FAX: (708) 450-3419
WEB: www.alberto.com
NO. OF EMPLOYEES: 16,100 (approx.)
SHAREHOLDERS: 898 (Class A com.); 898 (class B com.).
ANNUAL MEETING: In Jan.
INCORPORATED: DE, Jan., 1961

INSTITUTIONAL HOLDINGS:
No. of Institutions: 181
Shares Held: 17,145,081
% Held: 29.8

INDUSTRY: Toilet preparations (SIC: 2844).

TRANSFER AGENT(S): EquiServe L.P., Providence, RI

AIR PRODUCTS & CHEMICALS, INC.

YIELD 1.5%
P/E RATIO 23.2

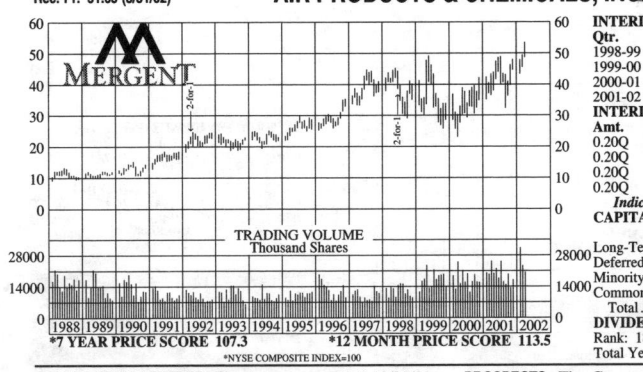

INTERIM EARNINGS (Per Share):

Qtr.	Dec.	Mar.	June	Sept.
1998-99	0.59	0.50	0.44	0.57
1999-00	0.23	0.22	d0.89	1.01
2000-01	0.62	0.43	0.60	0.68
2001-02	0.52	...	...	...

INTERIM DIVIDENDS (Per Share):

Amt.	Decl.	Ex.	Rec.	Pay.
0.20Q	5/17/01	6/28/01	7/02/01	8/13/01
0.20Q	9/20/01	9/27/01	10/01/01	11/12/01
0.20Q	11/15/01	12/28/01	1/02/02	2/11/02
0.20Q	3/21/02	3/27/02	4/01/02	5/13/02

Indicated div.: $0.80 (Div. Reinv. Plan)

CAPITALIZATION (9/30/01):

	($000)	(%)
Long-Term Debt	2,027,500	33.6
Deferred Income Tax	778,400	12.9
Minority Interest	118,000	2.0
Common & Surplus	3,105,800	51.5
Total	6,029,700	100.0

DIVIDEND ACHIEVER STATUS:
Rank: 180   10-Year Growth Rate: 7.60%
Total Years of Dividend Growth: 19

TRADING VOLUME Thousand Shares

*7 YEAR PRICE SCORE 107.3   *12 MONTH PRICE SCORE 113.5
*NYSE COMPOSITE INDEX=100

RECENT DEVELOPMENTS: For the quarter ended 12/31/01, net income decreased 16.2% to $113.7 million compared with $135.6 million in 2000. Sales amounted to $1.32 billion, down 10.8% from $1.48 billion in the prior-year period. Sales were negatively affected by weakness in the global electronics market and in U.S. manufacturing, which led to reduced volumes in most of the Company's gas and chemical product lines.

PROSPECTS: The Company expects market conditions to continue to be challenging. As a result, ADP anticipates operating earnings per share for the second quarter of fiscal 2002 to be between $2.35 and $2.45. Going forward, the Company will continue its efforts to lower costs and increase margins as well as refine its portfolio. Separately, on 1/3/02, ADP agreed to sell its U.S. packaged gas business to Airgas for an undisclosed amount.

BUSINESS

AIR PRODUCTS & CHEMICALS, INC. is an international supplier of industrial and specialty gas products.

Principal products of the industrial gases segment (69.0% of 2001 revenues) are oxygen, nitrogen, argon, hydrogen, carbon monoxide, carbon dioxide, synthesis gas, and helium. The chemical business (27.0%) consists of polymer chemicals, performance chemicals, and chemical intermediates. The equipment and services segment (4.0%) designs and manufactures cryogenic and gas processing equipment for air separation, gas processing, natural gas liquefaction, hydrogen purification, and nitrogen rejection. This segment also includes the continuing businesses from the environmental/energy segment.

ANNUAL FINANCIAL DATA

	9/30/01	9/30/00	9/30/99	9/30/98	9/30/97	9/30/96	9/30/95
Earnings Per Share	⑤ 2.33	④ 0.57	③ 2.09	①② 2.48	1.95	① 1.86	① 1.65
Cash Flow Per Share	4.58	3.24	4.53	4.71	4.04	3.71	3.35
Tang. Book Val. Per Share	13.67	9.07	11.39	11.08	20.08	11.22	10.34
Dividends Per Share	0.78	0.74	0.70	0.64	0.57	0.54	0.51
Dividend Payout %	33.5	129.8	33.5	25.8	29.5	28.8	30.7
INCOME STATEMENT (IN MILLIONS):							
Total Revenues	5,722.7	5,495.5	5,039.8	4,933.8	4,662.0	4,033.0	3,891.0
Costs & Expenses	4,404.3	4,089.0	3,787.9	3,599.4	3,477.5	3,030.0	2,907.0
Depreciation & Amort.	573.0	575.7	527.2	489.4	459.1	412.0	382.0
Operating Income	745.4	830.8	724.7	845.0	725.4	591.0	602.0
Net Interest Inc./(Exp.)	d191.2	d196.7	d159.1	d162.8	d161.3	d129.0	d100.0
Income Before Income Taxes	737.0	118.1	669.0	823.7	630.4	610.0	553.0
Income Taxes	219.0	cr13.7	203.4	276.9	201.1	193.0	185.0
Equity Earnings/Minority Int.	76.1	d7.6	d15.1	38.0	66.3	81.0	51.0
Net Income	⑤ 431.7	④ 124.2	③ 450.5	①② 546.8	429.3	① 417.0	① 368.0
Cash Flow	1,085.9	699.9	977.7	1,036.2	888.4	829.0	750.0
Average Shs. Outstg. (000)	219,300	216,200	216,000	220,100	220,100	223,400	224,000
BALANCE SHEET (IN MILLIONS):							
Cash & Cash Equivalents	66.2	94.1	132.0	61.5	52.5	79.0	87.0
Total Current Assets	1,684.8	1,805.0	1,782.4	1,641.7	1,624.3	1,375.0	1,332.0
Net Property	5,118.5	5,256.7	5,192.9	4,786.1	4,441.2	3,959.0	3,502.0
Total Assets	8,084.1	8,270.5	8,235.5	7,489.6	7,244.1	6,522.0	5,816.0
Total Current Liabilities	1,352.4	1,374.8	1,857.8	1,265.6	1,124.6	1,263.0	1,311.0
Long-Term Obligations	2,027.5	2,615.8	1,961.6	2,274.3	2,291.7	1,739.0	1,194.0
Net Stockholders' Equity	3,105.8	2,821.3	2,961.6	2,667.3	2,648.1	2,574.0	2,398.0
Net Working Capital	332.4	430.2	d75.4	376.1	499.7	112.0	21.0
Year-end Shs. Outstg. (000)	227,186	229,305	229,305	211,500	119,500	222,000	224,000
STATISTICAL RECORD:							
Operating Profit Margin %	13.0	15.1	14.4	17.1	15.6	14.7	15.5
Net Profit Margin %	7.5	2.3	8.9	11.1	9.2	10.3	9.5
Return on Equity %	13.9	4.4	15.2	20.5	16.2	16.2	15.3
Return on Assets %	5.3	1.5	5.5	7.3	5.9	6.4	6.3
Debt/Total Assets %	25.1	31.6	23.8	30.4	31.6	26.7	20.5
Price Range	49.00-32.25	42.25-23.00	49.25-25.69	45.34-29.00	44.81-33.19	35.31-25.19	29.81-21.94
P/E Ratio	21.0-13.8	74.1-40.3	23.6-12.3	18.3-11.7	23.0-17.0	19.0-13.5	18.1-13.3
Average Yield %	1.9	2.3	1.9	1.7	1.5	1.8	2.0

Statistics are as originally reported. Adj. for 2-for-1 split, 6/98. ① Incl. $35.0 mil aft-tx gn, 1998; aft-tx gn $41.0 mil, 1996; $6.6 mil gn gas plt. sale, 1995. ② Incl. $58.1 mil. aft-tax gn. ③ Incl. $28.3 mil. net chgs. & $23.6 mil. net gn. ④ Incl. $456.5 mil. aft-tax loss fr. curr. hedges & $126.8 mil. gn fr. sale of bus. ⑤ Incl. $67.3 mil. aft-tax chg., $3.7 mil. aft-tax lit. chg., $64.6 mil. aft-tax gn. & excl. $28.5 mil. aft-tax extraord. loss.

OFFICERS:
J. P. Jones III, Chmn., Pres., C.E.O.
L. J. Daley, V.P., Fin., C.F.O., Contr.

INVESTOR CONTACT: Alexander W. Massetti, Dir., Inv. Rel., (610) 481-5775

PRINCIPAL OFFICE: 7201 Hamilton Boulevard, Allentown, PA 18195-1501

TELEPHONE NUMBER: (610) 481-4911
FAX: (610) 481-5900
WEB: www.airproducts.com
NO. OF EMPLOYEES: 17,800 (approx.)
SHAREHOLDERS: 11,621
ANNUAL MEETING: In Jan.
INCORPORATED: MI, Oct., 1940; reincorp., DE, June, 1940

INSTITUTIONAL HOLDINGS:
No. of Institutions: 427
Shares Held: 185,693,940
% Held: 81.7

INDUSTRY: Industrial gases (SIC: 2813)

TRANSFER AGENT(S): First Chicago Trust Company of New York, Jersey City, NJ

AFLAC INCORPORATED

	YIELD	0.8%
	P/E RATIO	23.0

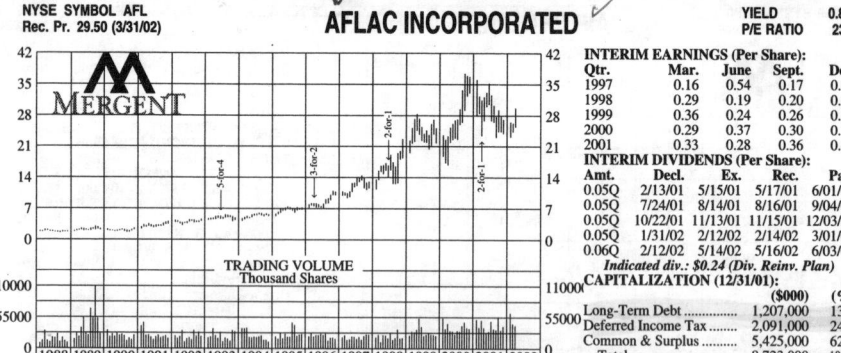

7 YEAR PRICE SCORE 132.5   **12 MONTH PRICE SCORE 96.5**
*NYSE COMPOSITE INDEX=100

INTERIM EARNINGS (Per Share):

Qtr.	Mar.	June	Sept.	Dec.
1997	0.16	0.54	0.17	0.18
1998	0.29	0.19	0.20	0.21
1999	0.36	0.24	0.26	0.19
2000	0.29	0.37	0.30	0.31
2001	0.33	0.28	0.36	0.31

INTERIM DIVIDENDS (Per Share):

Amt.	Decl.	Ex.	Rec.	Pay.
0.05Q	2/13/01	5/15/01	5/17/01	6/01/01
0.05Q	7/24/01	8/14/01	8/16/01	9/04/01
0.05Q	10/22/01	11/13/01	11/15/01	12/03/01
0.05Q	1/31/02	2/12/02	2/14/02	3/01/02
0.06Q	2/12/02	5/14/02	5/16/02	6/03/02

Indicated div.: $0.24 (Div. Reinv. Plan)

CAPITALIZATION (12/31/01):

	($000)	(%)
Long-Term Debt	1,207,000	13.8
Deferred Income Tax	2,091,000	24.0
Common & Surplus	5,425,000	62.2
Total	8,723,000	100.0

DIVIDEND ACHIEVER STATUS:
Rank: 54   10-Year Growth Rate: 15.90%
Total Years of Dividend Growth: 19

RECENT DEVELOPMENTS: For the year ended 12/31/01, earnings were flat compared with the prior year at $687.0 million. Earnings for 2001 included realized investment losses of $34.0 million, while earnings for 2000 included a one-time benefit of $99.0 million related to the termination of a retirement liability and realized investment losses of $69.0 million. Total revenues declined 1.1% to $9.60 billion from $9.70 billion in the prior year. Premiums revenue fell 2.0% to $8.06 billion from $8.22 billion a year earlier.

PROSPECTS: Looking ahead, AFL believes it is well positioned to achieve its objective of a 15.0% to 17.0% increase in operating earnings per share, excluding currency fluctuations, in 2002 and 2003. The Company's U.S. business should continue to benefit from positive sales momentum as it surpassed 200,000 payroll accounts during the year. Moreover, the Company should continue to benefit from the strong growth of its distribution system and gains in name and brand recognition.

BUSINESS

AFLAC Incorporated is an international insurance organization whose principal subsidiary is American Family Life Assurance Company of Columbus. In addition to life, and health & accident insurance, AFL has pioneered cancer-expense and intensive-care insurance coverage.

AFLAC's subsidiary Communicorp specializes in printing, advertising, audio-visuals, sales incentives, business meetings and mailings. As of 12/31/01, AFL insured more than 40.0 million people worldwide, and offered policies through more than 200,000 payroll accounts.

ANNUAL FINANCIAL DATA

	12/31/01	12/31/00	12/31/99	12/31/98	12/31/97	12/31/96	12/31/95
Earnings Per Share	③ 1.28	② 1.26	1.04	0.88	① 1.04	① 0.69	0.58
Tang. Book Val. Per Share	10.40	8.87	7.28	7.09	6.44	3.57	3.39
Dividends Per Share	0.19	0.17	0.14	0.13	0.11	0.10	0.08
Dividend Payout %	15.0	13.1	14.0	14.3	10.7	14.1	14.4
INCOME STATEMENT (IN MILLIONS):							
Total Premium Income	8,061.0	8,239.0	7,264.0	5,943.0	5,873.7	5,910.0	6,070.8
Net Investment Income	1,550.0	1,550.0	1,369.0	1,138.0	1,077.7	1,022.0	1,025.0
Other Income	d13.0	d69.0	7.0	23.0	299.3	168.2	94.8
Total Revenues	9,598.0	9,720.0	8,640.0	7,104.0	7,250.7	7,100.2	7,190.6
Policyholder Benefits	6,303.0	6,618.0	5,885.0	4,877.0	4,833.1	4,895.5	5,034.3
Income Before Income Taxes	1,081.0	1,012.0	778.0	551.0	864.8	650.0	601.0
Income Taxes	394.0	325.0	207.0	64.0	279.8	255.6	251.9
Net Income	③ 687.0	② 687.0	571.0	487.0	① 585.0	① 394.4	349.1
Average Shs. Outstg. (000)	537,380	544,906	550,846	551,744	563,192	578,048	598,160
BALANCE SHEET (IN MILLIONS):							
Cash & Cash Equivalents	852.0	609.0	616.0	374.0	279.0	261.7	236.3
Premiums Due	347.0	301.0	270.0	272.0	215.7	227.0	321.1
Invst. Assets: Fixed-term	25,817.0	25,817.0	25,248.0	21,564.0	22,437.8	20,327.7	19,675.0
Invst. Assets: Equities	245.0	236.0	215.0	177.0	146.3	136.3	108.1
Invst. Assets: Loans	...	...	...	16.7	17.8	22.2	
Invst. Assets: Total	31,941.0	31,558.0	31,408.0	26,620.0	22,644.2	20,746.5	20,040.8
Total Assets	37,860.0	37,232.0	37,041.0	31,183.0	29,454.0	25,022.8	25,338.0
Long-Term Obligations	1,207.0	1,079.0	1,111.0	596.0	523.2	353.5	327.3
Net Stockholders' Equity	5,425.0	4,694.0	3,868.0	3,770.0	3,430.5	2,125.6	2,134.1
Year-end Shs. Outstg. (000)	521,615	529,210	531,482	531,368	532,872	578,048	598,160
STATISTICAL RECORD:							
Return on Revenues %	7.2	7.1	6.6	6.9	8.1	5.6	4.9
Return on Equity %	12.7	14.6	14.8	12.9	17.1	18.6	16.4
Return on Assets %	1.8	1.8	1.5	1.6	2.0	1.6	1.4
Price Range	36.0-23.00	37.47-16.78	28.38-19.50	22.66-11.34	14.47-9.38	11.00-7.06	7.46-5.31
P/E Ratio	28.2-18.0	29.7-13.3	27.4-18.8	25.7-12.9	13.9-9.0	16.1-10.3	12.8-9.1
Average Yield %	0.7	0.6	0.6	0.7	1.0	1.1	1.3

Statistics are as originally reported. Adj. for stk. splits: 2-for-1, 3/01 & 6/98; 3-for-2, 3/96
① Incl. non-recurr. credit $267.2 mill., 12/97; $60.3 mill., 12/96 ② Incl. one-time benefit of $99.0 mill. & realized invest. loss of $69.0 mill. ③ Incl. realized invest. loss $34.0 mill.

OFFICERS:
D. P. Amos, Chmn., C.E.O.
K. Cloninger III, Pres., C.F.O., Treas.

INVESTOR CONTACT: Kenneth S. Janke, Jr., Sr. V.P., Inv. Rel., (800) 235-2667

PRINCIPAL OFFICE: 1932 Wynnton Road, Columbus, GA 31999

TELEPHONE NUMBER: (706) 323-3431
FAX: (706) 323-6330
WEB: www.aflac.com
NO. OF EMPLOYEES: 5,739
SHAREHOLDERS: 70,838 (registered); 182,700 (common approx.)
ANNUAL MEETING: In May
INCORPORATED: GA, 1973

INSTITUTIONAL HOLDINGS:
No. of Institutions: 458
Shares Held: 273,408,328
% Held: 52.8

INDUSTRY: Accident and health insurance (SIC: 6321)

TRANSFER AGENT(S): AFLAC Incorporated, Columbus, GA

ABM INDUSTRIES INCORPORATED

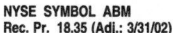
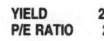

	YIELD	2.0%
	P/E RATIO	22.9

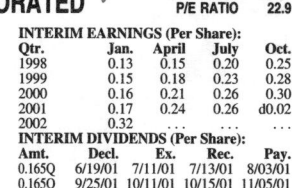

TRADING VOLUME
Thousand Shares

7 YEAR PRICE SCORE 112.7 **12 MONTH PRICE SCORE 107.3**

*NYSE COMPOSITE INDEX=100

INTERIM EARNINGS (Per Share):

Qtr.	Jan.	April	July	Oct.
1998	0.13	0.15	0.20	0.25
1999	0.15	0.18	0.23	0.28
2000	0.16	0.21	0.26	0.30
2001	0.17	0.24	0.26	d0.02
2002	0.32	...	...	...

INTERIM DIVIDENDS (Per Share):

Amt.	Decl.	Ex.	Rec.	Pay.
0.165Q	6/19/01	7/11/01	7/13/01	8/03/01
0.165Q	9/25/01	10/11/01	10/15/01	11/05/01
0.18Q	12/11/01	1/16/02	1/18/02	2/05/02
0.18Q	3/12/02	3/26/02	3/29/02	5/03/02
100% STK	3/12/02	5/07/02	3/29/02	5/06/02

Indicated div.: $0.36 (Adj.)

CAPITALIZATION (10/31/01):

	($000)	(%)
Long-Term Debt	942	0.3
Common & Surplus	361,177	99.7
Total	362,119	100.0

DIVIDEND ACHIEVER STATUS:

Rank: 121	10-Year Growth Rate: 10.82%	
Total Years of Dividend Growth:		37

RECENT DEVELOPMENTS: For the quarter ended 1/31/02, net income decreased 4.9% to $8.0 million compared with $8.4 million in the equivalent 2001 quarter. Results for 2001 included goodwill amortization of $2.9 million. The decline in earnings was primarily attributed to the loss of business related to the terrorist attacks on 9/11/01 and an increase of $3.0 million per quarter in ABM's pre-tax charge for self-insurance. Revenues increased 1.2% to $476.0 million from $470.4 million a year earlier.

PROSPECTS: On 2/19/02, ABM's subsidiary, AmTech Lighting Services, was awarded a multi-million dollar contract by Boston Properties, Inc. On 2/11/02, ABM's subsidiary, Ampco System Parking, was awarded a multi-million dollar contract renewal for San Francisco International Airport. On 1/17/02, ABM's subsidiary, Amtech Lighting Services, was awarded a multi-year, multi-million dollar contract with General Motors Dealership Identification Leasing Corporation.

BUSINESS

ABM INDUSTRIES INCORPORATED is engaged in the business of providing commercial, industrial and institutional janitorial, window cleaning, engineering and building maintenance services. The Company is also engaged in the business of air conditioning, heating equipment, elevator and escalator installation, repair and servicing; lighting and outdoor signage installation and maintenance; parking facility operations; building security services; and janitorial supplies and equipment sales. Amtech group offers a wide range of mechanical, electrical and elevator services to retail and commercial businesses. Contributions to sales for fiscal 2001 were as follows: ABM Janitorial, 65.8%; ABM Engineering, 9.7%; Ampco System Parking, 9.4%; Amtech Lighting, 8.2%; and Amtech Elevator, 6.9%.

ANNUAL FINANCIAL DATA

	10/31/01	10/31/00	10/31/99	10/31/98	10/31/97	10/31/96	10/31/95
Earnings Per Share	⑪ 0.65	0.93	0.83	0.72	0.67	0.56	0.46
Cash Flow Per Share	1.18	1.43	1.27	1.16	1.08	0.92	0.78
Tang. Book Val. Per Share	5.08	4.48	3.82	3.12	2.38	2.26	1.94
Dividends Per Share	0.33	0.31	0.28	0.24	0.20	0.17	0.15
Dividend Payout %	50.8	33.5	33.9	33.3	30.1	31.5	32.4
INCOME STATEMENT (IN MILLIONS):							
Total Revenues	1,950.0	1,807.6	1,629.7	1,501.8	1,252.5	1,086.9	965.4
Costs & Expenses	1,868.2	1,708.0	1,539.8	1,421.3	1,186.7	1,032.6	919.7
Depreciation & Amort.	26.3	23.5	20.7	19.6	16.1	13.7	11.5
Operating Income	55.5	76.0	69.2	61.0	49.6	40.7	34.2
Net Interest Inc./(Exp.)	d2.6	d3.3	d2.0	d3.5	d2.7	d2.6	d2.7
Income Before Income Taxes	52.9	72.7	67.2	57.5	47.0	38.1	31.4
Income Taxes	20.1	28.4	27.6	23.6	19.7	16.4	13.2
Net Income	⑪ 32.8	44.3	39.7	33.9	27.2	21.7	18.2
Cash Flow	58.7	67.4	59.9	53.0	42.8	34.9	29.2
Average Shs. Outstg. (000)	50,020	47,418	47,496	46,322	40,286	38,246	38,360
BALANCE SHEET (IN MILLIONS):							
Cash & Cash Equivalents	3.1	2.0	2.1	1.8	1.8	1.6	1.8
Total Current Assets	465.5	436.8	367.6	324.3	291.5	233.8	209.9
Net Property	42.9	40.7	35.2	27.3	26.6	22.6	22.6
Total Assets	683.1	642.0	563.4	501.4	464.3	379.8	335.0
Total Current Liabilities	236.0	212.6	183.3	157.8	153.8	113.8	114.2
Long-Term Obligations	0.9	36.8	28.9	33.7	38.4	33.7	22.6
Net Stockholders' Equity	361.2	316.3	277.0	237.5	197.8	164.3	141.8
Net Working Capital	229.5	224.2	184.3	166.5	137.8	120.0	95.6
Year-end Shs. Outstg. (000)	48,778	45,998	44,814	43,202	40,928	38,978	37,464
STATISTICAL RECORD:							
Operating Profit Margin %	2.8	4.2	4.2	4.1	4.0	3.7	3.5
Net Profit Margin %	1.7	2.5	2.4	2.3	2.2	2.0	1.9
Return on Equity %	9.1	14.0	14.3	14.3	13.8	13.2	12.8
Return on Assets %	4.8	6.9	7.0	6.8	5.9	5.7	5.4
Debt/Total Assets %	0.1	5.7	5.1	6.7	8.3	8.9	6.7
Price Range	19.10-12.48	16.06-9.63	17.25-10.00	18.50-12.50	15.75-8.69	10.09-6.75	7.13-5.25
P/E Ratio	29.4-19.2	17.4-10.4	20.9-12.1	25.7-17.4	23.7-13.1	18.2-12.2	15.4-11.4
Average Yield %	2.1	2.4	2.1	1.5	1.6	2.1	2.4

Statistics are as originally reported. Adj. for stk. split: 2-for-1, 7/92, 8/96 & 5/02. ⑪ Incl. a pre-tax charge of $20.0 million to strengthen the Company's self-insurance.

OFFICERS:
M. H. Mandles, Chmn., C.A.O.
H. Slipsager, Pres., C.E.O.
G. B. Sundby, Sr. V.P., C.F.O.

INVESTOR CONTACT: George B. Sundby, Sr. V.P., C.F.O., (415) 733-4000

PRINCIPAL OFFICE: 160 Pacific Avenue, Suite 222, San Francisco, CA 94111

TELEPHONE NUMBER: (415) 733-4000
FAX: (415) 733-7333
WEB: www.abm.com
NO. OF EMPLOYEES: 60,000 (approx.)
SHAREHOLDERS: 4,735 (approx.)
ANNUAL MEETING: In Mar.
INCORPORATED: CA, Apr., 1955; reincorp., DE, May, 1985

INSTITUTIONAL HOLDINGS:
No. of Institutions: 125
Shares Held: 30,396,732 (Adj.)
% Held: 62.2

INDUSTRY: Building maintenance services, nec (SIC: 7349)

TRANSFER AGENT(S): Mellon Investor Services LLC, San Francisco, CA

ABBOTT LABORATORIES

	YIELD	1.8%
	P/E RATIO	44.2

7 YEAR PRICE SCORE 121.4   **12 MONTH PRICE SCORE 109.2**
*NYSE COMPOSITE INDEX=100

INTERIM EARNINGS (Per Share):

Qtr.	Mar.	June	Sept.	Dec.
1997	0.35	0.34	0.31	0.37
1998	0.38	0.38	0.34	0.41
1999	0.43	0.42	0.38	0.43
2000	0.44	0.44	0.42	0.48
2001	0.06	0.34	0.40	0.39

INTERIM DIVIDENDS (Per Share):

Amt.	Decl.	Ex.	Rec.	Pay.
0.21Q	2/09/01	4/10/01	4/12/01	5/15/01
0.21Q	6/08/01	7/11/01	7/13/01	8/15/01
0.21Q	9/06/01	10/11/01	10/15/01	11/15/01
0.21Q	12/14/01	1/11/02	1/15/02	2/15/02
0.235Q	2/15/02	4/11/02	4/15/02	5/15/02

Indicated div.: $0.94 (Div. Reinv. Plan)

CAPITALIZATION (12/31/01):

	($000)	(%)
Long-Term Debt	4,335,493	32.4
Common & Surplus	9,059,432	67.6
Total	13,394,925	100.0

DIVIDEND ACHIEVER STATUS:
Rank: 85   10-Year Growth Rate: 13.07%
Total Years of Dividend Growth: 29

RECENT DEVELOPMENTS: For the twelve months ended 12/31/01, net earnings dropped 44.4% to $1.55 billion compared with $2.79 billion in the prior-year period. Results for 2001 included a pre-tax acquired in-process research and development charge of $1.33 billion. The 2000 results included a gain of $138.5 million on the sale of business. Net sales increased 18.5% to $16.29 billion from $13.75 billion in the previous year.

PROSPECTS: Going forward, ABT's pharmaceutical business is well positioned for continued double-digit growth. Separately, on 3/18/02, ABT agreed to acquire the cardiovascular stent business of Biocompatibles International plc for about $234.5 million in cash. In addition, ABT should benefit from its improved science and technology platforms, as well as its new-product pipeline.

BUSINESS

ABBOTT LABORATORIES' principal business is the discovery, development, manufacture, and sale of pharmaceuticals, nutritionals, and medical products, including devices and diagnostics. Pharmaceutical products include adult and pediatric pharmaceuticals and vitamins. This segment also includes consumer products, agricultural and chemical products, and bulk pharmaceuticals. Products in the hospital and laboratory segment include diagnostic systems, intravenous and irrigating fluids and related administration equipment, anesthetics, critical care equipment, and other specialty products. Products in the Ross segment include nutritional products such as SIMILAC and ENSURE. ABT also owns 50.0% of the joint venture, TAP Pharmaceutical Products Inc. On 2/8/01, ABT acquired BASF's pharmaceutical business, including the global operations of Knoll, for $6.90 billion in cash.

ANNUAL FINANCIAL DATA

	12/31/01	12/31/00	12/31/99	12/31/98	12/31/97	12/31/96	12/31/95
Earnings Per Share	③ 0.99	② 1.78	① 1.57	1.51	1.34	1.21	1.06
Cash Flow Per Share	1.74	2.31	2.10	2.02	1.81	1.64	1.42
Tang. Book Val. Per Share	1.14	4.54	3.78	2.88	2.54	2.48	2.69
Dividends Per Share	0.82	0.74	0.66	0.58	0.53	0.47	0.41
Dividend Payout %	82.8	41.6	42.0	38.7	39.2	38.6	38.7
INCOME STATEMENT (IN MILLIONS):							
Total Revenues	16,285.2	13,745.9	13,177.6	12,477.8	11,883.5	11,013.5	10,012.2
Costs & Expenses	13,223.2	9,517.9	9,200.2	8,575.7	8,305.3	7,710.3	7,062.9
Depreciation & Amort.	1,168.0	827.4	828.0	784.2	727.8	686.1	566.4
Operating Income	1,894.0	3,400.6	3,149.4	3,117.9	2,850.4	2,617.1	2,382.9
Net Interest Inc./(Exp.)	d234.8	d23.2	d81.8	d104.1	d86.8	d50.9	d17.7
Income Before Income Taxes	1,883.1	3,816.4	3,396.9	3,240.6	2,949.9	2,669.6	2,395.3
Income Taxes	332.8	1,030.4	951.1	907.4	855.5	787.5	706.6
Net Income	③ 1,550.4	② 2,786.0	① 2,445.8	2,333.2	2,094.5	1,882.0	1,688.7
Cash Flow	2,718.4	3,613.4	3,273.8	3,117.5	2,822.2	2,568.1	2,255.1
Average Inc. Outstg. (000)	1,565,963	1,565,579	1,557,655	1,545,658	1,561,462	1,562,494	1,590,724
BALANCE SHEET (IN MILLIONS):							
Cash & Cash Equivalents	713.5	1,156.7	723.3	383.3	259.0	123.1	315.7
Total Current Assets	8,419.2	7,376.2	6,419.8	5,553.1	5,038.2	4,480.9	4,226.7
Net Property	5,551.5	4,816.9	4,770.1	4,738.8	4,569.7	4,461.5	4,249.5
Total Assets	23,296.4	15,283.3	14,471.0	13,216.2	12,061.1	11,125.6	9,412.6
Total Current Liabilities	7,926.8	4,297.5	4,516.7	4,962.1	5,034.5	4,343.7	3,790.3
Long-Term Obligations	4,335.5	1,076.4	1,336.8	1,339.7	938.0	932.9	435.2
Net Stockholders' Equity	9,059.4	8,570.9	7,427.6	5,713.7	4,998.7	4,820.2	4,396.8
Net Working Capital	492.4	3,078.7	1,903.0	591.0	3.7	137.2	436.4
Year-end Shs. Outstg. (000)	1,554,530	1,545,934	1,547,020	1,516,063	1,528,188	1,548,898	1,574,614
STATISTICAL RECORD:							
Operating Profit Margin %	11.6	24.7	23.9	25.0	24.0	23.8	23.8
Net Profit Margin %	9.5	20.3	18.6	18.7	17.6	17.1	16.9
Return on Equity %	17.1	32.5	32.9	40.8	41.9	39.0	38.4
Return on Assets %	6.7	18.2	16.9	17.7	17.4	16.9	17.9
Debt/Total Assets %	18.6	7.0	9.2	10.1	7.8	8.4	4.6
Price Range	57.17-42.00	56.25-29.38	53.31-27.94	50.06-32.53	34.88-24.88	28.69-19.06	22.38-15.31
P/E Ratio	57.7-42.4	31.6-16.5	34.0-17.8	33.2-21.5	26.0-18.6	23.8-15.8	21.1-14.4
Average Yield %	1.7	1.7	1.6	1.4	1.8	1.9	2.2

Statistics are as originally reported. Adjusted for 2-for-1 stock split, 5/98. ① Incl. a nonrecurring pre-tax charge of $168.0 million relating to an FDA consent decree. ② Incl. pre-tax gain of $138.5 mill. on sale of bus. ③ Incl. pre-tax acq. in-process research & dev. chrg. of $1.33 bill.

OFFICERS:
M. D. White, Chmn., C.E.O.
T. C. Freyman, Sr. V.P., C.F.O.
T. C. Kearney, V.P., Treas.

INVESTOR CONTACT: Investor Relations,
(847) 937-6400

PRINCIPAL OFFICE: 100 Abbott Park Road,
Abbott Park, IL 60064-6400

TELEPHONE NUMBER: (847) 937-6100
FAX: (847) 937-1511
WEB: www.abbott.com

NO. OF EMPLOYEES: 71,426 (avg.)

SHAREHOLDERS: 97,760

ANNUAL MEETING: In Apr.

INCORPORATED: IL, Mar., 1900

INSTITUTIONAL HOLDINGS:
No. of Institutions: 1,056
Shares Held: 867,334,361
% Held: 55.7

INDUSTRY: Pharmaceutical preparations
(SIC: 2834)

TRANSFER AGENT(S): EquiServe,
Providence, RI

STATISTICAL RECORD:

Operating Profit Margin indicates operating profit as a percentage of net sales or revenues. **Net Profit Margin** is the percentage of total revenues remaining after the deduction of all non-extraordinary costs, including interest and taxes.

Return on Equity is one of several measures of profitability. It is the ratio of net income to net stockholders' equity, expressed as a percentage. This ratio illustrates how effectively the investment of the stockholders is being utilized to earn a profit.

Return on Assets is another means of measuring profitability. It is the ratio of net income to total assets, expressed as a percentage. This indicates how effectively the corporate assets are being used to generate profits.

Debt/Total Assets represents the ratio of long-term obligations to total assets as a percentage.

Price/Earnings Ratio is shown as a range. The figures are calculated by dividing the stock's highest price for the year and its lowest price by the year's earnings per share. Prices are for calendar years. Earnings used in the calculation for a particular calendar year are for the fiscal year in which the majority of the company's business took place. As a rule, for companies whose fiscal years end before June 30, the ratio is calculated by using the price range of the prior calendar year. For those with fiscal years ending on June 30 or later, the current year's price range is used.

Average Yield is the ratio (expressed as a percentage) of the annual dividend to the mean price of the common stock (average of the high and low for the year). Both prices and dividends are for calendar years.

EDITOR'S NOTE: In order to preserve the historical relationships between prices, earnings and dividends, figures are not restated to reflect subsequent events.

L. ADDITIONAL INFORMATION – For each stock, listings are provided for the company's officers, date of incorporation, its address, telephone number, fax number and website (when available), annual meeting date, the number of employees, the number of stockholders, institutional holdings, and transfer agent.

Institutional Holdings indicates the number of institutions holding the stock and the total number of shares held as last reported. Coverage includes investment companies, mutual funds, insurance companies, and banks. The percentage of shares outstanding held by institutions is also provided.

ABBREVIATIONS AND SYMBOLS

d	Deficit
E	Extra
M	Monthly
N.M.	Not Meaningful
p	Preliminary
P.F.	Pro Forma
Q	Quarterly
r	Revised
S	Semi-annual
Sp	Special Dividend
Y	Year-end Dividend

year shown as originally reported, provide the necessary historical perspective to intelligently review the various operating and financial trends. Generic definitions follow.

INCOME STATEMENT:

Total Revenues is the total income from operations including non-operating revenues.

Costs and Expenses is the total of all costs related to the operation of the business – including cost of sales, selling, and general and administrative expenses. Excluded items are depreciation, interest and non-operating expenses.

Depreciation and Amortization includes all non-cash charges such as depletion and amortization as well as depreciation.

Operating Income is the profit remaining after deducting depreciation as well as all operating costs and expenses from the company's net sales and revenues. This figure is *before* interest expenses, extraordinary gains and charges, and income and expense items of a non-operating nature.

Net Interest Income/(Expense) is the net amount of interest paid and received by a company during the fiscal year.

Income Before Income Taxes is the remaining income *after* deducting all costs, expenses, property charges, interest, etc. but *before* deducting income taxes.

Equity Earnings/Minority Interest is the net amount of profits allocated to minority owners or affiliates.

Income Taxes are shown as reported by the company and include both the amount of current taxes actually paid out and the amount deferred to future years.

Net Income is as reported by the corporation, before extraordinary gains and losses, discontinued operations and accounting changes, which are appropriately footnoted.

Cash Flow is the sum of net income and non-cash depreciation and amortization charges, less preferred dividends.

Average Shares Outstanding is the weighted average number of shares including common equivalent shares outstanding during the year, as reported by the corporation and fully

adjusted for all stock dividends and splits. The use of *average shares* minimizes the distortion in *earnings per share* which could result from issuance of a large amount of stock or the company's purchase of a large amount of its own stock during the year.

BALANCE SHEET:

All balance sheet items are shown as reported by the corporation in its annual report. Because of the limited amount of space available and in an effort to simplify and standardize accounts, some items have been combined. **Cash & Cash Equivalents** comprise unrestricted cash and temporary investments in marketable securities, such as U.S. Government securities, certificates of deposit and short-term investments.

Total Current Assets are all of the company's short-term assets, including cash, marketable securities, inventories, certain receivables, etc., as reported.

Net Property is total fixed assets, including all property, land, plants, buildings, equipment, fixtures, etc., less accumulated depreciation.

Total Assets represent the sum of all tangible and intangible assets as reported by the company.

Total Current Liabilities are all of the obligations of the company due within one year, as reported.

Long-term Obligations are total long-term debts (due beyond one year) reported by the company, including bonds, capital lease obligations, notes, mortgages, debentures, etc.

Net Stockholders' Equity is the sum of all capital stock accounts – stated values of preferred and common stock, paid-in capital, earned surplus (retained earnings), etc., net of all treasury stock.

Net Working Capital is derived by subtracting Current Liabilities from Current Assets.

Year-end Shares Outstanding are the number of shares outstanding as of the date of the company's annual report, exclusive of treasury stock and adjusted for subsequent stock dividends and splits.

HOW TO USE THIS BOOK (Continued)

shareholder had to have been a holder of record in order to have qualified for the dividend. The **Payable Date** indicates the date the company paid or intends to pay the dividend. The cash amount shown in the first column is followed by a letter (example "Q" for quarterly) to indicate the frequency of the dividend.

Indicated Dividend – This is the annualized amount (fully adjusted for splits) of the latest regular cash dividend. If the company has a dividend reinvestment plan, it is indicated here.

F. CAPITALIZATION – These are certain items in the company's capital account. Both the dollar amounts and their respective percentages are given.

Long-term Debt is the total amount of debt owed by the company which is due beyond one year.

Capital Lease Obligations is shown as a separate caption when indicated on the balance sheet as such.

Deferred Income Taxes represents the company's tax liability arising from accelerated depreciation and investment tax credit.

Preferred Stock is the sum of equity issues, exclusive of common stock, the holders of which have a prior claim, ahead of the common shareholders, to the income of the company while it continues to operate and to the assets in the event of dissolution.

Minority Interest in this instance is a capital item which reflects the share of ownership by an outside party in a consolidated subsidiary of the company.

Common and Surplus is the sum of the stated or par value of the common stock, plus additional paid-in capital and retained earnings less the dollar amount of treasury shares.

G. DIVIDEND ACHIEVER STATUS – The company's rank among the Dividend Achievers for dividend growth is indicated. Each company is ranked by its ten-year compound annual average cash dividend growth rate, which is also shown here, along with the total consecutive years of increases.

H. COMPANY BUSINESS – This section explains what the company does: the products or services it sells, its markets and production facilities.

I. RECENT DEVELOPMENTS – This section keeps you up to date on what has happened in the most recent quarter or fiscal year for which results are available. It provides analysis of recently released sales and earnings figures, including special charges and credits, and may also include results by sector, expense trends and ratios, and other current information.

J. ANNUAL FINANCIAL DATA – These figures are fully adjusted for all stock dividends and stock splits.

Earnings Per Share are as reported by the company except for adjustment for certain items as footnoted. Earnings per share reported after 12/15/97 are presented on a diluted basis, as described by Financial Accounting Standards Board Statement 128. Earnings per share reported prior to that date are shown on a primary basis.

Cash Flow Per Share is computed by dividing the total of net income and non-cash depreciation and amortization charges, less preferred dividends, by average shares outstanding.

Tangible Book Value Per Share is calculated by dividing stockholders equity minus intangibles by shares outstanding at fiscal year end. It demonstrates the underlying value of each common share if the company were to be liquidated as of that date.

Dividends Per Share represent the sum of all cash payments on a calendar year basis. Any fiscal year ending prior to June 30, for example, is shown with dividends for the prior calendar year.

Dividend Payout % is the percentage of cash paid out of **Earnings Per Share**.

K. INCOME STATEMENT, BALANCE SHEET AND STATISTICAL RECORD – Here is pertinent earnings and balance sheet information essential to analyzing a corporation's performance. The comparisons, each

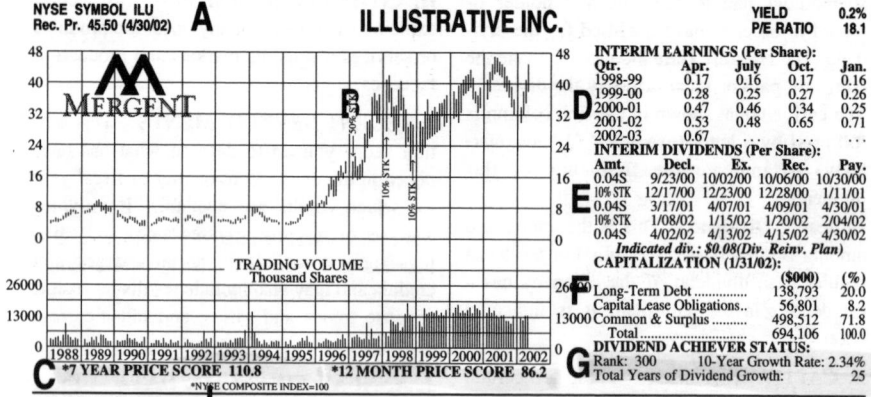

NYSE SYMBOL ILU **A**
Rec. Pr. 45.50 (4/30/02)

ILLUSTRATIVE INC.

YIELD 0.2%
P/E RATIO 18.1

D INTERIM EARNINGS (Per Share):

Qtr.	Apr.	July	Oct.	Jan.
1998-99	0.17	0.16	0.17	0.16
1999-00	0.28	0.25	0.27	0.26
2000-01	0.47	0.46	0.34	0.25
2001-02	0.53	0.48	0.65	0.71
2002-03	0.67	...	...	...

E INTERIM DIVIDENDS (Per Share):

Amt.	Decl.	Ex.	Rec.	Pay.
0.04S	9/23/00	10/02/00	10/06/00	10/30/00
10% STK	12/17/00	12/23/00	12/28/00	1/11/01
0.04S	3/17/01	4/07/01	4/09/01	4/30/01
10% STK	1/08/02	1/15/02	1/20/02	2/04/02
0.04S	4/02/02	4/13/02	4/15/02	4/30/02

Indicated div.: $0.08(Div. Reinv. Plan)

F CAPITALIZATION (1/31/02):

	($000)	(%)
Long-Term Debt	138,793	20.0
Capital Lease Obligations	56,801	8.2
Common & Surplus	498,512	71.8
Total	694,106	100.0

G DIVIDEND ACHIEVER STATUS:
Rank: 300 10-Year Growth Rate: 2.34%
Total Years of Dividend Growth: 25

TRADING VOLUME
Thousand Shares

C *7 YEAR PRICE SCORE 110.8 *12 MONTH PRICE SCORE 86.2
*NYSE COMPOSITE INDEX=100

RECENT DEVELOPMENTS: For the year ended 1/31/02, net income before an extraordinary gain improved to $46.8 million compared with net income of $22.3 million the year before. Total revenues increased to $1.15 billion from $614.1 million the year before. Increased revenues are contributing to improving margins at Bill's Burgers, Salads a Go Go, and Pizza Galore chains. Revenues from Company-owned restaurants climbed to $867.0 million from $712.8 billion.

PROSPECTS: Growing revenues per restaurant across all the Company's chains bode well for future results. The Company is planning to open an additional 60 Bill's Burgers restaurants in 2001 and another 90 in 2002. Meanwhile, 80 Pizza Galore and 40 Salad a Go Go restaurants are planned to open in the Midwest in the second half of 2001. The Company is predicting earnings per share of $1.10 to $1.20 for the current fiscal year.

H BUSINESS

ILLUSTRATIVE INC., through its subsidiaries and franchisees, owns and/or operates 1,576 Bill's Burgers restaurants, featuring the Company's patented vegetarian Bill Burgers. The restaurants are located in all 50 states. In addition, the Company owns 582 Salad a Go Go restaurants and take-out facilities in 14 eastern and southeastern states. The Company also owns and operates 312 Pizza Galore restaurants and 12 Seafood Symphony restaurants in North and South Carolina.

REVENUES

(01/31/02)	($000)	(%)
Co.-operated restaurants	1,022,453	88.9
Franchised & licensed	127,206	11.1
Total	1,149,659	100.0

J ANNUAL FINANCIAL DATA

	1/31/02	1/31/01	1/31/00	1/31/99	1/31/98	1/25/97	1/27/96
Earnings Per Share	2.37	1.52	1.06	0.66	0.54	0.51	0.48
Cash Flow Per Share	1.76	1.34	0.95	0.71	0.81	0.68	1.20
Tang. Book Val. Per Share	8.86	5.34	3.01	2.67	2.72	2.58	2.76
Dividends Per Share	0.07	0.06	0.05	0.04	0.03	0.02	0.01
Dividend Payout %	3.0	3.9	4.7	6.1	5.6	3.9	2.1
INCOME STATEMENT (IN MILLIONS):							
Total Revenues	1,149.7	614.1	465.4	443.7	460.4	502.6	533.6
Costs & Expenses	1,017.1	545.0	418.3	412.4	427.0	484.7	487.0
Depreciation & Amort.	46.4	27.1	21.4	22.8	22.8	25.2	26.6
Operating Income	86.2	42.0	25.7	8.6	10.5	27.3	20.0
Net Interest Inc./(Exp.)	d16.9	d9.9	d10.0	d9.2	d10.4	d13.6	d16.7
Income Before Income Taxes	76.6	36.7	18.0	2.4	6.3	27.3	18.9
Income Taxes	29.9	14.4	7.0	1.1	1.8	cr4.2	5.8
Net Income	46.8	22.3	11.0	1.3	4.4	d3.1	13.0
Cash Flow	93.2	49.4	32.3	24.0	27.3	22.1	39.6
Average Shs. Outstg. (000)	52,934	36,801	33,902	33,971	33,699	32,732	33,018
BALANCE SHEET (IN MILLIONS):							
Cash & Cash Equivalents	30.4	39.8	25.9	18.2	26.1	44.4	36.7
Total Current Assets	92.2	72.9	56.8	56.8	69.4	90.6	83.8
Net Property	674.6	242.9	155.7	163.8	146.8	150.6	175.0
Total Assets	957.4	401.2	246.8	244.3	242.1	268.9	292.6
Total Current Liabilities	176.5	83.9	61.3	71.6	66.6	91.4	92.3
Long-Term Obligations	195.6	81.9	70.6	69.9	63.3	80.3	102.1
Net Stockholders' Equity	498.5	214.8	101.2	88.5	92.1	84.7	89.7
Net Working Capital	d84.3	d11.0	d4.5	d14.7	2.9	d0.9	d8.5
Year-end Shs. Outstg. (000)	56,293	40,195	33,632	33,133	33,899	32,835	32,521
STATISTICAL RECORD: K							
Operating Profit Margin %	7.5	6.8	5.5	1.9	2.3	...	3.8
Net Profit Margin %	4.1	3.6	2.4	0.3	1.0	...	2.4
Return on Equity %	9.4	10.4	10.8	1.4	4.8	...	14.5
Return on Assets %	4.9	5.6	4.4	0.5	1.8	...	4.5
Debt/Total Assets %	20.4	20.4	28.6	28.6	26.1	29.8	34.9
Price Range	47.50-32	42.50-31	37.13-21.75	42-17.50	37.50-15.19	19.97-7.99	9.25-4.50
P/E Ratio	20-13.5	28-20.4	35-20.5	63.6-26.5	69.4-28.1	...	19.3-9.4
Average Yield %	0.2	0.2	0.2	0.1	0.1	0.2	0.2

Statistics are as originally reported. Adj. for stk. splits: 10% div., 1/99, 2/98; 3-for-2, 1/97

OFFICERS:
C. B. Dickens II, Chmn., C.E.O.
D. D. Alexander, President, C.O.O.
P. Patrick, Treas. & C.F.O.
B. I. Gussbus, Secretary
PRINCIPAL OFFICE: 800 N. Primrose Lane, Charlotte, NC 28200

TELEPHONE NUMBER: (704) 555-5796
FAX: (704) 555-3630
NO. OF EMPLOYEES: 46,500 (approx.)
SHAREHOLDERS: **L** 3,800 (approx.)
ANNUAL MEETING: In Jun.
INCORPORATED: NC, Dec., 1951

INSTITUTIONAL HOLDINGS:
No. of Institutions: 133
Shares Held: 44,571,077 (Adj.)
% Held: 78.2
INDUSTRY: Eating places (SIC: 5812)
TRANSFER AGENT(S): Wachovia Bank, Charlotte, NC

29a

MERGENT'S Dividend Achievers is a compact, easy-to-use reference that provides basic financial and business information on 282 companies that have increased their cash dividends annually over at least the past ten calendar years. The presentation of background information plus current and historical data provides the answers to three basic questions for each company:

1. What does the company do?
   (See G.)
2. How has it done in the past?
   (See B, D, E, I, J.)
3. How is it doing now?
   (See D, E, F, H.)

The following information is highlighted:

A. CAPSULE STOCK INFORMATION – This section shows the stock symbol, plus the approximate yield afforded by the indicated dividend, based on a recent price, and the price earnings ratio calculated on earnings from the most recent four quarters.

B. LONG-TERM PRICE CHART – This chart illustrates the pattern of monthly stock price movements, fully adjusted for stock dividends and splits. The chart points out the degree of volatility in the price movement of the company's stock and reveals its long-term trend. It indicates areas of price support and resistance, plus other technical points to be considered by the investor. The bars at the base of the long-term price chart indicate the monthly trading volume.

C. PRICE SCORES – Below each company's price/volume chart are its *Mergent's Price Scores*. These are basic measures of the stock's performance. Each stock is measured against the New York Stock Exchange Composite Index.

A score of 100 indicates that the stock did as well as the New York Stock Exchange Composite Index during the time period. A score of less than 100 means that the stock did not do as well; a score of more than 100 means that the stock outperformed the NYSE Com-

posite Index. All stock prices are adjusted for splits and stock dividends. The time periods measured for each company conclude with the date of the recent price shown in the top-left corner of each company's profile.

The *SEVEN-YEAR PRICE SCORE* mirrors the common stock's price growth over the previous seven years. The higher the price score, the better the relative performance. It is based on the ratio of the latest twelve-month average price to the current seven year average. This ratio is then indexed against the same ratio for the market as a whole (the New York Stock Exchange Composite Index), which is taken as 100.

The *TWELVE-MONTH PRICE SCORE* is a similar measurement but for a shorter period of time. It is based on the ratio of the latest two-month average price to the current twelve-month average. As was done for the Seven-Year Price Score, this ratio is also indexed to the same ratio for the market as a whole.

In both cases, all prices are adjusted for all stock dividends and splits.

D. INTERIM EARNINGS (Per Share) – Figures are reported before extraordinary items, discontinued operations and the cumulative effects of accounting changes (unless otherwise noted). Each figure is for the quarterly period indicated, unless otherwise noted. Prior to 12/15/97, primary earnings per share are shown. After that date, diluted earnings per share are displayed, as described in Financial Accounting Standards Board Statement 128. Figures are adjusted for all stock dividends and splits. See 'Earnings Per Share' below.

E. INTERIM DIVIDENDS (Per Share) – The cash dividends are the actual dollar amounts declared by the company. No adjustments have been made for stock dividends and splits. **Ex-Dividend Date**: a stockholder must purchase the stock prior to this date in order to be entitled to the dividend. The **Record Date** indicates the date on which the

SHOE MANUFACTURING
Weyco Group, Inc.

SOAPS & CLEANERS
* Clorox Co.
* Colgate-Palmolive Co.
* Procter & Gamble Co.

SOFT DRINKS
* The Coca-Cola Co.
* Pepsico, Inc.

STEEL
* Nucor Corp.

TELECOMMUNICATIONS
* ALLTEL Corp.
* CenturyTel, Inc.
  North Pittsburgh Systems, Inc.
* SBC Communications Inc.
* Telephone & Data Systems, Inc.

TIRES & RUBBER GOODS
* Bandag, Inc.

TOBACCO
* Philip Morris Companies, Inc.
* Universal Corp.

WATER COMPANIES
* American States Water Co.
* American Water Works Company, Inc.
* California Water Service Co.
* Connecticut Water Service, Inc.
* Middlesex Water Company
* Philadelphia Suburban Corp.
  SJW Corp.

WHOLESALERS - DISTRIBUTORS - JOBBERS
Grainger (W.W.), Inc.

*Designates companies offering dividend reinvestment plans

* Becton, Dickinson & Co.
* Johnson & Johnson
* Medtronic, Inc.
* Mine Safety Appliances Co.

METAL PRODUCTS
* Worthington Industries, Inc.

NATURAL GAS
* MDU Resources Group Inc.
* National Fuel Gas Co.
* Peoples Energy Corp.
* Vectren Corporation

NATURAL GAS - DISTRIBUTORS
* Atmos Energy Corp.
* Energen Corp.
* Energy West Inc.
* EnergySouth, Inc.
* Florida Public Utilities Co.
* NICOR Inc.
* Piedmont Natural Gas Co., Inc.
* Questar Corp.
* Semco Energy Inc.
* UGI Corp.
* WGL Holdings, Inc.

NEWSPAPERS
Belo Corp.
* Gannett Co., Inc.
* Lee Enterprises, Inc.

OFFICE EQUIPMENT & SUPPLIES
* Avery Dennison Corp.
* Diebold, Inc.
HON Industries Inc.
* Pitney Bowes Inc.

OIL
* ChevronTexaco Corp.
* Exxon Mobil Corp.

PAINTS & RELATED PRODUCTS
* RPM Inc.
* Sherwin-Williams Co.
* The Valspar Corp.

PAPER
* Bemis Co., Inc.
* Kimberly-Clark Corp.
* Pentair, Inc.
* Sonoco Products Co.
* Wausau-Mossinee Paper Corp.

POLLUTION CONTROL/ENVIRONMENT
* Pall Corp.

PRINTING & ENGRAVING
* Banta Corp.
* Donnelley (R. R.) & Sons Co.

PUBLISHING
* McGraw-Hill Companies, Inc.

RAILROAD EQUIPMENT
* GATX Corp.

REAL ESTATE INVESTMENT TRUSTS
* Commercial Net Lease Realty
* Cousins Properties Inc.
* Federal Realty Investment Trust
* Health Care Property Investors, Inc.
Health Care REIT, Inc.
* United Dominion Realty Trust, Inc.
* United Mobile Homes, Inc.
* Universal Health Realty Income Trust
* Washington Real Estate Investment Trust
* Weingarten Realty Investors

RECREATION
* Cedar Fair, L.P.

RESTAURANTS
Applebee's International, Inc.
Frisch's Restaurants, Inc.
* McDonald's Corp.

RETAIL DEPARTMENT STORES
* May Department Stores Co.
* Target Corp.

RETAIL - DISCOUNT & VARIETY STORES
* Dollar General Corporation
Family Dollar Stores, Inc.
* Wal-Mart Stores, Inc.

RETAIL - DRUG STORES
* Walgreen Co.

RETAIL - SPECIALTY STORES
Haverty Furniture Companies, Inc.
* Home Depot, Inc.
* Lowe's Companies, Inc.
* Pier 1 Imports, Inc.

SAVINGS & LOAN
* First Federal Capital Corp.
First Indiana Corp.
Golden West Financial Corp.
* Washington Mutual, Inc.
Wesco Financial Corp.

SECURITIES BROKERAGE
* Franklin Resources, Inc.
* Legg Mason, Inc.
* Merrill Lynch & Co., Inc.
* Raymond James Financial, Inc.
* Schwab (Charles) Corporation
SEI Investments Co.

SERVICES
Cintas Corporation
* Paychex, Inc.
* ServiceMaster Co.

* Progress Energy, Inc.
* TECO Energy, Inc.
* WPS Resources Corporation

ELECTRIC POWER - NORTHEASTERN REGION
* Consolidated Edison, Inc.
* DQE, Inc.

ELECTRIC POWER - WESTERN REGION
* Black Hills Corp.
* Northwestern Corp.
* Otter Tail Power Co.
  XCEL Energy, Inc.

ELECTRICAL EQUIPMENT
* Baldor Electric Co.
  Cohu, Inc.
* Emerson Electric Co.
* General Electric Co.
* Hubbell Inc.
* Raven Industries, Inc.

ENGINEERING & CONSTRUCTION
* Masco Corp.

EQUIPMENT LEASING
McGrath Rentcorp

FINANCE
* Fannie Mae
* Freddie Mac
* Household International, Inc.
* USA Education, Inc.

FINANCIAL SERVICES
Eaton Vance Corp.
* T. Rowe Price Group, Inc.
* Citigroup Inc.

FOOD - GRAIN & AGRICULTURE
Archer Daniels Midland Co.
* ConAgra Foods, Inc.

FOOD PROCESSING
* Heinz (H.J.) Co.
* Hormel Foods Corp.
* Kellogg Co.
* Lancaster Colony Corp.
* McCormick & Co., Inc.
* Sara Lee Corp.

FOOD WHOLESALERS
* SUPERVALU Inc.
* Sysco Corporation

FURNITURE & FIXTURES
* La-Z-Boy Incorporated
  Leggett & Platt, Inc.
  Virco Manufacturing Co.

GROCERY CHAINS
* Albertson's Inc.
* Weis Markets, Inc.

HARDWARE & TOOLS
* Illinois Tool Works Inc.
* The Stanley Works

INSURANCE - BROKERAGE
Gallagher (Arthur J.) & Co.
Hilb, Rogal & Hamilton Co.
* Marsh & McLennan Companies, Inc.

INSURANCE - COMBINED
American International Group, Inc.
* Aon Corp.
* Cincinnati Financial Corp.
  Crawford & Co.
* Jefferson-Pilot Corp.
* Lincoln National Corp.
* Midland Co.
* Old Republic International Corp.
  The Progressive Corp.

INSURANCE - LIFE
* AFLAC Inc.
* American National Insurance Co.
* Protective Life Corp.

INSURANCE - PROPERTY & CASUALTY
* Alfa Corp.
* The Chubb Co.
* Donegal Group Inc.
  Harleysville Group, Inc.
* Mercury General Corporation
  National Security Group, Inc.
* RLI Corp.
* St. Paul Cos., Inc.
* State Auto Financial Corp.
  Transatlantic Holdings, Inc.
  United Fire & Casualty Co.
  Unitrin, Inc.

INSURANCE - SPECIALTY
* Fidelity National Financial, Inc.
  MBIA Inc.

MACHINERY & EQUIPMENT
* Briggs & Stratton Corp.
* Dover Corp.
* Federal Signal Corp.
* Gorman-Rupp Co.
  Kaydon Corp.
* Modine Manufacturing Co.
  NACCO Industries Inc.
* Nordson Corporation
* Tennant Co.

MAINTENANCE & SECURITY SERVICES
ABM Industries, Inc.

MEASURING & CONTROL INSTRUMENTS
* Johnson Controls, Inc.
* Teleflex, Inc.

MEDICAL & DENTAL EQUIPMENT & SUPPLIES
* Abbott Laboratories
* Bard (C.R.), Inc.
  Beckman Coulter, Inc.

ADVERTISING
* Interpublic Group of Companies, Inc.

AMUSEMENTS
Bowl America Inc.

APPAREL
* VF Corp.

AUTOMOBILE PARTS
* Clarcor Inc.
* Genuine Parts Corp.
* Myers Industries, Inc.
* Superior Industries International, Inc.

BANKS - MAJOR
* Bank of America Corp.
MBNA Corp.
* Morgan (J.P.) Chase & Co., Inc.

BANKS - MID-ATLANTIC
* Community Trust Bancorp, Inc.
* First Commonwealth Financial Corp.
* First Virginia Banks, Inc.
* F.N.B. Corp.
* Fulton Financial Corp.
* Marshall & Ilsley Corp.
* Mercantile Bankshares Corp.
* Susquehanna Bancshares, Inc.
* WesBanco, Inc.

BANKS - MIDWEST
* Associated Banc-Corp.
* Charter One Financial, Inc.
* Citizens Banking Corp.
* Comerica, Inc.
* Commerce Bancshares, Inc.
Community First Bankshares, Inc.
Corus Bankshares, Inc.
* Fifth Third Bancorp
* First Financial Bancorp
1st Source Corp.
* FirstMerit Corp.
* Irwin Financial Corp.
* KeyCorp
* Northern Trust Corp.
* Old National Bancorp
* Park National Corp.
* United Bankshares, Inc.
* Wells Fargo & Co.

BANKS - NORTHEAST
* Chemical Financial Corp.
Commerce Bancorp, Inc.
* Community Bank System, Inc.
* Hudson United Bancorp
* Huntington Bancshares, Inc.
* M&T Bank Corp.
* National Penn Bancshares, Inc.
* PNC Financial Services Group, Inc.
S&T Bancorp, Inc.
* State Street Corp.
* Trustco Bank
* Valley National Bancorp
* Wilmington Trust Corporation

BANKS - SOUTH
* AmSouth Bancorporation
* BancorpSouth Inc.
* BB&T Corp.
* Compass Bancshares, Inc.
* National Commerce Financial Corp.
* Regions Financial Corp.
* SouthTrust Corp.
* SunTrust Banks, Inc.
* Synovus Financial Corp.
* Trustmark Corp.

BANKS - WEST
* CVB Financial Corp.
Pacific Capital Bancorp
* Pacific Century Financial Corp.
WestAmerica Bancorporation

BREWING
* Anheuser-Busch Companies, Inc.

CANDY & GUM
* Hershey Foods Corporation
Tootsie Roll Industries, Inc.
* Wrigley (Wm.) Jr. Co.

CHEMICALS
* Air Products & Chemicals, Inc.
* Brady Corp.
* Fuller (H.B.)
* PPG Industries, Inc.
* Quaker Chemical Corp.
* Rohm & Haas Co.
Sigma-Aldrich Corporation
Stepan Co.

COMPUTERS - SERVICES
* Automatic Data Processing, Inc.
* Jack Henry & Associates, Inc.

CONGLOMERATES
* Carlisle Companies, Inc.
* Hillenbrand Industries, Inc.
* Minnesota Mining & Manufacturing Co.

COSMETICS & TOILETRIES
Alberto-Culver Co.
* Avon Products, Inc.
* Gillette Co.

DEFENSE SYSTEMS & EQUIPMENT
* General Dynamics Corp.

DISTILLING
* Brown-Forman Corp.

DRUGS
* Bristol-Myers Squibb Co.
* Lilly (Eli) & Co.
* Merck & Co., Inc.
* Pfizer Inc.
* Schering-Plough Corp.

ELECTRIC POWER - CENTRAL & SOUTHEASTERN REGIONS
* CLECO Corp.
* Madison Gas & Electric Co.
* NiSource, Inc.

About Total Return

Total return represents one of the best measures of how well an investor in any given stock has fared because it reflects both dividend payments and price appreciation. Mergent has calculated total return for each Dividend Achiever company on the basis that cash dividends on each stock were reinvested in that company's shares at the end of the month in which the dividends were paid. Thus the preceding table demonstrates the effect of compounding as well as each stock's performance and the level of dividends paid. Figures have been adjusted for splits, stock dividends and spin-offs. In the case of a spin-off, shares in the spun-off company were assumed to be converted to cash and reinvested in the original company's stock.

How to read the rankings: On the preceding pages the Dividend Achiever companies are listed by one-year total return for calendar 2001. For example, an investor who bought shares at the end of December, 2000 in Raven Industries, Inc., and sold them at the end of December, 2001, would have realized a 112.9% gain on the original investment. Following each company's 2001 total return is its three-year total return and ranking and five-year total return and ranking. The three-year total return is based on an investment made at the end of December, 1998, and the five-year total return on an investment made at the end of December, 1996. The three- and five-year total-return percentages represent cumulative totals. Thus an investment made in Raven Industries at the end of December, 1998, would have increased 143.5% if the stock were sold at the end of December, 2001. If an investor had bought shares in Raven Industries at the end of December, 1996, and sold them at the end of December, 2001, his investment would have grown by 82.4%.

Total Returns (cont.)

2001 Rank	Company	2001 Tot. Return %	3-yr. Tot. Return %	3-yr. Rank	5-yr. Tot. Return %	5-yr. Rank
266.	Black Hills Corp.	-22.0	44.1	66	121.3	75
267.	Merrill Lynch & Co.	-22.7	61.8	36	171.8	38
268.	Weis Markets, Inc.	-24.5	-21.2	253	1.7	266
269.	Fidelity National Financial, Inc.	-25.0	-5.4	219	137.0	58
270.	Northern Trust Corp.	-25.4	41.9	70	251.0	17
271.	Emerson Electric Co.	-25.5	1.5	199	32.0	231
272.	Bristol-Myers Squibb Co.	-26.3	-16.1	244	113.3	82
273.	Semco Energy Inc.	-26.6	-21.1	252	-15.9	277
274.	Paychex, Inc.	-27.6	56.3	42	256.8	14
275.	Jack Henry & Associates, Inc.	-29.3	78.7	24	278.8	11
276.	Interpublic Group of Cos.	-29.6	-23.6	259	96.3	100
277.	AFLAC Inc.	-31.5	14.1	157	138.3	56
278.	GATX Corp.	-32.6	-5.5	220	56.2	183
279.	Schering-Plough Corp.	-35.9	-32.7	274	135.6	61
280.	Merck & Co., Inc.	-36.0	-16.2	245	60.5	170
281.	DQE, Inc.	-38.1	-50.1	281	-17.5	278
282.	Schwab (Charles) Corp.	-45.3	-17.0	247	231.0	23

Note: The three- and five-year returns for Vectren Corp. do not appear as sufficient pricing data were not available

Total Returns (cont.)

2001 Rank	Company	2001 Tot. Return %	3-yr. Tot. Return %	3-yr. Rank	5-yr. Tot. Return %	5-yr. Rank
221.	State Auto Financial Corp.	-8.4	35.0	86	88.2	114
222.	Protective Life Corp.	-8.7	-23.7	260	56.6	181
223.	KeyCorp	-8.9	-12.8	238	17.0	246
224.	Cousins Properties Inc.	-9.1	26.0	109	54.2	189
	Old National Bancorp	-9.1	-15.8	243	36.8	222
226.	Cintas Corp.	-9.3	3.6	191	150.7	47
227.	Colgate-Palmolive Co.	-9.5	28.9	99	167.6	39
228.	Heinz (H.J.) Co.	-10.0	-19.4	249	34.3	227
229.	Old Republic International	-10.6	34.9	87	75.5	145
	Peoples Energy Corp.	-10.6	12.5	162	47.0	202
231.	MDU Resources Group Inc.	-10.8	18.4	134	120.1	78
232.	Bandag, Inc.	-10.9	-2.0	213	-13.5	276
233.	Carlisle Companies Inc.	-11.7	-24.0	261	33.3	229
	Sysco Corp.	-11.7	98.0	10	243.5	20
235.	Tootsie Roll Industries, Inc.	-12.0	11.4	168	136.3	60
236.	Golden West Financial Corp.	-12.4	95.5	11	187.2	33
	Pfizer Inc.	-12.4	-1.7	212	201.8	29
238.	Kimberly-Clark Corp.	-13.8	15.8	146	37.8	218
	SJW Corp.	-13.8	57.4	41	113.6	80
240.	Questar Corp.	-14.2	42.6	69	60.2	171
241.	Lilly (Eli) & Co.	-14.4	-8.0	225	129.6	68
242.	Medtronic, Inc.	-14.8	39.6	76	207.9	28
243.	TECO Energy Inc.	-15.0	9.8	176	40.8	215
244.	General Electric Co.	-15.1	22.5	121	160.8	42
245.	State Street Corp.	-15.2	52.3	48	236.2	22
246.	SBC Communications Inc.	-16.0	-22.0	255	70.0	153
247.	Harleysville Group, Inc.	-16.4	0.7	200	78.0	138
	T. Rowe Price Group, Inc.	-16.4	5.7	184	69.8	154
249.	CLECO Corp.	-16.5	46.6	55	103.0	92
250.	St. Paul Cos., Inc.	-17.1	37.6	82	72.0	151
251.	Morgan (J.P.) Chase & Co.	-17.5	-17.2	248	37.6	219
252.	National Fuel Gas Co.	-18.4	23.0	119	45.8	203
253.	Chubb Corp.	-18.7	13.2	159	41.3	213
254.	Irwin Financial Corp.	-18.8	-35.1	276	44.7	207
255.	Walgreen Co.	-19.2	16.4	144	244.0	19
256.	American International Group	-19.3	54.9	44	212.8	27
	SEI Investments Co.	-19.3	175.0	4	1,149.5	1
258.	Wells Fargo & Co.	-20.2	15.8	146	121.1	76
259.	Dollar General Corporation	-20.4	0.5	202	82.9	127
260.	PNC Financial Services Group	-20.8	14.4	155	75.0	146
261.	Tennant Co.	-21.1	-1.5	210	49.6	199
262.	Coca-Cola Co. (The)	-21.4	-26.9	268	-5.3	269
	Energen Corp.	-21.4	38.5	79	90.8	110
264.	McDonald's Corp.	-21.5	-29.7	271	20.4	245
265.	NiSource, Inc.	-21.6	-12.4	237	45.3	204

Total Returns (cont.)

2001 Rank	Company	2001 Tot. Return %	3-yr. Tot. Return %	3-yr. Rank	5-yr. Tot. Return %	5-yr. Rank
176.	Minnesota Mining & Mfg. Co.	0.3	78.7	24	61.2	168
	Telephone & Data Systems	0.3	103.0	8	156.9	43
178.	Citigroup Inc.	0.1	110.5	7	252.9	15
179.	WGL Holdings, Inc.	-0.1	23.8	117	62.4	163
180.	California Water Service Co.	-0.4	-6.8	222	51.8	192
	Comerica, Inc.	-0.4	-8.3	226	87.1	118
182.	BB&T Corp.	-0.5	-3.0	216	125.8	72
	PepsiCo, Inc.	-0.5	24.1	115	92.9	107
184.	Briggs & Stratton Corp.	-0.8	-7.1	223	10.6	253
185.	Avon Products, Inc.	-1.2	11.1	170	79.0	135
186.	Cincinnati Financial Corp.	-1.5	10.7	173	94.4	104
187.	American States Water Co.	-1.6	44.7	63	100.3	95
188.	Piedmont Natural Gas Co., Inc.	-1.9	14.0	158	91.6	109
189.	Vectren Corporation	-2.0	----	----	----	----
190.	Commerce Bancshares, Inc.	-2.1	11.7	167	74.6	147
191.	National Security Group, Inc.	-2.3	48.0	54	72.2	150
	Rohm & Haas Co.	-2.3	22.8	120	42.0	212
193.	Masco Corp.	-2.4	-9.1	229	50.5	196
194.	Becton, Dickinson & Co.	-3.2	-19.6	250	61.3	167
195.	Charter One Financial, Inc.	-3.5	16.9	143	76.6	140
196.	MBNA Corp.	-3.7	46.2	57	201.0	30
197.	Progress Energy, Inc.	-3.8	12.5	162	59.8	172
198.	Brown-Forman Corp.	-3.9	-12.1	236	51.5	193
	Freddie Mac	-3.9	5.3	185	151.2	46
200.	Northwestern Corp.	-4.0	-7.5	224	55.4	185
201.	First Indiana Corp.	-4.2	18.4	134	38.5	217
202.	ConAgra Foods, Inc.	-4.5	-15.4	242	11.4	252
203.	Jefferson-Pilot Corp.	-5.0	-1.3	208	104.3	91
204.	Washington Mutual Inc.	-5.1	40.0	75	93.4	106
205.	Synovus Financial Corp.	-5.3	10.3	174	90.5	111
206.	Gillette Co. (The)	-5.6	-26.3	267	-7.6	271
207.	WestAmerica Bancorporation	-6.0	15.2	150	126.8	69
208.	WesBanco, Inc.	-6.2	-20.0	251	15.8	247
209.	Automatic Data Processing	-6.3	50.0	52	185.6	34
	Marsh & McLennan Cos. Inc.	-6.3	95.5	11	248.2	18
211.	Franklin Resources, Inc.	-6.8	12.3	165	59.2	175
212.	Kaydon Corp.	-6.9	-40.3	279	3.6	263
213.	Fannie Mae	-7.0	12.9	161	129.8	67
	Sara Lee Corp.	-7.0	-14.7	241	33.8	228
215.	Corus Bankshares, Inc.	-7.1	48.2	53	52.7	191
216.	Dover Corp.	-7.2	5.1	187	55.9	184
217.	Exxon Mobil Corp.	-7.5	14.8	153	80.1	133
218.	Legg Mason, Inc.	-7.6	62.1	34	261.0	13
219.	CenturyTel, Inc.	-7.7	-25.9	265	146.7	50
220.	Atmos Energy Corp.	-8.3	-22.9	258	12.2	251

Total Returns (cont.)

2001 Rank	Company	2001 Tot. Return %	3-yr. Tot. Return %	3-yr. Rank	5-yr. Tot. Return %	5-yr. Rank
131.	Teleflex Inc.	8.8	8.5	180	94.3	105
132.	M & T Bank Corp.	8.6	45.4	59	166.2	40
133.	Unitrin, Inc.	8.2	33.2	92	85.8	121
134.	Gannett Co., Inc.	8.1	8.4	182	92.1	108
135.	Valley National Bancorp	7.7	51.6	50	134.1	63
136.	Universal Corp.	7.5	18.2	137	37.1	221
137.	Weyco Group, Inc.	7.1	5.2	186	104.9	90
138.	Hershey Foods Corp.	7.0	15.2	150	68.6	156
	Otter Tail Power Co.	7.0	63.6	33	125.4	73
	Sherwin-Williams Co.	7.0	0.3	204	8.4	258
141.	Household International Inc.	6.8	53.0	47	102.9	93
142.	Park National Corp.	6.6	2.7	194	108.8	87
143.	Beckman Coulter, Inc.	6.5	68.5	31	144.3	53
144.	Aon Corp.	6.3	3.8	190	44.3	208
145.	Nordson Corp.	5.9	9.2	178	-9.2	274
146.	McGraw-Hill Cos., Inc.	5.7	25.7	112	189.6	32
	Stepan Co.	5.7	-0.5	206	35.4	225
148.	Frisch's Restaurants, Inc.	5.6	59.0	39	9.5	255
149.	Avery Dennison Corp.	5.5	33.2	92	75.8	144
150.	Crawford & Co.	5.4	-13.5	239	-7.7	273
151.	Alberto-Culver Co.	5.3	72.6	30	95.0	102
	Lincoln National Corp.	5.3	28.5	101	111.5	85
	Myers Industries Inc.	5.3	-33.6	275	26.8	239
	WPS Resources Corp.	5.3	26.0	109	76.3	141
155.	Wilmington Trust Corp.	5.2	13.1	160	86.6	119
156.	FirstMerit Corp.	5.1	11.9	166	77.8	139
157.	National Commerce Finl. Corp.	4.6	42.9	68	190.6	31
158.	ABM Industries Inc.	4.5	-3.2	218	87.5	116
159.	Fifth Third Bancorp	4.0	34.4	88	252.2	16
160.	General Dynamics Corp.	3.6	41.5	72	145.6	51
161.	Middlesex Water Co.	3.1	51.7	49	133.4	64
162.	Procter & Gamble Co.	3.0	-8.8	227	59.1	176
	Raymond James Finl. Inc.	3.0	74.6	28	181.5	36
164.	Mercantile Bankshares Corp.	2.5	21.7	123	131.3	66
165.	Fulton Financial Corp.	2.4	28.7	100	94.5	103
	Mercury General Corp.	2.4	9.0	179	87.3	117
167.	RLI Corp.	2.2	41.9	70	81.9	130
168.	Archer Daniels Midland Co.	2.0	1.8	197	-10.9	275
	SunTrust Banks, Inc.	2.0	-11.8	234	41.0	214
170.	Pacific Capital Bancorp	1.9	17.6	141	126.8	69
171.	Baldor Electric Co.	1.4	11.0	172	25.8	242
172.	ALLTEL Corp.	1.1	9.5	177	121.7	74
173.	Sigma-Aldrich Corp.	1.0	37.9	81	31.8	233
174.	Anheuser-Busch Cos., Inc.	0.9	44.6	64	147.8	49
175.	NICOR Inc.	0.8	12.5	162	43.1	211

Total Returns (cont.)

2001 Rank	Company	2001 Tot. Return %	3-yr. Tot. Return %	3-yr. Rank	5-yr. Tot. Return %	5-yr. Rank
86.	Trustmark Corp.	18.3	15.1	152	111.6	84
87.	Philadelphia Suburban Corp.	17.9	30.2	97	176.1	37
88.	Citizens Banking Corp.	17.6	10.0	175	23.6	244
	Federal Signal Corp.	17.6	-9.0	228	2.0	265
90.	Weingarten Realty Investors	17.5	33.3	91	65.4	162
91.	Modine Manufacturing Co.	17.0	-28.0	269	2.4	264
92.	Abbott Laboratories	16.9	19.5	131	138.2	57
	Commerce Bancorp, Inc.	16.9	74.8	27	301.4	10
94.	National Penn Bancshares, Inc.	16.6	2.1	196	87.9	115
	S&T Bancorp, Inc.	16.6	-1.6	211	86.1	120
96.	Air Products & Chemicals	16.5	24.6	114	48.9	200
97.	Pall Corp.	16.3	4.2	189	8.7	257
98.	Hubbell, Inc.	16.1	-11.8	234	-18.4	279
	May Department Stores Co.	16.1	0.3	204	35.6	224
100.	PPG Industries, Inc.	15.6	-2.2	214	6.1	260
101.	Illinois Tool Works, Inc.	15.2	20.9	127	78.6	136
102.	Quaker Chemical Corp.	14.6	31.8	96	57.6	179
103.	Clorox Co.	14.0	-28.2	270	72.7	149
	Johnson & Johnson	14.0	46.5	56	153.6	44
105.	Donegal Group Inc.	13.8	-24.8	262	5.9	262
	Regions Financial Corp.	13.8	-16.8	246	36.0	223
107.	Donnelley (R.R.) & Sons Co.	13.7	-25.1	263	9.0	256
	Virco Manufacturing Corp.	13.7	-25.6	264	58.5	177
109.	First Financial Bancorp	13.1	-22.4	257	76.3	141
110.	Florida Public Utilities Co.	12.7	14.2	156	110.0	86
111.	Wesco Financial Corp.	12.3	-10.0	232	71.9	152
112.	Home Depot, Inc. (The)	12.1	26.2	107	365.3	8
113.	First Federal Capital Corp	11.7	4.8	188	126.8	69
114.	Huntington Bancshares, Inc.	11.3	-22.2	256	13.0	250
	Washington R.E.I.T.	11.3	61.9	35	95.3	101
116.	Eaton Vance Corp.	11.1	250.3	1	531.0	2
117.	Consolidated Edison, Inc.	10.8	-9.2	230	83.3	126
118.	Brady Corp.	10.6	45.3	60	66.1	161
	HON Industries Inc.	10.6	21.9	122	81.0	131
	VF Corp.	10.6	-9.5	231	30.3	235
121.	Gallagher (Arthur J.) & Co.	10.4	235.5	2	412.0	5
122.	XCEL Energy, Inc.	10.3	19.7	130	61.5	166
123.	Community Bank System, Inc.	10.1	0.7	200	59.3	174
124.	MBIA Inc.	9.8	27.7	102	69.7	155
125.	ChevronTexaco Corp.	9.4	17.9	140	59.6	173
	First Virginia Banks Inc.	9.4	19.1	132	84.2	125
127.	Philip Morris Cos., Inc.	9.2	2.2	195	56.8	180
128.	Hillenbrand Industries, Inc.	9.1	3.2	193	66.6	160
129.	Wal-Mart Stores, Inc.	8.9	43.3	67	420.0	4
	Wrigley (Wm.) Jr. Co.	8.9	20.5	129	98.0	98

Total Returns (cont.)

2001 Rank	Company	2001 Tot. Return %	3-yr. Tot. Return %	3-yr. Rank	5-yr. Tot. Return %	5-yr. Rank
41.	Bard (C.R.) Inc.	40.7	36.8	83	152.3	45
42.	Chemical Financial Corp.	40.3	7.8	183	26.6	240
43.	Community First Bankshares, Inc.	40.1	34.0	89	112.9	83
44.	United Mobile Homes, Inc.	37.3	45.9	58	54.8	186
45.	F.N.B. Corp.	35.6	18.6	133	67.7	157
46.	Nucor Corp.	35.3	27.3	103	9.9	254
47.	Clarcor Inc.	33.8	45.2	61	106.9	89
	Grainger (W.W.) Inc.	33.8	21.2	125	29.0	236
49.	Federal Realty Invest. Trust	32.6	26.3	106	26.0	241
50.	Health Care Property Investors	32.5	58.7	40	61.2	168
51.	NACCO Industries, Inc.	31.9	-35.2	277	13.5	249
52.	Susquehanna Bancshares, Inc.	31.7	15.5	148	62.3	164
53.	AmSouth Bancorporation	29.9	-29.7	271	56.5	182
54.	Transatlantic Holdings, Inc.	29.5	83.7	19	161.5	41
55.	Lancaster Colony Corp.	29.4	18.3	136	27.8	238
56.	Superior Industries Int'l, Inc.	29.0	50.1	51	84.4	124
57.	Universal Health Realty Inc. Trust	28.5	59.3	38	80.6	132
58.	Target Corp.	28.1	54.3	46	335.1	9
59.	Sonoco Products Co.	27.1	-0.6	207	31.1	234
60.	Marshall & Ilsley Corp.	27.0	14.6	154	100.0	96
61.	UGI Corp.	26.6	54.9	44	84.5	123
62.	Alfa Corp.	25.3	0.4	203	102.5	94
63.	Valspar Corp.	25.1	11.1	170	50.1	198
64.	USA Education, Inc.	24.7	81.9	22	237.3	21
65.	Lee Enterprises, Inc.	24.6	23.4	118	74.1	148
66.	Leggett & Platt, Inc.	24.3	11.2	169	45.2	205
	ServiceMaster Co.	24.3	-31.5	273	35.3	226
68.	Trustco Bank	24.2	26.6	105	120.3	77
69.	SouthTrust Corp.	24.1	44.8	62	139.8	54
70.	Diebold, Inc.	23.5	20.9	127	6.1	260
71.	Energy West Inc.	23.1	39.6	76	82.7	128
	Madison Gas & Electric Co.	23.1	39.2	78	76.0	143
73.	Compass Bancshares Inc.	23.0	24.7	113	88.8	113
	Wausau-Mosinee Paper Corp.	23.0	-25.9	265	-26.8	280
75.	Albertson's, Inc.	21.7	-47.0	280	-2.4	268
76.	1st Source Corp.	21.2	-21.5	254	50.7	195
77.	First Commonwealth Financial	21.0	8.5	180	53.4	190
78.	Associated Banc-Corp.	20.4	27.2	104	62.2	165
79.	Pitney Bowes, Inc.	20.1	-36.9	278	58.3	178
80.	EnergySouth, Inc.	20.0	25.8	111	54.5	187
81.	American National Insurance	19.7	15.3	149	37.2	220
82.	Belo Corp.	19.2	-1.4	209	15.0	248
83.	Banta Corp.	18.7	16.3	145	44.2	209
	Kellogg Co.	18.7	-2.5	215	6.2	259
85.	McCormick & Co., Inc.	18.7	32.8	95	99.2	97

Ranking the Dividend Achievers
by Total Returns

For information about total returns, please see page 23a.

2001 Rank	Company	2001 Tot. Return %	3-yr. Tot. Return %	3-yr. Rank	5-yr. Tot. Return %	5-yr. Rank
1.	Raven Industries, Inc.	112.9	143.5	6	82.4	129
2.	Lowe's Cos., Inc.	109.0	82.7	21	430.1	3
3.	McGrath Rentcorp	98.7	85.4	15	228.6	24
4.	Worthington Industries, Inc.	85.9	32.9	94	-2.1	267
5.	RPM, Inc.	77.5	3.5	192	28.7	237
6.	North Pittsburgh Systems, Inc.	77.4	59.9	37	-5.9	270
7.	Pier 1 Imports, Inc.	70.3	86.7	14	134.9	62
8.	Haverty Furniture Cos., Inc.	70.1	65.2	32	218.0	25
9.	Community Trust Bancorp, Inc.	66.4	38.2	80	54.4	188
10.	Health Care REIT, Inc.	66.0	33.5	90	67.4	158
11.	SUPERVALU Inc.	64.5	-13.7	240	79.2	134
12.	Applebee's International, Inc.	63.7	151.6	5	90.1	112
13.	Mine Safety Appliances Co.	62.3	79.7	23	148.6	48
14.	Midland Co.	59.2	87.4	13	261.1	12
15.	Johnson Controls, Inc.	58.2	44.6	64	113.6	80
16.	CVB Financial Corp.	56.1	55.2	43	214.3	26
17.	Pentair, Inc.	54.1	-3.0	216	23.7	243
18.	Gorman-Rupp Co.	53.9	78.1	26	133.3	65
19.	Stanley Works	53.0	83.6	20	96.7	99
20.	Pacific Century Financial	51.0	18.0	139	44.9	206
21.	Bemis Co., Inc.	50.2	40.4	73	50.5	196
22.	Connecticut Water Service, Inc.	49.5	84.2	18	183.6	35
23.	United Fire & Casualty Co.	49.4	-6.4	221	-7.6	271
24.	Bowl America Inc.	48.5	101.0	9	139.5	55
25.	Fuller (H.B.) Co.	48.4	26.1	108	32.9	230
26.	Hormel Foods Corp.	46.5	72.9	29	119.9	79
27.	American Water Works Co.	46.2	36.3	84	137.0	58
28.	Genuine Parts Corp.	45.7	23.9	116	48.1	201
29.	Cedar Fair, L.P.	45.3	18.2	137	85.4	122
30.	United Dominion Realty Trust	44.7	85.1	16	43.3	210
31.	Progressive Corp.	44.2	-11.6	233	-122.5	281
32.	Cohu Inc.	43.2	84.8	17	78.4	137
33.	Hilb, Rogal & Hamilton Co.	42.8	200.7	3	384.5	6
34.	Bank of America Corp.	42.6	17.1	142	51.0	194
35.	Hudson United Bancorp	42.5	21.1	126	66.8	159
36.	BancorpSouth, Inc.	41.4	1.7	198	38.6	216
37.	La-Z-Boy Inc.	41.3	30.0	98	144.7	52
38.	Family Dollar Stores, Inc.	41.1	40.4	73	367.3	7
39.	Commercial Net Lease Realty	40.9	35.2	85	32.0	231
40.	United Bankshares, Inc.	40.8	21.5	124	107.5	88

Highest Twelve-Month Price Scores

Scores cover twelve months ending 3/31/02. Definitions of price scores may be found on page 28a.

Rank	Company	Price Score	Rank	Company	Price Score
1.	Pier 1 Imports, Inc.	142.6	11.	Cohu Inc.	123.7
2.	RPM, Inc.	135.9	12.	Bandag, Inc.	123.1
3.	Hilb, Rogal & Hamilton Co.	135.6	13.	Nucor Corp.	122.4
4.	Frisch's Restaurants, Inc.	133.2	14.	Procter & Gamble Co.	120.4
5.	La-Z-Boy Inc.	130.7	15.	BancorpSouth, Inc.	120.1
6.	Haverty Furniture Cos., Inc.	130.1		Raven Industries, Inc.	120.1
7.	Grainger (W.W.) Inc.	129.3	17.	Belo Corp.	119.2
8.	SUPERVALU Inc.	129.2	18.	Clorox Co.	119.1
9.	Valspar Corp.	124.9	19.	Stanley Works	118.8
10.	Bemis Co., Inc.	124.1	20.	Lowe's Cos., Inc.	118.7

Top 20 by Revenues

Rank	Company	Rev. ($Mil.)	Rank	Company	Rev. ($Mil.)
1.	Wal-Mart Stores, Inc.	219,812.0	11.	Morgan (J.P.) Chase & Co.	50,429.0
2.	Exxon Mobil Corp.	213,488.0	12.	Merck & Co., Inc.	47,715.7
3.	General Electric Co.	125,913.0	13.	SBC Communications Inc.	45,908.0
4.	Citigroup Inc.	112,022.0	14.	Target Corp.	39,888.0
5.	ChevronTexaco Corp.	106,245.0	15.	Procter & Gamble Co.	39,244.0
6.	Philip Morris Cos., Inc.	89,924.0	16.	Merrill Lynch & Co.	38,757.0
7.	American International Grp.	55,459.0	17.	Albertson's, Inc.	37,931.0
8.	Home Depot, Inc. (The)	53,553.0	18.	Freddie Mac	35,927.0
9.	Bank of America Corp.	52,641.0	19.	Johnson & Johnson	33,004.0
10.	Fannie Mae	50,803.0	20.	Pfizer Inc.	32,259.0

Top 20 by Net Income

Rank	Company	Net Inc. ($Mil.)	Rank	Company	Net Inc. ($Mil.)
1.	Exxon Mobil Corp.	15,105.0	11.	Johnson & Johnson	5,668.0
2.	Citigroup Inc.	14,284.0	12.	American International Grp.	5,499.0
3.	General Electric Co.	14,128.0	13.	Freddie Mac	4,373.0
4.	Philip Morris Cos., Inc.	8,566.0	14.	Coca-Cola Co. (The)	3,979.0
5.	Pfizer Inc.	7,752.0	15.	ChevronTexaco Corp.	3,931.0
6.	Merck & Co., Inc.	7,281.0	16.	Wells Fargo & Co.	3,423.0
7.	SBC Communications Inc.	7,260.0	17.	Home Depot, Inc. (The)	3,044.0
8.	Bank of America Corp.	6,792.0	18.	Procter & Gamble Co.	2,922.0
9.	Wal-Mart Stores, Inc.	6,671.0	19.	Lilly (Eli) & Co.	2,809.0
10.	Fannie Mae	6,067.0	20.	Washington Mutual Inc.	2,732.0

Highest Price/Earnings Ratios

Based on closing prices on 3/31/02.

Rank	Company	P/E Ratio	Rank	Company	P/E Ratio
1.	Transatlantic Holdings, Inc.	234.6	11.	Masco Corp.	65.4
2.	Schwab (Charles) Corp.	218.2	12.	Paychex, Inc.	54.4
3.	GATX Corp.	212.0	13.	Carlisle Companies Inc.	53.3
4.	Donnelley (R.R.) & Sons Co.	155.5	14.	Briggs & Stratton Corp.	51.7
5.	Merrill Lynch & Co.	135.1	15.	Dover Corp.	50.0
6.	Chubb Corp. (The)	130.5	16.	Aon Corp.	47.3
7.	Tennant Co.	80.6	17.	Hershey Foods Corp.	45.7
8.	KeyCorp	74.0	18.	Morgan (J.P.) Chase & Co.	44.6
9.	Wausau-Mosinee Paper Corp.	67.2	19.	Nordson Corp.	44.3
10.	Medtronic, Inc.	66.5		Nucor Corp.	44.3

Lowest Price/Earnings Ratios

Based on closing prices on 3/31/02.

Rank	Company	P/E Ratio	Rank	Company	P/E Ratio
1.	Unitrin, Inc.	7.2	11.	Old Republic International	11.1
2.	Fidelity National Financial	7.5		XCEL Energy, Inc.	11.1
3.	Energy West Inc.	7.8	13.	Weyco Group, Inc.	11.9
4.	National Security Group	8.3	14.	Frisch's Restaurants, Inc.	12.3
5.	Universal Corp.	9.1	15.	Golden West Financial Corp.	12.4
6.	Irwin Financial Corp.	9.4	16.	First Federal Capital Corp	12.5
7.	Black Hills Corp.	9.6	17.	Corus Bankshares, Inc.	12.6
8.	Sara Lee Corp.	10.5		Raven Industries, Inc.	12.6
9.	Freddie Mac	10.6	19.	TECO Energy Inc.	12.8
	Washington Mutual, Inc.	10.6	20.	1st Source Corp.	13.0

Highest Seven-Year Price Scores

Scores cover a seven-year period ending 3/31/02. Definitions of price scores may be found on page 28a.

Rank	Company	Price Score	Rank	Company	Price Score
1.	SEI Investments Co.	204.5	11.	Golden West Financial Corp.	151.4
2.	Eaton Vance Corp.	196.4	12.	Midland Co.	145.5
3.	Hilb, Rogal & Hamilton Co.	181.9	13.	Target Corp.	145.4
4.	Gallagher (Arthur J.) & Co.	177.2	14.	Paychex, Inc.	144.9
5.	Jack Henry & Associates, Inc.	176.2	15.	M & T Bank Corp.	143.2
6.	Commerce Bancorp, Inc.	168.0	16.	Fifth Third Bancorp	142.8
	Lowe's Cos., Inc.	168.0	17.	Walgreen Co.	141.5
8.	USA Education, Inc.	165.1	18.	Transatlantic Holdings, Inc.	140.8
9.	Family Dollar Stores, Inc.	156.3	19.	Philadelphia Suburban Corp.	140.2
10.	Sysco Corp.	154.9	20.	Citigroup Inc.	139.3

Top 20 by Return on Equity

Rank	Company	Return on Equity %	Rank	Company	Return on Equity %
1.	Sara Lee Corp.	142.9	11.	Lilly (Eli) & Co.	39.5
2.	Colgate-Palmolive Co.	135.5	12.	Eaton Vance Corp.	38.5
3.	Pitney Bowes, Inc.	57.7	13.	Heinz (H.J.) Co.	36.0
4.	Kellogg Co.	55.3	14.	Coca-Cola Co. (The)	35.0
5.	SEI Investments Co.	46.2	15.	Gallagher (Arthur J.) & Co.	33.7
6.	Merck & Co., Inc.	45.4	16.	Paychex, Inc.	33.6
7.	Philip Morris Cos., Inc.	43.7	17.	Fannie Mae	33.5
8.	Gillette Co. (The)	42.6	18.	McCormick & Co., Inc.	31.7
9.	Pfizer Inc.	42.4	19.	PepsiCo, Inc.	30.8
10.	Anheuser-Busch Cos., Inc.	42.0	20.	Kimberly-Clark Corp.	28.5

Top 20 by Return on Assets

Rank	Company	Return on Assets %	Rank	Company	Return on Assets %
1.	SEI Investments Co.	27.1		Sara Lee Corp.	15.8
2.	Wrigley (Wm.) Jr. Co.	20.6	12.	Medtronic, Inc.	14.9
3.	Pfizer Inc.	19.8		T. Rowe Price Group, Inc.	14.9
4.	Coca-Cola Co. (The)	17.7	14.	Johnson & Johnson	14.7
5.	Eaton Vance Corp.	17.2	15.	Avon Products, Inc.	13.5
6.	Lilly (Eli) & Co.	17.1		Family Dollar Stores, Inc.	13.5
7.	Merck & Co., Inc.	16.5	17.	Applebee's International, Inc.	13.1
8.	Colgate-Palmolive Co.	16.4	18.	Raven Industries, Inc.	13.0
9.	Schering-Plough Corp.	16.0	19.	Pier 1 Imports, Inc.	12.9
10.	Lancaster Colony Corp.	15.8	20.	Jack Henry & Associates, Inc.	12.8

Top 20 by Current Yield

Rank	Company	Current Yield %	Rank	Company	Current Yield %
1.	Commercial Net Lease Realty	9.0	11.	Weingarten Realty Investors	6.5
2.	SEMCO Energy, Inc.	8.8	12.	XCEL Energy, Inc.	5.9
3.	Health Care REIT, Inc.	8.4	13.	Northwestern Corp.	5.8
4.	DQE, Inc.	7.9	14.	Cousins Properties Inc.	5.7
	Health Care Property Investors	7.9		National Security Group, Inc.	5.7
	Universal Health Realty Income	7.9	16.	Consolidated Edison, Inc.	5.3
7.	Federal Realty Investment Trust	7.5		Peoples Energy Corp.	5.3
8.	United Dominion Realty Trust	7.0		WPS Resources Corp.	5.3
9.	Cedar Fair, L.P.	6.9	19.	NiSource, Inc.	5.1
	United Mobile Homes, Inc.	6.9		UGI Corp.	5.1

Dividend Achiever Name Changes

The following companies have changed their names in the last year.

Old Name	New Name
Belo (A.H.) Corp.	Belo Corp.
Chevron Corporation	ChevronTexaco Corporation
National Commerce Bancorporation	National Commerce Financial Corporation

Top 20 by Total Assets

Rank	Company	Assets ($Mil.)	Rank	Company	Assets ($Mil.)
1.	Citigroup Inc.	1,051,450.0	11.	Exxon Mobil Corp.	143,174.0
2.	Fannie Mae	799,791.0	12.	SunTrust Banks, Inc.	104,740.6
3.	Morgan (J.P.) Chase & Co.	693,575.0	13.	Lincoln National Corp.	98,001.3
4.	Bank of America Corp.	621,764.0	14.	SBC Communications Inc.	96,322.0
5.	Freddie Mac	617,340.0	15.	Household International Inc.	89,416.0
6.	General Electric Co.	495,023.0	16.	Philip Morris Cos., Inc.	84,968.0
7.	American International Grp.	492,982.0	17.	Wal-Mart Stores, Inc.	83,451.0
8.	Merrill Lynch & Co.	419,419.0	18.	KeyCorp	80,938.0
9.	Wells Fargo & Co.	307,569.0	19.	ChevronTexaco Corp.	77,752.0
10.	Washington Mutual Inc.	242,506.0	20.	Fifth Third Bancorp	71,026.0

Dividend Achiever Arrivals and Departures

The following companies, which recorded at least ten consecutive years of dividend increases in 2001, mark their debut as Dividend Achievers.

Applebee's International, Inc.
Beckman Coulter, Inc.
Briggs & Stratton Corp.
Chemical Financial Corp.
Commerce Bancorp, Inc.
Community Bank System, Inc.
Community First Bankshares, Inc.
Cousins Properties Inc.
First Federal Capital Corp
First Indiana Corp.
General Dynamics Corp.

Irwin Financial Corp.
MBNA Corp.
McGrath Rentcorp
Merrill Lynch & Co., Inc.
Morgan (J.P.) Chase & Co.
Philadelphia Suburban Corp.
Pier 1 Imports, Inc.
PNC Financial Services Group
SEI Investments Co.
State Auto Financial Corp.
Valley National Bancorp

According to Mergent's database, the following former Dividend Achievers did not increase their regular cash dividends in 2001 and dropped from the list.

Alliance Capital Management Holding
American Greetings Corp.
American Home Products Corp.
Berkley (W.R.) Corp.
First Tennessee National Corp.
First Union Corp.
Fleetwood Enterprises, Inc.
Hasbro, Inc.
Ingersoll-Rand Co.
Kelly Services Inc.
LESCO, Inc.
Liqui-Box Corp.

Mattel, Inc.
National Services Industries, Inc.
NBT Bancorp Inc.
Pep Boys-Manny, Moe & Jack
Reynolds & Reynolds Co.
SAFECO Corp.
Schulman (A.), Inc.
Sovereign Bancorp, Inc.
TRW Inc.
United National Bancorp
Wallace Computer Services

The following former Dividend Achiever companies have been merged or acquired.

American General Corp.
Dean Foods Co.
F&M National Corp.
GPU, Inc.

Harcourt General, Inc.
Houghton Mifflin Co.
Promistar Financial Corp.
Wachovia Corp.